WTO Appellate Body Repertory of Reports and Awards 1995–2005

The WTO Appellate Body is responsible for deciding appeals relating to disputes among the WTO's 148 Members. The Appellate Body Repertory is the definitive reference tool for practitioners of WTO law and anyone interested in international trade law. The Repertory contains excerpts from WTO Appellate Body Reports, dating from the first Appellate Body Report adopted in May 1996, through to the sixty-eighth Report adopted in May 2005. The excerpts are organized according to the particular provision of the WTO Agreements examined, and by subject-matter.

The Repertory also contains excerpts from Arbitration Awards issued pursuant to Article 21.3(c) of the *Understanding on Rules and Procedures Governing the Settlement of Disputes* determining the 'reasonable period' for implementation of Dispute Settlement Body rulings, for which Appellate Body Members have acted as Arbitrators.

Readers will also find useful the additional information relating to the Appellate Body and appellate proceedings set out in a number of Annexes, as well as the detailed indexes organized by subject-matter, by Appellate Body Report, and by Arbitration Award.

WTO Appellate Body Repertory of Reports and Awards

1995–2005

Compiled by the Appellate Body Secretariat

CAMBRIDGE
UNIVERSITY PRESS

CAMBRIDGE UNIVERSITY PRESS
Cambridge, New York, Melbourne, Madrid, Cape Town, Singapore, São Paulo

Cambridge University Press
The Edinburgh Building, Cambridge CB2 2RU, UK

Published in the United States of America by Cambridge University Press, New York

www.cambridge.org
Information on this title: www.cambridge.org/9780521866026

First published 2006

Printed in the United Kingdom at the University Press, Cambridge

A catalogue record for this publication is available from the British Library

ISBN-13 978-0-521-86602-6 hardback
ISBN-10 0-521-86602-2 hardback

Contents (outline)

Contents (detail)

Foreword to the 1995–2004 edition

The Appellate Body Repertory (the "Repertory") is intended to serve first and foremost as a source of information for those interested in the field of international trade law. It was initially developed as an internal research tool to assist the Appellate Body Secretariat in carrying out its duty to provide legal support to Appellate Body Members. The Repertory is now being made available to the public in the hope that it will become a practical tool for officials from WTO Members, and in particular for Members, including developing country Members, that may not have the resources to prepare similar compendiums in-house. We also hope that the Repertory will assist academics, students, private practitioners, and other followers of international trade law and dispute settlement.

Publication of the Repertory is also intended to mark the Tenth Anniversary of the establishment of the Appellate Body in 1995, and to commemorate the substantive body of case law developed by the Appellate Body during its first ten years. We salute in particular the founding Members of the Appellate Body, namely, James Bacchus, Christopher Beeby, Claus-Dieter Ehlermann, Said El-Naggar, Florentino P. Feliciano, Julio Lacarte-Muró, and Mitsuo Matsushita. We also pay tribute to those who currently serve on the Appellate Body, namely Georges Abi-Saab, Luiz Olavo Baptista, Arumugamangalam Venkatachalam Ganesan, Merit E. Janow, John Lockhart, Giorgio Sacerdoti, and Yasuhei Taniguchi.

This edition of the Repertory is divided into three parts. The first, and main, part consists of excerpts from Appellate Body Reports, which are organized according to the particular provision of the WTO Agreements examined and by subject-matter. The second part consists of excerpts from Arbitration Awards issued pursuant to Article 21.3(c) of the *Understanding on Rules and Procedures Governing the Settlement of Disputes* (the "DSU"), for which Appellate Body Members have acted in their individual capacities. Finally, a third part contains additional information relating to the Appellate Body and appellate proceedings, which is set out in a number of Annexes. In using the Repertory, readers should bear in mind that neither the choice of excerpts nor the choice of entries under which they are classified is intended to have legal significance.

The Repertory covers Appellate Body Reports and Article 21.3(c) Arbitration Awards circulated through 7 April 2004. The Appellate Body Secretariat and Cambridge University Press are committed to publishing updates on an annual basis. The first update is scheduled for publication in January 2006.

Credit for the initiative of creating the Repertory belongs to the staff of the Appellate Body Secretariat who preceded me. The Repertory itself has been laboriously compiled by former and current Appellate Body Secretariat staff, including Luan Aggersberg, Jan Bohanes, Stéphanie Cartier, Kaarlo Castren, Judy Cowell, Patricia Crawley, Victoria Donaldson, Lothar Ehring, Petina Gappah, Susan Hainsworth, Heather Lang, Simon Lester, Nicolas Lockhart, Vilaysoun Loungnarath, Peter Morrison, Joost Pauwelyn, Iain Sandford, Vicki Sharp, Debra Steger, Hector Torres, Peter Van den Bossche, Arun Venkataraman, Tania Voon, Alan Yanovich, and Werner Zdouc. I underline in particular the contribution of Werner Zdouc, who was responsible for the mammoth task of editing and preparing the Repertory for publication. I also acknowledge the significant efforts of Vicki Sharp, who processed the text and the numerous revisions, as well as of Iain Sandford and Alan Yanovich, who provided critical assistance with the publication project. The Repertory is published in English, French and Spanish, and we thank Marilita Pottié-Picon, Philippe Prevel, Juán Manuel Fernández Azpiroz, Juán Renard, Anibal Rubio, Fernando Prieto Ramos, and Neil Johnstone for their contributions to the French and Spanish translations. Finally, we thank Jean-Guy Carrier of the WTO Information and Media Relations Division and Finola O'Sullivan of Cambridge University Press, who provided valuable assistance in relation to the publication process, as well as Maureen MacGlashan, who undertook the indexing of the Repertory.

I trust that the Repertory will be a valuable resource. Comments and suggestions for improvement are welcome and should be addressed to the Appellate Body Secretariat at ABREPERTORY@wto.org.

Valerie Hughes
Director, Appellate Body Secretariat
World Trade Organization

Foreword to the 1995–2005 edition

The WTO Appellate Body Repertory of Reports and Awards 1995–2005 is an updated version of the first edition of the Repertory, published in early 2005. This new edition contains, in addition to all of the material found in the first edition, new material covering eight additional Appellate Body Reports adopted during 2004 and 2005. Thus, this volume contains excerpts from WTO Appellate Body Reports, dating from the first Appellate Body Report adopted in May 1996, through to the sixty-eighth Report, adopted in May 2005. A considerable amount of new material is included in this new edition covering the GATT 1994, the *Agreement on Agriculture*, the *Anti-Dumping Agreement*, the *Agreement on Subsidies and Countervailing Measures*, the *General Agreement on Trade in Services*, and the *Dispute Settlement Understanding*, reflecting the substantial volume of appeal work conducted by the Appellate Body during the period from May 2004 through May 2005.

The Repertory also contains excerpts from Arbitration Awards issued pursuant to Article 21.3(c) of the *Dispute Settlement Understanding* determining the "reasonable period of time" for implementation of Dispute Settlement Body rulings, for which Appellate Body Members have acted as Arbitrators. Material from three new Arbitration Awards is contained in this new edition.

I am grateful to the many people involved in the preparation and publication of this leading reference tool, especially my colleagues in the Appellate Body Secretariat and the WTO Language Services and Documentation Division. Special mention must be made of the contribution of Werner Zdouc, Iain Sandford and Vicki Sharp in preparing this new edition. I also thank those users who took the time to offer comments and suggestions in respect of the first edition of the Repertory. Comments and suggestions continue to be welcome and should be addressed to the Appellate Body Secretariat at ABREPERTORY@wto.org.

Valerie Hughes
Director, Appellate Body Secretariat
World Trade Organization

PART I

Appellate Body Reports

A

A.1 Agreement on Agriculture

A.1.1 Article 1(a) and Annex 3 – "Aggregate Measurement of Support"

A.1.1.1 *Korea – Various Measures on Beef*, para. 115
(WT/DS161/AB/R, WT/DS169/AB/R)

. . . for purposes of determining whether a Member has exceeded its commitment levels, Base Total AMS, and the commitment levels resulting or derived therefrom, are not themselves formulae to be worked out, but simply absolute figures set out in the Schedule of the Member concerned. As a result, Current Total AMS which is calculated according to Annex 3, is compared to the commitment level for a given year that is already specified as a given, absolute, figure in the Member's Schedule.

A.1.2 Article 1(a)(ii) and Annex 3 – "AMS commitments"

A.1.2.1 *Korea – Various Measures on Beef*, para. 112
(WT/DS161/AB/R, WT/DS169/AB/R)

Looking at the wording of Article 1(a)(ii) itself, it seems to us that this provision attributes higher priority to "the provisions of Annex 3" than to the "constituent data and methodology". From the viewpoint of ordinary meaning, the term "in accordance with" reflects a more rigorous standard than the term "taking into account".

A.1.2.2 *Korea – Various Measures on Beef*, para. 114
(WT/DS161/AB/R, WT/DS169/AB/R)

In the circumstances of the present case, it is not necessary to decide how a conflict between "the provisions of Annex 3" and the "constituent data and methodology used in the tables of supporting material incorporated by reference in Part IV of the Member's Schedule" would have to be resolved in principle. As the Panel has found, in this case, there simply are no constituent data and methodology for beef. Assuming *arguendo* that one would be justified – in spite of the wording of Article 1(a)(ii) – to give priority to constituent data and methodology used in the tables of supporting material over the guidance of Annex 3, for products entering into the calculation of the Base Total AMS, such a step would seem to us to be unwarranted in calculating Current AMS for a product which did *not* enter into the Base Total AMS calculation. . . .

A.1.3 Article 1(e) – "subsidy"

A.1.3.1 *Canada – Dairy*, para. 87
(WT/DS103/AB/R, WT/DS113/AB/R, WT/DS103/AB/R/Corr.1, WT/DS113/AB/R/Corr.1)

. . . Correspondingly, a "subsidy" involves a transfer of economic resources from the grantor to the recipient for less than full consideration. As we said in our Report in *Canada – Aircraft*, a "subsidy", within the meaning of Article 1.1 of the *SCM Agreement*, arises where the grantor makes a "financial contribution" which confers a "benefit" on the recipient, as compared with what would have been otherwise available to the recipient in the marketplace. . . .

A.1.3.2 *US – FSC*, para. 137
(WT/DS108/AB/R)

Therefore, in this case, we will consider, first, whether the FSC measure involves a transfer of economic resources by the grantor, which in this dispute is the government of the United States, and, second, whether any transfer of economic resources involves a benefit to the recipient.

A.1.3.3 *US – FSC (Article 21.5 – EC)*, para. 194
(WT/DS108/AB/RW)

. . . We have rejected the United States' appeal regarding the proper characterization of the measure under Article 3.1(a) of the *SCM Agreement*. The Panel held, and we have upheld, that the measure involves the foregoing of revenues that are otherwise due under Article 1.1(a)(ii) of the *SCM Agreement*. As we indicated in *US – FSC*, where a government foregoes revenues that are otherwise due in relation to agricultural products, a subsidy may arise under the *Agreement on Agriculture*. The fiscal treatment of agricultural products, under the measure, is not materially different from the fiscal treatment of products falling within the scope of the *SCM Agreement*. Accordingly, we see no reason to reach any conclusion under the *Agreement on Agriculture* that differs from our conclusion under the *SCM Agreement*. . . .

A.1.3.4 *EC – Export Subsidies on Sugar*, para. 269
(WT/DS265/AB/R, WT/DS266/AB/R, WT/DS283/AB/R)

The chapeau of Article 9.1 provides: "The following export subsidies are subject to reduction commitments". Hence, Article 9.1 sets forth a list of practices that, by definition, involve export subsidies. In other words, a measure falling within Article 9.1 is deemed to be an export subsidy within the meaning of Article 1(e) of the *Agreement on Agriculture*. We observe that Article 9.1(c) requires no independent enquiry into the existence of a "benefit".

A.1.4 Article 1(e) – "contingent upon export performance"

A.1.4.1 *US – FSC*, para. 141
(WT/DS108/AB/R)

... We see no reason, and none has been pointed out to us, to read the requirement of "contingent upon export performance" in the *Agreement on Agriculture* differently from the same requirement imposed by the *SCM Agreement*. The two Agreements use precisely the same words to define "export subsidies". Although there are differences between the export subsidy disciplines established under the two Agreements, those differences do not, in our view, affect the common substantive requirement relating to export contingency. Therefore, we think it appropriate to apply the interpretation of export contingency that we have adopted under the *SCM Agreement* to the interpretation of export contingency under the *Agreement on Agriculture*....

A.1.4.2 *US – Upland Cotton*, para. 571
(WT/DS267/AB/R)

Although an export subsidy granted to agricultural products must be examined, in the first place, under the *Agreement on Agriculture*, we find it appropriate, as has the Appellate Body in previous disputes, to rely on the *SCM Agreement* for guidance in interpreting provisions of the *Agreement on Agriculture*. Thus, we consider the export-contingency requirement in Article 1(e) of the *Agreement on Agriculture* having regard to that same requirement contained in Article 3.1(a) of the *SCM Agreement*.

A.1.4.3 *US – Upland Cotton*, para. 582
(WT/DS267/AB/R)

In sum, we agree with the Panel's view that Step 2 payments are export-contingent and, therefore, an export subsidy for purposes of Article 9 of the *Agreement on Agriculture* and Article 3.1(a) of the *SCM Agreement*. The statute and regulations pursuant to which Step 2 payments are granted, on their face, condition payments to exporters on exportation. In order to claim payment, an exporter must show proof of exportation. If an exporter does not provide proof of exportation, the exporter will not receive a payment. This is sufficient to establish that Step 2 payments to exporters of United States upland cotton are "conditional upon export performance" or "dependent for their existence on export performance". That domestic users may also be eligible to receive payments under different conditions does not eliminate the fact that an exporter will receive payment only upon proof of exportation.

A.1.4.4 *US – Upland Cotton*, para. 615
(WT/DS267/AB/R)

... Article 1(e) of the *Agreement on Agriculture* defines "export subsidies" as "subsidies contingent upon export performance, *including* the export subsidies listed in Article 9 of this Agreement". (emphasis added) The use of the word "including" suggests that the term "export subsidies" should be interpreted broadly and that the list of export subsidies in Article 9 is not exhaustive. Even though an export credit guarantee may not necessarily include a subsidy component, there is nothing inherent about export credit guarantees that precludes such measures from falling within the definition of a subsidy. An export credit guarantee that meets the definition of an export subsidy would be covered by Article 10.1 of the *Agreement on Agriculture* because it is not an export subsidy listed in Article 9.1 of that Agreement.

A.1.4A Article 3.1 – "export subsidy commitments"

A.1.4A.1 *EC – Export Subsidies on Sugar*, paras. 166–167
(WT/DS265/AB/R, WT/DS266/AB/R, WT/DS283/AB/R)

A preliminary question for our consideration is what rules apply in interpreting export subsidy commitments specified in a Member's Schedule under the *Agreement on Agriculture*. We observe that Article II:7 of the *General Agreement on Tariffs and Trade 1994* (the "GATT 1994") provides that the "Schedules annexed to this Agreement are hereby made an integral part of Part I of this Agreement." Furthermore, Article 3.1 of the *Agreement on Agriculture* provides that "export subsidy commitments in Part IV of each Member's Schedule ... are hereby made an integral part of [the] GATT 1994".

The applicable rules for interpreting the provisions of the GATT 1994 are the "customary rules of interpretation of public international law". The Appellate Body has held that these rules are codified in the *Vienna Convention on the Law of Treaties* (the "*Vienna Convention*"). As provisions of a Member's Schedule are "part of the terms of the treaty", they are subject to these same rules of treaty interpretation....

A.1.4B Article 3.1 – "commitments limiting subsidization"

A.1.4B.1 *EC – Export Subsidies on Sugar*, para. 209
(WT/DS265/AB/R, WT/DS266/AB/R, WT/DS283/AB/R)

... We do not see Article 3.1 as permitting a Member to limit subsidization to whatever commitment it chooses to specify in its Schedule without regard to Members' obligations under the *Agreement on Agriculture*. Rather, with respect to export subsidy commitments, we see Article 3.1 as requiring a Member to limit its subsidization to the budgetary outlay and quantity reduction commitments specified in its Schedule in accordance with the provisions of the *Agreement on Agriculture*....

A.1.5 Article 3.3 – "export subsidies"

A.1.5.1 *US – FSC*, para. 132
(WT/DS108/AB/R)

. . . A finding of inconsistency with Article 3.3 of the *Agreement on Agriculture* is dependent on the Member having provided export subsidies *listed in Article 9.1*. . . .

A.1.5.2 *US – FSC*, para. 152
(WT/DS108/AB/R)

As regards *scheduled* products, when the specific reduction commitment levels have been reached, the *limited authorization* to provide export subsidies as listed in Article 9.1 is transformed, effectively, into a *prohibition* against the provision of those subsidies. . . .

A.1.5A Article 3.3 – "budgetary outlay and quantity commitment levels"

A.1.5A.1 *EC – Export Subsidies on Sugar*, paras. 193–194
(WT/DS265/AB/R, WT/DS266/AB/R, WT/DS283/AB/R)

By its terms, Article 3.3 of the *Agreement on Agriculture* prohibits the granting of export subsidies (listed in Article 9.1) in excess of the budgetary outlay *and* quantity commitment levels specified in a Member's Schedule. Article 3.3 does not, however, explicitly state that export subsidy commitments must be specified in a Member's Schedule in terms of both budgetary outlay *and* quantity commitment levels. At the same time, Article 3.3 does not explicitly state that a Member may specify its commitment level in terms of either of the two forms of commitments. In our view, the use of the conjunctive "and", and the corresponding use of the word "levels" in the plural, suggest that the drafters of the Agreement intended that both types of commitments must be specified in a Member's Schedule in respect of any export subsidy listed in Article 9.1. Had the drafters intended that a Member could specify one or the other of the two forms of commitments, they would have chosen the disjunctive "or" and correspondingly used the word "level" in the singular. Given the choice, Members would choose only one or the other type of commitment, but not both, so as to minimize their obligations. Therefore, it appears to us that the drafters intended to ensure that export subsidy commitments are specified in Members' Schedules in terms of both budgetary outlay and quantity commitments, by using the word "and" as well as the word "levels" in the text of Article 3.3.

We find contextual support for the above interpretation in Article 9.2(b)(iv) of the *Agreement on Agriculture*, which provides:

> (iv) the Member's budgetary outlays for export subsidies and the quantities benefiting from such subsidies, at the conclusion of the implementation period, are no greater than 64 per cent and 79 per cent of the 1986–1990 base period levels, respectively. For developing country Members these percentages shall be 76 and 86 per cent, respectively.

This provision prescribes the export subsidy commitment levels to be reached at the conclusion of the implementation period (and to be maintained thereafter), and those commitment levels are expressed in terms of both budgetary outlays and quantities. We do not see how a Member could comply with Article 9.2(b)(iv), or for that matter Article 9.2(a), without having specified its export subsidy commitments in terms of both budgetary outlays and quantities. We also consider it significant that both Article 9.2(b)(iii) and Article 9.2(b)(iv) use the expression "budgetary outlays for export subsidies and the quantities *benefiting from such subsidies*". (emphasis added) This shows the drafters' recognition of the need to address the budgetary outlays and quantities together.

A.1.5A.2 *EC – Export Subsidies on Sugar*, para. 196
(WT/DS265/AB/R, WT/DS266/AB/R, WT/DS283/AB/R)

Our interpretation that Article 3.3 (as well as Article 9.2) requires that export subsidy commitments in a Member's Schedule must be expressed in terms of both budgetary outlay and quantity commitment levels is also in consonance with the object and purpose of the *Agreement on Agriculture*. We note, as did the Panel, that the third paragraph of the Preamble to the Agreement recognizes that the "long-term objective" of WTO Members, in initiating a reform process to deal with the distortions in the world agricultural markets, is "to provide for substantial progressive reductions in agricultural support and protection". Pursuant to this objective, the fourth paragraph of the Preamble expresses the commitment of the WTO Members "to achieving binding commitments" in the three specified areas, including "export competition". An interpretation that export subsidy commitments must be expressed in a Member's Schedule in terms of both budgetary outlay and quantity commitment levels is more in harmony with the objectives stated in the Preamble to the Agreement than an interpretation that a Member is only obliged to fulfil "whatever commitments" it chooses to specify in its Schedule.

A.1.5A.3 *EC – Export Subsidies on Sugar*, para. 197
(WT/DS265/AB/R, WT/DS266/AB/R, WT/DS283/AB/R)

We are also of the view that if an export subsidy commitment were allowed to be specified in only one form, budgetary outlay or quantity, as a Member may choose, and its conformity were measured on the basis of that one commitment alone, it would undermine the export subsidy disciplines of the *Agreement on Agriculture*. As we noted above, the drafters recognized the need to deal with budgetary outlays and quantities together in order to restrain subsidized exports. A commitment on budgetary outlay alone provides little predictability on export quantities, while a commitment on quantity alone could lead to subsidized exports taking place that would otherwise have not taken place but for the budgetary support. This is especially so given that the *Agreement on Agriculture* has initiated a reform process in an environment of high levels of export subsidies taking the form of budgetary outlays and quantities. . . .

A.1.5A.4 *EC – Export Subsidies on Sugar*, para. 200
(WT/DS265/AB/R, WT/DS266/AB/R, WT/DS283/AB/R)

. . . we agree with the Panel that Article 3.3 requires a Member to schedule both budgetary outlay and quantity commitment levels in respect of export subsidies listed in Article 9.1 of the *Agreement on Agriculture*. . . .

A.1.6 Articles 3.3 and 10.1 – "export subsidy commitments"

A.1.6.1 *US – FSC*, para. 145
(WT/DS108/AB/R)

Under Article 3, Members have undertaken two different types of "export subsidy commitments". Under the first clause of Article 3.3, Members have made a commitment that they will not "provide export subsidies listed in paragraph 1 of Article 9 in respect of the agricultural products or groups of products specified in Section II of Part IV of its Schedule in excess of the budgetary outlay and quantity commitments levels specified therein". . . .

A.1.6.2 *US – FSC*, paras. 146–147
(WT/DS108/AB/R)

Under the second clause of Article 3.3, Members have committed *not* to provide *any* export subsidies, *listed in Article 9.1*, with respect to *unscheduled* agricultural products. This clause clearly also involves "export subsidy commitments" within the meaning of Article 10.1. . . .

. . . The term "export subsidy commitments" has a wider reach that covers commitments and obligations relating to *both* scheduled and unscheduled agricultural products.

A.1.6.3 *EC – Export Subsidies on Sugar*, para. 211
(WT/DS265/AB/R, WT/DS266/AB/R, WT/DS283/AB/R)

. . . we examine whether the claimed commitment in Footnote 1 "limiting" subsidization of exports of sugar can prevail over the provisions of the *Agreement on Agriculture*, despite such a commitment being inconsistent with Articles 3.3 and 9.1 of the *Agreement on Agriculture*. . . .

A.1.6.4 *EC – Export Subsidies on Sugar*, para. 222
(WT/DS265/AB/R, WT/DS266/AB/R, WT/DS283/AB/R)

. . . Footnote 1, being part of the European Communities' Schedule, is an integral part of the GATT 1994 by virtue of Article 3.1 of the *Agreement on Agriculture*. Therefore, pursuant to Article 21 of the *Agreement on Agriculture*, the provisions of the *Agreement on Agriculture* prevail over Footnote 1. . . .

A.1.7 Article 4 – "market access"

A.1.7.1 *Chile – Price Band System*, para. 200
(WT/DS207/AB/R)

. . . we turn now to Article 4, which is the main provision of Part III of the *Agreement on Agriculture*. As its title indicates, Article 4 deals with "Market Access". During the course of the Uruguay Round, negotiators identified certain border measures which have in common that they restrict the volume or distort the price of imports of agricultural products. The negotiators decided that these border measures should be converted into ordinary customs duties, with a view to ensuring enhanced market access for such imports. Thus, they envisioned that ordinary customs duties would, in principle, become the only form of border protection. As ordinary customs duties are more transparent and more easily quantifiable than non-tariff barriers, they are also more easily compared between trading partners, and thus the maximum amount of such duties can be more easily reduced in future multilateral trade negotiations. The Uruguay Round negotiators agreed that market access would be improved – both in the short term and in the long term – through bindings and reductions of tariffs and minimum access requirements, which were to be recorded in Members' Schedules.

A.1.8 Article 4.1 – Market access commitments contained in Schedules.
See also Tariff Quotas – Non-discriminatory Administration (T.2)

A.1.8.1 *EC – Bananas III*, para. 156
(WT/DS27/AB/R)

Article 4.1 of the *Agreement on Agriculture* provides as follows:

> Market access concessions contained in Schedules relate to bindings and reductions of tariffs, and to other market access commitments as specified therein.

In our view, Article 4.1 does more than merely indicate where market access concessions and commitments for agricultural products are to be found. Article 4.1 acknowledges that significant, new market access concessions, in the form of new bindings and reductions of tariffs as well as other market access commitments (i.e. those made as a result of the tariffication process), were made as a result of the Uruguay Round negotiations on agriculture and included in Members' GATT 1994 Schedules. These concessions are fundamental to the agricultural reform process that is a fundamental objective of the *Agreement on Agriculture*.

A.1.8.2 *EC – Bananas III*, para. 157
(WT/DS27/AB/R)

. . . we do not see anything in Article 4.1 to suggest that market access concessions and commitments made as a result of the Uruguay Round negotiations on agriculture can be inconsistent with the provisions of Article XIII of the GATT 1994. There is nothing in Articles 4.1 or 4.2, or in any other article of the *Agreement on Agriculture*, that deals specifically with the allocation of tariff quotas on agricultural products. . . .

A.1.8.3 *US – Upland Cotton*, para. 548
(WT/DS267/AB/R)

Our approach in this case is consistent with the Appellate Body's approach in *EC – Bananas III*. In that case, the European Communities relied on Article 4.1 of the *Agreement on Agriculture* in arguing that the market access concessions it made for agricultural products pursuant to the *Agreement on Agriculture* prevailed over Article XIII of the GATT 1994. The Appellate Body, however, found that "[t]here is nothing in Articles 4.1 or 4.2, or in any other article of the *Agreement on Agriculture*, that deals specifically with the allocation of tariff quotas on agricultural products". It further explained that "[i]f the negotiators had intended to permit Members to act inconsistently with Article XIII of the GATT 1994, they would have said so explicitly". The situation before us is similar. We have found nothing in Article 6.3, paragraph 7 of Annex 3 or anywhere else in the *Agreement on Agriculture* that "deals specifically" with subsidies that are contingent on the use of domestic over imported agricultural products.

A.1.9 Article 4.2 and Footnote 1 – Conversion of certain border measures into ordinary customs duties

A.1.9.1 *Chile – Price Band System*, paras. 206–207
(WT/DS207/AB/R)

. . . Article 4.2 of the *Agreement on Agriculture* should be interpreted in a way that gives meaning to the use of the present perfect tense in that provision – particularly in the light of the fact that most of the other obligations in the *Agreement on Agriculture* and in the other covered agreements are expressed in the present, and not in the present perfect, tense. In general, requirements expressed in the present perfect tense impose obligations that came into being in the past, but may continue to apply at present. As used in Article 4.2, this temporal connotation relates to the date *by which* Members had to convert measures covered by Article 4.2 into ordinary customs duties, as well as to the date *from which* Members had to refrain from maintaining, reverting to, or resorting to, measures prohibited by Article 4.2. The conversion into ordinary customs duties of measures within the meaning of Article 4.2 began *during* the Uruguay Round multilateral trade negotiations, because ordinary customs duties that were to "compensate" for and replace converted border measures were to be recorded in Members' draft WTO Schedules by the *conclusion* of those negotiations. These draft Schedules, in turn, had to be verified before the signing of the *WTO Agreement* on 15 April 1994. Thereafter, there was no longer an option to replace measures covered by Article 4.2 with ordinary customs duties in excess of the levels of previously bound tariff rates. Moreover, as of the date of entry into force of the *WTO Agreement* on 1 January 1995, Members are required not to "maintain, revert to, or resort to" measures covered by Article 4.2 of the *Agreement on Agriculture*.

If Article 4.2 were to read "any measures of the kind which *are* required to be converted", this would imply that if a Member – for whatever reason – had failed, by the end of the Uruguay Round negotiations, to convert a measure within the meaning of Article 4.2, it could, *even today*, replace that measure with ordinary customs duties in excess of bound tariff rates. But, as Chile and Argentina have agreed, this is clearly not so. It seems to us that Article 4.2 was drafted in the present perfect tense to ensure that measures that were required to be converted as a result of the Uruguay Round – but were not converted – could not be maintained, by virtue of that Article, from the date of the entry into force of the *WTO Agreement* on 1 January 1995.

A.1.10 Article 4.2 and Footnote 1 – Measures of the kind

A.1.10.1 *Chile – Price Band System*, para. 208
(WT/DS207/AB/R)

Thus, contrary to what Chile argues, giving meaning and effect to the use of the present perfect tense in the phrase "have been required" does not suggest that the scope of the phrase "any measures of the kind which have been required to be converted into ordinary customs duties" must be limited only to those measures which were *actually* converted, or were *requested* to be converted, into ordinary customs duties by the end of the Uruguay Round. Indeed, in our view, such an interpretation would fail to give meaning and effect to the word "*any*" and the phrase "*of the kind*", which are descriptive of the word "measures" in that provision. A plain reading of these words suggests that the drafters intended to cover a broad category of measures. We do not see how proper meaning and effect could be accorded to the word "any" and the phrase "of the kind" in Article 4.2 if that provision were read to include only those specific measures that were singled out to be converted into ordinary customs duties by negotiating partners in the course of the Uruguay Round.

A.1.10.2 *Chile – Price Band System*, para. 209
(WT/DS207/AB/R)

The wording of footnote 1 to the *Agreement on Agriculture* confirms our interpretation.... the use of the word "include" in the footnote indicates that the list of measures is illustrative, not exhaustive. And, clearly, the existence of footnote 1 suggests that there will be "measures of the kind which have been required to be converted" that were *not* specifically identified during the Uruguay Round negotiations....

A.1.10.3 *Chile – Price Band System*, para. 216
(WT/DS207/AB/R)

Article 4.2 speaks of "measures of the kind which have been required to be *converted* into ordinary customs duties". The word "convert" means "undergo transformation". The word "converted" connotes "changed in their nature", "turned into something different". Thus, "measures which have been required to be converted into ordinary customs duties" had to be transformed into something they were not – namely, ordinary customs duties. The following example illustrates this point. The application of a "variable import levy", or a "minimum import price", as the terms are used in footnote 1, can result in the levying of a specific duty equal to the difference between a reference price and a target price, or minimum price. These resulting levies or specific duties take the same *form* as ordinary customs duties. However, the mere fact that a duty imposed on an import at the border is in the same *form* as an ordinary customs duty, does not mean that it is *not* a "variable import levy" or a "minimum import price". Clearly, as measures listed in footnote 1, "variable import levies" and "minimum import prices" had to be *converted into* ordinary customs duties by the end of the Uruguay Round. The mere fact that such measures result in the payment of duties does not exonerate a Member from the requirement not to maintain, resort to, or revert to those measures.

A.1.10.4 *Chile – Price Band System*, para. 278
(WT/DS207/AB/R)

. . . we disagree with the Panel's definition of "ordinary customs duties" and, therefore, we *reverse* the Panel's finding, in paragraph 7.52 of the Panel Report, that the term "ordinary customs duty", as used in Article 4.2 of the *Agreement on Agriculture*, is to be understood as "referring to a customs duty which is not applied to factors of an exogenous nature".

A.1.11 Article 4.2 and Footnote 1 – Minimum import price

A.1.11.1 *Chile – Price Band System*, paras. 236–237
(WT/DS207/AB/R)

The term "minimum import price" refers generally to the lowest price at which imports of a certain product may enter a Member's domestic market. Here, too, no definition has been provided by the drafters of the *Agreement on Agriculture*. However, the Panel described "minimum import prices" as follows:

> [these] schemes generally operate in relation to the actual transaction value of the imports. If the price of an individual consignment is below a specified minimum import price, an additional charge is imposed corresponding to the difference.

The Panel also said that minimum import prices "are generally not dissimilar from variable import levies in many respects, including in terms of their protective and stabilization effects, but that their mode of operation is generally less complicated." The main difference between minimum import prices and variable import levies is, according to the Panel, that "variable import levies are generally based on the difference between the *governmentally determined threshold* and the lowest world market offer price for the product concerned, while minimum import price schemes generally operate in relation to the *actual transaction value* of the imports." (emphasis added)

A.1.12 Article 4.2 and Footnote 1 – Similar border measures

A.1.12.1 *Chile – Price Band System*, para. 226
(WT/DS207/AB/R)

We agree with the first part of the Panel's definition of the term "similar" as "having a resemblance or likeness", "of the same nature or kind", and "having characteristics in common".... The better and appropriate approach is to determine similarity by asking the question whether two or more things have likeness or resemblance sufficient to be similar to each other. In our view, the task of determining whether something is similar to something else must be approached on an empirical basis.

A.1.13 Article 4.2 and Footnote 1 – Variable import levies

A.1.13.1 *Chile – Price Band System*, para. 233
(WT/DS207/AB/R)

To determine *what kind* of variability makes an import levy a "variable import levy", we turn to the immediate context of the other words in footnote 1. The term "variable import levies" appears after the introductory phrase "[t]hese *measures* include". Article 4.2 – to which the footnote is attached – also speaks of "*measures*". This suggests that at least one feature of "variable import levies" is the fact that the *measure* itself – as a mechanism – must impose the *variability* of the duties. Variability is inherent in a measure if the measure incorporates a scheme or formula that causes and ensures that levies change automatically and continuously. Ordinary customs duties, by contrast, are subject to discrete changes in applied tariff rates that occur independently, and unrelated to such an underlying scheme or formula. The level at which ordinary customs duties are applied can be *varied* by a legislature, but such duties will not be automatically and continuously *variable.* To vary the applied rate of duty in the case of ordinary customs duties will always require *separate* legislative or administrative action, whereas the ordinary meaning of the term "variable" implies that *no* such action is required.

A.1.13.2 *Chile – Price Band System*, para. 234
(WT/DS207/AB/R)

However, in our view, the presence of a formula causing automatic and continuous variability of duties is a *necessary*, but by no means a *sufficient*, condition for a particular measure to be a "variable import levy" within the meaning of footnote 1. "Variable import levies" have additional features that undermine the object and purpose of Article 4, which is to achieve improved market access conditions for imports of agricultural products by permitting only the application of ordinary customs duties. These additional features include a lack of transparency and a lack of predictability in the level of duties that will result from such measures. This lack of transparency and this lack of predictability are liable to restrict the volume of imports. As Argentina points out, an exporter is less likely to ship to a market if that exporter does not know and cannot reasonably predict what the amount of duties will be....

A.1.13.3 *Chile – Price Band System*, para. 254
(WT/DS207/AB/R)

. . . we find nothing in Article 4.2 to suggest that a measure prohibited by that provision would be rendered consistent with it if applied with a cap. Before the conclusion of the Uruguay Round, a measure could be recognized as a "variable import levy" even if the products to which the measure applied were subject to tariff bindings. And, there is nothing in the text of Article 4.2 to indicate that a measure, which was recognized as a "variable import levy" before the Uruguay Round, is exempt from the requirements of Article 4.2 simply because tariffs on some, or all, of the products to which that measure *now* applies were bound as a result of the Uruguay Round.

A.1.14 Article 5 – special safeguard

A.1.14.1 *EC – Poultry*, para. 153
(WT/DS69/AB/R)

. . . we interpret the "price at which the product concerned may enter the customs territory of the Member granting the concession, as determined on the basis of the c.i.f. import price" in Article 5.1(b) as the c.i.f. import price not including ordinary customs duties. . . .

A.1.14.2 *EC – Poultry*, para. 168
(WT/DS69/AB/R)

. . . neither the text nor the context of Article 5.5 of the *Agreement on Agriculture* permits us to conclude that the additional duties imposed under the special safeguard mechanism in Article 5 of the *Agreement on Agriculture* may be established by any method other than a comparison of the *c.i.f. price of the shipment* with the trigger price.

A.1.14.3 *Chile – Price Band System*, para. 217
(WT/DS207/AB/R)

Article 5, also found in Part III of the *Agreement on Agriculture* on "Market Access", lends contextual support to our interpretation of Article 4.2. In our view, the existence of a market access exemption in the form of a special safeguard provision under Article 5 implies that Article 4.2 should *not* be interpreted in a way that permits Members to maintain measures that a Member would not be permitted to maintain *but for* Article 5, and, much less, measures that are even more trade-distorting than special safeguards. In particular, if Article 4.2 were interpreted in a way that allowed Members to maintain measures that operate in a way similar to a special safeguard within the meaning of Article 5 – but without respecting the conditions set out in that provision for invoking such measures – it would be difficult to see how proper meaning and effect could be given to those conditions set forth in Article 5.

A.1.14A Article 6.3 – domestic support commitments

A.1.14A.1 *US – Upland Cotton*, para. 544
(WT/DS267/AB/R)

. . . Article 6.3 deals with domestic support. It establishes only a *quantitative* limitation on the amount of domestic support that a WTO Member can provide in a given year. The quantitative limitation in Article 6.3 applies generally to all domestic support measures that are included in a WTO Member's AMS. . . .

A.1.14A.2 *US – Upland Cotton*, para. 545
(WT/DS267/AB/R)

Article 6.3 does not authorize subsidies that are contingent on the use of domestic over imported goods. It only provides that a WTO Member shall be considered to be in compliance with its domestic support *reduction commitments* if its Current Total AMS does not exceed that Member's annual or final bound commitment level specified in its Schedule. It does not say that compliance with Article 6.3 of the *Agreement on Agriculture* insulates the subsidy from the prohibition in Article 3.1(b). . . .

A.1.14A.3 *US – Upland Cotton*, para. 546
(WT/DS267/AB/R)

. . . we find that paragraph 7 of Annex 3 and Article 6.3 of the *Agreement on Agriculture* do not deal specifically with the same matter as Article 3.1(b) of the *SCM Agreement*, that is, subsidies contingent upon the use of domestic over imported goods.

A.1.14B Article 8 – "export competition commitments"

A.1.14B.1 *EC – Export Subsidies on Sugar*, para. 216
(WT/DS265/AB/R, WT/DS266/AB/R, WT/DS283/AB/R)

It is clear from the plain wording of Article 8 that Members are prohibited from providing export subsidies otherwise than in conformity with the *Agreement on Agriculture* and the commitments as specified in their Schedules. Thus, compliance with both is obligatory. As compliance with the provisions of the *Agreement on Agriculture* is obligatory, it is clear that the commitments specified in a Member's Schedule must be in conformity with the provisions of the Agreement. . . .

A.1.14B.2 *EC – Export Subsidies on Sugar*, para. 220
(WT/DS265/AB/R, WT/DS266/AB/R, WT/DS283/AB/R)

. . . we find no provision under the *Agreement on Agriculture* that authorizes Members to depart, in their Schedules, from their obligations under that Agreement. Indeed, as we have noted, Article 8 requires that, in providing export subsidies, Members must comply with the provisions of both the *Agreement on Agriculture* and the export subsidy commitments specified in their Schedules. This is possible only if the commitments in the Schedules are in conformity with the provisions of the *Agreement on Agriculture*. Thus, we see no basis for the European Communities' assertion that it could depart from the obligations under the *Agreement on Agriculture* through the claimed commitment provided in Footnote 1.

A.1.14C Article 9.1 – "export subsidies"

A.1.14C.1 *EC – Export Subsidies on Sugar*, para. 269
(WT/DS265/AB/R, WT/DS266/AB/R, WT/DS283/AB/R)

The chapeau of Article 9.1 provides: "The following export subsidies are subject to reduction commitments". Hence, Article 9.1 sets forth a list of practices that, by definition, involve export subsidies. In other words, a measure falling within Article 9.1 is deemed to be an export subsidy within the meaning of Article 1(e) of the *Agreement on Agriculture*. We observe that Article 9.1(c) requires no independent enquiry into the existence of a "benefit".

Article 9.1 – Relationship with Article 10.1. *See* Agreement on Agriculture, Article 10.1 – Relationship with Article 9.1 (A.1.33)

A.1.14D Article 9.1 – "subject to reduction commitments"

A.1.14D.1 *EC – Export Subsidies on Sugar*, para. 206
(WT/DS265/AB/R, WT/DS266/AB/R, WT/DS283/AB/R)

The chapeau of Article 9.1 says that the subsidies listed in that Article "are subject to reduction commitments under this Agreement". The export subsidies given to ACP/India equivalent sugar, which admittedly fall within the ambit of Article 9.1(a), are therefore subject to reduction commitments. Furthermore, as noted by the Panel, the provisions of Article 9.2(b)(iv) apply to Members that take advantage of the flexibility provisions of Article 9.2(b). Article 9.2(b)(iv) specifies the reduction levels to be achieved at the conclusion of the implementation period with respect to both budgetary outlays and quantities. The provisions of Article 9.2(b)(iv) lend contextual support to the view that export subsidies listed in Article 9.1 are subject to reduction commitments. We further note that Article 9.2(a)(i) and (ii) also make it clear that both budgetary outlay and quantity commitments specified in a Member's Schedule for each year of the implementation period are "reduction" commitments. It follows that the export subsidies provided to ACP/India equivalent sugar are subject to reduction commitments in terms of Article 9.1 of the *Agreement on Agriculture*.

A.1.15 Article 9.1(a) – "direct subsidies, including payments-in-kind"

A.1.15.1 *Canada – Dairy*, para. 87
(WT/DS103/AB/R, WT/DS113/AB/R, WT/DS103/AB/R/Corr.1, WT/DS113/AB/R/Corr.1)

In our view, the term "payments-in-kind" describes one of the *forms* in which "direct subsidies" may be granted. Thus, Article 9.1(a) applies to "direct subsidies", *including* "direct subsidies" granted in the form of "payments-in-kind". We believe that, in its ordinary meaning, the word "payments", in the term "payments-in-kind", denotes a transfer of economic resources, in a form other than money, from the grantor of the payment to the recipient. However, the fact that a "payment-in-kind" has been made provides no indication as to the economic *value* of the transfer effected, either from the perspective of the grantor of the payment or from that of the recipient. A "payment-in-kind" may be made in exchange for full or partial consideration or it may be made gratuitously. Correspondingly, a "subsidy" involves a transfer of economic resources from the grantor to the recipient for less than full consideration. As we said in our Report in *Canada – Aircraft*, a "subsidy", within the meaning of Article 1.1 of the *SCM Agreement*, arises where the grantor makes a "financial contribution" which confers a "benefit" on the recipient, as compared with what would have been otherwise available to the recipient in the marketplace. Where the recipient gives full consideration in return for a "payment-in-kind" there can be no "subsidy", for the recipient is paying market-rates for what it receives. It follows, in our view, that the mere fact that a "payment-in-kind" has been made does not, *by itself*, imply that a "subsidy", "direct" or otherwise, has been granted.

A.1.16 Article 9.1(a) – "governments or their agencies"

A.1.16.1 *Canada – Dairy*, para. 97

(WT/DS103/AB/R, WT/DS113/AB/R, WT/DS103/AB/R/Corr.1, WT/DS113/AB/R/Corr.1)

. . . According to *Black's Law Dictionary*, "government" means, *inter alia*, "[t]he *regulation*, *restraint*, *supervision*, or *control* which is exercised upon the individual members of an organized jural society *by those invested with authority*". (emphasis added) This is similar to meanings given in other dictionaries. The essence of "government" is, therefore, that it enjoys the effective power to "regulate", "control" or "supervise" individuals, or otherwise "restrain" their conduct, through the exercise of lawful authority. This meaning is derived, in part, from the *functions* performed by a government and, in part, from the government having the *powers* and *authority* to perform those functions. A "government agency" is, in our view, an entity which exercises powers vested in it by a "government" for the purpose of performing functions of a "governmental" character, that is, to "regulate", "restrain", "supervise" or "control" the conduct of private citizens. As with any agency relationship, a "government agency" may enjoy a degree of discretion in the exercise of its functions.

A.1.16A Article 9.1(a) – "contingent on export performance"

A.1.16A.1 *US – Upland Cotton*, para. 582

(WT/DS267/AB/R)

In sum, we agree with the Panel's view that Step 2 payments are export-contingent and, therefore, an export subsidy for purposes of Article 9 of the *Agreement on Agriculture* and Article 3.1(a) of the *SCM Agreement*. The statute and regulations pursuant to which Step 2 payments are granted, on their face, condition payments to exporters on exportation. In order to claim payment, an exporter must show proof of exportation. If an exporter does not provide proof of exportation, the exporter will not receive a payment. This is sufficient to establish that Step 2 payments to exporters of United States upland cotton are "conditional upon export performance" or "dependent for their existence on export performance". That domestic users may also be eligible to receive payments under different conditions does not eliminate the fact that an exporter will receive payment only upon proof of exportation.

A.1.17 Article 9.1(c) – "payments"

A.1.17.1 *Canada – Dairy*, para. 107

(WT/DS103/AB/R, WT/DS113/AB/R, WT/DS103/AB/R/Corr.1, WT/DS113/AB/R/Corr.1)

We have found that the word "payments", in the term "payments-in-kind" in Article 9.1(a), denotes a transfer of economic resources. We believe that the same holds true for the word "payments" in Article 9.1(c). The question which we now address is whether, under Article 9.1(c), the economic resources that are transferred by way of a "payment" must be in the form of money, or whether the resources transferred may take other forms. As the Panel observed, the dictionary meaning of the word "payment" is not limited to payments made in monetary form. In support of this, the Panel cited the *Oxford English Dictionary*, which defines "payment" as "the remuneration of a person with money *or its equivalent*". (emphasis added) Similarly, the *Shorter Oxford English Dictionary* describes a "payment" as a "sum of money (*or other thing*) paid". (emphasis added) Thus, according to these meanings, a "payment" could be made in a form, other than money, that confers value, such as by way of goods or services. A "payment" which does not take the form of money is commonly referred to as a "payment in kind".

A.1.17.2 *Canada – Dairy*, para. 108

(WT/DS103/AB/R, WT/DS113/AB/R, WT/DS103/AB/R/Corr.1, WT/DS113/AB/R/Corr.1)

We agree with the Panel that the ordinary meaning of the word "payments" in Article 9.1(c) is consistent with the dictionary meaning of the word. Under Article 9.1(c), "payments" are "financed by virtue of governmental action" and they may or may not involve "a charge on the public account". Neither the word "financed" nor the term "a charge" suggests that the word "payments" should be interpreted to apply solely to money payments. A payment made in the form of goods or services is also "financed" in the same way as a money payment, and, likewise, "a charge on the public account" may arise as a result of a payment, or a legally binding commitment to make payment by way of goods or services, or as a result of revenue foregone.

A.1.17.3 *EC – Export Subsidies on Sugar*, paras. 262–265

(WT/DS265/AB/R, WT/DS266/AB/R, WT/DS283/AB/R)

Article 9.1(c) does not qualify the term "payments" by reference to the entity making, or the entity receiving the payment. This may be contrasted with, for instance, Articles 9.1(a) and 9.1(b) of the *Agreement on Agriculture*, which specifically refer to the entities making and also, in the case of Article 9.1(a), to the entity receiving the alleged export subsidy. Moreover, Article 9.1(c), on its face, does not qualify the meaning of the term "payments", other than by requiring that the alleged "payments" be "on the export of an agricultural product" and "financed by virtue of governmental action".

As we noted above, the European Communities submits, first, that a "payment" within the meaning of Article 9.1(c) requires, by definition, the presence of two distinct legal entities. We agree with the European Communities that a "payment", within the meaning of Article 9.1(c), certainly occurs when one entity transfers economic resources to another entity....

This, however, does not imply that the term "payment" necessarily requires, in each and every case, the presence of two distinct entities. In other words, contrary to the European Communities' argument, we do not see, *a priori*, any reason why "payments", within the meaning of Article 9.1(c), cannot include, in the particular circumstances of this dispute, transfers of resources within one economic entity. The "payment" in this case is not merely a "purely *notional*" one but, rather, reflects a very concrete transfer of economic resources to C sugar production. In the specific dispute before us, C sugar is being sold on the world market by European Communities' sugar producers/exporters at a price that does not "even remotely" cover its average total cost of production. In the light of the enormous difference between the price of C sugar and its average total cost of production, we do not see how the "payment" identified by the Panel was "purely notional".

The European Communities' approach is, in our view, too formalistic. To illustrate, one could envisage a scenario under which the producers of C sugar are legally distinct from the producers of A and B sugar. In this situation, the European Communities' approach could recognize that a "payment" under Article 9.1(c) could exist because there would be a transfer of economic resources between different parties. If, however, these same producers of A, B, and C sugar were integrated producers and organized as single legal entities, a payment under Article 9.1(c) would not exist, because the transfer would be merely "internal". We do not believe that the applicability of Article 9.1(c) should depend on how an economic entity is legally organized.

A.1.17.4 *EC – Export Subsidies on Sugar*, paras. 268–269

(WT/DS265/AB/R, WT/DS266/AB/R, WT/DS283/AB/R)

...The European Communities argues that, because the alleged "cross-subsidization" involves no "transfer of resources" to the sugar producers, it confers no *benefit* upon these producers and, therefore, cannot be considered to provide a subsidy. The European Communities disagrees with the Panel's finding that Article 9.1(c) does not require the demonstration of a benefit for a measure to constitute a "payment" within the meaning of that provision.

The chapeau of Article 9.1 provides: "The following export subsidies are subject to reduction commitments". Hence, Article 9.1 sets forth a list of practices that, by definition, involve export subsidies. In other words, a measure falling within Article 9.1 is deemed to be an export subsidy within the meaning of Article 1(e) of the

Agreement on Agriculture. We observe that Article 9.1(c) requires no independent enquiry into the existence of a "benefit".

A.1.18 Article 9.1(c) – Benchmark for payments-in-kind

A.1.18.1 *Canada – Dairy (Article 21.5 – New Zealand and US)*, para. 73 (WT/DS103/AB/RW, WT/DS113/AB/RW)

Although we did not have to examine whether the benchmarks used by the panel in the original proceedings were appropriate, our findings in those proceedings provide guidance in identifying when "payments" are made under Article 9.1(c). We recall that we upheld the original panel's finding that "the provision of *discounted* milk to processors or exporters under Special Classes 5(d) and 5(e) involves 'payments' within the meaning of Article 9.1(c) of the *Agreement on Agriculture*." (emphasis added) In reaching this conclusion, we noted that, where milk is sold at "*reduced* rates (that is, at *below market-rates*), 'payments' are, in effect, made to the recipient of the portion of the price that is not charged." (emphasis added) We noted that the producer of the milk "foregoes" the uncharged portion of the price. In short, we indicated that there are "payments" under Article 9.1(c) when the price charged by the producer of the milk is less than the milk's *proper value* to the producer.

A.1.18.2 *Canada – Dairy (Article 21.5 – New Zealand and US)*, para. 74 (WT/DS103/AB/RW, WT/DS113/AB/RW)

Thus, the determination of whether "payments" are involved requires a comparison between the price actually charged by the provider of the goods or services – the prices of CEM in this case – and some objective standard or benchmark which reflects the proper value of the goods or services to their provider – the milk producer in this case. We do not accept Canada's argument that as the producer negotiates freely the price with the processor, and CEM prices are, therefore, market-determined, it is not necessary to compare these prices with an objective standard.

A.1.18.3 *Canada – Dairy (Article 21.5 – New Zealand and US)*, para. 75 (WT/DS103/AB/RW, WT/DS113/AB/RW)

Article 9.1(c) of the *Agreement on Agriculture* does not expressly identify any standard for determining when a measure involves "payments" in the form of payments-in-kind. The absence of an express standard in Article 9.1(c) may be contrasted with several other provisions involving export subsidies which do provide an express standard. Thus, for instance, even within Article 9.1 itself, sub-paragraphs (b) and (e) expressly provide that the domestic market constitutes the appropriate basis for comparison.

A.1.18.4 *Canada – Dairy (Article 21.5 – New Zealand and US)*, para. 76 (WT/DS103/AB/RW, WT/DS113/AB/RW)

We believe that it is significant that Article 9.1(c) of the *Agreement on Agriculture* does not expressly identify a standard or benchmark for determining whether a measure involves "payments". It is clear that the notion of "payments" encompasses a diverse range of practices involving a transfer of resources, either monetary or in-kind. Moreover, the "payments" may take place in many different factual and regulatory settings. Accordingly, we believe that it is necessary to scrutinize carefully the facts and circumstances of a disputed measure, including the regulatory framework surrounding that measure, to determine the appropriate basis for comparison in assessing whether the measure involves "payments" under Article 9.1(c).

A.1.18.5 *Canada – Dairy (Article 21.5 – New Zealand and US)*, para. 81 (WT/DS103/AB/RW, WT/DS113/AB/RW)

... There can be little doubt, however, that the administered price is a price that is favourable to the domestic producers. Consequently, sale of CEM by the producer at less than the administered domestic price does not, necessarily, imply that the producer has foregone a portion of the proper value of the milk to it. In the situation where the producer, rather than the government, chooses to produce and sell CEM in the marketplace at a price it freely negotiates, we do not believe it is appropriate to use, as a basis for comparison, a domestic price that is fixed by the government.

A.1.19 Article 9.1(c) – Benchmark – world market prices vs. domestic prices

A.1.19.1 *Canada – Dairy (Article 21.5 – New Zealand and US)*, para. 83 (WT/DS103/AB/RW, WT/DS113/AB/RW)

... If a producer wishes to sell milk for export processing, it is obvious that the price of the milk to the processor must be competitive with world market prices. If it is not, the processor will not buy the milk, as it will not be able to produce a final product that is competitive in export markets. Accordingly, the range of world market prices determines the price which the producer can charge for milk destined for export markets. World market prices do, therefore, provide one possible measure of the value of the milk to the producer.

A.1.19.2 *Canada – Dairy (Article 21.5 – New Zealand and US)*, para. 84 (WT/DS103/AB/RW, WT/DS113/AB/RW)

However, world market prices do not provide a valid basis for determining whether there are "payments", under Article 9.1(c) of the *Agreement on Agriculture*, for, it remains possible that the reason CEM can be sold at prices competitive with world market prices is precisely because sales of CEM involve subsidies that make it competitive. Thus, a comparison between CEM prices and world market prices gives no indication on the crucial question, namely, whether Canadian export production has been given an advantage. Furthermore, if the basis for comparison were world market prices, it would be possible for WTO Members to subsidize domestic inputs for export processing, while taking care to maintain the price of these inputs to the processors at a level which equalled or marginally exceeded world market prices....

A.1.20 Article 9.1(c) – Benchmark – cost of production

A.1.20.1 *Canada – Dairy (Article 21.5 – New Zealand and US)*, para. 87
(WT/DS103/AB/RW, WT/DS113/AB/RW)

Although the proceeds from sales at domestic or world market prices represent two possible measures of the value of milk to the producer, we do not see these as the only possible measures of this value. For any economic operator, the production of goods or services involves an investment of economic resources. In the case of a milk producer, production requires an investment in fixed assets, such as land, cattle and milking facilities, and an outlay to meet variable costs, such as labour, animal feed and health-care, power and administration. These fixed and variable costs are the total amount which the producer must spend in order to produce the milk and the total amount it must recoup, in the long-term, to avoid making losses. To the extent that the producer charges prices that do not recoup the total cost of production, over time, it sustains a loss which must be financed from some other source, possibly "by virtue of governmental action".

A.1.20.2 *Canada – Dairy (Article 21.5 – New Zealand and US)*, para. 88
(WT/DS103/AB/RW, WT/DS113/AB/RW)

In our view, reliance upon the total cost of production, in this dispute, as a basis for determining whether there are "payments" within the meaning of Article 9.1(c), is in harmony with the domestic support and export subsidies disciplines of the *Agreement on Agriculture*. Under Article 3 of the *Agreement on Agriculture*, WTO Members are entitled to provide "*domestic support*" to agricultural producers within the limits of their domestic support commitments. The same Article establishes separate disciplines on *export subsidies* which prohibit WTO Members from providing such subsidies in excess of their export subsidy commitments.

A.1.20.3 *Canada – Dairy (Article 21.5 – New Zealand and US)*, para. 89
(WT/DS103/AB/RW, WT/DS113/AB/RW)

It is possible that the economic effects of WTO-consistent domestic support in favour of producers may "spill over" to provide certain benefits to export production, especially as many agricultural products result from a single line of production that does not distinguish whether the production is destined for consumption in the domestic or export market.

A.1.20.4 *Canada – Dairy (Article 21.5 – New Zealand and US)*, para. 90
(WT/DS103/AB/RW, WT/DS113/AB/RW)

We believe that it would erode the distinction between the domestic support and export subsidies disciplines of the *Agreement on Agriculture* if WTO-consistent domestic support measures were automatically characterized as export subsidies because they produced spill-over economic benefits for export production. Indeed, this is another reason why we do not agree with the Panel that sales of CEM at any price below the administered domestic price for milk can be regarded as "payments" under Article 9.1(c) of the *Agreement on Agriculture*. Such a basis for comparison would tend to collapse the distinction between these two different disciplines.

A.1.20.5 *Canada – Dairy (Article 21.5 – New Zealand and US)*, para. 91 (WT/DS103/AB/RW, WT/DS113/AB/RW)

However, we consider that the distinction between the domestic support and export subsidies disciplines in the *Agreement on Agriculture* would also be eroded if a WTO Member were entitled to use domestic support, without limit, to provide support for exports of agricultural products. Broadly stated, domestic support provisions of that Agreement, coupled with high levels of tariff protection, allow extensive support to producers, as compared with the limitations imposed through the export subsidies disciplines. Consequently, if domestic support could be used, without limit, to provide support for exports, it would undermine the benefits intended to accrue through a WTO Member's export subsidy commitments.

A.1.20.6 *Canada – Dairy (Article 21.5 – New Zealand and US)*, para. 92 (WT/DS103/AB/RW, WT/DS113/AB/RW)

In our view, by relying upon the total cost of production in this dispute, to determine whether there are "payments", the integrity of the two disciplines is best respected. The existence of "payments" is determined by reference to a standard that focuses upon the motivations of the independent economic operator who is making the alleged "payments" – here the producer – and not upon any government intervention in the marketplace. More importantly, using this basis for comparison, the potential for WTO Members to export their agricultural production is preserved, provided that any export-destined sales by a producer at below the total cost of production are not financed by virtue of governmental action. The export subsidy disciplines of the *Agreement on Agriculture* will also be maintained without erosion.

A.1.20.7 *Canada – Dairy (Article 21.5 – New Zealand and US)*, para. 93 (WT/DS103/AB/RW, WT/DS113/AB/RW)

Our approach is supported by the standards used in items (j) and (k) of the Illustrative List of the *SCM Agreement*. Item (j) is concerned with export subsidies that arise through the provision by the government of a variety of export credit guarantee and insurance programmes. Under item (j), the provision of such services by the government involves export subsidies when the premium rates charged do not "cover the *long-term operating costs and losses* of the programmes". (emphasis added) Thus, the measure of value under item (j) is the overall cost to the government, as the service provider, of providing the service. Likewise, in item (k), where the government provides export credits, the measure of the value of the service provided by the government is the amount "which [governments] actually have to pay for the funds so employed (or would have to pay if they borrowed on international capital markets . . .)". Again, the measure of value is by reference to the cost to the government, as the service provider, of providing the service. Therefore, items (j) and (k) give contextual support and *rationale*, for using the cost of production as a standard for determining whether there are "payments" under Article 9.1(c) of the *Agreement on Agriculture* in these proceedings.

A.1.20.8 *Canada – Dairy (Article 21.5 – New Zealand and US)*, paras. 94–95 (WT/DS103/AB/RW, WT/DS113/AB/RW)

A producer's cost of production may be measured in, at least, two ways. First, for any given unit of production, for instance a hectolitre of milk, there is an average total cost of production, which is the total cost of production divided by the total number of units produced, regardless of whether the production is destined for the domestic or export markets. The total cost of production includes *all* fixed and variable costs incurred in the production of all the units in question. Second, there is also the marginal cost of production which includes only the additional costs incurred by the producer in producing an extra unit of production. Generally, the marginal cost of production does not include any amount for the fixed costs of production. Although a producer may very well decide to sell goods or services if the sales price covers its marginal costs, the producer will make losses on such sales unless all of the remaining costs associated with making these sales, essentially the fixed costs, are financed through some other source, such as through highly profitable sales of the product in another market.

In the ordinary course of business, an economic operator chooses to invest, produce and sell, not only to recover the total cost of production, but also in the hope of making profits.

A.1.20.9 *Canada – Dairy (Article 21.5 – New Zealand and US)*, para. 96 (WT/DS103/AB/RW, WT/DS113/AB/RW)

Accordingly, in the circumstances of these proceedings, where the alleged payment is made by an independent economic operator and where the domestic price is administered, we believe that the average total cost of production represents the appropriate standard for determining whether sales of CEM involve "payments" under Article 9.1(c) of the *Agreement on Agriculture*. The average total cost of production would be determined by dividing the fixed and variable costs of producing *all* milk, whether destined for domestic or export markets, by the total number of units of milk produced for both these markets.

A.1.20.10 *Canada – Dairy (Article 21.5 – New Zealand and US)*, para. 97 (WT/DS103/AB/RW, WT/DS113/AB/RW)

. . . The export subsidy described in Article 9.1(c) comprises of several elements, the first of which is that there must be "payments". But the "payments" will be an export subsidy only when they are financed by virtue of governmental action. Thus, on the basis of the standard of average total cost of production, there will be an export subsidy only if the below-cost portion of an export sale is "financed by virtue of governmental action".

A.1.20.11 *EC – Export Subsidies on Sugar*, para. 266
(WT/DS265/AB/R, WT/DS266/AB/R, WT/DS283/AB/R)

. . . In this respect, we are also mindful of the fact that, in the ordinary course of business, an economic operator makes a decision to produce and sell a product expecting to recover the total cost of production and to make profits. Clearly, sales below total cost of production cannot be sustained in the long term, unless they are financed from some other sources. This is especially true when the volume of the loss-making sales is substantial. . . .

A.1.20.12 *EC – Export Subsidies on Sugar*, para. 267
(WT/DS265/AB/R, WT/DS266/AB/R, WT/DS283/AB/R)

Finally, we believe that the Panel did not err when it applied, in ascertaining the existence of "payments" under Article 9.1(c), the average total cost of production benchmark, which the Appellate Body held was appropriate in the circumstances in *Canada – Dairy (Article 21.5 – New Zealand and US)*. Given the huge volumes of C sugar exports and the price at which C sugar is being sold on the world market, we concur with the Panel that such production quantities cannot be deemed "incidental". We note in this context that C sugar represents between 11 and 21 per cent of the European Communities' total quota production, and that between 1997 and 2002, exports ranged between 1.3 and 3.3 million tonnes. As we have already noted, C sugar is being sold on the world market for prices that do not "even remotely" cover its average total cost of production.

A.1.20.13 *EC – Export Subsidies on Sugar*, paras. 287–288
(WT/DS265/AB/R, WT/DS266/AB/R, WT/DS283/AB/R)

The European Communities argues that, even if the Appellate Body were to conclude that "cross-subsidization" may constitute a "payment" within the meaning of Article 9.1(c), the Panel's finding is "seriously flawed". The European Communities contends that, in ascertaining the existence of "payments", the Panel erred in using as a benchmark the average total cost of production of *all* sugar. According to the European Communities, the Panel should have used, instead, the average total cost of producing *C sugar*, because the beet used in the production of C sugar is purchased at prices that are "generally lower" than the minimum prices for A and B beet.

The average total cost of production of sugar includes the cost of all economic resources used in sugar production, which means the cost of all economic resources invested in beet production, transport, and processing of beet into sugar, which is only notionally classified into A, B, and C sugar. It is for this reason that the Panel emphasized that "[s]ugar is sugar whether or not produced under an EC created designation of A, B or C sugar." The Panel further emphasized that "A, B or C sugar are part of the same line of production" and that "[t]here is no independent production of C sugar." It follows, in our view, that the average total cost of production of C sugar must be the same as the average total cost of production of all sugar. The European Communities' argument is flawed because the price of C beet does not determine the average total cost of production of C sugar. For these reasons, we do not agree with the European Communities that the Panel's use of the average total cost of production of *all* sugar as a benchmark for ascertaining the existence of payments was flawed in the particular circumstances of this case.

A.1.21 Article 9.1(c) – Industry-wide vs. Individual standard

A.1.21.1 *Canada – Dairy (Article 21.5 – New Zealand and US II)*, paras. 96–97 (WT/DS103/AB/RW2, WT/DS113/AB/RW2)

We believe that the standard for determining the existence of "payments", under Article 9.1(c), should reflect the fact that the obligation at issue is an international obligation imposed on Canada. The question is not whether one or more individual milk producers, efficient or not, are selling CEM at a price above or below their individual costs of production. The issue is whether Canada, on a national basis, has respected its WTO obligations and, in particular, its commitment levels. It, therefore, seems to us that the benchmark should be a single, industry-wide cost of production figure, rather than an indefinite number of cost of production figures for each individual producer. The industry-wide figure enables cost of production data for producers, as a whole, to be aggregated into a single, national standard that can be used to assess Canada's compliance with its international obligations.

By contrast, if the benchmark were to operate at the level of each individual producer, there would be a proliferation of standards, requiring individual-level inquiry and application of Article 9.1(c), as if the obligations under the *Agreement on Agriculture* involved rights and obligations of individual producers, rather than WTO Members.

A.1.22 Article 9.1(c) – "imputed" costs

A.1.22.1 *Canada – Dairy (Article 21.5 – New Zealand and US II)*, para. 102 (WT/DS103/AB/RW2, WT/DS113/AB/RW2)

. . . the purpose of the COP standard is precisely to determine whether supplies of CEM involve payments-in-kind that are made in a form other than money. If the COP standard were confined solely to cash costs, as Canada argues, this would overlook the possibility of "payments" being made in the form of non-cash resources invested in the production of milk. Thus, the COP standard must cover all of the economic resources invested in the production of milk and which may be transferred, irrespective of whether the resources involve an actual cash cost.

A.1.22.2 *Canada – Dairy (Article 21.5 – New Zealand and US II)*, para. 103 (WT/DS103/AB/RW2, WT/DS113/AB/RW2)

We are satisfied that any labour or management services provided by the farmer's family to the dairy enterprise are relevant economic resources invested in the production of milk and must be included in the COP standard. For the dairy farmer, and his or her family, the investment of services in the dairy enterprise has an economic cost, as those services cannot be put to an alternative remunerative use. . . .

Moreover, we believe that remuneration of family labour and management services is not part of the profits of the dairy farm. Rather, profits are the proceeds remaining after all costs, including such salary costs, have been accounted for.

A.1.22.3 *Canada – Dairy (Article 21.5 – New Zealand and US II)*, para. 104 (WT/DS103/AB/RW2, WT/DS113/AB/RW2)

The same is also true of any equity the owner invests in the dairy enterprise. The allocation of such capital is, clearly, an investment of economic resources and carries an economic opportunity cost to the owner because the capital cannot simultaneously be invested elsewhere. Again, the profits of the dairy enterprise are the proceeds after all costs, including the cost of equity, have been accounted for.

A.1.22.4 *Canada – Dairy (Article 21.5 – New Zealand and US II)*, paras. 107–108 (WT/DS103/AB/RW2, WT/DS113/AB/RW2)

Although it is clear that the COP standard includes all economic costs, even if they are non-cash costs, we acknowledge that a specific value cannot be as readily ascribed to non-cash costs as it can to cash costs....

In some situations, it may be appropriate for a panel to value non-monetary costs using a methodology set forth in a Member's Generally Accepted Accounting Principles ("GAAP"). In that respect, we observe that Canada did not contest the amounts the Canadian Dairy Commission (the "CDC") ascribed to depreciation using the rules in Canadian GAAP. However, although GAAP provide an objective valuation methodology for some non-monetary costs, they may not address all such costs. If GAAP rules do not provide an appropriate basis for valuing a particular cost, a panel should attempt to determine a value for relevant non-monetary costs using an objective methodology that is reasonable in the circumstances. Clearly, a panel must base itself on the evidence before it, applying the applicable rules on burden of proof.

A.1.23 Article 9.1(c) – Selling and quota costs

A.1.23.1 *Canada – Dairy (Article 21.5 – New Zealand and US II)*, paras. 113–114 (WT/DS103/AB/RW2, WT/DS113/AB/RW2)

We recall that the COP standard represents the producer's investment of economic resources in milk and, hence, in these proceedings, the proper value of the milk to the producer. In our view, costs incurred by the producer in selling milk are as much a part of the economic resources the producer invests in the milk as are farm-based production costs. Indeed, the costs incurred to make sales are a vital part of the process by which the producer earns revenues through producing milk....

In addition, we can see no reason to exclude the cost of quota from the COP standard. On the contrary, to the extent that the acquisition or retention of quota involves economic costs for the dairy producer, these costs should be reflected in the COP standard. In that respect, we are not persuaded by Canada that the cost of quota should be excluded from the COP standard because it relates solely to the domestic market. In the first Article 21.5 proceedings, we held that the COP standard must be determined for "all milk, whether destined for domestic or export markets". Thus, in principle, the costs of quota form part of the COP standard. . . .

A.1.24 Article 9.1(c) – "governmental action"

A.1.24.1 *Canada – Dairy (Article 21.5 – New Zealand and US)*, paras. 112–113 (WT/DS103/AB/RW, WT/DS113/AB/RW)

Although the phrase "financed by virtue of governmental action" must be understood as a whole, it is useful to consider separately the meaning of the different parts of this phrase. Taking the words "governmental action" first, we observe that the text of Article 9.1(c) does not place any qualifications on the types of "governmental action" which may be relevant under Article 9.1(c). In the original proceedings, we stated that "[t]he essence of 'government' is. . . that it enjoys the effective power to 'regulate', 'control' or 'supervise' individuals, or otherwise 'restrain' their conduct, through the exercise of lawful authority." In our opinion the word "action" embraces the full-range of these activities, including governmental action regulating the supply and price of milk in the domestic market.

Mere governmental action is not, however, sufficient for a finding that there is an export subsidy under Article 9.1(c). The words "by virtue of" indicate that there must be a demonstrable link between the *governmental action* at issue and the *financing* of the payments, whereby the payments are, in some way, financed as a result of, or as a consequence of, the governmental action. In our view, the link between governmental action and the financing of payments will be more difficult to establish, as an evidentiary matter, when the payment is in the form of a payment-in-kind rather than in monetary form, and all the more so when the payment-in-kind is made, not by the government, but by an independent economic operator. In any event, it will not be sufficient simply to demonstrate that a payment occurs as a consequence of governmental action because the word "financed", in Article 9.1(c), must also be given meaning.

A.1.24.2 *Canada – Dairy (Article 21.5 – New Zealand and US II)*, para. 87 (WT/DS103/AB/RW2, WT/DS113/AB/RW2)

. . . Article 9.1(c) of the *Agreement on Agriculture* describes an unusual form of subsidy in that "payments" can be made by private parties, and need not be made by government. Moreover, "payments" need not be funded from government resources, provided they are "financed by virtue of governmental action". Article 9.1(c), therefore, contemplates that "payments" may be made and funded by private parties, without the type of governmental involvement ordinarily associated with a subsidy. Furthermore, the notion of payments encompasses a diverse range of practices involving monetary transfers, or transfers-in-kind. We, therefore, determined that, in identifying whether "payments" are made, it is necessary to consider the particular features of the alleged "payments", by whom they are made, and in what circumstances. Thus, we found that the standard for determining the existence of "payments" under Article 9.1(c) must be identified after careful scrutiny of the factual and regulatory setting of the measure.

A.1.25 Article 9.1(c) – Governmental action vs. Private action

A.1.25.1 *Canada – Dairy (Article 21.5 – New Zealand and US II)*, para. 95 (WT/DS103/AB/RW2, WT/DS113/AB/RW2)

. . . under Article 9.1(c) of the *Agreement on Agriculture*, it is not solely the conduct of WTO Members that is relevant. We have noted that Article 9.1(c) describes an unusual form of export subsidy in that "payments" can be made and funded by private parties, and not just by government. The conduct of private parties, therefore, may play an important role in applying Article 9.1(c). Yet, irrespective of the role of private parties under Article 9.1(c), the obligations imposed in relation to Article 9.1(c) remain obligations imposed on Canada. It is Canada, and not private parties, which is responsible for ensuring that it respects its export subsidy commitments under the covered agreements. Thus, under the *Agreement on Agriculture*, any "export subsidies" provided through private party action in Canada are deemed to be provided by Canada, and count towards Canada's export subsidy commitment levels.

A.1.25.2 *Canada – Dairy (Article 21.5 – New Zealand and US II)*, para. 127 (WT/DS103/AB/RW2, WT/DS113/AB/RW2)

As regards "governmental action", we held in the first Article 21.5 proceedings that "the text of Article 9.1(c) does not place any qualifications on the types of 'governmental action' which may be relevant under Article 9.1(c)." Instead, the provision gives but one example of governmental action that is "included" in Article 9.1(c) – however, this example is merely illustrative. Accordingly, we stated that Article 9.1(c) "embraces the full-range" of activities by which governments "'regulate', 'control' or 'supervise' individuals". In particular, we said that governmental action "regulating the supply and price of milk in the domestic market" might be relevant "action" under Article 9.1(c). Moreover, the governmental action may be a single act or omission, or a series of acts or omissions.

A.1.25.3 *Canada – Dairy (Article 21.5 – New Zealand and US II)*, para. 128 and footnote 113 (WT/DS103/AB/RW2, WT/DS113/AB/RW2)

We observe that Article 9.1(c) does not require that payments be financed by virtue of government "mandate", or other "direction". Although the word "action" certainly covers situations where government mandates or directs that payments be made, it also covers other situations where no such compulsion is involved.[113]

[113] Article 9.1(c) of the *Agreement on Agriculture* may be contrasted with Article 9.1(e) of the *Agreement on Agriculture*, as well as with Article 1.1(a)(1)(iv) of the *SCM Agreement*, and items (c), (d), (j), and (k) of the Illustrative List of Export Subsidies (the "Illustrative List") of the *SCM Agreement*. In these provisions, some kind of government mandate, direction, or control is an element of a subsidy provided through a third party.

A.1.25.4 *Canada – Dairy (Article 21.5 – New Zealand and US II)*, para. 152
(WT/DS103/AB/RW2, WT/DS113/AB/RW2)

. . . Canada may act inconsistently with [its] commitments [under the *Agreement on Agriculture*] . . . even if some producers never make payments financed by virtue of governmental action.

A.1.26 Article 9.1(c) – "by virtue of"

A.1.26.1 *Canada – Dairy*, para. 119
(WT/DS103/AB/R, WT/DS113/AB/R, WT/DS103/AB/R/Corr.1, WT/DS113/AB/R/Corr.1)

In assessing whether the Panel erred in finding that the "payments" made under Special Classes 5(d) and 5(e) are "financed *by virtue of* governmental action", it is appropriate to look to the "governmental" involvement as a whole and not just to the role of the provincial milk marketing boards. The functioning of the system depends on a complex regulatory web involving the CDC and the CMSMC, acting together with the provincial milk marketing boards. It is, therefore, the "action" of all these bodies together which must be examined.

A.1.26.2 *Canada – Dairy*, para. 120
(WT/DS103/AB/R, WT/DS113/AB/R, WT/DS103/AB/R/Corr.1, WT/DS113/AB/R/Corr.1)

While the "cost of selling milk at a reduced price for export is not borne by the government", "governmental action" is, in our view, indispensable to the transfer of resources that takes place as a result of the operation of Special Classes 5(d) and 5(e). The factors relied upon by the Panel, which we have summarized above, demonstrate that at *every* stage in the supply of milk under Special Classes 5(d) and 5(e), from the determination of the volume and the authorization of the purchase of milk for processing for export, to the calculation of the price of the milk to the processors and the return to the producers, "governmental action" is not simply involved; it is, in fact, indispensable to enable the supply of milk to processors for export, and hence the transfer of resources, to take place. In the regulatory framework, "government agencies" stand so completely between the producers of the milk and the processors or the exporters that we have no doubt that the transfer of resources takes place "by virtue of governmental action".

A.1.26.3 *Canada – Dairy (Article 21.5 – New Zealand and US II)*, paras. 130–131
(WT/DS103/AB/RW2, WT/DS113/AB/RW2)

The words "by virtue of", therefore, express the relationship between "governmental action" and the "financing" of payments for the purpose of Article 9.1(c). The essence of that relationship is the "nexus" or "link" between "action" and "financing".

Thus, although Article 9.1(c) extends, in principle, to any "governmental action", not every governmental action will have the requisite nexus to the financing of payments. . . .

A.1.26.4 *Canada – Dairy (Article 21.5 – New Zealand and US II)*, para. 134 (WT/DS103/AB/RW2, WT/DS113/AB/RW2)

These general remarks illustrate well that "[i]t is extremely difficult . . . to define in the abstract the precise character of the required link between the governmental action and the financing of the payments, particularly where payments-in-kind are at issue." In each case, the alleged link must be examined taking account of the particular character of the governmental action at issue and its relationship to the payments made.

A.1.26.5 *Canada – Dairy (Article 21.5 – New Zealand and US II)*, para. 144 (WT/DS103/AB/RW2, WT/DS113/AB/RW2)

. . . We have agreed with the Panel that a significant percentage of producers are likely to finance sales of CEM at below the costs of production as a result of participation in the domestic market. Canadian "governmental action" controls virtually every aspect of domestic milk supply and management. In particular, government agencies fix the price of domestic milk that renders it highly remunerative to producers. Government action also controls the supply of domestic milk through quota, thereby protecting the administered price. The imposition by government of financial penalties on processors that divert CEM into the domestic market is another element of governmental control over the supply of milk. Further, the degree of government control over the domestic market is emphasized by the fact that government pools, allocates, and distributes revenues to producers from all domestic sales. Finally, governmental action also protects the domestic market from import competition through tariffs.

A.1.26.6 *Canada – Dairy (Article 21.5 – New Zealand and US II)*, para. 145 (WT/DS103/AB/RW2, WT/DS113/AB/RW2)

In our view, the effect of these different governmental actions is to secure a highly remunerative price for sales of domestic milk by producers. In turn, it is due to this price that a significant proportion of producers covers their fixed costs in the domestic market and, as a result, has the resources profitably to sell export milk at prices that are below the costs of production.

A.1.26.7 *Canada – Dairy (Article 21.5 – New Zealand and US II)*, para. 146 (WT/DS103/AB/RW2, WT/DS113/AB/RW2)

Accordingly, we agree with the Panel that "governmental action" in the domestic market plays a critical part in the "financing" of payments made by a significant percentage of producers on the sale of CEM. As such, we agree with the Panel that payments made through the supply of CEM at below the COP standard are financed by virtue of this governmental action. . . .

A.1.26.8 *Canada – Dairy (Article 21.5 – New Zealand and US II)*, para. 147 (WT/DS103/AB/RW2, WT/DS113/AB/RW2)

We do not agree with Canada that the circumstances indicate that the Canadian government has merely created a regulatory framework whereby it has enabled producers to sell CEM at prices that are below the costs of production. Certainly, producers decide for themselves whether and when to sell CEM. However, governmental action in the domestic market goes further than simply creating a regulatory environment in which producers choose to make export payments using their own resources. Rather, as we have said, Canadian governmental action is instrumental in providing a significant percentage of producers with the resources that enable them to sell CEM at below the costs of production.

A.1.26.9 *EC – Export Subsidies on Sugar*, para. 237 (WT/DS265/AB/R, WT/DS266/AB/R, WT/DS283/AB/R)

With respect to the words "by virtue of", the Appellate Body has previously held that there must be a "nexus" or "demonstrable link" between the governmental action at issue and the financing of payments. The Appellate Body clarified that not every governmental action will have the requisite "nexus" to the financing of payments. For instance, the Appellate Body held that the "demonstrable link" between "governmental action" and the "financing" of payments would not exist in a scenario in which "governmental action . . . establish[es] a regulatory framework merely *enabling* a third person freely to make and finance 'payments'." In this situation, the link between the governmental action and the financing of payments would be "too tenuous", such that the "payments" could not be regarded as "financed by virtue of governmental action" within the meaning of Article 9.1(c). Rather, according to the Appellate Body, there must be a "tighter nexus" between the mechanism or process by which the payments are financed (even if by a third person) and governmental action. In this respect, the Appellate Body clarified that, although governmental action is essential, Article 9.1(c) contemplates that "payments may be financed by virtue of governmental action even though significant aspects of the financing might not involve government." Thus, even if government does not fund the payments itself, it must play a sufficiently important part in the process by which a private party funds "payments", such that the requisite nexus exists between "governmental action" and the "financing". The alleged link must be examined on a case-by-case basis, taking account of the particular character of the governmental action at issue and its relationship to the payments made.

A.1.26.10 *EC – Export Subsidies on Sugar*, paras. 238–239 (WT/DS265/AB/R, WT/DS266/AB/R, WT/DS283/AB/R)

. . . in its finding that "payments" in the form of sales of C beet below its total cost of production are "financed by virtue of governmental action", the Panel relied on a number of aspects of the EC sugar regime. The Panel considered, *inter alia*, that: the EC sugar regime regulates prices of A and B beet and establishes a framework for the contractual relationships between beet growers and sugar producers with a view to ensuring a stable and adequate income for beet growers; C beet is invariably produced together with A and B beet in one single line of production; a significant percentage of beet growers are likely to finance sales of C beet below the total cost of production as a result of participation in the domestic market by making "highly remunerative" sales of A and B beet; the European Communities "controls virtually every aspect of domestic beet and sugar supply and management", including through financial penalties imposed on sugar producers that divert C sugar into the domestic market; the European Communities' Sugar Management Committee "overviews, supervises and protects the [European Communities'] domestic sugar through, *inter alia*, supply management"; the growing of C beet is not "incidental", but rather an "integral" part of the governmental regulation of the sugar market; and C sugar producers "*have incentives* to produce C sugar so as to maintain their share of the A and B quotas", while C beet growers "have an incentive to supply as much as is requested by C sugar producers with a view to receiving the high prices for A and B beet and their allocated amount of... C beet".

We agree with the Panel that, in the circumstances of the present case, all of these aspects of the EC sugar regime have a direct bearing on whether below-cost sales of C beet are financed by virtue of governmental action. As a result, we are unable to agree with the European Communities' first argument on appeal, namely, that the Panel applied a test under which an Article 9.1(c) subsidy was deemed to exist "simply because [governmental] action 'enabled' the beet growers to finance and make payments". Rather, we believe that the Panel relied on aspects of the EC sugar regime that go far beyond merely "enabling" or "permitting" beet growers to make payments to sugar producers....

A.1.26.11 *EC – Export Subsidies on Sugar*, para. 244

(WT/DS265/AB/R, WT/DS266/AB/R, WT/DS283/AB/R)

We now turn to the European Communities' argument that governmental action under the EC sugar regime is "less pervasive" than governmental action in *Canada – Dairy (Article 21.5 – New Zealand and the US II)*. We do not consider it inherently useful to compare the governmental action at issue and the governmental action in the context of a different dispute. The issue before us is not a comparison between two governmental regimes, but rather, whether "payments" under the EC sugar regime are "financed by virtue of governmental action". As the Appellate Body stated in *Canada – Dairy (Article 21.5 – New Zealand and the US)*, "the existence of... a demonstrable link [between governmental action and the financing of payments] must be identified *on a case-by-case basis, taking account of the particular governmental action at issue* and its effects on payments made by a third person." ...

A.1.27 Article 9.1(c) – "financed"

A.1.27.1 *Canada – Dairy (Article 21.5 – New Zealand and US)*, para. 114

(WT/DS103/AB/RW, WT/DS113/AB/RW)

The word "financed" might be given a rather specific meaning such that it would be confined to the financing of "payments" in monetary form or to the funding of "payments" from government resources. However, we have already recalled that "payments", under Article 9.1(c), include payments-in-kind, so the word "financed" needs to cover both the financing of monetary payments and payments-in-kind. In addition, Article 9.1(c) explicitly excludes a reading of the word "financed" whereby payments must be funded from government resources, as the provision states that payments can be financed by virtue of governmental action "whether or not a charge on the public account is involved". Thus, under Article 9.1(c), it is not necessary that the economic resources constituting the "payment" actually be paid by the government or even that they be paid from government resources. Accordingly, although the words "by virtue of" render governmental action essential, Article 9.1(c) contemplates that payments may be financed by virtue of governmental action even though significant aspects of the financing might not involve government.

A.1.27.2 *Canada – Dairy (Article 21.5 – New Zealand and US)*, para. 115 (WT/DS103/AB/RW, WT/DS113/AB/RW)

It is extremely difficult, however, to define in the abstract the precise character of the required link between the governmental action and the financing of the payments, particularly where payments-in-kind are at issue. Governments are constantly engaged in regulation of different kinds in pursuit of a variety of objectives. For instance, we can envisage that governmental action might establish a regulatory framework merely enabling a third person freely to make and finance "payments". In this situation, the link between the governmental action and the financing of the payments is too tenuous for the "payments" to be regarded as "*financed* by virtue of governmental action" (emphasis added) within the meaning of Article 9.1(c). Rather, there must be a tighter nexus between the mechanism or process by which the payments are *financed*, even if by a third person, and governmental action. In our opinion, the existence of such a demonstrable link must be identified on a case-by-case basis, taking account of the particular governmental action at issue and its effects on payments made by a third person.

A.1.27.3 *Canada – Dairy (Article 21.5 – New Zealand and US)*, para. 117 (WT/DS103/AB/RW, WT/DS113/AB/RW)

It is true that Canadian governmental action establishes a regulatory regime whereby some milk producers can make additional profits only if they choose to sell CEM. However, even though Canadian governmental action prevents further domestic sales, we do not see how producers are obliged or driven to produce additional milk for export sale. As we said above, each producer is free to decide whether or not to produce additional milk for sale as CEM. Furthermore, as we also said, the majority of Canadian milk producers choose not to sell CEM. For these reasons, we disagree with the Panel's characterization of the measure as "obliging producers, at least *de facto*, to sell outside-quota milk for export".

A.1.27.4 *Canada – Dairy (Article 21.5 – New Zealand and US II)*, paras. 132–133
(WT/DS103/AB/RW2, WT/DS113/AB/RW2)

. . . The word ["financing"] refers generally to the mechanism or process by which financial resources are provided to enable "payments" to be made. The word could, therefore, be read to mean that government itself must provide the resources for producers to make payments. However, Article 9.1(c) expressly precludes such a reading, as it states that "payments" need not involve "a charge on the public account". This is borne out by the fact that the text indicates that "financing" need only be "by virtue of governmental action", rather than "by government" itself. Article 9.1(c), therefore, contemplates that "payments may be financed by virtue of governmental action even though significant aspects of the financing might not involve government." Indeed, as we have said, payments may be made, and funded, by private parties.

The word "financing" must, nonetheless, be given meaning. Accordingly, even if government does not fund the payments itself, it must play a sufficiently important part in the process by which a private party funds "payments", such that the requisite nexus exists between "governmental action" and "financing".

A.1.27.5 *Canada – Dairy (Article 21.5 – New Zealand and US II)*, para. 139
(WT/DS103/AB/RW2, WT/DS113/AB/RW2)

Where fungible goods, such as milk, are produced using a single line of production, but sold in two different markets, the fixed costs of production are, in principle, shared between sales revenues from both markets. However, in the event that one of the two markets offers much higher revenues, a disproportionately large part, possibly even all, of the shared fixed costs may be borne by sales made in the more remunerative market.

A.1.27.6 *Canada – Dairy (Article 21.5 – New Zealand and US II)*, para. 140
(WT/DS103/AB/RW2, WT/DS113/AB/RW2)

Where sales in the more remunerative market bear more than their relative proportion of shared fixed costs, sales in the other market do not need to cover their relative proportion of the shared fixed costs in order to be profitable. Rather, these sales can be made profitably below the average total cost of production. If the more remunerative sales cover all fixed costs, sales in the other market can be made profitably at any price above marginal cost. In these situations, the higher revenue sales effectively "*finance*" a part of the lower revenue sales by funding the portion of the shared fixed costs attributable to the lower priced products.

A.1.27.7 *EC – Export Subsidies on Sugar*, para. 236
(WT/DS265/AB/R, WT/DS266/AB/R, WT/DS283/AB/R)

Addressing the word "financed", the Appellate Body held that this word generally refers to the "mechanism" or "process" by which financial resources are provided, such that payments are made. Article 9.1(c), by stating "whether or not a charge on the public account is involved", expressly provides that the *government itself* need *not* provide the resources for producers to make payments. Instead, payments may be made and funded by private parties.

A.1.28 Article 9.1(c) – Cross-subsidization

A.1.28.1 *Canada – Dairy (Article 21.5 – New Zealand and US II)*, para. 148
(WT/DS103/AB/RW2, WT/DS113/AB/RW2)

Canada also objects that this reasoning brings "cross-subsidization" under Article 9.1(c) of the *Agreement on Agriculture*. We have explained that the text of Article 9.1(c) applies to any "governmental action" which "finances" export "payments". The text does not exclude from the scope of the provision any particular governmental action, such as regulation of domestic markets, to the extent that this action may become an instrument for granting export subsidies. Nor does the text exclude any particular form of financing, such as "cross-subsidization". Moreover, the text focuses on the consequences of governmental action ("by virtue of which") and not the intent of government. Thus, the provision applies to governmental action that finances export payments, even if this result is not intended. As stated in our Report in the first Article 21.5 proceedings, this reading of Article 9.1(c) serves to preserve the legal "distinction between the domestic support and export subsidies disciplines of the *Agreement on Agriculture*". Subsidies may be granted in both the domestic and export markets, provided that the disciplines imposed by the Agreement on the levels of subsidization are respected. If governmental action in support of the domestic market could be applied to subsidize export sales, without respecting the commitments Members made to limit the level of export subsidies, the value of these commitments would be undermined. Article 9.1(c) addresses this possibility by bringing, in some circumstances, governmental action in the domestic market within the scope of the "export subsidies" disciplines of Article 3.3.

A.1.28.2 *EC – Export Subsidies on Sugar*, paras. 263–265
(WT/DS265/AB/R, WT/DS266/AB/R, WT/DS283/AB/R)

As we noted above, the European Communities submits, first, that a "payment" within the meaning of Article 9.1(c) requires, by definition, the presence of two distinct legal entities. We agree with the European Communities that a "payment", within the meaning of Article 9.1(c), certainly occurs when one entity transfers economic resources to another entity. . . .

This, however, does not imply that the term "payment" necessarily requires, in each and every case, the presence of two distinct entities. In other words, contrary to the European Communities' argument, we do not see, *a priori*, any reason why "payments", within the meaning of Article 9.1(c), cannot include, in the particular circumstances of this dispute, transfers of resources within one economic entity. The "payment" in this case is not merely a "purely *notional*" one but, rather, reflects a very concrete transfer of economic resources to C sugar production. In the specific dispute before us, C sugar is being sold on the world market by European

Communities' sugar producers/exporters at a price that does not "even remotely" cover its average total cost of production. In the light of the enormous difference between the price of C sugar and its average total cost of production, we do not see how the "payment" identified by the Panel was "purely notional".

The European Communities' approach is, in our view, too formalistic. To illustrate, one could envisage a scenario under which the producers of C sugar are legally distinct from the producers of A and B sugar. In this situation, the European Communities' approach could recognize that a "payment" under Article 9.1(c) could exist because there would be a transfer of economic resources between different parties. If, however, these same producers of A, B, and C sugar were integrated producers and organized as single legal entities, a payment under Article 9.1(c) would not exist, because the transfer would be merely "internal". We do not believe that the applicability of Article 9.1(c) should depend on how an economic entity is legally organized.

A.1.28.3 *EC – Export Subsidies on Sugar*, paras. 273–275
(WT/DS265/AB/R, WT/DS266/AB/R, WT/DS283/AB/R)

The European Communities argues that the Panel misinterpreted the requirement that a payment be "on the export" of an agricultural product, as contained in Article 9.1(c)....

...the Panel based its findings on the following reasoning:

> C sugar [can] only be sold for export. If not reclassified, C sugar "may not be disposed of in the Community's internal market and must be exported without further processing." Because of that legal requirement, advantages, payments or subsidies to C sugar, that must be exported, are subsidies "on the export" of that product.

We agree with the Panel. Under Article 13(1) of EC Regulation 1260/2001, C sugar "must be exported". It follows that payments in the form of "cross-subsidization" are, by definition, "payments" "on the export".

A.1.29 Article 9.1(d) – "costs of marketing"

A.1.29.1 *US – FSC*, paras. 130–131
(WT/DS108/AB/R)

The text of Article 9.1(d) lists "handling, upgrading and other processing costs, and the costs of international transport and freight" as examples of "costs of marketing". The text also states that "export promotion and advisory services" are covered by Article 9.1(d), provided that they are not "widely available". These are not examples of just *any* "cost of doing business" that "effectively reduce[s] the cost of marketing" products. Rather, they are specific types of costs that are incurred *as part of* and *during* the process of selling a product. They differ from general business costs, such as administrative overhead and debt financing costs, which are not specific to the process of putting a product on the market, and which are, therefore, related to the marketing of exports only in the broadest sense.

... Income tax liability under the FSC measure arises only when goods are actually sold for export, that is, *when they have been the subject of successful marketing*. Such liability arises *because* goods have, in fact, been sold, and not as *part of the process* of marketing them. Furthermore, at the time goods are sold, the costs associated with putting them on the market – costs such as handling, promotion and distribution costs – have already been incurred and the amount of these costs is not altered by the income tax, the amount of which is calculated by reference to the sale price of the goods. In our view, if income tax liability arising from export sales can be viewed as among the "costs of marketing exports", then so too can virtually any other cost incurred by a business engaged in exporting. . . .

A.1.29A Article 9.2 – Budgetary outlay and quantity commitment levels

A.1.29A.1 *EC – Export Subsidies on Sugar*, para. 194

(WT/DS265/AB/R, WT/DS266/AB/R, WT/DS283/AB/R)

We find contextual support for the above interpretation in Article 9.2(b)(iv) of the *Agreement on Agriculture*, which provides:

> (iv) the Member's budgetary outlays for export subsidies and the quantities benefiting from such subsidies, at the conclusion of the implementation period, are no greater than 64 per cent and 79 per cent of the 1986–1990 base period levels, respectively. For developing country Members these percentages shall be 76 and 86 per cent, respectively.

This provision prescribes the export subsidy commitment levels to be reached at the conclusion of the implementation period (and to be maintained thereafter), and those commitment levels are expressed in terms of both budgetary outlays and quantities. We do not see how a Member could comply with Article 9.2(b)(iv), or for that matter Article 9.2(a), without having specified its export subsidy commitments in terms of both budgetary outlays and quantities. We also consider it significant that both Article 9.2(b)(iii) and Article 9.2(b)(iv) use the expression "budgetary outlays for export subsidies and the quantities *benefiting from such subsidies*". (emphasis added) This shows the drafters' recognition of the need to address the budgetary outlays and quantities together.

A.1.29B Article 10 – General

A.1.29B.1 *US – Upland Cotton*, para. 616

(WT/DS267/AB/R)

We find it significant that paragraph 2 of Article 10 is included in an Article that is titled the "Prevention of Circumvention of Export Subsidy Commitments". As Brazil correctly points out, each paragraph in Article 10 pursues this aim. Article 10.1 provides that WTO Members shall not apply export subsidies not listed in Article 9.1 of the *Agreement on Agriculture* "in a manner which results in, or which threatens to lead to, circumvention of export subsidy commitments; nor shall non-commercial transactions be used to circumvent such commitments". Article 10.3 pursues the aim of preventing circumvention of export subsidy commitments by providing special rules on the reversal of burden of proof where a Member exports an agricultural product in quantities that exceed its reduction commitment level; in such a situation a WTO Member is treated as if it has granted WTO-*inconsistent* export subsidies for the excess quantities, unless the Member presents adequate evidence to "establish" the contrary. Article 10.4 provides disciplines to prevent WTO Members from circumventing their export subsidy commitments through food aid transactions. Similarly, Article 10.2 must be interpreted in a manner that is consistent with the aim of preventing circumvention of export subsidy commitments that pervades Article 10. Otherwise, it would not have been included in that provision.

A.1.30 Article 10.1 – "export subsidy commitments"

A.1.30.1 *US – FSC*, para. 144
(WT/DS108/AB/R)

The word "commitments" generally connotes "engagements" or "obligations". Thus, the term "export subsidy *commitments*" refers to commitments or obligations relating to export subsidies assumed by Members under provisions of the *Agreement on Agriculture*, in particular, under Articles 3, 8 and 9 of that Agreement.

A.1.31 Article 10.1 – "export subsidies" not listed in Article 9.1

A.1.31.1 *Canada – Dairy (Article 21.5 – New Zealand and US)*, para. 121
(WT/DS103/AB/RW, WT/DS113/AB/RW)

It is clear from the opening clause of Article 10.1 that this provision is residual in character to Article 9.1 of the *Agreement on Agriculture*. If a measure is an export subsidy listed in Article 9.1, it cannot simultaneously be an export subsidy under Article 10.1. In light of the facts available to us, we have found that we are unable to determine whether the measure at issue is an export subsidy listed in Article 9.1(c). However, it remains possible that the measure *is* such an export subsidy. Clearly, in that event, the opening clause of Article 10.1 means that the measure could not also be an export subsidy under Article 10.1. In these circumstances, where we are unable to determine the legal character of the measure under Article 9.1 of the *Agreement on Agriculture*, we are similarly unable to rule upon the legal character of the measure under Article 10.1 of that Agreement.

A.1.32 Article 10.1 – Actual circumvention

A.1.32.1 *US – FSC*, para. 148
(WT/DS108/AB/R)

... The verb "circumvent" means, *inter alia*, "find a way round, evade ...". Article 10.1 is designed to prevent Members from circumventing or "evading" their "export subsidy commitments". This may arise in many different ways....

A.1.32.1A *US – FSC*, para. 149
(WT/DS108/AB/R)

In determining whether the FSC measure in this case is "applied in a manner which... threatens to lead to circumvention of export subsidy commitments", it is important to consider the structure and other characteristics of that measure. The FSC measure creates, in itself, a *legal entitlement* for recipients to receive export subsidies, not listed in Article 9.1, with respect to agricultural products, both scheduled and unscheduled. As we understand it, that legal entitlement arises in the recipient when it complies with the statutory requirements and, at that point, the government of the United States must grant the FSC tax exemptions. There is, therefore, no discretionary element in the provision by the government of the FSC export subsidies. If the statutory eligibility requirements are met, then an FSC is entitled by law to the statutorily established tax exemption. Furthermore, there is no limitation on the amount of exempt foreign trade income that may be earned by an FSC. Therefore, the legal entitlement that the FSC measure establishes is unqualified as to the *amount* of export subsidies that may be claimed by FSCs. There is, in other words, no mechanism in the measure for stemming, or otherwise controlling, the flow of FSC subsidies that may be claimed with respect to any agricultural products. In this respect, the FSC measure is unlimited.

A.1.32.2 *US – FSC*, para. 150
(WT/DS108/AB/R)

With respect to *unscheduled* agricultural products, Members are *prohibited* under Article 3.3 from providing *any* export subsidies as listed in Article 9.1. Article 10.1 prevents the application of export subsidies which "*results in*, or which *threatens to lead to, circumvention*" of that prohibition. Members would certainly have "found a way round", a way to "evade", this prohibition if they could transfer, through tax exemptions, the very same economic resources that they are prohibited from providing in other forms under Articles 3.3 and 9.1....

A.1.32.3 *US – FSC*, para. 151
(WT/DS108/AB/R)

...Given that the nature of the "export subsidy commitment" differs as between scheduled and unscheduled products, we believe that what constitutes "circumvention" of those commitments, under Article 10.1, may also differ.

A.1.32.4 *US – FSC*, para. 152
(WT/DS108/AB/R)

...In our view, Members would have found "a way round", a way to "evade", their commitments under Articles 3.3 and 9.1, if they could transfer, through tax exemptions, the very same economic resources that they were, *at that time*, prohibited from providing through other methods under the first clause of Article 3.3 and under 9.1.

A.1.32.5 *US – Upland Cotton*, para. 626
(WT/DS267/AB/R)

. . . Export credit guarantees are subject to the export subsidy disciplines in the *Agreement on Agriculture* only to the extent that such measures include an export subsidy component. If no such export subsidy component exists, then the export credit guarantees are not subject to the Agreement's export subsidy disciplines. Moreover, even when export credit guarantees contain an export subsidy component, such an export credit guarantee would not be inconsistent with Article 10.1 of the *Agreement on Agriculture* unless the complaining party demonstrates that it is "applied in a manner which results in, or which threatens to lead to, circumvention of export subsidy commitments". Thus, under the *Agreement on Agriculture*, the complaining party must first demonstrate that an export credit guarantee program constitutes an export subsidy. If it succeeds, it must then demonstrate that such export credit guarantees are applied in a manner that results in, or threatens to lead to, circumvention of the responding party's export subsidy commitments within the meaning of Article 10.1 of the *Agreement on Agriculture*.

A.1.32.6 *US – Upland Cotton*, para. 692
(WT/DS267/AB/R)

We find nothing wrong in the Panel having relied on an admission by the United States relating to rice to conclude that the United States had failed to rebut Brazil's initial allegation of circumvention. This did not excuse the Panel, however, from specifically analyzing Brazil's claim in respect of the other products. Consequently, we find no basis to support the Panel's finding that "[i]t has not been established, however, that such actual circumvention has resulted in respect of the twelve other United States scheduled commodities".

A.1.32.7 *US – Upland Cotton*, para. 693
(WT/DS267/AB/R)

We must determine next whether there are sufficient uncontested facts in the record to permit us to complete the analysis with respect to the other commodities. In our view, there are not. First, the parties disagree about the time period covered by Brazil's claim. The United States asserts that Brazil's claim was limited to the period July 2001 to June 2002, while Brazil contends that its claim was not limited to that period. Second, as we noted previously, different time periods are used for the sets of data that have to be compared. The data regarding United States exports under the export credit guarantee programs are maintained on a fiscal year basis, which extends from 1 October to 30 September of the following year. The United States' export subsidy commitments are registered based on a year that extends from 1 July to 30 June of the following year. Both Brazil and the United States have sought to reconcile the data. In each case, Brazil and the United States assert that the data support their position. Given the differences between the participants in respect of the data that we would have to examine to determine whether the United States applied export credit guarantees in a manner that results in circumvention of its export subsidy commitments for pig meat and poultry meat, we do not believe there are sufficient undisputed facts in the record to enable us to complete the analysis.

A.1.32A Article 10.1 – Threat of circumvention

A.1.32A.1 *US – Upland Cotton*, para. 704
(WT/DS267/AB/R)

The Appellate Body has explained that "under Article 10.1, it is not necessary to demonstrate *actual* 'circumvention' of 'export subsidy commitments' ". It suffices that "export subsidies" are "applied in a manner which . . . threatens to lead to circumvention of export subsidy commitments". We note that the ordinary meaning of the term "threaten" includes "[c]onstitute a threat to", "be likely to injure" or "be a source of harm or danger". Article 10.1 is concerned not with injury, but rather with "circumvention". Accordingly, based on its ordinary meaning, the phrase "threaten[] to lead to . . . circumvention" would imply that the export subsidies are applied in a manner that is "likely to" lead to circumvention of a WTO Member's export subsidy commitments. Furthermore, we observe that the ordinary meaning of the term "threaten" refers to a *likelihood* of something happening; the ordinary meaning of "threaten" does not connote a sense of certainty.

A.1.32A.2 *US – Upland Cotton*, para. 705
(WT/DS267/AB/R)

The concept of "threat" has been discussed by the Appellate Body within the context of the *Agreement on Safeguards* and the *Anti-Dumping Agreement*. It has explained that "threat" refers to something that "has *not* yet occurred, but remains a future event whose actual materialization cannot, in fact, be assured with certainty". In *US – Line Pipe*, the Appellate Body stated that there is a continuum that ascends from a "threat of serious injury" up to the "serious injury" itself. We emphasize that the Appellate Body's discussion of the concept of "threat" in previous appeals related to the interpretation of other covered agreements that contain obligations relating to injury that differ from those relating to circumvention of export subsidy reduction commitments contained in Article 10.1 of the *Agreement on Agriculture*. Our interpretation of "threat" in Article 10.1 of the *Agreement on Agriculture* is consistent with the Appellate Body's interpretation of the term "threat" in these other contexts.

A.1.32A.3 *US – Upland Cotton*, para. 706
(WT/DS267/AB/R)

The Panel explained that, in its view, "threat" of circumvention under Article 10.1 requires that there be "an unconditional legal entitlement". We see no basis for this requirement in Article 10.1. The Panel also stated that "[i]n order to pose a 'threat' within the meaning of Article 10.1 of the *Agreement on Agriculture*, [it did] not believe that it is sufficient that an export credit guarantee programme might possibly, or theoretically, be used in a manner which threatens to lead to circumvention of export subsidy commitments". In both of these statements, the Panel seems to conflate the phrase "threaten to lead to . . . circumvention" with certainty that the circumvention will happen. We find it difficult, moreover, to reconcile the Panel's interpretation with the ordinary meaning of the term "threaten", which, as we indicated earlier, connotes that something is "likely" to happen. We also find it difficult to reconcile these statements of the Panel with its own view that it did "not believe that the 'mandatory/discretionary' distinction is the sole legally determinative one for our examination of whether or not 'threat' of circumvention of export subsidy commitments within the meaning of Article 10.1 of the *Agreement on Agriculture* has been proven to the required standard".

A.1.32A.4 *US – Upland Cotton*, para. 707

(WT/DS267/AB/R)

Nor are we prepared to accept Brazil's suggestion that the concept of "threat" in Article 10.1 should be read in a manner that requires WTO Members to take "anticipatory or precautionary action". The obligation not to apply export subsidies in a manner that "threatens to lead to" circumvention of their export subsidy commitments does not extend that far. There is no basis in Article 10.1 for requiring WTO Members to take affirmative, precautionary steps to ensure that circumvention of their export subsidy reduction commitments does not occur.

A.1.32A.5 *US – Upland Cotton*, para. 708

(WT/DS267/AB/R)

In concluding as it did, the Panel appears to have relied on the Appellate Body Report in *US – FSC* for guidance. In our view, however, the Panel misapplies that analysis. We recall that, in *US – FSC*, the Appellate Body underscored the importance of considering "the structure and other characteristics of [the] measure" when examining whether the specific measure at issue is "applied in a manner which . . . threatens to lead to circumvention of export subsidy commitments". The Appellate Body then went on to note that the specific measure at issue in that dispute created "a *legal entitlement* for recipients to receive export subsidies, not listed in Article 9.1, with respect to agricultural products, both scheduled and unscheduled". This meant that there was "no discretionary element in the provision by the government of the FSC export subsidies". Furthermore, the Appellate Body noted that the "legal entitlement that the FSC measure establishes is unqualified as to the *amount* of export subsidies that may be claimed". This meant that the measure was "unlimited" because there was "no mechanism in the measure for stemming, or otherwise controlling the flow of . . . subsidies that may be claimed with respect to any agricultural products".

A.1.32A.6 *US – Upland Cotton*, paras. 709–710

(WT/DS267/AB/R)

A proper reading of the Appellate Body's statement in *US – FSC*, however, reveals that it did not intend to provide an exhaustive interpretation of threat of circumvention under Article 10.1 of the *Agreement on Agriculture*. In noting that the measure at issue in that dispute created a "legal entitlement" and had no "discretionary element", the Appellate Body was merely describing characteristics of the measure at issue in that case that it found relevant for its analysis of "threat". In other words, the Appellate Body did not foreclose, in *US – FSC*, the possibility that a measure that does not create a "legal entitlement" or that has a "discretionary element" could be found to "threaten[] to lead to circumvention" under Article 10.1 of the *Agreement on Agriculture*.

We therefore modify the Panel's interpretation . . . of the phrase "threatens to lead to . . . circumvention" in Article 10.1 of the *Agreement on Agriculture* to the extent that the Panel's interpretation requires "an unconditional legal entitlement" to receive the relevant export subsidies as a condition for a finding of threat of circumvention.

A.1.32A.7 *US – Upland Cotton*, para. 713
(WT/DS267/AB/R)

We are not persuaded that the arguments put forward by Brazil establish that the United States' export credit guarantee programs are applied in a manner that threatens to lead to circumvention of the United States' export subsidy commitments in respect of scheduled products other than rice and unscheduled products not supported under the programs. In our view, the fact alone that exports of certain products are eligible for export credit guarantees is not sufficient to establish a threat of circumvention. This is particularly the case where there is no evidence in the record that exports of such products have been "supported" by export credit guarantees in the past. As we stated earlier, Article 10.1 of the *Agreement on Agriculture* does not require WTO Members to take affirmative, precautionary steps to ensure that circumvention of their export subsidy reduction commitments never happens. Nor is it sufficient for Brazil to have alleged that the United States has provided export credit guarantees to exports of *other* unscheduled products or to exports of scheduled products in excess of its export subsidy reduction commitments. Therefore, we agree with the Panel that Brazil has not established that the United States applies its export credit guarantee programs to scheduled agricultural products other than rice and other unscheduled agricultural products (not "supported" under the programs) "in a manner . . . which threatens to lead to . . . circumvention" of the United States' export subsidy commitments.

A.1.32A.8 *US – Upland Cotton*, para. 717
(WT/DS267/AB/R)

We believe the Panel was within its discretion in declining to examine whether scheduled products other than rice and unscheduled products supported by the programs are applied in a manner that "threatens to lead to" circumvention. The Panel had already found that the United States acted inconsistently with Article 10.1 of the *Agreement on Agriculture* because it applied its export credit guarantee program in a manner that "results in" (actual) circumvention of its export subsidy commitments for these products. We do not see why the Panel had to examine also whether the United States acted inconsistently with the *same* provision in respect of the *same* products, but on the basis of there being a *threat* of circumvention, rather than *actual* circumvention.

A.1.32B Article 10.1 – "non-commercial transactions"

A.1.32B.1 *US – Upland Cotton*, para. 619
(WT/DS267/AB/R)

... International food aid is covered by the second clause of Article 10.1 to the extent that it is a "non-commercial transaction". Article 10.4 provides specific disciplines that may be relied on to determine whether international food aid is being "used to circumvent" a WTO Member's export subsidy commitments.... WTO Members are free to grant as much food aid as they wish, provided that they do so consistently with Articles 10.1 and 10.4. Thus, Article 10.4 does not support the United States' reading of Article 10.2.

A.1.33 Article 10.1 – Relationship with Article 9.1

A.1.33.1 *Canada – Dairy (Article 21.5 – New Zealand and US II)*, para. 158
(WT/DS103/AB/RW2, WT/DS113/AB/RW2)

As we have concluded that the CEM scheme involves export subsidies under Article 9.1(c) of the *Agreement on Agriculture*, those subsidies cannot, by definition, simultaneously be export subsidies under Article 10.1.... In these circumstances, both the Panel's reasoning and its finding under Article 10.1 of the *Agreement on Agriculture* are moot and of no legal effect....

A.1.33.2 *US – Upland Cotton*, para. 615
(WT/DS267/AB/R)

Although Article 10.2 commits WTO Members to work toward the development of internationally agreed disciplines on export credit guarantees, export credits and insurance programs, it is in Article 10.1 that we find the disciplines that currently apply to export subsidies not listed in Article 9.1. A plain reading of Article 10.1 indicates that the only export subsidies that are excluded from its scope are those "listed in paragraph 1 of Article 9".... Thus, to the extent that an export credit guarantee meets the definition of an "export subsidy" under the *Agreement on Agriculture*, it would be covered by Article 10.1. Article 1(e) of the *Agreement on Agriculture* defines "export subsidies" as "subsidies contingent upon export performance, *including* the export subsidies listed in Article 9 of this Agreement". (emphasis added) The use of the word "including" suggests that the term "export subsidies" should be interpreted broadly and that the list of export subsidies in Article 9 is not exhaustive. Even though an export credit guarantee may not necessarily include a subsidy component, there is nothing inherent about export credit guarantees that precludes such measures from falling within the definition of a subsidy. An export credit guarantee that meets the definition of an export subsidy would be covered by Article 10.1 of the *Agreement on Agriculture* because it is not an export subsidy listed in Article 9.1 of that Agreement.

A.1.33A Article 10.2 – Export Credit Guarantees

A.1.33A.1 *US – Upland Cotton*, para. 607
(WT/DS267/AB/R)

Article 10.2 refers expressly to export credit guarantee programs, along with export credits and insurance programs. Under Article 10.2, WTO Members have taken on two distinct commitments in respect of these three types of measures: (i) to work toward the development of internationally agreed disciplines to govern their provision; and (ii) after agreement on such disciplines, to provide them only in conformity therewith. The text includes no temporal indication with respect to the first commitment. There is no deadline for beginning or ending the negotiations. The second commitment does have a temporal connotation, in the sense that it is triggered only "after agreement on such disciplines". This means that "after" international disciplines have been agreed upon, Members shall provide export credit guarantees, export credits and insurance programs only in conformity with those agreed disciplines. There is no dispute between the parties that, to date, no disciplines have been agreed internationally pursuant to Article 10.2.

A.1.33A.2 *US – Upland Cotton*, paras. 608–609
(WT/DS267/AB/R)

Article 10.2 does not, however, expressly define the disciplines that *currently* apply to export credits, export credit guarantees and insurance programs under the *Agreement on Agriculture*. . . .

We agree with the Panel's view that Article 10.2 does not expressly exclude export credit guarantees from the export subsidy disciplines in Article 10.1 of the *Agreement on Agriculture*. As the Panel observes, were such an exemption intended, it could have been easily achieved by, for example, inserting the words "[n]otwithstanding the provisions of Article 10.1", or other similar language at the beginning of Article 10.2. Article 10.2 does not include express language suggesting that it is intended as an exception, nor does it expressly state that the application of any export subsidy disciplines to export credits or export credit guarantees is "deferred", as the United States suggests. Given that the drafters were aware that subsidized export credit guarantees, export credits and insurance programs could fall within the export subsidy disciplines in the *Agreement on Agriculture* and the *SCM Agreement*, it would be expected that an exception would have been clearly provided had this been the drafters' intention.

A.1.33A.3 *US – Upland Cotton*, para. 615
(WT/DS267/AB/R)

Although Article 10.2 commits WTO Members to work toward the development of internationally agreed disciplines on export credit guarantees, export credits and insurance programs, it is in Article 10.1 that we find the disciplines that currently apply to export subsidies not listed in Article 9.1. A plain reading of Article 10.1 indicates that the only export subsidies that are excluded from its scope are those "listed in paragraph 1 of Article 9".... Thus, to the extent that an export credit guarantee meets the definition of an "export subsidy" under the *Agreement on Agriculture*, it would be covered by Article 10.1. Article 1(e) of the *Agreement on Agriculture* defines "export subsidies" as "subsidies contingent upon export performance, *including* the export subsidies listed in Article 9 of this Agreement". (emphasis added) The use of the word "including" suggests that the term "export subsidies" should be interpreted broadly and that the list of export subsidies in Article 9 is not exhaustive. Even though an export credit guarantee may not necessarily include a subsidy component, there is nothing inherent about export credit guarantees that precludes such measures from falling within the definition of a subsidy. An export credit guarantee that meets the definition of an export subsidy would be covered by Article 10.1 of the *Agreement on Agriculture* because it is not an export subsidy listed in Article 9.1 of that Agreement.

A.1.33A.4 *US – Upland Cotton*, para. 616
(WT/DS267/AB/R)

... Similarly, Article 10.2 must be interpreted in a manner that is consistent with the aim of preventing circumvention of export subsidy commitments that pervades Article 10. Otherwise, it would not have been included in that provision.

A.1.33A.5 *US – Upland Cotton*, para. 617
(WT/DS267/AB/R)

The United States submits that Article 10.2 contributes to the prevention of circumvention because it commits WTO Members to work toward the development of internationally agreed disciplines and to provide export credit guarantees, export credits and insurance programs only in conformity with these disciplines once an agreement has been reached. We are not persuaded by this argument. The necessary implication of the United States' interpretation of Article 10.2 is that, until WTO Members reach an agreement on international disciplines, export credit guarantees, export credits and insurance programs are subject to no disciplines *at all*. In other words, under the United States' interpretation, WTO Members are free to "circumvent" their export subsidy commitments through the use of export credit guarantees, export credits and insurance programs until internationally agreed disciplines are developed, whenever that may be. We find it difficult to believe that the negotiators would not have been aware of and did not seek to address the potential that subsidized export credit guarantees, export credits and insurance programs could be used to circumvent a WTO Member's export subsidy reduction commitments. Indeed, such an interpretation would *undermine* the objective of preventing circumvention of export subsidy commitments, which is central to the *Agreement on Agriculture*.

A.1.33A.6 *US – Upland Cotton*, para. 619
(WT/DS267/AB/R)

. . . Article 10.4 provides specific disciplines that may be relied on to determine whether international food aid is being "used to circumvent" a WTO Member's export subsidy commitments. There is no contradiction in the Panel's approach to Article 10.2 and its approach to Article 10.4. The measures in Article 10.2 and the transactions in Article 10.4 are both covered within the scope of Article 10.1. . . .

A.1.33A.7 *US – Upland Cotton*, para. 623
(WT/DS267/AB/R)

We agree with the Panel that the meaning of Article 10.2 is clear from the provision's text, in its context and in the light of the object and purpose of the *Agreement on Agriculture*, consistent with Article 31 of the *Vienna Convention*. The Panel did not think it necessary to resort to negotiating history for purposes of its interpretation of Article 10.2. Even if the negotiating history were relevant for our inquiry, we do not find that it supports the United States' position. This is because it does not indicate that the negotiators did not intend to discipline export credit guarantees, export credits and insurance programs *at all*. To the contrary, it shows that negotiators were aware of the need to impose disciplines on export credit guarantees, given their potential as a mechanism for subsidization and for circumvention of the export subsidy commitments under Article 9. Although the negotiating history reveals that the negotiators struggled with this issue, it does not indicate that the disagreement among them related to whether export credit guarantees, export credits and insurance programs were to be disciplined at all. In our view, the negotiating history suggests that the disagreement between the negotiators related to which kinds of specific disciplines were to apply to such measures. The fact that negotiators felt that internationally agreed disciplines were necessary for these three measures also suggests that the disciplines that currently exist in the *Agreement on Agriculture* must apply pending new disciplines because, otherwise, it would mean that subsidized export credit guarantees, export credits, and insurance programs could currently be extended without any limit or consequence.

A.1.33A.8 *US – Upland Cotton*, para. 625
(WT/DS267/AB/R)

We do not agree with the United States' submission in this regard. There could have been several reasons why Members chose not to include export credit guarantees, export credits and insurance programs under Article 9.1 of the *Agreement on*

Agriculture. One reason, for instance, may be that they considered that their export credit guarantee, export credit or insurance programs did not include a subsidy component, so that there was no need to subject them to export subsidy reduction commitments. There could have been other reasons. Thus, the fact that export credit guarantees, export credits and insurance programs were not included in Article 9.1 does not support the United States' interpretation of Article 10.2. We also observe that whether WTO Members with export credit guarantee programs have reported them in their export subsidy notifications is not determinative for purposes of our inquiry into the meaning of Article 10.2. In any event, the United States and Brazil disagree about whether such programs are subject to notification requirements.

A.1.33A.9 *US – Upland Cotton*, para. 626
(WT/DS267/AB/R)

Accordingly, we do not believe that Article 10.2 of the *Agreement on Agriculture* exempts export credit guarantees, export credits and insurance programs from the export subsidy disciplines in the *Agreement on Agriculture*. This does not mean that export credit guarantees, export credits and insurance programs will necessarily constitute export subsidies for purposes of the *Agreement on Agriculture*. Export credit guarantees are subject to the export subsidy disciplines in the *Agreement on Agriculture* only to the extent that such measures include an export subsidy component. If no such export subsidy component exists, then the export credit guarantees are not subject to the Agreement's export subsidy disciplines. Moreover, even when export credit guarantees contain an export subsidy component, such an export credit guarantee would not be inconsistent with Article 10.1 of the *Agreement on Agriculture* unless the complaining party demonstrates that it is "applied in a manner which results in, or which threatens to lead to, circumvention of export subsidy commitments". Thus, under the *Agreement on Agriculture*, the complaining party must first demonstrate that an export credit guarantee program constitutes an export subsidy. If it succeeds, it must then demonstrate that such export credit guarantees are applied in a manner that results in, or threatens to lead to, circumvention of the responding party's export subsidy commitments within the meaning of Article 10.1 of the *Agreement on Agriculture*.

A.1.33A.10 *US – Upland Cotton*, para. 628
(WT/DS267/AB/R)

Before proceeding further, we refer to the order followed by the Panel in its analysis of Brazil's claims against the United States' export credit guarantee programs. We do not find that the Panel's order of analysis was wrong or that it constituted legal error. Nor has the United States made such a claim on appeal. Nevertheless, we are struck by the fact that the Panel addressed Article 10.2 only at the end of its analysis, especially given that this provision constituted the core of the United States' defence that the disciplines of the *Agreement on Agriculture* currently do not apply to export credit guarantees at all.

A.1.34 Article 10.3 – Reversal of Burden of Proof. *See also* Burden of Proof, reversal (B.3.4)

A.1.34.1 *Canada – Dairy (Article 21.5 – New Zealand and US)*, para. 98 (WT/DS103/AB/RW, WT/DS113/AB/RW)

As we have reversed the Panel's findings regarding the standard for determining the existence of "payments" and have, instead, identified the appropriate standard for these proceedings, namely, the average total cost of production, we now consider whether we can resolve this aspect of the dispute by completing the analysis. The Panel found that, in these proceedings, Article 10.3 of the *Agreement on Agriculture* reverses the burden of proof so that Canada must establish "that no export subsidy ... has been granted". Although the burden of proof is on Canada, we must nonetheless complete the analysis solely on the basis of factual findings made by the Panel and uncontested facts in the Panel record.

A.1.34.2 *Canada – Dairy (Article 21.5 – New Zealand and US II)*, paras. 66, 68 (WT/DS103/AB/RW2, WT/DS113/AB/RW2)

... under the usual allocation of the burden of proof, a responding Member's measure will be treated as WTO-*consistent*, until sufficient evidence is presented to prove the contrary. We will not readily find that the usual rules on burden of proof do not apply, as they reflect a "canon of evidence" accepted and applied in international proceedings.

...

[Article 10.3] requires that a specific Member, in defined circumstances, "establish that no export subsidy ... has been granted". ... The provision refers to a Member making a "claim" that certain exports are "*not* [being] subsidized". Although the word "claim" usually refers to an assertion by a complaining Member that a measure is WTO-*inconsistent*, in this provision the word "claim" refers to an assertion by a responding Member that a measure is WTO-*consistent*. The "claim" to which Article 10.3 refers is, therefore, a defensive argument made by the responding Member.

A.1.34.3 *Canada – Dairy (Article 21.5 – New Zealand and US II)*, para. 69 (WT/DS103/AB/RW2, WT/DS113/AB/RW2)

Article 10.3 does not impose any substantive obligations regulating the grant of export subsidies under the *Agreement on Agriculture*. Rather, Article 10.3 provides a special rule for proof of export subsidies that applies in certain disputes under Articles 3, 8, 9, and 10 of the *Agreement on Agriculture*.

A.1.34.4 *Canada – Dairy (Article 21.5 – New Zealand and US II)*, para. 70 (WT/DS103/AB/RW2, WT/DS113/AB/RW2)

In identifying the nature of the special rule, it is useful to analyze the character of claims brought under these provisions. Pursuant to Article 3 of the *Agreement on Agriculture*, a Member is *entitled* to grant export subsidies within the limits of the reduction commitment specified in its Schedule. Where a Member claims that another Member has acted inconsistently with Article 3.3 by granting export subsidies in excess of a quantity commitment level, there are *two* separate parts to the claim. First, the responding Member must have exported an agricultural product in quantities exceeding its quantity commitment level. If the quantities exported do not reach the quantity commitment level, there can be no violation of that commitment, under Article 3.3. However, merely exporting a product in quantities that exceed the quantity commitment level is not inconsistent with the commitment. The commitment is an undertaking to limit the quantity of exports that may be *subsidized* and not a commitment to restrict the volume or quantity of exports *as such*. The second part of the claim is, therefore, that the responding Member must have granted export subsidies with respect to quantities exceeding the quantity commitment level. There is, in other words, a *quantitative* aspect and an *export subsidization* aspect to the claim.

A.1.34.5 *Canada – Dairy (Article 21.5 – New Zealand and US II)*, para. 71

(WT/DS103/AB/RW2, WT/DS113/AB/RW2)

Under the usual rules on burden of proof, the complaining Member would bear the burden of proving both parts of the claim. However, Article 10.3 of the *Agreement on Agriculture* partially alters the usual rules. The provision cleaves the complaining Member's claim in two, allocating to different parties the burden of proof with respect to the two parts of the claim we have described.

A.1.34.6 *Canada – Dairy (Article 21.5 – New Zealand and US II)*, para. 73

(WT/DS103/AB/RW2, WT/DS113/AB/RW2)

. . . The language of Article 10.3 is clearly intended to alter the generally-accepted rules on burden of proof. The verb "establish" is synonymous with the verbs "demonstrate" and "prove". Moreover, the auxiliary verb "must" conveys that the responding Member has an obligation – or legal burden – to "establish" or "prove" that "no export subsidy . . . has been granted".

A.1.34.7 *Canada – Dairy (Article 21.5 – New Zealand and US II)*, para. 74

(WT/DS103/AB/RW2, WT/DS113/AB/RW2)

. . . The significance of Article 10.3 is that, where a Member exports an agricultural product in quantities that exceed its quantity commitment level, that Member will be treated as if it has granted WTO-*inconsistent* export subsidies, for the excess quantities, unless the Member presents adequate evidence to "establish" the contrary. This reversal of the usual rules obliges the responding Member to bear the consequences of any doubts concerning the evidence of export subsidization. Article 10.3 thus acts as an incentive to Members to ensure that they are in a position to demonstrate compliance with their quantity commitments under Article 3.3.

A.1.34.8 *Canada – Dairy (Article 21.5 – New Zealand and US II)*, para. 75
(WT/DS103/AB/RW2, WT/DS113/AB/RW2)

With respect to the export subsidization part of the claim, the complaining Member, therefore, is relieved of its burden, under the usual rules, to establish a *prima facie* case of export subsidization of the excess quantity, provided that this Member has established the quantitative part of the claim. . . .

A.1.34.9 *US – Upland Cotton*, para. 616
(WT/DS267/AB/R)

. . . Article 10.3 pursues the aim of preventing circumvention of export subsidy commitments by providing special rules on the reversal of burden of proof where a Member exports an agricultural product in quantities that exceed its reduction commitment level; in such a situation a WTO Member is treated as if it has granted WTO-*inconsistent* export subsidies for the excess quantities, unless the Member presents adequate evidence to "establish" the contrary. . . .

A.1.34.10 *US – Upland Cotton*, para. 647
(WT/DS267/AB/R)

We agree with the United States that Article 10.3 of the *Agreement on Agriculture* does not apply to claims brought under the *SCM Agreement*. However, the Panel did not make the error attributed to it by the United States. The Panel made the statement relied on by the United States in the context of its assessment of the United States' export credit guarantee program under the *Agreement on Agriculture*. Although the Panel made use of the criteria set out in item (j) of the Illustrative List of Export Subsidies annexed to the *SCM Agreement* (providing these programs at premium rates inadequate to cover long-term operating costs and losses) it did so as contextual guidance for its analysis under the *Agreement on Agriculture*, and both the United States and Brazil appear to have agreed with the appropriateness of this approach. Thus, the Panel's reference to Article 10.3 did not relate to its assessment of the United States' export credit guarantee programs under the *SCM Agreement*.

A.1.34.11 *US – Upland Cotton*, para. 652
(WT/DS267/AB/R)

We disagree with the Panel's view that Article 10.3 applies to *unscheduled* products. Under the Panel's approach, the only thing a complainant would have to do to meet its burden of proof when bringing a claim against an *unscheduled* product is to demonstrate that the respondent has exported that product. Once that has been established, the respondent would have to demonstrate that it has not provided an export subsidy. This seems to us an extreme result. In effect, it would mean that any export of an unscheduled product is *presumed* to be subsidized. In our view, the presumption of subsidization when exported quantities exceed the reduction commitments makes sense in respect of a *scheduled* product because, by including it in its schedule, a WTO Member is reserving for itself the right to apply export subsidies to that product, within the limits in its schedule. In the case of *unscheduled* products, however, such a presumption appears inappropriate. Export subsidies for both unscheduled agricultural products and industrial products are completely prohibited under the *Agreement on Agriculture* and under the *SCM Agreement*, respectively. The Panel's interpretation implies that the burden of proof with regard to the same issue would apply differently, however, under each Agreement: it would be on the respondent under the *Agreement on Agriculture*, while it would be on the complainant under the *SCM Agreement*.

A.1.34A Article 10.3 – Relationship with Article 6.2 of the DSU

A.1.34A.1 *EC – Export Subsidies on Sugar*, para. 154

(WT/DS265/AB/R, WT/DS266/AB/R, WT/DS283/AB/R)

... Article 6.2 of the DSU and Article 10.3 of the *Agreement on Agriculture* address different matters and apply at different stages of panel proceedings. A panel request, on its face, must comply with the requirements of Article 6.2 of the DSU, whereas Article 10.3 of the *Agreement on Agriculture* relates to a Member's duty to adduce evidence to substantiate its assertions *during the course of the panel proceedings*. ...

A.1.34B Article 10.4 – "food aid"

A.1.34B.1 *US – Upland Cotton*, para. 616

(WT/DS267/AB/R)

... Article 10.4 provides disciplines to prevent WTO Members from circumventing their export subsidy commitments through food aid transactions. ...

A.1.34B.2 *US – Upland Cotton*, paras. 618–619

(WT/DS267/AB/R)

The United States submits that, under the Panel's approach, international food aid transactions would be subject to the "full array of export subsidy disciplines" because they are not expressly excluded from Article 10.1. ...

We are unable to subscribe to the United States' arguments because we do not see Article 10.4 as excluding international food aid from the scope of Article 10.1. International food aid is covered by the second clause of Article 10.1 to the extent that it is a "non-commercial transaction". Article 10.4 provides specific disciplines that may be relied on to determine whether international food aid is being "used to circumvent" a WTO Member's export subsidy commitments. There is no contradiction in the Panel's approach to Article 10.2 and its approach to Article 10.4. The measures in Article 10.2 and the transactions in Article 10.4 are both covered within the scope of Article 10.1. As Brazil submits, "Article 10.4 provides an example of specific disciplines that have been agreed upon for a particular type of measure and that complement the general export subsidy rules" but, like Article 10.2, it does not "establish any exceptions for the measures that [it] covers". WTO Members are free to grant as much food aid as they wish, provided that they do so consistently with Articles 10.1 and 10.4. Thus, Article 10.4 does not support the United States' reading of Article 10.2.

A.1.34C Article 13 – "due restraint" (peace clause). *See also* Agreement on Agriculture, Relationship between the Agreement on Agriculture and the GATT 1994 (A.1.37)

A.1.34C.1 SUBPARAGRAPH (A) – GREEN BOX

A.1.34C.1.1 *US – Upland Cotton*, para. 319
(WT/DS267/AB/R)

. . . domestic support that conforms fully to the provisions of Annex 2 – that is "green box" support, which is exempt from the domestic support reduction obligations of the *Agreement on Agriculture* – is also exempt, during the implementation period, from actions based on Article XVI of GATT 1994 and the actionable subsidies provisions of Part III of the *SCM Agreement*.

A.1.34C.1.2 *US – Upland Cotton*, para. 342
(WT/DS267/AB/R)

. . . production flexibility contract payments and direct payments are not "decoupled income support" within the meaning of paragraph 6, are not green box measures exempt from the reduction commitments by virtue of Annex 2 of the *Agreement on Agriculture*, and are not, therefore, sheltered from challenge by virtue of paragraph (a) of Article 13 of the *Agreement on Agriculture*. Rather, these measures are support covered by the chapeau to paragraph (b) of Article 13, and are to be taken into account in the analysis of that provision.

A.1.34C.2 SUBPARAGRAPH (B) – INTERPRETATION

A.1.34C.2.1 *US – Upland Cotton*, para. 347
(WT/DS267/AB/R)

Subparagraph (ii) to Article 13(b) exempts non-green box domestic support measures described in the chapeau from actions based on Article XVI:1 of GATT 1994 and Articles 5 and 6 of the *SCM Agreement*. This exemption is, however, subject to a proviso and is thus made conditional upon a requirement that "such measures do not grant support to a specific commodity in excess of that decided during the 1992 marketing year". . . .

A.1.34C.2.2 *US – Upland Cotton*, para. 361
(WT/DS267/AB/R)

We turn to our analysis of the phrase "such measures . . . grant[ing] support to a specific commodity" in Article 13(b)(ii). The Panel found and the participants do not dispute that the relevant United States measures grant "support"; similarly, the Panel found and the participants agree that upland cotton is a "commodity" in the sense of that provision.

A.1.34C.2.3 *US – Upland Cotton*, para. 362
(WT/DS267/AB/R)

The key element . . . is the significance of the qualifying word "specific" in this phrase. The Panel described the ordinary meaning of the term "specific" as "clearly or explicitly defined; precise; exact; definite" and as "specially or peculiarly pertaining to a particular thing or person, or a class of these; peculiar (*to*)". In our view, the term "specific" in the phrase "support to a specific commodity" means the "commodity" must be clearly identifiable. The use of term "to" connecting "support" with "a specific commodity" means that support must "specially pertain" to a particular commodity in the sense of being conferred on that commodity. In addition, the terms "such measures . . . grant" indicates that a discernible link must exist between "such measures" and the particular commodity to which support is granted. Thus, it is not sufficient that a commodity happens to benefit from support, or that support ends up flowing to that commodity by mere coincidence. Rather, the phrase "such measures" granting "support to a specific commodity" implies a discernible link between the support-conferring measure and the particular commodity to which support is granted.

A.1.34C.2.4 *US – Upland Cotton*, para. 363
(WT/DS267/AB/R)

Therefore, we agree with the Panel insofar as it found that the ordinary meaning of the phrase "such measures . . . grant[ing] support to a specific commodity" *includes* "non-green box measures that clearly or explicitly define a commodity as one to which they bestow or confer support". This is because the Panel's test requires that a commodity be specified in the measure, and that the support be conferred on that commodity. We believe, however, that the terms of this definition do not exhaust the scope of measures that may grant "support to a specific commodity". We note in this regard that the Panel looked, in applying its test, to factors such as eligibility criteria and payment rates, as well as the relationship between payments and current market prices of the commodity in question. In our view, the Panel was correct to consider such matters, as the requisite link between a measure granting support and a specific commodity may be discerned not just from an explicit specification of the commodity in the text of a measure, as the Panel's test – on its face – seems to imply, but also from an analysis of factors such as the characteristics, structure or design of that measure.

A.1.34C.2.5 *US – Upland Cotton*, para. 367
(WT/DS267/AB/R)

. . . The proviso to Article 13(b)(ii) mentions only the term "such measures" granting support; but the meaning of this term can be clarified by reference to the chapeau of Article 13(b) because, as the Panel noted, "[t]he chapeau of paragraph (b) and subparagraph (ii) form part of a single sentence." The chapeau identifies the categories of support measures covered by that provision. These are:

> ... domestic support measures that conform fully to the provisions of Article 6 of this Agreement including direct payments that conform to the requirements of paragraph 5 thereof, as reflected in each Member's Schedule, as well as domestic support within *de minimis* levels and in conformity with paragraph 2 of Article 6 ...

A.1.34C.2.6 *US – Upland Cotton*, para. 368
(WT/DS267/AB/R)

Measures covered by Article 6 include both product-specific and non-product-specific amber box support subject to reduction commitments. In addition, measures covered by the chapeau *also* include product-specific and non-product-specific support within *de minimis* levels. They further include blue box support provided in accordance with Article 6.5, as well as development box support, provided according to the provisions of Article 6.2, for both of which the distinction between product-specific and non-product specific support for purposes of the AMS calculation has little practical relevance. Like the Panel, we believe that the use of the term "such measures" in the proviso to Article 13(b)(ii) indicates that all such measures identified in the chapeau of Article 13(b) may qualify as granting "support to a specific commodity" and are eligible to be included in the analysis. By contrast, under the United States' argument, domestic support measures listed in the chapeau (with the exception of product-specific amber box support) could not be "support to a specific commodity" even if they confer support on a specific commodity and there is a discernible link between the measure and that commodity.

A.I.34C.3 SUBPARAGRAPH (B) – APPLICATION

A.1.34C.3.1 *US – Upland Cotton*, paras. 371–372
(WT/DS267/AB/R)

The proviso to Article 13(b)(ii) requires an assessment of whether the relevant United States non-green box domestic support measures grant, during the implementation period, "support to a specific commodity in excess of that decided during the 1992 marketing year".

As we have explained above, the term "such measures ... grant support to a specific commodity" comprises two elements: first, a non-green box measure actually confers support on the specific commodity in question; and second, there is a discernible link between the measure and the commodity, such that the measure is directed at supporting that commodity. Such a discernible link may be evident where a measure explicitly defines a specific commodity as one to which it bestows support. Such a link might also be ascertained, as a matter of fact, from the characteristics, structure or design of the measure under examination. Conversely, support that does not actually flow to a commodity or support that flows to a commodity by coincidence rather than by the inherent design of the measure cannot be regarded as falling within the ambit of the term "support to a specific commodity".

A.1.34C.3.2 *US – Upland Cotton*, paras. 375–376
(WT/DS267/AB/R)

We agree with the United States that payments made with respect to historical upland cotton base acres to commodities other than upland cotton or to producers who produced no commodities at all cannot be deemed to be support granted to upland cotton for purposes of the Article 13(b)(ii) comparison. The Article 13(b)(ii) assessment must be limited to support conferred on planted upland cotton; support flowing to other commodities that were planted, or support that was given where no commodities were produced must of course be removed from the assessment. We reject, therefore, the Panel's calculation methodology to the extent that it failed to limit the Article 13(b)(ii) calculation to payments with respect to upland cotton base acres corresponding to physical acres actually planted with upland cotton.

We observe, however, that the Panel acknowledged that a producer with upland cotton base acres may plant any crop other than the excluded fruits, vegetables, and wild rice, but it found that there was "a strongly positive relationship between those recipients who hold upland cotton base acres and those who continue to plant upland cotton, despite their entitlement to plant other crops"....

A.1.34C.3.3 *US – Upland Cotton*, paras. 377–378
(WT/DS267/AB/R)

... The "cotton to cotton" methodology limits the Article 13(b)(ii) calculation to payments with respect to cotton base acres corresponding to physical acres that were actually planted with upland cotton.

We turn next to the United States' contention that the mere fact that a measure is based on *historical* production of upland cotton is not a sufficient basis for a finding that the measure grants at present "support to [the] specific commodity" upland cotton. We agree that none of the base acre dependent programs expressly ties support to continued production of upland cotton. However, the absence of an express reference in the legislation to continued production of upland cotton does not mean that the payments do not grant support to upland cotton. This is because a link between the four measures at issue and the continued production of upland cotton is discernible from the characteristics, structure and operation of those measures.

A.1.34C.3.4 *US – Upland Cotton*, para. 380
(WT/DS267/AB/R)

We underline that these Panel findings do not pertain to *all* payments to *current* producers of upland cotton, but rather are limited to payments to producers with respect to historic *upland cotton* base acres. Indeed, we see little in the Panel's finding or on the record that would allow us to discern a link between the support-conferring measures with respect to non-cotton historical base acres and current production of upland cotton. We do not, therefore, accept the methodology submitted by Brazil that included, in the Article 13(b)(ii) calculation, payments with respect to both cotton and non-cotton base acres flowing to current production of upland cotton. We believe that only the "cotton to cotton" methodology, included by the Panel in "Attachment to Section VII:D" to its Report as an "appropriate" alternative calculation, sufficiently demonstrates a discernible link between payments under base acre dependent measures (related to upland cotton) and upland cotton.

A.I.34C.4 SUBPARAGRAPH (B) – "GRANT" VS. "DECIDED"

A.1.34C.4.1 *US – Upland Cotton*, paras. 381–382 (WT/DS267/AB/R)

Finally, we address the United States' argument that the calculation methodology under Article 13(b)(ii) must be based on only those factors that the government of a Member can control, excluding, for example, producer decisions regarding what crops to grow within the scope of production flexibility allowed by the measures. In advancing this contention, the United States relies upon the following statement of the Panel:

> [If] the proviso [to Article 13(b)(ii)] focused on where support was spent due to reasons beyond the control of the government, such as producer decisions on what to produce within a programme, it would introduce a major element of unpredictability into Article 13, and render it extremely difficult to ensure compliance.

The United States finds support for this view in the terms "grant" and "decided" in Article 13(b)(ii), and claims that "the focus of the Peace Clause comparison is on the support a Member decides". We note that the verbs "grant" and "decided" have distinct meanings. We agree with the observation of the Panel that " '[d]ecided' refers to what the government determines, but 'grant' refers to what its measures provide." In Article 13(b)(ii), each of these words has been chosen to govern one side of the comparison required by that proviso. In the light of the distinct meanings of these words, and the distinct roles they play in the context of Article 13(b)(ii), we reject the idea that the word "grant", which is applicable to implementation period support, must be read to mean the same thing as "decided", which is applicable to the 1992 benchmark level of support.

A.1.34C.4.2 *US – Upland Cotton*, para. 383 (WT/DS267/AB/R)

Moreover, we do not accept that unpredictability of producer decisions under planting flexibility rules, *per se*, could modify the specific requirements set out in the proviso to Article 13(b)(ii). What is relevant for the comparison is the support that the measure actually grants during the implementation period. Indeed, we agree with Brazil that a certain degree of unpredictability in the volume of the payments flowing to particular commodities is inherent in many of the support measures disciplined by the *Agreement on Agriculture*, including measures granting support to a specific commodity. The existence of such unpredictability cannot be a ground to alter the basis of comparison under the proviso to Article 13(b)(ii) from what is actually "grant[ed]" in the implementation period to what is only "decided".

A.1.34C.5 SUBPARAGRAPH (B) – CALCULATION METHOD

A.1.34C.5.1 *US – Upland Cotton*, paras. 388–389
(WT/DS267/AB/R)

In addressing this issue, we – like the Panel – note that Article 13(b)(ii) gives no specific guidance regarding *how* the "support" that measures granted in the implementation period or that was decided during the 1992 marketing year should be calculated. The Panel therefore turned to the broader context of the *Agreement on Agriculture* and chose to "apply the principles of AMS methodology" in accordance with Annex 3 of the *Agreement on Agriculture*, with certain modifications. We observe that, on appeal, neither of the participants, nor indeed any of the third participants that addressed this issue, suggested that the Panel erred in seeking guidance for its calculations in the principles set out in Annex 3.

Against this background, we observe that paragraph 10 of Annex 3 provides that "non-exempt direct payments . . . dependent on a price gap" may be measured using either price gap methodology or budgetary outlay methodology. . . .

A.1.34D Annex 2 – "green box"

A.1.34D.1 PARAGRAPH 1 – "FUNDAMENTAL REQUIREMENT"

A.1.34D.1.1 *US – Upland Cotton*, para. 333
(WT/DS267/AB/R)

We note that the first sentence of paragraph 1 of Annex 2 lays down a "fundamental requirement" for green box measures, such that they must have "no, or at most minimal, trade-distorting effects or effects on production". The second sentence of paragraph 1 provides that, "[a]ccordingly", green box measures must conform to the basic criteria stated in that sentence, "plus" the policy-specific criteria and conditions set out in the remaining paragraphs of Annex 2, including those in paragraph 6.

A.1.34D.1.2 *US – Upland Cotton*, para. 334
(WT/DS267/AB/R)

As we have noted, the Panel found that the planting flexibility limitations in this case "significantly constrain" production decisions. However one reads the "fundamental requirement" in paragraph 1 of Annex 2, given the factual findings of the Panel, the facts of this case do not present a situation in which the planting flexibility limitations demonstrably have "no, or at most minimal," trade-distorting effects or effects on production.

A.1.34D.2 PARAGRAPH 6 – "DECOUPLED INCOME SUPPORT"

A.1.34D.2.1 *US – Upland Cotton*, para. 321
(WT/DS267/AB/R)

Paragraph 6, entitled, "[d]ecoupled income support" applies to one type of "direct payment" to producers that may benefit from exemption from reduction commitments and protection under the peace clause. Paragraph 6(a) sets forth that eligibility for payments under a decoupled income support program must be determined by reference to certain "clearly-defined criteria" in a "defined and fixed base period". Paragraph 6(b) requires the severing of any link between the *amount of payments* under such a program and the *type or volume of production* undertaken by recipients of payments under that program in any year after the base period. Paragraphs 6(c) and 6(d) serve to require that payments are also decoupled from *prices* and *factors of production employed* after the base period. Paragraph 6(e) makes it clear that "[n]o production shall be required in order to receive . . . payments" under a decoupled income support program.

A.1.34D.2.2 *US – Upland Cotton*, para. 322
(WT/DS267/AB/R)

. . . the question before us regarding the consistency of production flexibility contract payments and direct payments with paragraph 6(b) of Annex 2 is a limited one. It does not concern a measure *requiring* producers to grow certain crops in order to receive payments; it also does not concern a measure with complete planting *flexibility* that provides payments without regard whatsoever to the crops that are grown. Indeed, it does not concern a measure that requires the production of any crop at all; nor does it involve a measure that totally *prohibits* the growing of any crops as a condition for payments. The question before us in this appeal thus concerns a measure with a *partial* exclusion combining planting flexibility and payments with the reduction or elimination of the payments when the excluded crops are produced, while providing payments even when no crops are produced at all.

A.1.34D.2.3 *US – Upland Cotton*, para. 323
(WT/DS267/AB/R)

In addressing the question of the consistency of such a measure with paragraph 6(b), we note that under this provision, for income support to be *decoupled*, the "amount of such payments . . . shall not be related to . . . the type or volume of production . . . undertaken by the producer in any year after the base period". . . .

A.1.34D.2.4 *US – Upland Cotton*, para. 324
(WT/DS267/AB/R)

The ordinary meaning of the term "related to" in paragraph 6(b) of Annex 2 denotes some degree of *relationship* or *connection* between two things, here the amount of payment, on the one hand, and the type or volume of production, on the other. It covers a broader set of connections than "based on", which term is also used to describe the relationship between two things covered by paragraph 6(b). Nothing in the ordinary meaning of the term "related to" suggests that the connections covered by this expression may not encompass connections of either a "positive" nature (including directions or requirements to do something) or a "negative" nature (including prohibitions or requirements not to do something) or a combination of both. . . .

A.1.34D.2.5 *US – Upland Cotton*, para. 325
(WT/DS267/AB/R)

Paragraph 6 of Annex 2, entitled "[d]ecoupled income support", seeks to decouple or de-link direct payments to producers from various aspects of their production decisions and thus aims at neutrality in this regard. Subparagraph (b) decouples the payments from production; subparagraph (c) decouples payments from prices; and subparagraph (d) decouples payments from factors of production. Subparagraph (e) completes the process by making it clear that no production shall be required in order to receive such payments. Decoupling of payments from production under paragraph 6(b) can only be ensured if the payments are not related to, or based upon, either a positive requirement to produce certain crops or a negative requirement not to produce certain crops or a combination of both positive and negative requirements on production of crops.

A.1.34D.2.6 *US – Upland Cotton*, para. 326
(WT/DS267/AB/R)

In contrast to the other subparagraphs of paragraph 6, paragraph 6(e) does explicitly distinguish between positive and negative production requirements, because it prohibits positive requirements to produce. The Panel reasoned that "[i]f paragraph 6(b) could be satisfied by ensuring that no production was required to receive payments, paragraph 6(e) would be redundant". We agree with the Panel that the context provided by paragraph 6(e) indicates that a measure that provided payments, even if a producer undertook no production at all, would not, for that reason alone, necessarily comply with paragraph 6(b). This is because other elements of that measure might still relate the amount of payments to the type or volume of production, contrary to the requirement of paragraph 6(b).

A.1.34D.2.7 *US – Upland Cotton*, para. 327
(WT/DS267/AB/R)

The United States seems to argue that the Panel's interpretation of the relationship between paragraphs 6(b) and 6(e) would subsume paragraph 6(e) within the scope of paragraph 6(b), thereby rendering it redundant. In our view, however, paragraph 6(e) continues to serve a purpose distinct from that of paragraph 6(b). It highlights a different aspect of decoupling income support. In prohibiting Members from making green-box measures contingent on production, paragraph 6(e) implies that Members are allowed, in principle, to require no production at all. Accordingly, payments conditioned on a total ban on any production may qualify as decoupled income support under paragraph 6(e). Even assuming that payments contingent on a total production ban could be seen to relate the amount of the payment to the *volume* of production within the meaning of paragraph 6(b) – the volume of production being nil – giving meaning and effect to both paragraphs 6(b) and 6(e) suggests a reading of paragraph 6(b) that would not disallow a total ban on any production.

A.1.34D.2.8 *US – Upland Cotton*, para. 329
(WT/DS267/AB/R)

We agree with the Panel that a partial exclusion of some crops from payments has the potential to channel production towards the production of crops that remain eligible for payments. In contrast to a total production ban, the channelling of production that may follow from a partial exclusion of some crops from payments will have *positive* production effects as regards crops eligible for payments. The extent of this will depend on the scope of the exclusion. . . .

A.1.34D.2.9 *US – Upland Cotton*, para. 340
(WT/DS267/AB/R)

. . . Our interpretation of paragraph 6(b) would not prevent a WTO Member from making illegal the production of certain crops. Nor would it prevent a Member from providing decoupled income support while at the same time making the production of certain crops illegal. As Brazil states, there is nothing in the *Agreement on Agriculture* to suggest that the term "production" in paragraph 6 of Annex 2 refers to anything other than *lawful* production. In addition, we observe that specific provisions of the *Agreement on Agriculture* recognize, and exempt from reduction commitments, domestic support programs that address the problem of production of illicit narcotic crops in developing countries or payments under certain environmental programs.

A.1.34D.3 PARAGRAPH 11 – "STRUCTURAL ADJUSTMENT ASSISTANCE"

A.1.34D.3.1 *US – Upland Cotton*, para. 335
(WT/DS267/AB/R)

We find further support for our interpretation of paragraph 6(b) in the context provided by paragraph 11 of Annex 2, entitled "Structural adjustment assistance provided through investment aids". Several of the subparagraphs of paragraph 11 are phrased in similar terms to those of paragraph 6. Indeed, like paragraph 6(b), paragraph 11(b) requires that the "amount of . . . payments . . . shall not be related to . . . the type or volume of production . . . undertaken by the producer in any year after the base period." However, unlike paragraph 6(b), paragraph 11(b) ends with the phrase "other than as provided for under criterion (e) below". Criterion 11(e) specifically envisages that "payments shall not mandate or in any way designate the agricultural products to be produced by the recipients except to require them not to produce a particular product".

A.1.34D.3.2 *US – Upland Cotton*, para. 336
(WT/DS267/AB/R)

We note that the exception provided by paragraph 11(e) and the link to paragraph 11(e) in paragraph 11(b) explicitly *authorize* the type of "negative" requirements not to produce that the United States argues is implicitly *permitted* by the terms of paragraph 6(b). In the light of the similarity of the language chosen in paragraphs 6(b) and 11(b), like the Panel, we attach significance to the fact that the drafters saw as necessary an explicit authorization of negative requirements not to produce under paragraph 11(b). In our view, this indicates that the ordinary meaning of the terms in paragraph 11(b) would otherwise exclude an interpretation allowing such negative requirements. The use of identical language in paragraphs 6(b) and 11(b), except for the reference in paragraph 11(b) to paragraph 11(e), suggests that the meaning of the terms in paragraph 6(b) must be the same as in paragraph 11(b). Accordingly, a comparison of these provisions confirms that the terms of paragraph 6(b) encompass both positive as well as negative connections between the amount of payments under a program and the type of production undertaken.

A.1.34E Annex 3, paragraph 7 – Measures directed at agricultural *processors* benefitting *producers* of agricultural products

A.1.34E.1 *US – Upland Cotton*, para. 537 and footnote 777
(WT/DS267/AB/R)

... we will proceed with our examination on the *assumption* that Step 2 payments to domestic users of United States cotton are contemplated by paragraph 7 of Annex 3 of the *Agreement on Agriculture*.[777]

[777] In this dispute we do not decide whether subsidies paid to textile manufacturers on their purchases of cotton could be regarded as measures directed at "agricultural processors" within the meaning of paragraph 7 of Annex 3.

A.1.34E.2 *US – Upland Cotton*, para. 540
(WT/DS267/AB/R)

... The second sentence of paragraph 7 recognizes situations where subsidies are not provided directly to the agricultural producer, but rather to an agricultural processor, yet the measures may benefit the producers of the basic agricultural good. This sentence also clarifies that only the portion of the subsidy that benefits the producers of the basic agricultural good, and not the entire amount, shall be included in a Member's AMS.

A.1.34E.3 *US – Upland Cotton*, para. 541
(WT/DS267/AB/R)

...There is nothing...in the text of paragraph 7 [of Annex 3 of the *Agreement on Agriculture*] that suggests that such measures, when they are import substitution subsidies, are exempt from the prohibition in Article 3.1(b) of the *SCM Agreement*....

A.1.34E.4 *US – Upland Cotton*, para. 542
(WT/DS267/AB/R)

...paragraph 7 of Annex 3 refers more broadly to measures directed at agricultural processors that benefit producers of a basic agricultural product and, contrary to the United States' assertion, it is not rendered inutile by the Panel's interpretation. WTO Members may still provide subsidies directed at agricultural processors that benefit producers of a basic agricultural commodity in accordance with the *Agreement on Agriculture*, as long as such subsidies do not include an import substitution component.

A.1.34E.5 *US – Upland Cotton*, para. 546
(WT/DS267/AB/R)

...we find that paragraph 7 of Annex 3 and Article 6.3 of the *Agreement on Agriculture* do not deal specifically with the same matter as Article 3.1(b) of the *SCM Agreement*, that is, subsidies contingent upon the use of domestic over imported goods.

A.1.35 Annex 3, paragraph 8 – "market price support"

A.1.35.1 *Korea – Various Measures on Beef*, para. 120
(WT/DS161/AB/R, WT/DS169/AB/R)

...the words "production *eligible* to receive the applied administered price" in paragraph 8 of Annex 3 have a different meaning in ordinary usage from "production *actually purchased*". The ordinary meaning of "eligible" is "fit or *entitled* to be chosen". Thus, "production eligible" refers to production that is "fit or entitled" to be purchased rather than production that was actually purchased. In establishing its program for future market price support, a government is able to define and to limit "eligible" production. Production actually purchased may often be less than eligible production.

A.1.36 Relationship between Domestic Support and Export Subsidies Disciplines

A.1.36.1 *Canada – Dairy (Article 21.5 – New Zealand and US)*, paras. 90–92
(WT/DS103/AB/RW, WT/DS113/AB/RW)

We believe that it would erode the distinction between the domestic support and export subsidies disciplines of the *Agreement on Agriculture* if WTO-consistent domestic support measures were automatically characterized as export subsidies because they produced spill-over economic benefits for export production. Indeed, this is another reason why we do not agree with the Panel that sales of CEM at any price below the administered domestic price for milk can be regarded as "payments" under Article 9.1(c) of the *Agreement on Agriculture*. Such a basis for comparison would tend to collapse the distinction between these two different disciplines.

However, we consider that the distinction between the domestic support and export subsidies disciplines in the *Agreement on Agriculture* would also be eroded if a WTO Member were entitled to use domestic support, without limit, to provide support for exports of agricultural products. Broadly stated, domestic support provisions of that Agreement, coupled with high levels of tariff protection, allow extensive support to producers, as compared with the limitations imposed through the export subsidies disciplines. Consequently, if domestic support could be used, without limit, to provide support for exports, it would undermine the benefits intended to accrue through a WTO Member's export subsidy commitments.

In our view, by relying upon the total cost of production in this dispute, to determine whether there are "payments", the integrity of the two disciplines is best respected. The existence of "payments" is determined by reference to a standard that focuses upon the motivations of the independent economic operator who is making the alleged "payments" – here the producer – and not upon any government intervention in the marketplace. More importantly, using this basis for comparison, the potential for WTO Members to export their agricultural production is preserved, provided that any export-destined sales by a producer at below the total cost of production are not financed by virtue of governmental action. The export subsidy disciplines of the *Agreement on Agriculture* will also be maintained without erosion.

A.1.36.2 *EC – Export Subsidies on Sugar*, paras. 279–282 (WT/DS265/AB/R, WT/DS266/AB/R, WT/DS283/AB/R)

... WTO Members are entitled to provide "*domestic support*" to agricultural producers within the limits of their domestic subsidy commitments. We observe, however, that the Appellate Body has also held that economic effects of WTO-consistent domestic support may "spill over" to benefit export production. Such spill-over effects may arise, in particular, in circumstances where agricultural products result from a single line of production that does not distinguish between production destined for the domestic market and production destined for the export market.

In this respect, the Appellate Body has cautioned that, "if domestic support could be used, without limit, to provide support for exports, it would undermine the benefits intended to accrue through a WTO Member's export subsidy commitments." We believe that these statements are relevant to the present case. In this case, we note that C sugar is produced and exported in huge quantities, and that there is a considerable difference between the world market price and the average total cost of production of sugar in the European Communities. As we have noted above, the subsidized production and export of C sugar is not the incidental effect of the domestic support system, but is a direct consequence of the EC sugar regime.

We also disagree with the European Communities' argument that the Panel's finding blurs the distinction between domestic support and export subsidies; we disagree, because the European Communities' legislation *requires* the exportation of C sugar, and prices obtained for C sugar on the world market are significantly below the average total cost of production of sugar in the European Communities. In our view, European Communities' legislation leaves the sugar producer wishing to sell C sugar with no choice but to export, short of the limited option of "carry over". We also note that the operation of the EC sugar regime enables sugar producers to cover the fixed costs of producing sugar and to sell C sugar profitably, even though the prices obtained for C sugar are significantly below the average total cost of production of sugar.

Thus, we do not consider that our interpretation erodes the boundary between "domestic support" and "export subsidies" recognized under the *Agreement on Agriculture*. Rather, our interpretation respects the boundary between the two and operates to ensure that Members provide domestic support and export subsidies in conformity with their obligations under the *Agreement on Agriculture*. As we noted earlier, our interpretation is based on the specific facts and circumstances of this dispute.

A.1.37 **Relationship between the Agreement on Agriculture and the GATT 1994.** *See also* Tariff Concessions, Relationship between Member's Schedules and the Agreement on Agriculture (T.1.4)

A.1.37.1 *EC – Bananas III*, para. 155
(WT/DS27/AB/R)

. . . The relationship between the provisions of the GATT 1994 and of the *Agreement on Agriculture* is set out in Article 21.1 of the *Agreement on Agriculture*:

> The provisions of GATT 1994 and of other Multilateral Trade Agreements in Annex 1A to the WTO Agreement shall apply subject to the provisions of this Agreement.

Therefore, the provisions of the GATT 1994, including Article XIII, apply to market-access commitments concerning agricultural products, except to the extent that the *Agreement on Agriculture* contains specific provisions dealing specifically with the same matter.

A.1.37.2 *EC – Bananas III*, para. 157
(WT/DS27/AB/R)

. . . we do not see anything in Article 4.1 to suggest that market access concessions and commitments made as a result of the Uruguay Round negotiations on agriculture can be inconsistent with the provisions of Article XIII of the GATT 1994. . . . we believe it is significant that Article 13 of the *Agreement on Agriculture* does not, by its terms, prevent dispute settlement actions relating to the consistency of market access concessions for agricultural products with Article XIII of the GATT 1994. As we have noted, the negotiators of the *Agreement on Agriculture* did not hesitate to specify such limitations elsewhere in that agreement; had they intended to do so with respect to Article XIII of the GATT 1994, they could, and presumably would, have done so. We note further that the *Agreement on Agriculture* makes no reference to the *Modalities* document or to any "common understanding" among the negotiators of the *Agreement on Agriculture* that the market-access commitments for agricultural products would not be subject to Article XIII of the GATT 1994.

A.1.37.3 *EC – Export Subsidies on Sugar*, para. 211
(WT/DS265/AB/R, WT/DS266/AB/R, WT/DS283/AB/R)

. . . we examine whether the claimed commitment in Footnote 1 "limiting" subsidization of exports of sugar can prevail over the provisions of the *Agreement on Agriculture*, despite such a commitment being inconsistent with Articles 3.3 and 9.1 of the *Agreement on Agriculture*. . . .

A.1.37.4 *EC – Export Subsidies on Sugar*, paras. 221–223
(WT/DS265/AB/R, WT/DS266/AB/R, WT/DS283/AB/R)

In any event, we note that Article 21 of the *Agreement on Agriculture* provides that: "[t]he provisions of [the] GATT 1994 and of other Multilateral Trade Agreements in Annex 1A to the WTO Agreement shall apply subject to the provisions of this Agreement." In other words, Members explicitly recognized that there may be conflicts between the *Agreement on Agriculture* and the GATT 1994, and explicitly provided, through Article 21, that the *Agreement on Agriculture* would prevail to the extent of such conflicts. Similarly, the *General interpretative note to Annex 1A* to the *WTO Agreement* states that, "[i]n the event of conflict between a provision of the [GATT 1994] and a provision of another agreement in Annex 1A. . . , the provision of the other agreement shall prevail to the extent of the conflict." The *Agreement on Agriculture* is contained in Annex 1A to the *WTO Agreement*.

As we noted above, Footnote 1, being part of the European Communities' Schedule, is an integral part of the GATT 1994 by virtue of Article 3.1 of the *Agreement on Agriculture*. Therefore, pursuant to Article 21 of the *Agreement on Agriculture*, the provisions of the *Agreement on Agriculture* prevail over Footnote 1 . . . .

As a separate matter, we note that the European Communities asserts that Footnote 1 was "negotiated" with its partners in the Uruguay Round negotiations and that it has been "respected". Accordingly, Footnote 1 forms part of the treaty ratified by the WTO Members. Similarly, the ACP Countries allege that Footnote 1 "was negotiated and agreed upon" or acquiesced in by the Complaining Parties before the end of the Uruguay Round. The Panel found, however, that "[t]he evidence and submissions produced by all parties show that the Complainants did not agree to any European Communities' deviations from the *Agreement on Agriculture*." The Panel concluded that "participants in the Uruguay Round and WTO Members did not agree to the European Communities' inclusion of Footnote 1 as an agreed departure from the European Communities' basic obligations under the *Agreement on Agriculture*." Accordingly, we see no basis in the Panel Reports for the contention of the European Communities and the ACP Countries that the Complaining Parties or the WTO Members negotiated or agreed to Footnote 1 as a departure from the European Communities' obligations under the *Agreement on Agriculture*.

A.1.37A Relationship between the Agreement on Agriculture and the Modalities Paper

A.1.37A.1 *EC – Bananas III*, para. 157
(WT/DS27/AB/R)

. . . We note further that the *Agreement on Agriculture* makes no reference to the *Modalities* document or to any "common understanding" among the negotiators of the *Agreement on Agriculture* that the market-access commitments for agricultural products would not be subject to Article XIII of the GATT 1994.

A.1.37A.2 *EC – Export Subsidies on Sugar*, para. 199
(WT/DS265/AB/R, WT/DS266/AB/R, WT/DS283/AB/R)

We do not find it necessary to decide in this appeal on the relevance of the "Modalities Paper". The "Modalities Paper" is not an agreement among the WTO Members and, by its terms, cannot be the basis of dispute settlement under the *Marrakesh Agreement Establishing the World Trade Organization* (the "*WTO Agreement*"). Furthermore, as the Appellate Body noted in *EC – Bananas III*, "the *Agreement on Agriculture* makes no reference to the *Modalities* document". . . .

A.1.38 Relationship between the Agreement on Agriculture and the SCM Agreement. *See also* Agreement on Agriculture, Article 1(e) – "subsidy" (A.1.3); SCM Agreement, Article 3.1 – "except as provided in the Agreement on Agriculture" (S.2.11)

A.1.38.1 *Canada – Dairy (Article 21.5 – New Zealand and US)*, paras. 123–124
(WT/DS103/AB/RW, WT/DS113/AB/RW)

The relationship between the *Agreement on Agriculture* and the *SCM Agreement* is defined, in part, by Article 3.1 of the *SCM Agreement*, which states that certain subsidies are "prohibited" "[e]xcept as provided in the Agreement on Agriculture". This clause, therefore, indicates that the WTO-consistency of an export subsidy for agricultural products has to be examined, in the first place, under the *Agreement on Agriculture*.

This is borne out by Article 13(c)(ii) of the *Agreement on Agriculture*, which provides that "export subsidies that conform fully to the [export subsidy] provisions of Part V" of the *Agreement on Agriculture*, "as reflected in each Member's Schedule, shall be . . . exempt from actions based on Article XVI of GATT 1994 or Articles 3, 5 and 6 of the Subsidies Agreement."

A.1.38.2 *US – Upland Cotton*, paras. 532–533
(WT/DS267/AB/R)

We agree that Article 21.1 could apply in the three situations described by the Panel, namely:

> . . . where, for example, the domestic support provisions of the *Agreement on Agriculture* would prevail in the event that an explicit carve-out or exemption from the disciplines in Article 3.1(b) of the *SCM Agreement* existed in the *text* of the *Agreement on Agriculture*. Another situation would be where it would be impossible for a Member to comply with its domestic support obligations under the *Agreement on Agriculture* and the Article 3.1(b) prohibition simultaneously. Another situation might be where there is an explicit authorization in the text of the *Agreement on Agriculture* that would authorize a measure that, in the absence of such an express authorization, would be prohibited by Article 3.1(b) of the *SCM Agreement*. [Panel Report, para. 7.1038 (original emphasis)]

The Appellate Body has interpreted Article 21.1 to mean that the provisions of the GATT 1994 and of other Multilateral Trade Agreements in Annex 1A apply, "except to the extent that the *Agreement on Agriculture* contains specific provisions dealing specifically with the same matter". There could be, therefore, situations other than those identified by the Panel where Article 21.1 of the *Agreement on Agriculture* may be applicable.

The key issue before us is whether the *Agreement on Agriculture* contains "specific provisions dealing specifically with the same matter" as Article 3.1(b) of the *SCM Agreement*, that is, subsidies contingent upon the use of domestic over imported goods. We, therefore, turn to the relevant provisions of the *Agreement on Agriculture*.

A.1.38.3 *US – Upland Cotton*, para. 536
(WT/DS267/AB/R)

Before determining whether Article 6.3 and paragraph 7 of Annex 3 of the *Agreement on Agriculture* deal specifically with the same matter as Article 3.1(b) of the *SCM Agreement*, we must address the question whether the Step 2 payments to domestic users of United States upland cotton fall within paragraph 7 of Annex 3 because the United States claims that they are "[m]easures directed at agricultural processors" and "benefit the producers of the basic agricultural products". . . .

A.1.38.4 *US – Upland Cotton*, para. 538
(WT/DS267/AB/R)

We thus turn to the issue raised by the United States' appeal, that is, whether Article 6.3 and paragraph 7 of Annex 3 of the *Agreement on Agriculture* are "specific provisions dealing specifically with the same matter" as Article 3.1(b) of the *SCM Agreement*, namely, subsidies contingent upon the use of domestic over imported goods.

A.1.38.5 *US – Upland Cotton*, para. 542
(WT/DS267/AB/R)

. . . Like the Panel, we do not believe that the scope of paragraph 7 is limited to measures that have an import substitution component in them. There could be other measures covered by paragraph 7 of Annex 3 that do not necessarily have such a component. Indeed, Brazil submits that if the Step 2 payments were provided to United States processors of cotton, regardless of the origin of the cotton, these processors "would still buy *at least* some U.S. upland cotton, so producers would continue to derive *some* benefit". Thus, paragraph 7 of Annex 3 refers more broadly to measures directed at agricultural processors that benefit producers of a basic agricultural product and, contrary to the United States' assertion, it is not rendered inutile by the Panel's interpretation. WTO Members may still provide subsidies directed at agricultural processors that benefit producers of a basic agricultural commodity in accordance with the *Agreement on Agriculture*, as long as such subsidies do not include an import substitution component.

A.1.38.6 *US – Upland Cotton*, para. 545
(WT/DS267/AB/R)

Article 6.3 does not authorize subsidies that are contingent on the use of domestic over imported goods. It only provides that a WTO Member shall be considered to be in compliance with its domestic support *reduction commitments* if its Current Total AMS does not exceed that Member's annual or final bound commitment level specified in its Schedule. It does not say that compliance with Article 6.3 of the *Agreement on Agriculture* insulates the subsidy from the prohibition in Article 3.1(b). . . .

A.1.38.7 *US – Upland Cotton*, para. 546
(WT/DS267/AB/R)

. . . we find that paragraph 7 of Annex 3 and Article 6.3 of the *Agreement on Agriculture* do not deal specifically with the same matter as Article 3.1(b) of the *SCM Agreement*, that is, subsidies contingent upon the use of domestic over imported goods.

A.1.38.8 *US – Upland Cotton*, para. 547
(WT/DS267/AB/R)

We are mindful that the introductory language of Article 3.1 of the *SCM Agreement* clarifies that this provision applies "[e]xcept as provided in the Agreement on Agriculture". Furthermore, as the United States has pointed out, this introductory language applies to both the export subsidy prohibition in paragraph (a) and to the prohibition on import substitution subsidies in paragraph (b) of Article 3.1. As we explained previously, in our review of the provisions of the *Agreement on Agriculture* [paragraph 7 of Annex 3 and Article 6.3 of the *Agreement on Agriculture*] relied on by the United States, we did not find a provision that deals specifically with subsidies that have an import substitution component. By contrast, the prohibition on the provision of subsidies contingent upon the use of domestic over imported goods in Article 3.1(b) of the *SCM Agreement* is explicit and clear. Because Article 3.1(b) treats subsidies contingent on the use of domestic over imported products as prohibited subsidies, it would be expected that the drafters would have included an equally explicit and clear provision in the *Agreement on Agriculture* if they had indeed intended to authorize such prohibited subsidies provided in connection with agricultural goods. We find no provision in the *Agreement on Agriculture* dealing specifically with subsidies contingent upon the use of domestic over imported agricultural goods.

A.1.38.9 *US – Upland Cotton*, para. 548
(WT/DS267/AB/R)

Our approach in this case is consistent with the Appellate Body's approach in *EC – Bananas III*. In that case, the European Communities relied on Article 4.1 of the *Agreement on Agriculture* in arguing that the market access concessions it made for agricultural products pursuant to the *Agreement on Agriculture* prevailed over Article XIII of the GATT 1994. The Appellate Body, however, found that "[t]here is nothing in Articles 4.1 or 4.2, or in any other article of the *Agreement on Agriculture*, that deals specifically with the allocation of tariff quotas on agricultural products". It further explained that "[i]f the negotiators had intended to permit Members to act inconsistently with Article XIII of the GATT 1994, they would have said so explicitly". The situation before us is similar. We have found nothing in Article 6.3, paragraph 7 of Annex 3 or anywhere else in the *Agreement on Agriculture* that "deals specifically" with subsidies that are contingent on the use of domestic over imported agricultural products.

A.1.38.10 *US – Upland Cotton*, para. 549
(WT/DS267/AB/R)

We recall that the *Agreement on Agriculture* and the *SCM Agreement* "are *both* Multilateral Agreements on Trade in Goods contained in Annex 1A of the *Marrakesh Agreement Establishing the World Trade Organization* (the '*WTO Agreement*'), and, as such, are both 'integral parts' of the same treaty, the *WTO Agreement*, that are 'binding on all Members'". Furthermore, as the Appellate Body has explained, "a treaty interpreter must read all applicable provisions of a treaty in a way that gives meaning to *all* of them, harmoniously". We agree with the Panel that "Article 3.1(b) of the *SCM Agreement* can be read together with the *Agreement on Agriculture* provisions relating to domestic support in a coherent and consistent manner which gives full and effective meaning to all of their terms".

A.1.38.11 *US – Upland Cotton*, para. 570
(WT/DS267/AB/R)

In previous appeals, the Appellate Body has explained that the WTO-consistency of an export subsidy for agricultural products has to be examined, in the first place, under the *Agreement on Agriculture*; the examination under the *SCM Agreement* would follow if necessary. Turning, then, to the *Agreement on Agriculture*, we note that Article 1(e) of that Agreement defines "export subsidies" as "subsidies contingent upon export performance, including the export subsidies listed in Article 9 of this Agreement".

A.1.38.12 *US – Upland Cotton*, para. 571
(WT/DS267/AB/R)

Although an export subsidy granted to agricultural products must be examined, in the first place, under the *Agreement on Agriculture*, we find it appropriate, as has the Appellate Body in previous disputes, to rely on the *SCM Agreement* for guidance in interpreting provisions of the *Agreement on Agriculture*. Thus, we consider the export-contingency requirement in Article 1(e) of the *Agreement on Agriculture* having regard to that same requirement contained in Article 3.1(a) of the *SCM Agreement*.

A.1.38.13 *US – Upland Cotton*, paras. 629–630
(WT/DS267/AB/R)

... According to the United States, "Article 3 of the *SCM Agreement*... is subject in its application to Article 21.1 of the *Agreement on Agriculture*". The United States then argues that, because "export credit guarantees are not subject to the disciplines of export subsidies for purposes of the *Agreement on Agriculture*, Article 21.1 of that Agreement renders Article 3.1(a) of the *SCM Agreement* inapplicable to such measures"....

... Therefore, because it is premised on an incorrect interpretation of Article 10.2 of the *Agreement on Agriculture*, we reject the United States' argument....

A.1.38.14 *US – Upland Cotton*, para. 647
(WT/DS267/AB/R)

We agree with the United States that Article 10.3 of the *Agreement on Agriculture* does not apply to claims brought under the *SCM Agreement*. However, the Panel did not make the error attributed to it by the United States. The Panel made the statement relied on by the United States in the context of its assessment of the United States' export credit guarantee program under the *Agreement on Agriculture*. Although the Panel made use of the criteria set out in item (j) of the Illustrative List of Export Subsidies annexed to the *SCM Agreement* (providing these programs at premium rates inadequate to cover long-term operating costs and losses) it did so as contextual guidance for its analysis under the *Agreement on Agriculture*, and both the United States and Brazil appear to have agreed with the appropriateness of this approach. Thus, the Panel's reference to Article 10.3 did not relate to its assessment of the United States' export credit guarantee programs under the *SCM Agreement*.

A.1.38.15 *EC – Export Subsidies on Sugar*, paras. 338–339 and footnote 537 to para. 339

(WT/DS265/AB/R, WT/DS266/AB/R, WT/DS283/AB/R)

Turning to the specific case before us, we note that the Complaining Parties argue that their claims under the *SCM Agreement* are closely related to their claims under the *Agreement on Agriculture*. We are not persuaded, however, that Articles 3, 8, and 9.1 of the *Agreement on Agriculture*, on the one hand, and Articles 3.1(a), 3.2, and items (a) and (d) of the Illustrative List of the *SCM Agreement*, on the other hand, are "closely related", because the issues presented under the two Agreements are different in several respects.

Furthermore, in the instant case, we note that the Panel made reference to the limited arguments made by the Complaining Parties under the *SCM Agreement*: . . . Although, on appeal, the Complaining Parties did argue their claims under the *SCM Agreement* to some extent, they did not address, in a sufficient manner, the question whether Article 3 of the *SCM Agreement* applies to export subsidies listed in Article 9.1 of the *Agreement on Agriculture* that are provided to *scheduled* agricultural products in excess of a responding Member's commitment levels. We believe that, in the light of Article 21 of the *Agreement on Agriculture* and the chapeau of Article 3 of the *SCM Agreement*, the question of the applicability of the *SCM Agreement* to the export subsidies in this dispute raises a number of complex issues.[537] We also consider that, in the absence of a full exploration of these issues, completing the analysis might affect the due process rights of the participants.

[537] These issues include, for instance, whether the *Agreement on Agriculture* contains "specific provisions dealing specifically with the same matter" (Appellate Body Report, *US – Upland Cotton*, paras. 532–533 (quoting Appellate Body Report, *EC – Bananas III*, para. 155; and referring to Appellate Body Report, *Chile – Price Band System*, para. 186)); whether the *SCM Agreement* applies to the subsidy as a whole, or whether it applies to the subsidy only to the extent that the subsidy exceeds the responding Members' commitment levels as specified in its Schedule; and whether, in the event the *SCM Agreement* applies, a panel could make a recommendation to withdraw the subsidy in whole, or whether that recommendation would apply to the subsidy only to the extent that it exceeds the responding Member's commitment levels.

Agreement on Implementation of Article VI of the GATT 1994. *See* Anti-Dumping Agreement (A.3)

Agreement on Import Licensing Procedures. *See* Licensing Agreement (L.2)

Agreement on Safeguards. *See* Safeguards Agreement (S.1)

Agreement on Subsidies and Countervailing Measures. *See* SCM Agreement (S.2)

Agreement on Technical Barriers to Trade. *See* TBT Agreement (T.4)

A.2 Amicus Curiae Briefs

A.2.1 Briefs submitted by NGOs

A.2.1.1 *US – Shrimp*, para. 89
(WT/DS58/AB/R)

We consider that the attaching of a brief or other material to the submission of either appellant or appellee, no matter how or where such material may have originated, renders that material at least *prima facie* an integral part of that participant's submission. On the one hand, it is of course for a participant in an appeal to determine for itself what to include in its submission. On the other hand, a participant filing a submission is properly regarded as assuming responsibility for the contents of that submission, including any annexes or other attachments.

A.2.1.2 *US – Shrimp*, para. 101
(WT/DS58/AB/R)

. . . access to the dispute settlement process of the WTO is limited to Members of the WTO. This access is not available, under the *WTO Agreement* and the covered agreements as they currently exist, to individuals or international organizations, whether governmental or non-governmental. Only Members may become parties to a dispute of which a panel may be seized, and only Members "having a substantial interest in a matter before a panel" may become third parties in the proceedings before that panel. Thus, under the DSU, only Members who are parties to a dispute, or who have notified their interest in becoming third parties in such a dispute to the DSB, have a *legal right* to make submissions to, and have a *legal right* to have those submissions considered by, a panel. Correlatively, a panel is *obliged* in law to accept and give due consideration only to submissions made by the parties and the third parties in a panel proceeding. . . .

A.2.1.3 *US – Shrimp*, para. 104
(WT/DS58/AB/R)

The comprehensive nature of the authority of a panel to "seek" information and technical advice from "any individual or body" it may consider appropriate, or from "any relevant source", should be underscored. This authority embraces more than merely the choice and evaluation of the *source* of the information or advice which it may seek. A panel's authority includes the authority to decide *not to seek* such information or advice at all. We consider that a panel also has the authority to *accept or reject* any information or advice which it may have sought and received, or to *make some other appropriate disposition* thereof. It is particularly within the province and the authority of a panel to determine *the need for information and advice* in a specific case, to ascertain the *acceptability* and *relevancy* of information or advice received, and to decide *what weight to ascribe to that information or advice* or to conclude that no weight at all should be given to what has been received.

A.2.1.4 *US – Shrimp*, para. 107
(WT/DS58/AB/R)

... If, in the exercise of its sound discretion in a particular case, a panel concludes *inter alia* that it could do so without "unduly delaying the panel process", it could grant permission to file a statement or a brief, subject to such conditions as it deems appropriate. The exercise of the panel's discretion could, of course, and perhaps should, include consultation with the parties to the dispute...

A.2.1.5 *US – Shrimp*, paras. 108–109
(WT/DS58/AB/R)

... authority to *seek* information is not properly equated with a *prohibition* on accepting information which has been submitted without having been requested by a panel. A panel has the discretionary authority either to accept and consider or to reject information and advice submitted to it, *whether requested by a panel or not*. The fact that a panel may *motu proprio* have initiated the request for information does not, by itself, bind the panel to accept and consider the information which is actually submitted. The amplitude of the authority vested in panels to shape the processes of fact-finding and legal interpretation makes clear that a panel will *not* be deluged, as it were, with non-requested material, *unless that panel allows itself to be so deluged.*

Moreover, acceptance and rejection of the information and advice of the kind here submitted to the Panel need not exhaust the universe of possible appropriate dispositions thereof....

A.2.1.6 *US – Shrimp*, para. 110
(WT/DS58/AB/R)

... we consider that the Panel acted within the scope of its authority under Articles 12 and 13 of the DSU in allowing any party to the dispute to attach the briefs by non-governmental organizations, or any portion thereof, to its own submissions.

A.2.1.7 *US – Lead and Bismuth II*, para. 39
(WT/DS138/AB/R)

In considering this matter, we first note that nothing in the DSU or the *Working Procedures* specifically provides that the Appellate Body may accept and consider submissions or briefs from sources other than the participants and third participants in an appeal. On the other hand, neither the DSU nor the *Working Procedures* explicitly prohibit acceptance or consideration of such briefs. However, Article 17.9 of the DSU provides:

> Working procedures shall be drawn up by the Appellate Body in consultation with the Chairman of the DSB and the Director-General, and communicated to the Members for their information.

This provision makes clear that the Appellate Body has broad authority to adopt procedural rules which do not conflict with any rules and procedures in the DSU or the covered agreements. Therefore, we are of the opinion that as long as we act consistently with the provisions of the DSU and the covered agreements, we have the legal authority to decide whether or not to accept and consider any information that we believe is pertinent and useful in an appeal.

A.2.1.8 *US – Lead and Bismuth II*, para. 40
(WT/DS138/AB/R)

We wish to emphasize that in the dispute settlement system of the WTO, the DSU envisages *participation* in panel or Appellate Body proceedings, as a matter of legal right, *only* by parties and third parties to a dispute. And, under the DSU, *only* Members of the WTO have a legal right to participate as parties or third parties in a particular dispute. . . .

A.2.1.9 *US – Lead and Bismuth II*, para. 41
(WT/DS138/AB/R)

Individuals and organizations, which are not Members of the WTO, have no legal *right* to make submissions to or to be heard by the Appellate Body. The Appellate Body has no legal *duty* to accept or consider unsolicited *amicus curiae* briefs submitted by individuals or organizations, not Members of the WTO. The Appellate Body has a legal *duty* to accept and consider *only* submissions from WTO Members which are parties or third parties in a particular dispute.

A.2.1.10 *US – Lead and Bismuth II*, para. 42
(WT/DS138/AB/R)

We are of the opinion that we have the legal authority under the DSU to accept and consider *amicus curiae* briefs in an appeal in which we find it pertinent and useful to do so. In this appeal, we have not found it necessary to take the two *amicus curiae* briefs filed into account in rendering our decision.

A.2.1.11 *US – Shrimp (Article 21.5 – Malaysia)*, para. 76
(WT/DS58/AB/RW)

As we have previously stated in our Report in *United States – Import Prohibition of Certain Shrimp and Shrimp Products* ("*United States – Shrimp*"), attaching a brief or other material to the submission of either an appellant or an appellee, no matter how or where such material may have originated, renders that material at least *prima facie* an integral part of that participant's submission. In that Report, we stated further that it is for a participant in an appeal to determine for itself what to include in its submission.

A.2.1.12 *EC – Sardines*, para. 160

(WT/DS231/AB/R)

. . . Accordingly, we believe that the objections of Peru with regard to the *amicus curiae* brief submitted by a private individual are unfounded. We find that we have the authority to accept the brief filed by a private individual, and to consider it. We also find that the brief submitted by a private individual does not assist us in this appeal.

A.2.1.13 *US – Softwood Lumber IV*, para. 9 and footnotes 21–22

(WT/DS257/AB/R)

The Appellate Body received two *amicus curiae* briefs during the course of these proceedings. The first, dated 21 October 2003, was received from the Indigenous Network on Economies and Trade (based in Vancouver, British Columbia, Canada).[21] The second, dated 7 November 2003, was a joint brief filed by Defenders of Wildlife (based in Washington, D.C., United States), Natural Resources Defense Council (based in Washington, D.C., United States) and Northwest Ecosystem Alliance (based in Bellingham, state of Washington, United States).[22] These briefs dealt with some questions not addressed in the submissions of the participants or third participants. No participant or third participant adopted the arguments made in these briefs. Ultimately, in this appeal, the Division did not find it necessary to take the two *amicus curiae* briefs into account in rendering its decision.

[21] This brief purported to add an indigenous dimension to the issues raised by this appeal.
[22] The organizations filing this brief commented on the environmental implications of the issues raised by this appeal.

A.2.2 Briefs submitted by WTO Members

A.2.2.1 *EC – Sardines*, para. 161

(WT/DS231/AB/R)

We turn now to the issue of the *amicus curiae* brief filed by Morocco, which raises a novel issue, as this is the first time that a WTO Member has submitted such a brief in any WTO dispute settlement proceeding. . . .

A.2.2.2 *EC – Sardines*, para. 162

(WT/DS231/AB/R)

. . . in *US – Lead and Bismuth II* . . . we did *not* distinguish between, on the one hand, submissions from WTO Members that are not participants or third participants in a particular appeal, and, on the other hand, submissions from *non*-WTO Members.

A.2.2.3 *EC – Sardines*, para. 164
(WT/DS231/AB/R)

... As we have already determined that we have the authority to receive an *amicus curiae* brief from a private individual or an organization, *a fortiori* we are entitled to accept such a brief from a WTO Member, provided there is no prohibition on doing so in the DSU. We find no such prohibition.

A.2.2.4 *EC – Sardines*, para. 165
(WT/DS231/AB/R)

... We have examined Articles 10.2 and 17.4, and we do not share Peru's view. Just because those provisions stipulate when a Member may participate in a dispute settlement proceeding as a third party or third participant, does not, in our view, lead inevitably to the conclusion that participation by a Member as an *amicus curiae* is prohibited.

A.2.2.5 *EC – Sardines*, para. 166
(WT/DS231/AB/R)

... By contrast, participation as *amici* in WTO appellate proceedings is not a legal *right*, and we have no duty to accept any *amicus curiae* brief. We may do so, however, based on our legal authority to regulate our own procedures as stipulated in Article 17.9 of the DSU. The fact that Morocco, as a sovereign State, has chosen not to exercise its *right* to participate in this dispute by availing itself of its third-party rights at the panel stage does not, in our opinion, undermine our *legal authority* under the DSU and our *Working Procedures* to accept and consider the *amicus curiae* brief submitted by Morocco.

A.2.2.6 *EC – Sardines*, para. 167
(WT/DS231/AB/R)

Therefore, we find that we are entitled to accept the *amicus curiae* brief submitted by Morocco, and to consider it.... To the contrary, acceptance of any *amicus curiae* brief is a matter of discretion, which we must exercise on a case-by-case basis....... Therefore, we could exercise our discretion to reject an *amicus curiae* brief if, by accepting it, this would interfere with the "fair, prompt and effective resolution of trade disputes." This could arise, for example, if a WTO Member were to seek to submit an *amicus curiae* brief at a very late stage in the appellate proceedings, with the result that accepting the brief would impose an undue burden on other participants.

A.2.2.7 *EC – Sardines*, para. 170
(WT/DS231/AB/R)

In sum, with the exception of the arguments relating to Article 2.1 of the *TBT Agreement* and the GATT 1994, to which we will return later, we find that Morocco's *amicus curiae* brief does not assist us in this appeal.

A.2.3 Additional Procedure

A.2.3.1 *EC – Asbestos*, para. 50
(WT/DS135/AB/R)

... we wrote to the parties and the third parties indicating that we were mindful that, in the proceedings before the Panel in this case, the Panel received five written submissions from non-governmental organizations, two of which the Panel decided to take into account. In our letter, we recognized the possibility that we might receive submissions in this appeal from persons other than the parties and the third parties to this dispute, and stated that we were of the view that the fair and orderly conduct of this appeal could be facilitated by the adoption of appropriate procedures, for the purposes of this appeal only, pursuant to Rule 16(1) of the *Working Procedures*, to deal with any possible submissions received from such persons. To this end, we invited the parties and the third parties in this appeal to submit their comments on a number of questions. These related to: whether we should adopt a "request for leave" procedure; what procedures would be needed to ensure that the parties and third parties would have a full and adequate opportunity to respond to submissions that might be received; and whether we should take any other points into consideration if we decided to adopt a "request for leave" procedure. . . .

A.2.3.2 *EC – Asbestos*, para. 51
(WT/DS135/AB/R)

... after consultations among all seven Members of the Appellate Body, we adopted, pursuant to Rule 16(1) of the *Working Procedures*, an additional procedure, *for the purposes of this appeal only*, to deal with written submissions received from persons other than the parties and third parties to this dispute (the "Additional Procedure"). The Additional Procedure was communicated to the parties and third parties. . . . the Chairman of the Appellate Body informed the Chairman of the Dispute Settlement Body, in writing, of the Additional Procedure adopted, and this letter was circulated, for information, as a dispute settlement document to the Members of the WTO. In that communication, the Chairman of the Appellate Body stated that:

> ... This additional procedure has been adopted by the Division hearing this appeal for the purposes of this appeal only pursuant to Rule 16(1) of the *Working Procedures for Appellate Review*, and is *not* a new working procedure drawn up by the Appellate Body pursuant to paragraph 9 of Article 17 of the *Understanding on Rules and Procedures Governing the Settlement of Disputes*. (original emphasis)

The Additional Procedure was posted on the WTO website...

A.2.3.3 *EC – Asbestos*, para. 52
(WT/DS135/AB/R)

The Additional Procedure provided:

> 1. In the interests of fairness and orderly procedure in the conduct of this appeal, the Division hearing this appeal has decided to adopt, pursuant to Rule 16(1) of the *Working Procedures for Appellate Review*,

and after consultations with the parties and third parties to this dispute, the following additional procedure for purposes of this appeal only.

2. Any person, whether natural or legal, other than a party or a third party to this dispute, wishing to file a written brief with the Appellate Body, must apply for leave to file such a brief from the Appellate Body *by noon* on *Thursday, 16 November 2000*.

3. An application for leave to file such a written brief shall:

(a) be made in writing, be dated and signed by the applicant, and include the address and other contact details of the applicant;
(b) be in no case longer than three typed pages;
(c) contain a description of the applicant, including a statement of the membership and legal status of the applicant, the general objectives pursued by the applicant, the nature of the activities of the applicant, and the sources of financing of the applicant;
(d) specify the nature of the interest the applicant has in this appeal;
(e) identify the specific issues of law covered in the Panel Report and legal interpretations developed by the Panel that are the subject of this appeal, as set forth in the Notice of Appeal (WT/DS135/8) dated 23 October 2000, which the applicant intends to address in its written brief;
(f) state why it would be desirable, in the interests of achieving a satisfactory settlement of the matter at issue, in accordance with the rights and obligations of WTO Members under the DSU and the other covered agreements, for the Appellate Body to grant the applicant leave to file a written brief in this appeal; and indicate, in particular, in what way the applicant will make a contribution to the resolution of this dispute that is not likely to be repetitive of what has been already submitted by a party or third party to this dispute; and
(g) contain a statement disclosing whether the applicant has any relationship, direct or indirect, with any party or any third party to this dispute, as well as whether it has, or will, receive any assistance, financial or otherwise, from a party or a third party to this dispute in the preparation of its application for leave or its written brief.

4. The Appellate Body will review and consider each application for leave to file a written brief and will, without delay, render a decision whether to grant or deny such leave.

5. The grant of leave to file a brief by the Appellate Body does not imply that the Appellate Body will address, in its Report, the legal arguments made in such a brief.

6. Any person, other than a party or a third party to this dispute, granted leave to file a written brief with the Appellate Body, must file its brief with the Appellate Body Secretariat *by noon* on *Monday, 27 November 2000*.

7. A written brief filed with the Appellate Body by an applicant granted leave to file such a brief shall:

(a) be dated and signed by the person filing the brief;
(b) be concise and in no case longer than 20 typed pages, including any appendices; and

> (c) set out a precise statement, strictly limited to legal arguments, supporting the applicant's legal position on the issues of law or legal interpretations in the Panel Report with respect to which the applicant has been granted leave to file a written brief.
>
> 8. An applicant granted leave shall, in addition to filing its written brief with the Appellate Body Secretariat, also serve a copy of its brief on all the parties and third parties to the dispute *by noon* on *Monday, 27 November 2000*.
>
> 9. The parties and the third parties to this dispute will be given a full and adequate opportunity by the Appellate Body to comment on and respond to any written brief filed with the Appellate Body by an applicant granted leave under this procedure. (original emphasis)

A.2.3.4 *EC – Asbestos*, para. 55
(WT/DS135/AB/R)

Pursuant to the Additional Procedure, the Appellate Body received 17 applications requesting leave to file a written brief in this appeal. Six of these 17 applications were received after the deadline specified in paragraph 2 of the Additional Procedure and, for this reason, leave to file a written brief was denied to these six applicants. Each such applicant was sent a copy of our decision denying its application for leave because the application was not filed in a timely manner.

A.2.3.5 *EC – Asbestos*, para. 56
(WT/DS135/AB/R)

The Appellate Body received 11 applications for leave to file a written brief in this appeal within the time limits specified in paragraph 2 of the Additional Procedure. We carefully reviewed and considered each of these applications in accordance with the Additional Procedure and, in each case, decided to deny leave to file a written brief. Each applicant was sent a copy of our decision denying its application for leave for failure to comply sufficiently with all the requirements set forth in paragraph 3 of the Additional Procedure.

A.3 Anti-Dumping Agreement

Article 1. *See* Anti-Dumping Agreement, Article VI of the GATT 1994 – Anti-Dumping duties (A.3.65)

A.3.1 Article 2 – Intent and effect of dumping

A.3.1.1 *US – 1916 Act*, para. 107
(WT/DS136/AB/R, WT/DS162/AB/R)

. . . under Article VI:1 of the GATT 1994 and Article 2 of the *Anti-Dumping Agreement*, neither the intent of the persons engaging in "dumping" nor the injurious effects that "dumping" may have on a Member's domestic industry are constituent elements of "dumping".

A.3.2 Article 2 – Period of investigation

A.3.2.1 *EC – Tube or Pipe*, para. 80

(WT/DS219/AB/R)

Permitting such discretionary selection of data from a period of time within the POI would defeat the objectives underlying investigating authorities' reliance on a POI for the purposes of a dumping determination. As the Panel correctly noted, the POI "form[s] the basis for an objective and unbiased determination by the investigating authority." Like the Panel and the parties to this dispute, we understand a POI to provide data collected over a sustained period of time, which period can allow the investigating authority to make a dumping determination that is less likely to be subject to market fluctuations or other vagaries that may distort a proper evaluation. We agree with the Panel that the standardized reliance on a POI, although not fixed in duration by the *Anti-Dumping Agreement*, assures the investigating authority and exporters of "a consistent and reasonable methodology for determining present dumping", which anti-dumping duties are intended to offset. In contrast to this consistency and reliability, Brazil's approach would introduce a significant level of subjectivity on the part of the investigating authority to determine when data from a subset of the POI may be a reliable indicator of an exporter's future pricing behaviour. . . .

A.3.3 Article 2.1 – "normal value . . . in the ordinary course of trade"

A.3.3.1 *US – Hot-Rolled Steel*, para. 139

(WT/DS184/AB/R)

Article 2.1 of the *Anti-Dumping Agreement* provides that normal value – the price of the like product in the home market of the exporter or producer – must be established on the basis of sales made "in the ordinary course of trade". Thus, sales which are *not* made "in the ordinary course of trade" must be excluded, by the investigating authorities, from the calculation of normal value. . . .

A.3.3.2 *US – Hot-Rolled Steel*, para. 140

(WT/DS184/AB/R)

In terms of the above definition, Article 2.1 requires investigating authorities to exclude sales not made "in the ordinary course of trade", from the calculation of normal value, precisely to ensure that normal value is, indeed, the "normal" price of the like product, in the home market of the exporter. Where a sales transaction is concluded on terms and conditions that are incompatible with "normal" commercial practice for sales of the like product, in the market in question, at the relevant time, the transaction is not an appropriate basis for calculating "normal" value.

A.3.3.3 *US – Hot-Rolled Steel*, para. 142

(WT/DS184/AB/R)

We note that determining whether a sales price is higher or lower than the "ordinary course" price is not simply a question of comparing prices. Price is merely one of the terms and conditions of a transaction. To determine whether the price is high or low, the price must be assessed in light of the other terms and conditions of the transaction. Thus, the volume of the sales transaction will affect whether a price is high or low. Or, the seller may undertake additional liability or responsibilities in some transactions, for instance for transport or insurance. These, and a number of other factors, may be expected to affect an assessment of the price.

A.3.3.4 *US – Hot-Rolled Steel*, para. 145
(WT/DS184/AB/R)

In our view, the duties of investigating authorities, under Article 2.1 of the *Anti-Dumping Agreement*, are precisely the *same*, whether the sales price is higher or lower than the "ordinary course" price, and irrespective of the reason why the transaction is not "in the ordinary course of trade". Investigating authorities must exclude, from the calculation of normal value, *all* sales which are not made "in the ordinary course of trade". To include such sales in the calculation, whether the price is high or low, would distort what is defined as "*normal* value".

A.3.3.5 *US – Hot-Rolled Steel*, para. 146
(WT/DS184/AB/R)

In view of the many different types of transaction not "in the ordinary course of trade" – some including affiliated parties, others not; some including high prices, others low prices; some including prices below cost, others not – investigating authorities need not, under the *Anti-Dumping Agreement*, scrutinize, according to *identical* rules, *each and every* category of sale that is potentially not "in the ordinary course of trade".

A.3.4 Article 2.1 – Sales below cost

A.3.4.1 *US – Hot-Rolled Steel*, para. 147
(WT/DS184/AB/R)

We note that Article 2.2.1 of the *Anti-Dumping Agreement* itself provides for a method for determining whether *sales below cost* are "in the ordinary course of trade". However, that provision does not purport to exhaust the range of methods for determining whether sales are "in the ordinary course of trade", nor even the range of possible methods for determining whether low-priced sales are "in the ordinary course of trade". Article 2.2.1 sets forth a method for determining whether sales between *any* two parties are "in the ordinary course of trade"; it does *not* address the more specific issue of transactions between affiliated parties. In transactions between such parties, the affiliation itself may signal that *sales above cost*, but below the usual market price, might not be in the ordinary course of trade. Such transactions may, therefore, be the subject of special scrutiny by the investigating authorities.

A.3.4.2 *US – Hot-Rolled Steel*, para. 148
(WT/DS184/AB/R)

Although we believe that the *Anti-Dumping Agreement* affords WTO Members discretion to determine how to ensure that normal value is not distorted through the inclusion of sales that are not "in the ordinary course of trade", that discretion is not without limits. In particular, the discretion must be exercised in an *even-handed* way that is fair to all parties affected by an anti-dumping investigation. If a Member elects to adopt general rules to prevent distortion of normal value through sales between affiliates, those rules must reflect, even-handedly, the fact that both high and low-priced sales between affiliates might not be "in the ordinary course of trade".

A.3.5 Article 2.1 – Calculation of normal value

A.3.5.1 *US – Hot-Rolled Steel*, para. 165
(WT/DS184/AB/R)

The text of Article 2.1 expressly imposes four conditions on sales transactions in order that they may be used to calculate normal value: first, the sale must be "in the ordinary course of trade"; second, it must be of the "like product"; third, the product must be "destined for consumption in the exporting country"; and, fourth, the price must be "comparable".

A.3.5.2 *US – Hot-Rolled Steel*, para. 166
(WT/DS184/AB/R)

The text of Article 2.1 is, however, silent as to *who* the parties to relevant sales transactions should be. Thus, Article 2.1 does not expressly mandate that the sale be made by the exporter for whom a margin of dumping is being calculated. Nor does Article 2.1 expressly preclude that relevant sales transactions might be made downstream, between affiliates of the exporter and independent buyers. In our view, provided that all of the explicit conditions in Article 2.1 of the *Anti-Dumping Agreement* are satisfied, the *identity* of the seller of the "like product" is not a ground for precluding the use of a downstream sales transaction when calculating normal value. In short, we see no reason to read into Article 2.1 an additional condition that is not expressed.

A.3.6 Article 2.1 – Fair comparison

A.3.6.1 *US – Hot-Rolled Steel*, para. 167
(WT/DS184/AB/R)

We do not mean to suggest that the identity of the seller is irrelevant in calculating normal value under Article 2.1 of the *Anti-Dumping Agreement*. However, to ensure that prices are "comparable", the *Anti-Dumping Agreement* provides a mechanism, in Article 2.4, which allows investigating authorities to take full account of the fact, as appropriate, that a relevant sale was not made by the exporter or producer itself, but was made by another party. Article 2.4 requires that a "fair comparison" be made between export price and normal value. This comparison "shall be made at the same level of trade, normally at the ex-factory level". In making a "fair comparison", Article 2.4 mandates that due account be taken of "differences which affect price comparability", such as differences in the "levels of trade" at which normal value and export price are calculated.

A.3.7 Article 2.1 – Volume of dumped imports

A.3.7.1 *EC – Bed Linen (Article 21.5 – India)*, para. 143
(WT/DS141/AB/RW)

. . . We see no conflict between the provisions requiring producer-specific determinations and the need to calculate, for purposes of determining injury, the total volume of dumped imports from producers or exporters originating in a particular exporting country as a whole. This can be done, and has to be done, by adding up the volume of imports attributable to producers or exporters that are dumping, whether on the basis of an individual examination or on the basis of an extrapolation. Further, we see nothing in the text of Article 2.1 that permits a derogation from the express requirements in paragraphs 1 and 2 of Article 3 to determine the volume of dumped imports on the basis of "positive evidence" and an "objective examination".

A.3.8 Article 2.1 – Relationship with Article 11.3. *See also* Anti-Dumping Agreement, Article 11.3 (A.3.45–52)

A.3.8.1 *A.3.8.1 US – Corrosion-Resistant Steel Sunset Review*, para. 109
(WT/DS244/AB/R)

We agree with Japan that the words "[f]or the purpose of this Agreement" in Article 2.1 indicate that this provision describes the circumstances in which a product is to be considered as being dumped for purposes of the entire *Anti-Dumping Agreement*, including Article 11.3. This interpretation is supported by the fact that Article 11.3 does not indicate, either expressly or by implication, that "dumping" has a different meaning in the context of sunset reviews than in the rest of the *Anti-Dumping Agreement*. Therefore, Article 2.1 of the *Anti-Dumping Agreement* and Article VI:1 of the GATT 1994 suggest that the question for investigating authorities, in making a likelihood determination in a sunset review pursuant to Article 11.3, is whether the expiry of the duty would be likely to lead to continuation or recurrence of dumping of the product subject to the duty (that is, to the introduction of that product into the commerce of the importing country at less than its normal value). . . .

A.3.9 Article 2.2.1 – Sales below cost and "ordinary course of trade"

A.3.9.1 *US – Hot-Rolled Steel*, para. 147
(WT/DS184/AB/R)

We note that Article 2.2.1 of the *Anti-Dumping Agreement* itself provides for a method for determining whether *sales below cost* are "in the ordinary course of trade". However, that provision does not purport to exhaust the range of methods for determining whether sales are "in the ordinary course of trade", nor even the range of possible methods for determining whether low-priced sales are "in the ordinary course of trade". Article 2.2.1 sets forth a method for determining whether sales between *any* two parties are "in the ordinary course of trade"; it does *not* address the more specific issue of transactions between affiliated parties. In transactions between such parties, the affiliation itself may signal that *sales above cost*, but below the usual market price, might not be in the ordinary course of trade. Such transactions may, therefore, be the subject of special scrutiny by the investigating authorities.

A.3.9A Article 2.2.1.1 – "consider all available evidence on the proper allocation of costs"

A.3.9A.1 *US – Softwood Lumber V*, paras. 133–135
(WT/DS264/AB/R)

. . . The ordinary meaning of the term "consider" is, *inter alia*, to "look at attentively", "reflect on", or to "weigh the merits of". In the context of the second sentence of Article 2.2.1.1, we read the term "consider" to mean that an investigating authority is required, when addressing the question of proper allocation of costs for a producer or exporter, to "reflect on" and to "weigh the merits of" "all available evidence on the proper allocation of costs". . . . the requirement to "consider" evidence would not be satisfied by simply "receiving evidence" or merely "tak[ing] notice of evidence".

. . . The word "*proper*", in our view, supports our reading of the word "consider", because it suggests some degree of deliberation on the part of the investigating authority in "consider[ing] all available evidence", so as to ensure that there is a proper allocation of costs. The nature of this deliberative process will depend on the facts of a particular case before the investigating authority.

We are aware that the term "comparison", which is derived from the verb "compare", is used in other provisions of the *Anti-Dumping Agreement*. For instance, Articles 2.4 and 2.4.2 refer to the "comparison" of export prices and normal value, for purposes of establishing the existence of margins of dumping. As both the word "consider" and the word "comparison" are used in the *Anti-Dumping Agreement*, it follows, in our view, that the non-inclusion, by the drafters of the *Anti-Dumping Agreement*, in Article 2.2.1.1 of the word "compare" is not a mere oversight, but rather a purposeful act of drafting. However, as we explain below, we do not believe that this requires an interpretation that the second sentence of Article 2.2.1.1 does not, *under any circumstances*, require an investigating authority to compare methodologies.

A.3.9A.2 *US – Softwood Lumber V*, paras. 137–138
(WT/DS264/AB/R)

The second sentence of Article 2.2.1.1 requires an investigating authority to "consider" all available evidence on the proper allocation of costs, which in certain circumstances may require the investigating authority to consider alternative allocation methodologies. Therefore, the issue before us is not simply whether the word "consider", in and of itself, entails a requirement to "compare". Rather, the issue before us is whether a requirement to "consider all available evidence on the proper allocation of costs" does or does not require an investigating authority to "compare" advantages and disadvantages of alternative cost allocation methodologies.

In our view, the parameters of the obligation to "consider all available evidence" will vary case-by-case. It may well be that, in the light of the facts of a particular case, the requirement to "consider all available evidence" may be satisfied by the investigating authority without comparing allocation methodologies or aspects thereof. However, in other instances – such as where there is compelling evidence available to the investigating authority that more than one allocation methodology potentially may be appropriate to ensure that there is a proper allocation of costs – the investigating authority may be required to "reflect on" and "weigh the merits of" evidence that relates to such alternative allocation methodologies, in order to satisfy the requirement to "consider all available evidence". Thus, although the second sentence of Article 2.2.1.1 does not, as a general rule, require investigating authorities to compare allocation methodologies to assess their respective advantages and disadvantages in each and every case, there may be particular instances in which the investigating authority may be required to compare them in order to satisfy the explicit requirement of the second sentence of Article 2.2.1.1 to "consider all available evidence on the proper allocation of costs".

A.3.9B Article 2.2.1.1 – "reasonably reflect" the cost of production

A.3.9B.1 *US – Softwood Lumber V*, para. 165
(WT/DS264/AB/R)

Canada argues that USDOC, in evaluating whether Tembec's records "reasonably reflect" the cost of production of the product under consideration (that is, softwood lumber), failed to exercise its discretion in an even-handed manner. . . .

A.3.9B.2 *US – Softwood Lumber V*, para. 163
(WT/DS264/AB/R)

. . . Whether a particular approach of an investigating authority is, or is not, even-handed is, ultimately, a matter of the "legal characterization" of facts and, as such, a matter of law. We are thus unable to agree with the United States that the issue raised by Canada with respect to the lack of even-handed treatment on the part of USDOC is beyond the scope of appellate review.

A.3.10 Article 2.2.2 – Low volume sales and "ordinary course of trade"

A.3.10.1 *EC – Tube or Pipe*, para. 98
(WT/DS219/AB/R)

As the Panel correctly observed, it is meaningful for the interpretation of Article 2.2.2 that Article 2.2 specifically identifies low-volume sales *in addition to* sales outside the ordinary course of trade. In contrast to Article 2.2, the chapeau of Article 2.2.2 explicitly excludes only sales outside the ordinary course of trade. The absence of any qualifying language related to low volumes in Article 2.2.2 implies that an exception for low-volume sales should not be read into Article 2.2.2. . . .

A.3.10.2 *EC – Tube or Pipe*, para. 101
(WT/DS219/AB/R)

. . . In our view, where, as in this investigation, low-volume sales are in the ordinary course of trade, an investigating authority does not act inconsistently with the chapeau of Article 2.2.2 by including actual data from those sales to derive SG&A and profits for the construction of normal value.

A.3.11 Article 2.2.2(ii) – Calculation of "weighted average"

A.3.11.1 *EC – Bed Linen*, para. 76
(WT/DS141/AB/R)

. . . the use of the phrase "weighted average", combined with the use of the words "amounts" and "exporters or producers" in the plural in the text of Article 2.2.2(ii), clearly anticipates the use of data from *more than one* exporter or producer. We conclude that the method for calculating amounts for SG&A and profits set out in this provision can only be used if data relating to more than one other exporter or producer is available.

A.3.11.2 *EC – Bed Linen*, para. 80
(WT/DS141/AB/R)

. . . in the calculation of the "weighted average", *all* of "the actual amounts incurred and realized" by other exporters or producers must be included, *regardless* of whether those amounts are incurred and realized on production and sales made in the ordinary course of trade or not. Thus, in our view, a Member is not allowed to exclude those sales that are not made in the ordinary course of trade from the calculation of the "weighted average" under Article 2.2.2(ii).

A.3.12 Article 2.4 – Identity of seller and "fair comparison"

A.3.12.1 *US – Hot-Rolled Steel*, para. 167
(WT/DS184/AB/R)

We do not mean to suggest that the identity of the seller is irrelevant in calculating normal value under Article 2.1 of the *Anti-Dumping Agreement*. However, to ensure that prices are "comparable", the *Anti-Dumping Agreement* provides a mechanism, in Article 2.4, which allows investigating authorities to take full account of the fact, as appropriate, that a relevant sale was not made by the exporter or producer itself, but was made by another party. Article 2.4 requires that a "fair comparison" be made between export price and normal value. This comparison "shall be made at the same level of trade, normally at the ex-factory level". In making a "fair comparison", Article 2.4 mandates that due account be taken of "differences which affect price comparability", such as differences in the "levels of trade" at which normal value and export price are calculated.

A.3.13 Article 2.4 – Calculation of dumping margins – Relationship with Article 11.3. *See also* Anti-Dumping Agreement, Article 11.3 (A.3.45–52)

A.3.13.1 *US – Corrosion-Resistant Steel Sunset Review*, paras. 127–128 (WT/DS244/AB/R)

Article 2 sets out the agreed disciplines in the *Anti-Dumping Agreement* for calculating dumping margins. As observed earlier, we see no obligation under Article 11.3 for investigating authorities to calculate or rely on dumping margins in determining the likelihood of continuation or recurrence of dumping. However, should investigating authorities choose to rely upon dumping margins in making their likelihood determination, the calculation of these margins must conform to the disciplines of Article 2.4.... USDOC chose to base its affirmative likelihood determination on positive dumping margins that had been previously calculated in two particular administrative reviews. If these margins were legally flawed because they were calculated in a manner inconsistent with Article 2.4, this could give rise to an inconsistency not only with Article 2.4, but also with Article 11.3 of the *Anti-Dumping Agreement*.

It follows that we disagree with the Panel's view that the disciplines in Article 2 regarding the calculation of dumping margins do not apply to the likelihood determination to be made in a sunset review under Article 11.3....

A.3.14 Article 2.4.2 – Calculation of dumping margins – "zeroing". *See also* Anti-Dumping Agreement, Article 2.2.1.1 – "consider all available evidence on the proper allocation of costs" (A.3.9A); Anti-Dumping Agreement, Article VI of the GATT 1994 (A.3.65)

A.3.14.1 *EC – Bed Linen*, para. 53 (WT/DS141/AB/R)

...We see nothing in Article 2.4.2 or in any other provision of the *Anti-Dumping Agreement* that provides for the establishment of "the existence of margins of dumping" for *types or models* of the product under investigation; to the contrary, all references to the establishment of "the existence of margins of dumping" are references to the *product* that is subject of the investigation.... Whatever the method used to calculate the margins of dumping, in our view, these margins must be, and can only be, established for the *product* under investigation as a whole....

A.3.14.2 *EC – Bed Linen*, para. 55 (WT/DS141/AB/R)

...the investigating authorities are required to compare the weighted average normal value with the weighted average of prices of *all* comparable export transactions. Here, we emphasize that Article 2.4.2 speaks of "all" comparable export transactions. As explained above, when "zeroing", the European Communities counted as zero the "dumping margins" for those models where the "dumping margin" was "negative". As the Panel correctly noted, for those models, the European

Communities counted "the weighted average export price to be equal to the weighted average normal value ... despite the fact that it was, in reality, higher than the weighted average normal value." By "zeroing" the "negative dumping margins", the European Communities, therefore, did *not* take fully into account the entirety of the prices of *some* export transactions, namely, those export transactions involving models of cotton-type bed linen where "negative dumping margins" were found.... Thus, the European Communities did *not* establish "the existence of margins of dumping" for cotton-type bed linen on the basis of a comparison of the weighted average normal value with the weighted average of prices of *all* comparable export transactions...

A.3.14.3 *EC – Bed Linen*, para. 58
(WT/DS141/AB/R)

Having defined the product at issue and the "like product" on the Community market as it did, the European Communities could not, at a subsequent stage of the proceeding, take the position that some types or models of that product had physical characteristics that were so different from each other that these types or models were not "comparable". All types or models falling within the scope of a "like" product must necessarily be "comparable", and export transactions involving those types or models must therefore be considered "comparable export transactions" within the meaning of Article 2.4.2.

A.3.14.4 *US – Corrosion-Resistant Steel Sunset Review*, paras. 135–136
(WT/DS244/AB/R)

When investigating authorities use a zeroing methodology such as that examined in *EC – Bed Linen* to calculate a dumping margin, whether in an original investigation or otherwise, that methodology will tend to inflate the margins calculated. Apart from inflating the margins, such a methodology could, in some instances, turn a negative margin of dumping into a positive margin of dumping. As the Panel itself recognized in the present dispute, "zeroing ... may lead to an affirmative determination that dumping exists where no dumping would have been established in the absence of zeroing." Thus, the inherent bias in a zeroing methodology of this kind may distort not only the magnitude of a dumping margin, but also a finding of the very existence of dumping.

... we note that the United States seemed to accept that USDOC's methodology in the administrative reviews was "a methodology in which no offset is granted to the respondent for negative differences between the normal value and export price (or constructed export price) of individual transactions"....

A.3.14.5 *EC – Tube or Pipe*, para. 76
(WT/DS219/AB/R)

... We fail to see how Article VI:2, by stating that the purpose of anti-dumping duties is "to offset or prevent dumping", imposes upon investigating authorities an obligation to select any particular methodology for comparing normal value and export prices under Article 2.4.2 of the *Anti-Dumping Agreement* when calculating a dumping margin. . . .

A.3.14.6 *US – Softwood Lumber V*, paras. 80–81 (WT/DS264/AB/R)

We note that there is no disagreement among the participants in this dispute as to the permissibility of "multiple averaging" under Article 2.4.2. All participants agree that an investigating authority may choose to divide the product under investigation into product types or models for purposes of calculating a weighted average normal value and a weighted average export price for the transactions involving each product type or model or sub-group of "comparable" transactions. . . .

We agree with the participants in this dispute that multiple averaging is permitted under Article 2.4.2 to establish the existence of margins of dumping for the product under investigation. We disagree with those who suggest that the Appellate Body Report in *EC – Bed Linen* is premised on an assumption that multiple averaging is prohibited. The issue of multiple averaging was not before the Appellate Body in *EC – Bed Linen* and the reasoning of the Appellate Body in that case should therefore not be read as prohibiting that practice. . . .

A.3.14.7 *US – Softwood Lumber V*, para. 86 (WT/DS264/AB/R)

Article 2.4.2 requires that the existence of margins of dumping "shall normally be established on the basis of a comparison of a weighted average normal value with a weighted average of prices of *all comparable export transactions*". (emphasis added) It is clear from the language of Article 2.4.2 that a weighted average normal value is to be compared with a weighted average of the prices of "comparable" export transactions, and not with prices of "non-comparable" export transactions. At the same time, the word "all" in "all comparable export transactions" makes it clear that Members cannot exclude from a comparison any transaction that is "comparable". Thus, we agree with the Panel that the term "all comparable export transactions" means that a Member "may only compare those export transactions which are comparable, but [] it must compare *all* such transactions."

A.3.14.8 *US – Softwood Lumber V*, para. 93 (WT/DS264/AB/R)

It is clear from the texts of [Article VI:1 of the GATT 1994 and Article 2.1 of the *Anti-Dumping Agreement*] that dumping is defined in relation to a product as a whole as defined by the investigating authority. Moreover, we note that the opening phrase of Article 2.1 – "[f]or the purpose of this Agreement" – indicates that the definition of "dumping" as contained in Article 2.1 applies to the entire Agreement, which includes, of course, Article 2.4.2. "Dumping", within the meaning of the *Anti-Dumping Agreement*, can therefore be found to exist only for the product under investigation as a whole, and cannot be found to exist only for a type, model, or category of that product.

A.3.14.9 *US – Softwood Lumber V*, paras. 96–98 (WT/DS264/AB/R)

The Appellate Body found in *EC – Bed Linen* that "[w]hatever the method used to calculate the margins of dumping . . . these margins must be, and can only be, established for the *product* under investigation as a whole." While "dumping" refers to the introduction of a product into the commerce of another country at less than its normal value, the term "margin of dumping" refers to the magnitude of dumping. As with dumping, "margins of dumping" can be found only for the product under investigation as a whole, and cannot be found to exist for a product type, model, or category of that product.

It is clear that an investigating authority may undertake multiple averaging to establish margins of dumping for a product under investigation. In our view, the results of the multiple comparisons at the sub-group level are, however, not "margins of dumping" within the meaning of Article 2.4.2. Rather, those results reflect only intermediate calculations made by an investigating authority in the context of establishing margins of dumping for the product under investigation. Thus, it is only on the basis of aggregating *all* these "intermediate values" that an investigating authority can establish margins of dumping for the product under investigation as a whole.

We fail to see how an investigating authority could properly establish margins of dumping for the product under investigation as a whole without aggregating *all* of the "results" of the multiple comparisons for *all* product types. There is no textual basis under Article 2.4.2 that would justify taking into account the "results" of only some multiple comparisons in the process of calculating margins of dumping, while disregarding other "results". If an investigating authority has chosen to undertake multiple comparisons, the investigating authority necessarily has to take into account the results of *all* those comparisons in order to establish margins of dumping for the product as a whole under Article 2.4.2. . . .

A.3.14.10 *US – Softwood Lumber V*, para. 100 (WT/DS264/AB/R)

. . . Article 2.4.2 contains no express language that permits an investigating authority to disregard the results of multiple comparisons at the aggregation stage. Other provisions of the *Anti-Dumping Agreement* are explicit regarding the permissibility of disregarding certain matters. For example, Article 2.2.1 of the *Anti-Dumping Agreement*, which deals with the calculation of normal value, sets forth the *only* circumstances under which sales of the like product may be disregarded. Similarly, Article 9.4 of the *Anti-Dumping Agreement* expressly directs investigating authorities to "disregard" zero and *de minimis* margins of dumping, under certain circumstances, when calculating the weighted average margin of dumping to be applied to exporters or producers that have not been individually investigated. Thus, when the negotiators sought to permit investigating authorities to disregard certain matters, they did so explicitly.

A.3.14.11 *US – Softwood Lumber V*, paras. 101–104
(WT/DS264/AB/R)

We now turn to the implications of zeroing as applied in this case. Zeroing means, *in effect*, that at least in the case of *some* export transactions, the export prices are treated as if they were less than what they actually are. Zeroing, therefore, does not take into account the *entirety* of the *prices* of *some* export transactions, namely, the prices of export transactions in those sub-groups in which the weighted average normal value is less than the weighted average export price. Zeroing thus inflates the margin of dumping for the product as a whole.

We understand the United States to argue that a prohibition of zeroing would amount to a requirement to compare "dumped" and "non-dumped" transactions at the aggregation stage. The United States contends that results of multiple comparisons in which the weighted average normal value exceeds the weighted average export price may be excluded because they do not involve "dumping". As we have stated earlier, the terms "dumping" and "margins of dumping" in Article VI of the GATT 1994 and the *Anti-Dumping Agreement* apply to the product under investigation as a whole and do not apply to sub-group levels. The treatment of comparisons for which the weighted average normal value is less than the weighted average export price as "non-dumped" comparisons is therefore not in accordance with the requirements of Article 2.4.2 of the *Anti-Dumping Agreement.*

For all these reasons, we do not agree with the United States that the results of comparisons at the sub-group level constitute margins of dumping. Nor do we agree with the United States that the results of the comparisons in which the weighted average normal value is less than the weighted average export price could be excluded in calculating a margin of dumping for the product under investigation as a whole.

We recall that the issue of whether zeroing is permitted under the transaction-to-transaction methodology or the average-to-individual methodology is not before us in this appeal....

A.3.15 Article 3.1 – general

A.3.15.1 *Thailand – H-Beams*, para. 106
(WT/DS122/AB/R)

Article 3 as a whole deals with obligations of Members with respect to the determination of injury. Article 3.1 is an overarching provision that sets forth a Member's fundamental, substantive obligation in this respect. Article 3.1 informs the more detailed obligations in succeeding paragraphs. These obligations concern the determination of the volume of dumped imports, and their effect on prices (Article 3.2), investigations of imports from more than one country (Article 3.3), the impact of dumped imports on the domestic industry (Article 3.4), causality between dumped imports and injury (Article 3.5), the assessment of the domestic production of the like product (Article 3.6), and the determination of the threat of material injury (Articles 3.7 and 3.8). The focus of Article 3 is thus on *substantive* obligations that a Member must fulfill in making an injury determination.

A.3.15A Footnote 9 to Article 3

A.3.15A.1 *US – Oil Country Tubular Goods Sunset Reviews*, para. 276 (WT/DS268/AB/R)

... we would agree with Argentina that, by virtue of its opening phrase, footnote 9 defines "injury" for the whole of the *Anti-Dumping Agreement*.... Therefore, when Article 11.3 requires a determination as to the likelihood of continuation or recurrence of "injury", the investigating authority must consider the continuation or recurrence of "injury" as defined in footnote 9.

A.3.16 Article 3.1 – "positive evidence"

A.3.16.1 *Thailand – H-Beams*, para. 107 (WT/DS122/AB/R)

... the ordinary meaning of [the terms of Article 3.1] does not suggest that an investigating authority is required to base an injury determination only upon evidence disclosed to, or discernible by, the parties to the investigation. An anti-dumping investigation involves the commercial behaviour of firms, and, under the provisions of the *Anti-Dumping Agreement*, involves the collection and assessment of *both* confidential and non confidential information. An injury determination conducted pursuant to the provisions of Article 3 of the *Anti-Dumping Agreement* must be based on the *totality* of that evidence. We see nothing in Article 3.1 which limits an investigating authority to base an injury determination only upon non-confidential information.

A.3.16.2 *Thailand – H-Beams*, para. 111 (WT/DS122/AB/R)

We consider, therefore, that the requirement in Article 3.1 that an injury determination be based on "positive" evidence and involve an "objective" examination of the required elements of injury does *not* imply that the determination must be based only on reasoning or facts that were disclosed to, or discernible by, the parties to an anti-dumping investigation. Article 3.1, on the contrary, permits an investigating authority making an injury determination to base its determination on *all* relevant reasoning and facts before it.

A.3.16.3 *US – Hot-Rolled Steel*, para. 192 (WT/DS184/AB/R)

... The thrust of the investigating authorities' obligation, in Article 3.1, lies in the requirement that they base their determination on "positive evidence" and conduct an "objective examination". The term "positive evidence" relates, in our view, to the quality of the evidence that authorities may rely upon in making a determination. The word "positive" means, to us, that the evidence must be of an affirmative, objective and verifiable character, and that it must be credible.

A.3.17 Article 3.1 – "objective examination"

A.3.17.1 *US – Hot-Rolled Steel*, para. 193
(WT/DS184/AB/R)

The term "objective examination" aims at a different aspect of the investigating authorities' determination. While the term "positive evidence" focuses on the facts underpinning and justifying the injury determination, the term "objective examination" is concerned with the investigative process itself. The word "examination" relates, in our view, to the way in which the evidence is gathered, inquired into and, subsequently, evaluated; that is, it relates to the conduct of the investigation generally. The word "objective", which qualifies the word "examination", indicates essentially that the "examination" process must conform to the dictates of the basic principles of good faith and fundamental fairness. In short, an "objective examination" requires that the domestic industry, and the effects of dumped imports, be investigated in an unbiased manner, without favouring the interests of any interested party, or group of interested parties, in the investigation. The duty of the investigating authorities to conduct an "objective examination" recognizes that the determination will be influenced by the objectivity, or any lack thereof, of the investigative process.

A.3.17.2 *US – Hot-Rolled Steel*, para. 196
(WT/DS184/AB/R)

However, the investigating authorities' evaluation of the relevant factors must respect the fundamental obligation, in Article 3.1, of those authorities to conduct an "objective examination". If an examination is to be "objective", the identification, investigation and evaluation of the relevant factors must be even-handed. Thus, investigating authorities are not entitled to conduct their investigation in such a way that it becomes more likely that, as a result of the fact-finding or evaluation process, they will determine that the domestic industry is injured.

A.3.17.3 *US – Hot-Rolled Steel*, paras. 204–205
(WT/DS184/AB/R)

We have already stated that it may be highly pertinent for investigating authorities to examine a domestic industry by part, sector or segment. However, as with all other aspects of the evaluation of the domestic industry, Article 3.1 of the *Anti-Dumping Agreement* requires that such a sectoral examination be conducted in an "objective" manner. In our view, this requirement means that, where investigating authorities undertake an examination of one part of a domestic industry, they should, in principle, examine, in like manner, all of the other parts that make up the industry, as well as examine the industry as a whole. Or, in the alternative, the investigating authorities should provide a satisfactory explanation as to why it is not necessary to examine directly or specifically the other parts of the domestic industry. Different parts of an industry may exhibit quite different economic performance during any given period. . . .

Moreover, by examining only one part of an industry, the investigating authorities may fail properly to appreciate the economic relationship between that part of the industry and the other parts of the industry, or between one or more of those parts and the whole industry. . . .

A.3.17.4 *US – Hot-Rolled Steel*, para. 206
(WT/DS184/AB/R)

Accordingly, an examination of only certain parts of a domestic industry does not ensure a proper evaluation of the state of the domestic industry as a whole, and does not, therefore, satisfy the requirements of "objectiv[ity]" in Article 3.1 of the *Anti-Dumping Agreement.*

A.3.18 Articles 3.1 and 3.2 – Method of calculating the "volume of the dumped imports"

A.3.18.1 *EC – Bed Linen (Article 21.5 – India)*, para. 113
(WT/DS141/AB/RW)

Although paragraphs 1 and 2 of Article 3 do not set out a *specific* methodology that investigating authorities are required to follow when calculating the volume of "dumped imports", this does not mean that paragraphs 1 and 2 of Article 3 confer unfettered discretion on investigating authorities to pick and choose whatever methodology they see fit for determining the volume and effects of the dumped imports. Paragraphs 1 and 2 of Article 3 require investigating authorities to make a determination of injury on the basis of "positive evidence" and to ensure that the injury determination results from an "objective examination" of the volume of dumped imports, the effects of the dumped imports on prices, and, ultimately, the state of the domestic industry. Thus, whatever methodology investigating authorities choose for determining the volume of dumped imports, if that methodology fails to ensure that a determination of injury is made on the basis of "positive evidence" and involves an "objective examination" of *dumped* imports – rather than imports that are found *not* to be dumped – it is not consistent with paragraphs 1 and 2 of Article 3.

A.3.18.2 *EC – Bed Linen (Article 21.5 – India)*, para. 117
(WT/DS141/AB/RW)

Thus, there is a right to conduct a limited examination in the circumstances described in the second sentence of Article 6.10. Paragraphs 1 and 2 of Article 3 must, accordingly, be interpreted in a way that permits investigating authorities to satisfy the requirements of "positive evidence" and an "objective examination" without having to investigate each producer or exporter individually. This does not, however, in any way, absolve investigating authorities from the absolute requirements in paragraphs 1 and 2 of Article 3 that the volume of dumped imports be determined on the basis of "positive evidence" and an "objective examination".

A.3.18.3 *EC – Bed Linen (Article 21.5 – India)*, para. 118 (WT/DS141/AB/RW)

. . . Still, whatever methodology investigating authorities choose for calculating the volume of "dumped imports", that calculation and, ultimately, the determination of injury under Article 3, clearly must be made on the basis of "positive evidence" and involve an "objective examination". . . .

A.3.19 Articles 3.1 and 3.2 – Calculation of the "volume of the dumped imports" without examining each producer or exporter individually. *See also* Anti-Dumping Agreement, Article 2.1 (A.3.3–8); Anti-Dumping Agreement, Article 3.3 (A.3.21); Anti-Dumping Agreement, Article 6.10 (A.3.37); Anti-Dumping Agreement, Article 9.4 (A.3.41–44)

A.3.19.1 *EC – Bed Linen (Article 21.5 – India)*, para. 130 (WT/DS141/AB/RW)

In this dispute, we agree with the participants that the evidence on dumping margins established for the producers that were examined individually is "positive" in the sense that we defined it in *US – Hot-Rolled Steel*,. . . We also agree . . . that evidence on *dumping* margins of more than *de minimis* for examined producers is relevant as "positive evidence" in this investigation for determining which import volumes may be attributed to *non*-examined producers that are *dumping*. In our view, both these qualities of evidence are probative of the existence of dumping in the circumstances of this investigation. Therefore, we conclude that the European Communities met the first requirement of paragraphs 1 and 2 of Article 3 by basing its determination on that "positive evidence".

A.3.19.2 *EC – Bed Linen (Article 21.5 – India)*, para. 132 (WT/DS141/AB/RW)

. . . The approach taken by the European Communities in determining the volume of dumped imports was not based on an "objective examination". The examination was not "objective" because its result is predetermined by the methodology itself. Under the approach used by the European Communities, whenever the investigating authorities decide to *limit* the examination to some, but not all, producers – as they are entitled to do under Article 6.10 – *all* imports from *all non*-examined producers will *necessarily always be included* in the volume of dumped imports under Article 3, as long as any of the producers examined individually were found to be dumping. . . . Moreover, such an approach tends to favour methodologies where *small numbers* of producers are examined individually. . . .

A.3.19.3 *EC – Bed Linen (Article 21.5 – India)*, para. 133
(WT/DS141/AB/RW)

For these reasons, we conclude that the European Communities' determination that *all* imports attributable to *non*-examined producers were dumped – even though the evidence from *examined* producers showed that producers accounting for 53 percent of imports attributed to examined producers were *not* dumping – did not lead to a result that was *unbiased*, *even-handed*, and *fair*. Therefore, the European Communities did not satisfy the requirements of paragraphs 1 and 2 of Article 3...

A.3.19.4 *EC – Bed Linen (Article 21.5 – India)*, para. 137
(WT/DS141/AB/RW)

...Article 6.10...does *not stipulate* that investigating authorities must follow a specific *methodology* when determining the *volume* of dumped imports under paragraphs 1 and 2 of Article 3. However, this does not mean that *evidence* emerging from the determination of margins of dumping for *individual* producers or exporters pursuant to Article 6.10 is irrelevant for the determination of the volume of dumped imports in paragraphs 1 and 2 of Article 3. To the contrary, such evidence may well form part of the "positive evidence" on which an "objective examination" of the volume of dumped imports for purposes of determining injury may be based. Indeed, in cases where the examination has been limited to a select number of producers under the authority of the second sentence of Article 6.10, it is difficult to conceive of a determination based on "positive evidence" and an "objective examination" that is made other than through some form of *extrapolation* of the evidence....

A.3.19.5 *EC – Bed Linen (Article 21.5 – India)*, para. 138
(WT/DS141/AB/RW)

India's suggestion that the investigating authorities should consider the *same* proportion of import volumes attributable to *non*-examined producers as *dumped*, as the proportion of import volumes attributed to *examined* producers that were found to be dumping, may be one way of adducing "positive evidence" from the record of an investigation and of conducting an "objective examination", especially if producers selected for individual examination constitute a statistically valid sample representative of all producers. Even if the producers selected for individual examination account, instead, for the *largest percentage of exports* that could reasonably be investigated, we do not exclude the possibility that the evidence from those *examined* producers could, nonetheless, qualify as part of the "positive evidence" that might serve as a basis for an "objective examination" of import volumes that can be attributed to the remaining *non*-examined producers. There may, indeed, be other ways of making these calculations that satisfy the requirements of paragraphs 1 and 2 of Article 3.

A.3.19.6 *EC – Bed Linen (Article 21.5 – India)*, para. 146
(WT/DS141/AB/RW)

. . . we agree with the Panel "that the [Anti-Dumping] Agreement does **not** require an investigating authority to determine the volume of imports from producers outside the sample that is properly considered 'dumped imports' for purposes of injury analysis on the basis of the proportion of imports from sampled producers that is found to be dumped" according to the *specific methodology* suggested by India in this appeal. . . .

A.3.20 Article 3.2 – No country-specific analysis of volume and prices of dumped imports

A.3.20.1 *EC – Tube or Pipe*, para. 111 and footnote 114
(WT/DS219/AB/R)

. . . There is no indication in the text of Article 3.2 that the analyses of volume and prices must be performed on a country-by-country basis where an investigation involves imports from several countries.[114]

[114] Brazil's thesis is further predicated on the assumption that if no significant increase in dumped imports (either in absolute terms or relative to production and consumption in the importing Member) were found originating from a specific country under Article 3.2, then those imports would have to be excluded from cumulative assessment under Article 3.3. (Brazil's response to questioning at the oral hearing) However, we find no support for this argument in the text of Article 3.2 itself: significant increases in imports have to be "consider[ed]" by investigating authorities under Article 3.2, but the text does not indicate that in the absence of such a significant increase, these imports could not be found to be causing injury.

A.3.20.2 *EC – Tube or Pipe*, para. 113
(WT/DS219/AB/R)

We also believe that cumulation without a country-specific analysis does not result in a "derog[ation]" of Article 3.2, as Brazil has asserted. We wish to emphasize that Article 3.2 plays a central role in the determination of injury and is a necessary step in any anti-dumping investigation. As the Panel correctly observed, it is possible for the analyses of volume and prices envisaged under Article 3.2 to be done on a cumulative basis, as opposed to an individual country basis, when dumped imports originate from more than one country.

A.3.21 Article 3.3 – Cumulative assessment of dumped imports.

See also Anti-Dumping Agreement, Article 3.2 (A.3.20)

A.3.21.1 *EC – Bed Linen (Article 21.5 – India)*, para. 145
(WT/DS141/AB/RW)

. . . The provisions regarding the cumulative assessment of imports pursuant to Article 3.3 must be interpreted consistently with the provisions of the *Anti-Dumping Agreement* that deal with the determinations of dumping margins or the application of anti-dumping duties with respect to specific producers or groups thereof.

Similarly, the right under Article 3.3 to conduct anti-dumping investigations with respect to imports from different exporting countries does not absolve investigating authorities from the requirements of paragraphs 1 and 2 of Article 3 to determine the volume of dumped imports on the basis of "positive evidence" and an "objective examination".

A.3.21.2 *EC – Tube or Pipe*, para. 110
(WT/DS219/AB/R)

We find no basis in the text of Article 3.3 for Brazil's assertion that a country-specific analysis of the potential negative effects of volumes and prices of dumped imports is a pre-condition for a cumulative assessment of the effects of all dumped imports. Article 3.3 sets out expressly the conditions that must be fulfilled before the investigating authorities may cumulatively assess the effects of dumped imports from more than one country. There is no reference to the country-by-country volume and price analyses that Brazil contends are pre-conditions to cumulation. In fact, Article 3.3 expressly requires an investigating authority to examine country-specific volumes, not in the manner suggested by Brazil, but for purposes of determining whether the "volume of imports from each country is not negligible".

A.3.21.3 *EC – Tube or Pipe*, para. 115
(WT/DS219/AB/R)

... Therefore, the text of Article 3 does not support Brazil's contention that volume and prices are deemed exclusively to be "factors", and not "effects", for the purposes of Article 3.3 of the *Anti-Dumping Agreement.*

A.3.21.4 *EC – Tube or Pipe*, para. 116
(WT/DS219/AB/R)

The apparent rationale behind the practice of cumulation confirms our interpretation that both volume and prices qualify as "effects" that may be cumulatively assessed under Article 3.3. A cumulative analysis logically is premised on a recognition that the domestic industry faces the impact of the "dumped imports" as a whole and that it may be injured by the total impact of the dumped imports, even though those imports originate from various countries. If, for example, the dumped imports from some countries are low in volume or are declining, an exclusively country-specific analysis may not identify the causal relationship between the dumped imports from those countries and the injury suffered by the domestic industry. The outcome may then be that, because imports from such countries could not *individually* be identified as causing injury, the dumped imports from these countries would not be subject to anti-dumping duties, even though they are in fact causing injury. In our view, therefore, by expressly providing for cumulation in Article 3.3 of the *Anti-Dumping Agreement*, the negotiators appear to have recognized that a domestic industry confronted with dumped imports originating from several countries may be injured by the cumulated effects of those imports, and that those effects may not be adequately taken into account in a country-specific analysis of the injurious effects of dumped imports. Consistent with the rationale behind cumulation, we consider that changes in import volumes from individual countries, and the effect of those country-specific volumes on prices in the importing country's market, are of little significance in determining whether injury is being caused to the domestic industry by the dumped imports as a whole.

A.3.21.5 *US – Oil Country Tubular Goods Sunset Reviews*, para. 300
(WT/DS268/AB/R)

Given the express intention of Members to permit cumulation in injury determinations in original investigations, and given the rationale behind cumulation in injury determinations, we do not read the *Anti-Dumping Agreement* as prohibiting cumulation in sunset reviews.

A.3.22 Article 3.4 – Evaluation of injury factors

A.3.22.1 *Thailand – H-Beams*, para. 125
(WT/DS122/AB/R)

. . . The Panel also examined, with respect to this issue, the interpretation by a previous panel of Article 3.4, and an earlier interpretation given by us of an analogous provision, Article 4.2(a) of the *Agreement on Safeguards*. The Panel concluded its comprehensive analysis by stating that "each of the fifteen individual factors listed in the mandatory list of factors in Article 3.4 must be evaluated by the investigating authorities. . . ". We agree with the Panel's analysis in its entirety, and with the Panel's interpretation of the mandatory nature of the factors mentioned in Article 3.4 of the *Anti-Dumping Agreement.*

A.3.22.2 *Thailand – H-Beams*, paras. 127–128
(WT/DS122/AB/R)

. . . Further, the Panel's interpretation that Article 3.4 requires a mandatory evaluation of all the individual factors listed in that Article clearly left no room for a "permissible" interpretation that all individual factors need *not* be considered.

We conclude that the Panel was correct in its interpretation that Article 3.4 requires a mandatory evaluation of all of the factors listed in that provision, and that, therefore, the Panel did not err in its application of the standard of review under Article 17.6(ii) of the *Anti-Dumping Agreement.*

A.3.22.3 *US – Hot-Rolled Steel*, para. 195
(WT/DS184/AB/R)

We see nothing in the *Anti-Dumping Agreement* which prevents a Member from requiring that its investigating authorities examine, in every investigation, the potential relevance of a particular "other factor", not listed in Article 3.4, as part of its overall "examination" of the state of the domestic industry. Similarly, it seems to us perfectly compatible with Article 3.4 for investigating authorities to undertake, or for a Member to require its investigating authorities to undertake, an evaluation of particular parts, sectors or segments within a domestic industry. Such a sectoral analysis may be highly pertinent, from an economic perspective, in assessing the state of an industry as a whole.

A.3.22.4 *US – Hot-Rolled Steel*, para. 196
(WT/DS184/AB/R)

However, the investigating authorities' evaluation of the relevant factors must respect the fundamental obligation, in Article 3.1, of those authorities to conduct an "objective examination". If an examination is to be "objective", the identification, investigation and evaluation of the relevant factors must be even-handed. Thus, investigating authorities are not entitled to conduct their investigation in such a way that it becomes more likely that, as a result of the fact-finding or evaluation process, they will determine that the domestic industry is injured.

A.3.22.5 *US – Hot-Rolled Steel*, para. 198
(WT/DS184/AB/R)

. . . In our opinion, nothing in the *Anti-Dumping Agreement* prevents the United States from directing its investigating authorities to evaluate the potential relevance of the structure of a domestic industry, and, in particular, the importance to that industry, as a whole, of the fact that the production of certain domestic producers is captively consumed, while the production of other domestic producers competes directly with imports in the merchant market. . . .

A.3.22.6 *US – Hot-Rolled Steel*, para. 206
(WT/DS184/AB/R)

Accordingly, an examination of only certain parts of a domestic industry does not ensure a proper evaluation of the state of the domestic industry as a whole, and does not, therefore, satisfy the requirements of "objectiv[ity]" in Article 3.1 of the *Anti-Dumping Agreement*.

A.3.22.7 *EC – Tube or Pipe*, para. 131
(WT/DS219/AB/R)

[Article 3.4 of the *Anti-Dumping Agreement*] requires an investigating authority to evaluate all relevant economic factors in its examination of the impact of the dumped imports. By its terms, it does not address the manner in which the results of this evaluation are to be set out, nor the type of evidence that may be produced before a panel for the purpose of demonstrating that this evaluation was indeed conducted. The provision simply requires Members to include an evaluation of all relevant economic factors in its examination of the impact of the dumped imports. . . .

A.3.22.8 *EC – Tube or Pipe*, para. 156
(WT/DS219/AB/R)

The participants in this appeal do not dispute that it is mandatory for investigating authorities to evaluate all of the fifteen injury factors listed in Article 3.4 of the *Anti-*

Dumping Agreement. One of the fifteen factors expressly listed in Article 3.4 is the "actual and potential negative effects on . . . growth". The issue raised by Brazil in this appeal is whether the requirements of Article 3.4 were satisfied in this case, even though the factor "growth" was evaluated only "implicitly" and no separate record of its evaluation was made.

A.3.22.9 *EC – Tube or Pipe*, para. 157
(WT/DS219/AB/R)

Looking first to the text of Article 3.4, we find that it calls for "an evaluation of all relevant economic factors and indices having a bearing on the state of the industry". The text, however, does not address the *manner* in which the results of the investigating authority's analysis of each injury factor are to be set out in the published documents.

A.3.23 Article 3.4 – Manner of evaluating injury factors

A.3.23.1 *EC – Tube or Pipe*, para. 160
(WT/DS219/AB/R)

. . . The obligation to evaluate all fifteen factors is distinct from the *manner* in which the evaluation is to be set out in the published documents. As the European Communities contends, that the analysis of a factor is implicit in the analyses of other factors does not necessarily lead to the conclusion that such a factor was not evaluated.

A.3.23.2 *EC – Tube or Pipe*, para. 161
(WT/DS219/AB/R)

Accordingly, because Articles 3.1 and 3.4 do not regulate the *manner* in which the results of the analysis of each injury factor are to be set out in the published documents, we share the Panel's conclusion that it is not required that in every anti-dumping investigation a separate record be made of the evaluation of each of the injury factors listed in Article 3.4. Whether a panel conducting an assessment of an anti-dumping measure is able to find in the record sufficient and credible evidence to satisfy itself that a factor has been evaluated, even though a separate record of the evaluation of that factor has not been made, will depend on the particular facts of each case. . . .

A.3.23.3 *EC – Tube or Pipe*, para. 162
(WT/DS219/AB/R)

Having regard to the nature of the factor "growth", we believe that an evaluation of that factor necessarily entails an analysis of certain other factors listed in Article 3.4. Consequently, the evaluation of those factors could cover also the evaluation of the factor "growth". . . .

A.3.23.4 *EC – Tube or Pipe*, para. 165
(WT/DS219/AB/R)

. . . From our perspective, the "declines" and "losses" observed with respect to several of the factors examined in this particular case necessarily relate to the issue of "growth" as well. To put it more precisely, the negative trends in these factors point to a lack of "growth". This, in turn, supports the conclusion that the European Commission evaluated this injury factor.

A.3.24 Article 3.5 – Non-attribution of injury caused by other known factors

A.3.24.1 *US – Hot-Rolled Steel*, para. 223
(WT/DS184/AB/R)

The non-attribution language in Article 3.5 of the *Anti-Dumping Agreement* applies solely in situations where dumped imports and other known factors are causing injury to the domestic industry *at the same time*. In order that investigating authorities, applying Article 3.5, are able to ensure that the injurious effects of the other known factors are not "attributed" to dumped imports, they must appropriately assess the injurious effects of those other factors. Logically, such an assessment must involve separating and distinguishing the injurious effects of the other factors from the injurious effects of the dumped imports. If the injurious effects of the dumped imports are not appropriately separated and distinguished from the injurious effects of the other factors, the authorities will be unable to conclude that the injury they ascribe to dumped imports is actually caused by those imports, rather than by the other factors. Thus, in the absence of such separation and distinction of the different injurious effects, the investigating authorities would have no rational basis to conclude that the dumped imports are indeed causing the injury which, under the *Anti-Dumping Agreement*, justifies the imposition of anti-dumping duties.

A.3.24.2 *US – Hot-Rolled Steel*, para. 224
(WT/DS184/AB/R)

We emphasize that the particular methods and approaches by which WTO Members choose to carry out the process of separating and distinguishing the injurious effects of dumped imports from the injurious effects of the other known causal factors are not prescribed by the *Anti-Dumping Agreement*. What the Agreement requires is simply that the obligations in Article 3.5 be respected when a determination of injury is made.

A.3.24.3 *US – Hot-Rolled Steel*, para. 226
(WT/DS184/AB/R)

It is clear to us that the interpretive approach adopted by the panel in *United States – Atlantic Salmon Anti-Dumping Duties* is at odds with the interpretive approach for Article 3.5 of the *Anti-Dumping Agreement* that we have just set forth. As we said, in order to comply with the non-attribution language in that provision, investigating authorities must make an appropriate assessment of the injury caused to the domestic industry by the other known factors, and they must separate and distinguish the injurious effects of the dumped imports from the injurious effects of those other factors. This requires a satisfactory explanation of the nature and extent of the injurious effects of the other factors, as distinguished from the injurious effects of the dumped imports. However, the panel in *United States – Atlantic Salmon Anti-Dumping Duties*, expressly disavowed any need to "identify" the injury caused by the other factors. According to that panel, such separate identification of the injurious effects of the other causal factors is not required.

A.3.24.4 *US – Hot-Rolled Steel*, para. 227
(WT/DS184/AB/R)

By following the panel in *United States – Atlantic Salmon Anti-Dumping Duties*, the Panel, in effect, took the view that the USITC was not required to separate and distinguish the injurious effects of the other factors from the injurious effects of dumped imports, and that the nature and extent of the injurious effects of the other known factors need not be identified at all. However, in our view, this is precisely what the non-attribution language in Article 3.5 of the *Anti-Dumping Agreement* requires, in order to ensure that determinations regarding dumped imports are not based on mere assumptions about the effects of those imports, as distinguished from the effects of the other factors.

A.3.24.5 *US – Hot-Rolled Steel*, para. 228
(WT/DS184/AB/R)

The United States contends that the panel in *United States – Atlantic Salmon Anti-Dumping Duties* correctly stated that there is no need to "isolate" the injurious effects of the other factors from the injurious effects of the dumped imports. We are not certain what the panel, in that dispute, intended to imply through the use of the word "isolation". Nevertheless, we agree with the United States that the different causal factors operating on a domestic industry may interact, and their effects may well be inter-related, such that they produce a *combined* effect on the domestic industry. We recognize, therefore, that it may not be easy, as a practical matter, to separate and distinguish the injurious effects of different causal factors. However, although this process may not be easy, this is precisely what is envisaged by the non-attribution language. If the injurious effects of the dumped imports and the other known factors remain lumped together and indistinguishable, there is simply no means of knowing whether injury ascribed to dumped imports was, in reality, caused by other factors. Article 3.5, therefore, requires investigating authorities to undertake the process of assessing appropriately, and separating and distinguishing, the injurious effects of dumped imports from those of other known causal factors.

A.3.24.6 *EC – Bed Linen (Article 21.5 – India)*, para. 112
(WT/DS141/AB/RW)

Article 3.5 continues in the same vein as the initial paragraphs of Article 3 by requiring a demonstration that dumped imports are causing injury to the domestic industry "through the *effects of dumping*", which, of course, depends upon there being imports from producers or exporters that *are dumped.* In addition, Article 3.5 lists "volume and prices of imports *not* sold at dumping prices" as an example of "known factors *other than the dumped* imports" that are injuring the domestic industry at the same time as the dumped imports. Article 3.5 requires that this injury *not* be attributed to the dumped imports. . . .

A.3.24.7 *EC – Tube or Pipe*, para. 188
(WT/DS219/AB/R)

. . . Non-attribution therefore requires separation and distinguishing of the effects of other causal factors from those of the dumped imports so that injuries caused by the dumped imports and those caused by other factors are not "lumped together" and made "indistinguishable".

A.3.24.8 *EC – Tube or Pipe*, para. 189
(WT/DS219/AB/R)

. . . Thus, provided that an investigating authority does not attribute the injuries of other causal factors to dumped imports, it is free to choose the methodology it will use in examining the "causal relationship" between dumped imports and injury.

A.3.25 Article 3.5 – Examination of other known factors

A.3.25.1 *EC – Tube or Pipe*, para. 175
(WT/DS219/AB/R)

. . . Critical to the effective operation of the non-attribution obligation, and indeed, the entire causality analysis, is the requirement of Article 3.5 to "examine any known factors other than the dumped imports which at the same time are injuring the domestic industry", for it is the "injuries" of those "known factors" that must not be attributed to dumped imports. In order for this obligation to be triggered, Article 3.5 requires that the factor at issue:

(a) be "known" to the investigating authority;
(b) be a factor "other than dumped imports"; and
(c) be injuring the domestic industry at the same time as the dumped imports.

A.3.25.2 *EC – Tube or Pipe*, para. 176
(WT/DS219/AB/R)

We are mindful that the *Anti-Dumping Agreement* does not expressly state how such factors should become "known" to the investigating authority, or if and in what manner they must be raised by interested parties, in order to qualify as "known".

We also recognize that the *Anti-Dumping Agreement* does not expressly state to what degree a factor must be unrelated to the dumped imports, or whether it must be extrinsic to the exporter and the dumped product, in order to constitute a factor "other than the dumped imports"....

A.3.25.3 *EC – Tube or Pipe*, para. 177
(WT/DS219/AB/R)

We note that Brazil's claim rests entirely on the assumption that there was a marked difference in the costs of production between the Brazilian exporter and the European Communities producers. Brazil's factual allegation regarding the difference in costs of production, however, was rejected by the European Commission.... Having rejected the Brazilian exporter's factual premise in the context of one phase of the investigation, the European Commission, in our view, had no reason to undertake an analysis in a subsequent phase of the investigation that would have been predicated upon the very correctness of the same premise. In other words, once the European Commission had determined that the allegation of the difference in cost of production was unfounded, it had no obligation to examine its effects on the domestic industry under Article 3.5.

A.3.25.4 *EC – Tube or Pipe*, para. 178
(WT/DS219/AB/R)

...However, we disagree with the Panel's apparent understanding of the term "known" in Article 3.5. We understand the Panel, in rejecting this aspect of Brazil's claim under Article 3.5, to have stated that the alleged causal factor *was* "known" to the European Commission in the context of its dumping and injury analyses, but that the factor was nevertheless *not* "known" in the context of its causality analysis. In our view, a factor is either "known" to the investigating authority, or it is not "known"; it cannot be "known" in one stage of the investigation and unknown in a subsequent stage....

A.3.26 Article 3.5 – Individual vs. Collective effects of other factors.

See also Anti-Dumping Agreement, Articles 3.1 and 3.2 (A.3.18–19)

A.3.26.1 *EC – Tube or Pipe*, para. 190
(WT/DS219/AB/R)

Turning to Brazil's arguments in this appeal, we do not read Article 3.5 as requiring, in each and every case, an examination of the *collective* effects of other causal factors *in addition to* examining those factors' individual effects. We observed in *US – Hot-Rolled Steel* that the non-attribution language of the *Anti-Dumping Agreement* necessarily requires that an investigating authority separate and distinguish the effects of other causal factors from the effects of dumped imports, because only by doing so can an investigating authority "conclude that the injury they ascribe to dumped imports is actually caused by those imports, rather than by the other factors."

A.3.26.2 *EC – Tube or Pipe*, para. 191
(WT/DS219/AB/R)

In contrast, we do not find that an examination of *collective* effects is necessarily required by the non-attribution language of the *Anti-Dumping Agreement.* In particular, we are of the view that Article 3.5 does not compel, *in every case*, an assessment of the *collective* effects of other causal factors, because such an assessment is not always necessary to conclude that injuries ascribed to dumped imports are actually caused by those imports and not by other factors.

A.3.26.3 *EC – Tube or Pipe*, para. 192
(WT/DS219/AB/R)

We believe that, depending on the facts at issue, an investigating authority could reasonably conclude, without further inquiry into *collective* effects, that "the injury . . . ascribe[d] to dumped imports is actually caused by those imports, rather than by the other factors." At the same time, we recognize that there may be cases where, because of the specific factual circumstances therein, the failure to undertake an examination of the collective impact of other causal factors would result in the investigating authority improperly attributing the effects of other causal factors to dumped imports. We are therefore of the view that an investigating authority is not required to examine the collective impact of other causal factors, provided that, under the specific factual circumstances of the case, it fulfils its obligation not to attribute to dumped imports the injuries caused by other causal factors.

A.3.26.4 *US – Steel Safeguards*, para. 491
(WT/DS248/AB/R, WT/DS249/AB/R, WT/DS251/AB/R, WT/DS252/AB/R, WT/DS253/AB/R, WT/DS254/AB/R, WT/DS258/AB/R, WT/DS259/AB/R)

Lastly, it may be useful to refer to our finding in *EC – Tube or Pipe Fittings* in respect of the relevance of factors that "had effectively been found not to exist". In that case, the competent authority had found, contrary to the submissions of the exporters, that the difference in costs of production between the imported product and the domestic product was virtually non-existent and thus did not constitute a "factor other than dumped imports" causing injury to the domestic industry under Article 3.5 of the *Anti-Dumping Agreement.* Consequently, we found that there was no reason for the investigating authority to undertake the analysis of whether the alleged "other factor" had any *effect* on the domestic industry under Article 3.5 because the alleged "other factor" "had effectively been found *not* to exist". In other words, we did not rule that minimal (or not significant) factors need not be considered by the competent authorities in conducting non-attribution analyses. Rather, we ruled that only factors that have been found to exist need be taken into account in the non-attribution analysis.

A.3.27 Article 3.7 – Threat of material injury

A.3.27.1 *Mexico – Corn Syrup (Article 21.5 – US)*, para. 83
(WT/DS132/AB/RW)

. . . Article 3.7 of the *Anti-Dumping Agreement* sets forth a number of requirements that must be respected in order to reach a valid determination of a threat of material injury. The third sentence of Article 3.7 explicitly recognizes that it is the *investigating authorities* who make a determination of threat of material injury, and that such determination – by the investigating authorities – "must be based on facts and not merely on allegation, conjecture or remote possibility". Consequently, Article 3.7 is not addressed to panels, but to the national investigating authorities which determine the existence of a threat of material injury.

A.3.27.2 *Mexico – Corn Syrup (Article 21.5 – US)*, para. 85
(WT/DS132/AB/RW)

In our view, the "establishment" of facts by investigating authorities includes both affirmative findings of events that took place during the period of investigation as well as assumptions relating to such events made by those authorities in the course of their analyses. In determining the existence of a *threat* of material injury, the investigating authorities will necessarily have to make assumptions relating to "the "occurrence of future events" since such *future* events "can never be definitively proven by facts". Notwithstanding this intrinsic uncertainty, a "proper establishment" of facts in a determination of threat of material injury must be based on events that, although they have not yet occurred, must be "clearly foreseen and imminent", in accordance with Article 3.7 of the *Anti-Dumping Agreement*.

A.3.28 Article 5.4 – Motives of domestic producers for supporting investigation

A.3.28.1 *US – Offset Act (Byrd Amendment)*, para. 283
(WT/DS217/AB/R, WT/DS234/AB/R)

A textual examination of Article 5.4 of the *Anti-Dumping Agreement* and Article 11.4 of the *SCM Agreement* reveals that those provisions contain no requirement that an investigating authority examine the motives of domestic producers that elect to support an investigation. Nor do they contain any explicit requirement that support be based on certain motives, rather than on others. The use of the terms "expressing support" and "expressly supporting" clarify that Articles 5.4 and 11.4 require only that authorities "determine" that support has been "expressed" by a sufficient number of domestic producers. Thus, in our view, an "examination" of the "degree" of support, and not the "nature" of support is required. In other words, it is the "quantity", rather than the "quality", of support that is the issue.

A.3.29 Article 6 – Evidentiary rules for anti-dumping investigations. *See also* Anti-Dumping Agreement, Article 11.3 (A.3.45–52)

A.3.29.1 *EC – Bed Linen (Article 21.5 – India)*, para. 136
(WT/DS141/AB/RW)

Article 6 is entitled "Evidence", and there is no indication in Article 6 – or elsewhere in the *Anti-Dumping Agreement* – that Article 6 does not apply generally to matters relating to "evidence" throughout that Agreement. Therefore, it seems to us that the subparagraphs of Article 6 set out evidentiary rules that apply throughout the course of an anti-dumping investigation, and provide also for due process rights that are enjoyed by "interested parties" throughout such an investigation.

A.3.30 Article 6.1 – "ample opportunity to present in writing all evidence". *See also* Anti-Dumping Agreement, Article 11.4 (A.3.53)

A.3.30.1 *A.3.30.1 US – Hot-Rolled Steel*, paras. 73–75
(WT/DS184/AB/R)

We observe that Article 6.1.1 does not explicitly use the word "deadlines". However, the *first* sentence of Article 6.1.1 clearly contemplates that investigating authorities may impose appropriate time-limits on interested parties for responses to questionnaires. That first sentence also prescribes an absolute minimum of 30 days for the initial response to a questionnaire. Article 6.1.1, therefore, recognizes that it is fully consistent with the *Anti-Dumping Agreement* for investigating authorities to impose time-limits for the submission of questionnaire responses. Investigating authorities must be able to control the conduct of their investigation and to carry out the multiple steps in an investigation required to reach a final determination. Indeed, in the absence of time-limits, authorities would effectively cede control of investigations to the interested parties, and could find themselves unable to complete their investigations within the time-limits mandated under the *Anti-Dumping Agreement*. . . .

. . . According to the express wording of the second sentence of Article 6.1.1, investigating authorities must extend the time-limit for responses to questionnaires "upon *cause shown*", where granting such an extension is "*practicable*". (emphasis added) This second sentence, therefore, indicates that the time-limits imposed by investigating authorities for responses to questionnaires are *not* necessarily absolute and immutable.

In sum, Article 6.1.1 establishes that investigating authorities may impose time-limits for questionnaire responses, and that in appropriate circumstances these time-limits must be extended. . . .

A.3.30.2 *US – Oil Country Tubular Goods Sunset Reviews*, para. 242
(WT/DS268/AB/R)

. . . the "ample" and "full" opportunities guaranteed by Articles 6.1 and 6.2, respectively, cannot extend indefinitely and must, at some point, legitimately cease to exist. This point must be determined by reference to the right of investigating authorities to rely on deadlines in the conduct of their investigations and reviews. Where the continued granting of opportunities to present evidence and attend hearings would impinge on an investigating authority's ability to "control the conduct" of its inquiry and to "carry out the multiple steps" required to reach a timely completion of the sunset review, a respondent will have reached the limit of the "ample" and "full" opportunities provided for in Articles 6.1 and 6.2 of the *Anti-Dumping Agreement*.

A.3.30.3 *US – Oil Country Tubular Goods Sunset Reviews*, para. 245 (WT/DS268/AB/R)

We consider, first, whether the due process rights of Articles 6.1 and 6.2 are denied to those respondents who file *incomplete submissions* in response to the USDOC notice of initiation. We recall that the Panel found that the USDOC considers submissions to be incomplete, for the purposes of Section 351.218(d)(2)(iii) of the USDOC Regulations, where *all* of the requested information is not contained in the respondent's submission. An incomplete submission might contain relevant evidence in support of the respondent's position, yet fall short of the information required by the USDOC Regulations in order to be considered "complete" by the USDOC. The Panel assumed *arguendo* that, as the United States claimed, the USDOC uses this "incomplete" information in making its *order-wide* sunset determination. Nevertheless, the Panel found, and the United States agrees on appeal, that "the USDOC is precluded from taking into consideration, in its determination *with respect to a given exporter*, the facts submitted by that exporter [in an incomplete response]". As the United States acknowledges, and as discussed above, the company-specific determination is "consider[ed]" by the USDOC when making its subsequent order-wide evaluation and is relevant to, even if not determinative of, the outcome of the sunset review.

A.3.30.4 *US – Oil Country Tubular Goods Sunset Reviews*, para. 246 (WT/DS268/AB/R)

. . . with respect to at least one part of the USDOC's analysis underlying the order-wide determination, evidence "presented" by a respondent is *disregarded* and an affirmative likelihood determination is made for that respondent. In our view, disregarding a respondent's evidence in this manner is incompatible with the respondent's right, under Article 6.1, to present evidence that it considers relevant in respect of the sunset review. The agency is clearly notified of a respondent's interest in participating in the sunset review by virtue of the respondent having filed a response – albeit an incomplete one. . . .

A.3.31 Article 6.2 – Opportunity for interested parties to defend their interests

A.3.31.1 *EC – Tube or Pipe*, para. 149 (WT/DS219/AB/R)

The European Communities recognized during the oral hearing that a finding of violation in this case under Article 6.4 would necessarily entail a violation of

Article 6.2. We are also of the view that, by failing to meet its legal obligation to disclose Exhibit EC-12, the European Communities did not afford the Brazilian exporter "a full opportunity for the defence of [its] interests" as required under Article 6.2 of the *Anti-Dumping Agreement*. One of the stated objectives of the disclosure of information required under Article 6.4 is to allow interested parties "to prepare presentations on the basis of this information". The "presentations" referred to in Article 6.4, whether written or oral, logically are the principal mechanisms through which an exporter subject to an anti-dumping investigation can defend its interests. Thus, by failing to disclose Exhibit EC-12 and thereby depriving the Brazilian exporter of an opportunity to present its defence, the European Communities did not act consistently with Article 6.2.

A.3.31.2 *US – Oil Country Tubular Goods Sunset Reviews*, para. 246 (WT/DS268/AB/R)

. . . the respondent will also be denied any opportunity to confront parties with adverse interests in a hearing, notwithstanding this respondent's clear expression of interest in participating in the sunset review. As a result, this respondent is denied its rights, pursuant to Article 6.2, to the "full opportunity for the defence of [its] interests". The United States claims that the USDOC "takes all record evidence into account, including evidence in incomplete submissions, when making the order-wide determination". This does not alter the fact that evidence in incomplete submissions is disregarded in the course of the USDOC's analysis, namely, when making company-specific determinations, thereby denying respondents their rights under Articles 6.1 and 6.2.

A.3.31.3 *US – Oil Country Tubular Goods Sunset Reviews*, para. 248 (WT/DS268/AB/R)

We now turn to evaluate whether those respondents that do not respond *at all* to the USDOC notice of initiation are also denied opportunities guaranteed by Articles 6.1 and 6.2. These respondents will also face automatic affirmative company-specific determinations, be precluded from submitting evidence in the remainder of the sunset proceeding, and not be allowed a hearing with adverse parties. Unlike the case of respondents who file *incomplete submissions*, however, there will be no evidence submitted by that respondent that the USDOC would disregard. Thus, the sole basis on which such respondents may claim a denial of rights under Articles 6.1 and 6.2 is the denial of the opportunity to participate in later stages of the proceeding, including the right to request a hearing and submit evidence subsequent to the filing deadline of the initial submission.

A.3.31.4 *US – Oil Country Tubular Goods Sunset Reviews*, para. 249 (WT/DS268/AB/R)

In this case, the claim under Article 6 centres on the *initiation* stage of the proceeding. In our view, an investigating authority may have at the initiation stage particular concerns about enforcing its deadline for receiving notifications of a respondent's interest in participating. The submissions filed by respondents and domestic interested parties frame the scope of the sunset review for the investigating authority. These submissions inform the agency as to the extent of the issues and company-specific data that may need to be investigated and adjudicated upon in the course of the sunset review. . . .

A.3.31.5 *US – Oil Country Tubular Goods Sunset Reviews*, para. 250
(WT/DS268/AB/R)

Respondents' initial submissions also serve to inform other interested parties of the critical issues in dispute in the sunset review. Particularly where company-specific behaviour is relevant to the final likelihood-of-dumping determination – for example, in respect of an individual respondent's dumping margins and volume and value of exports – respondents' submissions may provide factual information necessary for other interested parties to defend their interests adequately before the agency. . . . Because respondents' initial submissions effectively contribute to establishing the parameters of the sunset review – for the investigating authority as well as for other interested parties – the investigating authority has a significant interest in requiring respondents to comply with the deadline for notification of interest in participating at the initial stage of the proceeding.

A.3.31.6 *US – Oil Country Tubular Goods Sunset Reviews*, para. 252
(WT/DS268/AB/R)

. . . the rights to present evidence and request a hearing cannot be said to be "denied" to a respondent that is given an opportunity to submit an initial response to the notice of initiation simply because it must do so by a deadline that is conceded to be reasonable. We do not see it as an unreasonable burden on respondents to require them to file a timely submission in order to preserve their rights for the remainder of the sunset review. Indeed, even an incomplete submission will serve to preserve those rights. Accordingly, we are of the view that, if a respondent decides not to undertake the necessary initial steps to avail itself of the "ample" and "full" opportunities available for the defence of its interests, the fault lies with the respondent, and not with the deemed waiver provision.

A.3.32 Article 6.4 – Access to information relevant for interested parties to present their case. *See also* Anti-Dumping Agreement, Article 6.2 (A.3.31); Anti-Dumping Agreement, Article 11.4 (A.3.53)

A.3.32.1 *EC – Tube or Pipe*, para. 145
(WT/DS219/AB/R)

We turn first to the requirement that the information be "relevant". From the Panel's reasoning, it is apparent that it read this requirement to mean "relevant" from the perspective of the *investigating authority*. We disagree. Article 6.4 refers to "provid[ing] timely opportunities for all interested parties to see all information that is relevant to the presentation of *their* cases". (emphasis added) The possessive pronoun "their" clearly refers to the earlier reference in that sentence to "interested parties". The investigating authorities are not mentioned in Article 6.4 until later in the sentence, when the provision refers to the additional requirement that the information be "used by the authorities". Thus, whether or not the investigating authorities regarded the information in Exhibit EC-12 to be relevant does not determine whether the information would in fact have been "relevant" for the purposes of Article 6.4.

A.3.32.2 *EC – Tube or Pipe*, para. 146
(WT/DS219/AB/R)

This conclusion is supported by our reasoning in *US –+ Hot Rolled Steel*, where we explained that "Article 3.4 lists certain factors *which are deemed to be relevant in every investigation* and which must always be evaluated by the investigating authorities." Thus, because Exhibit EC-12 contains information on some of the injury factors listed in Article 3.4, and the injury factors listed in that provision "are deemed to be relevant in every investigation", Exhibit EC-12 must be considered to contain information that is relevant to the investigation carried out by the European Commission. As such, the information in Exhibit EC-12 was necessarily relevant to the presentation of the interested parties' cases and is, therefore, "relevant" for purposes of Article 6.4.

A.3.32.3 *EC – Tube or Pipe*, para. 147
(WT/DS219/AB/R)

. . . In our view, however, the Panel's reasoning overlooks the fact that the European Commission was required to evaluate all the injury factors listed in Article 3,4, and the evaluation of some of these factors is set out exclusively in Exhibit EC-12. In other words, Exhibit EC-12 relates to a required step in the anti-dumping investigation. The European Communities relies on Exhibit EC-12 as the *sole evidence* that it performed this required step. As we see it, this necessarily leads to the conclusion that the information in Exhibit EC-12 was in fact "used" by the European Commission in the anti-dumping investigation and that, therefore, Exhibit EC-12 also satisfies this criterion of Article 6.4. Thus, the European Communities was not entitled to exclude this information on the basis that it did not consider that it provided "value added" to the investigation.

A.3.33 Article 6.8 and Annex II – Facts available to investigating authorities

A.3.33.1 *US – Hot-Rolled Steel*, para. 77
(WT/DS184/AB/R)

Article 6.8 identifies the circumstances in which investigating authorities may overcome a lack of information, in the responses of the interested parties, by using "facts" which are otherwise "available" to the investigating authorities. According to Article 6.8, where the interested parties do not "significantly impede" the investigation, recourse may be had to facts available only if an interested party fails to submit necessary information "within a reasonable period". Thus, if information is, in fact, supplied "within a reasonable period", the investigating authorities *cannot* use facts available, but must use the information submitted by the interested party.

A.3.33.2 *US – Hot-Rolled Steel*, para. 79
(WT/DS184/AB/R)

Although this paragraph [Annex II, para. 1] is specifically concerned with ensuring that respondents receive proper notice of the rights of the investigating authorities to use facts available, it underscores that resort may be had to facts available only "if information is not supplied within a reasonable time". Like Article 6.8, paragraph 1 of Annex II indicates that determinations may *not* be based on facts available when information is supplied within a "reasonable time" but should, instead, be based on the information submitted.

A.3.34 Article 6.8 and Annex II – Timeliness of parties' submissions

A.3.34.1 *US – Hot-Rolled Steel*, para. 81
(WT/DS184/AB/R)

. . . according to paragraph 3 of Annex II, investigating authorities are directed to use information if three, and, in some circumstances, four, conditions are satisfied. In our view, it follows that if these conditions are met, investigating authorities are *not* entitled to reject information submitted, when making a determination. One of these conditions is that information must be submitted "in a *timely* fashion".

A.3.34.2 *US – Hot-Rolled Steel*, para. 82
(WT/DS184/AB/R)

. . . In our view, "timeliness" under paragraph 3 of Annex II must be read in light of the collective requirements, in Articles 6.1.1 and 6.8, and in Annex II, relating to the submission of information by interested parties. Taken together, these provisions establish a coherent framework for the treatment, by investigating authorities, of information submitted by interested parties. Article 6.1.1 establishes that investigating authorities may fix time-limits for responses to questionnaires, but indicates that, "upon cause shown", and if "practicable", these time-limits are to be extended. Article 6.8 and paragraph 1 of Annex II provide that investigating authorities may use facts available only if information is not submitted within a reasonable period of time, which, in turn, indicates that information which *is* submitted in a reasonable period of time should be used by the investigating authorities.

A.3.34.3 *US – Hot-Rolled Steel*, para. 83
(WT/DS184/AB/R)

That being so, we consider that, under paragraph 3 of Annex II, investigating authorities should not be entitled to reject information as untimely if the information is submitted within a reasonable period of time. In other words, we see, "in a timely fashion", in paragraph 3 of Annex II as a reference to a "reasonable period" or a "reasonable time". This reading of "timely" contributes to, and becomes part of, the coherent framework for fact-finding by investigating authorities. Investigating authorities *may* reject information under paragraph 3 of Annex II only in the same circumstances in which they are entitled to overcome the lack of this information through recourse to facts available, under Article 6.8 and paragraph 1 of Annex II of the *Anti-Dumping Agreement*. The coherence of this framework is also secured through the second sentence of Article 6.1.1, which requires investigating authorities to extend deadlines "upon cause shown", if "practicable". In short, if the investigating authorities determine that information was submitted within a reasonable period of time, Article 6.1.1 calls for the extension of the time-limits for the submission of information.

A.3.35 Article 6.8 and Annex II – "reasonable period" for submission of information

A.3.35.1 *US – Hot-Rolled Steel*, para. 84
(WT/DS184/AB/R)

. . . The word "reasonable" [in Article 6.8 and paragraph 1 of Annex II] implies a degree of flexibility that involves consideration of all of the circumstances of a particular case. What is "reasonable" in one set of circumstances may prove to be less than "reasonable" in different circumstances. This suggests that what constitutes a reasonable period or a reasonable time, under Article 6.8 and Annex II of the *Anti-Dumping Agreement*, should be defined on a case-by-case basis, in the light of the specific circumstances of each investigation.

A.3.35.2 *US – Hot-Rolled Steel*, para. 85
(WT/DS184/AB/R)

In sum, a "reasonable period" must be interpreted consistently with the notions of flexibility and balance that are inherent in the concept of "reasonableness", and in a manner that allows for account to be taken of the particular circumstances of each case. In considering whether information is submitted within a reasonable period of time, investigating authorities should consider, in the context of a particular case, factors such as: (i) the nature and quantity of the information submitted; (ii) the difficulties encountered by an investigated exporter in obtaining the information; (iii) the verifiability of the information and the ease with which it can be used by the investigating authorities in making their determination; (iv) whether other interested parties are likely to be prejudiced if the information is used; (v) whether acceptance of the information would compromise the ability of the investigating authorities to conduct the investigation expeditiously; and (vi) the numbers of days by which the investigated exporter missed the applicable time-limit.

A.3.35.3 *US – Hot-Rolled Steel*, para. 86
(WT/DS184/AB/R)

In determining whether information is submitted within a reasonable period of time, it is proper for investigating authorities to attach importance to the time-limit fixed for questionnaire responses, and to the need to ensure the conduct of the investigation in an orderly fashion. Article 6.8 and paragraph 1 of Annex II are not a license for interested parties simply to disregard the time-limits fixed by investigating authorities. Instead, Articles 6.1.1 and 6.8, and Annex II of the *Anti-Dumping Agreement*, must be read together as striking and requiring a balance between the rights of the investigating authorities to control and expedite the investigating process, and the legitimate interests of the parties to submit information and to have that information taken into account.

A.3.36 Article 6.8 and Annex II – Lack of cooperation by investigated parties. *See also* Anti-Dumping Agreement, Article 11.4 (A.3.53)

A.3.36.1 *US – Hot-Rolled Steel*, paras. 99–100
(WT/DS184/AB/R)

Paragraph 7 of Annex II indicates that a lack of "cooperation" by an interested party may, by virtue of the use made of facts available, lead to a result that is "less favourable" to the interested party than would have been the case had that interested party cooperated. . . . [P]arties may very well "cooperate" to a high degree, even though the requested information is, ultimately, not obtained. This is because the fact of "cooperating" is in itself not determinative of the end result of the cooperation. Thus, investigating authorities should not arrive at a "less favourable" outcome simply because an interested party fails to furnish requested information if, in fact, the interested party has "cooperated" with the investigating authorities, within the meaning of paragraph 7 of Annex II of the *Anti-Dumping Agreement*.

Paragraph 7 of Annex II does not indicate what *degree* of "cooperation" investigating authorities are entitled to expect from an interested party in order to preclude the possibility of such a "less favourable" outcome. To resolve this question we scrutinize the context found in Annex II. . . .

A.3.36.2 *US – Hot-Rolled Steel*, para. 102
(WT/DS184/AB/R)

We, therefore, see paragraphs 2 and 5 of Annex II of the *Anti-Dumping Agreement* as reflecting a careful balance between the interests of investigating authorities and exporters. In order to complete their investigations, investigating authorities are entitled to expect a very significant degree of effort – to the "best of their abilities" – from investigated exporters. At the same time, however, the investigating authorities are not entitled to insist upon *absolute* standards or impose *unreasonable* burdens upon those exporters.

A.3.36.3 *US – Hot-Rolled Steel*, paras. 119–120
(WT/DS184/AB/R)

. . . There is, however, no requirement in Article 6.8 that resort to facts available be limited to situations where there is *no* information whatsoever which can be used to calculate a margin. Thus, the application of Article 6.8, authorizing the use of facts available, is *not* confined to cases where the *entire* margin is established using *only* facts available. Rather, under Article 6.8, investigating authorities are entitled to have recourse to facts available *whenever* an interested party does not provide some necessary information within a reasonable period, or significantly impedes the investigation. Whenever such a situation exists, investigating authorities may remedy the lack of *any* necessary information by drawing appropriately from the "facts available". As the United States acknowledges, Article 6.8 may apply in situations where recourse to facts available is needed to cure the lack of even a very small amount of information.

In consequence, we are of the view that the "*circumstances* referred to" in Article 6.8 are the circumstances in which the investigating authorities properly have recourse to "facts available" to overcome a lack of necessary information in the record, and that these "circumstances" may, in fact, involve only a small amount of information to be used in the calculation of the individual margin of dumping for an exporter or producer.

A.3.37 Article 6.10 – No individual examination of all producers. *See also* Anti-Dumping Agreement, Articles 3.1 and 3.2 – Method of calculating the "volume of the dumped imports" (A.3.18); Anti-Dumping Agreement, Article 11.4 – Relationship with Article 6 (A.3.53)

A.3.37.1 *EC – Bed Linen (Article 21.5 – India)*, para. 116
(WT/DS141/AB/RW)

The issue raised in this appeal, however, does not relate to imports from producers or exporters that *were examined individually* in an investigation. Rather, it relates to the appropriate treatment of imports from producers or exporters that *were not examined individually* in such an investigation. The appeal before us involves an investigation in which *individual* margins of dumping have *not* been determined for *each* Indian producer exporting to the European Communities. It is, of course, not necessary under the *Anti-Dumping Agreement* for investigating authorities to examine *each* producer and exporter. The second sentence of Article 6.10 authorizes investigating authorities, when determining margins of dumping, to *limit their examination* where the number of producers or exporters of the product under investigation is so large that the determination of an *individual* margin of dumping for *each* of them would be *impracticable*. This limited examination may be conducted in one of two alternative ways identified in Article 6.10...

A.3.38 Article 6.13 – Cooperation between interested parties and investigation authorities

A.3.38.1 *US – Hot-Rolled Steel*, para. 104
(WT/DS184/AB/R)

Article 6.13 thus underscores that "cooperation" is, indeed, a two-way process involving joint effort. This provision requires investigating authorities to make certain allowances for, or take action to assist, interested parties in supplying information. If the investigating authorities fail to "take due account" of genuine "difficulties" experienced by interested parties, and made known to the investigating authorities, they cannot, in our view, fault the interested parties concerned for a lack of cooperation.

A.3.39 Article 9.1 – Imposition of anti-dumping duties – Relationship with Articles 2 and 3

A.3.39.1 *EC – Bed Linen (Article 21.5 – India)*, para. 123
(WT/DS141/AB/RW)

... In our view, too, the use by the drafters of the present perfect tense is significant; it indicates that the imposition and collection of anti-dumping duties under Article 9 is a separate and distinct phase of an anti-dumping action that necessarily occurs *after* the determination of dumping, injury, and causation under Articles 2 and 3 has been made. Members have the right to impose and collect anti-dumping duties only *after* the completion of an investigation in which it *has been established* that the requirements of dumping, injury, and causation "*have been fulfilled*". In other words, the right to impose anti-dumping duties under Article 9 is a *consequence* of the prior determination of the existence of dumping margins, injury, and a causal link. The determination, by the investigating authorities of a Member, that there is injury caused by a certain volume of dumping necessarily precedes and gives rise to the *consequential* right to impose and collect anti-dumping duties.

A.3.40 Article 9.2 – Product-specific vs. Company-specific anti-dumping determination. *See also* Anti-Dumping Agreement, Article 11.3 (A.3.45–52)

A.3.40.1 *US – Corrosion-Resistant Steel Sunset Review*, para. 150 and footnote 188
(WT/DS244/AB/R)

... Article 9.2 refers to the imposition of "an anti-dumping duty ... in respect of any product", rather than the imposition of a duty in respect of individual exporters or producers. We agree that this reference in Article 9.2 informs the interpretation of Article 11.3. We also note that Article 9.2 allows investigating authorities, in imposing a duty in respect of a product, to "name the supplier or suppliers of the product concerned" or, in certain circumstances, "the supplying country concerned." This suggests that authorities may use a single order to impose a "duty", even though the *amount* of the duty imposed on each exporter or producer may vary. Therefore, Article 9.2 confirms our initial view that Article 11.3 does not require investigating authorities to make their likelihood determination on a company-specific basis.[188]

[188] We have previously held that Article 9.4 is of little relevance for interpreting Articles 2 and 3 of the *Anti-Dumping Agreement* because "the right to impose anti-dumping duties under Article 9 is a *consequence* of the prior determination of the existence of dumping margins, injury, and a causal link." (Appellate Body Report, *EC – Bed Linen (Article 21.5 – India)*, paras. 123–124 (original emphasis), referring to Appellate Body Report, *EC – Bed Linen*, footnote 30 to para. 62) In contrast, the requirement to terminate an anti-dumping duty under Article 11.3 unless

investigating authorities make an affirmative likelihood determination in a sunset review is a *consequence* of the prior imposition of that duty under Article 9.

A.3.41 Article 9.4 – Calculation of the "all other" anti-dumping duty rate

A.3.41.1 *US – Hot-Rolled Steel*, para. 116
(WT/DS184/AB/R)

Article 9.4 does not prescribe any method that WTO Members must use to establish the "all others" rate that is actually applied to exporters or producers that are not investigated. Rather, Article 9.4 simply identifies a maximum limit, or ceiling, which investigating authorities "*shall not exceed*" in establishing an "all others" rate. Sub-paragraph (i) of Article 9.4 states the general rule that the relevant ceiling is to be established by calculating a "weighted average margin of dumping established" with respect to those exporters or producers who *were* investigated. However, the clause beginning with "provided that", which follows this sub-paragraph, qualifies this general rule. This qualifying language mandates that, "for the purpose of this paragraph", investigating authorities "*shall disregard*", first, zero and *de minimis* margins and, second, "margins established under the circumstances referred to in paragraph 8 of Article 6." Thus, in determining the amount of the ceiling for the "all others" rate, Article 9.4 establishes two *prohibitions*. The first prevents investigating authorities from calculating the "all others" ceiling using zero or *de minimis* margins; while the second precludes investigating authorities from calculating that ceiling using "margins established under the circumstances referred to" in Article 6.8.

A.3.42 Article 9.4 – Relationship with Article 2.4.2

A.3.42.1 *US – Hot-Rolled Steel*, para. 118
(WT/DS184/AB/R)

. . . we recall that the word "margins", which appears in Article 2.4.2 of that Agreement, has been interpreted in *European Communities – Bed Linen*. The Panel found, in that dispute, and we agreed, that "margins" means the individual margin of dumping determined for each of the investigated exporters and producers of the product under investigation, for that particular product. This margin reflects a comparison that is based upon examination of all of the relevant home market and export market transactions. We see no reason, in Article 9.4, to interpret the word "margins" differently from the meaning it has in Article 2.4.2, and the parties have not suggested one.

A.3.43 Article 9.4 – Relationship with Article 6.8

A.3.43.1 *US – Hot-Rolled Steel*, para. 122
(WT/DS184/AB/R)

We have noted that Article 9.4 establishes a prohibition, in calculating the ceiling for the all others rate, on using "margins established under the circumstances referred to" in Article 6.8. Nothing in the text of Article 9.4 supports the United States' argument that the scope of this prohibition should be narrowed so that it would be limited to excluding only margins established "entirely" on the basis of facts available. As noted earlier, Article 6.8 applies even in situations where only limited use is made of facts available. To read Article 9.4 in the way the United States does is to overlook the many situations where Article 6.8 allows a margin to be calculated, *in part*, using facts available. Yet, the text of Article 9.4 simply refers, in an open-ended fashion, to "margins established under the circumstances" in Article 6.8. Accordingly, we see no basis for limiting the scope of this prohibition in Article 9.4, by reading into it the word "entirely" as suggested by the United States. In our view, a margin does not cease to be "established under the circumstances referred to" in Article 6.8 simply because not every aspect of the calculation involved the use of "facts available".

A.3.43.2 *US – Hot-Rolled Steel*, para. 123
(WT/DS184/AB/R)

Our reading of Article 9.4 is consistent with the purpose of the provision. Article 6.8 authorizes investigating authorities to make determinations by remedying gaps in the record which are created, in essence, as a result of deficiencies in, or a lack of, information supplied by the investigated exporters. Indeed, in some circumstances, as set forth in paragraph 7 of Annex II of the *Anti-Dumping Agreement*, "if an interested party *does not cooperate* and thus relevant information is being withheld from the authorities, this situation could lead to a result which is *less favourable* to the party than if the party did cooperate." (emphasis added) Article 9.4 seeks to prevent the exporters, who were *not* asked to cooperate in the investigation, from being prejudiced by gaps or shortcomings in the information supplied by the investigated exporters. This objective would be compromised if the ceiling for the rate applied to "all others" were, as the United States suggests, calculated – due to the failure of investigated parties to supply certain information – using margins "established" even in part on the basis of the facts available.

A.3.43.3 *US – Hot-Rolled Steel*, para. 126
(WT/DS184/AB/R)

This *lacuna* arises because, while Article 9.4 *prohibits* the use of certain margins in the calculation of the ceiling for the "all others" rate, it does not expressly address the issue of *how* that ceiling should be calculated in the event that *all* margins are to be *excluded* from the calculation, under the prohibitions. This appeal does not raise the issue of how that *lacuna* might be overcome on the basis of the present text of the *Anti-Dumping Agreement*. Accordingly, it is not necessary for us to address that question.

A.3.44 Article 9.4 – Relationship with paragraphs 1 and 2 of Article 3

A.3.44.1 *EC – Bed Linen (Article 21.5 – India)*, para. 124
(WT/DS141/AB/RW)

...Similarly, in this implementation dispute, we are of the view that Article 9.4, which specifies what action may be taken only *after* certain prerequisites have been determined, is of little relevance for interpreting Article 3, which sets out those prerequisites. We do not see how Article 9.4, which authorizes the imposition of a certain maximum anti-dumping *duty* on imports from non-examined producers, is relevant for interpreting paragraphs 1 and 2 of Article 3, which deal with the determination of injury based on the *volume* of "dumped imports".... Likewise, Article 9.4 does not mention the term "dumped imports" or the "volume" of such imports. In our view, the right to impose a certain maximum amount of anti-dumping *duties* on imports attributable to *non*-examined producers under Article 9.4 cannot be read as permitting a derogation from the express and unambiguous requirements of paragraphs 1 and 2 of Article 3 to determine the *volume* of dumped imports – including dumped import volumes attributable to *non*-examined producers – on the basis of "positive evidence" and an "objective examination"....

A.3.44.2 *EC – Bed Linen (Article 21.5 – India)*, para. 125 (WT/DS141/AB/RW)

Moreover, Article 9.4, which relates to the imposition of anti-dumping duties on imports from non-examined producers, has, by its own terms, a limited purpose as an *exception* to the rule in Article 9.3.... In such cases, as an *exception* to the rule in Article 9.3, Article 9.4 permits the imposition of a certain maximum amount of anti-dumping duties on imports attributable to producers that were *not* examined individually, irrespective of whether those producers would have been found to be dumping had they been examined individually....

A.3.44.3 *EC – Bed Linen (Article 21.5 – India)*, para. 126 (WT/DS141/AB/RW)

In sum, Article 9.4 provides no guidance for determining the volume of dumped imports from producers that *were not* individually examined on the basis of "positive evidence" and an "objective examination" under Article 3.... we do not see why the volume of imports that has been found to be dumped by non-examined producers, for purposes of determining *injury* under paragraphs 1 and 2 of Article 3, must be *congruent* with the volume of imports from those non-examined producers that is subject to the *imposition of anti-dumping duties* under Article 9.4, as contended by the European Communities and the Panel.

A.3.45 **Article 11.3 – Sunset review – conditions.** *See also* Anti-Dumping Agreement, Article 6 (A.3.29–38); Anti-Dumping Agreement, Article 9.2 (A.3.40); Anti-Dumping Agreement, Article 11.4 (A.3.53)

A.3.45.1 *US – Corrosion-Resistant Steel Sunset Review*, para. 104 (WT/DS244/AB/R)

Article 11.3 imposes a temporal limitation on the maintenance of anti-dumping duties. It lays down a mandatory rule with an exception. Specifically, Members are required to terminate an anti-dumping duty within five years of its imposition "*unless*" the following conditions are satisfied: first, that a review be initiated before the expiry of five years from the date of the imposition of the duty; second, that in the review the authorities determine that the expiry of the duty would be likely to lead to continuation or recurrence of *dumping*; and third, that in the review the authorities determine that the expiry of the duty would be likely to lead to continuation or recurrence of *injury*. If any one of these conditions is not satisfied, the duty must be terminated.

A.3.46 Article 11.3 – Likelihood of continuation or recurrence of dumping

A.3.46.1 *US – Corrosion-Resistant Steel Sunset Review*, para. 105 (WT/DS244/AB/R)

This appeal concerns . . . the particular disciplines with which authorities must comply in determining, in accordance with Article 11.3, "that the expiry of the duty would be likely to lead to continuation or recurrence of dumping". In this Report, we refer to this determination as the "likelihood determination". The likelihood determination is a prospective determination. In other words, the authorities must undertake a forward-looking analysis and seek to resolve the issue of what would be likely to occur if the duty were terminated.

A.3.46.2 *US – Corrosion-Resistant Steel Sunset Review*, para. 107 (WT/DS244/AB/R)

. . . In an original anti-dumping investigation, investigating authorities must determine whether *dumping exists* during the period of investigation. In contrast, in a sunset review of an anti-dumping duty, investigating authorities must determine whether the expiry of the duty that was imposed at the conclusion of an original investigation would be *likely to lead to continuation or recurrence of dumping*.

A.3.46.3 *US – Oil Country Tubular Goods Sunset Reviews*, para. 323 (WT/DS268/AB/R)

Under Article 11.3 of the *Anti-Dumping Agreement*, a decision not to terminate an anti-dumping duty must be based on determinations of likelihood of continuation or recurrence of dumping and likelihood of continuation or recurrence of injury. We agree with the United States that the "likely" standard of Article 11.3 applies to the overall determinations regarding dumping and injury; it need not necessarily apply to each factor considered in rendering the overall determinations on dumping and injury. . . .

A.3.47 Article 11.3 – Standard of review

A.3.47.1 *US – Corrosion-Resistant Steel Sunset Review*, para. 111 (WT/DS244/AB/R)

This language in Article 11.3 makes clear that it envisages a process combining *both* investigatory and adjudicatory aspects. In other words, Article 11.3 assigns an active rather than a passive decision-making role to the authorities. The words "review" and "determine" in Article 11.3 suggest that authorities conducting a sunset review must act with an appropriate degree of diligence and arrive at a reasoned conclusion on the basis of information gathered as part of a process of reconsideration and examination. In view of the use of the word "likely" in Article 11.3, an affirmative likelihood determination may be made only if the evidence demonstrates that dumping would be probable if the duty were terminated – and not simply if the evidence suggests that such a result might be possible or plausible.

A.3.47.2 *US – Oil Country Tubular Goods Sunset Reviews*, para. 309 (WT/DS268/AB/R)

The Panel stated that the standard set out in Article 11.3 is the "likely" standard; this is plain from the text of the provision itself. Although the Panel did not elaborate with respect to the meaning of "likely", or expressly state that "likely" means "probable", we see nothing in the Panel Report to suggest that the Panel was of the view that "likely" does not mean "probable", or that "likely" means "anything less than probable".

A.3.47.3 *US – Oil Country Tubular Goods Sunset Reviews*, paras. 321–322 (WT/DS268/AB/R)

In *US – Corrosion-Resistant Steel Sunset Review*, the Appellate Body approved the description set out by the panel in that case of investigating authorities' obligations in a sunset review:

> The text of Article 11.3 contains an obligation "to determine" likelihood of continuation or recurrence of dumping and injury. The text of Article 11.3 does not, however, provide explicit guidance regarding the meaning of the term "determine". The ordinary meaning of the word "determine" is to "find out or establish precisely" or to "decide or settle". The requirement to make a "determination" concerning likelihood therefore precludes an investigating authority from simply assuming that likelihood exists. In order to continue the imposition of the measure after the expiry of the five-year application period, it is clear that *the investigating authority has to determine, on the basis of positive evidence*, that termination of the duty is likely to lead to continuation or recurrence of dumping and injury. *An investigating authority must have a sufficient factual basis* to allow it to draw reasoned and adequate conclusions concerning the likelihood of such continuation or recurrence. (emphasis added) [Appellate Body Report, para. 114]

These obligations of investigating authorities inform the task of a panel called upon to evaluate the consistency of an investigating authority's determination with Article 11.3 of the *Anti-Dumping Agreement*. The task of the panel is to assess whether the investigating authorities properly established the facts and evaluated them in an unbiased and objective manner. We agree with the Panel that "[its] task [was] not to perform a *de novo* review of the information and evidence on the record of the underlying sunset review, nor to substitute [its] judgment for that of the US authorities". If the panel is satisfied that an investigating authority's determination on continuation or recurrence of dumping or injury rests upon a sufficient factual basis to allow it to draw reasoned and adequate conclusions, it should conclude that the determination at issue is not inconsistent with Article 11.3 of the *Anti-Dumping Agreement*.

A.3.47.4 *US – Oil Country Tubular Goods Sunset Reviews*, paras. 340–341 (WT/DS268/AB/R)

We observe that most of the arguments put forward by Argentina on appeal with respect to the application by the USITC of the standard of likelihood is centred on the premise that some of the factors presented by the USITC are speculative. In particular, Argentina seems to assume that positive evidence requires absolute certainty on what is likely to occur in the future. We have some difficulty with this line of reasoning. Of course, we agree with Argentina that the investigating authority's likelihood determinations under Article 11.3 must be based on "positive evidence"....

The requirements of "positive evidence" must, however, be seen in the context that the determinations to be made under Article 11.3 are prospective in nature and that they involve a "forward-looking analysis". Such an analysis may inevitably entail assumptions about or projections into the future. Unavoidably, therefore, the inferences drawn from the evidence in the record will be, to a certain extent, speculative. In our view, that some of the inferences drawn from the evidence on record are projections into the future does not necessarily suggest that such inferences are not based on "positive evidence". The Panel considered that the five factors addressed by the USITC were supported by positive evidence in the USITC's record and, as we have explained, we see no reason to disagree with the Panel.

A.3.47A Article 11.3 – Nature of sunset review investigation

A.3.47A.1 *US – Corrosion-Resistant Steel Sunset Review*, para. 112 (WT/DS244/AB/R)

... Thus, even though the rules applicable to sunset reviews may not be identical in all respects to those applicable to original investigations, it is clear that the drafters of the *Anti-Dumping Agreement* intended a sunset review to include both full opportunity for all interested parties to defend their interests, and the right to receive notice of the process and reasons for the determination.

A.3.47A.2 *US – Corrosion-Resistant Steel Sunset Review*, para. 113 (WT/DS244/AB/R)

... the mandatory rule in Article 11.3 applies in addition to, and irrespective of, the obligations set out in the first two paragraphs of Article 11. This also suggests to us that authorities must conduct a rigorous examination in a sunset review before the exception (namely, the continuation of the duty) can apply. In addition, our view of the exacting nature of the obligations imposed on authorities under Article 11.3 is supported by a consideration of the implications of initiating a sunset review. The last sentence of Article 11.3 allows the relevant duty to continue while the review is underway, and Article 11.4 contemplates that the review process may take up to one year. These provisions create an additional exception to the requirement that anti-dumping duties will be terminated after five years, permitting a Member to maintain the duty for the period during which the review is ongoing, regardless of the outcome of that review. This, too, suggests that the drafters of the *Anti-Dumping Agreement* saw the sunset review as a rigorous process that can take up to one year, involving a number of procedural steps, and requiring an appropriate degree of diligence on the part of the national authorities.

A.3.48 Article 11.3 – Methodology for sunset review investigations

A.3.48.1 *US – Corrosion-Resistant Steel Sunset Review*, para. 123
(WT/DS244/AB/R)

In making its findings on this issue, the Panel correctly noted that Article 11.3 does not expressly prescribe any specific methodology for investigating authorities to use in making a likelihood determination in a sunset review. Nor does Article 11.3 identify any particular factors that authorities must take into account in making such a determination. Thus, Article 11.3 neither explicitly requires authorities in a sunset review to calculate fresh dumping margins, nor explicitly prohibits them from relying on dumping margins calculated in the past. This silence in the text of Article 11.3 suggests that no obligation is imposed on investigating authorities to calculate or rely on dumping margins in a sunset review.

A.3.48.2 *US – Corrosion-Resistant Steel Sunset Review*, para. 124
(WT/DS244/AB/R)

We consider that it is consistent with the different nature and purpose of original investigations, on the one hand, and sunset reviews, on the other hand, to interpret the *Anti-Dumping Agreement* as requiring investigating authorities to calculate dumping margins in an original investigation, but not in a sunset review. In an original investigation, if investigating authorities of a Member do not determine a positive dumping margin, the Member may not impose anti-dumping measures based on that investigation. In a sunset review, dumping margins may well be relevant to, but they will not necessarily be conclusive of, whether the expiry of the duty would be likely to lead to continuation or recurrence of dumping.

A.3.48A Article 11.3 – Cumulation in sunset reviews. *See also* Anti-Dumping Agreement, Article 3.3 – Cumulative assessment of dumped imports (A.3.21)

A.3.48A.1 *US – Oil Country Tubular Goods Sunset Reviews*, paras. 296–297
(WT/DS268/AB/R)

Although *EC – Tube or Pipe Fittings* concerned an original investigation, we are of the view that [the rationale behind the practice of cumulation] is equally applicable to likelihood-of-injury determinations in sunset reviews. Both an original investigation and a sunset review must consider possible sources of injury: in an original investigation, to determine whether to impose anti-dumping duties on products from those sources, and in a sunset review, to determine whether anti-dumping duties should *continue* to be imposed on products from those sources. Injury to the domestic industry – whether *existing* injury or *likely future* injury – might come from several sources simultaneously, and the cumulative impact of those imports would need to be analyzed for an injury determination.

Therefore, notwithstanding the differences between original investigations and sunset reviews, cumulation remains a useful tool for investigating authorities in both inquiries to ensure that all sources of injury and their cumulative impact on the domestic industry are taken into account in an investigating authority's determination as to whether to impose – or continue to impose – anti-dumping duties on products from those sources. Given the rationale for cumulation – a rationale that we consider applies to original investigations as well as to sunset reviews – we are of the view that it would be anomalous for Members to have limited authorization for cumulation in the *Anti-Dumping Agreement* to original investigations.

A.3.48A.2 *US – Oil Country Tubular Goods Sunset Reviews*, para. 300 (WT/DS268/AB/R)

Given the express intention of Members to permit cumulation in injury determinations in original investigations, and given the rationale behind cumulation in injury determinations, we do not read the *Anti-Dumping Agreement* as prohibiting cumulation in sunset reviews.

A.3.48A.3 *US – Oil Country Tubular Goods Sunset Reviews*, para. 302 (WT/DS268/AB/R)

. . . As the Appellate Body has observed, a sunset review determination under Article 11.3 must be based on a "rigorous examination" leading to a "reasoned conclusion". Such a determination must be supported by "positive evidence" and a "sufficient factual basis". These requirements govern all aspects of an investigating authority's likelihood determination, including the decision to resort to cumulation of the effects of likely dumped imports. As a result, Argentina's concerns that investigating authorities will be given "*carte blanche*" to resort to cumulation when making likelihood-of-injury determinations is unfounded. We, therefore, conclude that the conditions of Article 3.3 do not apply to likelihood-of-injury determinations in sunset reviews.

A.3.48A.4 *US – Oil Country Tubular Goods Sunset Reviews*, para. 328 (WT/DS268/AB/R)

We disagree with Argentina that the USITC's references to information gleaned in the original investigation rendered WTO-inconsistent its decision to cumulate the effects of dumped imports. In *US – Carbon Steel*, the Appellate Body clarified that, in a sunset review, a "fresh determination" on the *likelihood* of future injury is necessary because "[t]he nature of the determination to be made in a sunset review differs in certain essential respects from the nature of the determination to be made in an original investigation." Therefore, "[m]ere reliance by the authorities on the injury determination made in the original investigation will not be sufficient." *US – Carbon Steel* does not, however, establish a prohibition on investigating authorities from referring in a sunset review to information related to the original investigation. In this case, it seems to us that the information to which the USITC referred was relevant to the decision to cumulate imports and, ultimately, to the task of assessing the likelihood of continuation or recurrence of injury. Moreover, the USITC referred to this information in the context of a fresh determination as to whether the expiry of the orders would be likely to lead to continuation or recurrence of injury.

A.3.49 **Article 11.3 – Relationship with Article 2.** *See also* Anti-Dumping Agreement, Article 2.1 (A.3.3–8)

A.3.49.0 *US – Corrosion-Resistant Steel Sunset Review*, para. 109 (WT/DS244/AB/R)

We agree with Japan that the words "[f]or the purpose of this Agreement" in Article 2.1 indicate that this provision describes the circumstances in which a product is to be considered as being dumped for purposes of the entire *Anti-Dumping Agreement*, including Article 11.3. This interpretation is supported by the fact that Article 11.3 does not indicate, either expressly or by implication, that "dumping" has a different meaning in the context of sunset reviews than in the rest of the *Anti-Dumping Agreement*. Therefore, Article 2.1 of the *Anti-Dumping Agreement* and Article VI:1 of the GATT 1994 suggest that the question for investigating authorities, in making a likelihood determination in a sunset review pursuant to Article 11.3, is whether the expiry of the duty would be likely to lead to continuation or recurrence of dumping of the product subject to the duty (that is, to the introduction of that product into the commerce of the importing country at less than its normal value)....

A.3.49.1 *US – Corrosion-Resistant Steel Sunset Review*, paras. 126–128 (WT/DS244/AB/R)

...the opening words of Article 2.1 ("[f]or the purpose of this Agreement") go beyond a cross-reference and indicate that Article 2.1 applies to the entire *Anti-Dumping Agreement*. By virtue of these words, the word "dumping" as used in Article 11.3 has the meaning described in Article 2.1....

Article 2 sets out the agreed disciplines in the *Anti-Dumping Agreement* for calculating dumping margins. As observed earlier, we see no obligation under Article 11.3 for investigating authorities to calculate or rely on dumping margins in determining the likelihood of continuation or recurrence of dumping. However, should investigating authorities choose to rely upon dumping margins in making their likelihood determination, the calculation of these margins must conform to the disciplines of Article 2.4.... USDOC chose to base its affirmative likelihood determination on positive dumping margins that had been previously calculated in two particular administrative reviews. If these margins were legally flawed because they were calculated in a manner inconsistent with Article 2.4, this could give rise to an inconsistency not only with Article 2.4, but also with Article 11.3 of the *Anti-Dumping Agreement*.

It follows that we disagree with the Panel's view that the disciplines in Article 2 regarding the calculation of dumping margins do not apply to the likelihood determination to be made in a sunset review under Article 11.3. . . .

A.3.49.2 *US – Corrosion-Resistant Steel Sunset Review*, para. 130 (WT/DS244/AB/R)

. . . if a likelihood determination is based on a dumping margin calculated using a methodology inconsistent with Article 2.4, then this defect taints the likelihood determination too. Thus, the consistency with Article 2.4 of the methodology that USDOC used to calculate the dumping margins in the administrative reviews bears on the consistency with Article 11.3 of USDOC's likelihood determination in the CRS sunset review. In the CRS sunset review, USDOC based its determination that "dumping is likely to continue if the [CRS] order were revoked" on the "existence of dumping margins" calculated in the administrative reviews. If these margins were indeed calculated using a methodology that is inconsistent with Article 2.4 – an issue that we examine below – then USDOC's likelihood determination could not constitute a proper foundation for the continuation of anti-dumping duties under Article 11.3. Moreover, a legal defect of this kind cannot be cured by NSC's failure to take issue with it in the CRS sunset review or the administrative reviews. . . .

A.3.50 Article 11.3 – No duty to investigate each known producer and exporter individually. *See also* Anti-Dumping Agreement, Article 11.4 (A.3.53)

A.3.50.1 *US – Corrosion-Resistant Steel Sunset Review*, para. 149 (WT/DS244/AB/R)

. . . Article 11.3 does not prescribe any particular methodology to be used by investigating authorities in making a likelihood determination in a sunset review. In particular, Article 11.3 does not expressly state that investigating authorities must determine that the expiry of the duty would be likely to lead to dumping *by each known exporter or producer concerned*. In fact, Article 11.3 contains no express reference to individual exporters, producers, or interested parties. This contrasts with Article 11.2, which does refer to "any interested party" and "[i]nterested parties". We also note that Article 11.3 does not contain the word "margins", which might implicitly refer to individual exporters or producers. On its face, Article 11.3 therefore does not oblige investigating authorities in a sunset review to make "company-specific" likelihood determinations in the manner suggested by Japan.

A.3.50.2 *US – Oil Country Tubular Goods Sunset Reviews*, para. 231 (WT/DS268/AB/R)

. . . because the United States has chosen to make order-wide determinations in sunset reviews, an allegation that a measure prevents the United States from making a likelihood determination consistent with Article 11.3 must be evaluated by reference to the relevance of that measure for the *order-wide* determination.

A.3.50.3 *US – Oil Country Tubular Goods Sunset Reviews*, paras. 232–233 (WT/DS268/AB/R)

...As we have observed, the relevant inquiry in this dispute is whether the *order-wide* likelihood determination would be rendered inconsistent with Article 11.3 by virtue of the operation of the waiver provisions. It appears to us, therefore, that the Panel could not have properly arrived at a finding of consistency or inconsistency with Article 11.3 *until* it had examined how the operation of the waiver provisions could affect the order-wide determination. Had the Panel ceased its inquiry with the finding that the company-specific determinations are not "supported by reasoned and adequate conclusions based on the facts before an investigating authority", the Panel would not have had a basis to conclude that the waiver provisions are inconsistent, as such, with Article 11.3.

The Panel, however, did not base its ultimate conclusion of inconsistency with Article 11.3 on its assessment of only the *company-specific* determinations made pursuant to the waiver provisions. Instead, the Panel correctly continued its analysis and examined the impact of the company-specific determinations on the *order-wide* determination....

A.3.50.4 *US – Oil Country Tubular Goods Sunset Reviews*, para. 234 (WT/DS268/AB/R)

...even assuming that the USDOC takes into account the totality of record evidence in making its order-wide determination, it is clear that, as a result of the operation of the waiver provisions, certain *order-wide* likelihood determinations made by the USDOC will be based, at least in part, on statutorily-mandated *assumptions* about a company's likelihood of dumping. In our view, this result is inconsistent with the obligation of an investigating authority under Article 11.3 to "arrive at a reasoned conclusion" on the basis of "positive evidence".

A.3.51 Article 11.3 – Determination of dumping margins and import volumes

A.3.51.1 *US – Corrosion-Resistant Steel Sunset Review*, para. 158 (WT/DS244/AB/R)

Our conclusions regarding the consistency of this aspect of the Sunset Policy Bulletin "as such" with Article 11.3 do not imply that Article 11.3 precludes authorities from making separate likelihood determinations for individual exporters or producers in a sunset review and then continuing or terminating the relevant duty for each company according to the determination for that company. WTO Members are free to structure their anti-dumping systems as they choose, provided that those systems do not conflict with the provisions of the *Anti-Dumping Agreement*....

A.3.51.2 *US – Corrosion-Resistant Steel Sunset Review*, paras. 175–176 (WT/DS244/AB/R)

... We see no problem, in principle, with the United States instructing its investigating authorities to examine, in every sunset review, dumping margins and import volumes. These two factors will often be pertinent to the likelihood determination, and Japan itself does not dispute the relevance of at least one of them, namely dumping margins.

At issue, however, is whether Section II. A.3 goes further and instructs USDOC to attach decisive or preponderant weight to these two factors in every case. To us, the significance and probative value of the two factors for a likelihood determination in a sunset review will necessarily vary from case to case. The *degree* to which import volumes or dumping margins have decreased will be relevant in making an inference that dumping is likely to continue or recur. Whether the historical data is recent or not may affect its probative value, and *trends* in data over time may be significant for an assessment of likely future behaviour. Similarly, it is possible that in a particular case one of these factors may support an inference of likely future dumping, while the other factor supports a contrary inference.

A.3.51.3 *US – Corrosion-Resistant Steel Sunset Review*, para. 186 (WT/DS244/AB/R)

... a broad range of factors other than import volumes and dumping margins is potentially relevant to the authorities' likelihood determination....

A.3.51.4 *A.3.51.4 US – Oil Country Tubular Goods Sunset Reviews*, para. 208 (WT/DS268/AB/R)

In our view, "volume of dumped imports" and "dumping margins", before and after the issuance of anti-dumping duty orders, are highly important factors for any determination of likelihood of continuation or recurrence of dumping in sunset reviews, although other factors may also be as important, depending on the circumstances of the case. The three factual scenarios in Section II.A.3 of the SPB, which describe how these two factors will be considered in individual determinations, thus have certain probative value, the degree of which may vary from case to case. For example, if, under scenario (a) of Section II.A.3 of the SPB, dumping *continued* with substantial margins despite the existence of the anti-dumping duty order, this would be highly probative of the likelihood that dumping would continue if the anti-dumping order were revoked. Conversely, if, under scenarios (b) and (c) of Section II.A.3 of the SPB, imports ceased after issuance of the anti-dumping duty order, or imports continued but without dumping margins, the probative value of the scenarios may be much less, and other relevant factors may have to be examined to determine whether imports *with dumping margins* would "recur" if the anti-dumping duty order were revoked. The importance of the two underlying factors (import volumes and dumping margins) for a likelihood-of-dumping determination cannot be questioned; however, our concern here is with the possible mechanistic application of the three scenarios based on these factors, such that other factors that may be of equal importance are disregarded.

A.3.52 Article 11.3 – Likelihood determination based on evidence vs. presumptions

A.3.52.0 *US – Corrosion-Resistant Steel Sunset Review*, para. 97 (WT/DS244/AB/R)

Japan argued before the Panel that the repeated practice of USDOC, as demonstrated in its conduct of a large number of sunset reviews, serves to establish that the relevant provisions of the Sunset Policy Bulletin have the meaning and effect alleged by Japan, namely, that they unduly limit the factors that USDOC will take into account in making its determination. The Panel, however, did not make any factual findings as to the relevance or cogency of this evidence. Rather, the Panel opined that the Sunset Policy Bulletin, by itself, could not constitute "practice" because it was issued before any sunset review had occurred. The Panel also took the view that a repeated response to a particular set of circumstances could not "transform" the Bulletin into an "administrative procedure", or indicate that, "merely by repetition, the DOC would somehow become compelled to follow the Bulletin." In so doing, the Panel does not seem to have allowed for the possibility that Japan was not challenging the Sunset Policy Bulletin *as practice*, but was, rather, relying on the evidence of the consistent application of the Sunset Policy Bulletin in all sunset reviews so far conducted by USDOC to support its arguments that USDOC treats the "rules" in the Sunset Policy Bulletin as binding.

A.3.52.1 *US – Corrosion-Resistant Steel Sunset Review*, para. 178 (WT/DS244/AB/R)

We believe that a firm evidentiary foundation is required in each case for a proper determination under Article 11.3 of the likelihood of continuation or recurrence of dumping. Such a determination cannot be based solely on the mechanistic application of presumptions. . . .

A.3.52.2 *US – Corrosion-Resistant Steel Sunset Review*, para. 191 (WT/DS244/AB/R)

We acknowledge that these types of instructions to an executive agency may well serve as a useful tool to the agency as well as for all participants in administrative proceedings. They tend to promote transparency and consistency in decision-making, and can help authorities and participants to focus on the relevant issues and evidence. However, these considerations cannot override the obligation of investigating authorities, in a sunset review, to determine, on the basis of all relevant evidence, whether the expiry of the duty would be likely to lead to continuation or recurrence of dumping. As we have found in other situations, the use of presumptions may be inconsistent with an obligation to make a particular determination in each case using positive evidence. Provisions that create "irrebuttable" presumptions, or "predetermine" a particular result, run the risk of being found inconsistent with this type of obligation.

A.3.52.3 *US – Corrosion-Resistant Steel Sunset Review*, para. 199 and footnote 243 (WT/DS244/AB/R)

. . . Article 11.3 makes clear that the role of the authorities in a sunset review includes both investigatory and adjudicatory aspects. These authorities have a duty to seek out relevant information and to evaluate it in an objective manner.[243] At the same time, the *Anti-Dumping Agreement* assigns a prominent role to interested parties as well and contemplates that they will be a primary source of information in all proceedings conducted under that agreement. Company-specific data relevant to a likelihood determination under Article 11.3 can often be provided only by the companies themselves. For example, as the United States points out, it is the exporters or producers themselves who often possess the best evidence of their likely future pricing behaviour – a key element in the likelihood of future dumping.

[243] We have found a similar duty in the context of an investigation conducted in accordance with the *Agreement on Safeguards*: Appellate Body Report, *US – Wheat Gluten*, paras. 53–55.

A.3.52.4 *US – Oil Country Tubular Goods Sunset Reviews*, para. 180 (WT/DS268/AB/R)

The plain meaning of the terms "review" and "determine" in Article 11.3, therefore, compel an investigating authority in a sunset review to undertake an examination, on the basis of positive evidence, of the likelihood of continuation or recurrence of dumping and injury. In drawing conclusions from that examination, the investigating authority must arrive at a reasoned determination resting on a sufficient factual basis; it may not rely on assumptions or conjecture.

A.3.52.5 *US – Oil Country Tubular Goods Sunset Reviews*, paras. 209–210 (WT/DS268/AB/R)

In our view, therefore, in order to objectively assess, as required by Article 11 of the DSU, whether the three factual scenarios of Section II.A.3 of the SPB are regarded as determinative/conclusive, it is essential to examine concrete examples of cases where the likelihood determination of continuation or recurrence of dumping was based solely on one of the scenarios of Section II.A.3 of the SPB, even though the probative value of other factors might have outweighed that of the identified scenario. Such an examination requires a qualitative assessment of the likelihood determinations in individual cases.

We find that, in reaching its conclusion on the USDOC's consistent application of the SPB, the Panel relied solely on the overall statistics or aggregate results. The Panel did not undertake a qualitative analysis of at least some of the individual cases in Exhibit ARG-63 in order to see whether the USDOC's determinations in those cases were objective and rested on a sufficient factual basis.

A.3.52.6 *US – Oil Country Tubular Goods Sunset Reviews*, para. 211 (WT/DS268/AB/R)

A qualitative analysis of individual cases in all likelihood would have revealed a variety of circumstances. There could well have been cases where affirmative determinations were made objectively, based on one of the three scenarios. There could have been other cases where the affirmative determinations were flawed because the USDOC made its decisions relying solely on one of the scenarios of the SPB, even though the probative value of other factors outweighed it. There could have been yet other cases where the USDOC summarily rejected or ignored other factors introduced by foreign respondent parties, regardless of their probative value.

A.3.52.7 *US – Oil Country Tubular Goods Sunset Reviews*, para. 215 (WT/DS268/AB/R)

. . . we *reverse* the Panel's findings . . . that Section II.A.3 of the SPB is inconsistent, as such, with Article 11.3 of the *Anti-Dumping Agreement*. We wish to emphasize that we have not thereby concluded that Section II.A.3 of the SPB is consistent, as such, with Article 11.3 of the Anti-Dumping Agreement. Rather, we have found that the Panel's conclusion to the contrary must be reversed due to its failure to comply with Article 11 of the DSU. Thus, our reasoning here does not exclude the possibility that, in another case, it could be properly concluded that the three scenarios in Section II.A.3 of the SPB are regarded as determinative/conclusive of the likelihood of continuation or recurrence of dumping. However, such a conclusion would need to be supported by a rigorous analysis of the evidence regarding the manner in which Section II.A.3 of the SPB is applied by the USDOC.

A.3.52.8 *US – Oil Country Tubular Goods Sunset Reviews*, para. 234 (WT/DS268/AB/R)

We agree with the Panel's analysis of the impact of the waiver provisions on order-wide determinations. Because the waiver provisions require the USDOC to arrive at affirmative company-specific determinations without regard to any evidence on record, these determinations are merely *assumptions* made by the agency, rather than findings supported by evidence. The United States contends that respondents waiving the right to participate in a sunset review do so "intentionally", with full knowledge that, as a result of their failure to submit evidence, the evidence placed on the record by the domestic industry is likely to result in an unfavourable determination on an order-wide basis. In these circumstances, we see no fault in making an unfavourable order-wide determination by taking into account evidence provided by the domestic industry in support thereof. However, the USDOC also takes into account, in such circumstances, statutorily-mandated *assumptions*. Thus, even assuming that the USDOC takes into account the totality of record evidence in making its order-wide determination, it is clear that, as a result of the operation of the waiver provisions, certain *order-wide* likelihood determinations made by the USDOC will be based, at least in part, on statutorily-mandated *assumptions* about a company's likelihood of dumping. In our view, this result is inconsistent with the obligation of an investigating authority under Article 11.3 to "arrive at a reasoned conclusion" on the basis of "positive evidence".

A.3.52A Article 11.3 – Likelihood of continuation or recurrence of injury

A.3.52A.1 *US – Oil Country Tubular Goods Sunset Reviews*, para. 276
(WT/DS268/AB/R)

. . . we would agree with Argentina that, by virtue of its opening phrase, footnote 9 defines "injury" for the whole of the *Anti-Dumping Agreement*. . . . Therefore, when Article 11.3 requires a determination as to the likelihood of continuation or recurrence of "injury", the investigating authority must consider the continuation or recurrence of "injury" as defined in footnote 9.

A.3.52A.2 *US – Oil Country Tubular Goods Sunset Reviews*, para. 281
(WT/DS268/AB/R)

. . . we recall the following statement of the Appellate Body in *US – Corrosion-Resistant Steel Sunset Review*:

> Article 11.3 does not expressly prescribe any specific methodology for investigating authorities to use in making a likelihood determination in a sunset review. Nor does Article 11.3 identify any particular factors that authorities must take into account in making such a determination. [Appellate Body Report, para. 123]

Although the Appellate Body made this statement in the context of a likelihood-of-dumping determination, it applies equally with respect to a likelihood-of-injury determination.

A.3.52A.3 *US – Oil Country Tubular Goods Sunset Reviews*, para. 323
(WT/DS268/AB/R)

Under Article 11.3 of the *Anti-Dumping Agreement*, a decision not to terminate an anti-dumping duty must be based on determinations of likelihood of continuation or recurrence of dumping and likelihood of continuation or recurrence of injury. We agree with the United States that the "likely" standard of Article 11.3 applies to the overall determinations regarding dumping and injury; it need not necessarily apply to each factor considered in rendering the overall determinations on dumping and injury. . . .

A.3.52A.4 *US – Oil Country Tubular Goods Sunset Reviews*, para. 333 (WT/DS268/AB/R)

... the "likelihood" standard set out in Article 11.3 applies to a likelihood-of-injury determination as a whole, not to each and every factor that the investigating authority considers in the course of its analysis.

A.3.52B Article 11.3 – Relationship with Article 3

A.3.52B.1 *US – Oil Country Tubular Goods Sunset Reviews*, paras. 278–280 (WT/DS268/AB/R)

... In our view, however, the *Anti-Dumping Agreement* distinguishes between "determination[s] of injury", addressed in Article 3, and determinations of likelihood of "continuation or recurrence... of injury", addressed in Article 11.3. In addition, Article 11.3 does not contain any cross-reference to Article 3 to the effect that, in making the likelihood-of-injury determination, all the provisions of Article 3 – or any particular provisions of Article 3 – *must* be followed by investigating authorities. Nor does any provision of Article 3 indicate that, wherever the term "injury" appears in the *Anti-Dumping Agreement*, a determination of injury must be made following the provisions of Article 3.

The lack of a sufficient textual basis to apply Article 3 to likelihood-of-injury determinations is not surprising given "the different nature and purpose of original investigations, on the one hand, and sunset reviews, on the other hand", which the Appellate Body emphasized in *US – Corrosion-Resistant Steel Sunset Review*. Original investigations require an investigating authority, in order to *impose* an anti-dumping duty, to make a determination of the existence of dumping in accordance with Article 2, and subsequently to determine, in accordance with Article 3, whether the domestic industry is facing injury or a threat thereof at the time of the original investigation. In contrast, Article 11.3 requires an investigating authority, in order to *maintain* an anti-dumping duty, to review an anti-dumping duty order that has already been established – following the prerequisite determinations of dumping and injury – so as to determine whether that order should be continued or revoked.

Given the absence of textual cross-references, and given the different nature and purpose of these two determinations, we are of the view that, for the "review" of a determination of injury that has already been established in accordance with Article 3, Article 11.3 does not require that injury again be determined in accordance with Article 3. We therefore conclude that investigating authorities are not *mandated* to follow the provisions of Article 3 when making a likelihood-of-injury determination.

A.3.52B.2 *US – Oil Country Tubular Goods Sunset Reviews*, paras. 283–284 (WT/DS268/AB/R)

... We are not persuaded by the argument of Argentina that a likelihood-of-injury determination can rest on a "sufficient factual basis" and can be regarded as a "reasoned conclusion" *only* after undertaking all the analyses detailed in the paragraphs of Article 3.

This is not to say, however, that in a sunset review determination, an investigating authority is never required to examine any of the factors listed in the paragraphs of Article 3. Certain of the analyses mandated by Article 3 and necessarily relevant in an original investigation may prove to be probative, or possibly even required, in order for an investigating authority in a sunset review to arrive at a "reasoned conclusion". In this respect, we are of the view that the fundamental requirement of Article 3.1 that an injury determination be based on "positive evidence" and an "objective examination" would be equally relevant to likelihood determinations under Article 11.3. It seems to us that factors such as the volume, price effects, and the impact on the domestic industry of dumped imports, taking into account the conditions of competition, may be relevant to varying degrees in a given likelihood-of-injury determination. An investigating authority may also, in its own judgement, consider other factors contained in Article 3 when making a likelihood-of-injury determination. But the necessity of conducting such an analysis in a given case results from the requirement imposed by *Article 11.3* – not Article 3 – that a likelihood-of-injury determination rest on a "sufficient factual basis" that allows the agency to draw "reasoned and adequate conclusions".

A.3.52C Article 11.3 – Timeframe for likelihood of continuation or recurrence of injury

A.3.52C.1 *US – Oil Country Tubular Goods Sunset Reviews*, para. 356 (WT/DS268/AB/R)

The Panel noted that Article 11.3 of the *Anti-Dumping Agreement* does not prescribe any timeframe for likelihood of continuation or recurrence of injury; nor does it require investigating authorities to specify the timeframe on which their likelihood determination is based. The Panel consequently concluded that the standard of the "reasonably foreseeable time", set out in Sections 752(a)(1) and 752(a)(5), does not conflict with Article 11.3 of the *Anti-Dumping Agreement*.

A.3.52C.2 *US – Oil Country Tubular Goods Sunset Reviews*, paras. 359–360 (WT/DS268/AB/R)

As to the "impermissible gap" alluded to by Argentina, in our view, this argument is nothing more than a theoretical possibility, which Argentina builds from an abstract comparison between, on the one hand, the "imminent" manifestation of injury in the context of an original anti-dumping investigation and, on the other hand, the manifestation of injury within a "reasonably foreseeable time" in the context of a sunset review. The theoretical possibility of a "gap" would necessarily apply only to the situation of likelihood of "recurrence" of injury in the future, and not to the situation of "continuation" of injury. This mere theoretical possibility cannot justify the importation into Article 11.3 of an "imminent" standard for likelihood of recurrence of injury. Moreover, as the Appellate Body indicated in *US – Corrosion-Resistant Steel Sunset Review*, original investigations and sunset reviews are distinct processes with different purposes. The disciplines applicable to original investigations cannot, therefore, be automatically imported into review processes.

In our view, the Panel correctly analyzed the timeframe issue. We agree with the Panel that an assessment regarding whether injury is likely to recur that focuses "too far in the future would be highly speculative", and that it might be very difficult to justify such an assessment. However, like the Panel, we have no reason to believe that the standard of a "reasonably foreseeable time" set out in the United States statute is inconsistent with the requirements of Article 11.3.

A.3.53 Article 11.4 – Relationship with Article 6. *See also* Anti-Dumping Agreement – Article 6 (A.3.29–38)

A.3.53.1 *US – Corrosion-Resistant Steel Sunset Review*, para. 152 (WT/DS244/AB/R)

. . . several provisions of Article 6 refer expressly or by implication to individual exporters or producers. . . . [Article 6 and the particular provisions in Articles 6.1, 6.2, 6.4, and 6.9] suggest that, when the drafters of the *Anti-Dumping Agreement* intended to impose obligations on authorities regarding individual exporters or producers, they did so explicitly. These provisions of Article 6 apply to Article 11.3 by virtue of Article 11.4. They therefore confirm that investigating authorities have certain specific obligations towards each exporter or producer in a sunset review. However, these provisions of Article 6 are silent on whether the authorities must make a separate likelihood determination for each exporter or producer.

A.3.53.2 *US – Corrosion-Resistant Steel Sunset Review*, para. 155 (WT/DS244/AB/R)

We have already concluded that investigating authorities are not *required* to calculate or rely on *dumping margins* in making a likelihood determination in a sunset review under Article 11.3. This means that the requirement in Article 6.10 that dumping margins, "as a rule", be calculated "for each known exporter or producer concerned" is not, in principle, relevant to sunset reviews. Therefore, the reference in Article 11.4 to "[t]he provisions of Article 6 regarding evidence and procedure" does not import into Article 11.3 an obligation for investigating authorities to calculate dumping margins (on a company-specific basis or otherwise) in a sunset review. Nor does Article 11.4 import into Article 11.3 an obligation for investigating authorities to make their likelihood determination on a company-specific basis. We therefore agree with the Panel that "[t]he provisions of Article 6.10 concerning the calculation of individual margins of dumping in investigations do not require that the determination of *likelihood* of continuation or recurrence of dumping under Article 11.3 be made on a company-specific basis."

A.3.54 Article 17 – Dispute settlement. *See also* Special or Additional Rules and Procedures for Dispute Settlement (S.5)

A.3.54.1 *US – 1916 Act*, para. 62
(WT/DS136/AB/R, WT/DS162/AB/R)

Turning to the issue of the legal basis for claims brought under the *Anti-Dumping Agreement*, we note that Article 17 of the *Anti-Dumping Agreement* addresses dispute settlement under that Agreement. Just as Articles XXII and XXIII of the GATT 1994 create a legal basis for claims in disputes relating to provisions of the GATT 1994, so also Article 17 establishes the basis for dispute settlement claims relating to provisions of the *Anti-Dumping Agreement*. In the same way that Article XXIII of the GATT 1994 allows a WTO Member to challenge *legislation* as such, Article 17 of the *Anti-Dumping Agreement* is properly to be regarded as allowing a challenge to legislation as such, unless this possibility is excluded. No such *express* exclusion is found in Article 17 or elsewhere in the *Anti-Dumping Agreement*.

A.3.55 Article 17.3 – Consultations. *See also* Consultations (C.7); Legislation as such vs. Specific Application (L.1); Terms of Reference of Panels, specific measure at issue (T.6.3)

A.3.55.1 *Guatemala – Cement I*, para. 64
(WT/DS60/AB/R)

. . . Article 17.3 of the *Anti-Dumping Agreement* is not listed in Appendix 2 of the DSU as a special or additional rule and procedure. It is not listed precisely because it provides the legal basis for consultations to be requested by a complaining Member under the *Anti-Dumping Agreement*. Indeed, it is the equivalent provision in the *Anti-Dumping Agreement* to Articles XXII and XXIII of the GATT 1994, which serve as the basis for consultations and dispute settlement under the GATT 1994, under most of the other agreements in Annex 1A of the *Marrakesh Agreement Establishing the World Trade Organization* (the "*WTO Agreement*"), and under the *Agreement on Trade-Related Aspects of Intellectual Property Rights* (the "*TRIPS Agreement*").

A.3.55.2 *US – 1916 Act*, para. 68
(WT/DS136/AB/R, WT/DS162/AB/R)

Article 17.3 does not explicitly address challenges to legislation as such. As we have seen above, Articles XXII and XXIII allow challenges to be brought under the GATT 1994 against legislation as such. Since Article 17.3 is the "equivalent provision" to Articles XXII and XXIII of the GATT 1994, Article 17.3 provides further support for our view that challenges may be brought under the *Anti-Dumping Agreement* against legislation as such, unless such challenges are otherwise excluded.

A.3.55.3 *US – Corrosion-Resistant Steel Sunset Review*, para. 84
(WT/DS244/AB/R)

Our reasoning for concluding that the panel in *US – 1916 Act* had jurisdiction to consider *legislation*, as such, also applies in this case, where the relevant measures are specific provisions of an administrative instrument issued by an executive agency pursuant to statutory and regulatory provisions. That reasoning was based on the GATT *acquis* and the language of the *Anti-Dumping Agreement*, in particular Articles 17.3 and 18.4.

A.3.55.4 *US – Corrosion-Resistant Steel Sunset Review*, para. 86
(WT/DS244/AB/R)

The provisions of the *Anti-Dumping Agreement* setting forth a legal basis for matters to be referred to consultations and thus to dispute settlement, are also cast broadly. Article 17.3 establishes the principle that when a complaining Member "considers" that its benefits are being nullified or impaired "by another Member or Members", it may request consultations. This language underlines that a measure attributable to a Member may be submitted to dispute settlement provided only that another Member has taken the view, in good faith, that the measure nullifies or impairs benefits accruing to it under the *Anti-Dumping Agreement*. There is no threshold requirement, in Article 17.3, that the measure in question be of a certain type.

A.3.56 **Article 17.4 – "matter referred to the DSB".** *See also* Legislation as such vs. Specific Application (L.1); Terms of Reference of Panels (T.6)

A.3.56.1 *Guatemala – Cement I*, para. 72
(WT/DS60/AB/R)

. . . Thus, "the matter referred to the DSB" for the purposes of Article 7 of the DSU and Article 17.4 of the *Anti-Dumping Agreement* must be the "matter" identified in the request for the establishment of a panel under Article 6.2 of the DSU. . . .

A.3.56.2 *Guatemala – Cement I*, para. 79
(WT/DS60/AB/R)

Furthermore, Article 17.4 of the *Anti-Dumping Agreement* specifies the types of "measure" which may be referred as part of a "matter" to the DSB. Three types of anti-dumping measure are specified in Article 17.4: definitive anti-dumping duties, the acceptance of price undertakings, and provisional measures. According to Article 17.4, a "matter" may be referred to the DSB *only if* one of the relevant three anti-dumping measures is in place. This provision, when read together with Article 6.2 of the DSU, requires a panel request in a dispute brought under the *Anti-Dumping Agreement* to identify, as the specific measure at issue, either a definitive anti-dumping duty, the acceptance of a price undertaking, or a provisional measure. This requirement to identify a specific anti-dumping measure at issue in a panel request in no way limits the nature of the *claims* that may be brought concerning alleged nullification or impairment of benefits or the impeding of the achievement of any objective in a dispute under the *Anti-Dumping Agreement*. As we have observed earlier, there is a difference between the specific measures at issue – in the case of the *Anti-Dumping Agreement*, one of the three types of anti-dumping measure described in Article 17.4 – and the claims or the legal basis of the complaint referred to the DSB relating to those specific measures. In coming to this conclusion, we note that the language of Article 17.4 of the *Anti-Dumping Agreement* is unique to that Agreement.

A.3.56.3 *Guatemala – Cement I*, para. 80
(WT/DS60/AB/R)

For all of these reasons, we conclude that the Panel erred in finding that Mexico did not need to identify "specific measures at issue" in this dispute. We find that in disputes under the *Anti-Dumping Agreement* relating to the initiation and conduct of anti-dumping investigations, a definitive anti-dumping duty, the acceptance of a price undertaking or a provisional measure must be identified as part of the matter referred to the DSB pursuant to the provisions of Article 17.4 of the *Anti-Dumping Agreement* and Article 6.2 of the DSU.

A.3.56.4 *US – 1916 Act*, para. 72
(WT/DS136/AB/R, WT/DS162/AB/R)

Nothing in our Report in *Guatemala – Cement* suggests that Article 17.4 precludes review of anti-dumping legislation as such. Rather, in that case, we simply found that, for Mexico to challenge Guatemala's initiation and conduct of the anti-dumping investigation, Mexico was required to identify one of the three anti-dumping measures listed in Article 17.4 in its request for establishment of a panel. Since it did not do so, the panel in that case did not have jurisdiction.

A.3.56.5 *US – 1916 Act*, para. 73
(WT/DS136/AB/R, WT/DS162/AB/R)

Important considerations underlie the restriction contained in Article 17.4. In the context of dispute settlement proceedings regarding an anti-dumping investigation, there is tension between, on the one hand, a complaining Member's right to seek redress when illegal action affects its economic operators and, on the other hand, the risk that a responding Member may be harassed or its resources squandered if dispute settlement proceedings could be initiated against it in respect of each step, however small, taken in the course of an anti-dumping investigation, even before any concrete measure had been adopted. In our view, by limiting the availability of dispute settlement proceedings related to an anti-dumping investigation to cases in which a Member's request for establishment of a panel identifies a definitive anti-dumping duty, a price undertaking or a provisional measure, Article 17.4 strikes a balance between these competing considerations.

A.3.56.6 *US – 1916 Act*, para. 74
(WT/DS136/AB/R, WT/DS162/AB/R)

Therefore, Article 17.4 sets out certain conditions that must exist before a Member can challenge action taken by a national investigating authority in the context of an anti-dumping investigation. However, Article 17.4 does not address or affect a Member's right to bring a claim of inconsistency with the *Anti-Dumping Agreement* against anti-dumping legislation as such.

A.3.56.7 *US – 1916 Act*, para. 75
(WT/DS136/AB/R, WT/DS162/AB/R)

Moreover, as we have seen above, the GATT and WTO case law firmly establishes that dispute settlement proceedings may be brought based on the alleged inconsistency of a Member's legislation as such with that Member's obligations. We find nothing, and the United States has identified nothing, inherent in the nature of anti-dumping legislation that would rationally distinguish such legislation from other types of legislation for purposes of dispute settlement, or that would remove anti-dumping legislation from the ambit of the generally-accepted practice that a panel may examine legislation as such.

A.3.56.8 *US – Corrosion-Resistant Steel Sunset Review*, para. 83
(WT/DS244/AB/R)

... we have explained that Article 17.4 precludes a panel from addressing individual acts (as opposed to measures "as such") committed by an investigating authority in the context of the initiation and conduct of anti-dumping investigations *unless* one of the three types of measure listed in Article 17.4 is identified in the request for establishment of a panel. These measures are a definitive anti-dumping duty, the acceptance of a price undertaking, and a provisional measure. We have also found, in *US – 1916 Act,* that Article 17.4 does not place such a limit on a panel's jurisdiction to entertain claims against *legislation as such*. Indeed, we stated in that appeal that no provision of the *Anti-Dumping Agreement* precludes a panel from considering claims against legislation *as such*.

A.3.57 Article 17.5 – Facts made available to the investigating authority.
See also Request for the Establishment of a Panel (R.2)

A.3.57.1 *Guatemala – Cement I*, para. 75
(WT/DS60/AB/R)

... In our view, there is no *inconsistency* between Article 17.5 of the *Anti-Dumping Agreement* and the provisions of Article 6.2 of the DSU. On the contrary, they are complementary and should be applied together....

A.3.57.2 *Thailand – H-Beams*, para. 114
(WT/DS122/AB/R)

Articles 17.5 and 17.6 clarify the powers of review of a panel established under the *Anti-Dumping Agreement.* These provisions place limiting obligations on a panel, with respect to the review of the establishment and evaluation of facts by the investigating authority. Unlike Article 3.1, these provisions do not place obligations on WTO Members. Further, while the obligations in Article 3.1 apply to *all* injury determinations undertaken by Members, those in Articles 17.5 and 17.6 apply only when an injury determination is examined by a WTO panel. The obligations in Articles 17.5 and 17.6 are distinct from those in Article 3.1.

A.3.57.3 *Thailand – H-Beams*, para. 115
(WT/DS122/AB/R)

Article 17.5 specifies that a panel's examination must be based upon the "facts made available" to the domestic authorities. Anti-dumping investigations frequently involve both confidential and non-confidential information. The wording of Article 17.5 does not specifically exclude from panel examination facts made available to domestic authorities, but not disclosed or discernible to interested parties by the time of the final determination. Based on the wording of Article 17.5, we can conclude that a panel must examine the facts before it, whether in confidential documents or non-confidential documents.

A.3.57.4 *Thailand – H-Beams*, para. 118
(WT/DS122/AB/R)

Articles 17.5 and 17.6(i) require a panel to examine the facts made available to the investigating authority of the importing Member. These provisions do not prevent a panel from examining facts that were not disclosed to, or discernible by, the interested parties at the time of the final determination.

A.3.58 Article 17.6 – Standard of Review under the Anti-Dumping Agreement. *See also* Standard of Review, Article 11 of the DSU (S.7.2–7)

A.3.58.1 *US – Lead and Bismuth II*, para. 50
(WT/DS138/AB/R)

... [the *Decision on Review of Article 17.6 of the Agreement on Implementation of Article VI of the General Agreement on Tariffs and Trade 1994* (the "*Decision*")] provides for review of the standard of review in Article 17.6 of the *Anti-Dumping Agreement* to determine if it is "capable of general application" to other covered agreements, including the *SCM Agreement*. By implication, this *Decision* supports our conclusion that the Article 17.6 standard applies only to disputes arising under the *Anti-Dumping Agreement*, and not to disputes arising under other covered agreements, such as the *SCM Agreement*. To date, the DSB has not conducted the review contemplated in this *Decision*.

A.3.58.2 *Thailand – H-Beams*, para. 114
(WT/DS122/AB/R)

Articles 17.5 and 17.6 clarify the powers of review of a panel established under the *Anti-Dumping Agreement.* These provisions place limiting obligations on a panel, with respect to the review of the establishment and evaluation of facts by the investigating authority. Unlike Article 3.1, these provisions do not place obligations on WTO Members. Further, while the obligations in Article 3.1 apply to *all* injury determinations undertaken by Members, those in Articles 17.5 and 17.6 apply only when an injury determination is examined by a WTO panel. The obligations in Articles 17.5 and 17.6 are distinct from those in Article 3.1.

A.3.58.3 *US – Hot-Rolled Steel*, para. 54
(WT/DS184/AB/R)

. . . Article 17.6 is divided into two separate sub-paragraphs, each applying to different aspects of the panel's examination of the matter. The first sub-paragraph covers the *panel's* "*assessment* of the *facts* of the matter", whereas the second covers its "*interpret[ation* of] the *relevant provisions*". (emphasis added) The structure of Article 17.6, therefore, involves a clear distinction between a panel's assessment of the facts and its legal interpretation of the *Anti-Dumping Agreement*.

A.3.58.4 *Mexico – Corn Syrup (Article 21.5 – US)*, para. 130
(WT/DS132/AB/RW)

. . . The requirements of the standard of review provided for in Article 17.6(i) and 17.6(ii) are cumulative. In other words, a panel must find a determination made by the investigating authorities to be consistent with relevant provisions of the *Anti-Dumping Agreement* if it finds that those investigating authorities have properly established the facts and evaluated those facts in an unbiased and objective manner, *and* that the determination rests upon a "permissible" interpretation of the relevant provisions.

A.3.58.5 *EC – Bed Linen (Article 21.5 – India)*, para. 108
(WT/DS141/AB/RW)

. . . It is useful also to recall the specific standard of review under the *Anti-Dumping Agreement* that the Panel was required to follow in this dispute. This standard of review is set out in Article 17.6 of the *Anti-Dumping Agreement.* As to the facts, under Article 17.6(i), a panel "shall" determine whether the establishment of the facts by the investigating authorities was "proper" and whether the evaluation of those facts was "unbiased and objective". If the establishment of the facts was proper and the evaluation was unbiased and objective, then a panel "shall not" overturn that evaluation, even though it might have reached a different conclusion. As to the law, under Article 17.6(ii), first sentence, a panel "shall interpret the relevant provisions of the Agreement in accordance with customary rules of interpretation of public international law." Under Article 17.6(ii), second sentence, where a panel finds from such an interpretation that a relevant provision of the *Anti-Dumping Agreement* "admits of more than one permissible interpretation", the panel "shall find the [investigating] authorities' measure to be in conformity with the Agreement if it rests upon one of those permissible interpretations."...

A.3.59 **Article 17.6(i) – "assessment of the facts".** *See also* Seek Information and Technical Advice (S.4); Standard of Review, Article 11 of the DSU – Objective assessment of the facts (S.7.3)

A.3.59.1 *Thailand – H-Beams*, para. 116
(WT/DS122/AB/R)

Article 17.6(i) requires a panel, in its assessment of the facts of the matter, to determine whether the authorities' "establishment of the facts" was "proper". The ordinary meaning of "establishment" suggests an action to "place beyond dispute; ascertain, demonstrate, prove"; the ordinary meaning of "proper" suggests "accurate" or "correct". Based on the ordinary meaning of these words, the proper establishment of the facts appears to have no logical link to whether those facts are disclosed to, or discernible by, the parties to an anti-dumping investigation prior to the final determination. Article 17.6(i) requires a panel also to examine whether the evaluation of those facts was "unbiased and objective". The ordinary meaning of the words "unbiased" and "objective" also appears to have no logical link to whether those facts are disclosed to, or discernible by, the parties to an anti-dumping investigation at the time of the final determination.

A.3.59.2 *Thailand – H-Beams*, para. 118
(WT/DS122/AB/R)

Articles 17.5 and 17.6(i) require a panel to examine the facts made available to the investigating authority of the importing Member. These provisions do not prevent a panel from examining facts that were not disclosed to, or discernible by, the interested parties at the time of the final determination.

A.3.59.3 *Thailand – H-Beams*, para. 137
(WT/DS122/AB/R)

...Article 17.6(i) requires a panel, in its assessment of the facts, to determine "whether the authorities' establishment of the facts was proper" and to determine "whether their evaluation of those facts was unbiased and objective". Article 17.6(i) does *not* prevent a panel from examining whether a Member has complied with its obligations under Article 3.1. In evaluating whether a Member has complied with this obligation, a panel must examine whether the injury determination was based on positive evidence, and whether the injury determination involved an objective evaluation. Thus, to the extent that the Panel examined the facts in assessing whether Thailand's injury determination was consistent with Article 3.1, we are of the view that the Panel correctly conducted its examination consistently with the applicable standard of review under Article 17.6(i) of the *Anti-Dumping Agreement*.

A.3.59.4 *US – Hot-Rolled Steel*, para. 55
(WT/DS184/AB/R)

In considering Article 17.6(i) of the *Anti-Dumping Agreement*, it is important to bear in mind the different roles of panels and investigating authorities. Investigating authorities are charged, under the *Anti-Dumping Agreement*, with making factual determinations relevant to their overall determination of dumping and injury. Under Article 17.6(i), the task of panels is simply to review the investigating authorities' "establishment" and "evaluation" of the facts. To that end, Article 17.6(i) requires panels to make an "*assessment* of the *facts*". The language of this phrase reflects closely the obligation imposed on panels under Article 11 of the DSU to make an "*objective assessment* of the *facts*". Thus the text of both provisions requires panels to "assess" the facts and this, in our view, clearly necessitates an active review or examination of the pertinent facts. Article 17.6(i) of the *Anti-Dumping Agreement* does not expressly state that panels are obliged to make an assessment of the facts which is "*objective*". However, it is inconceivable that Article 17.6(i) should require anything other than that panels make an *objective* "assessment of the facts of the matter". In this respect, we see no "conflict" between Article 17.6(i) of the *Anti-Dumping Agreement* and Article 11 of the DSU.

A.3.59.5 *US – Hot-Rolled Steel*, para. 56
(WT/DS184/AB/R)

Article 17.6(i) of the *Anti-Dumping Agreement* also states that the panel is to determine, first, whether the investigating authorities' "*establishment* of the facts was *proper*" and, second, whether the authorities' "*evaluation* of those facts was *unbiased and objective*" (emphasis added) Although the text of Article 17.6(i) is couched in terms of an obligation on *panels* – panels "shall" make these determinations – the provision, at the same time, in effect defines when *investigating authorities* can be considered to have acted inconsistently with the *Anti-Dumping Agreement* in the course of their "establishment" and "evaluation" of the relevant facts. In other words, Article 17.6(i) sets forth the appropriate standard to be applied by *panels* in examining the WTO-consistency of the *investigating authorities'* establishment and evaluation of the facts under other provisions of the *Anti-Dumping Agreement*. Thus, panels must assess if the establishment of the facts by the investigating authorities was *proper* and if the evaluation of those facts by those authorities was *unbiased and objective*. If these broad standards have not been met, a panel must hold the investigating authorities' establishment or evaluation of the facts to be inconsistent with the *Anti-Dumping Agreement*.

A.3.59.6 *Mexico – Corn Syrup (Article 21.5 – US)*, para. 84
(WT/DS132/AB/RW)

The *Anti-Dumping Agreement* imposes a specific standard of review on *panels*. With respect to facts, Articles 17.5 and 17.6(i) of the *Anti-Dumping Agreement*, together with Article 11 of the DSU, set out the standard to be applied by panels when assessing whether a Member's investigating authorities have "established" and "evaluated" the facts consistently with that Member's obligations under the covered agreements. These provisions do not authorize panels to engage in a new and independent fact-finding exercise. Rather, in assessing the measure, panels must consider, in the light of the claims and arguments of the parties, whether, *inter alia*, the "establishment" of the facts by the investigating authorities was "proper", in accordance with the obligations imposed on such investigating authorities under the *Anti-Dumping Agreement.*

A.3.59.7 *Mexico – Corn Syrup (Article 21.5 – US)*, para. 90
(WT/DS132/AB/RW)

. . . [the investigating authority] *chose* to assume the existence and effectiveness of the alleged restraint agreement for purposes of its analysis of the likelihood of increased imports. We further note that none of the parties to this dispute challenged, before the Panel, SECOFI's decision to make such assumptions. In these circumstances, it was logical for the Panel to examine SECOFI's conclusions using the same premises. Indeed, we consider that it would have been improper for the Panel to have sought, on its own initiative, to go behind the assumptions made by SECOFI.

A.3.59.8 *EC – Bed Linen (Article 21.5 – India)*, para. 167
(WT/DS141/AB/RW)

. . . The mere fact that the Panel did not consider it necessary to seek information does not, by itself, imply that the Panel's exercise of its discretion was not "due". We, therefore, reject India's allegation that the Panel failed to comply with the requirements of Article 17.6 of the *Anti-Dumping Agreement* by not seeking information from the European Communities pursuant to Article 13 of the DSU.

A.3.59.9 *EC – Bed Linen (Article 21.5 – India)*, para. 169
(WT/DS141/AB/RW)

. . . in our view, the discretion that panels enjoy as triers of facts under Article 11 of the DSU is equally relevant to cases governed also by Article 17.6(i) of the *Anti-Dumping Agreement*. Thus, as under Article 11 of the DSU, we "will not interfere lightly with [a] panel's exercise of its discretion" under Article 17.6(i) of the *Anti-Dumping Agreement.*

A.3.59.10 *EC – Tube or Pipe*, para. 128
(WT/DS219/AB/R)

. . . In making such a claim under Article 17.6(i), it is not sufficient for Brazil simply to disagree with the Panel's weighing of the evidence, without substantiating its claim of error by the Panel. . . .

A.3.60 Article 17.6(ii) – "permissible interpretations". *See also* Interpretation, General rules of treaty interpretation – Article 31 of the Vienna Convention (I.3.1); Standard of Review, Article 11 of the DSU – Objective assessment of the facts (S.7.3)

A.3.60.1 *EC – Bed Linen*, para. 65
(WT/DS141/AB/R)

It appears clear to us from the emphatic and unqualified nature of this finding of inconsistency that the Panel did not view the interpretation given by the European Communities of Article 2.4.2 of the *Anti-Dumping Agreement* as a "permissible interpretation" within the meaning of Article 17.6(ii) of the *Anti-Dumping Agreement*. Thus, the Panel was not faced with a choice among multiple "permissible" interpretations which would have required it, under Article 17.6(ii), to give deference to the interpretation relied upon by the European Communities. Rather, the Panel was faced with a situation in which the interpretation relied upon by the European Communities was, to borrow a word from the European Communities, "impermissible". We do not share the view of the European Communities that the Panel failed to apply the standard of review set out in Article 17.6(ii) of the *Anti-Dumping Agreement*.

A.3.60.2 *US – Hot-Rolled Steel*, paras. 57, 59–60
(WT/DS184/AB/R)

. . . The *first* sentence of Article 17.6(ii), echoing closely Article 3.2 of the DSU, states that *panels* "shall" interpret the provisions of the *Anti-Dumping Agreement* "in accordance with customary rules of interpretation of public international law." Such customary rules are embodied in Articles 31 and 32 of the *Vienna Convention on the Law of Treaties* ("*Vienna Convention*"). Clearly, this aspect of Article 17.6(ii) involves no "conflict" with the DSU but, rather, confirms that the usual rules of treaty interpretation under the DSU also apply to the *Anti-Dumping Agreement*.

. . .

The *second* sentence of Article 17.6(ii) *presupposes* that application of the rules of treaty interpretation in Articles 31 and 32 of the *Vienna Convention* could give rise to, at least, two interpretations of some provisions of the *Anti-Dumping Agreement*, which, under that Convention, would both be "*permissible* interpretations". In that event, a measure is deemed to be in conformity with the *Anti-Dumping Agreement* "if it rests upon one of those permissible interpretations."

It follows that, under Article 17.6(ii) of the *Anti-Dumping Agreement*, panels are obliged to determine whether a measure rests upon an interpretation of the relevant provisions of the *Anti-Dumping Agreement* which is *permissible under the rules of treaty interpretation* in Articles 31 and 32 of the *Vienna Convention*. In other words, a permissible interpretation is one which is found to be appropriate *after* application of the pertinent rules of the *Vienna Convention*. We observe that the rules of treaty interpretation in Articles 31 and 32 of the *Vienna Convention* apply to *any* treaty, in *any* field of public international law, and not just to the WTO agreements. These rules of treaty interpretation impose certain common disciplines upon treaty interpreters, irrespective of the content of the treaty provision being examined and irrespective of the field of international law concerned.

A.3.60.3 *US – Hot-Rolled Steel*, para. 62
(WT/DS184/AB/R)

... although the second sentence of Article 17.6(ii) of the *Anti-Dumping Agreement* imposes obligations on panels which are not found in the DSU, we see Article 17.6(ii) as supplementing, rather than replacing, the DSU, and Article 11 in particular. Article 11 requires panels to make an "objective assessment of the matter" as a whole. Thus, under the DSU, in examining claims, panels must make an "objective assessment" of the legal provisions at issue, their "applicability" to the dispute, and the "conformity" of the measures at issue with the covered agreements. Nothing in Article 17.6(ii) of the *Anti-Dumping Agreement* suggests that panels examining claims under that Agreement should not conduct an "objective assessment" of the legal provisions of the Agreement, their applicability to the dispute, and the conformity of the measures at issue with the Agreement. Article 17.6(ii) simply adds that a panel shall find that a measure is in conformity with the *Anti-Dumping Agreement* if it rests upon one permissible interpretation of that Agreement.

A.3.60.4 *EC – Bed Linen (Article 21.5 – India)*, para. 118
(WT/DS141/AB/RW)

... Still, whatever methodology investigating authorities choose for calculating the volume of "dumped imports", that calculation and, ultimately, the determination of injury under Article 3, clearly must be made on the basis of "positive evidence" and involve an "objective examination". These requirements are not ambiguous, and they do not "admit of more than one permissible interpretation" within the meaning of the second sentence of Article 17.6(ii). Therefore, as in *US – Hot-Rolled Steel*, our interpretation of these requirements is based on customary rules of interpretation of public international law, as required by the first sentence of Article 17.6(ii). This leaves no room, in this appeal, for recourse to the second sentence of Article 17.6(ii) in interpreting paragraphs 1 and 2 of Article 3.

A.3.60.5 *US – Softwood Lumber V*, para. 116
(WT/DS264/AB/R)

The United States also claims that its interpretation of Article 2.4.2 is "permissible", *inter alia*, on the ground that "margins of dumping" within the meaning of Article 2.4.2 can be established for product types. In our view, the *Anti-Dumping Agreement*, when interpreted in accordance with customary rules of interpretation of public international law, as required by Article 17.6(ii), does not permit establishing margins of dumping for product types when the product as a whole is under investigation. The United States' interpretation of Article 2.4.2 is, therefore, *not* a "permissible interpretation" of that provision within the meaning of Article 17.6(ii). Hence, we see no error on the part of the Panel with respect to the Panel's obligations under Article 17.6(ii) of the *Anti-Dumping Agreement*.

A.3.61 Article 18.1 – Specific action against dumping. *See also* Anti-Dumping Agreement, Article VI of the GATT 1994 (A.3.65); SCM Agreement, Article 32.1 – Specific action against a subsidy (S.2.36)

A.3.61.1 *US – 1916 Act*, para. 122
(WT/DS136/AB/R, WT/DS162/AB/R)

In our view, the ordinary meaning of the phrase "specific action against dumping" of exports within the meaning of Article 18.1 is action that is taken in response to situations presenting the constituent elements of "dumping". "Specific action against dumping" of exports must, at a minimum, encompass action that may be taken *only* when the constituent elements of "dumping" are present. Since intent is not a constituent element of "dumping", the *intent* with which action against dumping is taken is not relevant to the determination of whether such action is "specific action against dumping" of exports within the meaning of Article 18.1 of the *Anti-Dumping Agreement.*

A.3.61.2 *US – 1916 Act*, para. 123
(WT/DS136/AB/R, WT/DS162/AB/R)

Footnote 24 to Article 18.1 of the *Anti-Dumping Agreement* states:

> This is not intended to preclude action under other relevant provisions of GATT 1994, as appropriate.

We note that footnote 24 refers generally to "action" and not, as does Article 18.1, to "specific action against dumping" of exports. "Action" within the meaning of footnote 24 is to be distinguished from "specific action against dumping" of exports, which is governed by Article 18.1 itself.

A.3.61.3 *US – 1916 Act*, para. 124
(WT/DS136/AB/R, WT/DS162/AB/R)

Article 18.1 of the *Anti-Dumping Agreement* contains a prohibition on the taking of any "specific action against dumping" of exports when such specific action is not "in accordance with the provisions of GATT 1994, as interpreted by this Agreement". Since the only provisions of the GATT 1994 "interpreted" by the *Anti-Dumping Agreement* are those provisions of Article VI concerning dumping, Article 18.1 should be read as requiring that any "specific action against dumping" of exports from another Member be in accordance with the relevant provisions of *Article VI* of the GATT 1994, as interpreted by the *Anti-Dumping Agreement*.

A.3.61.4 *US – 1916 Act*, para. 125
(WT/DS136/AB/R, WT/DS162/AB/R)

We recall that footnote 24 to Article 18.1 refers to "*other* relevant provisions of GATT 1994" (emphasis added). These terms can only refer to provisions other than the provisions of Article VI concerning dumping. Footnote 24 thus confirms that the "provisions of GATT 1994" referred to in Article 18.1 are in fact the provisions of Article VI of the GATT 1994 concerning dumping.

A.3.61.5 *US – Offset Act (Byrd Amendment)*, para. 236
(WT/DS217/AB/R, WT/DS234/AB/R)

Looking to the ordinary meaning of the words used in these provisions, we read them as establishing two conditions precedent that must be met in order for a measure to be governed by them. The first is that a measure must be "specific" to dumping or subsidization. The second is that a measure must be "against" dumping or subsidization. These two conditions operate together and complement each other. If they are not met, the measure will not be governed by Article 18.1 of the *Anti-Dumping Agreement* or by Article 32.1 of the *SCM Agreement*. If, however, it is established that a measure meets these two conditions, and thus falls within the scope of the prohibitions in those provisions, it would then be necessary to move to a further step in the analysis and to determine whether the measure has been "taken in accordance with the provisions of GATT 1994", as interpreted by the *Anti-Dumping Agreement* or the *SCM Agreement*. If it is determined that this is not the case, the measure would be inconsistent with Article 18.1 of the *Anti-Dumping Agreement* or Article 32.1 of the *SCM Agreement*.

A.3.61.6 *US – Offset Act (Byrd Amendment)*, para. 237
(WT/DS217/AB/R, WT/DS234/AB/R)

. . . The Panel analyzed the terms "specific" and "against" in Article 18.1 in the same manner as it did with respect to their use in Article 32.1. We agree with the Panel's approach. . . .

A.3.61.7 *US – Offset Act (Byrd Amendment)*, para. 239
(WT/DS217/AB/R, WT/DS234/AB/R)

. . . a measure that may be taken only when the constituent elements of dumping or a subsidy are present, is a "specific action" in response to dumping within the meaning of Article 18.1 of the *Anti-Dumping Agreement* or a "specific action" in response to subsidization within the meaning of Article 32.1 of the *SCM Agreement*. In other words, the measure must be inextricably linked to, or have a strong correlation with, the constituent elements of dumping or of a subsidy. Such link or correlation may, as in the 1916 Act, be derived from the text of the measure itself.

A.3.61.8 *US – Offset Act (Byrd Amendment)*, para. 240
(WT/DS217/AB/R, WT/DS234/AB/R)

. . . We recall that, in *US – 1916 Act*, we said the constituent elements of dumping are found in the definition of dumping in Article VI:1 of the GATT 1994, as elaborated in Article 2 of the *Anti-Dumping Agreement*. As regards the constituent elements of a subsidy, we are of the view that they are set out in the definition of a subsidy found in Article 1 of the *SCM Agreement*.

A.3.61.9 *US – Offset Act (Byrd Amendment)*, para. 244
(WT/DS217/AB/R, WT/DS234/AB/R)

...the "test" established in *US – 1916 Act* "is met not only when the constituent elements of dumping are 'explicitly built into' the action at issue, but also where... they are implicit in the express conditions for taking such action."...

A.3.61.10 *US – Offset Act (Byrd Amendment)*, para. 253
(WT/DS217/AB/R, WT/DS234/AB/R)

...in Article 18.1 of the *Anti-Dumping Agreement* and Article 32.1 of the *SCM Agreement*, there is no requirement that the measure must come into direct contact with the imported product, or entities connected to, or responsible for, the imported good such as the importer, exporter, or foreign producer....

A.3.61.11 *US – Offset Act (Byrd Amendment)*, para. 254
(WT/DS217/AB/R, WT/DS234/AB/R)

...to determine whether a measure is "against" dumping or a subsidy, we believe it is necessary to assess whether the design and structure of a measure is such that the measure is "opposed to", has an adverse bearing on, or, more specifically, has the effect of dissuading the practice of dumping or the practice of subsidization, or creates an incentive to terminate such practices. In our view, the CDSOA has exactly those effects because of its design and structure.

A.3.61.12 *US – Offset Act (Byrd Amendment)*, para. 257
(WT/DS217/AB/R, WT/DS234/AB/R)

...in order to determine whether the CDSOA is "against" dumping or subsidization, it was not necessary, nor relevant, for the Panel to examine the conditions of competition under which domestic products and dumped/subsidized imports compete, and to assess the impact of the measure on the competitive relationship between them. An analysis of the term "against", in our view, is more appropriately centred on the design and structure of the measure; such an analysis does not mandate an economic assessment of the implications of the measure on the conditions of competition under which domestic product and dumped/subsidized imports compete.

A.3.61.13 *US – Offset Act (Byrd Amendment)*, para. 258
(WT/DS217/AB/R, WT/DS234/AB/R)

...a measure cannot be against dumping or a subsidy simply because it facilitates or induces the exercise of rights that are WTO-consistent....

A.3.61.14 *US – Offset Act (Byrd Amendment)*, para. 262
(WT/DS217/AB/R, WT/DS234/AB/R)

...Footnotes 24 and 56 are clarifications of the main provisions, added to avoid ambiguity; they confirm what is implicit in Article 18.1 of the *Anti-Dumping*

Agreement and in Article 32.1 of the *SCM Agreement*, namely, that an action that is *not* "specific" within the meaning of Article 18.1 of the *Anti-Dumping Agreement* and of Article 32.1 of the *SCM Agreement*, but is nevertheless related to dumping or subsidization, is not prohibited by Article 18.1 of the *Anti-Dumping Agreement* or Article 32.1 of the *SCM Agreement*.

A.3.62 **Article 18.4 – Ensure conformity of domestic anti-dumping laws, regulations and procedures.** *See also* WTO Agreement, Article XVI:4 – WTO-conformity of laws, regulations and administrative procedures (W.4.3)

A.3.62.1 *US – 1916 Act*, para. 78
(WT/DS136/AB/R, WT/DS162/AB/R)

Article 18.4 imposes an affirmative obligation on each Member to bring its legislation into conformity with the provisions of the *Anti-Dumping Agreement* not later than the date of entry into force of the *WTO Agreement* for that Member. Nothing in Article 18.4 or elsewhere in the *Anti-Dumping Agreement* excludes the obligation set out in Article 18.4 from the scope of matters that may be submitted to dispute settlement.

A.3.62.2 *US – Corrosion-Resistant Steel Sunset Review*, para. 84
(WT/DS244/AB/R)

Our reasoning for concluding that the panel in *US – 1916 Act* had jurisdiction to consider *legislation*, as such, also applies in this case, where the relevant measures are specific provisions of an administrative instrument issued by an executive agency pursuant to statutory and regulatory provisions. That reasoning was based on the GATT *acquis* and the language of the *Anti-Dumping Agreement*, in particular Articles 17.3 and 18.4.

A.3.62.3 *US – Corrosion-Resistant Steel Sunset Review*, para. 87 and footnote 87
(WT/DS244/AB/R)

We also believe that the provisions of Article 18.4 of the *Anti-Dumping Agreement* are relevant to the question of the type of measures that may, as such, be submitted to dispute settlement under that Agreement. Article 18.4 contains an explicit obligation for Members to "take all necessary steps, of a general or particular character" to ensure that their "laws, regulations and administrative procedures" are in conformity with the obligations set forth in the *Anti-Dumping Agreement*. Taken as a whole, the phrase "laws, regulations and administrative procedures" seems to us to encompass the entire body of generally applicable rules, norms and standards adopted by Members in connection with the conduct of anti-dumping proceedings.[87] If some of these types of measure could not, as such, be subject to dispute settlement under the *Anti-Dumping Agreement*, it would frustrate the obligation of "conformity" set forth in Article 18.4.

[87] We observe that the scope of each element in the phrase "laws, regulations and administrative procedures" must be determined for purposes of WTO law and not simply by reference to the label given to various instruments under the domestic law of each WTO Member. This determination must be based on the content and substance of the instrument, and not merely on its form or nomenclature. Otherwise, the obligations set forth in Article 18.4 would vary from Member to Member depending on each Member's domestic law and practice.

A.3.62.4 *US – Corrosion-Resistant Steel Sunset Review*, para. 98
(WT/DS244/AB/R)

. . . the Panel did not consider the normative nature of the provisions of the Sunset Policy Bulletin, nor compare the type of norms that USDOC is required to publish in formal regulations with the type of norms it may set out in policy statements. These inquiries would have assisted the Panel in determining whether the Sunset Policy Bulletin is, in fact, an "administrative procedure" within the meaning of Article 18.4 of the *Anti-Dumping Agreement.*

Aggregate Investigations. *See* SCM Agreement, Article 19 (S.2.26–28)

A.3.63 Relationship between the Anti-Dumping Agreement and the SCM Agreement

A.3.63.1 *US – Lead and Bismuth II*, para. 49
(WT/DS138/AB/R)

. . . [the *Declaration on Dispute Settlement Pursuant to the Agreement on Implementation of Article VI of the General Agreement on Tariffs and Trade 1994 or Part V of the Agreement on Subsidies and Countervailing Measures* (the "*Declaration*")] does not impose an obligation to apply the standard of review contained in Article 17.6 of the *Anti-Dumping Agreement* to disputes involving countervailing duty measures under Part V of the *SCM Agreement*. The *Declaration* is couched in hortatory language; it uses the words "Ministers *recognize*". Furthermore, the *Declaration* merely acknowledges "the need for the consistent resolution of disputes arising from anti-dumping and countervailing duty measures." It does not specify any specific action to be taken. In particular, it does not prescribe a standard of review to be applied.

A.3.63.2 *US – Lead and Bismuth II*, para. 50
(WT/DS138/AB/R)

. . . [the *Decision on Review of Article 17.6 of the Agreement on Implementation of Article VI of the General Agreement on Tariffs and Trade 1994* (the "*Decision*")] provides for review of the standard of review in Article 17.6 of the *Anti-Dumping Agreement* to determine if it is "capable of general application" to other covered agreements, including the *SCM Agreement*. By implication, this *Decision* supports our conclusion that the Article 17.6 standard applies only to disputes arising under the *Anti-Dumping Agreement*, and not to disputes arising under other covered agreements, such as the *SCM Agreement*. To date, the DSB has not conducted the review contemplated in this *Decision*.

A.3.63.3 *US – Corrosion-Resistant Steel Sunset Review*, footnote 114 to para. 104
(WT/DS244/AB/R)

We note that Article 11.3 is textually identical to Article 21.3 of the *SCM Agreement*, except that, in Article 21.3, the word "countervailing" is used in place of the word "anti-dumping" and the word "subsidization" is used in place of the word "dumping". Given the parallel wording of these two articles, we believe that the explanation, in our Report in *US – Carbon Steel,* of the nature of the sunset review provision in the *SCM Agreement* also serves, *mutatis mutandis*, as an apt description of Article 11.3 of the *Anti-Dumping Agreement*. . . .

Relationship between the Anti-Dumping Agreement and the Safeguards Agreement. *See* Safeguards Agreement, Relationship between the Safeguards Agreement and the Anti-Dumping Agreement (S.1.43)

A.3.64 Relationship between the Anti-Dumping Agreement and the GATT 1994

A.3.64.1 *US – 1916 Act*, para. 114
(WT/DS136/AB/R, WT/DS162/AB/R)

. . . Article VI of the GATT 1994 and the *Anti-Dumping Agreement* are part of the same treaty, the *WTO Agreement*. As its full title indicates, the *Anti-Dumping Agreement* is an "Agreement on Implementation of Article VI of the General Agreement on Tariffs and Trade 1994". Accordingly, Article VI must be read in conjunction with the provisions of the *Anti-Dumping Agreement*, including Article 9.

A.3.64.2 *US – 1916 Act*, para. 133
(WT/DS136/AB/R, WT/DS162/AB/R)

. . . We also agree with the Panel that, having regard to the relationship between Article VI and the *Anti-Dumping Agreement*, "the applicability of Article VI to the 1916 Act also implies the applicability of the Anti-Dumping Agreement" to the 1916 Act.

A.3.65 Article VI of the GATT 1994 – Anti-dumping duties.

See also Anti-Dumping Agreement, Article 18.1 (A.3.61)

A.3.65.1 *US – 1916 Act*, para. 107
(WT/DS136/AB/R, WT/DS162/AB/R)

. . . under Article VI:1 of the GATT 1994 and Article 2 of the *Anti-Dumping Agreement*, neither the intent of the persons engaging in "dumping" nor the injurious effects that "dumping" may have on a Member's domestic industry are constituent elements of "dumping".

A.3.65.2 *US – 1916 Act*, para. 116
(WT/DS136/AB/R, WT/DS162/AB/R)

...the verb "may" in Article VI:2 of the GATT 1994 is, in our opinion, properly understood as giving Members a choice between imposing an anti-dumping duty *or not*, as well as a choice between imposing an anti-dumping duty equal to the dumping margin or imposing a lower duty. We find no support in Article VI:2, read in conjunction with Article 9 of the *Anti-Dumping Agreement*, for the United States' argument that the verb "may" indicates that Members, to counteract dumping, are permitted to take measures other than the imposition of anti-dumping duties.

A.3.65.3 *US – 1916 Act*, para. 117
(WT/DS136/AB/R, WT/DS162/AB/R)

...it appears to us that the text of Article VI is inconclusive as to whether Article VI regulates all possible measures which Members may take to counteract dumping, or whether it regulates only the imposition of anti-dumping duties.

A.3.65.4 *US – 1916 Act*, para. 121
(WT/DS136/AB/R, WT/DS162/AB/R)

We consider that the scope of application of Article VI is clarified, in particular, by Article 18.1 of the *Anti-Dumping Agreement*....

A.3.65.5 *US – 1916 Act*, para. 126
(WT/DS136/AB/R, WT/DS162/AB/R)

We have found that Article 18.1 of the *Anti-Dumping Agreement* requires that any "specific action against dumping" be in accordance with the provisions of Article VI of the GATT 1994 concerning dumping, as those provisions are interpreted by the *Anti-Dumping Agreement*. It follows that Article VI is applicable to any "specific action against dumping" of exports, i.e., action that is taken in response to situations presenting the constituent elements of "dumping".

A.3.65.6 *US – 1916 Act*, para. 130
(WT/DS136/AB/R, WT/DS162/AB/R)

...The constituent elements of "dumping" are built into the essential elements of civil and criminal liability under the 1916 Act. The wording of the 1916 Act also makes clear that these actions can be taken *only* with respect to conduct which presents the constituent elements of "dumping". It follows that the civil and criminal proceedings and penalties provided for in the 1916 Act are "specific action against dumping". We find, therefore, that Article VI of the GATT 1994 applies to the 1916 Act.

A.3.65.7 *US – 1916 Act*, para. 137
(WT/DS136/AB/R, WT/DS162/AB/R)

... Article VI, and, in particular, Article VI:2, read in conjunction with the *Anti-Dumping Agreement*, limit the permissible responses to dumping to definitive anti-dumping duties, provisional measures and price undertakings. Therefore, the 1916 Act is inconsistent with Article VI:2 and the *Anti-Dumping Agreement* to the extent that it provides for "specific action against dumping" in the form of civil and criminal proceedings and penalties.

A.3.65.8 *EC – Tube or Pipe*, para. 76
(WT/DS219/AB/R)

... We fail to see how Article VI:2, by stating that the purpose of anti-dumping duties is "to offset or prevent dumping", imposes upon investigating authorities an obligation to select any particular methodology for comparing normal value and export prices under Article 2.4.2 of the *Anti-Dumping Agreement* when calculating a dumping margin. As we see it, the obligation that flows from the purpose of "offset[ing] or prevent[ing] dumping" is clear from the text of Article VI:2 itself, namely, that an anti-dumping duty shall "not [be] greater in amount than the margin of dumping in respect of [the dumped] product". This limitation of anti-dumping duties to the margin of dumping is the only requirement imposed on investigating authorities by the first sentence of Article VI:2. The precise rules relating to the determination as to whether there is dumping and, if dumping exists, how the dumping margin is to be calculated, are set out, not in Article VI:2 of the GATT 1994, but rather in Article 2 of the *Anti-Dumping Agreement*, which is the agreement on the implementation of Article VI of the GATT 1994....

B

B.1 Balance-of-Payments Restrictions

B.1.1 Article XVIII:11 of the GATT 1994, Note Ad

B.1.1.1 *India – Quantitative Restrictions*, para. 114
(WT/DS90/AB/R)

We agree with the Panel that the Ad Note, and, in particular, the words "would thereupon produce", require a *causal link of a certain directness* between the removal of the balance-of-payments restrictions and the recurrence of one of the three conditions referred to in Article XVIII:9. . . .

B.1.1.2 *India – Quantitative Restrictions*, para. 115
(WT/DS90/AB/R)

We also agree with the Panel that the Ad Note and, in particular, the word "thereupon", expresses a *notion of temporal sequence* between the removal of the balance-of-payments restrictions and the recurrence of one of the conditions of Article XVIII:9. . . .

B.1.2 Article XVIII:11 of the GATT 1994, Proviso. *See also* Jurisdiction, General (J.2.1)

B.1.2.1 *India – Quantitative Restrictions*, paras. 126, 128
(WT/DS90/AB/R)

. . . we are of the opinion that the use of macroeconomic policy instruments is not related to any particular development policy, but is resorted to by all Members regardless of the type of development policy they pursue. . . .

. . .

We believe structural measures are different from macroeconomic instruments with respect to their relationship to development policy. If India were asked to implement agricultural reform or to scale back reservations on certain products for small-scale units as indispensable policy changes in order to overcome its balance-of-payments difficulties, such a requirement would probably have involved a change in India's development policy.

Benefit. *See* SCM Agreement, Article 14 (S.2.22–24)

B.2 Bilateral Settlements

B.2.1 *EC – Poultry*, para. 79

(WT/DS69/AB/R)

In our view, it is not necessary to have recourse to either Article 59.1 or Article 30.3 of the *Vienna Convention*, because the text of the *WTO Agreement* and the legal arrangements governing the transition from the GATT 1947 to the WTO resolve the issue of the relationship between Schedule LXXX and the Oilseeds Agreement in this case. Schedule LXXX is annexed to the *Marrakesh Protocol to the General Agreement on Tariffs and Trade 1994* (the "*Marrakesh Protocol*"), and is an integral part of the GATT 1994. As such, it forms part of the multilateral obligations under the *WTO Agreement*. The Oilseeds Agreement, in contrast, is a bilateral agreement negotiated by the European Communities and Brazil under Article XXVIII of the GATT 1947, as part of the resolution of the dispute in *EEC – Oilseeds*. As such, the Oilseeds Agreement is not a "covered agreement" within the meaning of Articles 1 and 2 of the DSU. Nor is the Oilseeds Agreement part of the multilateral obligations accepted by Brazil and the European Communities pursuant to the *WTO Agreement*, which came into effect on 1 January 1995. The Oilseeds Agreement is not cited in any Annex to the *WTO Agreement*. Although the provisions of certain legal instruments that entered into force under the GATT 1947 were made part of the GATT 1994 pursuant to the language in Annex 1A incorporating the GATT 1994 into the *WTO Agreement*, the Oilseeds Agreement is not one of those legal instruments.

B.3 Burden of Proof

B.3.1 General. *See also* Legislation as such vs. Specific Application (L.1)

B.3.1.1 *US – Wool Shirts and Blouses*, p. 14, DSR 1997:I, p. 323 at 335

(WT/DS33/AB/R, WT/DS33/AB/R/Corr.1)

. . . we find it difficult, indeed, to see how any system of judicial settlement could work if it incorporated the proposition that the mere assertion of a claim might amount to proof. It is, thus, hardly surprising that various international tribunals, including the International Court of Justice, have generally and consistently accepted and applied the rule that the party who asserts a fact, whether the claimant or the respondent, is responsible for providing proof thereof. Also, it is a generally-accepted canon of evidence in civil law, common law and, in fact, most jurisdictions, that the burden of proof rests upon the party, whether complaining or defending, who asserts the affirmative of a particular claim or defence. If that party adduces evidence sufficient to raise a presumption that what is claimed is true, the burden then shifts to the other party, who will fail unless it adduces sufficient evidence to rebut the presumption.

B.3.1.2 *US – Wool Shirts and Blouses*, p. 16, DSR 1997:I, p. 323 at 337
(WT/DS33/AB/R, WT/DS33/AB/R/Corr.1)

The transitional safeguard mechanism provided in Article 6 of the *ATC* is a fundamental part of the rights and obligations of WTO Members concerning non-integrated textile and clothing products covered by the *ATC* during the transitional period. Consequently, a party claiming a violation of a provision of the *WTO Agreement* by another Member must assert and prove its claim. . . .

B.3.1.3 *EC – Hormones*, para. 98
(WT/DS26/AB/R, WT/DS48/AB/R)

. . . The initial burden lies on the complaining party, which must establish a *prima facie* case of inconsistency with a particular provision of the *SPS Agreement* on the part of the defending party, or more precisely, of its SPS measure or measures complained about. When that *prima facie* case is made, the burden of proof moves to the defending party, which must in turn counter or refute the claimed inconsistency. . . .

B.3.1.4 *Japan – Apples*, para. 154
(WT/DS245/AB/R)

. . . the Appellate Body's statement in *EC – Hormones* [Appellate Body Report, para. 98] does not imply that the complaining party is responsible for providing proof of all facts raised in relation to the issue of determining whether a measure is consistent with a given provision of a covered agreement. In other words, although the complaining party bears the burden of proving its case, the responding party must prove the case it seeks to make in response. . . .

B.3.1.5 *India – Patents (US)*, para. 74
(WT/DS50/AB/R)

. . . it is not sufficient for a panel to enunciate the correct approach to burden of proof; a panel must also apply the burden of proof correctly. . . .

B.3.1.6 *Japan – Agricultural Products II*, para. 129
(WT/DS76/AB/R)

Article 13 of the DSU and Article 11.2 of the *SPS Agreement* suggest that panels have a significant investigative authority. However, this authority cannot be used by a panel to rule in favour of a complaining party which has not established a *prima facie* case of inconsistency based on specific legal claims asserted by it. A panel is entitled to seek information and advice from experts and from any other relevant source it chooses, pursuant to Article 13 of the DSU and, in an SPS case, Article 11.2 of the *SPS Agreement*, to help it to understand and evaluate the evidence submitted and the arguments made by the parties, but not to make the case for a complaining party.

B.3.1.7 *Japan – Apples*, para. 135 and footnote 230 (WT/DS245/AB/R)

The Panel determined that it was "legitimate to consider" the arguments and allegations of fact regarding apples other than mature, symptomless apples put forward by Japan in response to the claim pursued by the United States under Article 2.2. We agree with the Panel. A panel has the authority to make findings and draw conclusions on arguments and allegations of fact that are made by the respondent and *relevant* to a claim pursued by the complainant. The Panel's findings and conclusions with respect to apples other than mature, symptomless apples were in response to the arguments and allegations of fact that were "legitimately" raised by Japan. Therefore, when the Panel made findings and drew conclusions on apples other than mature, symptomless apple fruit, it duly acted within the limits of its authority.[230]

[230] In support of the argument that the Panel had no authority to make findings and draw conclusions with respect to immature apples, the United States relies on the finding of the Appellate Body in *Japan – Agricultural Products II* that a panel should not use its investigative authority "to rule in favour of a complaining party which has not established *a prima facie* case of inconsistency based on specific legal claims asserted by it." (Appellate Body Report, para. 129) The United States' reliance on *Japan – Agricultural Products II* is misplaced, for the facts and circumstances that led to the Appellate Body's finding are not the same as those present here. In *Japan – Agricultural Products II*, the Appellate Body found fault with the panel's reliance on expert evidence to rule in favour of the complainant in the absence of a case established by the complainant itself. The circumstances in the present case differ from those present in *Japan – Agricultural Products II*. Indeed, in the present case, the Panel made findings and drew conclusions on apples other than mature, symptomless apples in response to Japan's case.

B.3.1.8 *Canada – Aircraft*, para. 167 (WT/DS70/AB/R)

. . . There is a difference, however, in what evidence may be employed to prove that a subsidy is export contingent. *De jure* export contingency is demonstrated on the basis of the words of the relevant legislation, regulation or other legal instrument. Proving *de facto* export contingency is a much more difficult task. There is no single legal document which will demonstrate, on its face, that a subsidy is "contingent . . . in fact . . . upon export performance". Instead, the existence of this relationship of contingency, between the subsidy and export performance, must be *inferred* from the total configuration of the facts constituting and surrounding the granting of the subsidy, none of which on its own is likely to be decisive in any given case.

B.3.1.9 *India – Quantitative Restrictions*, para. 137 (WT/DS90/AB/R)

. . . The Panel thus appears to have considered that the burden of proof in respect of the Ad Note was on the United States. This is confirmed by the structure of the Panel's analysis in paragraphs 5.202 to 5.215 of its Report, in which the Panel begins its reasoning by considering the arguments advanced by the United States. . . . we do not consider that a panel is required to state *expressly* which party bears the burden of proof in respect of every claim made.

B.3.1.10 *Thailand – H-Beams*, para. 134 (WT/DS122/AB/R)

Thailand does not suggest that the Panel erred in its allocation and application of the burden of proof; it merely argues that the Panel did not make specific and explicit findings at every stage of its examination of Poland's claims under Article 3. In our view, a panel is not required to make a separate and specific finding, in each and every instance, that a party has met its burden of proof in respect of a particular claim, or that a party has rebutted a *prima facie* case. Thus, the Panel did not err to the extent that it made no specific findings on whether Poland had met its burden of proof.

B.3.1.11 *EC – Sardines*, para. 275 (WT/DS231/AB/R)

Given the conceptual similarities between, on the one hand, Articles 3.1 and 3.3 of the *SPS Agreement* and, on the other hand, Article 2.4 of the *TBT Agreement*, we see no reason why the Panel should not have relied on the principle we articulated in *EC – Hormones* to determine the allocation of the burden of proof under Article 2.4 of the *TBT Agreement*. In *EC – Hormones*, we found that a "general rule-exception" relationship between Articles 3.1 and 3.3 of the *SPS Agreement* does not exist, with the consequence that the complainant had to establish a case of inconsistency with *both* Articles 3.1 and 3.3. We reached this conclusion as a consequence of our finding there that "Article 3.1 of the *SPS Agreement* simply excludes from its scope of application the kinds of situations covered by Article 3.3 of that Agreement". [Appellate Body Report, *EC – Hormones*, para. 104] Similarly, the circumstances envisaged in the second part of Article 2.4 are excluded from the scope of application of the first part of Article 2.4. Accordingly, as with Articles 3.1 and 3.3 of the *SPS Agreement*, there is no "general rule-exception" relationship between the first and the second parts of Article 2.4. Hence, in this case, it is for Peru – as the complaining Member seeking a ruling on the inconsistency with Article 2.4 of the *TBT Agreement* of the measure applied by the European Communities – to bear the burden of proving its claim. This burden includes establishing that Codex Stan 94 has not been used "as a basis for" the EC Regulation, as well as establishing that Codex Stan 94 is effective and appropriate to fulfil the "legitimate objectives" pursued by the European Communities through the EC Regulation.

B.3.1.12 *EC – Sardines*, para. 281 (WT/DS231/AB/R)

. . . There is nothing in the WTO dispute settlement system to support the notion that the allocation of the burden of proof should be decided on the basis of a comparison between the respective difficulties that may possibly be encountered by the complainant and the respondent in collecting information to prove a case.

B.3.1.13 *US – Carbon Steel*, paras. 156–157
(WT/DS213/AB/R, WT/DS213/AB/R/Corr.1)

. . . in dispute settlement proceedings, Members may challenge the consistency with the covered agreements of another Member's laws, as such, as distinguished from any specific application of those laws. In both cases, the complaining Member bears the burden of proving its claim. . . .

Thus, a responding Member's law will be treated as WTO-*consistent* until proven otherwise. The party asserting that another party's municipal law, as such, is inconsistent with relevant treaty obligations bears the burden of introducing evidence as to the scope and meaning of such law to substantiate that assertion. Such evidence will typically be produced in the form of the text of the relevant legislation or legal instruments, which may be supported, as appropriate, by evidence of the consistent application of such laws, the pronouncements of domestic courts on the meaning of such laws, the opinions of legal experts and the writings of recognized scholars. The nature and extent of the evidence required to satisfy the burden of proof will vary from case to case.

B.3.1.14 *Canada – Dairy (Article 21.5 – New Zealand and US II)*, para. 66
(WT/DS103/AB/RW2, WT/DS113/AB/RW2)

. . . we have consistently held that, as a general matter, the burden of proof rests upon the complaining Member. That Member must make out a *prima facie* case by presenting sufficient evidence to raise a presumption in favour of its claim. If the complaining Member succeeds, the responding Member may then seek to rebut this presumption. Therefore, under the usual allocation of the burden of proof, a responding Member's measure will be treated as WTO-*consistent*, until sufficient evidence is presented to prove the contrary. We will not readily find that the usual rules on burden of proof do not apply, as they reflect a "canon of evidence" accepted and applied in international proceedings.

B.3.1.15 *EC – Tariff Preferences*, para. 98
(WT/DS246/AB/R)

. . . The status and relative importance of a given provision does not depend on whether it is characterized, for the purpose of allocating the burden of proof, as a claim to be proven by the complaining party, or as a defence to be established by the responding party. Whatever its characterization, a provision of the covered agreements must be interpreted in accordance with the "customary rules of interpretation of public international law", as required by Article 3.2 of the *Understanding on Rules and Procedures Governing the Settlement of Disputes* (the "DSU"). . . .

B.3.1.16 *Canada – Wheat Exports and Grain Imports*, para. 191
(WT/DS276/AB/R)

In our view, it is incumbent upon a party to identify in its submissions the relevance of the provisions of legislation – the evidence – on which it relies to support its arguments. It is not sufficient merely to file an entire piece of legislation and expect a panel to discover, on its own, what relevance the various provisions may or may not have for a party's legal position. We are not satisfied that the United States argued the relevance before the Panel of the various provisions of the *Canadian Wheat Board Act* on which it now relies.... Therefore, we do not agree with the United States that the Panel disregarded facts relevant to the independence of the CWB and we see no failure by the Panel in this respect to comply with its duty under Article 11 of the DSU.

B.3.1.17 *US – Upland Cotton*, para. 747
(WT/DS267/AB/R)

In this case, Brazil's claim on appeal is limited to the Panel's application of the burden of proof. Brazil has expressly stated that it is not requesting us to complete the analysis. In view of Brazil's request, our ruling would not result in recommendations or rulings by the DSB in respect of the ETI Act of 2000. In these circumstances, we fail to see how our examination of Brazil's claim would contribute to the "prompt" or "satisfactory settlement" of this matter or would contribute to "secure a positive solution" to this dispute. Even if we were to disagree with the manner in which the Panel applied the burden of proof, we would not make any findings in respect of the WTO-consistency of the ETI Act of 2000. We recognize that there may be cases in which it would be useful for us to make a finding on an issue, despite the fact that our decision would not result in rulings and recommendations by the DSB. In this case, however, we find no compelling reason for doing so on this particular issue.

B.3.2 Presumption – prima facie case

B.3.2.1 *US – Wool Shirts and Blouses*, p. 14, DSR 1997:I, p. 323 at 335
(WT/DS33/AB/R, WT/DS33/AB/R/Corr.1)

...precisely how much and precisely what kind of evidence will be required to establish such a presumption will necessarily vary from measure to measure, provision to provision, and case to case.

B.3.2.2 *EC – Hormones*, para. 104
(WT/DS26/AB/R, WT/DS48/AB/R)

...It is also well to remember that a *prima facie* case is one which, in the absence of effective refutation by the defending party, requires a panel, as a matter of law, to rule in favour of the complaining party presenting the *prima facie* case.

B.3.2.3 *Japan – Agricultural Products II*, para. 129
(WT/DS76/AB/R)

Article 13 of the DSU and Article 11.2 of the *SPS Agreement* suggest that panels have a significant investigative authority. However, this authority cannot be used by a panel to rule in favour of a complaining party which has not established a *prima facie* case of inconsistency based on specific legal claims asserted by it. A panel is entitled to seek information and advice from experts and from any other relevant source it chooses, pursuant to Article 13 of the DSU and, in an SPS case, Article 11.2 of the *SPS Agreement*, to help it to understand and evaluate the evidence submitted and the arguments made by the parties, but not to make the case for a complaining party.

B.3.2.4 *Canada – Aircraft*, para. 192
(WT/DS70/AB/R)

. . . A *prima facie* case, it is well to remember, is a case which, in the absence of effective refutation by the defending party (that is, in the present appeal, the Member requested to provide the information), requires a panel, as a matter of law, to rule in favour of the complaining party presenting the *prima facie* case. . . . a panel is vested with ample and extensive discretionary authority to determine *when* it needs information to resolve a dispute and *what* information it needs. A panel may need such information before or after a complaining or a responding Member has established its complaint or defence on a *prima facie* basis. A panel may, in fact, need the information sought in order to evaluate evidence already before it in the course of determining whether the claiming or the responding Member, as the case may be, has established a *prima facie* case or defence. Furthermore, a refusal to provide information requested on the basis that a *prima facie* case has not been made implies that the Member concerned believes that it is able to judge for itself whether the other party has made a *prima facie* case. However, no Member is free to determine for itself whether a *prima facie* case or defence has been established by the other party. That competence is necessarily vested in the panel under the DSU, and not in the Members that are parties to the dispute. . . .

B.3.2.5 *India – Quantitative Restrictions*, para. 142
(WT/DS90/AB/R)

We do not interpret the above statement as requiring a panel to conclude that a *prima facie* case is made before it considers the views of the IMF or any other experts that it consults. Such consideration may be useful in order to determine whether a *prima facie* case has been made. Moreover, we do not find it objectionable that the Panel took into account, in assessing whether the United States had made a *prima facie* case, the responses of India to the arguments of the United States. This way of proceeding does not imply, in our view, that the Panel shifted the burden of proof to India. We, therefore, are not of the opinion that the Panel erred in law in proceeding as it did.

B.3.2.6 *Korea – Dairy*, para. 145
(WT/DS98/AB/R)

We find no provision in the DSU or in the *Agreement on Safeguards* that requires a panel to make an explicit ruling on whether the complainant has established a *prima facie* case of violation before a panel may proceed to examine the respondent's defence and evidence. . . .

B.3.2.7 *US – Certain EC Products*, para. 114
(WT/DS165/AB/R)

... As the European Communities did not make a specific claim of inconsistency with Article 23.2(a), it did not adduce any evidence or arguments to demonstrate that the United States made a "determination as to the effect that a violation has occurred" in breach of Article 23.2(a) of the DSU. And, as the European Communities did not adduce any evidence or arguments in support of a claim of violation of Article 23.2(a) of the DSU, the European Communities could not have established, and did not establish, a *prima facie* case of violation of Article 23.2(a) of the DSU.

B.3.2.8 *Japan – Apples*, para. 157
(WT/DS245/AB/R)

It is important to distinguish, on the one hand, the principle that the complainant must establish a *prima facie* case of inconsistency with a provision of a covered agreement from, on the other hand, the principle that the party that asserts a fact is responsible for providing proof thereof. In fact, the two principles are distinct. In the present case, the burden of demonstrating a *prima facie* case that Japan's measure is maintained without sufficient scientific evidence, rested on the United States. Japan sought to counter the case put forward by the United States by putting arguments in respect of apples other than mature, symptomless apples being exported to Japan as a result of errors of handling or illegal actions. It was thus for Japan to substantiate those allegations; it was not for the United States to provide proof of the facts asserted by Japan. ...

B.3.2.9 *Japan – Apples*, para. 159
(WT/DS245/AB/R)

Japan also submits that, "in order to establish a *prima facie* case of insufficient scientific evidence under Article 2.2 of the SPS Agreement, the complaining party must establish that there is not sufficient scientific evidence for *any* of the perceived risks underlying the measure". According to Japan, the Panel should not have concluded that this *prima facie* case had been established unless the United States had first addressed *all* the possible hypotheses – including those for which the likelihood of occurrence is low or rests upon theoretical reasonings – and had shown for each of them that the risk of transmission of fire blight is negligible. We find no basis for the approach advocated by Japan. As the Appellate Body stated in *EC – Hormones* [Appellate Body Report, para. 104], "a *prima facie* case is one which, in the absence of effective refutation by the defending party, requires a panel, as a matter of law, to rule in favour of the complaining party presenting the *prima facie* case." In *US – Wool Shirts and Blouses* [Appellate Body Report, p. 14, DSR1997:I, p. 323 at 335], the Appellate Body stated that the nature and scope of evidence required to establish a *prima facie* case "will necessarily vary from measure to measure, provision to provision, and case to case." In the present case, the Panel appears to have concluded that in order to demonstrate a *prima facie* case that Japan's measure is maintained without sufficient scientific evidence, it sufficed for the United States to address only the question of whether mature, symptomless apples could serve as a pathway for fire blight.

B.3.2.10 *Japan – Apples*, para. 160
(WT/DS245/AB/R)

The Panel's conclusion seems appropriate to us for the following reasons. First, the claim pursued by the United States was that Japan's measure is maintained without sufficient scientific evidence to the extent that it applies to mature, symptomless apples exported from the United States to Japan. What is required to demonstrate a *prima facie* case is necessarily influenced by the nature and the scope of the claim pursued by the complainant. A complainant should not be required to prove a claim it does not seek to make. Secondly, the Panel found that mature, symptomless apple fruit is the commodity "normally exported" by the United States to Japan. The Panel indicated that the risk that apple fruit other than mature, symptomless apples may actually be imported into Japan would seem to arise primarily as a result of human or technical error, or illegal actions, and noted that the experts characterized errors of handling and illegal actions as "small" or "debatable" risks. Given the characterization of these risks, in our opinion it was legitimate for the Panel to consider that the United States could demonstrate a *prima facie* case of inconsistency with Article 2.2 of the *SPS Agreement* through argument based solely on mature, symptomless apples. Thirdly, the record contains no evidence to suggest that apples other than mature, symptomless ones have ever been exported to Japan from the United States as a result of errors of handling or illegal actions. Thus, we find no error in the Panel's approach that the United States could establish a *prima facie* case of inconsistency with Article 2.2 of the *SPS Agreement* in relation to apples exported from the United States to Japan, even though the United States confined its arguments to mature, symptomless apples.

B.3.2.11 *Japan – Apples*, para. 215
(WT/DS245/AB/R)

As Japan failed to establish that the Panel utilized subsequent scientific evidence in evaluating the risk assessment at issue, it is not necessary for us to express views on the question whether the conformity of a risk assessment with Article 5.1 should be evaluated solely against the scientific evidence available at the time of the risk assessment, to the exclusion of subsequent information. Resolution of such hypothetical claims would not serve "to secure a positive solution" to this dispute.

B.3.2.12 *US – Oil Country Tubular Goods Sunset Reviews*, para. 263
(WT/DS268/AB/R)

. . . As the Appellate Body indicated in *US – Carbon Steel*, the obligation to make out a *prima facie* case may be satisfied in certain cases simply by submitting the text of the measure or, particularly where the text may be unclear, with supporting materials. . . .

B.3.2.13 *US – Gambling*, paras. 138–140
(WT/DS285/AB/R)

The complaining party bears the burden of proving an inconsistency with specific provisions of the covered agreements. . . .

Where the complaining party has established its *prima facie* case, it is then for the responding party to rebut it. A panel errs when it rules on a claim for which the complaining party has failed to make a *prima facie* case.

A *prima facie* case must be based on "evidence *and* legal argument" put forward by the complaining party in relation to *each* of the elements of the claim. A complaining party may not simply submit evidence and expect the panel to divine from it a claim of WTO-inconsistency. Nor may a complaining party simply allege facts without relating them to its legal arguments.

B.3.2.14 *US – Gambling*, para. 141
(WT/DS285/AB/R)

. . . Given that . . . a requirement [to plainly connect the challenged measure(s) with the provision(s) of the covered agreements claimed to have been infringed, so that the respondent party is aware of the basis for the alleged nullification or impairment of the complaining party's benefits] applies to panel requests at the outset of a panel proceeding, we are of the view that a *prima facie* case – made in the course of submissions to the panel – demands no less of the complaining party. The evidence and arguments underlying a *prima facie* case, therefore, must be sufficient to identify the challenged measure and its basic import, identify the relevant WTO provision and obligation contained therein, and explain the basis for the claimed inconsistency of the measure with that provision.

B.3.2.15 *US – Gambling*, paras. 143–144
(WT/DS285/AB/R)

. . . Antigua was required to make its *prima facie* case by first alleging that the United States had undertaken a market access commitment in its GATS Schedule; and, secondly, by identifying, with supporting evidence, how the challenged laws constitute impermissible "limitations" falling within Article XVI:2(a) or XVI:2(c).

. . . Antigua was required to make its *prima facie* case with respect to *specific* federal and state laws identified in its panel request.

B.3.2.16 *US – Gambling*, para. 149
(WT/DS285/AB/R)

As to the eight state laws reviewed by the Panel, we note that Antigua made no mention of them in the course of its argument that the United States acts inconsistently with Article XVI of the GATS. In none of Antigua's submissions to the Panel was the way in which these measures operate explained in a manner that would have made it apparent to the Panel and to the United States that an inconsistency with Article XVI was being alleged with respect to these measures. Thus, we see no basis on which we can conclude that Antigua sufficiently connected the eight state laws with Article XVI and thereby established a *prima facie* case of inconsistency with that provision.

B.3.2.17 *US – Gambling*, paras. 153, 155
(WT/DS285/AB/R)

... with respect to the state laws ... Antigua failed to identify how these laws operated *and* how they were relevant to its claim of inconsistency with Article XVI:2.

...

... the Panel erred in ruling on claims relating to these state laws, where no *prima facie* case of inconsistency had been made out by Antigua ...

B.3.3 Defences and Exceptions. *See also* Request for the Establishment of a Panel, Article 6.2 of the DSU – Claims and legal basis of the complaint (R.2.2); SCM Agreement, Article 27 – Special and differential treatment for developing country Members (S.2.35); SPS Agreement, Article 3.2 – "measures which conform to international standards" (S.6.7)

B.3.3.1 *US – Gasoline*, pp. 22–23, DSR 1996:I, p. 3 at 21
(WT/DS2/AB/R)

The burden of demonstrating that a measure provisionally justified as being within one of the exceptions set out in the individual paragraphs of Article XX does not, in its application, constitute abuse of such exception under the chapeau, rests on the party invoking the exception. ...

B.3.3.2 *US – Wool Shirts and Blouses*, pp. 15–16, DSR 1997:I, p. 323 at 337
(WT/DS33/AB/R, WT/DS33/AB/R/Corr.1)

... We acknowledge that several GATT 1947 and WTO panels have required such proof of a party invoking a defence, such as those found in Article XX or Article XI:2(c)(i), to a claim of violation of a GATT obligation, such as those found in Articles I:1, II:1, III or XI:1. Articles XX and XI:(2)(c)(i) are limited exceptions from obligations under certain other provisions of the GATT 1994, not positive rules establishing obligations in themselves. They are in the nature of affirmative defences. It is only reasonable that the burden of establishing such a defence should rest on the party asserting it.

B.3.3.3 *EC – Hormones*, para. 104
(WT/DS26/AB/R, WT/DS48/AB/R)

... The general rule in a dispute settlement proceeding requiring a complaining party to establish a *prima facie* case of inconsistency with a provision of the *SPS Agreement* before the burden of showing consistency with that provision is taken on by the defending party, is *not* avoided by simply describing [Article 3.3] as an "exception". ...

B.3.3.4 *Brazil – Aircraft*, paras. 140–141
(WT/DS46/AB/R)

. . . On reading paragraphs 2(b) and 4 of Article 27 together, it is clear that the conditions set forth in paragraph 4 are *positive obligations* for developing country Members, *not* affirmative defences. If a developing country Member complies with the obligations in Article 27.4, the prohibition on export subsidies in Article 3.1(a) simply does not apply. However, if that developing country Member does *not* comply with those obligations, Article 3.1(a) *does* apply.

For these reasons, we agree with the Panel that the burden is on the complaining party . . . to demonstrate that the developing country Member . . . is not in compliance with at least one of the elements set forth in Article 27.4. . . .

B.3.3.5 *India – Quantitative Restrictions*, para. 136
(WT/DS90/AB/R)

. . . Assuming that the complaining party has successfully established a *prima facie* case of inconsistency with Article XVIII:11 and the Ad Note, the responding party may, in its defence, either rebut the evidence adduced in support of the inconsistency or invoke the proviso. In the latter case, it would have to demonstrate that the complaining party violated its obligation not to require the responding party to change its development policy. This is an assertion with respect to which the responding party must bear the burden of proof. . . .

B.3.3.6 *Brazil – Aircraft (Article 21.5 – Canada)*, para. 66
(WT/DS46/AB/RW)

. . . In our view, the fact that the measure at issue was "taken to comply" with the "recommendations and rulings" of the DSB does not alter the allocation of the burden of proving Brazil's "defence" under item (k). In this respect, we note that Brazil concedes that the revised PROEX measure is, in principle, prohibited under Article 3.1(a) of the *SCM Agreement*; yet Brazil asserts nonetheless that the PROEX measure is justified, under the first paragraph of item (k). Thus, in our view, Brazil is, clearly, using item (k) to make an affirmative claim in its defence. In *United States – Measure Affecting Imports of Woven Wool Shirts and Blouses from India*, we said: "It is only reasonable that the burden of establishing [an affirmative] defence should rest on the party asserting it." As it is Brazil that is asserting this "defence" using item (k) in these proceedings, we agree with the Article 21.5 Panel that Brazil has the burden of proving that the revised PROEX is justified under the first paragraph of item (k), including the burden of proving that payments under the revised PROEX are *not* "used to secure a material advantage in the field of export credit terms."

B.3.3.7 *US – FSC (Article 21.5 – EC)*, para. 133
(WT/DS108/AB/RW)

Accordingly, as we indicated in *US – FSC*, the fifth sentence of footnote 59 constitutes an affirmative defence that justifies a prohibited export subsidy when the measure in question is taken "to avoid the double taxation of foreign-source income". In such a situation, the burden of proving that a measure is justified by falling within the scope of the fifth sentence of footnote 59 rests upon the responding party.

B.3.3.8 *EC – Tariff Preferences*, para. 88
(WT/DS246/AB/R)

...In cases where one provision permits, in certain circumstances, behaviour that would otherwise be inconsistent with an obligation in another provision, and one of the two provisions refers to the other provision, the Appellate Body has found that the complaining party bears the burden of establishing that a challenged measure is inconsistent with the provision permitting particular behaviour *only* where one of the provisions suggests that the obligation is not applicable to the said measure. Otherwise, the permissive provision has been characterized as an exception, or defence, and the onus of invoking it and proving the consistency of the measure with its requirements has been placed on the responding party. However, this distinction may not always be evident or readily applicable.

B.3.3.9 *EC – Tariff Preferences*, para. 90
(WT/DS246/AB/R)

...By using the word "notwithstanding", paragraph 1 of the Enabling Clause permits Members to provide "differential and more favourable treatment" to developing countries "in spite of" the MFN obligation of Article I:1. Such treatment would otherwise be inconsistent with Article I:1 because that treatment is not extended to all Members of the WTO "immediately and unconditionally". Paragraph 1 thus excepts Members from complying with the obligation contained in Article I:1 for the purpose of providing differential and more favourable treatment to developing countries, provided that such treatment is in accordance with the conditions set out in the Enabling Clause. As such, the Enabling Clause operates as an "exception" to Article I:1.

B.3.3.10 *EC – Tariff Preferences*, para. 97
(WT/DS246/AB/R)

We do not consider it relevant, for the purposes of determining whether a provision is or is not in the nature of an exception, that the provision governs "trade measures" rather than measures of a primarily "non-trade" nature....

B.3.3.11 *EC – Tariff Preferences*, para. 98
(WT/DS246/AB/R)

...The status and relative importance of a given provision does not depend on whether it is characterized, for the purpose of allocating the burden of proof, as a claim to be proven by the complaining party, or as a defence to be established by the responding party. Whatever its characterization, a provision of the covered agreements must be interpreted in accordance with the "customary rules of interpretation of public international law", as required by Article 3.2 of the *Understanding on Rules and Procedures Governing the Settlement of Disputes* (the "DSU"). . . .

B.3.3.12 *EC – Tariff Preferences*, paras. 104–105
(WT/DS246/AB/R)

. . . it is normally for the respondent, first, to *raise* the defence and, second, to *prove* that the challenged measure meets the requirements of the defence provision.

We are therefore of the view that the European Communities must *prove* that the Drug Arrangements satisfy the conditions set out in the Enabling Clause. Consistent with the principle of *jura novit curia*, it is not the responsibility of the European Communities to provide us with the legal interpretation to be given to a particular provision in the Enabling Clause; instead, the burden of the European Communities is to adduce sufficient evidence to substantiate its assertion that the Drug Arrangements comply with the requirements of the Enabling Clause.

B.3.3.13 *EC – Tariff Preferences*, para. 110
(WT/DS246/AB/R)

. . . we are of the view that a complaining party challenging a measure taken pursuant to the Enabling Clause must allege more than mere inconsistency with Article I:1 of the GATT 1994, for to do only that would not convey the "legal basis of the complaint sufficient to present the problem clearly". In other words, it is insufficient in WTO dispute settlement for a complainant to allege inconsistency with Article I:1 of the GATT 1994 if the complainant seeks also to argue that the measure is not justified under the Enabling Clause. . . .

B.3.3.14 *EC – Tariff Preferences*, para. 118
(WT/DS246/AB/R)

. . . In the light of the above considerations, we are of the view that India was required to (i) identify, in its request for the establishment of a panel, which obligations in the Enabling Clause the Drug Arrangements are alleged to have contravened, and (ii) make written submissions in support of this allegation. The requirement to make such an argument, however, does not mean that India must prove inconsistency with a provision of the Enabling Clause, because the ultimate burden of establishing the consistency of the Drug Arrangements with the Enabling Clause lies with the European Communities.

B.3.3.15 *US – Gambling*, paras. 270–272
(WT/DS285/AB/R)

At the same time, the opportunity afforded to a Member to respond to claims and defences made against it is also a "fundamental tenet of due process". A party must not merely be given *an* opportunity to respond, but that opportunity must be meaningful in terms of that party's ability to defend itself adequately. A party that considers it was not afforded such an opportunity will often raise a due process objection before the panel. The Appellate Body has recognized in numerous cases that a Member's right to raise a claim or objection, as well as a panel's exercise of discretion, are circumscribed by the due process rights of other parties to a dispute. Those due process rights similarly serve to limit a responding party's right to set out its defence at *any* point during the panel proceedings.

Due process may be of particular concern in cases where a party raises *new facts* at a late stage of the panel proceedings. The Appellate Body has observed that, under the standard working procedures of panels, complaining parties should put forward their cases – with "a full presentation of the facts on the basis of submission of supporting evidence" – during the *first* stage of panel proceedings. We see no reason why this expectation would not apply equally to responding parties, which, once they have received the first written submission of a complaining party, are likely to be aware of the defences they might invoke and the evidence needed to support them.

It follows that the principles of good faith and due process oblige a responding party to articulate its defence promptly and clearly. This will enable the complaining party to understand that a specific defence has been made, "be aware of its dimensions, and have an adequate opportunity to address and respond to it."...

B.3.3.16 *US – Gambling*, para. 282
(WT/DS285/AB/R)

In the context of affirmative defences, then, a responding party must invoke a defence and put forward evidence and arguments in support of its assertion that the challenged measure satisfies the requirements of the defence. When a responding party fulfils this obligation, a panel may rule on whether the challenged measure is justified under the relevant defence, relying on arguments advanced by the parties or developing its own reasoning. The same applies to rebuttals. A panel may not take upon itself to rebut the claim (or defence) where the responding party (or complaining party) itself has not done so.

B.3.3.17 *US – Gambling*, paras. 309–310
(WT/DS285/AB/R)

It is well-established that a responding party invoking an affirmative defence bears the burden of demonstrating that its measure, found to be WTO-inconsistent, satisfies the requirements of the invoked defence. In the context of Article XIV(a), this means that the responding party must show that its measure is "necessary" to achieve objectives relating to public morals or public order. In our view, however, it is not the responding party's burden to show, in the first instance, that there are *no* reasonably available alternatives to achieve its objectives. In particular, a responding party need not identify the universe of less trade-restrictive alternative measures and then show that none of those measures achieves the desired objective. The WTO agreements do not contemplate such an impracticable and, indeed, often impossible burden.

Rather, it is for a responding party to make a *prima facie* case that its measure is "necessary" by putting forward evidence and arguments that enable a panel to assess the challenged measure in the light of the relevant factors to be "weighed and balanced" in a given case. The responding party may, in so doing, point out why alternative measures would not achieve the same objectives as the challenged measure, but it is under no obligation to do so in order to establish, in the first instance, that its measure is "necessary". If the panel concludes that the respondent has made a *prima facie* case that the challenged measure is "necessary" – that is, "significantly closer to the pole of 'indispensable' than to the opposite pole of simply 'making a contribution to' " – then a panel should find that challenged measure "necessary" within the terms of Article XIV(a) of the GATS.

B.3.3.18 *US – Gambling*, para. 311
(WT/DS285/AB/R)

If, however, the complaining party raises a WTO-consistent alternative measure that, in its view, the responding party should have taken, the responding party will be required to demonstrate why its challenged measure nevertheless remains "necessary" in the light of that alternative or, in other words, why the proposed alternative is not, in fact, "reasonably available". If a responding party demonstrates that the alternative is not "reasonably available", in the light of the interests or values being pursued and the party's desired level of protection, it follows that the challenged measure must be "necessary" within the terms of Article XIV(a) of the GATS.

B.3.3.19 *US – Gambling*, para. 323
(WT/DS285/AB/R)

. . . a responding party must make a *prima facie* case that its challenged measure is "necessary". A Panel determines whether this case is made through the identification, and weighing and balancing, of relevant factors, such as those in *Korea – Various Measures on Beef*, with respect to the measure challenged. . . .

B.3.4 Reversal of Burden of Proof. *See also* Agreement on Agriculture, Article 10.3 – Reversal of Burden of Proof (A.1.34)

B.3.4.1 *Canada – Dairy (Article 21.5 – New Zealand and US)*, para. 98
(WT/DS103/AB/RW, WT/DS113/AB/RW)

As we have reversed the Panel's findings regarding the standard for determining the existence of "payments" and have, instead, identified the appropriate standard for these proceedings, namely, the average total cost of production, we now consider whether we can resolve this aspect of the dispute by completing the analysis. The Panel found that, in these proceedings, Article 10.3 of the *Agreement on Agriculture* reverses the burden of proof so that Canada must establish "that no export subsidy . . . has been granted". Although the burden of proof is on Canada, we must nonetheless complete the analysis solely on the basis of factual findings made by the Panel and uncontested facts in the Panel record.

B.3.4.2 *Canada – Dairy (Article 21.5 – New Zealand and US II)*, para. 71 (WT/DS103/AB/RW2, WT/DS113/AB/RW2)

Under the usual rules on burden of proof, the complaining Member would bear the burden of proving both parts of the claim. However, Article 10.3 of the *Agreement on Agriculture* partially alters the usual rules. The provision cleaves the complaining Member's claim in two, allocating to different parties the burden of proof with respect to the two parts of the claim we have described.

B.3.4.3 *US – Upland Cotton*, paras. 647–648 (WT/DS267/AB/R)

We agree with the United States that Article 10.3 of the *Agreement on Agriculture* does not apply to claims brought under the *SCM Agreement*. However, the Panel did not make the error attributed to it by the United States. The Panel made the statement relied on by the United States in the context of its assessment of the United States' export credit guarantee program under the *Agreement on Agriculture*. Although the Panel made use of the criteria set out in item (j) of the Illustrative List of Export Subsidies annexed to the *SCM Agreement* (providing these programs at premium rates inadequate to cover long-term operating costs and losses) it did so as contextual guidance for its analysis under the *Agreement on Agriculture*, and both the United States and Brazil appear to have agreed with the appropriateness of this approach. Thus, the Panel's reference to Article 10.3 did not relate to its assessment of the United States' export credit guarantee programs under the *SCM Agreement*.

. . . It is clear from this paragraph that the Panel placed the burden of proof on Brazil and determined that Brazil met its burden of proving that the United States' export credit guarantees are provided at premium rates that are inadequate to cover long-term operating costs and losses. . . . The reference to Article 10.3 does not, by itself, change the fact that the Panel ultimately placed the burden of proof on Brazil.

B.3.4.4 *US – Upland Cotton*, para. 652 (WT/DS267/AB/R)

We disagree with the Panel's view that Article 10.3 applies to *unscheduled* products. Under the Panel's approach, the only thing a complainant would have to do to meet its burden of proof when bringing a claim against an *unscheduled* product is to demonstrate that the respondent has exported that product. Once that has been established, the respondent would have to demonstrate that it has not provided an export subsidy. This seems to us an extreme result. In effect, it would mean that any export of an unscheduled product is *presumed* to be subsidized. In our view, the presumption of subsidization when exported quantities exceed the reduction commitments makes sense in respect of a *scheduled* product because, by including it in its schedule, a WTO Member is reserving for itself the right to apply export subsidies to that product, within the limits in its schedule. In the case of *unscheduled* products, however, such a presumption appears inappropriate. Export subsidies for both unscheduled agricultural products and industrial products are completely prohibited under the *Agreement on Agriculture* and under the *SCM Agreement*, respectively. The Panel's interpretation implies that the burden of proof with regard to the same issue would apply differently, however, under each Agreement: it would be on the respondent under the *Agreement on Agriculture*, while it would be on the complainant under the *SCM Agreement*.

B.3.4.5 *US – Upland Cotton*, para. 656
(WT/DS267/AB/R)

In our view, none of these statements demonstrates that the Panel improperly applied the rules on burden of proof. The United States is selecting statements made by the Panel within its broader analysis of how the United States' export credit guarantee programs operate, reading them in isolation, and disregarding the context in which they were made. As indicated earlier, it is clear that the Panel imposed on Brazil the overall burden of proving that the premiums charged under the United States' export credit guarantee programs are inadequate to cover long-term operating costs and losses. This approach is consistent with the usual rules on the allocation of the burden of proof whereby the complaining party is responsible for proving its claim. . . .

B.4 Business Confidential Information. *See also* Confidentiality (C.6); Inferences drawn from the Refusal of a Party to Provide Information (I.1); Seek Information and Technical Advice (S.4)

B.4.1 *Brazil – Aircraft*, para. 9
(WT/DS46/AB/R)

. . . by joint letter of 27 May 1999, Brazil and Canada requested that the Appellate Body apply, *mutatis mutandis*, the Procedures Governing Business Confidential Information adopted by the Panel in this case. A preliminary hearing on this issue was held on 10 June 1999, with this Division sitting jointly with the Division of the Appellate Body hearing the appeal in *Canada – Measures Affecting the Export of Civilian Aircraft* ("*Canada – Aircraft*"), and a preliminary ruling was issued by this Division on 11 June 1999.

B.4.2 *Canada – Aircraft*, para. 6
(WT/DS70/AB/R)

. . . by joint letter of 27 May 1999, Brazil and Canada requested that the Appellate Body apply, *mutatis mutandis*, the Procedures Governing Business Confidential Information (the "BCI Procedures") adopted by the Panel in this case. A preliminary hearing on this issue was held on 10 June 1999, with this Division sitting jointly with the Division of the Appellate Body hearing the appeal in *Brazil – Export Financing Programme For Aircraft* ("*Brazil – Aircraft*"), and a preliminary ruling was issued by this Division on 11 June 1999.

B.4.3 *Brazil – Aircraft*, para. 119
(WT/DS46/AB/R)

Canada – Aircraft, para. 141
(WT/DS70/AB/R)

In our preliminary ruling of 11 June 1999, we concluded that it is not necessary, under all the circumstances of this case, to adopt *additional* procedures to protect business confidential information in these appellate proceedings. Our ruling was as follows:

> . . . We also note that *all* Members are obliged, by the provisions of the DSU, to treat these proceedings of the Appellate Body, including written submissions and other documents filed by the participants and the third participants, as confidential. We are confident that the participants and the third participants in this appeal will *fully respect* their obligations under the DSU, recognizing that a Member's obligation to maintain the confidentiality of these proceedings extends also to the individuals whom that Member selects to act as its representatives, counsel and consultants. . . .

B.4.4 *Brazil – Aircraft*, paras. 123–125
(WT/DS46/AB/R)

Canada – Aircraft, paras. 145–147
(WT/DS70/AB/R)

In our view, the provisions of Articles 17.10 and 18.2 apply to all Members of the WTO, and oblige them to maintain the confidentiality of any submissions or information submitted, or received, in an Appellate Body proceeding. Moreover, those provisions oblige Members to ensure that such confidentiality is fully respected by any person that a Member selects to act as its representative, counsel or consultant. In this respect, we note, with approval, the following statement made by the panel in [*Indonesia – Automobiles*]:

> We would like to emphasize that *all members of parties' delegations – whether or not they are government employees – are present as representatives of their governments, and as such are subject to the provisions of the DSU and of the standard working procedures, including Articles 18.1 and 18.2 of the DSU and paragraphs 2 and 3 of those procedures*. In particular, parties are required to treat as confidential all submissions to the Panel and all information so designated by other Members; and, in addition, the Panel meets in closed session. Accordingly, *we expect that all delegations will fully respect those obligations and will treat these proceedings with the utmost circumspection and discretion.* (emphasis added) [Panel Report, *Indonesia – Automobiles*, para. 14.1]

Finally, we wish to recall that Members of the Appellate Body and its staff are covered by Article VII:1 of the *Rules of Conduct*, which provides:

> Each covered person *shall at all times maintain the confidentiality of dispute settlement deliberations and proceedings together with any information identified by a party as confidential*. (emphasis added)

For these reasons, we do not consider that it is necessary, under all the circumstances of this case, to adopt *additional* procedures for the protection of business confidential information in these appellate proceedings. . . .

C

C.1 Claims and Arguments. *See also* Burden of Proof, General (B.3.1); Request for the Establishment of a Panel (R.2); Terms of Reference of Panels (T.6); Working Procedures for Appellate Review, Rule 20 – Notice of Appeal (W.2.7)

C.1.1 *Brazil – Desiccated Coconut*, p. 22, DSR 1997:I, p. 167 at 186 (WT/DS22/AB/R)

. . . the "matter" referred to a panel for consideration consists of the specific claims stated by the parties to the dispute in the relevant documents specified in the terms of reference. We agree with the approach taken in previous adopted panel reports that a matter, which includes the claims composing that matter, does not fall within a panel's terms of reference unless the claims are identified in the documents referred to or contained in the terms of reference.

C.1.2 *EC – Bananas III*, para. 141 (WT/DS27/AB/R)

. . . In our view, there is a significant difference between the *claims* identified in the request for the establishment of a panel, which establish the panel's terms of reference under Article 7 of the DSU, and the *arguments* supporting those claims, which are set out and progressively clarified in the first written submissions, the rebuttal submissions and the first and second panel meetings with the parties.

C.1.3 *EC – Bananas III*, para. 143 (WT/DS27/AB/R)

. . . Article 6.2 of the DSU requires that the *claims*, but not the *arguments*, must all be specified sufficiently in the request for the establishment of a panel in order to allow the defending party and any third parties to know the legal basis of the complaint. If a *claim* is not specified in the request for the establishment of a panel, then a faulty request cannot be subsequently "cured" by a complaining party's argumentation in its first written submission to the panel or in any other submission or statement made later in the panel proceeding.

C.1.4 *EC – Bananas III*, paras. 145, 147
(WT/DS27/AB/R)

. . . There is no requirement in the DSU or in GATT practice for arguments on all claims relating to the matter referred to the DSB to be set out in a complaining party's first written submission to the panel. It is the panel's terms of reference, governed by Article 7 of the DSU, which set out the claims of the complaining parties relating to the matter referred to the DSB.

. . .

. . . We do not agree with the Panel's statement that a "failure to make a claim in the first written submission cannot be remedied by later submissions or by incorporating the claims and arguments of other complainants". . . .

C.1.5 *India – Patents (US)*, para. 88
(WT/DS50/AB/R)

. . . we observed that there is a significant difference between the *claims* identified in the request for the establishment of a panel, which establish the panel's terms of reference under Article 7 of the DSU, and the *arguments* supporting those claims, which are set out and progressively clarified in the first written submissions, the rebuttal submissions, and the first and second panel meetings with the parties as a case proceeds. . . .

C.1.6 *Korea – Dairy*, para. 139
(WT/DS98/AB/R)

. . . By "*claim*" we mean a claim that the respondent party has violated, or nullified or impaired the benefits arising from, an identified provision of a particular agreement. Such a *claim of violation* must, as we have already noted, be distinguished from the *arguments* adduced by a complaining party to demonstrate that the responding party's measure does indeed infringe upon the identified treaty provision. Arguments supporting a claim are set out and progressively clarified in the first written submissions, the rebuttal submissions and the first and second panel meetings with the parties. . . .

. . . Both "claims" and "arguments" are distinct from the "evidence" which the complainant or respondent presents to support its assertions of fact and arguments.

C.1.7 *US – Lead and Bismuth II*, para. 73
(WT/DS138/AB/R)

In order to resolve the claim of the European Communities, the Panel deemed it necessary to address the two principal arguments made in support of this claim. In doing so, the Panel acted within the context of resolving this particular dispute and, therefore, within the scope of its mandate under the DSU.

C.1.8 *Chile – Price Band System*, para. 182
(WT/DS207/AB/R)

In our view, this distinction between claims and legal arguments under Article 6.2 of the DSU is also relevant to the distinction between "allegations of error" and legal arguments as contemplated by Rule 20 of the *Working Procedures*. Bearing this distinction in mind, we do *not* agree with Argentina that Chile's arguments regarding the order of analysis chosen by the Panel amount to a separate "allegation of error" that Chile *should have* – or *could have* – included in its Notice of Appeal. In fact, we do not see, nor has Argentina explained, what *separate* "allegation of error" could have been made, or what legal basis for such "allegation of error" there could have been. Rather than making a separate "allegation of error", Chile has, in our view, simply set out a *legal argument* in support of the issues it raised on appeal relating to Article 4.2 of the *Agreement on Agriculture* and Article II:1(b) of the GATT 1994.

C.1.9 *Dominican Republic – Import and Sale of Cigarettes*, para. 121
(WT/DS302/AB/R)

We also observe that the Appellate Body has consistently distinguished between the *claims* of a Member regarding the application of the various provisions of the *WTO Agreement*, and the *arguments* presented in support of those claims. Claims, which are typically allegations of violation of the substantive provisions of the *WTO Agreement*, must be set out clearly in the request for the establishment of a panel. Arguments, by contrast, are the means whereby a party progressively develops and supports its claims. These do not need to be set out in detail in a panel request; rather, they may be developed in the submissions made to the panel.

C.2 Claims and Panel Reasoning

C.2.1 *EC – Hormones*, para. 156
(WT/DS26/AB/R, WT/DS48/AB/R)

. . . Panels are inhibited from addressing legal claims falling outside their terms of reference. However, nothing in the DSU limits the faculty of a panel freely to use arguments submitted by any of the parties – or to develop its own legal reasoning – to support its own findings and conclusions on the matter under its consideration. A panel might well be unable to carry out an objective assessment of the matter, as mandated by Article 11 of the DSU, if in its reasoning it had to restrict itself solely to arguments presented by the parties to the dispute. Given that in this particular case both complainants claimed that the EC measures were inconsistent with Article 5.5 of the *SPS Agreement*, we conclude that the Panel did not make any legal finding beyond those requested by the parties.

C.2.2 *US – Certain EC Products*, para. 123
(WT/DS165/AB/R)

This appeal by the United States raises the question whether a panel is entitled to develop its own legal reasoning in reaching its findings and conclusions on the matter under its consideration. In our Report in *European Communities – Hormones*, we held:

> Panels are inhibited from addressing legal claims falling outside their terms of reference. However, nothing in the DSU limits the faculty of a panel freely to use arguments submitted by any of the parties – or to develop its own legal reasoning – to support its own findings and conclusions on the matter under its consideration.

The Panel in this case exercised its discretion to develop its own legal reasoning. Contrary to what the United States argues, the Panel was not obliged to limit its legal reasoning in reaching a finding to arguments presented by the European Communities. We, therefore, do not consider that the Panel committed a reversible error by developing its own legal reasoning.

C.2.3 *Chile – Price Band System*, paras. 167–168
(WT/DS207/AB/R)

However, Argentina's reliance on our ruling in *EC – Hormones* is misplaced. In *EC – Hormones*, and in *US – Certain EC Products*, we affirmed the capacity of panels to develop their own legal reasoning in a context in which it was clear that the complaining party had made a claim on the matter before the panel. It was also clear, in both those cases, that the complainant had advanced arguments in support of the finding made by the panel – even though the arguments in support of the claim were not the same as the interpretation eventually adopted by the Panel. The situation in this appeal is altogether different. No claim was properly made by Argentina under the *second* sentence of Article II:1(b). No legal arguments were advanced by Argentina under the *second* sentence of Article II:1(b). Therefore, those rulings have no relevance to the situation here.

Contrary to what Argentina argues, given our finding that Argentina has not made a *claim* under the *second* sentence of Article II:1(b), the Panel in this case had neither a "right" nor a "duty" to develop its own legal reasoning to support a claim under the second sentence. The Panel was not entitled to make a claim for Argentina, or to develop its own legal reasoning on a provision that was not at issue.

C.2.4 *Argentina – Footwear (EC)*, para. 74
(WT/DS121/AB/R)

We note that the very terms of Article 4.2(c) of the *Agreement on Safeguards* expressly incorporate the provisions of Article 3. Thus, we find it difficult to see how a panel could examine whether a Member had complied with Article 4.2(c) without also referring to the provisions of Article 3 of the *Agreement on Safeguards*. More particularly, given the express language of Article 4.2(c), we do not see how a panel could ignore the publication requirement set out in Article 3.1 when examining the publication requirement in Article 4.2(c) of the *Agreement on Safeguards*. And, generally, we fail to see how the Panel could have interpreted the requirements of Article 4.2(c) *without* taking into account in some way the provisions of Article 3. What is more, we fail to see how any panel could be expected to make an "objective assessment of the matter", as required by Article 11 of the DSU, if it could only refer in its reasoning to the specific provisions cited by the parties in their claims.

C.2.5 *Argentina – Footwear (EC)*, para. 75
(WT/DS121/AB/R)

Consequently, we conclude that the Panel did not exceed its terms of reference by referring in its reasoning to the provisions of Article 3 of the *Agreement on Safeguards*. On the contrary, we find that the Panel was *obliged* by the terms of Article 4.2(c) to take the provisions of Article 3 into account. Thus, we do not believe that the Panel erred in its reasoning relating to the provisions of Article 3 of the *Agreement on Safeguards* in making its findings under Article 4.2(c) of that Agreement.

C.2.6 *US – Gambling*, paras. 281–282
(WT/DS285/AB/R)

. . . a panel enjoys . . . discretion [freely to use arguments submitted by any of the parties – or to develop its own legal reasoning – to support its own findings and conclusions] only with respect to specific claims that are properly before it, for otherwise it would be considering a matter not within its jurisdiction. Moreover, when a panel rules on a claim in the absence of evidence and supporting arguments, it acts inconsistently with its obligations under Article 11 of the DSU.

In the context of affirmative defences, then, a responding party must invoke a defence and put forward evidence and arguments in support of its assertion that the challenged measure satisfies the requirements of the defence. When a responding party fulfils this obligation, a panel may rule on whether the challenged measure is justified under the relevant defence, relying on arguments advanced by the parties or developing its own reasoning. The same applies to rebuttals. A panel may not take upon itself to rebut the claim (or defence) where the responding party (or complaining party) itself has not done so.

C.2.7 *Dominican Republic – Import and Sale of Cigarettes*, para. 82
(WT/DS302/AB/R)

The Dominican Republic also submits that the Panel "misunderstood the proposition for which Exhibit DR-8 was offered", because "[t]he Panel . . . incorrectly focused on the relationship between smuggling and forgery", whereas "Exhibit DR-8 was offered as evidence of (a) smuggling and, separately, (b) forgery of tax stamps of a product in respect of which the Dominican Republic allows stamps to be affixed outside its territory." In our view, the Panel did not act in a manner inconsistent with Article 11 of the DSU in not finding that Memo DAT-No. 46 "adds any conclusive elements as relate to the relationship between the seizure of alcoholic beverages and the possible forgery of tax stamps". A panel does not act in a manner inconsistent with Article 11 of the DSU simply because it draws inferences from some of the evidence that do not coincide with the reason for which a party adduced it.

Coherence. *See* International Monetary Fund – "Coherence" (I.2)

C.3 Competence of Panels and the Appellate Body. *See also* Jurisdiction (J.2); Scope of Appellate Review (S.3); Terms of Reference of Panels (T.6)

C.3.1 Article 3.2 of the DSU – "clarify existing provisions"

C.3.1.1 *US – Certain EC Products*, para. 92
(WT/DS165/AB/R)

. . . we observe that it is certainly not the task of either panels or the Appellate Body to amend the DSU or to adopt interpretations within the meaning of Article IX:2 of the *WTO Agreement*. Only WTO Members have the authority to amend the DSU or to adopt such interpretations. Pursuant to Article 3.2 of the DSU, the task of panels and the Appellate Body in the dispute settlement system of the WTO is "to preserve the rights and obligations of Members under the covered agreements, and to *clarify the existing provisions* of those agreements in accordance with customary rules of interpretation of public international law." (emphasis added) Determining what the rules and procedures of the DSU ought to be is not our responsibility nor the responsibility of panels; it is clearly the responsibility solely of the Members of the WTO.

C.3.2 Articles 3.2 and 19.2 of the DSU – "not add to or diminish rights and obligations". *See also* Terms of Reference of Panels, Specific measure at issue (T.6.3)

C.3.2.1 *US – Wool Shirts and Blouses*, p. 19, DSR 1997:I, p. 323 at 340
(WT/DS33/AB/R, WT/DS33/AB/R/Corr.1)

. . . Given the explicit aim of dispute settlement that permeates the *DSU*, we do not consider that Article 3.2 of the *DSU* is meant to encourage either panels or the Appellate Body to "make law" by clarifying existing provisions of the *WTO Agreement* outside the context of resolving a particular dispute. A panel need only address those claims which must be addressed in order to resolve the matter in issue in the dispute.

C.3.2.2 *Chile – Alcoholic Beverages*, para. 79
(WT/DS87/AB/R, WT/DS110/AB/R)

. . . In this dispute, while we have rejected certain of the factors relied upon by the Panel, we have found that the Panel's legal conclusions are not tainted by any reversible error of law. In these circumstances, we do not consider that the Panel has added to the rights or obligations of any Member of the WTO. Moreover, we have difficulty in envisaging circumstances in which a panel could add to the rights and obligations of a Member of the WTO if its conclusions reflected a correct interpretation and application of provisions of the covered agreements. Chile's appeal under Articles 3.2 and 19.2 of the DSU must, therefore, be denied.

C.4 Completion of the Legal Analysis by the Appellate Body. *See also* Conditional Appeals (C.5); Judicial Economy (J.1); Scope of Appellate Review (S.3)

C.4.1 *US – Gasoline*, p. 19, DSR 1996:I, p. 3 at 18 (WT/DS2/AB/R)

The Panel did not find it necessary to deal with the issue of whether the baseline establishment rules "are made effective in conjunction with restrictions on domestic production or consumption", since it had earlier concluded that those rules had not even satisfied the preceding requirement of "relating to" in the sense of being "primarily aimed at" the conservation of clean air. Having been unable to concur with that earlier conclusion of the Panel, we must now address this second requirement of Article XX(g), the United States having, in effect, appealed from the failure of the Panel to proceed further with its inquiry into the availability of Article XX(g) as a justification for the baseline establishment rules.

C.4.2 *Canada – Periodicals*, p. 24, DSR 1997:I, p. 449 at 469 (WT/DS31/AB/R)

We believe the Appellate Body can, and should, complete the analysis of Article III:2 of the GATT 1994 in this case by examining the measure with reference to its consistency with the second sentence of Article III:2, provided that there is a sufficient basis in the Panel Report to allow us to do so. . . . An examination of the consistency of Part V.1 of the Excise Tax Act with Article III:2, second sentence, is therefore part of a logical continuum.

. . .

As the legal obligations in the first and second sentences are two closely-linked steps in determining the consistency of an internal tax measure with the national treatment obligations of Article III:2, the Appellate Body would be remiss in not completing the analysis of Article III:2. . . .

C.4.3 *EC – Hormones*, para. 222 (WT/DS26/AB/R, WT/DS48/AB/R)

. . . Because, however, we have reached a conclusion different from that of the Panel, we consider it appropriate to complete the Panel's analysis in order that we may be in a position to review the Panel's conclusion concerning consistency with Article 5.5 as a whole. The matter of therapeutic and zootechnical uses of hormones was fully argued before the Panel. Although the failure of the Panel to proceed with this comparison was not expressly appealed by the United States, the United States relies markedly upon the fact that the European Communities treats therapeutic and zootechnical uses of natural hormones differently from growth promotion use of the same hormones.

C.4.4 *EC – Hormones*, para. 251

(WT/DS26/AB/R, WT/DS48/AB/R)

We have . . . reversed the Panel's conclusion under Article 5.5 of the *SPS Agreement*. . . . However, it cannot be assumed that all the findings of fact necessary to proceed to a determination of consistency or inconsistency of the EC measures with the requirements of Article 5.6 have been made by the Panel . . .

C.4.5 *Australia – Salmon*, paras. 117–118

(WT/DS18/AB/R)

. . . In certain appeals, when we reverse a panel's finding on a legal issue, we may examine and decide an issue that was not specifically addressed by the panel, in order to complete the legal analysis and resolve the dispute between the parties. This occurred, for example, in the appeals in *United States – Gasoline*, *Canada – Certain Measures Concerning Periodicals*, *European Communities – Measures Affecting the Importation of Certain Poultry Products ("European Communities – Poultry")*, and *United States – Import Prohibition of Certain Shrimp and Shrimp Products*.

As we have reversed the Panel's finding that the SPS measure at issue, erroneously identified as the heat-treatment requirement, is not based on a risk assessment, we believe that – to the extent possible on the basis of the factual findings of the Panel and/or of undisputed facts in the Panel record – we should complete the legal analysis and determine whether the actual SPS measure at issue, i.e., Australia's *import prohibition* on fresh, chilled or frozen ocean-caught Pacific salmon, is based on a risk assessment.

C.4.6 *Argentina – Footwear (EC)*, para. 98

(WT/DS121/AB/R)

. . . we uphold the conclusions of the Panel that Argentina's investigation in this case was inconsistent with the requirements of Articles 2 and 4 of the *Agreement on Safeguards*. As a consequence, there is *no legal basis* for the safeguard measures imposed by Argentina. For this reason, we do not believe that it is necessary to complete the analysis of the Panel relating to the claim made by the European Communities under Article XIX of the GATT 1994 by ruling on whether the Argentine authorities have, in their investigation, demonstrated that the increased imports in this case occurred "as a result of unforeseen developments and of the effect of the obligations incurred by a Member under this Agreement, including tariff concessions . . . ".

C.4.7 *Korea – Dairy*, para. 92
(WT/DS98/AB/R)

... In the absence of any factual findings by the Panel or undisputed facts in the Panel record relating to whether the alleged increase in imports was, indeed, "a result of unforeseen developments and of the effect of the obligations incurred by a Member under this Agreement, including tariff concessions ...", we are not in a position, within the scope of our mandate set forth in Article 17 of the DSU, to complete the analysis and make a determination as to whether Korea acted inconsistently with its obligations under Article XIX:1(a). Accordingly, we are unable to come to a conclusion on whether or not Korea violated its obligations under Article XIX:1(a) of the GATT 1994.

C.4.8 *Korea – Dairy*, para. 102
(WT/DS98/AB/R)

... The Panel did not make any factual findings on the average level of imports of skimmed milk powder preparations in the last three representative years. The average level of imports in that period was also contested by the parties. Accordingly, we are not in a position, within the scope of our mandate under Article 17 of the DSU, to complete the analysis in this case and make a determination as to the consistency of Korea's safeguard measure with the second sentence of Article 5.1.

C.4.9 *Canada – Autos*, para. 133
(WT/DS139/AB/R, WT/DS142/AB/R)

In *Australia – Salmon*, we stated that where we have reversed a finding of a panel, we should attempt to complete a panel's legal analysis "to the extent possible on the basis of the factual findings of the Panel and/or of undisputed facts in the Panel record". Here, as we have stated, the Panel did not identify the precise levels of the CVA requirements applicable to specific manufacturers. In addition, there are not sufficient undisputed facts in the Panel record that would enable us to examine this issue ourselves. As a result, it is impossible for us to assess whether the use of domestic over imported goods is a condition "in law" for satisfying the CVA requirements, and, therefore, is a condition for receiving the import duty exemption.

C.4.10 *Canada – Autos*, para. 145
(WT/DS139/AB/R, WT/DS142/AB/R)

We stated earlier that the Panel's incomplete analysis of the operation of the CVA requirements leaves us with an insufficient basis on which to examine how the CVA requirements function. Furthermore, as the Panel concluded that Article 3.1(b) did not extend to contingency "in fact", the Panel did not examine the claims of the European Communities and Japan on this issue. As a result the Panel made *no* factual findings relating to the operation of the CVA requirements. In addition, there are not sufficient undisputed facts in the Panel record that would enable us to examine this issue ourselves. It is impossible for us to assess whether the use of domestic over imported goods is "in fact" a condition for satisfying the CVA requirements, and, therefore, is a condition for receiving the import duty exemption.

C.4.11 *EC – Asbestos*, paras. 78–79
(WT/DS135/AB/R)

. . . In previous appeals, we have, on occasion, completed the legal analysis with a view to facilitating the prompt settlement of the dispute, pursuant to Article 3.3 of the DSU. However, we have insisted that we can do so only if the factual findings of the panel and the undisputed facts in the panel record provide us with a sufficient basis for our own analysis. If that has not been the case, we have not completed the analysis.

The need for sufficient facts is not the only limit on our ability to complete the legal analysis in any given case. In *Canada – Periodicals*, we reversed the panel's conclusion that the measure at issue was inconsistent with Article III:2, first sentence, of the GATT 1994, and we then proceeded to examine the United States' claims under Article III:2, second sentence, which the panel had not examined at all. However, in embarking there on an analysis of a provision that the panel had not considered, we emphasized that "the first and second sentences of Article III:2 are *closely related*" and that those two sentences are "part of a *logical continuum*." (emphasis added)

C.4.12 *EC – Asbestos*, paras. 82–83
(WT/DS135/AB/R)

In light of their novel character, we consider that Canada's claims under the *TBT Agreement* have not been explored before us in depth. As the Panel did not address these claims, there are no "issues of law" or "legal interpretations" regarding them to be analyzed by the parties, and reviewed by us under Article 17.6 of the DSU. We also observe that the sufficiency of the facts on the record depends on the reach of the provisions of the *TBT Agreement* claimed to apply – a reach that has yet to be determined.

With this particular collection of circumstances in mind, we consider that we do not have an adequate basis properly to examine Canada's claims under Articles 2.1, 2.2, 2.4 and 2.8 of the *TBT Agreement* and, accordingly, we refrain from so doing.

C.4.13 *US – Hot-Rolled Steel*, paras. 174, 180
(WT/DS184/AB/R)

In these circumstances, Japan requests that we rule on its claim, under Article 2.4 of the *Anti-Dumping Agreement*, that, in relying on downstream sales, USDOC failed to make proper "allowances" in respect of the additional costs and profits of the downstream sellers, reflected in the price of these sales. . . .

. . .

Our examination of this issue must be based on the factual findings of the Panel or uncontested facts in the Panel record. As the Panel did not examine this issue, and as the parties do not agree on the relevant facts, we find that there is not an adequate factual record for us to complete the analysis by examining Japan's claim under Article 2.4 of the *Anti-Dumping Agreement*.

C.4.14 *US – Hot-Rolled Steel*, paras. 235–236 (WT/DS184/AB/R)

Having reversed the Panel's finding on Japan's claim, we must now consider whether it is appropriate for us to complete the analysis and facilitate the prompt settlement of the dispute, under Article 3.3 of the DSU, by examining Japan's claim ourselves. In previous Reports, we have emphasized that, after reversing a finding of the panel, we can complete the analysis only if the factual findings of the panel, or the undisputed facts in the panel record, provide us with a sufficient basis to do so.

... In our view, key aspects of these factual assertions were not the subject of findings by the Panel or were not agreed by the United States. We, therefore, find that, in the absence of an adequate factual record, there is no basis for us to complete the analysis of Japan's claim under Article 3.5 of the *Anti-Dumping Agreement*.

C.4.15 *Canada – Dairy (Article 21.5 – New Zealand and US)*, para. 98 (WT/DS103/AB/RW, WT/DS113/AB/RW)

As we have reversed the Panel's findings regarding the standard for determining the existence of "payments" and have, instead, identified the appropriate standard for these proceedings, namely, the average total cost of production, we now consider whether we can resolve this aspect of the dispute by completing the analysis. The Panel found that, in these proceedings, Article 10.3 of the *Agreement on Agriculture* reverses the burden of proof so that Canada must establish "that no export subsidy ... has been granted". Although the burden of proof is on Canada, we must nonetheless complete the analysis solely on the basis of factual findings made by the Panel and uncontested facts in the Panel record.

C.4.16 *Canada – Dairy (Article 21.5 – New Zealand and US)*, paras. 102–103 (WT/DS103/AB/RW, WT/DS113/AB/RW)

... the Panel did not find it necessary to make any factual findings on the costs of production and the facts relating to this issue were not the subject of agreement between the parties. Moreover, the Panel proceedings were conducted without the parties arguing their case, or the Panel making enquiries, from the perspective of the average total cost of production standard we have adopted.

In these circumstances, we are unable to complete the analysis by determining whether the supply of CEM involves "payments" under Article 9.1(c) of the *Agreement on Agriculture*. Yet, we do not wish to be understood as holding that the supply of CEM does *not* involve "payments" under Article 9.1(c). We are simply not in a position to make a ruling on this issue.

C.4.17 *US – Section 211 Appropriations Act*, para. 343
(WT/DS176/AB/R)

In the past, we have completed the analysis where there were sufficient factual findings in the panel report or undisputed facts in the panel record to enable us to do so, and we have not completed the analysis where there were not. In one instance, we declined to complete the analysis with respect to a "novel" issue that had not been argued in sufficient detail before the panel.

C.4.18 *US – Section 211 Appropriations Act*, para. 352
(WT/DS176/AB/R)

On the basis of:
– the fact that Sections 211(a)(2) and (b) do not distinguish on their face between trade marks and trade names;
– the participants' approach in submitting the same arguments and using the same analyses regarding trade name and trademark protection, suggesting that the obligations regarding protection of one are no different from those regarding protection of the other;
– the information in the Panel record about the participants' interpretation of Article 8 of the Paris Convention (1967); and
– the information in the Panel record about trade name protection under United States law;

we conclude that the Panel record contains sufficient factual findings and facts undisputed between the participants to permit us to complete the analysis regarding the consistency of Sections 211(a)(2) and (b) – in respect of trade names – with Article 2.1 of the *TRIPS Agreement* in conjunction with Article 2(1) of the Paris Convention (1967) and Article 3.1 of the *TRIPS Agreement*, with Article 4 of the *TRIPS Agreement*, with Article 42 of the *TRIPS Agreement*, and with Article 2.1 of that Agreement in conjunction with Article 8 of the Paris Convention (1967).

C.4.19 *US – Steel Safeguards*, para. 431
(WT/DS248/AB/R, WT/DS249/AB/R, WT/DS251/AB/R, WT/DS252/AB/R, WT/DS253/AB/R, WT/DS254/AB/R, WT/DS258/AB/R, WT/DS259/AB/R)

In previous appeals, we have, when appropriate, completed the legal analysis with a view to facilitating the prompt settlement of disputes. However, in the dispute before us, we have already upheld the Panel's finding that the United States acted inconsistently with Article XIX:1(a) of the GATT 1994, as well as with Article 3.1 of the *Agreement on Safeguards*, with regard to all ten measures at issue. We also find in the following section of this Report dealing with the issue of "parallelism", that the United States has acted inconsistently with Articles 2.1 and 4.2 of the *Agreement on Safeguards* with respect to all product categories, because the United States failed to establish that imports covered by the safeguard measures, *alone*, satisfy the conditions for the imposition of a safeguard measure. Therefore, the Panel's finding that the safeguard measures applied to tin mill products and stainless steel wire are both "deprived of a legal basis" remains undisturbed. As a result, it is not necessary for us to complete the analysis and determine whether the USITC report provided a reasoned and adequate explanation that imports of tin mill products and stainless steel wire had increased within the meaning of Article 2.1 of the *Agreement on Safeguards*.

C.4.20 *US – Softwood Lumber IV*, para. 118 (WT/DS257/AB/R)

. . . we are unable to complete the legal analysis of Canada's claim that the United States acted inconsistently with Article 14(d) of the *SCM Agreement*. We observe, in this regard, that panels sometimes make alternative factual findings that serve to assist the Appellate Body in completing the legal analysis should it disagree with legal interpretations developed by the panel, but this is not the case in the Panel Report before us.

C.4.21 *Canada – Wheat Exports and Grain Imports*, paras. 162–163 (WT/DS276/AB/R)

Canada states that it would welcome "guidance" from the Appellate Body as to whether a conditional request to complete the analysis of a particular issue should be raised in an appellee's submission filed pursuant to Rule 22 of the *Working Procedures*, or in another appellant's submission filed pursuant to Rule 23. . . .

As we have not reversed the Panel's interpretation of subparagraph (b) of Article XVII:1, the condition on which Canada's request to complete the analysis is made has not been satisfied. . . . In the circumstances of this appeal, it is neither necessary nor appropriate for us to provide "guidance" on the issue of how conditional requests to complete the analysis are properly brought before the Appellate Body.

C.4.22 *US – Oil Country Tubular Goods Sunset Reviews*, para. 219 (WT/DS268/AB/R)

. . . The factual premise of Argentina's claim under Article X:3(a) is thus not undisputed. We therefore *find* that the record does not allow us to complete the analysis of Argentina's conditional appeal with respect to Article X:3(a) of the GATT 1994.

C.4.23 *US – Oil Country Tubular Goods Sunset Reviews*, para. 220 (WT/DS268/AB/R)

We move now to Argentina's conditional appeal concerning the "practice" of the USDOC. . . . Here again, we note that the Panel record reveals no qualitative assessment of individual cases found in Exhibit ARG-63. As we noted above, this factual premise (particularly "without considering additional factors") is challenged by the United States and is not undisputed. Therefore, even assuming *arguendo* that a "practice" may be challenged as a "measure" in WTO dispute settlement – an issue on which we express no view here – we *find* that the record does not allow us to complete the analysis of Argentina's conditional appeal with respect to the "practice" of the USDOC regarding the likelihood determination in sunset reviews.

C.4.24 *US – Upland Cotton*, para. 693
(WT/DS267/AB/R)

We must determine next whether there are sufficient uncontested facts in the record to permit us to complete the analysis with respect to the other commodities. In our view, there are not. First, the parties disagree about the time period covered by Brazil's claim. The United States asserts that Brazil's claim was limited to the period July 2001 to June 2002, while Brazil contends that its claim was not limited to that period. Second, as we noted previously, different time periods are used for the sets of data that have to be compared. The data regarding United States exports under the export credit guarantee programs are maintained on a fiscal year basis, which extends from 1 October to 30 September of the following year. The United States' export subsidy commitments are registered based on a year that extends from 1 July to 30 June of the following year. Both Brazil and the United States have sought to reconcile the data. In each case, Brazil and the United States assert that the data support their position. Given the differences between the participants in respect of the data that we would have to examine to determine whether the United States applied export credit guarantees in a manner that results in circumvention of its export subsidy commitments for pig meat and poultry meat, we do not believe there are sufficient undisputed facts in the record to enable us to complete the analysis.

C.4.25 *US – Upland Cotton*, para. 747
(WT/DS267/AB/R)

In this case, Brazil's claim on appeal is limited to the Panel's application of the burden of proof. Brazil has expressly stated that it is not requesting us to complete the analysis. In view of Brazil's request, our ruling would not result in recommendations or rulings by the DSB in respect of the ETI Act of 2000. In these circumstances, we fail to see how our examination of Brazil's claim would contribute to the "prompt" or "satisfactory settlement" of this matter or would contribute to "secure a positive solution" to this dispute. Even if we were to disagree with the manner in which the Panel applied the burden of proof, we would not make any findings in respect of the WTO-consistency of the ETI Act of 2000. We recognize that there may be cases in which it would be useful for us to make a finding on an issue, despite the fact that our decision would not result in rulings and recommendations by the DSB. In this case, however, we find no compelling reason for doing so on this particular issue.

C.4.26 *US – Gambling*, para. 344
(WT/DS285/AB/R)

Provided that it complies with its duty to assess a matter objectively, a panel enjoys the freedom to decide *which legal issues* it must address in order to resolve a dispute. Moreover, in some instances, a panel's decision to continue its legal analysis and to make factual findings beyond those that are strictly necessary to resolve the dispute may assist the Appellate Body should it later be called upon to complete the analysis, as, for example, in this case.

C.4.27 *EC – Export Subsidies on Sugar*, paras. 337–341 and footnote 537 to para. 339 (WT/DS265/AB/R, WT/DS266/AB/R, WT/DS283/AB/R)

In several previous disputes, the Appellate Body examined an issue "not specifically addressed by the panel, in order to complete the legal analysis and resolve the dispute between the parties". However, the Appellate Body has declined to complete the legal analysis where "the factual findings of the panel and the undisputed facts in the panel record" did not provide a sufficient basis for the legal analysis by the Appellate Body. Moreover, as Article 17.6 of the DSU limits appeals to "issues of law covered in the panel report and legal interpretations developed by the panel", the Appellate Body has also previously declined to complete the legal analysis of a panel in circumstances where that would involve addressing claims "which the panel had not examined at all". In addition, the Appellate Body has indicated that it may complete the analysis only if the provision that a panel has not examined is "*closely related*" to a provision that the panel has examined, and that the two are "part of a *logical continuum*".

Turning to the specific case before us, we note that the Complaining Parties argue that their claims under the *SCM Agreement* are closely related to their claims under the *Agreement on Agriculture*. We are not persuaded, however, that Articles 3, 8, and 9.1 of the *Agreement on Agriculture*, on the one hand, and Articles 3.1(a), 3.2, and items (a) and (d) of the Illustrative List of the *SCM Agreement*, on the other hand, are "closely related", because the issues presented under the two Agreements are different in several respects.

Furthermore, in the instant case, we note that the Panel made reference to the limited arguments made by the Complaining Parties under the *SCM Agreement*: ...Although, on appeal, the Complaining Parties did argue their claims under the *SCM Agreement* to some extent, they did not address, in a sufficient manner, the question whether Article 3 of the *SCM Agreement* applies to export subsidies listed in Article 9.1 of the *Agreement on Agriculture* that are provided to *scheduled* agricultural products in excess of a responding Member's commitment levels. We believe that, in the light of Article 21 of the *Agreement on Agriculture* and the chapeau of Article 3 of the *SCM Agreement*, the question of the applicability of the *SCM Agreement* to the export subsidies in this dispute raises a number of complex issues.[537] We also consider that, in the absence of a full exploration of these issues, completing the analysis might affect the due process rights of the participants.

[537] These issues include, for instance, whether the *Agreement on Agriculture* contains "specific provisions dealing specifically with the same matter" (Appellate Body Report, *US – Upland Cotton*, paras. 532–533 (quoting Appellate Body Report, *EC – Bananas III*, para. 155; and referring to Appellate Body Report, *Chile – Price Band System*, para. 186)); whether the *SCM Agreement* applies to the subsidy as a whole, or whether it applies to the subsidy only to the extent that the subsidy exceeds the responding Members' commitment levels as specified in its Schedule; and whether, in the event the *SCM Agreement* applies, a panel could make a recommendation to withdraw the subsidy in whole, or whether that recommendation would apply to the subsidy only to the extent that it exceeds the responding Member's commitment levels.

Moreover, we do not have the requisite factual findings to complete the legal analysis. In particular, we do not have sufficient facts before us, as would be necessary to specify the period of time for withdrawal, as required by Article 4.7 of the *SCM Agreement*. We note in this respect that, when specifying what period would represent "without delay", panels have taken into account, *inter alia*, "the nature of the measures and the difficulties likely to be faced in implementing the recommendation". Based on our reading of the Panel Reports and the Panel record, we fail to see any evidence therein regarding the nature of the measures that would be required to "withdraw" the subsidy, which would permit us to make a recommendation under Article 4.7. Hence, *even if* we were able to examine the Complaining Parties' claims under the *SCM Agreement* and, *even if* we were to conclude that the *SCM Agreement* applies in the circumstances of this dispute and that the European Communities acted inconsistently with its obligations under the *SCM Agreement*, we would not necessarily be in a position to make a recommendation under Article 4.7 as to the time period for withdrawal of the subsidy.

For all these reasons, we are not in a position, and we therefore decline, to complete the legal analysis and to examine the Complaining Parties' claims under the *SCM Agreement* left unaddressed by the Panel.

C.5 Conditional Appeals

C.5.1 *US – 1916 Act*, paras. 153–154
(WT/DS136/AB/R, WT/DS162/AB/R)

In their joint other appellant's submission, the European Communities and Japan ask us to rule that the 1916 Act is inconsistent with United States' obligations under Articles III:4 and XI of the GATT 1994 and Article XVI:4 of the *WTO Agreement*. With respect to Articles III:4 and XI of the GATT 1994, their requests are conditioned on our reversal of the Panel's findings that the 1916 Act falls within the scope of Article VI of the GATT 1994 and the *Anti-Dumping Agreement*. With respect to Article XVI:4 of the *WTO Agreement*, their requests are conditioned on our reversal of the Panel's findings with respect to jurisdiction and the distinction between mandatory and discretionary legislation. Since, however, the conditions on which these requests are predicated have not been fulfilled, there is no need for us to examine the conditional appeals of the European Communities and Japan.

For these reasons, we decline to rule on the conditional appeals of the European Communities and Japan relating to Articles III:4 and XI of the GATT 1994 and Article XVI:4 of the *WTO Agreement*.

C.5.2 *Chile – Price Band System*, para. 286
(WT/DS207/AB/R)

Argentina asks us to rule that Chile's price band system is inconsistent with the *first* sentence of Article II:1(b). Argentina's request is, however, conditioned on our reversal of the Panel's finding that Chile's price band system is inconsistent with Article 4.2 of the *Agreement on Agriculture*. As this condition has not been fulfilled, and as Chile has not requested a finding with respect to the *first* sentence of Article II:1(b), we do not see it as necessary for us to rule on whether Chile's price band system is inconsistent with the first sentence of Article II:1(b) of the GATT 1994.

C.5.3 *Canada – Wheat Exports and Grain Imports*, paras. 162–163
(WT/DS276/AB/R)

Canada states that it would welcome "guidance" from the Appellate Body as to whether a conditional request to complete the analysis of a particular issue should be raised in an appellee's submission filed pursuant to Rule 22 of the *Working Procedures*, or in another appellant's submission filed pursuant to Rule 23. . . .

As we have not reversed the Panel's interpretation of subparagraph (b) of Article XVII:1, the condition on which Canada's request to complete the analysis is made has not been satisfied. . . . In the circumstances of this appeal, it is neither necessary nor appropriate for us to provide "guidance" on the issue of how conditional requests to complete the analysis are properly brought before the Appellate Body.

C.6 Confidentiality. *See also* Business Confidential Information (B.4); Consultations (C.7); Working Procedures for Appellate Review, Rule 8 – Rules of Conduct (W.2.4)

C.6.1 *Brazil – Aircraft*, para. 121
(WT/DS46/AB/R)

Canada – Aircraft, para. 143
(WT/DS70/AB/R)

With respect to appellate proceedings, in particular, the provisions of the DSU impose an obligation of confidentiality which applies to WTO Members generally as well as to Appellate Body Members and staff. In this respect, Article 17.10 of the DSU states, without qualification, that "[t]he *proceedings* of the Appellate Body *shall be confidential*." (emphasis added) The word "proceeding" has been defined as follows:

> In a general sense, the form and manner of conducting juridical business before a court or judicial officer. Regular and orderly progress in form of law, *including all possible steps in an action from its commencement to the execution of judgment.* (emphasis added)

More broadly, the word "proceedings" has been defined as "the business transacted by a court". In its ordinary meaning, we take "proceedings" to include, in an appellate proceeding, any written submissions, legal memoranda, written responses to questions, and oral statements by the participants and the third participants; the conduct of the oral hearing before the Appellate Body, including any transcripts or tapes of that hearing; and the deliberations, the exchange of views and internal workings of the Appellate Body.

C.6.2 *Brazil – Aircraft*, paras. 123–124
(WT/DS46/AB/R)

Canada – Aircraft, paras. 145–146
(WT/DS70/AB/R)

In our view, the provisions of Articles 17.10 and 18.2 apply to all Members of the WTO, and oblige them to maintain the confidentiality of any submissions or information submitted, or received, in an Appellate Body proceeding. Moreover, those provisions oblige Members to ensure that such confidentiality is fully respected by any person that a Member selects to act as its representative, counsel or consultant. In this respect, we note, with approval, the following statement made by the panel in *Indonesia – Automobiles*:

> We would like to emphasize that *all members of parties' delegations – whether or not they are government employees – are present as representatives of their governments, and as such are subject to the provisions of the DSU and of the standard working procedures, including Articles 18.1 and 18.2 of the DSU and paragraphs 2 and 3 of those procedures*. In particular, parties are required to treat as confidential all submissions to the Panel and all information so designated by other Members; and, in addition, the Panel meets in closed session. Accordingly, *we expect that all delegations will fully respect those obligations and will treat these proceedings with the utmost circumspection and discretion*. (emphasis added) [Panel Report, *Indonesia – Automobiles*, para. 14.1]

Finally, we wish to recall that Members of the Appellate Body and its staff are covered by Article VII:1 of the *Rules of Conduct*, which provides:

> Each covered person *shall at all times maintain the confidentiality of dispute settlement deliberations and proceedings together with any information identified by a party as confidential*. (emphasis added)

C.6.3 *Thailand – H-Beams*, para. 74
(WT/DS122/AB/R)

In our preliminary ruling of 14 December 2000, we stated:

> The terms of Article 17.10 of the DSU are clear and unequivocal: "[t]he proceedings of the Appellate Body shall be confidential". Like all obligations under the DSU, this is an obligation that all Members of the WTO, as well as the Appellate Body and its staff, must respect. WTO Members who are participants and third participants in an appeal are fully responsible under the DSU and the other covered agreements for any acts of their officials as well as their representatives, counsel or consultants. . . .
>
> We note that Poland has made substantial efforts to investigate this matter, and to gather information from its legal counsel, Hogan & Hartson L.L.P. We note as well the responses from the third participants, the European Communities, Japan and the United States. Furthermore, Poland has accepted the proposal made by Hogan & Hartson L.L.P. to withdraw as

Poland's legal counsel in this appeal. On the basis of the responses we have received from Poland and from the third participants, and on the basis of our own examination of the facts on the record in this appeal, we believe that there is *prima facie* evidence that CITAC received, or had access to, Thailand's appellant's submission in this appeal.

We see no reason to accept the written brief submitted by CITAC in this appeal. Accordingly, we have returned this brief to CITAC.

C.7 Consultations. *See also* Anti-Dumping Agreement, Article 17.3 – Consultations (A.3.55)

C.7.1 *India – Patents (US)*, para. 94

(WT/DS50/AB/R)

All parties engaged in dispute settlement under the DSU must be fully forthcoming from the very beginning both as to the claims involved in a dispute and as to the facts relating to those claims. Claims must be stated clearly. Facts must be disclosed freely. This must be so in consultations as well as in the more formal setting of panel proceedings. In fact, the demands of due process that are implicit in the DSU make this especially necessary during consultations. For the claims that are made and the facts that are established during consultations do much to shape the substance and the scope of subsequent panel proceedings. If, in the aftermath of consultations, any party believes that all the pertinent facts relating to a claim are, for any reason, not before the panel, then that party should ask the panel in that case to engage in additional fact-finding. But this additional fact-finding cannot alter the claims that are before the panel – because it cannot alter the panel's terms of reference. And, in the absence of the inclusion of a claim in the terms of reference, a panel must neither be expected nor permitted to modify rules in the DSU.

C.7.2 *Brazil – Aircraft*, para. 132

(WT/DS46/AB/R)

We do not believe, however, that Articles 4 and 6 of the DSU, or paragraphs 1 to 4 of Article 4 of the *SCM Agreement*, require a *precise and exact identity* between the specific measures that were the subject of consultations and the specific measures identified in the request for the establishment of a panel. As stated by the Panel, "[o]ne purpose of consultations, as set forth in Article 4.3 of the SCM Agreement, is to 'clarify the facts of the situation', and it can be expected that information obtained during the course of consultations may enable the complainant to focus the scope of the matter with respect to which it seeks establishment of a panel." We are confident that the specific measures at issue in this case are the Brazilian export subsidies for regional aircraft under PROEX. Consultations were held by the parties on these subsidies, and it is these same subsidies that were referred to the DSB for the establishment of a panel. . . .

C.7.3 *US – FSC*, para. 165
(WT/DS108/AB/R)

As we have said, a year passed between submission of the request for consultations by the European Communities and the first mention of this objection by the United States – despite the fact that the United States had numerous opportunities during that time to raise its objection. It seems to us that, by engaging in consultations on three separate occasions, and not even raising its objections in the two DSB meetings at which the request for establishment of a panel was on the agenda, the United States acted as if it had accepted the establishment of the Panel in this dispute, as well as the consultations preceding such establishment. In these circumstances, the United States cannot now, in our view, assert that the European Communities' claims under Article 3 of the *SCM Agreement* should have been dismissed and that the Panel's findings on these issues should be reversed. Accordingly, we decline the United States' appeal from the Panel's refusal to dismiss the European Communities' claim under Article 3 of the *SCM Agreement* due to the European Communities' alleged failure to comply with Article 4.2 of that Agreement. Thus, we do not find it necessary to rule on whether the European Communities' request for consultations includes a "statement of available evidence" that satisfies the requirements of Article 4.2 of the *SCM Agreement*.

C.7.4 *US – Certain EC Products*, para. 70
(WT/DS165/AB/R)

. . . in our Report in *Brazil – Export Financing Programme for Aircraft*, we stated that:

> Articles 4 and 6 of the DSU . . . set forth a process by which a complaining party must request consultations, and consultations must be held, before a matter may be referred to the DSB for the establishment of a panel.

The European Communities' request for consultations of 4 March 1999 did not, of course, refer to the action taken by the United States on 19 April 1999, because that action had not yet been taken at the time. At the oral hearing in this appeal, in response to questioning by the Division, the European Communities acknowledged that the 19 April action, *as such*, was not *formally* the subject of the consultations held on 21 April 1999. We, therefore, consider that the 19 April action is also, for that reason, not a measure at issue in this dispute and does not fall within the Panel's terms of reference.

C.7.5 *Mexico – Corn Syrup (Article 21.5 – US)*, para. 54
(WT/DS132/AB/RW)

. . . We agree with Mexico on the importance of consultations. Through consultations, parties exchange information, assess the strengths and weaknesses of their respective cases, narrow the scope of the differences between them and, in many cases, reach a mutually agreed solution in accordance with the explicit preference expressed in Article 3.7 of the DSU. Moreover, even where no such agreed solution is reached, consultations provide the parties an opportunity to define and delimit the scope of the dispute between them. Clearly, consultations afford many benefits to complaining and responding parties, as well as to third parties and to the dispute settlement system as a whole.

C.7.6 *Mexico – Corn Syrup (Article 21.5 – US)*, paras. 58–59 (WT/DS132/AB/RW)

. . . as a general matter, consultations are a prerequisite to panel proceedings. However, this general proposition is subject to certain limitations. . . .

Article 4.3 of the DSU relates the responding party's conduct towards consultations to the complaining party's right to request the establishment of a panel. When the responding party does not respond to a request for consultations, or declines to enter into consultations, the complaining party may dispense with consultations and proceed to request the establishment of a panel. In such a case, the responding party, by its own conduct, relinquishes the potential benefits that could be derived from those consultations.

C.7.7 *Mexico – Corn Syrup (Article 21.5 – US)*, para. 61 (WT/DS132/AB/RW)

Article 4.7 also relates the conduct of the responding party concerning consultations to the complaining party's right to request the establishment of a panel. This provision states that the responding party may agree with the complaining party to forgo the potential benefits that continued pursuit of consultations might bring. Thus, Article 4.7 contemplates that a panel may be validly established notwithstanding the shortened period for consultations, as long as the parties agree. Article 4.7 does not, however, specify any particular form that the agreement between the parties must take.

C.7.8 *Mexico – Corn Syrup (Article 21.5 – US)*, para. 62 (WT/DS132/AB/RW)

In addition, . . . [the requirement in Article 6.2 of the DSU to indicate] *whether* consultations were held . . . may be satisfied by an express statement that *no consultations were held*. In other words, Article 6.2 also envisages the possibility that a panel may be validly established without being preceded by consultations.

C.7.9 *Mexico – Corn Syrup (Article 21.5 – US)*, para. 63 (WT/DS132/AB/RW)

Thus, the DSU explicitly recognizes circumstances where the absence of consultations would *not* deprive the panel of its authority to consider the matter referred to it by the DSB. In our view, it follows that where the responding party does not object, explicitly and in a timely manner, to the failure of the complaining party to request or engage in consultations, the responding party may be deemed to have consented to the lack of consultations and, thereby, to have relinquished whatever right to consult it may have had.

C.7.10 *Mexico – Corn Syrup (Article 21.5 – US)*, para. 64
(WT/DS132/AB/RW)

As a result, we find that the lack of prior consultations is not a defect that, by its very nature, deprives a panel of its authority to deal with and dispose of a matter, and that, accordingly, such a defect is not one which a panel must examine even if both parties to the dispute remain silent thereon. . . .

C.7.11 *US – Upland Cotton*, para. 260
(WT/DS267/AB/R)

It is clear from Article 4.2 that, although a requested Member is under an obligation to engage in "consultation" on "any" representations made by another Member, such representations must pertain to "measures affecting the operation of any covered agreement". . . .

C.7.12 *US – Upland Cotton*, para. 261
(WT/DS267/AB/R)

We agree with the Panel that the word "affecting" refers primarily to "the way in which [measures] relate to a covered agreement". As the Appellate Body stated in *EC – Bananas III*, "[t]he ordinary meaning of the word 'affecting' implies a measure that has 'an effect on'" something else. At the same time, we also concur with the United States that the ordinary meaning of the word "affecting" suggests a temporal connotation. As the United States submits, the present tense of the phrase "affecting the operation of any covered agreement" denotes that the effects of such measures must relate to the present impact of those measures on the operation of a covered agreement. It is not sufficient that a Member alleges that challenged measures affected the operation of a covered agreement in the past; the representations of the Member requesting consultations must indicate that the effects are occurring in the present.

C.7.13 *US – Upland Cotton*, para. 262
(WT/DS267/AB/R)

Whether or not a measure is still in force is not dispositive of whether that measure is currently affecting the operation of any covered agreement. Therefore, we disagree with the United States' argument that measures whose legislative basis has expired are incapable of affecting the operation of a covered agreement in the present and that, accordingly, expired measures *cannot* be the subject of consultations under the DSU. In our view, the question of whether measures whose legislative basis has expired affect the operation of a covered agreement currently is an issue that must be resolved on the facts of each case. The outcome of such an analysis cannot be prejudged by excluding it from consultations and dispute settlement proceedings altogether.

C.7.14 *US – Upland Cotton*, para. 263
(WT/DS267/AB/R)

We consider that requesting Members should enjoy a degree of discretion to identify, in their request for consultations under Article 4.2, matters relating to the covered agreements for discussion in consultations. As the Appellate Body observed in *Mexico – Corn Syrup (Article 21.5 – US)*, consultations present an opportunity for clarifying factual and legal issues, and for narrowing the scope of a dispute, and for resolving differences between WTO Members. We do not think it would advance the purpose of consultations if Article 4.2 were interpreted as excluding *a priori* measures whose legislative basis may have expired, but whose effects are alleged to be impairing the benefits accruing to the requesting Member under a covered agreement. Nor, indeed, do we find textual support in the provision itself for doing so. Thus, we do not read Article 4.2 of the DSU as precluding a Member from making representations on measures whose legislative basis has expired, where that Member has reason to believe that such measures are still "affecting" the operation of a covered agreement.

C.7.15 *US – Upland Cotton*, para. 264
(WT/DS267/AB/R)

We find contextual support for this interpretation in Article 3.3 of the DSU, which underscores the importance of the "prompt settlement" of certain situations that, in the absence of settlement, could undermine the effective functioning of the WTO and the maintenance of a proper balance between the rights and obligations of Members. We note, first, that Article 3.3 focuses not upon "existing" measures, or measures that are "currently in force" but, rather, upon "measures taken" by a Member, which includes measures taken in the past. We also observe that Article 3.3 envisages that disputes arise when a Member "considers" that benefits accruing to it are being impaired by measures taken by another Member. By using the word "considers", Article 3.3 focuses on the perception or understanding of an aggrieved Member. This does not exclude the possibility that a Member requesting consultations may have reason to believe that a measure is still impairing benefits even though its legislative basis has expired.

C.7.16 *US – Upland Cotton*, paras. 286–287
(WT/DS267/AB/R)

In reviewing the Panel's analysis, we are faced with the question whether the scope of the consultations is determined by the written request for consultations or by what actually happens in the consultations. . . .

We believe that the Panel should have limited its analysis to the request for consultations because we are inclined to agree with the panel in *Korea – Alcoholic Beverages*, which stated that "[t]he only requirement under the DSU is that consultations were in fact held . . . [w]hat takes place in those consultations is not the concern of a panel". Examining what took place in the consultations would seem contrary to Article 4.6 of the DSU, which provides that "[c]onsultations shall be confidential, and without prejudice to the rights of any Member in any further proceedings." Moreover, it would seem at odds with the requirements in Article 4.4 of the DSU that the request for consultations be made in writing and that it be notified to the DSB. In addition, there is no public record of what actually transpires during consultations and parties will often disagree about what, precisely, was discussed. Ultimately, however, it is not necessary for us to inquire into this part of the Panel's analysis because the Panel also found "that export credit guarantee measures relating to all eligible agricultural commodities were included in Brazil's request for consultations, based on its reading of the text of the request itself"....

C.7.17 *US – Upland Cotton*, para. 291

(WT/DS267/AB/R)

We have examined carefully Brazil's request for consultations and we find that it provides a sufficient basis for the Panel to have concluded that the request included export credit guarantees to eligible agricultural commodities including, but not limited to, upland cotton....

C.7.18 *US – Upland Cotton*, para. 293

(WT/DS267/AB/R)

We emphasize that consultations are but the first step in the WTO dispute settlement process. They are intended to "provide the parties an opportunity to define and delimit the scope of the dispute between them". We also note that Article 4.2 of the DSU calls on a WTO Member that receives a request for consultations to "accord sympathetic consideration to and afford adequate opportunity for consultation regarding any representations made by another Member". As long as the complaining party does not expand the scope of the dispute, we hesitate to impose too rigid a standard for the "precise and exact identity" between the scope of consultations and the request for the establishment of a panel, as this would substitute the request for consultations for the panel request. According to Article 7 of the DSU, it is the request for the establishment of a panel that governs its terms of reference, unless the parties agree otherwise.

C.7.19 *US – Gambling*, paras. 120–123

(WT/DS285/AB/R)

The question before us, therefore, is whether an alleged "total prohibition" on the cross-border supply of gambling and betting services constitutes a measure that may be challenged under the GATS. The DSU provides for the "prompt settlement" of situations where Members consider that their benefits under the covered agreements "are being impaired by *measures* taken by another Member". Two elements of this reference to "measures" that may be the subject of dispute settlement are relevant. First, as the Appellate Body has stated, a "nexus" must exist between the responding Member and the "measure", such that the "measure" – whether an act or omission – must be "attributable" to that Member. Secondly, the "measure" must be the *source* of the alleged impairment, which is in turn the *effect* resulting from the existence or operation of the "measure".

Similarly [Article 4.2 of the DSU] contemplates that "measures" themselves will "affect" the operation of a covered agreement. Finally, we note that this distinction between measures and their effects is also evident in the scope of application of the GATS, namely, to "measures by Members affecting trade in services".

We are therefore of the view that the DSU and the GATS focus on "measures" as the subject of challenge in WTO dispute settlement. To the extent that a Member's complaint centres on the effects of an action taken by another Member, that complaint must nevertheless be brought as a challenge to the *measure* that is the source of the alleged effects.

Context. *See* Interpretation, General rules of treaty interpretation – Article 31 of the Vienna Convention (I.3.1)

Customary Rules of Interpretation. *See* Interpretation (I.3)

D

Development. *See* Enabling Clause (E.1); SCM Agreement, Article 27 – Special and differential treatment for developing country Members (S.2.35)

D.1 Directly Competitive or Substitutable Products. *See also* National Treatment, Article III:2 of the GATT 1994, second sentence – "directly competitive or substitutable" products (N.1.6); Textiles and Clothing Agreement, Article 6.2 – "directly competitive products" (T.7.4)

D.1.1 *Korea – Alcoholic Beverages*, para. 114

(WT/DS75/AB/R, WT/DS84/AB/R)

The term "directly competitive or substitutable" describes a particular type of relationship between two products, one imported and the other domestic. It is evident from the wording of the term that the essence of that relationship is that the products are in competition. This much is clear both from the word "competitive" which means "characterized by competition", and from the word "substitutable" which means "able to be substituted". The context of the competitive relationship is necessarily the marketplace since this is the forum where consumers choose between different products. Competition in the market place is a dynamic, evolving process. Accordingly, the wording of the term "directly competitive or substitutable" implies that the competitive relationship between products is *not* to be analyzed *exclusively* by reference to *current* consumer preferences. In our view, the word "substitutable" indicates that the requisite relationship *may* exist between products that are not, at a given moment, considered by consumers to be substitutes but which are, nonetheless, *capable* of being substituted for one another.

D.1.2 *Korea – Alcoholic Beverages*, para. 115

(WT/DS75/AB/R, WT/DS84/AB/R)

Thus, according to the ordinary meaning of the term, products are competitive or substitutable when they are interchangeable or if they offer, as the Panel noted, "alternative ways of satisfying a particular need or taste". Particularly in a market where there are regulatory barriers to trade or to competition, there may well be latent demand.

D.1.3 *Korea – Alcoholic Beverages*, para. 118
(WT/DS75/AB/R, WT/DS84/AB/R)

. . . "Like" products are a subset of directly competitive or substitutable products: all like products are, by definition, directly competitive or substitutable products, whereas not all "directly competitive or substitutable" products are "like". The notion of like products must be construed narrowly but the category of directly competitive or substitutable products is broader. While perfectly substitutable products fall within Article III:2, first sentence, imperfectly substitutable products can be assessed under Article III:2, second sentence.

D.1.4 *Korea – Alcoholic Beverages*, para. 120
(WT/DS75/AB/R, WT/DS84/AB/R)

In view of the objectives of avoiding protectionism, requiring equality of competitive conditions and protecting expectations of equal competitive relationships, we decline to take a static view of the term "directly competitive or substitutable." The object and purpose of Article III confirms that the scope of the term "directly competitive or substitutable" cannot be limited to situations where consumers *already* regard products as alternatives. If reliance could be placed only on current instances of substitution, the object and purpose of Article III:2 could be defeated by the protective taxation that the provision aims to prohibit. . . .

D.1.5 *Korea – Alcoholic Beverages*, para. 124
(WT/DS75/AB/R, WT/DS84/AB/R)

. . . the term "directly competitive or substitutable" does not prevent a panel from taking account of evidence of latent consumer demand as one of a range of factors to be considered when assessing the competitive relationship between imported and domestic products under Article III:2, second sentence, of the GATT 1994. . . .

D.1.6 *Korea – Alcoholic Beverages*, para. 127
(WT/DS75/AB/R, WT/DS84/AB/R)

. . . the object and purpose of Article III is the maintenance of equality of competitive conditions for imported and domestic products. It is, therefore, not only legitimate, but even necessary, to take account of this purpose in interpreting the term "directly competitive or substitutable product".

D.1.7 *Korea – Alcoholic Beverages*, para. 134
(WT/DS75/AB/R, WT/DS84/AB/R)

. . . we share the Panel's reluctance to rely unduly on quantitative analyses of the competitive relationship. In our view, an approach that focused solely on the quantitative overlap of competition would, in essence, make cross-price elasticity *the* decisive criterion in determining whether products are "directly competitive or substitutable"....

D.1.8 *Korea – Alcoholic Beverages*, para. 137
(WT/DS75/AB/R, WT/DS84/AB/R)

It is, of course, true that the "directly competitive or substitutable" relationship must be present in the market at issue.... It is also true that consumer responsiveness to products may vary from country to country. This does not, however, preclude consideration of consumer behaviour in a country other than the one at issue. It seems to us that evidence from other markets may be pertinent to the examination of the market at issue, particularly when demand on that market has been influenced by regulatory barriers to trade or to competition. Clearly, not every other market will be relevant to the market at issue. But if another market displays characteristics similar to the market at issue, then evidence of consumer demand in that other market may have some relevance to the market at issue. This, however, can only be determined on a case-by-case basis, taking account of all relevant facts.

D.1.9 *Korea – Alcoholic Beverages*, paras. 142–143
(WT/DS75/AB/R, WT/DS84/AB/R)

...Some grouping is almost always necessary in cases arising under Article III:2, second sentence, since generic categories commonly include products with *some* variation in composition, quality, function and price, and thus commonly give rise to sub-categories. From a slightly different perspective, we note that "grouping" of products involves at least a preliminary characterization by the treaty interpreter that certain products are sufficiently similar as to, for instance, composition, quality, function and price, to warrant treating them as a group for convenience in analysis. But, the use of such "analytical tools" does not relieve a panel of its duty to make an objective assessment of whether the components of a group of imported products are directly competitive or substitutable with the domestic products....

Whether, and to what extent, products can be grouped is a matter to be decided on a case-by-case basis....

D.1.10 *US – Cotton Yarn*, paras. 96–98
(WT/DS192/AB/R)

According to the ordinary meaning of the term "competitive", two products are in a competitive relationship if they are commercially interchangeable, or if they offer alternative ways of satisfying the same consumer demand in the marketplace. "Competitive" is a characteristic attached to a product and denotes the *capacity* of a product to compete both in a current or a future situation. The word "competitive" must be distinguished from the words "competing" or "being in actual competition". It has a wider connotation than "actually competing" and includes also the notion of a potential to compete. It is not necessary that two products be competing, or that they be in actual competition with each other, in the marketplace at a given moment in order for those products to be regarded as competitive. Indeed, products which are competitive may not be actually competing with each other in the marketplace at a given moment for a variety of reasons, such as regulatory restrictions or producers' decisions. Thus, a static view is incorrect, for it leads to the same products being regarded as competitive at one moment in time, and not so the next, depending upon whether or not they are in the marketplace.

It is significant that the word "competitive" is qualified by the word "directly", which emphasizes the degree of proximity that must obtain in the competitive relationship between the products under comparison. As noted earlier, a safeguard action under the *ATC* is permitted in order to protect the domestic industry against competition from an imported product. To ensure that such protection is reasonable, it is expressly provided that the domestic industry must be producing "like" and/or "directly competitive products"....

When ... the product produced by the domestic industry is not a "like product" as compared with the imported product, the question arises how close should be the competitive relationship between the imported product and the "unlike" domestic product. It is common knowledge that unlike or dissimilar products compete or can compete in the marketplace to varying degrees, ranging from direct or close competition to remote or indirect competition. The more unlike or dissimilar two products are, the more remote or indirect their competitive relationship will be in the marketplace. The term "competitive" has, therefore, purposely been qualified and limited by the word "directly" to signify the degree of proximity that must obtain in the competitive relationship when the products in question are unlike. Under this definition of "directly", a safeguard action will not extend to protecting a domestic industry that produces unlike products which have only a remote or tenuous competitive relationship with the imported product.

Discretionary and Mandatory Legislation. *See* Mandatory and Discretionary Legislation (M.1)

Dispute Settlement Understanding

Article 1.2. *See* Special or Additional Rules and Procedures for Dispute Settlement (S.5)

Article 3.2. *See* Competence of Panels and the Appellate Body (C.3); Interpretation (I.3)

Article 3.3. *See* Legislation as such vs. Specific Application (L.1); Review of Implementation of DSB Rulings, Article 21.5 of the DSU (R.4.1–3); Terms of Reference of Panels, Specific measure at issue (T.6.3)

Article 3.7. *See* Right to Bring Claims – Legal Interest (R.5); Suspension of Concessions or Other Obligations (S.9)

Domestic Law. *See* Municipal Law (M.5)

D.2 Due Process

D.2.1 Due process in the application of trade measures

D.2.1.1 *US – Shrimp*, para. 182
(WT/DS58/AB/R)

. . . Inasmuch as there are due process requirements generally for measures that are otherwise imposed in compliance with WTO obligations, it is only reasonable that rigorous compliance with the fundamental requirements of due process should be required in the application and administration of a measure which purports to be an exception to the treaty obligations of the Member imposing the measure and which effectively results in a suspension *pro hac vice* of the treaty rights of other Members.

D.2.2 Due process in WTO dispute settlement proceedings. *See also* Request for the Establishment of a Panel (R.2); Terms of Reference of Panels (T.6); Working Procedures for Appellate Review (W.2)

D.2.2.1 *Brazil – Desiccated Coconut*, p. 22, DSR 1997:I, p. 167 at 186
(WT/DS22/AB/R)

A panel's terms of reference are important for two reasons. First, terms of reference fulfil an important due process objective – they give the parties and third parties sufficient information concerning the claims at issue in the dispute in order to allow them an opportunity to respond to the complainant's case. Second, they establish the jurisdiction of the panel by defining the precise claims at issue in the dispute.

D.2.2.2 *EC – Hormones*, footnote 138 to para. 152
(WT/DS26/AB/R, WT/DS48/AB/R)

. . . the DSU, and in particular its Appendix 3, leave panels a margin of discretion to deal, always in accordance with due process, with specific situations that may arise in a particular case and that are not explicitly regulated. Within this context, an appellant requesting the Appellate Body to reverse a panel's ruling on matters of procedure must demonstrate the prejudice generated by such legal ruling.

D.2.2.3 *EC – Hormones*, para. 154
(WT/DS26/AB/R, WT/DS48/AB/R)

. . . Although Article 12.1 and Appendix 3 of the DSU do not specifically require the Panel to grant [the opportunity to participate in the second substantial meeting of the proceedings initiated by Canada] to the United States, we believe that this decision falls within the sound discretion and authority of the Panel, particularly if the Panel considers it necessary for ensuring to all parties due process of law. . . .

D.2.2.4 *India – Patents (US)*, para. 94
(WT/DS50/AB/R)

All parties engaged in dispute settlement under the DSU must be fully forthcoming from the very beginning both as to the claims involved in a dispute and as to the facts relating to those claims. Claims must be stated clearly. Facts must be disclosed freely. This must be so in consultations as well as in the more formal setting of panel proceedings. In fact, the demands of due process that are implicit in the DSU make this especially necessary during consultations. . . .

D.2.2.5 *India – Patents (US)*, para. 95
(WT/DS50/AB/R)

It is worth noting that, with respect to fact-finding, the dictates of due process could better be served if panels had standard working procedures that provided for appropriate factual discovery at an early stage in panel proceedings.

D.2.2.6 *Argentina – Textiles and Apparel*, footnote 68 to para. 79
(WT/DS56/AB/R, WT/DS56/AB/R/Corr.1)

As we have observed in two previous Appellate Body Reports, we believe that detailed, standard working procedures for panels would help to ensure due process and fairness in panel proceedings. See *European Communities – Regime for the Importation, Sale and Distribution of Bananas*, adopted 25 September 1997, WT/DS27/AB/R, para. 144; *India – Patent Protection for Pharmaceutical and Agricultural Chemical Products*, adopted 16 January 1998, WT/DS50/AB/R, para. 95.

D.2.2.7 *EC – Computer Equipment*, para. 70
(WT/DS62/AB/R, WT/DS67/AB/R, WT/DS68/AB/R)

. . . We do not see how the alleged lack of precision of the terms, LAN equipment and PCs with multimedia capability, in the request for the establishment of a panel affected the rights of defence of the European Communities *in the course* of the panel proceedings. As the ability of the European Communities to defend itself was not prejudiced by a lack of knowing the measures at issue, we do not believe that the fundamental rule of due process was violated by the Panel.

D.2.2.8 *US – FSC*, para. 166
(WT/DS108/AB/R)

. . . The procedural rules of WTO dispute settlement are designed to promote, not the development of litigation techniques, but simply the fair, prompt and effective resolution of trade disputes.

D.2.2.9 *Australia – Salmon*, para. 272
(WT/DS18/AB/R)

. . . We note that Article 12.2 of the DSU provides that "[p]anel procedures should provide sufficient flexibility so as to ensure high-quality panel reports, while not unduly delaying the panel process." However, a panel must also be careful to observe due process, which entails providing the parties adequate opportunity to respond to the evidence submitted....

D.2.2.10 *Australia – Salmon*, para. 278
(WT/DS18/AB/R)

... A fundamental tenet of due process is that a party be provided with an opportunity to respond to claims made against it. In this case, we believe that the Panel *did* accord Australia a proper opportunity to respond by allowing Australia to submit a third written submission. We cannot see how the Panel failed to accord due process to Australia by granting the extra time it had requested.

D.2.2.11 *US – 1916 Act*, para. 150
(WT/DS136/AB/R, WT/DS162/AB/R)

A panel's decision whether to grant "enhanced" participatory rights to third parties is thus a matter that falls within the discretionary authority of that panel. Such discretionary authority is, of course, not unlimited and is circumscribed, for example, by the requirements of due process. In the present cases, however, the European Communities and Japan have not shown that the Panel exceeded the limits of its discretionary authority....

D.2.2.12 *Mexico – Corn Syrup (Article 21.5 – US)*, para. 36
(WT/DS132/AB/RW)

... We believe that a panel comes under a duty to address issues in at least two instances. First, as a matter of due process, and the proper exercise of the judicial function, panels are required to address issues that are put before them by the parties to a dispute. Second, panels have to address and dispose of certain issues of a fundamental nature, even if the parties to the dispute remain silent on those issues. In this regard, we have previously observed that "[t]he vesting of jurisdiction in a panel is a fundamental prerequisite for lawful panel proceedings." For this reason, panels cannot simply ignore issues which go to the root of their jurisdiction – that is, to their authority to deal with and dispose of matters. Rather, panels must deal with such issues – if necessary, on their own motion – in order to satisfy themselves that they have authority to proceed.

D.2.2.13 *Mexico – Corn Syrup (Article 21.5 – US)*, para. 47
(WT/DS132/AB/RW)

... the "observations" raised by Mexico were not expressed in a fashion that indicated that Mexico was raising an objection to the authority of the Panel. The requirements of good faith, due process and orderly procedure dictate that objections, especially those of such potential significance, should be explicitly raised. Only in this way will the panel, the other party to the dispute, and the third parties, understand that a specific objection has been raised, and have an adequate opportunity to address and respond to it....

D.2.2.14 *Mexico – Corn Syrup (Article 21.5 – US)*, para. 49
(WT/DS132/AB/RW)

... had we been satisfied that Mexico did, in fact, explicitly raise its objections before the Panel, then the Panel may well have been required to "address" those objections, whether by virtue of Articles 7.2 and 12.7 of the DSU, or the requirements of due process....

D.2.2.15 *Mexico – Corn Syrup (Article 21.5 – US)*, para. 50
(WT/DS132/AB/RW)

... When a Member wishes to raise an objection in dispute settlement proceedings, it is always incumbent on that Member to do so promptly. A Member that fails to raise its objections in a timely manner, notwithstanding one or more opportunities to do so, may be deemed to have waived its right to have a panel consider such objections.

D.2.2.16 *US – FSC (Article 21.5 – EC)*, para. 243
(WT/DS108/AB/RW)

... the rights of third parties in panel proceedings are limited to the rights granted under Article 10 and Appendix 3 to the DSU. Beyond those minimum guarantees, panels enjoy a discretion to grant additional participatory rights to third parties in particular cases, as long as such "enhanced" rights are consistent with the provisions of the DSU and the principles of due process. However, panels have no discretion to circumscribe the rights guaranteed to third parties by the provisions of the DSU.

D.2.2.17 *Chile – Price Band System*, para. 144
(WT/DS207/AB/R)

We emphasize that we do not mean to condone a practice of amending measures during dispute settlement proceedings if such changes are made with a view to shielding a measure from scrutiny by a panel or by us. We do not suggest that this occurred in this case. However, generally speaking, the demands of due process are such that a complaining party should not have to adjust its pleadings throughout dispute settlement proceedings in order to deal with a disputed measure as a "moving target". If the terms of reference in a dispute are broad enough to include amendments to a measure – as they are in this case – and if it is necessary to consider an amendment in order to secure a positive solution to the dispute – as it is here – then it is appropriate to consider the measure *as amended* in coming to a decision in a dispute.

D.2.2.18 *US – Carbon Steel*, para. 123
(WT/DS213/AB/R, WT/DS213/AB/R/Corr.1)

... we have consistently held that, in the interests of due process, parties should bring alleged procedural deficiencies to the attention of a panel at the earliest possible opportunity. In this case, we see no reason to disagree with the Panel's view that the United States' objection was not raised in a timely manner. At the same time, however, as we have observed previously, certain issues going to the *jurisdiction* of a panel are so fundamental that they may be considered at any stage in a proceeding. In our view, the Panel was correct, therefore, in turning to consider its terms of reference and in satisfying itself as to its jurisdiction with respect to this matter.

D.2.2.19 *Canada – Wheat Exports and Grain Imports*, para. 177
(WT/DS276/AB/R)

Although an appellant is free to determine how to characterize its claims on appeal, at the same time due process requires that the legal basis of a claim be sufficiently clear to allow an appellee to respond effectively. This is especially the case when the claim is an allegation that the panel did not make an objective assessment of the matter as required by Article 11 of the DSU because, by definition, such a claim will not be found in the request for the establishment of the panel and, therefore, the panel will not have referred to it in the panel report.

D.2.2.20 *US – Gambling*, para. 269
(WT/DS285/AB/R)

. . . This does not mean that a responding party may put forward its defence whenever and in whatever manner it chooses. Article 3.10 of the DSU provides that "all Members will engage in these procedures in good faith in an effort to resolve the dispute", which implies the identification by each party of relevant legal and factual issues at the earliest opportunity, so as to provide other parties, including third parties, an opportunity to respond.

D.2.2.21 *US – Gambling*, para. 270
(WT/DS285/AB/R)

At the same time, the opportunity afforded to a Member to respond to claims and defences made against it is also a "fundamental tenet of due process". A party must not merely be given *an* opportunity to respond, but that opportunity must be meaningful in terms of that party's ability to defend itself adequately. A party that considers it was not afforded such an opportunity will often raise a due process objection before the panel. The Appellate Body has recognized in numerous cases that a Member's right to raise a claim or objection, as well as a panel's exercise of discretion, are circumscribed by the due process rights of other parties to a dispute. Those due process rights similarly serve to limit a responding party's right to set out its defence at *any* point during the panel proceedings.

D.2.2.22 *US – Gambling*, para. 271
(WT/DS285/AB/R)

Due process may be of particular concern in cases where a party raises *new facts* at a late stage of the panel proceedings. The Appellate Body has observed that, under the standard working procedures of panels, complaining parties should put forward their cases – with "a full presentation of the facts on the basis of submission of supporting evidence" – during the *first* stage of panel proceedings. We see no reason why this expectation would not apply equally to responding parties, which, once they have received the first written submission of a complaining party, are likely to be aware of the defences they might invoke and the evidence needed to support them.

D.2.2.23 *US – Gambling*, para. 272
(WT/DS285/AB/R)

It follows that the principles of good faith and due process oblige a responding party to articulate its defence promptly and clearly. This will enable the complaining party to understand that a specific defence has been made, "be aware of its dimensions, and have an adequate opportunity to address and respond to it." . . .

D.2.2.24 *US – Gambling*, para. 273
(WT/DS285/AB/R)

. . . as part of their duties, under Article 11 of the DSU, . . . panels must ensure that the due process rights of parties to a dispute are respected. A panel may act inconsistently with this duty if it addresses a defence that a responding party raised at such a late stage of the panel proceedings that the complaining party had no meaningful opportunity to respond to it. To this end, panels are endowed with "sufficient flexibility" in their working procedures, by virtue of Article 12.2 of the DSU, to regulate panel proceedings and, in particular, to adjust their timetables to allow for additional time to respond or for additional submissions where necessary.

D.2.2.25 *US – Gambling*, para. 276
(WT/DS285/AB/R)

. . . we are of the view that, although the United States could have raised its defence earlier, the Panel did not err in deciding to assess whether the United States' measures are justified under Article XIV. From the outset, Antigua was apparently aware that the United States might argue that its measures satisfy the requirements of Article XIV. Antigua admitted that it raised no objection to the timing of the United States' defence before the Panel. Antigua also acknowledged that it did have an opportunity to respond adequately to the United States' defence, albeit at a late stage of the proceeding. . . .

Duty of a Member to Comply with the Request of a Panel to Provide Information. *See* Inferences Drawn from the Refusal of a Party to Provide Information (I.1); Seek Information and Technical Advice (S.4)

E

E.1 Enabling Clause

E.1.1 Paragraph 1. *See also* Burden of Proof, Defences and Exceptions (B.3.3); Request for the Establishment of a Panel, Article 6.2 of the DSU – Claims and legal basis of the complaint (R.2.2)

E.1.1.1 *EC – Tariff Preferences*, para. 90
(WT/DS246/AB/R)

... By using the word "notwithstanding", paragraph 1 of the Enabling Clause permits Members to provide "differential and more favourable treatment" to developing countries "in spite of" the MFN obligation of Article I:1. Such treatment would otherwise be inconsistent with Article I:1 because that treatment is not extended to all Members of the WTO "immediately and unconditionally". Paragraph 1 thus excepts Members from complying with the obligation contained in Article I:1 for the purpose of providing differential and more favourable treatment to developing countries, provided that such treatment is in accordance with the conditions set out in the Enabling Clause. As such, the Enabling Clause operates as an "exception" to Article I:1.

E.1.1.2 *EC – Tariff Preferences*, paras. 101–102
(WT/DS246/AB/R)

... the text of paragraph 1 of the Enabling Clause ensures that, to the extent that there is a conflict between measures under the Enabling Clause and the MFN obligation in Article I:1, the Enabling Clause, as the more specific rule, prevails over Article I:1. In order to determine whether such a conflict exists, however, a dispute settlement panel should, as a first step, examine the consistency of a challenged measure with Article I:1, as the general rule. If the measure is considered at this stage to be inconsistent with Article I:1, the panel should then examine, as a second step, whether the measure is nevertheless justified by the Enabling Clause. It is only at this latter stage that a final determination of consistency with the Enabling Clause or inconsistency with Article I:1 can be made.

In other words, the Enabling Clause "does not exclude the applicability" of Article I:1 in the sense that, as a matter of procedure (or "order of examination", as the Panel stated), the challenged measure is submitted successively to the test of compatibility with the two provisions. But, as a matter of final determination – or *application* rather than *applicability* – it is clear that only one provision applies at a time. . . .

E.1.1.3 *EC – Tariff Preferences*, para. 109

(WT/DS246/AB/R)

We thus understand that, between the entry into force of the GATT and the adoption of the Enabling Clause, the Contracting Parties determined that the MFN obligation failed to secure adequate market access for developing countries so as to stimulate their economic development. Overcoming this required recognition by the multilateral trading system that certain obligations, applied to all Contracting Parties, could impede rather than facilitate the objective of ensuring that developing countries secure a share in the growth of world trade. This recognition came through an authorization for GSP schemes in the 1971 Waiver Decision and then in the broader authorization for preferential treatment for developing countries in the Enabling Clause.

E.1.1.4 *EC – Tariff Preferences*, para. 110

(WT/DS246/AB/R)

In our view, the special status of the Enabling Clause in the WTO system has particular implications for WTO dispute settlement. As we have explained, paragraph 1 of the Enabling Clause enhances market access for developing countries as a means of improving their economic development by authorizing preferential treatment for those countries, "notwithstanding" the obligations of Article I. It is evident that a Member cannot implement a measure authorized by the Enabling Clause without according an "advantage" to a developing country's products over those of a developed country. It follows, therefore, that every measure undertaken pursuant to the Enabling Clause would necessarily be inconsistent with Article I, if assessed on that basis alone, but it would be exempted from compliance with Article I because it meets the requirements of the Enabling Clause. Under these circumstances, we are of the view that a complaining party challenging a measure taken pursuant to the Enabling Clause must allege more than mere inconsistency with Article I:1 of the GATT 1994, for to do only that would not convey the "legal basis of the complaint sufficient to present the problem clearly". In other words, it is insufficient in WTO dispute settlement for a complainant to allege inconsistency with Article I:1 of the GATT 1994 if the complainant seeks also to argue that the measure is not justified under the Enabling Clause. This is especially so if the challenged measure, like that at issue here, is plainly taken pursuant to the Enabling Clause, as we discuss *infra*.

E.1.2 Paragraph 2(a)

E.1.2.1 *EC – Tariff Preferences*, para. 145

(WT/DS246/AB/R)

Paragraph 2(a) of the Enabling Clause provides . . . that, to be justified under that provision, preferential tariff treatment must be "in accordance" with the

GSP "as described" in the *Preamble* to the 1971 Waiver Decision. "Accordance" being defined in the dictionary as "conformity", only preferential tariff treatment that is in conformity with the description "generalized, non-reciprocal and non-discriminatory" treatment can be justified under paragraph 2(a).

E.1.2.2 *EC – Tariff Preferences*, paras. 152–153 (WT/DS246/AB/R)

. . . the ordinary meanings of "discriminate" point in conflicting directions with respect to the propriety of according differential treatment. Under India's reading, any differential treatment of GSP beneficiaries would be prohibited, because such treatment necessarily makes a distinction between beneficiaries. In contrast, under the European Communities' reading, differential treatment of GSP beneficiaries would not be prohibited *per se*. Rather, distinctions would be impermissible only where the basis for such distinctions was improper. Given these divergent meanings, we do not regard the term "non-discriminatory", on its own, as determinative of the permissibility of a preference-granting country according different tariff preferences to different beneficiaries of its GSP scheme.

Nevertheless, at this stage of our analysis, we are able to discern some of the content of the "non-discrimination" obligation based on the ordinary meanings of that term. Whether the drawing of distinctions is *per se* discriminatory, or whether it is discriminatory only if done on an improper basis, the ordinary meanings of "discriminate" converge in one important respect: they both suggest that distinguishing among similarly-situated beneficiaries is discriminatory. . . .

E.1.2.3 *EC – Tariff Preferences*, para. 154 (WT/DS246/AB/R)

Paragraph 2(a), on its face, does not explicitly authorize or prohibit the granting of different tariff preferences to different GSP beneficiaries. It is clear from the ordinary meanings of "non-discriminatory", however, that preference-granting countries must make available identical tariff preferences to all similarly-situated beneficiaries.

E.1.2.4 *EC – Tariff Preferences*, para. 155 (WT/DS246/AB/R)

. . . footnote 3 to paragraph 2(a) stipulates that, in addition to being "non-discriminatory", tariff preferences provided under GSP schemes must be "generalized". According to the ordinary meaning of that term, tariff preferences provided under GSP schemes must be "generalized" in the sense that they "apply more generally; [or] become extended in application". However, this ordinary meaning alone may not reflect the entire significance of the word "generalized" in the context of footnote 3 of the Enabling Clause, particularly because that word resulted from lengthy negotiations leading to the GSP. In this regard, we note the Panel's finding that, by requiring tariff preferences under the GSP to be "generalized", developed and developing countries together sought to eliminate existing "special" preferences that were granted only to certain designated developing countries. Similarly, in response to our questioning at the oral hearing, the participants agreed that one of the objectives of the 1971 Waiver Decision and the Enabling Clause was to eliminate the fragmented system of special preferences that were, in general, based on historical and political ties between developed countries and their former colonies.

E.1.2.5 *EC – Tariff Preferences*, para. 169
(WT/DS246/AB/R)

...We are of the view that the objective of improving developing countries' "share in the growth in international trade", and their "trade and export earnings", can be fulfilled by promoting preferential policies aimed at those interests that developing countries have in common, *as well as* at those interests shared by sub-categories of developing countries based on their particular needs. An interpretation of "non-discriminatory" that does not require the granting of "identical tariff preferences" allows not only for GSP schemes providing preferential market access to all beneficiaries, but also the possibility of additional preferences for developing countries with particular needs, provided that such additional preferences are not inconsistent with other provisions of the Enabling Clause, including the requirements that such preferences be "generalized" and "non-reciprocal". We therefore consider such an interpretation to be consistent with the object and purpose of the *WTO Agreement* and the Enabling Clause.

E.1.2.6 *EC – Tariff Preferences*, para. 173
(WT/DS246/AB/R)

Having examined the text and context of footnote 3 to paragraph 2(a) of the Enabling Clause, and the object and purpose of the *WTO Agreement* and the Enabling Clause, we conclude that the term "non-discriminatory" in footnote 3 does not prohibit developed-country Members from granting different tariffs to products originating in different GSP beneficiaries, provided that such differential tariff treatment meets the remaining conditions in the Enabling Clause. In granting such differential tariff treatment, however, preference-granting countries are required, by virtue of the term "non-discriminatory", to ensure that identical treatment is available to all similarly-situated GSP beneficiaries, that is, to all GSP beneficiaries that have the "development, financial and trade needs" to which the treatment in question is intended to respond.

E.1.2.7 *EC – Tariff Preferences*, paras. 187–188
(WT/DS246/AB/R)

We recall our conclusion that the term "non-discriminatory" in footnote 3 of the Enabling Clause requires that identical tariff treatment be available to all similarly-situated GSP beneficiaries. We find that the measure at issue fails to meet this requirement for the following reasons. First, as the European Communities itself acknowledges, according benefits under the Drug Arrangements to countries other than the 12 identified beneficiaries would require an amendment to the Regulation. Such a "closed list" of beneficiaries cannot ensure that the preferences under the Drug Arrangements are available to all GSP beneficiaries suffering from illicit drug production and trafficking.

Secondly, the Regulation contains no criteria or standards to provide a basis for distinguishing beneficiaries under the Drug Arrangements from other GSP beneficiaries. Nor did the European Communities point to any such criteria or standards anywhere else, despite the Panel's request to do so. As such, the European Communities cannot justify the Regulation under paragraph 2(a), because it does not provide a basis for establishing whether or not a developing country qualifies for preferences under the Drug Arrangements. Thus, although the European Communities claims that the Drug Arrangements are available to all developing countries that are "similarly affected by the drug problem", because the Regulation does not define the criteria or standards that a developing country must meet to qualify for preferences under the Drug Arrangements, there is no basis to determine whether those criteria or standards are discriminatory or not.

E.1.3 Paragraph 2(d)

E.1.3.1 *EC – Tariff Preferences*, para. 172
(WT/DS246/AB/R)

. . . The inclusion of paragraph 2(d), however, makes clear that developed countries may accord preferential treatment to least-developed countries distinct from the preferences granted to other developing countries under paragraph 2(a). Thus, pursuant to paragraph 2(d), preference-granting countries need not establish that differentiating between developing and least-developed countries is "non-discriminatory". This demonstrates that paragraph 2(d) does have an effect that is different and independent from that of paragraph 2(a), even if the term "non-discriminatory" does not require the granting of "identical tariff preferences" to all GSP beneficiaries.

E.1.4 Paragraph 3(a)

E.1.4.1 *EC – Tariff Preferences*, para. 167
(WT/DS246/AB/R)

. . . we note that, pursuant to paragraph 3(a) of the Enabling Clause, any "differential and more favourable treatment . . . shall be designed to facilitate and promote the trade of developing countries and not to raise barriers to or create undue difficulties for the trade of any other contracting parties." This requirement applies, *a fortiori*, to any preferential treatment granted to one GSP beneficiary that is not granted to another. . . .

E.1.5 Paragraph 3(c)

E.1.5.1 *EC – Tariff Preferences*, para. 161
(WT/DS246/AB/R)

. . . the Preamble to the *WTO Agreement*, which informs all the covered agreements including the GATT 1994 (and, hence, the Enabling Clause), explicitly recognizes the "need for positive efforts designed to ensure that developing countries, and especially the least developed among them, secure a share in the growth in international trade commensurate with the needs of their economic development". The word "commensurate" in this phrase appears to leave open the possibility that developing countries may have different needs according to their levels of development and particular circumstances. The Preamble to the *WTO Agreement* further recognizes that Members' "respective needs and concerns at different levels of economic development" may vary according to the different stages of development of different Members.

E.1.5.2 *EC – Tariff Preferences*, paras. 162–164
(WT/DS246/AB/R)

. . . we read paragraph 3(c) as authorizing preference-granting countries to "respond positively" to "needs" that are *not* necessarily common or shared by all developing countries. Responding to the "needs of developing countries" may thus entail treating different developing-country beneficiaries differently.

However, paragraph 3(c) does not authorize *any* kind of response to *any* claimed need of developing countries. First, we observe that the types of needs to which a response is envisaged are limited to "development, financial and trade needs". In our view, a "need" cannot be characterized as one of the specified "needs of developing countries" in the sense of paragraph 3(c) based merely on an assertion to that effect by, for instance, a preference-granting country or a beneficiary country. Rather, when a claim of inconsistency with paragraph 3(c) is made, the existence of a "development, financial [or] trade need" must be assessed according to an *objective* standard. Broad-based recognition of a particular need, set out in the *WTO Agreement* or in multilateral instruments adopted by international organizations, could serve as such a standard.

Secondly, paragraph 3(c) mandates that the response provided to the needs of developing countries be "positive". "Positive" is defined as "consisting in or characterized by constructive action or attitudes". This suggests that the response of a preference-granting country must be taken with a view to *improving* the development, financial or trade situation of a beneficiary country, based on the particular need at issue. As such, in our view, the expectation that developed countries will "respond positively" to the "needs of developing countries" suggests that a sufficient nexus should exist between, on the one hand, the preferential treatment provided under the respective measure authorized by paragraph 2, and, on the other hand, the likelihood of alleviating the relevant "development, financial [or] trade need". In the context of a GSP scheme, the particular need at issue must, by its nature, be such that it can be effectively addressed through tariff preferences. Therefore, only if a preference-granting country acts in the "positive" manner suggested, in "respon[se]" to a widely-recognized "development, financial [or] trade need", can such action satisfy the requirements of paragraph 3(c).

Enforcement of Intellectual Property Rights. *See* TRIPS Agreement, Article 42 (T.9.10)

E.2 Environmental Multilateral Agreements. *See also* General Exceptions: Article XX of the GATT 1994 (G.3)

E.2.1 *US – Shrimp (Article 21.5 – Malaysia)*, para. 122 (WT/DS58/AB/RW)

We concluded in *United States – Shrimp* that, to avoid "arbitrary or unjustifiable discrimination", the United States had to provide all exporting countries "similar opportunities to negotiate" an international agreement. Given the specific mandate contained in Section 609, and given the decided preference for multilateral approaches voiced by WTO Members and others in the international community in various international agreements for the protection and conservation of endangered sea turtles that were cited in our previous Report, the United States, in our view, would be expected to make good faith efforts to reach international agreements that are comparable from one forum of negotiation to the other. The negotiations need not be identical. Indeed, no two negotiations can ever be identical, or lead to identical results. Yet the negotiations must be *comparable* in the sense that comparable efforts are made, comparable resources are invested, and comparable energies are devoted to securing an international agreement. So long as such comparable efforts are made, it is more likely that "arbitrary or unjustifiable discrimination" will be avoided between countries where an importing Member concludes an agreement with one group of countries, but fails to do so with another group of countries.

E.2.2 *US – Shrimp (Article 21.5 – Malaysia)*, para. 123 (WT/DS58/AB/RW)

Under the chapeau of Article XX, an importing Member may not treat its trading partners in a manner that would constitute "arbitrary or unjustifiable discrimination". With respect to this measure, the United States could conceivably respect this obligation, and the conclusion of an international agreement might nevertheless not be possible despite the serious, good faith efforts of the United States. Requiring that a multilateral agreement be *concluded* by the United States in order to avoid "arbitrary or unjustifiable discrimination" in applying its measure would mean that any country party to the negotiations with the United States, whether a WTO Member or not, would have, in effect, a veto over whether the United States could fulfill its WTO obligations. Such a requirement would not be reasonable. For a variety of reasons, it may be possible to conclude an agreement with one group of countries but not another. The conclusion of a multilateral agreement requires the cooperation and commitment of many countries. In our view, the United States cannot be held to have engaged in "arbitrary or unjustifiable discrimination" under Article XX solely because one international negotiation resulted in an agreement while another did not.

E.2.3 *US – Shrimp (Article 21.5 – Malaysia)*, para. 124
(WT/DS58/AB/RW)

As we stated in *United States – Shrimp*, "the protection and conservation of highly migratory species of sea turtles . . . demands concerted and cooperative efforts on the part of the many countries whose waters are traversed in the course of recurrent sea turtle migrations". Further, the "need for, and the appropriateness of, such efforts have been recognized in the WTO itself as well as in a significant number of other international instruments and declarations". For example, Principle 12 of the Rio Declaration on Environment and Development states, in part, that "[e]nvironmental measures addressing transboundary or global environmental problems should, as far as possible, be based on international consensus". Clearly, and "as far as possible", a multilateral approach is strongly preferred. Yet it is one thing to *prefer* a multilateral approach in the application of a measure that is provisionally justified under one of the subparagraphs of Article XX of the GATT 1994; it is another to require the *conclusion* of a multilateral agreement as a condition of avoiding "arbitrary or unjustifiable discrimination" under the chapeau of Article XX. We see, in this case, no such requirement.

E.2.4 *US – Shrimp (Article 21.5 – Malaysia)*, para. 130
(WT/DS58/AB/RW)

At no time in *United States – Shrimp* did we refer to the Inter-American Convention as a "benchmark". The Panel might have chosen another and better word – perhaps, as suggested by Malaysia, "example". Yet it seems to us that the Panel did all that it should have done with respect to the Inter-American Convention, and did so consistently with our approach in *United States – Shrimp*. The Panel compared the efforts of the United States to negotiate the Inter-American Convention with one group of exporting WTO Members with the efforts made by the United States to negotiate a similar agreement with another group of exporting WTO Members. The Panel rightly used the Inter-American Convention as a factual reference in this exercise of comparison. It was all the more relevant to do so given that the Inter-American Convention was the only international agreement that the Panel could have used in such a comparison. As we read the Panel Report, it is clear to us that the Panel attached a relative value to the Inter-American Convention in making this comparison, but did not view the Inter-American Convention in any way as an absolute standard. Thus, we disagree with Malaysia's submission that the Panel raised the Inter-American Convention to the rank of a "legal standard". The mere use by the Panel of the Inter-American Convention *as a basis for a comparison* did not transform the Inter-American Convention into a "legal standard". Furthermore, although the Panel could have chosen a more appropriate word than "benchmark" to express its views, Malaysia is mistaken in equating the mere use of the word "benchmark", as it was used by the Panel, with the establishment of a legal standard.

E.3 Evidence. *See also* Burden of Proof (B.3); Business Confidential Information (B.4); Confidentiality (C.6); Inferences Drawn from the Refusal of a Party to Provide Information (I.1); Seek Information and Technical Advice (S.4); Standard of Review, Article 11 of the DSU (S.7.2–7)

E.3.1 *Argentina – Textiles and Apparel*, para. 79
(WT/DS56/AB/R, WT/DS56/AB/R/Corr.1)

Article 11 of the DSU does not establish time limits for the submission of evidence to a panel. Article 12.1 of the DSU directs a panel to follow the Working Procedures set out in Appendix 3 of the DSU, but at the same time authorizes a panel to do otherwise after consulting the parties to the dispute. The Working Procedures in Appendix 3 also do not establish precise deadlines for the presentation of evidence by a party to the dispute. It is true that the Working Procedures "do not prohibit" submission of additional evidence after the first substantive meeting of a panel with the parties. It is also true, however, that the Working Procedures in Appendix 3 do contemplate two distinguishable stages in a proceeding before a panel. . . .

. . . Under the Working Procedures in Appendix 3, the complaining party should set out its case in chief, including a full presentation of the facts on the basis of submission of supporting evidence, during the first stage. The second stage is generally designed to permit "rebuttals" by each party of the arguments and evidence submitted by the other parties.

E.3.2 *Argentina – Textiles and Apparel*, paras. 80–81
(WT/DS56/AB/R, WT/DS56/AB/R/Corr.1)

. . . the working procedures in their present form do not constrain panels with hard and fast rules on deadlines for submitting evidence. The Panel could have refused to admit the additional documentary evidence of the United States as unseasonably submitted. The Panel chose, instead, to admit that evidence, at the same time allowing Argentina two weeks to respond to it. . . . The Panel could well have granted Argentina more than two weeks to respond to the additional evidence. However, there is no indication in the panel record that Argentina explicitly requested from the Panel, at that time or at any later time, a longer period within which to respond to the additional documentary evidence of the United States. Argentina also did not submit any countering documents or comments in respect of any of the additional documents of the United States.

. . . while another panel could well have exercised its discretion differently, we do not believe that the Panel here committed an abuse of discretion amounting to a failure to render an objective assessment of the matter as mandated by Article 11 of the DSU.

E.3.3 *US – Shrimp*, para. 104
(WT/DS58/AB/R)

The comprehensive nature of the authority of a panel to "seek" information and technical advice from "any individual or body" it may consider appropriate, or from "any relevant source", should be underscored. This authority embraces more than merely the choice and evaluation of the *source* of the information or advice which it may seek. A panel's authority includes the authority to decide *not to seek* such information or advice at all. We consider that a panel also has the authority to *accept or reject* any information or advice which it may have sought and received, or to *make some other appropriate disposition* thereof. It is particularly within the province and the authority of a panel to determine *the need for information and advice* in a specific case, to ascertain the *acceptability* and *relevancy* of information or advice received, and to decide *what weight to ascribe to that information or advice* or to conclude that no weight at all should be given to what has been received.

E.3.4 *US – Shrimp*, para. 106
(WT/DS58/AB/R)

The thrust of Articles 12 and 13, taken together, is that the DSU accords to a panel established by the DSB, and engaged in a dispute settlement proceeding, ample and extensive authority to undertake and to control the process by which it informs itself both of the relevant facts of the dispute and of the legal norms and principles applicable to such facts. That authority, and the breadth thereof, is indispensably necessary to enable a panel to discharge its duty imposed by Article 11 of the DSU to "make an objective assessment of the matter before it, including an *objective assessment of the facts of the case* and the *applicability of and conformity with the relevant covered agreements. . . .*" (emphasis added).

E.3.5 *Australia – Salmon*, para. 272
(WT/DS18/AB/R)

. . . We note that Article 12.2 of the DSU provides that "[p]anel procedures should provide sufficient flexibility so as to ensure high-quality panel reports, while not unduly delaying the panel process." However, a panel must also be careful to observe due process, which entails providing the parties adequate opportunity to respond to the evidence submitted. . . .

E.3.5A *EC – Asbestos*, para. 161
(WT/DS135/AB/R)

The same holds true in this case. The Panel enjoyed a margin of discretion in assessing the value of the evidence, and the weight to be ascribed to that evidence. The Panel was entitled, in the exercise of its discretion, to determine that certain elements of evidence should be accorded more weight than other elements – that is the essence of the task of appreciating the evidence.

E.3.6 *US – Cotton Yarn*, paras. 77–78 and footnote 51 (WT/DS192/AB/R)

The exercise of due diligence by a Member cannot imply, however, the examination of evidence that did not exist and that, therefore, could not possibly have been taken into account when the Member made its determination. The demonstration by a Member that a particular product is being imported into its territory in such increased quantities as to cause serious damage (or actual threat thereof) to the domestic industry can be based only on facts and evidence which existed at the time the determination was made. The urgent nature of such an investigation may not permit the Member to delay its determination in order to take into account evidence that might be available only at a future date. Even a determination on the existence of threat of serious injury must be based on projections extrapolating from *existing* data.

In our view, a *panel* reviewing the due diligence exercised by a Member in making its determination under Article 6 of the *ATC* has to put itself in the place of that Member at the time it makes its determination. Consequently, a panel must not consider evidence which did not exist *at that point in time*.[51]

[51] We do not rule upon other forms of evidence, such as an expert opinion submitted to a panel that is based on data which existed when the Member made its determination. . . .

E.3.7 *EC – Tube or Pipe*, para. 131 (WT/DS219/AB/R)

[Article 3.4 of the *Anti-Dumping Agreement*] requires an investigating authority to evaluate all relevant economic factors in its examination of the impact of the dumped imports. By its terms, it does not address the manner in which the results of this evaluation are to be set out, nor the type of evidence that may be produced before a panel for the purpose of demonstrating that this evaluation was indeed conducted. The provision simply requires Members to include an evaluation of all relevant economic factors in its examination of the impact of the dumped imports. . . .

E.3.8 *Canada – Wheat Exports and Grain Imports*, para. 191 (WT/DS276/AB/R)

In our view, it is incumbent upon a party to identify in its submissions the relevance of the provisions of legislation – the evidence – on which it relies to support its arguments. It is not sufficient merely to file an entire piece of legislation and expect a panel to discover, on its own, what relevance the various provisions may or may not have for a party's legal position. We are not satisfied that the United States argued the relevance before the Panel of the various provisions of the *Canadian Wheat Board Act* on which it now relies. . . . Therefore, we do not agree with the United States that the Panel disregarded facts relevant to the independence of the CWB and we see no failure by the Panel in this respect to comply with its duty under Article 11 of the DSU.

E.3.9 *E.3.9 US – Oil Country Tubular Goods Sunset Reviews*, para. 312
(WT/DS268/AB/R)

We move now to the question whether the Panel erred in failing to consider the USITC's statements before United States courts or before a NAFTA panel regarding the meaning of "likely" as used in Article 11.3 of the Agreement. We agree with Argentina that the USITC's statements before United States courts or before a NAFTA panel are not, in principle, inadmissible evidence in WTO dispute settlement proceedings as such. However, we disagree with Argentina's understanding of the Panel's position. The task of the Panel was to decide whether the determination of "likely" future injury rested, in this specific case, on a sufficient factual basis to allow the USITC to draw reasoned and adequate conclusions. In order to perform this exercise properly, the Panel did not need to resort to the statements of the USITC before domestic courts or before a NAFTA panel, because the Panel's assessment necessarily had to be based on the meaning of "likely" within the WTO legal system – namely the meaning attributed to this term by the Appellate Body in *US – Corrosion-Resistant Steel Sunset Review*. Therefore, it was not unreasonable for the Panel to consider that the USITC's statements to which Argentina refers were "not relevant" in the task of assessing the application of the "likely" standard in Article 11.3 with respect to injury in the sunset review at issue.

E.3.10 *US – Oil Country Tubular Goods Sunset Reviews*, paras. 340–341
(WT/DS268/AB/R)

We observe that most of the arguments put forward by Argentina on appeal with respect to the application by the USITC of the standard of likelihood is centred on the premise that some of the factors presented by the USITC are speculative. In particular, Argentina seems to assume that positive evidence requires absolute certainty on what is likely to occur in the future. We have some difficulty with this line of reasoning. Of course, we agree with Argentina that the investigating authority's likelihood determinations under Article 11.3 must be based on "positive evidence"....

The requirements of "positive evidence" must, however, be seen in the context that the determinations to be made under Article 11.3 are prospective in nature and that they involve a "forward-looking analysis". Such an analysis may inevitably entail assumptions about or projections into the future. Unavoidably, therefore, the inferences drawn from the evidence in the record will be, to a certain extent, speculative. In our view, that some of the inferences drawn from the evidence on record are projections into the future does not necessarily suggest that such inferences are not based on "positive evidence". The Panel considered that the five factors addressed by the USITC were supported by positive evidence in the USITC's record and, as we have explained, we see no reason to disagree with the Panel.

E.3.11 *US – Upland Cotton*, para. 308
(WT/DS267/AB/R)

We recognize that the statement of available evidence plays an important role in WTO dispute settlement. The adequacy of the statement of available evidence must be determined on a case by case basis. As the Panel stated, moreover, the "statement of available evidence . . . is the starting point for consultations, and for the emergence of more evidence concerning the measures by reason of the clarification of the 'situation'". It is, therefore, important to bear in mind that the requirement to submit a statement of available evidence applies in the earliest stages of WTO dispute settlement, and that the requirement is to provide a "statement" of the evidence and not the evidence itself.

Exceptions. *See* Burden of Proof, Defences and Exceptions (B.3.3); General Exceptions: Article XX of the GATT 1994 (G.3)

Experts Advising a Panel. *See* Seek Information and Technical Advice (S.4)

F

G

G.1 GATS

G.1.1 **Article I: Scope of application – Measures affecting trade in services.** *See also* GATT 1994: Relationship between the GATT 1994 and the GATS (G.2.2)

G.1.1.1 *EC – Bananas III*, para. 220
(WT/DS27/AB/R)

. . . we note that Article I:1 of the GATS provides that "[t]his Agreement applies to measures by Members affecting trade in services". In our view, the use of the term "affecting" reflects the intent of the drafters to give a broad reach to the GATS. The ordinary meaning of the word "affecting" implies a measure that has "an effect on", which indicates a broad scope of application. This interpretation is further reinforced by the conclusions of previous panels that the term "affecting" in the context of Article III of the GATT is wider in scope than such terms as "regulating" or "governing". We also note that Article I:3(b) of the GATS provides that " 'services' includes *any service* in *any sector* except services supplied in the exercise of governmental authority" (emphasis added), and that Article XXVIII(b) of the GATS provides that the " 'supply of a service' includes the production, distribution, marketing, sale and delivery of a service". There is nothing at all in these provisions to suggest a limited scope of application for the GATS. . . .

G.1.1.2 *EC – Bananas III*, para. 221
(WT/DS27/AB/R)

. . . the GATS applies to the supply of services. It provides, *inter alia*, for both MFN treatment and national treatment for services and service suppliers. Given the respective scope of application of the two agreements, they may or may not overlap, depending on the nature of the measures at issue. Certain measures could be found to fall exclusively within the scope of the GATT 1994, when they affect trade in goods as goods. Certain measures could be found to fall exclusively within the scope of the GATS, when they affect the supply of services as services. There is yet a third category of measures that could be found to fall within the scope of both the GATT 1994 and the GATS. These are measures that involve a service relating to a particular good or a service supplied in conjunction with a particular good. In all such cases in this third category, the measure in question could be scrutinized under both the GATT 1994 and the GATS. However, while the same measure could be scrutinized under both agreements, the specific aspects of that measure examined under each agreement could be different. . . .

G.1.1.3 *Canada – Autos*, paras. 151–152 (WT/DS139/AB/R, WT/DS142/AB/R)

. . . Similarly, here, the fundamental structure and logic of Article I:1, in relation to the rest of the GATS, require that determination of whether a measure is, in fact, covered by the GATS must be made *before* the consistency of that measure with any substantive obligation of the GATS can be assessed.

. . . We find, therefore, that the Panel should have inquired, as a threshold question, into whether the measure is within the scope of the GATS by examining whether the import duty exemption is a measure "affecting trade in services" within the meaning of Article I. In failing to do so, the Panel erred in its interpretative approach.

G.1.1.4 *Canada – Autos*, para. 155 (WT/DS139/AB/R, WT/DS142/AB/R)

With these treaty provisions in mind, we believe that at least two key legal issues must be examined to determine whether a measure is one "affecting trade in services": first, whether there is "trade in services" in the sense of Article I:2; and, second, whether the measure in issue "affects" such trade in services within the meaning of Article I:1.

G.1.1.5 *Canada – Autos*, para. 165 (WT/DS139/AB/R, WT/DS142/AB/R)

We do not consider this statement of the Panel to be a sufficient basis for a legal finding that the import duty exemption "affects" wholesale trade services of motor vehicles *as services*, or wholesale trade service suppliers *in their capacity as service suppliers*. The Panel failed to analyze the evidence on the record relating to the provision of wholesale trade services of motor vehicles in the Canadian market. It also failed to articulate what it understood Article I:1 to require by the use of the term "affecting". Having interpreted Article I:1, the Panel should then have examined all the relevant facts, including *who* supplies wholesale trade services of motor vehicles through commercial presence in Canada, and *how* such services are supplied. It is not enough to make assumptions. Finally, the Panel should have applied its interpretation of "affecting trade in services" to the facts it should have found.

G.1.1.6 *Canada – Autos*, para. 166 (WT/DS139/AB/R, WT/DS142/AB/R)

The European Communities and Japan may well be correct in their assertions that the availability of the import duty exemption to certain manufacturer beneficiaries of the United States established in Canada, and the corresponding unavailability of this exemption to manufacturer beneficiaries of Europe and of Japan established in Canada, has an effect on the operations in Canada of wholesale trade service suppliers of motor vehicles and, therefore, "affects" those wholesale trade service suppliers in their capacity as service suppliers. However, the Panel did not examine this issue. The Panel merely asserted its conclusion, without explaining how or why it came to its conclusion. This is not good enough.

G.1.1.7 *Canada – Autos*, para. 167
(WT/DS139/AB/R, WT/DS142/AB/R)

For these reasons, we believe that the Panel has failed to examine whether the measure is one "affecting trade in services" as required under Article I:1 of the GATS. The Panel did not show that the measure at issue affects wholesale trade services of motor vehicles, as services, or wholesale trade service suppliers of motor vehicles, in their *capacity as service suppliers*. Nonetheless, we continue our analysis of the issues raised on appeal under Article II:1, and examine whether, in the terms of that provision, the measure accords treatment "no less favourable" to like services and service suppliers of other Members.

G.1.1.8 *US – Gambling*, paras. 120–123
(WT/DS285/AB/R)

The question before us, therefore, is whether an alleged "total prohibition" on the cross-border supply of gambling and betting services constitutes a measure that may be challenged under the GATS. The DSU provides for the "prompt settlement" of situations where Members consider that their benefits under the covered agreements "are being impaired by *measures* taken by another Member". Two elements of this reference to "measures" that may be the subject of dispute settlement are relevant. First, as the Appellate Body has stated, a "nexus" must exist between the responding Member and the "measure", such that the "measure" – whether an act or omission – must be "attributable" to that Member. Secondly, the "measure" must be the *source* of the alleged impairment, which is in turn the *effect* resulting from the existence or operation of the "measure".

Similarly [Article 4.2 of the DSU] contemplates that "measures" themselves will "affect" the operation of a covered agreement. Finally, we note that this distinction between measures and their effects is also evident in the scope of application of the GATS, namely, to "measures by Members affecting trade in services".

We are therefore of the view that the DSU and the GATS focus on "measures" as the subject of challenge in WTO dispute settlement. To the extent that a Member's complaint centres on the effects of an action taken by another Member, that complaint must nevertheless be brought as a challenge to the *measure* that is the source of the alleged effects.

G.1.1.9 *US – Gambling*, para. 180
(WT/DS285/AB/R)

We move . . . to examine the context provided by the structure of the GATS itself. . . . To us, the structure of the GATS necessarily implies two things. First, because the GATS covers *all* services except those supplied in the exercise of governmental authority, it follows that a Member may schedule a specific commitment in respect of *any* service. . . .

G.1.2 Schedules

G.1.2.1 INTERPRETATION OF SCHEDULES

G.1.2.1.1 *US – Gambling*, para. 160
(WT/DS285/AB/R)

In the context of the GATS, Article XX:3 explicitly provides that Members' Schedules are an "integral part" of that agreement. Here, too, the task of identifying the meaning of a concession in a GATS Schedule, like the task of interpreting any other treaty text, involves identifying the *common intention* of Members. . . . we consider that the meaning of the United States' GATS Schedule must be determined according to the rules codified in Article 31 and, to the extent appropriate, Article 32 of the *Vienna Convention.*

G.1.2.1.2 *US – Gambling*, para. 166
(WT/DS285/AB/R)

We have three reservations about the way in which the Panel determined the ordinary meaning of the word "sporting" in the United States' Schedule. First, to the extent that the Panel's reasoning simply equates the "ordinary meaning" with the meaning of words as defined in dictionaries, this is, in our view, too mechanical an approach. Secondly, the Panel failed to have due regard to the fact that its recourse to dictionaries revealed that gambling and betting can, at least in some contexts, be one of the meanings of the word "sporting". Thirdly, the Panel failed to explain the basis for its recourse to the meanings of the French and Spanish words "déportivos" and "sportifs" in the light of the fact that the United States' Schedule explicitly states, in a cover note, that it "is authentic in English only."

G.1.2.1.3 *US – Gambling*, para. 167
(WT/DS285/AB/R)

Overall, the Panel's finding concerning the word "sporting" was premature. In our view, the Panel should have taken note that, in the abstract, the range of possible meanings of the word "sporting" includes *both* the meaning claimed by Antigua and the meaning claimed by the United States, and then continued its inquiry into *which* of those meanings was to be attributed to the word as used in the United States' GATS Schedule.

G.1.2.2 RELEVANCE OF THE CENTRAL PRODUCT CLASSIFICATION (CPC), SERVICES SECTORAL CLASSIFICATION LIST (W/120) AND SCHEDULING GUIDELINES

G.1.2.2.1 *US – Gambling*, para. 175 (WT/DS285/AB/R)

We note that Article 31(2) refers to the *agreement* or *acceptance* of the parties. In this case, both W/120 and the 1993 Scheduling Guidelines were drafted by the GATT Secretariat rather than the parties to the negotiations. It may be true that, on its own, authorship by a delegated body would not preclude specific documents from falling within the scope of Article 31(2). However, we are not persuaded that in this case the Panel could find W/120 and the 1993 Scheduling Guidelines to be context. Such documents can be characterized as context only where there is sufficient evidence of their constituting an "agreement relating to the treaty" between the parties or of their "accept[ance by the parties] as an instrument related to the treaty".

G.1.2.2.2 *US – Gambling*, paras. 176, 178 (WT/DS285/AB/R)

We do not accept, as the Panel appears to have done, that, simply by requesting the preparation and circulation of these documents and using them in preparing their offers, the parties in the negotiations have accepted them as agreements or instruments related to the treaty. Indeed, there are indications to the contrary. As the United States pointed out before the Panel, the United States and several other parties to the negotiations clearly stated, at the time W/120 was proposed, that, although Members were encouraged to follow the broad structure of W/120, it was never meant to bind Members to the CPC definitions, nor to any other "specific nomenclature", and that "the composition of the list was not a matter for negotiations". Similarly, the Explanatory Note that prefaces the Scheduling Guidelines itself appears to contradict the Panel in this regard, as it expressly provides that, although it is intended to assist "persons responsible for scheduling commitments", that assistance "should not be considered as an authoritative legal interpretation of the GATS."

...

...therefore, the Panel erred in categorizing W/120 and the 1993 Scheduling Guidelines as "context" for the interpretation of the United States' GATS Schedule....

G.1.2.2.3 *US – Gambling*, para. 179 (WT/DS285/AB/R)

...the United States' Schedule ... makes no reference to CPC codes. The Schedule does, however, refer to W/120 in two instances, apparently in order to make clear that the United States' commitment corresponds to only *part* of a subsector listed in W/120. This suggests that, at least for some of its entries, the United States also expressly referred to W/120 in order to define the *content* of a Schedule entry and, thereby, limit the *scope* of its specific commitment....

G.1.2.2.4 *US – Gambling*, para. 180 (WT/DS285/AB/R)

We move . . . to examine the context provided by the structure of the GATS itself. . . . To us, the structure of the GATS necessarily implies two things. First, because the GATS covers *all* services except those supplied in the exercise of governmental authority, it follows that a Member may schedule a specific commitment in respect of *any* service. Secondly, because a Member's obligations regarding a particular service depend on the specific commitments that it has made with respect to the sector or subsector within which that service falls, a specific service cannot fall within two different sectors or subsectors. In other words, the sectors and subsectors in a Member's Schedule must be mutually exclusive. In the context of the United States' Schedule, this means that, notwithstanding the broad language used in sector 10 – for example, "recreational services", "sporting", and "entertainment services" – , gambling and betting services can *only* fall – if at all – within *one* of those service categories.

G.1.2.2.5 *US – Gambling*, para. 181 (WT/DS285/AB/R)

. . . Article 22.3(f) of the DSU provides that, for purposes of suspending concessions, "'sector' means . . . (ii) with respect to services, a principal sector as identified in the current 'Services Sectoral Classification List' which identifies such sectors". A footnote adds that "[t]he list in document MTN.GNS/W/120 identifies eleven sectors." This reference confirms the relevance of W/120 to the task of identifying service sectors in GATS Schedules, but does not appear to assist in the task of ascertaining within which *subsector* of a Member's Schedule a specific service falls.

G.1.2.2.6 *US – Gambling*, para. 182 (WT/DS285/AB/R)

. . . other Members' Schedules constitute relevant context for the interpretation of subsector 10.D of the United States' Schedule. . . . At the same time, as the Panel rightly acknowledged, use of other Members' Schedules as context must be tempered by the recognition that "[e]ach Schedule has its own intrinsic logic, which is different from the US Schedule."

G.1.2.2.7 *US – Gambling*, para. 183 (WT/DS285/AB/R)

. . . the United States' Schedule, like the Schedules of nearly all Members, generally follows the structure, and adopts the language, of W/120. These structural and linguistic similarities lead us to conclude, contrary to the United States submission, that the absence of references to CPC codes does not mean that words used in the United States' Schedule *must* have a different meaning and scope than the same words used in the Schedules of other Members.

G.1.2.2.8 *US – Gambling*, para. 186
(WT/DS285/AB/R)

... we find it significant that the entries made by many Members in sector 10 of their Schedules contain text additional to the text found in the headings and sub-headings used by the United States (and used in W/120). Such Members disaggregated their entries beyond the five subsectors identified in W/120 as falling within sector 10. There is a broad range of ways in which this was accomplished.... This context indicates that Members seeking to distinguish the commitments they were making regarding gambling and betting services from other commitments they were making in subsector 10.D used specific language and/or CPC codes to indicate this distinction....

G.1.2.2.9 *US – Gambling*, paras. 192–193
(WT/DS285/AB/R)

... in order for "practice" within the meaning of Article 31(3)(b) to be established: (i) there must be a common, consistent, discernible pattern of acts or pronouncements; *and* (ii) those acts or pronouncements must imply *agreement* on the interpretation of the relevant provision.

...Although the 2001 Guidelines were explicitly adopted by the Council for Trade in Services, this was in the context of the negotiation of *future* commitments and in order to assist in the preparation of offers and requests in respect of such commitments. As such, they do not constitute evidence of Members' understanding regarding the interpretation of *existing* commitments. Furthermore, as the United States emphasized before the Panel, in its Decision adopting the 2001 Guidelines, the Council for Trade in Services explicitly stated that they were to be "non-binding" and "shall not modify any rights or obligations of the Members under the GATS". Accordingly, we do not consider that the 2001 Guidelines, in and of themselves, constitute "subsequent practice" within the meaning of Article 31(3)(b) of the *Vienna Convention.*

G.1.2.2.10 *US – Gambling*, paras. 196–197
(WT/DS285/AB/R)

... this appeal does *not* raise the question whether W/120 and the 1993 Scheduling Guidelines constitute "supplementary means of interpretation, including the preparatory work of the treaty and the circumstances of its conclusion". Both participants agree that they do, and we see no reason to disagree.

... a proper interpretation pursuant to the principles codified in Article 31 of the *Vienna Convention* does not yield a clear meaning as to the scope of the commitment made by the United States in the entry "Other recreational services (except sporting)". Accordingly, it is appropriate to have recourse to the supplemental means of interpretation identified in Article 32 of the *Vienna Convention*. These means include W/120, the 1993 Scheduling Guidelines, and a cover note attached to drafts of the United States' Schedule.

G.1.2.2.11 *US – Gambling*, paras. 199–200
(WT/DS285/AB/R)

. . . W/120 does not, however, contain any explicit indication of: (i) whether the reference to Group 964 necessarily incorporates a reference to *each and every subcategory* of Group 964 within the CPC; or (ii) how W/120 relates to the GATS Schedules of individual Members.

. . . W/120 sets out a much more aggregated classification list than the one found in the CPC. . . . the CPC's level of disaggregation was one of the very reasons it was selected as a basis for a sectoral classification list. As the CPC is a decimal system, a reference to an aggregate category must be understood as a reference to all of the constituent parts of that category. . . .

G.1.2.2.12 *US – Gambling*, paras. 203–207
(WT/DS285/AB/R)

The Scheduling Guidelines thus underline the importance of using a common format and terminology in scheduling, and express a clear preference for parties to use W/120 and the CPC classifications in their Schedules. At the same time, the Guidelines make clear that parties wanting to use their own subsectoral classification or definitions – that is, to disaggregate in a way that diverges from W/120 and/or the CPC – were to do so in a "sufficiently detailed" way "to avoid any ambiguity as to the scope of the commitment." The example given in the Scheduling Guidelines illustrates how to make a positive commitment with respect to a discrete service that is more disaggregated than a service subsector identified in W/120. It is reasonable to assume that the parties to the negotiations expected the same technique to be applied to *exclude* a discrete service from the scope of a commitment, when the commitment is made in a subsector identified in W/120 and the excluded service is more disaggregated than that subsector.

In our view, the requisite clarity as to the scope of a commitment could not have been achieved through mere omission of CPC codes, particularly where a specific sector of a Member's Schedule, such as sector 10 of the United States' Schedule, follows the structure of W/120 in all other respects, and adopts *precisely* the same terminology as used in W/120. . . . W/120 and the 1993 Scheduling Guidelines were prepared and circulated . . . for the express purpose of assisting those parties in the preparation of their offers. These documents undoubtedly served, too, to assist parties in reviewing and evaluating the offers made by others. They provided a common language and structure which, although not obligatory, was widely used and relied upon. In such circumstances, and in the light of the specific guidance provided in the 1993 Scheduling Guidelines, it is reasonable to assume that parties to the negotiations examining a sector of a Schedule that tracked so closely the language of the same sector in W/120 would – absent a clear indication to the contrary – have expected the sector to have the same coverage as the corresponding W/120 sector. This is another way of stating that, as the Panel observed, "unless otherwise indicated in the Schedule, Members were assumed to have relied on W/120 and the corresponding CPC references."

Accordingly, the above excerpt from the 1993 Scheduling Guidelines, together with the linguistic similarities between the two subsectors, provide strong support for interpreting subsector 10.D of the United States' Schedule as corresponding to subsector 10.D of W/120, notwithstanding the absence of CPC codes in the United States' Schedule....

... another element of the preparatory work of the GATS suggests that the United States itself understood the Scheduling Guidelines in this way and sought to comply with them in the drafting of its GATS Schedule. Several drafts of the United States' Schedule included [a] cover note [which confirms] ...

... that the United States used W/120 and sought to follow the 1993 Scheduling Guidelines....

G.1.3 Article XVI – Market Access

G.1.3.1 GENERAL

G.1.3.1.1 *US – Gambling*, para. 214
(WT/DS285/AB/R)

Article XVI of the GATS sets out specific obligations for Members that apply insofar as a Member has undertaken "specific market access commitments" in its Schedule. The first paragraph of Article XVI obliges Members to accord services and service suppliers of other Members "no less favourable treatment than that provided for under the terms, limitations and conditions agreed and specified in its Schedule." The second paragraph of Article XVI defines, in six sub-paragraphs, measures that a Member, having undertaken a specific commitment, is not to adopt or maintain, "unless otherwise specified in its Schedule". The first four sub-paragraphs concern quantitative limitations on market access; the fifth sub-paragraph covers measures that restrict or require specific types of legal entity or joint venture through which a service supplier may supply a service; and the sixth sub-paragraph identifies limitations on the participation of foreign capital.

G.1.3.1.2 *US – Gambling*, para. 215
(WT/DS285/AB/R)

... the relevant entry for mode 1 supply in the market access column of subsector 10.D of the United States' Schedule reads "None". In other words, the United States has undertaken to provide full market access, within the meaning of Article XVI, in respect of the services included within the scope of its subsector 10.D commitment....

G.1.3.2 ARTICLE XVI:1 – RELATION TO PARAGRAPH 2

G.1.3.2.1 *US – Gambling*, para. 256
(WT/DS285/AB/R)

Antigua conditionally appeals [the Panel's finding that the restrictions on market access that are covered by Article XVI are only those listed in paragraph 2 of this

Article].... Having upheld the Panel's interpretation of sub-paragraphs (a) and (c) of Article XVI:2 and dismissed this ground of the United States' appeal, it follows that the condition on which this aspect of Antigua's appeal is made is not satisfied, and we *need not consider* it further. We thus leave the issue of the relationship between the first and second paragraphs of Article XVI to another day.

G.1.3.3 ARTICLE XVI:2 – CHAPEAU

G.1.3.3.1 *US – Gambling*, para. 233
(WT/DS285/AB/R)

...the chapeau to Article XVI:2 ...contemplates circumstances in which a Member's Schedule *includes* a commitment to allow market access, and points out that the function of the sub-paragraphs in Article XVI:2 is to define certain limitations that are prohibited unless specifically entered in the Member's Schedule. Plainly, the drafters of sub-paragraph (a) had in mind limitations that would impose a maximum limit of *above* zero. Similarly, Article II:1(b) of the GATT 1994 prohibits Members from imposing duties "in excess of" the bound duty rate. Such bound duty rate will usually be *above* zero. Yet this does not mean that Article II:1(b) does not also refer to bound rates set at zero.

G.1.3.4 ARTICLE XVI:2(A) – "LIMITATIONS ON THE NUMBER OF SERVICE SUPPLIERS"

G.1.3.4.1 *US – Gambling*, para. 225
(WT/DS285/AB/R)

Article XVI:2(a) ...refers to restrictions "on the *number* of service suppliers", as well as to "*numerical* quotas". These words reflect that the focus of Article XVI:2(a) is on limitations relating to numbers or, put differently, to *quantitative* limitations.

G.1.3.4.2 *US – Gambling*, para. 226
(WT/DS285/AB/R)

...dictionary definitions...suggest a degree of ambiguity as to the scope of the word "form". For example, "form" covers both the mode in which a thing "exists", as well as the mode in which it "manifests itself". This suggests a broad meaning for the term "form".

G.1.3.4.3 *US – Gambling*, para. 227
(WT/DS285/AB/R)

The words "in the form of" in sub-paragraph (a) relate to all four of the limitations identified in that provision. It follows, in our view, that the four types of limitations, themselves, impart meaning to "in the form of".... a "numerical quota" within Article XVI:2(a) appears to mean a quantitative limit on the number of service suppliers. The fact that the word "numerical" encompasses things which "have the characteristics of a number" suggests that limitations "in the form of a numerical quota" would encompass limitations which, even if not in themselves a number, have the characteristics of a number. Because zero is *quantitative* in nature, it can, in our view, be deemed to have the "characteristics of" a number – that is, to be "numerical".

G.1.3.4.4 *US – Gambling*, paras. 230–231 (WT/DS285/AB/R)

. . . [the definitions of a "monopoly supplier of a service" in Article XXVII(h) and of "exclusive service suppliers" in Article VIII:5] suggest that the reference, in Article XVI:2(a), to limitations on the number of service suppliers "in the form of monopolies and exclusive service suppliers" should be read to include limitations that are in form *or in effect*, monopolies or exclusive service suppliers.

. . . it is not clear that "limitations on the number of service suppliers . . . in the form of . . . the requirements of an economic needs test" must take a particular "form." Thus, this fourth type of limitation, too, suggests that the words "in the form of" must not be interpreted as prescribing a rigid mechanical formula.

G.1.3.4.5 *US – Gambling*, para. 232 (WT/DS285/AB/R)

This is not to say that the words "in the form of" should be ignored or replaced by the words "that have the effect of". Yet, at the same time, they cannot be read in isolation. Rather, when viewed as a whole, the text of sub-paragraph (a) supports the view that the words "in the form of" must be read in conjunction with the words that precede them – "limitations on the *number* of service suppliers" – as well as the words that follow them, including the words "*numerical* quotas". (emphasis added) Read in this way, it is clear that the thrust of sub-paragraph (a) is not on the *form* of limitations, but on their *numerical*, or *quantitative*, nature.

G.1.3.4.6 *US – Gambling*, paras. 236–238 (WT/DS285/AB/R)

. . . examination of the words of Article XVI:2(a) read in their context and in the light of the object and purpose of the GATS suggests that the words "in the form of" do not impose the type of precisely defined constraint that the United States suggests. Yet certain ambiguities about the meaning of the provision remain. The Panel, at this stage of its analysis, observed that any suggestion that the "form" requirement must be strictly interpreted to refer *only* to limitations "explicitly couched in numerical terms" leads to "absurdity". In either circumstance, this is an appropriate case in which to have recourse to supplementary means of interpretation, such as preparatory work.

. . . the 1993 Scheduling Guidelines . . . set out an example of the type of limitation that falls within the scope of sub-paragraph (a) of Article XVI:2 . . . That example is: "nationality requirements for suppliers of services (equivalent to zero quota)". This example confirms the view that measures equivalent to a zero quota fall within the scope of Article XVI:2(a).

. . . limitations amounting to a zero quota are quantitative limitations and fall within the scope of Article XVI:2(a).

G.1.3.5 ARTICLE XVI:2(C) – "LIMITATIONS ON THE TOTAL NUMBER OF SERVICE OPERATIONS"

G.1.3.5.1 *US – Gambling*, para. 245
(WT/DS285/AB/R)

. . . we are not persuaded that the key to the interpretation of this particular provision is to be found in a careful dissection of the use of commas within its grammatical structure. Regardless of which language version is analyzed, and of the implications of comma placement (or lack thereof), *all* three language versions are grammatically ambiguous. All three can arguably be read as identifying two limitations on the total number of service operations or on the total quantity of service output. All three can also arguably be read as identifying *three* limitations on the total number of service operations or on the total quantity of service output. The mere presence or absence of a comma in Article XVI:2(c) is not determinative of the issue before us.

G.1.3.5.2 *US – Gambling*, para. 246
(WT/DS285/AB/R)

We find it more useful, and appropriate, to look to the language of the provision itself for its meaning. Looking at the provision generally, we see that the first clause of sub-paragraph (c) deals with the *target* of the limitations covered by that provision. There are two such types of limitations: on the number of service operations; and on the quantity of service output. Both are *quantitative* in nature. The second part of the provision provides more detail as to the *type* of limitations – relating to those service operations or output – that fall within sub-paragraph (c). These are: "designated numerical units in the form of quotas or the requirement of an economic needs test". The second part of the provision clearly modifies the first part of the provision (service operations, service output). Yet certain elements of the second part apply differently to the two elements of the first part. For example, in its ordinary sense, the term "numerical units" is more naturally used to refer to "output" than to "operations".

G.1.3.5.3 *US – Gambling*, para. 247
(WT/DS285/AB/R)

In our view, by combining, in sub-paragraph (c), the elements of the first clause of Article XVI:2(c) and the elements in the second part of the provision, the parties to the negotiations sought to ensure that their provision covered certain types of limitations, but did not feel the need to clearly demarcate the scope of each such element. On the contrary, there is scope for overlap between such elements: between limitations on the number of service operations and limitations on the quantity of service output, for example, or between limitations in the form of quotas and limitations in the form of an economic needs test. That sub-paragraph (c) applies in respect of all four modes of supply under the GATS also suggests the limitations covered thereunder cannot take a single form, nor be constrained in a formulaic manner. Nonetheless, all types of limitations in sub-paragraph (c) are quantitative in nature, and all restrict market access. For these reasons, we are of the view that, *even if* sub-paragraph (c) is read as referring to only *two* types of limitations, as contended by the United States, it does not follow that sub-paragraph (c) would not catch a measure equivalent to a zero quota.

G.1.3.5.4 *US – Gambling*, para. 248
(WT/DS285/AB/R)

. . . we consider it useful to resort to supplementary means of interpretation. The market access obligations set forth in Article XVI were intended to be obligations in respect of *quantitative*, or "quantitative-type", measures. The difficulties faced by the negotiating parties concerned not *whether* Article XVI covered quantitative measures – for it was clear that it did – but rather how to "know where the line should be drawn between quantitative and qualitative measures".

G.1.3.5.5 *US – Gambling*, para. 250
(WT/DS285/AB/R)

The strict interpretation of Article XVI:2(c) advanced by the United States would imply that only limitations that contain an express reference to numbered units could fall within the scope of that provision. Under such an interpretation, sub-paragraph (c) could not cover, for example, a limitation expressed as a percentage or described using words such as "a majority". It is neither necessary nor appropriate for us to draw, in the abstract, the line between quantitative and qualitative measures, and we do not do so here. Yet we are satisfied that a prohibition on the supply of services in respect of which a full market access commitment has been undertaken is a quantitative limitation on the supply of such services.

G.1.3.6 ARTICLE XVI:2 – MEASURES DIRECTED AT CONSUMERS

G.1.3.6.1 *US – Gambling*, paras. 253–254
(WT/DS285/AB/R)

Antigua also appeals the Panel's findings that certain measures that prohibit *consumers* from purchasing cross-border gambling services are not caught by either sub-paragraph (a) or sub-paragraph (c) of Article XVI:2. The Panel applied its analysis of these provisions to find that four state laws directed at persons who engage in gambling – that is, to *consumers* of gambling services as opposed to *suppliers* of gambling services – had not been shown to be inconsistent with the United States' market access commitments.

. . . Having held that the Panel was not entitled to make findings on *any* of the eight state laws, including with respect to the four state laws directed at *consumers* rather than *suppliers* of gambling services, we need not, in resolving this appeal, consider the merits of Antigua's appeal of the Panel's findings with respect to restrictions on service *consumers* as opposed to service *suppliers.*

Article II. *See* MFN Treatment, Article II of the GATS (M.2.2)

Article XVII. *See* National Treatment, Article XVII of the GATS (N.1.13)

G.2 GATT 1994

Article I. *See* Enabling Clause, Paragraph 1 (E.1.1); MFN Treatment, Article I of the GATT 1994 (M.2.1)

Article II. *See* Tariff Concessions (T.1)

Article III. *See* National Treatment (N.1); SCM Agreement, Article III:8 of the GATT 1994 – Subsidies (S.2.42)

Article VI. *See* Anti-Dumping Agreement (A.3)

Article VI:3. *See* SCM Agreement, Article VI:3 of the GATT 1994 – Subsidies (S.2.43)

Article VIII. *See* International Monetary Fund – "Coherence" (I.2)

Article X. *See* Licensing Agreement (L.2); Publication and Administration of Trade Regulations (P.5)

Article XIII. *See* Tariff Quotas – Non-discriminatory Administration (T.2)

Article XV. *See* International Monetary Fund – "Coherence" (I.2); Seek Information and Technical Advice (S.4)

Article XVI. *See* SCM Agreement, Relationship between the SCM Agreement and the GATT 1994 (S.2.41)

Article XVIII:11, Note Ad. *See* Balance-of-Payments Restrictions (B.1)

Article XVIII:11, Proviso. *See* Balance-of-Payments Restrictions (B.1)

Article XIX. *See* Safeguards Agreement, Article XIX of the GATT 1994 (S.1.45–50); Safeguards Agreement, Relationship between the Safeguards Agreement and the GATT 1994 (S.1.44)

Article XX. *See* General Exceptions: Article XX of the GATT 1994 (G.3)

Article XXIV. *See* Regional Agreements (R.1)

G.2.1 Language of Annex 1A incorporating the GATT 1994 into the WTO Agreement. *See also* Status of Panel and Appellate Body Reports (S.8)

G.2.1.1 *Japan – Alcoholic Beverages II*, p. 14, DSR 1996:I, p. 97 at 107–108 (WT/DS8/AB/R, WT/DS10/AB/R, WT/DS11/AB/R)

Article XVI:1 of the *WTO Agreement* and paragraph 1(b)(iv) of the language of Annex 1A incorporating the GATT 1994 into the *WTO Agreement* bring the legal history and experience under the GATT 1947 into the new realm of the WTO in a way that ensures continuity and consistency in a smooth transition from the GATT 1947 system. This affirms the importance to the Members of the WTO of the experience acquired by the CONTRACTING PARTIES to the GATT 1947 – and acknowledges the continuing relevance of that experience to the new trading system served by the WTO. . . .

G.2.1.2 *Argentina – Footwear (EC)*, para. 80
(WT/DS121/AB/R)

We note that the GATT 1994 is the first agreement that appears in Annex 1A to the *WTO Agreement*, and that it consists of: the provisions of the GATT 1947, as rectified, amended or modified by the terms of legal instruments that entered into force before the entry into force of the *WTO Agreement*; the provisions of certain legal instruments, such as protocols and certifications, decisions on waivers and other decisions of the CONTRACTING PARTIES to the GATT 1947, that entered into force under the GATT 1947 before the entry into force of the *WTO Agreement*; certain Uruguay Round Understandings relating to specific GATT articles; and the Marrakesh Protocol to the GATT 1994 containing Members' Schedules of Concessions.

G.2.1.3 *Korea – Dairy*, para. 75
(WT/DS98/AB/R)

We note, furthermore, that the GATT 1994 was incorporated into the *WTO Agreement* as one of the Multilateral Agreements on Trade in Goods contained in Annex 1A to the *WTO Agreement*. The GATT 1994 consists of: (a) the provisions of the GATT 1947, as rectified, amended or modified before the entry into force of the *WTO Agreement*; (b) provisions of certain other legal instruments which entered into force under the GATT 1947 and before the date of entry into force of the *WTO Agreement*; (c) a number of Uruguay Round Understandings on the interpretation of certain GATT articles; and (d) the Marrakesh Protocol to GATT 1994. The *Agreement on Safeguards* is one of the thirteen Multilateral Agreements on Trade in Goods contained in Annex 1A of the *WTO Agreement*. It is important to understand that the *WTO Agreement* is *one* treaty. The GATT 1994 and the *Agreement on Safeguards* are both Multilateral Agreements on Trade in Goods contained in Annex 1A, which are integral parts of that treaty and are equally binding on all Members pursuant to Article II:2 of the *WTO Agreement*.

G.2.1.4 *US – FSC*, para. 107
(WT/DS108/AB/R)

. . . Paragraph 1(b) stipulates that the GATT 1994 includes certain "legal instruments . . . that entered into force under the GATT 1947", such as "other decisions of the CONTRACTING PARTIES to the GATT 1947" under sub-paragraph (b)(iv). As the Panel said, in terms of Article II:2 of the *WTO Agreement*, these various "legal instruments" are, in themselves, "integral parts" of the *WTO*

Agreement and are "binding on all Members". The inclusion of these "legal instruments" in the GATT 1994 recognizes that the legal character of the rights and obligations of the contracting parties under the GATT 1994 is not fully reflected by the text of the GATT 1994 because those rights and obligations are conditioned by the "protocols", "decisions" and other "legal instruments" to which paragraph 1(b) refers.

Relationship between the GATT 1994 and the Agreement on Agriculture. *See* Agreement on Agriculture, Relationship between the Agreement on Agriculture and the GATT 1994 (A.1.37)

Relationship between the GATT 1994 and the Anti-Dumping Agreement. *See* Anti-Dumping Agreement, Relationship between the Anti-Dumping Agreement and the GATT 1994 (A.3.64)

G.2.2 Relationship between the GATT 1994 and the GATS. *See also* GATS, Article I: Scope of application – Measures affecting trade in services (G.1.1)

G.2.2.1 *Canada – Periodicals*, p. 19, DSR 1997:I, p. 449 at 465
(WT/DS31/AB/R)

The entry into force of the GATS, as Annex 1B of the *WTO Agreement*, does not diminish the scope of application of the GATT 1994. . . .

We agree with the Panel's statement:

> The ordinary meaning of the texts of GATT 1994 and GATS as well as Article II:2 of the WTO Agreement, taken together, indicates that obligations under GATT 1994 and GATS can co-exist and that one does not override the other.

G.2.2.2 *EC – Bananas III*, para. 221
(WT/DS27/AB/R)

The second issue is whether the GATS and the GATT 1994 are mutually exclusive agreements. The GATS was not intended to deal with the same subject-matter as the GATT 1994. The GATS was intended to deal with a subject-matter not covered by the GATT 1994, that is, with trade in services. Thus, the GATS applies to the supply of services. It provides, *inter alia*, for both MFN treatment and national treatment for services and service suppliers. Given the respective scope of application of the two agreements, they may or may not overlap, depending on the nature of the measures at issue. Certain measures could be found to fall exclusively within the scope of the GATT 1994, when they affect trade in goods as goods. Certain measures could be found to fall exclusively within the scope of the GATS, when they affect the supply of services as services. There is yet a third category of measures that could be found to fall within the scope of both the GATT 1994 and the GATS. These are measures that involve a service relating to a particular good or a service supplied in conjunction with a particular good. In all such cases in this third category, the measure in question could be scrutinized under both the GATT 1994 and the GATS. However, while the same measure could be scrutinized under both agreements, the specific aspects of that measure examined under each agreement could be different. Under the GATT 1994, the focus is on how the measure affects the goods involved. Under the GATS, the focus is on how the measure affects the supply of the service or the service suppliers involved. Whether a certain measure affecting the supply of a service related to a particular good is scrutinized under the GATT 1994 or the GATS, or both, is a matter that can only be determined on a case-by-case basis. . . .

Relationship between the GATT 1994 and the Agreement on Import Licensing Procedures. *See* Licensing Agreement (L.2)

Relationship between the GATT 1994 and the Agreement on Safeguards. *See* Safeguards Agreement, Relationship between the Safeguards Agreement and the GATT 1994 (S.1.44)

Relationship between the GATT 1994 and the SCM Agreement. *See* SCM Agreement, Relationship between the SCM Agreement and the GATT 1994 (S.2.41)

Relationship between the GATT 1994 and the Schedules to the GATT 1994. *See* Tariff Concession (T.1)

G.3 General Exceptions: Article XX of the GATT 1994. *See also* General Exceptions: Article XIV of GATS (G.4)

G.3.1 Article XX – Two-tier analysis

G.3.1.1 *US – Gasoline*, p. 22, DSR 1996:I, p. 3 at 20
(WT/DS2/AB/R)

. . . In order that the justifying protection of Article XX may be extended to it, the measure at issue must not only come under one or another of the particular exceptions – paragraphs (a) to (j) – listed under Article XX; it must also satisfy the requirements imposed by the opening clauses of Article XX. The analysis is, in other words, two-tiered: first, provisional justification by reason of characterization of the measure under XX(g); second, further appraisal of the same measure under the introductory clauses of Article XX.

G.3.1.2 *US – Shrimp*, paras. 119–120
(WT/DS58/AB/R)

The sequence of steps indicated above in the analysis of a claim of justification under Article XX reflects, not inadvertence or random choice, but rather the fundamental structure and logic of Article XX. . . .

The task of interpreting the chapeau so as to prevent the abuse or misuse of the specific exemptions provided for in Article XX is rendered very difficult, if indeed it remains possible at all, where the interpreter (like the Panel in this case) has not first identified and examined the specific exception threatened with abuse....

G.3.2 Article XX(b) – Relationship with Article III

G.3.2.1 *EC – Asbestos*, para. 115
(WT/DS135/AB/R)

We do not agree with the Panel that considering evidence relating to the health risks associated with a product, under Article III:4, nullifies the effect of Article XX(b) of the GATT 1994. Article XX(b) allows a Member to "adopt and enforce" a measure, *inter alia*, necessary to protect human life or health, even though that measure is inconsistent with another provision of the GATT 1994. Article III:4 and Article XX(b) are distinct and independent provisions of the GATT 1994 each to be interpreted on its own. The scope and meaning of Article III:4 should not be broadened or restricted beyond what is required by the normal customary international law rules of treaty interpretation, simply because Article XX(b) exists and may be available to justify measures inconsistent with Article III:4. The fact that an interpretation of Article III:4, under those rules, implies a less frequent recourse to Article XX(b) does not deprive the exception in Article XX(b) of *effet utile*. Article XX(b) would only be deprived of *effet utile* if that provision could *not* serve to allow a Member to "adopt and enforce" measures "necessary to protect human ... life or health". Evaluating evidence relating to the health risks arising from the physical properties of a product does not prevent a measure which is inconsistent with Article III:4 from being justified under Article XX(b). We note, in this regard, that, different inquiries occur under these two very different Articles. Under Article III:4, evidence relating to health risks may be relevant in assessing the *competitive relationship in the marketplace* between allegedly "like" products. The same, or similar, evidence serves a different purpose under Article XX(b), namely, that of assessing whether a *Member* has a sufficient basis for "adopting or enforcing" a WTO-inconsistent measure on the grounds of human health.

G.3.3 Article XX(b) – Evidence. *See also* General Exceptions: Article XX of the GATT 1994, Article XX(d) – Necessity test (G.3.6)

G.3.3.1 *EC – Asbestos*, para. 178
(WT/DS135/AB/R)

... In justifying a measure under Article XX(b) of the GATT 1994, a Member may also rely, in good faith, on scientific sources which, at that time, may represent a divergent, but qualified and respected, opinion. A Member is not obliged, in setting health policy, automatically to follow what, at a given time, may constitute a majority scientific opinion. Therefore, a panel need not, necessarily, reach a decision under Article XX(b) of the GATT 1994 on the basis of the "preponderant" weight of the evidence.

G.3.4 Article XX(b) – Objective pursued – alternative measure

G.3.4.1 *EC – Asbestos*, para. 172
(WT/DS135/AB/R)

... In this case, the objective pursued by the measure is the preservation of human life and health through the elimination, or reduction, of the well-known, and life-threatening, health risks posed by asbestos fibres. The value pursued is both vital and important in the highest degree. The remaining question, then, is whether there is an alternative measure that would achieve the same end and that is less restrictive of trade than a prohibition.

G.3.5 Article XX(d) – Level of enforcement – alternative measure

G.3.5.1 *Korea – Various Measures on Beef*, para. 176
(WT/DS161/AB/R, WT/DS169/AB/R)

It is not open to doubt that Members of the WTO have the right to determine for themselves the level of enforcement of their WTO-consistent laws and regulations. We note that this has also been recognized by the panel in *United States – Section 337*, where it said: "The Panel wished to make it clear that this [the obligation to choose a reasonably available GATT-consistent or less inconsistent measure] does not mean that a contracting party could be asked to change its substantive patent law or its desired *level of enforcement* of that law....". (emphasis added) ...

G.3.6 Article XX(d) – Necessity test

G.3.6.1 *Korea – Various Measures on Beef*, para. 161
(WT/DS161/AB/R, WT/DS169/AB/R)

We believe that, as used in the context of Article XX(d), the reach of the word "necessary" is not limited to that which is "indispensable" or "of absolute necessity" or "inevitable". Measures which are indispensable or of absolute necessity or inevitable to secure compliance certainly fulfil the requirements of Article XX(d). But other measures, too, may fall within the ambit of this exception. As used in Article XX(d), the term "necessary" refers, in our view, to a range of degrees of necessity. At one end of this continuum lies "necessary" understood as "indispensable"; at the other end, is "necessary" taken to mean as "making a contribution to." We consider that a "necessary" measure is, in this continuum, located significantly closer to the pole of "indispensable" than to the opposite pole of simply "making a contribution to".

G.3.6.2 *Korea – Various Measures on Beef*, para. 162
(WT/DS161/AB/R, WT/DS169/AB/R)

... It seems to us that a treaty interpreter assessing a measure claimed to be necessary to secure compliance of a WTO-consistent law or regulation may, in appropriate cases, take into account the relative importance of the common interests or values that the law or regulation to be enforced is intended to protect. The more vital or important those common interests or values are, the easier it would be to accept as "necessary" a measure designed as an enforcement instrument.

G.3.6.3 *Korea – Various Measures on Beef*, para. 163
(WT/DS161/AB/R, WT/DS169/AB/R)

There are other aspects of the enforcement measure to be considered in evaluating that measure as "necessary". One is the extent to which the measure contributes to the realization of the end pursued, the securing of compliance with the law or regulation at issue. The greater the contribution, the more easily a measure might be considered to be "necessary". Another aspect is the extent to which the compliance measure produces restrictive effects on international commerce, that is, in respect of a measure inconsistent with Article III:4, restrictive effects *on imported goods*. A measure with a relatively slight impact upon imported products might more easily be considered as "necessary" than a measure with intense or broader restrictive effects.

G.3.6.4 *Korea – Various Measures on Beef*, para. 164
(WT/DS161/AB/R, WT/DS169/AB/R)

In sum, determination of whether a measure, which is not "indispensable", may nevertheless be "necessary" within the contemplation of Article XX(d), involves in every case a process of weighing and balancing a series of factors which prominently include the contribution made by the compliance measure to the enforcement of the law or regulation at issue, the importance of the common interests or values protected by that law or regulation, and the accompanying impact of the law or regulation on imports or exports.

G.3.6.5 *Dominican Republic – Import and Sale of Cigarettes*, para. 70
(WT/DS302/AB/R)

The Appellate Body Reports in *Korea – Various Measures on Beef, EC – Asbestos* and *US – Gambling* indicate that, in the assessment of whether a proposed alternative to the impugned measure is reasonably available, factors such as the trade impact of the measure, the importance of the interests protected by the measure, or the contribution of the measure to the realization of the end pursued, should be taken into account in the analysis. The weighing and balancing process of these three factors also informs the determination whether a WTO-consistent alternative measure which the Member concerned could reasonably be expected to employ is available, or whether a less WTO-inconsistent measure is reasonably available....

G.3.6.6 *Dominican Republic – Import and Sale of Cigarettes*, para. 72
(WT/DS302/AB/R)

Having assessed the importance of the interests protected by the tax stamp requirement, its trade impact, and its contribution to the realization of the end pursued, the Panel also considered whether a WTO-consistent alternative measure is reasonably available to secure compliance with the Dominican Republic's tax laws and regulations appropriate to the level of enforcement pursued by the Dominican

Republic. In the light of its analysis of the relevant factors, especially the measure's contribution to the realization of the end pursued, the Panel opined that the alternative of providing secure tax stamps to foreign exporters, so that those tax stamps could be affixed on cigarette packets in the course of their own production process, prior to importation, would be equivalent to the tax stamp requirement in terms of allowing the Dominican Republic to secure the high level of enforcement it pursues with regard to tax collection and the prevention of cigarette smuggling. The Panel gave substantial weight to its finding that the tax stamp requirement is of limited effectiveness in preventing tax evasion and cigarette smuggling; in particular, it found "no evidence to conclude that the tax stamp requirement secures a zero tolerance level of enforcement with regard to tax collection and the prevention of cigarette smuggling." We consider that the Panel conducted an appropriate analysis, following the approach set out in *Korea – Various Measures on Beef* and in *EC – Asbestos*, and affirmed in *US – Gambling*. We see no reason to disturb the Panel's conclusions in respect of the existence of a reasonably available alternative measure to the tax stamp requirement.

G.3.7 Article XX(g) – "conservation of exhaustible natural resources"

G.3.7.1 *US – Shrimp*, para. 128
(WT/DS58/AB/R)

. . . Textually, Article XX(g) is *not* limited to the conservation of "mineral" or "non-living" natural resources. The complainants' principal argument is rooted in the notion that "living" natural resources are "renewable" and therefore cannot be "exhaustible" natural resources. We do not believe that "exhaustible" natural resources and "renewable" natural resources are mutually exclusive. One lesson that modern biological sciences teach us is that living species, though in principle, capable of reproduction and, in that sense, "renewable", are in certain circumstances indeed susceptible of depletion, exhaustion and extinction, frequently because of human activities. Living resources are just as "finite" as petroleum, iron ore and other non-living resources.

G.3.7.2 *US – Shrimp*, para. 130
(WT/DS58/AB/R)

From the perspective embodied in the preamble of the *WTO Agreement*, we note that the generic term "natural resources" in Article XX(g) is not "static" in its content or reference but is rather "by definition, evolutionary". It is, therefore, pertinent to note that modern international conventions and declarations make frequent references to natural resources as embracing both living and non-living resources. . . .

G.3.7.3 *US – Shrimp*, para. 153
(WT/DS58/AB/R)

[The language of the Preamble of the *WTO Agreement*] demonstrates a recognition by WTO negotiators that optimal use of the world's resources should be made in accordance with the objective of sustainable development. As this preambular language reflects the intentions of negotiators of the *WTO Agreement*, we believe it must add colour, texture and shading to our interpretation of the agreements annexed to the *WTO Agreement*, in this case, the GATT 1994. We have already observed that Article XX(g) of the GATT 1994 is appropriately read with the perspective embodied in the above preamble.

G.3.8 Article XX(g) – "measures made effective in conjunction with"

G.3.8.1 *US – Gasoline*, pp. 20–21, DSR 1996:I, p. 3 at 19–20
(WT/DS2/AB/R)

. . . the clause "if such measures are made effective in conjunction with restrictions on domestic product or consumption" is appropriately read as a requirement that the measures concerned impose restrictions, not just in respect of imported gasoline but also with respect to domestic gasoline. The clause is a requirement of *even-handedness* in the imposition of restrictions, in the name of conservation, upon the production or consumption of exhaustible natural resources.

. . . if *no* restrictions on domestically-produced like products are imposed at all, and all limitations are placed upon imported products *alone*, the measure cannot be accepted as primarily or even substantially designed for implementing conservationist goals. The measure would simply be naked discrimination for protecting locally-produced goods.

We do not believe . . . that the clause "if made effective in conjunction with restrictions on domestic production or consumption" was intended to establish an empirical "effects test" for the availability of the Article XX(g) exception. . . .

G.3.8.2 *US – Shrimp*, paras. 144–145
(WT/DS58/AB/R)

. . . We believe that, in principle, Section 609 is an even-handed measure.

Accordingly, we hold that Section 609 is a measure made effective in conjunction with the restrictions on domestic harvesting of shrimp, as required by Article XX(g).

G.3.9 Article XX(g) – "relating to"

G.3.9.1 *US – Gasoline*, pp. 17–18, DSR 1996:I, p. 3 at 16
(WT/DS2/AB/R)

. . . In enumerating the various categories of governmental acts, laws or regulations which WTO Members may carry out or promulgate in pursuit of differing legitimate state policies or interests outside the realm of trade liberalization, Article XX uses different terms in respect of different categories:

> "necessary" – in paragraphs (a), (b) and (d); "essential" – in paragraph (j); "relating to" – in paragraphs (c), (e) and (g); "for the protection of" – in paragraph (f); "in pursuance of" – in paragraph (h); and "involving" – in paragraph (i).

It does not seem reasonable to suppose that the WTO Members intended to require, in respect of each and every category, the same kind or degree of connection or relationship between the measure under appraisal and the state interest or policy sought to be promoted or realized.

G.3.9.2 *US – Gasoline*, p. 18, DSR 1996:I, p. 3 at 16–17 (WT/DS2/AB/R)

. . . Article XX(g) and its phrase, "relating to the conservation of exhaustible natural resources," need to be read in context and in such a manner as to give effect to the purposes and objects of the *General Agreement*. The context of Article XX(g) includes the provisions of the rest of the *General Agreement*, including in particular Articles I, III and XI; conversely, the context of Articles I and III and XI includes Article XX. Accordingly, the phrase "relating to the conservation of exhaustible natural resources" may not be read so expansively as seriously to subvert the purpose and object of Article III:4. Nor may Article III:4 be given so broad a reach as effectively to emasculate Article XX(g) and the policies and interests it embodies. . . .

G.3.9.3 *US – Gasoline*, pp. 18–19, DSR 1996:I, p. 3 at 17 (WT/DS2/AB/R)

All the participants and the third participants in this appeal accept . . . that a measure must be "primarily aimed at" the conservation of exhaustible natural resources in order to fall within the scope of Article XX(g). Accordingly, we see no need to examine this point further, save, perhaps, to note that the phrase "primarily aimed at" is not itself treaty language and was not designed as a simple litmus test for inclusion or exclusion from Article XX(g).

G.3.9.4 *US – Gasoline*, p. 19, DSR 1996:I, p. 3 at 18 (WT/DS2/AB/R)

. . . We consider that, given that substantial relationship, the baseline establishment rules cannot be regarded as merely incidentally or inadvertently aimed at the conservation of clean air in the United States for the purposes of Article XX(g).

G.3.9.5 *US – Shrimp*, paras. 141–142 (WT/DS58/AB/R)

In its general design and structure, therefore, Section 609 is not a simple, blanket prohibition of the importation of shrimp imposed without regard to the consequences (or lack thereof) of the mode of harvesting employed upon the incidental capture and mortality of sea turtles. Focusing on the design of the measure here at stake, it appears to us that Section 609, *cum* implementing guidelines, is not disproportionately wide in its scope and reach in relation to the policy objective of protection and conservation of sea turtle species. The means are, in principle, reasonably related to the ends. The means and ends relationship between Section 609 and the legitimate policy of conserving an exhaustible, and, in fact, endangered species, is observably a close and real one....

In our view, therefore, Section 609 is a measure "relating to" the conservation of an exhaustible natural resource within the meaning of Article XX(g) of the GATT 1994.

G.3.10 Article XX(g) – Jurisdictional limitation. *See also* National Treatment, Relationship between Article III and Article XX (N.1.12)

G.3.10.1 *US – Shrimp*, para. 121
(WT/DS58/AB/R)

...conditioning access to a Member's domestic market on whether exporting Members comply with, or adopt, a policy or policies unilaterally prescribed by the importing Member may, to some degree, be a common aspect of measures falling within the scope of one or another of the exceptions (a) to (j) of Article XX. Paragraphs (a) to (j) comprise measures that are recognized as *exceptions to substantive obligations* established in the GATT 1994, because the domestic policies embodied in such measures have been recognized as important and legitimate in character. It is not necessary to assume that requiring from exporting countries compliance with, or adoption of, certain policies (although covered in principle by one or another of the exceptions) prescribed by the importing country, renders a measure *a priori* incapable of justification under Article XX. Such an interpretation renders most, if not all, of the specific exceptions of Article XX inutile, a result abhorrent to the principles of interpretation we are bound to apply.

G.3.10.2 *US – Shrimp (Article 21.5 – Malaysia)*, para. 138
(WT/DS58/AB/RW)

In our view, Malaysia overlooks the significance of this statement [in paragraph 121 of *US – Shrimp*]. Contrary to what Malaysia suggests, this statement is not "*dicta*". As we said before, it appears to us "that conditioning access to a Member's domestic market on whether exporting Members comply with, or adopt, a policy or policies unilaterally prescribed by the importing Member may, to some degree, be a common aspect of measures falling within the scope of one or another of the exceptions (a) to (j) of Article XX." This statement expresses a principle that was central to our ruling in *United States – Shrimp*.

G.3.10.3 *US – Shrimp*, para. 133
(WT/DS58/AB/R)

...We do not pass upon the question of whether there is an implied jurisdictional limitation in Article XX(g), and if so, the nature or extent of that limitation. We note only that in the specific circumstances of the case before us, there is a sufficient nexus between the migratory and endangered marine populations involved and the United States for purposes of Article XX(g).

G.3.11 Chapeau of Article XX – general

G.3.11.1 *US – Gasoline*, p. 22, DSR 1996:I, p. 3 at 20
(WT/DS2/AB/R)

The chapeau by its express terms addresses, not so much the questioned measure or its specific contents as such, but rather the manner in which that measure is applied. It is, accordingly, important to underscore that the purpose and object of the introductory clauses of Article XX is generally the prevention of "abuse of the exceptions. . . ." . . .

G.3.11.2 *US – Gasoline*, p. 22, DSR 1996:I, p. 3 at 21
(WT/DS2/AB/R)

. . . If those exceptions are not to be abused or misused, in other words, the measures falling within the particular exceptions must be applied reasonably, with due regard both to the legal duties of the party claiming the exception and the legal rights of the other parties concerned.

G.3.11.3 *US – Gasoline*, p. 23, DSR 1996:I, p. 3 at 21
(WT/DS2/AB/R)

. . . The provisions of the chapeau cannot logically refer to the same standard(s) by which a violation of a substantive rule has been determined to have occurred. . . .

G.3.11.4 *US – Gasoline*, p. 25, DSR 1996:I, p. 3 at 23
(WT/DS2/AB/R)

"Arbitrary discrimination", "unjustifiable discrimination" and "disguised restriction" on international trade may, accordingly, be read side-by-side; they impart meaning to one another. It is clear to us that "disguised restriction" includes disguised *discrimination* in international trade. It is equally clear that *concealed* or *unannounced* restriction or discrimination in international trade does *not* exhaust the meaning of "disguised restriction." . . .

G.3.11.5 *US – Shrimp*, para. 159
(WT/DS58/AB/R)

The task of interpreting and applying the chapeau is, hence, essentially the delicate one of locating and marking out a line of equilibrium between the right of a Member to invoke an exception under Article XX and the rights of the other Members under varying substantive provisions (e.g., Article XI) of the GATT 1994, so that neither of the competing rights will cancel out the other and thereby distort and nullify or impair the balance of rights and obligations constructed by the Members themselves in that Agreement. The location of the line of equilibrium, as expressed in the chapeau, is not fixed and unchanging; the line moves as the kind and the shape of the measures at stake vary and as the facts making up specific cases differ.

G.3.11.6 *US – Shrimp*, paras. 156–157
(WT/DS58/AB/R)

. . . we consider that [the chapeau of Article XX] embodies the recognition on the part of WTO Members of the need to maintain a balance of rights and obligations between the right of a Member to invoke one or another of the exceptions of Article XX, specified in paragraphs (a) to (j), on the one hand, and the substantive rights of the other Members under the GATT 1994, on the other hand. Exercise by one Member of its right to invoke an exception, such as Article XX(g), if abused or misused, will, to that extent, erode or render naught the substantive treaty rights in, for example, Article XI:1, of other Members. Similarly, because the GATT 1994 itself makes available the exceptions of Article XX, in recognition of the legitimate nature of the policies and interests there embodied, the right to invoke one of those exceptions is not to be rendered illusory. The same concept may be expressed from a slightly different angle of vision, thus, a balance must be struck between the *right* of a Member to invoke an exception under Article XX and the *duty* of that same Member to respect the treaty rights of the other Members. . . .

In our view, the language of the chapeau makes clear that each of the exceptions in paragraphs (a) to (j) of Article XX is a *limited and conditional* exception from the substantive obligations contained in the other provisions of the GATT 1994, that is to say, the ultimate availability of the exception is subject to the compliance by the invoking Member with the requirements of the chapeau. . . .

G.3.11.7 *US – Shrimp*, para. 160
(WT/DS58/AB/R)

. . . We note, preliminarily, that the application of a measure may be characterized as amounting to an abuse or misuse of an exception of Article XX not only when the detailed operating provisions of the measure prescribe the arbitrary or unjustifiable activity, but also where a measure, otherwise fair and just on its face, is actually applied in an arbitrary or unjustifiable manner. The standards of the chapeau, in our view, project both substantive and procedural requirements.

G.3.11.8 *US – Shrimp (Article 21.5 – Malaysia)*, para. 118
(WT/DS58/AB/RW)

The chapeau of Article XX establishes three standards regarding the *application* of measures for which justification under Article XX may be sought: first, there must be no "arbitrary" discrimination between countries where the same conditions prevail; second, there must be no "unjustifiable" discrimination between countries where the same conditions prevail; and, third, there must be no "disguised restriction on international trade". The Panel's findings appealed by Malaysia concern the first and second of these three standards.

G.3.12 Chapeau of Article XX – "arbitrary or unjustifiable discrimination between countries where the same conditions prevail"

G.3.12.1 *US – Gasoline*, pp. 23–24, DSR 1996:I, p. 3 at 22
(WT/DS2/AB/R)

. . . It was asked whether the words incorporated into the first two standards "between countries where the same conditions prevail" refer to conditions in importing and exporting countries, or only to conditions in exporting countries. The reply of the United States was to the effect that it interpreted that phrase as referring to both the exporting countries and importing countries and as between exporting countries. . . . At no point in the appeal was that assumption challenged by Venezuela or Brazil. . . .

. . . we see no need to decide the matter of the field of application of the standards set forth in the chapeau nor to make a ruling at variance with the common understanding of the participants.

G.3.12.2 *US – Shrimp*, para. 150
(WT/DS58/AB/R)

. . . In order for a measure to be applied in a manner which would constitute "arbitrary or unjustifiable discrimination between countries where the same conditions prevail", three elements must exist. First, the application of the measure must result in *discrimination*. As we stated in *United States – Gasoline*, the nature and quality of this discrimination is different from the discrimination in the treatment of products which was already found to be inconsistent with one of the substantive obligations of the GATT 1994, such as Articles I, III or XI. Second, the discrimination must be *arbitrary* or *unjustifiable* in character. We will examine this element of *arbitrariness* or *unjustifiability* in detail below. Third, this discrimination must occur *between countries where the same conditions prevail*. In *United States – Gasoline*, we accepted the assumption of the participants in that appeal that such discrimination could occur not only between different exporting Members, but also between exporting Members and the importing Member concerned. Thus, the standards embodied in the language of the chapeau are not only different from the requirements of Article XX(g); they are also different from the standard used in determining that Section 609 is violative of the substantive rules of Article XI:1 of the GATT 1994.

G.3.12.3 *US – Shrimp*, paras. 164–165
(WT/DS58/AB/R)

. . . It may be quite acceptable for a government, in adopting and implementing a domestic policy, to adopt a single standard applicable to all its citizens throughout that country. However, it is not acceptable, in international trade relations, for one WTO Member to use an economic embargo to "*require* other Members to adopt essentially the same comprehensive regulatory program, to achieve a certain policy goal, as that in force within that Member's territory, "*without* taking into consideration different conditions which may occur in the territories of those other Members.

... We believe that discrimination results not only when countries in which the same conditions prevail are differently treated, but also when the application of the measure at issue does not allow for any inquiry into the appropriateness of the regulatory program for the conditions prevailing in those exporting countries.

G.3.12.4 *US – Shrimp*, para. 177

(WT/DS58/AB/R)

... Section 609, in its application, imposes a single, rigid and unbending requirement that countries applying for certification ... adopt a comprehensive regulatory program that is essentially the same as the United States' program, without inquiring into the appropriateness of that program for the conditions prevailing in the exporting countries. Furthermore, there is little or no flexibility in how officials make the determination for certification pursuant to these provisions. In our view, this rigidity and inflexibility also constitute "arbitrary discrimination" within the meaning of the chapeau.

G.3.12.5 *US – Shrimp (Article 21.5 – Malaysia)*, paras. 122–123

(WT/DS58/AB/RW)

We concluded in *United States – Shrimp* that, to avoid "arbitrary or unjustifiable discrimination", the United States had to provide all exporting countries "similar opportunities to negotiate" an international agreement. Given the specific mandate contained in Section 609, and given the decided preference for multilateral approaches voiced by WTO Members and others in the international community in various international agreements for the protection and conservation of endangered sea turtles that were cited in our previous Report, the United States, in our view, would be expected to make good faith efforts to reach international agreements that are comparable from one forum of negotiation to the other. The negotiations need not be identical. Indeed, no two negotiations can ever be identical, or lead to identical results. Yet the negotiations must be *comparable* in the sense that comparable efforts are made, comparable resources are invested, and comparable energies are devoted to securing an international agreement. So long as such comparable efforts are made, it is more likely that "arbitrary or unjustifiable discrimination" will be avoided between countries where an importing Member concludes an agreement with one group of countries, but fails to do so with another group of countries.

Under the chapeau of Article XX, an importing Member may not treat its trading partners in a manner that would constitute "arbitrary or unjustifiable discrimination". With respect to this measure, the United States could conceivably respect this obligation, and the conclusion of an international agreement might nevertheless not be possible despite the serious, good faith efforts of the United States. Requiring that a multilateral agreement be *concluded* by the United States in order to avoid "arbitrary or unjustifiable discrimination" in applying its measure would mean that any country party to the negotiations with the United States, whether a WTO

Member or not, would have, in effect, a veto over whether the United States could fulfill its WTO obligations. Such a requirement would not be reasonable. For a variety of reasons, it may be possible to conclude an agreement with one group of countries but not another. The conclusion of a multilateral agreement requires the cooperation and commitment of many countries. In our view, the United States cannot be held to have engaged in "arbitrary or unjustifiable discrimination" under Article XX solely because one international negotiation resulted in an agreement while another did not.

G.3.12.6 *US – Shrimp (Article 21.5 – Malaysia)*, para. 124 (WT/DS58/AB/RW)

As we stated in *United States – Shrimp* [Appellate Body Report, para. 168], "the protection and conservation of highly migratory species of sea turtles . . . demands concerted and cooperative efforts on the part of the many countries whose waters are traversed in the course of recurrent sea turtle migrations". Further, the "need for, and the appropriateness of, such efforts have been recognized in the WTO itself as well as in a significant number of other international instruments and declarations". For example, Principle 12 of the Rio Declaration on Environment and Development states, in part, that "[e]nvironmental measures addressing transboundary or global environmental problems should, as far as possible, be based on international consensus". Clearly, and "as far as possible", a multilateral approach is strongly preferred. Yet it is one thing to *prefer* a multilateral approach in the application of a measure that is provisionally justified under one of the subparagraphs of Article XX of the GATT 1994; it is another to require the *conclusion* of a multilateral agreement as a condition of avoiding "arbitrary or unjustifiable discrimination" under the chapeau of Article XX. We see, in this case, no such requirement.

G.3.12.7 *US – Shrimp (Article 21.5 – Malaysia)*, para. 130 (WT/DS58/AB/RW)

. . . The Panel compared the efforts of the United States to negotiate the Inter-American Convention with one group of exporting WTO Members with the efforts made by the United States to negotiate a similar agreement with another group of exporting WTO Members. The Panel rightly used the Inter-American Convention as a factual reference in this exercise of comparison. It was all the more relevant to do so given that the Inter-American Convention was the only international agreement that the Panel could have used in such a comparison. As we read the Panel Report, it is clear to us that the Panel attached a relative value to the Inter-American Convention in making this comparison, but did not view the Inter-American Convention in any way as an absolute standard. Thus, we disagree with Malaysia's submission that the Panel raised the Inter-American Convention to the rank of a "legal standard". The mere use by the Panel of the Inter-American Convention *as a basis for a comparison* did not transform the Inter-American Convention into a "legal standard". Furthermore, although the Panel could have chosen a more appropriate word than "benchmark" to express its views, Malaysia is mistaken in equating the mere use of the word "benchmark", as it was used by the Panel, with the establishment of a legal standard.

G.3.12.8 *US – Shrimp (Article 21.5 – Malaysia)*, para. 144 (WT/DS58/AB/RW)

In our view, there is an important difference between conditioning market access on the adoption of essentially the same programme, and conditioning market access on the adoption of a programme *comparable in effectiveness*. Authorizing an importing Member to condition market access on exporting Members putting in place regulatory programmes *comparable in effectiveness* to that of the importing Member gives sufficient latitude to the exporting Member with respect to the programme it may adopt to achieve the level of effectiveness required. It allows the exporting Member to adopt a regulatory programme that is suitable to the specific conditions prevailing in its territory. As we see it, the Panel correctly reasoned and concluded that conditioning market access on the adoption of a programme *comparable in effectiveness*, allows for sufficient flexibility in the application of the measure so as to avoid "arbitrary or unjustifiable discrimination". We, therefore, agree with the conclusion of the Panel on "comparable effectiveness".

G.3.12.9 *US – Shrimp (Article 21.5 – Malaysia)*, paras. 149–150 (WT/DS58/AB/RW)

We need only say here that, in our view, a measure should be designed in such a manner that there is sufficient flexibility to take into account the specific conditions prevailing in *any* exporting Member, including, of course, Malaysia. Yet this is not the same as saying that there must be specific provisions in the measure aimed at addressing specifically the particular conditions prevailing in *every individual* exporting Member. Article XX of the GATT 1994 does not require a Member to anticipate and provide explicitly for the specific conditions prevailing and evolving in *every individual* Member.

We are, therefore, not persuaded by Malaysia's argument that the measure at issue is not flexible enough because the Revised Guidelines do not explicitly address the specific conditions prevailing in Malaysia.

G.3.13 Chapeau of Article XX – "disguised restriction on international trade"

G.3.13.1 *US – Gasoline*, p. 25, DSR 1996:I, p. 3 at 23 (WT/DS2/AB/R)

. . . It is equally clear that *concealed* or *unannounced* restriction or discrimination in international trade does *not* exhaust the meaning of "disguised restriction." We consider that "disguised restriction", whatever else it covers, may properly be read as embracing restrictions amounting to arbitrary or unjustifiable discrimination in international trade taken under the guise of a measure formally within the terms of an exception listed in Article XX. Put in a somewhat different manner, the kinds of considerations pertinent in deciding whether the application of a particular measure amounts to "arbitrary or unjustifiable discrimination", may also be taken into account in determining the presence of a "disguised restriction" on international trade. The fundamental theme is to be found in the purpose and object of avoiding abuse or illegitimate use of the exceptions to substantive rules available in Article XX.

G.4 General Exceptions: Article XIV of GATS

G.4.1 Relationship to Article XX of the GATT 1994

G.4.1.1 *US – Gambling*, para. 291
(WT/DS285/AB/R)

Article XIV of the GATS sets out the general exceptions from obligations under that Agreement in the same manner as does Article XX of the GATT 1994. Both of these provisions affirm the right of Members to pursue objectives identified in the paragraphs of these provisions even if, in doing so, Members act inconsistently with obligations set out in other provisions of the respective agreements, provided that all of the conditions set out therein are satisfied. Similar language is used in both provisions, notably the term "necessary" and the requirements set out in their respective chapeaux. Accordingly, like the Panel, we find previous decisions under Article XX of the GATT 1994 relevant for our analysis under Article XIV of the GATS.

G.4.1.2 *US – Gambling*, para. 292
(WT/DS285/AB/R)

Article XIV of the GATS, like Article XX of the GATT 1994, contemplates a "two-tier analysis" of a measure that a Member seeks to justify under that provision. A panel should first determine whether the challenged measure falls within the scope of one of the paragraphs of Article XIV. This requires that the challenged measure address the particular interest specified in that paragraph and that there be a sufficient nexus between the measure and the interest protected. The required nexus – or "degree of connection" – between the measure and the interest is specified in the language of the paragraphs themselves, through the use of terms such as "relating to" and "necessary to". Where the challenged measure has been found to fall within one of the paragraphs of Article XIV, a panel should then consider whether that measure satisfies the requirements of the chapeau of Article XIV.

G.4.2 Article XIV(a) – "public morals" and "public order"

G.4.2.1 *US – Gambling*, para. 296
(WT/DS285/AB/R)

In its analysis under Article XIV(a), the Panel found that "the term 'public morals' denotes standards of right and wrong conduct maintained by or on behalf of a community or nation." The Panel further found that the definition of the term "order", read in conjunction with footnote 5 of the GATS, "suggests that 'public order' refers to the preservation of the fundamental interests of a society, as reflected in public policy and law." The Panel then referred to Congressional reports and testimony establishing that "the government of the United States consider[s] [that the Wire Act, the Travel Act, and the IGBA] were adopted to address concerns such as those pertaining to money laundering, organized crime, fraud, underage gambling and pathological gambling." On this basis, the Panel found that the three federal statutes are "measures that are designed to 'protect public morals' and/or 'to maintain public order' within the meaning of Article XIV(a)."

G.4.2.2 *US – Gambling*, paras. 297–298
(WT/DS285/AB/R)

Antigua contests [the Panel's finding under Article XIV(a)] on a rather limited ground, namely that the Panel failed to determine whether the concerns identified by the United States satisfy the standard set out in footnote 5 to Article XIV(a) of the GATS, which reads:

> [t]he public order exception may be invoked only where a genuine and sufficiently serious threat is posed to one of the fundamental interests of society.

We see no basis to conclude that the Panel failed to assess whether the standard set out in footnote 5 had been satisfied. As Antigua acknowledges, the Panel expressly referred to footnote 5 in a way that demonstrated that it understood the requirement therein to be part of the meaning given to the term "public order". Although "*no further mention*" was made in the Panel Report of footnote 5 or of its text, this alone does not establish that the Panel failed to assess whether the interests served by the three federal statutes satisfy the footnote's criteria. Having defined "public order" to include the standard in footnote 5, and then applied that definition to the facts before it to conclude that the measures "are designed to 'protect public morals' and/or 'to maintain public order' ", the Panel was not required, in addition, to make a separate, explicit determination that the standard of footnote 5 had been met.

G.4.3 Article XIV(a) – Burden of proof

G.4.3.1 *US – Gambling*, paras. 309–310
(WT/DS285/AB/R)

It is well-established that a responding party invoking an affirmative defence bears the burden of demonstrating that its measure, found to be WTO-inconsistent, satisfies the requirements of the invoked defence. In the context of Article XIV(a), this means that the responding party must show that its measure is "necessary" to achieve objectives relating to public morals or public order. In our view, however, it is not the responding party's burden to show, in the first instance, that there are *no* reasonably available alternatives to achieve its objectives. In particular, a responding party need not identify the universe of less trade-restrictive alternative measures and then show that none of those measures achieves the desired objective. The WTO agreements do not contemplate such an impracticable and, indeed, often impossible burden.

Rather, it is for a responding party to make a *prima facie* case that its measure is "necessary" by putting forward evidence and arguments that enable a panel to assess the challenged measure in the light of the relevant factors to be "weighed and balanced" in a given case. The responding party may, in so doing, point out why alternative measures would not achieve the same objectives as the challenged measure, but it is under no obligation to do so in order to establish, in the first instance, that its measure is "necessary". If the panel concludes that the respondent has made a *prima facie* case that the challenged measure is "necessary" – that is, "significantly closer to the pole of 'indispensable' than to the opposite pole of simply 'making a contribution to' " – then a panel should find that challenged measure "necessary" within the terms of Article XIV(a) of the GATS.

G.4.3.2 *US – Gambling*, para. 311
(WT/DS285/AB/R)

If, however, the complaining party raises a WTO-consistent alternative measure that, in its view, the responding party should have taken, the responding party will be required to demonstrate why its challenged measure nevertheless remains "necessary" in the light of that alternative or, in other words, why the proposed alternative is not, in fact, "reasonably available". If a responding party demonstrates that the alternative is not "reasonably available", in the light of the interests or values being pursued and the party's desired level of protection, it follows that the challenged measure must be "necessary" within the terms of Article XIV(a) of the GATS.

G.4.3.3 *US – Gambling*, para. 323
(WT/DS285/AB/R)

. . . a responding party must make a *prima facie* case that its challenged measure is "necessary". A Panel determines whether this case is made through the identification, and weighing and balancing, of relevant factors, such as those in *Korea – Various Measures on Beef*, with respect to the measure challenged. . . .

G.4.4 Article XIV(a) – Necessity test – reasonably available alternative

G.4.4.1 *US – Gambling*, para. 304
(WT/DS285/AB/R)

. . . the standard of "necessity" provided for in the general exceptions provision is an *objective* standard. To be sure, a Member's characterization of a measure's objectives and of the effectiveness of its regulatory approach – as evidenced, for example, by texts of statutes, legislative history, and pronouncements of government agencies or officials – will be relevant in determining whether the measure is, objectively, "necessary". A panel is not bound by these characterizations, however, and may also find guidance in the structure and operation of the measure and in contrary evidence proffered by the complaining party. In any event, a panel must, on the basis of the evidence in the record, independently and objectively assess the "necessity" of the measure before it.

G.4.4.2 *US – Gambling*, paras. 306–308 (WT/DS285/AB/R)

The process [of weighing and balancing a series of factors in order to determine "necessity"] begins with an assessment of the "relative importance" of the interests or values furthered by the challenged measure. Having ascertained the importance of the particular interests at stake, a panel should then turn to the other factors that are to be "weighed and balanced". The Appellate Body has pointed to two factors that, in most cases, will be relevant to a panel's determination of the "necessity" of a measure, although not necessarily exhaustive of factors that might be considered. One factor is the contribution of the measure to the realization of the ends pursued by it; the other factor is the restrictive impact of the measure on international commerce.

A comparison between the challenged measure and possible alternatives should then be undertaken, and the results of such comparison should be considered in the light of the importance of the interests at issue. It is on the basis of this "weighing and balancing" and comparison of measures, taking into account the interests or values at stake, that a panel determines whether a measure is "necessary" or, alternatively, whether another, WTO-consistent measure is "reasonably available".

The requirement, under Article XIV(a), that a measure be "necessary" – that is, that there be no "reasonably available", WTO-consistent alternative – reflects the shared understanding of Members that substantive GATS obligations should not be deviated from lightly. An alternative measure may be found not to be "reasonably available", however, where it is merely theoretical in nature, for instance, where the responding Member is not capable of taking it, or where the measure imposes an undue burden on that Member, such as prohibitive costs or substantial technical difficulties. Moreover, a "reasonably available" alternative measure must be a measure that would preserve for the responding Member its right to achieve its desired level of protection with respect to the objective pursued under paragraph (a) of Article XIV.

G.4.4.3 *US – Gambling*, para. 315 (WT/DS285/AB/R)

In its "necessity" analysis under Article XIV(a), the Panel appeared to understand that, in order for a measure to be accepted as "necessary" under Article XIV(a), the responding Member must have first "*explored and exhausted*" all reasonably available WTO-compatible alternatives before adopting its WTO-inconsistent measure. This understanding led the Panel to conclude that, in this case, the United States had "an obligation to consult with Antigua before and while imposing its prohibition on the cross-border supply of gambling and betting services". Because the Panel found that the United States had not engaged in such consultations with Antigua, the Panel also found that the United States had not established that its measures are "necessary" and, therefore, provisionally justified under Article XIV(a).

G.4.4.4 *US – Gambling*, paras. 317–320 (WT/DS285/AB/R)

In our view, the Panel's "necessity" analysis was flawed because it did not focus on an alternative measure that was reasonably available to the United States to achieve the stated objectives regarding the protection of public morals or the maintenance of public order. Engaging in consultations with Antigua, with a view to arriving at a negotiated settlement that achieves the same objectives as the challenged United States' measures, was not an appropriate alternative for the Panel to consider because consultations are by definition a process, the results of which are uncertain and therefore not capable of comparison with the measures at issue in this case.

We note, in addition, that the Panel based its requirement of consultations, in part, on "the existence of [a] specific market access commitment [in the United States' GATS Schedule] with respect to cross-border trade of gambling and betting services". We do not see how the existence of a specific commitment in a Member's Schedule affects the "necessity" of a measure in terms of the protection of public morals or the maintenance of public order. For this reason as well, the Panel erred in relying on consultations as an alternative measure reasonably available to the United States.

. . . Antigua claims that the Panel "erred in limiting" its search for alternatives to the universe of *existing* United States regulatory measures. . . .

We observe, first, that the Panel did not state that it was limiting its search for alternatives in the manner alleged by Antigua. Secondly, although the Panel *began* its analysis of alternative measures by considering whether the United States already employs measures less restrictive than a prohibition to achieve the same objectives as the three federal statutes, its inquiry did not end there. The Panel obviously did consider alternatives *not* currently in place in the United States, as evidenced by its (ultimately erroneous) emphasis on the United States' alleged failure to pursue consultations with Antigua. Finally, we do not see why the Panel should have been expected to continue its analysis into additional alternative measures, which Antigua itself failed to identify. As we said above, it is not for the responding party to identify the universe of alternative measures against which its own measure should be compared. It is only if such an alternative is raised that this comparison is required. We therefore dismiss this aspect of Antigua's appeal.

G.4.4.5 *US – Gambling*, para. 332 (WT/DS285/AB/R)

Antigua additionally contends that the Panel acted inconsistently with Article 11 of the DSU because it undertook no assessment of factual evidence relating specifically to *Antiguan* gambling and betting services when evaluating whether the Wire Act, the Travel Act, and the IGBA are "necessary". To determine whether the statutes at issue are "necessary" under Article XIV(a), the Panel was called upon to assess the relationship between, on the one hand, the United States' restrictions on the remote supply of gambling, and, on the other hand, the "public moral"/"public order" interests identified by the United States as the reasons for the restrictions contained in the Wire Act, the Travel Act, and the IGBA. The United States did not explicitly identify either the *source of supply* or the *foreign nature* of the supply of gambling and betting services as a relevant concern. In other words, the evidence put before the Panel by the United States suggests that the nexus is with the remote supply of gambling services, regardless of its source or the national origin of the suppliers. Moreover, the statutes at issue make no distinction on their face as to gambling services from different origins; the Panel found simply that the statutes prohibit the remote supply of gambling and betting services. As a result, there was no need for the Panel to have analyzed evidence relating to the supply of gambling services specifically *from Antigua*, and we see no error in the Panel's decision not to make an assessment of the Antiguan industry.

G.4.5 Chapeau of Article XIV

G.4.5.1 *US – Gambling*, para. 339
(WT/DS285/AB/R)

. . . The focus of the chapeau, by its express terms, is on the *application* of a measure already found by the Panel to be inconsistent with one of the obligations under the GATS but falling within one of the paragraphs of Article XIV. By requiring that the measure be *applied* in a manner that does not . . . constitute "arbitrary" or "unjustifiable" discrimination, or a "disguised restriction on trade in services", the chapeau serves to ensure that Members' rights to avail themselves of exceptions are exercised reasonably, so as not to frustrate the rights accorded other Members by the substantive rules of the GATS.

G.4.5.2 *US – Gambling*, paras. 342–344
(WT/DS285/AB/R)

In deciding to assess whether the measures satisfied the requirements of the chapeau, the Panel explained that, even though such an examination was "not necessary", it wanted "to assist the parties in resolving the underlying dispute in this case." Antigua alleges that the Panel acted inconsistently with the Appellate Body's decision in *Korea – Various Measures on Beef* in determining whether the Wire Act, the Travel Act, and the IGBA meet the requirements of the chapeau after having found that they were not provisionally justified.

. . . [the statement by the Appellate Body at paragraph 156 of *Korea – Various Measures on Beef*] does not impose a *requirement* on panels to stop evaluating a responding party's defence once they have determined that a challenged measure is not provisionally justified under one of the paragraphs of the general exception provision.

Provided that it complies with its duty to assess a matter objectively, a panel enjoys the freedom to decide *which legal issues* it must address in order to resolve a dispute. Moreover, in some instances, a panel's decision to continue its legal analysis and to make factual findings beyond those that are strictly necessary to resolve the dispute may assist the Appellate Body should it later be called upon to complete the analysis, as, for example, in this case.

G.4.5.3 *US – Gambling*, paras. 349–351 (WT/DS285/AB/R)

The United States contends that . . . the Panel, in fact, assessed only whether the United States treats domestic service suppliers differently from foreign service suppliers. Such an assessment is inadequate, the United States argues, because the chapeau also requires a determination of whether differential treatment, or discrimination, is "arbitrary" or "unjustifiable".

The United States based its defence under the chapeau of Article XIV on the assertion that the measures at issue prohibit the remote supply of gambling and betting services by *any supplier*, whether domestic or foreign. In other words, the United States sought to justify the Wire Act, the Travel Act, and the IGBA on the basis that there is *no discrimination* in the manner in which the three federal statutes are applied to the remote supply of gambling and betting services. The United States could have, but did not, put forward an additional argument that *even if* such discrimination exists, it does not rise to the level of "arbitrary" or "unjustifiable" discrimination.

In the light of the arguments before it, we do not read the Panel to have ignored the requirement of "arbitrary" or "unjustifiable" discrimination by articulating the standard under the chapeau of Article XIV as one of "consistency". Rather, the Panel determined that Antigua had rebutted the United States' claim of no discrimination *at all* by showing that domestic service suppliers are permitted to provide remote gambling services in situations where foreign service suppliers are not so permitted. We see no error in the Panel's approach.

G.4.5.4 *US – Gambling*, para. 354 (WT/DS285/AB/R)

We observe, first, that none of the three federal statutes distinguishes, on its face, between domestic and foreign service suppliers. We agree with the Panel that, in the context of facially neutral measures, there may nevertheless be situations where the selective prosecution of persons rises to the level of discrimination. In our view, however, the evidence before the Panel could not justify finding that, notwithstanding the neutral language of the statute, the facts are "inconclusive" to establish "non-discrimination" in the United States' enforcement of the Wire Act. The Panel's conclusion rests, not only on an inadequate evidentiary foundation, but also on an incorrect understanding of the type of conduct that can, as a matter of law, be characterized as discrimination in the enforcement of measures.

I

Implementation of DSB Rulings Review. *See* Review of Implementation of DSB Rulings (R.4)

I.0 Implementation Recommendations – Article 19.1 of the DSU. *See also* SCM Agreement, Article 4.7 – "withdraw the subsidy without delay" (S.2.19); SCM Agreement, Article 7.8 – Remedies (S.2.19A)

I.0.1 *US – Upland Cotton*, paras. 272–273
(WT/DS267/AB/R)

The question whether an expired measure is susceptible to a recommendation under Article 19.1 of the DSU is a different matter. The Appellate Body in *US – Certain EC Products* confirmed that the 3 March Measure had ceased to exist. It noted that there was an obvious inconsistency between the finding of the panel that "the 3 March Measure is no longer in existence" and the panel's subsequent recommendation that the Dispute Settlement Body (the "DSB") request the United States to bring the 3 March Measure into conformity with its WTO obligations. Thus, the fact that a measure has expired may affect what recommendation a panel may make. It is not, however, dispositive of the preliminary question of whether a panel can address claims in respect of that measure.

. . . Article 7.8 of the *SCM Agreement* provides that, where it has been determined that "any subsidy has *resulted* in adverse effects to the interests of another Member", the subsidizing Member must "take appropriate steps *to remove the adverse effects* or . . . withdraw the subsidy". (emphasis added) The use of the word "resulted" suggests that there could be a time-lag between the payment of a subsidy and any consequential adverse effects. If expired measures underlying past payments could not be challenged in WTO dispute settlement proceedings, it would be difficult to seek a remedy for such adverse effects. Further – in contrast to Articles 3.7 and 19.1 of the DSU – the remedies under Article 7.8 of the *SCM Agreement* for adverse effects of a subsidy are (i) the withdrawal of the subsidy *or* (ii) the removal of adverse effects. Removal of adverse effects through actions other than the withdrawal of a subsidy could not occur if the expiration of a measure would automatically exclude it from a panel's terms of reference.

I.0.2 *EC – Export Subsidies on Sugar*, para. 332
(WT/DS265/AB/R, WT/DS266/AB/R, WT/DS283/AB/R)

Under Article 19.1 of the DSU, where a panel "concludes that a measure is inconsistent with a covered agreement, it shall recommend that the Member concerned bring the measure into conformity with that agreement". (footnote omitted) The panel is not required to make a recommendation as to how the Member should implement its obligations or as to the timeframe for implementation. However, Article 19.1 also provides that "[a] panel or [the] Appellate Body *may* suggest ways in which the Member concerned could implement the recommendations." (emphasis added)

Import Licensing. *See* Licensing Agreement (L.2)

Indirect Subsidization – Pass-Through. *See* SCM Agreement, Article VI:3 of the GATT 1994 – Subsidies (S.2.43)

I.1 Inferences Drawn from the Refusal of a Party to Provide Information. *See also* Business Confidential Information (B.4); Confidentiality (C.6); Seek Information and Technical Advice (S.4)

I.1.1 *Canada – Aircraft*, para. 187
(WT/DS70/AB/R)

. . . we are of the view that the word "should" in the third sentence of Article 13.1 is, in the context of the whole of Article 13, used in a normative, rather than a merely exhortative, sense. Members are, in other words, under a duty and an obligation to "respond promptly and fully" to requests made by panels for information under Article 13.1 of the DSU.

I.1.2 *Canada – Aircraft*, para. 203
(WT/DS70/AB/R)

Clearly, in our view, the Panel had the legal authority and the discretion to draw inferences from the facts before it – including the fact that Canada had refused to provide information sought by the Panel. . . .

I.1.3 *US – Wheat Gluten*, para. 171
(WT/DS166/AB/R)

. . . As the Appellate Body said in *Canada – Aircraft*, the refusal by a Member to provide information requested of it undermines seriously the ability of a panel to make an objective assessment of the facts and the matter, as required by Article 11 of the DSU. Such a refusal also undermines the ability of other Members of the WTO to seek the "prompt" and "satisfactory" resolution of disputes under the procedures "for which they bargained in concluding the DSU." . . .

I.1.4 *US – Wheat Gluten*, para. 173
(WT/DS166/AB/R)

We, therefore, characterized the drawing of inferences as a "discretionary" task falling within a panel's duties under Article 11 of the DSU. . . .

I.1.5 *US – Wheat Gluten*, para. 174
(WT/DS166/AB/R)

. . . As we emphasized in *Canada – Aircraft*, under Article 11 of the DSU, a panel must draw inferences on the basis of *all of the facts of record* relevant to the particular determination to be made. Where a party refuses to provide information requested by a panel under Article 13.1 of the DSU, that refusal will be one of the relevant facts of record, and indeed an important fact, to be taken into account in determining the appropriate inference to be drawn. However, if a panel were to ignore or disregard other relevant facts, it would fail to make an "objective assessment" under Article 11 of the DSU. In this case, as the Panel observed, there *were* other facts of record that the Panel was required to include in its "objective assessment". . . .

I.1.6 *US – Wheat Gluten*, para. 175
(WT/DS166/AB/R)

In reviewing the inferences the Panel drew from the facts of record, our task on appeal is not to redo afresh the Panel's assessment of those facts, and decide for ourselves what inferences we would draw from them. Rather, we must determine whether the Panel improperly exercised its discretion, under Article 11, by failing to draw certain inferences from the facts before it. In asking us to conduct such a review, an appellant must indicate clearly the manner in which a panel has improperly exercised its discretion. Taking into account the full *ensemble* of the facts, the appellant should, at least: identify the facts on the record from which the Panel should have drawn inferences; indicate the factual or legal inferences that the panel should have drawn from those facts; and, finally, explain why the failure of the panel to exercise its discretion by drawing these inferences amounts to an error of law under Article 11 of the DSU.

Internal Taxation Regulation. *See* National Treatment, Article III:2, first and second sentences (N.1.3–8); Taxation (T.3)

I.2 International Monetary Fund – "Coherence"

I.2.1 *Argentina – Textiles and Apparel*, para. 74
(WT/DS56/AB/R, WT/DS56/AB/R/Corr.1)

We agree, therefore, with the Panel that there is "nothing in the Agreement Between the IMF and the WTO, the Declaration on the Relationship of the World Trade Organization with the International Monetary Fund and the Declaration on the

Contribution of the World Trade Organization to Achieving Greater Coherence in Global Economic Policy-making" that modifies Argentina's obligations under Article VIII of the GATT 1994. We also agree with the Panel that there is "... no exception in the WTO Agreement that would excuse Argentina's compliance with the requirements of Article VIII of GATT." ...

I.2.2 *Argentina – Textiles and Apparel*, paras. 84–85 (WT/DS56/AB/R, WT/DS56/AB/R/Corr.1)

The only provision of the *WTO Agreement* that *requires* consultations with the IMF is Article XV:2 of the GATT 1994. This provision *requires* the WTO to consult with the IMF when dealing with "problems concerning monetary reserves, balances of payments or foreign exchange arrangements"....

As in the *WTO Agreement*, there are no provisions in the *Agreement Between the IMF and the WTO* that *require* a panel to consult with the IMF in a case such as this. Under paragraph 8 of this latter Agreement, in a case involving "exchange measures within the Fund's jurisdiction", the IMF "shall inform in writing the relevant WTO body (including dispute settlement panels) ... whether such measures are consistent with the Articles of Agreement of the Fund." This case does not, however, involve "exchange measures within the Fund's jurisdiction". Paragraph 8 also provides that the IMF "may communicate its views in writing on matters of mutual interest to the [WTO] or any of its organs or bodies (*excluding the WTO's dispute settlement panels*) ... " (emphasis added). Evidently, the IMF has not been authorized to provide its views to a WTO dispute settlement panel on matters *not* relating to exchange measures within its jurisdiction, unless it is requested to do so by a panel under Article 13 of the DSU.

I.2.3 *India – Quantitative Restrictions*, paras. 149, 151–152 (WT/DS90/AB/R)

On the basis of these provisions, the Panel submitted to the IMF a number of questions regarding India's balance-of-payments situation. The Panel gave considerable weight to the views expressed by the IMF in its reply to these questions. However, nothing in the Panel Report supports India's argument that the Panel delegated to the IMF its judicial function to make an objective assessment of the matter. A careful reading of the Panel Report makes clear that the Panel did not simply accept the views of the IMF. The Panel critically assessed these views and also considered other data and opinions in reaching its conclusions.

...

We conclude that the Panel made an objective assessment of the matter before it. Therefore, we do not agree with India that the Panel acted inconsistently with Article 11 of the DSU.

The question whether Article XV:2 of the GATT 1994 requires panels to consult with the IMF and to consider *as dispositive* specific determinations of the IMF was debated at length by the parties before the Panel. However, the Panel did not consider it necessary, for the purposes of this dispute, to decide this issue. As this finding of the Panel is not appealed, we abstain from taking any position on it.

I.3 Interpretation. *See also* Anti-Dumping Agreement, Article 17.6(ii) – "permissible interpretations" (A.3.60)

I.3.1 General rules of treaty interpretation – Article 31 of the Vienna Convention

I.3.1.1 *US – Gasoline,* p. 17, DSR 1996:I, p. 3 at 16
(WT/DS2/AB/R)

The general rule of interpretation [as set out in Article 31(1) of the Vienna Convention on the Law of Treaties] has attained the status of a rule of customary or general international law. As such, it forms part of the "customary rules of interpretation of public international law" which the Appellate Body has been directed, by Article 3(2) of the *DSU*, to apply in seeking to clarify the provisions of the *General Agreement* and the other "covered agreements" of the *Marrakesh Agreement Establishing the World Trade Organization* (the "*WTO Agreement*"). That direction reflects a measure of recognition that the *General Agreement* is not to be read in clinical isolation from public international law.

I.3.1.2 *Japan – Alcoholic Beverages II,* p. 34, DSR 1996:I, p. 97 at 122–123
(WT/DS8/AB/R, WT/DS10/AB/R, WT/DS11/AB/R)

. . . WTO rules are reliable, comprehensible and enforceable. WTO rules are not so rigid or so inflexible as not to leave room for reasoned judgements in confronting the endless and ever-changing ebb and flow of real facts in real cases in the real world. They will serve the multilateral trading system best if they are interpreted with that in mind. In that way, we will achieve the "security and predictability" sought for the multilateral trading system by the Members of the WTO through the establishment of the dispute settlement system.

I.3.1.3 *India – Patents (US)*, para. 46
(WT/DS50/AB/R)

. . . These rules must be respected and applied in interpreting the *TRIPS Agreement* or any other covered agreement. . . . Both panels and the Appellate Body must be guided by the rules of treaty interpretation set out in the *Vienna Convention*, and must not add to or diminish rights and obligations provided in the *WTO Agreement*.

I.3.1.4 *Argentina – Textiles and Apparel*, para. 42
(WT/DS56/AB/R, WT/DS56/AB/R/Corr.1)

. . . The Panel relies heavily on what it characterizes as "past GATT practice", without undertaking any analysis of the ordinary meaning of the terms of Article in their context and in the light of the object and purpose of the GATT 1994, in accordance with the general rules of treaty interpretation set out in Article 31 of the *Vienna Convention*. . . .

I.3.1.5 *US – Carbon Steel*, paras. 61–62
(WT/DS213/AB/R, WT/DS213/AB/R/Corr.1)

. . . we recall that Article 3.2 of the DSU recognizes that interpretative issues arising in WTO dispute settlement are to be resolved through the application of customary rules of interpretation of public international law. It is well settled in WTO case law that the principles codified in Articles 31 and 32 of the *Vienna Convention on the Law of Treaties* (the "*Vienna Convention*") are such customary rules. . . .

. . . the task of interpreting a treaty provision must begin with its specific terms. . . .

I.3.2 Text. *See also* Interpretation, Legitimate expectations (I.3.5); Municipal Law (M.5)

I.3.2.1 *Japan – Alcoholic Beverages II,* p. 12, DSR 1996:I, p. 97 at 105
(WT/DS8/AB/R, WT/DS10/AB/R, WT/DS11/AB/R)

Article 31 of the *Vienna Convention* provides that the words of the treaty form the foundation for the interpretive process: "interpretation must be based above all upon the text of the treaty". . . .

I.3.2.2 *EC – Hormones*, para. 181
(WT/DS26/AB/R, WT/DS48/AB/R)

. . . The fundamental rule of treaty interpretation requires a treaty interpreter to read and interpret the words actually used by the agreement under examination, not words the interpreter may feel should have been used.

I.3.2.3 *India – Patents (US)*, para. 45
(WT/DS50/AB/R)

. . . The duty of a treaty interpreter is to examine the words of the treaty to determine the intentions of the parties. This should be done in accordance with the principles of treaty interpretation set out in Article 31 of the *Vienna Convention*. But these principles of interpretation neither require nor condone the imputation into a treaty of words that are not there or the importation into a treaty of concepts that were not intended.

I.3.2.4 *US – Shrimp*, para. 114
(WT/DS58/AB/R)

. . . A treaty interpreter must begin with, and focus upon, the text of the particular provision to be interpreted. It is in the words constituting that provision, read in their context, that the object and purpose of the states parties to the treaty must first be sought. Where the meaning imparted by the text itself is equivocal or inconclusive, or where confirmation of the correctness of the reading of the text itself is desired, light from the object and purpose of the treaty as a whole may usefully be sought.

I.3.2.5 *Argentina – Footwear (EC)*, para. 91
(WT/DS121/AB/R)

To determine the meaning of the clause – "as a result of unforeseen developments and of the effect of the obligations incurred by a Member under this Agreement, including tariff concessions . . . " – in sub-paragraph (a) of Article XIX:1, we must examine these words in their ordinary meaning, in their context and in light of the object and purpose of Article XIX . . . .

I.3.2.6 *US – Line Pipe*, para. 251
(WT/DS202/AB/R)

We do not see the text of Article 5.1, first sentence, alone, as indicating one certain meaning. Therefore, in keeping with our customary approach, we must seek the meaning of the terms of this provision in their context and in the light of the object and purpose of the Agreement.

I.3.2.7 *US – Offset Act (Byrd Amendment)*, para. 248
(WT/DS217/AB/R, WT/DS234/AB/R)

. . . It should be remembered that dictionaries are important guides to, not dispositive statements of, definitions of words appearing in agreements and legal documents.

I.3.2.8 *US – Softwood Lumber IV*, paras. 58–59
(WT/DS257/AB/R)

The meaning of a treaty provision, properly construed, is rooted in the ordinary meaning of the terms used . . . .

. . . We note, . . . that dictionary definitions have their limitations in revealing the ordinary meaning of a term. This is especially true where the meanings of terms used in the different authentic texts of the *WTO Agreement* are susceptible to differences in scope . . . .

I.3.2.9 *US – Gambling*, para. 164 and footnote 191
(WT/DS285/AB/R)

. . . In order to identify the ordinary meaning, a Panel may start with the dictionary definitions of the terms to be interpreted.[191] But dictionaries, alone, are not necessarily capable of resolving complex questions of interpretation, as they typically aim to catalogue *all* meanings of words – be those meanings common or rare, universal or specialized.

[191] We note, in this regard, the words of the panel in *US – Section 301 Trade Act* [paragraph 7.22]:

For pragmatic reasons the normal usage . . . is to start the interpretation from the ordinary meaning of the "raw" text of the relevant treaty provisions and then seek to construe it in its context and in the light of the treaty's object and purpose.

I.3.2.10 *IUS – Gambling*, para. 166
(WT/DS285/AB/R)

We have three reservations about the way in which the Panel determined the ordinary meaning of the word "sporting" in the United States' Schedule. First, to the extent that the Panel's reasoning simply equates the "ordinary meaning" with the meaning of words as defined in dictionaries, this is, in our view, too mechanical an approach. Secondly, the Panel failed to have due regard to the fact that its recourse to dictionaries revealed that gambling and betting can, at least in some contexts, be one of the meanings of the word "sporting". Thirdly, the Panel failed to explain the basis for its recourse to the meanings of the French and Spanish words "déportivos" and "sportifs" in the light of the fact that the United States' Schedule explicitly states, in a cover note, that it "is authentic in English only."

I.3.2.11 *US – Gambling*, para. 167
(WT/DS285/AB/R)

Overall, the Panel's finding concerning the word "sporting" was premature. In our view, the Panel should have taken note that, in the abstract, the range of possible meanings of the word "sporting" includes *both* the meaning claimed by Antigua and the meaning claimed by the United States, and then continued its inquiry into *which* of those meanings was to be attributed to the word as used in the United States' GATS Schedule.

I.3.3 Context

I.3.3.1 *US – Carbon Steel*, para. 65
(WT/DS213/AB/R, WT/DS213/AB/R/Corr.1)

We have previously observed that the fact that a particular treaty provision is "silent" on a specific issue "must have some meaning". In this case, the lack of any indication, in the text of Article 21.3, that a *de minimis* standard must be applied in sunset reviews serves, at least at first blush, as an indication that no such requirement exists. However, as the Panel itself observed, the task of ascertaining the meaning of a treaty provision with respect to a specific requirement does not end once it has been determined that the text is silent on that requirement. Such silence does not exclude the possibility that the requirement was intended to be included by implication.

I.3.3.2 *US – Carbon Steel*, para. 69
(WT/DS213/AB/R, WT/DS213/AB/R/Corr.1)

... the technique of cross-referencing is frequently used in the *SCM Agreement*. ... These cross-references suggest to us that, when the negotiators of the *SCM Agreement* intended that the disciplines set forth in one provision be applied in another context, they did so expressly. In the light of the many express cross-references made in the *SCM Agreement*, we attach significance to the absence of any textual link between Article 21.3 reviews and the *de minimis* standard set forth in Article 11.9 . . . .

I.3.3.3 *US – Carbon Steel*, para. 104
(WT/DS213/AB/R, WT/DS213/AB/R/Corr.1)

In principle, when a provision refers, without qualification, to an action that a Member may take, this serves as an indication that no limitation is intended to be imposed on the manner or circumstances in which such action may be taken. However, because the task of interpreting a treaty provision does not end with a bare examination of its text, the absence of an express limitation on Members' ability to take a certain action is not dispositive of whether any such limitation exists.

I.3.3.4 *US – Gambling*, para. 175
(WT/DS285/AB/R)

We note that Article 31(2) refers to the *agreement* or *acceptance* of the parties. In this case, both W/120 and the 1993 Scheduling Guidelines were drafted by the GATT Secretariat rather than the parties to the negotiations. It may be true that, on its own, authorship by a delegated body would not preclude specific documents from falling within the scope of Article 31(2). However, we are not persuaded that in this case the Panel could find W/120 and the 1993 Scheduling Guidelines to be context. Such documents can be characterized as context only where there is sufficient evidence of their constituting an "agreement relating to the treaty" between the parties or of their "accept[ance by the parties] as an instrument related to the treaty".

I.3.3.5 *US – Gambling*, paras. 176, 178
(WT/DS285/AB/R)

We do not accept, as the Panel appears to have done, that, simply by requesting the preparation and circulation of these documents and using them in preparing their offers, the parties in the negotiations have accepted them as agreements or instruments related to the treaty. Indeed, there are indications to the contrary. As the United States pointed out before the Panel, the United States and several other parties to the negotiations clearly stated, at the time W/120 was proposed, that, although Members were encouraged to follow the broad structure of W/120, it was never meant to bind Members to the CPC definitions, nor to any other "specific nomenclature", and that "the composition of the list was not a matter for negotiations". Similarly, the Explanatory Note that prefaces the Scheduling Guidelines itself appears to contradict the Panel in this regard, as it expressly provides that, although it is intended to assist "persons responsible for scheduling commitments", that assistance "should not be considered as an authoritative legal interpretation of the GATS."

. . .

. . . therefore, the Panel erred in categorizing W/120 and the 1993 Scheduling Guidelines as "context" for the interpretation of the United States' GATS Schedule. . . .

I.3.4 Domestic legislative history

I.3.4.1 *US – FSC (Article 21.5 – EC)*, para. 150
(WT/DS108/AB/RW)

. . . The legislative history also states that the measure was adopted "to comply with decisions of a World Trade Organization dispute panel and Appellate Body." We take particular note of these statements, though we do not believe that it would be appropriate for us to end our inquiry here.

I.3.4.2 *US – Offset Act (Byrd Amendment)*, para. 259
(WT/DS217/AB/R, WT/DS234/AB/R)

. . . We note that the Panel referred to the "Findings of Congress", not as a *basis* for its conclusion that the CDSOA constitutes a specific action against dumping or subsidies, but rather as a consideration confirming that conclusion. We agree with the Panel that the intent, stated or otherwise, of the legislators is not conclusive as to whether a measure is "against" dumping or subsidies under Article 18.1 of the *Anti-Dumping Agreement* or Article 32.1 of the *SCM Agreement*. Thus, it was not necessary for the Panel to inquire into the intent pursued by United States legislators in enacting the CDSOA and to take this into account in the analysis. The text of the CDSOA provides sufficient information on the structure and design of the CDSOA, that is to say, on the manner in which it operates, to permit an analysis whether the measure is "against" dumping or a subsidy . . . .

I.3.5 Legitimate expectations

I.3.5.1 *India – Patents (US)*, para. 42
(WT/DS50/AB/R)

. . . the Panel's invocation of the "legitimate expectations" of Members relating to conditions of competition melds the legally-distinct bases for "violation" and "non-violation" complaints under Article XXIII of the GATT 1994 into one uniform cause of action. This is not consistent with either Article XXIII of the GATT 1994 or Article 64 of the *TRIPS Agreement* . . . .

I.3.5.2 *India – Patents (US)*, para. 45
(WT/DS50/AB/R)

. . . The legitimate expectations of the parties to a treaty are reflected in the language of the treaty itself. The duty of a treaty interpreter is to examine the words of the treaty to determine the intentions of the parties. This should be done in accordance with the principles of treaty interpretation set out in Article 31 of the *Vienna Convention*. But these principles of interpretation neither require nor condone the imputation into a treaty of words that are not there or the importation into a treaty of concepts that were not intended.

I.3.5.3 *India – Patents (US)*, para. 48
(WT/DS50/AB/R)

. . . we do not agree with the Panel that the legitimate expectations of Members and private rights holders concerning conditions of competition must always be taken into account in interpreting the *TRIPS Agreement*.

I.3.5.4 *EC – Computer Equipment*, para. 84
(WT/DS62/AB/R, WT/DS67/AB/R, WT/DS68/AB/R)

The purpose of treaty interpretation under Article 31 of the *Vienna Convention* is to ascertain the *common* intentions of the parties. These *common* intentions cannot be ascertained on the basis of the subjective and unilaterally determined "expectations" of *one* of the parties to a treaty. Tariff concessions provided for in a Member's Schedule – the interpretation of which is at issue here – are reciprocal and result from a mutually-advantageous negotiation between importing and exporting Members. A Schedule is made an integral part of the GATT 1994 by Article II:7 of the GATT 1994. Therefore, the concessions provided for in that Schedule are part of the terms of the treaty. As such, the only rules which may be applied in interpreting the meaning of a concession are the general rules of treaty interpretation set out in the *Vienna Convention*.

I.3.5.5 *EC – Computer Equipment*, para. 97
(WT/DS62/AB/R, WT/DS67/AB/R, WT/DS68/AB/R)

. . . we conclude that the Panel erred in finding that the "legitimate expectations" of an exporting Member are relevant for the purposes of interpreting the terms of Schedule LXXX and of determining whether the European Communities violated Article II:1 of the GATT 1994 . . . .

I.3.6 Preamble

I.3.6.1 *US – Shrimp*, para. 153
(WT/DS58/AB/R)

We note once more that the preamble of the *WTO Agreement* demonstrates a recognition by WTO negotiators that optimal use of the world's resources should be made in accordance with the objective of sustainable development. As this preambular language reflects the intentions of negotiators of the *WTO Agreement*, we believe it must add colour, texture and shading to our interpretation of the agreements annexed to the *WTO Agreement*, in this case, the GATT 1994. We have already observed that Article XX(g) of the GATT 1994 is appropriately read with the perspective embodied in the above preamble.

I.3.7 Principle of effectiveness

I.3.7.1 *US – Gasoline*, p. 23, DSR 1996:I, p. 3 at 21
(WT/DS2/AB/R)

. . . One of the corollaries of the "general rule of interpretation" in the *Vienna Convention* is that interpretation must give meaning and effect to all the terms of the treaty. An interpreter is not free to adopt a reading that would result in reducing whole clauses or paragraphs of a treaty to redundancy or inutility.

I.3.7.2 *Japan – Alcoholic Beverages II*, p. 12, DSR 1997:I, p. 97 at 106
(WT/DS8/AB/R, WT/DS10/AB/R, WT/DS11/AB/R)

. . . A fundamental tenet of treaty interpretation flowing from the general rule of interpretation set out in Article 31 is the principle of effectiveness (*ut res magis valeat quam pereat*) . . . .

I.3.7.3 *US – Underwear*, p. 16, DSR 1997:I, p. 11 at 24
(WT/DS24/AB/R)

. . . The common, day-to-day, implication which arises from this language is clear to us: the restraint is to be applied *in the future*, *after* the consultations, should these prove fruitless and the proposed measure not withdrawn. The principle of effectiveness in treaty interpretation sustains this implication.

I.3.7.4 *Canada – Dairy*, para. 133
(WT/DS103/AB/R, WT/DS113/AB/R, WT/DS103/AB/R/Corr.1, WT/DS113/AB/R/Corr.1)

. . . the task of the treaty interpreter is to ascertain and give effect to a legally operative meaning for the terms of the treaty. The applicable fundamental principle of *effet utile* is that a treaty interpreter is not free to adopt a meaning that would reduce parts of a treaty to redundancy or inutility.

I.3.7.5 *Argentina – Footwear (EC)*, para. 81
(WT/DS121/AB/R)

. . . Yet a treaty interpreter must read all applicable provisions of a treaty in a way that gives meaning to *all* of them, harmoniously. And, an appropriate reading of this "inseparable package of rights and disciplines" must, accordingly, be one that gives meaning to *all* the relevant provisions of these two equally binding agreements.

I.3.7.6 *Argentina – Footwear (EC)*, para. 95
(WT/DS121/AB/R)

Our reading of these prerequisites does precisely this, by making certain that *all* the relevant provisions of the *Agreement on Safeguards* and Article XIX of the GATT 1994 relating to safeguard measures are given their full meaning and their full legal effect . . . .

I.3.7.7 *Korea – Dairy*, para. 81
(WT/DS98/AB/R)

In light of the interpretive principle of effectiveness, it is the *duty* of any treaty interpreter to "read all applicable provisions of a treaty in a way that gives meaning to *all* of them, harmoniously." An important corollary of this principle is that a treaty should be interpreted as a whole, and, in particular, its sections and parts should be read as a whole. Article II:2 of the *WTO Agreement* expressly manifests the intention of the Uruguay Round negotiators that the provisions of the *WTO Agreement* and the Multilateral Trade Agreements included in its Annexes 1, 2 and 3 must be read as a whole.

I.3.7.8 *US – Section 211 Appropriations Act*, para. 338
(WT/DS176/AB/R)

Article 8 of the Paris Convention (1967) covers only the protection of trade names; Article 8 has no other subject. If the intention of the negotiators had been to exclude trade names from protection, there would have been no purpose whatsoever in including Article 8 in the list of Paris Convention (1967) provisions that were specifically incorporated into the *TRIPS Agreement.* To adopt the Panel's approach would be to deprive Article 8 of the Paris Convention (1967), as incorporated into the *TRIPS Agreement* by virtue of Article 2.1 of that Agreement, of any and all meaning and effect . . . .

I.3.7.9 *US – Offset Act (Byrd Amendment)*, para. 271
(WT/DS217/AB/R, WT/DS234/AB/R)

. . . The United States' reasoning would deprive Article 32.1 of the *SCM Agreement* of effectiveness. As we have stated on many occasions, the internationally recognized interpretive principle of effectiveness should guide the interpretation of the *WTO Agreement*, and, under this principle, provisions of the *WTO Agreement* should not be interpreted in such a manner that whole clauses or paragraphs of a treaty would be reduced to redundancy or inutility . . . .

I.3.7.10 *US – Upland Cotton*, para. 549
(WT/DS267/AB/R)

. . . Furthermore, as the Appellate Body has explained, "a treaty interpreter must read all applicable provisions of a treaty in a way that gives meaning to all of them, harmoniously". We agree with the Panel that "Article 3.1(b) of the SCM Agreement can be read together with the Agreement on Agriculture provisions relating to domestic support in a coherent and consistent manner which gives full and effective meaning to all of their terms".

I.3.8 Principle of in dubio mitius

I.3.8.1 *EC – Hormones*, para. 165 and footnote 154
(WT/DS26/AB/R, WT/DS48/AB/R)

. . . We cannot lightly assume that sovereign states intended to impose upon themselves the more onerous, rather than the less burdensome, obligation by mandating *conformity* or *compliance with* such standards, guidelines and recommendations.[154] To sustain such an assumption and to warrant such a far-reaching interpretation, treaty language far more specific and compelling than that found in Article 3 of the *SPS Agreement* would be necessary.

[154] The interpretative principle of *in dubio mitius*, widely recognized in international law as a "supplementary means of interpretation", has been expressed in the following terms:

> "The principle of in dubio mitius applies in interpreting treaties, in deference to the sovereignty of states. If the meaning of a term is ambiguous, that meaning is to be preferred which is less onerous to the party assuming an obligation, or which interferes less with the territorial and personal supremacy of a party, or involves less general restrictions upon the parties." . . .

I.3.9 Subsequent Practice

I.3.9.1 *Japan – Alcoholic Beverages II*, p. 13, DSR 1996:I, p. 97 at 106
(WT/DS8/AB/R, WT/DS10/AB/R, WT/DS11/AB/R)

. . . a "concordant, common and consistent" sequence of acts or pronouncements which is sufficient to establish a discernible pattern implying the agreement of the parties [to a treaty] regarding its interpretation . . . .

I.3.9.2 *Japan – Alcoholic Beverages II*, p. 15, DSR 1996:I, p. 97 at 108
(WT/DS8/AB/R, WT/DS10/AB/R, WT/DS11/AB/R)

. . . we do not agree with the Panel's conclusion in paragraph 6.10 of the Panel Report that "panel reports adopted by the GATT CONTRACTING PARTIES and the WTO Dispute Settlement Body constitute subsequent practice in a specific case" as the phrase "subsequent practice" is used in Article 31 of the *Vienna Convention* . . . .

I.3.9.3 *Chile – Price Band System*, paras. 213–214
(WT/DS207/AB/R)

Chile's argument that it is "highly relevant" that no country that had a price band system in place before the conclusion of the Uruguay Round actually converted it into ordinary customs duties gives rise to another question, namely: is this practice relevant in interpreting Article 4.2 because it constitutes "subsequent practice in the application of the treaty which establishes the agreement of the parties regarding its interpretation", within the meaning of the customary rule of interpretation codified in Article 31(3)(b) of the *Vienna Convention*? . . .

Neither the Panel record nor the participants' submissions on appeal suggests that there is a discernible pattern of acts or pronouncements implying an agreement among WTO Members on the interpretation of Article 4.2. Thus, in our view, this alleged practice of some Members does not amount to "subsequent practice" within the meaning of Article 31(3)(b) of the *Vienna Convention*.

I.3.9.4 *Chile – Price Band System*, para. 272
(WT/DS207/AB/R)

. . . The Schedule of one Member, and even the scheduling practice of a number of Members, is not relevant in interpreting the meaning of a treaty provision, unless that practice amounts to "subsequent practice in the application of the treaty" within the meaning of Article 31(3)(b) of the *Vienna Convention* ....

I.3.9.5 *US – Upland Cotton*, para. 625
(WT/DS267/AB/R)

... We also observe that whether WTO Members with export credit guarantee programs have reported them in their export subsidy notifications is not determinative for purposes of our inquiry into the meaning of Article 10.2. In any event, the United States and Brazil disagree about whether such programs are subject to notification requirements.

I.3.9.6 *US – Gambling*, paras. 192–193
(WT/DS285/AB/R)

... in order for "practice" within the meaning of Article 31(3)(b) to be established: (i) there must be a common, consistent, discernible pattern of acts or pronouncements; *and* (ii) those acts or pronouncements must imply *agreement* on the interpretation of the relevant provision.

... Although the 2001 Guidelines were explicitly adopted by the Council for Trade in Services, this was in the context of the negotiation of *future* commitments and in order to assist in the preparation of offers and requests in respect of such commitments. As such, they do not constitute evidence of Members' understanding regarding the interpretation of *existing* commitments. Furthermore, as the United States emphasized before the Panel, in its Decision adopting the 2001 Guidelines, the Council for Trade in Services explicitly stated that they were to be "non binding" and "shall not modify any rights or obligations of the Members under the GATS". Accordingly, we do not consider that the 2001 Guidelines, in and of themselves, constitute "subsequent practice" within the meaning of Article 31(3)(b) of the *Vienna Convention.*

I.3.10 Supplementary means of interpretation – Article 32 of the Vienna Convention

I.3.10.1 *Japan – Alcoholic Beverages II*, p. 10, DSR 1996:I, p. 97 at 104
(WT/DS8/AB/R, WT/DS10/AB/R, WT/DS11/AB/R)

... There can be no doubt that Article 32 of the *Vienna Convention*, dealing with the role of supplementary means of interpretation, has also attained the same status [of a rule of customary international law].

I.3.10.2 *EC – Computer Equipment*, para. 86
(WT/DS62/AB/R, WT/DS67/AB/R, WT/DS68/AB/R)

The application of these rules in Article 31 of the *Vienna Convention* will usually allow a treaty interpreter to establish the meaning of a term. However, if after applying Article 31 the meaning of the term remains ambiguous or obscure, or leads to a result which is manifestly absurd or unreasonable, Article 32 allows a treaty interpreter to have recourse to:

> ... supplementary means of interpretation, including the preparatory work of the treaty and the circumstances of its conclusion.

With regard to "the circumstances of [the] conclusion" of a treaty, this permits, in appropriate cases, the examination of the historical background against which the treaty was negotiated.

I.3.10.3 *EC – Computer Equipment*, para. 92
(WT/DS62/AB/R, WT/DS67/AB/R, WT/DS68/AB/R)

... In the light of our observations on "the circumstances of [the] conclusion" of a treaty as a supplementary means of interpretation under Article 32 of the *Vienna Convention*, we consider that the classification practice in the European Communities during the Uruguay Round is part of "the circumstances of [the] conclusion" of the *WTO Agreement* and may be used as a supplementary means of interpretation within the meaning of Article 32 of the *Vienna Convention* ....

I.3.10.4 *EC – Computer Equipment*, para. 93
(WT/DS62/AB/R, WT/DS67/AB/R, WT/DS68/AB/R)

... The purpose of treaty interpretation is to establish the *common* intention of the parties to the treaty. To establish this intention, the prior practice of only *one* of the parties may be relevant, but it is clearly of more limited value than the practice of all parties. In the specific case of the interpretation of a tariff concession in a Schedule, the classification practice of the importing Member, in fact, may be of great importance. However, the Panel was mistaken in finding that the classification practice of the United States was *not* relevant.

I.3.10.5 *EC – Computer Equipment*, para. 95
(WT/DS62/AB/R, WT/DS67/AB/R, WT/DS68/AB/R)

... Consistent prior classification practice may often be significant. Inconsistent classification practice, however, *cannot* be relevant in interpreting the meaning of a tariff concession ....

I.3.10.6 *EC – Poultry*, para. 83
(WT/DS69/AB/R)

... the Oilseeds Agreement may serve as a *supplementary means* of interpretation of Schedule LXXX pursuant to Article 32 of the *Vienna Convention*, as it is part of the historical background of the concessions of the European Communities for frozen poultry meat.

I.3.10.7 *India – Quantitative Restrictions*, para. 94
(WT/DS90/AB/R)

We note India's arguments relating to the negotiating history of the *BOP Understanding*. However, in the absence of a record of the negotiations on footnote 1 to the *BOP Understanding*, we find it difficult to give weight to these arguments. We do not exclude that footnote 1 to the *BOP Understanding* was "heavily negotiated", and that it tries to accommodate opposing views held by different parties to the negotiations on the *BOP Understanding*. We are convinced, however, that the second sentence of footnote 1 does not accord with the position held by India. To interpret the sentence as proposed by India would require us to read into the text words which are simply not there. Neither a panel nor the Appellate Body is allowed to do so.

I.3.10.8 *Canada – Dairy*, para. 138

(WT/DS103/AB/R, WT/DS113/AB/R, WT/DS103/AB/R/Corr.1, WT/DS113/AB/R/Corr.1)

In our view, the language in the notation in Canada's Schedule is *not* clear on its face. Indeed, the language is general and ambiguous, and, therefore, requires special care on the part of the treaty interpreter. For this reason, it is appropriate, indeed necessary, in this case, to turn to "supplementary means of interpretation" pursuant to Article 32 of the *Vienna Convention* ....

I.3.10.9 *US – Carbon Steel*, paras. 77–78 and footnote 76

(WT/DS213/AB/R, WT/DS213/AB/R/Corr.1)

... The Panel formed [its] opinion after examining a 1987 Note prepared by the Secretariat for the Uruguay Round Negotiating Group on Subsidies and Countervailing Measures ...

... in taking this approach, the Panel did not explain why it thought that it was appropriate to rely on the 1987 Note, but simply stated that "it is useful to consider the rationale for the application of a de minimis standard to investigations, as reflected in a Note by the Secretariat prepared in April 1987".[76] ... Even if it were appropriate to rely on the 1987 Note in interpreting the *SCM Agreement* in accordance with the rules of interpretation set forth in the *Vienna Convention*, selective reliance on such a document does not provide a proper basis for the conclusion reached by the Panel in this regard.

[76] Panel Report, para. 8.60. It is, for example, unclear to us whether the Panel considered the Note to form part of the preparatory work of the treaty and intended to use it as a supplementary means of treaty interpretation within the meaning of Article 32 of the *Vienna Convention*.

I.3.10.10 *US – Carbon Steel*, paras. 89–90

(WT/DS213/AB/R, WT/DS213/AB/R/Corr.1)

... we do not consider it strictly necessary to have recourse to the supplementary means of interpretation identified in Article 32 of the *Vienna Convention*.

In any event, we consider that recourse to the negotiating history of the *SCM Agreement* tends to confirm our view as to the meaning of Article 21.3. We note that the two issues, namely the application of a specific *de minimis* standard in investigations, and the introduction of a time-bound limitation on the maintenance of countervailing duties, were considered to be highly important and were the subject of protracted negotiations. Specific provisions dealing with each of these two issues were viewed as necessary to improve the existing disciplines of the GATT and of the Tokyo Round Subsidies Code. The final texts of Article 11.9 and of Article 21.3 were the result of a carefully negotiated compromise that drew from a number of different proposals, reflecting divergent interests and views. We further note in this respect that none of the participants in this appeal pointed to any document indicating that the inclusion of a *de minimis* threshold was ever considered in the negotiations on sunset review provisions leading to the text of Article 21.3.

I.3.10.11 *US – Upland Cotton*, para. 623
(WT/DS267/AB/R)

We agree with the Panel that the meaning of Article 10.2 is clear from the provision's text, in its context and in the light of the object and purpose of the *Agreement on Agriculture*, consistent with Article 31 of the *Vienna Convention*. The Panel did not think it necessary to resort to negotiating history for purposes of its interpretation of Article 10.2. Even if the negotiating history were relevant for our inquiry, we do not find that it supports the United States' position. This is because it does not indicate that the negotiators did not intend to discipline export credit guarantees, export credits and insurance programs *at all*. . . .

I.3.10.12 *US – Gambling*, para. 160
(WT/DS285/AB/R)

In the context of the GATS, Article XX:3 explicitly provides that Members' Schedules are an "integral part" of that agreement. Here, too, the task of identifying the meaning of a concession in a GATS Schedule, like the task of interpreting any other treaty text, involves identifying the *common intention* of Members. . . . we consider that the meaning of the United States' GATS Schedule must be determined according to the rules codified in Article 31 and, to the extent appropriate, Article 32 of the *Vienna Convention.*

I.3.10.13 *US – Gambling*, paras. 196–197
(WT/DS285/AB/R)

. . . this appeal does *not* raise the question whether W/120 and the 1993 Scheduling Guidelines constitute "supplementary means of interpretation, including the preparatory work of the treaty and the circumstances of its conclusion". Both participants agree that they do, and we see no reason to disagree.

. . . a proper interpretation pursuant to the principles codified in Article 31 of the *Vienna Convention* does not yield a clear meaning as to the scope of the commitment made by the United States in the entry "Other recreational services (except sporting)". Accordingly, it is appropriate to have recourse to the supplemental means of interpretation identified in Article 32 of the *Vienna Convention*. These means include W/120, the 1993 Scheduling Guidelines, and a cover note attached to drafts of the United States' Schedule.

I.3.10.14 *US – Gambling*, paras. 203–204
(WT/DS285/AB/R)

The Scheduling Guidelines thus underline the importance of using a common format and terminology in scheduling, and express a clear preference for parties to use W/120 and the CPC classifications in their Schedules. At the same time, the Guidelines make clear that parties wanting to use their own subsectoral classification or definitions – that is, to disaggregate in a way that diverges from W/120 and/or the CPC – were to do so in a "sufficiently detailed" way "to avoid any ambiguity as to the scope of the commitment." The example given in the Scheduling Guidelines illustrates how to make a positive commitment with respect to a discrete service that is more disaggregated than a service subsector identified in W/120. It is reasonable to assume that the parties to the negotiations expected the same technique to be applied to *exclude* a discrete service from the scope of a commitment, when the commitment is made in a subsector identified in W/120 and the excluded service is more disaggregated than that subsector.

In our view, the requisite clarity as to the scope of a commitment could not have been achieved through mere omission of CPC codes, particularly where a specific sector of a Member's Schedule, such as sector 10 of the United States' Schedule, follows the structure of W/120 in all other respects, and adopts *precisely* the same terminology as used in W/120. . . . W/120 and the 1993 Scheduling Guidelines were prepared and circulated . . . for the express purpose of assisting those parties in the preparation of their offers. These documents undoubtedly served, too, to assist parties in reviewing and evaluating the offers made by others. They provided a common language and structure which, although not obligatory, was widely used and relied upon. In such circumstances, and in the light of the specific guidance provided in the 1993 Scheduling Guidelines, it is reasonable to assume that parties to the negotiations examining a sector of a Schedule that tracked so closely the language of the same sector in W/120 would – absent a clear indication to the contrary – have expected the sector to have the same coverage as the corresponding W/120 sector. This is another way of stating that, as the Panel observed, "unless otherwise indicated in the Schedule, Members were assumed to have relied on W/120 and the corresponding CPC references."

I.3.10.15 *US – Gambling*, paras. 205–206
(WT/DS285/AB/R)

Accordingly, the above excerpt from the 1993 Scheduling Guidelines, together with the linguistic similarities between the two subsectors, provide strong support for interpreting subsector 10.D of the United States' Schedule as corresponding to subsector 10.D of W/120, notwithstanding the absence of CPC codes in the United States' Schedule. . . .

. . . another element of the preparatory work of the GATS suggests that the United States itself understood the Scheduling Guidelines in this way and sought to comply with them in the drafting of its GATS Schedule. Several drafts of the United States' Schedule included [a] cover note [which confirms] . . .

I.3.10.16 *US – Gambling*, para. 211
(WT/DS285/AB/R)

The Panel did not explain clearly how it used this document in interpreting the United States' Schedule. The Panel considered that, although the USITC Document did not constitute a "binding interpretation", it nevertheless "has probative value as to how the US government views the structure and the scope of the US Schedule, and, hence, its GATS obligations." The document was dealt with under the heading "Other supplementary means of interpretation". In this context, the Panel observed that "Article 32 of the *Vienna Convention* is not necessarily limited to preparatory material, but may allow treaty interpreters to take into consideration other relevant material". Yet the Panel also referred to the principle of "acquiescence" and to a commentator's statement that "Article 31:3(b) [of the *Vienna Convention*] might also apply". Notwithstanding these ambiguities, it is clear from the Panel's reasoning that it used the USITC publication to "confirm" its interpretation of subsector 10.D in the United States' Schedule. In other words, the Panel's interpretation did not depend on its treatment of the USITC document.

I.3.11 Multiple authentic languages – Article 33 of the Vienna Convention

I.3.11.1 *Chile – Price Band System*, para. 271
(WT/DS207/AB/R)

... Indeed, the Panel came to this conclusion by interpreting the French and Spanish versions of the term "ordinary customs duty" to mean something *different* from the ordinary meaning of the English version of that term. It is difficult to see how, in doing so, the Panel took into account the rule of interpretation codified in Article 33(4) of the *Vienna Convention* whereby "when a comparison of the authentic texts discloses a difference of meaning ..., the meaning which best *reconciles* the texts ... shall be adopted." (emphasis added).

I.3.11.2 *EC – Bed Linen (Article 21.5 – India)*, footnote 153 to para. 123
(WT/DS141/AB/RW)

According to Article 33.3 of the *Vienna Convention on the Law of Treaties*, where treaties have been authenticated in two or more languages, "[t]he terms of the treaty are presumed to have the same meaning in each authentic text." The Spanish terms ("se han cumplido" and "hayan limitado"), in paragraphs 1 and 4 of Article 9, have the same temporal meaning as the English terms ("have been fulfilled" and "have limited"). The French terms ("sont remplies" and "auront limité") can also accommodate this temporal meaning.

I.3.11.3 *US – Softwood Lumber IV*, para. 59 and footnote 50
(WT/DS257/AB/R)

... in accordance with the customary rule of treaty interpretation reflected in Article 33(3) of the *Vienna Convention on the Law of Treaties* (the "*Vienna Convention*"), the terms of a treaty authenticated in more than one language – like the *WTO*

Agreement – are presumed to have the same meaning in each authentic text. It follows that the treaty interpreter should seek the meaning that gives effect, simultaneously, to all the terms of the treaty, as they are used in each authentic language.[50]...

[50] See Appellate Body Report, *EC – Bed Linen (Article 21.5 – India)*, footnote 153 to para. 123. We also note that, in discussing the draft article that was later adopted as Article 33(3) of the *Vienna Convention*, the International Law Commission observed that the "presumption [that the terms of a treaty are intended to have the same meaning in each authentic text] requires that every effort should be made to find a common meaning for the texts before preferring one to another". (*Yearbook of the International Law Commission* (1966), Vol. II, p. 225) With regard to the application of customary rules of interpretation in respect of treaties authenticated in more than one language, see also International Court of Justice, Merits, *Case Concerning Elettronica Sicula S.p.A. (ELSI) (United States v. Italy)* 1989, ICJ Reports, para. 132, where, in interpreting a provision of the Treaty of Friendship, Commerce and Navigation between the United States of America and the Italian Republic of 1948, the International Court of Justice noted that it was possible to interpret the English and Italian versions "as meaning much the same thing", despite a potential divergence in scope.

I.3.11.4 *EC – Tariff Preferences*, para. 147
(WT/DS246/AB/R)

...In our view, the stronger, more obligatory language in both the French and Spanish texts – that is, using "as defined in" rather than "as described in" – lends support to our view that only preferential tariff treatment that is "generalized, non-reciprocal and non-discriminatory" is covered under paragraph 2(a) of the Enabling Clause.

I.3.11.5 *US – Upland Cotton*, para. 424 and footnote 510
(WT/DS267/AB/R)

...We agree, however, that the Panel's description of "price suppression" in paragraph 7.1277 of the Panel Report reflects the ordinary meaning of that term, particularly when read in conjunction with the French and Spanish versions of Article 6.3(c),[510] as required by Article 33(3) of the *Vienna Convention on the Law of Treaties* (the "*Vienna Convention*").

[510] The French version states, in part, "la subvention ... a pour effet d'*empêcher des hausses de prix* ou de déprimer les prix ... dans une mesure notable"; the Spanish version states, in part, "la subvención ... tenga un efecto significativo de contención de la *subida de los precios*, reducción de los precios". (emphasis added)

Issues of Fact/Law. *See* Scope of Appellate Review, Issues of law vs. Issues of fact (S.3.3)

J

J.1 Judicial Economy. *See also* Completion of the Legal Analysis by the Appellate Body (C.4)

J.1.1 *US – Wool Shirts and Blouses*, p. 18, DSR 1997:I, p. 323 at 339
(WT/DS33/AB/R, WT/DS33/AB/R/Corr.1)

Nothing in [Article 11 of the DSU] or in previous GATT practice *requires* a panel to examine *all* legal claims made by the complaining party. Previous GATT 1947 and WTO panels have frequently addressed only those issues that such panels considered necessary for the resolution of the matter between the parties, and have declined to decide other issues. Thus, if a panel found that a measure was inconsistent with a particular provision of the GATT 1947, it generally did not go on to examine whether the measure was also inconsistent with other GATT provisions that a complaining party may have argued were violated. In recent WTO practice, panels likewise have refrained from examining each and every claim made by the complaining party and have made findings only on those claims that such panels concluded were necessary to resolve the particular matter.

J.1.2 *US – Wool Shirts and Blouses*, p. 19, DSR 1997:I, p. 323 at 340
(WT/DS33/AB/R, WT/DS33/AB/R/Corr.1)

. . . Given the explicit aim of dispute settlement that permeates the *DSU*, we do not consider that Article 3.2 of the *DSU* is meant to encourage either panels or the Appellate Body to "make law" by clarifying existing provisions of the *WTO Agreement* outside the context of resolving a particular dispute. A panel need only address those claims which must be addressed in order to resolve the matter in issue in the dispute.

J.1.3 *US – Wool Shirts and Blouses*, p. 19, DSR 1997:I, p. 323 at 339–340
(WT/DS33/AB/R, WT/DS33/AB/R/Corr.1)

Although a few GATT 1947 and WTO panels did make broader rulings, by considering and deciding issues that were not absolutely necessary to dispose of the particular dispute, there is nothing anywhere in the *DSU* that requires panels to do so.

Furthermore, such a requirement is not consistent with the aim of the WTO dispute settlement system . . . .

J.1.4 *EC – Hormones*, para. 250

(WT/DS26/AB/R, WT/DS48/AB/R)

We agree with the Panel's application of the notion of judicial economy. We have affirmed the Panel's conclusion that the EC measures are inconsistent with Article 5.1 in view of the failure of the European Communities to provide a risk assessment that reasonably supports such measures. Under the circumstances, the necessity or propriety of proceeding to determine whether Article 2.2 of the *SPS Agreement* has also been violated is not at all clear to us . . . .

J.1.5 *India – Patents (US)*, para. 87

(WT/DS50/AB/R)

. . . a panel has the discretion to determine the claims it must address in order to resolve the dispute between the parties – provided that those claims are within that panel's terms of reference. . . .

J.1.6 *Australia – Salmon*, para. 223

(WT/DS18/AB/R)

The principle of judicial economy has to be applied keeping in mind the aim of the dispute settlement system. This aim is to resolve the matter at issue and "to secure a positive solution to a dispute". To provide only a partial resolution of the matter at issue would be false judicial economy. A panel has to address those claims on which a finding is necessary in order to enable the DSB to make sufficiently precise recommendations and rulings so as to allow for prompt compliance by a Member with those recommendations and rulings "in order to ensure effective resolution of disputes to the benefit of all Members."

J.1.7 *Japan – Agricultural Products II*, para. 111

(WT/DS76/AB/R)

. . . By not making a finding under Article 5.1 with regard to the varietal testing requirement as it applies to apricots, pears, plums and quince, the Panel improperly applied the principle of judicial economy. We believe that a finding under Article 5.1 with respect to apricots, pears, plums and quince is necessary "in order to ensure effective resolution" of the dispute.

J.1.8 *US – Lead and Bismuth II*, para. 71

(WT/DS138/AB/R)

The United States seems to consider that our Report in *United States – Shirts and Blouses* sets forth a general principle that panels may not address any issues that need not be addressed in order to resolve the dispute between the parties. We do not agree with this characterization of our findings. In that appeal, India had argued that it was entitled to a finding by the Panel on each of the legal claims that it had made. We, however, found that the principle of judicial economy allows a panel to decline to rule on certain claims.

J.1.9 *Canada – Autos*, paras. 112–114
(WT/DS139/AB/R, WT/DS142/AB/R)

In assessing this allegation of legal error made by the European Communities, we refer to the obligations of panels set out in very general terms in Article 11 of the DSU....

The standard terms of reference of a panel, set out in Article 7.1 of the DSU, speak in very similar terms. A panel should make "such findings as will assist the DSB" in making recommendations or rulings. Under Article 7.2 of the DSU, a panel "shall address the relevant provisions in any covered agreement or agreements cited by the parties to the dispute."

In discharging its functions under Articles 7 and 11 of the DSU, a panel is not, however, required to examine *all* legal claims made before it. A panel may exercise judicial economy....

J.1.10 *Canada – Autos*, paras. 116–117
(WT/DS139/AB/R, WT/DS142/AB/R)

In our view, it was not necessary for the Panel to make a determination on the European Communities' *alternative* claim relating to the CVA requirements under Article 3.1(a) of the *SCM Agreement* in order "to secure a positive solution" to this dispute. The Panel had already found that the CVA requirements violated both Article III:4 of the GATT 1994 and Article XVII of the GATS. Having made these findings, the Panel, in our view, exercising the discretion implicit in the principle of judicial economy, could properly decide not to examine the *alternative* claim of the European Communities that the CVA requirements are inconsistent with Article 3.1(a) of the *SCM Agreement*.

We are bound to add that, for purposes of transparency and fairness to the parties, a panel should, however, in all cases, address expressly those claims which it declines to examine and rule upon for reasons of judicial economy. Silence does not suffice for these purposes.

J.1.11 *US – Wheat Gluten*, para. 183
(WT/DS166/AB/R)

...The Panel found and we have upheld, albeit for different reasons, that the measure is inconsistent with Articles 2.1 and 4.2 of the *Agreement on Safeguards*. Thus, the Panel found, in effect, that the safeguard measure at issue in this case, like the measure at issue in *Argentina – Footwear Safeguard*, has no legal basis. The reasons for which the Panel found an inconsistency with Articles 2.1 and 4.2 of the *Agreement on Safeguards* do not alter that conclusion. The Panel was, therefore, entitled to decline to examine the claim of the European Communities regarding "unforeseen developments". A finding on that issue would not, in our view, have added anything to the ability of the DSB to make sufficiently precise recommendations and rulings in this dispute....

J.1.12 *US – Lamb*, para. 194
(WT/DS177/AB/R, WT/DS178/AB/R)

...Having found that the safeguard measure applied by the United States lacked a legal basis, the Panel was entitled to decline to address further claims that the same measure is inconsistent with other provisions of the *Agreement on Safeguards*. We also observe that a finding on New Zealand's claim under Article 5.1 of the *Agreement on Safeguards* would not have enhanced the ability of the DSB to make sufficiently precise recommendations and rulings in this dispute.

J.1.13 *Mexico – Corn Syrup (Article 21.5 – US)*, para. 36
(WT/DS132/AB/RW)

...We believe that a panel comes under a duty to address issues in at least two instances. First, as a matter of due process, and the proper exercise of the judicial function, panels are required to address issues that are put before them by the parties to a dispute. Second, panels have to address and dispose of certain issues of a fundamental nature, even if the parties to the dispute remain silent on those issues. In this regard, we have previously observed that "[t]he vesting of jurisdiction in a panel is a fundamental prerequisite for lawful panel proceedings." For this reason, panels cannot simply ignore issues which go to the root of their jurisdiction – that is, to their authority to deal with and dispose of matters. Rather, panels must deal with such issues – if necessary, on their own motion – in order to satisfy themselves that they have authority to proceed.

J.1.14 *Canada – Wheat Exports and Grain Imports*, paras. 133–134
(WT/DS276/AB/R)

The practice of judicial economy, which was first employed by a number of GATT panels, allows a panel to refrain from making multiple findings that the same measure is *inconsistent* with various provisions when a single, or a certain number of findings of inconsistency, would suffice to resolve the dispute. Although the doctrine of judicial economy *allows* a panel to refrain from addressing claims beyond those necessary to resolve the dispute, it does not *compel* a panel to exercise such restraint. At the same time, if a panel fails to make findings on claims where such findings are necessary to resolve the dispute, then this would constitute a false exercise of judicial economy and an error of law.

In this case, the Panel itself did not claim to be exercising judicial economy when it made an assumption concerning the relationship between subparagraphs (a) and (b) of Article XVII:1. The Panel made *no* finding of inconsistency with respect to the CWB Export Regime that would have entitled it to exercise judicial economy with respect to other claims. Moreover, neither Canada nor the United States argues that the Panel's approach is properly classified as an exercise of judicial economy, nor that the concept of judicial economy must be understood otherwise than as set out above. In sum, we see no reason to characterize the Panel's use of an assumption concerning the relationship between subparagraphs (a) and (b) of Article XVII:1 as an exercise of judicial economy....

J.1.15 *US – Upland Cotton*, para. 717
(WT/DS267/AB/R)

We believe the Panel was within its discretion in declining to examine whether scheduled products other than rice and unscheduled products supported by the programs are applied in a manner that "threatens to lead to" circumvention. The Panel had already found that the United States acted inconsistently with Article 10.1 of the *Agreement on Agriculture* because it applied its export credit guarantee program in a manner that "results in" (actual) circumvention of its export subsidy commitments for these products. We do not see why the Panel had to examine also whether the United States acted inconsistently with the *same* provision in respect of the *same* products, but on the basis of there being a *threat* of circumvention, rather than *actual* circumvention.

J.1.16 *US – Upland Cotton*, para. 718
(WT/DS267/AB/R)

The Appellate Body has stated that panels may exercise judicial economy and refrain from addressing claims beyond those necessary to resolve the dispute. In this case, the Panel did not expressly state it was exercising judicial economy. We agree with the United States, however, that the Panel's approach can be properly characterized as an exercise of judicial economy. Moreover, we believe that the Panel was within its discretion in refraining from making additional findings and it was not improper for the Panel to have exercised judicial economy given that its finding of *actual* circumvention resolved the matter.

J.1.17 *US – Upland Cotton*, para. 731
(WT/DS267/AB/R)

We need not decide, in this case, whether an export credit guarantee program that meets the standard of item (j) of the Illustrative List of Export Subsidies – because the premiums charged are adequate to cover long-term operating costs and losses – may nevertheless be challenged as a prohibited export subsidy under Article 3.1(a) on the basis that it confers a benefit. This is because, even if we were to assume that such a claim were possible, we would conclude that the Panel was within its discretion in exercising judicial economy in respect of Brazil's claim.

J.1.18 *US – Upland Cotton*, para. 732
(WT/DS267/AB/R)

As we explained earlier, panels may refrain from ruling on every claim as long as it does not lead to a "partial resolution of the matter". The Panel found that the United States' export credit guarantee programs constitute a prohibited export subsidy under Article 3.1(a) because they do not meet the criteria in item (j) of the Illustrative List of Export Subsidies. This finding, in our view, is sufficient to resolve the matter. Therefore, we are not persuaded that the Panel's exercise of judicial economy was improper, as Brazil has not demonstrated that it has led to "a partial resolution of the matter".

J.1.19 *US – Gambling*, paras. 342–344
(WT/DS285/AB/R)

In deciding to assess whether the measures satisfied the requirements of the chapeau, the Panel explained that, even though such an examination was "not necessary", it wanted "to assist the parties in resolving the underlying dispute in this case." Antigua alleges that the Panel acted inconsistently with the Appellate Body's decision in *Korea – Various Measures on Beef* in determining whether the Wire Act, the Travel Act, and the IGBA meet the requirements of the chapeau after having found that they were not provisionally justified.

... [the statement by the Appellate Body at paragraph 156 of *Korea – Various Measures on Beef*] does not impose a *requirement* on panels to stop evaluating a responding party's defence once they have determined that a challenged measure is not provisionally justified under one of the paragraphs of the general exception provision.

Provided that it complies with its duty to assess a matter objectively, a panel enjoys the freedom to decide *which legal issues* it must address in order to resolve a dispute. Moreover, in some instances, a panel's decision to continue its legal analysis and to make factual findings beyond those that are strictly necessary to resolve the dispute may assist the Appellate Body should it later be called upon to complete the analysis, as, for example, in this case.

J.1.20 *EC – Export Subsidies on Sugar*, para. 331
(WT/DS265/AB/R, WT/DS266/AB/R, WT/DS283/AB/R)

Thus, in addition to ruling on the matter before it, a panel is required [under Article 11 of the DSU] to "make such other findings as will assist the DSB in making the recommendations or in giving the rulings provided for in the covered agreements." Such "other findings" could, for instance, relate to implementation, to the extent that such findings "will assist the DSB in making the recommendations or in giving the rulings provided for in the covered agreements".

J.1.21 *EC – Export Subsidies on Sugar*, para. 335
(WT/DS265/AB/R, WT/DS266/AB/R, WT/DS283/AB/R)

In this case, the Panel's findings under Articles 3 and 8 of the *Agreement on Agriculture* were not sufficient to "fully resolve" the dispute. This is because, in declining to rule on the Complaining Parties' claims under Article 3 of the *SCM Agreement*, the Panel precluded the possibility of a remedy being made available to the Complaining Parties, pursuant to Article 4.7 of the *SCM Agreement*, in the event of the Panel finding in favour of the Complaining Parties with respect to their claims under Article 3 of the *SCM Agreement*. Moreover, in declining to rule on the Complaining Parties' claims under Article 3 of the *SCM Agreement*, the Panel failed to discharge its obligation under Article 11 of the DSU by failing to make "such other findings as will assist the DSB in making the recommendations or in giving the rulings provided for in the covered agreements", namely, a recommendation or ruling by the DSB pursuant to Article 4.7. This constitutes false judicial economy and legal error.

J.2 Jurisdiction

J.2.1 General. *See also* Anti-Dumping Agreement, Article 17.4 – "matter referred to the DSB" (A.3.56); Balance-of-Payments Restrictions (B.1); Legislation as such vs. Specific Application (L.1); Mandatory and Discretionary Legislation (M.1); Terms of Reference of Panels (T.6)

J.2.1.1 *Brazil – Desiccated Coconut*, p. 22, DSR 1997:I, p. 167 at 186
(WT/DS22/AB/R)

A panel's terms of reference are important for two reasons. First, terms of reference fulfil an important due process objective – they give the parties and third parties sufficient information concerning the claims at issue in the dispute in order to allow them an opportunity to respond to the complainant's case. Second, they establish the jurisdiction of the panel by defining the precise claims at issue in the dispute.

J.2.1.2 *Brazil – Desiccated Coconut*, p. 22, DSR 1997:I, p. 167 at 186
(WT/DS22/AB/R)

. . . the "matter" referred to a panel for consideration consists of the specific claims stated by the parties to the dispute in the relevant documents specified in the terms of reference. We agree with the approach taken in previous adopted panel reports that a matter, which includes the claims composing that matter, does not fall within a panel's terms of reference unless the claims are identified in the documents referred to or contained in the terms of reference.

J.2.1.3 *India – Patents (US)*, paras. 92–93
(WT/DS50/AB/R)

. . . Although panels enjoy some discretion in establishing their own working procedures, this discretion does not extend to modifying the substantive provisions of the DSU. To be sure, Article 12.1 of the DSU says: "Panels shall follow the Working Procedures in Appendix 3 unless the panel decides otherwise after consulting the parties to the dispute". Yet that is *all* that it says. Nothing in the DSU gives a panel the authority either to disregard or to modify other explicit provisions of the DSU. The jurisdiction of a panel is established by that panel's terms of reference, which are governed by Article 7 of the DSU. A panel may consider only those claims that it has the authority to consider under its terms of reference. A panel cannot assume jurisdiction that it does not have . . . .

. . . A panel is bound by its terms of reference.

J.2.1.4 *India – Quantitative Restrictions*, paras. 84–86
(WT/DS90/AB/R)

This dispute was brought pursuant to, *inter alia*, Article XXIII of the GATT 1994. According to Article XXIII, any Member which considers that a benefit accruing to it directly or indirectly under the GATT 1994 is being nullified or impaired as a result of the failure of another Member to carry out its obligations, may resort to the dispute settlement procedures of Article XXIII. The United States considers that a benefit accruing to it under the GATT 1994 was nullified or impaired as a result of India's alleged failure to carry out its obligations regarding balance-of-payments restrictions under Article XVIII: B of the GATT 1994. Therefore, the United States was entitled to have recourse to the dispute settlement procedures of Article XXIII with regard to this dispute.

Article XXIII is elaborated and applied by the DSU. The first sentence of Article 1.1 of the DSU provides:

> The rules and procedures of this Understanding shall apply to disputes brought pursuant to the consultation and dispute settlement provisions of the agreements listed in Appendix 1 to this Understanding (referred to in this Understanding as the "covered agreements").

We note that Appendix 1 to the DSU lists "Multilateral Agreements on Trade in Goods", to which the GATT 1994 belongs, among the agreements covered by the DSU. A dispute concerning Article XVIII:B is, therefore, covered by the DSU.

Article 1.2 of the DSU provides in relevant part:

> The rules and procedures of this Understanding shall apply subject to such special or additional rules and procedures on dispute settlement contained in the covered agreements as are identified in Appendix 2 to this Understanding.

Appendix 2 does not identify any special or additional dispute settlement rules or procedures relating to balance-of-payments restrictions. It does not mention Article XVIII:B of the GATT 1994, or any of its paragraphs. The DSU is, therefore, fully applicable to the current dispute.

J.2.1.5 *India – Quantitative Restrictions*, paras. 87–88 (WT/DS90/AB/R)

Any doubts that may have existed in the past as to whether the dispute settlement procedures under Article XXIII were available for disputes relating to balance-of-payments restrictions have been removed by the second sentence of footnote 1 to the *BOP Understanding*, ...

In our opinion, this provision makes it clear that the dispute settlement procedures under Article XXIII, as elaborated and applied by the DSU, *are* available for disputes relating to *any* matters concerning balance-of-payments restrictions.

J.2.1.6 *India – Quantitative Restrictions*, paras. 102–103 (WT/DS90/AB/R)

... Recourse to the dispute settlement procedures does not call into question either the availability or the utility of the procedures under Article XVIII:12 and the *BOP Understanding*. On the contrary, if panels refrained from reviewing the justification of balance-of-payments restrictions, they would diminish the explicit procedural rights of Members under Article XXIII and footnote 1 to the *BOP Understanding*, as well as their substantive rights under Article XVIII:11.

We are cognisant of the competence of the BOP Committee and the General Council with respect to balance-of-payments restrictions under Article XVIII:12 of the GATT 1994 and the *BOP Understanding*. However, we see no conflict between that competence and the competence of panels. Moreover, we are convinced that, in considering the justification of balance-of-payments restrictions, panels should take into account the deliberations and conclusions of the BOP Committee, as did the panel in *Korea – Beef*.

J.2.1.7 *India – Quantitative Restrictions*, para. 109
(WT/DS90/AB/R)

. . . we conclude that panels have the competence to review the justification of balance-of-payments restrictions. More generally, we conclude that the dispute settlement provisions of the GATT 1994, as elaborated and applied by the DSU, can be invoked with respect to any matters relating to balance-of-payments restrictions. . . .

J.2.1.8 *US – 1916 Act*, para. 54
(WT/DS136/AB/R, WT/DS162/AB/R)

We agree with the Panel that the interim review was not an appropriate stage in the Panel's proceedings to raise objections to the Panel's jurisdiction for the first time. An objection to jurisdiction should be raised as early as possible and panels must ensure that the requirements of due process are met. However, we also agree with the Panel's consideration that "some issues of jurisdiction may be of such a nature that they have to be addressed by the Panel at any time." We do not share the European Communities' view that objections to the jurisdiction of a panel are appropriately regarded as simply "procedural objections". The vesting of jurisdiction in a panel is a fundamental prerequisite for lawful panel proceedings. We, therefore, see no reason to accept the European Communities' argument that we must reject the United States' appeal because the United States did not raise its jurisdictional objection before the Panel in a timely manner.

J.2.1.9 *US – 1916 Act*, paras. 60–61
(WT/DS136/AB/R, WT/DS162/AB/R)

Prior to the entry into force of the *WTO Agreement*, it was firmly established that Article XXIII:1(a) of the GATT 1947 allowed a Contracting Party to challenge legislation as such, independently from the application of that legislation in specific instances. While the text of Article XXIII does not expressly address the matter, panels consistently considered that, under Article XXIII, they had the *jurisdiction* to deal with claims against legislation as such. In *examining* such claims, panels developed the concept that mandatory and discretionary legislation should be distinguished from each other, reasoning that only legislation that mandates a violation of GATT obligations can be found as such to be inconsistent with those obligations. We consider the application of this distinction to the present cases in section IV(B) below.

Thus, that a Contracting Party could challenge legislation as such before a panel was well-settled under the GATT 1947. We consider that the case law articulating and applying this practice forms part of the GATT *acquis* which, under Article XVI:1 of the *WTO Agreement*, provides guidance to the WTO and, therefore, to panels and the Appellate Body. Furthermore, in Article 3.1 of the DSU, Members affirm "their adherence to the principles for the management of disputes heretofore applied under Articles XXII and XXIII of GATT 1947". We note that, since the entry into force of the *WTO Agreement*, a number of panels have dealt with dispute settlement claims brought against a Member on the basis of its legislation as such, independently from the application of that legislation in specific instances.

J.2.1.10 *US – 1916 Act*, paras. 62, 68
(WT/DS136/AB/R, WT/DS162/AB/R)

Turning to the issue of the legal basis for claims brought under the *Anti-Dumping Agreement*, we note that Article 17 of the *Anti-Dumping Agreement* addresses dispute settlement under that Agreement. Just as Articles XXII and XXIII of the GATT 1994 create a legal basis for claims in disputes relating to provisions of the GATT 1994, so also Article 17 establishes the basis for dispute settlement claims relating to provisions of the *Anti-Dumping Agreement*. In the same way that Article XXIII of the GATT 1994 allows a WTO Member to challenge *legislation* as such, Article 17 of the *Anti-Dumping Agreement* is properly to be regarded as allowing a challenge to legislation as such, unless this possibility is excluded. No such *express* exclusion is found in Article 17 or elsewhere in the *Anti-Dumping Agreement*.

...

Article 17.3 does not explicitly address challenges to legislation as such. As we have seen above, Articles XXII and XXIII allow challenges to be brought under the GATT 1994 against legislation as such. Since Article 17.3 is the "equivalent provision" to Articles XXII and XXIII of the GATT 1994, Article 17.3 provides further support for our view that challenges may be brought under the *Anti-Dumping Agreement* against legislation as such, unless such challenges are otherwise excluded.

J.2.1.11 *US – 1916 Act*, para. 72
(WT/DS136/AB/R, WT/DS162/AB/R)

Nothing in our Report in *Guatemala – Cement* [Appellate Body Report, paras. 79–80] suggests that Article 17.4 precludes review of anti-dumping legislation as such. Rather, in that case, we simply found that, for Mexico to challenge Guatemala's initiation and conduct of the anti-dumping investigation, Mexico was required to identify one of the three anti-dumping measures listed in Article 17.4 in its request for establishment of a panel. Since it did not do so, the panel in that case did not have jurisdiction.

J.2.1.12 *Mexico – Corn Syrup (Article 21.5 – US)*, para. 36
(WT/DS132/AB/RW)

... We believe that a panel comes under a duty to address issues in at least two instances. First, as a matter of due process, and the proper exercise of the judicial function, panels are required to address issues that are put before them by the parties to a dispute. Second, panels have to address and dispose of certain issues of a fundamental nature, even if the parties to the dispute remain silent on those issues. In this regard, we have previously observed that "[t]he vesting of jurisdiction in a panel is a fundamental prerequisite for lawful panel proceedings." For this reason, panels cannot simply ignore issues which go to the root of their jurisdiction – that is, to their authority to deal with and dispose of matters. Rather, panels must deal with such issues – if necessary, on their own motion – in order to satisfy themselves that they have authority to proceed.

J.2.1.13 *Mexico – Corn Syrup (Article 21.5 – US)*, para. 53
(WT/DS132/AB/RW)

... our task is simply to determine whether the "objections" that Mexico now raises before us are of such a nature that they could have deprived the Panel of its authority to deal with and dispose of the matter. If so, then the Panel was bound to address them on its own motion....

J.2.1.14 *US – Carbon Steel*, para. 123
(WT/DS213/AB/R, WT/DS213/AB/R/Corr.1)

... we have consistently held that, in the interests of due process, parties should bring alleged procedural deficiencies to the attention of a panel at the earliest possible opportunity. In this case, we see no reason to disagree with the Panel's view that the United States' objection was not raised in a timely manner. At the same time, however, as we have observed previously, certain issues going to the *jurisdiction* of a panel are so fundamental that they may be considered at any stage in a proceeding. In our view, the Panel was correct, therefore, in turning to consider its terms of reference and in satisfying itself as to its jurisdiction with respect to this matter.

J.2.1.15 *US – Offset Act (Byrd Amendment)*, para. 208
(WT/DS217/AB/R, WT/DS234/AB/R)

... "[a]n objection to jurisdiction should be raised as early as possible" and it would be preferable, in the interests of due process, for the appellant to raise such issues in the Notice of Appeal, so that appellees will be aware that this claim will be advanced on appeal. However, in our view, the issue of a panel's jurisdiction is so fundamental that it is appropriate to consider claims that a panel has exceeded its jurisdiction even if such claims were not raised in the Notice of Appeal.

Appellate Body. *See* Scope of Appellate Review (S.3)

Panels. *See* Standard of Review (S.7); Terms of Reference of Panels (T.6)

L

Languages. *See* Interpretation, Multiple authentic languages – Article 33 of the Vienna Convention (I.3.11)

Law vs. Fact. *See* Scope of Appellate Review, Issues of law vs. Issues of fact (S.3.3)

L.0 Least-developed Countries

L.0.1 *US – Upland Cotton*, para. 512
(WT/DS267/AB/R)

. . . we recall that Article 24.1 of the DSU requires that "[a]t all stages of the determination of the causes of a dispute and of dispute settlement procedures involving a least-developed country Member, particular consideration shall be given to the special situation of least-developed country Members". We fully recognize the importance of this provision. . . .

L.1 Legislation as such vs. Specific Application. *See also* Anti-Dumping Agreement, Article 17.3 – consultations (A.3.55); Anti-Dumping Agreement, Article 17.4 – "matter referred to the DSB" (A.3.56); Mandatory and Discretionary Legislation (M.1); Municipal Law (M.5); Non-Violation Claims, Article XXIII:1(b) of the GATT 1994 – "any measure" (N.2.2); Terms of Reference of Panels, Specific measure at issue (T.6.3)

L.1.1 *US – 1916 Act*, paras. 60–61
(WT/DS136/AB/R, WT/DS162/AB/R)

Prior to the entry into force of the *WTO Agreement*, it was firmly established that Article XXIII:1(a) of the GATT 1947 allowed a Contracting Party to challenge legislation as such, independently from the application of that legislation in specific instances. While the text of Article XXIII does not expressly address the matter, panels consistently considered that, under Article XXIII, they had the *jurisdiction* to deal with claims against legislation as such. In *examining* such claims, panels developed the concept that mandatory and discretionary legislation should be distinguished from each other, reasoning that only legislation that mandates a violation of GATT obligations can be found as such to be inconsistent with those obligations. We consider the application of this distinction to the present cases in section IV(B) below.

Thus, that a Contracting Party could challenge legislation as such before a panel was well-settled under the GATT 1947. We consider that the case law articulating and applying this practice forms part of the GATT *acquis* which, under Article XVI:1 of the *WTO Agreement*, provides guidance to the WTO and, therefore, to panels and the Appellate Body. Furthermore, in Article 3.1 of the DSU, Members affirm "their adherence to the principles for the management of disputes heretofore applied under Articles XXII and XXIII of GATT 1947". We note that, since the entry into force of the *WTO Agreement*, a number of panels have dealt with dispute settlement claims brought against a Member on the basis of its legislation as such, independently from the application of that legislation in specific instances.

L.1.2 *US – 1916 Act*, paras. 62, 68
(WT/DS136/AB/R, WT/DS162/AB/R)

Turning to the issue of the legal basis for claims brought under the *Anti-Dumping Agreement*, we note that Article 17 of the *Anti-Dumping Agreement* addresses dispute settlement under that Agreement. Just as Articles XXII and XXIII of the GATT 1994 create a legal basis for claims in disputes relating to provisions of the GATT 1994, so also Article 17 establishes the basis for dispute settlement claims relating to provisions of the *Anti-Dumping Agreement*. In the same way that Article XXIII of the GATT 1994 allows a WTO Member to challenge *legislation* as such, Article 17 of the *Anti-Dumping Agreement* is properly to be regarded as allowing a challenge to legislation as such, unless this possibility is excluded. No such *express* exclusion is found in Article 17 or elsewhere in the *Anti-Dumping Agreement*.

...

Article 17.3 does not explicitly address challenges to legislation as such. As we have seen above, Articles XXII and XXIII allow challenges to be brought under the GATT 1994 against legislation as such. Since Article 17.3 is the "equivalent provision" to Articles XXII and XXIII of the GATT 1994, Article 17.3 provides further support for our view that challenges may be brought under the *Anti-Dumping Agreement* against legislation as such, unless such challenges are otherwise excluded.

L.1.3 *US – 1916 Act*, para. 75
(WT/DS136/AB/R, WT/DS162/AB/R)

Moreover, as we have seen above, the GATT and WTO case law firmly establishes that dispute settlement proceedings may be brought based on the alleged inconsistency of a Member's legislation as such with that Member's obligations. We find nothing, and the United States has identified nothing, inherent in the nature of anti-dumping legislation that would rationally distinguish such legislation from other types of legislation for purposes of dispute settlement, or that would remove anti-dumping legislation from the ambit of the generally-accepted practice that a panel may examine legislation as such.

L.1.4 *US – Corrosion-Resistant Steel Sunset Review*, para. 81 and footnote 79 (WT/DS244/AB/R)

. . . we start with the concept of "measure". Article 3.3 of the DSU refers to "situations in which a Member considers that any benefits accruing to it directly or indirectly under the covered agreements are being impaired by *measures taken by another Member*". (emphasis added) This phrase identifies the relevant nexus, for purposes of dispute settlement proceedings, between the "measure" and a "Member". In principle, any act or omission attributable to a WTO Member can be a measure of that Member for purposes of dispute settlement proceedings. The acts or omissions that are so attributable are, in the usual case, the acts or omissions of the organs of the state, including those of the executive branch.[79]

[79] Both specific determinations made by a Member's executive agencies and regulations issued by its executive branch can constitute acts attributable to that Member. . . .

L.1.5 *US – Corrosion-Resistant Steel Sunset Review*, para. 82 (WT/DS244/AB/R)

In addition, in GATT and WTO dispute settlement practice, panels have frequently examined measures consisting not only of particular acts applied only to a specific situation, but also of acts setting forth rules or norms that are intended to have general and prospective application. In other words, instruments of a Member containing rules or norms could constitute a "measure", irrespective of how or whether those rules or norms are applied in a particular instance. This is so because the disciplines of the GATT and the WTO, as well as the dispute settlement system, are intended to protect not only existing trade but also the security and predictability needed to conduct future trade. This objective would be frustrated if instruments setting out rules or norms inconsistent with a Member's obligations could not be brought before a panel once they have been adopted and irrespective of any particular instance of application of such rules or norms. It would also lead to a multiplicity of litigation if instruments embodying rules or norms could not be challenged as such, but only in the instances of their application. Thus, allowing claims against measures, as such, serves the purpose of preventing future disputes by allowing the root of WTO-inconsistent behaviour to be eliminated.

L.1.6 *US – Corrosion-Resistant Steel Sunset Review*, para. 83 (WT/DS244/AB/R)

. . . we have explained that Article 17.4 precludes a panel from addressing individual acts (as opposed to measures "as such") committed by an investigating authority in the context of the initiation and conduct of anti-dumping investigations *unless* one of the three types of measure listed in Article 17.4 is identified in the request for establishment of a panel. These measures are a definitive anti-dumping duty, the acceptance of a price undertaking, and a provisional measure. We have also found, in *US – 1916 Act*, that Article 17.4 does not place such a limit on a panel's jurisdiction to entertain claims against *legislation as such*. Indeed, we stated in that appeal that no provision of the *Anti-Dumping Agreement* precludes a panel from considering claims against legislation *as such*.

L.1.7 *US – Corrosion-Resistant Steel Sunset Review*, para. 86 (WT/DS244/AB/R)

The provisions of the *Anti-Dumping Agreement* setting forth a legal basis for matters to be referred to consultations and thus to dispute settlement, are also cast broadly. Article 17.3 establishes the principle that when a complaining Member "considers" that its benefits are being nullified or impaired "by another Member or Members", it may request consultations. This language underlines that a measure attributable to a Member may be submitted to dispute settlement provided only that another Member has taken the view, in good faith, that the measure nullifies or impairs benefits accruing to it under the *Anti-Dumping Agreement*. There is no threshold requirement, in Article 17.3, that the measure in question be of a certain type.

L.1.8 *US – Corrosion-Resistant Steel Sunset Review*, para. 87 and footnote 87 (WT/DS244/AB/R)

We also believe that the provisions of Article 18.4 of the *Anti-Dumping Agreement* are relevant to the question of the type of measures that may, as such, be submitted to dispute settlement under that Agreement. Article 18.4 contains an explicit obligation for Members to "take all necessary steps, of a general or particular character" to ensure that their "laws, regulations and administrative procedures" are in conformity with the obligations set forth in the *Anti-Dumping Agreement*. Taken as a whole, the phrase "laws, regulations and administrative procedures" seems to us to encompass the entire body of generally applicable rules, norms and standards adopted by Members in connection with the conduct of anti-dumping proceedings.[87] If some of these types of measure could not, as such, be subject to dispute settlement under the *Anti-Dumping Agreement*, it would frustrate the obligation of "conformity" set forth in Article 18.4.

[87] We observe that the scope of each element in the phrase "laws, regulations and administrative procedures" must be determined for purposes of WTO law and not simply by reference to the label given to various instruments under the domestic law of each WTO Member. This determination must be based on the content and substance of the instrument, and not merely on its form or nomenclature. Otherwise, the obligations set forth in Article 18.4 would vary from Member to Member depending on each Member's domestic law and practice.

L.1.9 *US – Corrosion-Resistant Steel Sunset Review*, para. 88 (WT/DS244/AB/R)

This analysis leads us to conclude that there is no basis, either in the practice of the GATT and the WTO generally or in the provisions of the *Anti-Dumping Agreement*, for finding that only certain types of measure can, as such, be challenged in dispute settlement proceedings under the *Anti-Dumping Agreement*. Hence we see no reason for concluding that, in principle, non-mandatory measures cannot be challenged "as such". . . .

L.1.10 *US – Corrosion-Resistant Steel Sunset Review*, para. 89 (WT/DS244/AB/R)

We observe, too, that allowing measures to be the subject of dispute settlement proceedings, whether or not they are of a mandatory character, is consistent with the comprehensive nature of the right of Members to resort to dispute settlement to "preserve [their] rights and obligations . . . under the covered agreements, and to clarify the existing provisions of those agreements". As long as a Member respects the principles set forth in Articles 3.7 and 3.10 of the DSU, namely, to exercise their "judgement as to whether action under these procedures would be fruitful" and to engage in dispute settlement in good faith, then that Member is entitled to request a panel to examine measures that the Member considers nullify or impair its benefits. We do not think that panels are obliged, as a preliminary jurisdictional matter, to examine whether the challenged measure is mandatory. This issue is relevant, if at all, only as part of the panel's assessment of whether the measure is, as such, inconsistent with particular obligations. It is to this issue that we now turn.

L.1.11 *US – Corrosion-Resistant Steel Sunset Review*, para. 168 (WT/DS244/AB/R)

When a measure is challenged "as such", the starting point for an analysis must be the measure on its face. If the meaning and content of the measure are clear on its face, then the consistency of the measure as such can be assessed on that basis alone. If, however, the meaning or content of the measure is not evident on its face, further examination is required. . . .

L.1.12 *US – Oil Country Tubular Goods Sunset Reviews*, para. 172 (WT/DS268/AB/R)

. . . In our view, "as such" challenges against a Member's measures in WTO dispute settlement proceedings are serious challenges. By definition, an "as such" claim challenges laws, regulations, or other instruments of a Member that have general and prospective application, asserting that a Member's conduct – not only in a particular instance that has occurred, but in future situations as well – will necessarily be inconsistent with that Member's WTO obligations. In essence, complaining parties bringing "as such" challenges seek to prevent Members *ex ante* from engaging in certain conduct. The implications of such challenges are obviously more far-reaching than "as applied" claims.

L.1.13 *US – Oil Country Tubular Goods Sunset Reviews*, para. 173 (WT/DS268/AB/R)

We also expect that measures subject to "as such" challenges would normally have undergone, under municipal law, thorough scrutiny through various deliberative processes to ensure consistency with the Member's international obligations, including those found in the covered agreements, and that the enactment of such a measure would implicitly reflect the conclusion of that Member that the measure is not inconsistent with those obligations. The presumption that WTO Members act in good faith in the implementation of their WTO commitments is particularly apt in the context of measures challenged "as such". We would therefore urge complaining parties to be *especially diligent* in setting out "as such" claims in their panel requests as clearly as possible. In particular, we would expect that "as such" claims state unambiguously the specific measures of municipal law challenged by the complaining party and the legal basis for the allegation that those measures are not consistent with particular provisions of the covered agreements. Through such straightforward presentations of "as such" claims, panel requests should leave respondent parties in little doubt that, notwithstanding their own considered views on the WTO-consistency of their measures, another Member intends to challenge those measures, as such, in WTO dispute settlement proceedings.

L.1.14 *US – Oil Country Tubular Goods Sunset Reviews*, para. 186 (WT/DS268/AB/R)

We turn first to the United States' understanding of the Appellate Body's finding in *US – Corrosion-Resistant Steel Sunset Review*. We disagree with the United States' assertion that, in that case, the Appellate Body left open the question whether the SPB is a measure. It is clear that by reversing the panel's finding that "the Sunset Policy Bulletin is not a measure that is challengeable, as such, under the *WTO Agreement*", the Appellate Body concluded that the SPB is a measure subject to WTO dispute settlement. . . .

L.1.15 *US – Oil Country Tubular Goods Sunset Reviews*, para. 187 (WT/DS268/AB/R)

. . . As noted by the United States, in *US – Corrosion-Resistant Steel Sunset Review*, the Appellate Body indicated that "acts setting forth rules or norms that are intended to have general and prospective application" are measures subject to WTO dispute settlement. We disagree with the United States' application of these criteria to the SPB. In our view, the SPB has normative value, as it provides administrative guidance and creates expectations among the public and among private actors. It is intended to have general application, as it is to apply to all the sunset reviews conducted in the United States. It is also intended to have prospective application, as it is intended to apply to sunset reviews taking place after its issuance. Thus, we confirm – once again – that the SPB, as such, is subject to WTO dispute settlement.

L.1.16 *Dominican Republic – Import and Sale of Cigarettes*, para. 107 (WT/DS302/AB/R)

. . . we observe that the Appellate Body has consistently affirmed the right of WTO Members to challenge legislation laying down norms or rules "as such", as well as their right to bring claims against the application of such measures in specific instances. . . .

Legitimate expectation. *See* Interpretation (I.3)

L.2 Licensing Agreement

L.2.1 *EC – Bananas III*, para. 193
(WT/DS27/AB/R)

. . . Although the precise terms of Article 1.1 do not say explicitly that licensing procedures for tariff quotas are within the scope of the *Licensing Agreement*, a careful reading of that provision leads inescapably to that conclusion. . . .

L.2.2 *EC – Bananas III*, para. 197
(WT/DS27/AB/R)

. . . By its very terms, Article 1.3 of the *Licensing Agreement* clearly applies to the *application* and *administration* of import licensing procedures, and requires that this application and administration be "neutral . . . fair and equitable". Article 1.3 of the *Licensing Agreement* does not require the import licensing *rules*, as such, to be neutral, fair and equitable. . . .

. . . none of the provisions of the *Licensing Agreement* concerns import licensing *rules, per se*. As is made clear by the title of the *Licensing Agreement*, it concerns import licensing *procedures*. The preamble of the *Licensing Agreement* indicates clearly that this agreement relates to import licensing procedures and their administration, not to import licensing rules. Article 1.1 of the *Licensing Agreement* defines its scope as the *administrative procedures* used for the operation of import licensing regimes.

L.2.3 *EC – Poultry*, para. 121
(WT/DS69/AB/R)

. . . The requirement to prevent trade distortion found in Articles 1.2 and 3.2 of the *Licensing Agreement* refers to *any* trade distortion that may be caused by the introduction or operation of licensing procedures, and is not necessarily limited to that part of trade to which the licensing procedures themselves apply. There may be situations where the operation of licensing procedures, in fact, have restrictive or distortive effects on that part of trade that is not strictly subject to those procedures.

L.2.4 *EC – Bananas III*, paras. 203–204
(WT/DS27/AB/R)

. . . We attach no significance to the difference in the phrases "neutral in application and administered in a fair and equitable manner" in Article 1.3 of the *Licensing Agreement* and "administer in a uniform, impartial and reasonable manner" in Article X:3(a) of the GATT 1994. In our view, the two phrases are, for all practical purposes, interchangeable. We agree, therefore, with the Panel's interpretation that the provisions of Article X:3(a) of the GATT 1994 and Article 1.3 of the *Licensing Agreement* have identical coverage.

Although Article X:3(a) of the GATT 1994 and Article 1.3 of the *Licensing Agreement* both apply, the Panel, in our view, should have applied the *Licensing Agreement* first, since this agreement deals specifically, and in detail, with the administration of import licensing procedures. If the Panel had done so, then there would have been no need for it to address the alleged inconsistency with Article X:3(a) of the GATT 1994.

Like products. *See* National Treatment, Article III:2 of the GATT 1994, first sentence – "like products" (N.1.3); National Treatment, Article III:4 of the GATT 1994 – Regulatory discrimination, "Like products" (N.1.9.1); Textiles and Clothing Agreement, Article 6.2 – "like products" (T.7.5)

L.3 Lomé Convention

L.3.1 *EC – Bananas III*, para. 167

(WT/DS27/AB/R)

The European Communities asserts that the Panel should not have conducted an objective examination of the requirements of the Lomé Convention, but instead should have deferred to the "common" EC and ACP views on the appropriate interpretation of the Lomé Convention. This assertion is without merit. The Panel was correct in stating:

> We note that since the GATT CONTRACTING PARTIES incorporated a reference to the Lomé Convention into the Lomé waiver, the meaning of the Lomé Convention became a GATT/WTO issue, at least to that extent. Thus, we have no alternative but to examine the provisions of the Lomé Convention ourselves in so far as it is necessary to interpret the Lomé waiver. . . .

M

M.1 Mandatory and Discretionary Legislation. *See also* Burden of Proof, General (B.3.1); Jurisdiction, General (J.2.1); Municipal Law (M.5); Terms of Reference of Panels, Specific measure at issue (T.6.3)

M.1.1 *US – 1916 Act*, paras. 60–61
(WT/DS136/AB/R, WT/DS162/AB/R)

Prior to the entry into force of the *WTO Agreement*, it was firmly established that Article XXIII:1(a) of the GATT 1947 allowed a Contracting Party to challenge legislation as such, independently from the application of that legislation in specific instances. While the text of Article XXIII does not expressly address the matter, panels consistently considered that, under Article XXIII, they had the *jurisdiction* to deal with claims against legislation as such. In *examining* such claims, panels developed the concept that mandatory and discretionary legislation should be distinguished from each other, reasoning that only legislation that mandates a violation of GATT obligations can be found as such to be inconsistent with those obligations. We consider the application of this distinction to the present cases in section IV(B) below.

Thus, that a Contracting Party could challenge legislation as such before a panel was well-settled under the GATT 1947. We consider that the case law articulating and applying this practice forms part of the GATT *acquis* which, under Article XVI:1 of the *WTO Agreement*, provides guidance to the WTO and, therefore, to panels and the Appellate Body. Furthermore, in Article 3.1 of the DSU, Members affirm "their adherence to the principles for the management of disputes heretofore applied under Articles XXII and XXIII of GATT 1947". We note that, since the entry into force of the *WTO Agreement*, a number of panels have dealt with dispute settlement claims brought against a Member on the basis of its legislation as such, independently from the application of that legislation in specific instances.

M.1.2 *US – 1916 Act*, paras. 88–91
(WT/DS136/AB/R, WT/DS162/AB/R)

. . . the concept of mandatory as distinguished from discretionary legislation was developed by a number of GATT panels as a threshold consideration in determining when legislation as such – rather than a specific application of that legislation – was inconsistent with a Contracting Party's GATT 1947 obligations. The practice of GATT panels was summed up in *United States – Tobacco* as follows:

> . . . panels had consistently ruled that legislation which mandated action inconsistent with the General Agreement could be challenged as such, whereas legislation which merely gave the discretion to the *executive authority* of a contracting party to act inconsistently with the General Agreement could not be challenged as such; only the actual application of such legislation inconsistent with the General Agreement could be subject to challenge. (emphasis added)

Thus, the relevant discretion, for purposes of distinguishing between mandatory and discretionary legislation, is a discretion vested in the *executive branch* of government.

The 1916 Act provides for two types of actions to be brought in a United States federal court: a civil action initiated by private parties, and a criminal action initiated by the United States Department of Justice. Turning first to the civil action, we note that there is no relevant discretion accorded to the executive branch of the United States' government with respect to such action. These civil actions are brought by private parties. A judge faced with such proceedings must simply *apply* the 1916 Act. In consequence, so far as the civil actions that may be brought under the 1916 Act are concerned, the 1916 Act is clearly mandatory legislation as that term has been understood for purposes of the distinction between mandatory and discretionary legislation.

The Panel, however, examined that part of the 1916 Act that provides for criminal prosecutions, and found that the discretion enjoyed by the United States Department of Justice to initiate or not to initiate criminal proceedings does not mean that the 1916 Act is a discretionary law. In light of the case law developing and applying the distinction between mandatory and discretionary legislation, we believe that the discretion enjoyed by the United States Department of Justice is not discretion of such a nature or of such breadth as to transform the 1916 Act into discretionary legislation, as this term has been understood for purposes of distinguishing between mandatory and discretionary legislation. We, therefore, agree with the Panel's finding on this point.

M.1.3 *US – 1916 Act*, para. 99
(WT/DS136/AB/R, WT/DS162/AB/R)

We note that answering the question of the continuing relevance of the distinction between mandatory and discretionary legislation for claims brought under the *Anti-Dumping Agreement* would have no impact upon the outcome of these appeals, because the 1916 Act is clearly not discretionary legislation, as that term has been understood for purposes of distinguishing between mandatory and discretionary legislation. Therefore, we do not find it necessary to consider, in these cases, whether Article 18.4, or any other provision of the *Anti-Dumping Agreement*, has supplanted or modified the distinction between mandatory and discretionary legislation. For the same reasons, the Panel did not, in the Japan Panel Report, need to opine on this issue.

M.1.4 *US – 1916 Act*, para. 100
(WT/DS136/AB/R, WT/DS162/AB/R)

. . . we note that, before the Panel and before us, the United States invoked the distinction between mandatory and discretionary legislation to argue that the 1916 Act cannot be mandatory legislation because United States' courts have interpreted or may interpret the 1916 Act in ways that would make it consistent with the WTO obligations of the United States. As we have seen, in the case law developed under the GATT 1947, the distinction between mandatory and discretionary legislation turns on whether there is relevant discretion vested in the *executive branch* of government. The United States, however, does not rely upon the discretion of the executive branch of the United States' government, but on the interpretation of the 1916 Act by the United States' courts. In our view, this argument does not relate to the distinction between mandatory and discretionary legislation.

M.1.5 *US – Section 211 Appropriations Act*, para. 259
(WT/DS176/AB/R)

. . . As the Panel rightly noted, in *US – 1916 Act*, we stated that a distinction should be made between legislation that mandates WTO-inconsistent behaviour, and legislation that gives rise to executive authority that can be exercised with discretion. We quoted with approval there the following statement of the panel in *US – Tobacco*:

> . . . panels had consistently ruled that legislation which mandated action inconsistent with the General Agreement could be challenged as such, whereas legislation which merely gave the discretion to the executive authority of a contracting party to act inconsistently with the General Agreement could not be challenged as such; only the actual application of such legislation inconsistent with the General Agreement could be subject to challenge.

Thus, where discretionary authority is vested in the executive branch of a WTO Member, it cannot be assumed that the WTO Member will fail to implement its obligations under the *WTO Agreement* in good faith. Relying on these rulings, and interpreting them correctly, the Panel concluded that it could not assume that OFAC would exercise its discretionary executive authority inconsistently with the obligations of the United States under the *WTO Agreement*. Here, too, we agree.

M.1.6 *US – Countervailing Measures on Certain EC Products*, para. 159 and footnote 334
(WT/DS212/AB/R)

There remains the question whether Section 1677(5)(F) is inconsistent *per se* with the WTO obligations of the United States because it mandates[334] a particular method of determining the existence of a "benefit" that is contrary to the *SCM Agreement*. We agree with both the appellant and appellee that "Section 1677(5)(F) does not

... prescribe any specific methodology", and, consequently, does not mandate the USDOC to apply the "same person" method. ...

[334] We are not, by implication, precluding the possibility that a Member could violate its WTO obligations by enacting legislation granting discretion to its authorities to act in violation of its WTO obligation. We make no finding in this respect.

M.1.7 *US – Corrosion–Resistant Steel Sunset Review*, para. 89 (WT/DS244/AB/R)

We observe, too, that allowing measures to be the subject of dispute settlement proceedings, whether or not they are of a mandatory character, is consistent with the comprehensive nature of the right of Members to resort to dispute settlement to "preserve [their] rights and obligations ... under the covered agreements, and to clarify the existing provisions of those agreements". As long as a Member respects the principles set forth in Articles 3.7 and 3.10 of the DSU, namely, to exercise their "judgement as to whether action under these procedures would be fruitful" and to engage in dispute settlement in good faith, then that Member is entitled to request a panel to examine measures that the Member considers nullify or impair its benefits. We do not think that panels are obliged, as a preliminary jurisdictional matter, to examine whether the challenged measure is mandatory. This issue is relevant, if at all, only as part of the panel's assessment of whether the measure is, as such, inconsistent with particular obligations. It is to this issue that we now turn.

M.1.8 *US – Corrosion–Resistant Steel Sunset Review*, para. 93 and footnote 94 (WT/DS244/AB/R)

In adopting this approach, the Panel was applying, as a preliminary consideration, the so-called "mandatory/discretionary distinction". We explained in *US – 1916 Act* that this analytical tool existed prior to the establishment of the WTO, and that a number of GATT panels had used it as a technique for evaluating claims brought against legislation as such. As the Panel seemed to acknowledge, we have not, as yet, been required to pronounce generally upon the continuing relevance or significance of the mandatory/discretionary distinction.[94] Nor do we consider that this appeal

[94] In our Report in *US – 1916 Act,* we examined the challenged legislation and found that the alleged "discretionary" elements of that legislation were not of a type that, *even under the mandatory/discretionary distinction*, would have led to the measure being classified as "discretionary" and therefore consistent with the *Anti-Dumping Agreement*. In other words, we *assumed* that the distinction could be applied because it did not, in any event, affect the outcome of our analysis. We specifically indicated that it was not necessary, in that appeal, for us to answer "the question of the continuing relevance of the distinction between mandatory and discretionary legislation for claims brought under the *Anti-Dumping Agreement*". (Appellate Body Report, *US – 1916 Act*, para. 99) We also expressly declined to answer this question in footnote 334 to paragraph 159 of our Report in *US – Countervailing Measures on Certain EC Products*. Furthermore, the appeal in *US – Section 211 Appropriations Act* presented a unique set of circumstances. In that case, in defending the measure challenged by the European Communities, the United States unsuccessfully argued that discretionary regulations, issued under a separate law, cured the discriminatory aspects of the measure at issue.

calls for us to undertake a comprehensive examination of this distinction. We do, nevertheless, wish to observe that, as with any such analytical tool, the import of the "mandatory/discretionary distinction" may vary from case to case. For this reason, we also wish to caution against the application of this distinction in a mechanistic fashion.

M.1.9 *US – Corrosion–Resistant Steel Sunset Review*, para. 98 (WT/DS244/AB/R)

The Panel adopted a similar narrow approach in finding that the Sunset Policy Bulletin is not an "administrative procedure" within the meaning of Article 18.4 of the *Anti-Dumping Agreement*. Having adopted the view that an administrative procedure is "a pre-established rule for the conduct of an anti-dumping investigation", the Panel assumed that a "rule" means a "mandatory rule" and used its previous finding that the Sunset Policy Bulletin is not a mandatory legal instrument to come to the conclusion that it therefore cannot be an administrative procedure. Again, the Panel did not consider the normative nature of the provisions of the Sunset Policy Bulletin, nor compare the type of norms that USDOC is required to publish in formal regulations with the type of norms it may set out in policy statements. These inquiries would have assisted the Panel in determining whether the Sunset Policy Bulletin is, in fact, an "administrative procedure" within the meaning of Article 18.4 of the *Anti-Dumping Agreement*.

M.1.10 *US – Upland Cotton*, para. 706 (WT/DS267/AB/R)

The Panel explained that, in its view, "threat" of circumvention under Article 10.1 requires that there be "an unconditional legal entitlement". We see no basis for this requirement in Article 10.1. The Panel also stated that "[i]n order to pose a 'threat' within the meaning of Article 10.1 of the *Agreement on Agriculture*, [it did] not believe that it is sufficient that an export credit guarantee programme might possibly, or theoretically, be used in a manner which threatens to lead to circumvention of export subsidy commitments". In both of these statements, the Panel seems to conflate the phrase "threaten to lead to . . . circumvention" with certainty that the circumvention will happen. We find it difficult, moreover, to reconcile the Panel's interpretation with the ordinary meaning of the term "threaten", which, as we indicated earlier, connotes that something is "likely" to happen. We also find it difficult to reconcile these statements of the Panel with its own view that it did "not believe that the 'mandatory/discretionary' distinction is the sole legally determinative one for our examination of whether or not 'threat' of circumvention of export subsidy commitments within the meaning of Article 10.1 of the *Agreement on Agriculture* has been proven to the required standard".

M.2 MFN Treatment. *See also* Enabling Clause (E.1); Tariff Quotas – Non-discriminatory Administration (T.2)

M.2.1 Article I of the GATT 1994

M.2.1.1 *EC – Bananas III*, para. 206
(WT/DS27/AB/R)

. . . we agree with the Panel that the activity function rules are an "advantage" granted to bananas imported from traditional ACP States, and not to bananas imported from other Members, within the meaning of Article I:1. Therefore, we uphold the Panel's finding that the activity function rules are inconsistent with Article I:1 of the GATT 1994.

M.2.1.2 *Canada – Autos*, para. 78
(WT/DS139/AB/R, WT/DS142/AB/R)

. . . we observe first that the words of Article I:1 do not restrict its scope only to cases in which the failure to accord an "advantage" to like products of all other Members appears *on the face* of the measure, or can be demonstrated on the basis of the words of the measure. Neither the words "*de jure*" nor "*de facto*" appear in Article I:1. Nevertheless, we observe that Article I:1 does not cover only "in law", or *de jure*, discrimination. As several GATT panel reports confirmed, Article I:1 covers also "in fact", or *de facto*, discrimination. Like the Panel, we cannot accept Canada's argument that Article I:1 does not apply to measures which, on their face, are "origin-neutral" . . . .

M.2.1.3 *Canada – Autos*, paras. 79, 81
(WT/DS139/AB/R, WT/DS142/AB/R)

We note next that Article I:1 requires that "*any advantage*, favour, privilege or immunity granted by any Member to *any product* originating in or destined for any other country shall be accorded immediately and unconditionally to the like product originating in or destined for the territories of *all other Members*." (emphasis added) The words of Article I:1 refer not to *some* advantages granted "with respect to" the subjects that fall within the defined scope of the Article, but to "*any advantage*"; not to *some* products, but to "*any product*"; and not to like products from *some* other Members, but to like products originating in or destined for "*all other*" Members.

...

Thus, from both the text of the measure and the Panel's conclusions about the practical operation of the measure, it is apparent to us that "[w]ith respect to customs duties ... imposed on or in connection with importation ...," Canada has granted an "advantage" to some products from some Members that Canada has not "accorded immediately and unconditionally" to "like" products "originating in or destined for the territories of *all other Members*." (emphasis added) And this, we conclude, is not consistent with Canada's obligations under Article I:1 of the GATT 1994.

M.2.1.4 *Canada – Autos*, para. 84
(WT/DS139/AB/R, WT/DS142/AB/R)

The object and purpose of Article I:1 supports our interpretation. That object and purpose is to prohibit discrimination among like products originating in or destined for different countries. The prohibition of discrimination in Article I:1 also serves as an incentive for concessions, negotiated reciprocally, to be extended to all other Members on an MFN basis.

M.2.1.5 *EC – Tariff Preferences*, para. 101
(WT/DS246/AB/R)

It is well settled that the MFN principle embodied in Article I:1 is a "cornerstone of the GATT" and "one of the pillars of the WTO trading system", which has consistently served as a key basis and impetus for concessions in trade negotiations....

M.2.2 Article II of the GATS

M.2.2.1 *EC – Bananas III*, paras. 233–234
(WT/DS27/AB/R)

... The question here is the meaning of "treatment no less favourable" with respect to the MFN obligation in Article II of the GATS. There is more than one way of writing a *de facto* non-discrimination provision. Article XVII of the GATS is merely one of many provisions in the *WTO Agreement* that require the obligation of providing "treatment no less favourable". The possibility that the two Articles may not have exactly the same meaning does *not* imply that the intention of the drafters of the GATS was that a *de jure*, or formal, standard should apply in Article II of the GATS. If that were the intention, why does Article II not say as much? The obligation imposed by Article II is unqualified. The ordinary meaning of this provision does not exclude *de facto* discrimination. Moreover, if Article II was not applicable to *de facto* discrimination, it would not be difficult – and, indeed, it would be a good deal easier in the case of trade in services, than in the case of trade in goods – to devise discriminatory measures aimed at circumventing the basic purpose of that Article.

For these reasons, we conclude that "treatment no less favourable" in Article II:1 of the GATS should be interpreted to include *de facto*, as well as *de jure*, discrimination. . . .

M.2.2.2 *EC – Bananas III*, para. 241
(WT/DS27/AB/R)

We see no specific authority either in Article II or in Article XVII of the GATS for the proposition that the "aims and effects" of a measure are in any way relevant in determining whether that measure is inconsistent with those provisions. In the GATT context, the "aims and effects" theory had its origins in the principle of Article III:1 that internal taxes or charges or other regulations "should not be applied to imported or domestic products so as to afford protection to domestic production". There is no comparable provision in the GATS. . . .

M.2.2.3 *Canada – Autos*, paras. 170–171
(WT/DS139/AB/R, WT/DS142/AB/R)

The wording of this provision suggests that analysis of the consistency of a measure with Article II:1 should proceed in several steps. First, as we have seen, a threshold determination must be made under Article I:1 that the measure is covered by the GATS. This determination requires that there be "trade in services" in one of the four modes of supply, and that there be also a measure which "affects" this trade in services. We have already held that the Panel failed to undertake this analysis.

If the threshold determination is that the measure *is* covered by the GATS, appraisal of the consistency of the measure with the requirements of Article II:1 is the next step. The text of Article II:1 requires, in essence, that treatment by one Member of "services and services suppliers" of any other Member be compared with treatment of "like" services and service suppliers of "any other country". Based on these core legal elements, the Panel should first have rendered its interpretation of Article II:1. It should then have made factual findings as to treatment of wholesale trade services and service suppliers of motor vehicles of different Members commercially present in Canada. Finally, the Panel should have applied its interpretation of Article II:1 to the facts as it found them.

M.2.2.4 *Canada – Autos*, para. 181
(WT/DS139/AB/R, WT/DS142/AB/R)

Clearly, here the Panel is confusing the *application* of the import duty exemption to *manufacturers* with its possible *effect* on *wholesalers*. In our view, the Panel has conducted a "goods" analysis of this measure, and has simply extrapolated its analysis of how the import duty exemption affects manufacturers to wholesale trade service suppliers of motor vehicles. The Panel surmised, without analyzing the effect of the measure on wholesalers *as service suppliers*, that the import duty exemption, granted to a limited number of manufacturers, *ipso facto* affects conditions of competition among wholesalers *in their capacity as service suppliers*. As we stated earlier in respect of whether the measure at issue "affects trade in services", the Panel failed to demonstrate how the import duty exemption granted to certain *manufacturers*, but not to other *manufacturers*, affects the supply of *wholesale trade services* and *the suppliers of wholesale trade services* of motor vehicles. In reaching its conclusions under Article II:1 of the GATS, the Panel has neither assessed the relevant facts – we see no analysis of any evidence relating to the supply of *wholesale trade services* of motor vehicles – nor has it interpreted Article II of the GATS and applied that interpretation to the facts it found.

M.2.3 Article 4 of the TRIPS Agreement

M.2.3.1 *US – Section 211 Appropriations Act*, para. 317
(WT/DS176/AB/R)

The fact that Section 515.201 of Title 31 CFR *could* also apply to a non-Cuban foreign national does not mean, however, that it would offset *in each and every case* the discriminatory treatment imposed by Sections 211(a)(2) and (b) on Cuban original owners. . . . We are, therefore, not satisfied that Section 515.201 would offset the inherently less favourable treatment present in Sections 211(a)(2) and (b) in each and every case.

Minimum Import Price. *See* Agreement on Agriculture, Article 4.2 and Footnote 1 (A.1.9–13)

Modalities Paper. *See* Agreement on Agriculture, Relationship between the Agreement on Agriculture and the Modalities Paper (A.1.37A)

M.3 Mootness of Panel Findings as a Consequence of Appellate Body Ruling. *See also* Completion of the Legal Analysis by the Appellate Body (C.4); Scope of Appellate Review (S.3)

M.3.1 *Brazil – Aircraft (Article 21.5 – Canada)*, para. 78
(WT/DS46/AB/RW)

. . . As Brazil has failed to prove one of the elements necessary to prove that payments made under the revised PROEX are justified by item (k), we do not believe it is necessary to examine the issue of whether export subsidies under the revised PROEX are "the payment [by governments] of all or part of the costs incurred by exporters or financial institutions in obtaining credits" within the meaning of the first paragraph of item (k). Therefore, we do not address the Article 21.5 Panel's findings on this issue. These findings of the Article 21.5 Panel are moot, and, thus, of no legal effect.

M.3.2 *US – Certain EC Products*, paras. 89–90 (WT/DS165/AB/R)

Having found that the 3 March Measure is the measure at issue in this dispute, and that the 19 April action is outside its terms of reference, the Panel should have limited its reasoning to issues that were relevant and pertinent to the 3 March Measure. By making statements on an issue that is only relevant to the 19 April action, the Panel failed to follow the logic of, and thus acted inconsistently with, its *own* finding on the measure at issue in this dispute. The Panel, therefore, erroneously made statements that relate to a measure which it had *itself* previously determined to be outside its terms of reference.

For these reasons, we conclude that the Panel erred by making the statements in paragraphs 6.121 to 6.126 of the Panel Report on the mandate of arbitrators appointed under Article 22.6 of the DSU. Therefore, these statements by the Panel have no legal effect.

M.3.3 *US – Cotton Yarn*, para. 127 (WT/DS192/AB/R)

We finally turn to the United States' appeal against the Panel's interpretation that Article 6.4 requires attribution to all Members the imports from whom cause serious damage or actual threat thereof. In this respect, we note that the scope of this dispute is defined by Pakistan's claims before the Panel. Pakistan claimed that the United States acted inconsistently with Article 6.4 because it "attributed serious damage to imports from Pakistan without making a comparative assessment of the imports from Pakistan and Mexico and their respective effects". The Panel considered it necessary, in its reasoning, to rule on the broader interpretative question of whether Article 6.4 requires attribution to all Members the imports from whom cause serious damage or actual threat thereof. The United States also appeals the Panel's interpretation on this broader question. However, our findings resolve the dispute as defined by Pakistan's claims before the Panel. We, therefore, do not rule on the issue of whether Article 6.4 requires attribution to all Members the imports from whom cause serious damage or actual threat thereof. In these circumstances, the Panel's interpretation on this question is of no legal effect.

M.3.4 *US – Upland Cotton*, para. 511 (WT/DS267/AB/R)

. . . we believe that an interpretation of the phrase "world market share" in Article 6.3(d) of the *SCM Agreement* is unnecessary for purposes of resolving this dispute. We emphasize that we neither uphold nor reverse the Panel's findings on the interpretation of the phrase "world market share" in Article 6.3(d) of the *SCM Agreement*.

M.3.5 *US – Upland Cotton*, para. 748
(WT/DS267/AB/R)

For these reasons, we decline Brazil's request that we reverse the Panel's conclusion that Brazil did not make a *prima facie* case that the ETI Act of 2000 is inconsistent with the United States' WTO obligations. In declining to rule on Brazil's request, we neither endorse nor reject the manner in which the Panel applied the burden of proof in the context of examining Brazil's claim against the ETI Act of 2000.

M.3.6 *US – Upland Cotton*, para. 762
(WT/DS267/AB/R)

We . . . believe that an interpretation of the phrase "any form of subsidy which operates to increase the export" in Article XVI:3 of the GATT 1994 is unnecessary for purposes of resolving this dispute. We emphasize that we neither uphold nor reverse the Panel's interpretation of this phrase in the second sentence of Article XVI:3.

Multiple Authentic Languages. *See* Interpretation (I.3)

M.4 Multiple Complainants. *See also* Panel Reports, Separate panel reports (P.1.3)

M.4.1 *EC – Hormones*, para. 152
(WT/DS26/AB/R, WT/DS48/AB/R)

. . . We consider [the Panel's] decision to hold a joint meeting with the scientific experts consistent with the letter and spirit of Article 9.3 of the DSU. Clearly, it would be an uneconomical use of time and resources to force the Panel to hold two successive but separate meetings gathering the same group of experts twice, expressing their views twice regarding the same scientific and technical matters related to the same contested EC measures. We do not believe that the Panel has erred by addressing the EC procedural objections only where the European Communities could make a precise claim of prejudice. It is evident to us that a procedural objection raised by a party to a dispute should be sufficiently specific to enable the panel to address it.

M.4.2 *EC – Hormones*, para. 153
(WT/DS26/AB/R, WT/DS48/AB/R)

. . . Having access to a common pool of information enables the panel and the parties to save time by avoiding duplication of the compilation and analysis of information already presented in the other proceeding . . . the Panel tried to avoid unnecessary delays, making an effort to comply with the letter and spirit of Article 9.3 of the DSU . . . .

M.4.3 *EC – Hormones*, para. 154
(WT/DS26/AB/R, WT/DS48/AB/R)

. . . Although Article 12.1 and Appendix 3 of the DSU do not specifically require the Panel to grant [the opportunity to participate in the second substantial meeting of the proceedings initiated by Canada] to the United States, we believe that this decision falls within the sound discretion and authority of the Panel, particularly if the Panel considers it necessary for ensuring to all parties due process of law....

M.5 Municipal Law. *See also* Mandatory and Discretionary Legislation (M.1)

M.5.1 *India – Patents (US)*, paras. 65–67
(WT/DS50/AB/R)

In public international law, an international tribunal may treat municipal law in several ways. Municipal law may serve as evidence of facts and may provide evidence of state practice. However, municipal law may also constitute evidence of compliance or non-compliance with international obligations. For example, in *Certain German Interests in Polish Upper Silesia*, the Permanent Court of International Justice observed:

> It might be asked whether a difficulty does not arise from the fact that the Court would have to deal with the Polish law of July 14th, 1920. This, however, does not appear to be the case. From the standpoint of International Law and of the Court which is its organ, municipal laws are merely facts which express the will and constitute the activities of States, in the same manner as do legal decisions and administrative measures. *The Court is certainly not called upon to interpret the Polish law as such; but there is nothing to prevent the Court's giving judgment on the question whether or not, in applying that law, Poland is acting in conformity with its obligations towards Germany under the Geneva Convention.* (emphasis added)

... It is clear that an examination of the relevant aspects of Indian municipal law ... is essential to determining whether India has complied with its obligations under Article 70.8(a). There was simply no way for the Panel to make this determination without engaging in an examination of Indian law. But, as in the case cited above before the Permanent Court of International Justice, in this case, the Panel was not interpreting Indian law "as such"; rather, the Panel was examining Indian law solely for the purpose of determining whether India had met its obligations under the *TRIPS Agreement*....

Previous GATT/WTO panels also have conducted a detailed examination of the domestic law of a Member in assessing the conformity of that domestic law with the relevant GATT/WTO obligations....

M.5.2 *Brazil – Aircraft (Article 21.5 – Canada)*, para. 46
(WT/DS46/AB/RW)

We note Brazil's argument before the Article 21.5 Panel that Brazil has a contractual obligation under domestic law to issue PROEX bonds pursuant to commitments that have already been made, and that Brazil could be liable for damages for breach of contract under Brazilian law if it failed to respect its contractual obligations. In response to a question from us at the oral hearing, however,

Brazil conceded that a WTO Member's domestic law does not excuse that Member from fulfilling its international obligations. Like the Article 21.5 Panel, we do not consider that any private contractual obligations, which Brazil may have under its domestic law, are relevant to the issue of whether the DSB's recommendation to "withdraw" the prohibited export subsidies permits the continued issuance of NTN-I bonds under letters of commitment issued before 18 November 1999.

M.5.3 *US – Shrimp (Article 21.5 – Malaysia)*, paras. 94–95

(WT/DS58/AB/RW)

The CIT ruling in the *Turtle Island* case addressed the Revised Guidelines: that ruling made no change to the interpretation of Section 609. Moreover, as stated by the Panel, the ruling in the *Turtle Island* case is declaratory: the CIT has not ordered the United States Department of State to modify either the content or the interpretation of the Revised Guidelines; in the legal interpretation of the United States authorities entrusted with enforcing them, the Revised Guidelines remain the same. Rightly, when examining the United States measure, the Panel took into account the status of municipal law at the time. In particular, the Panel took note of the fact that the CIT ruling in the *Turtle Island* case has not altered the content of the Revised Guidelines, and has not prevented the United States government from authorizing the importation of TED-caught shrimp from uncertified countries. In response to our questions at the oral hearing, the United States confirmed that the Department of State has received no order from the CIT to change its practice, and, therefore, the Department of State continues to apply the Revised Guidelines as before. Malaysia has not shown otherwise.

There is no way of knowing or predicting when or how that particular legal proceeding will conclude in the United States. The *Turtle Island* case has been appealed and could conceivably go as far as the Supreme Court of the United States. It would have been an exercise in speculation on the part of the Panel to predict either when or how that case may be concluded, or to assume that injunctive relief ultimately would be granted and that the United States Court of Appeals or the Supreme Court of the United States eventually would compel the Department of State to modify the Revised Guidelines. The Panel was correct not to indulge in such speculation, which would have been contrary to the duty of the Panel, under Article 11 of the DSU, to make "an objective assessment of the matter . . . including an objective assessment of the facts of the case".

M.5.4 *US – Hot-Rolled Steel*, para. 200

(WT/DS184/AB/R)

Although it is not the role of panels or the Appellate Body to interpret a Member's domestic legislation as such, it is permissible, indeed essential, to conduct a detailed examination of that legislation in assessing its consistency with WTO law. . . .

M.5.5 *US – Section 211 Appropriations Act*, paras. 105–106
(WT/DS176/AB/R)

Our rulings in these previous appeals are clear: the municipal law of WTO Members may serve not only as evidence of facts, but also as evidence of compliance or non-compliance with international obligations. Under the DSU, a panel may examine the municipal law of a WTO Member for the purpose of determining whether that Member has complied with its obligations under the *WTO Agreement*. Such an assessment is a legal characterization by a panel. And, therefore, a panel's assessment of municipal law as to its consistency with WTO obligations is subject to appellate review under Article 17.6 of the DSU.

To address the legal issues raised in this appeal, we must, therefore, necessarily examine the Panel's interpretation of the meaning of Section 211 under United States law. . . . The meaning given by the Panel to Section 211 is, thus, clearly within the scope of our review as set out in Article 17.6 of the DSU.

M.5.6 *US – Line Pipe*, para. 158
(WT/DS202/AB/R)

. . . we are not concerned with how the competent authorities of WTO Members reach their determinations in applying safeguard measures. The *Agreement on Safeguards* does not prescribe the internal decision-making process for making such a determination. That is entirely up to WTO Members in the exercise of their sovereignty. We are concerned only with the determination itself, which is a singular act for which a WTO Member may be accountable in WTO dispute settlement. It is of no matter to us whether that singular act results from a decision by one, one hundred, or – as here – six individual decision-makers under the municipal law of that WTO Member. What matters to us is whether the determination, however it is decided domestically, meets the requirements of the *Agreement on Safeguards*.

M.5.7 *US – Offset Act (Byrd Amendment)*, para. 259
(WT/DS217/AB/R, WT/DS234/AB/R)

. . . We note that the Panel referred to the "Findings of Congress", not as a *basis* for its conclusion that the CDSOA constitutes a specific action against dumping or subsidies, but rather as a consideration confirming that conclusion. We agree with the Panel that the intent, stated or otherwise, of the legislators is not conclusive as to whether a measure is "against" dumping or subsidies under Article 18.1 of the *Anti-Dumping Agreement* or Article 32.1 of the *SCM Agreement*. Thus, it was not necessary for the Panel to inquire into the intent pursued by United States legislators in enacting the CDSOA and to take this into account in the analysis. The text of the CDSOA provides sufficient information on the structure and design of the CDSOA, that is to say, on the manner in which it operates, to permit an analysis whether the measure is "against" dumping or a subsidy. . . .

M.5.8 *US – Carbon Steel*, para. 157
(WT/DS213/AB/R, WT/DS213/AB/R/Corr.1)

. . . a responding Member's law will be treated as WTO-*consistent* until proven otherwise. The party asserting that another party's municipal law, as such, is inconsistent with relevant treaty obligations bears the burden of introducing evidence as to the scope and meaning of such law to substantiate that assertion. Such evidence will typically be produced in the form of the text of the relevant legislation or legal instruments, which may be supported, as appropriate, by evidence of the consistent application of such laws, the pronouncements of domestic courts on the meaning of such laws, the opinions of legal experts and the writings of recognized scholars. The nature and extent of the evidence required to satisfy the burden of proof will vary from case to case.

M.5.9 *US – Corrosion–Resistant Steel Sunset Review*, para. 168
(WT/DS244/AB/R)

When a measure is challenged "as such", the starting point for an analysis must be the measure on its face. If the meaning and content of the measure are clear on its face, then the consistency of the measure as such can be assessed on that basis alone. If, however, the meaning or content of the measure is not evident on its face, further examination is required. . . .

M.5.10 *US – Softwood Lumber IV*, para. 56
(WT/DS257/AB/R)

. . . we observe that the arguments put forward by Canada relating to the nature of "personal property", raise issues concerning the relevance, for WTO dispute settlement, of the way in which the municipal law of a WTO Member classifies or regulates things or transactions. Previous Appellate Body Reports confirm that an examination of municipal law or particular transactions governed by it might be relevant, as evidence, in ascertaining whether a financial contribution exists. However, municipal laws – in particular those relating to property – vary amongst WTO Members. Clearly, it would be inappropriate to characterize, for purposes of applying any provisions of the WTO covered agreements, the same thing or transaction differently, depending on its legal categorization within the jurisdictions of different Members. Accordingly, we emphasize that municipal law classifications are not determinative of the issues raised in this appeal.

M.5.11 *US – Oil Country Tubular Goods Sunset Reviews*, para. 187
(WT/DS268/AB/R)

We note the argument of the United States that the SPB is not a legal instrument under United States law. This argument, however, is not relevant to the question before us. The issue is not whether the SPB is a legal instrument within the domestic legal system of the United States, but rather, whether the SPB is a measure that may be challenged within the WTO system. The United States has explained that, within the domestic legal system of the United States, the SPB does not bind the USDOC and that the USDOC "is entirely free to depart from [the] SPB at any time". However, it is not for us to opine on matters of United States domestic law. Our mandate is confined to clarifying the provisions of the *WTO Agreement* and to determining whether the challenged measures are consistent with those provisions. . . .

M.5.12 *US – Gambling*, paras. 361–362
(WT/DS285/AB/R)

. . . according to Antigua, the IHA, on its face, authorizes *domestic* service suppliers, but not *foreign* service suppliers, to offer remote betting services in relation to certain horse races. To this extent, in Antigua's view, the IHA "exempts" domestic service suppliers from the prohibitions of the Wire Act, the Travel Act, and the IGBA.

The United States disagreed, claiming that the IHA – a civil statute – cannot "repeal" the Wire Act, the Travel Act, or the IGBA – which are criminal statutes – *by implication*, that is, merely by virtue of the IHA's adoption *subsequent* to that of the Wire Act, the Travel Act, and the IGBA. Rather, under principles of statutory interpretation in the United States, such a repeal could be effective only if done *explicitly*, which was not the case with the IHA.

M.5.13 *US – Gambling*, para. 364
(WT/DS285/AB/R)

. . . the United States' appeal essentially challenges the Panel's failure to accord sufficient weight to the evidence submitted by the United States with respect to the relationship under United States law between the IHA and the measures at issue. The Panel had limited evidence before it, as submitted by the parties, on which to base its conclusion. This limitation, however, could not absolve the Panel of its responsibility to arrive at a conclusion as to the relationship between the IHA and the prohibitions in the Wire Act, the Travel Act, and the IGBA. The Panel found that the evidence provided by the United States was not sufficiently persuasive to conclude that, as regards wagering on horseracing, the remote supply of such services by *domestic* firms continues to be prohibited notwithstanding the plain language of the IHA. In this light, we are not persuaded that the Panel failed to make an objective assessment of the facts.

M.5.14 *Dominican Republic – Import and Sale of Cigarettes*, para. 112
(WT/DS302/AB/R)

Against this background, and consistent with the view expressed by the Appellate Body in *US – Carbon Steel*, we agree with Honduras that consideration of the express wording of the text of legislation establishing a measure is a fundamental element of an assessment of that legislation. That said, however, we see no merit in the proposition advanced by Honduras that a panel must limit itself, in considering a claim against legislation as such, *exclusively* to the wording of legislation itself. Indeed, in *US – Carbon Steel*, the Appellate Body recognized that different types of evidence may support assertions as to the meaning and scope of an impugned measure. A panel enjoys a margin of discretion in weighing such evidence, commensurate with its role as trier of fact.

M.5.15 *Dominican Republic – Import and Sale of Cigarettes*, para. 114 (WT/DS302/AB/R)

Finally, we observe that the situation in this appeal is different from that prevailing in *India – Patents (US)*, upon which Honduras relies. *India – Patents (US)* was a case in which certain "administrative instructions" were held to be insufficient evidence of India's compliance with its obligations under the "mailbox" requirements of the *TRIPS Agreement*, whereas certain legislative provisions were clearly inconsistent with those obligations. The panel and the Appellate Body were not required in *India – Patents (US)* to interpret the words of the relevant legislation *alone*, in isolation from other evidence, as Honduras would have had the Panel do in this case. Indeed, in *India – Patents (US)*, there was a considerable amount of evidence available regarding the proper interpretation of the express terms of the Indian Patents Act, which included, but was not limited to, the text of the legislation itself. The panel in that case was thus able to balance India's assertion that its "administrative instructions" – which required officials to disregard certain mandatory provisions of the Patents Act – were sufficient to implement India's WTO obligations, against evidence that the Indian government itself considered that legislative amendment was necessary. Thus, in *India – Patents (US)*, the panel made full use of the record that was before it. Although the record in that case appears to have been considerably richer than the one available in these proceedings (which appears to consist only of the text of the measure and the letter from the Director-General of Internal Taxes), it appears to us that the Panel in this case also considered all of the evidence that was before it. Accordingly, although the facts of this case differ from *India – Patents (US)*, the panels in each case followed the same – correct – approach in taking into account relevant factual information presented by the parties.

N

N.1 National Treatment

N.1.1 Article III:1 of the GATT 1994 – General Principle

N.1.1.1 *Japan – Alcoholic Beverages II*, pp. 16–17, DSR 1996:I, 97, at 109–110
(WT/DS8/AB/R, WT/DS10/AB/R, WT/DS11/AB/R)

The broad and fundamental purpose of Article III is to avoid protectionism in the application of internal tax and regulatory measures. More specifically, the purpose of Article III "is to ensure that internal measures 'not be applied to imported or domestic products so as to afford protection to domestic production' ". Toward this end, Article III obliges Members of the WTO to provide equality of competitive conditions for imported products in relation to domestic products.... It is irrelevant that "the trade effects" of the tax differential between imported and domestic products, as reflected in the volumes of imports, are insignificant or even non-existent; Article III protects expectations not of any particular trade volume but rather of the equal competitive relationship between imported and domestic products....

... The Article III national treatment obligation is a general prohibition on the use of internal taxes and other internal regulatory measures so as to afford protection to domestic production. This obligation clearly extends also to products not bound under Article II....

N.1.1.2 *Japan – Alcoholic Beverages II*, p. 18, DSR 1996:I, 97, at 111
(WT/DS8/AB/R, WT/DS10/AB/R, WT/DS11/AB/R)

... Article III:1 articulates a general principle that internal measures should not be applied so as to afford protection to domestic production. This general principle informs the rest of Article III. The purpose of Article III:1 is to establish this general principle as a guide to understanding and interpreting the specific obligations contained in Article III:2 and in the other paragraphs of Article III, while respecting, and not diminishing in any way, the meaning of the words actually used in the texts of those other paragraphs. In short, Article III:1 constitutes part of the context of Article III:2, in the same way that it constitutes part of the context of each of the other paragraphs in Article III. Any other reading of Article III would have the effect of rendering the words of Article III:1 meaningless, thereby violating the fundamental principle of effectiveness in treaty interpretation. Consistent with this principle of effectiveness, and with the textual differences in the two sentences, we believe that Article III:1 informs the first sentence and the second sentence of Article III:2 in different ways.

N.1.1.3 *Japan – Alcoholic Beverages II*, p. 18, DSR 1996:I, 97, at 111–112
(WT/DS8/AB/R, WT/DS10/AB/R, WT/DS11/AB/R)

. . . Article III:2, first sentence does not refer specifically to Article III:1. There is no specific invocation in this first sentence of the general principle in Article III:1 that admonishes Members of the WTO not to apply measures "so as to afford protection". This omission must have some meaning. We believe the meaning is simply that the presence of a protective application need not be established separately from the specific requirements that are included in the first sentence in order to show that a tax measure is inconsistent with the general principle set out in the first sentence. However, this does not mean that the general principle of Article III:1 does not apply to this sentence. To the contrary, we believe the first sentence of Article III:2 is, in effect, an application of this general principle. . . .

N.1.1.4 *EC – Asbestos*, para. 93
(WT/DS135/AB/R)

. . . However, both of these paragraphs of Article III constitute specific expressions of the overarching, "general principle", set forth in Article III:1 of the GATT 1994. As we have previously said, the "general principle" set forth in Article III:1 "informs" the rest of Article III and acts "as a guide to understanding and interpreting the specific obligations contained" in the other paragraphs of Article III, including paragraph 4. Thus, in our view, Article III:1 has particular contextual significance in interpreting Article III:4, as it sets forth the "general principle" pursued by that provision. Accordingly, in interpreting the term "like products" in Article III:4, we must turn, first, to the "general principle" in Article III:1, rather than to the term "like products" in Article III:2.

N.1.2 Article III:2 of the GATT 1994 – Tax discrimination

N.1.2.1 *Canada – Periodicals*, p. 19, DSR 1997:I, 449, at 464
(WT/DS31/AB/R)

Article III:2, first sentence, uses the words "directly or indirectly" in two different contexts: one in relation to the application of a tax to imported products and the other in relation to the application of a tax to like domestic products. Any measure that indirectly affects the conditions of competition between imported and like domestic products would come within the provisions of Article III:2, first sentence, or by implication, second sentence, given the broader application of the latter.

N.1.2.2 *Canada – Periodicals*, pp. 22–23, DSR 1997:I, 449, at 468
(WT/DS31/AB/R)

. . . there are two questions which need to be answered to determine whether there is a violation of Article III:2 of the GATT 1994: (a) whether imported and domestic products are like products; and (b) whether the imported products are taxed in excess of the domestic products. If the answers to both questions are affirmative, there is a violation of Article III:2, first sentence. If the answer to one question is negative, there is a need to examine further whether the measure is consistent with Article III:2, second sentence.

N.1.3 Article III:2 of the GATT 1994, first sentence – "like products"

N.1.3.1 SCOPE OF "LIKE PRODUCTS"

N.1.3.1.1 *Japan – Alcoholic Beverages II*, p. 19–20, DSR 1996:I, p. 97 at 112–113
(WT/DS8/AB/R, WT/DS10/AB/R, WT/DS11/AB/R)

Because the second sentence of Article III:2 provides for a separate and distinctive consideration of the protective aspect of a measure in examining its application to a broader category of products that are not "like products" as contemplated by the first sentence, we agree with the Panel that the first sentence of Article III:2 must be construed narrowly so as not to condemn measures that its strict terms are not meant to condemn. . . .

How narrowly is a matter that should be determined separately for each tax measure in each case. We agree with the practice under the GATT 1947 of determining whether imported and domestic products are "like" on a case-by-case basis. . . .

N.1.3.1.2 *Japan – Alcoholic Beverages II*, p. 21, DSR 1996:I, p. 97 at 114
(WT/DS8/AB/R, WT/DS10/AB/R, WT/DS11/AB/R)

No one approach to exercising judgement will be appropriate for all cases. The criteria in *Border Tax Adjustments* should be examined, but there can be no one precise and absolute definition of what is "like". The concept of "likeness" is a relative one that evokes the image of an accordion. The accordion of "likeness" stretches and squeezes in different places as different provisions of the *WTO Agreement* are applied. The width of the accordion in any one of those places must be determined by the particular provision in which the term "like" is encountered as well as by the context and the circumstances that prevail in any given case to which that provision may apply. . . .

N.1.3.1.3 *Canada – Periodicals*, p. 28, DSR 1997:I, p. 449 at 473
(WT/DS31/AB/R)

. . . A case of perfect substitutability would fall within Art. III:2, first sentence, while we are examining the broader prohibition of the second sentence. . . .

N.1.3.1.4 *EC – Asbestos*, paras. 94–95
(WT/DS135/AB/R)

…we observe that, although the obligations in Articles III:2 and III:4 both apply to "like products", the text of Article III:2 differs in one important respect from the text of Article III:4. Article III:2 contains *two separate* sentences, each imposing *distinct* obligations: the first lays down obligations in respect of "like products", while the second lays down obligations in respect of "directly competitive or substitutable" products. By contrast, Article III:4 applies only to "like products" and does not include a provision equivalent to the second sentence of Article III:2….

…this textual difference between paragraphs 2 and 4 of Article III has considerable implications for the meaning of the term "like products" in these two provisions. In *Japan – Alcoholic Beverages*, we concluded, in construing Article III:2, that the two separate obligations in the two sentences of Article III:2 must be interpreted in a harmonious manner that gives meaning to *both* sentences in that provision. We observed there that the interpretation of one of the sentences necessarily affects the interpretation of the other. Thus, the scope of the term "like products" in the first sentence of Article III:2 affects, and is affected by, the scope of the phrase "directly competitive or substitutable" products in the second sentence of that provision….

N.1.3.2 CRITERIA. *See also* National Treatment, Article III:4 of the GATT 1994 – Regulatory discrimination – Relation to Article III:2 (N.1.9.3); Textiles and Clothing Agreement, Article 6.2 – "like products" (T.7.5)

N.1.3.2.1 *Japan – Alcoholic Beverages II*, pp. 20–21, DSR 1996:I, p. 97 at 113–114
(WT/DS8/AB/R, WT/DS10/AB/R, WT/DS11/AB/R)

…In applying the criteria cited in *Border Tax Adjustments* to the facts of any particular case, and in considering other criteria that may also be relevant in certain cases, panels can only apply their best judgement in determining whether in fact products are "like". This will always involve an unavoidable element of individual, discretionary judgement… it is a discretionary decision that must be made in considering the various characteristics of products in individual cases.

N.1.3.2.2 *Japan – Alcoholic Beverages II*, p. 22, DSR 1996:I, p. 97 at 114–115
(WT/DS8/AB/R, WT/DS10/AB/R, WT/DS11/AB/R)

Uniform classification in tariff nomenclatures based on the Harmonized System (the "HS") was recognized in GATT 1947 practice as providing a useful basis for confirming "likeness" in products. However, there is a major difference between tariff classification nomenclature and tariff bindings or concessions made by Members of the WTO under Article of the GATT 1994….

…tariff bindings that include a wide range of products are not a reliable criterion for determining or confirming product "likeness" under Article III:2.

N.1.3.2.3 *Canada – Periodicals*, p. 21, DSR 1997:I, p. 449 at 466
(WT/DS31/AB/R)

. . . As the Panel recognized, the proper test is that a determination of "like products" for the purposes of Article III:2, first sentence, must be construed narrowly, on a case-by-case basis, by examining relevant factors including:
(i) the product's end-uses in a given market;
(ii) consumers' tastes and habits; and
(iii) the product's properties, nature and quality.

N.1.4 Article III:2 of the GATT 1994, first sentence – "in excess of"

N.1.4.1 *Japan – Alcoholic Beverages II*, pp. 18–19, DSR 1996:I, p. 97 at 112
(WT/DS8/AB/R, WT/DS10/AB/R, WT/DS11/AB/R)

. . . Read in their context and in the light of the overall object and purpose of the *WTO Agreement*, the words of the first sentence require an examination of the conformity of an internal tax measure with Article III by determining, first, whether the taxed imported and domestic products are "like" and, second, whether the taxes applied to the imported products are "in excess of" those applied to the like domestic products. If the imported and domestic products are "like products", and if the taxes applied to the imported products are "in excess of" those applied to the like domestic products, then the measure is inconsistent with Article III:2, first sentence.

N.1.4.2 *Japan – Alcoholic Beverages II*, p. 23, DSR 1996:I, p. 97 at 115
(WT/DS8/AB/R, WT/DS10/AB/R, WT/DS11/AB/R)

. . . Even the smallest amount of "excess" is too much. "The prohibition of discriminatory taxes in Article III:2, first sentence, is not conditional on a 'trade effects test' nor is it qualified by a *de minimis* standard." . . .

N.1.5 Article III:2 of the GATT 1994 – Notions of "like" and "directly competitive or substitutable" products

N.1.5.1 *Japan – Alcoholic Beverages II*, p. 25, DSR 1996:I, p. 97 at 117
(WT/DS8/AB/R, WT/DS10/AB/R, WT/DS11/AB/R)

. . . As with "like products" under the first sentence, the determination of the appropriate range of "directly competitive or substitutable products" under the second sentence must be made on a case-by-case basis.

In this case, the Panel emphasized the need to look not only at such matters as physical characteristics, common end-uses, and tariff classifications, but also at the "market-place". This seems appropriate. . . . It does not seem inappropriate to look at competition in the relevant markets as one among a number of means of identifying the broader category of products that might be described as "directly competitive or substitutable".

Nor does it seem inappropriate to examine elasticity of substitution as one means of examining those relevant markets.

N.1.5.2 *Canada – Periodicals*, p. 19, DSR 1997:I, p. 449 at 464–465 (WT/DS31/AB/R)

... Any measure that indirectly affects the conditions of competition between imported and like domestic products would come within the provisions of Article III:2, first sentence, or by implication, second sentence, given the broader application of the latter.

N.1.5.3 *Korea – Alcoholic Beverages*, para. 118 (WT/DS75/AB/R, WT/DS84/AB/R)

... "Like" products are a subset of directly competitive or substitutable products: all like products are, by definition, directly competitive or substitutable products, whereas not all "directly competitive or substitutable" products are "like". The notion of like products must be construed narrowly but the category of directly competitive or substitutable products is broader. While perfectly substitutable products fall within Article III:2, first sentence, imperfectly substitutable products can be assessed under Article III:2, second sentence.

N.1.6 Article III:2 of the GATT 1994, second sentence – "directly competitive or substitutable" products. *See also* Directly Competitive or Substitutable Products (D.1); Textiles and Clothing Agreement, Article 6.2 – "directly competitive products" (T.7.4)

N.1.6.1 *Korea – Alcoholic Beverages*, paras. 114–115 (WT/DS75/AB/R, WT/DS84/AB/R)

The term "directly competitive or substitutable" describes a particular type of relationship between two products, one imported and the other domestic. It is evident from the wording of the term that the essence of that relationship is that the products are in competition. This much is clear both from the word "competitive" which means "characterized by competition", and from the word "substitutable" which means "able to be substituted". The context of the competitive relationship is necessarily the marketplace since this is the forum where consumers choose between different products. Competition in the market-place is a dynamic, evolving process. Accordingly, the wording of the term "directly competitive or substitutable" implies that the competitive relationship between products is *not* to be analyzed *exclusively* by reference to *current* consumer preferences. In our view, the word "substitutable" indicates that the requisite relationship *may* exist between products that are not, at a given moment, considered by consumers to be substitutes but which are, nonetheless, *capable* of being substituted for one another.

Thus, according to the ordinary meaning of the term, products are competitive or substitutable when they are interchangeable or if they offer, as the Panel noted, "alternative ways of satisfying a particular need or taste". Particularly in a market where there are regulatory barriers to trade or to competition, there may well be latent demand.

N.1.6.2 *Korea – Alcoholic Beverages*, para. 120
(WT/DS75/AB/R, WT/DS84/AB/R)

In view of the objectives of avoiding protectionism, requiring equality of competitive conditions and protecting expectations of equal competitive relationships, we decline to take a static view of the term "directly competitive or substitutable." The object and purpose of Article III confirms that the scope of the term "directly competitive or substitutable" cannot be limited to situations where consumers *already* regard products as alternatives. If reliance could be placed only on current instances of substitution, the object and purpose of Article III:2 could be defeated by the protective taxation that the provision aims to prohibit. . . .

N.1.6.3 *Korea – Alcoholic Beverages*, para. 124
(WT/DS75/AB/R, WT/DS84/AB/R)

. . . the term "directly competitive or substitutable" does not prevent a panel from taking account of evidence of latent consumer demand as one of a range of factors to be considered when assessing the competitive relationship between imported and domestic products under Article III:2, second sentence, of the GATT 1994. . . .

N.1.6.4 *Korea – Alcoholic Beverages*, para. 127
(WT/DS75/AB/R, WT/DS84/AB/R)

. . . the object and purpose of Article III is the maintenance of equality of competitive conditions for imported and domestic products. It is, therefore, not only legitimate, but even necessary, to take account of this purpose in interpreting the term "directly competitive or substitutable product".

N.1.6.5 *Korea – Alcoholic Beverages*, para. 134
(WT/DS75/AB/R, WT/DS84/AB/R)

In taking issue with the use of the term "nature of competition", Korea, in effect, objects to the Panel's sceptical attitude to quantification of the competitive relationship between imported and domestic products. For the reasons set above, we share the Panel's reluctance to rely unduly on quantitative analyses of the competitive relationship. In our view, an approach that focused solely on the quantitative overlap of competition would, in essence, make cross-price elasticity *the* decisive criterion in determining whether products are "directly competitive or substitutable". . . .

N.1.6.6 *Korea – Alcoholic Beverages*, para. 137
(WT/DS75/AB/R, WT/DS84/AB/R)

It is, of course, true that the "directly competitive or substitutable" relationship must be present in the market at issue . . . . It is also true that consumer responsiveness to products may vary from country to country. This does not, however, preclude consideration of consumer behaviour in a country other than the one at issue. It seems to us that evidence from other markets may be pertinent to the examination of the market at issue, particularly when demand on that market has been influenced by regulatory barriers to trade or to competition. Clearly, not every other market will be relevant to the market at issue. But if another market displays characteristics similar to the market at issue, then evidence of consumer demand in that other market may have some relevance to the market at issue. This, however, can only be determined on a case-by-case basis, taking account of all relevant facts.

N.1.6.7 *Korea – Alcoholic Beverages*, paras. 142–143
(WT/DS75/AB/R, WT/DS84/AB/R)

. . . Some grouping is almost always necessary in cases arising under Article III:2, second sentence, since generic categories commonly include products with *some* variation in composition, quality, function and price, and thus commonly give rise to sub-categories. From a slightly different perspective, we note that "grouping" of products involves at least a preliminary characterization by the treaty interpreter that certain products are sufficiently similar as to, for instance, composition, quality, function and price, to warrant treating them as a group for convenience in analysis. But, the use of such "analytical tools" does not relieve a panel of its duty to make an objective assessment of whether the components of a group of imported products are directly competitive or substitutable with the domestic products. . . .

Whether, and to what extent, products can be grouped is a matter to be decided on a case-by-case basis. . . .

N.1.7 Article III:2 of the GATT 1994, second sentence – "not similarly taxed"

N.1.7.1 *Japan – Alcoholic Beverages II*, p. 27, DSR 1996:I, p. 97 at 118 119
(WT/DS8/AB/R, WT/DS10/AB/R, WT/DS11/AB/R)

To interpret "in excess of" and "not similarly taxed" identically would deny any distinction between the first and second sentences of Article III:2. Thus, in any given case, there may be some amount of taxation on imported products that may well be "in excess of" the tax on domestic "like products" but may not be so much as to compel a conclusion that "directly competitive or substitutable" imported and domestic products are "not similarly taxed" for the purposes of the *Ad* Article to Article III:2, second sentence. In other words, there may be an amount of excess taxation that may well be more of a burden on imported products than on domestic "directly competitive or substitutable products" but may nevertheless not be enough to justify a conclusion that such products are "not similarly taxed" for the purposes of Article III:2, second sentence. . . .

N.1.7.2 *Japan – Alcoholic Beverages II*, p. 27, DSR 1996:I, p. 97 at 119
(WT/DS8/AB/R, WT/DS10/AB/R, WT/DS11/AB/R)

. . . We agree with the Panel that this amount of differential taxation must be more than *de minimis* to be deemed "not similarly taxed" in any given case. And, like the Panel, we believe that whether any particular differential amount of taxation is *de minimis* or is not *de minimis* must, here too, be determined on a case-by-case basis. Thus, to be "not similarly taxed", the tax burden on imported products must be heavier than on "directly competitive or substitutable" domestic products, and that burden must be more than *de minimis* in any given case.

N.1.7.3 *Canada – Periodicals*, p. 29, DSR 1997:I, p. 449 at 474
(WT/DS31/AB/R)

. . . we find that the amount of the taxation is far above the *de minimis* threshold required by the Appellate Body Report in *Japan – Alcoholic Beverages*. The magnitude of this tax is sufficient to prevent the production and sale of split–run periodicals in Canada.

N.1.7.4 *Canada – Periodicals*, p. 32, DSR 1997:I, p. 449 at 476
(WT/DS31/AB/R)

We therefore conclude on the basis of the above reasons, including the magnitude of the differential taxation, the several statements of the Government of Canada's explicit policy objectives in introducing the measure and the demonstrated actual protective effect of the measure, that the design and structure of Part V.1 of the Excise Tax Act is clearly to afford protection to the production of Canadian periodicals.

N.1.7.5 *Chile – Alcoholic Beverages*, para. 49
(WT/DS87/AB/R, WT/DS110/AB/R)

. . . We must, therefore, assess the relative tax burden imposed on directly competitive or substitutable domestic and imported products.

N.1.7.6 *Chile – Alcoholic Beverages*, paras. 52–53
(WT/DS87/AB/R, WT/DS110/AB/R)

. . . The examination under the second issue must, therefore, take into account the fact that the group of directly competitive or substitutable domestic and imported products at issue in this case is not limited solely to beverages of a specific alcohol content, falling within a *particular* fiscal category, but covers *all* the distilled alcoholic beverages in *each and every* fiscal category under the New Chilean System.

A comprehensive examination of this nature, which looks at *all* of the directly competitive or substitutable domestic and imported products, shows that the tax burden on imported products, most of which will be subject to a tax rate of 47 per cent, will be heavier than the tax burden on domestic products, most of which will be subject to a tax rate of 27 per cent. . . .

N.1.8 Article III:2 of the GATT 1994, second sentence – "so as to afford protection"

N.1.8.1 *Japan – Alcoholic Beverages II*, pp. 27–28, DSR 1996:I, p. 97 at 119
(WT/DS8/AB/R, WT/DS10/AB/R, WT/DS11/AB/R)

This third inquiry under Article III:2, second sentence, must determine whether "directly competitive or substitutable products" are "not similarly taxed" in a way that affords protection. This is not an issue of intent. It is not necessary for a panel to sort through the many reasons legislators and regulators often have for what they do and weigh the relative significance of those reasons to establish legislative or regulatory intent. If the measure is applied to imported or domestic products so as to afford protection to domestic production, then it does not matter that there may not have been any desire to engage in protectionism in the minds of the legislators or the regulators who imposed the measure. It is irrelevant that protectionism was not an intended objective if the particular tax measure in question is nevertheless, to echo Article III:1, "*applied* to imported or domestic products so as to afford protection to domestic production". This is an issue of how the measure in question is *applied.*

N.1.8.2 *Japan – Alcoholic Beverages II*, p. 29, DSR 1996:I, p. 97 at 120
(WT/DS8/AB/R, WT/DS10/AB/R, WT/DS11/AB/R)

Although it is true that the aim of a measure may not be easily ascertained, nevertheless its protective application can most often be discerned from the design, the architecture, and the revealing structure of a measure. . . .

N.1.8.3 *Japan – Alcoholic Beverages II*, p. 29, DSR 1996:I, p. 97 at 120
(WT/DS8/AB/R, WT/DS10/AB/R, WT/DS11/AB/R)

. . . The very magnitude of the dissimilar taxation in a particular case may be evidence of such a protective application, as the Panel rightly concluded in this case. Most often, there will be other factors to be considered as well. In conducting this inquiry, panels should give full consideration to all the relevant facts and all the relevant circumstances in any given case.

N.1.9 Article III:4 of the GATT 1994 – Regulatory discrimination

N.1.9.1 "LIKE PRODUCTS"

N.1.9.1.1 *EC – Asbestos*, para. 89
(WT/DS135/AB/R)

. . . while the meaning attributed to the term "like products" in other provisions of the GATT 1994, or in other covered agreements, may be relevant context in interpreting Article III:4 of the GATT 1994, the interpretation of "like products" in Article III:4 need not be identical, in all respects, to those other meanings.

N.1.9.1.2 *EC – Asbestos*, paras. 91–92
(WT/DS135/AB/R)

This meaning suggests that "like" products are products that share a number of identical or similar characteristics or qualities. The reference to "similar" as a synonym of "like" also echoes the language of the French version of Article III:4, "*produits similaires*", and the Spanish version, "*productos similares*", which, together with the English version, are equally authentic.

However, as we have previously observed, "dictionary meanings leave many interpretive questions open." In particular, this definition does not resolve three issues of interpretation. First, this dictionary definition of "like" does not indicate *which characteristics or qualities are important* in assessing the "likeness" of products under Article III:4. For instance, most products will have many qualities and characteristics, ranging from physical properties such as composition, size, shape, texture, and possibly taste and smell, to the end-uses and applications of the product. Second, this dictionary definition provides no guidance in determining the *degree or extent to which products must share qualities or characteristics* in order to be "like products" under Article III:4. Products may share only very few characteristics or qualities, or they may share many. Thus, in the abstract, the term "like" can encompass a spectrum of differing degrees of "likeness" or "similarity". Third, this dictionary definition of "like" does not indicate *from whose perspective* "likeness" should be judged. For instance, ultimate consumers may have a view about the "likeness" of two products that is very different from that of the inventors or producers of those products.

N.1.9.2 RELATION TO GENERAL PRINCIPLE IN ARTICLE III:1

N.1.9.2.1 *EC – Asbestos*, para. 93
(WT/DS135/AB/R)

. . . However, both of these paragraphs of Article III constitute specific expressions of the overarching, "general principle", set forth in Article III:1 of the GATT 1994. As we have previously said, the "general principle" set forth in Article III:1 "informs" the rest of Article III and acts "as a guide to understanding and interpreting the specific obligations contained" in the other paragraphs of Article III, including paragraph 4. Thus, in our view, Article III:1 has particular contextual significance in interpreting Article III:4, as it sets forth the "general principle" pursued by that provision. Accordingly, in interpreting the term "like products" in Article III:4, we must turn, first, to the "general principle" in Article III:1, rather than to the term "like products" in Article III:2.

N.1.9.2.2 *EC – Asbestos*, para. 96
(WT/DS135/AB/R)

In construing Article III:4, the same interpretive considerations do not arise, because the "general principle" articulated in Article III:1 is expressed in Article III:4, not through two distinct obligations, as in the two sentences in Article III:2, but instead through a single obligation that applies solely to "like products". Therefore, the harmony that we have attributed to the two sentences of Article III:2 need not and, indeed, cannot be replicated in interpreting Article III:4. Thus, we conclude that, given the textual difference between Articles III:2 and III:4, the "accordion" of "likeness" stretches in a different way in Article III:4.

N.1.9.2.3 *EC – Asbestos*, para. 98
(WT/DS135/AB/R)

As we have said, although this "general principle" is not explicitly invoked in Article III:4, nevertheless, it "informs" that provision. Therefore, the term "like product" in Article III:4 must be interpreted to give proper scope and meaning to this principle. In short, there must be consonance between the objective pursued by Article III, as enunciated in the "general principle" articulated in Article III:1, and the interpretation of the specific expression of this principle in the text of Article III:4. This interpretation must, therefore, reflect that, in endeavouring to ensure "equality of competitive conditions", the "general principle" in Article III seeks to prevent Members from applying internal taxes and regulations in a manner which affects the competitive relationship, in the marketplace, *between the domestic and imported products involved*, "so as to afford protection to domestic production."

N.1.9.3 RELATION TO ARTICLE III:2

N.1.9.3.1 *EC – Asbestos*, paras. 94–95
(WT/DS135/AB/R)

. . . we observe that, although the obligations in Articles III:2 and III:4 both apply to "like products", the text of Article III:2 differs in one important respect from the text of Article III:4. Article III:2 contains *two separate* sentences, each imposing *distinct* obligations: the first lays down obligations in respect of "like products", while the second lays down obligations in respect of "directly competitive or substitutable" products. By contrast, Article III:4 applies only to "like products" and does not include a provision equivalent to the second sentence of Article III:2. . . .

. . . this textual difference between paragraphs 2 and 4 of Article III has considerable implications for the meaning of the term "like products" in these two provisions. . . .

N.1.9.3.2 *EC – Asbestos*, para. 99
(WT/DS135/AB/R)

As products that are in a competitive relationship in the marketplace could be affected through treatment of *imports* "less favourable" than the treatment accorded to *domestic* products, it follows that the word "like" in Article III:4 is to be interpreted to apply to products that are in such a competitive relationship. Thus, a determination of "likeness" under Article III:4 is, fundamentally, a determination about the nature and extent of a competitive relationship between and among products. In saying this, we are mindful that there is a spectrum of degrees of "competitiveness" or "substitutability" of products in the marketplace, and that it is difficult, if not impossible, in the abstract, to indicate precisely where on this spectrum the word "like" in Article III:4 of the GATT 1994 falls. We are not saying that *all* products which are in *some* competitive relationship are "like products" under Article III:4. In ruling on the measure at issue, we also do not attempt to define the precise scope of the word "like" in Article III:4. Nor do we wish to decide if the scope of "like products" in Article III:4 is co-extensive with the combined scope of "like" and "directly competitive or substitutable" products in Article III:2. However, we recognize that the relationship between these two provisions is important, because there is no sharp distinction between fiscal regulation, covered by Article III:2, and non-fiscal regulation, covered by Article III:4. Both forms of regulation can often be used to achieve the same ends. It would be incongruous if, due to a significant difference in the product scope of these two provisions, Members were prevented from using one form of regulation – for instance, fiscal – to protect domestic production of certain products, but were able to use another form of regulation – for instance, non-fiscal – to achieve those ends. This would frustrate a consistent application of the "general principle" in Article III:1. For these reasons, we conclude that the scope of "like" in Article III:4 is broader than the scope of "like" in Article III:2, first sentence. Nonetheless, we note, once more, that Article III:2 extends not only to "like products", but also to products which are "directly competitive or substitutable", and that Article III:4 extends only to "like products". In view of this different language, and although we need not rule, and do not rule, on the precise product scope of Article III:4, we do conclude that the product scope of Article III:4, although broader than the *first* sentence of Article III:2, is certainly *not* broader than the *combined* product scope of the *two* sentences of Article III:2 of the GATT 1994.

N.I.9.4 LIKENESS CRITERIA

N.1.9.4.1 *EC – Asbestos*, paras. 101–102
(WT/DS135/AB/R)

. . . The Report of the Working Party on *Border Tax Adjustments* outlined an approach for analyzing "likeness" that has been followed and developed since by several panels and the Appellate Body. . . .

These general criteria, or groupings of potentially shared characteristics, provide a framework for analyzing the "likeness" of particular products on a case-by-case basis. These criteria are, it is well to bear in mind, simply tools to assist in the task of sorting and examining the relevant evidence. They are neither a treaty–mandated nor a closed list of criteria that will determine the legal characterization of products. More important, the adoption of a particular framework to aid in the examination of evidence does not dissolve the duty or the need to examine, in each case, *all* of the pertinent evidence. In addition, although each criterion addresses, in principle, a different aspect of the products involved, which should be examined separately, the different criteria are interrelated. For instance, the physical properties of a product shape and limit the end-uses to which the products can be devoted. Consumer perceptions may similarly influence – modify or even render obsolete – traditional uses of the products. Tariff classification clearly reflects the physical properties of a product.

N.1.9.4.2 *EC – Asbestos*, para. 111
(WT/DS135/AB/R)

We believe that physical properties deserve a separate examination that should not be confused with the examination of end-uses. Although not decisive, the extent to which products share common physical properties may be a useful indicator of "likeness". Furthermore, the physical properties of a product may also influence how the product can be used, consumer attitudes about the product, and tariff classification. It is, therefore, important for a panel to examine fully the physical character of a product. . . .

N.1.9.4.3 *EC – Asbestos*, para. 114
(WT/DS135/AB/R)

Panels must examine fully the physical properties of products. In particular, panels must examine those physical properties of products that are likely to influence the competitive relationship between products in the marketplace. . . .

N.1.9.4.4 *EC – Asbestos*, paras. 117–118
(WT/DS135/AB/R)

Before examining the Panel's findings under the second and third criteria, we note that these two criteria involve certain of the key elements relating to the competitive relationship between products: first, the extent to which products are capable of performing the same, or similar, functions (end-uses), and, second, the extent to which consumers are willing to use the products to perform these functions (consumers' tastes and habits). Evidence of this type is of particular importance under Article III of the GATT 1994, precisely because that provision is concerned with competitive relationships in the marketplace. If there is – or could be – *no* competitive relationship between products, a Member cannot intervene, through internal taxation or regulation, to protect domestic production. Thus, evidence about the extent to which products can serve the same end-uses, and the extent to which consumers are – or would be – willing to choose one product instead of another to perform those end-uses, is highly relevant evidence in assessing the "likeness" of those products under Article III:4 of the GATT 1994.

We consider this to be especially so in cases where the evidence relating to properties establishes that the products at issue are physically quite different. In such cases, in order to overcome this indication that products are *not* "like", a higher burden is placed on complaining Members to establish that, despite the pronounced physical differences, there is a competitive relationship between the products such that *all* of the evidence, taken together, demonstrates that the products are "like" under Article III:4 of the GATT 1994. In this case, where it is clear that the fibres have very different properties, in particular, because chrysotile is a known carcinogen, a very heavy burden is placed on Canada to show, under the second and third criteria, that the chrysotile asbestos and PCG fibres are in such a competitive relationship.

N.1.9.4.5 *EC – Asbestos*, para. 119
(WT/DS135/AB/R)

. . . the Panel stated that "[i]t suffices that, for a *given utilization*, the properties are the same to the extent that one product can replace the other." (emphasis added) Although we agree that it is certainly relevant that products have similar end-uses for a "small number of . . . applications", or even for a "given utilization", we think that a panel must also examine the other, *different* end-uses for products. It is only by forming a complete picture of the various end-uses of a product that a panel can assess the significance of the fact that products share a limited number of end-uses. In this case, the Panel did not provide such a complete picture of the various end-uses of the different fibres. The Panel did not explain, or elaborate in any way on, the "small number of . . . applications" for which the various fibres have similar end-uses. Nor did the Panel examine the end-uses for these products which were not similar. . . .

N.1.9.4.6 *EC – Asbestos*, para. 120
(WT/DS135/AB/R)

. . . There will be few situations where the evidence on the "likeness" of products will lend itself to "clear results". In many cases, the evidence will give conflicting indications, possibly within each of the four criteria. For instance, there may be some evidence of similar physical properties and some evidence of differing physical properties. Or the physical properties may differ completely, yet there may be strong evidence of similar end-uses and a high degree of substitutability of the products from the perspective of the consumer. A panel cannot decline to inquire into relevant evidence simply because it suspects that evidence may not be "clear" or, for that matter, because the parties agree that certain evidence is not relevant. . . .

N.1.9.4.7 *EC – Asbestos*, para. 121
(WT/DS135/AB/R)

Furthermore, in a case such as this, where the fibres are physically very different, a panel *cannot* conclude that they are "like products" if it *does not examine* evidence relating to consumers' tastes and habits. In such a situation, if there is *no* inquiry into this aspect of the nature and extent of the competitive relationship between the products, there is no basis for overcoming the inference, drawn from the different physical properties of the products, that the products are not "like".

N.1.9.4.8 *EC – Asbestos*, para. 138
(WT/DS135/AB/R)

. . . Where products have a wide range of end-uses, only some of which overlap, we do not believe that it is sufficient to rely solely on evidence regarding the overlapping end-uses, without also examining evidence of the nature and importance of these end-uses in relation to all of the other possible end-uses for the products. In the absence of such evidence, we cannot determine the significance of the fact that chrysotile asbestos and PCG fibres share a small number of similar end-uses.

N.1.9.5 EVIDENCE

N.1.9.5.1 *EC – Asbestos*, para. 103
(WT/DS135/AB/R)

The kind of evidence to be examined in assessing the "likeness" of products will, necessarily, depend upon the particular products and the legal provision at issue. When all the relevant evidence has been examined, panels must determine whether that evidence, as a whole, indicates that the products in question are "like" in terms of the legal provision at issue. We have noted that, under Article III:4 of the GATT 1994, the term "like products" is concerned with competitive relationships between and among products. Accordingly, whether the *Border Tax Adjustments* framework is adopted or not, it is important under Article III:4 to take account of evidence which indicates whether, and to what extent, the products involved are – or could be – in a competitive relationship in the marketplace.

N.1.9.5.2 *EC – Asbestos*, para. 113
(WT/DS135/AB/R)

. . . In reviewing this finding by the Panel, we note that neither the text of Article III:4 nor the practice of panels and the Appellate Body suggest that any evidence should be excluded *a priori* from a panel's examination of "likeness". Moreover, as we have said, in examining the "likeness" of products, panels must evaluate *all* of the relevant evidence. We are very much of the view that evidence relating to the health risks associated with a product may be pertinent in an examination of "likeness" under Article III:4 of the GATT 1994. We do not, however, consider that the evidence relating to the health risks associated with chrysotile asbestos fibres need be examined under a *separate* criterion, because we believe that this evidence can be evaluated under the existing criteria of physical properties, and of consumers' tastes and habits, to which we will come below.

N.1.10 Article III:4 of the GATT 1994 – "affecting"

N.1.10.1 *EC – Bananas III*, para. 211
(WT/DS27/AB/R)

At issue in this appeal is not whether *any* import licensing requirement, as such, is within the scope of Article III:4, but whether the EC procedures and requirements for the *distribution* of import licences for imported bananas among eligible operators *within* the European Communities are within the scope of this provision. . . . These rules go far beyond the mere import licence requirements needed to administer the tariff quota for third-country and non-traditional ACP bananas or Lomé Convention requirements for the importation of bananas. These rules are intended, among other things, to cross-subsidize distributors of EC (and ACP) bananas and to ensure that EC banana ripeners obtain a share of the quota rents. As such, these rules affect "the internal sale, offering for sale, purchase, . . . " within the meaning of Article III:4, and therefore fall within the scope of this provision. . . .

N.1.10.2 *US – FSC (Article 21.5 – EC)*, paras. 208–210
(WT/DS108/AB/RW)

. . . the word "affecting" assists in defining the types of measure that must conform to the obligation not to accord "less favourable treatment" to like imported products, which is set out in Article III:4.

The word "affecting" serves a similar function in Article I:1 of the *General Agreement on Trade in Services* (the "GATS"), where it also defines the types of measure that are subject to the disciplines set forth elsewhere in the GATS but does not, in itself, impose any obligation. . . .

In view of the similar function of the identical word, "affecting", in Article III:4 of the GATT 1994, we also interpret this word, in this provision, as having a "broad scope of application".

N.1.11 Article III:4 of the GATT 1994 – "less favourable treatment"

N.1.11.1 *EC – Bananas III*, paras. 213–214
(WT/DS27/AB/R)

. . . the practice of issuing hurricane licences constitutes an incentive for operators to market EC bananas to the exclusion of third-country and non-traditional ACP bananas. This practice therefore affects the competitive conditions in the market in favour of EC bananas. . . .

. . . we agree with the Panel that the EC practice of issuing hurricane licences is inconsistent with Article III:4 of the GATT 1994.

N.1.11.2 *EC – Bananas III*, para. 216
(WT/DS27/AB/R)

. . . we stated that "Article III:1 articulates a general principle" which "informs the rest of Article III". However, we also said in that Report that Article III:1 "informs the first sentence and the second sentence of Article III:2 in different ways". With respect to Article III:2, first sentence, we noted that it does not refer specifically to Article III:1. . . .

. . .

. . . Article III:4 does *not* specifically refer to Article III:1. Therefore, a determination of whether there has been a violation of Article III:4 does *not* require a separate consideration of whether a measure "afford[s] protection to domestic production".

N.1.11.3 *Korea – Various Measures on Beef*, para. 137
(WT/DS161/AB/R, WT/DS169/AB/R)

A formal difference in treatment between imported and like domestic products is thus neither necessary, nor sufficient, to show a violation of Article III:4. Whether or not imported products are treated "less favourably" than like domestic products should be assessed instead by examining whether a measure modifies the *conditions of competition* in the relevant market to the detriment of imported products.

N.1.11.4 *Korea – Various Measures on Beef*, para. 144
(WT/DS161/AB/R, WT/DS169/AB/R)

. . . the Korean measure formally separates the selling of imported beef and domestic beef. However, that formal separation, *in and of itself*, does not necessarily compel the conclusion that the treatment thus accorded to imported beef is less favourable than the treatment accorded to domestic beef. To determine whether the treatment given to imported beef is less favourable than that given to domestic beef, we must, as earlier indicated, inquire into whether or not the Korean dual retail system for beef modifies the *conditions of competition* in the Korean beef market to the disadvantage of the imported product.

N.1.11.5 *Korea – Various Measures on Beef*, para. 149
(WT/DS161/AB/R, WT/DS169/AB/R)

. . . We are *not* holding that a dual or parallel distribution system that is *not* imposed directly or indirectly by law or governmental regulation, but is rather solely the result of private entrepreneurs acting on their own calculations of comparative costs and benefits of differentiated distribution systems, is unlawful under Article III:4 of the GATT 1994. . . .

N.1.11.6 *Korea – Various Measures on Beef*, paras. 150–151
(WT/DS161/AB/R, WT/DS169/AB/R)

. . . Korea requires that imported beef be sold in a store displaying a sign declaring "Specialized Imported Beef Store". . . .

Without a system of specialized imported beef stores, the sign requirement would have no meaning and would not be required. When considered independently from a dual retail system, a sign requirement might or might not be characterized legally as consistent with Article III:4 of the GATT 1994. . . .

N.1.11.7 *EC – Asbestos*, para. 100
(WT/DS135/AB/R)

We recognize that, by interpreting the term "like products" in Article III:4 in this way, we give that provision a relatively broad product scope – although no broader than the product scope of Article III:2. In so doing, we observe that there is a second element that must be established before a measure can be held to be inconsistent with Article III:4. Thus, even if two products are "like", that does not mean that a measure is inconsistent with Article III:4. A complaining Member must still establish that the measure accords to the group of "like" *imported* products "less favourable treatment" than it accords to the group of "like" *domestic* products. The term "less favourable treatment" expresses the general principle, in Article III:1, that internal regulations "should not be applied . . . so as to afford protection to domestic production". If there is "less favourable treatment" of the group of "like" imported products, there is, conversely, "protection" of the group of "like" domestic products. However, a Member may draw distinctions between products which have been found to be "like", without, for this reason alone, according to the group of "like" *imported* products "less favourable treatment" than that accorded to the group of "like" *domestic* products. In this case, we do not examine further the interpretation of the term "treatment no less favourable" in Article III:4, as the Panel's findings on this issue have not been appealed or, indeed, argued before us.

N.1.11.8 *US – FSC (Article 21.5 – EC)*, para. 215
(WT/DS108/AB/RW)

The examination of whether a measure involves "less favourable treatment" of imported products within the meaning of Article III:4 of the GATT 1994 must be grounded in close scrutiny of the "fundamental thrust and effect of the measure itself". This examination cannot rest on simple assertion, but must be founded on a careful analysis of the contested measure and of its implications in the marketplace. At the same time, however, the examination need not be based on the *actual effects* of the contested measure in the marketplace.

N.1.11.9 *US – FSC (Article 21.5 – EC)*, para. 221
(WT/DS108/AB/RW)

In our view, the above conclusion is not nullified by the fact that the fair market value rule will not give rise to less favourable treatment for like imported products in each and every case. . . .

N.1.11.10 *Dominican Republic – Import and Sale of Cigarettes*, para. 96
(WT/DS302/AB/R)

Nor do we accept Honduras' argument that the bond requirement accords "less favourable treatment" to imported cigarettes because, as the sales of domestic cigarettes are greater than those of imported cigarettes on the Dominican Republic market, the per-unit cost of the bond requirement for imported cigarettes is higher than for domestic products. The Appellate Body indicated in *Korea – Various Measures on Beef* that imported products are treated less favourably than like products if a measure modifies the conditions of competition in the relevant market *to the detriment of imported products*. However, the existence of a detrimental effect on a given imported product resulting from a measure does not necessarily imply that this measure accords less favourable treatment to imports if the detrimental effect is explained by factors or circumstances unrelated to the foreign origin of the product, such as the market share of the importer in this case. In this specific case, the mere demonstration that the per-unit cost of the bond requirement for imported cigarettes was higher than for some domestic cigarettes during a particular period is not, in our view, *sufficient* to establish "less favourable treatment" under Article III:4 of the GATT 1994. Indeed, the difference between the per-unit costs of the bond requirement alleged by Honduras is explained by the fact that the importer of Honduran cigarettes has a smaller market share than two domestic producers (the per-unit cost of the bond requirement being the result of dividing the cost of the bond by the number of cigarettes sold on the Dominican Republic market). In this case, the difference between the per-unit costs of the bond requirement alleged by Honduras does not depend on the foreign origin of the imported cigarettes. Therefore, in our view, the Panel was correct in dismissing the argument that the bond requirement accords less favourable treatment to imported cigarettes because the per-unit cost of the bond was higher for the importer of Honduran cigarettes than for two domestic producers.

N.1.12 Relationship between Article III and Article XX

N.1.12.1 *EC – Asbestos*, para. 115
(WT/DS135/AB/R)

We do not agree with the Panel that considering evidence relating to the health risks associated with a product, under Article III:4, nullifies the effect of Article XX(b) of the GATT 1994. Article XX(b) allows a Member to "adopt and enforce" a measure, *inter alia*, necessary to protect human life or health, even though that measure is inconsistent with another provision of the GATT 1994. Article III:4 and Article XX(b) are distinct and independent provisions of the GATT 1994 each to be interpreted on its own. The scope and meaning of Article III:4 should not be broadened or restricted beyond what is required by the normal customary international law rules of treaty interpretation, simply because Article XX(b) exists and may be available to justify measures inconsistent with Article III:4. The fact that an interpretation of Article III:4, under those rules, implies a less frequent recourse to Article XX(b) does not deprive the exception in Article XX(b) of *effet utile*. Article XX(b) would only be deprived of *effet utile* if that provision could *not* serve to allow a Member to "adopt and enforce" measures "necessary to protect human . . . life or health". Evaluating evidence relating to the health risks arising from the physical properties of a product does not prevent a measure which is inconsistent with Article III:4 from being justified under Article XX(b). We note, in this regard, that, different inquiries occur under these two very different Articles. Under Article III:4, evidence relating to health risks may be relevant in assessing the *competitive relationship in the marketplace* between allegedly "like" products. The same, or similar, evidence serves a different purpose under Article XX(b), namely, that of assessing whether a *Member* has a sufficient basis for "adopting or enforcing" a WTO–inconsistent measure on the grounds of human health.

N.1.13 Article XVII of the GATS. *See also* MFN Treatment, Article II of the GATS (M.2.2)

N.1.13.1 *EC – Bananas III*, para. 241
(WT/DS27/AB/R)

We see no specific authority either in Article or in Article XVII of the GATS for the proposition that the "aims and effects" of a measure are in any way relevant in determining whether that measure is inconsistent with those provisions. In the GATT context, the "aims and effects" theory had its origins in the principle of Article III:1 that internal taxes or charges or other regulations "should not be applied to imported or domestic products so as to afford protection to domestic production". There is no comparable provision in the GATS. Furthermore, in our Report in *Japan – Alcoholic Beverages* the Appellate Body rejected the "aims and effects" theory with respect to Article III:2 of the GATT 1994. The European Communities cites an unadopted panel report dealing with Article III of the GATT 1947, *United States – Taxes on Automobiles* as authority for its proposition, despite our recent ruling.

N.1.14 Article 3.1 of the TRIPS Agreement

N.1.14.1 *US – Section 211 Appropriations Act*, paras. 242–243
(WT/DS176/AB/R)

As we see it, the national treatment obligation is a fundamental principle underlying the *TRIPS Agreement*, just as it has been in what is now the GATT 1994. The

Panel was correct in concluding that, as the language of Article 3.1 of the *TRIPS Agreement*, in particular, is similar to that of Article III:4 of the GATT 1994, the jurisprudence on Article III:4 of the GATT 1994 may be useful in interpreting the national treatment obligation in the *TRIPS Agreement*.

As articulated in Article 3.1 of the *TRIPS Agreement*, the national treatment principle calls on WTO Members to accord no less favourable treatment to non-nationals than to nationals in the "protection" of trade-related intellectual property rights. The footnote to Article 3.1 clarifies that this "protection" extends to "matters affecting the availability, acquisition, scope, maintenance and enforcement of intellectual property rights as well as those matters affecting the use of intellectual property rights specifically addressed" in the *TRIPS Agreement*. . . .

N.1.14.2 *US – Section 211 Appropriations Act*, paras. 261–265 (WT/DS176/AB/R)

. . . the report of the panel in *US – Section 337*. That panel reasoned that "the mere fact that imported products are subject under Section 337 to legal provisions that are different from those applying to products of national origin is in itself not conclusive in establishing inconsistency with Article III:4."

That panel stated further that:

> [I]t would follow . . . that any unfavourable elements of treatment of imported products could be offset by more favourable elements of treatment, provided that the results, as shown in past cases, have not been less favourable. *[E]lements of less and more favourable treatment could thus only be offset against each other to the extent that they always would arise in the same cases and necessarily would have an offsetting influence on the other*. (emphasis added) [BISD 36S/345, para. 5.12]

And that panel, importantly for our purposes, concluded that:

> . . . while the likelihood of having to defend imported products in two fora is small, the existence of the possibility is inherently less favourable than being faced with having to conduct a defence in only one of those fora. (emphasis added) [BISD 36S/345, para. 5.19]

. . . It is likewise not disputed that, under Section 211(a)(2), in *every individual situation* where a non-United States successor-in-interest seeks to assert its rights without the express consent of the original owner or its *bona fide* successor-in-interest, the United States courts are required not to recognize, enforce or otherwise validate any assertion of rights. We emphasize that this situation exists under the statute *on its face*, and that, therefore, unlike the situation with respect to the granting of a special licence to United States successors-in-interest by OFAC, this situation assumes no action by OFAC or by any other agency of the United States Government.

The United States may be right that the likelihood of having to overcome the hurdles of both Section 515.201 of Title 31 CFR and Section 211(a)(2) may, echoing the panel in *US – Section 337*, be *small*. But, again echoing that panel, even the *possibility* that non-United States successors-in-interest face two hurdles is *inherently less favourable* than the undisputed fact that United States successors-in-interest face only one.

N.1.14.3 *US – Section 211 Appropriations Act*, para. 267 (WT/DS176/AB/R)

The United States has not shown, as required under the national treatment obligation, that, in every individual case, the courts of the United States would not validate the assertion of rights by a United States successor-in-interest. Moreover, even if there is, as the United States argues, a *likelihood* that United States courts would not enforce rights asserted by a United States successor-in-interest, the fact remains, nevertheless, that non-United States successors-in-interest are placed by the measure, *on its face*, in an inherently less favourable situation than that faced by United States successors-in-interest. And, even if we were to accept the United States argument about the doctrine of non-recognition of foreign confiscation, presumably that doctrine would apply to those who are not nationals of the United States as well as to those who are. Any application of this doctrine would therefore not offset the discrimination in Section 211(a)(2), because it would constitute yet another, separate obstacle faced by nationals and non-nationals alike. Hence, it would not offset the effect of Section 211(a)(2), which applies only to successors-in-interest who are not United States nationals.

N.1.14.4 *US – Section 211 Appropriations Act*, para. 286 (WT/DS176/AB/R)

. . . to fulfill the national treatment obligation, less favourable treatment must be offset, and thereby eliminated, in *every* individual situation that exists under a measure. Therefore, for this argument by the United States to succeed, it must hold true for *all* Cuban original owners of United States trademarks, and not merely for *some* of them.

N.1.14.5 *US – Section 211 Appropriations Act*, para. 289 (WT/DS176/AB/R)

. . . the very existence of the additional "hurdle" that is imposed by requiring application to OFAC is, in itself, inherently less favourable. Sections 211(a)(2) and (b) do not apply to United States original owners; no application to OFAC is required. But Cuban original owners residing in the "authorized trade territory" must apply to OFAC. Thus, such Cuban original owners must comply with an administrative requirement that does not apply to United States original owners. . . .

N.1.14.6 *US – Section 211 Appropriations Act*, para. 294 (WT/DS176/AB/R)

. . . We are, therefore, not satisfied that Section 515.201 would offset the inherently less favourable treatment present in Sections 211(a)(2) and (b) in each and every case. And, because it has not been shown by the United States that it would do so in each and every case, the less favourable treatment that exists under the measure cannot be said to have been offset and, thus, eliminated.

Non-Discrimination. *See* Enabling Clause (E.1); MFN Treatment (M.2); National Treatment (N.1); State Trading Enterprises (S.7A); Tariff Quotas – Non-discriminatory Administration (T.2)

Non-Governmental Organizations. *See* Amicus Curiae Briefs, Briefs submitted by NGOs (A.2.1)

N.2 Non-Violation Claims. See also Interpretation, Legitimate expectations (I.3.5); Legislation as such vs. Specific Application (L.1)

N.2.1 Article XXIII:1(b) of the GATT 1994 – General

N.2.1.1 *EC – Asbestos*, paras. 185–186
(WT/DS135/AB/R)

. . . Article XXIII:1(a) sets forth a cause of action for a claim that a Member has failed to carry out one or more of its obligations under the GATT 1994. A claim under Article XXIII:1(a), therefore, lies when a Member is alleged to have acted inconsistently with a provision of the GATT 1994. Article XXIII:1(b) sets forth a separate cause of action for a claim that, through the application of a measure, a Member has "nullified or impaired" "benefits" accruing to another Member, "whether or not that measure conflicts with the provisions" of the GATT 1994. Thus, it is not necessary, under Article XXIII:1(b), to establish that the measure involved is inconsistent with, or violates, a provision of the GATT 1994. Cases under Article XXIII:1(b) are, for this reason, sometimes described as "non-violation" cases; we note, though, that the word "non-violation" does not appear in this provision. The purpose of this rather unusual remedy was described by the panel in *European Economic Community – Payments and Subsidies Paid to Processors and Producers of Oilseeds and Related Animal-Feed Proteins* ("*EEC – Oilseeds*") in the following terms:

> The idea underlying [the provisions of Article XXIII:1(b)] is that *the improved competitive opportunities that can legitimately be expected from a tariff concession can be frustrated not only by measures proscribed by the General Agreement but also by measures consistent with that Agreement. In order to encourage contracting parties to make tariff concessions* they must therefore be given a right of redress when a reciprocal concession is impaired by another contracting party as a result of the application of any measure, whether or not it conflicts with the General Agreement. (emphasis added) [BISD 37S/86, para. 144]

Like the panel in *Japan –Measures Affecting Consumer Photographic Film and Paper* ("*Japan –Film*") [Panel Report, para. 10.37], we consider that the remedy in Article XXIII:1(b) "should be approached with caution and should remain an exceptional remedy"....

N.2.2 Article XXIII:1(b) of the GATT 1994 – "any measure"

N.2.2.1 *EC – Asbestos*, paras. 187–188
(WT/DS135/AB/R)

...The wording of the provision, therefore, clearly states that a claim may succeed, under Article XXIII:1(b), *even if the measure "conflicts" with some substantive provisions of the GATT* 1994. It follows that a measure may, *at one and the same time*, be inconsistent with, or in breach of, a provision of the GATT 1994 *and*, nonetheless, give rise to a cause of action under Article XXIII:1(b). Of course, if a measure "conflicts" with a provision of the GATT 1994, that measure must actually fall within the scope of application of that provision of the GATT 1994. We agree with the Panel that this reading of Article XXIII:1(b) is consistent with the panel reports in *Japan – Film* and *EEC – Oilseeds*, which both support the view that Article XXIII:1(b) applies to measures which simultaneously fall within the scope of application of other provisions of the GATT 1994....

...The use of the word "any" suggests that measures of all types may give rise to such a cause of action. The text does not distinguish between, or exclude, certain types of measure. Clearly, therefore, the text of Article XXIII:1(b) contradicts the European Communities' argument that certain types of measure, namely, those with health objectives, are excluded from the scope of application of Article XXIII:1(b).

Notice of Appeal. *See* Claims and Arguments (C.1); Request for the Establishment of a Panel (R.2); Scope of Appellate Review (S.3); Standard of Review, Article 11 of the DSU (S.7.2–7); Working Procedures for Appellate Review, Rule 20 – Notice of appeal (W.2.7)

N.3 Nullification or Impairment. *See also* Non-Violation Claims (N.2)

N.3.1 *EC – Bananas III*, paras. 252–253
(WT/DS27/AB/R)

So, too, is the panel report in *United States –Superfund*, to which the Panel referred. In that case, the panel examined whether measures with "only an insignificant effect on the volume of exports do nullify or impair benefits under Article III:2 ...". The panel concluded (and in so doing, confirmed the views of previous panels) that:

> Article III:2, first sentence, cannot be interpreted to protect expectations on export volumes; it protects expectations on the competitive relationship between imported and domestic products. A change in the competitive relationship contrary to that provision must consequently be regarded *ipso*

> *facto* as a nullification or impairment of benefits accruing under the General Agreement. A demonstration that a measure inconsistent with Article III:2, first sentence, has no or insignificant effects would therefore in the view of the Panel not be a sufficient demonstration that the benefits accruing under that provision had not been nullified or impaired even if such a rebuttal were in principle permitted. [BISD 34S/136, para. 5.1.9]

The panel in *United States –Superfund* subsequently decided "not to examine the submissions of the parties on the trade effects of the tax differential" on the basis of the legal grounds it had enunciated. The reasoning in *United States –Superfund* applies equally in this case.

N.3.2 *EC – Export Subsidies on Sugar*, para. 296
(WT/DS265/AB/R, WT/DS266/AB/R, WT/DS283/AB/R)

. . . pursuant to Article 3.8, where a Member has acted inconsistently with a covered agreement, the inconsistency is presumed to nullify or impair benefits accruing to other Members. In such a case, the burden falls on the defending Member to rebut this presumption by demonstrating that the inconsistency did not result in nullification or impairment. We observe that Article 3.8 equates the concept of "nullification or impairment" with "adverse impact on other Members", although the DSU does not define "adverse impact".

N.3.3 *EC – Export Subsidies on Sugar*, para. 299
(WT/DS265/AB/R, WT/DS266/AB/R, WT/DS283/AB/R)

The text of Article 3.8 of the DSU suggests that a Member may rebut the presumption of nullification or impairment by demonstrating that its breach of WTO rules has no adverse impact on other Members. Trade losses represent an obvious example of adverse impact under Article 3.8. Unless a Member demonstrates that there are no adverse trade effects arising as a consequence of WTO-inconsistent export subsidies, we do not believe that a complaining Member's expectations would have a bearing on a finding pursuant to Article 3.8 of the DSU. Therefore, the European Communities has failed to rebut the presumption of nullification or impairment pursuant to Article 3.8 of the DSU.

O

O.1 Objections. *See also* Terms of Reference of Panels (T.6)

O.1.1 *EC – Hormones*, para. 152 and footnote 138
(WT/DS26/AB/R, WT/DS48/AB/R)

. . . It is evident to us that a procedural objection raised by a party to a dispute should be sufficiently specific to enable the panel to address it.[138]

[138] Furthermore, the DSU, and in particular its Appendix 3, leave panels a margin of discretion to deal, always in accordance with due process, with specific situations that may arise in a particular case and that are not explicitly regulated. Within this context, an appellant requesting the Appellate Body to reverse a panel's ruling on matters of procedure must demonstrate the prejudice generated by such legal ruling.

O.1.2 *US – FSC*, para. 165
(WT/DS108/AB/R)

As we have said, a year passed between submission of the request for consultations by the European Communities and the first mention of this objection by the United States – despite the fact that the United States had numerous opportunities during that time to raise its objection. It seems to us that, by engaging in consultations on three separate occasions, and not even raising its objections in the two DSB meetings at which the request for establishment of a panel was on the agenda, the United States acted as if it had accepted the establishment of the Panel in this dispute, as well as the consultations preceding such establishment. In these circumstances, the United States cannot now, in our view, assert that the European Communities' claims under Article 3 of the *SCM Agreement* should have been dismissed and that the Panel's findings on these issues should be reversed. Accordingly, we decline the United States' appeal from the Panel's refusal to dismiss the European Communities' claim under Article 3 of the *SCM Agreement* due to the European Communities' alleged failure to comply with Article 4.2 of that Agreement. Thus, we do not find it necessary to rule on whether the European Communities' request for consultations includes a "statement of available evidence" that satisfies the requirements of Article 4.2 of the *SCM Agreement*.

O.1.3 *US – FSC*, para. 166
(WT/DS108/AB/R)

. . . The same principle of good faith requires that responding Members seasonably and promptly bring claimed procedural deficiencies to the attention of the complaining Member, and to the DSB or the Panel, so that corrections, if needed, can be made to resolve disputes. The procedural rules of WTO dispute settlement are designed to promote, not the development of litigation techniques, but simply the fair, prompt and effective resolution of trade disputes.

O.1.4 *Thailand – H–Beams*, para. 97
(WT/DS122/AB/R)

. . . We also note that nothing in the DSU prevents a defending party from requesting further clarification on the claims raised in a panel request from the complaining party, even before the filing of the first written submission. In this regard, we point to Article 3.10 of the DSU which enjoins Members of the WTO, if a dispute arises, to engage in dispute settlement procedures "in good faith in an effort to resolve the dispute". As we have previously stated, the "procedural rules of WTO dispute settlement are designed to promote, not the development of litigation techniques, but simply the fair, prompt and effective resolution of trade disputes".

O.1.5 *Mexico – Corn Syrup (Article 21.5 – US)*, para. 47
(WT/DS132/AB/RW)

. . . the "observations" raised by Mexico were not expressed in a fashion that indicated that Mexico was raising an objection to the authority of the Panel. The requirements of good faith, due process and orderly procedure dictate that objections, especially those of such potential significance, should be explicitly raised. Only in this way will the panel, the other party to the dispute, and the third parties, understand that a specific objection has been raised, and have an adequate opportunity to address and respond to it. . . .

O.1.6 *Mexico – Corn Syrup (Article 21.5 – US)*, paras. 49–50
(WT/DS132/AB/RW)

. . . had we been satisfied that Mexico did, in fact, explicitly raise its objections before the Panel, then the Panel may well have been required to "address" those objections, whether by virtue of Articles 7.2 and 12.7 of the DSU, or the requirements of due process. . . .

. . . When a Member wishes to raise an objection in dispute settlement proceedings, it is always incumbent on that Member to do so promptly. A Member that fails to raise its objections in a timely manner, notwithstanding one or more opportunities to do so, may be deemed to have waived its right to have a panel consider such objections.

O.1.7 *Mexico – Corn Syrup (Article 21.5 – US)*, para. 53
(WT/DS132/AB/RW)

... our task is simply to determine whether the "objections" that Mexico now raises before us are of such a nature that they could have deprived the Panel of its authority to deal with and dispose of the matter. If so, then the Panel was bound to address them on its own motion....

O.1.8 *US – Offset Act (Byrd Amendment)*, para. 208
(WT/DS217/AB/R, WT/DS234/AB/R)

..."[a]n objection to jurisdiction should be raised as early as possible" and it would be preferable, in the interests of due process, for the appellant to raise such issues in the Notice of Appeal, so that appellees will be aware that this claim will be advanced on appeal. However, in our view, the issue of a panel's jurisdiction is so fundamental that it is appropriate to consider claims that a panel has exceeded its jurisdiction even if such claims were not raised in the Notice of Appeal.

O.1.9 *Canada – Wheat Exports and Grain Imports*, para. 206
(WT/DS276/AB/R)

As regards objections to the *adequacy* of panel requests, the Appellate Body has stated that compliance with the requirements of Article 6.2 of the DSU must be determined on the merits of each case. Similarly, it would appear to us that a determination as to the *timeliness* of an objection raised under Article 6.2 must be examined on a case-by-case basis. This is consistent with the discretion given to panels, under the DSU, to deal with specific situations that may arise in a particular case and that are not explicitly regulated. Furthermore, under Article 12 of the DSU, it is the panel that sets the timetable for the panel proceedings and, therefore, it is the panel that is in the best position to determine whether, under the particular circumstances of each case, an objection is raised in a timely manner.

O.1.10 *Canada – Wheat Exports and Grain Imports*, para. 207
(WT/DS276/AB/R)

Having said this, we agree with the March Panel that, in the particular circumstances of this case, Canada's objection was not filed in an untimely manner. Canada raised its written objection only one day after the composition of the March Panel was determined. We see no error in the March Panel's view that this constituted the "earliest possible opportunity" in which Canada could have raised its objection and sought a ruling from the Panel. Indeed, only a month and a half had passed between the establishment and the composition of the March Panel, and a little over two months had passed since the request for the establishment of the panel was submitted by the United States.

O.1.11 *Canada – Wheat Exports and Grain Imports*, para. 210
(WT/DS276/AB/R)

For all these reasons, we find that, in the particular circumstances of this case, the Panel did not err in declining to dismiss Canada's preliminary objection on the grounds that it was untimely.

O.1.12 *Canada – Wheat Exports and Grain Imports*, para. 211
(WT/DS276/AB/R)

We do not mean to suggest that a responding party is foreclosed from seeking clarification of a panel request during the DSB meetings at which the panel request is considered, or that it would never be useful to do so. In the particular circumstances of this case, however, the March Panel found that it would have been unreasonable to conclude that Canada's objection was untimely *solely* because Canada had not raised the objection at the DSB meetings. . . .

O.1.13 *US – Gambling*, para. 269
(WT/DS285/AB/R)

Article 6.2 of the DSU requires that the legal basis for a dispute, that is, the *claims*, be identified in a panel request with specificity sufficient "to present the problem clearly," so that a responding party will be aware, at the time of the establishment of a panel, of the claims raised by the complaining party to which it might seek to respond in the course of the panel proceedings. In contrast, the DSU is silent about a deadline or a method by which a responding party must state the legal basis for its defence. This does not mean that a responding party may put forward its defence whenever and in whatever manner it chooses. Article 3.10 of the DSU provides that "all Members will engage in these procedures in good faith in an effort to resolve the dispute", which implies the identification by each party of relevant legal and factual issues at the earliest opportunity, so as to provide other parties, including third parties, an opportunity to respond.

O.1.14 *US – Gambling*, para. 270
(WT/DS285/AB/R)

At the same time, the opportunity afforded to a Member to respond to claims and defences made against it is also a "fundamental tenet of due process". A party must not merely be given *an* opportunity to respond, but that opportunity must be meaningful in terms of that party's ability to defend itself adequately. A party that considers it was not afforded such an opportunity will often raise a due process objection before the panel. The Appellate Body has recognized in numerous cases that a Member's right to raise a claim or objection, as well as a panel's exercise of discretion, are circumscribed by the due process rights of other parties to a dispute. Those due process rights similarly serve to limit a responding party's right to set out its defence at *any* point during the panel proceedings.

O.1.15 *US – Gambling*, para. 272
(WT/DS285/AB/R)

It follows that the principles of good faith and due process oblige a responding party to articulate its defence promptly and clearly. This will enable the complaining party to understand that a specific defence has been made, "be aware of its dimensions, and have an adequate opportunity to address and respond to it." ...

O.1.16 *US – Gambling*, para. 276
(WT/DS285/AB/R)

... we are of the view that, although the United States could have raised its defence earlier, the Panel did not err in deciding to assess whether the United States' measures are justified under Article XIV. From the outset, Antigua was apparently aware that the United States might argue that its measures satisfy the requirements of Article XIV. Antigua admitted that it raised no objection to the timing of the United States' defence before the Panel. Antigua also acknowledged that it did have an opportunity to respond adequately to the United States' defence, albeit at a late stage of the proceeding. ...

Objective assessment of the Matter. *See* Legislation as such vs. Specific Application (L.1); Request for the Establishment of a Panel (R.2); Scope of Appellate Review, Review of "objective assessment" by the panel – Article 11 of the DSU (S.3.2); Standard of Review, Article 11 of the DSU (S.7.2–7); Terms of Reference of Panels (T.6); Working Procedures for Appellate Review, Rule 20 – Notice of appeal, Article 11 of the DSU – Allegation of the panel's failure to objectively assess (W.2.7.6)

Omission to Act. *See* Legislation as such vs. Specific Application (L.1)

O.2 Order of Analysis – Use of Assumptions

O.2.1 *US – Gasoline*, p. 22, DSR 1996:I, p. 3 at 20
(WT/DS2/AB/R)

... In order that the justifying protection of Article XX may be extended to it, the measure at issue must not only come under one or another of the particular exceptions – paragraphs (a) to (j) – listed under Article XX; it must also satisfy the requirements imposed by the opening clauses of Article XX. The analysis is, in other words, two-tiered: first, provisional justification by reason of characterization of the measure under XX(g); second, further appraisal of the same measure under the introductory clauses of Article XX.

O.2.2 *US – Shrimp*, para. 119
(WT/DS58/AB/R)

The sequence of steps indicated above in the analysis of a claim of justification under Article XX reflects, not inadvertence or random choice, but rather the fundamental structure and logic of Article XX. The Panel appears to suggest, albeit indirectly, that following the indicated sequence of steps, or the inverse thereof, does not make any difference. To the Panel, reversing the sequence set out in *United States – Gasoline* "seems equally appropriate." We do not agree.

O.2.3 *US – FSC*, para. 89 and footnote 99
(WT/DS108/AB/R)

We start with the United States' argument that the Panel erred by failing to begin its examination of the European Communities' claim under Article 3.1(a) of the *SCM Agreement* with footnote 59 of that Agreement. Instead, the Panel began its examination with the general definition of a "subsidy" that is set forth in Article 1.1 of the *SCM Agreement*. This definition applies throughout the *SCM Agreement*, to all the different types of "subsidy" covered by that Agreement. In our view, it was not a legal error for the Panel to begin its examination of whether the FSC measure involves export *subsidies* by examining the general definition of a "*subsidy*" that is applicable to export *subsidies* in Article 3.1(a). In any event, whether the examination begins with the general definition of a "subsidy" in Article 1.1 or with footnote 59, we believe that the outcome of the European Communities' claim under Article 3.1(a) would be the same. The appropriate meaning of both provisions can be established and can be given effect, irrespective of whether the examination of the claim of the European Communities under Article 3.1(a) begins with Article 1.1 or with footnote 59.[99]

[99] We note that the relationship between Article 1.1 and footnote 59 of the *SCM Agreement* is, therefore, different in this way from the relationship between the chapeau of Article XX of the GATT 1994 and the particular exceptions listed in sub-paragraphs (a) to (j) of that Article. In our Report in *United States – Import Prohibitions of Certain Shrimp and Shrimp Products* ("*United States – Shrimp*"), we observed that the application of the general standards of the chapeau of Article XX of the GATT 1994 is rendered very difficult, if not impossible, if the treaty interpreter does not, first, identify and examine the specific exception at issue (WT/DS58/AB/R, adopted 6 November 1998, para. 120).

O.2.4 *Canada – Autos*, para. 151
(WT/DS139/AB/R, WT/DS142/AB/R)

In *United States – Import Prohibition of Certain Shrimp and Shrimp Products*, we said, in the context of Article XX of the GATT 1994, that a panel may not ignore the "fundamental structure and logic" of a provision in deciding the proper sequence of steps in its analysis, save at the peril of reaching flawed results. Similarly, here, the fundamental structure and logic of Article I:1, in relation to the rest of the GATS, require that determination of whether a measure is, in fact, covered by the GATS must be made *before* the consistency of that measure with any substantive obligation of the GATS can be assessed.

O.2.5 *US – Steel Safeguards*, footnote 494 to para. 481
(WT/DS248/AB/R, WT/DS249/AB/R, WT/DS251/AB/R, WT/DS252/AB/R, WT/DS253/AB/R, WT/DS254/AB/R, WT/DS258/AB/R, WT/DS259/AB/R)

In paragraph 10.278 of the Panel Reports, the Panel stated that it "assumed for the purposes of its consideration of the issue of causation", that the relevant domestic producers had been correctly defined and that serious injury or threat thereof existed. We note that the Panel found no "increased imports" for five product categories – CCFRS, hot-rolled bar, stainless steel rod, tin mill, and stainless steel wire. However, the Panel must also have assumed, tacitly, that, for the purposes of its causation analysis, imports had increased for those five products. We do not see anything improper *per se* in panels making such assumptions, especially when doing so enables panels to make findings they otherwise would not have made, thereby facilitating appellate review. We are mindful that the volume and complexity of this case may have prompted the Panel to exercise judicial economy on several issues and to rely on the corresponding inter-dependent assumptions. We note, however, that the cumulation of several inter-related assumptions could have affected our ability to complete the Panel's legal analysis had we pursued a ruling on causation.

O.2.6 *Canada – Wheat Exports and Grain Imports*, para. 109
(WT/DS276/AB/R)

Thus, in each case it is the nature of the relationship between two provisions that will determine whether there exists a mandatory sequence of analysis which, if not followed, would amount to an error of law. In some cases, this relationship is such that a failure to structure the analysis in the proper logical sequence will have repercussions for the substance of the analysis itself. . . .

O.2.7 *Canada – Wheat Exports and Grain Imports*, para. 122
(WT/DS276/AB/R)

. . . the approach taken by the Panel in this case must be distinguished from the approach taken by the panels in *US – Shrimp* and *Canada – Autos*. Those panels proceeded directly to an analysis under one provision, without having engaged in *any* analysis under, or made any assumptions relating to, a provision setting forth a logically prior analytical step.

O.2.8 *Canada – Wheat Exports and Grain Imports*, paras. 126–129
(WT/DS276/AB/R)

. . . we wish to express some concern about the manner in which the Panel conducted its analysis of the consistency of the CWB Export Regime with Article XVII:1(a) and (b). As a general principle, panels are free to structure the order of their analysis as they see fit. In so doing, panels may find it useful to take account of the manner in which a claim is presented to them by a complaining Member. Furthermore, panels may choose to use assumptions in order to facilitate resolution of a particular issue or to enable themselves to make additional and alternative factual findings and thereby assist in the resolution of a dispute should it proceed to the appellate level.

At the same time, panels must ensure that they proceed on the basis of a properly structured analysis to interpret the substantive provisions at issue. As the Appellate Body found in *US – Shrimp* and *Canada – Autos*, panels that ignore or jump over a prior logical step of the analysis run the risk of compromising or invalidating later findings. This risk is compounded in the case of two legally interrelated provisions, where one of those provisions must, as a matter of logic and analytical coherence, be analyzed before the other, as is the case with subparagraphs (a) and (b) of Article XVII:1 of the GATT 1994.

Furthermore, an over-reliance on the use of assumptions as an aid to analysis can detract from the clarity of a panel's analysis or have other adverse effects at the appellate stage. . . .

The intertwining of analysis and assumption may, in some cases, create a degree of uncertainty as to the precise findings that a panel did make. This could pose difficulties for parties in deciding whether and what to appeal. We thus recommend that when using assumptions as a tool to facilitate analysis – which we recognize can be useful – panels ensure that they are clear and explicit as to exactly what is assumed and what they have concluded based on these assumptions.

O.2.9 *US – Upland Cotton*, paras. 431–433
(WT/DS267/AB/R)

As noted above, Article 6.3(c) is silent as to the sequence of steps to be followed in assessing whether the effect of a subsidy is significant price suppression. We note that Article 6.8 indicates that the existence of serious prejudice pursuant to Articles 5(c) and 6.3(c) is to be determined on the basis of information submitted to or obtained by the panel, including information submitted in accordance with Annex V of the *SCM Agreement*. Annex V provides some limited guidance about the type of information on which a panel might base its assessment under Article 6.3(c). But we find little other guidance on this issue. The text of Article 6.3(c) does not, however, preclude the approach taken by the Panel to examine first whether significant price suppression exists and then, if it is found to exist, to proceed further to examine whether the significant price suppression is the effect of the subsidy. The Panel evidently considered that, in the absence of significant price suppression, it would not need to proceed to analyze the effect of the subsidy. We see no legal error in this approach.

One might contend that, having decided to separate its analysis of significant price suppression from its analysis of the effects of the challenged subsidies, the Panel's price suppression analysis should have addressed prices without reference to the subsidies and their effects. . . .

However, the ordinary meaning of the transitive verb "suppress" implies the existence of a subject (the challenged subsidies) and an object (in this case, prices in the world market for upland cotton). This suggests that it would be difficult to make a judgement on significant price *suppression* without taking into account the effect of the subsidies. The Panel's definition of price suppression, explained above, reflects this problem; it includes the notion that prices "do not increase when they *otherwise* would have" or "they do actually increase, but the increase is less than it *otherwise* would have been". The word "otherwise" in this context refers to the hypothetical situation in which the challenged subsidies are absent. Therefore, the fact that the Panel may have addressed some of the same or similar factors in its reasoning as to significant price suppression and its reasoning as to "effects" is not necessarily wrong.

O.2.10 *US – Upland Cotton*, para. 628
(WT/DS267/AB/R)

Before proceeding further, we refer to the order followed by the Panel in its analysis of Brazil's claims against the United States' export credit guarantee programs. We do not find that the Panel's order of analysis was wrong or that it constituted legal error. Nor has the United States made such a claim on appeal. Nevertheless, we are struck by the fact that the Panel addressed Article 10.2 only at the end of its analysis, especially given that this provision constituted the core of the United States' defence that the disciplines of the *Agreement on Agriculture* currently do not apply to export credit guarantees at all.

O.2.11 *US – Gambling*, para. 292
(WT/DS285/AB/R)

Article XIV of the GATS, like Article XX of the GATT 1994, contemplates a "two-tier analysis" of a measure that a Member seeks to justify under that provision. A panel should first determine whether the challenged measure falls within the scope of one of the paragraphs of Article XIV. This requires that the challenged measure address the particular interest specified in that paragraph and that there be a sufficient nexus between the measure and the interest protected. The required nexus – or "degree of connection" – between the measure and the interest is specified in the language of the paragraphs themselves, through the use of terms such as "relating to" and "necessary to". Where the challenged measure has been found to fall within one of the paragraphs of Article XIV, a panel should then consider whether that measure satisfies the requirements of the chapeau of Article XIV.

Ordinary Meaning. *See* Interpretation, Text (I.3.2)

P

P.1 Panel Reports

P.1.1 Basic rationale behind findings and conclusions. *See also* Claims and Arguments (C.1); Claims and Panel Reasoning (C.2); Standard of Review (S.7)

P.1.1.1 *Korea – Alcoholic Beverages*, paras. 166, 168
(WT/DS75/AB/R, WT/DS84/AB/R)

Korea claims that the Panel has failed to fulfil its obligation under Article 12.7 of the DSU to set out the basic rationale behind its findings and recommendations. . . .

. . .

In this case, we do not consider it either necessary, or desirable, to attempt to define the scope of the obligation provided for in Article 12.7 of the DSU. It suffices to state that the Panel has set out a detailed and thorough rationale for its findings and recommendations in this case. The Panel went to some length to take account of competing considerations and to explain why, nonetheless, it made the findings and recommendations it did. . . .

P.1.1.2 *Chile – Alcoholic Beverages*, para. 78
(WT/DS87/AB/R, WT/DS110/AB/R)

. . . In our view, in this case, the Panel did "set out" a "basic rationale" for its finding and recommendation on the issue of "not similarly taxed", as required by Article 12.7 of the DSU. The Panel identified the legal standard it applied, examined the relevant facts, and provided reasons for its conclusion that dissimilar taxation existed. . . .

P.1.1.3 *Argentina – Footwear (EC)*, para. 149
(WT/DS121/AB/R)

. . . In this case, the Panel conducted *extensive* factual and legal analyses of the competing claims made by the parties, set out numerous factual findings based on detailed consideration of the evidence before the Argentine authorities as well as other evidence presented to the Panel, and provided extensive explanations of how and why it reached its factual and legal conclusions. Although Argentina may not agree with the rationale provided by the Panel, and we do not ourselves agree with all of its reasoning, we have no doubt that the Panel set out, in its Report, a "basic rationale" consistent with the requirements of Article 12.7 of the DSU.

P.1.1.4 *Mexico – Corn Syrup (Article 21.5 – US)*, paras. 106–109 (WT/DS132/AB/RW)

. . . Article 12.7 establishes a minimum standard for the reasoning that panels must provide in support of their findings and recommendations. Panels must set forth explanations and reasons sufficient to disclose the essential, or fundamental, justification for those findings and recommendations.

. . . the duty of panels under Article 12.7 of the DSU to provide a "basic rationale" reflects and conforms with the principles of fundamental fairness and due process that underlie and inform the provisions of the DSU. In particular, in cases where a Member has been found to have acted inconsistently with its obligations under the covered agreements, that Member is entitled to know the reasons for such finding as a matter of due process. In addition, the requirement to set out a "basic rationale" in the panel report assists such Member to understand the nature of its obligations and to make informed decisions about: (i) what must be done in order to implement the eventual rulings and recommendations made by the DSB; and (ii) whether and what to appeal. Article 12.7 also furthers the objectives, expressed in Article 3.2 of the DSU, of promoting security and predictability in the multilateral trading system and of clarifying the existing provisions of the covered agreements, because the requirement to provide "basic" reasons contributes to other WTO Members' understanding of the nature and scope of the rights and obligations in the covered agreements.

. . . Whether a panel has articulated adequately the "basic rationale" for its findings and recommendations must be determined on a case-by-case basis, taking into account the facts of the case, the specific legal provisions at issue, and the particular findings and recommendations made by a panel. Panels must identify the relevant facts and the applicable legal norms. In applying those legal norms to the relevant facts, the reasoning of the panel must reveal how and why the law applies to the facts. In this way, panels will, in their reports, disclose the essential or fundamental justification for their findings and recommendations.

This does not, however, necessarily imply that Article 12.7 requires panels to expound at length on the reasons for their findings and recommendations. We can, for example, envisage cases in which a panel's "basic rationale" might be found in reasoning that is set out in other documents, such as in previous panel or Appellate Body reports – provided that such reasoning is quoted or, at a minimum, incorporated by reference. Indeed, a panel acting pursuant to Article 21.5 of the DSU would be expected to refer to the initial panel report, particularly in cases where the implementing measure is closely related to the original measure, and where the claims made in the proceeding under Article 21.5 closely resemble the claims made in the initial panel proceedings.

P.1.1.5 *Mexico – Corn Syrup (Article 21.5 – US)*, paras. 124, 126
(WT/DS132/AB/RW)

Having regard to these circumstances, we are of the view that the Panel Report, read together with the original panel report, leaves no doubt about the reasons for the Panel's additional finding under Article 3.1 of the *Anti-Dumping Agreement*. . . .

. . .

We wish to add that for purposes of transparency and fairness to the parties, even a panel proceeding under Article 21.5 of the DSU should strive to present the essential justification for its findings and recommendations in its own report. In this case, in particular, we consider that the Panel's finding under Article 3.1 of the *Anti-Dumping Agreement* would have been better supported by a direct quotation from or, at least, an explicit reference to, the relevant reasoning set out in the original panel report.

P.1.1.6 *US – Steel Safeguards*, paras. 503–504
(WT/DS248/AB/R, WT/DS249/AB/R, WT/DS251/AB/R, WT/DS252/AB/R, WT/DS253/AB/R, WT/DS254/AB/R, WT/DS258/AB/R, WT/DS259/AB/R)

. . . Based on our review of the Panel's reasoning, it appears to us that the Panel considered in detail the evidence that was before the USITC, and provided detailed explanations of how and why it concluded that the USITC had failed to demonstrate, through a reasoned and adequate explanation, that the alleged "unforeseen developments" *resulted* in increased imports of *each* product subject to a safeguard measure. . . .

In our view, in making these statements, the Panel has sufficiently set out in its Reports the "basic rationale" for its finding that the USITC failed to explain how, though "plausible", the "unforeseen developments" identified in the report in fact *resulted* in increased imports of the specific products subject to the safeguard measures at issue.

Duty to address issues. *See* Completion of the Legal Analysis by the Appellate Body (C.4); Judicial Economy (J.1); Jurisdiction (J.2); Objections (O.1)

P.1.2 **Panel findings not appealed.** *See also* Review of Implementation of DSB Rulings, Article 21.5 of the DSU – Effect of DSB rulings in the original dispute (R.4.3)

P.1.2.1 *Canada – Periodicals*, footnote 28 to p. 19, DSR 1997:I, p. 449 at 464
(WT/DS31/AB/R)

. . . a Panel finding that has not been specifically appealed in a particular case should not be considered to have been endorsed by the Appellate Body. Such a finding may be examined by the Appellate Body when the issue is raised properly in a subsequent appeal.

P.1.3 Separate panel reports

P.1.3.1 *US – Offset Act (Byrd Amendment)*, para. 311
(WT/DS217/AB/R, WT/DS234/AB/R)

Having made these observations, we note that Article 9.2 must not be read in isolation from other provisions of the DSU, and without taking into account the overall object and purpose of that Agreement. The overall object and purpose of the DSU is expressed in Article 3.3 of that Agreement which provides, relevantly, that the "prompt settlement" of disputes is "essential to the effective functioning of the WTO." If the right to a separate panel report under Article 9.2 were "unqualified", this would mean that a panel would have the obligation to submit a separate panel report, pursuant to the request of a party to the dispute, *at any time during the panel proceedings*. Moreover, a request for such a report could be made for whatever reason – or indeed, *without any reason* – even on the day that immediately precedes the day the panel report is due to be circulated to WTO Members at large. Such an interpretation would clearly undermine the overall object and purpose of the DSU to ensure the "prompt settlement" of disputes.

P.1.3.2 *US – Offset Act (Byrd Amendment)*, paras. 315–316
(WT/DS217/AB/R, WT/DS234/AB/R)

. . . we note that the first sentence in Article 9.2 provides that it is for the panel to "organize its examination and present its findings in such a manner that the rights which the parties to the dispute would have enjoyed had separate panels examined the complaints are in no way impaired." Our comments in *EC – Hormones* about panels' discretion in dealing with procedural issues are pertinent here:

> . . . the DSU and in particular its Appendix 3, leave panels a *margin of discretion* to deal, always in accordance with due process, with specific situations that may arise in a particular case and that are not explicitly regulated. Within this context, an appellant requesting the Appellate Body to reverse a panel's ruling on matters of procedure must demonstrate the prejudice generated by such legal ruling. (emphasis added)

In our view, the Panel acted within its "margin of discretion" by denying the United States' request for a separate panel report. We do not believe that we should lightly disturb panels' decisions on their procedure, particularly in cases such as the one at hand, in which the Panel's decision appears to have been reasonable and in accordance with due process. We observe that, on appeal, the United States is not claiming that it suffered any prejudice from the denial of its request for a separate panel report. We also note that the first sentence of Article 9.2 refers to the rights of all the parties to the dispute. The Panel correctly based its decision on an assessment of the rights of all the parties, and not of one alone.

P.2 Paris Convention (1967). *See also* TRIPS Agreement, Article 2.1 (T.9.2); TRIPS Agreement, Article 15.2 (T.9.4)

P.2.1 Article 6(1) – Trademarks

P.2.1.1 *US – Section 211 Appropriations Act*, paras. 130, 132–133 (WT/DS176/AB/R)

Before examining the text of Article 6*quinquies*, we note that the Paris Convention (1967) provides two ways in which a national of a country of the Paris Union may obtain registration of a trademark in a country of that Union other than the country of the applicant's origin: one way is by registration under Article 6 of the Paris Convention (1967); the other is by registration under Article 6*quinquies* of that same Convention.

. . .

Article 6(1) states the general rule, namely, that each country of the Paris Union has the right to determine the *conditions* for filing and registration of trademarks in its domestic legislation. This is a reservation of considerable discretion to the countries of the Paris Union – and now, by incorporation, the Members of the WTO – to continue, in principle, to determine for themselves the conditions for filing and registration of trademarks. Thus, in our view, the general rule under the Paris Convention (1967) is that national laws apply with respect to trademark registrations within the *territory* of each country of the Paris Union, subject to the requirements of other provisions of that Convention. And, likewise, through incorporation, this is also now the general rule for all WTO Members under the *TRIPS Agreement*.

Therefore, an applicant who chooses to seek registration of a trademark in a particular foreign country under Article 6 must comply with the conditions for filing and registration specified in that country's legislation. Such an applicant is *not* obliged to register a trademark first in its country of origin in order to register that trademark in another country of the Paris Union. However, that applicant must comply with the conditions of that other country where registration is sought.

P.2.2 Article 6quinquies – Trademarks

P.2.2.1 *US – Section 211 Appropriations Act*, paras. 135–136 (WT/DS176/AB/R)

This alternative way of seeking acceptance in another country of the Paris Union of a trademark registered in the applicant's country of origin, afforded by Article 6*quinquies* A(1), is subject to two prerequisites. First, that trademark must be *duly registered* according to the domestic legislation of the country of origin, and, second, it must be registered in the applicant's *country of origin*, as defined in Article 6*quinquies* A(2)...

By virtue of Article 6*quinquies* A(1), WTO Members are obliged to confer an exceptional right on an applicant in a Paris Union country other than its country of origin, one that is over and above whatever rights the other country grants to its own nationals in its domestic law....

P.2.2.2 *US – Section 211 Appropriations Act*, paras. 137, 139 (WT/DS176/AB/R)

The participants to this dispute disagree on the scope of the requirement imposed by Article 6*quinquies* A(1) to accept for filing and protect trademarks duly registered in the country of origin "as is". Looking first to the text of Article 6*quinquies* A(1), we see that the words "as is" (or, in French, "telle quelle") relate to the trademark to be "accepted for filing and protected" in another country based on registration in the applicant's country of origin. The ordinary meaning of the words "as is" is "in the existing state". The French term "telle quelle" can be defined as "sans arrangement, sans modification." This suggests to us that the requirement of Article 6*quinquies* A(1) to accept for filing and protect a trademark duly registered in the applicant's country of origin relates at least to the *form* of the trademark as registered in the applicant's country of origin. The question before us is whether the scope of this requirement also encompasses other features and aspects of that trademark as registered in the country of origin.

...

... We find that there is considerable contextual support for the view that the requirement to register a trademark "as is" under Article 6*quinquies* A(1) does *not* encompass all the features and aspects of that trademark....

P.2.2.3 *US – Section 211 Appropriations Act*, para. 147 (WT/DS176/AB/R)

... We also agree that the obligation of countries of the Paris Union under Article 6*quinquies* A(1) to accept for filing and protect a trademark duly registered in the country of origin "as is" does not encompass matters related to ownership.

P.2.3 Article 8 – Trade names

P.2.3.1 *US – Section 211 Appropriations Act*, para. 338
(WT/DS176/AB/R)

Article 8 of the Paris Convention (1967) covers only the protection of trade names; Article 8 has no other subject. If the intention of the negotiators had been to exclude trade names from protection, there would have been no purpose whatsoever in including Article 8 in the list of Paris Convention (1967) provisions that were specifically incorporated into the *TRIPS Agreement*. . . .

P.2.3.2 *US – Section 211 Appropriations Act*, para. 341
(WT/DS176/AB/R)

. . . we reverse the Panel's finding in paragraph 8.41 of the Panel Report that trade names are not covered under the *TRIPS Agreement* and find that WTO Members do have an obligation under the *TRIPS Agreement* to provide protection to trade names.

Pass-Through of Indirect Subsidization. *See* SCM Agreement, Article VI:3 of the GATT 1994 – Subsidies (S.2.43)

Patents. *See* TRIPS Agreement, Article 33 (T.9.7–9)

P.3 Principles and Concepts of General Public International Law

P.3.1 Good faith – Pacta sunt servanda

P.3.1.1 *US – Shrimp*, para. 158
(WT/DS58/AB/R)

The chapeau of Article XX is, in fact, but one expression of the principle of good faith. This principle, at once a general principle of law and a general principle of international law, controls the exercise of rights by states. One application of this general principle, the application widely known as the doctrine of *abus de droit*, prohibits the abusive exercise of a state's rights and enjoins that whenever the assertion of a right "impinges on the field covered by [a] treaty obligation, it must be exercised bona fide, that is to say, reasonably." An abusive exercise by a Member of its own treaty right thus results in a breach of the treaty rights of the other Members and, as well, a violation of the treaty obligation of the Member so acting. . . .

P.3.1.2 *US – FSC*, para. 166
(WT/DS108/AB/R)

Article 3.10 of the DSU commits Members of the WTO, if a dispute arises, to engage in dispute settlement procedures "in good faith in an effort to resolve the dispute". This is another specific manifestation of the principle of good faith which, we have pointed out, is at once a general principle of law and a principle of general international law. This pervasive principle requires both complaining and responding Members to comply with the requirements of the DSU (and related requirements in other covered agreements) in good faith. By good faith compliance, complaining Members accord to the responding Members the full measure of protection and opportunity to defend, contemplated by the letter and spirit of the procedural rules. The same principle of good faith requires that responding Members seasonably and promptly bring claimed procedural deficiencies to the attention of the complaining Member, and to the DSB or the Panel, so that corrections, if needed, can be made to resolve disputes. The procedural rules of WTO dispute settlement are designed to promote, not the development of litigation techniques, but simply the fair, prompt and effective resolution of trade disputes.

P.3.1.3 *Thailand – H-Beams*, para. 97
(WT/DS122/AB/R)

. . . We also note that nothing in the DSU prevents a defending party from requesting further clarification on the claims raised in a panel request from the complaining party, even before the filing of the first written submission. In this regard, we point to Article 3.10 of the DSU which enjoins Members of the WTO, if a dispute arises, to engage in dispute settlement procedures "in good faith in an effort to resolve the dispute". As we have previously stated, the "procedural rules of WTO dispute settlement are designed to promote, not the development of litigation techniques, but simply the fair, prompt and effective resolution of trade disputes".

P.3.1.4 *US – Lamb*, para. 115
(WT/DS177/AB/R, WT/DS178/AB/R)

We wish to emphasize that the discretion that WTO Members enjoy to argue dispute settlement claims in the manner they deem appropriate does not, of course, detract from their obligation, under Article 3.10 of the DSU, "to engage in dispute settlement procedures 'in good faith in an effort to resolve the dispute'." It follows that WTO Members cannot improperly withhold arguments from competent authorities with a view to raising those arguments later before a panel. . . .

P.3.1.5 *US – Hot-Rolled Steel*, para. 101
(WT/DS184/AB/R)

. . . This provision requires investigating authorities to strike a balance between the effort that they can expect interested parties to make in responding to questionnaires, and the practical ability of those interested parties to comply fully with all demands made of them by the investigating authorities. We see this provision as another detailed expression of the principle of good faith, which is, at once, a general principle of law and a principle of general international law, that informs the provisions of the *Anti-Dumping Agreement*, as well as the other covered agreements. This organic principle of good faith, in this particular context, restrains investigating authorities from imposing on exporters burdens which, in the circumstances, are not reasonable.

P.3.1.6 *US – Cotton Yarn*, para. 81
(WT/DS192/AB/R)

There is no need for the purpose of this appeal to express a view on the question whether an importing Member would be under an *obligation*, flowing from the "pervasive" general principle of *good faith* that underlies all treaties, to *withdraw* a safeguard measure if post-determination evidence relating to pre-determination facts were to emerge revealing that a determination was based on such a critical factual error that one of the conditions required by Article 6 turns out never to have been met.

P.3.1.7 *Mexico – Corn Syrup (Article 21.5 – US)*, para. 47
(WT/DS132/AB/RW)

. . . the "observations" raised by Mexico were not expressed in a fashion that indicated that Mexico was raising an objection to the authority of the Panel. The requirements of good faith, due process and orderly procedure dictate that objections, especially those of such potential significance, should be explicitly raised. Only in this way will the panel, the other party to the dispute, and the third parties, understand that a specific objection has been raised, and have an adequate opportunity to address and respond to it. . . .

P.3.1.8 *US – Shrimp (Article 21.5 – Malaysia)*, footnote 97 to para. 134
(WT/DS58/AB/RW)

. . . We do wish to note, though, that there is one observation by the Panel with which we do not agree. In assessing the good faith efforts made by the United States, the Panel stated that:

> The United States is a demandeur in this field and given its scientific, diplomatic and financial means, it is reasonable to expect rather more than less from that Member in terms of serious good faith efforts. Indeed, the capacity of persuasion of the United States is illustrated by the successful negotiation of the Inter-American Convention. (Panel Report, para. 5.76)

We are not persuaded by this line of reasoning. As we stated in our previous Report, the chapeau of Article XX is "but one expression of the principle of good faith". (Appellate Body Report, *United States – Shrimp, supra*, footnote 24, para. 158) This good faith notion applies to all WTO Members equally.

P.3.1.9 *EC – Sardines*, para. 278
(WT/DS231/AB/R)

. . . We must assume that Members of the WTO will abide by their treaty obligations in good faith, as required by the principle of *pacta sunt servanda* articulated in Article 26 of the *Vienna Convention*. And, always in dispute settlement, every Member of the WTO must assume the good faith of every other Member.

P.3.1.10 *US – Offset Act (Byrd Amendment)*, paras. 296–298
(WT/DS217/AB/R, WT/DS234/AB/R)

. . . Article 26 of the *Vienna Convention*, entitled *Pacta Sunt Servanda*, to which several appellees referred in their submissions, provides that "[e]very treaty in force is binding upon the parties to it and must be performed by them in good faith." The United States itself affirmed "that WTO Members must uphold their obligations under the covered agreements in good faith".

. . . Clearly, therefore, there is a basis for a dispute settlement panel to determine, in an appropriate case, whether a Member has not acted in good faith.

Nothing, however, in the covered agreements supports the conclusion that simply because a WTO Member is found to have violated a substantive treaty provision, it has therefore not acted in good faith. In our view, it would be necessary to prove more than mere violation to support such a conclusion.

P.3.1.11 *EC – Tube or Pipe*, para. 127
(WT/DS219/AB/R)

This excerpt . . . indicates that the Panel did not rely exclusively on the presumption of good faith, as Brazil suggests, given that some of the Panel's questions were directed at the *validity* of Exhibit EC-12. If the Panel had placed total reliance on the presumption of good faith, it would have simply accepted the European Communities' assertion that Exhibit EC-12 formed part of the record of the investigation and would not have posed questions to assess the consistency of Exhibit EC-12 with other evidence contained in the record. . . .

P.3.1.12 *US – Corrosion-Resistant Steel Sunset Review*, para. 86
(WT/DS244/AB/R)

. . . a measure attributable to a Member may be submitted to dispute settlement provided only that another Member has taken the view, in good faith, that the measure nullifies or impairs benefits accruing to it under the *Anti-Dumping Agreement*. . . .

P.3.1.13 *US – Corrosion-Resistant Steel Sunset Review*, para. 89
(WT/DS244/AB/R)

. . . As long as a Member respects the principles set forth in Articles 3.7 and 3.10 of the DSU, namely, to exercise their "judgement as to whether action under these procedures would be fruitful" and to engage in dispute settlement in good faith, then that Member is entitled to request a panel to examine measures that the Member considers nullify or impair its benefits. . . .

P.3.1.14 *US – Gambling*, para. 269
(WT/DS285/AB/R)

. . . This does not mean that a responding party may put forward its defence whenever and in whatever manner it chooses. Article 3.10 of the DSU provides that "all Members will engage in these procedures in good faith in an effort to resolve the dispute", which implies the identification by each party of relevant legal and factual issues at the earliest opportunity, so as to provide other parties, including third parties, an opportunity to respond.

P.3.1.15 *US – Gambling*, para. 272
(WT/DS285/AB/R)

It follows that the principles of good faith and due process oblige a responding party to articulate its defence promptly and clearly. This will enable the complaining party to understand that a specific defence has been made, "be aware of its dimensions, and have an adequate opportunity to address and respond to it." . . .

P.3.1.16 *EC – Export Subsidies on Sugar*, para. 307
(WT/DS265/AB/R, WT/DS266/AB/R, WT/DS283/AB/R)

. . . we observe that, to the extent that this concept [of estoppel] applies at all, it is reasonable for a panel to examine estoppel in the context of determining whether a Member has engaged "in these procedures in good faith", as required under Article 3.10 of the DSU. Hence, not only do we believe that the Panel's examination did not fail to address the European Communities' contention on Article 3.10 and good faith, but the Panel made no error in addressing this issue together with the issue of estoppel. We therefore see no error in the Panel's approach. . . .

P.3.2 Jura novit curia

P.3.2.1 *EC – Tariff Preferences*, para. 105
(WT/DS246/AB/R)

We are therefore of the view that the European Communities must *prove* that the Drug Arrangements satisfy the conditions set out in the Enabling Clause. Consistent with the principle of *jura novit curia*, it is not the responsibility of the European Communities to provide us with the legal interpretation to be given to a particular provision in the Enabling Clause; instead, the burden of the European Communities is to adduce sufficient evidence to substantiate its assertion that the Drug Arrangements comply with the requirements of the Enabling Clause.

P.3.3 Non-recognition of foreign expropriations

P.3.3.1 *US – Section 211 Appropriations Act*, para. 267
(WT/DS176/AB/R)

. . . even if we were to accept the United States argument about the doctrine of non-recognition of foreign confiscation, presumably that doctrine would apply to those who are not nationals of the United States as well as to those who are....

P.3.3.2 *US – Section 211 Appropriations Act*, para. 295
(WT/DS176/AB/R)

... the United States referred to its longstanding doctrine of non-recognition of foreign confiscations. However, this policy could not possibly apply to trademarks that existed *in the United States* when a business or assets connected with a trademark composed of the same or substantially similar signs were confiscated *in Cuba*.

P.3.4 No retroactive application of treaties. *See also* Temporal Application of Rights and Obligations (T.5)

P.3.4.1 *Brazil – Desiccated Coconut*, p. 15, DSR 1997:I, p. 167 at 179–180
(WT/DS22/AB/R)

Article 28 [of the *Vienna Convention on the Law of Treaties*] states the general principle that a treaty shall not be applied retroactively unless a different intention appears from the treaty or is otherwise established". Absent a contrary intention, a treaty cannot apply to acts or facts which took place, or situations which ceased to exist, before the date of its entry into force....

P.3.4.2 *EC – Bananas III*, paras. 235, 237
(WT/DS27/AB/R)

The European Communities also raises the question whether the Panel erred in giving retroactive effect to Articles and XVII of the GATS, contrary to the principle stated in Article 28 of the *Vienna Convention*. Article 28 states the general principle of international law that "[u]nless a different intention appears from the treaty or is otherwise established, its provisions do not bind a party in relation to ... any situation which ceased to exist before the date of entry into force of the treaty ...". The Panel stated in its finding on this issue that:

> ... the scope of our legal examination includes only actions which the EC took or continued to take, or measures that remained in force or continued to be applied by the EC, and thus did not cease to exist after the entry into force of the GATS. Likewise, any finding of consistency or inconsistency with the requirements of Articles and XVII of GATS would be made with respect to the period after the entry into force of the GATS. [Panel Report, para. 7.308]

The Panel stated, further, in a footnote to this finding, that "the EC measures at issue may be considered as continuing measures, which in some cases were enacted before the entry into force of the GATS but which did *not* cease to exist after that date (the opposite of the situation envisaged in Article 28)".

...

It is ... evident from the terms of its finding that the Panel concluded, as a matter of fact, that the *de facto* discrimination did continue to exist after the entry into force of the GATS. This factual finding is beyond review by the Appellate Body. Thus, we do not reverse or modify the Panel's conclusion in paragraph 7.308 of the Panel Reports.

P.3.4.3 *Canada – Patent Term*, para. 72
(WT/DS170/AB/R)

. . . Article 28 [of the *Vienna Convention on the Law of Treaties*] establishes that, in the absence of a contrary intention, treaty provisions do *not* apply to "any situation which ceased to exist" before the treaty's entry into force for a party to the treaty. Logically, it seems to us that Article 28 also necessarily implies that, absent a contrary intention, treaty obligations *do* apply to any "situation" which has *not* ceased to exist – that is, to any situation that arose in the past, but continues to exist under the new treaty. . . .

P.3.4.4 *Canada – Patent Term*, para. 70
(WT/DS170/AB/R)

. . . A treaty applies to existing rights, even when those rights result from "acts which occurred" [in the wording of Article 70.1 of the *TRIPS Agreement*] before the treaty entered into force.

P.3.4.5 *EC – Sardines*, para. 200
(WT/DS231/AB/R)

We recall that Article 28 of the *Vienna Convention on the Law of Treaties* (the "*Vienna Convention*") provides that treaties generally do not apply retroactively. . . .
. . . As we have said in previous disputes, the interpretation principle codified in Article 28 is relevant to the interpretation of the covered agreements. . . .

P.3.5 **Precautionary principle.** *See also* SPS Agreement, Article 5.7 – Precautionary principle (S.6.23)

P.3.5.1 *EC – Hormones*, paras. 123–124
(WT/DS26/AB/R, WT/DS48/AB/R)

The status of the precautionary principle in international law continues to be the subject of debate among academics, law practitioners, regulators and judges. The precautionary principle is regarded by some as having crystallized into a general principle of customary international *environmental* law. Whether it has been widely accepted by Members as a principle of *general* or *customary international law* appears less than clear. We consider, however, that it is unnecessary, and probably imprudent, for the Appellate Body in this appeal to take a position on this important, but abstract, question. We note that the Panel itself did not make any definitive finding with regard to the status of the precautionary principle in international law and that the precautionary principle, at least outside the field of international environmental law, still awaits authoritative formulation.

It appears to us important, nevertheless, to note some aspects of the relationship of the precautionary principle to the *SPS Agreement*. First, the principle has not been written into the *SPS Agreement* as a ground for justifying SPS measures that are otherwise inconsistent with the obligations of Members set out in particular provisions of that Agreement. Secondly, the precautionary principle indeed finds reflection in Article 5.7 of the *SPS Agreement*. We agree, at the same time, with the European Communities, that there is no need to assume that Article 5.7 exhausts the relevance of a precautionary principle. It is reflected also in the sixth paragraph of the preamble and in Article 3.3. These explicitly recognize the right of Members to establish their own appropriate level of sanitary protection, which level may be higher (i.e., more cautious) than that implied in existing international standards, guidelines and recommendations. Thirdly, a panel charged with determining, for instance, whether "sufficient scientific evidence" exists to warrant the maintenance by a Member of a particular SPS measure may, of course, and should, bear in mind that responsible, representative governments commonly act from perspectives of prudence and precaution where risks of irreversible, e.g. life-terminating, damage to human health are concerned. Lastly, however, the precautionary principle does not, by itself, and without a clear textual directive to that effect, relieve a panel from the duty of applying the normal (i.e. customary international law) principles of treaty interpretation in reading the provisions of the *SPS Agreement*.

P.3.6 Proportionality

P.3.6.1 *US – Cotton Yarn*, paras. 119–120
(WT/DS192/AB/R)

... the part of the total serious damage attributed to an exporting Member must be proportionate to the damage caused by the imports from that Member. Contrary to the view of the United States, we believe that Article 6.4, second sentence, does not permit the attribution of the totality of serious damage to one Member, unless the imports from that Member alone have caused all the serious damage.

Our view is supported further by the rules of general international law on state responsibility, which require that countermeasures in response to breaches by states of their international obligations be commensurate with the injury suffered. In the same vein, we note that Article 22.4 of the DSU stipulates that the suspension of concessions shall be equivalent to the level of nullification or impairment. This provision of the DSU has been interpreted consistently as not justifying punitive damages. These two examples illustrate the consequences of breaches by states of their international obligations, whereas a safeguard action is merely a remedy to WTO-consistent "fair trade" activity. It would be absurd if the breach of an international obligation were sanctioned by proportionate countermeasures, while, in the absence of such breach, a WTO Member would be subject to a disproportionate and, hence, "punitive", attribution of serious damage not wholly caused by its exports. In our view, such an exorbitant derogation from the principle of proportionality in respect of the attribution of serious damage could be justified only if the drafters of the *ATC* had expressly provided for it, which is not the case.

P.3.6.2 *US – Line Pipe*, para. 257
(WT/DS202/AB/R)

. . . If the pain inflicted on exporters by a safeguard measure were permitted to have effects beyond the share of injury caused by increased imports, this would imply that an exceptional remedy, which is not meant to protect the industry of the importing country from unfair or illegal trade practices, could be applied in a more trade-restrictive manner than countervailing and anti-dumping duties. On what basis should the *WTO Agreement* be interpreted to limit a countermeasure to the extent of the injury caused by unfair practices or a violation of the treaty but not so limit a countermeasure when there has not even been an allegation of a violation or an unfair practice?

P.3.6.3 *US – Line Pipe*, para. 259
(WT/DS202/AB/R)

We note as well the customary international law rules on state responsibility, to which we also referred in *US – Cotton Yarn*. We recalled there that the rules of general international law on state responsibility require that countermeasures in response to breaches by States of their international obligations be proportionate to such breaches. Article 51 of the International Law Commission's Draft Articles on Responsibility of States for Internationally Wrongful Acts provides that "countermeasures must be commensurate with the injury suffered, taking into account the gravity of the internationally wrongful act and the rights in question". Although Article 51 is part of the International Law Commission's Draft Articles, which do not constitute a binding legal instrument as such, this provision sets out a recognized principle of customary international law. We observe also that the United States has acknowledged this principle elsewhere. In its comments on the International Law Commission's Draft Articles, the United States stated that "under customary international law a rule of proportionality applies to the exercise of countermeasures".

P.3.7 Estoppel

P.3.7.1 *EC – Export Subsidies on Sugar*, para. 310
(WT/DS265/AB/R, WT/DS266/AB/R, WT/DS283/AB/R)

We agree with the Panel that it is far from clear that the estoppel principle applies in the context of WTO dispute settlement. . . .

P.3.7.2 *EC – Export Subsidies on Sugar*, para. 312
(WT/DS265/AB/R, WT/DS266/AB/R, WT/DS283/AB/R)

The principle of estoppel has never been applied by the Appellate Body. Moreover, the notion of estoppel, as advanced by the European Communities, would appear to inhibit the ability of WTO Members to initiate a WTO dispute settlement proceeding. We see little in the DSU that explicitly limits the rights of WTO Members to bring an action; WTO Members must exercise their "judgement as to whether action under these procedures would be fruitful", by virtue of Article 3.7 of the DSU, and they must engage in dispute settlement procedures in good faith, by virtue of Article 3.10 of the DSU. This latter obligation covers, in our view, the entire spectrum of dispute settlement, from the point of initiation of a case through implementation. Thus, even assuming *arguendo* that the principle of estoppel could apply in the WTO, its application would fall within these narrow parameters set out in the DSU.

P.4 Private Counsel Participation in Dispute Settlement Proceedings

P.4.1 *EC – Bananas III*, para. 10

(WT/DS27/AB/R)

. . . we can find nothing in the *Marrakesh Agreement Establishing the World Trade Organization* (the "*WTO Agreement*"), the DSU or the Working Procedures, nor in customary international law or the prevailing practice of international tribunals, which prevents a WTO Member from determining the composition of its delegation in Appellate Body proceedings. . . . we rule that it is for a WTO Member to decide who should represent it as members of its delegation in an oral hearing of the Appellate Body.

P.4.2 *EC – Bananas III*, para. 12

(WT/DS27/AB/R)

. . . We also note that representation by counsel of a government's own choice may well be a matter of particular significance – especially for developing-country Members – to enable them to participate fully in dispute settlement proceedings. Moreover, given the Appellate Body's mandate to review only issues of law or legal interpretation in panel reports, it is particularly important that governments be represented by qualified counsel in Appellate Body proceedings.

P.5 Publication and Administration of Trade Regulations. *See also* Safeguards Agreement, Article 3.1 (S.1.18–22); Safeguards Agreement, Article XIX of the GATT 1994 – General (S.1.45)

P.5.1 Article X:1 of the GATT 1994 – Publication of laws, regulations, judicial decisions and administrative rulings of general application

P.5.1.1 *EC – Poultry*, para. 111

(WT/DS69/AB/R)

Article X:1 of the GATT 1994 makes it clear that Article X does not deal with specific transactions, but rather with rules "of general application". . . .

P.5.1.2 *EC – Poultry*, para. 113
(WT/DS69/AB/R)

. . . Although it is true, as Brazil contends, that any measure of general application will always have to be applied in specific cases, nevertheless, the particular treatment accorded to each individual shipment cannot be considered a measure "of general application" within the meaning of Article X. . . .

P.5.1.3 *EC – Poultry*, para. 115
(WT/DS69/AB/R)

. . . Thus, to the extent that Brazil's appeal relates to the *substantive content* of the EC rules themselves, and not to their *publication* or *administration*, that appeal falls outside the scope of Article X of the GATT 1994. The WTO-consistency of such substantive content must be determined by reference to provisions of the covered agreements other than Article X of the GATT 1994.

P.5.2 Article X:2 of the GATT 1994 – Publication of measures of general application

P.5.2.1 *US – Underwear*, p. 21, DSR 1997:I, p. 3 at 29
(WT/DS24/AB/R)

The Panel found that the safeguard restraint measure imposed by the United States is "a measure of general application" within the contemplation of Article X:2. We agree with this finding. . . .

P.5.3 Article X:3 of the GATT 1994 – Uniform, impartial and reasonable administration

P.5.3.1 *EC – Bananas III*, para. 200
(WT/DS27/AB/R)

. . . The text of Article X:3(a) clearly indicates that the requirements of "uniformity, impartiality and reasonableness" do not apply to the laws, regulations, decisions and rulings *themselves*, but rather to the *administration* of those laws, regulations, decisions and rulings. The context of Article X:3(a) within Article X, which is entitled "Publication and Administration of Trade Regulations", and a reading of the other paragraphs of Article X, make it clear that Article X applies to the *administration* of laws, regulations, decisions and rulings. To the extent that the laws, regulations, decisions and rulings themselves are discriminatory, they can be examined for their consistency with the relevant provisions of the GATT 1994.

P.5.3.2 *US – Oil Country Tubular Goods Sunset Reviews*, para. 217
(WT/DS268/AB/R)

Argentina claims that the USDOC has conducted sunset reviews in a biased and unreasonable manner, in violation of Article X:3(a) of the GATT 1994. This provision states that every WTO Member "shall administer in a uniform, impartial and reasonable manner all its laws, regulations, decisions and rulings". We observe, first, that allegations that the conduct of a WTO Member is biased or unreasonable are serious under any circumstances. Such allegations should not be brought lightly, or in a subsidiary fashion. A claim under Article X:3(a) of the GATT 1994 must be supported by solid evidence; the nature and the scope of the claim, and the evidence adduced by the complainant in support of it, should reflect the gravity of the accusations inherent in claims under Article X:3(a) of the GATT 1994.

P.5.4 SPS Agreement, Annex B on "Transparency of SPS Regulations", paragraph 1

P.5.4.1 *Japan – Agricultural Products II*, paras. 105–106
(WT/DS76/AB/R)

We consider that the list of instruments contained in the footnote to paragraph 1 of Annex B is, as is indicated by the words "such as", not exhaustive in nature. The scope of application of the publication requirement is not limited to "laws, decrees or ordinances", but also includes, in our opinion, other instruments which are applicable generally and are similar in character to the instruments explicitly referred to in the illustrative list of the footnote to paragraph 1 of Annex B.

The object and purpose of paragraph 1 of Annex B is "to enable interested Members to become acquainted with" the sanitary and phytosanitary regulations adopted or maintained by other Members and thus to enhance transparency regarding these measures. In our opinion, the scope of application of the publication requirement of paragraph 1 of Annex B should be interpreted in the light of the object and purpose of this provision.

R

Refusal of a Party to Provide Information. *See* Inferences Drawn from the Refusal of a Party to Provide Information (I.1)

R.1 Regional Trade Agreements

R.1.1 Article XXIV:4 – Purpose of trade integration

R.1.1.1 *Turkey – Textiles*, para. 57
(WT/DS34/AB/R)

According to paragraph 4, the purpose of a customs union is "to facilitate trade" between the constituent members and "not to raise barriers to the trade" with third countries. This objective demands that a balance be struck by the constituent members of a customs union. A customs union should facilitate trade within the customs union, but it should *not* do so in a way that raises barriers to trade with third countries. We note that the *Understanding on Article XXIV* explicitly reaffirms this purpose of a customs union, and states that in the formation or enlargement of a customs union, the constituent members should "to the greatest possible extent avoid creating adverse affects on the trade of other Members". Paragraph 4 contains purposive, and not operative, language. It does not set forth a separate obligation itself but, rather, sets forth the overriding and pervasive purpose for Article XXIV which is manifested in operative language in the specific obligations that are found elsewhere in Article XXIV. Thus, the purpose set forth in paragraph 4 informs the other relevant paragraphs of Article XXIV, including the chapeau of paragraph 5. For this reason, the chapeau of paragraph 5, and the conditions set forth therein for establishing the availability of a defence under Article XXIV, must be interpreted in the light of the purpose of customs unions set forth in paragraph 4. The chapeau cannot be interpreted correctly without constant reference to this purpose.

R.1.2 Article XXIV:5 – Chapeau

R.1.2.1 *Turkey – Textiles*, para. 45
(WT/DS34/AB/R)

First, in examining the text of the chapeau to establish its ordinary meaning, we note that the chapeau states that the provisions of the GATT 1994 "*shall not prevent*" the formation of a customs union. We read this to mean that the provisions of the GATT 1994 *shall not make impossible* the formation of a customs union. Thus, the chapeau makes it clear that Article XXIV may, under certain conditions, justify the adoption of a measure which is inconsistent with certain other GATT provisions, and may be invoked as a possible "defence" to a finding of inconsistency.

R.1.2.2 *Turkey – Textiles*, para. 58
(WT/DS34/AB/R)

... in a case involving the formation of a customs union, this "defence" is available only when two conditions are fulfilled. First, the party claiming the benefit of this defence must demonstrate that the measure at issue is introduced upon the formation of a customs union that fully meets the requirements of sub-paragraphs 8(a) and 5(a) of Article XXIV. And, second, that party must demonstrate that the formation of that customs union would be prevented if it were not allowed to introduce the measure at issue. Again, *both* these conditions must be met to have the benefit of the defence under Article XXIV.

R.1.3 Article XXIV:5(a) – Duties and other trade regulations on trade with non-parties "not on the whole" higher or more trade restrictive than prior to customs union formation

R.1.3.1 *Turkey – Textiles*, paras. 53–55
(WT/DS34/AB/R)

With respect to "duties", Article XXIV:5(a) requires that the duties applied by the constituent members of the customs union *after* the formation of the customs union "shall *not* on the whole be *higher* ... than the *general incidence*" of the duties that were applied by each of the constituent members before the formation of the customs union. Paragraph 2 of the *Understanding on Article XXIV* requires that the evaluation under Article XXIV:5(a) of the *general incidence of the duties* applied before and after the formation of a customs union "shall ... be based upon an overall assessment of weighted average tariff rates and of customs duties collected." Before the agreement on this Understanding, there were different views among the GATT Contracting Parties as to whether one should consider, when applying the test of Article XXIV:5(a), the *bound* rates of duty or the *applied* rates of duty. This issue has been resolved by paragraph 2 of the *Understanding on Article XXIV*, which clearly states that the *applied* rate of duty must be used.

With respect to "other regulations of commerce", Article XXIV:5(a) requires that those applied by the constituent members *after* the formation of the customs union "shall *not* on the whole be... *more restrictive* than the *general incidence*" of the regulations of commerce that were applied by each of the constituent members *before* the formation of the customs union. Paragraph 2 of the *Understanding on Article XXIV* explicitly recognizes that the quantification and aggregation of regulations of commerce other than duties may be difficult, and, therefore, states that "for the purpose of the overall assessment of the incidence of other regulations of commerce for which quantification and aggregation are difficult, the examination of individual measures, regulations, products covered and trade flows affected may be required."

We agree with the Panel that the terms of Article XXIV:5(a), as elaborated and clarified by paragraph 2 of the *Understanding on Article XXIV*, provide:

> . . . that the effects of the resulting trade measures and policies of the new regional agreement shall not be more trade restrictive, overall, than were the constituent countries' previous trade policies. . . .

R.1.4 Article XXIV:8(a)(i) – Elimination of duties and other trade restrictions on "substantially all" internal trade

R.1.4.1 *Turkey – Textiles*, para. 48
(WT/DS34/AB/R)

Sub-paragraph 8(a)(i) of Article XXIV establishes the standard for the *internal trade* between constituent members in order to satisfy the definition of a "customs union". It requires the constituent members of a customs union to eliminate "duties and other restrictive regulations of commerce" with respect to "substantially all the trade" between them. Neither the GATT CONTRACTING PARTIES nor the WTO Members have ever reached an agreement on the interpretation of the term "substantially" in this provision. It is clear, though, that "substantially all the trade" is not the same as *all* the trade, and also that "substantially all the trade" is something considerably more than merely *some* of the trade. We note also that the terms of sub-paragraph 8(a)(i) provide that members of a customs union may maintain, where necessary, in their internal trade, certain restrictive regulations of commerce that are otherwise permitted under Articles IX through XV; and under Article XX of the GATT 1994. Thus, we agree with the Panel that the terms of sub-paragraph 8(a)(i) offer "some flexibility" to the constituent members of a customs union when liberalizing their internal trade in accordance with this sub-paragraph. Yet we caution that the degree of "flexibility" that sub-paragraph 8(a)(i) allows is limited by the requirement that "duties and other restrictive regulations of commerce" be "eliminated with respect to substantially all" internal trade.

R.1.5 Article XXIV: 8(a)(ii) – "substantially the same" duties and other regulations on external trade

R.1.5.1 *Turkey – Textiles*, para. 49
(WT/DS34/AB/R)

Sub-paragraph 8(a)(ii) establishes the standard for the trade of constituent members *with third countries* in order to satisfy the definition of a "customs union". It requires the constituent members of a customs union to apply "substantially the same" duties and other regulations of commerce to external trade with third countries. The constituent members of a customs union are thus required to apply a common external trade regime, relating to both duties and other regulations of commerce. However, sub-paragraph 8(a)(ii) does *not* require each constituent member of a customs union to apply *the same* duties and other regulations of commerce as other constituent members with respect to trade with third countries; instead, it requires that *substantially the same* duties and other regulations of commerce shall be applied. We agree with the Panel that:

> [t]he ordinary meaning of the term "substantially" in the context of sub-paragraph 8(a) appears to provide for both qualitative and quantitative components. The expression "substantially the same duties and other regulations of commerce are applied by each of the Members of the [customs] union" would appear to encompass both quantitative and qualitative elements, the quantitative aspect more emphasized in relation to duties.

R.1.5.2 *Turkey – Textiles*, para. 50
(WT/DS34/AB/R)

We also believe that the Panel was correct in its statement that the terms of sub-paragraph 8(a)(ii), and, in particular, the phrase "substantially the same" offer a certain degree of "flexibility" to the constituent members of a customs union in "the creation of a common commercial policy." Here too we would caution that this "flexibility" is limited. It must not be forgotten that the word "substantially" qualifies the words "the same". Therefore, in our view, something closely approximating "sameness" is required by Article XXIV:8(a)(ii). We do not agree with the Panel that:

> . . . as a general rule, a situation where constituent members have "comparable" trade regulations having similar effects with respect to the trade with third countries, would generally meet the qualitative dimension of the requirements of sub-paragraph 8(a)(ii).

Sub-paragraph 8(a)(ii) requires the constituent members of a customs union to adopt "substantially the same" trade regulations. In our view, "comparable trade regulations having similar effects" do not meet this standard. A higher degree of "sameness" is required by the terms of sub-paragraph 8(a)(ii).

R.1.6 Relationship between Article XXIV of the GATT 1994 and the Safeguards Agreement. *See also* Safeguards Agreement, Article 2 – Parallelism (S.1.13)

R.1.6.1 *Argentina – Footwear (EC)*, para. 109
(WT/DS121/AB/R)

. . . we also are not persuaded that an analysis of Article XXIV of the GATT 1994 was relevant to the specific issue that was before the Panel. This issue, as the Panel itself observed, is whether Argentina, after including imports from all sources in its investigation of "increased imports" of footwear products into its territory and the consequent effects of such imports on its domestic footwear industry, was justified in excluding other MERCOSUR member States from the application of the safeguard measures. In our Report in *Turkey – Restrictions on Imports of Textile and Clothing Products* [Appellate Body Report, para. 58], we stated that under certain conditions, "Article XXIV may justify a measure which is inconsistent with certain other GATT provisions." We indicated, however, that this defence is available only when it is demonstrated by the Member imposing the measure that "the measure at issue is introduced upon the formation of a customs union that fully meets the requirements of sub-paragraphs 8(a) and 5(a) of Article XXIV" and "that the formation of that customs union would be prevented if it were not allowed to introduce the measure at issue."

R.1.6.2 *US – Line Pipe*, para. 198
(WT/DS202/AB/R)

. . . we do not prejudge whether Article 2.2 of the *Agreement on Safeguards* permits a Member to exclude imports originating in member states of a free-trade area from the scope of a safeguard measure. We need not, and so do not, rule on the question whether Article XXIV of the GATT 1994 permits exempting imports originating in a partner of a free-trade area from a measure in departure from Article 2.2 of the *Agreement on Safeguards*. The question of whether Article XXIV of the GATT 1994 serves as an exception to Article 2.2 of the *Agreement on Safeguards* becomes relevant in only two possible circumstances. One is when, in the investigation by the competent authorities of a WTO Member, the imports that are exempted from the safeguard measure *are not considered* in the determination of serious injury. The other is when, in such an investigation, the imports that are exempted from the safeguard measure *are considered* in the determination of serious injury, *and* the competent authorities have *also* established explicitly, through a reasoned and adequate explanation, that imports from sources outside the free-trade area, alone, satisfied the conditions for the application of a safeguard measure, as set out in Article 2.1 and elaborated in Article 4.2. . . .

R.2 Request for the Establishment of a Panel. *See also* Claims and Arguments (C.1); Legislation as such vs. Specific Application (L.1); Standard of Review, Article 11 of the DSU (S.7.2–7); Terms of Reference of Panels (T.6); Working Procedures for Appellate Review (W.2)

R.2.1 Article 6.2 of the DSU – General

R.2.1.1 *Brazil – Desiccated Coconut*, p. 22, DSR 1997:I, p.167, at 186
(WT/DS22/AB/R)

A panel's terms of reference are important for two reasons. First, terms of reference fulfil an important due process objective – they give the parties and third parties sufficient information concerning the claims at issue in the dispute in order to allow them an opportunity to respond to the complainant's case. Second, they establish the jurisdiction of the panel by defining the precise claims at issue in the dispute.

R.2.1.2 *Brazil – Desiccated Coconut*, p. 22, DSR 1997:I, p. 167 at 186 (WT/DS22/AB/R)

... the "matter" referred to a panel for consideration consists of the specific claims stated by the parties to the dispute in the relevant documents specified in the terms of reference. We agree with the approach taken in previous adopted panel reports that a matter, which includes the claims composing that matter, does not fall within a panel's terms of reference unless the claims are identified in the documents referred to or contained in the terms of reference.

R.2.1.3 *EC – Bananas III*, para. 142 (WT/DS27/AB/R)

We recognize that a panel request will usually be approved automatically at the DSB meeting following the meeting at which the request first appears on the DSB's agenda. As a panel request is normally not subjected to detailed scrutiny by the DSB, it is incumbent upon a panel to examine the request for the establishment of the panel very carefully to ensure its compliance with both the letter and the spirit of Article 6.2 of the DSU. It is important that a panel request be sufficiently precise for two reasons: first, it often forms the basis for the terms of reference of the panel pursuant to Article 7 of the DSU; and, second, it informs the defending party and the third parties of the legal basis of the complaint.

R.2.1.4 *Guatemala – Cement I*, para. 72 (WT/DS60/AB/R)

... Article 6.2 specifies the requirements under which a complaining Member may refer a "matter" to the DSB: in order to establish a panel to hear its complaint, a Member must make, in writing, a "request for the establishment of a panel" (a "panel request"). In addition to being the document which enables the DSB to establish a panel, the panel request is also usually identified in the panel's terms of reference as the document setting out "the matter referred to the DSB". Thus, "the matter referred to the DSB" for the purposes of Article 7 of the DSU and Article 17.4 of the *Anti-Dumping Agreement* must be the "matter" identified in the request for the establishment of a panel under Article 6.2 of the DSU. That provision requires the complaining Member, in a panel request, to "identify the *specific measures at issue* and provide a brief summary of the *legal basis of the complaint* sufficient to present the problem clearly." (emphasis added) The "*matter* referred to the DSB", therefore, consists of two elements: the specific *measures* at issue and the *legal basis of the complaint* (or the *claims*).

R.2.1.5 *Guatemala – Cement I*, paras. 75–76 (WT/DS60/AB/R)

... In our view, there is no *inconsistency* between Article 17.5 of the *Anti-Dumping Agreement* and the provisions of Article 6.2 of the DSU. On the contrary, they are complementary and should be applied together. A panel request made concerning a dispute brought under the *Anti-Dumping Agreement* must therefore comply with the relevant dispute settlement provisions of both that Agreement and the DSU. Thus, when a "matter" is referred to the DSB by a complaining party under Article 17.4 of the *Anti-Dumping Agreement*, the panel request must meet the requirements of Articles 17.4 and 17.5 of the *Anti-Dumping Agreement* as well as Article 6.2 of the DSU.

... the word "matter" has the same meaning in Article 17 of the *Anti-Dumping Agreement* as it has in Article 7 of the DSU. It consists of two elements: the specific "measure" and the "claims" relating to it, both of which must be properly identified in a panel request as required by Article 6.2 of the DSU.

R.2.1.6 *Korea – Dairy*, para. 120 (WT/DS98/AB/R)

. . . When parsed into its constituent parts, Article 6.2 may be seen to impose the following requirements. The request must: (i) be in writing; (ii) indicate whether consultations were held; (iii) identify the specific measures at issue; and (iv) provide a brief summary of the legal basis of the complaint sufficient to present the problem clearly. In its fourth requirement, Article 6.2 demands only a summary – and it may be a brief one – of the legal basis of the complaint; but the summary must, in any event, be one that is "sufficient to present the problem clearly". It is not enough, in other words, that "the legal basis of the complaint" is summarily identified; the identification must "present the problem clearly".

R.2.1.7 *US – Carbon Steel*, paras. 125–126 (WT/DS213/AB/R)

There are, therefore, two distinct requirements, namely identification of *the specific measures at issue*, and the provision of a *brief summary of the legal basis of the complaint* (or the *claims*). Together, they comprise the "matter referred to the DSB", which forms the basis for a panel's terms of reference under Article 7.1 of the DSU.

The requirements of precision in the request for the establishment of a panel flow from the two essential purposes of the terms of reference. First, the terms of reference define the scope of the dispute. Secondly, the terms of reference, and the request for the establishment of a panel on which they are based, serve the *due process* objective of notifying the parties and third parties of the nature of a complainant's case. When faced with an issue relating to the scope of its terms of reference, a panel must scrutinize carefully the request for establishment of a panel "to ensure its compliance with both the letter and the spirit of Article 6.2 of the DSU."

R.2.1.8 *Canada – Wheat Exports and Grain Imports*, para. 206 (WT/DS276/AB/R)

As regards objections to the *adequacy* of panel requests, the Appellate Body has stated that compliance with the requirements of Article 6.2 of the DSU must be determined on the merits of each case. Similarly, it would appear to us that a determination as to the *timeliness* of an objection raised under Article 6.2 must be examined on a case-by-case basis. This is consistent with the discretion given to panels, under the DSU, to deal with specific situations that may arise in a particular case and that are not explicitly regulated. Furthermore, under Article 12 of the DSU, it is the panel that sets the timetable for the panel proceedings and, therefore, it is the panel that is in the best position to determine whether, under the particular circumstances of each case, an objection is raised in a timely manner.

R.2.1.9 *Canada – Wheat Exports and Grain Imports*, para. 211 (WT/DS276/AB/R)

We do not mean to suggest that a responding party is foreclosed from seeking clarification of a panel request during the DSB meetings at which the panel request is considered, or that it would never be useful to do so. In the particular circumstances of this case, however, the March Panel found that it would have been unreasonable to conclude that Canada's objection was untimely *solely* because Canada had not raised the objection at the DSB meetings....

R.2.1.10 *Canada – Wheat Exports and Grain Imports*, para. 212 (WT/DS276/AB/R)

Before leaving this issue, we turn to the United States' assertion that the March Panel erred by implying that "if the United States had responded to Canada's letter of April 7, 2003 ... the United States could have cured the alleged procedural defect in that panel request"....

...

We do not find that this statement carries the "implication" alleged by the United States. In fact, as the United States acknowledges, the March Panel expressly rejected such an implication when it stated that "the United States *could not have 'cured'* any inconsistencies with Article 6.2 of its panel request subsequent to the establishment of this Panel".

R.2.1.11 *US – Oil Country Tubular Goods Sunset Reviews*, para. 162 (WT/DS268/AB/R)

... in order for a panel request to "present the problem clearly", it must plainly connect the challenged measure(s) with the provision(s) of the covered agreements claimed to have been infringed, so that the respondent party is aware of the basis for the alleged nullification or impairment of the complaining party's benefits. Only by such connection between the measure(s) and the relevant provision(s) can a respondent "know what case it has to answer, and ... begin preparing its defence".

R.2.1.12 *US – Upland Cotton*, para. 293
(WT/DS267/AB/R)

We emphasize that consultations are but the first step in the WTO dispute settlement process. They are intended to "provide the parties an opportunity to define and delimit the scope of the dispute between them". We also note that Article 4.2 of the DSU calls on a WTO Member that receives a request for consultations to "accord sympathetic consideration to and afford adequate opportunity for consultation regarding any representations made by another Member". As long as the complaining party does not expand the scope of the dispute, we hesitate to impose too rigid a standard for the "precise and exact identity" between the scope of consultations and the request for the establishment of a panel, as this would substitute the request for consultations for the panel request. According to Article 7 of the DSU, it is the request for the establishment of a panel that governs its terms of reference, unless the parties agree otherwise.

R.2.1.13 *Dominican Republic – Import and Sale of Cigarettes*, para. 120
(WT/DS302/AB/R)

. . . The Appellate Body has consistently maintained that, where a panel request fails to identify adequately particular measures or fails to specify a particular claim, then such measures or claims will not form part of the matter covered by the panel's terms of reference.

R.2.2 Article 6.2 of the DSU – Claims and legal basis of the complaint.
See also Burden of Proof, General (B.3.1); Claims and Arguments (C.1); Claims and Panel Reasoning (C.2); Enabling Clause (E.1)

R.2.2.1 *EC – Bananas III*, para. 141
(WT/DS27/AB/R)

. . . We accept the Panel's view that it was sufficient for the Complaining Parties to list the provisions of the specific agreements alleged to have been violated without setting out detailed arguments as to which specific aspects of the measures at issue relate to which specific provisions of those agreements. In our view, there is a significant difference between the *claims* identified in the request for the establishment of a panel, which establish the panel's terms of reference under Article 7 of the DSU, and the *arguments* supporting those claims, which are set out and progressively clarified in the first written submissions, the rebuttal submissions and the first and second panel meetings with the parties.

R.2.2.2 *EC – Bananas III*, para. 143
(WT/DS27/AB/R)

. . . Article 6.2 of the DSU requires that the *claims*, but not the *arguments*, must all be specified sufficiently in the request for the establishment of a panel in order to allow the defending party and any third parties to know the legal basis of the complaint. If a *claim* is not specified in the request for the establishment of a panel, then a faulty request cannot be subsequently "cured" by a complaining party's argumentation in its first written submission to the panel or in any other submission or statement made later in the panel proceeding.

R.2.2.3 *EC – Bananas III*, para. 145
(WT/DS27/AB/R)

We do not agree with the Panel's decisions to exclude certain claims under Article XVII of the GATS made by Mexico and all of the GATS claims made by Guatemala and Honduras from the scope of this case. There is no requirement in the DSU or in GATT practice for arguments on all claims relating to the matter referred to the DSB to be set out in a complaining party's first written submission to the panel. It is the panel's terms of reference, governed by Article 7 of the DSU, which set out the claims of the complaining parties relating to the matter referred to the DSB.

R.2.2.4 *EC – Bananas III*, para. 147
(WT/DS27/AB/R)

. . . We do not agree with the Panel's statement that a "failure to make a claim in the first written submission cannot be remedied by later submissions or by incorporating the claims and arguments of other complainants". . . .

R.2.2.5 *India – Patents (US)*, para. 90
(WT/DS50/AB/R)

. . . the convenient phrase, "including but not necessarily limited to", is simply not adequate to "identify the specific measures at issue and provide a brief summary of the legal basis of the complaint sufficient to present the problem clearly" as required by Article 6.2 of the DSU. If this phrase incorporates Article 63, what article of the *TRIPS Agreement* does it not incorporate? Therefore, this phrase is not sufficient to bring a claim relating to Article 63 within the terms of reference of the Panel.

R.2.2.6 *Korea – Dairy*, paras. 123–124
(WT/DS98/AB/R)

. . . we did not purport in *European Communities – Bananas* to establish the mere listing of the articles of an agreement alleged to have been breached as a standard of precision, observance of which would *always* constitute sufficient compliance with the requirements of Article 6.2, *in each and every case*, without regard to the particular circumstances of such cases. . . . Close scrutiny of what we in fact said in *European Communities – Bananas* shows that we, firstly, restated the reasons why precision is necessary in a request for a panel; secondly, we stressed that claims, not detailed arguments, are what need to be set out with sufficient clarity; and thirdly, we agreed with the conclusion of the panel that, in that case, the listing of the articles of the agreements claimed to have been violated satisfied the *minimum* requirements of Article 6.2 of the DSU. . . .

Identification of the treaty provisions claimed to have been violated by the respondent is always necessary both for purposes of defining the terms of reference of a panel and for informing the respondent and the third parties of the claims made by the complainant; such identification is a minimum prerequisite if the legal basis of the complaint is to be presented at all. But it may not always be enough. There may be situations where the simple listing of the articles of the agreement or agreements involved may, in the light of attendant circumstances, suffice to meet the standard of *clarity* in the statement of the legal basis of the complaint. However, there may also be situations in which the circumstances are such that the mere listing of treaty articles would not satisfy the standard of Article 6.2. This may be the case, for instance, where the articles listed establish not one single, distinct obligation, but rather multiple obligations. In such a situation, the listing of articles of an agreement, in and of itself, may fall short of the standard of Article 6.2.

R.2.2.7 *Korea – Dairy*, para. 127
(WT/DS98/AB/R)

. . . we consider that whether the mere listing of the articles claimed to have been violated meets the standard of Article 6.2 must be examined on a case-by-case basis. In resolving that question, we take into account whether the ability of the respondent to defend itself was prejudiced, given the actual course of the panel proceedings, by the fact that the panel request simply listed the provisions claimed to have been violated.

R.2.2.8 *Thailand – H-Beams*, para. 88
(WT/DS122/AB/R)

Article 6.2 of the DSU calls for sufficient clarity with respect to the legal basis of the complaint, that is, with respect to the "claims" that are being asserted by the complaining party. A defending party is entitled to know what case it has to answer, and what violations have been alleged so that it can begin preparing its defence. Likewise, those Members of the WTO who intend to participate as third parties in panel proceedings must be informed of the legal basis of the complaint. This requirement of due process is fundamental to ensuring a fair and orderly conduct of dispute settlement proceedings.

R.2.2.9 *Thailand – H-Beams*, para. 90
(WT/DS122/AB/R)

. . . Article 3.1, which requires that an injury determination be based on positive evidence, and that it involve an objective examination of the relevant injury factors, is a fundamental and substantial obligation that functions as a chapeau, and informs the rest of Article 3. Thus, in citing the language of Article 3.1 and in referring to certain key factors enumerated in Article 3, Poland has sufficiently provided a "brief summary of the legal basis of the complaint sufficient to present the problem clearly", as required by Article 6.2 of the DSU.

R.2.2.10 *Thailand – H-Beams*, paras. 92–95
(WT/DS122/AB/R)

In the facts and circumstances of this case, therefore, we consider that the reference in Poland's panel request to the "[calculation of] an alleged dumping margin" was sufficient to bring Poland's claims under Article 2 within the panel's terms of reference, and to inform Thailand of the nature of Poland's claims. Thus, with respect to the claims relating to Article 2 of the *Anti-Dumping Agreement*, Poland's panel request was sufficient to meet the requirements of Article 6.2 of the DSU.

... Article 5 sets out various but closely related procedural steps that investigating authorities must comply with in initiating and conducting an anti-dumping investigation. In view of the interlinked nature of the obligations in Article 5, we are of the view that, in the facts and circumstances of this case, Poland's reference to "the procedural ... requirements" of Article 5 was sufficient to meet the minimum requirements of Article 6.2 of the DSU.

In assessing the sufficiency of Poland's panel request with respect to the claims relating to Articles 2 and 5, the Panel put considerable emphasis on the fact that the dispute involved "several issues that were raised before the Thai investigating authorities". The Panel's reasoning seems to assume that there is always continuity between claims raised in an underlying anti-dumping investigation and claims raised by a complaining party in a related dispute brought before the WTO. This is not necessarily the case. The parties involved in an underlying anti-dumping investigation are generally exporters, importers and other commercial entities, while those involved in WTO dispute settlement are the Members of the WTO. Therefore, it cannot be assumed that the range of issues raised in an anti-dumping investigation will be the same as the claims that a Member chooses to bring before the WTO in a dispute. Furthermore, although the defending party will be aware of the issues raised in an underlying investigation, other parties may not. Thus, the underlying investigation cannot normally, in and of itself, be determinative in assessing the sufficiency of the claims made in a request for the establishment of a panel. We, therefore, are of the view that, in this case, the Panel erred to the extent that it relied mainly on issues raised in the underlying anti-dumping investigation in assessing the sufficiency of Poland's panel request under Articles 2 and 5.

Thailand argues that it was prejudiced by the lack of clarity of Poland's panel request. The fundamental issue in assessing claims of prejudice is whether a defending party was made aware of the claims presented by the complaining party, sufficient to allow it to defend itself. In assessing Thailand's claims of prejudice, we consider it relevant that, although Thailand asked the Panel for a preliminary ruling on the sufficiency of Poland's panel request with respect to Articles 5 and 6 of the *Anti-Dumping Agreement* at the time of filing of its first written submission, it did not do so at that time with respect to Poland's claims under Articles 2 and 3 of that Agreement. We must, therefore, conclude that Thailand did not feel at that time that it required additional clarity with respect to these claims, particularly as we note that Poland had further clarified its claims in its first written submission. This is a strong indication to us that Thailand did not suffer any prejudice on account of any lack of clarity in the panel request.

R.2.2.11 *Korea – Various Measures on Beef*, para. 87
(WT/DS161/AB/R, WT/DS169/AB/R)

. . . Although the "commitment levels" in Korea's Schedule and "Annex 3" of the *Agreement on Agriculture* were *not explicitly* referred to in the panel requests in this dispute, it is clear that Articles 3 and 6 of the *Agreement on Agriculture*, which *were referred* to in the panel requests, incorporate those terms, either directly through Articles 3.2 and 6.3, in the case of the "commitment levels", or indirectly through Article 1(a)(ii), in the case of "Annex 3". In our view, the commitment levels in Korea's Schedule and the provisions of Annex 3 were in effect referred to in the complaining parties' panel requests, and were, therefore, within the Panel's terms of reference.

R.2.2.12 *US – Certain EC Products*, paras. 111–112
(WT/DS165/AB/R)

Article 23.1 of the DSU imposes a general obligation of Members to redress a violation of obligations or other nullification or impairment of benefits under the covered agreements only by recourse to the rules and procedures of the DSU, and not through unilateral action. Subparagraphs (a), (b) and (c) of Article 23.2 articulate specific and clearly-defined forms of prohibited unilateral action contrary to Article 23.1 of the DSU. There is a close relationship between the obligations set out in paragraphs 1 and 2 of Article 23. They *all* concern the obligation of Members of the WTO not to have recourse to unilateral action. We therefore consider that, as the request for the establishment of a panel of the European Communities included a claim of inconsistency with Article 23, a claim of inconsistency with Article 23.2(a) is within the Panel's terms of reference.

However, the fact that a claim of inconsistency with Article 23.2(a) of the DSU can be considered to be within the Panel's terms of reference does not mean that the European Communities actually made such a claim. An analysis of the Panel record shows that, with the exception of two instances during the Panel proceedings, the European Communities did not refer *specifically* to Article 23.2(a) of the DSU. Furthermore, in response to a request from the United States to clarify the scope of its claim under Article 23, the European Communities asserted only claims of violation of Articles 23.1 and 23.2(c) of the DSU; no mention was made of Article 23.2(a). Our reading of the Panel record shows us that, throughout the Panel proceedings in this case, the European Communities made arguments relating only to its claims that the United States acted inconsistently with Article 23.1 and Article 23.2(c) of the DSU.

R.2.2.13 *Chile – Price Band System*, paras. 150–151
(WT/DS207/AB/R)

The Panel request refers to Article of the GATT 1994 in general terms. No specific reference is made to any of the seven paragraphs or eight subparagraphs of Article of the GATT 1994. Argentina's request clearly does not limit the scope of Argentina's claims to the *first* sentence of Article II:1(b). Therefore, we find that Article in its entirety – including the second sentence of Article II:1(b) – is within the Panel's terms of reference.

This, however, is not the end of our inquiry on this issue. Chile does not dispute that Argentina included Article II:1(b) in the request for the establishment of a panel. However, Chile submits that making a general reference to Article in the Panel request is not dispositive of whether Argentina *has actually made a claim* under the *second* sentence of Article II:1(b), and, thus, of whether the Panel was entitled to make a finding under that provision.

R.2.2.14 *Chile – Price Band System*, para. 164
(WT/DS207/AB/R)

... Argentina appears to suggest that a claim may be made implicitly, and need not be made explicitly. We do not agree. The requirements of due process and orderly procedure dictate that claims must be made explicitly in WTO dispute settlement. Only in this way will the panel, other parties, and third parties understand that a specific claim has been made, be aware of its dimensions, and have an adequate opportunity to address and respond to it. WTO Members must not be left to wonder what specific claims have been made against them in dispute settlement....

R.2.2.15 *US – Carbon Steel*, para. 127
(WT/DS213/AB/R, WT/DS213/AB/R/Corr.1)

As we have said previously, compliance with the requirements of Article 6.2 must be demonstrated on the face of the request for the establishment of a panel. Defects in the request for the establishment of a panel cannot be "cured" in the subsequent submissions of the parties during the panel proceedings. Nevertheless, in considering the sufficiency of a panel request, submissions and statements made during the course of the panel proceedings, in particular the first written submission of the complaining party, may be consulted in order to confirm the meaning of the words used in the panel request and as part of the assessment of whether the ability of the respondent to defend itself was prejudiced. Moreover, compliance with the requirements of Article 6.2 must be determined on the merits of each case, having considered the panel request as a whole, and in the light of attendant circumstances.

R.2.2.16 *US – Carbon Steel*, para. 130
(WT/DS213/AB/R, WT/DS213/AB/R/Corr.1)

... As we have observed, although the listing of the treaty provisions allegedly violated is always a *necessary* "minimum prerequisite" for compliance with Article 6.2, whether such a listing is *sufficient* to constitute a "brief summary of the legal basis of the complaint sufficient to present the problem clearly" within the meaning of Article 6.2 will depend on the circumstances of each case, and in particular on the extent to which mere reference to a treaty provision sheds light on the nature of the obligation at issue....

R.2.2.17 *EC – Tariff Preferences*, para. 110
(WT/DS246/AB/R)

. . . we are of the view that a complaining party challenging a measure taken pursuant to the Enabling Clause must allege more than mere inconsistency with Article I:1 of the GATT 1994, for to do only that would not convey the "legal basis of the complaint sufficient to present the problem clearly". In other words, it is insufficient in WTO dispute settlement for a complainant to allege inconsistency with Article I:1 of the GATT 1994 if the complainant seeks also to argue that the measure is not justified under the Enabling Clause. . . .

R.2.2.18 *EC – Tariff Preferences*, para. 113
(WT/DS246/AB/R)

In the light of the extensive requirements set forth in the Enabling Clause, we are of the view that, when a complaining party considers that a preference scheme of another Member does not meet one or more of those requirements, the specific provisions of the Enabling Clause with which the scheme allegedly falls afoul, form critical components of the "legal basis of the complaint" and, therefore, of the "matter" in dispute. Accordingly, a complaining party cannot, in good faith, ignore those provisions and must, in its request for the establishment of a panel, identify them and thereby "notif[y] the parties and third parties of the nature of [its] case". For the failure of such a complaining party to raise the relevant provisions of the Enabling Clause would place an unwarranted burden on the responding party. This due process consideration applies equally to the elaboration of a complaining party's case in its written submissions, which must "explicitly" articulate a claim so that the panel and all parties to a dispute "understand that a specific claim has been made, [are] aware of its dimensions, and have an adequate opportunity to address and respond to it".

R.2.2.19 *EC – Tariff Preferences*, para. 118
(WT/DS246/AB/R)

. . . In the light of the above considerations, we are of the view that India was required to (i) identify, in its request for the establishment of a panel, which obligations in the Enabling Clause the Drug Arrangements are alleged to have contravened, and (ii) make written submissions in support of this allegation. The requirement to make such an argument, however, does not mean that India must prove inconsistency with a provision of the Enabling Clause, because the ultimate burden of establishing the consistency of the Drug Arrangements with the Enabling Clause lies with the European Communities.

R.2.2.20 *US – Gambling*, para. 269
(WT/DS285/AB/R)

Article 6.2 of the DSU requires that the legal basis for a dispute, that is, the *claims*, be identified in a panel request with specificity sufficient "to present the problem clearly," so that a responding party will be aware, at the time of the establishment of a panel, of the claims raised by the complaining party to which it might seek to respond in the course of the panel proceedings. In contrast, the DSU is silent about a deadline or a method by which a responding party must state the legal basis for its defence. This does not mean that a responding party may put forward its defence whenever and in whatever manner it chooses. Article 3.10 of the DSU provides that "all Members will engage in these procedures in good faith in an effort to resolve the dispute", which implies the identification by each party of relevant legal and factual issues at the earliest opportunity, so as to provide other parties, including third parties, an opportunity to respond.

R.2.3 Article 6.2 of the DSU – Specific measures at issue. *See also* Legislation as such vs. Specific Application (L.1); Mandatory and Discretionary Legislation (M.1); Terms of Reference of Panels, Specific measure at issue (T.6.3)

R.2.3.1 *Australia – Salmon*, para. 103
(WT/DS18/AB/R)

... In our view, the ... measure at issue can only be the measure which is *actually* applied to the product at issue....

R.2.3.2 *Guatemala – Cement I*, para. 77
(WT/DS60/AB/R)

... Where a complaining Member wishes to make any claims concerning an action taken, or not taken, in the course of an anti-dumping investigation under the provisions of the *Anti-Dumping Agreement*, Article 6.2 of the DSU requires "the specific measures at issue" to be identified in the panel request.

R.2.3.3 *Guatemala – Cement I*, para. 80
(WT/DS60/AB/R)

... We find that in disputes under the *Anti-Dumping Agreement* relating to the initiation and conduct of anti-dumping investigations, a definitive anti-dumping duty, the acceptance of a price undertaking or a provisional measure must be identified as part of the matter referred to the DSB pursuant to the provisions of Article 17.4 of the *Anti-Dumping Agreement* and Article 6.2 of the DSU.

R.2.3.4 *EC – Computer Equipment*, para. 65
(WT/DS62/AB/R, WT/DS67/AB/R, WT/DS68/AB/R)

We consider that "measures" within the meaning of Article 6.2 of the DSU are not only measures of general application, i.e., normative rules, but also can be the application of tariffs by customs authorities....

R.2.3.5 *EC – Computer Equipment*, para. 67
(WT/DS62/AB/R, WT/DS67/AB/R, WT/DS68/AB/R)

... Article 6.2 of the DSU does *not* explicitly require that the products to which the "specific measures at issue" apply be identified. However with respect to certain WTO obligations, in order to identify "the specific measures at issue" it may also be necessary to identify the products subject to the measures in dispute.

R.2.3.6 *EC – Computer Equipment*, para. 68
(WT/DS62/AB/R, WT/DS67/AB/R, WT/DS68/AB/R)

LAN equipment and PCs with multimedia capacity are both generic terms. Whether these terms are sufficiently precise to "identify the specific measure at issue" under Article 6.2 of the DSU depends, in our view, upon whether they satisfy the purposes of the requirements of that provision.

R.2.3.7 *EC – Computer Equipment*, para. 70
(WT/DS62/AB/R, WT/DS67/AB/R, WT/DS68/AB/R)

... As the ability of the European Communities to defend itself was not prejudiced by a lack of knowing the measures at issue, we do not believe that the fundamental rule of due process was violated by the Panel.

R.2.3.8 *Brazil – Aircraft*, para. 132
(WT/DS46/AB/R)

We do not believe, however, that Articles 4 and 6 of the DSU, or paragraphs 1 to 4 of Article 4 of the *SCM Agreement*, require a *precise and exact identity* between the specific measures that were the subject of consultations and the specific measures identified in the request for the establishment of a panel. ...

R.2.3.9 *Chile – Price Band System*, para. 139
(WT/DS207/AB/R)

... Chile's price band system remains essentially the same after the enactment of Law 19.772. The measure is not, in its essence, any different because of that Amendment. Therefore, we conclude that the measure before us in this appeal includes Law 19.772, because that law amends Chile's price band system without *changing its essence*.

R.2.3.10 *Chile – Price Band System*, para. 144
(WT/DS207/AB/R)

We emphasize that we do not mean to condone a practice of amending measures during dispute settlement proceedings if such changes are made with a view to shielding a measure from scrutiny by a panel or by us. We do not suggest that this occurred in this case. However, generally speaking, the demands of due process are such that a complaining party should not have to adjust its pleadings throughout dispute settlement proceedings in order to deal with a disputed measure as a "moving target". If the terms of reference in a dispute are broad enough to include amendments to a measure – as they are in this case – and if it is necessary to consider an amendment in order to secure a positive solution to the dispute – as it is here – then it is appropriate to consider the measure *as amended* in coming to a decision in a dispute.

R.2.3.11 *US – Carbon Steel*, para. 171
(WT/DS213/AB/R, WT/DS213/AB/R/Corr.1)

In our view, the references in the panel request to "certain aspects of the sunset review procedure", to the United States statutory provisions governing sunset reviews, to related regulatory provisions, and to the Sunset Policy Bulletin, can be read to refer, generally, to United States law regarding the determination to be made in a sunset review. However, we do not believe they can be read to refer to *distinct* measures, consisting of United States law, as such, and as applied, relating to the submission of evidence. Accordingly, we agree with the Panel that the matters relating to the submission of evidence in a sunset review were not within its terms of reference because the *specific measures at issue were not adequately identified* in the request for the establishment of the panel, as required by Article 6.2 of the DSU.

R.2.3.12 *US – Oil Country Tubular Goods Sunset Reviews*, para. 173
(WT/DS268/AB/R)

We also expect that measures subject to "as such" challenges would normally have undergone, under municipal law, thorough scrutiny through various deliberative processes to ensure consistency with the Member's international obligations, including those found in the covered agreements, and that the enactment of such a measure would implicitly reflect the conclusion of that Member that the measure is not inconsistent with those obligations. The presumption that WTO Members act in good faith in the implementation of their WTO commitments is particularly apt in the context of measures challenged "as such". We would therefore urge complaining parties to be *especially diligent* in setting out "as such" claims in their panel requests as clearly as possible. In particular, we would expect that "as such" claims state unambiguously the specific measures of municipal law challenged by the complaining party and the legal basis for the allegation that those measures are not consistent with particular provisions of the covered agreements. Through such straightforward presentations of "as such" claims, panel requests should leave respondent parties in little doubt that, notwithstanding their own considered views on the WTO-consistency of their measures, another Member intends to challenge those measures, as such, in WTO dispute settlement proceedings.

R.2.3.13 *US – Upland Cotton*, para. 262
(WT/DS267/AB/R)

Whether or not a measure is still in force is not dispositive of whether that measure is currently affecting the operation of any covered agreement. Therefore, we disagree with the United States' argument that measures whose legislative basis has expired are incapable of affecting the operation of a covered agreement in the present and that, accordingly, expired measures *cannot* be the subject of consultations under the DSU. In our view, the question of whether measures whose legislative basis has expired affect the operation of a covered agreement currently is an issue that must be resolved on the facts of each case. The outcome of such an analysis cannot be prejudged by excluding it from consultations and dispute settlement proceedings altogether.

R.2.3.14 *US – Upland Cotton*, para. 269
(WT/DS267/AB/R)

The only temporal connotation contained in the ordinary meaning of the expression "at issue", as used in Article 6.2 of the DSU, is expressed by its present tense: measures must be "at issue" – or, putting it another way, "in dispute" – at the time the request is made. Certainly, nothing inherent in the term "at issue" sheds light on whether measures at issue must be currently in force, or whether they may be measures whose legislative basis has expired.

R.2.3.15 *US – Gambling*, paras. 120–123
(WT/DS285/AB/R)

The question before us, therefore, is whether an alleged "total prohibition" on the cross-border supply of gambling and betting services constitutes a measure that may be challenged under the GATS. The DSU provides for the "prompt settlement" of situations where Members consider that their benefits under the covered agreements "are being impaired by *measures* taken by another Member". Two elements of this reference to "measures" that may be the subject of dispute settlement are relevant. First, as the Appellate Body has stated, a "nexus" must exist between the responding Member and the "measure", such that the "measure" – whether an act or omission – must be "attributable" to that Member. Secondly, the "measure" must be the *source* of the alleged impairment, which is in turn the *effect* resulting from the existence or operation of the "measure".

Similarly [Article 4.2 of the DSU] contemplates that "measures" themselves will "affect" the operation of a covered agreement. Finally, we note that this distinction between measures and their effects is also evident in the scope of application of the GATS, namely, to "measures by Members affecting trade in services".

We are therefore of the view that the DSU and the GATS focus on "measures" as the subject of challenge in WTO dispute settlement. To the extent that a Member's complaint centres on the effects of an action taken by another Member, that complaint must nevertheless be brought as a challenge to the *measure* that is the source of the alleged effects.

R.2.3.16 *US – Gambling*, paras. 125–126
(WT/DS285/AB/R)

We note also that, if the "total prohibition" were a measure, a complaining party could fulfil its obligation to identify the "specific measure at issue", pursuant to Article 6.2 of the DSU, merely by explicitly mentioning the "prohibition".

Yet, without knowing the precise source of the "prohibition", a responding party would not be in a position to prepare adequately its defence, particularly where, as here, it is alleged that numerous federal and state laws underlie the "total prohibition".

Therefore, we conclude that, without demonstrating the source of the prohibition, a complaining party may not challenge a "total prohibition" as a "measure", *per se*, in dispute settlement proceedings under the GATS. . . .

R.2.3.17 *US – Gambling*, paras. 129, 131–132

(WT/DS285/AB/R)

. . . the Panel relied on certain Appellate Body decisions in support of its view that "'practice' can be considered as an autonomous measure that can be challenged in and of itself". . . .

. . .

We disagree with the participants' characterization of the Panel's statement on "practice", in paragraph 6.197 of the Panel Report, as a "finding" of the Panel. The Panel itself acknowledged that, in any case, Antigua was not challenging a practice, as such. In this light, the Panel's statement on "practice", in our view, was a mere *obiter dictum*, and we need not rule on it.

We nevertheless express our disagreement with the Panel's understanding of previous Appellate Body decisions. The Appellate Body has *not*, to date, pronounced upon the issue of whether "practice" may be challenged, as such, as a "measure" in WTO dispute settlement.

R.2.4 Article 6.2 of the DSU – "whether consultations were held"

R.2.4.1 *Brazil – Aircraft*, para. 131

(WT/DS46/AB/R)

In our view, Articles 4 and 6 of the DSU, as well as paragraphs 1 to 4 of Article 4 of the *SCM Agreement*, set forth a process by which a complaining party must request consultations, and consultations must be held, before a matter may be referred to the DSB for the establishment of a panel. Under Article 4.3 of the *SCM Agreement*, moreover, the purpose of consultations is "to clarify the facts of the situation and to arrive at a mutually agreed solution."

R.2.4.2 *Mexico – Corn Syrup (Article 21.5 – US)*, paras. 69–70

(WT/DS132/AB/RW)

. . . in previous appeals, we have observed that Article 6.2 imposes four requirements on Members requesting establishment of a panel, one of which obliges Members requesting the establishment of a panel to "indicate", in that request, "whether consultations were held". The issue which we examine here is not whether Members come under such an obligation, for it is clear that they do. Rather, we must consider the nature of that obligation, and the consequences that ensue when a requesting

Member does not "indicate whether consultations were held" in its request for establishment of a panel and a responding Member does not object to that omission. . . .

. . . we observe that the requirement will be satisfied by the inclusion, in the request for establishment of a panel, of a statement as to whether consultations occurred *or not*. The purpose of the requirement seems to be primarily informational – to inform the DSB and Members as to whether consultations took place. We also recall that the DSU expressly contemplates that, in certain circumstances, a panel can deal with and dispose of the matter referred to it even if no consultations took place. Similarly, the authority of the panel cannot be invalidated by the absence, in the request for establishment of the panel, of an indication "whether consultations were held". Indeed, it would be curious if the requirement in Article 6.2 to inform the DSB whether consultations were held was accorded more importance in the dispute settlement process than the requirement actually to hold those consultations.

Resolution of a Dispute. *See* Review of Implementation of DSB Rulings (R.4); Working Procedures for Appellate Review, Rule 30 – Withdrawal (W.2.13)

R.3 Retroactive Application of Trade Measures

R.3.1 *US – Underwear*, p. 14, DSR 1997:I, p. 11 at 22 (WT/DS24/AB/R)

It is essential to note that, under the express terms of Article 6.10, *ATC*, the restraint measure may be "applied" only "after the expiry of the period of 60 days" for consultations, without success, and only within the "window" of 30 days immediately following the 60-day period. Accordingly, we believe that, in the absence of an express authorization in Article 6.10, *ATC*, to backdate the effectivity of a safeguard restraint measure, a presumption arises from the very text of Article 6.10 that such a measure may be applied only prospectively. . . .

R.3.2 *US – Underwear*, pp. 19–20, DSR 1997:I, p. 11 at 28 (WT/DS24/AB/R)

The conclusion we have arrived at, in respect of the issue of permissibility of backdating, is that the giving of retroactive effect to a safeguard restraint measure is no longer permissible under the regime of Article 6 of the *ATC* and is in fact prohibited under Article 6.10 of that *Agreement*. The presumption of prospective effect only, has not been overturned; it is a proposition not simply presumptively correct but one requiring our assent. . . . The importing Member is, however, not defenceless against a speculative "flood of imports" where it is confronted with the circumstances contemplated in Article 6.11. Its appropriate recourse is, in other words, to action under Article 6.11 of the *ATC*, complying in the process with the requirements of Article 6.10 and Article 6.11.

R.4 Review of Implementation of DSB Rulings

R.4.1 Article 21.5 of the DSU – "measures taken to comply"

R.4.1.1 *Canada – Aircraft (Article 21.5 – Brazil)*, para. 36
(WT/DS70/AB/RW)

Proceedings under Article 21.5 do not concern just *any* measure of a Member of the WTO; rather, Article 21.5 proceedings are limited to those "measures *taken to comply* with the recommendations and rulings" of the DSB. In our view, the phrase "measures taken to comply" refers to measures which have been, or which should be, adopted by a Member to bring about compliance with the recommendations and rulings of the DSB. In principle, a measure which has been "taken to comply with the recommendations and rulings" of the DSB will *not* be the same measure as the measure which was the subject of the original dispute, so that, in principle, there would be two separate and distinct measures: the original measure which *gave rise* to the recommendations and rulings of the DSB, and the "measures taken to comply" which are – or should be – adopted to *implement* those recommendations and rulings. In these Article 21.5 proceedings, the measure at issue is a new measure, the *revised* TPC programme, which became effective on 18 November 1999 and which Canada presents as a "measure taken to comply with the recommendations and rulings" of the DSB.

R.4.1.2 *Canada – Aircraft (Article 21.5 – Brazil)*, para. 38
(WT/DS70/AB/RW)

We add also that the examination of "measures taken to comply" is based on the relevant facts proved, by the complainant, to the Article 21.5 panel, during the panel proceedings. Therefore, the "minimum implementation standard" that the Article 21.5 Panel expressed and which, it said, was "effectively" agreed between the parties, should be viewed with caution. The Article 21.5 Panel said that Canada's implementation should " '*ensure*' that *future* TPC assistance to the Canadian regional aircraft industry will not be *de facto* contingent on export performance." (emphasis added) The use in this standard of the words "ensure" and "future", if taken too literally, might be read to mean that the Panel was seeking a strict guarantee or absolute assurance as to the *future* application of the revised TPC programme. A standard which, if so read, would, however, be very difficult, if not impossible, to satisfy since no one can predict how unknown administrators would apply, in the unknowable future, even the most conscientiously crafted compliance measure.

R.4.1.3 *EC – Bed Linen (Article 21.5 – India)*, para. 78
(WT/DS141/AB/RW)

. . . As in *original* dispute settlement proceedings, the "matter" in Article 21.5 proceedings consists of two elements: the specific *measures* at issue and the legal basis of the complaint (that is, the *claims*). If a *claim* challenges a *measure* which is not a "measure taken to comply", that *claim* cannot properly be raised in Article 21.5 proceedings. We agree with the Panel that it is, ultimately, for an Article 21.5 panel –

and not for the complainant or the respondent – to determine which of the measures listed in the request for its establishment are "measures taken to comply"....

R.4.1.4 *EC – Bed Linen (Article 21.5 – India)*, para. 79 (WT/DS141/AB/RW)

... We explained there that the mandate of Article 21.5 panels is to examine either the "existence" of "measures taken to comply" or, more frequently, the "*consistency with a covered agreement*" of implementing measures. This implies that an Article 21.5 panel is not confined to examining the "measures taken to comply" from the perspective of the claims, arguments, and factual circumstances relating to the measure that was the subject of the *original* proceedings. Moreover, the relevant facts bearing upon the "measure taken to comply" may be different from the facts relevant to the measure at issue in the original proceedings. It is to be expected, therefore, that the claims, arguments, and factual circumstances relating to the "measure taken to comply" will not, necessarily, be the same as those relating to the measure in the original dispute. Indeed, a complainant in Article 21.5 proceedings may well raise *new* claims, arguments, and factual circumstances different from those raised in the original proceedings, because a "measure taken to comply" may be *inconsistent* with WTO obligations in ways different from the original measure. In our view, therefore, an Article 21.5 panel could not properly carry out its mandate to assess whether a "measure taken to comply" is *fully consistent* with WTO obligations if it were precluded from examining claims additional to, and different from, the claims raised in the original proceedings.

R.4.2 Article 21.5 of the DSU – "new claims"

R.4.2.1 *Canada – Aircraft (Article 21.5 – Brazil)*, paras. 40–41 (WT/DS70/AB/RW)

We have already noted that these proceedings, under Article 21.5 of the DSU, concern the "consistency" of the revised TPC programme with Article 3.1(a) of the *SCM Agreement*. Therefore, we disagree with the Article 21.5 Panel that the scope of these Article 21.5 dispute settlement proceedings is limited to "the issue of whether or not Canada *has implemented the DSB recommendation*".... It follows then that the task of the Article 21.5 Panel in this case is, in fact, to determine whether the new measure – the revised TPC programme – is consistent with Article 3.1(a) of the *SCM Agreement*.

Accordingly, in carrying out its review under Article 21.5 of the DSU, a panel is not confined to examining the "measures taken to comply" from the perspective of the claims, arguments and factual circumstances that related to the measure that was the subject of the original proceedings. Although these may have some relevance in proceedings under Article 21.5 of the DSU, Article 21.5 proceedings involve, in principle, not the original measure, but rather a new and different measure which was not before the original panel. In addition, the relevant facts bearing upon the "measure taken to comply" may be different from the relevant facts relating to the measure at issue in the original proceedings. It is natural, therefore, that the claims, arguments and factual circumstances which are pertinent to the "measure taken to comply" will not, necessarily, be the same as those which were pertinent in the original dispute. Indeed, the utility of the review envisaged under Article 21.5 of the DSU would be seriously undermined if a panel were restricted to examining the new measure from the perspective of the claims, arguments and factual circumstances that related to the original measure, because an Article 21.5 panel would then be unable to examine fully the "consistency with a covered agreement of the measures taken to comply", as required by Article 21.5 of the DSU.

R.4.2.2 *US – Shrimp (Article 21.5 – Malaysia)*, paras. 86–88 (WT/DS58/AB/RW)

As we ruled in our Report in *Canada – Aircraft (21.5)*, panel proceedings pursuant to Article 21.5 of the DSU involve, in principle, not the original measure, but a new and different measure that was not before the original panel. Therefore, "in carrying out its review under Article 21.5 of the DSU, a panel is not confined to examining the 'measure[] taken to comply' from the perspective of the claims, arguments and factual circumstances that related to the measure that was the subject of the original proceedings."

When the issue concerns the consistency of a new measure "taken to comply", the task of a panel in a matter referred to it by the DSB for an Article 21.5 proceeding is to consider that new measure in its totality. The fulfilment of this task requires that a panel consider both the measure itself and the measure's application. As the title of Article 21 makes clear, the task of panels under Article 21.5 forms part of the process of the "*Surveillance of Implementation of the Recommendations and Rulings*" of the DSB. Toward that end, the task of a panel under Article 21.5 is to examine the "consistency with a covered agreement of measures taken to comply with the recommendations and rulings" of the DSB. That task is circumscribed by the specific claims made by the complainant when the matter is referred by the DSB for an Article 21.5 proceeding. It is not part of the task of a panel under Article 21.5 to address a claim that has not been made.

Malaysia relies in this appeal on our ruling in *Canada – Aircraft (21.5)*. We understand Malaysia to argue, based in part on our ruling in *Canada – Aircraft (21.5)*, that the Panel in this case had a duty to review the *totality* of the United States measure, and to assess it for its consistency with the relevant provisions of the GATT 1994. That is indeed a panel's task under Article 21.5 of the DSU. Yet, as we have said, it is not part of a panel's task to go beyond the particular claims that have been made with respect to the consistency of a new measure with a covered agreement when a matter is referred to it by the DSB for an Article 21.5 proceeding. Thus, it would not have been appropriate in this case for the Panel to address a claim that was *not* made by Malaysia when requesting that this matter be referred by the DSB for an Article 21.5 proceeding.

R.4.2.3 *EC – Bed Linen (Article 21.5 – India)*, paras. 80, 87 (WT/DS141/AB/RW)

This appeal, however, raises an issue different from the issue that was before us in *Canada – Aircraft (Article 21.5 – Brazil)*. Here, India did not raise a *new* claim before the Article 21.5 Panel; rather, India reasserted in the Article 21.5 proceedings the *same* claim that it had raised before the *original* panel in respect of a component of the implementation measure which was the same as in the original measure. . . .

. . .

We conclude, therefore, that, in these Article 21.5 proceedings, India has raised the *same* claim under Article 3.5 relating to "other factors" as it did in the original proceedings. In doing so, India seeks to challenge an aspect of the original measure which has not changed, and which the European Communities did not have to change, in order to comply with the DSB recommendations and rulings to make that measure consistent with the European Communities' WTO obligations.

R.4.2.4 *EC – Bed Linen (Article 21.5 – India)*, paras. 88–89
(WT/DS141/AB/RW)

. . . We agree with the Panel that the *Canada – Aircraft (Article 21.5 – Brazil)* dispute involved a *new* claim challenging a *new* component of the measure taken to comply which was not part of the original measure. The situation in *Canada – Aircraft (Article 21.5 – Brazil)* was thus different from the situation in this appeal.

. . . In other words, the *US – FSC (Article 21.5 – EC)* dispute involved a *new* claim challenging a *changed* component of the measure taken to comply, while this dispute, by contrast, concerns the *same* claim against an *unchanged* component of the implementation measure that was part of the original measure and that was not found to be inconsistent with WTO obligations. Therefore, the situation in *US – FSC (Article 21.5 – EC)* was different from the situation in this appeal.

R.4.3 Article 21.5 of the DSU – Effect of DSB rulings in the original dispute. *See also* Status of Panel and Appellate Body Reports (S.8)

R.4.3.1 *US – Shrimp (Article 21.5 – Malaysia)*, paras. 89, 96–97
(WT/DS58/AB/RW)

With respect to a claim that *has* been made when a matter is referred by the DSB for an Article 21.5 proceeding, Malaysia seems to suggest as well that a panel must re-examine, for WTO-consistency, even those aspects of a new measure that were part of a previous measure that was the subject of a dispute, and were found by the Appellate Body to be *WTO-consistent* in that dispute, and that remain unchanged as part of the new measure.

. . .

As we see it, then, the Panel properly examined Section 609 as part of its examination of the totality of the new measure, correctly found that Section 609 had not been changed since the original proceedings, and rightly concluded that our ruling in *United States – Shrimp* with respect to the consistency of Section 609, therefore, still stands.

We wish to recall that panel proceedings under Article 21.5 of the DSU are, as the title of Article 21 states, part of the process of the "*Surveillance of Implementation of*

Recommendations and Rulings" of the DSB. This includes Appellate Body Reports. To be sure, the right of WTO Members to have recourse to the DSU, including under Article 21.5, must be respected. Even so, it must also be kept in mind that Article 17.14 of the DSU provides not only that Reports of the Appellate Body "shall be" adopted by the DSB, by consensus, but also that such Reports "shall be ... unconditionally accepted by the parties to the dispute. ..." Thus, Appellate Body Reports that are adopted by the DSB are, as Article 17.14 provides, "... unconditionally accepted by the parties to the dispute", and, therefore, must be treated by the parties to a particular dispute as a final resolution to that dispute. In this regard, we recall, too, that Article 3.3 of the DSU states that the "prompt settlement" of disputes "is essential to the effective functioning of the WTO".

R.4.3.2 *Mexico – Corn Syrup (Article 21.5 – US)*, para. 79 (WT/DS132/AB/RW)

With respect to the first element, we note that the original panel report, regarding the *initial* measure (SECOFI's original determination), has been adopted and that these Article 21.5 proceedings concern a *subsequent* measure (SECOFI's redetermination). We also note that Mexico did not appeal the original panel's report, and that Articles 3.2 and 3.3 of the DSU reflect the importance to the multilateral trading system of security, predictability and the prompt settlement of disputes. We see no basis for us to examine the original panel's treatment of the alleged restraint agreement.

R.4.3.3 *Mexico – Corn Syrup (Article 21.5 – US)*, para. 121 (WT/DS132/AB/RW)

The Panel was charged, under Article 21.5 of the DSU, with assessing the claims made by the United States with respect to the consistency of the redetermination with Mexico's obligations under the *Anti-Dumping Agreement.* In proceeding under Article 21.5 of the DSU, the Panel conducted its work against the background of the original proceedings, and with full cognizance of the reasons provided by the original panel. The original determination and original panel proceedings, as well as the redetermination and the panel proceedings under Article 21.5, form part of a continuum of events. We consider that the Panel Report cannot be read in isolation from those events.

R.4.3.4 *EC – Bed Linen (Article 21.5 – India)*, paras. 92–93 (WT/DS141/AB/RW)

The issue raised in this appeal is similar to the issue we resolved in *US – Shrimp (Article 21.5 – Malaysia)*. In this appeal, however, the original panel's finding on India's claim under Article 3.5 relating to "other factors" was *not appealed* in the original dispute. Accordingly, the finding of the original panel relating to that claim was adopted by the DSB as part of a *panel* report, and, therefore, Article 17.14, which deals with the adoption of *Appellate Body* Reports, does not dispose of the issue before us.

All the same, in our view, an *unappealed* finding included in a panel report that is *adopted* by the DSB must be treated as a *final resolution* to a dispute between the parties in respect of the *particular* claim and the *specific* component of a measure that is the subject of that claim. This conclusion is supported by Articles 16.4 and 19.1, paragraphs 1 and 3 of Article 21, and Article 22.1 of the DSU. Where a panel concludes that a measure is inconsistent with a covered agreement, that panel shall *recommend*, according to Article 19.1, that the Member concerned bring that measure into conformity with that agreement. A panel report, including the *recommendations* contained therein, shall be *adopted* by the DSB within the time period specified in Article 16.4 – unless appealed. Members are to *comply* with recommendations and rulings *adopted* by the DSB promptly, or within a reasonable period of time, in accordance with paragraphs 1 and 3 of Article 21 of the DSU. A Member that does not comply with the recommendations and rulings adopted by the DSB within these time periods must face the consequences set out in Article 22.1, relating to compensation and suspension of concessions. Thus, a reading of Articles 16.4 and 19.1, paragraphs 1 and 3 of Article 21, and Article 22.1, taken together, makes it abundantly clear that a panel finding which is not appealed, and which is included in a panel report *adopted* by the DSB, must be accepted by the parties as a *final* resolution to the dispute between them, in the same way and with the same finality as a finding included in an Appellate Body Report adopted by the DSB – with respect to the particular claim and the specific component of the measure that is the subject of the claim. . . .

R.4.3.5 *EC – Bed Linen (Article 21.5 – India)*, para. 96
(WT/DS141/AB/RW)

We consider next whether the fact that the Panel dismissed India's claim because India had not established a *prima facie* case has any relevance for our decision on the effect of the adoption by the DSB of a finding of a panel report that was not appealed. . . . Here, however, the original panel ruled that India had failed to present a *prima facie* case in respect of its claim under Article 3.5 relating to "other factors". In our view, the effect, for the parties, of findings adopted by the DSB as part of a panel report is the same, regardless of whether a panel found that the complainant failed to establish a *prima facie* case that the measure is inconsistent with WTO obligations, that the Panel found that the measure is fully consistent with WTO obligations, or that the Panel found that the measure is not consistent with WTO obligations. . . .

R.4.3.6 *EC – Bed Linen (Article 21.5 – India)*, paras. 98–99
(WT/DS141/AB/RW)

. . . It would be incompatible with the function and purpose of the WTO dispute settlement system if a claim could be reasserted in Article 21.5 proceedings after the original panel or the Appellate Body has made a finding that the challenged aspect of the original measure is *not* inconsistent with WTO obligations, and that report has been adopted by the DSB. At some point, disputes must be viewed as definitely *settled* by the WTO dispute settlement system.

In the light of the foregoing, we conclude that the original panel's finding on India's claim under Article 3.5 relating to "other factors" provides a "final resolution" to the dispute in this respect between the parties, because it was not appealed, and forms part of a panel report adopted by the DSB....

Review of Countervailing Duty Measures. *See* SCM Agreement, Article 21 (S.2.29–33)

R.5 Right to Bring Claims – Legal Interest

R.5.1 *EC – Bananas III*, para. 132
(WT/DS27/AB/R)

We agree with the Panel that "neither Article 3.3 nor 3.7 of the DSU nor any other provision of the DSU contain any explicit requirement that a Member must have a 'legal interest' as a prerequisite for requesting a panel". We do not accept that the need for a "legal interest" is implied in the DSU or in any other provision of the *WTO Agreement*....

R.5.2 *EC – Bananas III*, para. 135
(WT/DS27/AB/R)

...we believe that a Member has broad discretion in deciding whether to bring a case against another Member under the DSU. The language of Article XXIII:1 of the GATT 1994 and of Article 3.7 of the DSU suggests, furthermore, that a Member is expected to be largely self-regulating in deciding whether any such action would be "fruitful".

R.5.3 *EC – Bananas III*, paras. 136–138
(WT/DS27/AB/R)

We are satisfied that the United States was justified in bringing its claims under the GATT 1994 in this case. The United States is a producer of bananas, and a potential export interest by the United States cannot be excluded. The internal market of the United States for bananas could be affected by the EC banana regime, in particular, by the effects of that regime on world supplies and world prices of bananas. We also agree with the Panel's statement that:

> ...with the increased interdependence of the global economy, ...Members have a greater stake in enforcing WTO rules than in the past since any deviation from the negotiated balance of rights and obligations is more likely than ever to affect them, directly or indirectly.

We note, too, that there is no challenge here to the standing of the United States under the GATS, and that the claims under the GATS and the GATT 1994 relating to the EC import licensing regime are inextricably interwoven in this case.

Taken together, these reasons are sufficient justification for the United States to have brought its claims against the EC banana import regime under the GATT 1994. This does not mean, though, that one or more of the factors we have noted in this case would necessarily be dispositive in another case. . . .

R.5.4 *Mexico – Corn Syrup (Article 21.5 – US)*, paras. 73–74 (WT/DS132/AB/RW)

. . . [the first sentence of Article 3.7 of the DSU] reflects a basic principle that Members should have recourse to WTO dispute settlement in good faith, and not frivolously set in motion the procedures contemplated in the DSU. . . .

Given the "largely self-regulating" nature of the requirement in the first sentence of Article 3.7, panels and the Appellate Body must presume, whenever a Member submits a request for establishment of a panel, that such Member does so in good faith, having duly exercised its judgement as to whether recourse to that panel would be "fruitful". Article 3.7 neither requires nor authorizes a panel to look behind that Member's decision and to question its exercise of judgement. Therefore, the Panel was not obliged to consider this issue on its own motion.

R.5.5 *US – Corrosion-Resistant Steel Sunset Review*, para. 86 (WT/DS244/AB/R)

. . . a measure attributable to a Member may be submitted to dispute settlement provided only that another Member has taken the view, in good faith, that the measure nullifies or impairs benefits accruing to it under the *Anti-Dumping Agreement*. . . .

R.5.6 *US – Corrosion-Resistant Steel Sunset Review*, para. 89 (WT/DS244/AB/R)

We observe, too, that allowing measures to be the subject of dispute settlement proceedings, whether or not they are of a mandatory character, is consistent with the comprehensive nature of the right of Members to resort to dispute settlement to "preserve [their] rights and obligations . . . under the covered agreements, and to clarify the existing provisions of those agreements". As long as a Member respects the principles set forth in Articles 3.7 and 3.10 of the DSU, namely, to exercise their "judgement as to whether action under these procedures would be fruitful" and to engage in dispute settlement in good faith, then that Member is entitled to request a panel to examine measures that the Member considers nullify or impair its benefits. . . .

S

S.1 Safeguards Agreement

S.1.1 General

S.1.1.1 *US – Line Pipe*, paras. 80, 82–84
(WT/DS202/AB/R)

. . . it is useful to recall that safeguard measures are extraordinary remedies to be taken only in emergency situations. Furthermore, they are remedies that are imposed in the form of import restrictions in the absence of any allegation of an unfair trade practice. In this, safeguard measures differ from, for example, anti-dumping duties and countervailing duties to counter subsidies, which are both measures taken in response to unfair trade practices. . . .

. . .

. . . part of the *raison d'être* of Article XIX of the GATT 1994 and the *Agreement on Safeguards* is, unquestionably, that of giving a WTO Member the possibility, as trade is liberalized, of resorting to an effective remedy in an extraordinary emergency situation that, in the judgement of that Member, makes it necessary to protect a domestic industry temporarily.

There is, therefore, a natural tension between, on the one hand, defining the appropriate and legitimate scope of the right to apply safeguard measures and, on the other hand, ensuring that safeguard measures are not applied against "fair trade" beyond what is necessary to provide extraordinary and temporary relief. A WTO Member seeking to apply a safeguard measure will argue, correctly, that the *right* to apply such measures must be respected in order to maintain the *domestic* momentum and motivation for ongoing trade liberalization. In turn, a WTO Member whose trade is affected by a safeguard measure will argue, correctly, that the *application* of such measures must be limited in order to maintain the *multilateral* integrity of ongoing trade concessions. The balance struck by the WTO Members in reconciling this natural tension relating to safeguard measures is found in the provisions of the *Agreement on Safeguards*.

This natural tension is likewise inherent in two basic inquiries that are conducted in interpreting the *Agreement on Safeguards*. These two basic inquiries are: *first*, is there a right to apply a safeguard measure? And, *second*, if so, has that right been exercised, through the application of such a measure, within the limits set out in the treaty? These two inquiries are separate and distinct. They must not be confused by the treaty interpreter. One necessarily precedes and leads to the other. . . .

S.1.1.2 *US – Steel Safeguards*, para. 264
(WT/DS248/AB/R, WT/DS249/AB/R, WT/DS251/AB/R, WT/DS252/AB/R, WT/DS253/AB/R, WT/DS254/AB/R, WT/DS258/AB/R, WT/DS259/AB/R)

. . . Article XIX and the *Agreement on Safeguards* confirm the right of WTO Members to apply safeguard measures when, as a result of unforeseen developments and of the effect of obligations incurred, including tariff concessions, a product is being imported in such increased quantities and under such conditions as to cause or threaten to cause serious injury to the domestic industry that produces like or directly competitive products. However, as Article 2.1 of the *Agreement on Safeguards* makes clear, the right to apply such measures arises "*only*" if these prerequisites are shown to exist.

S.1.2 Standard of review. *See also* Standard of Review, Article 11 of the DSU (S.7.2–7)

S.1.2.1 *US – Lamb*, para. 103
(WT/DS177/AB/R, WT/DS178/AB/R)

Thus, an "objective assessment" of a claim under Article 4.2(a) of the *Agreement on Safeguards* has, in principle, two elements. First, a panel must review whether competent authorities have evaluated *all relevant factors*, and, second, a panel must review whether the authorities have provided a *reasoned and adequate explanation* of how the facts support their determination. Thus, the panel's objective assessment involves a *formal* aspect and a *substantive* aspect. The formal aspect is whether the competent authorities have evaluated "all relevant factors". The substantive aspect is whether the competent authorities have given a reasoned and adequate explanation for their determination.

S.1.2.2 *US – Lamb*, paras. 106–107
(WT/DS177/AB/R, WT/DS178/AB/R)

We wish to emphasize that, although panels are not entitled to conduct a *de novo* review of the evidence, nor to *substitute* their own conclusions for those of the competent authorities, this does *not* mean that panels must simply *accept* the conclusions of the competent authorities. To the contrary, in our view, in examining a claim under Article 4.2(a), a panel can assess whether the competent authorities' explanation for its determination is reasoned and adequate *only* if the panel critically examines that explanation, in depth, and in the light of the facts before the panel. Panels must, therefore, review whether the competent authorities' explanation fully addresses the nature, and, especially, the complexities, of the data, and responds to other plausible interpretations of that data. A panel must find, in particular, that an explanation is not reasoned, or is not adequate, if some *alternative explanation* of the facts is plausible, and if the competent authorities' explanation does not seem adequate in the light of that alternative explanation. Thus, in making an "objective assessment" of a claim under Article 4.2(a), panels must be open to the possibility that the explanation given by the competent authorities is not reasoned or adequate.

In this respect, the phrase "*de novo* review" should not be used loosely. If a panel concludes that the competent authorities, in a particular case, have *not* provided a reasoned or adequate explanation for their determination, that panel has not, thereby, engaged in a *de novo* review. Nor has that panel substituted its own conclusions for those of the competent authorities. Rather, the panel has, consistent with its obligations under the DSU, simply reached a conclusion that the determination made by the competent authorities is inconsistent with the specific requirements of Article 4.2 of the *Agreement on Safeguards*.

S.1.2.3 *US – Steel Safeguards*, para. 276
(WT/DS248/AB/R, WT/DS249/AB/R, WT/DS251/AB/R, WT/DS252/AB/R, WT/DS253/AB/R, WT/DS254/AB/R, WT/DS258/AB/R, WT/DS259/AB/R)

We explained in *US – Lamb*, in the context of a claim under Article 4.2(a) of the *Agreement on Safeguards*, that the competent authorities must provide a "*reasoned and adequate explanation* of how the facts support their determination". More recently, in *US – Line Pipe*, in the context of a claim under Article 4.2(b) of the *Agreement on Safeguards*, we said that the competent authorities must, similarly, provide a "*reasoned and adequate explanation*, that injury caused by factors other than increased imports is not attributed to increased imports". Our findings in those cases did not purport to address *solely* the standard of review that is appropriate for claims arising under Article 4.2 of the *Agreement on Safeguards*. We see no reason not to apply the same standard generally to the obligations under the *Agreement on Safeguards* as well as to the obligations in Article XIX of the GATT 1994.

S.1.3 Article 2.1 – "like or directly competitive products". *See also* Safeguards Agreement, Article 4.1(c) – Domestic industry (S.1.25)

S.1.3.1 *US – Lamb*, para. 86
(WT/DS177/AB/R, WT/DS178/AB/R)

Thus, a safeguard measure is imposed on a specific "*product*", namely, the imported product. The measure may only be imposed if that specific product ("such *product*") is having the stated effects upon the "domestic industry *that produces like or directly competitive products*." (emphasis added) The conditions in Article 2.1, therefore, relate in several important respects to *specific products*. In particular, according to Article 2.1, the legal basis for imposing a safeguard measure exists *only* when imports of a specific product have prejudicial effects on domestic producers of products that are "like or directly competitive" with that imported product. In our view, it would be a clear departure from the text of Article 2.1 if a safeguard measure could be imposed because of the prejudicial effects that an imported product has on domestic producers of products that are *not* "like or directly competitive products" in relation to the imported product.

S.1.4 Article 2.1 – Domestic decision-making

S.1.4.1 *US – Line Pipe*, para. 158
(WT/DS202/AB/R)

... we are not concerned with how the competent authorities of WTO Members reach their determinations in applying safeguard measures. The *Agreement on Safeguards* does not prescribe the internal decision-making process for making such a determination. That is entirely up to WTO Members in the exercise of their sovereignty. We are concerned only with the determination itself, which is a singular act for which a WTO Member may be accountable in WTO dispute settlement. It is of no matter to us whether that singular act results from a decision by one, one hundred, or – as here – six individual decision-makers under the municipal law of that WTO Member. What matters to us is whether the determination, however it is decided domestically, meets the requirements of the *Agreement on Safeguards*.

S.1.5 Articles 2.1 and 4.1(c) – Territorial application of safeguard measure

S.1.5.1 *Argentina – Footwear (EC)*, para. 111
(WT/DS121/AB/R)

... Taken together, the provisions of Articles 2.1 and 4.1(c) of the *Agreement on Safeguards* demonstrate that a Member of the WTO may only apply a safeguard measure after that Member has determined that a product is being imported *into its territory* in such increased quantities and under such conditions as to cause or threaten to cause serious injury to *its* domestic industry *within its territory*. According to Articles 2.1 and 4.1(c), therefore, all of the relevant aspects of a safeguard investigation must be conducted by the Member that ultimately applies the safeguard measure, on the basis of increased imports entering its territory and causing or threatening to cause serious injury to the domestic industry within its territory.

S.1.6 Article 2.1 – Increased imports

S.1.6.1 *Argentina – Footwear (EC)*, para. 131
(WT/DS121/AB/R)

We recall here our reasoning and conclusions above on the meaning of the phrase "as a result of unforeseen developments" in Article XIX:1(a) of the GATT 1994. We concluded there that the increased quantities of imports should have been "unforeseen" or "unexpected". We also believe that the phrase "in *such* increased quantities" in Article 2.1 of the *Agreement on Safeguards* and Article XIX:1(a) of the GATT 1994 is meaningful to this determination. In our view, the determination of whether the requirement of imports "in such increased quantities" is met is not a merely mathematical or technical determination. In other words, it is not enough for an investigation to show simply that imports of the product this year were more than last year – or five years ago. Again, and it bears repeating, not just *any* increased quantities of imports will suffice. There must be "*such* increased quantities" as to cause or threaten to cause serious injury to the domestic industry in order to fulfil this requirement for applying a safeguard measure. And this language in both Article 2.1 of the *Agreement on Safeguards* and Article XIX:1(a) of the GATT 1994, we believe, requires that the increase in imports must have been recent enough, sudden enough, sharp enough, and significant enough, both quantitatively and qualitatively, to cause or threaten to cause "serious injury".

S.1.6.2 *US – Steel Safeguards*, para. 346

(WT/DS248/AB/R, WT/DS249/AB/R, WT/DS251/AB/R, WT/DS252/AB/R, WT/DS253/AB/R, WT/DS254/AB/R, WT/DS258/AB/R, WT/DS259/AB/R)

... In [*Argentina – Footwear (EC)*] we underlined the importance of reading the requirement of "such increased quantities" in the context in which it appears in both Article XIX:1(a) of the GATT 1994 and Article 2.1 of the *Agreement on Safeguards*. That context includes the words "to cause or threaten to cause serious injury". Read in context, it is apparent that "there must be 'such increased quantities' as to cause or threaten to cause serious injury to the domestic industry in order to fulfill this requirement for applying a safeguard measure." Indeed, in our view, the term "such", which appears in the phrase "such increased quantities" in Articles XIX:1(a) and 2.1, clearly links the relevant increased imports to their ability to cause serious injury or the threat thereof. Accordingly, we agree with the United States that our statement in *Argentina – Footwear (EC)* that the "increase in imports must have been recent enough, sudden enough, sharp enough and significant enough ... to cause or threaten to cause serious injury", was a statement about "the entire investigative responsibility of the competent authorities under the Safeguards Agreement", and that "[w]hether an increase in imports is recent, sudden, sharp and significant enough to cause or threaten serious injury are questions that are answered as the competent authorities proceed with the remainder of their analysis (i.e., their consideration of serious injury/threat and causation)."

S.1.6.3 *US – Steel Safeguards*, para. 350

(WT/DS248/AB/R, WT/DS249/AB/R, WT/DS251/AB/R, WT/DS252/AB/R, WT/DS253/AB/R, WT/DS254/AB/R, WT/DS258/AB/R, WT/DS259/AB/R)

... we said in *Argentina – Footwear (EC)* that "the increased quantities of imports should have been 'unforeseen' or 'unexpected'." In doing so, we were referring to the fact that the increased imports must, under Article XIX:1(a), result from "unforeseen developments" in order to justify the application of a safeguard measure. Because the "increased imports" must be "as a result" of an event that was "unforeseen" or "unexpected", it follows that the increased imports must also be "unforeseen" or "unexpected". Thus, the "extraordinary nature" of the domestic response to increased imports does not depend on the absolute or relative quantities of the product being imported. Rather, it depends on the fact that the increased imports were unforeseen or unexpected.

S.1.7 Article 2.1 – Examination of trends

S.1.7.1 *Argentina – Footwear (EC)*, para. 129
(WT/DS121/AB/R)

We agree with the Panel that Articles 2.1 and 4.2(a) of the *Agreement on Safeguards* require a demonstration not merely of *any* increase in imports, but, instead, of imports "in such increased quantities . . . and under such conditions as to cause or threaten to cause serious injury." In addition, we agree with the Panel that the specific provisions of Article 4.2(a) require that "the *rate* and *amount* of the increase in imports . . . in absolute and relative terms" (emphasis added) must be evaluated. Thus, we do not dispute the Panel's view and ultimate conclusion that the competent authorities are required to consider the *trends* in imports over the period of investigation (rather than just comparing the end points) under Article 4.2(a). . . .

S.1.7.2 *US – Steel Safeguards*, para. 354
(WT/DS248/AB/R, WT/DS249/AB/R, WT/DS251/AB/R, WT/DS252/AB/R, WT/DS253/AB/R, WT/DS254/AB/R, WT/DS258/AB/R, WT/DS259/AB/R)

We concluded in *Argentina – Footwear (EC)* that "the competent authorities are required to consider the *trends* in imports over the period of investigation (rather than just comparing the end points) under Article 4.2(a)." A determination of whether there is an increase in imports cannot, therefore, be made merely by comparing the end points of the period of investigation. Indeed, in cases where an examination does not demonstrate, for instance, a clear and uninterrupted upward trend in import volumes, a simple end-point-to-end-point analysis could easily be manipulated to lead to different results, depending on the choice of end points. A comparison could support either a finding of an increase or a decrease in import volumes simply by choosing different starting and ending points.

S.1.7.3 *US – Steel Safeguards*, paras. 355–356
(WT/DS248/AB/R, WT/DS249/AB/R, WT/DS251/AB/R, WT/DS252/AB/R, WT/DS253/AB/R, WT/DS254/AB/R, WT/DS258/AB/R, WT/DS259/AB/R)

. . . a demonstration of "any increase" in imports between any two points in time is not sufficient to demonstrate "increased imports" for purposes of Articles XIX and 2.1. Rather, as we have said, competent authorities are required to examine the trends in imports over the entire period of investigation.

We, therefore, reject the United States' assertion that "the phrase 'in such increased quantities' simply states the requirement that, in general, the level of imports at (or reasonably near to) the end of a period of investigation be higher than at some unspecified earlier point in time." . . .

S.1.7.4 *US – Steel Safeguards*, para. 374
(WT/DS248/AB/R, WT/DS249/AB/R, WT/DS251/AB/R, WT/DS252/AB/R, WT/DS253/AB/R, WT/DS254/AB/R, WT/DS258/AB/R, WT/DS259/AB/R)

In our view, what is called for in every case is an *explanation* of how the *trend* in imports supports the competent authority's finding that the requirement of "such increased quantities" within the meaning of Articles XIX:1(a) and 2.1 has been fulfilled. It is this *explanation* concerning the *trend* in imports – over the entire period of investigation – that allows a competent authority to *demonstrate* that "a product is being imported in such increased quantities".

S.1.8 Article 2.1 – Decrease at the end of an investigation period

S.1.8.1 *Argentina – Footwear (EC)*, para. 130

(WT/DS121/AB/R)

. . . In our view, the use of the present tense of the verb phrase "is being imported" in both Article 2.1 of the *Agreement on Safeguards* and Article XIX:1(a) of the GATT 1994 indicates that it is necessary for the competent authorities to examine recent imports, and not simply trends in imports during the past five years – or, for that matter, during any other period of several years. In our view, the phrase "is being imported" implies that the increase in imports must have been sudden and recent.

S.1.8.2 *US – Steel Safeguards*, para. 367

(WT/DS248/AB/R, WT/DS249/AB/R, WT/DS251/AB/R, WT/DS252/AB/R, WT/DS253/AB/R, WT/DS254/AB/R, WT/DS258/AB/R, WT/DS259/AB/R)

. . . Article 2.1 does *not* require that imports need to be increasing at the time of the determination. Rather, the plain meaning of the phrase "is being imported in such increased quantities" suggests merely that imports must *have* increased, and that the relevant products continue "being imported" in (such) increased quantities. We also do *not* believe that a decrease in imports at the end of the period of investigation would necessarily prevent an investigating authority from finding that, nevertheless, products continue to be imported "in such increased quantities."

S.1.8.3 *US – Steel Safeguards*, para. 388

(WT/DS248/AB/R, WT/DS249/AB/R, WT/DS251/AB/R, WT/DS252/AB/R, WT/DS253/AB/R, WT/DS254/AB/R, WT/DS258/AB/R, WT/DS259/AB/R)

. . . we note here also that, in not explaining the "most recent decrease" in absolute imports, the USITC did *not*, in our view, provide an explanation concerning the overall *trend* in imports that occurred during the period of investigation. . . . In our view, by failing to address the decrease in imports that occurred between interim 2000 and interim 2001, the United States did not – and could not – provide a reasoned and adequate explanation of how the facts supported its finding that imports of hot-rolled bar "increased", as required by Article 2.1 of the *Agreement on Safeguards*. This failure to account for the decrease in absolute imports is all the more serious in the light of the fact that the intervening trend that was not addressed by the USITC occurred at the very end of the period of investigation. In *US – Lamb*, we found that the competent authority "must assess" the data from the most recent past "in the context of the data for the entire investigative period". As the Panel found, it is, precisely, those most recent data that the USITC failed to account for with respect to absolute imports.

S.1.9 Article 2.1 – Increase relative to domestic production

S.1.9.1 *US – Steel Safeguards*, para. 390
(WT/DS248/AB/R, WT/DS249/AB/R, WT/DS251/AB/R, WT/DS252/AB/R, WT/DS253/AB/R, WT/DS254/AB/R, WT/DS258/AB/R, WT/DS259/AB/R)

... Article 2.1 provides that a Member may apply a safeguard measure after a determination that the relevant product is "being imported ... in such increased quantities, absolute *or* relative to domestic production ... as to cause or threaten to cause serious injury" (emphasis added). Therefore, a determination of either an absolute or relative increase in imports causing serious injury is sufficient to authorize a Member to apply safeguard measures. Accordingly, the increased imports requirement *can* be met not only if there is an absolute increase in imports, but also if there is an increase relative to domestic production.

S.1.10 Article 2.1 – Serious injury or threat thereof. *See also* Safeguards Agreement, Article 4.1(b) – Threat of serious injury (S.1.24)

S.1.10.1 *US – Line Pipe*, para. 161
(WT/DS202/AB/R)

... precisely what kind of "finding" on this "pertinent issue of law" must appear in the published report of the competent authorities? The question is: should the phrase "*cause or threaten to cause*" in Article 2.1 be read as "cause or threaten to cause" in the sense of either *one* ("cause") *or the other* ("threaten to cause"), *but not both*? Or should this phrase be read rather as "cause or threaten to cause" in the sense of *either one or the other, or both in combination* ("cause or threaten to cause")?

S.1.10.2 *US – Line Pipe*, paras. 163–164
(WT/DS202/AB/R)

Our view is that the phrase "cause or threaten to cause" can be read either way. As we read it, the dictionary definition of "or" supports either conclusion. ...

... "or" can be exclusive, and "or" can also be inclusive. The text of Article 2.1 does not provide decisive interpretative guidance in this respect. This is not to say that we believe that "serious injury" and "threat of serious injury" are the same thing, or that competent authorities may make a finding that both exist at the same time. Rather, we believe that the text of Article 2.1 lends itself to either interpretation.

S.1.10.3 *US – Line Pipe*, para. 167
(WT/DS202/AB/R)

... we agree with the Panel that the respective definitions of "serious injury" and "threat of serious injury" are two distinct concepts that must be given distinctive meanings in interpreting the *Agreement on Safeguards*. Yet, although we agree with the Panel that the *Agreement on Safeguards* establishes a distinction between "serious injury" and "threat of serious injury", we do not agree with the Panel that a requirement follows from such a distinction to make a discrete finding either of "serious injury" or of "threat of serious injury" when making a determination relating to the application of a safeguard measure.

S.1.10.4 *US – Line Pipe*, paras. 170–171
(WT/DS202/AB/R)

. . . The question at issue is whether the right [to apply a safeguard measure] exists in this particular case. And, as the right exists if there is a finding by the competent authorities of a "threat of serious injury" or – something *beyond* – "serious injury", then it seems to us that it is irrelevant, *in determining whether the right exists*, if there is "serious injury" or only "threat of serious injury" – so long as there is a determination that there is *at least* a "threat". In terms of the rising continuum of an injurious condition of a domestic industry that ascends from a "threat of serious injury" up to "serious injury", we see "serious injury" – because it is something *beyond* a "threat" – as necessarily *including* the concept of a "threat" and *exceeding* the presence of a "threat" for purposes of answering the relevant inquiry: is there a right to apply a safeguard measure?

Based on this analysis of the most relevant context of the phrase "cause or threaten to cause" in Article 2.1, we do not see that phrase as necessarily meaning *one or the other, but not both*. Rather, that clause could also mean *either one or the other, or both in combination*. Therefore, for the reasons we have set out, we do not see that it matters – for the purpose of determining whether there is a right to apply a safeguard measure under the *Agreement on Safeguards* – whether a domestic authority finds that there is "serious injury", "threat of serious injury", or, as the USITC found here, "serious injury or threat of serious injury". In any of those events, the right to apply a safeguard is, in our view, established.

S.1.11 Article 2.1 – Causation. *See also* Safeguards Agreement, Article 4.2(b) – Causation (S.1.29–32)

S.1.11.1 *US – Wheat Gluten*, para. 76
(WT/DS166/AB/R)

. . . Thus, under Article 2.1, the causation analysis embraces two elements: the first relating to increased "imports" specifically and the second to the "conditions" under which imports are occurring.

S.1.12 Article 2.1 – "under such conditions"

S.1.12.1 *US – Wheat Gluten*, para. 78
(WT/DS166/AB/R)

. . . Thus, the phrase "under such conditions" refers generally to the prevailing "conditions", in the marketplace for the product concerned, when the increase in imports occurs. Interpreted in this way, the phrase "under such conditions" is a shorthand reference to the remaining factors listed in Article 4.2(a), which relate to the overall state of the domestic industry and the domestic market, as well as to other factors "having a bearing on the situation of [the] industry". The phrase "under such conditions", therefore, supports the view that, under Articles 4.2(a) and 4.2(b) of the *Agreement on Safeguards*, the competent authorities should determine whether the increase in imports, not alone, but in conjunction with the other relevant factors, cause serious injury.

S.1.13 Article 2 – Parallelism

S.1.13.1 GENERAL

S.1.13.1.1 *US – Wheat Gluten*, para. 96
(WT/DS166/AB/R)

The same phrase – "product . . . being imported" – appears in *both* these paragraphs of Article 2. In view of the identity of the language in the two provisions, and in the absence of any contrary indication in the context, we believe that it is appropriate to ascribe the *same* meaning to this phrase in both Articles 2.1 and 2.2. To include imports from all sources in the determination that increased imports are causing serious injury, and then to exclude imports from one source from the application of the measure, would be to give the phrase "product being imported" a *different* meaning in Articles 2.1 and 2.2 of the *Agreement on Safeguards*. In Article 2.1, the phrase would embrace imports from *all* sources whereas, in Article 2.2, it would exclude imports from certain sources. This would be incongruous and unwarranted. In the usual course, therefore, the imports included in the determinations made under Articles 2.1 and 4.2 should correspond to the imports included in the application of the measure, under Article 2.2.

S.1.13.1.2 *US – Line Pipe*, paras. 179, 181, 194
(WT/DS202/AB/R)

The concept of parallelism is derived from the parallel language used in the first and second paragraphs of Article 2 of the *Agreement on Safeguards*. . . .

. . .

As we then stated in *US – Wheat Gluten*, "the imports included in the determinations made under Articles 2.1 and 4.2 should correspond to the imports included in the application of the measure, under Article 2.2." We added that a gap between imports covered under the investigation and imports falling within the scope of the measure can be justified only if the competent authorities "establish explicitly" that imports from sources covered by the measure "satisf[y] the conditions for the application of a safeguard measure, as set out in Article 2.1 and elaborated in Article 4.2 of the *Agreement on Safeguards*." And, as we explained further in *US – Lamb*, in the context of a claim under Article 4.2(a) of the *Agreement on Safeguards*, "establish[ing] explicitly" implies that the competent authorities must provide a "*reasoned and adequate explanation* of how the facts support their determination".

. . .

. . . To be explicit, a statement must express distinctly all that is meant; it must leave nothing merely implied or suggested; it must be clear and unambiguous.

S.1.13.1.3 *US – Steel Safeguards*, para. 441
(WT/DS248/AB/R, WT/DS249/AB/R, WT/DS251/AB/R, WT/DS252/AB/R, WT/DS253/AB/R, WT/DS254/AB/R, WT/DS258/AB/R, WT/DS259/AB/R)

. . . where, for purposes of applying a safeguard measure, a Member has conducted an investigation considering imports from *all* sources (that is, *including* any members of a free-trade area), that Member may not, subsequently, without any further analysis, exclude imports from free-trade area partners from the application of the resulting safeguard measure. As we stated in *US – Line Pipe*, if a Member were to do so, there would be a "gap" between, on the one hand, imports covered by the investigation and, on the other hand, imports falling within the scope of the safeguard measure. . . .

S.1.13.2 PRIMA FACIE CASE

S.1.13.2.1 *US – Line Pipe*, para. 187
(WT/DS202/AB/R)

. . . Korea has demonstrated that the USITC considered imports from all sources in its investigation. Korea has also shown that exports from Canada and Mexico were excluded from the safeguard measure at issue. And, in our view, this *is* enough to have made a *prima facie* case of the absence of parallelism in the line pipe measure. . . .

S.1.14 Article 2 – "factors other than increased imports"

S.1.14.1 *US – Steel Safeguards*, para. 450
(WT/DS248/AB/R, WT/DS249/AB/R, WT/DS251/AB/R, WT/DS252/AB/R, WT/DS253/AB/R, WT/DS254/AB/R, WT/DS258/AB/R, WT/DS259/AB/R)

. . . the phrase "increased imports" in Articles 4.2(a) and 4.2(b) must, in our view, be read as referring to the same set of imports envisaged in Article 2.1, that is, *to imports included in the safeguard measure*. Consequently, imports *excluded* from the application of the safeguard measure must be considered a factor "other than increased imports" within the meaning of Article 4.2(b). The possible injurious effects that these excluded imports may have on the domestic industry must not be attributed to imports included in the safeguard measure pursuant to Article 4.2(b). The requirement articulated by the Panel "to account for the fact that excluded imports may have some injurious impact on the domestic industry" is, therefore, not, as the United States argues, an "extra analytical step" that the Panel added to the analysis of imports from all sources. To the contrary, this requirement necessarily follows from the obligation in Article 4.2(b) for the competent authority to ensure that the effects of factors other than increased imports – a set of factors that subsumes *imports excluded from the safeguard measure* – are not attributed to imports included in the measure, in establishing a causal link between imports included in the measure and serious injury or threat thereof.

S.1.14.2 *US – Steel Safeguards*, para. 452

(WT/DS248/AB/R, WT/DS249/AB/R, WT/DS251/AB/R, WT/DS252/AB/R, WT/DS253/AB/R, WT/DS254/AB/R, WT/DS258/AB/R, WT/DS259/AB/R)

In order to provide such a reasoned and adequate explanation, the competent authority must explain how it ensured that it did not attribute the injurious effects of *factors other than included imports* – which subsume "excluded imports" – to the imports included in the measure. As we explained in *US – Line Pipe* in the context of Article 3.1 and "unforeseen developments" in this Report, if the competent authority does not provide such an explanation, a panel is not in a position to find that the competent authority ensured compliance with the clear and express requirement of non-attribution under Article 4.2(b) of the *Agreement on Safeguards*.

S.1.15 Article 2 – Separate determinations

S.1.15.1 *US – Steel Safeguards*, paras. 465–466

(WT/DS248/AB/R, WT/DS249/AB/R, WT/DS251/AB/R, WT/DS252/AB/R, WT/DS253/AB/R, WT/DS254/AB/R, WT/DS258/AB/R, WT/DS259/AB/R)

. . . the USITC made *two separate determinations* – one determination that the exclusion of imports from *Canada and Mexico* would not change the "injury analysis" of the USITC, and another *separate* determination that the exclusion of imports from *Israel and Jordan* would not change the conclusions of the USITC.

The requirement of the *Agreement on Safeguards* to establish explicitly that imports from sources covered by a measure, *alone*, satisfy the conditions for the application of a safeguard measure cannot be fulfilled by conducting a *series of separate and partial* determinations. For example, where a WTO Member seeks to establish explicitly that imports from *sources other than A and B* satisfy the conditions for the application of a safeguard measure, if that Member conducts a separate investigation, and makes a separate determination, on whether imports from sources *other than A* satisfy the relevant conditions, and then, subsequently, conducts *another* separate and distinct investigation, and makes a separate determination, on whether imports from sources *other than B* satisfy the relevant conditions, then these *two separate* determinations, in our view, do not demonstrate that imports from sources other than *A and B together* satisfy the requirements for the imposition of a safeguard measure. By making these two separate determinations, that Member will, logically, for each of them, be basing its determination, in part, either on imports from A or on imports from B. If this were permitted, a determination on the application of a safeguard measure could be easily subjected to mathematical manipulation. This could not have been the intent of the Members of the WTO in drafting and agreeing on the *Agreement on Safeguards*.

S.1.15.2 *US – Steel Safeguards*, para. 468
(WT/DS248/AB/R, WT/DS249/AB/R, WT/DS251/AB/R, WT/DS252/AB/R, WT/DS253/AB/R, WT/DS254/AB/R, WT/DS258/AB/R, WT/DS259/AB/R)

It may not have made a practical difference in the application of the safeguard measures at issue in this appeal, in as much as, on the facts, the quantity of imports from the excluded countries was negligible or virtually non-existent. However, we are of the view that, rather than making *two separate determinations* – excluding either Canada and Mexico, or, alternatively, Israel and Jordan – from the underlying data on which it based its overall determination, the USITC should have, as the Panel found, provided *one single joint* determination, supported explicitly by a reasoned and adequate explanation, on whether imports from sources *other than Canada, Israel, Jordan, and Mexico*, by themselves, satisfied the conditions for the application of a safeguard measure.

S.1.15.3 *US – Steel Safeguards*, para. 471
(WT/DS248/AB/R, WT/DS249/AB/R, WT/DS251/AB/R, WT/DS252/AB/R, WT/DS253/AB/R, WT/DS254/AB/R, WT/DS258/AB/R, WT/DS259/AB/R)

As for the argument that the USITC's findings on imports from sources other than Canada and Mexico should have been read by the Panel as applying simultaneously to imports from sources other than Canada, Israel, Jordan, and Mexico *by virtue of the small import volumes at issue*, we observe that the *Agreement on Safeguards* does not provide for any different application of the parallelism requirement based on the volume of imports. With this argument, the United States is asking us to read something into the *Agreement on Safeguards* that is not there, and this we cannot do.

S.1.16 **Article 2.1, Footnote 1 – Customs union.** *See also* Regional Trade Agreements, Relationship between Article XXIV of the GATT 1994 and the Safeguards Agreement (R.1.6)

S.1.16.1 *Argentina – Footwear (EC)*, para. 108
(WT/DS121/AB/R)

. . . at the time the safeguard measures at issue in this case were imposed by the Government of Argentina, these measures were not applied by MERCOSUR "on behalf of" Argentina, but rather, they were applied by Argentina. It is Argentina that is a Member of the WTO for the purposes of Article 2 of the *Agreement on Safeguards*, and it is Argentina that applied the safeguard measures after conducting an investigation of products being imported into *its* territory and the effects of those imports on *its* domestic industry. For these reasons, we do not believe that footnote 1 to Article 2.1 applies to the safeguard measures imposed by Argentina in this case. . . .

S.1.16.2 *Argentina – Footwear (EC)*, para. 109
(WT/DS121/AB/R)

. . . we also are not persuaded that an analysis of Article XXIV of the GATT 1994 was relevant to the specific issue that was before the Panel. This issue, as the Panel itself observed, is whether Argentina, after including imports from all sources in its investigation of "increased imports" of footwear products into its territory and the consequent effects of such imports on its domestic footwear industry, was justified in excluding other MERCOSUR member States from the application of the safeguard measures. In our Report in *Turkey – Restrictions on Imports of Textile and Clothing Products* [Appellate Body Report, para. 58], we stated that under certain conditions, "Article XXIV may justify a measure which is inconsistent with certain other GATT provisions." We indicated, however, that this defence is available only when it is demonstrated by the Member imposing the measure that "the measure at issue is introduced upon the formation of a customs union that fully meets the requirements of sub-paragraphs 8(a) and 5(a) of Article XXIV" and "that the formation of that customs union would be prevented if it were not allowed to introduce the measure at issue."

S.1.16.3 *Argentina – Footwear (EC)*, para. 114
(WT/DS121/AB/R)

... We conclude that Argentina, on the facts of this case, cannot justify the imposition of its safeguard measures only on non-MERCOSUR third country sources of supply on the basis of an investigation that found serious injury or threat thereof caused by imports from all sources, including imports from other MERCOSUR member States. However, as we have stated, we do not agree that the Panel was dealing, on the facts of this case, with a safeguard measure applied by a customs union *on behalf of* a member State. And we wish to underscore that, as the issue is not raised in this appeal, we make no ruling on whether, as a general principle, a member of a customs union can exclude other members of that customs union from the application of a safeguard measure.

S.1.17 **Article 2.2 – Free trade area.** *See also* Regional Trade Agreements, Relationship between Article XXIV of the GATT 1994 and the Safeguards Agreement (R.1.6)

S.1.17.1 *US – Line Pipe*, para. 198
(WT/DS202/AB/R)

... we do not prejudge whether Article 2.2 of the *Agreement on Safeguards* permits a Member to exclude imports originating in member states of a free-trade area from the scope of a safeguard measure. We need not, and so do not, rule on the question whether Article XXIV of the GATT 1994 permits exempting imports originating in a partner of a free-trade area from a measure in departure from Article 2.2 of the *Agreement on Safeguards*. The question of whether Article XXIV of the GATT 1994 serves as an exception to Article 2.2 of the *Agreement on Safeguards* becomes relevant in only two possible circumstances. One is when, in the investigation by the competent authorities of a WTO Member, the imports that are exempted from the safeguard measure *are not considered* in the determination of serious injury. The other is when, in such an investigation, the imports that are exempted from the safeguard measure *are considered* in the determination of serious injury, *and* the competent authorities have *also* established explicitly, through a reasoned and adequate explanation, that imports from sources outside the free-trade area, alone, satisfied the conditions for the application of a safeguard measure, as set out in Article 2.1 and elaborated in Article 4.2. . . .

S.1.18 Article 3.1 – General

S.1.18.1 *US – Steel Safeguards*, para. 304

(WT/DS248/AB/R, WT/DS249/AB/R, WT/DS251/AB/R, WT/DS252/AB/R, WT/DS253/AB/R, WT/DS254/AB/R, WT/DS258/AB/R, WT/DS259/AB/R)

. . . Members may suspend trade concessions temporarily by applying safeguard measures "*only*" in accordance with Article XIX of the GATT 1994 and with the *Agreement on Safeguards*, including Article 3.1 of that Agreement. The last sentence of the latter provision, as elaborated by Article 4.2(c) of that Agreement, requires that:

(a) the "competent authorities . . . publish a report";
(b) the report contain "a detailed analysis of the case";
(c) the report "demonstrat[e] . . . the relevance of the factors examined";
(d) the report "set[] forth findings and reasoned conclusions"; and
(e) the "findings and reasoned conclusions" cover "all pertinent issues of fact and law" prescribed in Article XIX of the GATT 1994 and the relevant provisions of the *Agreement on Safeguards*.

S.1.18.2 *US – Steel Safeguards*, para. 331

(WT/DS248/AB/R, WT/DS249/AB/R, WT/DS251/AB/R, WT/DS252/AB/R, WT/DS253/AB/R, WT/DS254/AB/R, WT/DS258/AB/R, WT/DS259/AB/R)

. . . under Article 2.1 of the *Agreement on Safeguards*, safeguard measures can be justified "*only*" when, as a result of unforeseen developments and of the effect of obligations incurred, including tariff concessions, a product is being imported in such increased quantities and under such conditions as to cause or threaten to cause serious injury to the domestic industry that produces like or directly competitive products. It is "*only*" if these prerequisites set forth in Article XIX:1(a) of the GATT 1994 and the *Agreement on Safeguards* are shown to exist that the right to apply a safeguard measure arises. The fulfilment of each of these prerequisites is a "pertinent issue[] of fact and law" for which "finding[s] and reasoned conclusion[s]" must be included in the published report of the competent authorities, as required by Article 3.1 of the *Agreement on Safeguards*. . . .

S.1.19 Article 3.1 – Investigation

S.1.19.1 *US – Wheat Gluten*, para. 53

(WT/DS166/AB/R)

. . . The ordinary meaning of the word "investigation" suggests that the competent authorities should carry out a "systematic inquiry" or a "careful study" into the matter before them. The word, therefore, suggests a proper degree of activity on the part of the competent authorities because authorities charged with conducting an inquiry or a study – to use the treaty language, an "investigation" – must actively seek out pertinent information.

S.1.19.2 *US – Wheat Gluten*, para. 54
(WT/DS166/AB/R)

. . . The focus of the investigative steps mentioned in Article 3.1 is on "interested parties", who must be notified of the investigation, and who must be given an opportunity to submit "evidence", as well as their "views", to the competent authorities. The interested parties are also to be given an opportunity to "respond to the presentations of other parties". The *Agreement on Safeguards*, therefore, envisages that the interested parties play a central role in the investigation and that they will be a primary source of information for the competent authorities.

S.1.19.3 *US – Wheat Gluten*, para. 55
(WT/DS166/AB/R)

. . . we note that the competent authorities' "investigation" under Article 3.1 is *not limited* to the investigative steps mentioned in that provision, but must simply "*include*" these steps. Therefore, the competent authorities must undertake additional investigative steps, when the circumstances so require, in order to fulfill their obligation to evaluate all relevant factors.

S.1.19.4 *US – Lamb*, para. 113
(WT/DS177/AB/R, WT/DS178/AB/R)

. . . In arguing claims in dispute settlement, a *WTO Member* is not confined merely to rehearsing arguments that were made to the competent authorities by the *interested parties* during the domestic investigation, even if the WTO Member was itself an interested party in that investigation. Likewise, panels are not obliged to determine, and confirm themselves the nature and character of the arguments made by the interested parties to the competent authorities. Arguments before national competent authorities may be influenced by, and focused on, the requirements of the national laws, regulations and procedures. On the other hand, dispute settlement proceedings brought under the DSU concerning safeguard measures imposed under the *Agreement on Safeguards* may involve arguments that were not submitted to the competent authorities by the interested parties.

S.1.19.5 *US – Lamb*, para. 115
(WT/DS177/AB/R, WT/DS178/AB/R)

We wish to emphasize that the discretion that WTO Members enjoy to argue dispute settlement claims in the manner they deem appropriate does not, of course, detract from their obligation, under Article 3.10 of the DSU, "to engage in dispute settlement procedures 'in good faith in an effort to resolve the dispute'." It follows that WTO Members cannot improperly withhold arguments from competent authorities with a view to raising those arguments later before a panel. . . .

S.1.20 Article 3.1 – Multiple findings

S.1.20.1 *US – Steel Safeguards*, para. 414

(WT/DS248/AB/R, WT/DS249/AB/R, WT/DS251/AB/R, WT/DS252/AB/R, WT/DS253/AB/R, WT/DS254/AB/R, WT/DS258/AB/R, WT/DS259/AB/R)

. . . we note that Article 3.1 of the *Agreement on Safeguards* requires the competent authority, *inter alia*, to "publish a report setting forth their findings and reasoned conclusions reached on all pertinent issues of fact and law". We do not read Article 3.1 as necessarily precluding the possibility of providing multiple findings instead of a single finding in order to support a determination under Articles 2.1 and 4 of the *Agreement on Safeguards*. Nor does any other provision of the *Agreement on Safeguards* expressly preclude such a possibility. The *Agreement on Safeguards*, therefore, in our view, does not interfere with the discretion of a WTO Member to choose whether to support the determination of its competent authority by a single explanation or, alternatively, by multiple explanations by members of the competent authority. This discretion reflects the fact that, as we stated in *US – Line Pipe* [Appellate Body Report, para. 158], "the *Agreement on Safeguards* does not prescribe the internal decision-making process for making [] a determination [in a domestic safeguard investigation]".

S.1.20.2 *US – Steel Safeguards*, para. 418 and footnote 388

(WT/DS248/AB/R, WT/DS249/AB/R, WT/DS251/AB/R, WT/DS252/AB/R, WT/DS253/AB/R, WT/DS254/AB/R, WT/DS258/AB/R, WT/DS259/AB/R)

. . . in examining whether one of the multiple sets of explanations set forth by the competent authority, taken individually, provides a reasoned and adequate explanation for the competent authority's determination, a panel may have to address, *inter alia*, the question whether, *as a matter of WTO obligations*, findings by individual Commissioners made on the basis of a *broad* product grouping can provide a reasoned and adequate explanation for a "single institutional determination" of the USITC concerning a *narrow* product grouping.[388] Accordingly, we do *not* suggest that the product scope of an affirmative finding by an individual Commissioner is *not* relevant for the enquiry whether this finding does or does not provide a reasoned and adequate explanation for the competent authority's determination. Rather, our finding implies that a panel may not conclude that there is no reasoned and adequate explanation for a competent authority's determination by relying merely on the fact that distinct multiple explanations given by the competent authority are not based on an identically-defined like product.

[388] In this regard, we note that the fact that, pursuant to the domestic law of a WTO Member, a finding made on the basis of a *broad* product grouping is deemed to support a competent authority's determination which relates to a *narrower* product, does not, in and of itself, imply that this conclusion holds true also for the purposes of the *Agreement on Safeguards*.

S.1.21 Article 3.1 – Published report

S.1.21.1 *US – Lamb*, para. 72
(WT/DS177/AB/R, WT/DS178/AB/R)

. . . The first clause [of Article XIX:1(a) of the GATT 1994], as we noted, contains, in part, the "circumstance" of "unforeseen developments". The second clause, as we said, relates to the three "conditions" for the application of safeguard measures, which are also reiterated in Article 2.1 of the *Agreement on Safeguards*. Clearly, the fulfilment of these conditions must be the central element of the report of the competent authorities, which must be published under Article 3.1 of the *Agreement on Safeguards*. . . .

S.1.21.2 *US – Lamb*, para. 76
(WT/DS177/AB/R, WT/DS178/AB/R)

. . . we observe that Article 3.1 requires competent authorities to set forth findings and reasoned conclusions on "all pertinent issues of fact and law" in their published report. As Article XIX:1(a) of the GATT 1994 requires that "unforeseen developments" must be demonstrated, as a matter of fact, for a safeguard measure to be applied, the existence of "unforeseen developments" is, in our view, a "pertinent issue[] of fact and law", under Article 3.1, for the application of a safeguard measure, and it follows that the published report of the competent authorities, under that Article, must contain a "finding" or "reasoned conclusion" on "unforeseen developments".

S.1.21.3 *US – Line Pipe*, para. 160
(WT/DS202/AB/R)

We agree with the Panel that the fulfilment of the basic conditions set out in Article 2.1 is a "pertinent issue[] of law" for which "finding[s]" or "reasoned conclusion[s]" must be included in the published report of the competent authorities, as required by Article 3.1. We agree with the Panel also that among those "issues" is the condition that the "product" must be "imported . . . in such increased quantities, . . . and under such conditions as *to cause or threaten to cause serious injury*".

S.1.21.4 *US – Steel Safeguards*, para. 295
(WT/DS248/AB/R, WT/DS249/AB/R, WT/DS251/AB/R, WT/DS252/AB/R, WT/DS253/AB/R, WT/DS254/AB/R, WT/DS258/AB/R, WT/DS259/AB/R)

. . . Although we agree with the United States that competent authorities "may choose any structure, any order of analysis, and any format for [the] explanation that they see fit, as long as the report complies" with Article 3.1, we do not agree that the Panel was requiring that a report be in a certain form. . . .

S.1.22 Article 3.1 – Reasoned conclusions

S.1.22.1 *US – Steel Safeguards*, paras. 286–288

(WT/DS248/AB/R, WT/DS249/AB/R, WT/DS251/AB/R, WT/DS252/AB/R, WT/DS253/AB/R, WT/DS254/AB/R, WT/DS258/AB/R, WT/DS259/AB/R)

. . . The requirement of Article 3.1 is that "competent authorities shall publish a report setting forth their findings and reasoned conclusions reached on all pertinent issues of fact and law." The meaning of Article 3.1 must be established through an examination of the ordinary meaning of the terms of Article 3.1, read in their context and in the light of the object and purpose of the *Agreement on Safeguards*. Thus, instead of basing an interpretation of Article 3.1 – as the United States does – entirely on the meaning of *one* word – "reasoned" – in that provision, it is, in our view, appropriate to interpret Article 3.1 by examining the ordinary meaning of *all* of the words that together prescribe the relevant obligation in that Article.

In doing so, we note that the definition of "conclusion" is "the result of a discussion or an examination of an issue" or a "judgement or statement arrived at by reasoning: an inference; a deduction". Thus, the "conclusion" required by Article 3.1 is a "judgement or statement arrived at by reasoning". We further note that the word "reasoned", which the United States defines in terms of the verb "to reason", is, in fact, used in Article 3.1, last sentence, as an adjective to qualify the term "conclusion". The relevant definition of the intransitive verb "to reason" is "to think in a connected or logical manner; use one's reason in forming conclusions". The definition of the transitive verb "to reason" is "to arrange the thought of in a logical manner, embody reason in; express in a logical form". Thus, to be a "reasoned" conclusion, the "judgement or statement" must be one which is reached in a connected or logical manner or expressed in a logical form. Article 3.1 further requires that competent authorities must "set forth" the "reasoned conclusion" in their report. The definition of the phrase "set forth" is "give an account of, esp. in order, distinctly, or in detail; expound, relate, narrate, state, describe". Thus, the competent authorities are required by Article 3.1, last sentence, to "give an account of" a "judgement or statement which is reached in a connected or logical manner or expressed in a logical form", "distinctly, or in detail."

Panels have a responsibility in WTO dispute settlement to assess whether a competent authority has complied with its obligation under Article 3.1 of the *Agreement on Safeguards* to "set forth" "findings and reasoned conclusions" for their determinations. The European Communities and Norway argue that panels could not fulfill this responsibility if they were left to "deduce for themselves" from the report of that competent authority the "rationale for the determinations from the facts and data contained in the report of the competent authority." We agree.

S.1.22.2 *US – Steel Safeguards*, paras. 326, 329

(WT/DS248/AB/R, WT/DS249/AB/R, WT/DS251/AB/R, WT/DS252/AB/R, WT/DS253/AB/R, WT/DS254/AB/R, WT/DS258/AB/R, WT/DS259/AB/R)

Article 3.1 of the *Agreement on Safeguards* requires that the competent authority set out "reasoned conclusions" on all "pertinent issues of fact and law". One of those "issues of law" is the requirement to demonstrate the existence of "unforeseen developments" that have resulted in increased imports causing serious injury. In our view, therefore, it was for the USITC to provide a "reasoned conclusion" on "unforeseen developments". ...

...

... It is not for the Panel to do the reasoning for, or instead of, the competent authority, but rather to assess the adequacy of that reasoning to satisfy the relevant requirement. In consequence, we cannot agree with the United States that the Panel was "required" to consider the relevant data to which the USITC referred in other sections of its report to support the USITC's finding that "unforeseen developments" had resulted in increased imports; ...

S.1.22.3 *US – Steel Safeguards*, para. 506
(WT/DS248/AB/R, WT/DS249/AB/R, WT/DS251/AB/R, WT/DS252/AB/R, WT/DS253/AB/R, WT/DS254/AB/R, WT/DS258/AB/R, WT/DS259/AB/R)

... As the United States itself acknowledges, "Article 3.1 assigns the competent authorities – not the panel – the obligation to 'publish a report setting forth *their* findings and reasoned conclusions reached on all pertinent issues of fact and law'." Therefore, it was for the USITC, and not for the Panel, to explain how the facts supported its determination with respect to "unforeseen developments". The argument of the United States in this appeal seeks to shift the burden of this demonstration to the Panel, whose function, in this regard, is confined to assessing the adequacy of the "reasoned conclusions" put forward by the competent authority. We agree with the Panel that the USITC's demonstration was insufficient, and we find no error in the Panel's explanation of that finding.

S.1.23 Article 4.1(a) – Serious injury

S.1.23.1 *US – Lamb*, para. 124
(WT/DS177/AB/R, WT/DS178/AB/R)

The standard of "serious injury" set forth in Article 4.1(a) is, on its face, very high. Indeed, in *United States – Wheat Gluten Safeguard* [Appellate Body Report, para. 149], we referred to this standard as "exacting". Further, in this respect, we note that the word "injury" is qualified by the adjective "serious", which, in our view, underscores the extent and degree of "significant overall impairment" that the domestic industry must be suffering, or must be about to suffer, for the standard to be met. We are fortified in our view that the standard of "serious injury" in the *Agreement on Safeguards* is a very high one when we contrast this standard with the standard of "material injury" envisaged under the *Anti-Dumping Agreement*, the *Agreement on Subsidies and Countervailing Measures* (the "*SCM Agreement*") and the GATT 1994. We believe that the word "serious" connotes a much higher standard of injury than the word "material". Moreover, we submit that it accords with the object and purpose of the *Agreement on Safeguards* that the injury standard for the application of a safeguard measure should be higher than the injury standard for anti-dumping or countervailing measures ...

S.1.23.2 *US – Line Pipe*, para. 168
(WT/DS202/AB/R)

. . . In the sequence of events facing a domestic industry, it is fair to assume that, often, there is a continuous progression of injurious effects eventually rising and culminating in what can be determined to be "serious injury". Serious injury does not generally occur suddenly. Present serious injury is often preceded in time by an injury that threatens clearly and imminently to become serious injury, as we indicated in *US – Lamb*. Serious injury is, in other words, often the realization of a threat of serious injury. Although, in each case, the investigating authority will come to the conclusion that follows from the investigation carried out in compliance with Article 3 of the *Agreement on Safeguards*, the precise point where a "threat of serious injury" becomes "serious injury" may sometimes be difficult to discern. But, clearly, "serious injury" is something *beyond* a "threat of serious injury".

S.1.23.3 *US – Line Pipe*, para. 170
(WT/DS202/AB/R)

. . . In terms of the rising continuum of an injurious condition of a domestic industry that ascends from a "threat of serious injury" up to "serious injury", we see "serious injury" – because it is something *beyond* a "threat" – as necessarily *including* the concept of a "threat" and *exceeding* the presence of a "threat". . . .

S.1.24 Article 4.1(b) – Threat of serious injury. *See also* Safeguards Agreement, Article 2.1 – Serious injury or threat thereof (S.1.10)

S.1.24.1 *US – Lamb*, para. 125
(WT/DS177/AB/R, WT/DS178/AB/R)

Returning now to the term "*threat* of serious injury", we note that this term is concerned with "serious injury" which has *not* yet occurred, but remains a future event whose actual materialization cannot, in fact, be assured with certainty. We note, too, that Article 4.1(b) builds on the definition of "serious injury" by providing that, in order to constitute a "threat", the serious injury must be "*clearly imminent*". The word "imminent" relates to the moment in time when the "threat" is likely to materialize. The use of this word implies that the anticipated "serious injury" must be on the very verge of occurring. Moreover, we see the word "clearly", which qualifies the word "imminent", as an indication that there must be a high degree of likelihood that the anticipated serious injury will materialize in the very near future. We also note that Article 4.1(b) provides that any determination of a threat of serious injury "shall be based on facts and not merely on allegation, conjecture or *remote possibility*." (emphasis added) To us, the word "clearly" relates also to the *factual* demonstration of the existence of the "threat". Thus, the phrase "clearly imminent" indicates that, as a matter of fact, it must be manifest that the domestic industry is on the brink of suffering serious injury.

S.1.24.2 *US – Line Pipe*, para. 169
(WT/DS202/AB/R)

In our view, defining "threat of serious injury" separately from "serious injury" serves the purpose of setting a *lower threshold* for establishing the *right* to apply a safeguard measure. Our reading of the balance struck in the *Agreement on Safeguards* leads us to conclude that this was done by the Members in concluding the Agreement so that an importing Member may act sooner to take preventive action when increased imports pose a "threat" of "serious injury" to a domestic industry, but have not yet caused "serious injury". And, since a "threat" of "serious injury" is defined as "serious injury" that is "clearly imminent", it logically follows, to us, that "serious injury" is a condition that is above that *lower threshold* of a "threat". A "serious injury" is *beyond* a "threat", and, therefore, is *above* the threshold of a "threat" that is required to establish a right to apply a safeguard measure.

S.1.25 Article 4.1(c) – Domestic industry

S.1.25.1 *US – Lamb*, para. 84
(WT/DS177/AB/R, WT/DS178/AB/R)

The definition of "domestic industry" in this provision refers to two elements. First, the industry consists of "producers". As the Panel indicated, "producers" are those who grow or manufacture an Article; "producers" are those who bring a thing into existence. This meaning of "producers" is, however, qualified by the second element in the definition of "domestic industry". This element identifies the particular products that must be produced by the domestic "producers" in order to qualify for inclusion in the "domestic industry". According to the clear and express wording of the text of Article 4.1(c), the term "domestic industry" extends solely to the "producers . . . *of the like or directly competitive* products". (emphasis added) The definition, therefore, focuses exclusively on the producers of a very specific group of products. Producers of products that are *not* "like or directly competitive products" do not, according to the text of the treaty, form part of the domestic industry.

S.1.25.2 *US – Lamb*, para. 86
(WT/DS177/AB/R, WT/DS178/AB/R)

Thus, a safeguard measure is imposed on a specific "*product*", namely, the imported product. The measure may only be imposed if that specific product ("such *product*") is having the stated effects upon the "domestic industry *that produces like or directly competitive products*." (emphasis added) The conditions in Article 2.1, therefore, relate in several important respects to *specific products*. In particular, according to Article 2.1, the legal basis for imposing a safeguard measure exists *only* when imports of a specific product have prejudicial effects on domestic producers of products that are "like or directly competitive" with that imported product. In our view, it would be a clear departure from the text of Article 2.1 if a safeguard measure could be imposed because of the prejudicial effects that an imported product has on domestic producers of products that are *not* "like or directly competitive products" in relation to the imported product.

S.1.25.3 *US – Lamb*, para. 87
(WT/DS177/AB/R, WT/DS178/AB/R)

Accordingly, the first step in determining the scope of the domestic industry is the identification of the products which are "like or directly competitive" with the imported product. Only when those products have been identified is it possible then to identify the "producers" of those products.

S.1.25.4 *US – Lamb*, para. 90
(WT/DS177/AB/R, WT/DS178/AB/R)

... If an input product and an end-product are not "like" or "directly competitive", then it is irrelevant, under the *Agreement on Safeguards*, that there is a continuous line of production between an input product and an end-product, that the input product represents a high proportion of the value of the end-product, that there is no use for the input product other than as an input for the particular end-product, or that there is a substantial coincidence of economic interests between the producers of these products. In the absence of a "like or directly competitive" relationship, we see no justification, in Article 4.1(c) or any other provision of the *Agreement on Safeguards*, for giving credence to any of these criteria in defining a "domestic industry".

S.1.25.5 *US – Lamb*, para. 91
(WT/DS177/AB/R, WT/DS178/AB/R)

... The words "as a whole" [in Article 4.1(c)] apply to "producers" and, when read together with the terms "collective output" and "major proportion" which follow, clearly address the *number* and the *representative nature* of producers making up the domestic industry. ...

Article 4.2(a) – "increase in imports". *See* Safeguards Agreement, Article 2.1 – Increased imports (S.1.6)

S.1.26 Article 4.2(a) – Evaluation of relevant injury factors. *See also* Standard of Review, Article 11 of the DSU – Objective assessment of whether the investigating authority's explanation is reasoned and adequate (S.7.4)

S.1.26.1 *Argentina – Footwear (EC)*, para. 139
(WT/DS121/AB/R)

In our view, it is only when the *overall position* of the domestic industry is evaluated, in light of all the relevant factors having a bearing on a situation of that industry, that it can be determined whether there is "a significant overall impairment" in the position of that industry. Although Article 4.2(a) technically requires that certain listed factors must be evaluated, and that all other relevant factors must be evaluated, that provision does not specify what such an evaluation must demonstrate. Obviously, any such evaluation will be different for different industries in different cases, depending on the facts of the particular case and the situation of the industry concerned. An evaluation of each listed factor will not necessarily have to show that each such factor is "declining". In one case, for example, there may be significant declines in sales, employment and productivity that will show "significant overall impairment" in the position of the industry, and therefore will justify a finding of serious injury. In another case, a certain factor may not be declining, but the overall picture may nevertheless demonstrate "significant overall impairment" of the industry. Thus, in addition to a technical examination of whether the competent authorities in a particular case have evaluated all the listed factors and any other relevant factors, we believe that it is essential for a panel to take the definition of "serious injury" in Article 4.1(a) of the *Agreement on Safeguards* into account in its review of any determination of "serious injury".

S.1.26.2 *US – Wheat Gluten*, para. 55

(WT/DS166/AB/R)

. . . The competent authorities must, in every case, carry out a full investigation to enable them to conduct a proper evaluation of all of the relevant factors expressly mentioned in Article 4.2(a) of the *Agreement on Safeguards*. Moreover, Article 4.2(a) requires the competent authorities – and *not the interested parties* – to evaluate fully the relevance, if any, of "other factors". If the competent authorities consider that a particular "other factor" may be relevant to the situation of the domestic industry, under Article 4.2(a), their duties of investigation and evaluation preclude them from remaining passive in the face of possible short-comings in the evidence submitted, and views expressed, by the interested parties. In such cases, where the competent authorities do not have sufficient information before them to evaluate the possible relevance of such an "other factor", they must investigate fully that "other factor", so that they can fulfill their obligations of evaluation under Article 4.2(a). In that respect, we note that the competent authorities' "investigation" under Article 3.1 is *not limited* to the investigative steps mentioned in that provision, but must simply "*include*" these steps. Therefore, the competent authorities must undertake additional investigative steps, when the circumstances so require, in order to fulfill their obligation to evaluate all relevant factors.

S.1.26.3 *US – Wheat Gluten*, para. 71

(WT/DS166/AB/R)

. . . In evaluating the relevance of a particular factor, the competent authorities must, therefore, assess the "bearing", or the "influence" or "effect" that factor has on the overall situation of the domestic industry, against the background of all the other relevant factors.

S.1.26.4 *US – Wheat Gluten*, para. 72
(WT/DS166/AB/R)

... Thus, we consider that Article 4.2(a) does not support the Panel's conclusion that some of the "relevant factors" – those related exclusively to increased imports – should be counted towards an affirmative determination of serious injury, while others – those not related to increased imports – should be excluded from that determination.

S.1.26.5 *US – Lamb*, para. 103
(WT/DS177/AB/R, WT/DS178/AB/R)

... an "objective assessment" of a claim under Article 4.2(a) of the *Agreement on Safeguards* has, in principle, two elements. First, a panel must review whether competent authorities have evaluated *all relevant factors*, and, second, a panel must review whether the authorities have provided a *reasoned and adequate explanation* of how the facts support their determination. Thus, the panel's objective assessment involves a *formal* aspect and a *substantive* aspect. The formal aspect is whether the competent authorities have evaluated "all relevant factors". The substantive aspect is whether the competent authorities have given a reasoned and adequate explanation for their determination.

S.1.26.6 *US – Lamb*, para. 104
(WT/DS177/AB/R, WT/DS178/AB/R)

... Under Article 4.2(a), competent authorities must, as a formal matter, evaluate "all relevant factors". However, that evaluation is not simply a matter of form, and the list of relevant factors to be evaluated is not a mere "check list". ...

S.1.27 Article 4.2(a) – Data for the injury evaluation

S.1.27.1 *US – Lamb*, para. 130
(WT/DS177/AB/R, WT/DS178/AB/R)

We recognize that the clause "of an objective and quantifiable nature" refers expressly to "factors", but not expressly to data. We are, however, convinced that factors can only be "of an objective and quantifiable nature" if they allow a determination to be made, as required by Article 4.2(b) of the *Agreement on Safeguards*, on the basis of "objective evidence". Such evidence is, in principle, objective data. The words "factors of an objective and quantifiable nature" imply, therefore, an evaluation of objective *data* which enables the measurement and quantification of these factors.

S.1.27.2 *US – Lamb*, para. 131
(WT/DS177/AB/R, WT/DS178/AB/R)

... competent authorities must have a *sufficient* factual basis to allow them to draw reasoned and adequate conclusions concerning the situation of the "domestic industry". The need for such a sufficient factual basis, in turn, implies that the data examined, concerning the relevant factors, must be representative of the "domestic industry". Indeed, a determination made on the basis of insufficient data would not be a determination about the state of the "domestic industry", as defined in the Agreement, but would, in reality, be a determination pertaining to producers of something less than "a major proportion of the total domestic production" of the products at issue. . . .

S.1.27.3 *US – Lamb*, para. 132
(WT/DS177/AB/R, WT/DS178/AB/R)

We do not wish to suggest that competent authorities must, in every case, actually have before them data pertaining to *all* those domestic producers whose production, taken together, constitutes a major proportion of the domestic industry. In some instances, no doubt, such a requirement would be both impractical and unrealistic. Rather, the data before the competent authorities must be sufficiently representative to give a true picture of the "domestic industry". What is sufficient in any given case will depend on the particularities of the "domestic industry" at issue. . . .

S.1.27.4 *US – Lamb*, footnote 99 to para. 144
(WT/DS177/AB/R, WT/DS178/AB/R)

. . . We note that, earlier in its Report, the Panel stated that competent authorities "may arrive at a threat determination *even if the majority of firms within the relevant industry is not facing declining profitability*, provided that an evaluation of the injury factors *as a whole* indicates threat of serious injury." (Panel Report, para. 7.188, emphasis added) In *Argentina – Footwear Safeguard*, we said that the competent authorities' determination of "serious injury" must be based on "the overall picture" of the domestic industry and that the determination must be made "in light of all the relevant factors". Accordingly, in evaluating "the overall position of the domestic industry", no single relevant factor can be accorded decisive importance and, instead, all of the factors must be examined and weighed together. (Appellate Body Report, *Argentina – Footwear Safeguard*, *supra*, footnote 15, para. 139)

It follows that the Panel was correct to state that the competent authorities' determination must be based on "an evaluation of the injury factors *as a whole*". Moreover, it is theoretically possible, as the Panel said, that an industry *might* be threatened with serious injury, even though "a majority of firms . . . is not facing declining profitability". Profits are simply one of the relevant factors mentioned in Article 4.2(a) and to accord that factor decisive importance would be to disregard the other relevant factors. However, in our view, it will be a rare case, indeed, where the relevant factors as a whole indicate that there is a threat of serious injury, even though the "majority of firms in the industry" is not facing declining profitability.

S.1.28 Article 4.2(a) – Injury data relating to the most recent past

S.1.28.1 *US – Lamb*, para. 137
(WT/DS177/AB/R, WT/DS178/AB/R)

. . . we note that the *Agreement on Safeguards* provides no particular methodology to be followed in making determinations of serious injury or threat thereof. However, whatever methodology is chosen, we believe that data relating to the most recent past will provide competent authorities with an essential, and, usually, the most reliable, basis for a determination of a threat of serious injury. The likely state of the domestic industry in the very near future can best be gauged from data from the most recent past. . . .

S.1.28.2 *US – Lamb*, para. 138
(WT/DS177/AB/R, WT/DS178/AB/R)

However, we believe that, although data from the most recent past has special importance, competent authorities should not consider such data in isolation from the data pertaining to the entire period of investigation. The real significance of the short-term trends in the most recent data, evident at the end of the period of investigation, may only emerge when those short-term trends are assessed in the light of the longer-term trends in the data for the whole period of investigation. If the most recent data is evaluated in isolation, the resulting picture of the domestic industry may be quite misleading. . . .

S.1.29 Article 4.2(b) – Causation of injury by increased imports

S.1.29.1 *Argentina – Footwear (EC)*, para. 144
(WT/DS121/AB/R)

We note that Article 4.2(a) requires the competent authorities to evaluate "the rate and amount of the increase in imports", "the share of the domestic market taken by increased imports", as well as the "changes" in the level of factors such as sales, production, productivity, capacity utilization, and others. We see no reason to disagree with the Panel's interpretation that the words "rate and amount" and "changes" in Article 4.2(a) mean that "the *trends* – in both the injury factors and the imports – matter as much as their absolute levels." We also agree with the Panel that, in an analysis of causation, "it is the *relationship* between the *movements* in imports (volume and market share) and the *movements* in injury factors that must be central to a causation analysis and determination." (emphasis added) . . .

S.1.29.2 *US – Wheat Gluten*, para. 67
(WT/DS166/AB/R)

. . . Article 4.2(b) does *not* suggest that increased imports be *the sole* cause of the serious injury, or that "*other* factors" causing injury must be excluded from the determination of serious injury. To the contrary, the language of Article 4.2(b), as a whole, suggests that "the causal link" between increased imports and serious injury may exist, *even though other factors are also contributing, "at the same time", to the situation of the domestic industry.*

S.1.29.3 *US – Wheat Gluten*, para. 70
(WT/DS166/AB/R)

... the need to distinguish between the effects caused by increased imports and the effects caused by other factors does *not* necessarily imply, as the Panel said, that increased imports *on their own* must be capable of causing serious injury, nor that injury caused by other factors must be *excluded* from the determination of serious injury.

S.1.30 Article 4.2(b) – Causation of injury by increased imports vs. other factors

S.1.30.1 *US – Wheat Gluten*, para. 69
(WT/DS166/AB/R)

Article 4.2(b) presupposes, therefore, as a first step in the competent authorities' examination of causation, that the injurious effects caused to the domestic industry by increased imports are *distinguished from* the injurious effects caused by other factors. The competent authorities can then, as a second step in their examination, attribute to increased imports, on the one hand, and, by implication, to other relevant factors, on the other hand, "injury" caused by all of these different factors, including increased imports. Through this two stage process, the competent authorities comply with Article 4.2(b) by ensuring that any injury to the domestic industry that was *actually* caused by factors other than increased imports is not "attributed" to increased imports and is, therefore, not treated as if it were injury caused by increased imports, when it is not. In this way, the competent authorities determine, as a final step, whether "the causal link" exists between increased imports and serious injury, and whether this causal link involves a genuine and substantial relationship of cause and effect between these two elements, as required by the *Agreement on Safeguards*.

S.1.30.2 *US – Lamb*, paras. 178–181
(WT/DS177/AB/R, WT/DS178/AB/R)

We emphasize that these three steps simply describe a logical process for complying with the obligations relating to causation set forth in Article 4.2(b). These steps are not legal "tests" mandated by the text of the *Agreement on Safeguards*, nor is it imperative that each step be the subject of a separate finding or a reasoned conclusion by the competent authorities. Indeed, these steps leave unanswered many methodological questions relating to the non-attribution requirement found in the second sentence of Article 4.2(b).

The primary objective of the process we described in *United States – Wheat Gluten Safeguard* is, of course, to determine whether there is "a genuine and substantial relationship of cause and effect" between increased imports and serious injury or threat thereof. As part of that determination, Article 4.2(b) states expressly that injury caused to the domestic industry by factors other than increased imports "shall not be attributed to increased imports." In a situation where *several factors* are causing injury "at the same time", a final determination about the injurious effects caused by *increased imports* can only be made if the injurious effects caused by all the different causal factors are distinguished and separated. Otherwise, any conclusion based exclusively on an assessment of only one of the causal factors – increased imports – rests on an uncertain foundation, because it *assumes* that the other causal factors are *not* causing the injury which has been ascribed to increased imports. The non-attribution language in Article 4.2(b) precludes such an assumption and, instead, requires that the competent authorities assess appropriately the injurious effects of the other factors, so that those effects may be disentangled from the injurious effects of the increased imports. In this way, the final determination rests, properly, on the genuine and substantial relationship of cause and effect between increased imports and serious injury.

As we said in our Report in *United States – Wheat Gluten Safeguard*, the non-attribution language in Article 4.2(b) indicates that, logically, the final identification of the injurious effects caused by increased imports must follow a prior separation of the injurious effects of the different causal factors. If the effects of the different factors are not separated and distinguished from the effects of increased imports, there can be no proper assessment of the injury caused by that single and decisive factor. As we also indicated, the final determination about the existence of "the causal link" between increased imports and serious injury can only be made *after* the effects of increased imports have been properly assessed, and this assessment, in turn, follows the separation of the effects caused by all the different causal factors.

We emphasize that the method and approach WTO Members choose to carry out the process of separating the effects of increased imports and the effects of the other causal factors is not specified by the *Agreement on Safeguards*. What the Agreement requires is simply that the obligations in Article 4.2 must be respected when a safeguard measure is applied.

S.1.31 Article 4.2(b) – Non-attribution of injury caused by other factors

S.1.31.1 *US – Line Pipe*, para. 208
(WT/DS202/AB/R)

Article 4.2(b) of the *Agreement on Safeguards* establishes two distinct legal requirements for competent authorities in the application of a safeguard measure. First, there must be a demonstration of the "existence of the causal link between increased imports of the product concerned and serious injury or threat thereof". Second, the injury caused by factors other than the increased imports must not be attributed to increased imports.

S.1.31.2 *US – Wheat Gluten*, para. 68
(WT/DS166/AB/R)

...Clearly, the process of attributing "injury", envisaged by this sentence, can only be made following a separation of the "injury" that must then be properly "attributed". What is important in this process is separating or distinguishing the *effects* caused by the different factors in bringing about the "injury".

S.1.31.3 *US – Lamb*, para. 185
(WT/DS177/AB/R, WT/DS178/AB/R)

... to be certain that the injury caused by these other factors, whatever its magnitude, was not attributed to increased imports, the USITC should also have assessed, to some extent, the injurious effects of these other factors. ...

S.1.31.4 *US – Lamb*, para. 186
(WT/DS177/AB/R, WT/DS178/AB/R)

In the absence of any meaningful explanation of the nature and extent of the injurious effects of these six "other" factors, it is impossible to determine whether the USITC properly separated the injurious effects of these other factors from the injurious effects of the increased imports. It is, therefore, also impossible to determine whether injury caused by these other factors has been attributed to increased imports. In short, without knowing anything about the nature and extent of the injury caused by the six other factors, we cannot satisfy ourselves that the injury deemed by the USITC to have been caused by increased imports does not include injury which, in reality, was caused by these factors.

S.1.31.5 *US – Line Pipe*, paras. 215, 217
(WT/DS202/AB/R)

... competent authorities must separate and distinguish the injurious effects of the increased imports from the injurious effects of the other factors ... competent authorities are required to identify the nature and extent of the injurious effects of the known factors other than increased imports, as well as explain satisfactorily the nature and extent of the injurious effects of those other factors as distinguished from the injurious effects of the increased imports.

...

Thus, to fulfill the requirement of Article 4.2(b), last sentence, the competent authorities must establish explicitly, through a reasoned and adequate explanation, that injury caused by factors other than increased imports is not attributed to increased imports. This explanation must be clear and unambiguous. It must not merely imply or suggest an explanation. It must be a straightforward explanation in express terms.

S.1.31.6 *US – Line Pipe*, para. 262
(WT/DS202/AB/R)

... even if the USITC failed to separate and distinguish the injurious effects of the increased imports from the injurious effects of the other factors, it is still possible that the safeguard measure may have been applied in such a manner that it addressed only a portion of the identified injurious effects, namely, the portion that is equal to or less than the injurious effects of increased imports. The United States did not rebut Korea's *prima facie* case by showing that this was so. We offer this observation only to emphasize that we are not stating that a violation of the last sentence of

Article 4.2(b) implies an *automatic* violation of the first sentence of Article 5.1 of the *Agreement on Safeguards*.

S.1.31.7 *US – Steel Safeguards*, para. 489
(WT/DS248/AB/R, WT/DS249/AB/R, WT/DS251/AB/R, WT/DS252/AB/R, WT/DS253/AB/R, WT/DS254/AB/R, WT/DS258/AB/R, WT/DS259/AB/R)

. . . the *Agreement on Safeguards* – in Article 2.1, as elaborated by Article 4.2, and in combination with Article 3.1 – requires that competent authorities demonstrate the *existence* of a "causal link" between "increased imports" and "serious injury" (or the threat thereof) on the basis of "objective evidence". In addition, the competent authorities must provide a reasoned and adequate explanation of how facts (that is, the aforementioned "objective evidence") support their determination. If these requirements are not met, the right to apply a safeguard measure does not arise.

S.1.32 Article 4.2(b) – Causation – assumptions regarding increased imports and injury

S.1.32.1 *US – Steel Safeguards*, footnote 494 to para. 481
(WT/DS248/AB/R, WT/DS249/AB/R, WT/DS251/AB/R, WT/DS252/AB/R, WT/DS253/AB/R, WT/DS254/AB/R, WT/DS258/AB/R, WT/DS259/AB/R)

In paragraph 10.278 of the Panel Reports, the Panel stated that it "assumed for the purposes of its consideration of the issue of causation", that the relevant domestic producers had been correctly defined and that serious injury or threat thereof existed. We note that the Panel found no "increased imports" for five product categories – CCFRS, hot-rolled bar, stainless steel rod, tin mill, and stainless steel wire. However, the Panel must also have assumed, tacitly, that, for the purposes of its causation analysis, imports had increased for those five products. We do not see anything improper *per se* in panels making such assumptions, especially when doing so enables panels to make findings they otherwise would not have made, thereby facilitating appellate review. We are mindful that the volume and complexity of this case may have prompted the Panel to exercise judicial economy on several issues and to rely on the corresponding inter-dependent assumptions. We note, however, that the cumulation of several inter-related assumptions could have affected our ability to complete the Panel's legal analysis had we pursued a ruling on causation.

S.1.32.2 *US – Steel Safeguards*, footnote 495 to para. 481
(WT/DS248/AB/R, WT/DS249/AB/R, WT/DS251/AB/R, WT/DS252/AB/R, WT/DS253/AB/R, WT/DS254/AB/R, WT/DS258/AB/R, WT/DS259/AB/R)

. . . We note that "serious injury" is the purported effect that should be causally linked by the competent authority to "increased imports". When the determination of "serious injury" is challenged, a panel may only conclude definitively that "the existence of the causal link" has been adequately demonstrated *after* having established that "increased imports" *and* "serious injury" were adequately determined in the investigation.

S.1.32.3 *US – Steel Safeguards*, para. 483
(WT/DS248/AB/R, WT/DS249/AB/R, WT/DS251/AB/R, WT/DS252/AB/R, WT/DS253/AB/R, WT/DS254/AB/R, WT/DS258/AB/R, WT/DS259/AB/R)

As we have already found that the measures before us are inconsistent with Article XIX:1(a) of the GATT 1994 and with Articles 2.1, 3.1, and 4.2 of the *Agreement on Safeguards*, it is unnecessary, for the purposes of resolving this dispute, to rule on whether the Panel was correct in finding that the United States also acted inconsistently with Articles 2.1 and 4.2 of the *Agreement on Safeguards* because the USITC report failed to demonstrate the existence of a "causal link" between increased imports from *all* sources (that is, imports covered by the measures *and* imports not covered by the measures) and serious injury to the domestic industry. We, therefore, decline to rule on the issue of causation. Accordingly, and as we have not examined the Panel's findings on causation for the seven products that are the focus of this claim by the United States – CCFRS, hot-rolled bar, cold-finished bar, rebar, welded pipe, FFTJ, and stainless steel bar – we neither reverse nor uphold those findings.

S.1.33 Article 4.2(c) – Publication of a detailed analysis. *See also* Safeguards Agreement, Article 3.1 – General (S.1.18); Safeguards Agreement, Relationship between Article XIX of the GATT 1994 and Article 3.1 of the Safeguards Agreement (S.1.46); Safeguards Agreement, Relationship between Article XIX of the GATT 1994 and Article 4.2(c) of the Safeguards Agreement (S.1.47)

S.1.33.1 *US – Steel Safeguards*, paras. 289–290
(WT/DS248/AB/R, WT/DS249/AB/R, WT/DS251/AB/R, WT/DS252/AB/R, WT/DS253/AB/R, WT/DS254/AB/R, WT/DS258/AB/R, WT/DS259/AB/R)

. . . we see Article 4.2(c) as an elaboration of the requirement set out in Article 3.1, last sentence, to provide a "reasoned conclusion" in a published report.

The United States argued at the oral hearing that "Article 4.2(c) does not apply to the competent authorities' demonstration of unforeseen developments" under Article XIX:1(a) of the GATT 1994. We disagree. Article 4.2(c) is an elaboration of Article 3; moreover "unforeseen developments" under Article XIX:1(a) of the GATT 1994 is one of the "pertinent issues of fact and law" to which the last sentence of Article 3.1 refers. It follows that Article 4.2(c) also applies to the competent authorities' demonstration of "unforeseen developments" under Article XIX:1(a).

S.1.34 Article 5.1 – Application of the safeguard measure to the extent necessary to prevent or remedy serious injury and to facilitate adjustment. *See also* Principles and Concepts of General Public International Law, Proportionality (P.3.6)

S.1.34.1 *Korea – Dairy*, para. 96
(WT/DS98/AB/R)

. . . We agree with the Panel that the wording of this provision leaves no room for doubt that it imposes an *obligation* on a Member applying a safeguard measure to ensure that the measure applied is commensurate with the goals of preventing or remedying serious injury and of facilitating adjustment. We also agree that this obligation applies regardless of the particular form that a safeguard measure might take. Whether it takes the form of a quantitative restriction, a tariff or a tariff rate quota, the measure in question must be applied "only to the extent necessary" to achieve the goals set forth in the first sentence of Article 5.1.

S.1.34.2 *US – Line Pipe*, para. 84
(WT/DS202/AB/R)

. . . [if] there *is* a right to apply a safeguard measure in that particular case, then the interpreter must next consider whether the Member has applied that safeguard measure "only to the extent necessary to prevent or remedy serious injury and to facilitate adjustment", as required by Article 5.1, first sentence, of the *Agreement on Safeguards*. Thus, the right to apply a safeguard measure – even where it has been found to exist in a particular case and thus can be exercised – is not unlimited. . . .

S.1.34.3 *US – Line Pipe*, para. 172
(WT/DS202/AB/R)

. . . the permissible extent of a safeguard measure is defined by the share of serious injury that is attributed to increased imports, not by the characterization the competent authority ascribes to the situation of the industry. . . .

S.1.35 Article 5.1 – Justification of the necessary extent of the application

S.1.35.1 *US – Line Pipe*, paras. 233–234, 236
(WT/DS202/AB/R)

. . . apart from one exception, Article 5.1, including the first sentence, does not oblige a Member to justify, at the time of application, that the safeguard measure at issue is applied "only to the extent necessary". The exception we identified in *Korea – Dairy* lies in the second sentence of Article 5.1. [Appellate Body Report, paras. 98–99] That exception concerns safeguard measures in the form of quantitative restrictions, which reduce the quantity of imports below the average of imports in the last three representative years. That exception does not apply to the line pipe measure.

Thus, our findings in *Korea – Dairy* establish that Article 5.1 imposes a general substantive obligation, namely, to apply safeguard measures only to the permissible extent, and also a particular procedural obligation, namely, to provide a clear justification in the specific case of quantitative restrictions reducing the volume of imports below the average of imports in the last three representative years. Article 5.1 does not establish a general procedural obligation to demonstrate compliance with Article 5.1, first sentence, at the time a measure is applied.

. . .

This does not imply, as Korea seems to assert, that the measure may be devoid of justification or that the multilateral verification of the consistency of the measure with the *Agreement on Safeguards* is impeded. The Member imposing a safeguard measure must, in any event, meet several obligations under the *Agreement on Safeguards*. And, meeting those obligations should have the effect of clearly explaining and "justifying" the extent of the application of the measure. By separating and distinguishing the injurious effects of factors other than increased imports from those caused by increased imports, as required by Article 4.2(b), and by including this detailed analysis in the report that sets forth the findings and reasoned conclusions, as required by Articles 3.1 and 4.2(c), a Member proposing to apply a safeguard measure should provide sufficient motivation for that measure. Compliance with Articles 3.1, 4.2(b) and 4.2(c) of the *Agreement on Safeguards* should have the incidental effect of providing sufficient "justification" for a measure and, as we will explain, should also provide a benchmark against which the permissible extent of the measure should be determined.

S.1.35.2 *US – Line Pipe*, paras. 242–243
(WT/DS202/AB/R)

... In stating that Article 4.2(b) should not be read as necessarily implying that increased imports, *on their own*, must be capable of causing serious injury, or that injury caused by other factors must be *excluded* from the determination of serious injury, we were addressing the question of whether there is a right to apply a safeguard measure; we were not addressing the permissible extent of the application of a safeguard measure.

The United States is, therefore, mistaken in maintaining that our ruling in *US – Wheat Gluten* supports the proposition that Article 5.1, first sentence, permits a Member to apply a safeguard measure to prevent or remedy "the *entirety* of the serious injury experienced by the domestic industry". The United States submits that because we "decided that in accordance with Article 4.2(a) serious injury was the entirety of the condition of the industry", it follows that the serious injury to which Article 5.1, first sentence, refers must be the "entirety" of the serious injury. But, our ruling in *US – Wheat Gluten* makes no mention of the permissible extent to which a safeguard measure may be applied, nor of the "entirety" of serious injury as it relates to that permissible extent. The permissible extent of a safeguard measure is the subject of Article 5.1, first sentence. The meaning of Article 5.1, first sentence, was not at issue in *US – Wheat Gluten*; it is at issue here.

S.1.35.3 *US – Line Pipe*, para. 257
(WT/DS202/AB/R)

... If the pain inflicted on exporters by a safeguard measure were permitted to have effects beyond the share of injury caused by increased imports, this would imply that an exceptional remedy, which is not meant to protect the industry of the importing country from unfair or illegal trade practices, could be applied in a more trade-restrictive manner than countervailing and anti-dumping duties. On what basis should the *WTO Agreement* be interpreted to limit a countermeasure to the extent of the injury caused by unfair practices or a violation of the treaty but not so limit a countermeasure when there has not even been an allegation of a violation or an unfair practice?

S.1.35.4 *US – Line Pipe*, para. 258
(WT/DS202/AB/R)

The object and purpose of the *Agreement on Safeguards* support this reading of the context of Article 5.1, first sentence. The *Agreement on Safeguards* deals only with *imports*. It deals only with measures that, under certain conditions, can be applied to *imports*. The title of Article XIX of the GATT 1994 is "Emergency Action on *Imports* of Particular Products". (emphasis added) It seems apparent to us that the object and purpose of both Article XIX of the GATT 1994 and the *Agreement on Safeguards* support the conclusion that safeguard measures should be applied so as to address only the consequences of *imports*. And, therefore, it seems apparent to us as well that the limited objective of Article 5.1, first sentence, is limited by the consequences of *imports*.

S.1.36 Relationship between Articles 5.1 and 4.2(b) of the Safeguards Agreement

S.1.36.1 *US – Line Pipe*, paras. 234, 236
(WT/DS202/AB/R)

. . . Article 5.1 does not establish a general procedural obligation to demonstrate compliance with Article 5.1, first sentence, at the time a measure is applied.

. . .

This does not imply, as Korea seems to assert, that the measure may be devoid of justification or that the multilateral verification of the consistency of the measure with the *Agreement on Safeguards* is impeded. The Member imposing a safeguard measure must, in any event, meet several obligations under the *Agreement on Safeguards*. And, meeting those obligations should have the effect of clearly explaining and "justifying" the extent of the application of the measure. By separating and distinguishing the injurious effects of factors other than increased imports from those caused by increased imports, as required by Article 4.2(b), and by including this detailed analysis in the report that sets forth the findings and reasoned conclusions, as required by Articles 3.1 and 4.2(c), a Member proposing to apply a safeguard measure should provide sufficient motivation for that measure. Compliance with Articles 3.1, 4.2(b) and 4.2(c) of the *Agreement on Safeguards* should have the incidental effect of providing sufficient "justification" for a measure and, as we will explain, should also provide a benchmark against which the permissible extent of the measure should be determined.

S.1.36.2 *US – Line Pipe*, para. 252
(WT/DS202/AB/R)

. . . the non-attribution language of the second sentence of Article 4.2(b) has two objectives. First, it seeks, in situations where several factors cause injury at the same time, to prevent investigating authorities from inferring the required "causal link" between increased imports and serious injury or threat thereof on the basis of the injurious effects caused by factors other than increased imports. Second, it is a benchmark for ensuring that only an appropriate share of the overall injury is attributed to increased imports. As we read the Agreement, this latter objective, in turn, informs the permissible extent to which the safeguard measure may be applied pursuant to Article 5.1, first sentence. Indeed, as we see it, this is the only possible interpretation of the obligation set out in Article 4.2(b), last sentence, that ensures its consistency with Article 5.1, first sentence. It would be illogical to require an investigating authority to ensure that the "causal link" between increased imports and serious injury not be based on the share of injury attributed to factors other than increased imports while, at the same time, permitting a Member to apply a safeguard measure addressing injury caused by all factors.

S.1.36.3 *US – Line Pipe*, paras. 261–262
(WT/DS202/AB/R)

. . . we conclude that, by establishing that the United States violated Article 4.2(b) of the *Agreement on Safeguards*, Korea has made a *prima facie* case that the application of the line pipe measure was not limited to the extent permissible under Article 5.1. In the absence of a rebuttal by the United States of this *prima facie* case by Korea, we find that the United States applied the line pipe measure beyond the "extent necessary to prevent or remedy serious injury and to facilitate adjustment". . . .

. . . even if the USITC failed to separate and distinguish the injurious effects of the increased imports from the injurious effects of the other factors, it is still possible that the safeguard measure may have been applied in such a manner that it addressed only a portion of the identified injurious effects, namely, the portion that is equal to or less than the injurious effects of increased imports. The United States did not rebut Korea's *prima facie* case by showing that this was so. We offer this observation only to emphasize that we are not stating that a violation of the last sentence of Article 4.2(b) implies an *automatic* violation of the first sentence of Article 5.1 of the *Agreement on Safeguards*.

S.1.37 Article 5.2(b) – Quota modulation

S.1.37.1 *US – Line Pipe*, para. 173
(WT/DS202/AB/R)

. . . we disagree with the support the Panel finds for its conclusions on this issue in the context of Article 5.2(b) of the *Agreement on Safeguards*. Article 5.2(b) excludes quota modulation in the case of threat of serious injury. It is, in our view, the only provision in the *Agreement on Safeguards* that establishes a difference in the legal effects of "serious injury" and "threat of serious injury". Under Article 5.2(b), in order for an importing Member to adopt a safeguard measure in the form of a quota to be allocated in a manner departing from the general rule contained in Article 5.2(a), that Member must have determined that there is "serious injury". A Member cannot engage in quota modulations if there is only a "threat of serious injury". This is an exception that must be respected. But we do not think it appropriate to generalize from such a limited exception to justify a general rule. In any event, this exceptional circumstance is not relevant to the line pipe measure. We find nothing in Article 5.2(b), viewed as part of the context of Article 2.1, that would support a finding that, in this case, the USITC acted inconsistently with the *Agreement on Safeguards* by making a non-discrete determination in this case.

S.1.38 Article 8.1 – Equivalent level of concessions

S.1.38.1 *US – Wheat Gluten*, paras. 145–146
(WT/DS166/AB/R)

Article 8.1 imposes an obligation on Members to "endeavour to maintain" equivalent concessions with affected exporting Members. The efforts made by a Member to this end must be "in accordance with the provisions of" Article 12.3 of the *Agreement on Safeguards*.

In view of this explicit link between Articles 8.1 and 12.3 of the *Agreement on Safeguards*, a Member cannot, in our view, "endeavour to maintain" an adequate balance of concessions unless it has, as a first step, provided an adequate opportunity for prior consultations on a proposed measure. ...

S.1.38.2 *US – Line Pipe*, para. 109
(WT/DS202/AB/R)

We note that reaching such an "understanding" [on ways to achieve the objective set out in paragraph 1 of Article 8] serves the interests not only of the exporting Members, but also of the importing Member, who will wish to avoid excessive compensatory measures in response to the safeguard action. As we have said, the *Agreement on Safeguards* permits Members to impose measures against "fair trade". As a result, Members against whom such measures are imposed are prevented from enjoying the full benefit of trade concessions. For this reason, Article 8.1 of the *Agreement on Safeguards* provides that "Members concerned may agree on any adequate means of trade compensation for the adverse effects of the measure on their trade." If no agreement on compensation is reached, Article 8.2 provides that "the affected ... Members shall be free, not later than 90 days after the measure is applied, to suspend ... the application of substantially equivalent concessions or other obligations under GATT 1994, to the trade of the Member applying the safeguard measure". Thus, there is an interest on the part of both the exporting Member and the importing Member applying the safeguard measure to engage in "prior consultations" with a view to reaching an understanding on the import of the measure.

S.1.38.3 *US – Line Pipe*, para. 119
(WT/DS202/AB/R)

In our view, our reasoning in *US – Wheat Gluten* is also applicable in this case. Therefore, we agree with the Panel that the United States, "by failing to comply with its obligations under Article 12.3, has also acted inconsistently with its obligations under Article 8.1 to endeavour to maintain a substantially equivalent level of concessions. . . . " . . .

S.1.39 Article 9.1 – Exclusion of developing country Members from the application of safeguards

S.1.39.1 *US – Line Pipe*, paras. 127–128
(WT/DS202/AB/R)

. . . Article 9.1 does not indicate how a Member must comply with this obligation. There is nothing, for example, in the text of Article 9.1 to the effect that countries to which the measure will not apply must be expressly excluded from the measure. Although the Panel may have a point in saying that it is "reasonable to expect" an express exclusion, we see nothing in Article 9.1 that requires one.

. . . it is possible to comply with Article 9.1 without providing a specific list of the Members that are either included in, or excluded from, the measure. Although such a list could, and would, be both useful and helpful by providing transparency for the benefit of all Members concerned, we see nothing in Article 9.1 that mandates one.

S.1.39.2 *US – Line Pipe*, para. 129
(WT/DS202/AB/R)

. . . we note that Article 9.1 is concerned with the application of a safeguard measure on a *product*. And we note, too, that a duty, such as the supplemental duty imposed by the line pipe measure, does not need actually to be enforced and collected to be "applied" to a product. In our view, duties are "applied against a *product*" when a Member imposes conditions under which that product can enter that Member's market – including when that Member establishes, as the United States did here, a duty to be imposed on over-quota imports. Thus, in our view, duties are "applied" irrespective of whether they result in making imports more expensive, in discouraging imports because they become more expensive, or in preventing imports altogether.

S.1.39.3 *US – Line Pipe*, paras. 130–131
(WT/DS202/AB/R)

. . . according to the latest data available at the time the line pipe measure took effect – data found in the Panel record and not disputed by the United States – the 9,000 short-ton exemption from the over-quota duty imposed by the line pipe measure did *not* represent three percent of the total imports. Rather, the exemption represented only 2.7 percent of total imports . . . The exemption . . . was, on the evidence, too small.

. . . the United States argued before the Panel that it "expected" the measure would result in a decrease from the total volume of imports . . . But expectations are not realized "automatically". The facts indicate that, when the measure was adopted, the 9,000 ton exclusion represented less than three percent of total imports into the

United States market. The over-quota duty applied to imports that exceeded the 9,000 short-ton exemption, irrespective of their origin.

S.1.40 Article 12.1 – Immediate notification

S.1.40.1 *US – Wheat Gluten*, para. 102
(WT/DS166/AB/R)

. . . Article 12.1 of the *Agreement on Safeguards* sets out three separate obligations to make notification to the Committee on Safeguards, each of which is triggered "upon" the occurrence of an event specified in one of the three subparagraphs. The chapeau to Article 12.1 stipulates that the notifications must be made "*immediately* . . . upon" the occurrence of the triggering events. (emphasis added)

S.1.40.2 *US – Wheat Gluten*, paras. 105–106
(WT/DS166/AB/R)

As regards the meaning of the word "immediately" in the chapeau to Article 12.1, we agree with the Panel that the ordinary meaning of the word "implies a certain urgency". The degree of urgency or immediacy required depends on a case-by-case assessment, account being taken of the administrative difficulties involved in preparing the notification, and also of the character of the information supplied. As previous panels have recognized, relevant factors in this regard may include the complexity of the notification and the need for translation into one of the WTO's official languages. Clearly, however, the amount of time taken to prepare the notification must, in all cases, be kept to a minimum, as the underlying obligation is to notify "immediately".

"Immediate" notification is that which allows the Committee on Safeguards, and Members, the *fullest possible period* to reflect upon and react to an ongoing safeguard investigation. Anything less than "immediate" notification curtails this period. We do not, therefore, agree with the United States that the requirement of "*immediate*" notification is satisfied as long as the Committee on Safeguards and Members of the WTO have *sufficient* time to review that notification. In our view, whether a Member has made an "immediate" notification does not depend on evidence as to how the Committee on Safeguards and individual Members of the WTO actually use that notification. Nor can the requirement of "immediate" notification depend on an *ex post facto* assessment of whether individual Members suffered actual prejudice through an insufficiency in the notification period.

S.1.40.3 *US – Wheat Gluten*, para. 120
(WT/DS166/AB/R)

In examining the ordinary meaning of Article 12.1(c), we observe that the relevant triggering event is the "*taking*" of a decision. To us, Article 12.1(c) is focused upon whether a "decision" has *occurred*, or has been "taken", and not on whether that decision has been *given effect*. On the face of the text, the timeliness of a notification under Article 12.1(c) depends only on whether the notification was immediate.

S.1.41 Article 12.2 – Notification of all pertinent information

S.1.41.1 *Korea – Dairy*, para. 107
(WT/DS98/AB/R)

...The text of Article 12.2 makes it clear that a Member proposing to apply a safeguard measure is required to provide the Committee on Safeguards with *all* pertinent, not just *any* pertinent, information. Moreover, it provides that such information *shall* include certain items listed immediately after the phrase "all pertinent information", namely, evidence of serious injury or threat thereof caused by increased imports, a precise description of the product involved and the proposed measure, the proposed date of introduction, the expected duration of the measure and a timetable for progressive liberalization. These items, which are listed as mandatory components of "all pertinent information", constitute a minimum notification requirement that must be met if a notification is to comply with the requirements of Article 12.

S.1.41.2 *Korea – Dairy*, para. 108
(WT/DS98/AB/R)

...We believe that "evidence of serious injury" in the sense of Article 12.2 should refer, at a minimum, to the injury factors required to be evaluated under Article 4.2(a). In other words, according to the text and the context of Article 12.2, a Member must, *at a minimum*, address in its notifications, pursuant to paragraphs 1(b) and 1(c) of Article 12, all the items specified in Article 12.2 as constituting "all pertinent information", as well as the factors listed in Article 4.2 that are required to be evaluated in a safeguards investigation. We believe that the standard set by Article 12 with respect to the content of "all pertinent information" to be notified to the Committee on Safeguards is an objective standard independent of the subjective assessment of the notifying Member.

S.1.41.3 *US – Wheat Gluten*, paras. 123–125
(WT/DS166/AB/R)

Article 12.2 is related to, and complements, Article 12.1 of the *Agreement on Safeguards*. Whereas Article 12.1 sets forth *when* notifications must be made during an investigation, Article 12.2 clarifies *what* detailed information must be contained in the notifications under Articles 12.1(b) and 12.1(c). We do not, however, see the content requirements of Article 12.2 as prescribing *when* the notification under 12.1(c) must take place. Rather, in our view, timeliness under 12.1(c) is determined by whether a decision to apply or extend a safeguard measure is notified "immediately". A *separate* question arises as to whether notifications made by the Member satisfy the content requirements of Article 12.2. Answering this separate question requires examination of whether, in its notifications under *either* Article 12.1(b) *or* Article 12.1(c), the Member proposing to apply a safeguard measure has notified "all pertinent information", including the "mandatory components" specifically enumerated in Article 12.2.

Thus, the obligations set forth under Articles 12.1(b), 12.1(c) and 12.2 relate to different aspects of the notification process. Although related, these obligations are discrete. A Member could notify "all pertinent information" in its Articles 12.1(b) and 12.1(c) notifications, and thereby satisfy Article 12.2, but still act inconsistently with Article 12.1 because the relevant notifications were not made "immediately". Similarly, a Member could satisfy the Article 12.1 requirement of "immediate" notification, but act inconsistently with Article 12.2 if the content of its notifications was deficient.

In our view, in finding that the United States acted inconsistently with Article 12.1(c) *solely because* the decision to apply a safeguard measure was notified after that decision had been implemented, the Panel confused the separate obligations imposed on Members pursuant to Article 12.1(c) and Article 12.2 and, thereby, added another layer to the timeliness requirements in Article 12.1(c). Instead of insisting on "immediate" notification, as stipulated by Article 12.1(c), the Panel required notification to be made *both* "immediately" *and* before implementation of the safeguard measure. We see no basis in Article 12.1(c) for this conclusion.

S.1.42 Article 12.3 – "adequate opportunity for prior consultations"

S.1.42.1 *US – Wheat Gluten*, paras. 136–137
(WT/DS166/AB/R)

We note, first, that Article 12.3 requires a Member proposing to apply a safeguard measure to provide an "adequate opportunity for prior consultations" with Members with a substantial interest in exporting the product concerned. Article 12.3 states that an "adequate opportunity" for consultations is to be provided "with a view to": reviewing the information furnished pursuant to Article 12.2; exchanging views on the measure; and reaching an understanding with exporting Members on an equivalent level of concessions. In view of these objectives, we consider that Article 12.3 requires a Member proposing to apply a safeguard measure to provide exporting Members with sufficient information and time to allow for the possibility, through consultations, for a meaningful exchange on the issues identified. To us, it follows from the text of Article 12.3 itself that information on the *proposed* measure must be provided in *advance* of the consultations, so that the consultations can adequately address that measure. Moreover, the reference, in Article 12.3, to "the information provided under" Article 12.2, indicates that Article 12.2 identifies the information that is needed to enable meaningful consultations to occur under Article 12.3. Among the list of "mandatory components" regarding information identified in Article 12.2 are: a precise description of the *proposed* measure, and its *proposed* date of introduction.

Thus, in our view, an exporting Member will not have an "adequate opportunity" under Article 12.3 to negotiate overall equivalent concessions through consultations unless, prior to those consultations, it has obtained, *inter alia*, sufficiently detailed information on the form of the proposed measure, including the nature of the remedy.

S.1.42.2 *US – Line Pipe*, paras. 103–104
(WT/DS202/AB/R)

The notifications that informed the consultations held on 24 January 2000 described the measures proposed by the USITC. The Panel found, as a matter of fact, that these proposed measures "differed substantially" from the one announced by the President on 11 February 2000 and eventually applied by the United States, effective as of 1 March 2000. For this reason, we do not believe that the notifications by the United States under Article 12.1(b) in this case were sufficiently precise to allow Korea to conduct meaningful consultations on the measure at issue.

We do not mean by this to imply that the "prior consultations" envisioned by Article 12.3 must be on a proposed measure that is identical, in every respect, to the one that is eventually applied. Presumably, the "prior consultations" will, from time to time, result in some changes in a proposed measure. But where, as here, the proposed measure "differed substantially" from the measure that was later applied, and not as a consequence of "prior consultations", we fail to see how meaningful "prior consultations" could have occurred, as required by Article 12.3. . . .

S.1.42.3 *US – Line Pipe*, paras. 106–108
(WT/DS202/AB/R)

. . . Article 12.3 requires "a Member proposing to apply a safeguard measure to provide exporting Members with *sufficient information and time* to allow for the possibility, through consultations, for a *meaningful exchange*". . . .

Article 12.3 does not specify precisely how much time should be made available for consultations. Therefore, a finding on the adequacy of time in any particular case must necessarily be addressed on a case-by-case basis. . . .

. . . there must be sufficient time "to allow for the possibility . . . for a meaningful exchange". This requirement presupposes that exporting Members will obtain the relevant information sufficiently in advance to permit analysis of the measure, and assumes further that exporting Members will have an adequate opportunity to consider the likely consequences of the measure before the measure takes effect. For it is only in such circumstances that an exporting Member will be in a position, as required by Article 12.3, to "reach[] an understanding on ways to achieve the objective set out in paragraph 1 of Article 8" of "maintain[ing] a substantially equivalent level of concessions and other obligations to that existing under GATT 1994". We see this specific textual link between Article 12.3 and paragraph 1 of Article 8 as especially significant.

S.1.42.4 *US – Line Pipe*, paras. 109–110
(WT/DS202/AB/R)

We note that reaching such an "understanding" serves the interests not only of the exporting Members, but also of the importing Member, who will wish to avoid excessive compensatory measures in response to the safeguard action. As we have said, the *Agreement on Safeguards* permits Members to impose measures against "fair trade". As a result, Members against whom such measures are imposed are prevented from enjoying the full benefit of trade concessions. For this reason, Article 8.1 of the *Agreement on Safeguards* provides that "Members concerned may agree on any adequate means of trade compensation for the adverse effects of the measure on their trade." If no agreement on compensation is reached, Article 8.2 provides that "the affected . . . Members shall be free, not later than 90 days after the measure is applied, to suspend . . . the application of substantially equivalent concessions or other obligations under GATT 1994, to the trade of the Member applying the safeguard measure". Thus, there is an interest on the part of both the exporting Member and the importing Member applying the safeguard measure to engage in "prior consultations" with a view to reaching an understanding on the import of the measure.

Finally, the notion of a *meaningful exchange*, as we see it, assumes that the importing Member will enter into consultations in good faith and will take the time appropriate to give due consideration to any comments received from exporting Members before implementing the measure. As always, we must assume that WTO Members seek to carry out their WTO obligations in good faith.

S.1.43 Relationship between the Safeguards Agreement and the Anti-Dumping Agreement

S.1.43.1 *US – Line Pipe*, para. 214
(WT/DS202/AB/R)

. . . As we noted in that appeal [*US – Hot-Rolled Steel*]: "[a]lthough the text of the *Agreement on Safeguards* on causation is by no means identical to that of the *Anti-Dumping Agreement*, there are considerable similarities between the two Agreements as regards the non-attribution language." [Appellate Body Report, para. 230] We then went on to say that "adopted panel and Appellate Body reports relating to the non-attribution language in the *Agreement on Safeguards* can provide guidance in interpreting the non-attribution language in Article 3.5 of the *Anti-Dumping Agreement*." We are of the view that this reasoning applies both ways. Our statements in *US – Hot-Rolled Steel* on Article 3.5 of the *Anti-Dumping Agreement* likewise provide guidance in interpreting the similar language in Article 4.2(b) of the *Agreement on Safeguards*.

S.1.44 Relationship between the Safeguards Agreement and the GATT 1994

S.1.44.1 *Argentina – Footwear (EC)*, para. 81
(WT/DS121/AB/R)

Thus, the GATT 1994 is *not* the GATT 1947. It is "legally distinct" from the GATT 1947. The GATT 1994 and the *Agreement on Safeguards* are *both* Multilateral Agreements on Trade in Goods contained in Annex 1A of the *WTO Agreement*, and, as such, are *both* "integral parts" of the same treaty, the *WTO Agreement*, that are "binding on all Members". Therefore, the provisions of Article XIX of the GATT 1994 *and* the provisions of the *Agreement on Safeguards* are *all* provisions of one treaty, the *WTO Agreement*. They entered into force as part of that treaty at the same time. They apply equally and are equally binding on all WTO Members. And, as these provisions relate to the same thing, namely the application by Members of safeguard measures, the Panel was correct in saying that "Article XIX of GATT and the Safeguards Agreement must *a fortiori* be read as representing an *inseparable package* of rights and disciplines which have to be considered in conjunction." Yet a treaty interpreter must read all applicable provisions of a treaty in a way that gives meaning to *all* of them, harmoniously. And, an appropriate reading of this "inseparable package of rights and disciplines" must, accordingly, be one that gives meaning to *all* the relevant provisions of these two equally binding agreements.

S.1.44.2 *Argentina – Footwear (EC)*, paras. 83–84
(WT/DS121/AB/R)

We see nothing in the language of either Article 1 or Article 11.1(a) of the *Agreement on Safeguards* that suggests an intention by the Uruguay Round negotiators to *subsume* the requirements of Article XIX of the GATT 1994 within the *Agreement on Safeguards* and thus to render those requirements no longer applicable. Article 1 states that the purpose of the *Agreement on Safeguards* is to establish "rules for the application of safeguard measures which shall be understood to mean *those measures provided for* in Article XIX of GATT 1994." (emphasis added) This suggests that Article XIX continues in full force and effect, and, in fact, establishes certain prerequisites for the imposition of safeguard measures. Furthermore, in Article 11.1(a), the ordinary meaning of the language "unless such action *conforms with the provisions of that Article applied in accordance with this Agreement*" (emphasis added) clearly is that any safeguard action must *conform with* the provisions of Article XIX of the GATT 1994 *as well as* with the provisions of the *Agreement on Safeguards*. Neither of these provisions states that any safeguard action taken after the entry into force of the *WTO Agreement* need only conform with the provisions of the *Agreement on Safeguards*.

Thus, we conclude that any safeguard measure imposed after the entry into force of the *WTO Agreement* must comply with the provisions of *both* the *Agreement on Safeguards and* Article XIX of the GATT 1994.

S.1.44.3 *Korea – Dairy*, para. 75
(WT/DS98/AB/R)

. . . The *Agreement on Safeguards* is one of the thirteen Multilateral Agreements on Trade in Goods contained in Annex 1A of the *WTO Agreement*. It is important to understand that the *WTO Agreement* is *one* treaty. The GATT 1994 and the *Agreement on Safeguards* are both Multilateral Agreements on Trade in Goods contained in Annex 1A, which are integral parts of that treaty and are equally binding on all Members pursuant to Article II:2 of the *WTO Agreement*.

S.1.44.4 *Korea – Dairy*, para. 77
(WT/DS98/AB/R)

Article 1 states that the purpose of the *Agreement on Safeguards* is to establish "rules for the application of safeguard measures which shall be understood to mean *those measures provided for in* Article XIX of GATT 1994." (emphasis added) The ordinary meaning of the language in Article 11.1(a) – "unless such action conforms with the provisions of that Article applied in accordance with this Agreement" – is that any safeguard action *must conform* with the provisions of Article XIX of the GATT 1994 *as well as* with the provisions of the *Agreement on Safeguards*. Thus, any safeguard measure imposed after the entry into force of the *WTO Agreement* must comply with the provisions of *both* the *Agreement on Safeguards* and Article XIX of the GATT 1994.

S.1.45 Article XIX of the GATT 1994 – General. *See also* Agreement on Agriculture, Article 5 – Special safeguard (A.1.14); Safeguards Agreement, General (S.1.1); Textiles and Clothing Agreement, Article 6 – Transitional safeguard (T.7.1)

S.1.45.1 *Korea – Dairy*, para. 86
(WT/DS98/AB/R)

. . . In our view, the text of Article XIX:1(a) of the GATT 1994, read in its ordinary meaning and in its context, demonstrates that safeguard measures were intended by the drafters of the GATT to be matters out of the ordinary, to be matters of urgency, to be, in short, "emergency actions." And, such "emergency actions" are to be invoked only in situations when, as a result of obligations incurred under the GATT 1994, an importing Member finds itself confronted with developments it had not "foreseen" or "expected" when it incurred that obligation. The remedy that Article XIX:1(a) allows in this situation is temporarily to "suspend the obligation in whole or in part or to withdraw or modify the concession". Thus, Article XIX is clearly an extraordinary remedy.

S.1.45.2 *US – Steel Safeguards*, para. 347
(WT/DS248/AB/R, WT/DS249/AB/R, WT/DS251/AB/R, WT/DS252/AB/R, WT/DS253/AB/R, WT/DS254/AB/R, WT/DS258/AB/R, WT/DS259/AB/R)

. . . Because safeguard measures are "emergency actions", we have noted as well that "when construing the prerequisites for taking such actions, their extraordinary nature must be taken into account." The requirement relating to "increased imports" in Articles XIX:1(a) and 2.1 must, therefore, be read in the context of the "extraordinary nature" of the "emergency action" that is authorized by Article XIX:1(a) of the GATT 1994. Even so, the fact that safeguard actions are "emergency actions", and that the prerequisites for taking such actions should therefore be construed while taking into account the "extraordinary nature" of safeguard measures, does not imply that the prerequisites for taking such actions, *in and of themselves*, must necessarily be "abnormal" or "extraordinary". The question is one of the "conditions" under which "such" increased quantities of imports occur.

S.1.46 Relationship between Article XIX of the GATT 1994 and Article 3.1 of the Safeguards Agreement

S.1.46.1 *US – Lamb*, para. 76

(WT/DS177/AB/R, WT/DS178/AB/R)

...we observe that Article 3.1 requires competent authorities to set forth findings and reasoned conclusions on "all pertinent issues of fact and law" in their published report. As Article XIX:1(a) of the GATT 1994 requires that "unforeseen developments" must be demonstrated, as a matter of fact, for a safeguard measure to be applied, the existence of "unforeseen developments" is, in our view, a "pertinent issue[] of fact and law", under Article 3.1, for the application of a safeguard measure, and it follows that the published report of the competent authorities, under that Article, must contain a "finding" or "reasoned conclusion" on "unforeseen developments".

S.1.46.2 *US – Steel Safeguards*, para. 279

(WT/DS248/AB/R, WT/DS249/AB/R, WT/DS251/AB/R, WT/DS252/AB/R, WT/DS253/AB/R, WT/DS254/AB/R, WT/DS258/AB/R, WT/DS259/AB/R)

We do not see how a panel could examine objectively the consistency of a determination with Article XIX of the GATT 1994 if the competent authority had not set out an explanation supporting its conclusions on "unforeseen developments". Indeed, to enable a panel to determine whether there was compliance with the prerequisites that must be demonstrated before the application of a safeguard measure, the competent authority must provide a "reasoned and adequate explanation" of how the facts support its determination for those prerequisites, including "unforeseen developments" under Article XIX:1(a) of the GATT 1994.

S.1.46.3 *US – Steel Safeguards*, paras. 326, 329

(WT/DS248/AB/R, WT/DS249/AB/R, WT/DS251/AB/R, WT/DS252/AB/R, WT/DS253/AB/R, WT/DS254/AB/R, WT/DS258/AB/R, WT/DS259/AB/R)

Article 3.1 of the *Agreement on Safeguards* requires that the competent authority set out "reasoned conclusions" on all "pertinent issues of fact and law". One of those "issues of law" is the requirement to demonstrate the existence of "unforeseen developments" that have resulted in increased imports causing serious injury. In our view, therefore, it was for the USITC to provide a "reasoned conclusion" on "unforeseen developments"....

...

...It is not for the Panel to do the reasoning for, or instead of, the competent authority, but rather to assess the adequacy of that reasoning to satisfy the relevant requirement. In consequence, we cannot agree with the United States that the Panel was "required" to consider the relevant data to which the USITC referred in other sections of its report to support the USITC's finding that "unforeseen developments" had resulted in increased imports; ...

S.1.47 Relationship between Article XIX of the GATT 1994 and Article 4.2(c) of the Safeguards Agreement

S.1.47.1 *US – Steel Safeguards*, paras. 289–290
(WT/DS248/AB/R, WT/DS249/AB/R, WT/DS251/AB/R, WT/DS252/AB/R, WT/DS253/AB/R, WT/DS254/AB/R, WT/DS258/AB/R, WT/DS259/AB/R)

... we see Article 4.2(c) as an elaboration of the requirement set out in Article 3.1, last sentence, to provide a "reasoned conclusion" in a published report.

The United States argued at the oral hearing that "Article 4.2(c) does not apply to the competent authorities' demonstration of unforeseen developments" under Article XIX:1(a) of the GATT 1994. We disagree. Article 4.2(c) is an elaboration of Article 3; moreover "unforeseen developments" under Article XIX:1(a) of the GATT 1994 is one of the "pertinent issues of fact and law" to which the last sentence of Article 3.1 refers. It follows that Article 4.2(c) also applies to the competent authorities' demonstration of "unforeseen developments" under Article XIX:1(a).

S.1.48 Article XIX of the GATT 1994 – "as a result of"

S.1.48.1 *US – Steel Safeguards*, para. 315
(WT/DS248/AB/R, WT/DS249/AB/R, WT/DS251/AB/R, WT/DS252/AB/R, WT/DS253/AB/R, WT/DS254/AB/R, WT/DS258/AB/R, WT/DS259/AB/R)

Turning to the term "as a result of" that is also found in Article XIX:1(a), we note that the ordinary meaning of "result" is, as defined in the dictionary, "an effect, issue, or outcome *from* some action, process or design". The increased imports to which this provision refers must therefore be an "effect, or outcome" of the "unforeseen developments". Put differently, the "unforeseen developments" must "result" in increased imports of the product ("such product") that is subject to a safeguard measure.

S.1.48.2 *US – Steel Safeguards*, para. 350
(WT/DS248/AB/R, WT/DS249/AB/R, WT/DS251/AB/R, WT/DS252/AB/R, WT/DS253/AB/R, WT/DS254/AB/R, WT/DS258/AB/R, WT/DS259/AB/R)

... we said in *Argentina – Footwear (EC)* that "the increased quantities of imports should have been 'unforeseen' or 'unexpected'." In doing so, we were referring to the fact that the increased imports must, under Article XIX:1(a), result from "unforeseen developments" in order to justify the application of a safeguard measure. Because the "increased imports" must be "as a result" of an event that was "unforeseen" or "unexpected", it follows that the increased imports must also be "unforeseen" or "unexpected". Thus, the "extraordinary nature" of the domestic response to increased imports does not depend on the absolute or relative quantities of the product being imported. Rather, it depends on the fact that the increased imports were unforeseen or unexpected.

S.1.49 Article XIX of the GATT 1994 – "such product"

S.1.49.1 *US – Steel Safeguards*, para. 314
(WT/DS248/AB/R, WT/DS249/AB/R, WT/DS251/AB/R, WT/DS252/AB/R, WT/DS253/AB/R, WT/DS254/AB/R, WT/DS258/AB/R, WT/DS259/AB/R)

The term "such product" in Article XIX:1(a) refers to the product that may be subject to a safeguard measure. That product is, necessarily, *the product* that "is being imported in such increased quantities". Read in its entirety, Article XIX:1(a) clearly requires that safeguard measures be applied to the product that "is being imported in such increased quantities", and that those "increased quantities" are being imported "as a result" of "unforeseen developments".

S.1.49.2 *US – Steel Safeguards*, para. 316
(WT/DS248/AB/R, WT/DS249/AB/R, WT/DS251/AB/R, WT/DS252/AB/R, WT/DS253/AB/R, WT/DS254/AB/R, WT/DS258/AB/R, WT/DS259/AB/R)

It is evident . . . that not just any development that is "unforeseen" will do. To trigger the right to apply a safeguard measure, the development must be such as to *result* in increased imports of *the product* ("such product") that is subject to the safeguard measure. Moreover, *any* product, as Article XIX:1(a) provides, may, potentially, be subject to that safeguard measure, provided that the alleged "unforeseen developments" *result* in increased imports of that *specific product* ("such product"). We, therefore, agree with the Panel that, with respect to the specific products subject to the respective determinations, the competent authorities are required by Article XIX:1(a) of the GATT 1994 to demonstrate that the "unforeseen developments identified . . . have <u>resulted</u> in increased imports [of the specific products subject to] . . . <u>each</u> safeguard measure at issue."

S.1.49.3 *US – Steel Safeguards*, paras. 318–319
(WT/DS248/AB/R, WT/DS249/AB/R, WT/DS251/AB/R, WT/DS252/AB/R, WT/DS253/AB/R, WT/DS254/AB/R, WT/DS258/AB/R, WT/DS259/AB/R)

There must . . . be a "logical connection" linking the "unforeseen developments" and an increase in imports of the product that is causing, or threatening to cause, serious injury. Without such a "logical connection" between the "unforeseen developments" and *the product* on which safeguard measures may be applied, it could not be determined, as Article XIX:1(a) requires, that the increased imports of "such product" were "a result of" the relevant "unforeseen development". Consequently, the right to apply a safeguard measure to *that product* would not arise.

. . . when an importing Member wishes to apply safeguard measures on imports of several products, it is not sufficient merely to demonstrate that "unforeseen developments" resulted in increased imports of a broad category of products that included the specific products subject to the respective determinations by the competent authority. If that could be done, a Member could make a determination and apply a safeguard measure to a broad category of products even if imports of one or more of those products did not increase and did not result from the "unforeseen developments" at issue. Accordingly, we agree with the Panel that such an approach does not meet the requirements of Article XIX:1(a), and that the demonstration of "unforeseen developments" must be performed for *each* product subject to a safeguard measure.

S.1.50 Article XIX of the GATT 1994 – "unforeseen developments"

S.1.50.1 *Argentina – Footwear (EC)*, para. 92
(WT/DS121/AB/R)

. . . The first clause in Article XIX:1(a) – "as a result of unforeseen developments and of the obligations incurred by a Member under the Agreement, including tariff concessions . . . " – is a dependent clause which, in our view, is linked grammatically to the verb phrase "is being imported" in the second clause of that paragraph. Although we do not view the first clause in Article XIX:1(a) as establishing independent *conditions* for the application of a safeguard measure, additional to the *conditions* set forth in the second clause of that paragraph, we do believe that the first clause describes certain *circumstances* which must be demonstrated as a matter of fact in order for a safeguard measure to be applied consistently with the provisions of Article XIX of the GATT 1994. In this sense, we believe that there is a logical connection between the circumstances described in the first clause – "as a result of unforeseen developments and of the effect of the obligations incurred by a Member under this Agreement, including tariff concessions . . . " – and the conditions set forth in the second clause of Article XIX:1(a) for the imposition of a safeguard measure.

S.1.50.2 *Korea – Dairy*, para. 85
(WT/DS98/AB/R)

. . . The first clause in Article XIX:1(a) – "as a result of unforeseen developments and of the obligations incurred by a Member under the Agreement, including tariff concessions . . . " – is a dependent clause which, in our view, is linked grammatically to the verb phrase "is being imported" in the second clause of that paragraph. Although we do not view the first clause in Article XIX:1(a) as establishing independent *conditions* for the application of a safeguard measure, additional to the *conditions* set forth in the second clause of that paragraph, we do believe that the first clause describes certain *circumstances* which must be demonstrated as a matter of fact in order for a safeguard measure to be applied consistently with the provisions of Article XIX of the GATT 1994. In this sense, we believe that there is a logical connection between the circumstances described in the first clause – "as a result of unforeseen developments and of the effect of the obligations incurred by a Member under this Agreement, including tariff concessions . . . " – and the conditions set forth in the second clause of Article XIX:1(a) for the imposition of a safeguard measure.

S.1.50.3 *US – Lamb*, para. 72
(WT/DS177/AB/R, WT/DS178/AB/R)

Although we stated in these two Reports that, under Article XIX:1(a) of the GATT 1994, unforeseen developments "must be demonstrated as a matter of fact", we did not have occasion, in those two appeals, to examine when, where or how that demonstration should occur. In conducting such an examination now, we note that the text of Article XIX provides no express guidance on this issue. However, as the existence of unforeseen developments is a prerequisite that must be demonstrated, as we have stated, "in order for a safeguard measure to be applied" consistently with Article XIX of the GATT 1994, it follows that this demonstration must be made *before* the safeguard measure is applied. Otherwise, the legal basis for the measure is flawed. We find instructive guidance for where and when the "demonstration" should occur in the "logical connection" that we observed previously between the two clauses of Article XIX:1(a). The first clause, as we noted, contains, in part, the "circumstance" of "unforeseen developments". The second clause, as we said, relates to the three "conditions" for the application of safeguard measures, which are also reiterated in Article 2.1 of the *Agreement on Safeguards*. Clearly, the fulfilment of these conditions must be the central element of the report of the competent authorities, which must be published under Article 3.1 of the *Agreement on Safeguards*. In our view, the logical connection between the "conditions" identified in the second clause of Article XIX:1(a) and the "circumstances" outlined in the first clause of that provision dictates that the demonstration of the existence of these circumstances must also feature in the same report of the competent authorities. Any other approach would sever the "logical connection" between these two clauses, and would also leave vague and uncertain how compliance with the first clause of Article XIX:1(a) would be fulfilled.

S.1.50.4 *US – Steel Safeguards*, paras. 289–290

(WT/DS248/AB/R, WT/DS249/AB/R, WT/DS251/AB/R, WT/DS252/AB/R, WT/DS253/AB/R, WT/DS254/AB/R, WT/DS258/AB/R, WT/DS259/AB/R)

. . . we see Article 4.2(c) as an elaboration of the requirement set out in Article 3.1, last sentence, to provide a "reasoned conclusion" in a published report.

The United States argued at the oral hearing that "Article 4.2(c) does not apply to the competent authorities' demonstration of unforeseen developments" under Article XIX:1(a) of the GATT 1994. We disagree. Article 4.2(c) is an elaboration of Article 3; moreover "unforeseen developments" under Article XIX:1(a) of the GATT 1994 is one of the "pertinent issues of fact and law" to which the last sentence of Article 3.1 refers. It follows that Article 4.2(c) also applies to the competent authorities' demonstration of "unforeseen developments" under Article XIX:1(a).

S.1.50.5 *US – Steel Safeguards*, para. 506

(WT/DS248/AB/R, WT/DS249/AB/R, WT/DS251/AB/R, WT/DS252/AB/R, WT/DS253/AB/R, WT/DS254/AB/R, WT/DS258/AB/R, WT/DS259/AB/R)

In our view, the Panel did not simply *assume*, but rather clearly pointed to, a deficiency in the USITC's reasoning. The Panel reviewed the USITC's findings and found that the USITC failed to demonstrate that the "plausible" unforeseen developments did, in fact, result in increased imports of the specific products subject to the safeguard measures at issue. Because the USITC, according to the United States, relied on macroeconomic events having effects across the respective industries, it was for the USITC to show how those events were relevant to each product covered by each of the safeguard measures at issue. As the United States itself acknowledges, "Article 3.1 assigns the competent authorities – not the panel – the obligation to 'publish a report setting forth *their* findings and reasoned conclusions reached on all pertinent issues of fact and law'." Therefore, it was for the USITC, and not for the Panel, to explain how the facts supported its determination with respect to "unforeseen developments". The argument of the United States in this appeal seeks to shift the burden of this demonstration to the Panel, whose function, in this regard, is confined to assessing the adequacy of the "reasoned conclusions" put forward by the competent authority. We agree with the Panel that the USITC's demonstration was insufficient, and we find no error in the Panel's explanation of that finding.

Schedules of Concessions. *See* Tariff Concessions (T.1)

S.2 SCM Agreement

S.2.1 Object and Purpose

S.2.1.1 *US – Carbon Steel*, paras. 73–74
(WT/DS213/AB/R, WT/DS213/AB/R/Corr.1)

. . . we turn to the object and purpose of the *SCM Agreement*. We note, first, that the Agreement contains no preamble to guide us in the task of ascertaining its object and purpose. In *Brazil – Desiccated Coconut* [Appellate Body Report, p. 17, DSR 1997:I, p. 167 at 181], we observed that the "*SCM Agreement* contains a set of rights and obligations that go well beyond merely applying and interpreting Articles VI, XVI and XXIII of the GATT 1947." The *SCM Agreement* defines the concept of "subsidy", as well as the conditions under which Members may not employ subsidies. It establishes remedies when Members employ prohibited subsidies, and sets out additional remedies available to Members whose trading interests are harmed by another Member's subsidization practices. Part V of the *SCM Agreement* deals with one such remedy, permitting Members to levy countervailing duties on imported products to offset the benefits of specific subsidies bestowed on the manufacture, production or export of those goods. However, Part V also conditions the right to apply such duties on the demonstrated existence of three substantive conditions (subsidization, injury, and a causal link between the two) and on compliance with its procedural and substantive rules, notably the requirement that the countervailing duty cannot exceed the amount of the subsidy. Taken as a whole, the main object and purpose of the *SCM Agreement* is to increase and improve GATT disciplines relating to the use of both subsidies and countervailing measures.

We thus believe that the Panel properly identified, as among the objectives of the *SCM Agreement*, the establishment of a framework of rights and obligations relating to countervailing duties, and the creation of a set of rules which WTO Members must respect in the use of such duties. Part V of the Agreement is aimed at striking a balance between the right to impose countervailing duties to offset subsidization that is causing injury, and the obligations that Members must respect in order to do so. . . .

S.2.1.2 *US – Softwood Lumber IV*, para. 64
(WT/DS257/AB/R)

Moreover, to accept Canada's interpretation of the term "goods" would, in our view, undermine the object and purpose of the *SCM Agreement*, which is to strengthen and improve GATT disciplines relating to the use of both subsidies and countervailing measures, while, recognizing at the same time, the right of Members to impose such measures under certain conditions. It is in furtherance of this object and purpose that Article 1.1(a)(1)(iii) recognizes that subsidies may be conferred, not only through monetary transfers, but also by the provision of non-monetary inputs. Thus, to interpret the term "goods" in Article 1.1(a)(1)(iii) narrowly, as Canada would have us do, would permit the circumvention of subsidy disciplines in cases of financial contributions granted in a form other than money, such as through the provision of standing timber for the sole purpose of severing it from land and processing it.

S.2.1.3 *US – Softwood Lumber IV*, para. 95
(WT/DS257/AB/R)

. . . the Panel's restrictive interpretation . . . frustrates the object and purpose of the *SCM Agreement*, which includes disciplining the use of subsidies and countervailing measures while, at the same time, enabling WTO Members whose domestic industries are harmed by subsidized imports to use such remedies . . . If the calculation of the benefit yields a result that is artificially low, or even zero, as could be the case under the Panel's approach, then a WTO Member could not fully offset, by applying countervailing duties, the effect of the subsidy as permitted by the Agreement.

S.2.1.4 *US – Softwood Lumber IV*, para. 109
(WT/DS257/AB/R)

. . . This is because countervailing measures may be used only for the purpose of offsetting a subsidy bestowed upon a product, provided that it causes injury to the domestic industry producing the like product. They must not be used to offset differences in comparative advantages between countries.

S.2.2 **Article 1.1 – "subsidy".** *See also* SCM Agreement, Article 15 – Determination of injury (S.2.25)

S.2.2.1 *US – FSC*, para. 89
(WT/DS108/AB/R)

We start with the United States' argument that the Panel erred by failing to begin its examination of the European Communities' claim under Article 3.1(a) of the

SCM Agreement with footnote 59 of that Agreement. Instead, the Panel began its examination with the general definition of a "subsidy" that is set forth in Article 1.1 of the *SCM Agreement*. This definition applies throughout the *SCM Agreement*, to all the different types of "subsidy" covered by that Agreement. In our view, it was not a legal error for the Panel to begin its examination of whether the FSC measure involves export *subsidies* by examining the general definition of a "*subsidy*" that is applicable to export *subsidies* in Article 3.1(a). . . .

S.2.2.2 *US – FSC*, para. 93
(WT/DS108/AB/R)

Article 1.1 sets forth the general definition of the term "subsidy" which applies "for the purpose of this Agreement". This definition, therefore, applies wherever the word "subsidy" occurs throughout the *SCM Agreement* and conditions the application of the provisions of that Agreement regarding *prohibited* subsidies in Part II, *actionable* subsidies in Part III, *non-actionable* subsidies in Part IV and countervailing measures in Part V. By contrast, footnote 59 relates to one item in the Illustrative List of Export Subsidies. . . .

S.2.2.3 *US – FSC (Article 21.5 – EC)*, paras. 85–86
(WT/DS108/AB/RW)

. . . Article 1.1 itself does not impose any obligation on Members with respect to the subsidies it defines. It is the provisions of the *SCM Agreement* which follow Article 1, such as Articles 3 and 5, which impose obligations on Members with respect to subsidies falling within the definition set forth in Article 1.1. . . .

. . . Article 1.1 of the *SCM Agreement* does not prohibit a Member from foregoing revenue that is otherwise due under its rules of taxation, even if this also confers a benefit under Article 1.1(b) of the *SCM Agreement*. . . .

S.2.2.4 *US – Carbon Steel*, paras. 80–81
(WT/DS213/AB/R, WT/DS213/AB/R/Corr.1)

. . . Article 1 of the *SCM Agreement* sets out a definition of "subsidy" that applies to the whole of that Agreement. This definition includes *all* such subsidies, regardless of their amount. None of the provisions in the *SCM Agreement* that uses the term "subsidization" confines the meaning of "subsidization" to subsidization at a rate equal to or in excess of 1 percent *ad valorem*, or to any other *de minimis* threshold. It is also worth noting that, under Part of the *SCM Agreement*, prohibited subsidies are prohibited regardless of the amount of the subsidy.

Thus, in our view, the terms "subsidization" and "injury" each have an independent meaning in the *SCM Agreement* which is not derived by reference to the other. It is *unlikely* that very low levels of subsidization could be demonstrated to *cause* "material" injury. Yet such a possibility is not, *per se*, precluded by the Agreement itself, as injury is not defined in the *SCM Agreement* in relation to any specific level of subsidization.

S.2.3 Article 1.1(a)(1) – "financial contribution"

S.2.3.1 *US – Softwood Lumber IV*, para. 52 and footnote 35
(WT/DS257/AB/R)

An evaluation of the existence of a financial contribution involves consideration of the nature of the transaction through which something of economic value is transferred by a government. A wide range of transactions falls within the meaning of "financial contribution" in Article 1.1(a)(1). According to paragraphs (i) and (ii) of Article 1.1(a)(1), a financial contribution may be made through a direct transfer of funds by a government, or the foregoing of government revenue that is otherwise due. Paragraph (iii) of Article 1.1(a)(1) recognizes that, in addition to such monetary contributions, a contribution having financial value can also be made *in kind* through governments providing goods or services, or through government purchases. Paragraph (iv) of Article 1.1(a)(1) recognizes that paragraphs (i) – (iii) could be circumvented by a government making payments to a funding mechanism or through entrusting or directing a private body to make a financial contribution. It accordingly specifies that these kinds of actions are financial contributions as well. This range of government measures capable of providing subsidies is broadened still further by the concept of "income or price support" in paragraph (2) of Article 1.1(a).[35]

[35] We note, however, that not all government measures capable of conferring benefits would necessarily fall within Article 1.1(a). If that were the case, there would be no need for Article 1.1(a), because all government measures conferring benefits, *per se*, would be subsidies. In this regard, we find informative the discussion of the negotiating history of the *SCM Agreement* contained in the panel report in *US – Export Restraints*, which was not appealed. That panel, at paragraph 8.65 of the panel report, said that the:

> . . . negotiating history demonstrates . . . that the requirement of a financial contribution from the outset was intended by its proponents precisely to ensure that not all government measures that conferred benefits could be deemed to be subsidies. This point was extensively discussed during the negotiations, with many participants consistently maintaining that only government actions constituting financial contributions should be subject to the multilateral rules on subsidies and countervailing measures. (footnote omitted)

S.2.4 Article 1.1(a)(1)(ii) – "government revenue . . . otherwise due"

S.2.4.1 *US – FSC*, para. 90
(WT/DS108/AB/R)

. . . In our view, the "*foregoing*" of revenue "*otherwise* due" implies that less revenue has been raised by the government than would have been raised in a different situation, or, that is, "otherwise". Moreover, the word "foregone" suggests that the government has given up an entitlement to raise revenue that it could "otherwise" have raised. This cannot, however, be an entitlement in the abstract, because governments, in theory, could tax *all* revenues. There must, therefore, be some defined, normative benchmark against which a comparison can be made between the revenue actually raised and the revenue that would have been raised "otherwise". We, therefore, agree with the Panel that the term "otherwise due" implies some kind of comparison between the revenues due under the contested measure and revenues that would be due in some other situation. We also agree with the Panel that the basis of comparison must be the tax rules applied by the Member in question. . . .

S.2.4.2 *US – FSC*, para. 91
(WT/DS108/AB/R)

The Panel found that the term "otherwise due" establishes a "but for" test, in terms of which the appropriate basis of comparison for determining whether revenues are "otherwise due" is "the situation that would prevail but for the measures in question". In the present case, this legal standard provides a sound basis for comparison because it is not difficult to establish in what way the foreign-source income of an FSC would be taxed "but for" the contested measure. However, we have certain abiding reservations about applying any legal standard, such as this "but for" test, in the place of the actual treaty language. Moreover, we would have particular misgivings about using a "but for" test if its application were limited to situations where there actually existed an alternative measure, under which the revenues in question would be taxed, absent the contested measure. It would, we believe, not be difficult to circumvent such a test by designing a tax regime under which there would be *no* general rule that applied formally to the revenues in question, absent the contested measures. We observe, therefore, that, although the Panel's "but for" test works in this case, it may not work in other cases. . . .

S.2.4.3 *Canada – Autos*, para. 91
(WT/DS139/AB/R, WT/DS142/AB/R)

. . . We note, once more, that Canada has established a normal MFN duty rate for imports of motor vehicles of 6.1 per cent. Absent the import duty exemption, this duty would be paid on imports of motor vehicles. Thus, through the measure in dispute, the Government of Canada has, in the words of *United States – FSC*, "given up an entitlement to raise revenue that it could 'otherwise' have raised." More specifically, through the import duty exemption, Canada has ignored the "defined, normative benchmark" that it established for itself for import duties on motor vehicles under its normal MFN rate and, in so doing, has foregone "government revenue that is otherwise due".

S.2.4.4 *US – FSC (Article 21.5 – EC)*, paras. 88–89
(WT/DS108/AB/RW)

. . . the mere fact that revenues are not "due" from a fiscal perspective does not determine that the revenues are or are not "otherwise due" within the meaning of Article 1.1(a)(1)(ii) of the *SCM Agreement.*

. . . the treaty phrase "otherwise due" implies a comparison with a "defined, normative benchmark". . . . the comparison under Article 1.1(a)(1)(ii) of the *SCM Agreement* must necessarily be between the rules of taxation contained in the contested measure and other rules of taxation of the Member in question. . . .

S.2.4.5 *US – FSC (Article 21.5 – EC)*, para. 90
(WT/DS108/AB/RW)

. . . In identifying the appropriate benchmark for comparison [under Article 1.1(a)(1)(ii)], panels must obviously ensure that they identify and examine fiscal situations which it is legitimate to compare. In other words, there must be a rational basis for comparing the fiscal treatment of the income subject to the contested measure and the fiscal treatment of certain other income. In general terms, in this comparison, like will be compared with like. . . .

S.2.4.6 *S.2.4.6 US – FSC (Article 21.5 – EC)*, para. 91
(WT/DS108/AB/RW)

. . . We do not, however, consider that Article 1.1(a)(1)(ii) always *requires* panels to identify, with respect to any particular income, the "general" rule of taxation prevailing in a Member. Given the variety and complexity of domestic tax systems, it will usually be very difficult to isolate a "general" rule of taxation and"exceptions" to that "general" rule. Instead, we believe that panels should seek to compare the fiscal treatment of legitimately comparable income to determine whether the contested measure involves the foregoing of revenue which is "otherwise due", in relation to the income in question.

S.2.5 Article 1.1(a)(1)(ii), Footnote 1 – Exemption from or remission of internal taxes upon exportation

S.2.5.1 *Canada – Autos*, para. 92
(WT/DS139/AB/R, WT/DS142/AB/R)

Canada argues that the measure is "analogous" to the situation described in footnote 1 to the *SCM Agreement*, which provides that "the exemption of an exported product from duties or taxes borne by the like product when destined for domestic consumption, or the remission of such duties or taxes in amounts not in excess of those which have accrued, shall not be deemed to be a subsidy." We do not share Canada's view. Footnote 1 to the *SCM Agreement* deals with duty and tax exemptions or remissions for *exported* products. The measure at issue applies, in contrast, to *imports* of motor vehicles which are sold for consumption in Canada. For this reason, we do not consider that footnote 1 bears upon the import duty exemption at issue in this case.

S.2.6 Article 1.1(a)(1)(iii) – "Goods" provided by the government

S.2.6.1 *US – Softwood Lumber IV*, para. 53
(WT/DS257/AB/R)

Article 1.1(a)(1)(iii) of the *SCM Agreement*, . . . sets forth that a financial contribution exists where a government "provides goods or services other than general infrastructure, or purchases goods". As such, the Article contemplates two distinct types of transaction. The first is where a government provides goods or services other than general infrastructure. Such transactions have the potential to lower artificially the cost of producing a product by providing, to an enterprise, inputs having a financial value. The second type of transaction falling within Article 1.1(a)(1)(iii) is where a government purchases goods from an enterprise. This type of transaction has the potential to increase artificially the revenues gained from selling the product.

S.2.6.2 *US – Softwood Lumber IV*, para. 59
(WT/DS257/AB/R)

... we find that the ordinary meaning of the term "goods" in the English version of Article 1.1(a)(1)(iii) of the *SCM Agreement* should not be read so as to exclude tangible items of property, like trees, that are severable from land.

S.2.6.3 *US – Softwood Lumber IV*, para. 60
(WT/DS257/AB/R)

We find that terms that accompany the word "goods" in Article 1.1(a)(1)(iii) support [an interpretation of that term that does not exclude tangible items of property, like trees, that are severable from land.] In Article 1.1(a)(1)(iii), the only explicit exception to the general principle that the provision of "goods" by a government will result in a financial contribution is when those goods are provided in the form of "general infrastructure". In the context of Article 1.1(a)(1)(iii), all goods that might be used by an enterprise to its benefit – including even goods that might be considered *infrastructure* – are to be considered "goods" within the meaning of the provision, unless they are infrastructure of a *general* nature.

S.2.6.4 *US – Softwood Lumber IV*, para. 64
(WT/DS257/AB/R)

Moreover, to accept Canada's interpretation of the term "goods" would, in our view, undermine the object and purpose of the *SCM Agreement*, which is to strengthen and improve GATT disciplines relating to the use of both subsidies and countervailing measures, while, recognizing at the same time, the right of Members to impose such measures under certain conditions. It is in furtherance of this object and purpose that Article 1.1(a)(1)(iii) recognizes that subsidies may be conferred, not only through monetary transfers, but also by the provision of non-monetary inputs. Thus, to interpret the term "goods" in Article 1.1(a)(1)(iii) narrowly, as Canada would have us do, would permit the circumvention of subsidy disciplines in cases of financial contributions granted in a form other than money, such as through the provision of standing timber for the sole purpose of severing it from land and processing it.

S.2.7 Article 1.1(a)(1)(iii) – "Provision" of goods

S.2.7.1 *US – Softwood Lumber IV*, paras. 68, 71
(WT/DS257/AB/R)

... we now turn to consider what it means to "provide" goods, for purposes of Article 1.1(a)(1)(iii) of the *SCM Agreement*. ...

...

... we do not see how the general governmental acts referred to by Canada would necessarily fall within the concept of a government "making available" services or goods. In our view, such actions would be too remote from the concept of "making available" or "putting at the disposal of", which requires there to be a reasonably proximate relationship between the action of the government providing the good or service on the one hand, and the use or enjoyment of the good or service by the recipient on the other. Indeed, a government must have some control over the *availability* of a specific thing being "made available".

S.2.7.2 *US – Softwood Lumber IV*, paras. 73, 75
(WT/DS257/AB/R)

... in our view, it does not make a difference, for purposes of applying the requirements of Article 1.1(a)(1)(iii) of the *SCM Agreement* to the facts of this case, if "provides" is interpreted as "supplies", "makes available" or "puts at the disposal of". What matters for determining the existence of a subsidy is whether all elements of the subsidy definition are fulfilled as a result of the transaction, irrespective of whether all elements are fulfilled *simultaneously*.

...

... what matters, for purposes of determining whether a government "provides goods" in the sense of Article 1.1(a)(1)(iii), is the consequence of the transaction. Rights over felled trees or logs crystallize as a natural and inevitable consequence of the harvesters' exercise of their harvesting rights. Indeed, as the Panel indicated, the evidence suggests that making available timber is the *raison d'être* of the stumpage arrangements. Accordingly, like the Panel, we believe that, by granting a right to harvest standing timber, governments provide that standing timber to timber harvesters. ...

S.2.8 Article 1.1(a)(1)(iv) – Payments to a funding mechanism

S.2.8.1 *Canada – Dairy (Article 21.5 – New Zealand and US II)*, para. 128 and footnote 113
(WT/DS103/AB/RW2, WT/DS113/AB/RW2)

We observe that Article 9.1(c) does not require that payments be financed by virtue of government "mandate", or other "direction". Although the word "action" certainly covers situations where government mandates or directs that payments be made, it also covers other situations where no such compulsion is involved.[113]

[113] Article 9.1(c) of the *Agreement on Agriculture* may be contrasted with Article 9.1(e) of the *Agreement on Agriculture*, as well as with Article 1.1(a)(1)(iv) of the *SCM Agreement*, and items (c), (d), (j), and (k) of the Illustrative List of Export Subsidies (the "Illustrative List") of the *SCM Agreement*. In these provisions, some kind of government mandate, direction, or control is an element of a subsidy provided through a third party.

S.2.9 Article 1.1(b) – Conferral of a benefit to a recipient. *See also* SCM Agreement, Article 14 – Chapeau – Calculation of the benefit to the "recipient" (S.2.22)

S.2.9.1 *Canada – Aircraft*, para. 154
(WT/DS70/AB/R)

A "benefit" does not exist in the abstract, but must be received and enjoyed by a beneficiary or a recipient. Logically, a "benefit" can be said to arise only if a person, natural or legal, or a group of persons, has in fact received something. The term "benefit", therefore, implies that there must be a recipient. . . .

S.2.9.2 *Canada – Aircraft*, para. 157
(WT/DS70/AB/R)

We also believe that the word "benefit", as used in Article 1.1(b), implies some kind of comparison. This must be so, for there can be no "benefit" to the recipient unless the "financial contribution" makes the recipient "better off" than it would otherwise have been, absent that contribution. In our view, the marketplace provides an appropriate basis for comparison in determining whether a "benefit" has been "conferred", because the trade-distorting potential of a "financial contribution" can be identified by determining whether the recipient has received a "financial contribution" on terms more favourable than those available to the recipient in the market.

S.2.9.3 *US – Lead and Bismuth II*, para. 58
(WT/DS138/AB/R)

We . . . agree with the Panel's findings that benefit as used in Article 1.1(b) is concerned with the "benefit to the recipient", [and] that such recipient must be a natural or legal person. . .

S.2.9.4 *US – Lead and Bismuth II*, para. 68
(WT/DS138/AB/R)

The question whether a "financial contribution" confers a "benefit" depends, therefore, on whether the recipient has received a "financial contribution" on terms more favourable than those available to the recipient in the market. In the present case, the Panel made factual findings that UES and BSplc/BSES paid fair market value for all the productive assets, goodwill, etc., they acquired from BSC and subsequently used in the production of leaded bars imported into the United States in 1994, 1995 and 1996. We, therefore, see no error in the Panel's conclusion that, in the specific circumstances of this case, the "financial contributions" bestowed on BSC between 1977 and 1986 could not be deemed to confer a "benefit" on UES and BSplc/BSES.

S.2.9.5 *US – Countervailing Measures on Certain EC Products*, para. 102
(WT/DS212/AB/R)

We agree with the United States that, irrespective of the price paid by the new private owner, privatization does not *remove* the equipment that a state-owned enterprise may have acquired (or received) with a financial contribution and that, consequently, the same firm may "continue[] to make the same products on the same equipment". However, this observation serves only to illustrate that, following privatization, the *utility value* of equipment acquired as a result of a financial contribution is not extinguished, because it is transferred to the newly-privatized firm. But, the *utility value* of such equipment to the newly-privatized firm is legally irrelevant for purposes of determining the continued existence of a "benefit" under the *SCM Agreement*. As we found in *Canada – Aircraft* [Appellate Body Report, para. 157], the value of the "benefit" under the *SCM Agreement* is to be assessed using the *marketplace* as the basis for comparison. It follows, therefore, that once a fair market price is paid for the equipment, its *market value* is redeemed, regardless of the utility the firm may derive from the equipment. Accordingly, it is the *market value* of the equipment that is the focal point of analysis, and not the equipment's *utility value* to the privatized firm.

S.2.9.6 *US – Countervailing Measures on Certain EC Products*, paras. 108, 110 (WT/DS212/AB/R)

. . . In *Canada – Aircraft*, we were asked whether the "cost to government" was relevant to the interpretation of "benefit" within the meaning of Article 1.1(b) of the *SCM Agreement*. In finding the "cost to government" not to be the relevant benchmark for identifying the "benefit", we said that Article 14 of the *SCM Agreement* prescribes the guidelines required to "calculate the benefit *to the recipient* conferred pursuant to paragraph 1 of Article 1". (emphasis added) We concluded that this phrase in Article 14 necessarily provides relevant context for interpreting Article 1.1, and we found that:

> [a] "benefit" does not exist in the abstract, but must be *received and enjoyed* by a beneficiary or a recipient. Logically, a "benefit" can be said to arise only if a person, natural or legal, or *a group of persons*, has in fact received something. The term "benefit", therefore, implies that there must be a recipient. (emphasis added) [Appellate Body Report, para. 154]

Contrary to what has been argued here by the United States, when referring to "a recipient" in *Canada – Aircraft*, we did not exclude the possibility that "a recipient" could include both a firm and its owner. A "group of persons" could include a group of "natural persons", or a group of "natural and legal persons", or a group exclusively of "legal persons".

. . .

Contrary to the reading that has been suggested by the United States, when we referred, in *US – Lead and Bismuth II* [paragraphs 56 and 58], to "legal or natural persons", we were *not* seeking to distinguish between a firm and its owners. . . . In our reasoning, we simply explained that the focus of any analysis of whether a "benefit" exists should be on "legal or natural persons" *instead of* on productive operations; we did not rely in our reasoning on what the United States describes as "normal corporate law principles". Moreover, there is nothing in these findings indicating that the "benefit" of a financial contribution, as contemplated in

Article 1.1(b) of the *SCM Agreement*, should necessarily be "received and enjoyed" by the *same* person or, put differently, there is nothing indicating that the "benefit" cannot be "received and enjoyed" by two or more distinct persons.

S.2.9.7 *US – Countervailing Measures on Certain EC Products*, paras. 112–113 (WT/DS212/AB/R)

The *SCM Agreement* does not include a specific definition of the "recipient" of a "benefit". However, several terms are used to refer to the "recipient" of a "benefit" in the Agreement. Article 2 refers to "an enterprise or industry or group of enterprises or industries"; Article 6.1(b) refers to "an industry"; footnote 36 to Article 10 refers to subsidies "bestowed directly or indirectly upon the manufacture, production or export of any merchandise"; Article 14 refers to "the firm"; Article 11.2(ii) refers to "exporter or foreign producer"; Article 19.3 refers to "sources found to be subsidized"; Annex I refers to "a firm or an industry"; and Annex IV refers to the "recipient firm". This is not an exhaustive list, but it certainly indicates that the *SCM Agreement* does not identify the "recipient" of a "benefit" by using any particular legal term of art. Rather, the *SCM Agreement* uses several terms to describe the economic entity that receives a "benefit". Thus, the reliance by the United States on the list of financial contributions in Article 1.1(a)(1) is not persuasive, because, when viewed in the context of the *SCM Agreement* as a whole, that list cannot be read to imply that the "recipient" is necessarily defined as a "legal person".

In addition, we observe that a transfer of funds could be provided directly from the government to the legal person that is the producer of the subsidized product, or it could be provided indirectly, say, through an income tax concession to the natural persons that own the firm (inasmuch as they invest in the legal person's productive activities). In both cases, the cost of raising capital for the legal person that is the producer would be reduced. Hence, contrary to the contention of the United States, it is possible to confer a "benefit" on a firm by providing a financial contribution to its owners, whether natural or legal persons, possibly holding property by means of shares. Moreover, we note that Article VI:3 of the GATT 1994 and footnote 36 of Article 10 of the *SCM Agreement* contemplate this possibility by providing that a subsidy may be bestowed "*indirectly*" upon the manufacture, production or export of merchandise. (emphasis added)

S.2.9.8 *US – Countervailing Measures on Certain EC Products*, paras. 115–116, 118 (WT/DS212/AB/R)

. . . the legal distinction between firms and their owners that may be recognized in a domestic legal context is not necessarily relevant, and certainly not conclusive, for the purpose of determining whether a "benefit" exists under the *SCM Agreement*, because a financial contribution bestowed on those investing in a firm may confer a benefit "upon the manufacture, production or export of any merchandise, as provided for in paragraph 3 of Article VI of GATT 1994."

> ... we are of the view that the Panel went too far in stating, in paragraph 7.54 of the Panel Report, that, "for the purpose of the benefit determination under the SCM Agreement, *no distinction* should be made [because] ... [w]hen the SCM Agreement refers to the recipient of a benefit it means the company and its shareholders together". (emphasis added) In so finding, the Panel adopted too sweeping an interpretation of the *SCM Agreement*.
>
> ...
>
> ... we note that the Panel's overly broad finding that a firm and its owners are, for *all* purposes of the *SCM Agreement*, virtually the same, could be interpreted as entitling investigating authorities to assume, in *all* cases, that, for the purpose of calculating the benefit, and irrespective of the means and conditions imposed by a government for the provision of a financial contribution to owners of the firm, that firm will receive a benefit equivalent to the full financial contribution. This may or may not be so in all cases. We do not express an opinion on this question, but we caution that this finding of the Panel must not be interpreted as entitling authorities to overlook the possibility that some of the financial contribution provided to owners may not flow into the firm....

S.2.9.9 *US – Countervailing Measures on Certain EC Products*, paras. 126–127 (WT/DS212/AB/R)

We understand the Panel to be stating that privatization at arm's length and for fair market value privatization *presumptively* extinguishes any benefit received from the non-recurring financial contribution bestowed upon a state-owned firm. The effect of such a privatization is to shift to the investigating authority the burden of identifying evidence which establishes that the benefit from the previous financial contribution does indeed continue beyond privatization. In the absence of such proof, the fact of the arm's-length, fair market value privatization is sufficient to compel a conclusion that the "benefit" no longer exists for the privatized firm, and, therefore, that countervailing duties should not be levied. This is an accurate characterization of a Member's obligations under the *SCM Agreement*.

Therefore, we find that the Panel erred in concluding that "[p]rivatizations at arm's length and for fair market value *must* lead to the conclusion that the privatized producer paid for what he got and thus did not get any benefit or advantage from the prior financial contribution bestowed upon the state-owned producer." (emphasis added) Privatization at arm's length and for fair market value *may* result in extinguishing the benefit. Indeed, we find that there is a rebuttable presumption that a benefit ceases to exist after such a privatization. Nevertheless, it does not *necessarily* do so. There is no inflexible rule *requiring* that investigating authorities, in future cases, *automatically* determine that a "benefit" derived from pre-privatization financial contributions expires following privatization at arm's length and for fair market value. It depends on the facts of each case....

S.2.9.10 *US – Upland Cotton*, para. 731
(WT/DS267/AB/R)

We need not decide, in this case, whether an export credit guarantee program that meets the standard of item (j) of the Illustrative List of Export Subsidies – because the premiums charged are adequate to cover long-term operating costs and losses – may nevertheless be challenged as a prohibited export subsidy under Article 3.1(a) on the basis that it confers a benefit. This is because, even if we were to assume that such a claim were possible, we would conclude that the Panel was within its discretion in exercising judicial economy in respect of Brazil's claim.

S.2.10 Article 1.1 – Pass-through of indirect subsidies. *See also* SCM Agreement, Article VI.3 of the GATT 1994 – Subsidies (S.2.43)

S.2.10.1 *US – Softwood Lumber IV*, para. 142
(WT/DS257/AB/R)

[According to] the general definition of a "subsidy" in Article 1 of the *SCM Agreement*... a subsidy shall be deemed to exist only if there is both a *financial contribution* by a government within the meaning of Article 1.1(a)(1), and a *benefit* is thereby conferred within the meaning of Article 1.1(b). If countervailing duties are intended to offset a subsidy granted to the producer of an input product, but the duties are to be imposed on the *processed product* (and not the input product), it is *not* sufficient for an investigating authority to establish only for the *input* product the existence of a financial contribution and the conferral of a benefit to the input producer. In such a case, the cumulative conditions set out in Article 1 must be established with respect to the processed product, especially when the producers of the input and the processed product are not the same entity. The investigating authority must establish that a *financial contribution* exists; and it must also establish that the benefit resulting from the subsidy has passed through, at least in part, from the input downstream, so as to *benefit* indirectly the processed product to be countervailed.

S.2.10.2 *US – Softwood Lumber IV*, para. 143
(WT/DS257/AB/R)

... Thus, for a potentially countervailable subsidy to exist, there must be a financial contribution by the government that confers a benefit to a *recipient*. Where a subsidy is conferred on input products, and the countervailing duty is imposed on processed products, the initial recipient of the subsidy and the producer of the eventually countervailed product, may not be the same. In such a case, there is a *direct recipient* of the benefit – the producer of the *input* product. When the input is subsequently processed, the producer of the *processed product* is an *indirect recipient* of the benefit – provided it can be established that the benefit flowing from the input subsidy is passed through, at least in part, to the processed product. Where the input producers and producers of the processed products operate at *arm's length*, the pass-through of input subsidy benefits from the direct recipients to the indirect recipients downstream cannot simply be presumed; it must be established by the investigating authority. In the absence of such analysis, it cannot be shown that the essential elements of the subsidy definition in Article 1 are present in respect of the *processed product*. In turn, the right to impose a countervailing duty on the processed product for the purpose of offsetting an input subsidy, would not have been established in accordance with Article VI:3 of the GATT 1994, and, consequently, would also not have been in accordance with Articles 10 and 32.1 of the *SCM Agreement*.

S.2.10.3 *US – Upland Cotton*, para. 471
(WT/DS267/AB/R)

The United States contends that the Appellate Body's reasoning in *US – Softwood Lumber IV* indicates that it cannot be presumed that a "subsidy", as defined in Article 1.1 of the *SCM Agreement*, provided to a producer of an input (such as raw cotton) "passes through" to the producer of the processed product (in this case, upland cotton lint). However, the Appellate Body's reasoning in that dispute focuses not on the requirements for establishing serious prejudice under Articles 5(c) and 6.3(c) of the *SCM Agreement*, but on the conduct of countervailing duty investigations pursuant to Part V of the *SCM Agreement*.

S.2.11 Article 3.1(a) – "except as provided in the Agreement on Agriculture" – export subsidies

S.2.11.1 *Canada – Dairy (Article 21.5 – New Zealand and US)*, paras. 123–125
(WT/DS103/AB/RW, WT/DS113/AB/RW)

The relationship between the *Agreement on Agriculture* and the *SCM Agreement* is defined, in part, by Article 3.1 of the *SCM Agreement*, which states that certain subsidies are "prohibited" "[e]xcept as provided in the Agreement on Agriculture". This clause, therefore, indicates that the WTO-consistency of an export subsidy for agricultural products has to be examined, in the first place, under the *Agreement on Agriculture*.

This is borne out by Article 13(c)(ii) of the *Agreement on Agriculture*, which provides that "export subsidies that conform fully to the [export subsidy] provisions of Part V" of the *Agreement on Agriculture*, "as reflected in each Member's Schedule, shall be . . . exempt from actions based on Article XVI of GATT 1994 or Articles 3, 5 and 6 of the Subsidies Agreement."

In this appeal, we are unable to determine whether the measure at issue "conforms fully" to Articles 9.1(c) or 10.1 of Part V of the *Agreement on Agriculture*. In these circumstances, we decline to examine the claim made by the United States that the measure is inconsistent with Article 3.1 of the *SCM Agreement*.

S.2.11.2 *US – Upland Cotton*, paras. 629–630
(WT/DS267/AB/R)

. . . According to the United States, "Article 3 of the *SCM Agreement* . . . is subject in its application to Article 21.1 of the *Agreement on Agriculture*". The United States then argues that, because "export credit guarantees are not subject to the disciplines of export subsidies for purposes of the *Agreement on Agriculture*, Article 21.1 of that Agreement renders Article 3.1(a) of the *SCM Agreement* inapplicable to such measures"....

...Therefore, because it is premised on an incorrect interpretation of Article 10.2 of the *Agreement on Agriculture*, we reject the United States' argument....

S.2.12 Article 3.1(a) – "contingent, in law or in fact, ... upon export performance"

S.2.12.1 *Canada – Aircraft*, para. 166
(WT/DS70/AB/R)

...In our view, the key word in Article 3.1(a) is "contingent". As the Panel observed, the ordinary connotation of "contingent" is "conditional" or "dependent for its existence on something else". This common understanding of the word "contingent" is borne out by the text of Article 3.1(a), which makes an explicit link between "contingency" and "conditionality" in stating that export contingency can be the sole or "one of several other *conditions*".

S.2.12.2 *Canada – Aircraft*, para. 167
(WT/DS70/AB/R)

Article 3.1(a) prohibits *any* subsidy that is contingent upon export performance, whether that subsidy is contingent "in law or in fact". The Uruguay Round negotiators have, through the prohibition against export subsidies that are contingent *in fact* upon export performance, sought to prevent circumvention of the prohibition against subsidies contingent *in law* upon export performance. In our view, the legal standard expressed by the word "contingent" is the same for both *de jure* or *de facto* contingency. There is a difference, however, in what evidence may be employed to prove that a subsidy is export contingent....

S.2.12.2A *Canada – Aircraft*, para. 171
(WT/DS70/AB/R)

The second substantive element in footnote 4 is "tied to". The ordinary meaning of "tied to" confirms the linkage of "contingency" with "conditionality" in Article 3.1(a). Among the many meanings of the verb "tie", we believe that, in this instance, because the word "tie" is immediately followed by the word "to" in footnote 4, the relevant ordinary meaning of "tie" must be to "limit or restrict as to...conditions". This element of the standard set forth in footnote 4, therefore, emphasizes that a relationship of conditionality or dependence must be demonstrated. The second substantive element is at the very heart of the legal standard in footnote 4 and cannot be overlooked. In any given case, the facts must "demonstrate" that the granting of a subsidy is *tied to* or *contingent upon* actual or anticipated exports. It does *not* suffice to demonstrate solely that a government granting a subsidy *anticipated* that exports would result. The prohibition in Article 3.1(a) applies to subsidies that are *contingent* upon export performance.

S.2.12.3 *Canada – Aircraft (Article 21.5 – Brazil)*, para. 47
(WT/DS70/AB/RW)

It is worth recalling that the granting of a subsidy is not, in and of itself, prohibited under the *SCM Agreement*. Nor does granting a "subsidy", without more, constitute an inconsistency with that Agreement. The universe of subsidies is vast. Not all subsidies are inconsistent with the *SCM Agreement*. The only "prohibited" subsidies are those identified in Article 3 of the *SCM Agreement*; Article 3.1(a) of that Agreement prohibits those subsidies that are "contingent, in law or in fact, upon export performance". We have stated previously that "a subsidy is prohibited under Article 3.1(a) if it is 'conditional' upon export performance, that is, if it is 'dependent for its existence on' export performance." We have also emphasized that a "relationship of conditionality or dependence", namely that the granting of a subsidy should be "tied to" the export performance, lies at the "very heart" of the legal standard in Article 3.1(a) of the *SCM Agreement*.

S.2.12.4 *Canada – Aircraft (Article 21.5 – Brazil)*, paras. 48, 51
(WT/DS70/AB/RW)

To demonstrate the existence of this "relationship of conditionality or dependence", we have also stated that it is *not* sufficient to show that a subsidy is granted in the knowledge, or with the anticipation, that exports will result. Such knowledge or anticipation does not, taken alone, demonstrate that the granting of the subsidy is "contingent upon" export performance. The second sentence of footnote 4 of the *SCM Agreement* stipulates, in this regard, that the "*mere fact* that a subsidy is granted to enterprises which export shall not *for that reason alone* be considered to be an export subsidy . . . ". (emphasis added) That fact, by itself, does not, therefore, compel the conclusion that there is a "relationship of conditionality or dependence", such that the granting of a subsidy is "tied to" export performance. However, we have also said that the export-orientation of a recipient "may be taken into account as *a* relevant fact, provided it is one of several facts which are considered and is not the only fact supporting a finding" of export contingency. (underlining added)

. . .

For all these reasons, we find that Brazil has not sufficiently established that the Canadian regional aircraft industry is "specifically targeted" *because of* its high export-orientation.

S.2.12.4A *US – FSC (Article 21.5 – EC)*, para. 110
(WT/DS108/AB/RW)

The United States appeals the Panel's finding that the measure involves the grant of a subsidy "contingent . . . upon export performance". The United States contends that, under Article 3.1(a) of the *SCM Agreement*, export contingency is a *necessary* condition of grant if a subsidy is to be export contingent. It points out that the ETI measure is export-neutral as the tax exclusion is available with respect to property that is *not* produced in the United States and, therefore, not exported from the United States. Thus, it is argued, the tax exclusion can be obtained without exportation so that export performance is not a condition that must be satisfied in order to obtain this exclusion. The Panel, however, overlooked this fact and "artificially bifurcat[ed]" the ETI measure, examining it only as it relates to property produced in the United States. The United States insists that no such distinction exists under the ETI measure.

S.2.12.5 *US – FSC (Article 21.5 – EC)*, paras. 114–115

(WT/DS108/AB/RW)

... The conditions for the grant of subsidy with respect to property produced *outside* the United States are distinct from those governing the grant of subsidy in respect of property produced *within* the United States.

In our view, it is hence appropriate, indeed necessary, under Article 3.1(a) of the *SCM Agreement*, to examine separately the conditions pertaining to the grant of the subsidy in the two different situations addressed by the measure.... The measure itself identifies the two situations which must be different since the very same property cannot be produced both within and outside the United States.

S.2.12.6 *US – FSC (Article 21.5 – EC)*, para. 119

(WT/DS108/AB/RW)

... Our conclusion that the ETI measure grants subsidies that are export contingent in the first set of circumstances is not affected by the fact that the subsidy can also be obtained in the second set of circumstances. The fact that the subsidies granted in the second set of circumstances *might* not be export contingent does not dissolve the export contingency arising in the first set of circumstances. Conversely, the export contingency arising in these circumstances has no bearing on whether there is an export contingent subsidy in the second set of circumstances....

S.2.12.7 *US – Upland Cotton*, para. 571

(WT/DS267/AB/R)

Although an export subsidy granted to agricultural products must be examined, in the first place, under the *Agreement on Agriculture*, we find it appropriate, as has the Appellate Body in previous disputes, to rely on the *SCM Agreement* for guidance in interpreting provisions of the *Agreement on Agriculture*. Thus, we consider the export-contingency requirement in Article 1(e) of the *Agreement on Agriculture* having regard to that same requirement contained in Article 3.1(a) of the *SCM Agreement*.

S.2.12.8 *US – Upland Cotton*, para. 572

(WT/DS267/AB/R)

The Appellate Body has indicated, in this regard, that the ordinary meaning of "contingent" is "conditional" or "dependent" and that Article 3.1(a) of the *SCM*

Agreement prohibits subsidies that are conditional upon export performance, or are dependent for their existence on export performance. It has also emphasized that "a 'relationship of conditionality or dependence', namely that the granting of a subsidy should be 'tied to' the export performance, lies at the 'very heart' of the legal standard in Article 3.1(a) of the *SCM Agreement*". . . .

S.2.12.9 *US – Upland Cotton*, para. 578
(WT/DS267/AB/R)

Furthermore, we agree with the Panel's conclusion that the fact that the subsidy is also available to domestic users of upland cotton does not "dissolve" the export-contingent nature of the Step 2 payments to exporters. The Panel's reasoning is consistent with the approach taken by the Appellate Body in *US – FSC (Article 21.5 – EC)*. In that case, the United States argued that the tax exclusion at issue was not an export-contingent subsidy because it was available for both (i) property produced within the United States and held for use outside the United States and (ii) property produced outside the United States and held for use outside the United States. The United States asserted that, as the tax exemption was available in both circumstances, it was "export-neutral". According to the United States, the panel's separate examination of each situation in which the tax exemption was available "artificially bifurcat[ed]" the measure.

S.2.12.10 *US – Upland Cotton*, para. 579
(WT/DS267/AB/R)

The Appellate Body rejected the United States' contention in *US – FSC (Article 21.5 – EC)* because it considered it necessary, under Article 3.1(a) of the *SCM Agreement*, "to examine separately the conditions pertaining to the grant of the subsidy in the two different situations". [Appellate Body Report, *US – FSC (Article 21.5 – EC)*, para. 115] It then confirmed the Panel's finding that the tax exemption in the first situation, namely for property produced within the United States and held for use outside the United States, is an export-contingent subsidy. In its reasoning, the Appellate Body explained that whether or not the subsidies were export-contingent in both situations envisaged by the measure would not alter the conclusion that the tax exemption in the first situation was contingent upon export . . .

S.2.12.11 *US – Upland Cotton*, para. 580
(WT/DS267/AB/R)

As in *US – FSC (Article 21.5 – EC)*, the Panel in this case found that Step 2 payments are available in two situations, only one of which involves export contingency. The Panel's conclusion, therefore, is consistent with the Appellate Body's holding in *US – FSC (Article 21.5 – EC)* quoted above that "the fact that the subsidies granted in the second set of circumstances *might* not be export contingent does not dissolve the export contingency arising in the first set of circumstances".

S.2.12.12 *US – Upland Cotton*, para. 582
(WT/DS267/AB/R)

In sum, we agree with the Panel's view that Step 2 payments are export-contingent and, therefore, an export subsidy for purposes of Article 9 of the *Agreement on Agriculture* and Article 3.1(a) of the *SCM Agreement*. The statute and regulations pursuant to which Step 2 payments are granted, on their face, condition payments to exporters on exportation. In order to claim payment, an exporter must show proof of exportation. If an exporter does not provide proof of exportation, the exporter will not receive a payment. This is sufficient to establish that Step 2 payments to exporters of United States upland cotton are "conditional upon export performance" or "dependent for their existence on export performance". That domestic users may also be eligible to receive payments under different conditions does not eliminate the fact that an exporter will receive payment only upon proof of exportation.

S.2.13 Article 3.1(a) – Contingency in law

S.2.13.1 *Canada – Autos*, para. 100
(WT/DS139/AB/R, WT/DS142/AB/R)

. . . In our view, a subsidy is contingent "in law" upon export performance when the existence of that condition can be demonstrated on the basis of the very words of the relevant legislation, regulation or other legal instrument constituting the measure. The simplest, and hence, perhaps, the uncommon, case is one in which the condition of exportation is set out expressly, in so many words, on the face of the law, regulation or other legal instrument. We believe, however, that a subsidy is also properly held to be *de jure* export contingent where the condition to export is clearly, though implicitly, in the instrument comprising the measure. Thus, for a subsidy to be *de jure* export contingent, the underlying legal instrument does not always have to provide *expressis verbis* that the subsidy is available only upon fulfillment of the condition of export performance. Such conditionality can also be derived by necessary implication from the words actually used in the measure.

S.2.13.2 *Canada – Autos*, para. 104
(WT/DS139/AB/R, WT/DS142/AB/R)

. . . Like the Panel, we fail to see how a manufacturer with a production-to-sales ratio of 100:100 could obtain access to the import duty exemption – and still maintain its required production-to-sales ratio – without exporting. . . . In our view, as the import duty exemption is simply not available to a manufacturer unless it exports motor vehicles, the import duty exemption is clearly conditional, or dependent upon, exportation and, therefore, is contrary to Article 3.1(a) of the SCM Agreement.

S.2.13.3 *Canada – Autos*, para. 107
(WT/DS139/AB/R, WT/DS142/AB/R)

Although we are not examining whether the subsidy in this case is contingent "in fact" upon export performance, we note that footnote 4 to Article 3.1(a) uses the words "tied to" as a synonym for "contingent" or "conditional". As the legal standard is the same for *de facto* and *de jure* export contingency, we believe that a "tie", amounting to the relationship of contingency, between the granting of the subsidy and actual or anticipated exportation meets the legal standard of "contingent" in Article 3.1(a) of the *SCM Agreement*.

S.2.13.4 *Canada – Autos*, para. 108
(WT/DS139/AB/R, WT/DS142/AB/R)

Even where the ratio requirement for a particular manufacturer is set at less than 100:100, in our view, there is contingency "in law" upon export performance because, as a result of the operation of the MVTO 1998 and the SROs themselves, the granting of, or the entitlement to, the import duty exemption is tied to the exportation of motor vehicles by the manufacturer beneficiaries. By the very operation of the measure, the more motor vehicles that a manufacturer exports, the more motor vehicles it can import duty-free. In other words, a clear relationship of dependency or conditionality exists between the granting of the import duty exemption and the exportation of motor vehicles by manufacturer beneficiaries. We find, therefore, that, even when the ratio requirements are less than 100:100, the measure is "contingent . . . in law . . . upon export performance".

S.2.13.5 *US – Upland Cotton*, para. 572
(WT/DS267/AB/R)

. . . We are also mindful that in demonstrating export contingency in the case of subsidies that are contingent in law upon export performance, the "existence of that condition can be demonstrated on the basis of the very words of the relevant legislation, regulation or other legal instrument constituting the measure".

S.2.14 Article 3.1(a) – Contingency in fact

S.2.14.1 *Canada – Aircraft*, para. 169
(WT/DS70/AB/R)

. . . We note that satisfaction of the standard for determining *de facto* export contingency set out in footnote 4 requires proof of three different substantive elements: first, the "*granting* of a subsidy"; second, "is . . . *tied to*. . . "; and, third, "actual or anticipated exportation or export earnings". (emphasis added) . . .

S.2.14.2 *Canada – Aircraft*, para. 175
(WT/DS70/AB/R)

Having examined the legal standard set forth in footnote 4 for determining *de facto* export contingency under Article 3.1(a), we turn next to the Panel's application of that legal standard to the facts relating to assistance provided by TPC to the Canadian regional aircraft industry. The Panel set out in some detail the various facts that it took into account in concluding that TPC assistance was "contingent . . . in fact . . . upon export performance". Indeed, the Panel took into account sixteen different factual elements, which covered a variety of matters, including: TPC's statement of its overall objectives; types of information called for in applications for TPC funding; the considerations, or eligibility criteria, employed by TPC in deciding whether to grant assistance; factors to be identified by TPC officials in making recommendations about applications for funding; TPC's record of funding in the export field, generally, and in the aerospace and defence sector, in particular; the nearness-to-the-export-market of the projects funded; the importance of projected export sales by applicants to TPC's funding decisions; and the export orientation of the firms or the industry supported.

S.2.14A Article 3.1(b) – "except as provided in the Agreement on Agriculture" – import substitution subsidies

S.2.14A.1 *US – Upland Cotton*, para. 541
(WT/DS267/AB/R)

It may well be that a measure that is an import substitution subsidy could fall within the second sentence of paragraph 7 as "[m]easures directed at agricultural processors [that] shall be included [in the AMS calculation] to the extent that such measures benefit the producers of the basic agricultural products". There is nothing, however, in the text of paragraph 7 [of Annex 3 of the *Agreement on Agriculture*] that suggests that such measures, when they are import substitution subsidies, are exempt from the prohibition in Article 3.1(b) of the *SCM Agreement*. We agree with the Panel that there is a clear distinction between a provision that requires a Member to include a certain type of payment (or part thereof) in its AMS calculation and one that would authorize subsidies that are contingent on the use of domestic over imported goods.

S.2.14A.2 *US – Upland Cotton*, para. 542
(WT/DS267/AB/R)

. . . Like the Panel, we do not believe that the scope of paragraph 7 is limited to measures that have an import substitution component in them. There could be other measures covered by paragraph 7 of Annex 3 that do not necessarily have such a component. Indeed, Brazil submits that if the Step 2 payments were provided to United States processors of cotton, regardless of the origin of the cotton, these processors "would still buy *at least* some U.S. upland cotton, so producers would continue to derive *some* benefit". Thus, paragraph 7 of Annex 3 refers more broadly to measures directed at agricultural processors that benefit producers of a basic agricultural product and, contrary to the United States' assertion, it is not rendered inutile by the Panel's interpretation. WTO Members may still provide subsidies directed at agricultural processors that benefit producers of a basic agricultural commodity in accordance with the *Agreement on Agriculture*, as long as such subsidies do not include an import substitution component.

S.2.14A.3 *US – Upland Cotton*, para. 545
(WT/DS267/AB/R)

Article 6.3 does not authorize subsidies that are contingent on the use of domestic over imported goods. It only provides that a WTO Member shall be considered to be in compliance with its domestic support *reduction commitments* if its Current Total AMS does not exceed that Member's annual or final bound commitment level specified in its Schedule. It does not say that compliance with Article 6.3 of the *Agreement on Agriculture* insulates the subsidy from the prohibition in Article 3.1(b). . . .

S.2.14A.4 *US – Upland Cotton*, para. 546
(WT/DS267/AB/R)

. . . we find that paragraph 7 of Annex 3 and Article 6.3 of the *Agreement on Agriculture* do not deal specifically with the same matter as Article 3.1(b) of the *SCM Agreement*, that is, subsidies contingent upon the use of domestic over imported goods.

S.2.14A.5 *US – Upland Cotton*, para. 547
(WT/DS267/AB/R)

We are mindful that the introductory language of Article 3.1 of the *SCM Agreement* clarifies that this provision applies "[e]xcept as provided in the Agreement on Agriculture". Furthermore, as the United States has pointed out, this introductory language applies to both the export subsidy prohibition in paragraph (a) and to the prohibition on import substitution subsidies in paragraph (b) of Article 3.1. As we explained previously, in our review of the provisions of the *Agreement on Agriculture* [paragraph 7 of Annex 3 and Article 6.3 of the *Agreement on Agriculture*] relied on by the United States, we did not find a provision that deals specifically with subsidies that have an import substitution component. By contrast, the prohibition on the provision of subsidies contingent upon the use of domestic over imported goods in Article 3.1(b) of the *SCM Agreement* is explicit and clear. Because Article 3.1(b) treats subsidies contingent on the use of domestic over imported products as prohibited subsidies, it would be expected that the drafters would have included an equally explicit and clear provision in the *Agreement on Agriculture* if they had indeed intended to authorize such prohibited subsidies provided in connection with agricultural goods. We find no provision in the *Agreement on Agriculture* dealing specifically with subsidies contingent upon the use of domestic over imported agricultural goods.

S.2.14A.6 *US – Upland Cotton*, para. 549
(WT/DS267/AB/R)

. . . Furthermore, as the Appellate Body has explained, "a treaty interpreter must read all applicable provisions of a treaty in a way that gives meaning *to all* of them, harmoniously". We agree with the Panel that "Article 3.1(b) of the *SCM Agreement* can be read together with the *Agreement on Agriculture* provisions relating to domestic support in a coherent and consistent manner which gives full and effective meaning to all of their terms".

S.2.14A.7 *US – Upland Cotton*, para. 550
(WT/DS267/AB/R)

In sum, we are not persuaded by the United States' submission that the prohibition in Article 3.1(b) of the *SCM Agreement* is inapplicable to import substitution subsidies provided in connection with products falling under the *Agreement on Agriculture*. WTO Members may still provide domestic support that is consistent with their reduction commitments under the *Agreement on Agriculture*. In providing such domestic support, however, WTO Members must be mindful of their other WTO obligations, including the prohibition in Article 3.1(b) of the *SCM Agreement* on the provision of subsidies that are contingent on the use of domestic over imported goods.

S.2.15 Article 3.1(b) – "contingent upon the use of domestic over imported products"

S.2.15.1 *Canada – Autos*, para. 123
(WT/DS139/AB/R, WT/DS142/AB/R)

In our discussion of Article 3.1(a) in Section VI of this Report, we recalled that in *Canada – Aircraft* [Appellate Body Report, para. 166] we stated that "the ordinary connotation of 'contingent' is 'conditional' or 'dependent for its existence on something else'." Thus, a subsidy is prohibited under Article 3.1(a) if it is "conditional" upon export performance, that is, if it is "dependent for its existence on" export performance. In addition, in *Canada – Aircraft*, we stated that contingency "in law" is demonstrated "on the basis of the *words* of the relevant legislation, regulation or other legal instrument." (emphasis added) As we have already explained, such conditionality can be derived by necessary implication from the words actually used in the measure. We believe that this legal standard applies not only to "contingency" under Article 3.1(a), but also to "contingency" under Article 3.1(b) of the *SCM Agreement*.

S.2.15.2 *Canada – Autos*, paras. 131–132
(WT/DS139/AB/R, WT/DS142/AB/R)

In our view, the Panel's examination of the CVA requirements for specific manufacturers was insufficient for a reasoned determination of whether contingency "in law" on the use of domestic over imported goods exists. For the MVTO 1998 manufacturers and most SRO manufacturers, the Panel did not make findings as to what the actual CVA requirements are and how they operate for individual manufacturers. Without this vital information, we do not believe the Panel knew enough about the measure to determine whether the CVA requirements were contingent "in law" upon the use of domestic over imported goods. We recall that the Panel did make a finding as to the level of the CVA requirements for one company, CAMI. The Panel stated that the CVA requirements for CAMI are 60 per cent of the cost of sales of vehicles sold in Canada. At this level, it may well be that the CVA requirements operate as a condition for using domestic over imported goods. However, the Panel did *not* examine how the CVA requirements would actually operate at a level of 60 per cent.

The Panel's failure to examine fully the legal instruments at issue here and their implications for individual manufacturers vitiates its conclusion that the CVA requirements do not make the import duty exemption contingent "in law" upon the use of domestic over imported goods. In the absence of an examination of the operation of the applicable CVA requirements for individual manufacturers, the Panel simply did not have a sufficient basis for its finding on the issue of "in law" contingency. Thus, we conclude that the Panel erred in conducting its "in law" contingency analysis.

S.2.15.3 *US – Upland Cotton*, para. 544

(WT/DS267/AB/R)

. . . Article 3.1(b) of the *SCM Agreement* prohibits subsidies that are contingent – that is, "conditional" – on the use of domestic over imported goods.

S.2.16 Article 3.1(b) – Contingent in law and contingent in fact

S.2.16.1 *Canada – Autos*, paras. 139–143

(WT/DS139/AB/R, WT/DS142/AB/R)

. . . we observe that the ordinary meaning of the phrase "contingent . . . upon the use of domestic over imported goods" is not conclusive as to whether Article 3.1(b) covers both subsidies contingent "in law" and subsidies contingent "in fact" upon the use of domestic over imported goods. Just as there is nothing in the language of Article 3.1(b) that specifically *includes* subsidies contingent "in fact", so, too, is there nothing in that language that specifically *excludes* subsidies contingent "in fact" from the scope of coverage of this provision. As the text of the provision is not conclusive on this point, we must turn to additional means of interpretation. Accordingly, we look for guidance to the relevant context of the provision.

Although we agree with the Panel that Article 3.1(a) is relevant context, we believe that other contextual aspects should also be examined. First, we note that Article III:4 of the GATT 1994 also addresses measures that favour the use of domestic over imported goods, albeit with different legal terms and with a different scope. Nevertheless, both Article III:4 of the GATT 1994 and Article 3.1(b) of the *SCM Agreement* apply to measures that require the use of domestic goods over imports. Article III:4 of the GATT 1994 covers both *de jure* and *de facto* inconsistency. Thus, it would be most surprising if a similar provision in the *SCM Agreement* applied only to situations involving *de jure* inconsistency.

Second, we recall our findings in *European Communities – Regime for the Importation, Sale and Distribution of Bananas* ("*European Communities – Bananas*") on whether or not Article of the GATS covers cases of *de facto* discrimination. In that case, the Panel found that Article XVII of the GATS provides relevant context for determining whether Article of the GATS applies to both *de jure* and *de facto* discrimination. On this issue, we said:

> Article XVII of the GATS is merely one of many provisions in the *WTO Agreement* that require the obligation of providing "treatment no less favourable". The possibility that the two Articles may not have exactly the same meaning does *not* imply that the intention of the drafters of the GATS was that a *de jure*, or formal, standard should apply in Article of the GATS. If that were the intention, why does Article not say as much? The obligation imposed by Article is unqualified. The ordinary meaning of this provision does not exclude *de facto* discrimination. [Appellate Body Report, para. 233]

We believe the same reasoning is applicable here. The fact that Article 3.1(a) refers to "in law or in fact", while those words are absent from Article 3.1(b), does not necessarily mean that Article 3.1(b) extends only to *de jure* contingency.

Finally, we believe that a finding that Article 3.1(b) extends only to contingency "in law" upon the use of domestic over imported goods would be contrary to the object and purpose of the *SCM Agreement* because it would make circumvention of obligations by Members too easy. We expressed a similar concern with respect to the GATS in *European Communities – Bananas* when we said:

> Moreover, if Article was not applicable to *de facto* discrimination, it would not be difficult – and, indeed, it would be a good deal easier in the case of trade in services, than in the case of trade in goods – to devise discriminatory measures aimed at circumventing the basic purpose of that Article. [Appellate Body Report, para. 233]

For all these reasons, we believe that the Panel erred in finding that Article 3.1(b) does not extend to subsidies contingent "in fact" upon the use of domestic over imported goods. We, therefore, reverse the Panel's broad conclusion that "Article 3.1(b) extends only to contingency in law."

S.2.17 Article 4, paragraphs 1 to 4 – Consultations

S.2.17.1 *Brazil – Aircraft*, paras. 131–132

(WT/DS46/AB/R)

In our view, Articles 4 and 6 of the DSU, as well as paragraphs 1 to 4 of Article 4 of the *SCM Agreement*, set forth a process by which a complaining party must request consultations, and consultations must be held, before a matter may be referred to the DSB for the establishment of a panel. Under Article 4.3 of the *SCM Agreement*, moreover, the purpose of consultations is "to clarify the facts of the situation and to arrive at a mutually agreed solution."

We do not believe, however, that Articles 4 and 6 of the DSU, or paragraphs 1 to 4 of Article 4 of the *SCM Agreement*, require a *precise and exact identity* between the specific measures that were the subject of consultations and the specific measures identified in the request for the establishment of a panel. . . .

S.2.18 Article 4.2 – "statement of available evidence"

S.2.18.1 *US – FSC*, para. 159
(WT/DS108/AB/R)

. . . It is clear to us that Article 4.4 of the DSU and Article 4.2 of the *SCM Agreement* can and should be read and applied together, so that a request for consultations relating to a prohibited subsidy claim under the *SCM Agreement* must satisfy the requirements of both provisions.

S.2.18.2 *US – FSC*, para. 161
(WT/DS108/AB/R)

We emphasize that this additional requirement of "a statement of available evidence" under Article 4.2 of the *SCM Agreement* is distinct from – and not satisfied by compliance with – the requirements of Article 4.4 of the DSU. . . .

S.2.18.3 *US – Upland Cotton*, para. 308
(WT/DS267/AB/R)

We recognize that the statement of available evidence plays an important role in WTO dispute settlement. The adequacy of the statement of available evidence must be determined on a case by case basis. As the Panel stated, moreover, the "statement of available evidence . . . is the starting point for consultations, and for the emergence of more evidence concerning the measures by reason of the clarification of the 'situation' ". It is, therefore, important to bear in mind that the requirement to submit a statement of available evidence applies in the earliest stages of WTO dispute settlement, and that the requirement is to provide a "statement" of the evidence and not the evidence itself.

S.2.19 Article 4.7 – "withdraw the subsidy without delay"

S.2.19.1 *Brazil – Aircraft (Article 21.5 – Canada)*, para. 45
(WT/DS46/AB/RW)

Turning to the ordinary meaning of "withdraw", we observe first that this word has been defined as "remove" or "take away", and as "to take away what has been enjoyed; to take from." This definition suggests that "withdrawal" of a subsidy, under Article 4.7 of the *SCM Agreement*, refers to the "removal" or "taking away" of that subsidy . . . In our view, to continue to make payments under an export subsidy measure found to be prohibited is not consistent with the obligation to "withdraw" prohibited export subsidies, in the sense of "removing" or "taking away". . . .

S.2.19.2 *US – FSC (Article 21.5 – EC)*, para. 230
(WT/DS108/AB/RW)

. . . a Member's obligation under Article 4.7 of the *SCM Agreement* to withdraw prohibited subsidies "without delay" is unaffected by contractual obligations that the Member itself may have assumed under municipal law. Likewise, a Member's obligation to withdraw prohibited export subsidies, under Article 4.7 of the *SCM Agreement*, cannot be affected by contractual obligations which private parties may have assumed *inter se* in reliance on laws conferring prohibited export subsidies. . . .

S.2.19.3 *Brazil – Aircraft*, para. 192
(WT/DS46/AB/R)

With respect to implementation of the recommendations or rulings of the DSB in a dispute brought under Article 4 of the *SCM Agreement*, there is a significant difference between the relevant rules and procedures of the DSU and the special or additional rules and procedures set forth in Article 4.7 of the *SCM Agreement*. Therefore, the provisions of Article 21.3 of the DSU are not relevant in determining the period of time for implementation of a finding of inconsistency with the prohibited subsidies provisions of Part of the *SCM Agreement*. . . Article 4.7 of the *SCM Agreement*, which is applicable to this case, stipulates a time-period. . . .

S.2.19.4 *EC – Export Subsidies on Sugar*, paras. 333–335
(WT/DS265/AB/R, WT/DS266/AB/R, WT/DS283/AB/R)

Pursuant to Article 1.2 of the DSU, the situation is different for disputes brought under Part II of the *SCM Agreement*. The *SCM Agreement* contains "special rules and additional procedures on dispute settlement" in respect of subsidies prohibited under Article 3 of the *SCM Agreement*. . . .

Thus, where a panel finds that a complaining Member has established that the subsidy in question is prohibited within the meaning of Article 3 of the *SCM Agreement*, it shall make an additional recommendation as described in Article 4.7. Upon adoption, this additional recommendation – that the subsidizing Member "withdraw the subsidy without delay" – will become a recommendation or ruling of the DSB.

In this case, the Panel's findings under Articles 3 and 8 of the *Agreement on Agriculture* were not sufficient to "fully resolve" the dispute. This is because, in declining to rule on the Complaining Parties' claims under Article 3 of the *SCM Agreement*, the Panel precluded the possibility of a remedy being made available to the Complaining Parties, pursuant to Article 4.7 of the *SCM Agreement*, in the event of the Panel finding in favour of the Complaining Parties with respect to their claims under Article 3 of the *SCM Agreement*. Moreover, in declining to rule on the Complaining Parties' claims under Article 3 of the *SCM Agreement*, the Panel failed to discharge its obligation under Article 11 of the DSU by failing to make "such other findings as will assist the DSB in making the recommendations or in giving the rulings provided for in the covered agreements", namely, a recommendation or ruling by the DSB pursuant to Article 4.7. This constitutes false judicial economy and legal error.

S.2.19.5 *EC – Export Subsidies on Sugar*, para. 340
(WT/DS265/AB/R, WT/DS266/AB/R, WT/DS283/AB/R)

Moreover, we do not have the requisite factual findings to complete the legal analysis. In particular, we do not have sufficient facts before us, as would be necessary to specify the period of time for withdrawal, as required by Article 4.7 of the *SCM Agreement*. We note in this respect that, when specifying what period would represent "without delay", panels have taken into account, *inter alia*, "the nature of the measures and the difficulties likely to be faced in implementing the recommendation". Based on our reading of the Panel Reports and the Panel record, we fail to see any evidence therein regarding the nature of the measures that would be required to "withdraw" the subsidy, which would permit us to make a recommendation under Article 4.7. Hence, *even if* we were able to examine the Complaining Parties' claims under the *SCM Agreement* and, *even if* we were to conclude that the *SCM Agreement* applies in the circumstances of this dispute and that the European Communities acted inconsistently with its obligations under the *SCM Agreement*, we would not necessarily be in a position to make a recommendation under Article 4.7 as to the time period for withdrawal of the subsidy.

S.2.19A Article 5 – "adverse effects" – Relationship with Article 6.3(c)

S.2.19A.1 *US – Upland Cotton*, paras. 485–486
(WT/DS267/AB/R)

Having found that the effect of the price-contingent subsidies is significant price suppression within the meaning of Article 6.3(c) of the *SCM Agreement*, the Panel then considered whether the United States had caused adverse effects in the form of serious prejudice to the interests of Brazil through the use of these subsidies, contrary to Article 5(c) of the *SCM Agreement*. The Panel found that the significant price suppression it had found under Article 6.3(c) of the *SCM Agreement* amounted to serious prejudice within the meaning of the Article 5(c) of the *SCM Agreement*, based on [two alternative reasons] . . .

. . . The Panel's primary reason was that if the effect of a subsidy is significant price suppression within the meaning of Article 6.3(c), this is sufficient, without more, to conclude that the subsidizing Member has caused serious prejudice to the interests of another Member within the meaning of Article 5(c). The Panel's alternative reason was that, even if this is not sufficient, Brazil had fulfilled the burden of demonstrating that the United States had caused serious prejudice to the interests of Brazil within the meaning of Article 5(c).

S.2.19A.2 *US – Upland Cotton*, para. 488
(WT/DS267/AB/R)

As neither party has appealed the Panel's finding . . . (regarding the sufficiency of a finding of an effect under Article 6.3(c) for a finding of serious prejudice under Article 5(c), in general terms) or the Panel's alternative finding . . . (regarding serious prejudice to the interests of Brazil in the particular circumstances of this dispute), we express no opinion on either of those findings. Nor do we address the Panel's consequential finding that the significant price suppression that it had found to be the effect of the price-contingent subsidies under Article 6.3(c) of the *SCM Agreement* amounted to serious prejudice within the meaning of Article 5(c) of the *SCM Agreement*. Accordingly, upon adoption of the Panel Report by the DSB, the Panel's findings in paragraphs 7.1390 and 7.1391 of the Panel Report as mentioned above would stand, without endorsement or rejection by the Appellate Body.

S.2.19B Article 6.3(c) – Serious Prejudice

S.2.19B.1 RELEVANT MARKET

S.2.19B.1.1 *US – Upland Cotton*, para. 400
(WT/DS267/AB/R)

Turning to the question of the relevant "market", we observe that Article 6.3(c) of the *SCM Agreement* addresses the situation where "the effect of the subsidy is . . . significant price suppression . . . in the same *market*". (emphasis added) As the Panel suggested, and the parties agree, it is up to the complaining Member to identify the market in which it alleges that the effect of a subsidy is significant price suppression and to demonstrate that the subsidy has that effect within the meaning of Article 6.3(c). . . .

S.2.19B.1.2 *US – Upland Cotton*, para. 402
(WT/DS267/AB/R)

On appeal, the United States submits that the Panel erred in interpreting the words "same market" in Article 6.3(c) of the *SCM Agreement* as including a "world market". It also submits that the Panel's finding that a "world market" exists for upland cotton is inconsistent with certain of its other findings. The United States also argues that, in any case, the Panel did not make a finding that United States and Brazilian upland cotton compete in the world market that it had identified for upland cotton. Brazil contends that significant price suppression under Article 6.3(c) "may apply to *any* 'market,' from local to global, and everything in between".

S.2.19B.1.3 *US – Upland Cotton*, paras. 404–405
(WT/DS267/AB/R)

The Panel described the ordinary meaning of the word "market" as:

> "a place . . . with a demand for a commodity or service";[1355] "a geographical area of demand for commodities or services"; "the area of economic activity in which buyers and sellers come together and the forces of supply and demand affect prices".[1356] [Panel Report, para. 7.1236]

[1355] *The New Shorter Oxford English Dictionary* (1993).
[1356] *Merriam-Webster Dictionary online*.

We accept that this is an adequate description of the ordinary meaning of the word "market" for the purposes of this dispute, and we do not understand the parties to dispute it. This ordinary meaning does not, of itself, impose any limitation on the "geographical area" that makes up any given market. Nor does it indicate that a "world market" cannot exist for a given product. As the Panel indicated, the "degree to which a market is limited by geography will depend on the product itself and its ability to be traded across distances".

S.2.19B.1.4 *US – Upland Cotton*, para. 406
(WT/DS267/AB/R)

The only express qualification on the type of "market" referred to in Article 6.3(c) is that it must be "the same" market. Aside from this qualification (to which we return below), Article 6.3(c) imposes no explicit geographical limitation on the scope of the relevant market. This contrasts with the other paragraphs of Article 6.3: paragraph (a) restricts the relevant market to "the market of the subsidizing Member"; paragraph (b) restricts the relevant market to "a third country market"; and paragraph (d) refers specifically to the "world market share". We agree with the Panel that this difference may indicate that the drafters did not intend to confine, *a priori*, the market examined under Article 6.3(c) to any particular area. Thus, the ordinary meaning of the word "market" in Article 6.3(c), when read in the context of the other paragraphs of Article 6.3, neither requires nor excludes the possibility of a national market or a world market.

S.2.19B.1.5 *US – Upland Cotton*, para. 407
(WT/DS267/AB/R)

Turning to the phrase "in the same market", it is clear to us from a plain reading of Article 6.3(c) that this phrase applies to all four situations covered in that provision, namely, "significant price undercutting", "significant price suppression, price depression [and] lost sales". We read the Panel Report and the participants' submissions as endorsing this interpretation. The phrase "in the same market" suggests that the subsidized product in question (United States upland cotton in this case) and the relevant product of the complaining Member must be "in the same market". In this appeal, the Panel and the participants agree that United States upland cotton and Brazilian upland cotton must be "in the same market" for Brazil's claim under Article 6.3(c) to succeed. Furthermore, the participants agree that these are like products.

S.2.19B.1.6 *US – Upland Cotton*, para. 408
(WT/DS267/AB/R)

When can two products be considered to be "in the same market" for the purposes of a claim of significant price suppression under Article 6.3(c)? Article 6.3(c) does not provide an explicit answer. However, recalling that one accepted definition of "market" is "the area of economic activity in which buyers and sellers come together and the forces of supply and demand affect prices", it seems reasonable to conclude that two products would be in the same market if they were engaged in actual or potential competition in that market. Thus, two products may be "in the same market" even if they are not necessarily sold at the same time and in the same place or country. As the Panel correctly pointed out, the scope of the "market", for determining the area of competition between two products, may depend on several factors such as the nature of the product, the homogeneity of the conditions of competition, and transport costs. This market for a particular product could well be a "world market". However, we agree with the Panel that the fact that a world market exists for one product does not necessarily mean that such a market exists for every product. Thus the determination of the relevant market under Article 6.3(c) of the *SCM Agreement* depends on the subsidized product in question. If a world market exists for the product in question, Article 6.3(c) does not exclude the possibility of this "world market" being the "same market" for the purposes of a significant price suppression analysis under that Article.

S.2.19B.2 RELEVANT PRICE

S.2.19B.2.1 *US – Upland Cotton*, paras. 416–417 (WT/DS267/AB/R)

...The question before us is whether it was sufficient for the Panel to analyze the price of upland cotton in general in the world market or whether the Panel was required to analyze the price of Brazilian upland cotton in the world market and find significant price suppression with respect to that price.

...Therefore, the Panel found that the A-Index adequately reflected prices in the world market for upland cotton. The Panel also found that "developments in the world upland cotton price would inevitably affect prices" wherever Brazilian and United States upland cotton compete, "due to the nature of the world prices in question and the nature of the world upland cotton market, and the relative proportion of that market enjoyed by the United States and Brazil". It was not necessary, in these circumstances, for the Panel to proceed to a separate analysis of the prices of Brazilian upland cotton in the world market.

S.2.19B.3 ORDER OF ANALYSIS

S.2.19B.3.1 *US – Upland Cotton*, paras. 431–433 (WT/DS267/AB/R)

As noted above, Article 6.3(c) is silent as to the sequence of steps to be followed in assessing whether the effect of a subsidy is significant price suppression. We note that Article 6.8 indicates that the existence of serious prejudice pursuant to Articles 5(c) and 6.3(c) is to be determined on the basis of information submitted to or obtained by the panel, including information submitted in accordance with Annex V of the *SCM Agreement*. Annex V provides some limited guidance about the type of information on which a panel might base its assessment under Article 6.3(c). But we find little other guidance on this issue. The text of Article 6.3(c) does not, however, preclude the approach taken by the Panel to examine first whether significant price suppression exists and then, if it is found to exist, to proceed further to examine whether the significant price suppression is the effect of the subsidy. The Panel evidently considered that, in the absence of significant price suppression, it would not need to proceed to analyze the effect of the subsidy. We see no legal error in this approach.

One might contend that, having decided to separate its analysis of significant price suppression from its analysis of the effects of the challenged subsidies, the Panel's price suppression analysis should have addressed prices without reference to the subsidies and their effects. ...

However, the ordinary meaning of the transitive verb "suppress" implies the existence of a subject (the challenged subsidies) and an object (in this case, prices in the world market for upland cotton). This suggests that it would be difficult to make a judgement on significant price *suppression* without taking into account the effect of the subsidies. The Panel's definition of price suppression, explained above, reflects this problem; it includes the notion that prices "do not increase when they *otherwise* would have" or "they do actually increase, but the increase is less than it *otherwise* would have been". The word "otherwise" in this context refers to the hypothetical situation in which the challenged subsidies are absent. Therefore, the fact that the Panel may have addressed some of the same or similar factors in its reasoning as to significant price suppression and its reasoning as to "effects" is not necessarily wrong.

S.2.19B.4 SIGNIFICANT PRICE SUPPRESSION

S.2.19B.4.1 *US – Upland Cotton*, paras. 423–427 (WT/DS267/AB/R)

... In explaining [the term "price suppression"], the Panel stated, in paragraph 7.1277 of the Panel Report:

> Thus, "*price suppression*" refers to the situation where "prices" – in terms of the "amount of money set for sale of upland cotton" or the "value or worth" of upland cotton – either are prevented or inhibited from rising (i.e. they do not increase when they otherwise would have) or they do actually increase, but the increase is less than it otherwise would have been. *Price depression* refers to the situation where "prices" are pressed down, or reduced.[1388]

[1388] In the remainder of our analysis, we use the term "price suppression" to refer both to an actual decline (which otherwise would not have declined, or would have done so to a lesser degree) and an increase in prices (which otherwise would have increased to a greater degree). (emphasis added)

Although the Panel first identified "price suppression" and "price depression" as two separate concepts in paragraph 7.1277, footnote 1388 of the Panel Report suggests that, for its analysis, the Panel used the term "price suppression" to refer to both price suppression and price depression. We recognize that "the situation where 'prices' ... are prevented or inhibited from rising" and "the situation where 'prices' are pressed down, or reduced" may overlap. Nevertheless, it would have been preferable, in our view, for the Panel to avoid using the term "price suppression" as short-hand for both price suppression and price depression, given that Article 6.3(c) of the *SCM Agreement* refers to "price suppression" and "price depression" as distinct concepts. We agree, however, that the Panel's description of "price suppression" in paragraph 7.1277 of the Panel Report reflects the ordinary meaning of that term, particularly when read in conjunction with the French and Spanish versions of Article 6.3(c), as required by Article 33(3) of the *Vienna Convention on the Law of Treaties* (the "*Vienna Convention*").

The Panel described its task in assessing "price suppression" under Article 6.3(c) as follows:

> We need to examine whether these prices were suppressed, that is, lower than they would have been without the United States subsidies in respect of upland cotton. [Panel Report, para. 7.1288]

As regards the word "significant" in the context of "significant price suppression" in Article 6.3(c), the Panel found that this word means "important, notable or consequential".

Article 6.3(c) does not set forth any specific methodology for determining whether the effect of a subsidy is significant price suppression. There may well be different ways to make this determination. However, we find no difficulty with the Panel's approach in the particular circumstances of this dispute. We therefore turn to an examination of how the Panel carried out its assessment.

S.2.19B.4.2 *US – Upland Cotton*, para. 434
(WT/DS267/AB/R)

The specific factors that the Panel examined in determining whether or not "price suppression" had occurred were: "(a) the relative magnitude of the United States' production and exports in the world upland cotton market; (b) general price trends; and (c) the nature of the subsidies at issue, and in particular, whether or not the nature of these subsidies is such as to have discernible price suppressive effects". In the absence of explicit guidance on assessing significant price suppression in the text of Article 6.3(c), we have no reason to reject the relevance of these factors for the Panel's assessment in the present case. An assessment of "general price trends" is clearly relevant to significant price suppression (although, as the Panel itself recognized, price trends alone are not conclusive). The two other factors – the nature of the subsidies and the relative magnitude of the United States' production and exports of upland cotton – are also relevant for this assessment. We are not persuaded that the fact that these latter factors were also considered in connection with the Panel's analysis of "the effect of the subsidy" amounts to legal error for that reason alone.

S.2.19B.5 EFFECT OF THE SUBSIDY – CAUSATION AND NON-ATTRIBUTION

S.2.19B.5.1 *US – Upland Cotton*, paras. 435–436
(WT/DS267/AB/R)

Turning to the Panel's assessment of the "effect of the subsidy", the Panel addressed the question whether there was a "causal link" between the price-contingent subsidies and the significant price suppression it had found. It then addressed the impact of "[o]ther alleged causal factors". We observe that Article 6.3(c) does not use the word "cause"; rather, it states that "the effect of the subsidy is . . . significant price suppression". However, the ordinary meaning of the noun "effect" is "[s]omething . . . caused or produced; a result, a consequence". The "something" in this context is significant price suppression, and thus the question is whether significant price suppression is "caused" by or is a "result" or "consequence" of the challenged subsidy. The Panel's conclusion that "[t]he text of the treaty requires the establishment of a causal link between the subsidy and the significant price suppression" is thus consistent with this ordinary meaning of the term "effect". This is also confirmed by the context provided by Article 5(c) of the *SCM Agreement* . . .

As the Panel pointed out, "Articles 5 and 6.3 . . . do not contain the more elaborate and precise 'causation' and non-attribution language" found in the trade remedy provisions of the *SCM Agreement*. Part V of the *SCM Agreement*, which relates to the imposition of countervailing duties, requires, *inter alia*, an examination of "any known factors other than the subsidized imports which at the same time are injuring the domestic industry". However, such causation requirements have not been expressly prescribed for an examination of *serious prejudice* under Article 5(c) and Article 6.3(c) in Part III of the *SCM Agreement*. This suggests that a panel has a certain degree of discretion in selecting an appropriate methodology for determining whether the "effect" of a subsidy is significant price suppression under Article 6.3(c).

S.2.19B.5.2 *US – Upland Cotton*, para. 437
(WT/DS267/AB/R)

Nevertheless, we agree with the Panel that it is necessary to ensure that the effects of other factors on prices are not improperly attributed to the challenged subsidies. Pursuant to Article 6.3(c) of the *SCM Agreement*, "[s]erious prejudice in the sense of paragraph (c) of Article 5 may arise" when "the effect of *the subsidy* is . . . significant price suppression". (emphasis added) If the significant price suppression found in the world market for upland cotton were caused by factors other than the challenged subsidies, then that price suppression would not be "the effect of" the challenged subsidies in the sense of Article 6.3(c). Therefore, we do not find fault with the Panel's approach of "examin[ing] whether or not 'the effect of the subsidy' is the significant price suppression which [it had] found to exist in the same world market" and separately "consider[ing] the role of other alleged causal factors in the record before [it] which may affect [the] analysis of the causal link between the United States subsidies and the significant price suppression."

S.2.19B.5.3 *US – Upland Cotton*, para. 438
(WT/DS267/AB/R)

The Panel's approach with respect to causation and non-attribution is similar to that reflected in Appellate Body decisions in the context of other WTO agreements. . . . It must be borne in mind that these provisions of the *Agreement on Safeguards* and the *Anti-Dumping Agreement*, as well as the provisions of Part V of the *SCM Agreement*, relate to a determination of "injury" rather than "serious prejudice", and they apply in different contexts and with different purposes. Therefore, they must not be automatically transposed into Part III of the *SCM Agreement*. Nevertheless, they may suggest ways of assessing whether the effect of a subsidy is significant price suppression rather than it being the effect of other factors.

S.2.19B.5.4 *US – Upland Cotton*, para. 451
(WT/DS267/AB/R)

. . . in our view, one would normally expect a discernible correlation between significantly suppressed prices and the challenged subsidies if the effect of these subsidies is significant price suppression. Accordingly, this is an important factor in any analysis of whether the effect of a subsidy is significant price suppression within the meaning of Article 6.3(c). However, we recognize that mere correlation between payment of subsidies and significantly suppressed prices would be insufficient, without more, to prove that the effect of the subsidies is significant price suppression.

S.2.19B.5.5 *US – Upland Cotton*, para. 453
(WT/DS267/AB/R)

We agree with the general proposition of the United States that variable costs may play a role in farmers' decision-making as to whether to plant upland cotton or some alternative crop, and how much of each crop to plant. From a short-term perspective, variable costs may be particularly important. However, from a longer-term perspective, total costs may be relevant. . . . In the circumstances of this dispute, we do not consider that the Panel's reliance on total rather than variable costs of production amounts to an error vitiating the Panel's analysis under Article 6.3(c).

S.2.19B.5.6 *US – Upland Cotton*, paras. 457–458
(WT/DS267/AB/R)

. . . In sum, the Panel Report shows that it examined the other factors raised by the United States. Although the Panel found that some of them had price-suppressive effects, it did not attribute those effects to the United States' price-contingent subsidies.

Unlike in certain other instances under the WTO agreements, a panel conducting an analysis under Article 6.3(c) of the *SCM Agreement* is the first trier of facts, rather than a reviewer of factual determinations made by a domestic investigating authority. Bearing this in mind, we underline the responsibility of panels in gathering and analyzing relevant factual data and information in assessing claims under Article 6.3(c) in order to arrive at reasoned conclusions. In this case, the voluminous evidentiary record before the Panel included several economic studies, and substantial data and information. For its part, the Panel posed a large number of questions to which the parties submitted detailed answers. Overall, the Panel evidently conducted an extensive analysis, but we believe that, in its reasoning, the Panel could have provided a more detailed explanation of its analysis of the complex facts and economic arguments arising in this dispute. The Panel could have done so in order to demonstrate precisely how it evaluated the different factors bearing on the relationship between the price-contingent subsidies and significant price suppression. Nevertheless, in the light of the Panel's examination of the relevant evidence, coupled with its legal reasoning, we find no legal error in the Panel's causation analysis.

S.2.19B.6 MAGNITUDE OF SUBSIDIES

S.2.19B.6.1 *US – Upland Cotton*, para. 461
(WT/DS267/AB/R)

Beginning with the text of Article 6.3(c), we note that this provision does not state explicitly that a panel needs to quantify the amount of the challenged subsidy. However, in assessing whether "the effect of the subsidy is . . . significant price suppression", and ultimately serious prejudice, a panel will need to consider the effects of the subsidy on prices. The magnitude of the subsidy is an important factor in this analysis. A large subsidy that is closely linked to prices of the relevant product is likely to have a greater impact on prices than a small subsidy that is less closely linked to prices. All other things being equal, the smaller the subsidy for a given product, the smaller the degree to which it will affect the costs or revenue of the recipient, and the smaller its likely impact on the prices charged by the recipient for the product. However, the size of a subsidy is only one of the factors that may be relevant to the determination of the effects of a challenged subsidy. A panel needs to assess the effect of the subsidy taking into account all relevant factors.

S.2.19B.6.2 *US – Upland Cotton*, paras. 463–464
(WT/DS267/AB/R)

In order for a panel to find that a subsidy has the effect of significant price suppression, or some other effect mentioned in Article 6.3(c), the panel must determine that the payment is a specific subsidy within the meaning of Articles 1 and 2 of the *SCM Agreement*. The Panel did so in this dispute, and we do not understand the United States to contest this conclusion. Rather, the United States argues that a panel needs to quantify the amount of the "benefit" conferred on the subsidized product by a challenged subsidy. However, the definitions of a specific subsidy in Articles 1 and 2 do not expressly require the quantification of the "benefit" conferred by the subsidy on any particular product.

Turning to the context of Article 6.3(c), we note that Article 6.1(a) – which has now expired – contains the only reference in Part III of the *SCM Agreement* to a calculation of *ad valorem* subsidization of a product. Footnote 14 to Article 6.1(a) explains that this calculation is to be performed in accordance with Annex IV on the "Calculation of the Total *Ad Valorem* Subsidization (Paragraph 1(a) of Article 6)". No similar provisions are found in Article 6.3(c), which suggests that no precise quantification is envisaged in that provision.

S.2.19B.6.3 *US – Upland Cotton*, paras. 465–466
(WT/DS267/AB/R)

The provisions of the *SCM Agreement* regarding quantification of subsidies reveal that the methodological approaches to quantification may be quite different, depending on the context and purpose of quantification. The absence of any indication in Article 6.3(c) as to whether one of these methods, or any other method, should be used suggests to us that no such precise quantification was envisaged as a necessary prerequisite for a panel's analysis under Article 6.3(c).

Pursuant to Article 6.8, "the existence of serious prejudice" under Article 6.3(c) "should be determined on the basis of the information submitted to or obtained by the panel, including information submitted in accordance with the provisions of Annex V" of the *SCM Agreement*. The United States is correct that Annex V refers to "information . . . as necessary to establish the existence and amount of subsidization" (in paragraph 2) and "data concerning the amount of the subsidy in question" (in paragraph 5), but Annex V also refers to other information. This demonstrates that the amount of the subsidy, as well as other elements, are relevant for the assessment of whether price suppression exists. But we do not read Annex V as mandating the precise quantification of subsidies in order to determine their effect under Article 6.3(c).

S.2.19B.6.4 *US – Upland Cotton*, para. 467
(WT/DS267/AB/R)

In sum, reading Article 6.3(c) in the context of Article 6.8 and Annex V suggests that a panel should have regard to the magnitude of the challenged subsidy and its relationship to prices of the product in the relevant market when analyzing whether the effect of a subsidy is significant price suppression. In many cases, it may be difficult to decide this question in the absence of such an assessment. Nevertheless, this does not mean that Article 6.3(c) imposes an obligation on panels to quantify precisely the amount of a subsidy benefiting the product at issue in every case. A precise, definitive quantification of the subsidy is not required.

S.2.19B.7 "PASS-THROUGH" ANALYSIS

S.2.19B.7.1 *US – Upland Cotton*, para. 471
(WT/DS267/AB/R)

The United States contends that the Appellate Body's reasoning in *US – Softwood Lumber IV* [Appellate Body Report, *US – Softwood Lumber IV*, paras. 140–142] indicates that it cannot be presumed that a "subsidy", as defined in Article 1.1 of the *SCM Agreement*, provided to a producer of an input (such as raw cotton) "passes through" to the producer of the processed product (in this case, upland cotton lint). However, the Appellate Body's reasoning in that dispute focuses not on the requirements for establishing serious prejudice under Articles 5(c) and 6.3(c) of the *SCM Agreement*, but on the conduct of countervailing duty investigations pursuant to Part V of the *SCM Agreement*.

S.2.19B.7.2 *US – Upland Cotton*, para. 472
(WT/DS267/AB/R)

As we have already noted, the requirement in Article VI:3 of the GATT 1994 and Article 19.4 of the *SCM Agreement* that countervailing duties on a product be limited to the amount of the subsidy accruing to that product finds no parallel in the provisions on actionable subsidies and pertinent remedies under Part III of the *SCM Agreement*. Therefore, the need for a "pass-through" analysis under Part V of the *SCM Agreement* is not critical for an assessment of significant price suppression under Article 6.3(c) in Part III of the *SCM Agreement*. Nevertheless, we acknowledge that the "subsidized product" must be properly identified for purposes of significant price suppression under Article 6.3(c) of the *SCM Agreement*. And if the challenged payments do not, in fact, subsidize that product, this may undermine the conclusion that the effect of the subsidy is significant suppression of prices of that product in the relevant market.

S.2.19B.8 EFFECT OF SUBSIDIES OVER TIME

S.2.19B.8.1 *US – Upland Cotton*, para. 475
(WT/DS267/AB/R)

We observe that the United States' contention that the effect of a subsidy must be "allocated" or "expensed" to the year in which it is paid is confined to "recurring" subsidies, that is, subsidies paid on an annual basis. The United States acknowledges that "non-recurring" subsidies could be "allocated" to subsequent years as well. Article 6.3(c) of the *SCM Agreement* applies to a subsidy whether it is "recurring" or "non-recurring". This Article does not suggest that the effect of a subsidy is limited to or continues only for a specified period of time.

S.2.19B.8.2 *US – Upland Cotton*, para. 476
(WT/DS267/AB/R)

In this appeal, we are asked to address the limited question of whether the effect of a subsidy may continue beyond the year in which it was paid, in the context of a significant price suppression analysis under Article 6.3(c) of the *SCM Agreement*. Whether the effect of a subsidy begins and expires in the year in which it is paid or begins in one year and continues in any subsequent year, and how long a subsidy can be regarded as having effects, are fact-specific questions. The answers to these questions may depend on the nature of the subsidy and the product in question. We see nothing in the text of Article 6.3(c) that excludes *a priori* the possibility that the effect of a "recurring" subsidy may continue after the year in which it is paid. Article 6.3(c) deals with the "effect" of a subsidy, and not with the financial accounting of the amount of the subsidy.

S.2.19B.8.3 *US – Upland Cotton*, para. 477
(WT/DS267/AB/R)

The context of Article 6.3(c) within Part III of the *SCM Agreement* does not support the suggestion that the effect of a subsidy is immediate, short-lived, or limited to one year, regardless of whether or not it is paid every year. Article 6.2 of the *SCM Agreement* refers to the possibility of the subsidizing Member demonstrating that "the subsidy in question *has not resulted* in any of the effects enumerated in paragraph 3". (emphasis added) The word "resulted" in this sentence highlights the temporal relationship between the subsidy and the effect, in that one might expect a time lag between the provision of the subsidy and the resulting effect. In addition, the use of the present perfect tense in this provision implies that some time may have passed between the granting of the subsidy and the demonstration of the absence of its effects.

S.2.19B.8.4 *US – Upland Cotton*, para. 478
(WT/DS267/AB/R)

Article 6.4 of the *SCM Agreement* is also relevant context for interpreting Article 6.3(c). Article 6.4 requires that the displacement or impeding of exports be demonstrated "over an appropriately representative period", which "shall be at least one year", so that "clear trends" in changes in market share can be demonstrated. This suggests that the effect of a subsidy under Article 6.4 must be examined over a sufficiently long period of time and is not limited to the year in which it was paid. As the Panel has also pointed out in the context of Article 6.3(c), "[c]onsideration of developments over a period of longer than one year . . . provides a more robust basis for a serious prejudice evaluation than merely paying attention to developments in a single recent year".

S.2.19B.8.5 *US – Upland Cotton*, para. 482
(WT/DS267/AB/R)

For these reasons, we are not persuaded by the United States' contention that the effect of annually paid subsidies must be "allocated" or "expensed" solely to the year in which they are paid and that, therefore, the effect of such subsidies cannot be significant price suppression in any subsequent year. We do not agree with the proposition that, if subsidies are paid annually, their effects are also necessarily extinguished annually.

S.2.19C **Article 7.8 – Remedies.** *See also* Implementation Recommendations – Article 19.1 of the DSU (I.0)

S.2.19C.1 *US – Upland Cotton*, para. 273
(WT/DS267/AB/R)

. . . Article 7.8 of the *SCM Agreement* provides that, where it has been determined that "any subsidy has *resulted* in adverse effects to the interests of another Member", the subsidizing Member must "take appropriate steps *to remove the adverse effects* or . . . withdraw the subsidy". (emphasis added) The use of the word "resulted" suggests that there could be a time-lag between the payment of a subsidy and any consequential adverse effects. If expired measures underlying past payments could not be challenged in WTO dispute settlement proceedings, it would be difficult to seek a remedy for such adverse effects. Further – in contrast to Articles 3.7 and 19.1 of the DSU – the remedies under Article 7.8 of the *SCM Agreement* for adverse effects of a subsidy are (i) the withdrawal of the subsidy *or* (ii) the removal of adverse effects. Removal of adverse effects through actions other than the withdrawal of a subsidy could not occur if the expiration of a measure would automatically exclude it from a panel's terms of reference.

Article 10 and Footnote 36 – Application of Article VI of the GATT 1994. *See* SCM Agreement, Article 1.1 – Pass-through of indirect subsidies (S.2.10); SCM Agreement, Article VI:3 of the GATT 1994 – Subsidies (S.2.43)

Article 11 – Initiation and subsequent investigation. *See* SCM Agreement, Article 21.4 – Relationship with Articles 11 and 12 (S.2.33)

S.2.20 Article 11.4 – Initiation of an investigation

S.2.20.1 *US – Offset Act (Byrd Amendment)*, para. 283

(WT/DS217/AB/R, WT/DS234/AB/R)

A textual examination of Article 5.4 of the *Anti-Dumping Agreement* and Article 11.4 of the *SCM Agreement* reveals that those provisions contain no requirement that an investigating authority examine the motives of domestic producers that elect to support an investigation. Nor do they contain any explicit requirement that support be based on certain motives, rather than on others. The use of the terms "expressing support" and "expressly supporting" clarify that Articles 5.4 and 11.4 require only that authorities "determine" that support has been "expressed" by a sufficient number of domestic producers. Thus, in our view, an "examination" of the "degree" of support, and not the "nature" of support is required. In other words, it is the "quantity", rather than the "quality", of support that is the issue.

S.2.21 Article 11.9 – Termination of an investigation

S.2.21.1 *US – Carbon Steel*, paras. 67–68 and footnote 58

(WT/DS213/AB/R, WT/DS213/AB/R/Corr.1)

[Paragraph 9] is one of the eleven paragraphs of Article 11. The various paragraphs set forth rules of a mainly procedural and evidentiary nature. All of them relate to the authorities' initiation and conduct of a countervailing duty *investigation*, as would be expected given the overall title of Article 11 – "*Initiation and Subsequent Investigation*". Paragraph 9 of Article 11 requires authorities to terminate immediately investigative action in three situations. One of these is when the authorities are satisfied that the amount of the subsidy is less than 1 percent *ad valorem*.

Although the terms of Article 11.9 are detailed as regards the obligations imposed on authorities thereunder, none of the words in Article 11.9 suggests that the *de minimis* standard that it contains is applicable *beyond* the investigation phase of a countervailing duty proceeding.[58] In particular, Article 11.9 does *not* refer to Article 21.3, nor to reviews that may follow the imposition of a countervailing duty.

[58] We do not subscribe to the view, expressed by Japan, that the use of the word "cases" (rather than the word "investigation") in the second sentence of Article 11.9 means that the application of the *de minimis* standard set forth in that provision must be applied in *all* phases of countervailing duty proceedings – not only in investigations. The use of the word "cases" does not alter the fact that the terms of Article 11.9 apply the *de minimis* standard only to the investigation phase. We note further that the panel in *US – DRAMS* rejected a similar argument with respect to the meaning of the word "cases" in Article 5.8 of the *Anti-Dumping Agreement*, a provision almost identical to Article 11.9 of the *SCM Agreement*. (Panel Report, *US – DRAMS*, para. 6.87)

S.2.21.2 *US – Carbon Steel*, para. 69
(WT/DS213/AB/R, WT/DS213/AB/R/Corr.1)

. . . the technique of cross-referencing is frequently used in the *SCM Agreement* . . . These cross-references suggest to us that, when the negotiators of the *SCM Agreement* intended that the disciplines set forth in one provision be applied in another context, they did so expressly. In the light of the many express cross-references made in the *SCM Agreement*, we attach significance to the absence of any textual link between Article 21.3 reviews and the *de minimis* standard set forth in Article 11.9. . . .

S.2.21.3 *US – Carbon Steel*, para. 83
(WT/DS213/AB/R, WT/DS213/AB/R/Corr.1)

To us, there is nothing in Article 11.9 to suggest that its *de minimis* standard was intended to create a special category of "*non-injurious*" subsidization, or that it reflects a concept that subsidization at less than a *de minimis* threshold *can never* cause injury. For us, the *de minimis* standard in Article 11.9 does no more than lay down an agreed rule that if *de minimis* subsidization is found to exist in an original investigation, authorities are obliged to terminate their investigation, with the result that no countervailing duty can be imposed in such cases.

Article 12 – Evidence. *See* SCM Agreement, Article 21.4 – Relationship with Articles 11 and 12 (S.2.33)

S.2.22 **Article 14 – Chapeau – Calculation of the benefit to the "recipient".** *See also* SCM Agreement, Article 1.1(b) – Conferral of a benefit to a recipient (S.2.9)

S.2.22.1 *US – Softwood Lumber IV*, para. 91
(WT/DS257/AB/R)

. . . The chapeau of Article 14 requires that "*any*" method used by investigating authorities to calculate the benefit to the recipient shall be provided for in a WTO Member's legislation or regulations, and it requires that its application be transparent and adequately explained. The reference to "*any*" method in the chapeau clearly implies that more than one method consistent with Article 14 is available to investigating authorities for purposes of calculating the benefit to the recipient. . . .

S.2.22.2 *US – Softwood Lumber IV*, para. 92
(WT/DS257/AB/R)

. . . We agree with the Panel that the term "shall" in the last sentence of the chapeau of Article 14 suggests that calculating benefit consistently with the guidelines is mandatory. We also agree that the term "guidelines" suggests that Article 14 provides the "framework within which this calculation is to performed", although the "precise detailed method of calculation is not determined". Taken together, these terms establish mandatory parameters within which the benefit must be calculated, but they do not require using only one methodology for determining the adequacy of remuneration for the provision of goods by a government. . . .

S.2.23 Article 14(d) – Calculation of adequacy of remuneration

S.2.23.1 *US – Softwood Lumber IV*, para. 84
(WT/DS257/AB/R)

. . . Article 14(d) establishes that the provision of goods by a government shall not be considered as conferring a benefit unless the provision is made for less than adequate remuneration. As the Panel observed, the term "adequate" in this context means "sufficient, satisfactory". "Remuneration" is defined as "reward, recompense; payment, pay". Thus, a benefit is conferred when a government provides goods to a recipient and, in return, receives insufficient payment or compensation for those goods.

S.2.23.2 *US – Softwood Lumber IV*, para. 87
(WT/DS257/AB/R)

Turning first to the text of Article 14(d), we consider the submission of the United States that the term "market conditions" necessarily implies a market undistorted by the government's financial contribution . . . We agree with the Panel that "[t]he text of Article 14(d) [of the] SCM Agreement does not qualify in any way the 'market' conditions which are to be used as the benchmark . . . [a]s such, the text does not explicitly refer to a 'pure' market, to a market 'undistorted by government intervention', or to a 'fair market value'." . . .

S.2.23.3 *US – Softwood Lumber IV*, para. 89
(WT/DS257/AB/R)

As we see it, the phrase "in relation to" implies a comparative exercise, but its meaning is not limited to "in comparison with". The phrase "in relation to" has a meaning similar to the phrases "as regards" and "with respect to". These phrases do not denote the rigid comparison suggested by the Panel, but may imply a broader sense of "relation, connection, reference". Thus, the use of the phrase "in relation to" in Article 14(d) suggests that, contrary to the Panel's understanding, the drafters did not intend to exclude any possibility of using as a benchmark something other than private prices in the market of the country of provision. This is not to say, however, that private prices in the market of provision may be disregarded. Rather, it must be demonstrated that, based on the facts of the case, the benchmark chosen relates or refers to, or is connected with, the conditions prevailing in the market of the country of provision.

S.2.23.4 *US – Softwood Lumber IV*, para. 90
(WT/DS257/AB/R)

Although Article 14(d) does not dictate that private prices are to be used as the *exclusive* benchmark in all situations, it does emphasize by its terms that prices of similar goods sold by private suppliers in the country of provision are the primary benchmark that investigating authorities must use when determining whether goods have been provided by a government for less than adequate remuneration. In this case, both participants and the third participants agree that the starting-point, when determining adequacy of remuneration, is the prices at which the same or similar goods are sold by private suppliers in arm's length transactions in the country of provision. This approach reflects the fact that private prices in the market of provision will generally represent an appropriate measure of the "adequacy of remuneration" for the provision of goods. However, this may not always be the case. As will be explained below, investigating authorities may use a benchmark other than private prices in the country of provision under Article 14(d), if it is first established that private prices in that country are distorted because of the government's predominant role in providing those goods.

S.2.23.5 *US – Softwood Lumber IV*, para. 93
(WT/DS257/AB/R)

Furthermore, the Panel's interpretation is not supported by the objective of Article 14 . . . Under the approach advocated by the Panel (that is, private prices in the country of provision must be used whenever they exist), however, there may be situations in which there is no way of telling whether the recipient is "better off" *absent the financial contribution*. . . .

S.2.24 Article 14(d) – Alternative benchmark for calculating the adequacy of remuneration

S.2.24.1 *US – Softwood Lumber IV*, paras. 97–98
(WT/DS257/AB/R)

Having established that prices in the market of the country of provision are the primary, but not the exclusive, benchmark for calculating benefit, we come to the next question that arises in our analysis, namely, when an investigating authority may use a benchmark other than private prices in the country of provision for purposes of calculating the benefit under Article 14(d).

. . . the Panel . . . acknowledged that "it will in certain situations not be possible to use in-country prices" as a benchmark, and gave two examples of such situations . . . (i) where the government is the only supplier of the particular goods in the country; and, (ii) where the government administratively controls all of the prices for those goods in the country. . . .

S.2.24.2 *US – Softwood Lumber IV*, para. 100
(WT/DS257/AB/R)

In analyzing this question, we have some difficulty with the Panel's approach of treating a situation in which the government is the sole supplier of certain goods differently from a situation in which the government is the predominant supplier of those goods. In terms of market distortion and effect on prices, there may be little difference between situations where the government is the sole provider of certain goods and situations where the government has a predominant role in the market as a provider of those goods. . . .

S.2.24.3 *US – Softwood Lumber IV*, paras. 101–102
(WT/DS257/AB/R)

. . . When private prices are distorted because the government's participation in the market as a provider of the same or similar goods is so predominant that private suppliers will align their prices with those of the government-provided goods, it will not be possible to calculate benefit having regard exclusively to such prices.

We emphasize . . . the possibility under Article 14(d) for investigating authorities to consider a benchmark other than private prices in the country of provision is very limited . . . an allegation that a government is a significant supplier would not, on its own, prove distortion and allow an investigating authority to choose a benchmark other than private prices in the country of provision. The determination of whether private prices are distorted because of the government's predominant role in the market, as a provider of certain goods, must be made on a case-by-case basis, according to the particular facts underlying each countervailing duty investigation.

S.2.24.4 *US – Softwood Lumber IV*, para. 106
(WT/DS257/AB/R)

We agree with the submissions of the participants and third participants that alternative methods for determining the adequacy of remuneration could include proxies that take into account prices for similar goods quoted on world markets, or proxies constructed on the basis of production costs. We emphasize, however, that where an investigating authority proceeds in this manner, it is under an obligation to ensure that the resulting benchmark relates or refers to, or is connected with, prevailing market conditions in the country of provision, and must reflect price, quality, availability, marketability, transportation and other conditions of purchase or sale, as required by Article 14(d) . . . Nor are we required to determine the consistency with Article 14(d) of all the alternative methods mentioned by the participants and third participants; such assessment will depend on how any such method is applied in a particular case. We, therefore, make no findings on the WTO-consistency of any of these methods in the abstract.

S.2.24.5 *US – Softwood Lumber IV*, para. 108
(WT/DS257/AB/R)

. . . we observe that, when choosing an alternative method for determining the adequacy of remuneration, it has to be kept in mind that prices in the market of a WTO Member would be expected to reflect prevailing market conditions in that Member; they are unlikely to reflect conditions prevailing in another Member. Therefore, it cannot be presumed that market conditions prevailing in one Member, for instance the United States, relate or refer to, or are connected with, market conditions prevailing in another Member, such as Canada for example. Indeed, it seems to us that it would be difficult, from a practical point of view, for investigating authorities to replicate reliably market conditions prevailing in one country on the basis of market conditions prevailing in another country. First, there are numerous factors to be taken into account in making adjustments to market conditions prevailing in one country so as to replicate those prevailing in another country; secondly, it would be difficult to ensure that all necessary adjustments are made to prices in one country in order to develop a benchmark that relates or refers to, or is connected with, prevailing market conditions in another country, so as to reflect price, quality, availability, marketability, transportation and other conditions of purchase or sale in that other country.

S.2.24.6 *US – Softwood Lumber IV*, para. 109
(WT/DS257/AB/R)

It is clear, in the abstract, that different factors can result in one country having a comparative advantage over another with respect to the production of certain goods. In any event, any comparative advantage would be reflected in the market conditions prevailing in the country of provision and, therefore, would have to be taken into account and reflected in the adjustments made to any method used for the determination of adequacy of remuneration, if it is to relate or refer to, or be connected with, prevailing market conditions in the market of provision. This is because countervailing measures may be used only for the purpose of offsetting a subsidy bestowed upon a product, provided that it causes injury to the domestic industry producing the like product. They must not be used to offset differences in comparative advantages between countries.

S.2.24.7 *US – Softwood Lumber IV*, paras. 119–120
(WT/DS257/AB/R)

. . . we . . . find . . . that an investigating authority may use a benchmark other than private prices in the country of provision, when it has been established that private prices of the goods in question in that country are distorted, because of the predominant role of the government in the market as a provider of the same or similar goods.

We emphasize, however, that when an investigating authority proceeds in this manner, it is obliged, pursuant to Article 14(d), to ensure that the alternative benchmark it uses relates or refers to, or is connected with, prevailing market conditions in the country of provision, (including price, quality, availability, marketability, transportation and other conditions of purchase or sale), with a view to determining, ultimately, whether the goods at issue were provided by the government for less than adequate remuneration.

S.2.25 Article 15 – Determination of injury

S.2.25.1 *US – Carbon Steel*, paras. 79, 81

(WT/DS213/AB/R, WT/DS213/AB/R/Corr.1)

. . . Article 15 of the *SCM Agreement*, which deals with injury and how it is to be determined, refers, in its paragraph 3, to the *de minimis* standard in Article 11.9 only for the purpose of cumulation of imports. Moreover, . . .

. . . In defining the concept of injury, footnote 45 does not make any reference to the amount of subsidy involved.

. . .

Thus, in our view, the terms "subsidization" and "injury" each have an independent meaning in the *SCM Agreement* which is not derived by reference to the other. It is *unlikely* that very low levels of subsidization could be demonstrated to *cause* "material" injury. Yet such a possibility is not, *per se*, precluded by the Agreement itself, as injury is not defined in the *SCM Agreement* in relation to any specific level of subsidization.

S.2.26 Article 19.1 – Conditions for the imposition of countervailing duties

S.2.26.1 *US – Countervailing Measures on Certain EC Products*, para. 147

(WT/DS212/AB/R)

. . . In an original investigation, an investigating authority must establish all conditions set out in the *SCM Agreement* for the imposition of countervailing duties. Those obligations, identified in Article 19.1 of the *SCM Agreement*, read in conjunction with Article 1, include a determination of the existence of a "benefit". . . .

S.2.27 Article 19.3 – Imposition of countervailing duties on a non-discriminatory basis after aggregate investigation

S.2.27.1 *US – Softwood Lumber IV*, para. 152 and footnote 189

(WT/DS257/AB/R)

We agree with the United States that Article 19 of the *SCM Agreement* authorizes Members to perform an investigation on an *aggregate* basis. Article 19.3 requires that countervailing duties "shall be levied, in the appropriate amounts in each case, on a *non-discriminatory basis* on imports of such product from *all sources* found to be subsidized and causing injury". (emphasis added) Article 19.3 further provides that "[a]ny exporter whose exports are subject to a definitive countervailing duty *but who was not actually investigated* . . . shall be entitled to an expedited *review* in order that the investigating authorities promptly establish an *individual* countervailing duty rate for that exporter." (emphasis added) Accordingly, countervailing duties shall be imposed, on a non-discriminatory basis, on *all sources* found to be subsidized, although *no prior* investigation of all *individual* exporters or producers is required by Article 19. This implies that countervailing duties may be imposed on imports of products subject to the investigation, even though specific shipments from exporters or producers that were not investigated individually might not at all be subsidized, or not subsidized to an extent equal to a countervailing duty rate calculated on an aggregate (country-wide) basis.[189]

[189] We note, in this respect, as pointed out by the European Communities, that the first sentence of Article 6.10 of the *Anti-Dumping Agreement* requires, as a rule, a determination of an individual margin of dumping for each known producer or exporter of the product under investigation, unless this is rendered impracticable due to the high number of producers and exporters or of the types of products involved. If that is the case, the second sentence of Article 6.10 permits investigating authorities to limit the investigation to a statistically valid sample, or the largest percentage of the volume of exports that can reasonably be investigated. By contrast, the *SCM Agreement* does not contain a similar rule requiring Members, in principle, to determine an individual margin of subsidization for each known producer or exporter of the subsidized good. . . .

S.2.27.2 *US – Softwood Lumber IV*, para. 154

(WT/DS257/AB/R)

We note, however, that country-wide or company-specific countervailing duty rates may be imposed under Part V of the *SCM Agreement* only *after* the investigating authority has determined the existence of subsidization, injury to the domestic industry, and a causal link between them. In other words, the fact that Article 19 permits the imposition of countervailing duties on imports from producers or exporters not investigated individually, does not exonerate a Member from the obligation to determine the total amount of subsidy and the countervailing duty rate consistently with the provisions of the *SCM Agreement* and Article VI of the GATT 1994. In this respect, as the panel in *US – Countervailing Measures on Certain EC Products* correctly stated, the "determination of a benefit (as a component of subsidization) must be made *before* countervailing duties can be imposed." Therefore, turning to the issue in this case, before being entitled to impose countervailing duties on a processed product, for the purpose of offsetting an input subsidy, a Member must first determine, in accordance with Article 1.1, that a financial contribution exists, and that the benefit conferred directly on the input producer has been passed through, at least in part, to the producer of the processed product. . . .

S.2.28 Article 19.4 – Calculation of countervailing duty rates on per unit basis

S.2.28.1 *US – Softwood Lumber IV*, para. 153

(WT/DS257/AB/R)

We also observe that Article 19.4 requires the calculation of countervailing duties in terms of "subsidization *per unit* of the subsidized and exported product". (emphasis added) In our view, the reference to calculation of countervailing duty rates on a per unit basis under Article 19.4 supports the interpretation that an investigating authority is permitted to calculate the total amount and the rate of subsidization on an aggregate basis.

S.2.29 Article 21 – Duration and review of countervailing duties

S.2.29.1 *US – Countervailing Measures on Certain EC Products*, para. 139 (WT/DS212/AB/R)

In considering these arguments, we begin by recalling that, under Article 1.1 of the *SCM Agreement*, a "subsidy" is "deemed to exist" only if a "financial contribution" confers a "benefit". Also, under Article VI:3 of the GATT 1994, investigating authorities, before imposing countervailing duties, must ascertain the precise amount of a subsidy attributed to the imported products under investigation. In furtherance of this obligation, Article 10 of the *SCM Agreement* provides that Members must "ensure" that duties levied for the purpose of offsetting a subsidy are imposed only "in accordance with" the provisions of Article VI:3 of the GATT 1994 and the *SCM Agreement*. Moreover, Article 19.4 of the *SCM Agreement*, consistent with the language of Article VI:3 of the GATT 1994, requires that "[*n*]*o countervailing duty* shall be levied on any imported product in excess of the amount of the *subsidy found to exist*". (emphasis added) Finally, Article 21.1 of the *SCM Agreement* provides that "[a] countervailing duty shall remain in force *only as long as and to the extent necessary* to counteract subsidization which is causing injury." (emphasis added) In sum, these provisions set out the obligation of Members to limit countervailing duties to the amount and duration of the subsidy found to exist by the investigating authority. These obligations apply to original investigations as well as to administrative and sunset reviews covered under Article 21 of the *SCM Agreement*.

S.2.30 Article 21.1 – "only as long and to the extent necessary"

S.2.30.1 *US – Carbon Steel*, para. 70 (WT/DS213/AB/R, WT/DS213/AB/R/Corr.1)

. . . The first paragraph of Article 21 stipulates that a countervailing duty "shall remain in force only as long as and to the extent necessary to counteract subsidization which is causing injury". We see this as a general rule that, after the imposition of a countervailing duty, the continued application of that duty is subject to certain disciplines. These disciplines relate to the *duration* of the countervailing duty ("only as long as . . . necessary"), its *magnitude* ("only . . . to the extent necessary"), and its *purpose* ("to counteract subsidization which is causing injury"). Thus, the general rule of Article 21.1 underlines the requirement for periodic review of countervailing duties and highlights the factors that must inform such reviews. . . .

S.2.31 Article 21.2 – Review of the need for continued imposition

S.2.31.1 *US – Lead and Bismuth II*, paras. 53–54
(WT/DS138/AB/R)

. . . Pursuant to [paragraph 2 of Article 21], the authorities of a Member applying a countervailing duty must, where warranted, "review the need for the continued imposition of the duty". In carrying out such a review, the authorities must "examine whether the continued imposition of the duty is necessary to offset subsidization" and/or "whether the injury would be likely to continue or recur if the duty were removed or varied". Article 21.2 provides a review mechanism to ensure that Members comply with the rule set out in Article 21.1 of the *SCM Agreement*, which stipulates:

> A countervailing duty shall remain in force only as long as and to the extent necessary to counteract subsidization which is causing injury.

Setting aside the issue of injury, which does not arise in this case, we note that in order to establish the continued need for countervailing duties, an investigating authority will have to make a finding on *subsidization*, i.e., whether or not the subsidy continues to exist. If there is no longer a subsidy, there would no longer be any need for a countervailing duty.

S.2.31.2 *US – Lead and Bismuth II*, paras. 61–62
(WT/DS138/AB/R)

. . . In an administrative review pursuant to Article 21.2, the investigating authority may be presented with "positive information" that the "financial contribution" has been repaid or withdrawn and/or that the "benefit" no longer accrues. On the basis of its assessment of the information presented to it by interested parties, as well as of other evidence before it relating to the period of review, the investigating authority must determine whether there is a continuing need for the application of countervailing duties. The investigating authority is not free to ignore such information. If it were free to ignore this information, the review mechanism under Article 21.2 would have no purpose.

Therefore, we agree with the Panel that while an investigating authority may presume, in the context of an administrative review under Article 21.2, that a "benefit" continues to flow from an untied, non-recurring "financial contribution", this presumption can never be "irrebuttable". . . .

S.2.31.3 *US – Lead and Bismuth II*, para. 63
(WT/DS138/AB/R)

. . . We do not agree with the Panel's implied view that, in the context of an administrative review under Article 21.2, an investigating authority must *always* establish the existence of a "benefit" during the period of review *in the same way as* an investigating authority must establish a "benefit" in an original investigation. We believe that it is important to distinguish between the original investigation leading to the imposition of countervailing duties and the administrative review. In an original investigation, the investigating authority must establish that *all* conditions set out in the *SCM Agreement* for the imposition of countervailing duties are fulfilled. In an administrative review, however, the investigating authority must address those issues which have been raised before it by the interested parties or, in the case of an investigation conducted on its own initiative, those issues which warranted the examination.

S.2.31.4 *US – Carbon Steel*, para. 71
(WT/DS213/AB/R, WT/DS213/AB/R/Corr.1)

. . . the last sentence of Article 21.2 emphasizes the principle that the countervailing duty must be terminated "immediately" when "the authorities determine that the countervailing duty is no longer warranted". As we explained in our Report in *US – Lead and Bismuth II*, the determination made in a review under Article 21.2 must be a meaningful one . . .

. . . the requirement of a rigorous review cannot be denied . . .

S.2.31.5 *US – Carbon Steel*, para. 108
(WT/DS213/AB/R, WT/DS213/AB/R/Corr.1)

Article 21.2 differs from Article 21.3 in that the former identifies certain circumstances in which the authorities are under an *obligation* to review ("shall review") whether the continued imposition of the countervailing duty is necessary. In contrast, the principal obligation in Article 21.3 is not, *per se*, to conduct a review, but rather to *terminate* a countervailing duty *unless* a specific determination is made in a review. We note that Article 21.2 sets down an explicit evidentiary standard for requests by interested parties for a review under that provision. In order to trigger the authorities' obligation to conduct a review, such requests must, *inter alia*, include "positive information substantiating the need for review". Article 21.2 does not, on its face, apply this same standard to the initiation by authorities "on their own initiative" of a review carried out under that provision. Thus, Article 21.2 contemplates that, for reviews carried out pursuant to that provision, the self-initiation by the authorities of a review is not governed by the same standards that apply to initiation upon request by other parties.

S.2.31.6 *US – Countervailing Measures on Certain EC Products*, paras. 144, 146
(WT/DS212/AB/R)

. . . we reaffirm our finding in [*US – Lead and Bismuth II*] that an investigating authority, in an administrative review, when presented with information directed at proving that a "benefit" no longer exists following a privatization, *must* determine whether the continued imposition of countervailing duties is warranted in the light of that information. This obligation is premised, *not* on the creation of a new legal person, as the United States insists, but on the possibility that such a change in ownership has affected the continued existence of a benefit.

. . .

...under the "same person" method, when the USDOC determines that no new legal person is created as a result of privatization, the USDOC will conclude from this determination, *without any further analysis*, and irrespective of the price paid by the new owners for the newly-privatized enterprise, that the newly-privatized enterprise continues to receive the benefit of a previous financial contribution. This approach is contrary to the obligation in Article 21.2 of the *SCM Agreement* that the investigating authority must take into account in an administrative review "positive information substantiating the need for a review." Such information could relate to developments with respect to the subsidy, privatization at arm's length and for fair market value, or some other information....

S.2.31.7 *US – Countervailing Measures on Certain EC Products*, para. 149
(WT/DS212/AB/R)

...[Article 21.2 of the *SCM Agreement*] requires an investigating authority in an *administrative* review, upon receiving information of a privatization resulting in a change in ownership, to determine whether a "benefit" continues to exist. In our view, the *SCM Agreement*, by virtue of Articles 10, 19.4, and 21.1, also imposes an obligation to conduct such a determination on an investigating authority conducting a *sunset* review. As we observed earlier, the interplay of GATT Article VI:3 and Articles 10, 19.4 and 21.1 of the *SCM Agreement* prescribes an obligation applicable to original investigations as well as to reviews covered under Article 21 of the *SCM Agreement* to limit countervailing duties to the amount and duration of the subsidy found to exist by the investigating authority....

S.2.32 Article 21.3 – Termination of countervailing duties unless continued or recurrent subsidization and injury likely

S.2.32.1 *US – Carbon Steel*, para. 63
(WT/DS213/AB/R, WT/DS213/AB/R/Corr.1)

Article 21.3 imposes an explicit temporal limit on the maintenance of countervailing duties. For countervailing duties that have been in place for five years, the terms of Article 21.3 require their termination *unless* certain specified conditions are met. Specifically, a Member is permitted *not* to terminate such duties only if it conducts a review and, in that review, determines that the prescribed conditions for the continued application of the duty are satisfied. The prescribed conditions are "that the expiry of the duty would be likely to lead to continuation or recurrence of subsidization and injury". If, in a sunset review, a Member makes an affirmative determination that these conditions are satisfied, it may continue to apply countervailing duties beyond the five-year period set forth in Article 21.3. If it does not conduct a sunset review, or, having conducted such a review, it does not make such a positive determination, the duties must be terminated.

S.2.32.2 *US – Carbon Steel*, para. 69
(WT/DS213/AB/R, WT/DS213/AB/R/Corr.1)

. . . the technique of cross-referencing is frequently used in the *SCM Agreement*. . . . These cross-references suggest to us that, when the negotiators of the *SCM Agreement* intended that the disciplines set forth in one provision be applied in another context, they did so expressly. In the light of the many express cross-references made in the *SCM Agreement*, we attach significance to the absence of any textual link between Article 21.3 reviews and the *de minimis* standard set forth in Article 11.9. . . .

S.2.32.3 *US – Carbon Steel*, para. 87
(WT/DS213/AB/R, WT/DS213/AB/R/Corr.1)

. . . original investigations and sunset reviews are distinct processes with different purposes. The nature of the determination to be made in a sunset review differs in certain essential respects from the nature of the determination to be made in an original investigation. For example, in a sunset review, the authorities are called upon to focus their inquiry on what would happen if an existing countervailing duty were to be removed. In contrast, in an original investigation, the authorities must investigate the existence, degree and effect of any alleged subsidy in order to determine whether a subsidy exists and whether such subsidy is causing injury to the domestic industry so as to warrant the imposition of a countervailing duty. . . .

S.2.32.4 *US – Carbon Steel*, para. 88
(WT/DS213/AB/R, WT/DS213/AB/R/Corr.1)

. . . we wish to underline the thrust of Article 21.3 of the *SCM Agreement*. An automatic time-bound termination of countervailing duties that have been in place for five years from the original investigation or a subsequent comprehensive review is at the heart of this provision. Termination of a countervailing duty is the rule and its continuation is the exception. The continuation of a countervailing duty must therefore be based on a properly conducted review and a positive determination that the revocation of the countervailing duty would "be likely to lead to continuation or recurrence of subsidization and injury." Where the level of subsidization at the time of the review is very low, there must be persuasive evidence that revocation of the duty would nevertheless lead to injury to the domestic industry. Mere reliance by the authorities on the injury determination made in the original investigation will not be sufficient. Rather, a fresh determination, based on credible evidence, will be necessary to establish that the continuation of the countervailing duty is warranted to remove the injury to the domestic industry.

S.2.32.5 *US – Carbon Steel*, para. 92
(WT/DS213/AB/R, WT/DS213/AB/R/Corr.1)

. . . we are unable to conclude that the *de minimis* standard set forth in Article 11.9 of the *SCM Agreement* is implied in Article 21.3 of the Agreement. . . .

S.2.32.6 *US – Carbon Steel*, para. 103
(WT/DS213/AB/R, WT/DS213/AB/R/Corr.1)

... Article 21.3 requires the termination of countervailing duties within five years unless the prescribed determination is made in a review. Article 21.3 contemplates initiation of this review in one of two alternative ways, as is made clear through the use of the word "or". Either the authorities may make their determination "in a review initiated ... on their own initiative"; *or, alternatively*, the authorities may make the determination "in a review initiated ... upon a *duly substantiated* request made by or on behalf of the domestic industry ... ". The words "duly substantiated" qualify only the authorization to initiate a review upon request made by or on behalf of the domestic industry. No such language qualifies the first method for initiating a sunset review, namely self-initiation of a review by the authorities.

S.2.32.7 *US – Carbon Steel*, paras. 116–117
(WT/DS213/AB/R, WT/DS213/AB/R/Corr.1)

In sum, our review of the context of Article 21.3 of the *SCM Agreement* reveals no indication that the ability of authorities to self-initiate a sunset review under that provision is conditioned on compliance with the evidentiary standards set forth in Article 11 of the *SCM Agreement* relating to initiation of investigations. Nor do we consider that any other evidentiary standard is prescribed for the self-initiation of a sunset review under Article 21.3.

This is not to say that authorities may continue the countervailing duties after five years in the absence of evidence that the expiry of the duty would be likely to lead to continuation or recurrence of subsidization and injury. Article 21.3 prohibits the continuation of countervailing duties unless a review is undertaken and the prescribed determination, based on adequate evidence, is made.

S.2.33 Article 21.4 – Relationship with Articles 11 and 12

S.2.33.1 *US – Carbon Steel*, para. 72
(WT/DS213/AB/R, WT/DS213/AB/R/Corr.1)

... Article 12 sets out obligations, primarily of an evidentiary and procedural nature, that apply to the conduct of an *investigation*. It comes immediately after Article 11, which sets forth a number of procedural, evidentiary as well as substantive rules related to the initiation and conduct of an *investigation*. Given that the requirements of Articles 11 and 12 are placed consecutively in the Agreement, and the fact that both Articles expressly set out obligations in relation to *investigations*, we read the express reference in Article 21.4 to Article 12, but not to Article 11, as an indication that the drafters intended that the obligations in Article 12, but not those in Article 11, would apply to reviews carried out under Article 21.3.

S.2.34 Article 22 – Public notice and explanation of determinations

S.2.34.1 *US – Carbon Steel*, paras. 111–112
(WT/DS213/AB/R, WT/DS213/AB/R/Corr.1)

Article 22.1 imposes *notification and public notice obligations* upon Members that have decided, in accordance with all the requirements of Article 11, that the initiation of a countervailing duty investigation is justified. Article 22.1 does not itself establish any evidentiary rule, but only refers to a standard established in Article 11.9.

Article 22.7 applies the provisions of Article 22 "*mutatis mutandis* to the initiation and completion of reviews pursuant to Article 21". To us, in the same way that Article 22.1 imposes notification and public notice requirements on investigating authorities that have decided, in accordance with the standards set out in Article 11, to initiate an *investigation*, Article 22.1 (by virtue of Article 22.7) also operates to impose notification and public notice requirements on investigating authorities that have decided, in accordance with Article 21, to initiate a *review*. Similarly, in the same way that Article 22.1 does *not* itself establish evidentiary standards applicable to the initiation of an *investigation*, it does *not* itself establish evidentiary standards applicable to the initiation of sunset reviews. Such standards, if they exist, must be found elsewhere.

S.2.35 Article 27 – Special and differential treatment for developing country Members

S.2.35.1 PARAGRAPH 4 – PHASE-OUT OR STANDSTILL OF EXPORT SUBSIDIES

S.2.35.1.1 *Brazil – Aircraft*, para. 140
(WT/DS46/AB/R)

The title of Article 27 is "Special and Differential Treatment of Developing Country Members". Paragraph 1 of that Article provides that "Members recognize that subsidies may play an important role in economic development programmes of developing country Members." Both from its title and from its terms, it is clear that Article 27 is intended to provide special and differential treatment for developing country Members, under certain specified conditions. In our view, too, paragraph 4 of Article 27 provides certain obligations that developing country Members must fulfill if they are to benefit from this special and differential treatment during the transitional period. On reading paragraphs 2(b) and 4 of Article 27 together, it is clear that the conditions set forth in paragraph 4 are *positive obligations* for developing country Members, *not* affirmative defences. If a developing country Member complies with the obligations in Article 27.4, the prohibition on export subsidies in Article 3.1(a) simply does not apply. However, if that developing country Member does *not* comply with those obligations, Article 3.1(a) *does* apply.

S.2.35.1.2 *Brazil – Aircraft*, para. 150
(WT/DS46/AB/R)

...we uphold the finding of the Panel that the "proper point of reference" in determining whether a Member has increased the level of its export subsidies under Article 27.4 is actual expenditures, rather than budgeted amounts or appropriations.

S.2.35.1.3 *Brazil – Aircraft*, para. 156
(WT/DS46/AB/R)

. . . It is pursuant to the provisions of Article 27.4 that Brazil is obliged not to increase "the level of its export subsidies". And, to ascertain the meaning of this phrase, it is necessary to look, again, at footnote 55, which is affixed to Article 27.4 and which speaks of "the level of export subsidies *granted*" (emphasis added) by a developing country Member. . . .

S.2.35.1.4 *Brazil – Aircraft*, para. 163
(WT/DS46/AB/R)

. . . in our view, to take no account of inflation in assessing the level of export subsidies granted by a developing country Member would render the special and differential treatment provisions of Article 27 meaningless. . . .

S.2.35.2 PARAGRAPHS 10 AND 11 – HIGHER *DE MINIMIS* SUBSIDIZATION THRESHOLD

S.2.35.2.1 *US – Carbon Steel*, para. 82
(WT/DS213/AB/R, WT/DS213/AB/R/Corr.1)

. . . Articles 27.10 and 27.11 of the *SCM Agreement* . . . require authorities, in a countervailing duty investigation, to apply a higher *de minimis* subsidization threshold to imports from developing country Members. To accept the Panel's reasoning – that *de minimis* subsidization is non-injurious subsidization – would imply that, for the same product, imported into the same country, and affecting the same domestic industry, the *SCM Agreement* establishes different thresholds at which the same industry can be said to suffer injury, depending on the origin of the product. . . .

S.2.36 Article 32.1 – Specific action against a subsidy. *See also* Anti-Dumping Agreement, Article 18.1 – Specific action against dumping (A.3.61); SCM Agreement, Article 1.1 – Pass-through of indirect subsidies (S.2.10); SCM Agreement, Article VI:3 of the GATT 1994 – Subsidies (S.2.43)

S.2.36.1 *US – Offset Act (Byrd Amendment)*, para. 236
(WT/DS217/AB/R, WT/DS234/AB/R)

Looking to the ordinary meaning of the words used in these provisions, we read them as establishing two conditions precedent that must be met in order for a measure to be governed by them. The first is that a measure must be "specific" to dumping or subsidization. The second is that a measure must be "against" dumping or subsidization. These two conditions operate together and complement each other. If they are not met, the measure will not be governed by Article 18.1 of the *Anti-Dumping Agreement* or by Article 32.1 of the *SCM Agreement*. If, however, it is established that a measure meets these two conditions, and thus falls within the scope of the prohibitions in those provisions, it would then be necessary to move to a further step in the analysis and to determine whether the measure has been "taken in accordance with the provisions of GATT 1994", as interpreted by the *Anti-Dumping Agreement* or the *SCM Agreement*. If it is determined that this is not the case, the measure would be inconsistent with Article 18.1 of the *Anti-Dumping Agreement* or Article 32.1 of the *SCM Agreement*.

S.2.36.2 *US – Offset Act (Byrd Amendment)*, para. 237
(WT/DS217/AB/R, WT/DS234/AB/R)

. . . The Panel analyzed the terms "specific" and "against" in Article 18.1 in the same manner as it did with respect to their use in Article 32.1. We agree with the Panel's approach. . . .

S.2.36.3 *US – Offset Act (Byrd Amendment)*, para. 239
(WT/DS217/AB/R, WT/DS234/AB/R)

. . . a measure that may be taken only when the constituent elements of dumping or a subsidy are present, is a "specific action" in response to dumping within the meaning of Article 18.1 of the *Anti-Dumping Agreement* or a "specific action" in response to subsidization within the meaning of Article 32.1 of the *SCM Agreement*. In other words, the measure must be inextricably linked to, or have a strong correlation with, the constituent elements of dumping or of a subsidy. Such link or correlation may, as in the 1916 Act, be derived from the text of the measure itself.

S.2.36.4 *US – Offset Act (Byrd Amendment)*, para. 240
(WT/DS217/AB/R, WT/DS234/AB/R)

. . . We recall that, in *US – 1916 Act*, we said the constituent elements of dumping are found in the definition of dumping in Article VI:1 of the GATT 1994, as elaborated in Article 2 of the *Anti-Dumping Agreement*. As regards the constituent elements of a subsidy, we are of the view that they are set out in the definition of a subsidy found in Article 1 of the *SCM Agreement*.

S.2.36.5 *US – Offset Act (Byrd Amendment)*, para. 253
(WT/DS217/AB/R, WT/DS234/AB/R)

. . . in Article 18.1 of the *Anti-Dumping Agreement* and Article 32.1 of the *SCM Agreement*, there is no requirement that the measure must come into direct contact with the imported product, or entities connected to, or responsible for, the imported good such as the importer, exporter, or foreign producer. . . .

S.2.36.6 *US – Offset Act (Byrd Amendment)*, para. 254
(WT/DS217/AB/R, WT/DS234/AB/R)

Recalling the other two elements of the definition of "against" from the *New Shorter Oxford Dictionary* relied upon by the United States, namely "of motion or action in opposition" and "in hostility or active opposition to", to determine whether a measure is "against" dumping or a subsidy, we believe it is necessary to assess whether the design and structure of a measure is such that the measure is "opposed to", has an adverse bearing on, or, more specifically, has the effect of dissuading the practice of dumping or the practice of subsidization, or creates an incentive to terminate such practices. In our view, the CDSOA has exactly those effects because of its design and structure.

S.2.36.7 *US – Offset Act (Byrd Amendment)*, para. 257
(WT/DS217/AB/R, WT/DS234/AB/R)

... in order to determine whether the CDSOA is "against" dumping or subsidization, it was not necessary, nor relevant, for the Panel to examine the conditions of competition under which domestic products and dumped/subsidized imports compete, and to assess the impact of the measure on the competitive relationship between them. An analysis of the term "against", in our view, is more appropriately centred on the design and structure of the measure; such an analysis does not mandate an economic assessment of the implications of the measure on the conditions of competition under which domestic product and dumped/subsidized imports compete.

S.2.36.8 *US – Offset Act (Byrd Amendment)*, para. 258
(WT/DS217/AB/R, WT/DS234/AB/R)

... a measure cannot be against dumping or a subsidy simply because it facilitates or induces the exercise of rights that are WTO-consistent. ...

S.2.36.9 *US – Offset Act (Byrd Amendment)*, para. 262
(WT/DS217/AB/R, WT/DS234/AB/R)

... Footnotes 24 and 56 are clarifications of the main provisions, added to avoid ambiguity; they confirm what is implicit in Article 18.1 of the *Anti-Dumping Agreement* and in Article 32.1 of the *SCM Agreement*, namely, that an action that is *not* "specific" within the meaning of Article 18.1 of the *Anti-Dumping Agreement* and of Article 32.1 of the *SCM Agreement*, but is nevertheless related to dumping or subsidization, is not prohibited by Article 18.1 of the *Anti-Dumping Agreement* or Article 32.1 of the *SCM Agreement*.

S.2.36.10 *US – Offset Act (Byrd Amendment)*, para. 269
(WT/DS217/AB/R, WT/DS234/AB/R)

... The GATT 1994 and the *SCM Agreement* provide four responses to a countervailable subsidy: (i) definitive countervailing duties; (ii) provisional measures; (iii) price undertakings; and (iv) multilaterally-sanctioned countermeasures under the dispute settlement system. No other response to subsidization is envisaged in the text of the GATT 1994, or in the text of the *SCM Agreement*. Therefore, to be "in accordance with the GATT 1994, as interpreted by" the *SCM Agreement*, a response to subsidization must be in one of those four forms.

S.2.36.11 *US – Offset Act (Byrd Amendment)*, para. 273
(WT/DS217/AB/R, WT/DS234/AB/R)

In our view, Article VI:3 of the GATT 1994 and Part V of the *SCM Agreement* encompass *all* measures taken against subsidization. To be in accordance with the GATT 1994, as interpreted by the *SCM Agreement*, a response to subsidization must be either in the form of definitive countervailing duties, provisional measures or price undertakings, or in the form of multilaterally-sanctioned countermeasures resulting from resort to the dispute settlement system. . . .

Article 32.3 – Temporal Scope of Application. *See* SCM Agreement, Relationship between the SCM Agreement and the GATT 1994 (S.2.41); Temporal Application of Rights and Obligations, SCM Agreement (T.5.1)

Illustrative List of Export Subsidies: Items (c) and (d). *See* Agreement on Agriculture, Article 9.1(c) – Governmental action vs. Private action (A.1.25)

S.2.37 Illustrative List of Export Subsidies: Item (e), footnote 59, first sentence – "remission or deferral of direct taxes"

S.2.37.1 *US – FSC*, para. 97
(WT/DS108/AB/R)

. . . The first sentence of footnote 59 is specifically related to the statement in item (e) of the Illustrative List that the "full or partial exemption remission, or deferral specifically related to exports, of direct taxes" is an export subsidy. The first sentence of footnote 59 qualifies this by stating that "deferral need not amount to an export subsidy where, for example, appropriate interest charges are collected." . . .

S.2.38 Illustrative List of Export Subsidies: Item (e), footnote 59, fifth sentence – "double taxation"

S.2.38.1 *US – FSC (Article 21.5 – EC)*, para. 132
(WT/DS108/AB/RW)

The import of the fifth sentence of footnote 59 is that Members are entitled to "take", or "adopt" measures to avoid double taxation of foreign-source income, notwithstanding that they may be, in principle, export subsidies within the meaning of Article 3.1(a). The fifth sentence of footnote 59, therefore, constitutes an exception to the legal regime applicable to export subsidies under Article 3.1(a) by explicitly providing that when a measure is taken to avoid the double taxation of foreign-source income, a Member is entitled to adopt it.

S.2.38.2 *US – FSC (Article 21.5 – EC)*, para. 133
(WT/DS108/AB/RW)

Accordingly, as we indicated in *US – FSC* [Appellate Body Report, para. 101], the fifth sentence of footnote 59 constitutes an affirmative defence that justifies a prohibited export subsidy when the measure in question is taken "to avoid the double taxation of foreign-source income". In such a situation, the burden of proving that a measure is justified by falling within the scope of the fifth sentence of footnote 59 rests upon the responding party.

S.2.38.3 *US – FSC (Article 21.5 – EC)*, para. 137
(WT/DS108/AB/RW)

We note at the outset that "double taxation" occurs when the same income, in the hands of the same taxpayer, is liable to tax in different States. The fifth sentence of footnote 59 applies to a measure taken by a Member to avoid such double taxation of "foreign-source income". In examining the phrase "foreign-source income", we observe that, in ordinary usage, the word "source" can refer to the place where a thing originates, and that the words "source" and "origin" can be synonyms. We consider, therefore, that the word "source", in the context of the fifth sentence of footnote 59, has a meaning akin to "origin" and refers to the place where the income is earned. This reading is supported by the combination of the words "foreign" and "source" as "foreign" also refers to the place where the income is earned. Used in this way, the word "foreign" indicates a source which is external to the Member adopting the measure at stake. Footnote 59, therefore, applies to measures taken by a Member to avoid the double taxation of income earned by a taxpayer of that Member in a "foreign" State.

S.2.38.4 *US – FSC (Article 21.5 – EC)*, para. 138
(WT/DS108/AB/RW)

. . . the term "foreign-source income" in footnote 59 refers to income which is susceptible of being taxed in two States. . . .

S.2.38.5 *US – FSC (Article 21.5 – EC)*, paras. 139–140
(WT/DS108/AB/RW)

. . . We have emphasized in previous appeals that Members have the sovereign authority to determine their own rules of taxation, provided that they respect their WTO obligations. Thus, subject to this important proviso, each Member is free to determine the rules it will use to identify the source of income and the fiscal consequences – to tax or not to tax the income – flowing from the identification of source. We see nothing in footnote 59 to the *SCM Agreement* which is intended to alter this situation. We, therefore, agree with the Panel that footnote 59 does not oblige Members to adopt any particular legal standard to determine whether income is foreign-source for the purposes of their double taxation-avoidance measures.

. . . however, footnote 59 does not give Members an unfettered discretion to avoid double taxation of "foreign-source income" through the grant of export subsidies. As the fifth sentence of footnote 59 to the *SCM Agreement* constitutes an exception to the prohibition on export subsidies, great care must be taken in defining its scope. . . .

S.2.38.6 *US – FSC (Article 21.5 – EC)*, para. 142
(WT/DS108/AB/RW)

. . . In seeking to give meaning to the term "foreign-source income" in footnote 59 to the *SCM Agreement*, which is a tax-related provision in an international trade treaty, we believe that it is appropriate for us to derive assistance from these widely recognized principles which many States generally apply in the field of taxation. . . .

S.2.38.7 *US – FSC (Article 21.5 – EC)*, para. 143
(WT/DS108/AB/RW)

We recognize, of course, that the detailed rules on taxation of non-residents differ considerably from State-to-State, with some States applying rules which may be more likely to tax the income of non-residents than the rules applied by other States. However, despite the differences, there seems to us to be a widely accepted common element to these rules. The common element is that a "foreign" State will tax a non-resident on income which is generated by activities of the non-resident that have some link with that State. Thus, whether a "foreign" State decides to tax non-residents on income generated by a permanent establishment or whether, absent such an establishment, it decides to tax a non-resident on income generated by the conduct of a trade or business on its territory, the "foreign" State taxes a non-resident only on income generated by activities linked to the territory of that State. As a result of this link, the "foreign" State treats the income in question as domestic-source, under its source rules, and taxes it. Conversely, where the income of a non-resident does not have any links with a "foreign" State, it is widely accepted that the income will be subject to tax only in the taxpayer's State of residence, and that this income will not be subject to taxation by a "foreign" State.

S.2.38.8 *US – FSC (Article 21.5 – EC)*, para. 145
(WT/DS108/AB/RW)

Accordingly, in our view, "foreign-source income", in footnote 59 to the *SCM Agreement*, refers to income generated by activities of a non-resident taxpayer in a "foreign" State which have such links with that State so that the income could properly be subject to tax in that State.

S.2.38.9 *US – FSC (Article 21.5 – EC)*, para. 146
(WT/DS108/AB/RW)

. . . The avoidance of double taxation is not an exact science. Indeed, the income exempted from taxation in the State of residence of the taxpayer might not be subject to a corresponding, or any, tax in a "foreign" State. Yet, this does not necessarily mean that the measure is not taken to avoid double taxation of foreign-source income. Thus, we agree with the Panel, and the United States, that measures falling under footnote 59 are not required to be perfectly tailored to the actual double tax burden.

S.2.38.10 *US – FSC (Article 21.5 – EC)*, para. 148
(WT/DS108/AB/RW)

We also recognize that Members are not obliged by the covered agreements to provide relief from double taxation. Footnote 59 to the *SCM Agreement* simply preserves the prerogative of Members to grant such relief, at their discretion, for "foreign-source income". Accordingly, we do not believe that measures falling under footnote 59 must grant relief from *all* double tax burdens. Rather, Members retain the sovereign authority to determine for themselves whether, and to what extent, they will grant such relief.

S.2.38.11 *US – FSC (Article 21.5 – EC)*, para. 175
(WT/DS108/AB/RW)

... However, in the absence of an established link between the income of such taxpayers and their activities in a "foreign" State, we do not believe that there is "foreign-source income" within the meaning of footnote 59 of the *SCM Agreement*.

S.2.38.12 *US – FSC (Article 21.5 – EC)*, para. 176
(WT/DS108/AB/RW)

... In our view, however, sales income cannot be regarded as "foreign-source income", under footnote 59, for the sole reason that the property, subject-matter of the sale, is exported to another State, for use there. The mere fact that the buyer uses property outside the United States does not mean that the seller undertook activities in a "foreign" State generating income there. Such an interpretation of footnote 59 would, in effect, allow Members to grant a tax exemption in favour of export related income on the ground that the exportation by itself of the property renders the income "foreign-source". In our view, this reading would allow Members easily to evade the prohibition on export subsidies in Article 3.1(a) of the *SCM Agreement* and render this prohibition meaningless.

S.2.38.13 *US – FSC (Article 21.5 – EC)*, para. 185
(WT/DS108/AB/RW)

Certainly, if the ETI measure were confined to those aspects which grant a tax exemption for "foreign-source income", it would fall within footnote 59. However, the ETI measure is not so confined ... We have said that avoiding double taxation is not an exact science and we recognize that Members must have a degree of flexibility in tackling double taxation. However, in our view, the flexibility under footnote 59 to the *SCM Agreement* does not properly extend to allowing

Members to adopt allocation rules that systematically result in a tax exemption for income that has no link with a "foreign" State and that would not be regarded as foreign-source under any of the widely accepted principles of taxation we have reviewed.

S.2.39 **Illustrative List of Export Subsidies: Item (j) – Export credit guarantee or insurance.** *See also* Agreement on Agriculture, Article 9.1(c) – Governmental action vs. Private action (A.1.25)

S.2.39.1 *Canada – Dairy (Article 21.5 – New Zealand and US)*, para. 93
(WT/DS103/AB/RW, WT/DS113/AB/RW)

Our approach is supported by the standards used in items (j) and (k) of the Illustrative List of the *SCM Agreement*. Item (j) is concerned with export subsidies that arise through the provision by the government of a variety of export credit guarantee and insurance programmes. Under item (j), the provision of such services by the government involves export subsidies when the premium rates charged do not "cover the *long-term operating costs and losses* of the programmes". (emphasis added) Thus, the measure of value under item (j) is the overall cost to the government, as the service provider, of providing the service. Likewise, in item (k), where the government provides export credits, the measure of the value of the service provided by the government is the amount "which [governments] actually have to pay for the funds so employed (or would have to pay if they borrowed on international capital markets . . .)". Again, the measure of value is by reference to the cost to the government, as the service provider, of providing the service. Therefore, items (j) and (k) give contextual support and *rationale*, for using the cost of production as a standard for determining whether there are "payments" under Article 9.1(c) of the *Agreement on Agriculture* in these proceedings.

S.2.39.2 *US – Upland Cotton*, para. 647
(WT/DS267/AB/R)

We agree with the United States that Article 10.3 of the *Agreement on Agriculture* does not apply to claims brought under the *SCM Agreement*. However, the Panel did not make the error attributed to it by the United States. The Panel made the statement relied on by the United States in the context of its assessment of the United States' export credit guarantee program under the *Agreement on Agriculture*. Although the Panel made use of the criteria set out in item (j) of the Illustrative List of Export Subsidies annexed to the *SCM Agreement* (providing these programs at premium rates inadequate to cover long-term operating costs and losses) it did so as contextual guidance for its analysis under the *Agreement on Agriculture*, and both the United States and Brazil appear to have agreed with the appropriateness of this approach. Thus, the Panel's reference to Article 10.3 did not relate to its assessment of the United States' export credit guarantee programs under the *SCM Agreement*.

S.2.39.3 *US – Upland Cotton*, para. 648
(WT/DS267/AB/R)

. . . It is clear from this paragraph that the Panel placed the burden of proof on Brazil and determined that Brazil met its burden of proving that the United States' export credit guarantees are provided at premium rates that are inadequate to cover long-term operating costs and losses. . . . The reference to Article 10.3 does not, by itself, change the fact that the Panel ultimately placed the burden of proof on Brazil.

S.2.39.4 *US – Upland Cotton*, para. 656
(WT/DS267/AB/R)

In our view, none of these statements demonstrates that the Panel improperly applied the rules on burden of proof. The United States is selecting statements made by the Panel within its broader analysis of how the United States' export credit guarantee programs operate, reading them in isolation, and disregarding the context in which they were made. As indicated earlier, it is clear that the Panel imposed on Brazil the overall burden of proving that the premiums charged under the United States' export credit guarantee programs are inadequate to cover long-term operating costs and losses. This approach is consistent with the usual rules on the allocation of the burden of proof whereby the complaining party is responsible for proving its claim. . . .

S.2.39.5 *US – Upland Cotton*, para. 663
(WT/DS267/AB/R)

The United States has styled its claim as related to the interpretation and application of item (j) of the Illustrative List of Export Subsidies annexed to the *SCM Agreement*. According to the United States, the Panel could not have reached a legal conclusion under item (j) without having necessarily determined what were the long-term operating costs and losses of the United States' export credit guarantee programs, and more specifically, made a determination in respect of the treatment of rescheduled debt. We find no difficulty with the United States' approach. Its claim relates to the Panel's application of item (j) to the specific facts of the case. The United States is not asking us to review the Panel's factual findings, nor is it arguing that the Panel's assessment of the matter was not objective. Instead, the United States' claim relates to the application of the legal standard set out in item (j) of the Illustrative List of Export Subsidies to the specific facts of this case. It is an issue of legal characterization. . . .

S.2.39.6 *US – Upland Cotton*, paras. 665–666
(WT/DS267/AB/R)

The Panel provided the following explanation of the examination that is required under item (j) of the Illustrative List of Export Subsidies:

> . . . item (j) calls for an examination of whether the premium rates of the export credit guarantee programme at issue are inadequate to cover the

> long-term operating costs and losses of the programmes. Beyond that, item (j) does not set forth, or require us to use, any one particular methodological approach nor accounting philosophy in conducting our examination. Nor are we required to quantify precisely the amount by which costs and losses exceeded premiums paid. [Panel Report, para. 7.804]

We agree with the Panel's approach. The text of item (j) does not suggest that this provision requires a Panel to choose one particular basis for the calculation and then to make a precise quantification of the difference between premiums and long-term operating costs and losses on that basis. Indeed, at the oral hearing, the United States acknowledged that the text of item (j) does not, by its own terms, require precise quantification, but asserted that the Panel should have precisely quantified the long-term operating costs and losses "in this particular case".

In our view, the focus of item (j) is on the inadequacy of the premiums. To us, this focus suggests that what is required is a finding on whether the premiums are insufficient and thus whether the specific export credit guarantee program at issue constitutes an export subsidy, and not a finding of the precise difference between premiums and long-term operating costs and losses.

S.2.39.7 *US – Upland Cotton*, para. 672
(WT/DS267/AB/R)

In the light of the above, it is clear that the Panel undertook a sufficiently detailed examination of the financial performance of the United States' export credit guarantee programs. Its analysis showed that none of the methods proposed by the parties indicated that the premiums charged under the United States' export credit guarantee programs are adequate to cover long-term costs and losses. In these circumstances, we agree with the Panel that, in this particular case, it was not necessary to choose a particular method nor determine the precise amount by which long-term operating costs and losses exceeded premiums. Although it did not provide a final figure for the long-term operating costs and losses of the United States' export credit guarantee programs, as the United States suggests it should have, the Panel found that the various methods put forward by the parties led to the same conclusion, namely, that the premiums for the United States' export credit guarantee programs are inadequate to cover the programs' long-term operating costs and losses. The Panel's decision not to choose between methods or make a finding on the precise difference between premiums and long-term costs and losses does not, in our view, invalidate the Panel's ultimate findings under Articles 3.1(a) and 3.2 of the *SCM Agreement*.

S.2.39.8 *US – Upland Cotton*, para. 731
(WT/DS267/AB/R)

We need not decide, in this case, whether an export credit guarantee program that meets the standard of item (j) of the Illustrative List of Export Subsidies – because the premiums charged are adequate to cover long-term operating costs and losses – may nevertheless be challenged as a prohibited export subsidy under Article 3.1(a) on the basis that it confers a benefit. This is because, even if we were to assume that such a claim were possible, we would conclude that the Panel was within its discretion in exercising judicial economy in respect of Brazil's claim.

S.2.40 Illustrative List of Export Subsidies: Item (k) – Export credits.

See also Agreement on Agriculture, Article 9.1(c) – Governmental action vs. Private action (A.1.25); SCM Agreement, Illustrative List of Export Subsidies: Item (j) (S.2.39)

S.2.40.1 *Brazil – Aircraft*, para. 181

(WT/DS46/AB/R)

. . . the issue here is whether the export subsidies for regional aircraft under PROEX "are used to secure" for Brazil "a material advantage in the field of export credit terms" . . . the *OECD Arrangement* can be appropriately viewed as one example of an international undertaking providing a specific market benchmark by which to assess whether payments by governments, coming within the provisions of item (k), are "used to secure a material advantage in the field of export credit terms". . . in our view, the appropriate comparison to be made in determining whether a payment is "used to secure a material advantage", within the meaning of item (k), is between the actual interest rate applicable in a particular export sales transaction after deduction of the government payment (the "*net* interest rate") and the relevant CIRR [Commercial Interest Reference Rate].

S.2.40.2 *Brazil – Aircraft (Article 21.5 – Canada)*, para. 64

(WT/DS46/AB/RW)

. . . the CIRR is "*one example*" of a "market benchmark" that may be used to determine whether a "payment" is used to "secure a material advantage". (emphasis added) The CIRR is a constructed interest rate for a particular currency, at a particular time, that does not always necessarily reflect the actual state of the credit markets. Where the CIRR does not, in fact, reflect the rates available in the marketplace, we believe that a Member should be able, in principle, to rely on evidence from the marketplace itself in order to establish an alternative "market benchmark", on which it might rely in one or more transactions. Thus, the CIRR is not, necessarily, the *sole* "market benchmark" that may be used to determine whether a payment "is used to secure a material advantage in the field of export credit terms", within the meaning of item (k) of the Illustrative List.

S.2.40.3 *Brazil – Aircraft (Article 21.5 – Canada)*, paras. 68–69

(WT/DS46/AB/RW)

. . . Brazil contends, on this basis, that the revised PROEX is *not* "used to secure a material advantage in the field of export credit terms" within the meaning of the first paragraph of item (k) of the Illustrative List.

To prove this argument, Brazil must establish *both* of two elements: first, Brazil must prove that it has identified an appropriate "market benchmark"; and, second, Brazil must prove that the net interest rates under the revised PROEX are at or above that benchmark.

S.2.40.4 *Brazil – Aircraft (Article 21.5 – Canada)*, para. 80
(WT/DS46/AB/RW)

If Brazil had demonstrated that the payments made under the revised PROEX were not "used to secure a material advantage in the field of export credit terms", and that such payments were "payments" by Brazil of "all or part of the costs incurred by exporters or financial institutions in obtaining credits", then we would have been prepared to find that the payments made under the revised PROEX are justified under item (k) of the Illustrative List. However, Brazil has not demonstrated that those conditions of item (k) are met in this case. In making this observation, we wish to emphasize that we are not interpreting footnote 5 of the *SCM Agreement*, and we do not opine on the scope of footnote 5, or on the meaning of any other items in the Illustrative List.

Relationship between the SCM Agreement and the Anti-Dumping Agreement. *See* Anti-Dumping Agreement, Relationship between the Anti-Dumping Agreement and the SCM Agreement (A.3.63)

S.2.41 Relationship between the SCM Agreement and the GATT 1994

S.2.41.1 *Brazil – Desiccated Coconut*, p. 16, DSR 1997:I, p. 167 at 181
(WT/DS22/AB/R)

. . . The ordinary meaning of these provisions taken in their context leads us to the conclusion that the negotiators of the *SCM Agreement* clearly intended that, under the integrated *WTO Agreement*, countervailing duties may only be imposed in accordance with the provisions of Part V of the *SCM Agreement and* Article VI of the GATT 1994, taken together. If there is a conflict between the provisions of the *SCM Agreement* and Article VI of the GATT 1994, furthermore, the provisions of the *SCM Agreement* would prevail as a result of the general interpretative note to Annex 1A.

S.2.41.2 *Brazil – Desiccated Coconut*, pp. 18–19, DSR 1997:I, p. 167 at 182–183
(WT/DS22/AB/R)

The fact that Article VI of the GATT 1947 could be invoked independently of the *Tokyo Round SCM Code* under the previous GATT system does not mean that Article VI of GATT 1994 can be applied independently of the *SCM Agreement* in the context of the WTO. The authors of the new WTO regime intended to put an end to the fragmentation that had characterized the previous system. This can be seen from the preamble to the *WTO Agreement* which states, in pertinent part:

> *Resolved*, therefore, to develop an integrated, more viable and durable multilateral trading system encompassing the General Agreement on Tariffs and Trade, the results of past trade liberalization efforts, and all of the results of the Uruguay Round of Multilateral Trade Negotiations.

Article II:2 of the *WTO Agreement* also provides that the Multilateral Trade Agreements are "integral parts" of the *WTO Agreement*, "binding on all Members". The single undertaking is further reflected in the Articles of the *WTO Agreement* on original membership, accession, non-application, acceptance and withdrawal. Furthermore, the *DSU* establishes an integrated dispute settlement system which applies to all the "covered agreements", allowing all the provisions of the *WTO Agreement* relevant to a particular dispute to be examined in one proceeding.

The Appellate Body sees Article 32.3 of the *SCM Agreement* as a clear statement that for countervailing duty investigations or reviews, the dividing line between the application of the GATT 1947 system of agreements and the *WTO Agreement* is to be determined by the date on which the application was made for the countervailing duty investigation or review. Article 32.3 has limited application only in specific circumstances where a countervailing duty proceeding, either an investigation or a review, was underway at the time of entry into force of the *WTO Agreement*. This does not mean that the *WTO Agreement* does not apply as of 1 January 1995 to all other acts, facts and situations which come within the provisions of the *SCM Agreement* and Article VI of the GATT 1994. However, the Uruguay Round negotiators expressed an explicit intention to draw the line of application of the new *WTO Agreement* to countervailing duty investigations and reviews at a different point in time from that for other general measures. . . .

S.2.41.3 *US – FSC*, para. 117
(WT/DS108/AB/R)

. . . the provisions of the *SCM Agreement* do not provide explicit assistance as to the relationship between the export subsidy provisions of the *SCM Agreement* and Article XVI:4 of the GATT 1994. In the absence of any such specific textual guidance, we must determine the relationship between Articles 1.1(a)(1) and 3.1(a) of the *SCM Agreement* and Article XVI:4 of the GATT 1994 on the basis of the texts of the relevant provisions as a whole. It is clear from even a cursory examination of Article XVI:4 of the GATT 1994 that it differs very substantially from the subsidy provisions of the *SCM Agreement*, and, in particular, from the export subsidy provisions of both the *SCM Agreement* and the *Agreement on Agriculture*. First of all, the *SCM Agreement* contains an express definition of the term "subsidy" which is not contained in Article XVI:4. In fact, as we have observed previously, the *SCM Agreement* contains a broad package of new export subsidy disciplines that "go well beyond merely applying and interpreting Articles VI, XVI and XXIII of the GATT 1947". Next, Article XVI:4 prohibits export subsidies only when they result in the export sale of a product at a price lower than the "comparable price charged for the like product to buyers in the domestic market." In contrast, the *SCM Agreement* establishes a much broader prohibition against *any* subsidy which is "contingent upon export performance". To say the least, the rule contained in Article 3.1(a) of the *SCM Agreement* that all subsidies which are "contingent upon export performance" are prohibited is significantly different from a rule that prohibits only those subsidies which result in a lower price for the exported product than the comparable price for that product when sold in the domestic market. Thus, whether or not a measure is an export subsidy under Article XVI:4 of the GATT 1947 provides no guidance in determining whether that measure is a prohibited export subsidy under Article 3.1(a) of the *SCM Agreement*. Also, and significantly, Article XVI:4 of the GATT 1994 does not apply to "primary products", which include agricultural products. Unquestionably, the explicit export subsidy disciplines, relating to agricultural products, contained in Articles 3, 8, 9 and 10 of the *Agreement on Agriculture* must clearly take precedence over the *exemption* of primary products from export subsidy disciplines in Article XVI:4 of the GATT 1994.

S.2.41.4 *US – Softwood Lumber IV*, para. 134
(WT/DS257/AB/R)

. . . we observe that provisions in both the GATT 1994 and the *SCM Agreement* are relevant to this dispute. We note the Appellate Body's earlier ruling that a provision of an agreement included in Annex 1A of the *WTO Agreement* (including the *SCM Agreement*), and a provision of the GATT 1994, that have identical coverage, both apply, but that the provision of the agreement that "deals specifically, and in detail" with a question should be examined first. . . . No conflict between Articles 10 and 32.1 of the *SCM Agreement* on the one hand, and Article VI:3 of the GATT 1994 on the other hand, is alleged in this appeal, nor do we see any such conflict. Therefore, the requirements of these provisions of the *SCM Agreement* and the GATT 1994 apply on a cumulative basis.

S.2.41.5 *US – Softwood Lumber IV*, para. 138
(WT/DS257/AB/R)

We note that, if we were to find that USDOC's final determination and the imposition of countervailing duties on Canadian imports of softwood lumber products contravene the requirements of Article VI:3 of the GATT 1994, the United States necessarily would *not* have "take[n] all necessary steps to ensure that the imposition of a countervailing duty . . . is in accordance with the provisions of Article VI of GATT 1994", as required by Article 10 of the *SCM Agreement*. The "specific action against a subsidy" taken by the United States would also *not*, as required by Article 32.1 of the *SCM Agreement*, be "in accordance with the provisions of GATT 1994, as interpreted by the [SCM] Agreement". Consequently, any inconsistency of the United States' imposition of countervailing duties on Canadian imports of softwood lumber products with Article VI:3 of the GATT 1994, would necessarily render this measure inconsistent *also* with Articles 10 and 32.1 of the *SCM Agreement*.

S.2.42 Article III:8 of the GATT 1994 – Subsidies

S.2.42.1 *Canada – Periodicals*, p. 34, DSR 1997:I, p. 449 at 478
(WT/DS31/AB/R)

. . . Indeed, an examination of the text, context, and object and purpose of Article III:8(b) suggests that it was intended to exempt from the obligations of Article III only the payment of subsidies which involves the expenditure of revenue by a government.

S.2.43 Article VI:3 of the GATT 1994 – Subsidies. *See also* Anti-Dumping Agreement, Article 18.1 – Specific action against dumping (A.3.61); SCM Agreement, Article 1.1 – Pass-through of indirect subsidies (S.2.10); SCM Agreement, Article 32.1 – Specific action against a subsidy (S.2.36)

S.2.43.1 *US – Softwood Lumber IV*, para. 139
(WT/DS257/AB/R)

The Panel described the pass-through problem as follows: "[w]here the subsidies at issue are received by someone other than the producer of the investigated product, the question arises whether there is subsidization in respect of that product." In addressing this question, we note that Article VI:3 prohibits levying countervailing duties on an imported product "*in excess* of an amount equal to the estimated . . . subsidy determined to have been granted, directly or indirectly, on the manufacture, production or export of such product". (emphasis added) According to Article VI:3, countervailing duties are "levied for the purpose of offsetting . . . subsid[ies] bestowed, *directly or indirectly*, upon the *manufacture*, *production or export* of any *merchandise*". (emphasis added) The definition of the term "countervailing duties" in footnote 36 to Article 10 of the *SCM Agreement* is along the same lines.

S.2.43.2 *US – Softwood Lumber IV*, para. 140
(WT/DS257/AB/R)

The phrase "subsid[ies] bestowed . . . *indirectly*", as used in Article VI:3, implies that financial contributions by the government to the production of *inputs* used in manufacturing products subject to an investigation are not, in principle, excluded from the amount of subsidies that may be offset through the imposition of countervailing duties on the *processed product*. Where the producer of the input is not the same entity as the producer of the processed product, it cannot be presumed, however, that the subsidy bestowed on the input passes through to the processed product. In such case, it is necessary to analyze to what extent subsidies on inputs may be included in the determination of the total amount of subsidies bestowed upon processed products. For it is only the subsidies determined to have been granted upon the *processed products* that may be offset by levying countervailing duties on those products.

S.2.43.3 *US – Softwood Lumber IV*, para. 141
(WT/DS257/AB/R)

In our view, it would not be possible to determine whether countervailing duties levied on the processed product are *in excess* of the amount of the total subsidy accruing to that product, without establishing whether, and in what amount, subsidies bestowed on the producer of the input flowed through, downstream, to the producer of the product processed from that input. Because Article VI:3 permits *offsetting*, through countervailing duties, no more than the "subsidy determined to have been granted . . . directly or indirectly, on the manufacture [or] production . . . of such *product*", it follows that Members must not impose duties to offset an amount of the input subsidy that has *not* passed through to the countervailed processed products. It is only the amount by which an indirect subsidy granted to producers of inputs flows through to the processed product, together with the amount of subsidy bestowed directly on producers of the processed product, that may be offset through the imposition of countervailing duties. The definition of "countervailing duties" in footnote 36 to Article 10 of the *SCM Agreement* supports this interpretation of the requirements of Article VI:3 of the GATT 1994.

S.3 Scope of Appellate Review. *See also* Competence of Panels and the Appellate Body (C.3); Completion of the Legal Analysis by the Appellate Body (C.4); Conditional Appeals (C.5); Judicial Economy (J.1); Jurisdiction (J.2); Legislation as such vs. Specific Application (L.1); Standard of Review, Article 11 of the DSU (S.7.2–7); Terms of Reference of Panels (T.6); Working Procedures for Appellate Review (W.2)

S.3.1 General

S.3.1.1 *US – Gasoline*, p. 12, DSR 1996:I, p. 3 at 11
(WT/DS2/AB/R)

. . . to deal with those two issues [i.e. the clean air issue and the application of the TBT Agreement], under the circumstances of this appeal, would have required the Appellate Body casually to disregard its own *Working Procedures* and to do so in the absence of a compelling reason grounded on, for instance, fundamental fairness or *force majeure*. Venezuela and Brazil could have appealed the Panel's finding and non-finding on the two matters by taking advantage of Rules 23(1) or 23(4) of the *Working Procedures* and thereby placing the Appellate Body in a position to dispose of those issues directly in one and the same appellate proceeding.

. . . the route they chose for addressing the two issues in question is not contemplated by the *Working Procedures*, and therefore, these issues are not properly the subject of this appeal.

S.3.1.2 *US – Wool Shirts and Blouses*, p. 17, DSR 1997:I, p. 323 at 338
(WT/DS33/AB/R, WT/DS33/AB/R/Corr.1)

In our view, this statement by the Panel is purely a descriptive and gratuitous comment providing background concerning the Panel's understanding of how the TMB functions. We do not consider this comment by the Panel to be "a legal finding or conclusion" which the Appellate Body "may uphold, modify or reverse".

S.3.1.3 *EC – Poultry*, para. 107
(WT/DS69/AB/R)

. . . It is true that in footnote 140 of the Panel Report, the Panel states that paragraph 7.75 of the *European Communities – Bananas* panel reports and "particularly the use of the phrase 'all suppliers other than Members with a substantial interest in supplying the product' . . . indicates that the *Banana III* panel did not take the view that allocation of quota shares to non-Members under Article XIII:2(d) was not permitted". We do not consider this comment made in a footnote by the Panel to be either a "legal interpretation developed by the panel" within the meaning of Article 17.6 of the DSU or a "legal finding" or "conclusion" that the Appellate Body may "uphold, modify or reverse" under Article 17.13 of the DSU. It is undisputed in this case that there is no *allocation* of a country-specific share in the tariff-rate quota to a non-Member. There is, therefore, no finding nor any "legal interpretation developed by the panel" that may be the subject of an appeal of which the Appellate Body may take cognizance.

S.3.1.4 *Canada – Aircraft*, para. 211
(WT/DS70/AB/R)

In our view, this new argument raised by Brazil is beyond the scope of appellate review. Article 17.6 of the DSU provides that "[a]n appeal shall be limited to issues of law covered in the panel report and legal interpretations developed by the panel." In principle, new arguments are not *per se* excluded from the scope of appellate review, simply because they are new. However, for us to rule on Brazil's new argument, we would have to solicit, receive and review new facts that were not before the Panel, and were not considered by it. In our view, Article 17.6 of the DSU manifestly precludes us from engaging in any such enterprise. . . .

S.3.1.5 *US – FSC*, para. 103
(WT/DS108/AB/R)

. . . The argument which the United States asks us to address under the fifth sentence of footnote 59 involves two separate legal issues: first, that the FSC measure is a measure "to avoid double taxation of foreign-source income" within the meaning of footnote 59; and second, that, in consequence, the FSC measure is *excluded* from the prohibition in Article 3.1(a) of the *SCM Agreement* against export subsidies. In our view, examination of the substantive issues raised by this particular argument would be outside the scope of our mandate under Article 17.6 of the DSU, as this argument does not involve either an "issue of law covered in the panel report" or "legal interpretations developed by the panel". The Panel was simply not asked to address the issues raised by the United States' new argument. Further, the new argument now made before us would require us to address legal issues quite different from those which confronted the Panel and which may well require proof of new facts. ...

S.3.1.6 *US – Upland Cotton*, para. 745
(WT/DS267/AB/R)

At the outset, we observe that Article 17.6 of the DSU provides that appeals "shall be limited to issues of law covered in the panel report and legal interpretations developed by the panel". Furthermore, Article 17.12 of the DSU states that "[t]he Appellate Body shall address each of the issues raised in accordance with paragraph 6 during the appellate proceeding". The United States does not argue that Brazil has failed to appeal an issue of law or a legal interpretation. Thus, the United States is not asserting that Brazil could not have brought this claim on appeal or that we are legally precluded from addressing it. The United States' assertion is that it is not *necessary* for us to resolve Brazil's claim because Brazil is not requesting us to make findings that would result in DSB rulings and recommendations.

S.3.1.7 *EC – Export Subsidies on Sugar*, paras. 240–242
(WT/DS265/AB/R, WT/DS266/AB/R, WT/DS283/AB/R)

... the European Communities did *not* argue before the Panel that sales of A and B beet are "largely insufficient to cover all the fixed costs of producing C beet", in the manner in which it is arguing this point on appeal.

The Appellate Body previously held, in *Canada – Aircraft*, that new arguments are not excluded from the scope of appellate review "simply because they are new". However, in that case, the Appellate Body also said:

> ... for us to rule on [the] new argument [at issue], we would have to solicit, receive and review new facts that were not before the Panel, and were not considered by it. In our view, Article 17.6 of the DSU manifestly precludes us from engaging in any such enterprise.

In this respect, we note that the European Communities supports its argument on appeal with a table containing calculations ... This table was not placed before the Panel, but uses data drawn from Exhibits presented to the Panel by the Complaining Parties. We also note that the Complaining Parties, in their respective appellee's submissions and at the oral hearing, contested the accuracy of some of the calculations, as well as certain concepts underlying the European Communities' calculations.

S.3.2 Review of "objective assessment" by the panel – Article 11 of the DSU. *See also* Standard of Review, Article 11 of the DSU (S.7.2–7)

S.3.2.1 *EC – Hormones*, para. 132
(WT/DS26/AB/R, WT/DS48/AB/R)

...Whether or not a panel has made an objective assessment of the facts before it, as required by Article 11 of the DSU, is also a legal question which, if properly raised on appeal, would fall within the scope of appellate review.

S.3.2.2 *US – Countervailing Measures on Certain EC Products*, para. 74
(WT/DS212/AB/R)

...A *claim* of error by a panel under Article 11 of the DSU is possible only in the context of an appeal. By definition, this *claim* will not be found in requests for establishment of a panel, and panels therefore will not have referred to it in panel reports. Accordingly, if appellants intend to argue that issue on appeal, they must refer to it in Notices of Appeal in a way that will enable appellees to discern it and know the case they have to meet.

S.3.2.3 *EC – Poultry*, para. 133
(WT/DS69/AB/R)

An allegation that a panel has failed to conduct the "objective assessment of the matter before it" required by Article 11 of the DSU is a very serious allegation. Such an allegation goes to the very core of the integrity of the WTO dispute settlement process itself. ...

S.3.2.4 *US – Upland Cotton*, para. 398
(WT/DS267/AB/R)

In its opening statement delivered at the oral hearing, the United States confirmed that it has not made an Article 11 claim in this appeal.... Under these circumstances, there is no need for us to rule that the United States makes no Article 11 claim. We also refrain from ruling on whether the Panel complied with Article 11 of the DSU....

S.3.2.5 *US – Upland Cotton*, para. 399
(WT/DS267/AB/R)

We are nevertheless mindful of the scope of appellate review with respect to legal and factual matters. Pursuant to Article 17.6 of the DSU, appeals are "limited to issues of law covered in the panel report and legal interpretations developed by the panel". To the extent that the United States' arguments concern the Panel's appreciation and weighing of the evidence, we note from the outset that the Appellate Body will not interfere lightly with the Panel's discretion "as the trier of facts". At the same time, the Appellate Body has previously pointed out that the "consistency or inconsistency of a given fact or set of facts with the requirements of a given treaty provision is . . . a legal characterization issue". Whether the Panel properly interpreted the requirements of Article 6.3(c) of the *SCM Agreement* and properly applied that interpretation to the facts in this case is a legal question. This question is different from whether the Panel made "an objective assessment of the matter before it, including an objective assessment of the facts of the case", in accordance with Article 11 of the DSU. Therefore, the Panel's application of the legal requirements of Article 6.3(c) of the *SCM Agreement* to the facts of this case falls within the scope of our review in this appeal, despite the fact that the United States does not claim that the Panel erred under Article 11 of the DSU.

S.3.2.6 *US – Upland Cotton*, para. 695
(WT/DS267/AB/R)

Brazil has made an additional claim that the Panel failed to make an objective assessment of the matter, as required by Article 11 of the DSU. Having reversed the Panel's ultimate finding, we find that it is not necessary for us to rule on Brazil's additional claim under Article 11 of the DSU. This is because, even if we were to agree with Brazil, it would lead to the same result that we have reached after examining the Panel's application of Article 10.1 of the *Agreement on Agriculture* to the facts before it.

S.3.3 **Issues of law vs. Issues of fact.** *See also* Completion of the Legal Analysis by the Appellate Body (C.4); Mootness of Panel Findings as a Consequence of Appellate Body Rulings (M.3)

S.3.3.1 *Canada – Periodicals*, p. 22, DSR 1997:I, p. 449 at 468
(WT/DS31/AB/R)

We are mindful of the limitation of our mandate in Articles 17.6 and 17.13 of the *DSU*. According to Article 17.6, an appeal shall be limited to issues of law covered in the Panel Report and legal interpretations developed by the Panel. The determination of whether imported and domestic products are "like products" is a process by which legal rules have to be applied to facts. In any analysis of Article III:2, first sentence, this process is particularly delicate, since "likeness" must be construed narrowly and on a case-by-case basis. . . .

S.3.3.2 *EC – Bananas III*, paras. 206, 237, 239
(WT/DS27/AB/R)

On the first issue, the Panel found that the procedural and administrative requirements of the activity function rules for importing third-country and non-traditional ACP bananas differ from, and go significantly beyond, those required for importing traditional ACP bananas. This is a factual finding. . . .

. . .

It is, however, evident from the terms of its finding that the Panel concluded, as a matter of fact, that the *de facto* discrimination did continue to exist after the entry into force of the GATS. This factual finding is beyond review by the Appellate

Body. Thus, we do not reverse or modify the Panel's conclusion in paragraph 7.308 of the Panel Reports.

. . .

In our view, the conclusions by the Panel on whether Del Monte is a Mexican company, the ownership and control of companies established in the European Communities that provide wholesale trade services in bananas, the market shares of suppliers of Complaining Parties' origin as compared with suppliers of EC (or ACP) origin, and the nationality of the majority of operators that "include or directly represent" EC (or ACP) producers, are all factual conclusions. Therefore, we decline to rule on these arguments made by the European Communities.

S.3.3.3 *EC – Hormones*, para. 132
(WT/DS26/AB/R, WT/DS48/AB/R)

Under Article 17.6 of the DSU, appellate review is limited to appeals on questions of law covered in a panel report and legal interpretations developed by the panel. Findings of fact, as distinguished from legal interpretations or legal conclusions, by a panel are, in principle, not subject to review by the Appellate Body. The determination of whether or not a certain event did occur in time and space is typically a question of fact; for example, the question of whether or not Codex has adopted an international standard, guideline or recommendation on MGA is a factual question. Determination of the credibility and weight properly to be ascribed to (that is, the appreciation of) a given piece of evidence is part and parcel of the fact finding process and is, in principle, left to the discretion of a panel as the trier of facts. The consistency or inconsistency of a given fact or set of facts with the requirements of a given treaty provision is, however, a legal characterization issue. It is a legal question. . . .

S.3.3.4 *Australia – Salmon*, para. 261
(WT/DS18/AB/R)

The Panel's consideration and weighing of the evidence in support of Canada's claims relates to its assessment of the facts and, therefore, falls outside the scope of appellate review under Article 17.6 of the DSU.

S.3.3.5 *Korea – Alcoholic Beverages*, paras. 161–162
(WT/DS75/AB/R, WT/DS84/AB/R)

The Panel's examination and weighing of the evidence submitted fall, in principle, within the scope of the Panel's discretion as the trier of facts and, accordingly, outside the scope of appellate review. This is true, for instance, with respect to the Panel's treatment of the Dodwell Study, the Sofres Report and the Nielsen Study. We cannot second-guess the Panel in appreciating either the evidentiary value of such studies or the consequences, if any, of alleged defects in those studies. Similarly, it is not for us to review the relative weight ascribed to evidence on such matters as marketing studies, methods of production, taste, colour, places of consumption, consumption with "meals" or with "snacks", and prices.

A panel's discretion as trier of facts is not, of course, unlimited. That discretion is always subject to, and is circumscribed by, among other things, the panel's duty to render an objective assessment of the matter before it. . . .

S.3.3.6 *India – Quantitative Restrictions*, paras. 143–144 (WT/DS90/AB/R)

As to the second alleged mistake, namely, that the evidence introduced by the United States could not, as a matter of law, have constituted a *prima facie* case that India's balance-of-payments restrictions were not justified under the Ad Note, . . .

We believe that this second mistake alleged by India relates to the weighing and assessing of the evidence adduced by the United States, and is, therefore, outside the scope of appellate review.

S.3.3.7 *US – Wheat Gluten*, paras. 150–151 (WT/DS166/AB/R)

. . . we recall that, in previous appeals, we have emphasized that the role of the Appellate Body differs from the role of panels. Under Article 17.6 of the DSU, appeals are "limited to *issues of law* covered in the panel report and *legal* interpretations developed by the panel". (emphasis added) By contrast, we have previously stated that, under Article 11 of the DSU, panels are:

> . . . charged with the mandate to determine the *facts* of the case and to arrive at *factual findings*. In carrying out this mandate, a panel has the duty to examine and consider all the evidence before it, not just the evidence submitted by one or the other party, and to evaluate the relevance and probative force of each piece thereof. (emphasis added)

We have also stated previously that, although the task of panels under Article 11 relates, in part, to its assessment of the *facts*, the question whether a panel has made an "objective assessment" of the facts is a *legal* one, that may be the subject of an appeal. (emphasis added) However, in view of the distinction between the respective roles of the Appellate Body and panels, we have taken care to emphasize that a panel's appreciation of the evidence falls, in principle, "within the *scope of the panel's discretion as the trier of facts*". (emphasis added) In assessing the panel's appreciation of the evidence, we cannot base a finding of inconsistency under Article 11 simply on the conclusion that we might have reached a different factual finding from the one the panel reached. Rather, we must be satisfied that the panel has exceeded the bounds of its discretion, as the trier of facts, in its appreciation of the evidence. As is clear from previous appeals, we will not interfere lightly with the panel's exercise of its discretion.

S.3.3.8 *US – Section 211 Appropriations Act*, paras. 105–106 (WT/DS176/AB/R)

Our rulings in these previous appeals are clear: the municipal law of WTO Members may serve not only as evidence of facts, but also as evidence of compliance or non-compliance with international obligations. Under the DSU, a panel may examine the municipal law of a WTO Member for the purpose of determining whether that Member has complied with its obligations under the *WTO Agreement*. Such an assessment is a legal characterization by a panel. And, therefore, a panel's assessment of municipal law as to its consistency with WTO obligations is subject to appellate review under Article 17.6 of the DSU.

To address the legal issues raised in this appeal, we must, therefore, necessarily examine the Panel's interpretation of the meaning of Section 211 under United States law . . . The meaning given by the Panel to Section 211 is, thus, clearly within the scope of our review as set out in Article 17.6 of the DSU.

S.3.3.9 *EC – Sardines*, para. 299 (WT/DS231/AB/R)

. . . As we have stated in several previous appeals, panels enjoy a discretion as the trier of facts; they enjoy "a margin of discretion in assessing the value of the evidence, and the weight to be ascribed to that evidence." We have also said that we will not "interfere lightly" with the Panel's appreciation of the evidence: we will not intervene solely because we might have reached a different factual finding from the one the panel reached; we will intervene only if we are "satisfied that the panel has exceeded the bounds of its discretion, as the trier of facts, in its appreciation of the evidence".

S.3.3.10 *Chile Price Band System*, para. 224 (WT/DS207/AB/R)

. . . the Panel's characterization of its finding "as a factual matter" does not mean that the issue whether Chile's price band system is a border measure similar to a variable import levy or a minimum import price is shielded from appellate review. This is a question of law, and not of fact, and thus is clearly within our jurisdiction under Article 17.6 of the DSU. As we said in our Report in *EC – Hormones* [in paragraph 132], the assessment of the consistency or inconsistency of a given fact or set of facts with the requirements of a given treaty provision is an issue of legal characterization. The mere assertion by a panel that its conclusion is a "factual matter" does not make it so. Here, the Panel's interpretation of the terms "variable import levies", "minimum import prices", and "similar border measures other than ordinary customs duties", as these terms are used in footnote 1, constitutes, not a *factual* determination, but rather a *legal* interpretation of the words of Article 4.2. Hence, these interpretations are within the purview of appellate review under Article 17.6 of the DSU. Moreover, the Panel's appraisal of Chile's price band system in the light of its legal interpretation is an application of the law to the facts of the case. All the same, in reviewing the Panel's assessment of Chile's price band system, we are mindful of the need to give due deference to the discretion of the Panel, as the "trier of fact", to weigh the evidence before it.

S.3.3.11 *US – Offset Act (Byrd Amendment)*, para. 222
(WT/DS217/AB/R, WT/DS234/AB/R)

. . . Article 17.6 is clear in limiting our jurisdiction to issues of law covered in panel reports and legal interpretations developed by panels. We have no authority to consider new facts on appeal. The fact that the documents are "available on the public record" does not excuse us from the limitations imposed by Article 17.6. We note that the other participants have not had an opportunity to comment on those documents and, in order to do so, may feel required to adduce yet more evidence. We would also be precluded from considering such evidence. . . .

S.3.3.12 *US – Upland Cotton*, para. 399
(WT/DS267/AB/R)

We are nevertheless mindful of the scope of appellate review with respect to legal and factual matters. Pursuant to Article 17.6 of the DSU, appeals are "limited to issues of law covered in the panel report and legal interpretations developed by the panel". To the extent that the United States' arguments concern the Panel's appreciation and weighing of the evidence, we note from the outset that the Appellate Body will not interfere lightly with the Panel's discretion "as the trier of facts". At the same time, the Appellate Body has previously pointed out that the "consistency or inconsistency of a given fact or set of facts with the requirements of a given treaty provision is . . . a legal characterization issue". Whether the Panel properly interpreted the requirements of Article 6.3(c) of the *SCM Agreement* and properly applied that interpretation to the facts in this case is a legal question. This question is different from whether the Panel made "an objective assessment of the matter before it, including an objective assessment of the facts of the case", in accordance with Article 11 of the DSU. Therefore, the Panel's application of the legal requirements of Article 6.3(c) of the *SCM Agreement* to the facts of this case falls within the scope of our review in this appeal, despite the fact that the United States does not claim that the Panel erred under Article 11 of the DSU.

S.3.3.13 *US – Upland Cotton*, para. 411
(WT/DS267/AB/R)

. . . In our view, whether a world market for upland cotton and a world price for upland cotton exist in the circumstances of this case are factual questions. . . .

S.3.3.14 *US – Upland Cotton*, para. 413
(WT/DS267/AB/R)

Whether or not Brazilian and United States upland cotton competed in the "world market for upland cotton" during the period the Panel examined is a factual question. . . .

S.3.3.15 *US – Upland Cotton*, para. 445
(WT/DS267/AB/R)

. . . We are . . . satisfied that the Panel adopted a plausible view of the facts in connection with expected prices and planting decisions, even though it attributed to these factors a different weight or meaning than did the United States. As the Appellate Body has said, it is not necessary for panels to "accord to factual evidence of the parties the same meaning and weight as do the parties".

S.3.3.16 *US – Upland Cotton*, para. 446
(WT/DS267/AB/R)

. . . It would not amount to an error in the application of Article 6.3(c) to the facts of this case for the Panel not to address specifically in its Report every item of evidence provided and to refer explicitly to every argument made by the parties, if the Panel considered certain items or arguments less significant for its reasoning than others.

S.3.3.17 *US – Upland Cotton*, para. 663
(WT/DS267/AB/R)

The United States has styled its claim as related to the interpretation and application of item (j) of the Illustrative List of Export Subsidies annexed to the *SCM Agreement*. According to the United States, the Panel could not have reached a legal conclusion under item (j) without having necessarily determined what were the long-term operating costs and losses of the United States' export credit guarantee programs, and more specifically, made a determination in respect of the treatment of rescheduled debt. We find no difficulty with the United States' approach. Its claim relates to the Panel's application of item (j) to the specific facts of the case. The United States is not asking us to review the Panel's factual findings, nor is it arguing that the Panel's assessment of the matter was not objective. Instead, the United States' claim relates to the application of the legal standard set out in item (j) of the Illustrative List of Export Subsidies to the specific facts of this case. It is an issue of legal characterization. Thus, we do not agree with Brazil's contention that the United States was under an obligation to bring its claim under Article 11 of the DSU. Consequently, our inquiry will be limited to the Panel's application of the law to the facts in this case.

S.3.4 Need to Address Each Issue Raised (Article 17.12 of the DSU)

S.3.4.1 *US – Upland Cotton*, paras. 508, 510–511
(WT/DS267/AB/R)

Nor do we believe that it is necessary to make a finding on the interpretation of the phrase "world market share" in Article 6.3(d) of the *SCM Agreement*. We recall that Article 17.12 of the DSU requires that the "Appellate Body shall address each of the issues raised in accordance with paragraph 6 [of Article 17] during the appellate proceeding". . . . For its part, Article 3.4 of the DSU provides that "[r]ecommendations or rulings made by the DSB shall be aimed at achieving a satisfactory settlement of the matter". Similarly, Article 3.7 states that "[t]he aim of the dispute settlement mechanism is to secure a positive solution to a dispute".

. . .

With this in mind, we observe that although an interpretation by the Appellate Body, in the abstract, of the meaning of the phrase "world market share" in Article 6.3(d) of the *SCM Agreement* might offer at best some degree of "guidance" on that issue, it would not affect the resolution of this particular dispute. Indeed, irrespective of whether we were to uphold or reverse the Panel's finding on this issue, upon adoption of the recommendations and rulings by the DSB, the United States would be under no additional obligation regarding implementation. Thus, although we recognize that there may be cases in which it would be useful for us to review an issue, despite the fact that our ruling would not result in rulings and recommendations by the DSB, we find no compelling reason for doing so in this case.

Accordingly, we believe that an interpretation of the phrase "world market share" in Article 6.3(d) of the *SCM Agreement* is unnecessary for purposes of resolving this dispute. We emphasize that we neither uphold nor reverse the Panel's findings on the interpretation of the phrase "world market share" in Article 6.3(d) of the *SCM Agreement.*

S.3.4.2 *US – Upland Cotton*, para. 695
(WT/DS267/AB/R)

Brazil has made an additional claim that the Panel failed to make an objective assessment of the matter, as required by Article 11 of the DSU. Having reversed the Panel's ultimate finding, we find that it is not necessary for us to rule on Brazil's additional claim under Article 11 of the DSU. This is because, even if we were to agree with Brazil, it would lead to the same result that we have reached after examining the Panel's application of Article 10.1 of the *Agreement on Agriculture* to the facts before it.

S.3.4.3 *US – Upland Cotton*, para. 745
(WT/DS267/AB/R)

At the outset, we observe that Article 17.6 of the DSU provides that appeals "shall be limited to issues of law covered in the panel report and legal interpretations developed by the panel". Furthermore, Article 17.12 of the DSU states that "[t]he Appellate Body shall address each of the issues raised in accordance with paragraph 6 during the appellate proceeding". The United States does not argue that Brazil has failed to appeal an issue of law or a legal interpretation. Thus, the United States is not asserting that Brazil could not have brought this claim on appeal or that we are legally precluded from addressing it. The United States' assertion is that it is not *necessary* for us to resolve Brazil's claim because Brazil is not requesting us to make findings that would result in DSB rulings and recommendations.

S.3.4.4 *US – Upland Cotton*, para. 746
(WT/DS267/AB/R)

We agree. Article 3.3 of the DSU explains that the aim of the WTO's dispute settlement system is the "prompt settlement of situations in which a Member considers that any benefits accruing to it directly or indirectly under the covered agreements are being impaired by measures taken by another Member". For its part, Article 3.4 of the DSU provides that "[r]ecommendations or rulings made by the DSB shall be aimed at achieving a satisfactory settlement of the matter". Similarly, Article 3.7 states that "[t]he aim of the dispute settlement mechanism is to secure a positive solution to a dispute". The Appellate Body, moreover, has cautioned that "[g]iven the explicit aim of dispute settlement that permeates the *DSU*, ... Article 3.2 of the *DSU* is [not] meant to encourage either panels or the Appellate Body to 'make law' by clarifying existing provisions of the *WTO Agreement* outside the context of resolving a particular dispute".

S.3.4.5 *US – Upland Cotton*, para. 747
(WT/DS267/AB/R)

In this case, Brazil's claim on appeal is limited to the Panel's application of the burden of proof. Brazil has expressly stated that it is not requesting us to complete the analysis. In view of Brazil's request, our ruling would not result in recommendations or rulings by the DSB in respect of the ETI Act of 2000. In these circumstances, we fail to see how our examination of Brazil's claim would contribute to the "prompt" or "satisfactory settlement" of this matter or would contribute to "secure a positive solution" to this dispute. Even if we were to disagree with the manner in which the Panel applied the burden of proof, we would not make any findings in respect of the WTO-consistency of the ETI Act of 2000. We recognize that there may be cases in which it would be useful for us to make a finding on an issue, despite the fact that our decision would not result in rulings and recommendations by the DSB. In this case, however, we find no compelling reason for doing so on this particular issue.

S.3.4.6 *US – Upland Cotton*, para. 748
(WT/DS267/AB/R)

For these reasons, we decline Brazil's request that we reverse the Panel's conclusion that Brazil did not make a *prima facie* case that the ETI Act of 2000 is inconsistent with the United States' WTO obligations. In declining to rule on Brazil's request, we neither endorse nor reject the manner in which the Panel applied the burden of proof in the context of examining Brazil's claim against the ETI Act of 2000.

S.3.4.7 *US – Upland Cotton*, paras. 761–762
(WT/DS267/AB/R)

Nor do we believe that it is necessary to make a finding on the interpretation of the phrase "any form of subsidy which operates to increase the export of any primary product" in the second sentence of Article XVI:3 of the GATT 1994 in order to resolve this dispute. Given our ruling under Article 6.3(c) of the *SCM*

Agreement, we observe that, although any ruling by the Appellate Body on the scope of the subsidies covered by Article XVI:3 of the GATT 1994 in the abstract might at best offer some degree of "guidance", it would not affect the resolution of this dispute. Indeed, irrespective of whether we were to uphold or reverse the Panel's finding on this issue, upon adoption of the recommendations and rulings by the DSB, the United States would be under no additional obligation regarding implementation. Thus, although we recognize that there may be cases in which it would be useful for us to make a finding on an issue, despite the fact that our finding would not result in recommendations and rulings by the DSB, we find no compelling reason for doing so in this case in respect of this particular issue.

We therefore believe that an interpretation of the phrase "any form of subsidy which operates to increase the export" in Article XVI:3 of the GATT 1994 is unnecessary for purposes of resolving this dispute. We emphasize that we neither uphold nor reverse the Panel's interpretation of this phrase in the second sentence of Article XVI:3.

S.4 Seek Information and Technical Advice. *See also* Amicus Curiae briefs (A.2); Burden of Proof (B.3); Evidence (E.3); Inferences Drawn from the Refusal of a Party to Provide Information (I.1); Standard of Review, Article 11 of the DSU (S.7.2–7)

S.4.1 *EC – Hormones*, para. 147

(WT/DS26/AB/R, WT/DS48/AB/R)

. . . Both Article 11.2 of the *SPS Agreement* and Article 13 of the DSU enable panels to seek information and advice as they deem appropriate in a particular case. . . .

. . . We find that in disputes involving scientific or technical issues, neither Article 11.2 of the *SPS Agreement*, nor Article 13 of the DSU prevents panels from consulting with individual experts. Rather, both the *SPS Agreement* and the DSU leave to the sound discretion of a panel the determination of whether the establishment of an expert review group is necessary or appropriate.

S.4.2 *EC – Hormones*, para. 148

(WT/DS26/AB/R, WT/DS48/AB/R)

. . . The rules and procedures set forth in Appendix 4 of the DSU apply in situations in which expert review groups have been established. However, this is not the situation in this particular case. Consequently, once the panel has decided to request the opinion of individual scientific experts, there is no legal obstacle to the panel drawing up, in consultation with the parties to the dispute, *ad hoc* rules for those particular proceedings.

S.4.3 *Argentina – Textiles and Apparel*, paras. 82, 84
(WT/DS56/AB/R, WT/DS56/AB/R/Corr.1)

...The DSU gives panels different means or instruments for complying with Article 11; among these is the right to "seek information and technical advice" provided in Article 13 of the DSU. ...

...

The only provision of the *WTO Agreement* that *requires* consultations with the IMF is Article XV:2 of the GATT 1994. This provision *requires* the WTO to consult with the IMF when dealing with "problems concerning monetary reserves, balances of payments or foreign exchange arrangements". However, this case does not relate to these matters. Article 13.1 of the DSU gives a panel "... the right to seek information and technical advice from any individual or body which it *deems appropriate*." (emphasis added) Pursuant to Article 13.2 of the DSU, a panel may seek information from any relevant source and may consult experts to obtain their opinions on certain aspects of the matter at issue. This is a grant of discretionary authority: a panel is not duty-bound to seek information in each and every case or to consult particular experts under this provision. ...

S.4.4 *US – Shrimp*, para. 104
(WT/DS58/AB/R)

The comprehensive nature of the authority of a panel to "seek" information and technical advice from "any individual or body" it may consider appropriate, or from "any relevant source", should be underscored. This authority embraces more than merely the choice and evaluation of the *source* of the information or advice which it may seek. A panel's authority includes the authority to decide *not to seek* such information or advice at all. We consider that a panel also has the authority to *accept or reject* any information or advice which it may have sought and received, or to *make some other appropriate disposition* thereof. It is particularly within the province and the authority of a panel to determine *the need for information and advice* in a specific case, to ascertain the *acceptability* and *relevancy* of information or advice received, and to decide *what weight to ascribe to that information or advice* or to conclude that no weight at all should be given to what has been received.

S.4.5 *US – Shrimp*, paras. 108–109
(WT/DS58/AB/R)

... authority to *seek* information is not properly equated with a *prohibition* on accepting information which has been submitted without having been requested by a panel. A panel has the discretionary authority either to accept and consider or to reject information and advice submitted to it, *whether requested by a panel or not*. The fact that a panel may *motu proprio* have initiated the request for information does not, by itself, bind the panel to accept and consider the information which is actually submitted. The amplitude of the authority vested in panels to shape the processes of fact-finding and legal interpretation makes clear that a panel will *not* be deluged, as it were, with non-requested material, *unless that panel allows itself to be so deluged*.

Moreover, acceptance and rejection of the information and advice of the kind here submitted to the Panel need not exhaust the universe of possible appropriate dispositions thereof. . . .

S.4.6 *Japan – Agricultural Products II*, paras. 127–128
(WT/DS76/AB/R)

. . . Article 13 of the DSU allows a panel to seek *information* from any relevant source and to consult individual experts or expert bodies to obtain their *opinion* on certain aspects of the matter before it. In our Report in *United States – Import Prohibition of Certain Shrimp and Shrimp Products* ("*United States – Shrimp*") [Appellate Body Report, para. 104], we noted the "comprehensive nature" of this authority, and stated that this authority is "indispensably necessary" to enable a panel to discharge its duty imposed by Article 11 of the DSU to "make an objective assessment of the matter before it, including an *objective assessment of the facts of the case* and the *applicability of and conformity with the relevant covered agreements. . . .*"

Furthermore, we note that the present dispute is a dispute under the *SPS Agreement*. Article 11.2 of the *SPS Agreement* explicitly *instructs* panels in disputes under this Agreement involving scientific and technical issues to "seek advice from experts".

S.4.7 *Japan – Agricultural Products II*, para. 129
(WT/DS76/AB/R)

Article 13 of the DSU and Article 11.2 of the *SPS Agreement* suggest that panels have a significant investigative authority. However, this authority cannot be used by a panel to rule in favour of a complaining party which has not established a *prima facie* case of inconsistency based on specific legal claims asserted by it. A panel is entitled to seek information and advice from experts and from any other relevant source it chooses, pursuant to Article 13 of the DSU and, in an SPS case, Article 11.2 of the *SPS Agreement*, to help it to understand and evaluate the evidence submitted and the arguments made by the parties, but not to make the case for a complaining party.

S.4.8 *Canada – Aircraft*, para. 185
(WT/DS70/AB/R)

It is clear from the language of Article 13 that the discretionary authority of a panel may be exercised to request and obtain information, not just "from any individual or body" within the jurisdiction of a Member of the WTO, but also from *any Member*, including *a fortiori* a Member who is a party to a dispute before a panel. This is made crystal clear by the third sentence of Article 13.1, which states: "*A Member* should respond promptly and fully to *any request by a panel for such information as the panel considers necessary and appropriate*." (emphasis added) It is equally important to stress that this discretionary authority to seek and obtain information is *not* made conditional by this, or any other provision, of the DSU upon the other party to the dispute having previously established, on a *prima facie* basis, such other party's claim or defence. Indeed, Article 13.1 imposes *no conditions* on the exercise of this discretionary authority. Canada argues that the Panel in this case had *no authority to request* the submission of information relating to the EDC's financing of the ASA transaction because Brazil had not previously established a *prima facie* case that the financial contribution offered by such financing conferred a "benefit" on ASA and therefore satisfied that other prerequisite of a prohibited export subsidy. This argument is, quite simply, bereft of any textual or logical basis. There is nothing in either the DSU or the *SCM Agreement* to sustain it. Nor can any support for this argument be derived from a consideration of the nature of the functions and responsibilities entrusted to panels in the WTO dispute settlement system – a consideration which we essay below. . . .

S.4.9 *Canada – Aircraft*, para. 187
(WT/DS70/AB/R)

. . . we are of the view that the word "should" in the third sentence of Article 13.1 is, in the context of the whole of Article 13, used in a normative, rather than a merely exhortative, sense. Members are, in other words, under a duty and an obligation to "respond promptly and fully" to requests made by panels for information under Article 13.1 of the DSU.

S.4.10 *Canada – Aircraft*, para. 203
(WT/DS70/AB/R)

Clearly, in our view, the Panel had the legal authority and the discretion to draw inferences from the facts before it – including the fact that Canada had refused to provide information sought by the Panel. . . .

S.4.11 *Thailand – H-Beams*, para. 135
(WT/DS122/AB/R)

With respect to Thailand's argument that the claims of Poland were not sufficiently clear, and that the Panel, therefore, overstepped the limits of its authority in asking questions of the parties, we note that we have previously stated that panels are entitled to ask questions of the parties that they deem relevant to the consideration of the issues before them. In our Report in *Canada – Measures Affecting the Export of Civilian Aircraft*, we dismissed the view that a panel has no authority to ask a question relating to claims for which the complaining party had not first established a *prima facie* case, and stated that such an argument was "bereft of any textual or logical basis".

S.4.12 *EC – Sardines*, para. 302
(WT/DS231/AB/R)

. . . Article 13.2 of the DSU provides that "[p]anels may seek information from any relevant source and may consult experts to obtain their opinion on certain aspects of the matter." This provision is clearly phrased in a manner that attributes discretion to panels, and we have interpreted it in this vein. Our statements in *EC – Hormones*, *Argentina – Measures Affecting Imports of Footwear, Textiles, Apparel and Other Items* ("*Argentina – Textiles and Apparel*"), and *US – Shrimp*, all support the conclusion that, under Article 13.2 of the DSU, panels enjoy discretion as to *whether or not* to seek information from external sources. In this case, the Panel evidently concluded that it did not need to request information from the Codex Commission, and conducted itself accordingly. We believe that, in doing so, the Panel acted within the limits of Article 13.2 of the DSU. A contravention of the duty under Article 11 of the DSU to make an objective assessment of the facts of the case cannot result from the due exercise of the discretion permitted by another provision of the DSU, in this instance Article 13.2 of the DSU.

S.4.13 *US – Carbon Steel*, para. 153
(WT/DS213/AB/R, WT/DS213/AB/R/Corr.1)

We also wish to underline that although panels enjoy a *discretion*, pursuant to Article 13 of the DSU, to seek information "from any relevant source", Article 11 of the DSU imposes no *obligation* on panels to conduct their own fact-finding exercise, or to fill in gaps in the arguments made by parties. In consequence, given that the European Communities itself had submitted no evidence – other than the text of the provision – on this point, the Panel did not act inconsistently with Article 11 in refraining from seeking additional information on its own initiative.

S.4.14 *EC – Bed Linen (Article 21.5 – India)*, para. 167
(WT/DS141/AB/RW)

. . . a panel's duty to "actively review the pertinent facts" in order to comply with Article 17.6(i) of the *Anti-Dumping Agreement* does not, in our view, imply that a panel *must* exercise its right to seek information under Article 13 of the DSU, which explicitly states that the exercise of that right is *discretionary*. Indeed, there is nothing in the texts of Article 17.6(i) of the *Anti-Dumping Agreement* or Article 13 of the DSU to suggest that a reading of these provisions, in combination, would render *mandatory* the exercise of a panel's *discretionary* power under Article 13 of the DSU . . . The mere fact that the Panel did not consider it necessary to seek information does not, by itself, imply that the Panel's exercise of its discretion was not "due". We, therefore, reject India's allegation that the Panel failed to comply with the requirements of Article 17.6 of the *Anti-Dumping Agreement* by not seeking information from the European Communities pursuant to Article 13 of the DSU.

Separate Panel Reports. *See* Panel Reports, Separate Panel Reports (P.1.3)

Special and Differential Treatment. *See* Enabling Clause (E.1); SCM Agreement, Article 27 – Special and differential treatment for developing country Members (S.2.35)

S.5 Special or Additional Rules and Procedures for Dispute Settlement. *See also* Anti-Dumping Agreement, Article 17 (A.3.54)

S.5.1 *S.5.1 Guatemala – Cement I*, para. 64
(WT/DS60/AB/R)

. . . Article 17.3 of the *Anti-Dumping Agreement* is not listed in Appendix 2 of the DSU as a special or additional rule and procedure. It is not listed precisely because it provides the legal basis for consultations to be requested by a complaining Member under the *Anti-Dumping Agreement*. Indeed, it is the equivalent provision in the *Anti-Dumping Agreement* to Articles XXII and XXIII of the GATT 1994, which serve as the basis for consultations and dispute settlement under the GATT 1994, under most of the other agreements in Annex 1A of the *Marrakesh Agreement Establishing the World Trade Organization* (the "*WTO Agreement*"), and under the *Agreement on Trade-Related Aspects of Intellectual Property Rights* (the "*TRIPS Agreement*").

S.5.2 *Guatemala – Cement I*, para. 65
(WT/DS60/AB/R)

. . . it is only where the provisions of the DSU and the special or additional rules and procedures of a covered agreement *cannot* be read as *complementing* each other that the special or additional provisions are to *prevail*. A special or additional provision should only be found to *prevail* over a provision of the DSU in a situation where adherence to the one provision will lead to a violation of the other provision, that is, in the case of a *conflict* between them. An interpreter must, therefore, identify an *inconsistency* or a *difference* between a provision of the DSU and a special or additional provision of a covered agreement *before* concluding that the latter *prevails* and that the provision of the DSU does not apply.

S.5.3 *Guatemala – Cement I*, paras. 67–68
(WT/DS60/AB/R)

Clearly, the consultation and dispute settlement provisions of a covered agreement are not meant to *replace*, as a coherent system of dispute settlement for that agreement, the rules and procedures of the DSU. To read Article 17 of the *Anti-Dumping Agreement* as *replacing* the DSU system as a whole is to deny the integrated nature of the WTO dispute settlement system established by Article 1.1 of the DSU. . . .

... we conclude that the Panel erred in finding that Article 17 of the *Anti-Dumping Agreement* "provides for a coherent set of rules for dispute settlement specific to anti-dumping cases ... that replaces the more general approach of the DSU."

S.5.4 *US – Corrosion-Resistant Steel Sunset Review*, footnote 82 to para. 83 (WT/DS244/AB/R)

... We recall, that Article 1.1 of the DSU applies the rules and procedures contained in the DSU to "disputes brought pursuant to the consultation and dispute settlement provisions of the agreements listed in Appendix 1", but that this general rule is, under Article 1.2 of the DSU, subject to the special or additional rules and procedures on dispute settlement identified in Appendix 2 to the DSU. The *Anti-Dumping Agreement* is listed as a covered agreement in Appendix 1 of the DSU. Articles 17.4 through 17.7 of the *Anti-Dumping Agreement* are listed as special or additional rules in Appendix 2 to the DSU.

S.6 SPS Agreement

S.6.1 Difference between the appropriate level of protection and the SPS measure chosen to implement. *See also* SPS Agreement, Article 5 (S.6.9–23)

S.6.1.1 *Australia – Salmon*, para. 199 (WT/DS18/AB/R)

We do not believe that Article 11 of the DSU, or any other provision of the DSU or of the *SPS Agreement*, entitles the Panel or the Appellate Body, for the purpose of applying Article 5.6 in the present case, to substitute its own reasoning about the implied level of protection for that expressed consistently by Australia. The determination of the appropriate level of protection, a notion defined in paragraph 5 of Annex A, as "the level of protection deemed appropriate by the Member establishing a sanitary... measure", is a *prerogative* of the Member concerned and not of a panel or of the Appellate Body.

S.6.1.2 *Australia – Salmon*, paras. 200–201 (WT/DS18/AB/R)

The "appropriate level of protection" established by a Member and the "SPS measure" have to be clearly distinguished. They are not one and the same thing. The first is an *objective*, the second is an *instrument* chosen to attain or implement that objective.

It can be deduced from the provisions of the *SPS Agreement* that the determination by a Member of the "appropriate level of protection" logically precedes the establishment or decision on maintenance of an "SPS measure". The provisions of the *SPS Agreement* also clarify the correlation between the "appropriate level of protection" and the "SPS measure".

S.6.1.3 *Australia – Salmon*, para. 203
(WT/DS18/AB/R)

...The words of Article 5.6, in particular the terms "*when establishing or maintaining* sanitary ... protection", demonstrate that the determination of the level of protection is an element in the decision-making process which logically *precedes* and is *separate* from the establishment or maintenance of the SPS measure. It is the appropriate level of protection which determines the SPS measure to be introduced or maintained, not the SPS measure introduced or maintained which determines the appropriate level of protection. To imply the appropriate level of protection from the existing SPS measure would be to assume that the measure always achieves the appropriate level of protection determined by the Member. That clearly cannot be the case.

S.6.1.4 *Australia – Salmon*, para. 206
(WT/DS18/AB/R)

We thus believe that the *SPS Agreement* contains an implicit obligation to determine the appropriate level of protection. We do not believe that there is an obligation to determine the appropriate level of protection in quantitative terms. This does not mean, however, that an importing Member is free to determine its level of protection with such vagueness or equivocation that the application of the relevant provisions of the *SPS Agreement*, such as Article 5.6, becomes impossible. It would obviously be wrong to interpret the *SPS Agreement* in a way that would render nugatory entire Articles or paragraphs of Articles of this Agreement and allow Members to escape from their obligations under this Agreement.

S.6.1.5 *Australia – Salmon*, para. 207
(WT/DS18/AB/R)

...we believe that in cases where a Member does not determine its appropriate level of protection, or does so with insufficient precision, the appropriate level of protection may be established by panels on the basis of the level of protection reflected in the SPS measure actually applied. Otherwise, a Member's failure to comply with the implicit obligation to determine its appropriate level of protection – with sufficient precision – would allow it to escape from its obligations under this Agreement and, in particular, its obligations under Articles 5.5 and 5.6.

S.6.2 Article 2 – Basic rights and obligations. *See also* SPS Agreement, Article 5.1 (S.6.9–14)

S.6.2.1 *EC – Hormones*, para. 250
(WT/DS26/AB/R, WT/DS48/AB/R)

...We are, of course, surprised by the fact that the Panel did not begin its analysis of this whole case by focusing on Article 2 that is captioned "Basic Rights and Obligations", an approach that appears logically attractive. We recall the reading that we have given above to Articles 2 and 5 – that Article 2.2 informs Article 5.1, and that similarly Article 2.3 informs Article 5.5 – but believe that further analysis of their relationship should await another case.

S.6.3 **Article 2.2 – "sufficient scientific evidence".** *See also* Burden of Proof, Presumption – prima facie case (B.3.2); SPS Agreement, Article 5.1 (S.6.9–14); SPS Agreement, Article 5.7 (S.6.19–23)

S.6.3.1 *EC – Hormones*, para. 177
(WT/DS26/AB/R, WT/DS48/AB/R)

. . . The requirements of a risk assessment under Article 5.1, as well as of "sufficient scientific evidence" under Article 2.2, are essential for the maintenance of the delicate and carefully negotiated balance in the *SPS Agreement* between the shared, but sometimes competing, interests of promoting international trade and of protecting the life and health of human beings. . . .

S.6.3.2 *EC – Hormones*, para. 180
(WT/DS26/AB/R, WT/DS48/AB/R)

. . . the Panel considered that Article 5.1 may be viewed as a specific application of the basic obligations contained in Article 2.2 of the *SPS Agreement* . . .

. . . We agree with this general consideration and would also stress that Articles 2.2 and 5.1 should constantly be read together. Article 2.2 informs Article 5.1: the elements that define the basic obligation set out in Article 2.2 impart meaning to Article 5.1.

S.6.3.3 *Australia – Salmon*, para. 138
(WT/DS18/AB/R)

. . . by maintaining an import prohibition . . . in violation of Article 5.1, Australia has, by implication, also acted inconsistently with Article 2.2 of the SPS Agreement.

S.6.3.4 *Japan – Agricultural Products II*, paras. 73–74
(WT/DS76/AB/R)

. . . we can conclude that "sufficiency" is a relational concept. "Sufficiency" requires the existence of a sufficient or adequate relationship between two elements, *in casu*, between the SPS measure and the scientific evidence.

The context of the word "sufficient" or, more generally, the phrase "maintained without sufficient scientific evidence" in Article 2.2, includes Article 5.1 as well as Articles 3.3 and 5.7 of the *SPS Agreement*.

S.6.3.5 *Japan – Agricultural Products II*, para. 84
(WT/DS76/AB/R)

. . . we agree with the Panel that the obligation in Article 2.2 that an SPS measure not be maintained without sufficient scientific evidence requires that there be a rational or objective relationship between the SPS measure and the scientific evidence. Whether there is a rational relationship between an SPS measure and the scientific evidence is to be determined on a case-by-case basis and will depend upon the particular circumstances of the case, including the characteristics of the measure at issue and the quality and quantity of the scientific evidence.

S.6.3.6 *Japan – Agricultural Products II*, para. 80
(WT/DS76/AB/R)

. . . Article 5.7 allows Members to adopt provisional SPS measures "[i]n cases where relevant scientific evidence is insufficient" and certain other requirements are fulfilled. Article 5.7 operates as a *qualified* exemption from the obligation under Article 2.2 not to maintain SPS measures without sufficient scientific evidence. An overly broad and flexible interpretation of that obligation would render Article 5.7 meaningless.

S.6.3.7 *Japan – Apples*, paras. 163–164
(WT/DS245/AB/R)

As we see it, the Panel examined the evidence adduced by the parties and considered the opinions of the experts. It concluded as a matter of fact that it is not likely that apple fruit would serve as a pathway for the entry, establishment or spread of fire blight in Japan. The Panel then contrasted the extent of the risk and the nature of the elements composing the measure, and concluded that the measure was "clearly disproportionate to the risk identified on the basis of the scientific evidence available." For the Panel, such "clear disproportion" implies that a "rational or objective relationship" does not exist between the measure and the relevant scientific evidence, and, therefore, the Panel concluded that the measure is maintained "without sufficient scientific evidence" within the meaning of Article 2.2 of the *SPS Agreement*. We note that the "clear disproportion" to which the Panel refers, relates to the application in this case of the requirement of a "rational or objective relationship between an SPS measure and the scientific evidence".

We emphasize, following the Appellate Body's statement in *Japan – Agricultural Products II* [paragraph 84], that whether a given approach or methodology is appropriate in order to assess whether a measure is maintained "without sufficient scientific evidence", within the meaning of Article 2.2, depends on the "particular circumstances of the case", and must be "determined on a case-by-case basis". Thus, the approach followed by the Panel in this case – disassembling the sequence of events to identify the risk and comparing it with the measure – does not exhaust the range of methodologies available to determine whether a measure is maintained "without sufficient scientific evidence" within the meaning of Article 2.2. Approaches different from that followed by the Panel in this case could also prove appropriate to evaluate whether a measure is maintained without sufficient scientific evidence within the meaning of Article 2.2. Whether or not a particular approach is appropriate will depend on the "particular circumstances of the case". The methodology adopted by the Panel was appropriate to the particular circumstances of the case before it and, therefore, we see no error in the Panel's reliance on it.

S.6.4 Article 2.3 – "not arbitrarily or unjustifiably discriminate between Members where identical or similar conditions prevail". *See also* SPS Agreement, Article 5.5 (S.6.15–17)

S.6.4.1 *Australia – Salmon*, para. 252
(WT/DS18/AB/R)

. . . a finding of violation of Article 5.5 will necessarily imply a violation of Article 2.3, first sentence, or Article 2.3, second sentence. Discrimination "between Members, including their own territory and that of others Members" within the meaning of Article 2.3, first sentence, can be established by following the complex and indirect route worked out and elaborated by Article 5.5. However, it is clear that this route is not the only route leading to a finding that an SPS measure constitutes arbitrary or unjustifiable discrimination according to Article 2.3, first sentence. Arbitrary or unjustifiable discrimination in the sense of Article 2.3, first sentence, can be found to exist without any examination under Article 5.5.

S.6.5 Article 3 – Level of protection and harmonization of SPS measures

S.6.5.1 *EC – Hormones*, para. 104
(WT/DS26/AB/R, WT/DS48/AB/R)

. . . It appears to us that the Panel has misconceived the relationship between Articles 3.1, 3.2 and 3.3, a relationship discussed below, which is qualitatively different from the relationship between, for instance, Articles I or III and Article XX of the GATT 1994. Article 3.1 of the *SPS Agreement* simply excludes from its scope of application the kinds of situations covered by Article 3.3 of that Agreement, that is, where a Member has projected for itself a higher level of sanitary protection than would be achieved by a measure based on an international standard. . . .

S.6.5.2 *EC – Hormones*, para. 177
(WT/DS26/AB/R, WT/DS48/AB/R)

. . . In generalized terms, the object and purpose of Article 3 is to promote the harmonization of the SPS measures of Members on as wide a basis as possible, while recognizing and safeguarding, at the same time, the right and duty of Members to protect the life and health of their people. The ultimate goal of the harmonization of SPS measures is to prevent the use of such measures for arbitrary or unjustifiable discrimination between Members or as a disguised restriction on international trade, without preventing Members from adopting or enforcing measures which are both "necessary to protect" human life or health and "based on scientific principles", and without requiring them to change their appropriate level of protection. . . .

S.6.6 Article 3.1 – "measures based on . . . international standards"

S.6.6.1 *EC – Hormones*, para. 102
(WT/DS26/AB/R, WT/DS48/AB/R)

. . . The presumption of consistency with relevant provisions of the *SPS Agreement* that arises under Article 3.2 in respect of measures that conform to international standards may well be an *incentive* for Members so to conform their SPS measures with such standards. It is clear, however, that a decision of a Member not to conform a particular measure with an international standard does not authorize imposition of a special or generalized burden of proof upon that Member, which may, more often than not, amount to a *penalty*.

S.6.6.2 *EC – Hormones*, paras. 165–166
(WT/DS26/AB/R, WT/DS48/AB/R)

. . . We cannot lightly assume that sovereign states intended to impose upon themselves the more onerous, rather than the less burdensome, obligation by mandating *conformity* or *compliance with* such standards, guidelines and recommendations. To sustain such an assumption and to warrant such a far-reaching interpretation, treaty language far more specific and compelling than that found in Article 3 of the *SPS Agreement* would be necessary.

. . . we disagree with the Panel's interpretation that "based on" means the same thing as "conform to".

S.6.6.3 *EC – Hormones*, para. 171
(WT/DS26/AB/R, WT/DS48/AB/R)

Under Article 3.1 of the *SPS Agreement*, a Member may choose to establish an SPS measure that is based on the existing relevant international standard, guideline or recommendation. Such a measure may adopt some, not necessarily all, of the elements of the international standard. The Member imposing this measure does not benefit from the presumption of consistency set up in Article 3.2; but, as earlier observed, the Member is not penalized by exemption of a complaining Member from the normal burden of showing a *prima facie* case of inconsistency with Article 3.1 or any other relevant Article of the *SPS Agreement* or of the GATT 1994.

S.6.7 Article 3.2 – "measures which conform to international standards"

S.6.7.1 *EC – Hormones*, para. 102
(WT/DS26/AB/R, WT/DS48/AB/R)

. . . The presumption of consistency with relevant provisions of the *SPS Agreement* that arises under Article 3.2 in respect of measures that conform to international standards may well be an *incentive* for Members so to conform their SPS measures with such standards. It is clear, however, that a decision of a Member not to conform a particular measure with an international standard does not authorize imposition of a special or generalized burden of proof upon that Member, which may, more often than not, amount to a *penalty*.

S.6.7.2 *EC – Hormones*, para. 170
(WT/DS26/AB/R, WT/DS48/AB/R)

Under Article 3.2 of the *SPS Agreement*, a Member may decide to promulgate an SPS measure that conforms to an international standard. Such a measure would embody the international standard completely and, for practical purposes, converts it into a municipal standard. Such a measure enjoys the benefit of a presumption (albeit a rebuttable one) that it is consistent with the relevant provisions of the *SPS Agreement* and of the GATT 1994.

S.6.8 Article 3.3 – "measures which result in a higher level of ... protection"

S.6.8.1 *EC – Hormones*, para. 104
(WT/DS26/AB/R, WT/DS48/AB/R)

... It appears to us that the Panel has misconceived the relationship between Articles 3.1, 3.2 and 3.3, a relationship discussed below, which is qualitatively different from the relationship between, for instance, Articles I or and Article XX of the GATT 1994 ... Article 3.3 recognizes the autonomous right of a Member to establish such higher level of protection, provided that that Member complies with certain requirements in promulgating SPS measures to achieve that level. ...

S.6.8.2 *EC – Hormones*, para. 172
(WT/DS26/AB/R, WT/DS48/AB/R)

Under Article 3.3 of the *SPS Agreement*, a Member may decide to set for itself a level of protection different from that implicit in the international standard, and to implement or embody that level of protection in a measure not "based on" the international standard. The Member's appropriate level of protection may be higher than that implied in the international standard. The right of a Member to determine its own appropriate level of sanitary protection is an important right. This is made clear in the sixth preambular paragraph of the *SPS Agreement*: ...

... [the] right of a Member to establish its own level of sanitary protection under Article 3.3 of the *SPS Agreement* is an autonomous right and *not* an "exception" from a "general obligation" under Article 3.1.

S.6.8.3 *EC – Hormones*, para. 173
(WT/DS26/AB/R, WT/DS48/AB/R)

The right of a Member to define its appropriate level of protection is, however, not an absolute or unqualified right. ...

S.6.8.4 *EC – Hormones*, para. 175
(WT/DS26/AB/R, WT/DS48/AB/R)

Article 3.3 is evidently not a model of clarity in drafting and communication. The use of the disjunctive "or" does indicate that two situations are intended to be covered. These are the introduction or maintenance of SPS measures which result in a higher level of protection:

(a) "if there is a scientific justification"; or
(b) "as a consequence of the level of . . . protection a Member determines to be appropriate in accordance with the relevant provisions of paragraphs 1 through 8 of Article 5".

It is true that situation (a) does not speak of Articles 5.1 through 5.8. Nevertheless, two points need to be noted. First, the last sentence of Article 3.3 requires that "all measures which result in a [higher] level of . . . protection", that is to say, measures falling within situation (a) as well as those falling within situation (b), be "not inconsistent with any other provision of [the SPS] Agreement". "Any other provision of this Agreement" textually includes Article 5. Secondly, the footnote to Article 3.3, while attached to the end of the first sentence, defines "scientific justification" as an "examination and evaluation of available scientific information in conformity with relevant provisions of this Agreement . . . ". This examination and evaluation would appear to partake of the nature of the risk assessment required in Article 5.1 and defined in paragraph 4 of Annex A of the *SPS Agreement.*

S.6.8.5 *EC – Hormones*, para. 177
(WT/DS26/AB/R, WT/DS48/AB/R)

. . . the Panel's finding that the European Communities is required by Article 3.3 to comply with the requirements of Article 5.1 is correct . . .

S.6.9 Article 5.1 and Annex A, paragraph 4 – Concept of risk assessment

S.6.9.1 *EC – Hormones*, para. 177
(WT/DS26/AB/R, WT/DS48/AB/R)

. . . The requirements of a risk assessment under Article 5.1, as well as of "sufficient scientific evidence" under Article 2.2, are essential for the maintenance of the carefully negotiated balance achieved in the *SPS Agreement* between the shared, but sometimes competing, interests of promoting international trade and protecting the health of human beings. . . .

S.6.9.2 *EC – Hormones*, para. 180
(WT/DS26/AB/R, WT/DS48/AB/R)

. . . the Panel considered that Article 5.1 may be viewed as a specific application of the basic obligations contained in Article 2.2 of the *SPS Agreement* . . .

. . . We agree with this general consideration and would also stress that Articles 2.2 and 5.1 should constantly be read together. Article 2.2 informs Article 5.1: the elements that define the basic obligation set out in Article 2.2 impart meaning to Article 5.1.

S.6.9.3 *EC – Hormones*, para. 181
(WT/DS26/AB/R, WT/DS48/AB/R)

. . . We must stress . . . that Article 5 and Annex A of the *SPS Agreement* speak of "risk assessment" only and that the term "risk management" is not to be found either in Article 5 or in any other provision of the *SPS Agreement.* Thus, the Panel's distinction, which it apparently employs to achieve or support what appears to be a restrictive notion of risk assessment, has no textual basis. . . .

S.6.9.4 *EC – Hormones*, paras. 183–184
(WT/DS26/AB/R, WT/DS48/AB/R)

Interpreting [paragraph 4 of Annex A of the *SPS Agreement*], the Panel elaborates risk assessment as a two-step process that "should (i) *identify* the *adverse effects* on human health (if any) arising from the presence of the hormones at issue when used as growth promoters *in meat* . . . , and (ii) if any such adverse effects exist, *evaluate* the *potential* or probability of occurrence of such effects".

. . . Although the utility of a two-step analysis may be debated, it does not appear to us to be substantially wrong. What needs to be pointed out at this stage is that the Panel's use of "probability" as an alternative term for "potential" creates a significant concern. The ordinary meaning of "potential" relates to "possibility" and is different from the ordinary meaning of "probability". "Probability" implies a higher degree or a threshold of potentiality or possibility. It thus appears that here the Panel introduces a quantitative dimension to the notion of risk.

S.6.9.5 *EC – Hormones*, para. 190
(WT/DS26/AB/R, WT/DS48/AB/R)

Article 5.1 does not insist that a Member that adopts a sanitary measure shall have carried out its own risk assessment. It only requires that the SPS measures be "based on an assessment, as appropriate for the circumstances . . . ". The SPS measure might well find its objective justification in a risk assessment carried out by another Member, or an international organization. . . .

S.6.10 Article 5.1 – Ascertainable risk

S.6.10.1 *EC – Hormones*, para. 186
(WT/DS26/AB/R, WT/DS48/AB/R)

. . . In one part of its Reports, the Panel opposes a requirement of an "identifiable risk" to the uncertainty that theoretically always remains since science can *never* provide *absolute* certainty that a given substance will not *ever* have adverse health effects. We agree with the Panel that this theoretical uncertainty is not the kind of risk which, under Article 5.1, is to be assessed....

S.6.10.2 *EC – Hormones*, para. 187
(WT/DS26/AB/R, WT/DS48/AB/R)

...It is essential to bear in mind that the risk that is to be evaluated in a risk assessment under Article 5.1 is not only risk ascertainable in a science laboratory operating under strictly controlled conditions, but also risk in human societies as they actually exist, in other words, the actual potential for adverse effects on human health in the real world where people live and work and die.

S.6.10.3 *Australia – Salmon*, para. 125
(WT/DS18/AB/R)

...As stated in our Report in *European Communities – Hormones*, the "risk" evaluated in a risk assessment must be an ascertainable risk; theoretical uncertainty is "not the kind of risk which, under Article 5.1, is to be assessed." This does not mean, however, that a Member cannot determine its own appropriate level of protection to be "zero risk".

S.6.10.4 *Japan – Apples*, para. 241
(WT/DS245/AB/R)

The comments of the Panel in response to the argument of the United States on "theoretical risk" should be viewed in their appropriate context. In *EC – Hormones*, the Appellate Body referred to the notion of "theoretical uncertainty" in the context of Article 5.1 of the *SPS Agreement*. The Appellate Body indicated that Article 5.1 does not address theoretical uncertainty, that is to say, "uncertainty that theoretically always remains since science can *never* provide *absolute* certainty that a given substance will not *ever* have adverse health effects." [Appellate Body Report, para. 186] We understand that the "scientific prudence" displayed by the experts in this case related to the risks that might arise from radical changes in Japan's current system of phytosanitary controls, taking into account Japan's island environment and climate. The scientific prudence displayed by the experts did not relate to the "theoretical uncertainty" that is inherent in the scientific method and which stems from the intrinsic limits of experiments, methodologies, or instruments deployed by scientists to explain a given phenomenon. Therefore, we agree with the Panel that the scientific prudence displayed by the experts should not be "completely assimilated" to the "theoretical uncertainty" that the Appellate Body discussed in *EC – Hormones* as being beyond the purview of risks to be addressed by measures subject to the *SPS Agreement*....

S.6.11 Article 5.1 – Types of risk assessment

S.6.11.1 *Australia – Salmon*, para. 121
(WT/DS18/AB/R)

. . . in this case a risk assessment within the meaning of Article 5.1 must:

(1) *identify* the diseases whose entry, establishment or spread a Member wants to prevent within its territory, as well as the potential biological and economic consequences associated with the entry, establishment or spread of these diseases;

(2) evaluate the likelihood of entry, establishment or spread of these diseases, as well as the associated potential biological and economic consequences; and

(3) evaluate the likelihood of entry, establishment or spread of these diseases *according to the SPS measures which might be applied.*

S.6.12 Article 5.1 – Degree of risk

S.6.12.1 *Australia – Salmon*, footnote 69 to para. 123
(WT/DS18/AB/R)

We note that the first type of risk assessment in paragraph 4 of Annex A is substantially different from the second type of risk assessment contained in the same paragraph. While the second requires only the evaluation of the *potential* for adverse effects on human or animal health, the first type of risk assessment demands an evaluation of the *likelihood* of entry, establishment or spread of a disease, and of the associated potential biological and economic consequences. In view of the very different language used in paragraph 4 of Annex A for the two types of risk assessment, we do not believe that it is correct to diminish the substantial differences between these two types of risk assessments . . .

S.6.12.2 *Australia – Salmon*, para. 123
(WT/DS18/AB/R)

. . . for a risk assessment to fall within the meaning of Article 5.1 and the first definition in paragraph 4 of Annex A, it is not sufficient that a risk assessment conclude that there is a *possibility* of entry, establishment or spread of diseases and associated biological and economic consequences. A proper risk assessment of this type must evaluate the "likelihood", i.e., the "probability", of entry, establishment or spread of diseases and associated biological and economic consequences as well as the "likelihood", i.e., "probability", of entry, establishment or spread of diseases *according to the SPS measures which might be applied.*

S.6.12.3 *Australia – Salmon*, para. 124
(WT/DS18/AB/R)

. . . We do not agree with the Panel that a risk assessment of this type needs only *some* evaluation of the likelihood or probability. The definition of this type of risk assessment in paragraph 4 of Annex A refers to "the evaluation of the likelihood" and not to *some* evaluation of the likelihood. We agree, however, ... that the *SPS Agreement* does not require that the evaluation of the likelihood needs to be done quantitatively. The likelihood may be expressed either quantitatively or qualitatively ... there is no requirement for a risk assessment to establish a certain magnitude or threshold level of degree of risk.

S.6.12.4 *Japan – Apples*, para. 208
(WT/DS245/AB/R)

The definition of "risk assessment" in the *SPS Agreement* requires that the evaluation of the entry, establishment or spread of a disease be conducted "according to the sanitary or phytosanitary measures which might be applied". We agree with the Panel that this phrase "refers to the measures *which might* be applied, not merely to the measures which *are being* applied." The phrase "which might be applied" is used in the conditional tense. In this sense, "might" means: "were or would be or have been able to, were or would be or have been allowed to, were or would perhaps". We understand this phrase to imply that a risk assessment should not be limited to an examination of the measure already in place or favoured by the importing Member. In other words, the evaluation contemplated in paragraph 4 of Annex A to the *SPS Agreement* should not be distorted by preconceived views on the nature and the content of the measure to be taken; nor should it develop into an exercise tailored to and carried out for the purpose of justifying decisions *ex post facto*.

S.6.13 Articles 5.1 and 5.2 – Risk assessment – specific to the risk identified

S.6.13.1 *EC – Hormones*, para. 199
(WT/DS26/AB/R, WT/DS48/AB/R)

The European Communities laid particular emphasis on the 1987 IARC Monographs and the Articles and opinions of individual scientists referred to above. The Panel notes, however, that the scientific evidence set out in these Monographs and these Articles and opinions relates to the carcinogenic potential of entire *categories* of hormones, or of the hormones at issue *in general*. The Monographs and the Articles and opinions are, in other words, in the nature of general studies of or statements on the carcinogenic potential of the named hormones. The Monographs and the Articles and opinions of individual scientists have not evaluated the carcinogenic potential of those hormones when used specifically *for growth promotion purposes*. Moreover, they do not evaluate the specific potential for carcinogenic effects arising from the presence *in "food"*, more specifically, "meat or meat products" of residues of the hormones in dispute. The Panel also notes that, according to the scientific experts advising the Panel, the data and studies set out in these 1987 Monographs have been taken into account in the 1988 and 1989 JECFA Reports and that the conclusions reached by the 1987 IARC Monographs are complementary to, rather than contradictory of, the conclusions of the JECFA Reports. The Panel concludes that these Monographs and these Articles and opinions are insufficient to support the EC measures at issue in this case.

S.6.13.2 *EC – Hormones*, para. 206 (WT/DS26/AB/R, WT/DS48/AB/R)

. . . The *SPS Agreement* requires assessment of the potential for adverse effects on human health arising from the presence of contaminants and toxins in food. We consider that the object and purpose of the *SPS Agreement* justify the examination and evaluation of all such risks for human health whatever their precise and immediate origin may be. We do not mean to suggest that risks arising from potential abuse in the administration of controlled substances and from control problems need to be, or should be, evaluated by risk assessors in each and every case. When and if risks of these types do in fact arise, risk assessors may examine and evaluate them. Clearly, the necessity or propriety of examination and evaluation of such risks would have to be addressed on a case-by-case basis. What, in our view, is a fundamental legal error is to exclude, on an *a priori* basis, any such risks from the scope of application of Articles 5.1 and 5.2. . . .

S.6.13.3 *Japan – Apples*, para. 202 and footnote 372 (WT/DS245/AB/R)

. . . Under the *SPS Agreement*, the obligation to conduct an assessment of "risk" is not satisfied merely by a general discussion of the disease sought to be avoided by the imposition of a phytosanitary measure.[372] The Appellate Body found the risk assessment at issue in *EC – Hormones* not to be "sufficiently specific" even though the scientific Articles cited by the importing Member had evaluated the "carcinogenic potential of entire *categories* of hormones, or of the hormones at issue *in general*." In order to constitute a "risk assessment" as defined in the *SPS Agreement*, the Appellate Body concluded, the risk assessment should have reviewed the carcinogenic potential, not of the relevant hormones in general, but of "residues of those hormones found in meat derived from cattle to which the hormones had been administered for growth promotion purposes". Therefore, when discussing the risk to be specified in the risk assessment in *EC – Hormones*, the Appellate Body referred in general to the harm concerned (cancer or genetic damage) *as well as* to the precise agent that may possibly cause the harm (that is, the specific hormones when used in a specific manner and for specific purposes).

[372] Indeed, we are of the view that, as a general matter, "risk" cannot usually be understood only in terms of the disease or adverse effects that may result. Rather, an evaluation of risk must connect the possibility of adverse effects with an antecedent or cause. For example, the abstract reference to the "risk of cancer" has no significance, in and of itself, under the *SPS Agreement*; but when one refers to the "risk of cancer from smoking cigarettes", the particular risk is given content.

S.6.13.4 *Japan – Apples*, para. 203 and footnote 379
(WT/DS245/AB/R)

In this case, the Panel found that the conclusion of the 1999 PRA with respect to fire blight was "based on an overall assessment of possible modes of contamination, where apple fruit is only one of the possible hosts/vectors considered." The Panel further found, on the basis of the scientific evidence, that the risk of entry, establishment or spread of the disease varies significantly depending on the vector, or specific host plant, being evaluated. Given that the measure at issue relates to the risk of transmission of fire blight through apple fruit, in an evaluation of whether the risk assessment is "sufficiently specific to the case at hand", the nature of the risk addressed by the measure at issue is a factor to be taken into account. In the light of these considerations, we are of the view that the Panel properly determined that the 1999 PRA "evaluat[ion of] the risks associated with all possible hosts taken together" was not sufficiently specific to qualify as a "risk assessment" under the *SPS Agreement* for the evaluation of the likelihood of entry, establishment or spread of fire blight in Japan through apple fruit.[379]

[379] We note our understanding that the Panel did not base its finding on, nor make any reference to, whether the *SPS Agreement* requires a risk assessment to analyze the importation of products on a *country-specific* basis. Neither participant in this appeal has asked us to find that the definition of "risk assessment" in the *SPS Agreement* mandates an analysis of risk specific to *each country* of exportation. As a result, we make no findings with respect to whether such a *country-specific* analysis is required in order to satisfy a Member's obligations under Article 5.1 of the *SPS Agreement*.

S.6.14 Article 5.1 – Requirement to *base* measure on the risk assessment

S.6.14.1 *EC – Hormones*, para. 186
(WT/DS26/AB/R, WT/DS48/AB/R)

. . . To the extent that the Panel purported to require a risk assessment to establish a minimum magnitude of risk, we must note that imposition of such a quantitative requirement finds no basis in the *SPS Agreement*. A panel is authorized only to determine whether a given SPS measure is "based on" a risk assessment. . . .

S.6.14.2 *EC – Hormones*, para. 193
(WT/DS26/AB/R, WT/DS48/AB/R)

. . . We believe that Article 5.1, when contextually read as it should be, in conjunction with and as informed by Article 2.2 of the *SPS Agreement*, requires that the results of the risk assessment must sufficiently warrant – that is to say, reasonably support – the SPS measure at stake. The requirement that an SPS measure be "based on" a risk assessment is a substantive requirement that there be a rational relationship between the measure and the risk assessment.

S.6.14.3 *Japan – Agricultural Products II*, para. 84
(WT/DS76/AB/R)

. . . we agree with the Panel that the obligation in Article 2.2 that an SPS measure not be maintained without sufficient scientific evidence requires that there be a rational or objective relationship between the SPS measure and the scientific evidence. Whether there is a rational relationship between an SPS measure and the scientific evidence is to be determined on a case-by-case basis and will depend upon the particular circumstances of the case, including the characteristics of the measure at issue and the quality and quantity of the scientific evidence.

S.6.14.4 *EC – Hormones*, para. 194
(WT/DS26/AB/R, WT/DS48/AB/R)

We do not believe that a risk assessment has to come to a monolithic conclusion that coincides with the scientific conclusion or view implicit in the SPS measure. The risk assessment could set out both the prevailing view representing the "mainstream" of scientific opinion, as well as the opinions of scientists taking a divergent view. Article 5.1 does not require that the risk assessment must necessarily embody only the view of a majority of the relevant scientific community . . . In most cases, responsible and representative governments tend to base their legislative and administrative measures on "mainstream" scientific opinion. In other cases, equally responsible and representative governments may act in good faith on the basis of what, at a given time, may be a divergent opinion coming from qualified and respected sources. By itself, this does not necessarily signal the absence of a reasonable relationship between the SPS measure and the risk assessment, especially where the risk involved is life-threatening in character and is perceived to constitute a clear and imminent threat to public health and safety. Determination of the presence or absence of that relationship can only be done on a case-to-case basis, after account is taken of all considerations rationally bearing upon the issue of potential adverse health effects.

S.6.14.5 *Japan – Apples*, para. 215
(WT/DS245/AB/R)

As Japan failed to establish that the Panel utilized subsequent scientific evidence in evaluating the risk assessment at issue, it is not necessary for us to express views on the question whether the conformity of a risk assessment with Article 5.1 should be evaluated solely against the scientific evidence available at the time of the risk assessment, to the exclusion of subsequent information. Resolution of such hypothetical claims would not serve "to secure a positive solution" to this dispute.

S.6.15 Article 5.5 – Consistency in the application of the appropriate level of protection

S.6.15.1 *EC – Hormones*, para. 213
(WT/DS26/AB/R, WT/DS48/AB/R)

The objective of Article 5.5 is formulated as the "achieving [of] consistency in the application of the concept of appropriate level of sanitary or phytosanitary protection". Clearly, the desired consistency is defined as a goal to be achieved in the future . . . Thus, we agree with the Panel's view that the statement of that goal does not establish a *legal obligation* of consistency of appropriate levels of protection. We think, too, that the goal set is not absolute or perfect consistency, since governments establish their appropriate levels of protection frequently on an *ad hoc* basis and over time, as different risks present themselves at different times. It is only arbitrary or unjustifiable inconsistencies that are to be avoided.

S.6.15.2 *EC – Hormones*, paras. 214–215
(WT/DS26/AB/R, WT/DS48/AB/R)

Close inspection of Article 5.5 indicates that a complaint of violation of this Article must show the presence of three distinct elements. The first element is that the Member imposing the measure complained of has adopted its own appropriate levels of sanitary protection against risks to human life or health in several different situations. The second element to be shown is that those *levels of protection* exhibit arbitrary or unjustifiable differences ("distinctions" in the language of Article 5.5) in their treatment of different situations. The last element requires that the arbitrary or unjustifiable differences result in discrimination or a disguised restriction of international trade. We understand the last element to be referring to the *measure* embodying or implementing a particular level of protection as resulting, in its application, in discrimination or a disguised restriction on international trade.

We consider the above three elements of Article 5.5 to be cumulative in nature; all of them must be demonstrated to be present if violation of Article 5.5 is to be found. In particular, both the second and third elements must be found. The second element alone would not suffice. The third element must also be demonstrably present: the implementing measure must be shown to be applied in such a manner as to result in discrimination or a disguised restriction on international trade. The presence of the second element – the arbitrary or unjustifiable character of differences in *levels of protection* considered by a Member as appropriate in differing situations – may in practical effect operate as a "warning" signal that the implementing *measure* in its application *might* be a discriminatory measure or *might* be a restriction on international trade disguised as an SPS measure for the protection of human life or health. Nevertheless, the measure itself needs to be examined and appraised and, in the context of the differing levels of protection, shown to result in discrimination or a disguised restriction on international trade.

S.6.16 Article 5.5 – "distinctions in the level of protection in different situations"

S.6.16.1 *EC – Hormones*, para. 217
(WT/DS26/AB/R, WT/DS48/AB/R)

...The situations exhibiting differing levels of protection cannot, of course, be compared unless they are comparable, that is, unless they present some common element or elements sufficient to render them comparable. If the situations proposed to be examined are *totally* different from one another, they would not be rationally comparable and the differences in levels of protection cannot be examined for arbitrariness.

S.6.16.2 *Australia – Salmon*, para. 146
(WT/DS18/AB/R)

...the Panel was correct in stating that situations can be compared under Article 5.5 if these situations involve *either* a risk of entry, establishment or spread of the same or a similar disease, *or* a risk of the same or similar "associated potential biological and economic consequences".

S.6.16.3 *Australia – Salmon*, para. 152
(WT/DS18/AB/R)

...we believe that for situations to be comparable under Article 5.5, it is sufficient for these situations to have in common a risk of entry, establishment or spread of *one* disease of concern. There is no need for these situations to have in common a risk of entry, establishment or spread of *all* diseases of concern....

S.6.17 Article 5.5 – "result in discrimination or a disguised restriction"

S.6.17.1 *EC – Hormones*, para. 212
(WT/DS26/AB/R, WT/DS48/AB/R)

Article 5.5 must be read in context. An important part of that context is Article 2.3 of the *SPS Agreement*, which provides as follows:

> Members shall ensure that their sanitary and phytosanitary measures do not arbitrarily or unjustifiably discriminate between Members where identical or similar conditions prevail, including between their own territory and that of other Members. Sanitary and phytosanitary measures shall not be applied in a manner which would constitute a disguised restriction on international trade.

When read together with Article 2.3, Article 5.5 may be seen to be marking out and elaborating a particular route leading to the same destination set out in Article 2.3.

S.6.17.2 *EC – Hormones*, para. 238
(WT/DS26/AB/R, WT/DS48/AB/R)

We agree with the Panel's view that "all three elements [of Article 5.5] need to be distinguished and addressed separately". We also recall our interpretation that Article 5.5 and, in particular, the terms "discrimination or a disguised restriction on international trade", have to be read in the context of the basic obligations contained in Article 2.3, which requires that "sanitary . . . *measures* shall not be *applied in a manner which would constitute a disguised restriction on international trade*". (emphasis added)

S.6.17.3 *EC – Hormones*, para. 240
(WT/DS26/AB/R, WT/DS48/AB/R)

In our view, the degree of difference, or the extent of the discrepancy, in the levels of protection, is only one kind of factor which, along with others, may cumulatively lead to the conclusion that discrimination or a disguised restriction on international trade in fact results from the application of a measure or measures embodying one or more of those different levels of protection . . . It is well to bear in mind that, after all, the difference in levels of protection that is characterizable as arbitrary or unjustifiable is only an element of (indirect) proof that a Member may actually be applying an SPS measure in a manner that discriminates between Members or constitutes a disguised restriction on international trade, prohibited by the basic obligations set out in Article 2.3 of the *SPS Agreement*. . . .

S.6.17.4 *EC – Hormones*, para. 246
(WT/DS26/AB/R, WT/DS48/AB/R)

Our conclusion, therefore, is that the Panel's finding that the "arbitrary or unjustifiable" difference in the EC levels of protection in respect of the hormones at issue on the one hand and in respect of carbadox and olaquindox on the other hand, "result in discrimination or a disguised restriction on international trade", is not supported either by the architecture and structure of the EC Directives here at stake or of the subsequent Directive on carbadox and olaquindox, or by the evidence submitted by the United States and Canada to the Panel. . . .

S.6.17.5 *Australia – Salmon*, para. 164
(WT/DS18/AB/R)

. . . in this case the degree of difference in the levels of protection (prohibition *versus* tolerance) is indeed, as the Panel stated, "rather substantial". We, therefore, consider it legitimate to treat this difference as a separate warning signal.

S.6.17.6 *Australia – Salmon*, para. 166
(WT/DS18/AB/R)

. . . We note that a finding that an SPS measure is not based on an assessment of the risks to human, animal or plant life or health – either because there was no risk assessment at all or because there is an insufficient risk assessment – is a strong indication that this measure is not really concerned with the protection of human, animal or plant life or health but is instead a trade-restrictive measure taken in the guise of an SPS measure, i.e., a "disguised restriction on international trade". We, therefore, consider that the finding of inconsistency with Article 5.1 is an appropriate warning signal for a "disguised restriction on international trade".

S.6.18 Article 5.6 – Not more trade restrictive than required to achieve the appropriate level of protection

S.6.18.1 *Australia – Salmon*, para. 194

(WT/DS18/AB/R)

We agree with the Panel that Article 5.6 and, in particular, the footnote to this provision, clearly provides a three-pronged test to establish a violation of Article 5.6. As already noted, the three elements of this test under Article 5.6 are that there is an SPS measure which:

(1) is reasonably available taking into account technical and economic feasibility;
(2) achieves the Member's appropriate level of sanitary or phytosanitary protection; and
(3) is significantly less restrictive to trade than the SPS measure contested.

These three elements are cumulative in the sense that, to establish inconsistency with Article 5.6, all of them have to be met. If any of these elements is not fulfilled, the measure in dispute would be consistent with Article 5.6. . . .

S.6.18.2 *Japan – Agricultural Products II*, para. 95

(WT/DS76/AB/R)

Article 5.6 of the SPS Agreement prohibits SPS measures that are more trade-restrictive than required to achieve a Member's appropriate level of protection. According to the footnote to Article 5.6, a measure is considered more trade-restrictive than required if there is another SPS measure which:

(1) is reasonably available taking into account technical and economic feasibility;
(2) achieves the Member's appropriate level of sanitary or phytosanitary protection; and
(3) is significantly less restrictive to trade than the SPS measure contested.

As we have stated in our Report in *Australia – Salmon*, these three elements are cumulative in nature.

S.6.19 Article 5.7 – Provisional adoption of SPS measures

S.6.19.1 *Japan – Agricultural Products II*, para. 80

(WT/DS76/AB/R)

. . . Article 5.7 allows Members to adopt provisional SPS measures "[i]n cases where relevant scientific evidence is insufficient" and certain other requirements are fulfilled. Article 5.7 operates as a *qualified* exemption from the obligation under Article 2.2 not to maintain SPS measures without sufficient scientific evidence. An overly broad and flexible interpretation of that obligation would render Article 5.7 meaningless.

S.6.19.2 *Japan – Agricultural Products II*, para. 89
(WT/DS76/AB/R)

Article 5.7 of the *SPS Agreement* sets out four requirements which must be met in order to adopt and maintain a provisional SPS measure. Pursuant to the first sentence of Article 5.7, a Member may provisionally adopt an SPS measure if this measure is:

(1) imposed in respect of a situation where "relevant scientific information is insufficient"; and
(2) adopted "on the basis of available pertinent information".

Pursuant to the second sentence of Article 5.7, such a provisional measure may not be maintained unless the Member which adopted the measure:

(1) "seek[s] to obtain the additional information necessary for a more objective assessment of risk"; and
(2) "review[s] the ... measure accordingly within a reasonable period of time".

These four requirements are clearly cumulative in nature and are equally important for the purpose of determining consistency with this provision. Whenever *one* of these four requirements is not met, the measure at issue is inconsistent with Article 5.7.

S.6.19.3 *Japan – Agricultural Products II*, para. 91
(WT/DS76/AB/R)

We, therefore, conclude that the Panel did not err in its application of Article 5.7 by first examining whether the varietal testing requirement meets the requirements of the second sentence of Article 5.7. Having established that the requirements of the second sentence of Article 5.7 are not met, there was no need for the Panel to examine the requirements of the first sentence.

S.6.20 Article 5.7 – "where relevant scientific evidence is insufficient"

S.6.20.1 *Japan – Apples*, para. 179
(WT/DS245/AB/R)

... The first requirement of Article 5.7 is that there must be insufficient scientific evidence. When a panel reviews a measure claimed by a Member to be provisional, that panel must assess whether "relevant scientific evidence is insufficient". This evaluation must be carried out, not in the abstract, but in the light of a particular inquiry. The notions of "relevance" and "insufficiency" in the introductory phrase of Article 5.7 imply a relationship between the scientific evidence and something else. Reading this introductory phrase in the broader context of Article 5 of the *SPS Agreement*, which is entitled "Assessment of Risk and Determination of the Appropriate Level of Sanitary or Phytosanitary Protection", is instructive in ascertaining the nature of the relationship to be established. Article 5.1 sets out a key discipline under Article 5, namely that "Members shall ensure that their sanitary or phytosanitary measures are based on an assessment . . . of the risks to human, animal or plant life or health". This discipline informs the other provisions of Article 5, including Article 5.7. We note, as well, that the second sentence of Article 5.7 refers to a "more objective assessment of risks". These contextual elements militate in favour of a link or relationship between the first requirement under Article 5.7 and the obligation to perform a risk assessment under Article 5.1: "relevant scientific evidence" will be "insufficient" within the meaning of Article 5.7 if the body of available scientific evidence does not allow, in quantitative or qualitative terms, the performance of an adequate assessment of risks as required under Article 5.1 and as defined in Annex A to the *SPS Agreement*. Thus, the question is not whether there is sufficient evidence of a general nature or whether there is sufficient evidence related to a specific aspect of a phytosanitary problem, or a specific risk. The question is whether the relevant evidence, be it "general" or "specific", in the Panel's parlance, is sufficient to permit the evaluation of the likelihood of entry, establishment or spread of, in this case, fire blight in Japan.

S.6.20.2 *Japan – Apples*, para. 184
(WT/DS245/AB/R)

. . . The application of Article 5.7 is triggered not by the existence of scientific uncertainty, but rather by the insufficiency of scientific evidence. The text of Article 5.7 is clear: it refers to "cases where relevant scientific evidence is insufficient", not to "scientific uncertainty". The two concepts are not interchangeable. Therefore, we are unable to endorse Japan's approach of interpreting Article 5.7 through the prism of "scientific uncertainty".

S.6.21 Article 5.7 – "seek to obtain additional information"

S.6.21.1 *Japan – Agricultural Products II*, para. 92
(WT/DS76/AB/R)

. . . we note that the first part of the second sentence stipulates that the Member adopting a provisional SPS measure "shall seek to obtain the additional information necessary for a more objective assessment of risk". Neither Article 5.7 nor any other provision of the *SPS Agreement* sets out explicit prerequisites regarding the additional information to be collected or a specific collection procedure. Furthermore, Article 5.7 does not specify what actual results must be achieved; the obligation is to "seek to obtain" additional information. However, Article 5.7 states that the additional information is to be sought in order to allow the Member to conduct "a more objective assessment of risk". Therefore, the information sought must be germane to conducting such a risk assessment, i.e., the evaluation of the likelihood of entry, establishment or spread of, *in casu*, a pest, according to the SPS measures which might be applied. . . .

S.6.22 Article 5.7 – "review . . . within a reasonable period of time"

S.6.22.1 *Japan – Agricultural Products II*, para. 93
(WT/DS76/AB/R)

. . . In our view, what constitutes a "reasonable period of time" has to be established on a case-by-case basis and depends on the specific circumstances of each case, including the difficulty of obtaining the additional information necessary for the review *and* the characteristics of the provisional SPS measure. . . .

S.6.23 Article 5.7 – Precautionary principle

S.6.23.1 *EC – Hormones*, paras. 123–125
(WT/DS26/AB/R, WT/DS48/AB/R)

The status of the precautionary principle in international law continues to be the subject of debate among academics, law practitioners, regulators and judges. The precautionary principle is regarded by some as having crystallized into a general principle of customary international *environmental* law. Whether it has been widely accepted by Members as a principle of *general* or *customary international law* appears less than clear. We consider, however, that it is unnecessary, and probably imprudent, for the Appellate Body in this appeal to take a position on this important, but abstract, question. We note that the Panel itself did not make any definitive finding with regard to the status of the precautionary principle in international law and that the precautionary principle, at least outside the field of international environmental law, still awaits authoritative formulation.

It appears to us important, nevertheless, to note some aspects of the relationship of the precautionary principle to the *SPS Agreement*. First, the principle has not been written into the *SPS Agreement* as a ground for justifying SPS measures that are otherwise inconsistent with the obligations of Members set out in particular provisions of that Agreement. Secondly, the precautionary principle indeed finds reflection in Article 5.7 of the *SPS Agreement*. We agree, at the same time, with the European Communities, that there is no need to assume that Article 5.7 exhausts the relevance of a precautionary principle. It is reflected also in the sixth paragraph of the preamble and in Article 3.3. These explicitly recognize the right of Members to establish their own appropriate level of sanitary protection, which level may be higher (i.e., more cautious) than that implied in existing international standards, guidelines and recommendations. Thirdly, a panel charged with determining, for instance, whether "sufficient scientific evidence" exists to warrant the maintenance by a Member of a particular SPS measure may, of course, and should, bear in mind that responsible, representative governments commonly act from perspectives of prudence and precaution where risks of irreversible, e.g. life-terminating, damage to human health are concerned. Lastly, however, the precautionary principle does not, by itself, and without a clear textual directive to that effect, relieve a panel from the duty of applying the normal (i.e. customary international law) principles of treaty interpretation in reading the provisions of the *SPS Agreement*.

We accordingly agree with the finding of the Panel that the precautionary principle does not override the provisions of Articles 5.1 and 5.2 of the *SPS Agreement*.

S.6.24 Annex B on "Transparency of SPS Regulations", paragraph 1 – "publication of laws, decrees or ordinances"

S.6.24.1 *Japan – Agricultural Products II*, paras. 105–106
(WT/DS76/AB/R)

We consider that the list of instruments contained in the footnote to paragraph 1 of Annex B is, as is indicated by the words "such as", not exhaustive in nature. The scope of application of the publication requirement is not limited to "laws, decrees or ordinances", but also includes, in our opinion, other instruments which are applicable generally and are similar in character to the instruments explicitly referred to in the illustrative list of the footnote to paragraph 1 of Annex B.

The object and purpose of paragraph 1 of Annex B is "to enable interested Members to become acquainted with" the sanitary and phytosanitary regulations adopted or maintained by other Members and thus to enhance transparency regarding these measures. In our opinion, the scope of application of the publication requirement of paragraph 1 of Annex B should be interpreted in the light of the object and purpose of this provision.

S.7 Standard of Review. *See also* Anti-Dumping Agreement, Article 17.6 – Standard of Review under the Anti-Dumping Agreement (A.3.58); Safeguards Agreement, General (S.1.1); Scope of Appellate Review (S.3); Seek Information and Technical Advice (S.4); Working Procedures for Appellate Review, Rule 20 – Notice of appeal (W.2.7)

S.7.1 General

S.7.1.1 *EC – Hormones*, para. 114
(WT/DS26/AB/R, WT/DS48/AB/R)

...Only Article 17.6(i) of the *Anti-Dumping Agreement* has language on the standard of review to be employed by panels engaged in the "assessment of the facts of the matter". We find no indication in the *SPS Agreement* of an intent on the part of the Members to adopt or incorporate into that Agreement the standard set out in Article 17.6(i) of the *Anti-Dumping Agreement*. Textually, Article 17.6(i) is specific to the *Anti-Dumping Agreement*.

S.7.1.2 *Argentina – Footwear (EC)*, para. 118
(WT/DS121/AB/R)

We have stated, on more than one occasion, that, for all but one of the covered agreements, Article 11 of the DSU sets forth the appropriate standard of review for panels. The only exception is the *Agreement on Implementation of Article VI of the General Agreement on Tariffs and Trade 1994*, in which a specific provision, Article 17.6, sets out a special standard of review for disputes arising under that Agreement.

S.7.1.3 *Argentina – Footwear (EC)*, para. 120
(WT/DS121/AB/R)

. . . The *Agreement on Safeguards*, like the *Agreement on the Application of Sanitary and Phytosanitary Measures*, is silent as to the appropriate standard of review. Therefore, Article 11 of the DSU, and, in particular, its requirement that ". . . a panel should make an objective assessment of the matter before it, including an objective assessment of the facts of the case and the applicability of and conformity with the relevant covered agreements", sets forth the appropriate standard of review for examining the consistency of a safeguard measure with the provisions of the *Agreement on Safeguards*.

S.7.1.4 *US – Lead and Bismuth II*, para. 49
(WT/DS138/AB/R)

. . . [the *Declaration on Dispute Settlement Pursuant to the Agreement on Implementation of Article VI of the General Agreement on Tariffs and Trade 1994 or Part V of the Agreement on Subsidies and Countervailing Measures* (the "*Declaration*")] does not impose an obligation to apply the standard of review contained in Article 17.6 of the *Anti-Dumping Agreement* to disputes involving countervailing duty measures under Part V of the *SCM Agreement*. The *Declaration* is couched in hortatory language; it uses the words "Ministers *recognize*". Furthermore, the *Declaration* merely acknowledges "the need for the consistent resolution of disputes arising from anti-dumping and countervailing duty measures." It does not specify any specific action to be taken. In particular, it does not prescribe a standard of review to be applied.

S.7.1.5 *US – Hot-Rolled Steel*, para. 54
(WT/DS184/AB/R)

Article 11 of the DSU imposes upon panels a comprehensive obligation to make an "objective assessment of the matter", an obligation which embraces all aspects of a panel's examination of the "matter", both factual and legal. Thus, panels make an "objective assessment of the facts", of the "applicability" of the covered agreements, and of the "conformity" of the measure at stake with those covered agreements. Article 17.6 is divided into two separate sub-paragraphs, each applying to different aspects of the panel's examination of the matter. The first sub-paragraph covers the *panel's* "*assessment* of the *facts* of the matter", whereas the second covers its "*interpret[ation* of] the *relevant provisions*". (emphasis added) The structure of Article 17.6, therefore, involves a clear distinction between a panel's assessment of the facts and its legal interpretation of the *Anti-Dumping Agreement*.

S.7.1.6 *US – Hot-Rolled Steel*, para. 55
(WT/DS184/AB/R)

In considering Article 17.6(i) of the *Anti-Dumping Agreement*, it is important to bear in mind the different roles of panels and investigating authorities. Investigating authorities are charged, under the *Anti-Dumping Agreement*, with making factual determinations relevant to their overall determination of dumping and injury. Under Article 17.6(i), the task of panels is simply to review the investigating authorities' "establishment" and "evaluation" of the facts. To that end, Article 17.6(i) requires panels to make an "*assessment* of the *facts*". The language of this phrase reflects closely the obligation imposed on panels under Article 11 of the DSU to make an "*objective assessment* of the *facts*". Thus the text of both provisions requires panels to "assess" the facts and this, in our view, clearly necessitates an active review or examination of the pertinent facts. Article 17.6(i) of the *Anti-Dumping Agreement* does not expressly state that panels are obliged to make an assessment of the facts which is "*objective*". However, it is inconceivable that Article 17.6(i) should require anything other than that panels make an *objective* "assessment of the facts of the matter". In this respect, we see no "conflict" between Article 17.6(i) of the *Anti-Dumping Agreement* and Article 11 of the DSU.

S.7.1.7 *US – Hot-Rolled Steel*, para. 62
(WT/DS184/AB/R)

. . . although the second sentence of Article 17.6(ii) of the *Anti-Dumping Agreement* imposes obligations on panels which are not found in the DSU, we see Article 17.6(ii) as supplementing, rather than replacing, the DSU, and Article 11 in particular. Article 11 requires panels to make an "objective assessment of the matter" as a whole. Thus, under the DSU, in examining claims, panels must make an "objective assessment" of the legal provisions at issue, their "applicability" to the dispute, and the "conformity" of the measures at issue with the covered agreements. Nothing in Article 17.6(ii) of the *Anti-Dumping Agreement* suggests that panels examining claims under that Agreement should not conduct an "objective assessment" of the legal provisions of the Agreement, their applicability to the dispute, and the conformity of the measures at issue with the Agreement. Article 17.6(ii) simply adds that a panel shall find that a measure is in conformity with the *Anti-Dumping Agreement* if it rests upon one permissible interpretation of that Agreement.

S.7.1.8 *US – Cotton Yarn*, para. 68
(WT/DS192/AB/R)

Article 11 of the DSU lays down the standard of review for panels in disputes under the covered agreements . . .

S.7.2 Article 11 of the DSU – Objective assessment of the matter

S.7.2.1 *EC – Hormones*, paras. 116–119
(WT/DS26/AB/R, WT/DS48/AB/R)

. . . Article 11 of the DSU bears directly on this matter and, in effect, articulates with great succinctness but with sufficient clarity the appropriate standard of review for panels in respect of both the ascertainment of facts and the legal characterization of such facts under the relevant agreements. . . .

So far as fact-finding by panels is concerned, their activities are always constrained by the mandate of Article 11 of the DSU: the applicable standard is neither *de novo* review as such, nor "total deference", but rather the "objective assessment of the facts". Many panels have in the past refused to undertake *de novo* review, wisely, since under current practice and systems, they are in any case poorly suited to engage in such a review. On the other hand, "total deference to the findings of the national authorities", it has been well said, "could not ensure an 'objective assessment' as foreseen by Article 11 of the DSU".

In so far as legal questions are concerned – that is, consistency or inconsistency of a Member's measure with the provisions of the applicable agreement – a standard not found in the text of the *SPS Agreement* itself cannot absolve a panel (or the Appellate Body) from the duty to apply the customary rules of interpretation of public international law. It may be noted that the European Communities refrained from suggesting that Article 17.6 of the *Anti-Dumping Agreement* in its entirety was applicable to the present case. Nevertheless, it is appropriate to stress that here again Article 11 of the DSU is directly on point, requiring a panel to "make an objective assessment of the matter before it, including an objective assessment of the facts of the case and the applicability of and conformity with the relevant covered agreements . . . ".

We consider, therefore, that the issue of failure to apply an appropriate standard of review, raised by the European Communities, resolves itself into the issue of whether or not the Panel, in making the above and other findings referred to and appealed by the European Communities, had made an "objective assessment of the matter before it, including *an objective assessment of the facts* . . . ". . . .

S.7.2.2 *EC – Poultry*, para. 133
(WT/DS69/AB/R)

An allegation that a panel has failed to conduct the "objective assessment of the matter before it" required by Article 11 of the DSU is a very serious allegation. Such an allegation goes to the very core of the integrity of the WTO dispute settlement process itself. . . .

S.7.2.3 *EC – Poultry*, para. 135
(WT/DS69/AB/R)

. . . Just as a panel has the discretion to address only those *claims* which must be addressed in order to dispose of the matter at issue in a dispute, so too does a panel have the discretion to address only those *arguments* it deems necessary to resolve a particular claim. So long as it is clear in a panel report that a panel has reasonably considered a claim, the fact that a particular argument relating to that claim is not specifically addressed in the "Findings" section of a panel report will not, in and of itself, lead to the conclusion that that panel has failed to make the "objective assessment of the matter before it" required by Article 11 of the DSU.

S.7.2.4 *Chile – Price Band System*, para. 173
(WT/DS207/AB/R)

... Because it made a finding on a provision that was not before it, the Panel, therefore, did not make an objective assessment *of the matter before it*, as required by Article 11. Rather, the Panel made a finding on a matter that was *not* before it. In doing so, the Panel acted *ultra petita* and inconsistently with Article 11 of the DSU.

S.7.2.5 *US – Gambling*, para. 273
(WT/DS285/AB/R)

... as part of their duties, under Article 11 of the DSU, ... panels must ensure that the due process rights of parties to a dispute are respected. A panel may act inconsistently with this duty if it addresses a defence that a responding party raised at such a late stage of the panel proceedings that the complaining party had no meaningful opportunity to respond to it. To this end, panels are endowed with "sufficient flexibility" in their working procedures, by virtue of Article 12.2 of the DSU, to regulate panel proceedings and, in particular, to adjust their timetables to allow for additional time to respond or for additional submissions where necessary.

S.7.2.6 *US – Gambling*, paras. 281–282
(WT/DS285/AB/R)

... a panel enjoys ... discretion [freely to use arguments submitted by any of the parties – or to develop its own legal reasoning – to support its own findings and conclusions] only with respect to specific claims that are properly before it, for otherwise it would be considering a matter not within its jurisdiction. Moreover, when a panel rules on a claim in the absence of evidence and supporting arguments, it acts inconsistently with its obligations under Article 11 of the DSU.

In the context of affirmative defences, then, a responding party must invoke a defence and put forward evidence and arguments in support of its assertion that the challenged measure satisfies the requirements of the defence. When a responding party fulfils this obligation, a panel may rule on whether the challenged measure is justified under the relevant defence, relying on arguments advanced by the parties or developing its own reasoning. The same applies to rebuttals. A panel may not take upon itself to rebut the claim (or defence) where the responding party (or complaining party) itself has not done so.

S.7.2.7 *US – Gambling*, paras. 342–344 (WT/DS285/AB/R)

In deciding to assess whether the measures satisfied the requirements of the chapeau, the Panel explained that, even though such an examination was "not necessary", it wanted "to assist the parties in resolving the underlying dispute in this case." Antigua alleges that the Panel acted inconsistently with the Appellate Body's decision in *Korea – Various Measures on Beef* in determining whether the Wire Act, the Travel Act, and the IGBA meet the requirements of the chapeau after having found that they were not provisionally justified.

... [the statement by the Appellate Body at paragraph 156 of *Korea – Various Measures on Beef*] does not impose a *requirement* on panels to stop evaluating a responding party's defence once they have determined that a challenged measure is not provisionally justified under one of the paragraphs of the general exception provision.

Provided that it complies with its duty to assess a matter objectively, a panel enjoys the freedom to decide *which legal issues* it must address in order to resolve a dispute. Moreover, in some instances, a panel's decision to continue its legal analysis and to make factual findings beyond those that are strictly necessary to resolve the dispute may assist the Appellate Body should it later be called upon to complete the analysis, as, for example, in this case.

S.7.2.8 *Dominican Republic – Import and Sale of Cigarettes*, para. 105 (WT/DS302/AB/R)

Article 11 of the DSU provides that a panel "should make an objective assessment of the matter before it, including an objective assessment of the facts of the case and the applicability of and conformity with the relevant covered agreements". The Appellate Body underlined in *Chile – Price Band System* that "Article 11 obliges panels not only to make 'an objective assessment of the facts of the case', but also 'an objective assessment of the matter before it' ". The "matter" is constituted by both the facts of the case (and, in particular, the specific measures at issue) as well as the legal claims raised. The corollary is that a panel is not entitled to make an assessment of a matter that is *not* before it, for example, by making findings on a claim not raised by the complainant.

S.7.2.9 *Dominican Republic – Import and Sale of Cigarettes*, para. 125 (WT/DS302/AB/R)

In any event, we note that there is no obligation upon a panel to consider each and every argument put forward by the parties in support of their respective cases, so long as it completes an objective assessment of the matter before it, in accordance with Article 11 of the DSU.

S.7.2A Article 11 of the DSU – Objective assessment of the measure

S.7.2A.1 *Canada – Wheat Exports and Grain Imports*, paras. 176–177 (WT/DS276/AB/R)

We agree with Canada that [the United States' claim that the Panel did not examine the measure in its entirety] of error fits more properly under Article 11 of the DSU [than under Article XVII:1 of the GATT 1994]. The Appellate Body has stated previously that the measure at issue (and the claims made by the complaining Member) make up the "*matter* referred to the DSB" for the purpose of Article 7 of the DSU. In this sense, the United States' argument that the Panel did not examine the measure in its entirety relates to the Panel's examination of the "matter". Article 11 of the DSU sets out the duties of a panel, including that it "should make an objective assessment of the *matter* before it". (emphasis added) Therefore, as we see it, the United States' allegation that the Panel did not examine the measure in its entirety amounts to an allegation that the Panel did not "make an objective assessment of the matter" under Article 11 of the DSU.

Although an appellant is free to determine how to characterize its claims on appeal, at the same time due process requires that the legal basis of a claim be sufficiently clear to allow an appellee to respond effectively. This is especially the case when the claim is an allegation that the panel did not make an objective assessment of the matter as required by Article 11 of the DSU because, by definition, such a claim will not be found in the request for the establishment of the panel and, therefore, the panel will not have referred to it in the panel report.

S.7.2A.2 *Canada – Wheat Exports and Grain Imports*, para. 191 (WT/DS276/AB/R)

In our view, it is incumbent upon a party to identify in its submissions the relevance of the provisions of legislation – the evidence – on which it relies to support its arguments. It is not sufficient merely to file an entire piece of legislation and expect a panel to discover, on its own, what relevance the various provisions may or may not have for a party's legal position. We are not satisfied that the United States argued the relevance before the Panel of the various provisions of the *Canadian Wheat Board Act* on which it now relies.... Therefore, we do not agree with the United States that the Panel disregarded facts relevant to the independence of the CWB and we see no failure by the Panel in this respect to comply with its duty under Article 11 of the DSU.

S.7.2A.3 *US – Oil Country Tubular Goods Sunset Reviews*, paras. 209–210 (WT/DS268/AB/R)

In our view, therefore, in order to objectively assess, as required by Article 11 of the DSU, whether the three factual scenarios of Section II.A.3 of the SPB are regarded as determinative/conclusive, it is essential to examine concrete examples of cases where the likelihood determination of continuation or recurrence of dumping was based solely on one of the scenarios of Section II.A.3 of the SPB, even though the probative value of other factors might have outweighed that of the identified scenario. Such an examination requires a qualitative assessment of the likelihood determinations in individual cases.

We find that, in reaching its conclusion on the USDOC's consistent application of the SPB, the Panel relied solely on the overall statistics or aggregate results. The Panel did not undertake a qualitative analysis of at least some of the individual cases in Exhibit ARG-63 in order to see whether the USDOC's determinations in those cases were objective and rested on a sufficient factual basis.

S.7.2A.4 *US – Oil Country Tubular Goods Sunset Reviews*, para. 212 (WT/DS268/AB/R)

The Panel record does not show that the Panel undertook any such qualitative assessment of at least some of the cases of Exhibit ARG-63 with a view to discerning whether the USDOC regarded the existence of one of the factual scenarios of the SPB as determinative/conclusive for its determinations. The Panel also appears not to have examined in how many cases the foreign respondent parties participated in the proceedings, in how many they introduced other "good cause" factors, and how the USDOC dealt with those factors when they were introduced. Such an inquiry would have enabled the Panel to identify and undertake a qualitative analysis of at least some of those cases to see whether the affirmative determinations were made solely on the basis of one of the scenarios to the exclusion of other factors. The Panel failed to undertake any such qualitative assessment and relied exclusively on the overall statistics or aggregated results of Exhibit ARG-63. The fact that affirmative determinations were made in reliance on one of the three scenarios in all the sunset reviews of anti-dumping duty orders where domestic interested parties took part strongly suggests that these scenarios are mechanistically applied. However, without a qualitative examination of the reasons leading to such determinations, it is not possible to conclude definitively that these determinations were based exclusively on these scenarios in disregard of other factors.

S.7.2A.5 *US – Oil Country Tubular Goods Sunset Reviews*, para. 215 (WT/DS268/AB/R)

In the light of the above, we *find* that the Panel did not "make an objective assessment of the matter", as required by Article 11 of the DSU. It apparently reached its conclusion – that the three scenarios in Section II.A.3 of the SPB are perceived by the USDOC to be determinative/conclusive of the likelihood of continuation or recurrence of dumping – on the sole basis of the overall statistics in Exhibit ARG-63. The Panel record reveals no qualitative analysis of even some of the cases in Exhibit ARG-63, and the Panel Report contains only a single sentence justifying its conclusion based on the overall statistics. . . .

S.7.2A.6 *US – Gambling*, paras. 356–357
(WT/DS285/AB/R)

In our view, the proper significance to be attached to isolated instances of enforcement, or lack thereof, cannot be determined in the absence of evidence allowing such instances to be placed in their proper context. Such evidence might include evidence on the *overall* number of suppliers, and on *patterns* of enforcement, and on the reasons for particular instances of non-enforcement. Indeed, enforcement agencies may refrain from prosecution in many instances for reasons unrelated to discriminatory intent and without discriminatory effect.

Faced with the limited evidence the parties put before it with respect to enforcement, the Panel should rather have focused, as a matter of law, on the wording of the measures at issue. These measures, on their face, do *not* discriminate between United States and foreign suppliers of remote gambling services. . . .

S.7.2A.7 *US – Gambling*, para. 364
(WT/DS285/AB/R)

. . . the United States' appeal essentially challenges the Panel's failure to accord sufficient weight to the evidence submitted by the United States with respect to the relationship under United States law between the IHA and the measures at issue. The Panel had limited evidence before it, as submitted by the parties, on which to base its conclusion. This limitation, however, could not absolve the Panel of its responsibility to arrive at a conclusion as to the relationship between the IHA and the prohibitions in the Wire Act, the Travel Act, and the IGBA. The Panel found that the evidence provided by the United States was not sufficiently persuasive to conclude that, as regards wagering on horseracing, the remote supply of such services by *domestic* firms continues to be prohibited notwithstanding the plain language of the IHA. In this light, we are not persuaded that the Panel failed to make an objective assessment of the facts.

S.7.3 Article 11 of the DSU – Objective assessment of the facts

S.7.3.1 *EC – Hormones*, para. 132
(WT/DS26/AB/R, WT/DS48/AB/R)

Under Article 17.6 of the DSU, appellate review is limited to appeals on questions of law covered in a panel report and legal interpretations developed by the panel. Findings of fact, as distinguished from legal interpretations or legal conclusions, by a panel are, in principle, not subject to review by the Appellate Body. The determination of whether or not a certain event did occur in time and space is typically a question of fact; for example, the question of whether or not Codex has adopted an international standard, guideline or recommendation on MGA is a factual question. Determination of the credibility and weight properly to be ascribed to (that is, the appreciation of) a given piece of evidence is part and parcel of the fact finding process and is, in principle, left to the discretion of a panel as the trier of facts. The consistency or inconsistency of a given fact or set of facts with the requirements of a given treaty provision is, however, a legal characterization issue. It is a legal question. . . .

S.7.3.2 *EC – Hormones*, para. 133

(WT/DS26/AB/R, WT/DS48/AB/R)

. . . when may a panel be regarded as having failed to discharge its duty under Article 11 of the DSU to make an objective assessment of the facts before it? Clearly, not every error in the appreciation of the evidence (although it may give rise to a question of law) may be characterized as a failure to make an objective assessment of the facts . . . The duty to make an objective assessment of the facts is, among other things, an obligation to consider the evidence presented to a panel and to make factual findings on the basis of that evidence. The deliberate disregard of, or refusal to consider, the evidence submitted to a panel is incompatible with a panel's duty to make an objective assessment of the facts. The wilful distortion or misrepresentation of the evidence put before a panel is similarly inconsistent with an objective assessment of the facts. "Disregard" and "distortion" and "misrepresentation" of the evidence, in their ordinary signification in judicial and quasi-judicial processes, imply not simply an error of judgment in the appreciation of evidence but rather an egregious error that calls into question the good faith of a panel. A claim that a panel disregarded or distorted the evidence submitted to it is, in effect, a claim that the panel, to a greater or lesser degree, denied the party submitting the evidence fundamental fairness, or what in many jurisdictions is known as due process of law or natural justice.

S.7.3.3 *EC – Hormones*, paras. 135–136

(WT/DS26/AB/R, WT/DS48/AB/R)

. . . it is generally within the discretion of the Panel to decide which evidence it chooses to utilize in making findings. . . .

The European Communities argues that the Panel failed to request the submission of data on MGA and contends that this failure constituted a violation of Article 11 of the DSU. However, we see nothing in Article 11 to suggest that there is an obligation on the Panel to gather data relating to MGA and that it was therefore required to request the submission of this data.

S.7.3.4 *EC – Hormones*, para. 138

(WT/DS26/AB/R, WT/DS48/AB/R)

. . . The Panel cannot realistically refer to all statements made by the experts advising it and should be allowed a substantial margin of discretion as to which statements are useful to refer to explicitly. . . .

S.7.3.5 *Australia – Salmon*, para. 267
(WT/DS18/AB/R)

... in response to Australia's contention that the Panel failed to accord "due deference" to matters of fact it put forward, we note that Article 11 of the DSU calls upon panels to "make an objective assessment of the matter before it, including an objective assessment of the facts of the case and the applicability of and conformity with the relevant covered agreements". Therefore, the function of this Panel was to assess the facts in a manner consistent with its obligation to make such an "objective assessment of the matter before it". We believe the Panel has done so in this case. Panels, however, are not required to accord to factual evidence of the parties the same meaning and weight as do the parties.

S.7.3.6 *Korea – Alcoholic Beverages*, para. 164
(WT/DS75/AB/R, WT/DS84/AB/R)

We are bound to conclude that Korea has not succeeded in showing that the Panel has committed any egregious errors that can be characterized as a failure to make an objective assessment of the matter before it. Korea's arguments, when read together with the Panel Report and the record of the Panel proceedings, do not disclose that the Panel has distorted, misrepresented or disregarded evidence, or has applied a "double standard" of proof in this case. It is not an error, let alone an egregious error, for the Panel to fail to accord the weight to the evidence that one of the parties believes should be accorded to it.

S.7.3.7 *Japan – Agricultural Products II*, para. 127
(WT/DS76/AB/R)

... Article 13 of the DSU allows a panel to seek *information* from any relevant source and to consult individual experts or expert bodies to obtain their *opinion* on certain aspects of the matter before it. In our Report in *United States – Import Prohibition of Certain Shrimp and Shrimp Products* ("*United States – Shrimp*"), we noted the "comprehensive nature" of this authority, and stated that this authority is "indispensably necessary" to enable a panel to discharge its duty imposed by Article 11 of the DSU to "make an objective assessment of the matter before it, including an *objective assessment of the facts of the case* and the *applicability of and conformity with the relevant covered agreements....*" [Appellate Body Report, para. 106]

S.7.3.8 *Japan – Agricultural Products II*, para. 129
(WT/DS76/AB/R)

Article 13 of the DSU and Article 11.2 of the *SPS Agreement* suggest that panels have a significant investigative authority. However, this authority cannot be used by a panel to rule in favour of a complaining party which has not established a *prima facie* case of inconsistency based on specific legal claims asserted by it. A panel is entitled to seek information and advice from experts and from any other relevant source it chooses, pursuant to Article 13 of the DSU and, in an SPS case, Article 11.2 of the *SPS Agreement*, to help it to understand and evaluate the evidence submitted and the arguments made by the parties, but not to make the case for a complaining party.

S.7.3.9 *Japan – Agricultural Products II*, para. 141
(WT/DS76/AB/R)

. . . not every failure by the Panel in the appreciation of the evidence before it can be characterized as failure to make an objective assessment of the facts as required by Article 11 of the DSU. Only egregious errors constitute a failure to make an objective assessment of the facts as required by Article 11 of the DSU.

S.7.3.10 *India – Quantitative Restrictions*, paras. 149, 151
(WT/DS90/AB/R)

. . . The Panel gave considerable weight to the views expressed by the IMF in its reply to these questions. However, nothing in the Panel Report supports India's argument that the Panel delegated to the IMF its judicial function to make an objective assessment of the matter. A careful reading of the Panel Report makes clear that the Panel did not simply accept the views of the IMF. The Panel critically assessed these views and also considered other data and opinions in reaching its conclusions.

. . .

We conclude that the Panel made an objective assessment of the matter before it. . . .

S.7.3.11 *Korea – Dairy*, para. 137
(WT/DS98/AB/R)

. . . However, under Article 11 of the DSU, a panel is charged with the mandate to determine the facts of the case and to arrive at factual findings. In carrying out this mandate, a panel has the duty to examine and consider all the evidence before it, not just the evidence submitted by one or the other party, and to evaluate the relevance and probative force of each piece thereof. . . .

. . . The determination of the significance and weight properly pertaining to the evidence presented by one party is a function of a panel's appreciation of the probative value of all the evidence submitted by both parties considered together.

S.7.3.11A *US – Wheat Gluten*, para. 151
(WT/DS166/AB/R)

. . . although the task of panels under Article 11 relates, in part, to its assessment of the *facts*, the question whether a panel has made an "objective assessment" of the facts is a *legal* one, that may be the subject of an appeal. (emphasis added) However, in view of the distinction between the respective roles of the Appellate Body and panels, we have taken care to emphasize that a panel's appreciation of the evidence falls, in principle, "within the *scope of the panel's discretion as the trier of facts*". (emphasis added) In assessing the panel's appreciation of the evidence, we cannot base a finding of inconsistency under Article 11 simply on the conclusion that we might have reached a different factual finding from the one the panel reached. Rather, we must be satisfied that the panel has exceeded the bounds of its discretion, as the trier of facts, in its appreciation of the evidence. As is clear from previous appeals, we will not interfere lightly with the panel's exercise of its discretion.

S.7.3.12 *US – Shrimp (Article 21.5 – Malaysia)*, para. 95
(WT/DS58/AB/RW)

There is no way of knowing or predicting when or how that particular legal proceeding will conclude in the United States. The *Turtle Island* case has been appealed and could conceivably go as far as the Supreme Court of the United States. It would have been an exercise in speculation on the part of the Panel to predict either when or how that case may be concluded, or to assume that injunctive relief ultimately would be granted and that the United States Court of Appeals or the Supreme Court of the United States eventually would compel the Department of State to modify the Revised Guidelines. The Panel was correct not to indulge in such speculation, which would have been contrary to the duty of the Panel, under Article 11 of the DSU, to make "an objective assessment of the matter . . . including an objective assessment of the facts of the case".

S.7.3.12A *EC – Asbestos*, para. 161
(WT/DS135/AB/R)

The same holds true in this case. The Panel enjoyed a margin of discretion in assessing the value of the evidence, and the weight to be ascribed to that evidence. The Panel was entitled, in the exercise of its discretion, to determine that certain elements of evidence should be accorded more weight than other elements – that is the essence of the task of appreciating the evidence.

S.7.3.12B *EC – Sardines*, para. 299
(WT/DS231/AB/R)

. . . As we have stated in several previous appeals, panels enjoy a discretion as the trier of facts; they enjoy "a margin of discretion in assessing the value of the evidence, and the weight to be ascribed to that evidence." We have also said that we will not "interfere lightly" with the Panel's appreciation of the evidence: we will not intervene solely because we might have reached a different factual finding from the one the panel reached; we will intervene only if we are "satisfied that the panel has exceeded the bounds of its discretion, as the trier of facts, in its appreciation of the evidence".

S.7.3.13 *EC – Sardines*, para. 301
(WT/DS231/AB/R)

. . . The interim review stage is not an appropriate time to introduce new evidence. We recall that Article 15 of the DSU governs the interim review. Article 15 permits parties, during that stage of the proceedings, to submit comments on the draft report issued by the panel, and to make requests "for the panel to review precise aspects of the interim report". At that time, the panel process is all but completed; it is only – in the words of Article 15 – "precise aspects" of the report that must be verified during the interim review. And this, in our view, cannot properly include an assessment of new and unanswered evidence. Therefore, we are of the view that the Panel acted properly in refusing to take into account the new evidence during the interim review, and did not thereby act inconsistently with Article 11 of the DSU.

S.7.3.14 *US – Carbon Steel*, para. 142
(WT/DS213/AB/R, WT/DS213/AB/R/Corr.1)

. . . Article 11 requires panels to take account of the evidence put before them and forbids them to wilfully disregard or distort such evidence. Nor may panels make affirmative findings that lack a basis in the evidence contained in the panel record. Provided that panels' actions remain within these parameters, however, we have said that "it is generally within the discretion of the Panel to decide which evidence it chooses to utilize in making findings", and, on appeal, we "will not interfere lightly with a panel's exercise of its discretion".

S.7.3.15 *US – Carbon Steel*, para. 153
(WT/DS213/AB/R, WT/DS213/AB/R/Corr.1)

We also wish to underline that although panels enjoy a *discretion*, pursuant to Article 13 of the DSU, to seek information "from any relevant source", Article 11 of the DSU imposes no *obligation* on panels to conduct their own fact-finding exercise, or to fill in gaps in the arguments made by parties. In consequence, given that the European Communities itself had submitted no evidence – other than the text of the provision – on this point, the Panel did not act inconsistently with Article 11 in refraining from seeking additional information on its own initiative.

S.7.3.16 *EC – Bed Linen (Article 21.5 – India)*, para. 177
(WT/DS141/AB/RW)

India has not persuaded us that the Panel in this case exceeded its discretion as the trier of facts. In our view, the Panel assessed and weighed the evidence submitted by both parties, and ultimately concluded that the European Communities had information on all relevant economic factors listed in Article 3.4. It is not "an error, let alone an egregious error", for the Panel to have declined to accord to the evidence the weight that India sought to have accorded to it. We, therefore, reject India's argument that, by failing to *shift* the burden of proof, the Panel did not properly discharge its duty to assess objectively the facts of the case as required by Article 11 of the DSU.

S.7.3.17 *EC – Bed Linen (Article 21.5 – India)*, para. 181
(WT/DS141/AB/RW)

. . . Specifically, India argues that the Panel did not make an objective assessment of the facts of the case because the Panel *distorted* the evidence by placing greater weight on the statements made by the European Communities than on those made by India. As we stated earlier, the weighing of the evidence is within the discretion of the Panel as the trier of facts, and there is no indication in this case that the Panel exceeded the bounds of this discretion. . . .

S.7.3.18 *Japan – Apples*, para. 221
(WT/DS245/AB/R)

. . . Since *EC – Hormones*, the Appellate Body has consistently emphasized that, within the bounds of their obligation under Article 11 to make an objective assessment of the facts of the case, panels enjoy a "margin of discretion" as triers of fact. Panels are thus "not required to accord to factual evidence of the parties the same meaning and weight as do the parties" and may properly "determine that certain elements of evidence should be accorded more weight than other elements".

S.7.3.19 *Japan – Apples*, para. 222
(WT/DS245/AB/R)

Consistent with this margin of discretion, the Appellate Body has recognized that "not every error in the appreciation of the evidence (although it may give rise to a question of law) may be characterized as a failure to make an objective assessment of the facts." When addressing claims under Article 11 of the DSU, the Appellate Body does not "second-guess the Panel in appreciating either the evidentiary value of . . . studies or the consequences, if any, of alleged defects in [the evidence]". . . .

. . . Where parties challenging a panel's fact-finding under Article 11 have failed to establish that a panel exceeded the bounds of its discretion as the trier of facts, the Appellate Body has not "interfere[d]" with the findings of the panel.

S.7.3.20 *US – Oil Country Tubular Goods Sunset Reviews*, para. 313
(WT/DS268/AB/R)

In any event, we consider that the Panel's decision not to rely on the statements of the USITC before domestic courts and before a NAFTA panel relates to the weighing of evidence. . . .

. . .

The Appellate Body has consistently emphasized that, within the confines of their obligation under Article 11 of the DSU to make "an objective assessment of the facts of the case", panels enjoy a "margin of discretion" as triers of facts. Accordingly, we see no reason to interfere with the Panel's treatment of the USITC's statements before domestic courts and before a NAFTA panel.

S.7.3.21 *US – Upland Cotton*, para. 399
(WT/DS267/AB/R)

. . . Pursuant to Article 17.6 of the DSU, appeals are "limited to issues of law covered in the panel report and legal interpretations developed by the panel". To the extent that the United States' arguments concern the Panel's appreciation and weighing of the evidence, we note from the outset that the Appellate Body will not interfere lightly with the Panel's discretion "as the trier of facts". At the same time, the Appellate Body has previously pointed out that the "consistency or inconsistency of a given fact or set of facts with the requirements of a given treaty provision is . . . a legal characterization issue". Whether the Panel properly interpreted the requirements of Article 6.3(c) of the *SCM Agreement* and properly applied that interpretation to the facts in this case is a legal question. This question is different from whether the Panel made "an objective assessment of the matter before it, including an objective assessment of the facts of the case", in accordance with Article 11 of the DSU. Therefore, the Panel's application of the legal requirements of Article 6.3(c) of the *SCM Agreement* to the facts of this case falls within the scope of our review in this appeal, despite the fact that the United States does not claim that the Panel erred under Article 11 of the DSU.

S.7.3.22 *US – Upland Cotton*, para. 458
(WT/DS267/AB/R)

Unlike in certain other instances under the WTO agreements, a panel conducting an analysis under Article 6.3(c) of the *SCM Agreement* is the first trier of facts, rather than a reviewer of factual determinations made by a domestic investigating authority. Bearing this in mind, we underline the responsibility of panels in gathering and analyzing relevant factual data and information in assessing claims under Article 6.3(c) in order to arrive at reasoned conclusions. In this case, the voluminous evidentiary record before the Panel included several economic studies, and substantial data and information. For its part, the Panel posed a large number of questions to which the parties submitted detailed answers. Overall, the Panel evidently conducted an extensive analysis, but we believe that, in its reasoning, the Panel could have provided a more detailed explanation of its analysis of the complex facts and economic arguments arising in this dispute. The Panel could have done so in order to demonstrate precisely how it evaluated the different factors bearing on the relationship between the price-contingent subsidies and significant price suppression. Nevertheless, in the light of the Panel's examination of the relevant evidence, coupled with its legal reasoning, we find no legal error in the Panel's causation analysis.

S.7.3.23 *US – Upland Cotton*, para. 663
(WT/DS267/AB/R)

... The United States is not asking us to review the Panel's factual findings, nor is it arguing that the Panel's assessment of the matter was not objective. Instead, the United States' claim relates to the application of the legal standard set out in item (j) of the Illustrative List of Export Subsidies to the specific facts of this case. It is an issue of legal characterization. Thus, we do not agree with Brazil's contention that the United States was under an obligation to bring its claim under Article 11 of the DSU. Consequently, our inquiry will be limited to the Panel's application of the law to the facts in this case.

S.7.3.24 *US – Upland Cotton*, para. 686
(WT/DS267/AB/R)

We understand Brazil to argue that the Panel erred both in the application of Article 10.1 of the *Agreement on Agriculture* and in its assessment of the matter pursuant to Article 11 of the DSU. As we explained earlier, the application of a legal rule to the specific facts of a case is an issue of legal characterization. In this case, we understand that Brazil's claim under Article 11 of the DSU is additional to its claim of legal error in respect of Article 10.1. We thus turn first to Brazil's claim that the Panel erred in its application of Article 10.1 of the *Agreement on Agriculture* to the facts before it.

S.7.3.25 *US – Gambling*, para. 363
(WT/DS285/AB/R)

... the Panel had before it conflicting evidence as to the relationship between the IHA, on the one hand, and the measures at issue, on the other. We have already referred to the discretion accorded to panels, as fact-finders, in the assessment of the evidence. As the Appellate Body has observed on previous occasions, "not every error in the appreciation of the evidence (although it may give rise to a question of law) may be characterized as a failure to make an objective assessment of the facts."

S.7.3.26 *Dominican Republic – Import and Sale of Cigarettes*, para. 82
(WT/DS302/AB/R)

The Dominican Republic also submits that the Panel "misunderstood the proposition for which Exhibit DR-8 was offered", because "[t]he Panel ... incorrectly focused on the relationship between smuggling and forgery", whereas "Exhibit DR-8 was offered as evidence of (a) smuggling and, separately, (b) forgery of tax stamps of a product in respect of which the Dominican Republic allows stamps to be affixed outside its territory." In our view, the Panel did not act in a manner inconsistent with Article 11 of the DSU in not finding that Memo DAT-No. 46 "adds any conclusive elements as relate to the relationship between the seizure of alcoholic beverages and the possible forgery of tax stamps". A panel does not act in a manner inconsistent with Article 11 of the DSU simply because it draws inferences from some of the evidence that do not coincide with the reason for which a party adduced it.

S.7.3.27 *Dominican Republic – Import and Sale of Cigarettes*, para. 84
(WT/DS302/AB/R)

The Dominican Republic disagrees with the Panel's position that Exhibits DR-8 and DR-29 do not establish a causal link between allowing stamps to be affixed abroad and forgery of tax stamps. It contends that such a causal link exists, basing its contention on an inference it draws from evidence of smuggling and forgery of tax stamps with respect to alcohol products. However, a mere divergence of views between a party and a panel on the inferences to be drawn from pieces of evidence is not a sufficient ground to conclude that the Panel failed to "make . . . an objective assessment of the facts of the case". . . .

S.7.4 Article 11 of the DSU – Objective assessment of whether the investigating authority's explanation is reasoned and adequate

S.7.4.1 *US – Wheat Gluten*, paras. 161–162
(WT/DS166/AB/R)

. . . We consider that the Panel's conclusion is at odds with its treatment and description of the evidence supporting that conclusion. We do not see how the Panel could conclude that the USITC Report *did* provide an adequate explanation of the allocation methodologies, when it is clear that the Panel itself saw such deficiencies in that Report that it placed extensive reliance on "clarifications" that were not contained in the USITC Report.

By reaching a conclusion regarding the USITC Report, which relied so heavily on supplementary information provided by the United States during the Panel proceedings – information not contained in the USITC Report – the Panel applied a standard of review which falls short of what is required by Article 11 of the DSU.

S.7.4.2 *US – Lamb*, para. 103
(WT/DS177/AB/R, WT/DS178/AB/R)

Thus, an "objective assessment" of a claim under Article 4.2(a) of the *Agreement on Safeguards* has, in principle, two elements. First, a panel must review whether competent authorities have evaluated *all relevant factors*, and, second, a panel must review whether the authorities have provided a *reasoned and adequate explanation* of how the facts support their determination. Thus, the panel's objective assessment involves a *formal* aspect and a *substantive* aspect. The formal aspect is whether the competent authorities have evaluated "all relevant factors". The substantive aspect is whether the competent authorities have given a reasoned and adequate explanation for their determination.

S.7.4.3 *US – Lamb*, para. 104
(WT/DS177/AB/R, WT/DS178/AB/R)

... Under Article 4.2(a), competent authorities must, as a formal matter, evaluate "all relevant factors". However, that evaluation is not simply a matter of form, and the list of relevant factors to be evaluated is not a mere "check-list". ...

S.7.4.4 *US – Lamb*, para. 105
(WT/DS177/AB/R, WT/DS178/AB/R)

It follows that the precise nature of the examination to be conducted by a panel, in reviewing a claim under Article 4.2 of the *Agreement on Safeguards*, stems, in part, from the panel's obligation to make an "objective assessment of the matter" under Article 11 of the DSU and, in part, from the obligations imposed by Article 4.2, to the extent that those obligations are part of the claim. Thus, as with any claim under the provisions of a covered agreement, panels are required to examine, in accordance with Article 11 of the DSU, whether the Member has complied with the obligations imposed by the particular provisions identified in the claim. By examining whether the explanation given by the competent authorities in their published report is reasoned and adequate, panels can determine whether those authorities have acted consistently with the obligations imposed by Article 4.2 of the *Agreement on Safeguards*.

S.7.4.5 *US – Cotton Yarn*, para. 74
(WT/DS192/AB/R)

Our Reports in ... disputes under the *Agreement on Safeguards* spell out key elements of a panel's standard of review under Article 11 of the DSU in assessing whether the competent authorities complied with their obligations in making their determinations. This standard may be summarized as follows: panels must examine whether the competent authority has evaluated all relevant factors; they must assess whether the competent authority has examined all the pertinent facts and assessed whether an adequate explanation has been provided as to how those facts support the determination; and they must also consider whether the competent authority's explanation addresses fully the nature and complexities of the data and responds to other plausible interpretations of the data. However, panels must not conduct a *de novo* review of the evidence nor substitute their judgement for that of the competent authority.

S.7.5 Article 11 of the DSU – No de novo review

S.7.5.1 *US – Lamb*, paras. 106–107
(WT/DS177/AB/R, WT/DS178/AB/R)

We wish to emphasize that, although panels are not entitled to conduct a *de novo* review of the evidence, nor to *substitute* their own conclusions for those of the competent authorities, this does *not* mean that panels must simply *accept* the conclusions of the competent authorities. To the contrary, in our view, in examining a claim under Article 4.2(a), a panel can assess whether the competent authorities' explanation for its determination is reasoned and adequate *only* if the panel critically examines that explanation, in depth, and in the light of the facts before the panel. Panels must, therefore, review whether the competent authorities' explanation fully addresses the nature, and, especially, the complexities, of the data, and responds to other plausible interpretations of that data. A panel must find, in particular, that an explanation is not reasoned, or is not adequate, if some *alternative explanation* of the facts is plausible, and if the competent authorities' explanation does not seem adequate in the light of that alternative explanation. Thus, in making an "objective assessment" of a claim under Article 4.2(a), panels must be open to the possibility that the explanation given by the competent authorities is not reasoned or adequate.

In this respect, the phrase "*de novo* review" should not be used loosely. If a panel concludes that the competent authorities, in a particular case, have *not* provided a reasoned or adequate explanation for their determination, that panel has not, thereby, engaged in a *de novo* review. Nor has that panel substituted its own conclusions for those of the competent authorities. Rather, the panel has, consistent with its obligations under the DSU, simply reached a conclusion that the determination made by the competent authorities is inconsistent with the specific requirements of Article 4.2 of the *Agreement on Safeguards*.

S.7.5.2 *US – Lamb*, para. 113
(WT/DS177/AB/R, WT/DS178/AB/R)

. . . In arguing claims in dispute settlement, a *WTO Member* is not confined merely to rehearsing arguments that were made to the competent authorities by the *interested parties* during the domestic investigation, even if the WTO Member was itself an interested party in that investigation. Likewise, panels are not obliged to determine, and confirm themselves the nature and character of the arguments made by the interested parties to the competent authorities. Arguments before national competent authorities may be influenced by, and focused on, the requirements of the national laws, regulations and procedures. On the other hand, dispute settlement proceedings brought under the DSU concerning safeguard measures imposed under the *Agreement on Safeguards* may involve arguments that were not submitted to the competent authorities by the interested parties.

S.7.5.3 *US – Steel Safeguards*, paras. 298–299
(WT/DS248/AB/R, WT/DS249/AB/R, WT/DS251/AB/R, WT/DS252/AB/R, WT/DS253/AB/R, WT/DS254/AB/R, WT/DS258/AB/R, WT/DS259/AB/R)

. . . A panel must not be left to *wonder* why a safeguard measure has been applied.

It is precisely by "setting forth findings and reasoned conclusions on all pertinent issues of fact and law", under Article 3.1, and by providing "a detailed analysis of the case under investigation as well as a demonstration of the relevance of the factors examined", under Article 4.2(c), that competent authorities provide panels with the basis to "make an objective assessment of the matter before it" in accordance with Article 11. As we have said before, a panel may not conduct a *de novo* review of the evidence or substitute its judgement for that of the competent authorities. Therefore, the "reasoned conclusions" and "detailed analysis" as well as "a demonstration of the relevance of the factors examined" that are contained in the report of a competent authority, are the only bases on which a panel may assess whether a competent authority has complied with its obligations under the *Agreement on Safeguards* and Article XIX:1(a) of the GATT 1994. This is all the more reason why they must be made explicit by a competent authority.

S.7.5.4 *US – Steel Safeguards*, para. 303

(WT/DS248/AB/R, WT/DS249/AB/R, WT/DS251/AB/R, WT/DS252/AB/R, WT/DS253/AB/R, WT/DS254/AB/R, WT/DS258/AB/R, WT/DS259/AB/R)

. . . we cannot accept the United States' interpretation that a failure to explain a finding does not support the conclusion that the USITC "did not actually *perform* the analysis correctly, thereby breaching Article 2.1, 4.2, or 4.2(b) [of the *Agreement on Safeguards*]". As we stated above, because a panel may not conduct a *de novo* review of the evidence before the competent authority, it is the *explanation* given by the competent authority for its determination that alone enables panels to determine whether there has been compliance with the requirements of Article XIX of the GATT 1994 and of Articles 2 and 4 of the *Agreement on Safeguards*. It may well be that, as the United States argues, the competent authorities have performed the appropriate analysis correctly. However, where a competent authority has not provided a reasoned and adequate explanation to support its determination, the panel is not in a position to conclude that the relevant requirement for applying a safeguard measure has been fulfilled by that competent authority. . . .

S.7.6 Article 11 of the DSU – Temporal scope of review

S.7.6.1 *US – Cotton Yarn*, paras. 76–79

(WT/DS192/AB/R)

Unlike Article 3 of the *Agreement on Safeguards*, which provides explicitly for an investigation by competent authorities of a Member, Article 6 of the *ATC* does not specify either the organ or the procedure through which a Member makes its "determination". Nevertheless, the above principles concerning the standard of review under Article 11 of the DSU with respect to the *Agreement on Safeguards* apply equally, in our view, to a panel's review of a Member's determination under Article 6 of the *ATC*. We note that Article 6 does not require the participation of all interested parties in the process leading to the determination. We consider, therefore, that the exercise of due diligence by a Member is all the more important in reaching a determination under Article 6 of the *ATC*.

The exercise of due diligence by a Member cannot imply, however, the examination of evidence that did not exist and that, therefore, could not possibly have been taken into account when the Member made its determination. The demonstration by a Member that a particular product is being imported into its territory in such increased quantities as to cause serious damage (or actual threat thereof) to the domestic industry can be based only on facts and evidence which existed at the time the determination was made. The urgent nature of such an investigation may not permit the Member to delay its determination in order to take into account evidence that might be available only at a future date. Even a determination on the existence of threat of serious injury must be based on projections extrapolating from *existing* data.

In our view, a *panel* reviewing the due diligence exercised by a Member in making its determination under Article 6 of the *ATC* has to put itself in the place of that Member at the time it makes its determination. Consequently, a panel must not consider evidence which did not exist *at that point in time*. A Member cannot, of course, be faulted for not having taken into account what it could not have known when making its determination. If a panel were to examine such evidence, the panel would, in effect, be conducting a *de novo* review and it would be doing so without having had the benefit of the views of the interested parties. The panel would be assessing the due diligence of a Member in reaching its conclusions and making its projections with the benefit of hindsight and would, in effect, be reinvestigating the market situation and substituting its own judgement for that of the Member. In our view, this would be inconsistent with the standard of a panel's review under Article 11 of the DSU.

Moreover, if a Member that has exercised due diligence in complying with its obligations of investigation, evaluation and explanation, were held responsible before a panel for what it *could not have known* at the time it made its determination, this would undermine the right afforded to importing Members under Article 6 to take transitional safeguard action when the determination demonstrates the fulfilment of the specific conditions provided for in this Article.

S.7.7 Article 11 of the DSU – "make such other findings [to] assist the DSB . . . in giving the rulings"

S.7.7.1 *EC – Export Subsidies on Sugar*, para. 331
(WT/DS265/AB/R, WT/DS266/AB/R, WT/DS283/AB/R)

Thus, in addition to ruling on the matter before it, a panel is required [under Article 11 of the DSU] to "make such other findings as will assist the DSB in making the recommendations or in giving the rulings provided for in the covered agreements." Such "other findings" could, for instance, relate to implementation, to the extent that such findings "will assist the DSB in making the recommendations or in giving the rulings provided for in the covered agreements".

S.7.7.2 *EC – Export Subsidies on Sugar*, para. 335
(WT/DS265/AB/R, WT/DS266/AB/R, WT/DS283/AB/R)

In this case, the Panel's findings under Articles 3 and 8 of the *Agreement on Agriculture* were not sufficient to "fully resolve" the dispute. This is because, in declining to rule on the Complaining Parties' claims under Article 3 of the *SCM Agreement*, the Panel precluded the possibility of a remedy being made available to the Complaining Parties, pursuant to Article 4.7 of the *SCM Agreement*, in the event of the Panel finding in favour of the Complaining Parties with respect to their claims under Article 3 of the *SCM Agreement*. Moreover, in declining to rule on the Complaining Parties' claims under Article 3 of the *SCM Agreement*, the Panel failed to discharge its obligation under Article 11 of the DSU by failing to make "such other findings as will assist the DSB in making the recommendations or in giving the rulings provided for in the covered agreements", namely, a recommendation or ruling by the DSB pursuant to Article 4.7. This constitutes false judicial economy and legal error.

Standing. *See* Right to Bring Claims – Legal Interest (R.5)

S.7A State Trading Enterprises: Article XVII of the GATT 1994

S.7A.1 Article XVII of the GATT 1994 – "principles of non-discriminatory treatment"

S.7A.1.1 *Canada – Wheat Exports and Grain Imports*, para. 85
(WT/DS276/AB/R)

Subparagraph (a) of Article XVII:1 contains a number of different elements, including both an acknowledgement and an obligation. It recognizes that Members may establish or maintain State enterprises or grant exclusive or special privileges to private enterprises, but requires that, *if they do so*, such enterprises must, when they are involved in certain types of transactions ("purchases or sales involving either imports or exports"), comply with a specific requirement. That requirement is to act consistently with certain principles contained in the GATT 1994 ("general principles of non-discriminatory treatment . . . for governmental measures affecting imports or exports by private traders"). Subparagraph (a) seeks to ensure that a Member cannot, through the creation or maintenance of a State enterprise or the grant of exclusive or special privileges to any enterprise, engage in or facilitate conduct that would be condemned as discriminatory under the GATT 1994 if such conduct were undertaken directly by the Member itself. In other words, subparagraph (a) is an "anti-circumvention" provision.

S.7A.1.2 *Canada – Wheat Exports and Grain Imports*, para. 87
(WT/DS276/AB/R)

This requirement, which lies at the core of subparagraph (a), is a requirement that STEs not engage in certain types of discriminatory conduct. When viewed in the abstract, the concept of discrimination may encompass both the making of distinctions between similar situations, as well as treating dissimilar situations in a formally identical manner. The Appellate Body has previously dealt with the concept of discrimination and the meaning of the term "non-discriminatory", and acknowledged that, at least insofar as the making of distinctions between similar situations is concerned, the ordinary meaning of discrimination can accommodate both drawing distinctions *per se*, and drawing distinctions *on an improper basis.* Only a full and proper interpretation of a provision containing a prohibition on discrimination will reveal which type of differential treatment is prohibited. In all cases, a claimant alleging *discrimination* will need to establish that differential treatment has occurred in order to succeed in its claim.

S.7A.1.3 *Canada – Wheat Exports and Grain Imports*, para. 98 and footnote 104 (WT/DS276/AB/R)

As we have seen, through its reference to the "general principles of non-discriminatory treatment prescribed in this Agreement for governmental measures affecting imports or exports by private traders", Article XVII:1 imposes an obligation on Members not to use STEs in order to discriminate in ways that would be prohibited if undertaken directly by Members. Yet even if Article XVII:1 itself did not exist, this would not imply that STEs would be subject to no disciplines under the GATT 1994. For example, the express provisions of Article II:4 of the GATT 1994 and the *ad* Note to Articles XI, XII, XIII, XIV and XVIII constrain the behaviour of STEs. Other provisions of the GATT 1994, notably Article VI, also apply to the activities of STEs.[104] We need not identify, for purposes of this appeal, all of the provisions of the GATT 1994 that may apply to STEs, nor consider how these disciplines interact with and reinforce each other. We do, however, believe that these other provisions reveal that, even in 1947, the negotiators of the GATT created a number of complementary requirements to address the different ways in which STEs could be used by a contracting party to seek to circumvent its obligations under the GATT. The existence of these other provisions of the GATT 1994 also supports the view that Article XVII was never intended to be the sole source of the disciplines imposed on STEs under that Agreement. This is also consistent with the view that Article XVII:1 was intended to impose disciplines on one particular type of STE behaviour, namely discriminatory behaviour, rather than to constitute a comprehensive code of conduct for STEs. Moreover, as the Panel observed, since the conclusion of the Uruguay Round, a number of additional obligations, under different covered agreements, operate to further constrain the behaviour of STEs.

[104] We note that different views exist as to whether, or the extent to which, Article III of the GATT 1994 would also apply to STEs, although we take no view on this issue for purposes of this appeal. . . .

S.7A.1.4 *Canada – Wheat Exports and Grain Imports*, para. 145 (WT/DS276/AB/R)

. . . The disciplines of Article XVII:1 are aimed at preventing certain types of discriminatory behaviour. We see no basis for interpreting that provision as imposing comprehensive competition-law-type obligations on STEs, as the United States would have us do.

S.7A.2 Article XVII of the GATT 1994, Note Ad – differential prices for commercial reasons

S.7A.2.1 *Canada – Wheat Exports and Grain Imports*, para. 94 (WT/DS276/AB/R)

. . . This *ad* Note is attached to Article XVII:1 as a whole, rather than to either subparagraph (a) or subparagraph (b) alone. This sentence of the *ad* Note confirms that at least one type of differential treatment – price differentiation – is consistent with Article XVII:1 *provided that* the reasons for such differential prices are commercial in nature, and gives an example of such commercial reasons ("to meet conditions of supply and demand in export markets"). Thus, this Note also contemplates that determining the consistency or inconsistency of an STE's conduct with Article XVII:1 will involve an examination of *both* differential treatment and of commercial considerations.

S.7A.3 Article XVII:1 of the GATT 1994 – Relationship between subparagraphs (a) and (b)

S.7A.3.1 *Canada – Wheat Exports and Grain Imports*, para. 89 (WT/DS276/AB/R)

. . . the question we are asked to consider is how subparagraph (a) relates to subparagraph (b) of Article XVII:1. In our view, the answer to that inquiry is not found in the text of subparagraph (a). Rather, the words that bear most directly on the relationship between the first two paragraphs of Article XVII:1 are found in the opening phrase of subparagraph (b), which states that the "provisions of subparagraph (*a*) of this paragraph *shall be understood to require* that such enterprises shall . . .". (emphasis added) This phrase makes it abundantly clear that the remainder of subparagraph (b) is dependent upon the content of subparagraph (a), and operates to clarify the scope of the requirement not to discriminate in subparagraph (a). . . . Thus, the opening phrase in subparagraph (b) of Article XVII:1 supports Canada's view that the *principal source* of the relevant obligation(s) in Article XVII:1(a) and (b) is, indeed, found in "[t]he provisions of subparagraph (*a*)".

S.7A.3.2 *Canada – Wheat Exports and Grain Imports*, para. 91 (WT/DS276/AB/R)

Having examined the text of subparagraphs (a) and (b) of Article XVII:1, it is our view that subparagraph (b), by defining and clarifying the requirement in subparagraph (a), is dependent upon, rather than separate and independent from, subparagraph (a). . . .

S.7A.3.3 *Canada – Wheat Exports and Grain Imports*, paras. 99–100 (WT/DS276/AB/R)

. . . subparagraphs (a) and (b) are necessarily related to each other. Subparagraph (a) is the general and principal provision, and subparagraph (b) explains it by identifying types of differential treatment in commercial transactions. It appears to us that these types of differential treatment would be the most likely to occur in practice and, therefore, that most if not all cases under Article XVII:1 will involve an analysis of both subparagraphs (a) and (b).

For all these reasons, we are of the view that subparagraph (a) of Article XVII:1 of the GATT 1994 sets out an obligation of non-discrimination, and that subparagraph (b) clarifies the scope of that obligation. We therefore disagree with the United

States that subparagraph (b) establishes separate requirements that are independent of subparagraph (a).

S.7A.3.4 *Canada – Wheat Exports and Grain Imports*, para. 106 and footnote 115
(WT/DS276/AB/R)

Our conclusions regarding the relationship between subparagraphs (a) and (b) imply that a panel confronted with a claim that an STE has acted inconsistently with Article XVII:1 will need to begin its analysis of that claim under subparagraph (a), because it is that provision which contains the principal obligation of Article XVII:1, namely the requirement not to act in a manner contrary to the "general principles of non-discriminatory treatment prescribed in [the GATT 1994] for governmental measures affecting imports or exports by private traders." At the same time, because both subparagraphs (a) and (b) define the scope of that non-discrimination obligation, we would expect that panels, in most if not all cases, would not be in a position to make any finding of violation of Article XVII:1 until they have properly interpreted and applied both provisions.[115]

[115] We are not asked, in this appeal, to rule on whether it might be possible for a panel to find a violation of Article XVII:1 based solely on an analysis undertaken under subparagraph (a) – without conducting any analysis under subparagraph (b) – and we make no finding in this regard. The question before us is, rather, whether it might be possible for a panel to find a violation of Article XVII:1 based solely on an analysis undertaken under subparagraph (b) – without conducting any analysis under subparagraph (a). In other words, although we accept that subparagraph (b) identifies two examples of conduct *consistent* with the obligation set forth in subparagraph (a), we make no finding as to whether subparagraph (b) also serves to define, exhaustively, the type of conduct that is *inconsistent* with the obligation in subparagraph (a).

S.7A.3.5 *Canada – Wheat Exports and Grain Imports*, para. 109
(WT/DS276/AB/R)

Thus, in each case it is the nature of the relationship between two provisions that will determine whether there exists a mandatory sequence of analysis which, if not followed, would amount to an error of law. In some cases, this relationship is such that a failure to structure the analysis in the proper logical sequence will have repercussions for the substance of the analysis itself.

S.7A.3.6 *Canada – Wheat Exports and Grain Imports*, paras. 110–111
(WT/DS276/AB/R)

. . . a panel faced with a claim of inconsistency with Article XVII:1(a) and (b) will, in most if not all cases, need to analyze and apply *both* provisions in order to assess the consistency of the measure at issue. Subparagraph (b) sets forth two specific conditions with which an STE must comply if allegedly discriminatory conduct falling, *prima facie*, within the scope of subparagraph (a) is to be found consistent with Article XVII:1. Yet, in order to know whether the conditions in (b) are satisfied, a panel must know *what* constitutes the conduct alleged to be inconsistent with the principles of non-discriminatory treatment in the GATT 1994. A panel will need to identify at least the differential treatment at issue. The outcome of an assessment under subparagraph (b) of whether the differential treatment is consistent with commercial considerations may depend, in part, upon whether the alleged discrimination relates to pricing, quality, or conditions of sale, and whether it is discrimination between export markets or some other form of discrimination.

It follows that, logically, a panel cannot assess whether particular practices of an allegedly discriminatory nature accord with commercial considerations without first identifying the key elements of the alleged discrimination. We emphasize that we are *not* suggesting that panels are always obliged to make specific factual and legal findings with respect to each element of a claim of discrimination under subparagraph (a) before undertaking *any* analysis under subparagraph (b). Rather, because a panel's analysis and application of subparagraph (b) to the facts of the case is, like subparagraph (b) itself, dependent on the obligation set forth in subparagraph (a), panels must identify the differential treatment alleged to be discriminatory under subparagraph (a) in order to ensure that they are undertaking a proper inquiry under subparagraph (b).

S.7A.3.7 *Canada – Wheat Exports and Grain Imports*, paras. 124–125 (WT/DS276/AB/R)

. . . although the Panel refrained from explicitly defining the relationship between the first two subparagraphs of Article XVII:1, its approach was consistent with our interpretation of that relationship.

In sum, we find that, in the particular circumstances of this case, the Panel did not err in not considering the "proper" relationship between subparagraphs (a) and (b) of Article XVII:1 of the GATT 1994, or in proceeding to examine the consistency of the CWB Export Regime with Article XVII:1(b) without first having found a breach of Article XVII:1(a). . . .

S.7A.4 Article XVII:1(b) of the GATT 1994 – "commercial considerations"

S.7A.4.1 *Canada – Wheat Exports and Grain Imports*, paras. 140–141 (WT/DS276/AB/R)

. . . The Panel began its analysis by considering the meaning of the term "commercial considerations" in subparagraph (b) and found that this term should be understood as meaning "considerations pertaining to commerce and trade, or considerations which involve regarding purchases or sales 'as mere matters of business'." The Panel also determined that the requirement that STEs act solely in accordance with such considerations "must imply that they should seek to purchase or sell on terms which are economically advantageous for themselves and/or their owners, members, beneficiaries, etc." Thus, the Panel interpreted the term "commercial considerations" as encompassing a range of different considerations that are defined in any given case by the type of "business" involved (purchases or sales), and by the economic considerations that motivate actors engaged in business in the relevant market(s).

The Panel then turned to address several arguments advanced by the United States with respect to the interpretation of the first clause of subparagraph (b). It was in responding to the United States' assertion that the requirement that STEs act "solely in accordance with commercial considerations" is equivalent to a requirement that STEs act like "commercial actors" that the Panel made the statement that "the requirement in question is simply intended to prevent STEs from behaving like 'political' actors". Yet in so doing the Panel expressly stated that it was *not*, as the United States now suggests that it did, equating "non-commercial" actors with political actors. . . .

S.7A.4.2 *Canada – Wheat Exports and Grain Imports*, paras. 144–145 (WT/DS276/AB/R)

. . . it is important to observe that the Panel's interpretation of the term "commercial considerations" necessarily implies that the determination of whether or not a particular STE's conduct is consistent with the requirements of the first clause of subparagraph (b) of Article XVII:1 must be undertaken on a case-by-case basis, and must involve a careful analysis of the relevant market(s). We see no error in the Panel's approach; only such an analysis will reveal the type and range of considerations properly considered "commercial" as regards purchases and sales made in those markets, as well as how those considerations influence the actions of participants in the market(s).

At the same time, our interpretation of the relationship between subparagraphs (a) and (b) of Article XVII:1 necessarily implies that . . . a panel inquiring whether an STE has acted solely in accordance with commercial considerations must undertake this inquiry with respect to the market(s) in which the STE is alleged to be engaging in discriminatory conduct. Subparagraph (b) does not give panels a mandate to engage in a broader inquiry into whether, in the abstract, STEs are acting "commercially". . . .

S.7A.4.3 *Canada – Wheat Exports and Grain Imports*, para. 146 (WT/DS276/AB/R)

. . . For the United States, because commercial actors naturally conduct their business on the basis of commercial considerations, the first clause of Article XVII:1(b) necessarily must prevent an STE from using its privileges in a way that creates serious obstacles to trade and disadvantages such commercial actors. . . .

S.7A.4.4 *Canada – Wheat Exports and Grain Imports*, para. 149 (WT/DS276/AB/R)

. . . the Panel's approach emphasizes that whether an STE is in compliance with the disciplines in Article XVII:1 must be assessed by means of a market-based analysis, rather than simply by determining whether an STE has used the privileges that it has been granted. In arguing that Article XVII:1(b) must be interpreted as prohibiting STEs from using their exclusive or special privileges to the disadvantage of "commercial actors", the United States appears to construe Article XVII:1(b) as requiring STEs to act not only as commercial actors in the marketplace, but as *virtuous* commercial actors, by tying their own hands. We do not see how such an interpretation can be reconciled with an analysis of "commercial considerations" based on market forces. In other words, we cannot accept that the first clause of subparagraph (b) would, as a general rule, require STEs to refrain from using the privileges and advantages that they enjoy because such use might "disadvantage" private enterprises. STEs, like private enterprises, are entitled to exploit the advantages they may enjoy to their economic benefit. Article XVII:1(b) merely prohibits STEs from making purchases or sales on the basis of non-commercial considerations.

S.7A.5 Article XVII:1(b) of the GATT 1994 – Afford adequate opportunity to compete for participation in purchases or sales

S.7A.5.1 *Canada – Wheat Exports and Grain Imports*, para. 153 (WT/DS276/AB/R)

. . . The United States asserts that the Panel's incorrect interpretative approach led it to the erroneous conclusion that this term [afford the enterprises of the other Member adequate opportunity . . . to compete for participation in such purchases or sales] referred to enterprises that wish to *buy* from an STE, but not to enterprises that wish to *sell* in competition with an STE. . . .

S.7A.5.2 *Canada – Wheat Exports and Grain Imports*, paras. 156–157 (WT/DS276/AB/R)

In the abstract, competition to participate in purchases and sales could include competition to participate as a buyer, as a seller, or both. However, the clause under examination does not refer, in the abstract, to *any* purchases and sales. Rather, it refers to "*such* purchases or sales", repeating the phrase found in the first clause of subparagraph (b). As discussed in our analysis above, this phrase in subparagraph (b) of Article XVII:1 refers back to the activities identified in subparagraph (a), namely the purchases and sales of an STE involving imports or exports.

In other words, the second clause of subparagraph (b) refers to purchases and sales transactions where: (i) one of the parties involved in the transaction is an STE; and (ii) the transaction involves imports to or exports from the Member maintaining the STE. Thus, the requirement to afford an adequate opportunity to compete for participation (*i.e.*, taking part with others) in "such" purchases and sales (import or export transactions involving an STE) must refer to the opportunity to become the STE's counterpart in the transaction, *not* to an opportunity to replace the STE as a participant in the transaction. If it were otherwise, the transaction would no longer be the type of transaction described by the phrase "*such* purchases or sales" in the second clause of Article XVII:1(b), because it would not involve an STE as a party. Thus, in transactions involving two parties, one of whom is an STE seller, the word "enterprises" in the second clause of Article XVII:1(b) can refer *only* to buyers.

S.7A.5.3 *Canada – Wheat Exports and Grain Imports*, para. 160
(WT/DS276/AB/R)

... The Panel did not determine the full ambit of the requirement to "afford adequate opportunity ... to compete for participation" in relevant purchases and sales. Nor do we. The Panel expressly recognized the possibility that, in other circumstances, particular enterprises could act both as a buyer and as a seller. The Panel also explicitly stated that it was not asked to, and was *not*, ruling on the scope of the obligation in this clause with respect to STEs that act as *purchasers*, rather than as *sellers*.

S.7A.6 Article XVII:3 of the GATT 1994

S.7A.6.1 *Canada – Wheat Exports and Grain Imports*, para. 97
(WT/DS276/AB/R)

To us, [Article XVII:3] explicitly recognizes that, *notwithstanding* the existence of certain disciplines on STEs in Article XVII:1, these alone may not suffice to prevent the various ways in which STEs might create obstacles to trade, and that additional measures to limit or reduce such obstacles should therefore be pursued through negotiation. Thus, this provision constitutes acknowledgement by the GATT contracting parties of the *limitations* inherent in Article XVII:1, and recognizes that Article XVII:1 cannot serve as the sole legal basis for eliminating *all* potential obstacles to trade relating to STEs....

S.8 Status of Panel and Appellate Body Reports. *See also* Panel Reports (P.1); Review of Implementation of DSB Rulings, Article 21.5 of the DSU – Effect of DSB rulings in original dispute (R.4.3)

S.8.1 *Japan – Alcoholic Beverages II*, pp. 14–15, DSR 1996:I, p. 97 at 107–108
(WT/DS8/AB/R, WT/DS10/AB/R, WT/DS11/AB/R)

Article XVI:1 of the *WTO Agreement* and paragraph 1(b)(iv) of the language of Annex 1A incorporating the GATT 1994 into the *WTO Agreement* bring the legal history and experience under the GATT 1947 into the new realm of the WTO in a way that ensures continuity and consistency in a smooth transition from the GATT 1947 system. This affirms the importance to the Members of the WTO of the experience acquired by the CONTRACTING PARTIES to the GATT 1947 – and acknowledges the continuing relevance of that experience to the new trading system served by the WTO. Adopted panel reports are an important part of the GATT *acquis*. They are often considered by subsequent panels. They create legitimate expectations among WTO Members, and, therefore, should be taken into account where they are relevant to any dispute. However, they are not binding, except with respect to resolving the particular dispute between the parties to that dispute. In short, their character and their legal status have not been changed by the coming into force of the *WTO Agreement*.

For these reasons, we do not agree with the Panel's conclusion in paragraph 6.10 of the Panel Report that "panel reports adopted by the GATT CONTRACTING PARTIES and the WTO Dispute Settlement Body constitute subsequent practice in a specific case" as the phrase "subsequent practice" is used in Article 31 of the *Vienna Convention*. Further, we do not agree with the Panel's conclusion in the same paragraph of the Panel Report that adopted panel reports in themselves constitute "other decisions of the CONTRACTING PARTIES to GATT 1947" for the purposes of paragraph 1(b)(iv) of the language of Annex 1A incorporating the GATT 1994 into the *WTO Agreement*.

However, we agree with the Panel's conclusion in that same paragraph of the Panel Report that *unadopted* panel reports "have no legal status in the GATT or WTO system since they have not been endorsed through decisions by the CONTRACTING PARTIES to GATT or WTO Members". Likewise, we agree that "a panel could nevertheless find useful guidance in the reasoning of an unadopted panel report that it considered to be relevant".

S.8.2 *US – Shrimp (Article 21.5 – Malaysia)*, paras. 107–109 (WT/DS58/AB/RW)

Malaysia also objects to the frequent references made by the Panel to our reasoning in our Report in *United States – Shrimp*. The reasoning in our Report in *United States – Shrimp* on which the Panel relied was not *dicta*; it was essential to our ruling. The Panel was right to use it, and right to rely on it. Nor are we surprised that the Panel made frequent references to our Report in *United States – Shrimp*. Indeed, we would have expected the Panel to do so. The Panel had, necessarily, to consider our views on this subject, as we had overruled certain aspects of the findings of the original panel on this issue and, more important, had provided interpretative guidance for future panels, such as the Panel in this case.

. . . we note that in our Report in *Japan – Taxes on Alcoholic Beverages*, we stated that:

> Adopted panel reports are an important part of the GATT *acquis*. They are often considered by subsequent panels. They create legitimate expectations among WTO Members, and, therefore, should be taken into account where they are relevant to any dispute.

This reasoning applies to adopted Appellate Body Reports as well. Thus, in taking into account the reasoning in an adopted Appellate Body Report – a Report, moreover, that was directly relevant to the Panel's disposition of the issues before it – the Panel did not err. The Panel was correct in using our findings as a tool for its own reasoning. Further, we see no indication that, in doing so, the Panel limited itself merely to examining the new measure from the perspective of the recommendations and rulings of the DSB.

S.8.3 *US – Softwood Lumber V*, para. 112
(WT/DS264/AB/R)

Bearing [the findings in *Japan – Alcoholic Beverages II* and *US – Shrimp (Article 21.5 – Malaysia)*] in mind, and noting Article 3.2 of the *Understanding on Rules and Procedures Governing the Settlement of Disputes* (the "DSU"), which states that "the dispute settlement system of the WTO is a central element in providing security and predictability to the multilateral trading system," we have given full consideration to the particular facts of this case and to the arguments raised by the United States on appeal, as well as to those raised by Canada and the third participants. In doing so, we have taken into account the reasoning and findings contained in the Appellate Body Report in *EC – Bed Linen*, as appropriate.

S.8.4 *US – Oil Country Tubular Goods Sunset Reviews*, para. 188
(WT/DS268/AB/R)

. . . The Panel had before it exactly the same instrument that had been examined by the Appellate Body in *US – Corrosion-Resistant Steel Sunset Review*; thus, it was appropriate for the Panel, in determining whether the SPB is a measure, to rely on the Appellate Body's conclusion in that case. Indeed, following the Appellate Body's conclusions in earlier disputes is not only appropriate, but is what would be expected from panels, especially where the issues are the same. . . .

Subsequent Practice. *See* Interpretation (I.3)

Subsidies. *See* SCM Agreement (S.2)

Supplementary Means of Interpretation. *See* Interpretation, Supplementary means of interpretation – Article 32 of the Vienna Convention (I.3.10)

S.9 Suspension of Concessions or Other Obligations

S.9.1 *US – Certain EC Products*, para. 120
(WT/DS165/AB/R)

The *obligation* of WTO Members not to suspend concessions or other obligations *without* prior DSB authorization is explicitly set out in Articles 22.6 and 23.2(c), not in Article 3.7 of the DSU . . . We consider, however, that if a Member has acted in breach of Articles 22.6 and 23.2(c) of the DSU, that Member has also, in view of the nature and content of Article 3.7, last sentence, necessarily acted contrary to the latter provision.

S.9.2 *US – Cotton Yarn*, para. 120
(WT/DS192/AB/R)

Our view is supported further by the rules of general international law on state responsibility, which require that countermeasures in response to breaches by states of their international obligations be commensurate with the injury suffered. In the same vein, we note that Article 22.4 of the DSU stipulates that the suspension of concessions shall be equivalent to the level of nullification or impairment. This provision of the DSU has been interpreted consistently as not justifying punitive damages. These two examples illustrate the consequences of breaches by states of their international obligations, whereas a safeguard action is merely a remedy to WTO-consistent "fair trade" activity. It would be absurd if the breach of an international obligation were sanctioned by proportionate countermeasures, while, in the absence of such breach, a WTO Member would be subject to a disproportionate and, hence, "punitive", attribution of serious damage not wholly caused by its exports. In our view, such an exorbitant derogation from the principle of proportionality in respect of the attribution of serious damage could be justified only if the drafters of the *ATC* had expressly provided for it, which is not the case.

T

T.1 Tariff Concessions

T.1.1 Article II:1 of the GATT 1994. *See also* Agreement on Agriculture, Article 4.2 and Footnote 1 (A.1.9–13)

T.1.1.1 *Argentina – Textiles and Apparel*, para. 45
(WT/DS56/AB/R, WT/DS56/AB/R/Corr.1)

. . . Paragraph (a) of Article II:1 contains a general prohibition against according treatment less favourable to imports than that provided for in a Member's Schedule. Paragraph (b) prohibits a specific kind of practice that will always be inconsistent with paragraph (a): that is, the application of ordinary customs duties in excess of those provided for in the Schedule. Because the language of Article II:1(b), first sentence, is more specific and germane to the case at hand, our interpretative analysis begins with, and focuses on, that provision.

T.1.1.2 *Argentina – Textiles and Apparel*, para. 55
(WT/DS56/AB/R, WT/DS56/AB/R/Corr.1)

We conclude that the application of a type of duty different from the type provided for in a Member's Schedule is inconsistent with Article II:1(b), first sentence, of the GATT 1994 to the extent that it results in ordinary customs duties being levied in excess of those provided for in that Member's Schedule. In this case, we find that Argentina has acted inconsistently with its obligations under Article II:1(b), first sentence, of the GATT 1994, because the DIEM regime, by its structure and design, results, with respect to a certain range of import prices in any relevant tariff category to which it applies, in the levying of customs duties in excess of the bound rate of 35 per cent *ad valorem* in Argentina's Schedule.

T.1.1.3 *Canada – Dairy*, para. 134
(WT/DS103/AB/R, WT/DS113/AB/R, WT/DS103/AB/R/Corr.1, WT/DS113/AB/R/Corr.1)

. . . Under Article II:1(b) of the GATT 1994, the market access concessions granted by a Member are "*subject to*" the "terms, conditions or qualifications set forth in [its] Schedule". (emphasis added) In our view, the ordinary meaning of the phrase "subject to" is that such concessions are without prejudice to and are *subordinated to*, and are, therefore, *qualified by*, any "terms, conditions or qualifications" inscribed in a Member's Schedule. . . . The phrase "terms and conditions" is a composite one which, in its ordinary meaning, denotes the imposition of qualifying restrictions or conditions. A strong presumption arises that the language which is inscribed in a Member's Schedule under the heading, "Other Terms and Conditions", has some *qualifying* or *limiting* effect on the substantive content or scope of the concession or commitment.

T.1.2 Interpretation and clarification of tariff concessions

T.1.2.1 *EC – Computer Equipment*, para. 84
(WT/DS62/AB/R, WT/DS67/AB/R, WT/DS68/AB/R)

The purpose of treaty interpretation under Article 31 of the *Vienna Convention* is to ascertain the *common* intentions of the parties. These *common* intentions cannot be ascertained on the basis of the subjective and unilaterally determined "expectations" of *one* of the parties to a treaty. Tariff concessions provided for in a Member's Schedule – the interpretation of which is at issue here – are reciprocal and result from a mutually-advantageous negotiation between importing and exporting Members. A Schedule is made an integral part of the GATT 1994 by Article II:7 of the GATT 1994. Therefore, the concessions provided for in that Schedule are part of the terms of the treaty. As such, the only rules which may be applied in interpreting the meaning of a concession are the general rules of treaty interpretation set out in the *Vienna Convention*.

T.1.2.2 *EC – Computer Equipment*, paras. 89–90
(WT/DS62/AB/R, WT/DS67/AB/R, WT/DS68/AB/R)

. . . We believe, however, that a proper interpretation of Schedule LXXX should have included an examination of the *Harmonized System* and its *Explanatory Notes*.

. . . we consider that in interpreting the tariff concessions in Schedule LXXX, decisions of the WCO may be relevant . . .

T.1.2.3 *EC – Computer Equipment*, para. 92
(WT/DS62/AB/R, WT/DS67/AB/R, WT/DS68/AB/R)

. . . In the light of our observations on "the circumstances of [the] conclusion" of a treaty as a supplementary means of interpretation under Article 32 of the *Vienna Convention*, we consider that the classification practice in the European Communities during the Uruguay Round is part of "the circumstances of [the] conclusion" of the *WTO Agreement* and may be used as a supplementary means of interpretation within the meaning of Article 32 of the *Vienna Convention*. . . .

T.1.2.4 *EC – Computer Equipment*, para. 93
(WT/DS62/AB/R, WT/DS67/AB/R, WT/DS68/AB/R)

. . . The purpose of treaty interpretation is to establish the *common* intention of the parties to the treaty. To establish this intention, the prior practice of only *one* of the parties may be relevant, but it is clearly of more limited value than the practice of all parties. In the specific case of the interpretation of a tariff concession in a Schedule, the classification practice of the importing Member, in fact, may be of great importance. However, the Panel was mistaken in finding that the classification practice of the United States was *not* relevant.

T.1.2.5 *EC – Computer Equipment*, para. 95

(WT/DS62/AB/R, WT/DS67/AB/R, WT/DS68/AB/R)

. . . Consistent prior classification practice may often be significant. Inconsistent classification practice, however, *cannot* be relevant in interpreting the meaning of a tariff concession. . . .

T.1.2.6 *EC – Computer Equipment*, para. 97

(WT/DS62/AB/R, WT/DS67/AB/R, WT/DS68/AB/R)

. . . we conclude that the Panel erred in finding that the "legitimate expectations" of an exporting Member are relevant for the purposes of interpreting the terms of Schedule LXXX and of determining whether the European Communities violated Article II:1 of the GATT 1994 . . .

T.1.2.7 *EC – Computer Equipment*, paras. 109–110

(WT/DS62/AB/R, WT/DS67/AB/R, WT/DS68/AB/R)

. . . Tariff negotiations are a process of reciprocal demands and concessions, of "give and take". It is only normal that importing Members define their offers (and their ensuing obligations) in terms which suit their needs. On the other hand, exporting Members have to ensure that their corresponding rights are described in such a manner in the Schedules of importing Members that their export interests, as agreed in the negotiations, are guaranteed. There was a special arrangement made for this in the Uruguay Round. For this purpose, a process of verification of tariff schedules took place from 15 February through 25 March 1994, which allowed Uruguay Round participants to check and control, through consultations with their negotiating partners, the scope and definition of tariff concessions. Indeed, the fact that Members' Schedules are an integral part of the GATT 1994 indicates that, while each Schedule represents the tariff commitments made by *one* Member, they represent a common agreement among *all* Members.

. . . We consider that any clarification of the scope of tariff concessions that may be required during the negotiations is a task for *all* interested parties.

T.1.2.8 *US – Gambling*, para. 233

(WT/DS285/AB/R)

. . . the chapeau to Article XVI:2 . . . contemplates circumstances in which a Member's Schedule *includes* a commitment to allow market access, and points out that the function of the sub-paragraphs in Article XVI:2 is to define certain limitations that are prohibited unless specifically entered in the Member's Schedule. Plainly, the drafters of sub-paragraph (a) had in mind limitations that would impose a maximum limit of *above* zero. Similarly, Article II:1(b) of the GATT 1994 prohibits Members from imposing duties "in excess of" the bound duty rate. Such bound duty rate will usually be *above* zero. Yet this does not mean that Article II:1(b) does not also refer to bound rates set at zero.

T.1.3 Relationship between Schedules of concessions and the GATT 1994

T.1.3.1 *EC – Bananas III*, paras. 154–155
(WT/DS27/AB/R)

The market access concessions for agricultural products that were made in the Uruguay Round of multilateral trade negotiations are set out in Members' Schedules annexed to the *Marrakesh Protocol,* and are an integral part of the GATT 1994. By the terms of the *Marrakesh Protocol*, the Schedules are "Schedules to the GATT 1994", and Article II:7 of the GATT 1994 provides that "Schedules annexed to this Agreement are hereby made an integral part of Part I of this Agreement". With respect to concessions contained in the Schedules annexed to the GATT 1947, the panel in *United States – Restrictions on Importation of Sugar* ("*United States – Sugar Headnote*") found that:

> . . . Article permits contracting parties to incorporate into their Schedules acts yielding rights under the General Agreement but not acts diminishing obligations under that Agreement.

This principle is equally valid for the market access concessions and commitments for agricultural products contained in the Schedules annexed to the GATT 1994. The ordinary meaning of the term "concessions" suggests that a Member may yield rights and grant benefits, but it cannot diminish its obligations. This interpretation is confirmed by paragraph 3 of the *Marrakesh Protocol* which provides:

> The implementation of the concessions and commitments contained in the schedules annexed to this Protocol shall, upon request, be subject to multilateral examination by the Members. This would be *without prejudice to the rights and obligations of Members under Agreements in Annex 1A of the WTO Agreement*. (emphasis added)

The question remains whether the provisions of the *Agreement on Agriculture* allow market access concessions on agricultural products to deviate from Article XIII of the GATT 1994. The preamble of the *Agreement on Agriculture* states that it establishes "a basis for initiating a process of reform of trade in agriculture" and that this reform process "should be initiated through the negotiation of commitments on support and protection and through the establishment of strengthened and more operationally effective GATT rules and disciplines". The relationship between the provisions of the GATT 1994 and of the *Agreement on Agriculture* is set out in Article 21.1 of the *Agreement on Agriculture*:

> The provisions of GATT 1994 and of other Multilateral Trade Agreements in Annex 1A to the WTO Agreement shall apply subject to the provisions of this Agreement.

Therefore, the provisions of the GATT 1994, including Article XIII, apply to market-access commitments concerning agricultural products, except to the extent that the

Agreement on Agriculture contains specific provisions dealing specifically with the same matter.

T.1.3.2 *EC – Poultry*, para. 98
(WT/DS69/AB/R)

. . . The ordinary meaning of the term "concessions" suggests that a Member may yield or waive some of its own rights and grant benefits to other Members, but that it cannot unilaterally diminish its own obligations. . . .

T.1.3.3 *EC – Poultry*, para. 99
(WT/DS69/AB/R)

Therefore, the concessions contained in Schedule LXXX pertaining to the tariff-rate quota for frozen poultry meat must be consistent with Articles I and XIII of the GATT 1994.

T.1.4 Relationship between Members' Schedules and the Agreement on Agriculture. *See also* Agreement on Agriculture, Relationship between the Agreement on Agriculture and the GATT 1994 (A.1.37)

T.1.4.1 *EC – Export Subsidies on Sugar*, paras. 220–223
(WT/DS265/AB/R, WT/DS266/AB/R, WT/DS283/AB/R)

. . . we find no provision under the *Agreement on Agriculture* that authorizes Members to depart, in their Schedules, from their obligations under that Agreement. Indeed, as we have noted, Article 8 requires that, in providing export subsidies, Members must comply with the provisions of both the *Agreement on Agriculture* and the export subsidy commitments specified in their Schedules. This is possible only if the commitments in the Schedules are in conformity with the provisions of the *Agreement on Agriculture*. Thus, we see no basis for the European Communities' assertion that it could depart from the obligations under the *Agreement on Agriculture* through the claimed commitment provided in Footnote 1.

In any event, we note that Article 21 of the *Agreement on Agriculture* provides that: "[t]he provisions of [the] GATT 1994 and of other Multilateral Trade Agreements in Annex 1A to the WTO Agreement shall apply subject to the provisions of this Agreement." In other words, Members explicitly recognized that there may be conflicts between the *Agreement on Agriculture* and the GATT 1994, and explicitly provided, through Article 21, that the *Agreement on Agriculture* would prevail to the extent of such conflicts. Similarly, the *General interpretative note to Annex 1A* to the *WTO Agreement* states that, "[i]n the event of conflict between a provision of the [GATT 1994] and a provision of another agreement in Annex 1A . . . , the provision of the other agreement shall prevail to the extent of the conflict." The *Agreement on Agriculture* is contained in Annex 1A to the *WTO Agreement*.

As we noted above, Footnote 1, being part of the European Communities' Schedule, is an integral part of the GATT 1994 by virtue of Article 3.1 of the *Agreement on Agriculture*. Therefore, pursuant to Article 21 of the *Agreement on Agriculture*, the provisions of the *Agreement on Agriculture* prevail over Footnote 1. . . .

As a separate matter, we note that the European Communities asserts that Footnote 1 was "negotiated" with its partners in the Uruguay Round negotiations and that it has been "respected". Accordingly, Footnote 1 forms part of the treaty ratified by the WTO Members. Similarly, the ACP Countries allege that Footnote 1 "was negotiated and agreed upon" or acquiesced in by the Complaining Parties before the end of the Uruguay Round. The Panel found, however, that "[t]he evidence and submissions produced by all parties show that the Complainants did not agree to any European Communities' deviations from the *Agreement on Agriculture*." The Panel concluded that "participants in the Uruguay Round and WTO Members did not agree to the European Communities' inclusion of Footnote 1 as an agreed departure from the European Communities' basic obligations under the *Agreement on Agriculture*." Accordingly, we see no basis in the Panel Reports for the contention of the European Communities and the ACP Countries that the Complaining Parties or the WTO Members negotiated or agreed to Footnote 1 as a departure from the European Communities' obligations under the *Agreement on Agriculture*.

T.1.5 **Interpretation of Members' Schedules.** *See also* GATS, Schedules, Interpretation of Schedules (G.1.2.1)

T.1.5.1 *EC – Computer Equipment*, para. 84
(WT/DS62/AB/R, WT/DS67/AB/R, WT/DS68/AB/R)

The purpose of treaty interpretation under Article 31 of the *Vienna Convention* is to ascertain the *common* intentions of the parties. These *common* intentions cannot be ascertained on the basis of the subjective and unilaterally determined "expectations" of *one* of the parties to a treaty. Tariff concessions provided for in a Member's Schedule – the interpretation of which is at issue here – are reciprocal and result from a mutually-advantageous negotiation between importing and exporting Members. A Schedule is made an integral part of the GATT 1994 by Article II:7 of the GATT 1994. Therefore, the concessions provided for in that Schedule are part of the terms of the treaty. As such, the only rules which may be applied in interpreting the meaning of a concession are the general rules of treaty interpretation set out in the *Vienna Convention*.

T.1.5.2 *EC – Computer Equipment*, para. 93
(WT/DS62/AB/R, WT/DS67/AB/R, WT/DS68/AB/R)

. . . The purpose of treaty interpretation is to establish the *common* intention of the parties to the treaty. To establish this intention, the prior practice of only *one* of the parties may be relevant, but it is clearly of more limited value than the practice of all parties. In the specific case of the interpretation of a tariff concession in a Schedule, the classification practice of the importing Member, in fact, may be of great importance. However, the Panel was mistaken in finding that the classification practice of the United States was *not* relevant.

T.1.5.3 *EC – Computer Equipment*, para. 95

(WT/DS62/AB/R, WT/DS67/AB/R, WT/DS68/AB/R)

. . . Consistent prior classification practice may often be significant. Inconsistent classification practice, however, *cannot* be relevant in interpreting the meaning of a tariff concession. . . .

T.1.5.4 *EC – Export Subsidies on Sugar*, paras. 166–167

(WT/DS265/AB/R, WT/DS266/AB/R, WT/DS283/AB/R)

A preliminary question for our consideration is what rules apply in interpreting export subsidy commitments specified in a Member's Schedule under the *Agreement on Agriculture*. We observe that Article II:7 of the *General Agreement on Tariffs and Trade 1994* (the "GATT 1994") provides that the "Schedules annexed to this Agreement are hereby made an integral part of Part I of this Agreement." Furthermore, Article 3.1 of the *Agreement on Agriculture* provides that "export subsidy commitments in Part IV of each Member's Schedule . . . are hereby made an integral part of [the] GATT 1994."

The applicable rules for interpreting the provisions of the GATT 1994 are the "customary rules of interpretation of public international law". The Appellate Body has held that these rules are codified in the *Vienna Convention on the Law of Treaties* (the "*Vienna Convention*"). As provisions of a Member's Schedule are "part of the terms of the treaty", they are subject to these same rules of treaty interpretation. . . .

T.2 Tariff Quotas – Non-discriminatory Administration. *See also* Agreement on Agriculture, Article 4.1 – Market access commitments contained in Schedules (A.1.8); Licensing Agreement (L.2); Waivers (W.1)

T.2.1 *EC – Bananas III*, para. 161

(WT/DS27/AB/R)

. . . allocation to Members not having a substantial interest must be subject to the basic principle of non-discrimination. When this principle of non-discrimination is applied to the allocation of tariff quota shares to Members not having a substantial interest, it is clear that a Member cannot, whether by agreement or by assignment, allocate tariff quota shares to some Members not having a substantial interest while not allocating shares to other Members who likewise do not have a substantial interest. To do so is clearly inconsistent with the requirement in Article XIII:1 that a Member cannot restrict the importation of any product from another Member unless the importation of the like product from all third countries is "similarly" restricted.

T.2.2 *EC – Bananas III*, para. 163
(WT/DS27/AB/R)

...the reallocation of unused portions of a tariff quota share exclusively to other BFA countries, and not to other non-BFA banana-supplying Members, does not result in an allocation of tariff quota shares which approaches "as closely as possible the shares which the various Members might be expected to obtain in the absence of the restrictions". Therefore, the tariff quota reallocation rules of the BFA are also inconsistent with the chapeau of Article XIII:2 of the GATT 1994.

T.2.3 *EC – Bananas III*, para. 190
(WT/DS27/AB/R)

...The essence of the non-discrimination obligations is that like products should be treated equally, irrespective of their origin. As no participant disputes that all bananas are like products, the non-discrimination provisions apply to *all* imports of bananas, irrespective of whether and how a Member categorizes or subdivides these imports for administrative or other reasons. If, by choosing a different legal basis for imposing import restrictions, or by applying different tariff rates, a Member could avoid the application of the non-discrimination provisions to the imports of like products from different Members, the object and purpose of the non-discrimination provisions would be defeated. It would be very easy for a Member to circumvent the non-discrimination provisions of the GATT 1994 and the other Annex 1A agreements, if these provisions apply only *within* regulatory regimes established by that Member.

T.2.4 *EC – Bananas III*, para. 200
(WT/DS27/AB/R)

...The text of Article X:3(a) clearly indicates that the requirements of "uniformity, impartiality and reasonableness" do not apply to the laws, regulations, decisions and rulings *themselves*, but rather to the *administration* of those laws, regulations, decisions and rulings. The context of Article X:3(a) within Article X, which is entitled "Publication and Administration of Trade Regulations", and a reading of the other paragraphs of Article X, make it clear that Article X applies to the *administration* of laws, regulations, decisions and rulings. To the extent that the laws, regulations, decisions and rulings themselves are discriminatory, they can be examined for their consistency with the relevant provisions of the GATT 1994.

T.2.5 *EC – Poultry*, para. 93
(WT/DS69/AB/R)

...As the European Communities did not seek an agreement with Thailand, the other contracting party having a substantial interest in the supply of frozen poultry meat to the European Communities at that time, the Oilseeds Agreement cannot be considered an agreement within the meaning of Article XIII:2(d) of the GATT 1994.

T.2.6 *EC – Poultry*, para. 100
(WT/DS69/AB/R)

. . . We see nothing in Article XXVIII to suggest that compensation negotiated within its framework may be exempt from compliance with the non-discrimination principle inscribed in Articles I and XIII of the GATT 1994. . . .

T.2.7 *EC – Poultry*, para. 106
(WT/DS69/AB/R)

We agree with the Panel that the calculation of shares must be based on the total imports of the product in question – whether those imports originate from Members or non-Members. Otherwise, it would not be possible to comply with the requirement in the chapeau of Article XIII:2 that:

> In applying import restrictions to any product, Members shall aim at a distribution of trade in such product approaching as closely as possible the shares which the various Members might be expected to obtain in the absence of such restrictions. . . .

T.3 Taxation. *See also* National treatment, Article III:2 of the GATT 1994, first and second sentences (N.1.3–8)

T.3.1 *Japan – Alcoholic Beverages II*, p. 16, DSR 1996:I, p. 97 at 110
(WT/DS8/AB/R, WT/DS10/AB/R, WT/DS11/AB/R)

. . . Members of the WTO are free to pursue their own domestic goals through internal taxation or regulation so long as they do not do so in a way that violates Article III or any of the other commitments they have made in the *WTO Agreement*.

T.3.2 *Chile – Alcoholic Beverages*, para. 60
(WT/DS87/AB/R, WT/DS110/AB/R)

Members of the WTO have sovereign authority to determine the basis or bases on which they will tax goods, such as, for example, distilled alcoholic beverages, and to classify such goods accordingly, provided of course that the Members respect their WTO commitments. The reference in *Ad* Article III:2, second sentence, of the GATT 1994 to "not similarly taxed" is not in itself a prohibition against classifying goods for revenue and regulatory purposes that Members set for themselves as legitimate and desirable. Members of the WTO are free to tax distilled alcoholic beverages on the basis of their alcohol content and price, as long as the tax classification is not applied so as to protect domestic production over imports. Alcohol content, like any other basis or criterion of taxation, is subject to the legal standard embodied in Article III:2 of the GATT 1994.

T.3.3 *US – FSC*, para. 90
(WT/DS108/AB/R)

. . . A Member, in principle, has the sovereign authority to tax any particular categories of revenue it wishes. It is also free *not* to tax any particular categories of revenues. . . .

T.3.4 *US – FSC*, para. 98
(WT/DS108/AB/R)

. . . Members of the WTO are *not* obliged, by WTO rules, to tax *any* categories of income, whether foreign- or domestic-source income. . . .

T.4 TBT Agreement

T.4.1 Annex 1.1 – "technical regulation" definition

T.4.1.1 *EC – Asbestos*, para. 67
(WT/DS135/AB/R)

The heart of the definition of a "technical regulation" is that a "document" must "lay down" – that is, set forth, stipulate or provide – "product *characteristics*". The word "characteristic" has a number of synonyms that are helpful in understanding the ordinary meaning of that word, in this context. Thus, the "characteristics" of a product include, in our view, any objectively definable "features", "qualities", "attributes", or other "distinguishing mark" of a product. Such "characteristics" might relate, *inter alia*, to a product's composition, size, shape, colour, texture, hardness, tensile strength, flammability, conductivity, density, or viscosity. In the definition of a "technical regulation" in Annex 1.1, the *TBT Agreement* itself gives certain examples of "product characteristics" – "terminology, symbols, packaging, marking or labelling requirements". These examples indicate that "product characteristics" include, not only features and qualities intrinsic to the product itself, but also related "characteristics", such as the means of identification, the presentation and the appearance of a product. In addition, according to the definition in Annex 1.1 of the *TBT Agreement*, a "technical regulation" may set forth the "applicable administrative provisions" for products which have certain "characteristics". Further, we note that the definition of a "technical regulation" provides that such a regulation "may also include or deal *exclusively* with terminology, symbols, packaging, marking *or* labelling requirements". (emphasis added) The use here of the word "exclusively" and the disjunctive word "or" indicates that a "technical regulation" may be confined to laying down only one or a few "product characteristics".

T.4.1.2 *EC – Asbestos*, para. 68
(WT/DS135/AB/R)

The definition of a "technical regulation" in Annex 1.1 of the *TBT Agreement* also states that "*compliance*" with the "product characteristics" laid down in the "document" must be "*mandatory*". A "technical regulation" must, in other words, regulate the "characteristics" of products in a binding or compulsory fashion. It follows that, with respect to products, a "technical regulation" has the effect of *prescribing* or *imposing* one or more "characteristics" – "features", "qualities", "attributes", or other "distinguishing mark".

T.4.1.3 *EC – Asbestos*, para. 69
(WT/DS135/AB/R)

"Product characteristics" may, in our view, be prescribed or imposed with respect to products in either a positive or a negative form. That is, the document may provide, positively, that products *must possess* certain "characteristics", or the document may require, negatively, that products *must not possess* certain "characteristics". In both cases, the legal result is the same: the document "lays down" certain binding "characteristics" for products, in one case affirmatively, and in the other by negative implication.

T.4.1.4 *EC – Asbestos*, para. 70
(WT/DS135/AB/R)

A "technical regulation" must, of course, be applicable to an *identifiable* product, or group of products. Otherwise, enforcement of the regulation will, in practical terms, be impossible. This consideration also underlies the formal obligation, in Article 2.9.2 of the *TBT Agreement*, for Members to notify other Members, through the WTO Secretariat, "of the *products to be covered*" by a proposed "technical regulation". (emphasis added) Clearly, compliance with this obligation requires identification of the product coverage of a technical regulation. However, in contrast to what the Panel suggested, this does not mean that a "technical regulation" must apply to "*given*" products which are actually *named*, *identified* or *specified* in the regulation. (emphasis added) Although the *TBT Agreement* clearly applies to "products" generally, nothing in the text of that Agreement suggests that those products need be named or otherwise *expressly* identified in a "technical regulation". Moreover, there may be perfectly sound administrative reasons for formulating a "technical regulation" in a way that does *not* expressly identify products by name, but simply makes them identifiable – for instance, through the "characteristic" that is the subject of regulation.

T.4.1.5 *EC – Asbestos*, para. 72
(WT/DS135/AB/R)

. . . It is important to note here that, although formulated *negatively* – products containing asbestos are prohibited – the measure, in this respect, effectively prescribes or imposes certain objective features, qualities or "characteristics" on *all* products. That is, in effect, the measure provides that *all* products must *not* contain asbestos fibres. Although this prohibition against products containing asbestos applies to a large number of products, and although it is, indeed, true that the products to which this prohibition applies cannot be determined from the terms of the measure itself, it seems to us that the products covered by the measure are *identifiable*: all products must be asbestos free; any products containing asbestos are prohibited....

T.4.1.6 *EC – Sardines*, paras. 175–176
(WT/DS231/AB/R)

As we explained in *EC – Asbestos* [paragraph 59], whether a measure is a "technical regulation" is a threshold issue because the outcome of this issue determines whether the *TBT Agreement* is applicable. If the measure before us is not a "technical regulation", then it does not fall within the scope of the *TBT Agreement*....

We interpreted this definition in *EC – Asbestos* [paragraphs 66-70]. In doing so, we set out *three criteria* that a document must meet to fall within the definition of "technical regulation" in the *TBT Agreement*. *First*, the document must apply to an identifiable product or group of products. The *identifiable* product or group of products need not, however, be expressly *identified* in the document. *Second*, the document must lay down one or more characteristics of the product. These product characteristics may be intrinsic, or they may be related to the product. They may be prescribed or imposed in either a positive or a negative form. *Third*, compliance with the product characteristics must be mandatory....

T.4.1.7 *EC – Sardines*, para. 180
(WT/DS231/AB/R)

...Thus, a product does not necessarily have to be mentioned *explicitly* in a document for that product to be an *identifiable* product. *Identifiable* does not mean expressly identified.

T.4.1.8 *EC – Sardines*, para. 183
(WT/DS231/AB/R)

...We observe that the EC Regulation does not expressly identify *Sardinops sagax*. However, this does not necessarily mean that *Sardinops sagax* is not an *identifiable* product. As we stated in *EC – Asbestos* [paragraph 70], a product need not be expressly identified in the document for it to be *identifiable*.

T.4.1.9 *EC – Sardines*, paras. 190–191
(WT/DS231/AB/R)

We do not find it necessary, in this case, to decide whether the definition of "technical regulation" in the *TBT Agreement* makes a distinction between "naming" and labelling.... We are of the view that this requirement – to be prepared exclusively from fish of the species *Sardina pilchardus* – is a product characteristic "intrinsic to" preserved sardines that is laid down by the EC Regulation....

In any event, as we said in *EC – Asbestos* [paragraph 67], a "means of identification" *is* a product characteristic. A name clearly identifies a product; indeed, the European Communities concedes that a name is a "means of identification"...

T.4.2 Annex 1.2 – Standards

T.4.2.1 *EC – Sardines*, paras. 222–223
(WT/DS231/AB/R)

. . . In our view, the text of the Explanatory note supports the conclusion that consensus is not required for standards adopted by the international standardizing community. The last sentence of the Explanatory note refers to "documents". The term "document" is also used in the singular in the first sentence of the definition of a "standard". We believe that "document(s)" must be interpreted as having the same meaning in both the definition and the Explanatory note. The European Communities agrees. Interpreted in this way, the term "documents" in the last sentence of the Explanatory note must refer to standards *in general*, and not only to those adopted by entities *other than* international bodies, as the European Communities claims.

Moreover, the text of the last sentence of the Explanatory note, referring to documents not based on consensus, gives no indication whatsoever that it is departing from the subject of the immediately preceding sentence, which deals with standards adopted by international bodies. . . .

Article 2.2 – "not be more trade-restrictive than necessary to fulfil a legitimate objective". *See* TBT Agreement, Article 2.4 – "international standards . . . as a basis for technical regulation" (T.4.3)

T.4.3 Article 2.4 – "international standards . . . as a basis for technical regulation". *See also* Burden of Proof, General (B.3.1); Temporal Application of Rights and Obligations, TBT Agreement (T.5.3)

T.4.3.1 *EC – Sardines*, para. 248
(WT/DS231/AB/R)

We see no need here to define in general the nature of the relationship that must exist for an international standard to serve "as a basis for" a technical regulation. Here we need only examine this measure to determine if it fulfils this obligation. In our view, it can certainly be said – at a minimum – that something cannot be considered a "basis" for something else if the two are *contradictory*. Therefore, under Article 2.4, if the technical regulation and the international standard *contradict* each other, it cannot properly be concluded that the international standard has been used "as a basis for" the technical regulation.

T.4.3.2 *EC – Sardines*, para. 250
(WT/DS231/AB/R)

In making this determination, we note at the outset that Article 2.4 of the *TBT Agreement* provides that "Members shall use [relevant international standards], *or the relevant parts of them*, as a basis for their technical regulations". (emphasis added) In our view, the phrase "*relevant parts of them*" defines the appropriate focus of an analysis to determine whether a relevant international standard has been used "as a basis for" a technical regulation. In other words, the examination must be limited to those parts of the relevant international standards that relate to the subject-matter of the challenged prescriptions or requirements. In addition, the examination must be broad enough to address *all* of those relevant parts; the regulating Member is not permitted to select only *some* of the "relevant parts" of an international standard. If a "part" is "relevant", then it must be one of the elements which is "a basis for" the technical regulation.

T.4.4 Article 2.4 – "except when such international standards or relevant parts would be an ineffective or inappropriate means"

T.4.4.1 *EC – Sardines*, para. 285
(WT/DS231/AB/R)

... we noted earlier the Panel's view that the term "ineffective or inappropriate means" refers to two questions – the question of the *effectiveness* of the measure and the question of the *appropriateness* of the measure – and that these two questions, although closely related, are different in nature. The Panel pointed out that the term "ineffective" "refers to something which is not 'having the function of accomplishing', 'having a result', or 'brought to bear', whereas [the term] 'inappropriate' refers to something which is not 'specially suitable', 'proper', or 'fitting' ". The Panel also stated that:

> Thus, in the context of Article 2.4, an ineffective means is a means which does not have the function of accomplishing the legitimate objective pursued, whereas an inappropriate means is a means which is not specially suitable for the fulfilment of the legitimate objective pursued. ... The question of effectiveness bears upon the *results* of the means employed, whereas the question of appropriateness relates more to the *nature* of the means employed. (original emphasis)

We agree with the Panel's interpretation.

T.4.4.2 *EC – Sardines*, para. 286
(WT/DS231/AB/R)

As to the second question, we are of the view that the Panel was also correct in concluding that "the 'legitimate objectives' referred to in Article 2.4 must be interpreted in the context of Article 2.2", which refers also to "legitimate objectives", and includes a description of what the nature of some such objectives can be. Two implications flow from the Panel's interpretation. First, the term "legitimate objectives" in Article 2.4, as the Panel concluded, must cover the objectives explicitly mentioned in Article 2.2, namely: "national security requirements; the prevention of deceptive practices; protection of human health or safety, animal or plant life or health, or the environment." Second, given the use of the term "*inter alia*" in Article 2.2, the objectives covered by the term "legitimate objectives" in Article 2.4 extend beyond the list of the objectives specifically mentioned in Article 2.2. Furthermore, we share the view of the Panel that the second part of Article 2.4

implies that there must be an examination and a determination on the legitimacy of the objectives of the measure.

T.4.5 Article 2.4 – Preparation, adoption and continued application of existing regulations

T.4.5.1 *EC – Sardines*, para. 205
(WT/DS231/AB/R)

. . . We fail to see how the terms "where technical regulations are required", "exist", "imminent", "use", and "as a basis for" give any indication that Article 2.4 applies only to the two stages of *preparation* and *adoption* of technical regulations. To the contrary, as the Panel noted, the use of the present tense suggests a continuing obligation for existing measures, and not one limited to regulations prepared and adopted after the *TBT Agreement* entered into force. . . .

T.4.5.2 *EC – Sardines*, para. 208
(WT/DS231/AB/R)

Furthermore, like Articles 5.1 and 5.5 of the *SPS Agreement*, Article 2.4 is a "central provision" of the *TBT Agreement*, and it cannot just be assumed that such a central provision does not apply to existing measures. Again, following our reasoning in *EC – Hormones*, we must conclude that, if the negotiators had wanted to exempt the very large group of existing technical regulations from the disciplines of a provision as important as Article 2.4 of the *TBT Agreement*, they would have said so explicitly. No such explicit exemption is found in the terms "where technical regulations are required", "exist", "imminent", "use", or "as a basis for".

T.4.5.3 *EC – Sardines*, para. 215
(WT/DS231/AB/R)

. . . In our view, excluding existing technical regulations from the obligations set out in Article 2.4 would undermine the important role of international standards in furthering these objectives of the *TBT Agreement*. Indeed, it would go precisely in the opposite direction.

T.5 Temporal Application of Rights and Obligations. *See also* WTO Agreement, Article XVI:4 – WTO-conformity of laws, regulations and administrative procedures (W.4.3)

T.5.1 SCM Agreement

T.5.1.1 *Brazil – Desiccated Coconut*, p. 15, DSR 1997:I, p. 167 at 179–180
(WT/DS22/AB/R)

Article 28 [of the *Vienna Convention on the Law of Treaties*] states the general principle that a treaty shall not be applied retroactively "unless a different intention appears from the treaty or is otherwise established". Absent a contrary intention, a treaty cannot apply to acts or facts which took place, or situations which ceased to exist, before the date of its entry into force. Article 32.3 of the *SCM Agreement* is an express statement of intention which we will now examine.

T.5.1.2 *Brazil – Desiccated Coconut*, pp. 18–19, DSR 1997:I, p. 167 at 182–183
(WT/DS22/AB/R)

The Appellate Body sees Article 32.3 of the *SCM Agreement* as a clear statement that for countervailing duty investigations or reviews, the dividing line between the application of the GATT 1947 system of agreements and the *WTO Agreement* is to be determined by the date on which the application was made for the countervailing duty investigation or review. Article 32.3 has limited application only in specific circumstances where a countervailing duty proceeding, either an investigation or a review, was underway at the time of entry into force of the *WTO Agreement*. This does not mean that the *WTO Agreement* does not apply as of 1 January 1995 to all other acts, facts and situations which come within the provisions of the *SCM Agreement* and Article VI of the GATT 1994. However, the Uruguay Round negotiators expressed an explicit intention to draw the line of application of the new *WTO Agreement* to countervailing duty investigations and reviews at a different point in time from that for other general measures. . . .

T.5.2 SPS Agreement

T.5.2.1 *EC – Hormones*, para. 128
(WT/DS26/AB/R, WT/DS48/AB/R)

. . . We agree with the Panel that the *SPS Agreement* would apply to situations or measures that did not cease to exist, such as the 1981 and 1988 Directives, unless the *SPS Agreement* reveals a contrary intention. We also agree with the Panel that the *SPS Agreement* does not reveal such an intention. The *SPS Agreement* does not contain any provision limiting the temporal application of the *SPS Agreement*, or of any provision thereof, to SPS measures adopted after 1 January 1995. . . .

T.5.3 TBT Agreement. *See also* Principles and Concepts of General Public International Law, No retroactive application of treaties (P.3.4)

T.5.3.1 *EC – Sardines*, para. 200
(WT/DS231/AB/R)

We recall that Article 28 of the *Vienna Convention on the Law of Treaties* (the "*Vienna Convention*") provides that treaties generally do not apply retroactively. . . .
. . . As we have said in previous disputes, the interpretation principle codified in Article 28 is relevant to the interpretation of the covered agreements.

T.5.3.2 *EC – Sardines*, para. 205
(WT/DS231/AB/R)

. . . We fail to see how the terms "where technical regulations are required", "exist", "imminent", "use", and "as a basis for" give any indication that Article 2.4 applies only to the two stages of *preparation* and *adoption* of technical regulations. To the contrary, as the Panel noted, the use of the present tense suggests a continuing obligation for existing measures, and not one limited to regulations prepared and adopted after the *TBT Agreement* entered into force. . . .

TRIPS Agreement. *See* TRIPS Agreement, Article 70 (T.9.11–15)

T.6 Terms of Reference of Panels. *See also* Claims and Arguments (C.1); Claims and Panel Reasoning (C.2); Competence of Panels and the Appellate Body (C.3); Judicial Economy (J.1); Jurisdiction (J.2); Legislation as such vs. Specific Application (L.1); Request for the Establishment of a Panel (R.2); Standard of Review – General (S.7.1)

T.6.1 General

T.6.1.1 *Brazil – Desiccated Coconut*, p. 22, DSR 1997:I, p. 167 at 186
(WT/DS22/AB/R)

A panel's terms of reference are important for two reasons. First, terms of reference fulfil an important due process objective – they give the parties and third parties sufficient information concerning the claims at issue in the dispute in order to allow them an opportunity to respond to the complainant's case. Second, they establish the jurisdiction of the panel by defining the precise claims at issue in the dispute.

T.6.1.2 *Brazil – Desiccated Coconut*, p. 22, DSR 1997:I, p. 167 at 186
(WT/DS22/AB/R)

. . . the "matter" referred to a panel for consideration consists of the specific claims stated by the parties to the dispute in the relevant documents specified in the terms of reference. We agree with the approach taken in previous adopted panel reports that a matter, which includes the claims composing that matter, does not fall within a panel's terms of reference unless the claims are identified in the documents referred to or contained in the terms of reference.

T.6.1.3 *EC – Bananas III*, para. 142
(WT/DS27/AB/R)

We recognize that a panel request will usually be approved automatically at the DSB meeting following the meeting at which the request first appears on the DSB's agenda. As a panel request is normally not subjected to detailed scrutiny by the DSB, it is incumbent upon a panel to examine the request for the establishment of the panel very carefully to ensure its compliance with both the letter and the spirit of Article 6.2 of the DSU. It is important that a panel request be sufficiently precise for two reasons: first, it often forms the basis for the terms of reference of the panel pursuant to Article 7 of the DSU; and, second, it informs the defending party and the third parties of the legal basis of the complaint.

T.6.1.4 *India – Patents (US)*, para. 94
(WT/DS50/AB/R)

All parties engaged in dispute settlement under the DSU must be fully forthcoming from the very beginning both as to the claims involved in a dispute and as to the facts relating to those claims. Claims must be stated clearly. Facts must be disclosed freely. This must be so in consultations as well as in the more formal setting of panel proceedings. In fact, the demands of due process that are implicit in the DSU make this especially necessary during consultations. For the claims that are made and the facts that are established during consultations do much to shape the substance and the scope of subsequent panel proceedings. If, in the aftermath of consultations, any party believes that all the pertinent facts relating to a claim are, for any reason, not before the panel, then that party should ask the panel in that case to engage in additional fact-finding. But this additional fact-finding cannot alter the claims that are before the panel – because it cannot alter the panel's terms of reference. And, in the absence of the inclusion of a claim in the terms of reference, a panel must neither be expected nor permitted to modify rules in the DSU.

T.6.1.5 *Guatemala – Cement I*, para. 72
(WT/DS60/AB/R)

. . . Thus, "the matter referred to the DSB" for the purposes of Article 7 of the DSU and Article 17.4 of the *Anti-Dumping Agreement* must be the "matter" identified in the request for the establishment of a panel under Article 6.2 of the DSU. That provision requires the complaining Member, in a panel request, to "identify the *specific measures at issue* and provide a brief summary of the *legal basis of the complaint* sufficient to present the problem clearly." (emphasis added) The "*matter* referred to the DSB", therefore, consists of two elements: the specific *measures* at issue and the *legal basis of the complaint* (or the *claims*).

T.6.1.6 *Guatemala – Cement I*, para. 76
(WT/DS60/AB/R)

. . . the word "matter" has the same meaning in Article 17 of the *Anti-Dumping Agreement* as it has in Article 7 of the DSU. It consists of two elements: the specific "measure" and the "claims" relating to it, both of which must be properly identified in a panel request as required by Article 6.2 of the DSU.

T.6.1.7 *Korea – Dairy*, para. 120
(WT/DS98/AB/R)

. . . When parsed into its constituent parts, Article 6.2 may be seen to impose the following requirements. The request must: (i) be in writing; (ii) indicate whether consultations were held; (ii) identify the specific measures at issue; and (iii) provide a brief summary of the legal basis of the complaint sufficient to present the problem clearly. In its fourth requirement, Article 6.2 demands only a summary – and it may be a brief one – of the legal basis of the complaint; but the summary must, in any event, be one that is "sufficient to present the problem clearly". It is not enough, in other words, that "the legal basis of the complaint" is summarily identified; the identification must "present the problem clearly".

T.6.1.8 *US – Carbon Steel*, para. 123
(WT/DS213/AB/R, WT/DS213/AB/R/Corr.1)

... we have consistently held that, in the interests of due process, parties should bring alleged procedural deficiencies to the attention of a panel at the earliest possible opportunity. In this case, we see no reason to disagree with the Panel's view that the United States' objection was not raised in a timely manner. At the same time, however, as we have observed previously, certain issues going to the *jurisdiction* of a panel are so fundamental that they may be considered at any stage in a proceeding. In our view, the Panel was correct, therefore, in turning to consider its terms of reference and in satisfying itself as to its jurisdiction with respect to this matter.

T.6.1.9 *US – Carbon Steel*, paras. 124–125
(WT/DS213/AB/R, WT/DS213/AB/R/Corr.1)

... pursuant to Article 7 of the DSU, a panel's terms of reference are governed by the request for establishment of a panel. Article 6.2 of the DSU sets forth the requirements applicable to such requests. ...

There are ... two distinct requirements, namely identification of *the specific measures at issue*, and the provision of a *brief summary of the legal basis of the complaint* (or the *claims*). Together, they comprise the "matter referred to the DSB", which forms the basis for a panel's terms of reference under Article 7.1 of the DSU.

T.6.1.10 *US – Carbon Steel*, para. 126
(WT/DS213/AB/R, WT/DS213/AB/R/Corr.1)

The requirements of precision in the request for the establishment of a panel flow from the two essential purposes of the terms of reference. First, the terms of reference define the scope of the dispute. Secondly, the terms of reference, and the request for the establishment of a panel on which they are based, serve the *due process* objective of notifying the parties and third parties of the nature of a complainant's case. When faced with an issue relating to the scope of its terms of reference, a panel must scrutinize carefully the request for establishment of a panel "to ensure its compliance with both the letter and the spirit of Article 6.2 of the DSU."

T.6.1.11 *US – Offset Act (Byrd Amendment)*, para. 208
(WT/DS217/AB/R, WT/DS234/AB/R)

... "[a]n objection to jurisdiction should be raised as early as possible" and it would be preferable, in the interests of due process, for the appellant to raise such issues in the Notice of Appeal, so that appellees will be aware that this claim will be advanced on appeal. However, in our view, the issue of a panel's jurisdiction is so fundamental that it is appropriate to consider claims that a panel has exceeded its jurisdiction even if such claims were not raised in the Notice of Appeal.

T.6.2 Claims and legal basis of the complaint. *See also* Burden of Proof, General (B.3.1); Claims and Arguments (C.1); Enabling Clause (E.1); Judicial Economy (J.1); Jurisdiction (J.2); Request for the Establishment of a Panel, Article 6.2 of the DSU – Claims and legal basis of the complaint (R.2.2)

T.6.2.1 *EC – Bananas III*, para. 141
(WT/DS27/AB/R)

. . . We accept the Panel's view that it was sufficient for the Complaining Parties to list the provisions of the specific agreements alleged to have been violated without setting out detailed arguments as to which specific aspects of the measures at issue relate to which specific provisions of those agreements. In our view, there is a significant difference between the *claims* identified in the request for the establishment of a panel, which establish the panel's terms of reference under Article 7 of the DSU, and the *arguments* supporting those claims, which are set out and progressively clarified in the first written submissions, the rebuttal submissions and the first and second panel meetings with the parties.

T.6.2.2 *EC – Bananas III*, para. 143
(WT/DS27/AB/R)

. . . Article 6.2 of the DSU requires that the *claims*, but not the *arguments*, must all be specified sufficiently in the request for the establishment of a panel in order to allow the defending party and any third parties to know the legal basis of the complaint. If a *claim* is not specified in the request for the establishment of a panel, then a faulty request cannot be subsequently "cured" by a complaining party's argumentation in its first written submission to the panel or in any other submission or statement made later in the panel proceeding.

T.6.2.3 *EC – Bananas III*, paras. 145, 147
(WT/DS27/AB/R)

. . . There is no requirement in the DSU or in GATT practice for arguments on all claims relating to the matter referred to the DSB to be set out in a complaining party's first written submission to the panel. It is the panel's terms of reference, governed by Article 7 of the DSU, which set out the claims of the complaining parties relating to the matter referred to the DSB.

. . .

. . . We do not agree with the Panel's statement that a "failure to make a claim in the first written submission cannot be remedied by later submissions or by incorporating the claims and arguments of other complainants". . . .

T.6.2.4 *US – Carbon Steel*, para. 127
(WT/DS213/AB/R, WT/DS213/AB/R/Corr.1)

As we have said previously, compliance with the requirements of Article 6.2 must be demonstrated on the face of the request for the establishment of a panel. Defects in the request for the establishment of a panel cannot be "cured" in the subsequent submissions of the parties during the panel proceedings. Nevertheless, in considering the sufficiency of a panel request, submissions and statements made during the course of the panel proceedings, in particular the first written submission of the complaining party, may be consulted in order to confirm the meaning of the words used in the panel request and as part of the assessment of whether the ability of the respondent to defend itself was prejudiced. Moreover, compliance with the requirements of Article 6.2 must be determined on the merits of each case, having considered the panel request as a whole, and in the light of attendant circumstances.

T.6.2.5 *US – Carbon Steel*, para. 130
(WT/DS213/AB/R, WT/DS213/AB/R/Corr.1)

. . . As we have observed, although the listing of the treaty provisions allegedly violated is always a *necessary* "minimum prerequisite" for compliance with Article 6.2, whether such a listing is *sufficient* to constitute a "brief summary of the legal basis of the complaint sufficient to present the problem clearly" within the meaning of Article 6.2 will depend on the circumstances of each case, and in particular on the extent to which mere reference to a treaty provision sheds light on the nature of the obligation at issue. . . .

T.6.2.6 *India – Patents (US)*, paras. 89–90
(WT/DS50/AB/R)

. . . a claim *must* be included in the request for establishment of a panel in order to come within a panel's terms of reference in a given case. . . .

. . . the convenient phrase, "including but not necessarily limited to", is simply not adequate to "identify the specific measures at issue and provide a brief summary of the legal basis of the complaint sufficient to present the problem clearly" as required by Article 6.2 of the DSU. If this phrase incorporates Article 63, what article of the *TRIPS Agreement* does it not incorporate? Therefore, this phrase is not sufficient to bring a claim relating to Article 63 within the terms of reference of the Panel.

T.6.2.7 *Korea – Dairy*, para. 124
(WT/DS98/AB/R)

Identification of the treaty provisions claimed to have been violated by the respondent is always necessary both for purposes of defining the terms of reference of a panel and for informing the respondent and the third parties of the claims made by the complainant; such identification is a minimum prerequisite if the legal basis of the complaint is to be presented at all. But it may not always be enough. There may be situations where the simple listing of the articles of the agreement or agreements involved may, in the light of attendant circumstances, suffice to meet the standard of *clarity* in the statement of the legal basis of the complaint. However, there may also be situations in which the circumstances are such that the mere listing of treaty articles would not satisfy the standard of Article 6.2. This may be the case, for instance, where the articles listed establish not one single, distinct obligation, but rather multiple obligations. In such a situation, the listing of articles of an agreement, in and of itself, may fall short of the standard of Article 6.2.

T.6.2.8 *Korea – Dairy*, para. 127
(WT/DS98/AB/R)

Along the same lines, we consider that whether the mere listing of the articles claimed to have been violated meets the standard of Article 6.2 must be examined on a case-by-case basis. In resolving that question, we take into account whether the ability of the respondent to defend itself was prejudiced, given the actual course of the panel proceedings, by the fact that the panel request simply listed the provisions claimed to have been violated.

T.6.2.9 *Thailand – H-Beams*, para. 88
(WT/DS122/AB/R)

Article 6.2 of the DSU calls for sufficient clarity with respect to the legal basis of the complaint, that is, with respect to the "claims" that are being asserted by the complaining party. A defending party is entitled to know what case it has to answer, and what violations have been alleged so that it can begin preparing its defence. Likewise, those Members of the WTO who intend to participate as third parties in panel proceedings must be informed of the legal basis of the complaint. This requirement of due process is fundamental to ensuring a fair and orderly conduct of dispute settlement proceedings.

T.6.2.10 *Thailand – H-Beams*, para. 92
(WT/DS122/AB/R)

In the facts and circumstances of this case, therefore, we consider that the reference in Poland's panel request to the "[calculation of] an alleged dumping margin" was sufficient to bring Poland's claims under Article 2 within the panel's terms of reference, and to inform Thailand of the nature of Poland's claims. Thus, with respect to the claims relating to Article 2 of the *Anti-Dumping Agreement*, Poland's panel request was sufficient to meet the requirements of Article 6.2 of the DSU.

T.6.2.11 *Korea – Various Measures on Beef*, para. 87
(WT/DS161/AB/R, WT/DS169/AB/R)

. . . Although the "commitment levels" in Korea's Schedule and "Annex 3" of the *Agreement on Agriculture* were *not explicitly* referred to in the panel requests in this dispute, it is clear that Articles 3 and 6 of the *Agreement on Agriculture*, which *were referred* to in the panel requests, incorporate those terms, either directly through

Articles 3.2 and 6.3, in the case of the "commitment levels", or indirectly through Article 1(a)(i), in the case of "Annex 3". In our view, the commitment levels in Korea's Schedule and the provisions of Annex 3 were in effect referred to in the complaining parties' panel requests, and were, therefore, within the Panel's terms of reference.

T.6.2.12 *US – Certain EC Products*, para. 111
(WT/DS165/AB/R)

Article 23.1 of the DSU imposes a general obligation of Members to redress a violation of obligations or other nullification or impairment of benefits under the covered agreements only by recourse to the rules and procedures of the DSU, and not through unilateral action. Subparagraphs (a), (b) and (c) of Article 23.2 articulate specific and clearly-defined forms of prohibited unilateral action contrary to Article 23.1 of the DSU. There is a close relationship between the obligations set out in paragraphs 1 and 2 of Article 23. They *all* concern the obligation of Members of the WTO not to have recourse to unilateral action. We therefore consider that, as the request for the establishment of a panel of the European Communities included a claim of inconsistency with Article 23, a claim of inconsistency with Article 23.2(a) is within the Panel's terms of reference.

T.6.2.13 *US – Certain EC Products*, para. 112
(WT/DS165/AB/R)

However, the fact that a claim of inconsistency with Article 23.2(a) of the DSU can be considered to be within the Panel's terms of reference does not mean that the European Communities actually made such a claim. An analysis of the Panel record shows that, with the exception of two instances during the Panel proceedings, the European Communities did not refer *specifically* to Article 23.2(a) of the DSU. Furthermore, in response to a request from the United States to clarify the scope of its claim under Article 23, the European Communities asserted only claims of violation of Articles 23.1 and 23.2(c) of the DSU; no mention was made of Article 23.2(a). Our reading of the Panel record shows us that, throughout the Panel proceedings in this case, the European Communities made arguments relating only to its claims that the United States acted inconsistently with Article 23.1 and Article 23.2(c) of the DSU.

T.6.2.14 *US – Certain EC Products*, para. 113
(WT/DS165/AB/R)

The Panel record does show that the European Communities made several references to what it termed the "unilateral determination" of the United States. However, in those references, the European Communities did not specifically link the alleged "unilateral determination" to a claim of violation of Article 23.2(a) *per se*. The European Communities' arguments relating to the alleged "unilateral determination" of the United States were made with reference to the alleged failure on the part of the United States to redress a perceived WTO violation through recourse to the DSU as required by Article 23.1 of the DSU. At no point did the European Communities link the notion of a "unilateral determination" on the part of the United States with a violation of Article 23.2(a).

T.6.2.15 *US – Certain EC Products*, para. 114
(WT/DS165/AB/R)

On the basis of our review of the European Communities' submissions and statements to the Panel, we conclude that the European Communities did not specifically claim before the Panel that, by adopting the 3 March Measure, the United States acted inconsistently with Article 23.2(a) of the DSU. As the European Communities did not make a specific claim of inconsistency with Article 23.2(a), it did not adduce any evidence or arguments to demonstrate that the United States made a "determination as to the effect that a violation has occurred" in breach of Article 23.2(a) of the DSU. And, as the European Communities did not adduce any evidence or arguments in support of a claim of violation of Article 23.2(a) of the DSU, the European Communities could not have established, and did not establish, a *prima facie* case of violation of Article 23.2(a) of the DSU.

T.6.2.16 *Chile – Price Band System*, paras. 150–151
(WT/DS207/AB/R)

The Panel request refers to Article of the GATT 1994 in general terms. No specific reference is made to any of the seven paragraphs or eight subparagraphs of Article of the GATT 1994. Argentina's request clearly does not limit the scope of Argentina's claims to the *first* sentence of Article II:1(b). Therefore, we find that Article in its entirety – including the second sentence of Article II:1(b) – is within the Panel's terms of reference.

This, however, is not the end of our inquiry on this issue. Chile does not dispute that Argentina included Article II:1(b) in the request for the establishment of a panel. However, Chile submits that making a general reference to Article in the Panel request is not dispositive of whether Argentina *has actually made a claim* under the *second* sentence of Article II:1(b), and, thus, of whether the Panel was entitled to make a finding under that provision.

T.6.2.17 *Chile – Price Band System*, para. 164
(WT/DS207/AB/R)

. . . Argentina appears to suggest that a claim may be made implicitly, and need not be made explicitly. We do not agree. The requirements of due process and orderly procedure dictate that claims must be made explicitly in WTO dispute settlement. Only in this way will the panel, other parties, and third parties understand that a specific claim has been made, be aware of its dimensions, and have an adequate opportunity to address and respond to it. WTO Members must not be left to wonder what specific claims have been made against them in dispute settlement. . . .

T.6.2.18 *US – Offset Act (Byrd Amendment)*, para. 212
(WT/DS217/AB/R, WT/DS234/AB/R)

In our view, these statements do not constitute a finding by the Panel that was outside its terms of reference. The Panel was merely reflecting in its reasoning the fact that the CDSOA does not operate in a vacuum but, rather, operates in a context that includes other laws and regulations. The Panel's view was that the combination of anti-dumping duties (or countervailing duties) and CDSOA offset payments distorts the competitive relationship between dumped (subsidized) and domestic products, to the detriment of dumped (subsidized) products. This led the Panel to find that the CDSOA – alone – has an adverse bearing on dumping (subsidization) and, therefore, operates "against" dumping (subsidies) within the meaning of Article 18.1 of the *Anti-Dumping Agreement* (and Article 32.1 of the *SCM Agreement*). Therefore, we dismiss the claim of the United States that the Panel exceeded its terms of reference by examining claims concerning the CDSOA "in combination" with other United States laws and regulations.

T.6.2.19 *EC – Tariff Preferences*, para. 113
(WT/DS246/AB/R)

In the light of the extensive requirements set forth in the Enabling Clause, we are of the view that, when a complaining party considers that a preference scheme of another Member does not meet one or more of those requirements, the specific provisions of the Enabling Clause with which the scheme allegedly falls afoul, form critical components of the "legal basis of the complaint" and, therefore, of the "matter" in dispute. Accordingly, a complaining party cannot, in good faith, ignore those provisions and must, in its request for the establishment of a panel, identify them and thereby "notif[y] the parties and third parties of the nature of [its] case". For the failure of such a complaining party to raise the relevant provisions of the Enabling Clause would place an unwarranted burden on the responding party. This due process consideration applies equally to the elaboration of a complaining party's case in its written submissions, which must "explicitly" articulate a claim so that the panel and all parties to a dispute "understand that a specific claim has been made, [are] aware of its dimensions, and have an adequate opportunity to address and respond to it".

T.6.3 Specific measure at issue. *See also* Burden of Proof (B.3); Jurisdiction (J.2); Legislation as such vs. Specific Application (L.1); Mandatory and Discretionary Legislation (M.1); Request for the Establishment of a Panel – Specific measures at issue (R.2.3)

T.6.3.1 *Japan – Alcoholic Beverages II*, p. 26, DSR 1996:I, p. 97 at 117–118
(WT/DS8/AB/R, WT/DS10/AB/R, WT/DS11/AB/R)

We note that the Panel's conclusions on "like products" and on "directly competitive or substitutable products"... fail to address the full range of alcoholic beverages included in the Panel's Terms of Reference.... We consider this failure to incorporate into its conclusions all the products referred to in the Terms of Reference, consistent with the matters referred to the DSB in WT/DS8/5, WT/DS10/5 and WT/DS11/2, to be an error of law by the Panel.

T.6.3.2 *Australia – Salmon*, para. 103
(WT/DS18/AB/R)

. . . In our view, the . . . measure at issue can only be the measure which is *actually* applied to the product at issue. . . .

T.6.3.3 *US – Certain EC Products*, para. 70
(WT/DS165/AB/R)

. . . in our Report in *Brazil – Export Financing Programme for Aircraft*, we stated that:

> Articles 4 and 6 of the DSU . . . set forth a process by which a complaining party must request consultations, and consultations must be held, before a matter may be referred to the DSB for the establishment of a panel.

The European Communities' request for consultations of 4 March 1999 did not, of course, refer to the action taken by the United States on 19 April 1999, because that action had not yet been taken at the time. At the oral hearing in this appeal, in response to questioning by the Division, the European Communities acknowledged that the 19 April action, *as such*, was not *formally* the subject of the consultations held on 21 April 1999. We, therefore, consider that the 19 April action is also, for that reason, not a measure at issue in this dispute and does not fall within the Panel's terms of reference.

T.6.3.4 *US – Carbon Steel*, para. 171
(WT/DS213/AB/R, WT/DS213/AB/R/Corr.1)

. . . the references in the panel request to "certain aspects of the sunset review procedure", to the United States statutory provisions governing sunset reviews, to related regulatory provisions, and to the Sunset Policy Bulletin, can be read to refer, generally, to United States law regarding the determination to be made in a sunset review. However, we do not believe they can be read to refer to *distinct* measures, consisting of United States law, as such, and as applied, relating to the submission of evidence. Accordingly, we agree with the Panel that the matters relating to the submission of evidence in a sunset review were not within its terms of reference because the *specific measures at issue were not adequately identified* in the request for the establishment of the panel, as required by Article 6.2 of the DSU.

T.6.3.5 *Chile – Price Band System*, para. 139
(WT/DS207/AB/R)

. . . Chile's price band system remains essentially the same after the enactment of Law 19.772. The measure is not, in its essence, any different because of that

Amendment. Therefore, we conclude that the measure before us in this appeal includes Law 19.772, because that law amends Chile's price band system without *changing its essence*.

T.6.3.6 *Chile – Price Band System*, para. 144 (WT/DS207/AB/R)

We emphasize that we do not mean to condone a practice of amending measures during dispute settlement proceedings if such changes are made with a view to shielding a measure from scrutiny by a panel or by us. We do not suggest that this occurred in this case. However, generally speaking, the demands of due process are such that a complaining party should not have to adjust its pleadings throughout dispute settlement proceedings in order to deal with a disputed measure as a "moving target". If the terms of reference in a dispute are broad enough to include amendments to a measure – as they are in this case – and if it is necessary to consider an amendment in order to secure a positive solution to the dispute – as it is here – then it is appropriate to consider the measure *as amended* in coming to a decision in a dispute.

T.6.3.7 *US – Oil Country Tubular Goods Sunset Reviews*, para. 173 (WT/DS268/AB/R)

We also expect that measures subject to "as such" challenges would normally have undergone, under municipal law, thorough scrutiny through various deliberative processes to ensure consistency with the Member's international obligations, including those found in the covered agreements, and that the enactment of such a measure would implicitly reflect the conclusion of that Member that the measure is not inconsistent with those obligations. The presumption that WTO Members act in good faith in the implementation of their WTO commitments is particularly apt in the context of measures challenged "as such". We would therefore urge complaining parties to be *especially diligent* in setting out "as such" claims in their panel requests as clearly as possible. In particular, we would expect that "as such" claims state unambiguously the specific measures of municipal law challenged by the complaining party and the legal basis for the allegation that those measures are not consistent with particular provisions of the covered agreements. Through such straightforward presentations of "as such" claims, panel requests should leave respondent parties in little doubt that, notwithstanding their own considered views on the WTO-consistency of their measures, another Member intends to challenge those measures, as such, in WTO dispute settlement proceedings.

T.6.3.8 *US – Oil Country Tubular Goods Sunset Reviews*, para. 220 (WT/DS268/AB/R)

...Therefore, even assuming *arguendo* that a "practice" may be challenged as a "measure" in WTO dispute settlement – an issue on which we express no view here – we *find* that the record does not allow us to complete the analysis of Argentina's conditional appeal with respect to the "practice" of the USDOC regarding the likelihood determination in sunset reviews.

T.6.3.9 *US – Upland Cotton*, para. 262
(WT/DS267/AB/R)

Whether or not a measure is still in force is not dispositive of whether that measure is currently affecting the operation of any covered agreement. Therefore, we disagree with the United States' argument that measures whose legislative basis has expired are incapable of affecting the operation of a covered agreement in the present and that, accordingly, expired measures *cannot* be the subject of consultations under the DSU. In our view, the question of whether measures whose legislative basis has expired affect the operation of a covered agreement currently is an issue that must be resolved on the facts of each case. The outcome of such an analysis cannot be prejudged by excluding it from consultations and dispute settlement proceedings altogether.

T.6.3.10 *US – Upland Cotton*, para. 269
(WT/DS267/AB/R)

The only temporal connotation contained in the ordinary meaning of the expression "at issue", as used in Article 6.2 of the DSU, is expressed by its present tense: measures must be "at issue" – or, putting it another way, "in dispute" – at the time the request is made. Certainly, nothing inherent in the term "at issue" sheds light on whether measures at issue must be currently in force, or whether they may be measures whose legislative basis has expired.

T.6.3.11 *US – Gambling*, paras. 121–123
(WT/DS285/AB/R)

The DSU provides for the "prompt settlement" of situations where Members consider that their benefits under the covered agreements "are being impaired by *measures* taken by another Member". Two elements of this reference to "measures" that may be the subject of dispute settlement are relevant. First, as the Appellate Body has stated, a "nexus" must exist between the responding Member and the "measure", such that the "measure" – whether an act or omission – must be "attributable" to that Member. Secondly, the "measure" must be the *source* of the alleged impairment, which is in turn the *effect* resulting from the existence or operation of the "measure".

Similarly [Article 4.2 of the DSU] contemplates that "measures" themselves will "affect" the operation of a covered agreement. Finally, we note that this distinction between measures and their effects is also evident in the scope of application of the GATS, namely, to "measures by Members affecting trade in services".

We are therefore of the view that the DSU and the GATS focus on "measures" as the subject of challenge in WTO dispute settlement. To the extent that a Member's complaint centres on the effects of an action taken by another Member, that complaint must nevertheless be brought as a challenge to the *measure* that is the source of the alleged effects.

T.6.3.12 *US – Gambling*, paras. 129, 131–132
(WT/DS285/AB/R)

. . . the Panel relied on certain Appellate Body decisions in support of its view that " 'practice' can be considered as an autonomous measure that can be challenged in and of itself". . . .

. . .

We disagree with the participants' characterization of the Panel's statement on "practice", in paragraph 6.197 of the Panel Report, as a "finding" of the Panel. The Panel itself acknowledged that, in any case, Antigua was not challenging a practice, as such. In this light, the Panel's statement on "practice", in our view, was a mere *obiter dictum*, and we need not rule on it.

We nevertheless express our disagreement with the Panel's understanding of previous Appellate Body decisions. The Appellate Body has *not*, to date, pronounced upon the issue of whether "practice" may be challenged, as such, as a "measure" in WTO dispute settlement.

Text. *See* Interpretation (I.3)

T.7 Textiles and Clothing Agreement

T.7.1 Article 6 – Transitional safeguard

T.7.1.1 *US – Wool Shirts and Blouses*, p. 16, DSR 1997:I, p. 323 at 337
(WT/DS33/AB/R, WT/DS33/AB/R/Corr.1)

We do not believe that these particular previous GATT 1947 panel reports are relevant in this case. This case concerns Article 6 of the *ATC*. The *ATC* is a transitional arrangement that, by its own terms, will terminate when trade in textiles and clothing is fully integrated into the multilateral trading system. Article 6 of the *ATC* is an integral part of the transitional arrangement manifested in the *ATC* and should be interpreted accordingly. As the Appellate Body observed in *United States – Restrictions on Imports of Cotton and Man-made Fibre Underwear* with respect to Article 6.10 of the *ATC*, we believe Article 6 is "carefully negotiated language . . . which reflects an equally carefully drawn balance of rights and obligations of Members. . . ." That balance must be respected.

T.7.1.2 *US – Cotton Yarn*, para. 81
(WT/DS192/AB/R)

There is no need for the purpose of this appeal to express a view on the question whether an importing Member would be under an *obligation*, flowing from the "pervasive" general principle of *good faith* that underlies all treaties, to *withdraw* a safeguard measure if post-determination evidence relating to pre-determination facts were to emerge revealing that a determination was based on such a critical factual error that one of the conditions required by Article 6 turns out never to have been met.

T.7.2 Article 6.2 – "determination"

T.7.2.1 *US – Cotton Yarn*, para. 76
(WT/DS192/AB/R)

Unlike Article 3 of the *Agreement on Safeguards*, which provides explicitly for an investigation by competent authorities of a Member, Article 6 of the *ATC* does not specify either the organ or the procedure through which a Member makes its "determination"....

T.7.2.2 *US – Cotton Yarn*, para. 77
(WT/DS192/AB/R)

...The demonstration by a Member that a particular product is being imported into its territory in such increased quantities as to cause serious damage (or actual threat thereof) to the domestic industry can be based only on facts and evidence which existed at the time the determination was made. The urgent nature of such an investigation may not permit the Member to delay its determination in order to take into account evidence that might be available only at a future date....

T.7.3 Article 6.2 – "domestic industry"

T.7.3.1 *US – Cotton Yarn*, para. 86
(WT/DS192/AB/R)

A plain reading of the phrase "domestic industry producing like and/or directly competitive products" shows clearly that the terms "like" and "directly competitive" are characteristics attached to the domestic products that are to be compared with the imported product. We are, therefore, of the view that the definition of the *domestic industry* must be product-oriented and not producer-oriented, and that the definition must be based on the products produced by the *domestic industry* which are to be compared with the imported product in terms of their being like or directly competitive.

T.7.3.2 *US – Cotton Yarn*, para. 95
(WT/DS192/AB/R)

...Article 6.2 permits a safeguard action to be taken in order to protect a domestic industry from serious damage (or actual threat thereof) caused by a surge in imports, provided the domestic industry is identified as the industry producing "like and/or directly competitive products" in comparison with the imported product. The criteria of "like" and "directly competitive" are characteristics attached to the domestic product in order to ensure that the domestic industry is the appropriate industry in relation to the imported product. The degree of proximity between the imported and domestic products in their competitive relationship is thus critical to underpin the reasonableness of a safeguard action against an imported product.

T.7.4 Article 6.2 – "directly competitive products". *See also* Directly Competitive or Substitutable Products (D.1)

T.7.4.1 *US – Cotton Yarn*, paras. 96–98
(WT/DS192/AB/R)

According to the ordinary meaning of the term "competitive", two products are in a competitive relationship if they are commercially interchangeable, or if they offer alternative ways of satisfying the same consumer demand in the marketplace. "Competitive" is a characteristic attached to a product and denotes the *capacity* of a product to compete both in a current or a future situation. The word "competitive" must be distinguished from the words "competing" or "being in actual competition". It has a wider connotation than "actually competing" and includes also the notion of a potential to compete. It is not necessary that two products be competing, or that they be in actual competition with each other, in the marketplace at a given moment in order for those products to be regarded as competitive. Indeed, products which are competitive may not be actually competing with each other in the marketplace at a given moment for a variety of reasons, such as regulatory restrictions or producers' decisions. Thus, a static view is incorrect, for it leads to the same products being regarded as competitive at one moment in time, and not so the next, depending upon whether or not they are in the marketplace.

It is significant that the word "competitive" is qualified by the word "directly", which emphasizes the degree of proximity that must obtain in the competitive relationship between the products under comparison. As noted earlier, a safeguard action under the *ATC* is permitted in order to protect the domestic industry against competition from an imported product. To ensure that such protection is reasonable, it is expressly provided that the domestic industry must be producing "like" and/or "directly competitive products"....

When . . . the product produced by the domestic industry is not a "like product" as compared with the imported product, the question arises how close should be the competitive relationship between the imported product and the "unlike" domestic product. It is common knowledge that unlike or dissimilar products compete or can compete in the marketplace to varying degrees, ranging from direct or close competition to remote or indirect competition. The more unlike or dissimilar two products are, the more remote or indirect their competitive relationship will be in the marketplace. The term "competitive" has, therefore, purposely been qualified and limited by the word "directly" to signify the degree of proximity that must obtain in the competitive relationship when the products in question are unlike. Under this definition of "directly", a safeguard action will not extend to protecting a domestic industry that produces unlike products which have only a remote or tenuous competitive relationship with the imported product.

T.7.4.2 *US – Cotton Yarn*, para. 105
(WT/DS192/AB/R)

... we find that combed cotton yarn produced by vertically integrated fabric producers for their internal consumption is "directly competitive" with combed cotton yarn imported from Pakistan....

T.7.5 Article 6.2 – "like products"

T.7.5.1 *US – Cotton Yarn*, para. 97
(WT/DS192/AB/R)

... Like products are, necessarily, in the highest degree of competitive relationship in the marketplace. In permitting a safeguard action, the first consideration is, therefore, whether the domestic industry is producing a like product as compared with the imported product in question. If this is so, there can be no doubt as to the reasonableness of the safeguard action against the imported product.

T.7.6 Article 6.4 – Attribution of serious damage. *See also* Principles and Concepts of General Public International Law, Proportionality (P.3.6)

T.7.6.1 *US – Cotton Yarn*, paras. 114–115
(WT/DS192/AB/R)

The first requirement is that the attribution be confined to only those Members from whom imports have shown a sharp and substantial increase. Such Members will be identified on an individual basis by virtue of the wording in Article 6.4, second sentence, "on the basis of a sharp and substantial increase in imports, actual or imminent, from such a Member or Members individually". (footnote omitted) The Panel interpreted the term "sharp" to refer to the rate of the import increase, and the term "substantial" to the amount of that increase. These interpretations of the Panel have not been appealed and are, therefore, not before us.

The second requirement of Article 6.4, second sentence, is a comparative analysis, in the event that there is more than one Member from whom imports have shown a sharp and substantial increase in its imports. The conduct of the comparative analysis is governed by the latter part of the second sentence of Article 6.4...

T.7.6.2 *US – Cotton Yarn*, paras. 118–119
(WT/DS192/AB/R)

Article 6.4 provides, in relevant part, that "[t]he Member or Members to whom serious damage... is attributed, shall be *determined on the basis* of a sharp and substantial *increase in imports... from such a Member or Members*". (emphasis added) The clear inference from this phrase is that the sharp and substantial increase of imports from *such a* Member determines not only the basis, but also the *scope* of attribution of serious damage to that Member.

In consequence, where imports from more than one Member contribute to serious damage, it is only that *part* of the total damage which is actually caused by imports from such a Member that can be attributed to that Member under Article 6.4, second sentence. Damage that is actually caused to the domestic industry by imports from one Member cannot, in our view, be attributed to a different Member imports from whom were not the cause of that part of the damage. This would amount to a "mis-attribution" of damage and would be inconsistent with the interpretation in good faith of the terms of Article 6.4. Therefore, the part of the total serious damage attributed to an exporting Member must be proportionate to the damage caused by the imports from that Member. Contrary to the view of the United States, we believe that Article 6.4, second sentence, does not permit the attribution of the totality of serious damage to one Member, unless the imports from that Member alone have caused all the serious damage.

T.7.6.3 *US – Cotton Yarn*, para. 121
(WT/DS192/AB/R)

. . . most significantly, if the totality of serious damage could be attributed to only one of those Members the imports from whom have contributed to it, there would be no need to undertake a comparative analysis of the effects of imports from that one Member, once the imports from that Member have been found to have increased sharply and substantially; such an interpretation would reduce a whole segment of Article 6.4 to inutility.

T.7.6.4 *US – Cotton Yarn*, paras. 122–124
(WT/DS192/AB/R)

We now turn to the question of how to conduct the comparative analysis required by Article 6.4. This analysis is to be seen in the light of the principle of proportionality as the means of determining the scope or assessing the part of the total serious damage that can be attributed to an exporting Member. We recall that Article 6.4 enjoins the importing Member to conduct this comparative analysis on a multi factor basis including "levels of imports", "market share" and "prices", while specifying that none of these factors alone or in combination with other factors can necessarily give decisive guidance. The comparison is to take place between the effects of imports from the Member in question, on the one hand, and those of imports from other sources, on the other. The comparison must thus be based on a variety of factors, each of which has a different significance and weight, and is to be measured on a different scale.

It is of course possible to compare the level of imports of one Member with the level of imports from other sources taken together. Likewise, it is possible to establish the market share of one Member in comparison with all other imports and the output of the domestic industry. However, the full effects of the level of imports from, and the market share of, one Member can only be assessed if this level and this share are compared *individually* with the level of imports from, and the market share of, the other Members from whom imports have also increased sharply and substantially. This conclusion is even more obvious for the comparison of import and domestic prices. The price of imports from one Member can be compared with the average price of imports from other sources and with domestic prices. However, prices of imports from the other Members may vary widely from one another. A fair assessment of the effects of the price of imports from one Member will therefore require a comparison with the price of imports from other Members taken individually. Moreover, these different factors interact in different ways, producing different effects, under different circumstances, not to mention the possible existence of other relevant factors (and their effects) that must be taken into account in the comparison according to the proviso at the end of Article 6.4, second sentence.

An assessment of the share of total serious damage, which is proportionate to the damage actually caused by imports from a particular Member, requires, therefore, a comparison according to the factors envisaged in Article 6.4 with all other Members (from whom imports have also increased sharply and substantially) taken individually.

T.7.7 Article 6.10 – No backdating of safeguard

T.7.7.1 *US – Underwear*, p. 14, DSR 1997:I, p. 11 at 22 (WT/DS24/AB/R)

It is essential to note that, under the express terms of Article 6.10, *ATC*, the restraint measure may be "applied" only "after the expiry of the period of 60 days" for consultations, without success, and only within the "window" of 30 days immediately following the 60-day period. Accordingly, we believe that, in the absence of an express authorization in Article 6.10, *ATC*, to backdate the effectivity of a safeguard restraint measure, a presumption arises from the very text of Article 6.10 that such a measure may be applied only prospectively. . . .

T.7.7.2 *US – Underwear*, p. 19, DSR 1997:I, p. 11 at 28 (WT/DS24/AB/R)

The conclusion we have arrived at, in respect of the issue of permissibility of backdating, is that the giving of retroactive effect to a safeguard restraint measure is no longer permissible under the regime of Article 6 of the *ATC* and is in fact prohibited under Article 6.10 of that *Agreement*. The presumption of prospective effect only, has not been overturned; it is a proposition not simply presumptively correct but one requiring our assent. . . .

T.7.8 Article 6.11 – Provisional application of a safeguard

T.7.8.1 *US – Underwear*, p. 20, DSR 1997:I, p. 11 at 28 (WT/DS24/AB/R)

. . . The importing Member is, however, not defenceless against a speculative "flood of imports" where it is confronted with the circumstances contemplated in Article 6.11. Its appropriate recourse is, in other words, to action under Article 6.11 of the *ATC*, complying in the process with the requirements of Article 6.10 and Article 6.11.

T.8 Third Party Rights. *See also* Amicus Curiae Briefs, Briefs submitted by WTO Members (A.2.2); Working Procedures for Appellate Review, Rule 24 – Third participants (W.2.9)

T.8.1 *EC – Hormones*, para. 154
(WT/DS26/AB/R, WT/DS48/AB/R)

... Although Article 12.1 and Appendix 3 of the DSU do not specifically require the Panel to grant ... ["enhanced" third party rights] to the United States, we believe that this decision falls within the sound discretion and authority of the Panel, particularly if the Panel considers it necessary for ensuring to all parties due process of law....

T.8.2 *US – 1916 Act*, para. 150
(WT/DS136/AB/R, WT/DS162/AB/R)

A panel's decision whether to grant "enhanced" participatory rights to third parties is thus a matter that falls within the discretionary authority of that panel. Such discretionary authority is, of course, not unlimited and is circumscribed, for example, by the requirements of due process. In the present cases, however, the European Communities and Japan have not shown that the Panel exceeded the limits of its discretionary authority....

T.8.3 *US – FSC (Article 21.5 – EC)*, para. 243
(WT/DS108/AB/RW)

... the rights of third parties in panel proceedings are limited to the rights granted under Article 10 and Appendix 3 to the DSU. Beyond those minimum guarantees, panels enjoy a discretion to grant additional participatory rights to third parties in particular cases, as long as such "enhanced" rights are consistent with the provisions of the DSU and the principles of due process. However, panels have no discretion to circumscribe the rights guaranteed to third parties by the provisions of the DSU.

T.8.4 *US – FSC (Article 21.5 – EC)*, para. 245
(WT/DS108/AB/RW)

Article 10.3 of the DSU is couched in mandatory language. By its terms, third parties "shall" receive "the submissions of the parties to the *first* meeting of the panels". (emphasis added) Article 10.3 does *not* say that third parties shall receive "the *first* submissions" of the parties, but rather that they shall receive "*the* submissions" of the parties. (emphasis added) The number of submissions that third parties are entitled to receive is *not* stated. Rather, Article 10.3 defines the submissions that third parties are entitled to receive by reference to a specific step in the proceedings – the first meeting of the panel. It follows, in our view, that, under this provision, third parties must be given all of the submissions that have been made by the parties to the panel up to the first meeting of the panel, irrespective of the number of such submissions which are made, including any rebuttal submissions filed in advance of the first meeting.

T.8.5 *US – FSC (Article 21.5 – EC)*, para. 249
(WT/DS108/AB/RW)

. . . Article 10.1 directs panels "fully" to take into account the interests of Members other than the parties to the dispute, and Article 10.2 requires panels to grant to third parties "an opportunity to be heard". Article 10.3 ensures that, up to a defined stage in the panel proceedings, third parties can participate fully in the proceedings, on the basis of the same written submissions as the parties themselves. Article 10.3 thereby seeks to guarantee that the third parties can participate at a session of the first meeting with the panel in a full and meaningful fashion that would not be possible if the third parties were denied written submissions made to the panel before that meeting. Moreover, panels themselves will thereby benefit more from the contributions made by third parties and will, therefore, be better able "fully" to take into account the interests of Members, as directed by Article 10.1 of the DSU.

T.8.6 *Chile – Price Band System*, para. 163
(WT/DS207/AB/R)

. . . Third parties to a dispute cannot make claims. It was for Argentina, as the claimant, to make its claim; Argentina cannot rely on third parties to do so on its behalf. Moreover, we note that Argentina did not adopt these arguments of the third parties in subsequent proceedings.

Trademarks. *See* Paris Convention (1967), Articles 6(1) and 6(quinquies) (P.2.1–2); TRIPS Agreement, Articles 15 and 16 (T.9.3–6)

Trade Names. *See* Paris Convention (1967), Article 8 (P.2.3); TRIPS Agreement, Article 2.1 (T.9.2)

Transparency. *See* Business Confidential Information (B.4); Confidentiality (C.6); Inferences Drawn from the Refusal of a Party to Provide Information (I.1); Publication and Administration of Trade Regulations (P.5); Seek Information and Technical Advice (S.4)

Treaties Incorporated into the TRIPS Agreement. *See* Paris Convention (1967) (P.2)

T.9 TRIPS Agreement

T.9.1 Article 1.2 – Definition of "intellectual property"

T.9.1.1 *US – Section 211 Appropriations Act*, para. 335
(WT/DS176/AB/R)

The Panel interpreted the phrase "'intellectual property' refers to all categories of intellectual property that are the *subject* of Sections 1 through 7 of Part II" (emphasis added) as if that phrase read "intellectual property means those categories of intellectual property appearing in the *titles* of Sections 1 through 7 of Part II." To our mind, the Panel's interpretation ignores the plain words of Article 1.2, for it fails to take into account that the phrase "the subject of Sections 1 through 7 of Part II" deals not only with the categories of intellectual property indicated in each section *title*, but with other *subjects* as well. . . .

T.9.1.2 *US – Section 211 Appropriations Act*, para. 341 (WT/DS176/AB/R)

. . . we reverse the Panel's finding in paragraph 8.41 of the Panel Report that trade names are not covered under the *TRIPS Agreement* and find that WTO Members do have an obligation under the *TRIPS Agreement* to provide protection to trade names.

T.9.2 Article 2.1 – Intellectual Property Law Conventions. *See also* Paris Convention (1967) (P.2)

T.9.2.1 *US – Section 211 Appropriations Act*, para. 331 (WT/DS176/AB/R)

. . . the Panel interpreted the words "in respect of" in Article 2.1 as limiting the incorporation of the provisions of the Paris Convention (1967), including Article 8, to Parts II, III and IV of the *TRIPS Agreement*. . . .

T.9.2.2 *US – Section 211 Appropriations Act*, paras. 336–338 (WT/DS176/AB/R)

. . . Article 2.1 explicitly incorporates Article 8 of the Paris Convention (1967) into the *TRIPS Agreement*.

The Panel was of the view that the words "in respect of" in Article 2.1 have the effect of "conditioning" Members' obligations under the Articles of the Paris Convention (1967) incorporated into the *TRIPS Agreement*, with the result that trade names are not covered. We disagree.

Article 8 of the Paris Convention (1967) covers only the protection of trade names; Article 8 has no other subject. If the intention of the negotiators had been to exclude trade names from protection, there would have been no purpose whatsoever in including Article 8 in the list of Paris Convention (1967) provisions that were specifically incorporated into the *TRIPS Agreement*. To adopt the Panel's approach would be to deprive Article 8 of the Paris Convention (1967), as incorporated into the *TRIPS Agreement* by virtue of Article 2.1 of that Agreement, of any and all meaning and effect. . . .

T.9.2.3 *US – Section 211 Appropriations Act*, para. 341 (WT/DS176/AB/R)

. . . we reverse the Panel's finding in paragraph 8.41 of the Panel Report that trade names are not covered under the *TRIPS Agreement* and find that WTO Members do have an obligation under the *TRIPS Agreement* to provide protection to trade names.

Article 3.1 – National treatment. *See* National Treatment, Article 3.1 of the TRIPS Agreement (N.1.14)

Article 4 – MFN treatment. *See* MFN Treatment, Article 4 of the TRIPS Agreement (M.2.3)

T.9.3 Article 15.1 – Trademarks – "protectable subject-matter"

T.9.3.1 *US – Section 211 Appropriations Act*, paras. 154–156 (WT/DS176/AB/R)

. . . To us, the title of Article 15.1 – "Protectable Subject-matter" – indicates that Article 15.1 embodies a *definition* of what can constitute a trademark. WTO Members are obliged under Article 15.1 to ensure that those signs or combinations of signs that meet the distinctiveness criteria set forth in Article 15.1 – and are, thus, *capable of constituting a trademark* – are *eligible for registration* as trademarks within their domestic legislation.

. . . Identifying certain signs that are *capable of* registration and imposing on WTO Members an obligation to make those signs *eligible for* registration in their domestic legislation is not the same as imposing on those Members an obligation to register *automatically* each and every sign or combination of signs that are *capable of* and *eligible for* registration under Article 15.1. . . . In this way, the title of Article 15 expresses the notion that the subject-matter covered by the provision is subject-matter that *qualifies* for, but is not necessarily *entitled to*, protection.

It follows that the wording of Article 15.1 allows WTO Members to set forth in their domestic legislation conditions for the registration of trademarks that do *not* address the definition of either "protectable subject-matter" or of what constitutes a trademark.

T.9.4 Article 15.2 – Trademarks – Denial of protection on other grounds

T.9.4.1 *US – Section 211 Appropriations Act*, paras. 171, 174, 177 (WT/DS176/AB/R)

The specific reference to Article 15.1 in Article 15.2 makes it clear that the "other grounds" for denial of registration to which Article 15.2 refers are different from those mentioned in Article 15.1. Given this, the key phrase relating to the issue before us is the limitation found in the final phrase of Article 15.2, which requires that those grounds "do not derogate from the provisions of the Paris Convention (1967)."

. . .

. . . the question before us with respect to Article 15.2 is the extent to which, if at all, Members are permitted to deny trademark registration on grounds *other than those expressly provided for* in the *TRIPS Agreement* and the Paris Convention (1967).

. . .

Therefore, a condition need not be expressly mentioned in the Paris Convention (1967) in order not to "derogate" from it. Denial of registration on "other grounds" would derogate from the Paris Convention (1967) only if the denial were on grounds that are inconsistent with the provisions of that Convention.

T.9.5 Article 16.1 – Trademarks – Exclusive rights conferred on the owner

T.9.5.1 *US – Section 211 Appropriations Act*, paras. 186–188 (WT/DS176/AB/R)

. . . Article 16 confers on the *owner* of a registered trademark an internationally agreed minimum level of "exclusive rights" that all WTO Members must guarantee in their domestic legislation. These exclusive rights protect the owner against infringement of the registered trademark by unauthorized third parties.

We underscore that Article 16.1 confers these exclusive rights on the "owner" of a registered trademark. As used in this treaty provision, the ordinary meaning of "owner" can be defined as the proprietor or the person who holds the title or dominion of the property constituted by the trademark. We agree with the Panel that this ordinary meaning does not clarify how the ownership of a trademark is to be determined. Also, we agree with the Panel that Article 16.1 does not, in express terms, define how ownership of a registered trademark is to be determined. Article 16.1 confers exclusive rights on the "owner", but Article 16.1 does not tell us who the "owner" *is*.

As the United States reminds us, and as the European Communities concedes, the last sentence of Article 16.1 acknowledges that WTO Members may make the rights available "on the basis of use" of the trademark. We read this to permit WTO Members to make the "exclusive rights" contemplated by Article 16.1 available within their respective jurisdictions on the basis of registration or use. The Panel concluded that Article 16.1 contemplates that different forms of entitlement may exist under the laws of different Members, and we agree. However, the *TRIPS Agreement* does not establish or prescribe a regime of ownership of trademarks.

T.9.6 Article 16.1 – Trademarks – Determination of ownership

T.9.6.1 *US – Section 211 Appropriations Act*, para. 195 (WT/DS176/AB/R)

. . . we conclude that neither Article 16.1 of the *TRIPS Agreement*, nor any other provision of either the *TRIPS Agreement* and the Paris Convention (1967), determines who owns or who does not own a trademark.

T.9.6.2 *US – Section 211 Appropriations Act*, para. 199 (WT/DS176/AB/R)

We recall that the European Communities contends that the Panel created an artificial distinction between the owner of a registered trademark and the trademark itself. We disagree with the apparent equation by the European Communities of trademark registration with trademark ownership. Here, again, the European Communities appears to us to overlook the necessary legal distinction between a trademark system in which ownership is based on registration and a trademark system in which ownership is based on use. As we have noted more than once, United States law confers exclusive trademark rights, not on the basis of registration, but on the basis of use. There is nothing in Article 16.1 that compels the United States to base the protection of exclusive rights on registration. Indeed, as we have also observed more than once, the last sentence of Article 16.1 confirms that WTO Members may make such rights available on the basis of use. The United States has done so. Therefore, it necessarily follows that, under United States law, registration is *not* conclusive of ownership of a trademark. Granted, under United States law, the registration of a trademark does confer a *prima facie* presumption of the registrant's ownership of the registered trademark and of the registrant's exclusive right to use that trademark in commerce. But, while we agree with the Panel that the presumptive owner of the *registered* trademark must be entitled, under United States law, to the exclusive rights flowing from Article 16.1 unless and until the presumption arising from registration is successfully challenged through court or administrative proceedings, we do not agree with the European Communities' evident equation of registration with ownership.

T.9.7 Article 33 – Patents – "term of protection"

T.9.7.1 *Canada – Patent Term*, para. 90

(WT/DS170/AB/R)

We agree with the Panel that, in Article 33 of the *TRIPS Agreement*, the word "available" means "available, as a matter of right", that is to say, available as a matter of legal right and certainty.

T.9.7.2 *Canada – Patent Term*, para. 91

(WT/DS170/AB/R)

. . . The fact that the patent term required under Article 33 can be a by-product of possible delays in the patent-granting process does not imply that this term is available, as a matter of legal right and certainty, to each and every Old Act patent applicant in Canada.

T.9.7.3 *Canada – Patent Term*, para. 92

(WT/DS170/AB/R)

To demonstrate that the patent term in Article 33 is "available", it is not sufficient to point, as Canada does, to a combination of procedures that, when used in a particular sequence or in a particular way, *may* add up to twenty years. The opportunity to obtain a twenty-year patent term must not be "available" only to those who are somehow able to meander successfully through a maze of administrative procedures. The opportunity to obtain a twenty-year term must be a readily discernible and specific right, and it must be clearly seen as such by the patent applicant when a patent application is filed. The grant of the patent must be sufficient *in itself* to obtain the minimum term mandated by Article 33. The use of the word "available" in Article 33 does not undermine but, rather, underscores this obligation.

T.9.7.4 *Canada – Patent Term*, para. 95
(WT/DS170/AB/R)

The text of Article 33 gives no support to the notion of an "effective" term of protection as distinguished from a "nominal" term of protection. On the contrary, the obligation in Article 33 is straightforward and mandatory: to provide, as a specific right, a term of protection that does not end before the expiry of a period of twenty years counted from the filing date.

T.9.8 Article 33 – Relationship with Article 62.2

T.9.8.1 *Canada – Patent Term*, para. 97
(WT/DS170/AB/R)

. . . Article 62.2 deals with procedures relating to the acquisition of intellectual property rights. Article 62.2 does not deal with the duration of those rights once they are acquired. . . . This purely procedural Article cannot be used to modify the clear and substantive standard set out in Article 33 so as to conjecture a new standard of "effective" protection. Each Member of the WTO may well have its own subjective judgement about what constitutes a "reasonable period of time" not only for granting patents in general, but also for granting patents in specific sectors or fields of complexity. If Canada's arguments were accepted, each and every Member of the WTO would be free to adopt a term of "effective" protection for patents that, in its judgement, meets the criteria of "reasonable period of time" and "unwarranted curtailment of the period of protection", and to claim that its term of protection is substantively "equivalent" to the term of protection envisaged by Article 33. . . .

T.9.9 Article 33 – Relationship with Article 70.2

T.9.9.1 *Canada – Patent Term*, para. 77
(WT/DS170/AB/R)

. . . Article 70.2 applies the obligations of the *TRIPS Agreement* to "all subject-matter existing . . . and which is protected" on the date of application of the *TRIPS Agreement* for a Member. A Member is required, as from that date, to implement *all* obligations under the *TRIPS Agreement* in respect of such existing subject-matter. This includes the obligation in Article 33. We see no basis in the text for isolating or insulating the obligation in Article 33 relating to the duration of a patent term from the other obligations relating to patents that are also found in Section 5 of the *TRIPS Agreement*. . . .

T.9.10 Article 42 – Civil and administrative procedures and remedies

T.9.10.1 *US – Section 211 Appropriations Act*, para. 205
(WT/DS176/AB/R)

Article 42 forms part of Part III on "Enforcement of Intellectual Property Rights". Part III has broad coverage. It applies to all intellectual property rights covered by the *TRIPS Agreement*. According to Article 1.2 of the *TRIPS Agreement*, the term "intellectual property" refers to "all categories of intellectual property that are the subject of Sections 1 through 7 of Part II" of that Agreement.

T.9.10.2 *US – Section 211 Appropriations Act*, para. 206
(WT/DS176/AB/R)

Section 1 of Part III lays out "General Obligations" of Members. According to Article 41.1 of Section 1, Members are required to ensure that enforcement procedures as specified in Part III are available under their domestic law "so as to permit effective action against any act of infringement of intellectual property rights covered by [the TRIPS] Agreement". These enforcement procedures must include expeditious remedies to prevent infringements and remedies which constitute a deterrent to further infringements. At the same time, these procedures must be applied in such a manner as to avoid the creation of barriers to legitimate trade and to provide safeguards against their abuse. These procedures provide for an internationally-agreed minimum standard which Members are bound to implement in their domestic legislation.

T.9.10.3 *US – Section 211 Appropriations Act*, para. 207
(WT/DS176/AB/R)

Section 2 of Part III is entitled "Civil and Administrative Procedures and Remedies". Article 42 deals with enforcement action in judicial proceedings, and contains detailed requirements which ensure that "civil judicial procedures" are "fair and equitable". Like Section 1 of Part III, Section 2 introduces an international minimum standard which Members are bound to implement in their domestic legislation.

T.9.10.4 *US – Section 211 Appropriations Act*, para. 215
(WT/DS176/AB/R)

The first sentence of Article 42 requires Members to make certain civil judicial procedures "available" to right holders. Making something *available* means making it "obtainable", putting it "within one's reach" and "at one's disposal" in a way that has sufficient force or efficacy. We agree with the Panel that the ordinary meaning of the term "make available" suggests that "right holders" are entitled under Article 42 to have *access* to civil judicial procedures that are effective in bringing about the enforcement of their rights covered by the Agreement.

T.9.10.5 *US – Section 211 Appropriations Act*, para. 216
(WT/DS176/AB/R)

Article 42, first sentence, does not define what the term "civil judicial procedures" in that sentence encompasses. The *TRIPS Agreement* thus reserves, subject to the procedural minimum standards set out in that Agreement, a degree of discretion to Members on this, taking into account "differences in national legal systems"....

T.9.10.6 *US – Section 211 Appropriations Act*, para. 217 (WT/DS176/AB/R)

Pursuant to the first sentence of Article 42, civil judicial procedures must be made available to "right holders" of intellectual property rights covered by the *TRIPS Agreement* so as to enable them to protect those rights against infringement. . . . We agree with the Panel that the term "right holders" as used in Article 42 is not limited to persons who have been established as owners of trademarks. Where the *TRIPS Agreement* confers rights exclusively on "owners" of a right, it does so in express terms, such as in Article 16.1, which refers to the "owner of a registered trademark". By contrast, the term "right holders" within the meaning of Article 42 also includes persons who claim to have legal standing to assert rights. . . .

T.9.10.7 *US – Section 211 Appropriations Act*, paras. 218–221 (WT/DS176/AB/R)

. . . we agree with the Panel that the "right holders" to whom Members must make the procedural rights of Article 42 available include trademark registrants who are presumptive owners under United States law. In our view, these procedural rights extend as well to all other "right holders".

WTO Members must also guarantee to all "parties" the right to "substantiate their claims", as required by the fourth sentence of Article 42. The use of the words "their claims" suggests that, under Article 42, the choice of which claims or how many issues to raise in civil judicial procedures is left to each party. The use of the word "substantiate" implies that litigants have the right to do more than simply initiate claims; Members must duly entitle all litigants to "give substance" to, or "give good grounds" for, their claims in order to prove the truth of a charge, and to demonstrate or verify it by evidence.

Litigants are also entitled under the fourth sentence of Article 42 to "present all relevant evidence" in such procedures. These words indicate that parties have the right to file "all relevant evidence" in support of their claims with the courts.

From all this, we understand that the rights which Article 42 obliges Members to make available to right holders are *procedural* in nature. These *procedural* rights guarantee an international minimum standard for nationals of other Members within the meaning of Article 1.3 of the *TRIPS Agreement.*

T.9.10.8 *US – Section 211 Appropriations Act*, para. 226 (WT/DS176/AB/R)

In our view, a conclusion by a court on the basis of Section 211, after applying the Federal Rules of Civil Procedure and the Federal Rules of Evidence, that an enforcement proceeding has failed to establish ownership – a requirement of substantive law – with the result that it is impossible for the court to rule in favour of that claimant's or that defendant's claim to a trademark right, does not constitute a violation of Article 42. There is nothing in the *procedural* obligations of Article 42 that prevents a Member, in such a situation, from legislating whether or not its courts must examine *each and every* requirement of substantive law at issue before making a ruling.

T.9.11 Article 70 – Relationship between paragraphs 1 and 2

T.9.11.1 *Canada – Patent Term*, para. 69
(WT/DS170/AB/R)

Like the Panel, we see Articles 70.1 and 70.2 as dealing with two distinct and separate matters. The former deals with past "acts", while the latter deals with "subject-matter" existing on the applicable date of the *TRIPS Agreement*. Article 70.1 of the *TRIPS Agreement* operates only to exclude obligations in respect of "acts which occurred" before the date of application of the *TRIPS Agreement*, but does *not* exclude rights and obligations in respect of *continuing situations*. On the contrary, "subject-matter existing . . . which is protected" is clearly a continuing situation, whether viewed as protected inventions, or as the patent rights attached to them. "Subject-matter existing . . . which is protected" is not within the scope of Article 70.1, and, therefore, the "[e]xcept as otherwise provided for" clause in Article 70.2 can have no application to it. . . .

T.9.11.2 *Canada – Patent Term*, para. 70
(WT/DS170/AB/R)

We wish to point out that our interpretation of Article 70 does not lead to a "retroactive" application of the *TRIPS Agreement*. Article 70.1 alone addresses "retroactive" circumstances, and it excludes them generally from the scope of the Agreement. The application of Article 33 to inventions protected under Old Act patents is justified under Article 70.2, not Article 70.1. A treaty applies to existing rights, even when those rights result from "acts which occurred" before the treaty entered into force.

T.9.12 Article 70.1 – Acts which occurred before the date of TRIPS application

T.9.12.1 *Canada – Patent Term*, paras. 55–56
(WT/DS170/AB/R)

Article 70.1 provides that, where such "acts" "occurred" before the date of application of the *TRIPS Agreement* for a Member, that is to say, where such "acts" were done, carried out or completed before that date, no obligation of the *TRIPS Agreement* is to be imposed on a Member in respect of those "acts". Those "acts" themselves cannot be called in question after the date of application of the *TRIPS Agreement* for a Member. In this regard, we note that, in this dispute, the United States has repeatedly emphasized that it is not challenging or complaining against any "act" of any Canadian public authority or private party that took place before 1 January 1996, the date of application of the *TRIPS Agreement* for Canada.

However, in the realm of intellectual property rights, it is of fundamental importance to distinguish between "acts" and the "rights" created by those "acts". . . .

T.9.12.2 *Canada – Patent Term*, para. 57
(WT/DS170/AB/R)

With respect to Article 70.1, the crucial question for consideration before us is, therefore: if patents created by "acts" of public authorities under the Old Act continue to be in force on the date of application of the *TRIPS Agreement* for Canada (that is, on 1 January 1996), can Article 70.1 operate to exclude those patents from the scope of the *TRIPS Agreement*, on the ground that they were created by "acts which occurred" before that date?

T.9.12.3 *Canada – Patent Term*, para. 58
(WT/DS170/AB/R)

. . . An "act" is something that is "done", and the use of the phrase "acts which occurred" suggests that what was done is now complete or ended. This excludes situations, including existing rights and obligations, that have *not* ended. . . .

T.9.12.4 *Canada – Patent Term*, para. 59
(WT/DS170/AB/R)

A contrary interpretation would seriously erode the scope of the other provisions of Article 70, especially the explicit provisions of Article 70.2. Almost any existing situation or right can be said to have arisen from one or more past "acts". For example, virtually all contractual and property rights could be said to arise from "acts which occurred" in the past. If the phrase "acts which occurred" were interpreted to cover all *continuing* situations involving patents which were granted before the date of application of the *TRIPS Agreement* for a Member [. . .] then Article 70.1 would preclude the application of virtually the whole of the *TRIPS Agreement* to rights conferred by the patents arising from such "acts". This is not consistent with the object and purpose of the *TRIPS Agreement*, as reflected in the preamble of the Agreement.

T.9.12.5 *Canada – Patent Term*, para. 60
(WT/DS170/AB/R)

We conclude, therefore, that Article 70.1 of the *TRIPS Agreement* cannot be interpreted to exclude existing rights, such as patent rights, even if such rights arose through acts which occurred before the date of application of the *TRIPS Agreement* for a Member. . . .

T.9.13 Article 70.2 – "protection of existing subject-matter"

T.9.13.1 *Canada – Patent Term*, para. 65
(WT/DS170/AB/R)

. . . We can deduce, therefore, that the "subject-matter", for purposes of Article 70.2, is that which is "protected", or "meets the criteria for protection", under the terms of the *TRIPS Agreement*. As, in the present case, patents are the means of protection, then whatever patents protect must be the "subject-matter" to which Article 70.2 refers.

T.9.13.2 *Canada – Patent Term*, para. 66
(WT/DS170/AB/R)

...These Articles [28, 31 and 34] confirm that *inventions* are the relevant "subject-matter" in the case of patents, and that the "subject-matter" in Article 70.2 means, in the case of patents, patentable or patented inventions. Article 70.2 thus gives rise to obligations in respect of all such inventions existing on the date of application of the *TRIPS Agreement* for a Member....

T.9.13.3 *Canada – Patent Term*, para. 77
(WT/DS170/AB/R)

...Article 70.2 applies the obligations of the *TRIPS Agreement* to "all subject-matter existing... and which is protected" on the date of application of the *TRIPS Agreement* for a Member. A Member is required, as from that date, to implement *all* obligations under the *TRIPS Agreement* in respect of such existing subject-matter....

T.9.14 Article 70.8(a) – Filing of "mailbox" applications

T.9.14.1 *India – Patents (US)*, para. 58
(WT/DS50/AB/R)

...we do *not* agree with the Panel that Article 70.8(a) requires a Member to establish a means "so as to eliminate any reasonable doubts regarding whether mailbox applications and eventual patents based on them could be rejected or invalidated because, at the filing or priority date, the matter for which protection was sought was unpatentable in the country in question". India is *entitled*, by the "transitional arrangements" in paragraphs 1, 2 and 4 of Article 65, to delay application of Article 27 for patents for pharmaceutical and agricultural chemical products until 1 January 2005. In our view, India is obliged, by Article 70.8(a), to provide a legal mechanism for the filing of mailbox applications that provides a sound legal basis to preserve both the novelty of the inventions and the priority of the applications as of the relevant filing and priority dates. No more.

T.9.14.2 *India – Patents (US)*, paras. 70–71
(WT/DS50/AB/R)

...we are not persuaded that India's "administrative instructions" would survive a legal challenge under the Patents Act. And, consequently, we are not persuaded that India's "administrative instructions" provide a sound legal basis to preserve novelty of inventions and priority of applications as of the relevant filing and priority dates.

For these reasons, we agree with the Panel's conclusion that India's "administrative instructions" for receiving mailbox applications are inconsistent with Article 70.8(a) of the *TRIPS Agreement*.

T.9.15 Article 70.9 – Exclusive marketing rights

T.9.15.1 *India – Patents (US)*, para. 84

(WT/DS50/AB/R)

. . . we agree with the Panel that India should have had a mechanism in place to provide for the grant of exclusive marketing rights effective as from the date of entry into force of the *WTO Agreement*, and, therefore, we agree with the Panel that India is in violation of Article 70.9 of the *TRIPS Agreement*.

V

W

W.1 Waivers

W.1.1 *EC – Bananas III*, para. 183
(WT/DS27/AB/R)

. . . Neither the circumstances surrounding the negotiation of the Lomé Waiver, nor the need to interpret it so as to permit it to achieve its objectives, allow us to disregard the clear and plain wording of the Lomé Waiver by extending its scope to include a waiver from the obligations under Article XIII. Moreover, although Articles I and XIII of the GATT 1994 are both non-discrimination provisions, their relationship is not such that a waiver from the obligations under Article I implies a waiver from the obligations under Article XIII.

W.1.2 *EC – Bananas III*, para. 184
(WT/DS27/AB/R)

The Panel's interpretation of the Lomé Waiver as including a waiver from the GATT 1994 obligations relating to the allocation of tariff quotas is difficult to reconcile with the limited GATT practice in the interpretation of waivers, the strict disciplines to which waivers are subjected under the *WTO Agreement*, the history of the negotiations of this particular waiver and the limited GATT practice relating to granting waivers from the obligations of Article XIII.

W.1.3 *EC – Bananas III*, para. 185
(WT/DS27/AB/R)

. . . Although the *WTO Agreement* does not provide any specific rules on the interpretation of waivers, Article IX of the *WTO Agreement* and the *Understanding in Respect of Waivers of Obligations under the General Agreement on Tariffs and Trade 1994*, which provide requirements for granting and renewing waivers, stress the exceptional nature of waivers and subject waivers to strict disciplines. Thus, waivers should be interpreted with great care.

Withdrawal of an Appeal. *See* Working Procedures for Appellate Review, Rule 30 – Withdrawal (W.2.13)

W.2 Working Procedures for Appellate Review

W.2.1 General

W.2.1.1 *US – FSC*, para. 166
(WT/DS108/AB/R)

. . . The procedural rules of WTO dispute settlement are designed to promote, not the development of litigation techniques, but simply the fair, prompt and effective resolution of trade disputes.

W.2.1.2 *EC – Sardines*, para. 139
(WT/DS231/AB/R)

. . . we emphasize that the *Working Procedures* must not be interpreted in a way that could undermine the effectiveness of the dispute settlement system, for they have been drawn up pursuant to the DSU and as a means of ensuring that the dispute settlement mechanism achieves the aim of securing a positive solution to a dispute. . . .

W.2.2 Rule 3.1 – Decision making

W.2.2.1 *EC – Asbestos*, para. 51
(WT/DS135/AB/R)

. . . after consultations among all seven Members of the Appellate Body, we adopted, pursuant to Rule 16(1) of the *Working Procedures*, an additional procedure, *for the purposes of this appeal only*, to deal with written submissions received from persons other than the parties and third parties to this dispute (the "Additional Procedure"). . . .

W.2.3 Rule 3.2 – Concurring opinion – Article 17.11 of the DSU

W.2.3.1 *EC – Asbestos*, para. 149
(WT/DS135/AB/R)

One Member of the Division hearing this appeal wishes to make a concurring statement. At the outset, I would like to make it abundantly clear that I agree with the findings and conclusions reached, and the reasoning set out in support thereof, by the Division, in: Section V (*TBT Agreement*); Section VII (Article XX(b) of the GATT 1994 and Article 11 of the DSU); Section VIII (Article XXIII:1(b) of the GATT 1994); and Section IX (Findings and Conclusions) of the Report. This concurring statement, in other words, relates only to Section VI ("Like Products" in Article III:4 of the GATT 1994) of the Report.

W.2.3.2 *EC – Asbestos*, para. 150
(WT/DS135/AB/R)

More particularly, in respect of Section VI of the Report, I join in the findings and conclusions set out in: paragraphs 116, 126, 128, 131, 132, 141, 147 and 148. I am bound to say that, in truth, I agree with a great deal more than just the bare findings and conclusions contained in these eight paragraphs of the Report. It is, however, as a practical matter, not feasible to sort out and identify which part of which paragraph, of the sixty-odd paragraphs comprising Section VI of our Report in which I join. Nor is it feasible to offer a detailed statement with respect to the portions that would then remain. Accordingly, I set out only two related matters below.

W.2.3.3 *EC – Asbestos*, para. 154
(WT/DS135/AB/R)

. . . Moreover, in future concrete contexts, the line between a "fundamentally" and "exclusively" economic view of "like products" under Article III:4 may well prove very difficult, as a practical matter, to identify. It seems to me the better part of valour to reserve one's opinion on such an important, indeed, philosophical matter, which may have unforeseeable implications, and to leave that matter for another appeal and another day, or perhaps other appeals and other days. I so reserve my opinion on this matter.

W.2.3A Rule 3.2 – Separate opinion – Article 17.11 of the DSU

W.2.3A.1 *US – Upland Cotton*, para. 631
(WT/DS267/AB/R)

One Member of the Division hearing this appeal wishes to set out a brief separate opinion. At the outset, I would like to make it absolutely clear that I agree with the findings and conclusions and reasoning set out in all preceding Sections of this Report, but one, namely, Section C above, which relates to Article 10.2 of the *Agreement on Agriculture*. It is only on the interpretation of Article 10.2 that I must respectfully disagree.

W.2.3A.2 *US – Upland Cotton*, para. 641 and footnote 952
(WT/DS267/AB/R)

I also recognize that this interpretation of Article 10.2 has consequential results for some of the other claims on appeal brought by both the United States and Brazil in connection with the United States' export credit guarantee programs. As to the other Sections of this Report dealing with export credit guarantees, I agree that the legal interpretation and analyses contained therein follow logically from the view of my colleagues on the Division with respect to Article 10.2, as set forth in paragraphs 605 through 630 of this Report.[952]

[952] The relevant findings and conclusions for purposes of the recommendations and rulings to be adopted by the DSB in this dispute, pursuant to Article 17.14 of the DSU, are those set out in paragraph 763(e) and (f) of this Report.

W.2.4 Rule 8 – Rules of conduct – confidentiality. *See also* Business Confidential Information (B.4); Confidentiality (C.6)

W.2.4.1 *Brazil – Aircraft*, para. 124
(WT/DS46/AB/R)

Canada – Aircraft, para. 146
(WT/DS70/AB/R)

. . . Members of the Appellate Body and its staff are covered by Article VII:1 of the *Rules of Conduct*, which provides:

> Each covered person *shall at all times maintain the confidentiality of dispute settlement deliberations and proceedings together with any information identified by a party as confidential.* (emphasis added)

W.2.5 Rule 13 – Replacement of Appellate Body Member on Division. *See also* Working Procedures for Appellate Review, Rule 16 – Process (W.2.6)

W.2.5.1 *US – Lead and Bismuth II*, para. 8
(WT/DS138/AB/R)

On 19 March 2000, Mr. Christopher Beeby, a Member of the Division hearing this appeal, passed away. On 20 March 2000, the Appellate Body, pursuant to Rule 13 of the *Working Procedures*, selected Mr. Julio Lacarte-Muró to replace Mr. Beeby . . . .

W.2.5.2 *US – Offset Act (Byrd Amendment)*, para. 8
(WT/DS217/AB/R, WT/DS234/AB/R)

In a letter dated 22 November 2002, the Director of the Appellate Body Secretariat informed the participants and third participants that, in accordance with Rule 13 of the *Working Procedures*, the Appellate Body had selected Mr. Giorgio Sacerdoti to replace Mr. A.V. Ganesan as Presiding Member of the Division hearing this appeal. The latter was prevented from continuing to serve on the Division for serious personal reasons.

W.2.5.3 *US – Softwood Lumber IV*, para. 10
(WT/DS257/AB/R)

In a letter dated 12 November 2003, the Director of the Appellate Body Secretariat informed the participants and third participants that, in accordance with Rule 13 of the *Working Procedures*, the Appellate Body had selected Mr. Giorgio Sacerdoti to replace Mr. A.V. Ganesan as a Member of the Division hearing this appeal because the latter was prevented from continuing to serve on the Division for serious personal reasons.

W.2.6 **Rule 16 – Process.** *See also* Amicus Curiae Briefs, Additional Procedure (A.2.3); Working Procedures for Appellate Review, Rule 26 – Working Schedule (W.2.10); Working Procedures for Appellate Review, Rule 27 – Oral hearing (W.2.11)

W.2.6.1 *EC – Bananas III*, para. 10
(WT/DS27/AB/R)

On 15 July 1997, the Appellate Body notified the participants and third participants in this appeal of its ruling that the request by Saint Lucia would be allowed. The Appellate Body said the following:

> . . . we can find nothing in the *Marrakesh Agreement Establishing the World Trade Organization (the "WTO Agreement")*, the *DSU* or the *Working Procedures*, nor in customary international law or the prevailing practice of international tribunals, which prevents a WTO Member from determining the composition of its delegation in Appellate Body proceedings. Having carefully considered the request made by the government of Saint Lucia, and the responses dated 14 July 1997 received from Canada; Jamaica; Ecuador, Guatemala, Honduras, Mexico and the United States, we rule that it is for a WTO Member to decide who should represent it as members of its delegation in an oral hearing of the Appellate Body.

W.2.6.2 *Guatemala – Cement I*, para. 4
(WT/DS60/AB/R)

. . . On 14 August 1998, Guatemala filed an appellant's submission drafted in Spanish. On 31 August 1998, Mexico filed an appellee's submission also drafted in Spanish. In order to ensure that the third participant would have time to prepare its submission after receiving an English version of the appellant's submission, the Appellate Body granted the United States additional time to file its third participant's submission. The United States filed that submission on 14 September 1998. By our ruling of 31 August 1998, we declined Mexico's request that its appellee's submission be withheld from Guatemala and the United States until the end of the time-period allowed to the United States to file its third participant's submission . . . .

W.2.6.3 *Brazil – Aircraft*, para. 9; *mutatis mutandis*
(WT/DS46/AB/R)

Canada – Aircraft, para. 6
(WT/DS70/AB/R)

. . . by joint letter of 27 May 1999, Brazil and Canada requested that the Appellate Body apply, *mutatis mutandis*, the Procedures Governing Business Confidential Information adopted by the Panel in this case. A preliminary hearing on this issue was held on 10 June 1999, with this Division sitting jointly with the Division of the Appellate Body hearing the appeal in *Canada – Measures Affecting the Export of Civilian Aircraft* ("*Canada – Aircraft*"), and a preliminary ruling was issued by this Division on 11 June 1999.

W.2.6.4 *Brazil – Aircraft*, para. 104; *mutatis mutandis*
(WT/DS46/AB/R)

Canada – Aircraft, para. 126
(WT/DS70/AB/R)

By letter of 31 May 1999, we invited the participants to file legal memoranda in support of their request, and offered each an opportunity to respond to the legal memorandum submitted by the other. The third participants were also given an opportunity to file legal memoranda. Brazil and Canada submitted legal memoranda on 2 June 1999. On 4 June 1999, the third participants, the European Communities and the United States, also filed legal memoranda. On the same date, Brazil and Canada each filed a written response to the memorandum previously submitted by the other on 2 June 1999. A preliminary hearing on this issue was held on 10 June 1999, with this Division sitting jointly with the Division of the Appellate Body hearing the appeal in *Canada – Aircraft*.

W.2.6.5 *Brazil – Aircraft*, para. 119
(WT/DS46/AB/R)

Canada – Aircraft, para. 141
(WT/DS70/AB/R)

In our preliminary ruling of 11 June 1999, we concluded that it is not necessary, under all the circumstances of this case, to adopt *additional* procedures to protect business confidential information in these appellate proceedings . . . .

W.2.6.6 *EC – Asbestos*, para. 51
(WT/DS135/AB/R)

. . . after consultations among all seven Members of the Appellate Body, we adopted, pursuant to Rule 16(1) of the *Working Procedures*, an additional procedure, *for the purposes of this appeal only*, to deal with written submissions received from persons other than the parties and third parties to this dispute (the "Additional Procedure"). The Additional Procedure was communicated to the parties and third parties . . . . the Chairman of the Appellate Body informed the Chairman of the Dispute Settlement Body, in writing, of the Additional Procedure adopted, and this letter was circulated, for information, as a dispute settlement document to the Members of the WTO . . . .

W.2.6.7 *US – FSC (Article 21.5 – EC)*, para. 8
(WT/DS108/AB/RW)

By letter of 22 October 2001, the United States requested the Appellate Body pursuant to Rule 16(2) of the *Working Procedures* to modify the timetable set out in the Working Schedule for Appeal for the filing of the appellant's submissions by the United States. The United States stated that suspected bioterrorist attacks had compromised the ability of the United States to conduct the necessary consultations with the United States Congress with regard to this appeal. According to the

United States, the effect of these circumstances was such that adhering to the original timetable would result in manifest unfairness to the United States. In its letter of 23 October 2001, the European Communities did not object to the request made by the United States, but requested that, in order to preserve the balance of procedural rights afforded to the participants in this appeal, the Appellate Body extend the deadline for the filing of the European Communities' appellee's submission by 14 days. In a letter dated 23 October 2001, the Division of the Appellate Body hearing the appeal accepted that the circumstances identified by the United States constituted "exceptional circumstances" within the meaning of Rule 16(2) of the *Working Procedures* and that maintaining the deadline for submission of the appellants' submission would result in "manifest unfairness" to the United States. Accordingly, the Division agreed to modify the Working Schedule for this appeal to allow the United States an additional seven days for the filing of its appellant's submission. In the same letter, the Division also extended by seven days the deadlines for the filing of the other appellant's submissions, the appellee's submission, and the third participants' submissions.

W.2.6.8 *US – Lead and Bismuth II*, para. 8
(WT/DS138/AB/R)

On 19 March 2000, Mr. Christopher Beeby, a Member of the Division hearing this appeal, passed away. On 20 March 2000, the Appellate Body, pursuant to Rule 13 of the *Working Procedures*, selected Mr. Julio Lacarte-Muró to replace Mr. Beeby. In view of these extraordinary circumstances, the newly-constituted Division decided, pursuant to Rule 16(1) of the *Working Procedures*, and in the interests of fairness and orderly procedure in the conduct of this appeal, to hold another oral hearing on 4 April 2000. On that date, the participants and third participants presented oral arguments and responded to questions put to them by the Members of the newly-constituted Division. Due to these same extraordinary circumstances, the participants in this appeal, the European Communities and the United States, agreed to a two week extension of the 90-day time limit for the consideration of this appeal, and thus agreed that this Report should be circulated no later than 10 May 2000.

W.2.6.9 *US – Countervailing Measures on Certain EC Products*, para. 52
(WT/DS212/AB/R)

On 10 September 2002, the European Communities the filed a Request for a Preliminary Ruling (the "Request"), alleging that the United States' Notice of Appeal "is manifestly not in conformity with Rule 20(2)(d) of the *Working Procedures for Appellate Review*" because it "fails to identify the findings or the legal interpretations that it considers to be erroneous." The European Communities argued that "[a]s a consequence, the European Communities is unable to prepare its response to the appeal." The European Communities asked us to "order the United States, pursuant to Rule 16(1) of the Working Procedures, immediately to file further and better particulars to its notice of appeal identifying the precise legal findings and legal interpretations that it is challenging."

W.2.6.10 *US – Countervailing Measures on Certain EC Products*, para. 55 (WT/DS212/AB/R)

On 12 September 2002, we invited the United States "to identify the precise findings and interpretations of the Panel which are alleged, in the Notice of Appeal filed on 9 September 2002, to constitute errors." The United States responded by letter dated 13 September 2002. In an attachment to that letter, the United States quoted in full the paragraphs of the Panel Report to which it had merely referred by number in the Notice of Appeal. The United States also provided information as to legal errors allegedly committed by the Panel.

W.2.7 Rule 20 – Notice of appeal

W.2.7.1 GENERAL

W.2.7.1.1 *US – Countervailing Measures on Certain EC Products*, para. 62 (WT/DS212/AB/R)

. . . [we] have underscored the important balance that must be maintained between the right of Members to exercise the right of appeal meaningfully and effectively, and the right of appellees to receive notice through the Notice of Appeal of the findings under appeal, so that they may exercise their right of defence effectively. Hence, we disagree with the contention of the United States here that the Notice of Appeal "serves a limited purpose" as "simply a formal trigger for initiating the appeal." Indeed, if this were the only objective of the notice, our *Working Procedures* would have included only the first paragraph of Rule 20, which refers to commencement of an appeal through written notification to the Dispute Settlement Body and Appellate Body Secretariat. However, Rule 20 also prescribes additional requirements for commencing an appeal; it provides that the Notice of Appeal must include "a brief statement of the nature of the appeal, including the allegations of errors in the issues of law covered in the panel report and legal interpretations developed by the panel." The notification under Rule 20(1) serves as the "trigger" to which the United States refers. The additional requirements under Rule 20(2) serve to ensure that the appellee also receives notice, albeit brief, of the "nature of the appeal" and the "allegations of errors" by the panel.

W.2.7.1.2 *US – Offset Act (Byrd Amendment)*, para. 200 (WT/DS217/AB/R, WT/DS234/AB/R)

. . . the Notice of Appeal "serve[s] to ensure that the appellee also receives notice, albeit brief, of the 'nature of the appeal' and the 'allegations of errors' by the panel." Generic statements such as that relied upon by the United States cannot serve to give the appellees adequate notice that they will be required to defend against a claim that the Panel exceeded its terms of reference. This is particularly so for procedural errors; it can be especially difficult to discern a claim of procedural error by a panel from general references to panel findings or from extracts of a panel report, because allegations of procedural error by a panel may not necessarily be raised until the appellate stage.

W.2.7.1.3 *US – Offset Act (Byrd Amendment)*, para. 208
(WT/DS217/AB/R, WT/DS234/AB/R)

... we have said, "[a]n objection to jurisdiction should be raised as early as possible" and it would be preferable, in the interests of due process, for the appellant to raise such issues in the Notice of Appeal, so that appellees will be aware that this claim will be advanced on appeal. However, in our view, the issue of a panel's jurisdiction is so fundamental that it is appropriate to consider claims that a panel has exceeded its jurisdiction even if such claims were not raised in the Notice of Appeal.

W.2.7.2 CONTENT. *See also* Claims and Arguments (C.1)

W.2.7.2.1 *US – Shrimp*, para. 95
(WT/DS58/AB/R)

... The *Working Procedures for Appellate Review* enjoin the appellant to be *brief* in its notice of appeal in setting out "the nature of the appeal, including the allegations of errors". We believe that, in principle, the "nature of the appeal" and "the allegations of errors" are sufficiently set out where the notice of appeal adequately identifies the findings or legal interpretations of the Panel which are being appealed as erroneous. The notice of appeal is not expected to contain the reasons why the appellant regards those findings or interpretations as erroneous. The notice of appeal is not designed to be a summary or outline of the arguments to be made by the appellant. The legal arguments in support of the allegations of error are, of course, to be set out and developed in the appellant's submission.

W.2.7.2.2 *Chile – Price Band System*, para. 182
(WT/DS207/AB/R)

In our view, this distinction between claims and legal arguments under Article 6.2 of the DSU is also relevant to the distinction between "allegations of error" and legal arguments as contemplated by Rule 20 of the *Working Procedures*. Bearing this distinction in mind, we do *not* agree with Argentina that Chile's arguments regarding the order of analysis chosen by the Panel amount to a separate "allegation of error" that Chile *should have* – or *could have* – included in its Notice of Appeal. In fact, we do not see, nor has Argentina explained, what *separate* "allegation of error" could have been made, or what legal basis for such "allegation of error" there could have been. Rather than making a separate "allegation of error", Chile has, in our view, simply set out a *legal argument* in support of the issues it raised on appeal relating to Article 4.2 of the *Agreement on Agriculture* and Article II:1(b) of the GATT 1994.

W.2.7.3 INSUFFICIENT NOTICE

W.2.7.3.1 *EC – Bananas III*, para. 152
(WT/DS27/AB/R)

In our view, the claims of error by the European Communities set out in paragraphs (c) and (d) of the Notice of Appeal do not cover the Panel's finding in paragraph 7.93 of the Panel Reports. The finding in that paragraph explicitly deals with Ecuador's right to invoke Article XIII:2 or XIII:4 of the GATT 1994, given that Ecuador acceded to the WTO *after* the *WTO Agreement* entered into force and *after* the tariff quota for the BFA countries had been negotiated and inscribed in the EC Schedule to the GATT 1994. There is no specific mention of this Panel finding in either the Notice of Appeal or in the main arguments of the appellant's submission by the European Communities. Therefore, Ecuador had no notice that the European Communities was appealing this finding. For these reasons, we conclude that the Panel's finding in paragraph 7.93 of the Panel Reports should be excluded from the scope of this appeal.

W.2.7.3.2 *US – Countervailing Measures on Certain EC Products*, para. 70
(WT/DS212/AB/R)

We observe that, in coming to these conclusions, we have before us a rather unusual example of the "Conclusions and Recommendations" section of a panel report. In most panel reports, the "Conclusions and Recommendations" section is relatively brief, setting out findings in summary fashion. Detailed legal interpretations and reasoning upon which panels rely are usually found only in the "Findings" sections of panel reports. In this case, however, the Panel's "Conclusions and Recommendations" are more detailed than usual. Paragraphs 8.1(a)–8.1(d) of the Panel Report include, not only the Panel's findings, but also certain of the reasons leading to those findings. Hence, in this case, it is possible, by reading the "Conclusions and Recommendations" section from the Panel Report, to discern alleged errors of law appealed by the United States. We emphasize, however, that generally, a Notice of Appeal that refers simply to the paragraph numbers found in the "Conclusions and Recommendations" section of a panel report, or that quotes them in full, will be insufficient to provide adequate notice of the allegations of error on appeal, and, hence, will fall short of the requirements set out in Rule 20(2)(d) of the *Working Procedures*.

W.2.7.3.3 *US – Upland Cotton*, para. 495
(WT/DS267/AB/R)

We acknowledge that the wording of paragraph 10 of the United States' Notice of Appeal (and, in particular, the use of the words "for example") suggests that the findings listed in this paragraph are simply *examples* of findings challenged in connection with Article 12.7 of the DSU, and that the United States' claim of error under Article 12.7 extends to other Panel findings. In other words, paragraph 10 purports to provide an illustrative rather than exhaustive list of the findings that the

United States intends to challenge under Article 12.7 of the DSU. However, the fact that paragraph 10 purports to provide an illustrative list is not conclusive as to whether the Notice of Appeal contains a sufficient reference to the Panel's findings described in paragraph 493 above for us to conclude that these findings are included in the United States' appeal. The significance of terms such as "for example" is likely to depend on the particular claim in question and the particular context in which the term is used in a given appeal. In our view, the United States' Notice of Appeal did not provide adequate notice to Brazil, as contemplated by Rule 20(2) of the *Working Procedures for Appellate Review* (the "*Working Procedures*"), that the United States intended to make a claim of error under Article 12.7 of the DSU with respect to the Panel's findings described in paragraph 493 above. We therefore decline to rule on these findings in connection with Article 12.7 of the DSU.

W.2.7.3.4 *EC – Export Subsidies on Sugar*, para. 344
(WT/DS265/AB/R, WT/DS266/AB/R, WT/DS283/AB/R)

In its Notice of Appeal, the European Communities "seeks review" of six "conclusion[s]" and "related legal findings and interpretations" set out in certain specified paragraphs of the Panel Reports. The European Communities summarizes the substance of each contested conclusion and the related legal findings and interpretations. The Notice of Appeal also contains a list of the legal provisions of the covered agreements that the Panel is alleged to have erred in interpreting or applying. In our view, the Notice of Appeal gives adequate notice to the Complaining Parties of the content of its appeal so as to allow them to make a proper defence, as required by Rule 20(2)(d) of the *Working Procedures.*

W.2.7.4 AMENDMENT. *See also* Working Procedures for Appellate Review, Rule 30 – Withdrawal, Withdrawal and re-filing notice of appeal (W.2.13.1)

W.2.7.4.1 *US – Countervailing Measures on Certain EC Products*, para. 52
(WT/DS212/AB/R)

On 10 September 2002, the European Communities the filed a Request for a Preliminary Ruling (the "Request"), alleging that the United States' Notice of Appeal "is manifestly not in conformity with Rule 20(2)(d) of the *Working Procedures for Appellate Review*" because it "fails to identify the findings or the legal interpretations that it considers to be erroneous." The European Communities argued that "[a]s a consequence, the European Communities is unable to prepare its response to the appeal." The European Communities asked us to "order the United States, pursuant to Rule 16(1) of the Working Procedures, immediately to file further and better particulars to its notice of appeal identifying the precise legal findings and legal interpretations that it is challenging."

W.2.7.4.2 *US – Countervailing Measures on Certain EC Products*, para. 64 (WT/DS212/AB/R)

In conducting our analysis, we will examine both the Notice of Appeal and the letter of 13 September 2002 supplementing the Notice of Appeal. Although the *Working Procedures* do not expressly provide for the filing of clarifications or further particulars or supplementary or amended Notices of Appeal, we consider it appropriate, in the particular circumstances of this case, to examine both documents with a view to giving "full meaning and effect to the right of appeal." We note in particular that the additional document was filed by the United States in response to our invitation to do so, based in part on a request for additional particulars filed by the European Communities. Moreover, the additional document was filed shortly after the filing of the Notice of Appeal (three days). Finally, we note that the European Communities referred to both the Notice of Appeal and the letter of 13 September 2002 in its arguments on this issue.

W.2.7.5 ARTICLE 11 OF THE DSU – ALLEGATION OF THE PANEL'S FAILURE TO OBJECTIVELY ASSESS. *See also* Standard of Review, Article 11 of the DSU (S.7.2–7)

W.2.7.5.1 *US – Countervailing Measures on Certain EC Products*, para. 74 (WT/DS212/AB/R)

...A *claim* of error by a panel under Article 11 of the DSU is possible only in the context of an appeal. By definition, this *claim* will not be found in requests for establishment of a panel, and panels therefore will not have referred to it in panel reports. Accordingly, if appellants intend to argue that issue on appeal, they must refer to it in Notices of Appeal in a way that will enable appellees to discern it and know the case they have to meet.

W.2.7.5.2 *Japan – Apples*, paras. 126–127 (WT/DS245/AB/R)

By referring to the Panel's alleged failure to comply with Article 11 of the DSU only in the context of Article 2.2, Japan did not enable the United States to "know the case [it had] to meet" as to the Article 11 claim related to Article 5.1 of the *SPS Agreement*. The Appellate Body has consistently emphasized that due process requires that a Notice of Appeal place an appellee on notice of the issues raised on appeal. It is this concern with due process, reflected in Rule 20 of the *Working Procedures*, that underlay the Appellate Body's ruling on the sufficiency of the Notice of Appeal in *US – Countervailing Measures on Certain EC Products*.

...the Appellate Body determined in *US – Countervailing Measures on Certain EC Products* that Article 11 claims are distinct from those raised under substantive provisions of other covered agreements. It follows from this distinction that notice of an Article 11 challenge cannot be "assumed" merely because there is a challenge to a panel's analysis of a substantive provision of a WTO agreement. Rather, an Article 11 claim constitutes a "separate 'allegation of error'" that must be included in a Notice of Appeal. We therefore reject Japan's assertion that an Article 11 challenge is only a "legal argument" underlying the issues raised on appeal.

W.2.7.5.3 *US – Corrosion-Resistant Steel Sunset Review*, footnote 60 to para. 71 (WT/DS244/AB/R)

We have already held that a claim, by an appellant, that a panel erred under Article 11 of the DSU, and a request for a finding to this effect, must be included in the Notice of Appeal, and clearly articulated and substantiated in an appellant's submission with specific arguments....

W.2.7.5.4 *US – Steel Safeguards*, paras. 498–499 (WT/DS248/AB/R, WT/DS249/AB/R, WT/DS251/AB/R, WT/DS252/AB/R, WT/DS253/AB/R, WT/DS254/AB/R, WT/DS258/AB/R, WT/DS259/AB/R)

A challenge under Article 11 of the DSU must not be vague or ambiguous. On the contrary, such a challenge must be clearly articulated and substantiated with specific arguments. An Article 11 claim is not to be made lightly, or merely as a subsidiary argument or claim in support of a claim of a panel's failure to construe or apply correctly a particular provision of a covered agreement. A claim under Article 11 of the DSU must stand by itself and be substantiated, as such, and not as subsidiary to another alleged violation.

The United States' arguments on Article 11 of the DSU are mentioned only in passing in its appellant's submission. Nowhere do we find a clearly articulated claim or specific arguments that would support such a claim. Moreover, the United States did not clarify its challenge under Article 11 of the DSU during the oral hearing. In sum, the United Stated has not substantiated its claim that the Panel acted inconsistently with Article 11 of the DSU, and this claim must therefore fail.

W.2.7.5.5 *Canada – Wheat Exports and Grain Imports*, paras. 176–177 (WT/DS276/AB/R)

We agree with Canada that [the United States' claim that the Panel did not examine the measure in its entirety] of error fits more properly under Article 11 of the DSU [than under Article XVII:1 of the GATT 1994]. The Appellate Body has stated previously that the measure at issue (and the claims made by the complaining Member) make up the "*matter* referred to the DSB" for the purpose of Article 7 of the DSU. In this sense, the United States' argument that the Panel did not examine the measure in its entirety relates to the Panel's examination of the "matter". Article 11 of the DSU sets out the duties of a panel, including that it "should make an objective assessment of the *matter* before it". (emphasis added) Therefore, as we see it, the United States' allegation that the Panel did not examine the measure in its entirety amounts to an allegation that the Panel did not "make an objective assessment of the matter" under Article 11 of the DSU.

Although an appellant is free to determine how to characterize its claims on appeal, at the same time due process requires that the legal basis of a claim be sufficiently clear to allow an appellee to respond effectively. This is especially the case when the claim is an allegation that the panel did not make an objective assessment of the matter as required by Article 11 of the DSU because, by definition, such a claim will not be found in the request for the establishment of the panel and, therefore, the panel will not have referred to it in the panel report.

W.2.7.5.6 *US – Upland Cotton*, para. 398
(WT/DS267/AB/R)

In its opening statement delivered at the oral hearing, the United States confirmed that it has not made an Article 11 claim in this appeal. Rather, the United States claims that the Panel erred in its interpretation of Article 6.3(c) of the *SCM Agreement* and in applying this interpretation to the facts in this dispute. The United States also requests us not to dismiss certain of its arguments as requested by Brazil. Under these circumstances, there is no need for us to rule that the United States makes no Article 11 claim. We also refrain from ruling on whether the Panel complied with Article 11 of the DSU. Moreover, we decline to dismiss the United States' arguments that Brazil lists in Annex A to its appellee's submission on the basis that an Article 11 claim was not properly set out by the United States.

W.2.7A Rule 22 – Appellee's submission

W.2.7A.1 *Canada – Wheat Exports and Grain Imports*, paras. 162–163 and footnote 190
(WT/DS276/AB/R)

Canada states that it would welcome "guidance" from the Appellate Body as to whether a conditional request to complete the analysis of a particular issue should be raised in an appellee's submission filed pursuant to Rule 22 of the *Working Procedures*, or in another appellant's submission filed pursuant to Rule 23. . . .

As we have not reversed the Panel's interpretation of subparagraph (b) of Article XVII:1, the condition on which Canada's request to complete the analysis is made has not been satisfied. . . . In the circumstances of this appeal, it is neither necessary nor appropriate for us to provide "guidance" on the issue of how conditional requests to complete the analysis are properly brought before the Appellate Body.[190]

[190] We observe, in this respect, that Article 17.9 of the DSU provides for the Appellate Body to consult with the Director-General of the WTO and the Chair of the DSB in amending its *Working Procedures*. In accordance with the DSB Decision of 19 December 2002 (WT/DSB/31), the DSB Chair also consults with WTO Members on amendments proposed by the Appellate Body. The Appellate Body monitors the operation of the *Working Procedures* closely, and recognizes that a need for revision may arise from time to time. We believe that issues such as the one referred to by Canada in this appeal could usefully be addressed in the context of future revision.

W.2.8 **Rule 23 – Multiple appeals – (cross appeal).** *See also* Working Procedures for Appellate Review, Rule 20 – Notice of appeal (W.2.7); Working Procedures for Appellate Review, Rule 22 – Appellee's submission (W.2.7A)

W.2.8.1 *US – Gasoline*, p. 12, DSR 1996:I, p. 3 at 11
(WT/DS2/AB/R)

. . . to deal with those two issues [i.e. the clean air issue and the application of the *TBT Agreement*], under the circumstances of this appeal, would have required the Appellate Body casually to disregard its own *Working Procedures* and to do so in the absence of a compelling reason grounded on, for instance, fundamental fairness or *force majeure*. Venezuela and Brazil could have appealed the Panel's finding and non-finding on the two matters by taking advantage of Rules 23(1) or 23(4) of the *Working Procedures* and thereby placing the Appellate Body in a position to dispose of those issues directly in one and the same appellate proceeding.

. . . the route they chose for addressing the two issues in question is not contemplated by the *Working Procedures*, and therefore, these issues are not properly the subject of this appeal.

W.2.9 **Rule 24 – Third participants.** *See also* Third Party Rights (T.8); Working Procedures for Appellate Review, Rule 26 – Working schedule (W.2.10); Working Procedures for Appellate Review, Rule 27 – Oral hearing (W.2.11)

W.2.9.1 *Argentina – Footwear (EC)*, para. 7
(WT/DS121/AB/R)

On 19 October 1999, the Appellate Body received a letter from the Government of Paraguay indicating its interest "in attending" the oral hearing in this appeal. On 25 October 1999, the Appellate Body received a second letter from Paraguay clarifying that it was not requesting an opportunity to "make oral arguments or presentations at the oral hearing" as set forth in Rule 27.3 of the *Working Procedures*. Rather, Paraguay maintained that, as a third party which had notified its interest to the Dispute Settlement Body under Article 10.2 of the DSU, it had the right to "participate passively" in the oral hearing before the Appellate Body in the present dispute. No participant or third participant objected to the participation of Paraguay on a "passive" basis. On 26 October 1999, the Members of the Division hearing this appeal informed Paraguay, the participants and third participants that, having regard to the provisions of Articles 10.2 and 17.4 of the DSU as well as the provisions of Rules 24 and 27 of the *Working Procedures*, Paraguay would be allowed to attend the oral hearing as a "passive observer".

W.2.9.2 *EC – Asbestos*, para. 7
(WT/DS135/AB/R)

On 21 November 2000, the Appellate Body received a letter from Zimbabwe indicating its interest in attending the oral hearing in this appeal. Zimbabwe participated in the proceedings before the Panel as a third party which had notified its interest to the DSB under Article 10.2 of the DSU, but it did not file a third participant's submission in the appeal. No participant or third participant objected to Zimbabwe's request. On 15 December 2000, the Members of the Division hearing this appeal informed Zimbabwe, the participants and third participants, that Zimbabwe would be allowed to attend the oral hearing as a passive observer.

W.2.9.3 *US – Lamb*, paras. 8–9
(WT/DS177/AB/R, WT/DS178/AB/R)

On 26 February 2001, the Appellate Body received letters from Canada and Japan indicating that they would not be filing written submissions in this appeal. Canada stated that it "reserve[d] the right to intervene, as appropriate, during the oral hearing" and Japan indicated that it wished "to reserve its right to present its views at the oral hearing." On 6 March 2001, the Appellate Body Secretariat replied to Canada and Japan that the Division hearing this appeal wished to have clarification as to whether Canada and Japan wanted to attend the oral hearing simply as "passive observers" or to participate actively in the oral hearing. By their letters dated 9 March 2001, Canada stated that it wished to attend the oral hearing as a "passive observer", while Japan stated that it "would like to hear the arguments made by the parties to the dispute, and to intervene when necessary and [when] given an opportunity to do so by the Appellate Body."

On 9 March 2001, the Appellate Body Secretariat informed the participants and third participants that the Division hearing this appeal was "inclined to allow Canada and Japan to attend the oral hearing as passive observers, if none of the participants or third participants object." No such objection was received. On 14 March 2001, the Division hearing this appeal informed Canada, Japan, the participants and the European Communities, that Canada and Japan would be allowed to attend the oral hearing as passive observers, that is, to hear the oral statements and responses to questioning by Australia, the European Communities, New Zealand and the United States.

W.2.9.4 *US – Shrimp (Article 21.5 – Malaysia)*, footnote 16 to para. 10
(WT/DS58/AB/RW)

Pursuant to Rule 24 of the *Working Procedures*, Ecuador, a third party in the proceedings before the Panel, did not file a third participant's submission, but requested permission to attend the oral hearing as a "passive observer". After consulting the participants and third participants, the Division hearing this appeal granted Ecuador permission to attend the oral hearing in this capacity.

W.2.9.5 *India – Autos*, paras. 12–13
(WT/DS146/AB/R, WT/DS175/AB/R)

On 25 February 2002, the Appellate Body received a letter from Japan indicating that Japan would not be filing a written submission in this appeal, but that Japan wished to attend the oral hearing. By letter dated 27 February 2002, the Appellate

Body Secretariat informed Japan, the participants and the third participant that the Division hearing this appeal was "inclined to allow Japan to attend the oral hearing as a passive observer, if none of the participants or third participants object." On 1 March 2002 and 4 March 2002, respectively, the Appellate Body received written responses from the European Communities and the United States.

Taking account of the views expressed by the European Communities and the United States, the Division on 5 March 2002 informed Japan, the participants, and the third participant, that although Japan had not filed a written submission as a third participant, Japan would be allowed to attend the oral hearing as a passive observer, that is, to attend the oral hearing and hear the oral statements and responses to questioning by the participants and the third participant in this appeal.

W.2.9.6 *Chile – Price Band System*, para. 6
(WT/DS207/AB/R)

On 19 July 2002, the Appellate Body received communications from Japan and Nicaragua stating that they wished to attend the oral hearing in this appeal, although neither wished to file a written submission in accordance with Rule 24 of the *Working Procedures*. On 22 July 2002, the Appellate Body notified the participants and third participants that it was inclined to allow Japan and Nicaragua to attend the oral hearing as passive observers, if none of the participants or other third participants objected. No participant or third participant objected to Japan and Nicaragua *attending* the oral hearing. However, the European Communities considered that Japan and Nicaragua should be allowed to attend the oral hearing as third participants and not as passive observers. On 30 July 2002, the participants and third participants were informed that Japan and Nicaragua would be allowed to attend the oral hearing as passive observers.

W.2.9.7 *EC – Sardines*, para. 18
(WT/DS231/AB/R)

On 23 July 2002, we received a letter from Colombia indicating that, although it would not file a third participant's submission, it had an interest in attending the oral hearing in this appeal. Colombia had participated in the proceedings before the Panel as a third party which had notified its interest to the DSB under Article 10.2 of the DSU. By letter of 7 August 2002, we informed the participants and third participants that we were inclined to allow Colombia to attend the oral hearing as a passive observer, and to notify us if they had any objection. The European Communities had no objection to Colombia attending the oral hearing as a third participant, but did object to Colombia attending as a passive observer. Ecuador had no objection to Colombia attending the hearing, but found there was no legal basis to apply a passive observer status and deny them the right to attend as a third participant. On 9 August 2002, we informed the participants and third participants that Colombia would be permitted to attend the oral hearing as a passive observer.

W.2.9.8 *EC – Tariff Preferences*, para. 7
(WT/DS246/AB/R)

. . . on 2 February 2004, Brazil notified its intention to make a statement at the oral hearing as a third participant, and Mauritius notified its intention to appear at the oral hearing as a third participant. Finally, on 2 February 2004, El Salvador, Guatemala, Honduras, and Nicaragua jointly notified their intention to make a statement at the oral hearing as third participants. On 4 February 2004, Cuba notified its intention to appear at the oral hearing as a third participant. By letter dated 16 February 2004, Pakistan submitted a request to make a statement at the oral hearing. No participant objected to Pakistan's request, which was authorized by the Division hearing the appeal on 18 February 2004.

W.2.10 Rule 26 – Working schedule

W.2.10.1 EXTENSION OF DEADLINE FOR SUBMISSIONS OF PARTICIPANTS OR THIRD PARTICIPANTS

W.2.10.1.1 *EC – Bananas III*, para. 3
(WT/DS27/AB/R)

. . . In accordance with Rule 16(2) of the *Working Procedures*, and at the request of the Complaining Parties, the Appellate Body granted a two-day extension for the filing of appellees' and third participants' submissions . . . .

W.2.10.1.2 *Guatemala – Cement I*, para. 4
(WT/DS60/AB/R)

. . . On 14 August 1998, Guatemala filed an appellant's submission drafted in Spanish. On 31 August 1998, Mexico filed an appellee's submission also drafted in Spanish. In order to ensure that the third participant would have time to prepare its submission after receiving an English version of the appellant's submission, the Appellate Body granted the United States additional time to file its third participant's submission. The United States filed that submission on 14 September 1998. By our ruling of 31 August 1998, we declined Mexico's request that its appellee's submission be withheld from Guatemala and the United States until the end of the time-period allowed to the United States to file its third participant's submission . . . .

W.2.10.1.3 *EC – Bed Linen*, footnote 12 to para. 6
(WT/DS141/AB/R)

Following a joint request by the European Communities and India, the Division hearing the appeal decided on 12 December 2000, pursuant to Rule 16(2) of the *Working Procedures* and in the light of the "exceptional circumstances" in this appeal, to extend the time-period for filing the appellee's and third participant's submissions from 2 January 2001 to 8 January 2001.

W.2.10.1.4 *US – Softwood Lumber IV*, paras. 6–7 and footnotes 16–17 (WT/DS257/AB/R)

. . . On 3 October 2003, for scheduling reasons, the United States withdrew its Notice of Appeal pursuant to Rule 30 of the *Working Procedures*, conditional on its right to re-file the Notice of Appeal at a later date. On 21 October 2003, the United States re-filed a substantively identical Notice of Appeal pursuant to Rule 20 of the *Working Procedures*. On that same day, the United States filed its appellant's submission in accordance with the *Working Schedule* drawn up by the Division for this appeal.

On 23 October 2003, the European Communities, a third participant in these proceedings, requested the Appellate Body to modify the *Working Schedule*.[16] On 24 October 2003, the Appellate Body declined the European Communities' request, noting that extending the date for the filing of third participants' submissions would significantly reduce the time available for the Division to consider carefully the arguments raised therein as well as the time available to the participants to respond to those arguments.[17] The Division also observed that the new Notice of Appeal filed by the United States on 21 October 2003 was, in all relevant respects, identical to the one submitted on 2 October 2003, and that the critical time-period for third participants and appellees to prepare their responses to arguments raised by appellants and other appellants is the period between the receipt of the appellant's or other appellant's submissions, which contains the appellants' arguments, and the due date for the filing of the third participants' submissions. The Division noted that the time-period between the receipt of the appellant's submission and the due date for third participants' submissions in this case was the same as it would have been, had the Notice of Appeal of 21 October 2003 been filed 10 days before the date of the appellant's submission, as normally occurs.

[16] In a letter from the Permanent Delegation of the European Commission dated 23 October 2003, the European Communities argued that the time-period within which it had to file its third participant's submission was contrary to Rule 24(1) of the *Working Procedures* because it was less than 25 days from the date of the re-filing of the Notice of Appeal.

[17] Letter from the Director of the Appellate Body Secretariat dated 24 October 2003.

W.2.10.2 EXTENSION OF DEADLINE FOR CIRCULATION OF APPELLATE BODY REPORT

W.2.10.2.1 *EC – Hormones* (Communication from the Appellate Body – WT/DS26/11, WT/DS48/9)

. . . I am writing to inform you that the Appellate Body will not be able to circulate its Report in this appeal by 23 December 1997, due to the exceptional nature of this case, the time needed for translation and the intervention of the Christmas holiday period. As a result, the Appellate Body Report in this appeal will be circulated to WTO Members by Friday, 16 January 1998.

W.2.10.2.2 *US – Lead and Bismuth II*, para. 8 (WT/DS138/AB/R)

On 19 March 2000, Mr. Christopher Beeby, a Member of the Division hearing this appeal, passed away . . . . Due to these same extraordinary circumstances, the participants in this appeal, the European Communities and the United States, agreed to a two week extension of the 90-day time limit for the consideration of this appeal, and thus agreed that this Report should be circulated no later than 10 May 2000.

W.2.10.2.3 *EC – Asbestos*, para. 8
(WT/DS135/AB/R)

On 20 December 2000, the Appellate Body informed the DSB that, due to the exceptional workload of the Appellate Body, and in light of the agreement of the participants, Canada and the European Communities, the Appellate Body Report in this appeal would be circulated to WTO Members no later than Monday, 12 March 2001.

W.2.10.2.4 *Thailand – H-Beams*, para. 7
(WT/DS122/AB/R)

...On 20 December 2000, the Appellate Body informed the DSB that, due to the exceptional workload of the Appellate Body, and in light of the agreement of the participants in this appeal, the Appellate Body Report in the appeal would be circulated to Members of the WTO no later than 12 March 2001.

W.2.10.2.5 *US – Upland Cotton*, para. 8
(WT/DS267/AB/R)

After consultation with the Appellate Body Secretariat, Brazil and the United States noted, in letters filed on 10 December 2004, that it would not be possible for the Appellate Body to circulate its Report in this appeal within the 90-day time limit referred to in Article 17.5 of the DSU. Brazil and the United States agreed that additional time was needed for several reasons: the issues arising in this appeal were particularly numerous and complex compared to prior appeals, which increased the burden on the Appellate Body and WTO translation services; WTO translation services were unavailable during the WTO holiday period; and the Appellate Body was likely to be considering two or three other appeals during the same period. Brazil and the United States accordingly confirmed that they would deem the Appellate Body Report in this proceeding, issued no later than 3 March 2005, to be an Appellate Body Report circulated pursuant to Article 17.5 of the DSU.

W.2.11 Rule 27 – Oral hearing. *See also* Business Confidential Information (B.4); Confidentiality (C.6)

W.2.11.1 CHANGE OF DATE

W.2.11.1.1 *EC – Bananas III*, para. 4
(WT/DS27/AB/R)

On 10 July 1997, pursuant to Rule 16(2) of the *Working Procedures*, the Government of Jamaica asked the Appellate Body to postpone the dates of the oral hearing, set out in the working schedule for 21 and 22 July 1997, to 4 and 5 August 1997.

This request was not granted as the Appellate Body was not persuaded that there were exceptional circumstances resulting in manifest unfairness to any participant or third participant that justified the postponement of the oral hearing in this appeal.

W.2.11.1.2 *US – Shrimp (Article 21.5 – Malaysia)*, para. 11
(WT/DS58/AB/RW)

On 13 August 2001, the United States requested that the Division hearing this appeal change the date of the oral hearing set out in the working schedule for this appeal. After inviting the participants to make their views known with respect to this request, the Division ruled that it would not change the date of the oral hearing. Accordingly, the oral hearing in the appeal was held on 4 September 2001....

W.2.11.2 JOINT ORAL HEARING

W.2.11.2.1 *US – 1916 Act*, para. 8
(WT/DS136/AB/R, WT/DS162/AB/R)

The oral hearing in the two appeals was held on 19 July 2000. The participants and third participants presented oral arguments and responded to questions put to them by the Members of the Division hearing the appeals.

W.2.12 Rule 28 – Written responses

W.2.12.1 *US – Gasoline*, p. 3, DSR 1996:I, p. 3 at 4
(WT/DS2/AB/R)

The oral hearing contemplated by Rule 27 of the *Working Procedures* was held on 27 and 28 March 1996. At the hearing, oral arguments were made respectively by the participants and the third participants. Questions were put to them by the Members of the Appellate Body hearing the appeal. Most of these questions were answered orally, and some were responded to in writing with the responses being furnished both to the Appellate Body and the other participants and third participants. In addition, the participants and third participants were invited to provide, and did provide, the Appellate Body and each other with final written statements of their respective positions. All the participants and third participants responded positively and punctually, which was a source of satisfaction for the Appellate Body.

W.2.12.2 *Japan – Alcoholic Beverages II*, p. 2, DSR 1996:I, p. 97 at 98
(WT/DS8/AB/R, WT/DS10/AB/R, WT/DS11/AB/R)

The oral hearing contemplated by Rule 27 of the *Working Procedures* was held on 9 September 1996. The participants presented their arguments and answered questions from the Division of the Appellate Body hearing the appeal (the "Division"). The participants answered most of these questions orally at the hearing. They answered some in writing. The Division gave each participant an opportunity to respond to the written post-hearing memoranda of the other participants.

W.2.12.3 *US – Underwear*, p. 5, DSR 1997:I, p. 11 at 13–14
(WT/DS24/AB/R)

The oral hearing contemplated by Rule 27 of the *Working Procedures* was held on 16 December 1996. At the hearing, oral arguments were made respectively by the participants and the third participant. Questions were put to them by the Division. All of these questions were answered orally. The participants and third participant did not take advantage of an invitation by the Division to submit post-hearing memoranda. On 18 December 1996, the United States submitted a written clarification and amplification of its oral response to one of the Division's questions. The next day, Costa Rica responded in writing to the United States' clarification.

W.2.12.4 *EC – Poultry*, para. 6
(WT/DS69/AB/R)

The oral hearing in the appeal was held on 9 June 1998. The participants and third participants presented oral arguments and responded to questions put to them by the Members of the Division hearing the appeal. The participants and third participants also gave oral concluding statements. At the request of the Members of the Division, the participants and third participants submitted, on 12 June 1998, written post-hearing memoranda on particular issues relating to the appeal. The participants submitted their respective written replies to these post-hearing memoranda on 15 June 1998.

W.2.12.5 *US – Shrimp*, para. 8
(WT/DS58/AB/R)

. . . At the invitation of the Appellate Body, the United States, India, Pakistan, Thailand and Malaysia filed additional submissions on certain issues arising under Article XX(b) and Article XX(g) of the GATT 1994 on 17 August 1998. The oral hearing in the appeal was held on 19–20 August 1998 . . . .

W.2.12.6 *Canada – Patent Term*, para. 8
(WT/DS170/AB/R)

. . . On 29 June 2000, Canada filed an appellant's submission. The United States filed an appellee's submission on 14 July 2000. On 25 July 2000, at the request of the Appellate Body Division hearing the appeal, the participants submitted additional memoranda on certain issues of legal interpretation arising under Articles 70.1 and 70.2 of the *TRIPS Agreement*. The Division afforded each participant an opportunity to respond to the additional memoranda submitted by the other participant.

W.2.12.7 *US – Section 211 Appropriations Act*, para. 13
(WT/DS176/AB/R)

On 2 November 2001, pursuant to Rule 28(1) of the *Working Procedure*s, the Division hearing the appeal requested that the participants submit additional written memoranda on the interpretation by domestic courts of Article 6*quinquies* of the Paris Convention (1967), or the interpretation by domestic courts of legislation incorporating Article 6*quinquies*. Both participants filed the additional written memoranda on 6 November 2001, and served these memoranda on each other. Pursuant to Rule 28(2) of the *Working Procedures*, the Division gave the participants an opportunity to respond to these memoranda at the oral hearing in this appeal.

W.2.12.8 *US – FSC (Article 21.5 – EC)*, para. 11
(WT/DS108/AB/RW)

At the oral hearing, the Division requested the United States to reduce to writing, by 28 November 2001, certain of its responses to questioning. The Division also authorized the European Communities and the third participants, if they wished, to respond in writing by 30 November 2001. In response to this request, the United States filed an additional written memorandum on 28 November 2001. The European Communities filed a response to this additional written memorandum on 30 November 2001.

W.2.13 Rule 30 – Withdrawal

W.2.13.1 WITHDRAWAL AND RE-FILING NOTICE OF APPEAL

W.2.13.1.1 *US – FSC*, para. 4
(WT/DS108/AB/R)

. . . For scheduling reasons, and pursuant to an agreement it had reached with the European Communities, on 2 November 1999 the United States notified the Chairman of the Appellate Body and the Chairman of the DSB of its decision to withdraw its 28 October 1999 notice of appeal. This withdrawal was made pursuant to Rule 30(1) of the *Working Procedures*, and was conditional upon the right of the United States to file a new notice of appeal pursuant to Rule 20 of the *Working Procedures* . . . .

W.2.13.1.2 *US – Line Pipe*, para. 13
(WT/DS202/AB/R)

On 6 November 2001, the United States notified the DSB of its intention to appeal certain issues of law covered in the Panel Report and certain legal interpretations developed by the Panel, pursuant to paragraph 4 of Article 16 of the DSU, and filed a notice of appeal pursuant to Rule 20 of the *Working Procedures for Appellate Review* (the "*Working Procedures*"). For scheduling reasons, on 13 November 2001, the United States notified the Chairman of the Appellate Body and the Chairman of the DSB of its decision to withdraw the notice of appeal filed on 6 November 2001. The withdrawal was made pursuant to Rule 30(1) of the *Working Procedures*, and was conditional on the right to file a new notice of appeal. On 19 November 2001, the United States again notified the DSB of its intention to appeal certain issues of law covered in the Panel Report and certain legal interpretations developed by the Panel, pursuant to paragraph 4 of Article 16 of the DSU, and filed a new notice of appeal pursuant to Rule 20 of the *Working Procedures* . . . .

W.2.13.1.3 *EC – Sardines*, paras. 137–138
(WT/DS231/AB/R)

...Rule 30(1) of the *Working Procedures for Appellate Review* (the "*Working Procedures*"), which governs the withdrawal of an appeal...

...accords to the appellant a broad right to withdraw an appeal at any time. This right appears, on its face, to be unfettered: an appellant is not subject to any deadline by which to withdraw its appeal; an appellant need not provide any reason for the withdrawal; and an appellant need not provide any notice thereof to other participants in an appeal. More significantly for this appeal, there is nothing in the Rule prohibiting the attachment of conditions to a withdrawal....

W.2.13.1.4 *EC – Sardines*, paras. 140–141
(WT/DS231/AB/R)

This obligation to interpret the *Working Procedures* in a way that promotes the effective resolution of disputes is complemented by the obligation of Members, set out in Article 3.10 of the DSU, to "engage in [dispute settlement] procedures in good faith in an effort to resolve the dispute." Hence, the right to withdraw an appeal must be exercised subject to these limitations, which are applicable generally to the dispute settlement process.

...While it is true that nothing in the text of Rule 30(1) explicitly permits an appellant to exercise its right subject to conditions, it is also true that nothing in the same text prohibits an appellant from doing so. As we have just explained, in our view, the right to withdraw a notice of appeal under Rule 30(1) is broad, subject only to the limitations we have described.... Rather, the correct interpretation, in our view, is that Rule 30(1) permits conditional withdrawals, unless the condition imposed undermines the "fair, prompt and effective resolution of trade disputes", or unless the Member attaching the condition is not "engag[ing] in [dispute settlement] procedures in good faith in an effort to resolve the dispute." Therefore, it is necessary to examine any such conditions attached to withdrawals on a case-by-case basis to determine whether, in fact, the particular condition in a particular case in any way obstructs the dispute settlement process, or in some way diminishes the rights of the appellee or other participants in the appeal.

W.2.13.1.5 *EC – Sardines*, paras. 145–147
(WT/DS231/AB/R)

...Thus, for the reasons explained, we find that the withdrawal of the original Notice on condition of filing a replacement Notice was appropriate and had the effect of conditionally withdrawing the original Notice.

...We agree with Peru that there may be situations where the withdrawal of an appeal on condition of refiling a new notice, and the filing thereafter of a new notice, could be abusive and disruptive. However, in such cases, we would have the right to reject the condition, and also to reject any filing of a new notice of appeal, on the grounds either that the Member seeking to file such a new notice would not be engaging in dispute settlement proceedings in good faith, or that Rule 30(1) of the *Working Procedures* must not be used to undermine the fair, prompt, and effective resolution of trade disputes....

In addition, we believe there are circumstances that, although not constituting "abusive practices", would be in violation of the DSU, and would, thus, compel us to disallow the conditional withdrawal of a notice of appeal as well as the filing of a replacement notice. For example, if the conditional withdrawal or the filing of a new notice were to take place after the 60-day deadline in Article 16.4 of the DSU for adoption of panel reports, this would effectively circumvent the requirement to file appeals within 60 days of circulation of panel reports. In such circumstances, we would reject the conditional withdrawal and the new notice of appeal.

W.2.13.1.6 *EC – Sardines*, paras. 149–150
(WT/DS231/AB/R)

...we agree with the European Communities that the replacement Notice of Appeal contains no additional grounds of appeal, and that it merely added information to the paragraphs in the initial Notice that Peru considered deficient.

...We are, however, not creating a new procedural right; we are only upholding the right to withdraw an appeal....

...In the circumstances of this case, we believe that Peru has been accorded the full measure of its due process rights, because the withdrawal of the original Notice and the filing of a replacement Notice were carried out in response to objections raised by Peru, the replacement Notice was filed in a timely manner and early in the process, and the replacement Notice contained no new or modified grounds of appeal. Also, Peru has not demonstrated that it suffered prejudice as a result. Moreover, Peru was given an adequate opportunity to address its concerns about the European Communities' actions during the course of the appeal.

W.2.13.1.7 *US – Softwood Lumber IV*, para. 6
(WT/DS257/AB/R)

On 2 October 2003, the United States notified the DSB of its intention to appeal certain issues of law covered in the Panel Report and certain legal interpretations developed by the Panel, pursuant to paragraph 4 of Article 16 of the *Understanding on Rules and Procedures Governing the Settlement of Disputes* (the "DSU"), and filed a Notice of Appeal pursuant to Rule 20 of the *Working Procedures for Appellate Review* (the "*Working Procedures*"). On 3 October 2003, for scheduling reasons, the United States withdrew its Notice of Appeal pursuant to Rule 30 of the *Working Procedures*, conditional on its right to re-file the Notice of Appeal at a later date. On 21 October 2003, the United States re-filed a substantively identical Notice of Appeal pursuant to Rule 20 of the *Working Procedures*. On that same day, the United States filed its appellant's submission in accordance with the *Working Schedule* drawn up by the Division for this appeal.

W.2.13.2 WITHDRAWAL OF APPEAL

W.2.13.2.1 *India – Autos*, paras. 15, 17–18
(WT/DS146/AB/R, WT/DS175/AB/R)

On 14 March 2002, the Appellate Body received a letter from India, in which India stated that:

> Pursuant to Rule 30(1) of the *Working Procedures for Appellate Review*, this is to inform the Appellate Body that India is withdrawing the above-mentioned appeal; oral hearing on this is scheduled for 15 March 2002. Inconvenience caused to the Appellate Body, Secretariat, the other parties and the third participants is deeply regretted.

...

Upon receipt of India's letter of 14 March 2002, the Appellate Body on the same day notified the DSB, pursuant to Rule 30(1) of the *Working Procedures*, that India "has notified the Appellate Body that India is withdrawing its appeal" in this dispute, and simultaneously informed India, the European Communities, the United States, Korea and Japan that the oral hearing in this appeal was cancelled.

In view of India's withdrawal of the appeal by its letter of 14 March 2002, the Appellate Body hereby completes its work in this appeal.

Rules of Conduct – Annex II. *See* Confidentiality (C.6); Working Procedures for Appellate Review, Rule 3 (W.2.2–3); Working Procedures for Appellate Review, Rule 8 (W.2.4); Working Procedures for Appellate Review, Rule 27 (W.2.11)

W.3 Working Procedures for Panels

W.3.1 *EC – Bananas III*, paras. 143–144
(WT/DS27/AB/R)

... Article 6.2 of the DSU requires that the *claims*, but not the *arguments*, must all be specified sufficiently in the request for the establishment of a panel in order to allow the defending party and any third parties to know the legal basis of the complaint. If a *claim* is not specified in the request for the establishment of a panel, then a faulty request cannot be subsequently "cured" by a complaining party's argumentation in its first written submission to the panel or in any other submission or statement made later in the panel proceeding.

We note, in passing, that this kind of issue could be decided early in panel proceedings, without causing prejudice or unfairness to any party or third party, if panels had detailed, standard working procedures that allowed, *inter alia*, for preliminary rulings.

W.3.2 *EC – Hormones*, para. 148
(WT/DS26/AB/R, WT/DS48/AB/R)

... The rules and procedures set forth in Appendix 4 of the DSU apply in situations in which expert review groups have been established. However, this is not the situation in this particular case. Consequently, once the panel has decided to request the opinion of individual scientific experts, there is no legal obstacle to the panel drawing up, in consultation with the parties to the dispute, *ad hoc* rules for those particular proceedings.

W.3.3 *EC – Hormones*, footnote 138 to para. 152

(WT/DS26/AB/R, WT/DS48/AB/R)

. . . the DSU, and in particular its Appendix 3, leave panels a margin of discretion to deal, always in accordance with due process, with specific situations that may arise in a particular case and that are not explicitly regulated. Within this context, an appellant requesting the Appellate Body to reverse a panel's ruling on matters of procedure must demonstrate the prejudice generated by such legal ruling.

W.3.4 *India – Patents (US)*, para. 92

(WT/DS50/AB/R)

. . . Although panels enjoy some discretion in establishing their own working procedures, this discretion does not extend to modifying the substantive provisions of the DSU. To be sure, Article 12.1 of the DSU says: "Panels shall follow the Working Procedures in Appendix 3 unless the panel decides otherwise after consulting the parties to the dispute". Yet that is *all* that it says. Nothing in the DSU gives a panel the authority either to disregard or to modify other explicit provisions of the DSU. The jurisdiction of a panel is established by that panel's terms of reference, which are governed by Article 7 of the DSU. A panel may consider only those claims that it has the authority to consider under its terms of reference. . . .

W.3.5 *India – Patents (US)*, para. 95

(WT/DS50/AB/R)

It is worth noting that, with respect to fact-finding, the dictates of due process could better be served if panels had standard working procedures that provided for appropriate factual discovery at an early stage in panel proceedings.

W.3.6 *Argentina – Textiles and Apparel*, para. 79 and footnote 68

(WT/DS56/AB/R, WT/DS56/AB/R/Corr.1)

Article 11 of the DSU does not establish time limits for the submission of evidence to a panel. Article 12.1 of the DSU directs a panel to follow the Working Procedures set out in Appendix 3 of the DSU, but at the same time authorizes a panel to do otherwise after consulting the parties to the dispute. The Working Procedures in Appendix 3 also do not establish precise deadlines for the presentation of evidence by a party to the dispute.[68] It is true that the Working Procedures "do not prohibit" submission of additional evidence after the first substantive meeting of a panel with the parties. It is also true, however, that the Working Procedures in Appendix 3 do contemplate two distinguishable stages in a proceeding before a panel. . . .

[68] As we have observed in two previous Appellate Body Reports, we believe that detailed, standard working procedures for panels would help to ensure due process and fairness in panel proceedings. See *European Communities – Regime for the Importation, Sale and Distribution of Bananas*, adopted 25 September 1997, WT/DS27/AB/R, para. 144; *India – Patent Protection for Pharmaceutical and Agricultural Chemical Products*, adopted 16 January 1998, WT/DS50/AB/R, para. 95.

W.3.7 *US – FSC (Article 21.5 – EC)*, para. 240
(WT/DS108/AB/RW)

. . . We observe, first, that the DSU and, in particular, paragraphs 5, 6 and 7 of Appendix 3 to the DSU, "contemplate two distinguishable stages in a proceeding before a panel." The "first stage" comprises the first written submissions by the parties and the first meeting of the panel, while the "second stage" consists of the second written submissions – or "rebuttal" submissions – and the second meeting with the panel. However, no provision of the DSU explicitly requires panels to hold two meetings with the parties, or to oblige the parties to submit two written submissions.

W.3.8 *US – FSC (Article 21.5 – EC)*, para. 247
(WT/DS108/AB/RW)

. . . The DSU allows panels the flexibility, in determining their procedures, to request more than one submission in advance of the first meeting, and the DSU also allows for the possibility that panels may, ultimately, hold only one meeting. . . .

W.4 WTO Agreement. *See also* GATT 1994, Language of Annex 1A incorporating the GATT 1994 into the WTO Agreement (G.2.1); Temporal Application of Rights and Obligations (T.5)

W.4.1 Preamble

W.4.1.1 *EC – Tariff Preferences*, para. 161
(WT/DS246/AB/R)

. . . the Preamble to the *WTO Agreement*, which informs all the covered agreements including the GATT 1994 (and, hence, the Enabling Clause), explicitly recognizes the "need for positive efforts designed to ensure that developing countries, and especially the least developed among them, secure a share in the growth in international trade commensurate with the needs of their economic development". The word "commensurate" in this phrase appears to leave open the possibility that developing countries may have different needs according to their levels of development and particular circumstances. The Preamble to the *WTO Agreement* further recognizes that Members' "respective needs and concerns at different levels of economic development" may vary according to the different stages of development of different Members.

Article IX – Decision-making. *See* Waivers (W.1)

W.4.2 Article XVI:1 – Relevance to GATT 1947 decisions, procedures and customary practices

W.4.2.1 *Japan – Alcoholic Beverages II*, p. 14, DSR 1996:I, p. 97 at 107–108
(WT/DS8/AB/R, WT/DS10/AB/R, WT/DS11/AB/R)

Article XVI:1 of the *WTO Agreement* and paragraph 1(b)(iv) of the language of Annex 1A incorporating the GATT 1994 into the *WTO Agreement* bring the legal history and experience under the GATT 1947 into the new realm of the WTO in a way that ensures continuity and consistency in a smooth transition from the GATT 1947 system. This affirms the importance to the Members of the WTO of the experience acquired by the CONTRACTING PARTIES to the GATT 1947 – and acknowledges the continuing relevance of that experience to the new trading system served by the WTO. . . .

W.4.3 Article XVI:4 – WTO-conformity of laws, regulations and administrative procedures. *See also* Anti-Dumping Agreement, Article 18.4 – Ensure conformity of domestic anti-dumping laws, regulations and procedures (A.3.62)

W.4.3.1 *EC – Sardines*, para. 213
(WT/DS231/AB/R)

Moreover, as general context for all the covered agreements, Article XVI:4 of the *Marrakesh Agreement Establishing the World Trade Organization* is of great significance. . . .

. . . This provision establishes a clear obligation for all WTO Members to ensure the conformity of their existing laws, regulations, and administrative procedures with the obligations in the covered agreements.

PART II

Arbitration Awards under Article 21.3(c) of the DSU

ARB.1 Mandate of Arbitrator Under Article 21.3(c)

ARB.1.1 *EC – Hormones*, paras. 32, 38
(WTDS26/15, WT/DS48/13)

There is an issue in this arbitration as to what constitutes "implementation of the recommendations and rulings of the DSB" under Article 21.3 of the DSU. . . .

. . .

It is not within my mandate under Article 21.3(c) of the DSU, to suggest ways or means to the European Communities to implement the recommendations and rulings of the Appellate Body Report and Panel Reports. My task is to determine the reasonable period of time within which implementation must be completed. Article 3.7 of the DSU provides, in relevant part, that "the first objective of the dispute settlement mechanism is *usually to secure the withdrawal of the measures concerned* if these are found to be inconsistent with the provisions of any of the covered agreements" (emphasis added). Although withdrawal of an inconsistent measure is the *preferred* means of complying with the recommendations and rulings of the DSB in a violation case, it is not necessarily the *only* means of implementation consistent with the covered agreements. An implementing Member, therefore, has a measure of discretion in choosing the *means* of implementation, as long as the means chosen are consistent with the recommendations and rulings of the DSB and with the covered agreements.

ARB.1.2 *Australia – Salmon*, para. 35
(WT/DS18/9)

I am mindful of the limits of my mandate in this arbitration. I am particularly aware that suggesting ways and means of implementation is not part of my mandate and that my task is confined to the determination of the "reasonable period of time". Choosing the means of implementation is, and should be, the prerogative of the implementing Member. . . .

ARB.1.3 *Korea – Alcoholic Beverages*, para. 45
(WT/DS75/16, WT/DS84/14)

My mandate in this arbitration relates exclusively to determining the reasonable period of time for implementation under Article 21.3(c) of the DSU. It is not within my mandate to suggest ways and means to implement the recommendations and rulings of the DSB. Choosing the means of implementation is, and should be, the prerogative of the implementing Member, as long as the means chosen are consistent with the recommendations and rulings of the DSB and the provisions of the covered agreements. I consider it, therefore, inappropriate to determine whether, and to what extent, amendments to various regulatory instruments are required before the new tax legislation comes into effect.

ARB.1.4 *Canada – Pharmaceutical Patents*, para. 40
(WT/DS114/13)

Moreover, I am of the view that whether the means of implementation chosen by a Member is consistent with that Member's obligations under the WTO covered agreements is not a question that falls within the jurisdiction of an arbitrator under Article 21.3(c). As the text of the provision makes clear, the sole task of an arbitrator under Article 21.3(c) is to determine a "reasonable period of time" in which a Member must complete implementation....

ARB.1.5 *Canada – Pharmaceutical Patents*, para. 41
(WT/DS114/13)

As an arbitrator under Article 21.3(c), certainly my responsibility includes examining closely the relevance and duration of each of the necessary steps leading to implementation to determine when a "reasonable period of time" for implementation will end. My responsibility does not, however, include in any respect a determination of the *consistency* of the proposed implementing measure with the recommendations and rulings of the DSB. The proper concern of an arbitrator under Article 21.3(c) is with *when*, not *what*.

ARB.1.6 *Canada – Pharmaceutical Patents*, para. 42
(WT/DS114/13)

...If there is any question about whether *what* a Member chooses as a means of implementation is sufficient to comply with the recommendations and rulings of the DSB, as opposed to *when* that Member proposes to do it, then Article 21.5 applies, not Article 21.3. The reasons are many and obvious. For example, if the consistency of implementing measures could also be examined during arbitrations under Article 21.3(c), then Article 21.5 would lose much of its effect. Parties would have little to lose in requesting also from an arbitrator under Article 21.3(c) an immediate ruling on the consistency of a proposed measure. Also, the more elaborate Article 21.5 procedures, involving a panel of three or five members and a report adopted by the DSB, seem more suitable than the more constrained legal domain of Article 21.3(c) for assessing the consistency of substantive obligations under WTO covered agreements.

ARB.1.7 *Canada – Pharmaceutical Patents*, para. 43
(WT/DS114/13)

. . . Accordingly, I conclude that the "reasonable period of time" for implementation that must be determined in this Article 21.3 proceeding is the "reasonable period of time" for implementing what has been *proposed by Canada*, and nothing else. Thus, Ioffer no opinion whatsoever on whether Canada's proposed regulatory change is sufficient, or whether legislative change may be required instead for consistency with the recommendations and rulings of the DSB.

ARB.1.8 *Canada – Pharmaceutical Patents*, footnote 30 to para. 52
(WT/DS114/13)

In paras. 3 and 10 of its submission, the European Communities stated that, during earlier consultations, Canada had offered to implement the recommendations and rulings of the DSB in nine months. Canada argued in the oral hearing in this arbitration that this offer had been made without prejudice during confidential consultations, and that, by submitting this evidence to me, the European Communities wasin breach of Article 4.6 of the DSU. . . . It is not clear to me that my mandate allows me to rule on whether submission by the European Communities of evidence of an earlier offer by Canada on defining "a reasonable period of time" in this case is inconsistent with Article 4.6 of the DSU. . . . Therefore, I make no ruling on Canada's argument relating to Article 4.6.

ARB.1.9 *US – Hot-Rolled Steel*, para. 30
(WT/DS184/13)

. . . I do not believe that an arbitrator acting under Article 21.3(c) of the DSU is vested with jurisdiction to make any determination of the proper scope and content of implementing legislation, and hence do not propose to deal with it. The degree of complexity of the contemplated implementing legislation may be relevant for the arbitrator, to the extent that such complexity bears upon the length of time that may reasonably be allocated to the enactment of such legislation. But the proper scope and content of anticipated legislation are, in principle, left to the implementing WTO Member to determine.

ARB.1.10 *US – Offset Act (Byrd Amendment)*, para. 48
(WT/DS217/14, WT/DS234/22)

I recall that my mandate, under Article 21.3(c), is confined to the determination of the reasonable period of time for implementation of the recommendations and rulings of the DSB. I am particularly aware that it is *not* part of my mandate to determine or even to suggest the manner in which the United States is to implement the recommendations and rulings of the DSB. . . .

ARB.1.11 *EC – Tariff Preferences*, para. 30
(WT/DS246/14)

It is, of course, beyond the scope of my mandate to determine *how* the European Communities should implement the recommendations and rulings of the DSB. It is for the European Communities to choose the method of implementation, provided that the method chosen is consistent with the relevant recommendations and rulings and with the provisions of the covered agreements. Within these limitations, the European Communities is thus entitled to bring the Drug Arrangements into conformity through whatever method it deems appropriate, be it at the same time and within the same instrument as its GSP scheme, or otherwise.

ARB.2 Prompt Compliance

ARB.2.1 *Japan – Alcoholic Beverages II*, para. 11
(WT/DS8/15, WT/DS10/15, WT/DS11/13)

Article 21(1) of the *DSU* stipulates that "*prompt compliance* with recommendations and rulings of the DSB is essential in order to ensure effective resolution of disputes to the benefit of all Members" (emphasis added). This obligation is further elaborated in Article 21(3) of the *DSU*, where it is stipulated that "if it is impracticable to comply *immediately* with the recommendations and rulings, the Member concerned shall have a reasonable period of time in which to do so" (emphasis added)....

ARB.2.2 *EC – Hormones*, para. 39
(WTDS26/15, WT/DS48/13)

Withdrawal is the *preferred* means of implementation under Article 3.7 of the DSU, and *prompt compliance* with the recommendations and rulings of the DSB is essential under Article 21.1. It would not be in keeping with the requirement of *prompt* compliance to include in the reasonable period of time, time to conduct studies or to consult experts to demonstrate the *consistency* of a measure already judged to be *inconsistent*....

ARB.2.3 *EC – Hormones*, para. 41
(WTDS26/15, WT/DS48/13)

To grant the European Communities a further two years, from the date of adoption by the DSB of the Appellate Body Report and Panel Reports, to conduct the risk assessment that was required as of 1 January 1995 would not be consistent with the provisions of the DSU requiring prompt compliance with DSB recommendations and rulings, nor with the obligations of the European Communities under the *SPS Agreement*.

ARB.2.4 *Chile – Alcoholic Beverages*, para. 38
(WT/DS87/15, WT/DS110/14)

The DSU clearly stressed the systemic interest of all WTO Members in the Member concerned complying "immediately" with the recommendations and rulings of the

DSB. Reading Articles 21.1 and 21.3 together, "prompt" compliance is, in principle, "immediate" compliance. At the same time, however, should "immediate" compliance be "impracticable" – it may be noted that the DSU does not use the far more rigorous term "impossible" – the Member concerned becomes entitled to a "reasonable period of time" to bring itself into a state of conformity with its WTO obligations. Clearly, a certain element of flexibility in respect of time is built into the notion of compliance with the recommendations and rulings of the DSB. That element would appear to be essential if "prompt" compliance, in a world of sovereign states, is to be a balanced conception and objective.

ARB.2.5 *Canada – Autos*, paras. 47–48
(WT/DS139/12, WT/DS142/12)

After examining Canada's arguments concerning the "reasonable period of time", it is clear that certain of the steps proposed by Canada for implementation of the DSB's recommendations and rulings in this dispute are not fixed either by law or by regulation. Rather, they are estimates made by the Government of Canada. The actual time taken to implement the DSB's recommendations and rulings in this case is subject to the discretion of the Government of Canada, and Canada has considerable flexibility in this regard. I recall the guidance provided by Article 21.1 of the DSU, which states that "[*p*]*rompt* compliance with recommendations or rulings of the DSB is essential in order to ensure effective resolution of disputes to the benefit of all Members." (emphasis added) Thus, it is incumbent upon the Government of Canada to use its discretion to ensure that compliance with the DSB's recommendations at issue is "prompt".

I am not persuaded that the implementation schedule proposed by Canada properly reflects the objective of "prompt" compliance. In particular, it appears that the Government of Canada could use the discretion inherent in its Regulatory Policy to implement the recommendations of the DSB in this case in a shorter period of time while still following the normal procedures for modifying regulations. . . .

ARB.2.6 *US – Section 110(5) Copyright Act*, para. 38
(WT/DS160/12)

With regard to the specific proposal of the United States, it seems to me that the United States has proposed a longer period of time than is reasonable for implementation in this case. In this regard, I note that the United States Congress appears to have flexibility with regard to the amount of time it takes to enact legislation. In response to questioning at the oral hearing, the United States acknowledged that Congress has "a fair amount of flexibility" in the scheduling of its work. Furthermore, the "vast majority" of steps in the legislative process, according to the United States, are not subject to mandatory time-frames. Thus, when the United States Congress wants to act promptly on a matter, its normal legislative procedures allow it the flexibility to do so. In my view, the time-period proposed by the United States does not take sufficient account of this flexibility.

ARB.2.7 *Argentina – Hides and Leather*, para. 49
(WT/DS155/10)

A final point that should be made is that to build into the concept of a "reasonable period of time" to comply with DSB recommendations and rulings, time or opportunity to control and manage economic or social conditions which antedate or are contemporaneous with the adoption of the WTO-inconsistent governmental measure, may, in the generality of instances, be to defer to an indefinitely receding future the duty of compliance. The implications for the multilateral trading system as we know it today, of such an interpretation of "reasonable period of time" for compliance are clear and far-reaching and ominous. Such an interpretation would tend to reduce the fundamental duty of "immediate" or "prompt" compliance to a figure of speech.

ARB.2.8 *Chile – Price Band System*, para. 33
(WT/DS207/13)

Article 21.1 of the DSU, which provides relevant context for understanding the remaining paragraphs of Article 21, states that "[p]rompt compliance with recommendations or rulings of the DSB is essential in order to ensure effective resolution of disputes to the benefit of all Members." Recognizing that "prompt compliance" may not always be "immediate" compliance, however, the chapeau of Article 21.3 provides, "If it is impracticable to comply immediately with the recommendations and rulings [of the DSB], the Member concerned shall have a reasonable period of time in which to do so." The allowance of a "reasonable period of time" for implementation, therefore, is premised on it being impracticable for the Member to comply "immediately".

ARB.2.9 *US – Offset Act (Byrd Amendment)*, para. 40
(WT/DS217/14, WT/DS234/22)

Article 21.3 . . . makes clear that "prompt compliance", in principle, implies "immediate[]" compliance. Thus, a "reasonable period of time" for implementation is not available unconditionally to an implementing Member. Rather, an implementing Member is entitled to a reasonable period of time for implementation only where, pursuant to Article 21.3, "it is impracticable to comply immediately with the recommendations and rulings" of the DSB.

ARB.2.10 *US – Oil Country Tubular Goods Sunset Reviews*, para. 27
(WT/DS268/12)

. . . whatever be the method of implementation chosen by the implementing Member, that Member must take advantage of the flexibility and discretion available within its legal and administrative system to implement the recommendations and rulings of the DSB as speedily as possible.

ARB.3 Withdrawal or Modification of the Measure

ARB.3.1 General

ARB.3.1.1 *Australia – Salmon*, para. 30
(WT/DS18/9)

Taken together, these provisions clearly define the rights and obligations of the Member concerned with respect to the implementation of the recommendations and rulings of the DSB. In the absence of a mutually agreed solution, the first objective is usually the *immediate withdrawal* of the measure judged to be inconsistent with any of the covered agreements. Only if it is impracticable to do so, is the Member concerned entitled to a reasonable period of time for implementation. . . .

ARB.3.1.2 *Argentina – Hides and Leather*, para. 40
(WT/DS155/10)

. . . Implementation, in essence, consists of bringing the measure held to be inconsistent with the obligations of the WTO Member concerned under particular provisions of a particular covered agreement, into conformity with those same provisions. Article 3.7 of the DSU stresses that "the *first objective* of the dispute settlement mechanism is usually to secure *withdrawal of the WTO-inconsistent measure*". (emphasis added) The DSU goes on to state that compensation may be resorted to only if "the immediate *withdrawal* of the measure is impracticable and then only as "a *temporary* measure *pending the withdrawal of the WTO-inconsistent measure*." (emphasis added) Suspension of concessions or other obligations under the covered agreements is explicitly designated as a "*last resort*" mode of compliance "subject to authorization by the DSB", but it too remains a "*temporary*" remedy allowed under Article 22.8 of the DSU only until the non-conforming measure is "*removed*" or a "*mutually satisfactory solution*" is achieved. Moreover, and at any rate, Article 22.1 of the DSU cautions that neither compensation nor suspension of concessions or other obligations is to be "preferred to full implementation of a recommendation to bring a measure into conformity with the covered agreements." . . .

ARB.3.1.3 *US – Offset Act (Byrd Amendment)*, para. 50
(WT/DS217/14, WT/DS234/22)

Thus, in my view, the United States may choose either to *withdraw* or *modify* the CDSOA so as to bring it into conformity with its obligations under the covered agreements. I therefore do not see any basis for the claim of the Complaining Parties that deliberations as to different, WTO-consistent methods for distributing collected anti-dumping or countervailing duties should *not* be considered as part of the implementation process.

ARB.3.1.4 *US – Offset Act (Byrd Amendment)*, para. 53
(WT/DS217/14, WT/DS234/22)

With respect to the proposal by the United States Executive branch to the United States Congress, I do not believe that it would be appropriate for an arbitrator acting under Article 21.3(c) to attach any particular weight to any individual proposal. As I and other arbitrators have said, it is not for the arbitrator acting under Article 21.3(c) to impose any particular means for implementing the recommendations and rulings of the DSB. The means of implementation is left to the discretion of the implementing Member, which is bound to implement the recommendations and rulings of the DSB within "the shortest period possible within the legal system of the Member." Thus, my task is not to look at *how* implementation will be carried out, but to determine *when* it is to be done. For this reason, individual proposals under consideration by the implementing Member cannot be determinative in my inquiry.

ARB.3.2 Panel Recommendations

ARB.3.2.1 *US – Offset Act (Byrd Amendment)*, para. 52
(WT/DS217/14, WT/DS234/22)

With respect to the suggestion of the Panel that the United States repeal the CDSOA, I note, first, that the Panel, in making its suggestion, also recognized that "there could potentially be a number of ways in which the United States could bring the CDSOA into conformity". Moreover, although the suggestion by the Panel, as part of a panel report adopted by the DSB, could serve as a useful contribution to the decisionmaking process in the implementing Member, I do not believe that the existence of such a suggestion ultimately affects the well-established principle that "choosing the means of implementation is, and should be, the prerogative of the implementing Member".

ARB.4 "Reasonable Period of Time"

ARB.4.1 General

ARB.4.1.1 *Canada – Pharmaceutical Patents*, para. 45
(WT/DS114/13)

. . . Further, and significantly, a "reasonable period of time" is not available unconditionally. Article 21.3 makes it clear that a reasonable period of time is available for implementation only "[i]f it is impracticable to comply *immediately* with the recommendations and rulings" of the DSB. Implicit in the wording of Article 21.3 seems to me to be the assumption that, ordinarily, Members will comply with recommendations and rulings of the DSB "immediately". The "reasonable period of time" to which Article 21.3 refers is, thus, a period of time in what is implicitly not the ordinary circumstance, but a circumstance in which "it is impracticable to comply *immediately* . . . ".

ARB.4.1.2 *Canada – Pharmaceutical Patents*, para. 63
(WT/DS114/13)

. . . As I see it, the commitment made by Canada to the DSB to comply fully with the recommendations and rulings of the DSB in this case, and thereby to fulfill

Canada's international obligations as a Member of the WTO, should give rise to, if not equal, then comparable, urgency in Canada. Whatever their disagreements on a "reasonable period of time" for implementation in this dispute, doubtless Canada and the European Communities will agree on this: the desire of a WTO Member to comply with its treaty obligations under the *WTO Agreement* should occasion, domestically, some modicum of dispatch.

ARB.4.1.3 *US – Hot-Rolled Steel*, para. 26
(WT/DS184/13)

Although, in [paragraphs 84 and 85 of the Appellate Body Report] the Appellate Body dealt with the *Anti-Dumping Agreement*, and not the DSU, the essence of "reasonableness" so articulated is, in my view, equally pertinent for an arbitrator faced with the task of determining what constitutes "a reasonable period of time" in the context of the DSU.

ARB.4.1.4 *US – Hot-Rolled Steel*, para. 39
(WT/DS184/13)

... It appears to me that whether the actions of the DSB in those two instances have any precedential value in respect of the present arbitration proceedings, is open to substantial debate. The present proceedings have been precipitated precisely by the failure of the parties to the dispute to reach an agreement on a reasonable period of time to comply under Article 21.3(b) of the DSU.

ARB.4.1.5 *US – Offset Act (Byrd Amendment)*, para. 42
(WT/DS217/14, WT/DS234/22)

The final sentence of Article 21.3(c), moreover, makes clear that the "reasonable period of time" cannot be determined in the abstract, but rather has to be established on the basis of the particular circumstances of each case. I therefore agree, in principle, with the Arbitrator in *US – Hot-Rolled Steel*, who found that the term "reasonable" should be interpreted as including "the notions of flexibility and balance", in a manner which allows for account to be taken of the particular circumstances of each case....

ARB.4.1.6 *EC – Tariff Preferences*, para. 25
(WT/DS246/14)

In determining the reasonable period of time for implementation, I am guided by several provisions of the DSU, including Article 21 in particular. To begin with, Article 21.1 provides that "[p]rompt compliance with recommendations or rulings of the DSB is essential in order to ensure effective resolution of disputes to the benefit of all Members". This is consistent with the expectation in Article 21.3... that compliance will be immediate, unless this is impracticable....

ARB.4.2 15 month guideline

ARB.4.2.1 *EC – Hormones*, para. 25
(WT/DS26/15, WT/DS48/13)

The ordinary meaning of the terms of Article 21.3(c) indicates that 15 months is a "guideline for the arbitrator", and not a rule. This guideline is stated expressly to be that "the reasonable period of time ... *should not exceed* 15 months from the date of adoption of a panel or Appellate Body report" (emphasis added). In other words, the 15-month guideline is an outer limit or a maximum in the usual case. Forexample, when implementation can be effected by administrative means, the reasonable period of time should be considerably shorter than 15 months. However, the reasonable period of time could be shorter or longer, depending upon the particular circumstances, as specified in Article 21.3(c).

ARB.4.2.2 *Australia – Salmon*, para. 30
(WT/DS18/9)

... When the reasonable period of time is determined through arbitration, the guideline for the arbitrator is that it should not exceed 15 months from the date of adoption of the panel and/or Appellate Body reports. This does not mean, however, that the arbitrator is obliged to grant 15 months in all cases. The reasonable period of time may be shorter or longer, depending upon the particular circumstances.

ARB.4.2.3 *Korea – Alcoholic Beverages*, para. 36
(WT/DS75/16, WT/DS84/14)

... When the reasonable period of time is determined through arbitration, the guideline for the arbitrator is that it should not exceed 15 months from the date of adoption of the panel and/or Appellate Body reports. This does not mean, however, that the arbitrator is obliged to grant 15 months in all cases. The reasonable period of time may be shorter or longer, depending upon the particular circumstances.

ARB.4.2.4 *Chile – Alcoholic Beverages*, para. 39
(WT/DS87/15, WT/DS110/14)

... What Article 21.3(c) of the DSU provides arbitrators with is a "*guide*line", not a fixed command, that the reasonable period should be not more than 15 months from the date of adoption by the DSB of the pertinent Panel and Appellate Body Reports. Article 21.3(c) evidently contemplates a case-specific approach and authorizes the consideration of the "particular circumstances" of a given case, which may warrant a longer or shorter period.

ARB.4.2.5 *Canada – Pharmaceutical Patents*, para. 45
(WT/DS114/13)

I note that the 15-month period is a "guideline", and not an average, or usual, period. It is expressed also as a *maximum* period, subject only to any "particular circumstances" mentioned in the second sentence....

ARB.4.2.6 *Canada – Autos*, para. 39
(WT/DS139/12, WT/DS142/12)

. . . when the "reasonable period of time" is determined through arbitration, the guideline for the arbitrator is that this period should not exceed 15 months from the date of adoption of the panel report and/or the Appellate Body report. This does not mean, however, that the arbitrator is obliged to grant 15 months in all cases. Article 21.3(c) makes clear that the "reasonable period of time" may be shorter or longer, depending upon the "particular circumstances". The "particular circumstances" of a dispute may influence the determination of what is a "reasonable period of time" for implementation, as has been stated by previous Arbitrators.

ARB.4.2.7 *US – Hot-Rolled Steel*, para. 25
(WT/DS184/13)

. . . I do not see any basis for reading the 15-month guideline as establishing a fixed maximum or "*outer* limit" for "a reasonable period of time." . . .

ARB.4.2.8 *Chile – Price Band System*, para. 34
(WT/DS207/13)

Article 21.3(c) provides for an arbitrator a "guideline" of a maximum of 15 months from the date of adoption of the panel and Appellate Body reports when establishing a "reasonable period of time" for implementation. Notwithstanding this "guideline", I must ultimately be informed, as Article 21.3(c) instructs, by the "particular circumstances" of a given case, which may counsel in favour of shorter or longer periods. . . .

ARB.4.2.9 *US – Offset Act (Byrd Amendment)*, para. 41
(WT/DS217/14, WT/DS234/22)

The 15-month period set forth in Article 21.3(c) is a "guideline", expressed as a maximum period, and does not represent an average, or usual, period. Rather, as previous arbitrators have recognized, it is ultimately the relevant "particular circumstances" that influence what is a "reasonable period of time" for implementation.

ARB.4.2.10 *EC – Tariff Preferences*, para. 27
(WT/DS246/14)

India has argued that the implementing Member – in this case, the European Communities – bears the burden of demonstrating that the period it proposes is reasonable and that "the already great burden becomes even greater" if this period is more than 15 months. In my view, the European Communities must demonstrate that the period it proposes is reasonable; but I do not find it necessary in this arbitration to determine whether the burden of proof becomes greater if the period proposed is more than 15 months. I have found the evidence and arguments presented by both the European Communities and India very helpful in determining whether, in the particular circumstances of this case, the period of time for implementation should be 15 months or a shorter or longer period.

ARB.4.3 Shortest period possible within a Member's legal system

ARB.4.3.1 *EC – Hormones*, para. 26
(WTDS26/15, WT/DS48/13)

Article 21.3(c) also should be interpreted in its context and in light of the object and purpose of the DSU. Relevant considerations in this respect include other provisions of the DSU, including, in particular, Articles 21.1 and 3.3.... Read in context, it is clear that the reasonable period of time, as determined under Article 21.3(c), should be the shortest period possible within the legal system of the Member to implement the recommendations and rulings of the DSB. In the usual case, this should not be greater than 15 months, but could also be less.

ARB.4.3.2 *Korea – Alcoholic Beverages*, para. 42
(WT/DS75/16, WT/DS84/14)

Although the reasonable period of time should be the shortest period possible within the legal system of the Member to implement the recommendations and rulings of the DSB, this does not require a Member, in my view, to utilize an *extraordinary* legislative procedure, rather than the *normal* legislative procedure, in every case. Taking into account all of the circumstances of the present case, I believe that it is reasonable to allow Korea to follow its *normal* legislative procedure for the consideration and adoption of a tax bill with budgetary implications....

ARB.4.3.3 *Chile – Alcoholic Beverages*, para. 39
(WT/DS87/15, WT/DS110/14)

...Thus, the shortest period of time *theoretically* possible for the completion of the legislative process, even assuming the bill enjoys the necessary parliamentary majority from the beginning and is never the subject of serious debate, is not the *sole* criterion that I should take into account in determining the reasonable period....

ARB.4.3.4 *Canada – Pharmaceutical Patents*, para. 47
(WT/DS114/13)

Based on the wording of Articles 21.3, and on the context provided in Articles 3.3, 21.1 and 21.4 of the DSU, I agree with the arbitrator in *European Communities – Hormones* that "the reasonable period of time, as determined under Article 21.3(c), should be the shortest period possible within the legal system of the Member to implement the recommendations and rulings of the DSB."...

ARB.4.3.5 *US – Section 110(5) Copyright Act*, para. 32
(WT/DS160/12)

The "shortest period possible within the legal system of the Member" generally refers to the "normal legislative procedures", and does not require a Member to utilize an "*extraordinary* legislative procedure" in every case.

ARB.4.3.6 *Chile – Price Band System*, para. 34
(WT/DS207/13)

. . . the controlling principle is that the "reasonable period of time" should be "the shortest period possible within the legal system of the Member to implement the relevant recommendations and rulings of the DSB", in the light of the "particular circumstances" of the dispute.

ARB.4.3.7 *Chile – Price Band System*, para. 51
(WT/DS207/13)

I referred earlier to the special status of the PBS in Chile's agricultural policy and the consequent difficulties imposed on the formulation of legislation to implement the recommendations and rulings of the DSB in this case. Having recognized the need for thorough discussion on any implementing measure modifying the PBS, it would not be right for me to *expect* that the President of Chile will necessarily seek truncated review of such a measure in the very legislative body intended for deliberation and debate on behalf of the public it represents. This severe reduction of legislative deliberation is precisely what Argentina seeks when suggesting that I factor the strict time limits of the "urgency procedure" into my determination of the "reasonable period of time" for implementation. Therefore, I find it unreasonable for me to *expect* or assume that Chile will necessarily make use of the "flexibility" arguably provided by the extraordinary "urgency procedure" when implementing legislation that modifies the PBS. Indeed, there is sufficient flexibility within the *ordinary* legislative procedure of Chile to enable it to implement the recommendations and rulings of the DSB in this case within a time frame of less than the 18 months which it seeks.

ARB.4.3.8 *US – Offset Act (Byrd Amendment)*, para. 43
(WT/DS217/14, WT/DS234/22)

I recall that the "shortest period possible within the legal system of the Member" generally refers, in the case of implementation by legislative means, to normal legislative procedures. Therefore, I concur with the view of previous arbitrators that, when implementing recommendations and rulings of the DSB, a Member is not required to have recourse to extraordinary legislative procedures in every case.

ARB.4.3.9 *US – Offset Act (Byrd Amendment)*, para. 74
(WT/DS217/14, WT/DS234/22)

. . . it is . . . important to recall that an implementing Member, in principle, is to use its "normal" legislative procedure and should not be required to utilize "extraordinary legislative procedures" in every case. In the light of this principle, I confirm that I do not, in this case, propose the United States to utilize extraordinary legislative procedures. . . .

ARB.4.3.10 *EC – Tariff Preferences*, para. 26
(WT/DS246/14)

Reading Article 21.3(c) together with Article 21.1, and referring for guidance to the Awards issued in previous arbitrations under Article 21.3(c), it is clear that the reasonable period of time should be "the shortest period possible within the legal system of the Member to implement the relevant recommendations and rulings of the DSB", in the light of the "particular circumstances" of the dispute....

ARB.4.3.11 *EC – Tariff Preferences*, para. 31
(WT/DS246/14)

However, as the European Communities itself acknowledges, the relevant recommendations and rulings of the DSB require the European Communities to bring into conformity solely the Drug Arrangements, and not any other part of the European Communities' GSP scheme. Therefore, my determination as to the reasonable period of time for implementation in this arbitration must have regard only to the shortest period possible within the legal system of the European Communities to bring the Drug Arrangements into conformity with its WTO obligations. The mere fact that the European Communities has decided to incorporate the task of implementation within the larger objective of reforming its overall GSP scheme cannot lead to a determination of a shorter, or longer, period of time. In other words, my task is not to determine the reasonable period of time for reforming the overall GSP scheme. Rather, my determination must be confined to the reasonable period of time for implementing the recommendations and rulings of the DSB with respect to the Drug Arrangements.

ARB.4.3.12 *US – Oil Country Tubular Goods Sunset Reviews*, para. 27
(WT/DS268/12)

... whatever be the method of implementation chosen by the implementing Member, that Member must take advantage of the flexibility and discretion available within its legal and administrative system to implement the recommendations and rulings of the DSB as speedily as possible.

ARB.5 "Particular Circumstances"

ARB.5.1 General

ARB.5.1.1 *Japan – Alcoholic Beverages II*, para. 11
(WT/DS8/15, WT/DS10/15, WT/DS11/13)

... Article 21(3)(c) of the *DSU* also stipulates, however, that the "reasonable period of time" may be shorter or longer than 15 months, depending upon the "particular circumstances". The term, "particular circumstances", is not defined in the *DSU*.

ARB.5.1.2 *Japan – Alcoholic Beverages II*, para. 27
(WT/DS8/15, WT/DS10/15, WT/DS11/13)

As stated in Article 3(2) of the *DSU*, the dispute settlement system of the WTO is a central element in providing security and predictability to the multilateral trading system. Therefore, all WTO Members have a strong interest in prompt compliance with and full implementation of the recommendations and rulings of the DSB. This interest is clearly reflected in the provisions of the *DSU*, and in particular in Article 21(3)(c), which stipulates that a "reasonable period of time" for implementation should not exceed 15 months unless there are "particular circumstances" justifying a longer or shorter period. In this case, I am not persuaded that the "particular circumstances" advanced by Japan and the United States justify a departure from the 15-month "guideline" either way....

ARB.5.1.3 *Australia – Salmon*, para. 38
(WT/DS18/9)

It has been pointed out that the arbitrator is not obliged to grant 15 months as the reasonable period for implementation in all cases. "Particular circumstances" justifying a longer or shorter period must be taken into account on a case-by-case basis. In the present case, there are certain considerations which persuade me that the reasonable period of time should be significantly less than 15 months....

ARB.5.1.4 *Chile – Alcoholic Beverages*, para. 39
(WT/DS87/15, WT/DS110/14)

The concept of reasonableness, which is, of course, built into the notion of "a reasonable period of time" for implementation, inherently involves taking into account the relevant circumstances. In some cases these circumstances may be singular or few in number but in other cases they may be multiple. Determination of a "reasonable period of time" is not, in principle, appropriately carried out by ascribing decisive or exclusive relevance to one single or even a few *a priori* factors and eschewing consideration of everything else as non-pertinent....

ARB.5.1.5 *Canada – Pharmaceutical Patents*, para. 48
(WT/DS114/13)

The "particular circumstances" mentioned in Article 21.3 are, therefore, those that can influence what the shortest period possible for implementation may be within the legal system of the implementing Member. Conceivably, several such "particular circumstances", depending on the facts, could be relevant to a case such as the one before me.

ARB.5.1.6 *Canada – Pharmaceutical Patents*, para. 52
(WT/DS114/13)

...There may well be other "particular circumstances" that may be relevant to a particular case. However, in my view, the "particular circumstances" mentioned in Article 21.3 do *not* include factors unrelated to an assessment of the shortest period possible for implementation within the legal system of a Member. Any such unrelated factors are irrelevant to determining the "reasonable period of time" for implementation. For example, as others have ruled in previous Article 21.3 arbitrations, any proposed period intended to allow for the "structural adjustment" of an affected domestic industry will not be relevant to an assessment of the legal process. The determination of a "reasonable period of time" must be a legal judgement based on an examination of relevant legal requirements.

ARB.5.1.7 *Canada – Autos*, paras. 54–55
(WT/DS139/12, WT/DS142/12)

Canada has placed great emphasis on the "significant implications" that implementation of the DSB's recommendations in this case will have for the "administration of Canada's customs regime"....

Regardless of Canada's specific argument on this issue, I wish to emphasize that factors unrelated to an assessment of the shortest period of time possible for a Member to implement, within its legal system, the recommendations and rulings of the DSB in a particular case are irrelevant to determining the "reasonable period of time" under Article 21.3(c) of the DSU. While it might be more convenient for Canada to implement the DSB's recommendations in this case on the same timeline as it has planned for the reform of its customs administration regime, this factor is not relevant in determining the "shortest period possible" within Canada's legal system for implementation of the DSB's recommendations.... the determination of the "reasonable period of time" for implementation must be a legal judgment based on an examination of relevant legal requirements.

ARB.5.1.8 *US – 1916 Act*, para. 40
(WT/DS136/11, WT/DS162/14)

The United States also urges me to take account of the "additional special circumstances" involved in this case, that is, the need for a period of transition to a new President, a new Administration, and a new Congress, and the accompanying shifts in the balance of power between the two principal political parties in the United States. Even allowing for these unusual circumstances, I note that what is significant for the case at hand is that the first session of the 107th United States Congress has been in progress since 3 January 2001. It is, therefore, possible for the United States to introduce a legislative proposal and have it passed by the Congress as speedily as possible, using, as I have stated earlier, all the flexibility available within its normal legislative procedures.

ARB.5.1.9 *Canada – Patent Term*, paras. 59–60
(WT/DS170/10)

While Canada invokes the controversial character of any amendment to its *Patent Act* which will have an impact on the Canadian health care system, the United States emphasizes that under Canada's parliamentary system, the Government of Canada controls the majority in both Houses of Parliament, the House of Commons and the Senate. According to the United States, with this majority, the government controls the legislative process, and sets the timetable for both Houses of Parliament from start to finish; the Government of Canada can essentially pass any legislation it wishes in whatever time it likes.

It may well be possible that Canada's political system and the actual distribution of seats among the political parties in Canada's Parliament facilitate the passage of legislative initiatives taken by the present Canadian government. I am, however, very reluctant to take these factors into account in determining the "reasonable period of time". These factors vary from country to country, and from constitution to constitution. Even within a given country, they will change over time. In addition, their evaluation will often be difficult and highly speculative. I also note that such factors have never been considered as "particular circumstances" in any of the earlier awards under Article 21.3 (c) of the DSU. Thus, the political factors mentioned in the preceding paragraph, and invoked by the United States in support of its request for a "reasonable period of time" of six months, are not relevant to my task.

ARB.5.1.10 *Chile – Price Band System*, para. 34
(WT/DS207/13)

Article 21.3(c) provides for an arbitrator a "guideline" of a maximum of 15 months from the date of adoption of the panel and Appellate Body reports when establishing a "reasonable period of time" for implementation. Notwithstanding this "guideline", I must ultimately be informed, as Article 21.3(c) instructs, by the "particular circumstances" of a given case, which may counsel in favour of shorter or longer periods. . . .

ARB.5.2 Actions taken since DSB adoption of Report(s)

ARB.5.2.1 *US – Section 110(5) Copyright Act*, para. 46
(WT/DS160/12)

. . . Article 21.3(c) makes clear that the "reasonable period of time" for implementation is measured as from the "date of adoption of a panel or Appellate Body report". I recall that Article 21.1 establishes that "prompt compliance" is essential in order to ensure effective resolution of disputes to the benefit of all Members. Clearly, timeliness is of the essence. Thus, an implementing Member must use the time after adoption of a panel and/or Appellate Body report to begin to implement the recommendations and rulings of the DSB. Arbitrators will scrutinize very carefully the actions an implementing Member takes in respect of implementation during the period after adoption of a panel and/or Appellate Body report and prior to any arbitration proceeding. If it is perceived by an arbitrator that an implementing Member has not adequately begun implementation after adoption so as to effect "prompt compliance", it is to be expected that the arbitrator will take this into account in determining the "reasonable period of time".

ARB.5.2.2 *Chile – Price Band System*, paras. 43, 45
(WT/DS207/13)

. . . A Member's obligation to implement the recommendations and rulings of the DSB is triggered by the DSB's adoption of the relevant panel and/or Appellate Body reports. Although Article 21.3 acknowledges circumstances where *immediate* implementation is "impracticable", in my view the implementation process should not be prolonged through a Member's inaction (or insufficient action) in the first months following adoption. In other words, whether or not a Member is able to *complete* implementation promptly, it must at the very least promptly *commence* and continue concrete steps towards implementation. Otherwise, inaction or dilatory conduct by the implementing Member would exacerbate the nullification or impairment of the rights of other Members caused by the inconsistent measure. It is for this reason that arbitral awards under Article 21.3(c) calculate "reasonable period[s] of time" as from the date of adoption of panel and/or Appellate Body reports.

...

...I realize the value of thorough pre-legislative activities, particularly so as to ensure passage of final legislation and thereby achieve "full implementation". I also recognize that consultations, discussions and deliberations, by their very nature, are indeterminate and cannot be subject to arbitrary time limits, particularly because the extensiveness of these activities may change with each measure in issue. Nevertheless, for purposes of calculating a "reasonable period of time" under Article 21.3(c), such activities should not be assumed to be without reasonable limits. I do not suggest that Chile's pre-legislative activities in this case should necessarily have concluded by this time; but, in my view, this phase should reasonably have proceeded further than it has.

ARB.5.3 Complexity of implementing measures

ARB.5.3.1 *US – 1916 Act*, para. 36
(WT/DS136/11, WT/DS162/14)

At the oral hearing, I enquired whether, although it is not within the mandate of an arbitrator to determine or suggest the precise means of implementation, it is necessary for the arbitrator to know the scope and complexity of the implementing measure, as distinguished from the complexity of the Member's legislative process, in order to assess the "reasonable period of time" required to put in place the proposed implementing measure.... The United States explained, however, that regardless of the complexity of the legislation required to implement the rulings and recommendations of the DSB, this would be taken care of through the normal legislative process, and the United States does not argue for or seek any additional time on the basis of the scope, content or complexity of the implementing legislation in this case. In view of the explicit acknowledgement of the United States that it is not relying on the complexity of the implementing legislation as a particular circumstance to justify or lengthen the period of time needed for implementation in this case, it is not necessary for me to examine this issue.

ARB.5.3.2 *Canada – Pharmaceutical Patents*, para. 50
(WT/DS114/13)

Likewise, the *complexity* of the proposed implementation can be a relevant factor. If implementation is accomplished through extensive new regulations affecting many sectors of activity, then adequate time will be required to draft the changes, consult affected parties, and make any consequent modifications as needed. On the other hand, if the proposed implementation is the simple repeal of a single provision of perhaps a sentence or two, then, obviously, less time will be needed for drafting, consulting, and finalizing the procedure. To be sure, complexity is not merely a matter of the number of pages in a proposed regulation; yet it seems reasonable to assume that, in most cases, the shorter a proposed regulation, the less its likely complexity.

ARB.5.3.3 *US – Hot-Rolled Steel*, para. 30
(WT/DS184/13)

. . . I do not believe that an arbitrator acting under Article 21.3(c) of the DSU is vested with jurisdiction to make any determination of the proper scope and content of implementing legislation, and hence do not propose to deal with it. The degree of complexity of the contemplated implementing legislation may be relevant for the arbitrator, to the extent that such complexity bears upon the length of time that may reasonably be allocated to the enactment of such legislation. But the proper scope and content of anticipated legislation are, in principle, left to the implementing WTO Member to determine.

ARB.5.3.4 *US – Offset Act (Byrd Amendment)*, para. 60
(WT/DS217/14, WT/DS234/22)

Similarly, the need to distinguish, in the light of Panel and the Appellate Body findings in this dispute, between WTO-consistent and WTO-inconsistent implementation options would appear to be the typical content, and concomitant aspect, of every legislative process aiming at implementing recommendations and rulings of the DSB. I do agree with previous arbitrators that, in principle, the complex nature of implementing measures can be a relevant factor for the determination of the reasonable period of time. Nevertheless, I do not believe that the need to take into account international treaty obligations in the process of drafting implementing legislation, in and of itself, gives rise to the kind of complexity that would warrant additional time for implementation. *Each and every* piece of legislation enacted with a view to implementing recommendations and rulings of the DSB must be designed and drafted in the light of the implementing Member's rights and obligations under the covered agreements. If the need to distinguish between WTO-consistent and WTO-inconsistent implementation options were to qualify, *per se*, as "complexity", and, therefore, were to give rise to "particular circumstances" relevant for the determination of the reasonable period of time, then *every* implementation measure under consideration in proceedings pursuant to Article 21.3(c) would have to be considered complex. In other words, "complexity" would not be a "particular circumstance"; rather, it would be a standard aspect of every implementation.

ARB.5.4 Complexity of implementation process

ARB.5.4.1 *EC – Bananas III*, para. 19
(WT/DS27/15)

The Complaining Parties have not persuaded me that there are "particular circumstances" in this case to justify a shorter period of time than stipulated by the guideline in Article 21.3(c) of the DSU. At the same time, the complexity of the implementation process, demonstrated by the European Communities, would suggest adherence to the guideline, with a slight modification, so that the "reasonable period" of time for implementation would expire by 1 January 1999.

ARB.5.4.2 *EC – Hormones*, para. 39
(WTDS26/15, WT/DS48/13)

. . . It would not be in keeping with the requirement of *prompt* compliance to include in the reasonable period of time, time to conduct studies or to consult experts to demonstrate the *consistency* of a measure already judged to be *inconsistent*. That cannot be considered as "particular circumstances" justifying a longer period than the guideline suggested in Article 21.3(c). This is not to say that the commissioning of scientific studies or consultations with experts *cannot* form part of a domestic implementation process in a particular case. However, such considerations are not pertinent to the determination of the reasonable period of time.

ARB.5.4.3 *EC – Hormones*, paras. 41–42
(WTDS26/15, WT/DS48/13)

To grant the European Communities a further two years, from the date of adoption by the DSB of the Appellate Body Report and Panel Reports, to conduct the risk assessment that was required as of 1 January 1995 would not be consistent with the provisions of the DSU requiring prompt compliance with DSB recommendations and rulings, nor with the obligations of the European Communities under the *SPS Agreement*.

For the foregoing reasons, it would not be proper to include in the reasonable period of time granted to the European Communities under Article 21.3(c) of the DSU, an initial phase of two years for the conduct and completion of scientific studies to determine if there is a risk to human health from hormone-treated beef.

ARB.5.4.4 *US – 1916 Act*, para. 38
(WT/DS136/11, WT/DS162/14)

In my view, factors such as the volume of legislation brought before the United States Congress, and the high percentage of bills that never become law, are not relevant to my determination of the "reasonable period of time" for implementation of the recommendations and rulings of the DSB in this case. Information of this nature may be of general interest in examining how a legislative system operates in practice, not only in the United States, but in many other countries as well. What is relevant for my determination in this case is the treaty obligations explicitly undertaken by Members pursuant to the covered agreements.... In view of these fundamental obligations assumed by the Members of the WTO, factors such as the volume of legislation proposed, and the high percentage of bills that never become law, cannot be considered to extend the period of time needed for implementation. As for the argument that legislation passed by the United States Congress is usually passed at the end of the legislative session, this again may be the usual practice in the United States Congress, but it is not the outcome of a legal requirement. Where an international treaty obligation is required to be complied with in the shortest period of time possible, as in this case, this cannot be a relevant consideration for extending the period of implementation.

ARB.5.4.5 *US – 1916 Act*, para. 39
(WT/DS136/11, WT/DS162/14)

Turning to the complexity of the United States' legislative process, I note that the United States has explained, in sufficient detail, the multiple and time-consuming steps involved in the enactment of legislation within the specific context of the legislative system of the United States. It is generally accepted that certain of these steps are not required by law, and that the majority of these steps are not subject to compulsory minimum time limits. In other words, the United States' legislative process, while complex, is characterized by a considerable degree of flexibility. That this flexibility is exercised to achieve the prompt passage of legislation when this is considered necessary and appropriate is revealed by the fact that bills have been passed by the United States Congress within short periods of time, using its "normal" legislative process. The United States has stated that it "will make every effort to promptly implement the DSB's recommendations and rulings" in this case. Since this is a case where the United States has to enact a piece of legislation to bring it into compliance with its international treaty obligations under the covered agreements, the United States Congress may reasonably be expected to use all the flexibility available within its normal legislative procedures to enact the required legislation as speedily as possible.

ARB.5.4.6 *Chile – Price Band System*, para. 38
(WT/DS207/13)

Chile identifies a "pre-legislative" phase followed by an extensive lawmaking procedure through which any law implementing the DSB's recommendations and rulings must pass. The multi-step process of legislating, which involves the participation of several legislative committees with at least two rounds of review ("general" and "specific", as labelled by Chile) by not only those committees, but also by each house of Congress itself, highlights the complexity of the *process* Chile will undergo during implementation....

ARB.5.4.7 *Chile – Price Band System*, para. 39
(WT/DS207/13)

...I am also conscious of the fact that most steps in Chile's lawmaking procedure, while required by law, are not subject to statutory or constitutional time limits.

Therefore, there appears to be a certain amount of "flexibility" within the normal legislative process, particularly in terms of steps such as the "general discussions" and Presidential endorsement, that Chile may fairly be expected to utilize in good faith so that it may promptly develop a new law repealing or modifying the PBS and otherwise ensure that it conforms with its WTO obligations.

ARB.5.4.8 *Chile – Price Band System*, para. 42
(WT/DS207/13)

The absence of a requirement under Chile's laws to engage in pre-legislative consultations is not sufficient, in my view, to dismiss the relevance of such consultations for purposes of this Article 21.3(c) arbitration. As other arbitrators have noted, and as Chile has emphasized, the consultation phase is important for laying the foundation upon which a proposed law passes through the legislative process. Although not mandated by law, consultations within government agencies as well as with the affected sectors of society are typically a concomitant of lawmaking in contemporary polities, and such consultations should be taken into account when fixing a "reasonable period of time" for implementation.

ARB.5.4.9 *Chile – Price Band System*, para. 52
(WT/DS207/13)

Nevertheless, the relevant laws of Chile, namely, the Constitution and Law 18.918, appear to enable Chile to resort to this "extraordinary" legislative procedure when proposing a law to modify the PBS. Because of the significant passage of time since adoption of the panel and Appellate Body reports in this case, and the lack of progress made thus far in implementing the recommendations and rulings of the DSB, Chile may itself decide to resort to the "urgency procedure" at certain stages of the legislative process. Chile recognizes that it must implement those recommendations and rulings in good faith towards other Members of the WTO. It must therefore do everything it reasonably can to act expeditiously in this process of implementation. Perhaps this will call for Chile to invoke its "urgency procedure". Perhaps it will not. On the facts of this case and the evidence before me, I believe that whether and at what stages Chile utilizes the "urgency procedure" are questions for Chile to determine for itself. But, whatever it does, Chile must implement the recommendations and rulings of the DSB promptly.

ARB.5.4.10 *US – Offset Act (Byrd Amendment)*, para. 64
(WT/DS217/14, WT/DS234/22)

I am aware that the component steps of the United States' legislative process, as pointed out by the United States, are numerous and potentially time-consuming. However, I note that legislative bills have been passed by the United States Congress within short periods of time; for instance, the CDSOA itself appears to have been passed in a period of only 25 days. Moreover, the United States has described itself as a "strong advocate [ ] of prompt compliance". Finally, I also agree with the arbitrators in *US – Section 110(5) Copyright Act* and in *US – 1916 Act*, respectively, who noted that, where the United States is obliged to enact a piece of legislation in order to bring itself into compliance with its obligations under an international treaty, the United States Congress may be expected to take advantage of the flexibility available within the legislative procedures to implement such legislation as speedily as possible.

ARB.5.4.11 *EC – Tariff Preferences*, para. 53
(WT/DS246/14)

To start with the European enlargement, the European Communities argues that considerable time will be needed to translate into the 20 official languages certain instruments connected with implementation. I agree that this circumstance is likely to increase the period of time reasonably required to complete certain steps in the implementation process. Therefore, I have taken this into account in my determination. I also agree with the European Communities that, if a member State of the European Union requested verification that the Council adopted the implementing regulation by a qualified majority representing at least 62% of the population of the European Union, this could add to the time required for implementation.

ARB.5.4.12 *EC – Tariff Preferences*, para. 54
(WT/DS246/14)

I turn to the election of a new European Parliament in June 2004 and the commencement of a new Commission on 1 November 2004. According to the European Communities' estimates, the Commission will complete its proposal on a Council regulation modifying the Drug Arrangements, and that proposal will be transmitted to the European Parliament, in October 2004. The fact that a new Commission takes charge on 1 November 2004 would not appear to increase the time required to complete that proposal. Similarly, if the Commission's proposal is transmitted to the European Parliament in October 2004, this should allow sufficient time for the European Parliament to become "operational" before it examines the proposal.

ARB.5.5 Relevance of contentiousness

ARB.5.5.1 *Chile – Alcoholic Beverages*, para. 43
(WT/DS87/15, WT/DS110/14)

Two aspects of the Chilean legislative process may be usefully noted. One is the set of practices designated as the "pre-legislative" phase of the law-making process in Chile, during which phase a specific revised tax scheme is developed and proposed on the basis of consultations and technical assessments. These consultations will include discussions aimed at building and organizing the broad support necessary for the adoption of the proposed bill, by both Chambers of the National Congress. The duration of this "pre-legislative" phase may differ from bill to bill; no maximum period is set by law but it is clearly an important phase if the success of the legislative effort is important. . . .

ARB.5.5.2 *Canada – Pharmaceutical Patents*, para. 58
(WT/DS114/13)

. . . I see nothing in this proposed regulatory change that can be described as complex. What is more, in this case, comments from the public could not be expected to result in much alteration of the one substantive sentence of Canada's proposed regulatory change, which merely repeals the existing regulation. After all, how many other ways could this one sentence be written? Likewise, in this case, any consideration of any changes that might conceivably be needed in the solitary substantive sentence of the proposed regulatory change could not be expected to take very long. . . . If this proposed regulatory change were more complex, I might reach a different conclusion. Yet it is not complex at all. And, given the sheer simplicity of the wording, function and purpose of this proposed regulation, I consider it implausible that this particular implementation step in this case should take as much time as claimed by Canada.

ARB.5.5.3 *Canada – Pharmaceutical Patents*, para. 60
(WT/DS114/13)

. . . I see nothing in Article 21.3 to indicate that the supposed domestic "contentiousness" of a measure taken to comply with a WTO ruling should in any way be a factor to be considered in determining a "reasonable period of time" for implementation. . . .

ARB.5.5.4 *US – Section 110(5) Copyright Act*, paras. 41–42
(WT/DS160/12)

. . . one of the factors listed by the United States as support for the period it has proposed is not relevant for the determination of a "reasonable period of time" for implementation. The United States refers to the "controversy" surrounding the legislation, and the "divergent views of stakeholders". . . .

. . . any argument as to the "controversy", in the sense of domestic "contentiousness", regarding the measure at issue is not relevant. . . . While I agree that this is an important issue, I do not see how it will add any *additional* time to the legislative process, as the *content* of the legislation effecting implementation is precisely the issue that Congress will decide through its normal procedures.

ARB.5.5.5 *Canada – Patent Term*, para. 49
(WT/DS170/10)

I now turn to Canada's main argument in support of its request for a "reasonable period of time" of 14 months and two days. I recall Canada's observation that the required amendment of its *Patent Act* will have an economic impact on Canada's health care system, so that it can be expected that there will be significant debate which is likely to be divisive, and that, therefore, the Government of Canada will have to carefully manage the legislative process. . . .

ARB.5.5.6 *Canada – Patent Term*, para. 53
(WT/DS170/10)

The issue raised by Canada is of great importance, both from the point of view of the implementation of recommendations and rulings of the DSB, that is, the respect of international treaty obligations, and from the point of view of fundamental principles of the democratic process. I do not believe, however, that I have to decide the controversy between the parties for the implementation through legislation in general. My only task is to determine the "reasonable period of time" for the case before me. My reasoning, therefore, applies to this case only.

ARB.5.5.7 *Canada – Patent Term*, para. 58
(WT/DS170/10)

The treatment of existing patents which benefit from a longer period of protection than the period prescribed by Article 33 of the *TRIPS Agreement* may be highly controversial and closely connected politically with the amendment of Article 45 of the Canadian *Patent Act*. However, as I have already said, this issue is outside the strict boundaries of the implementation of the recommendations and rulings of the DSB. Consequently, the "contentiousness" of this issue is certainly not a "particular circumstance" which I should take into account in determining the "reasonable period of time" in the present case. Therefore, Canada cannot invoke legislative choices and the likely divisiveness of the debate in the Canadian Parliament to justify its request for a "reasonable period of time" of 14 months and two days.

ARB.5.5.8 *US – Hot-Rolled Steel*, para. 38
(WT/DS184/13)

. . . Even so, it does not seem unreasonable to infer that the formal proceedings are likely to be carried out with more dispatch in view of the "pre-legislative", informal consultations already undertaken. In *Chile – Taxes on Alcoholic Beverages – Arbitration under Article 21.3(c) of the DSU* ("*Chile – Alcoholic Beverages*"), the Arbitrator noted that the "pre-legislative" phase is "an important phase if the success of the legislative effort is important."

ARB.5.5.9 *Chile – Price Band System*, paras. 47–48
(WT/DS207/13)

. . . it has been rightly said that "[a]ll WTO disputes are 'contentious' domestically at least to some extent; if they were not, there would be no need for recourse by WTO Members to dispute settlement." Simple contentiousness may thus not be a sufficient consideration under Article 21.3(c) for a longer period of time.

Nevertheless, the facts of this dispute, as identified by Chile and uncontested by Argentina, raise special concerns that warrant my taking them into account in my determination. I am of the view that the PBS is so fundamentally integrated into the policies of Chile, that domestic opposition to repeal or modification of those measures reflects, not simply opposition by interest groups to the loss of protection, but also reflects serious debate, within and outside the legislature of Chile, over the means of devising an implementation measure when confronted with a DSB ruling against the original law. In the light of the longstanding nature of the PBS, its fundamental integration into the central agricultural policies of Chile, its price-determinative regulatory position in Chile's agricultural policy, and its intricacy, I find its unique role and impact on Chilean society is a relevant factor in my determination of the "reasonable period of time" for implementation.

ARB.5.5.10 *US – Offset Act (Byrd Amendment)*, para. 61
(WT/DS217/14, WT/DS234/22)

I do not mean to suggest that I am of the view that the dispute between the United States and the eleven Complaining Parties in *US – Offset Act (Byrd Amendment)* does not involve important questions under WTO law. Moreover, I am fully aware of the high level of economic and political interest in this particular dispute, as evidenced by the significant number of WTO Members involved in all stages of this dispute, including in these arbitration proceedings. Nevertheless, "complexity" of implementing legislation as a particular circumstance, within the meaning of Article 21.3(c), is a *legal* criterion, to be examined without regard for political contentiousness or other non-legal factors that may surround a measure at issue. I am precluded, by my mandate under Article 21.3(c), from giving consideration to these non-legal factors.

ARB.5.5.11 *EC – Tariff Preferences*, para. 56
(WT/DS246/14)

I am not persuaded by the statements of the European Communities that the particular nature of the Drug Arrangements within the GSP scheme and the development policy of the European Communities warrants any increase in the reasonable period of time for implementation. Although a modification to the Drug Arrangements may well be described as "politically sensitive", this factor does not distinguish the Drug Arrangements from any other measure that is likely to be the subject of a WTO dispute. The measure examined in *Chile – Price Band System* was quite different. That measure had a "unique ... impact on Chilean society" (that is, the society of the *implementing* Member); "domestic opposition" to its repeal or modification reflected "serious debate, within and outside the legislature of Chile, over the means of devising an implementation measure" and "not simply opposition by interest groups to the loss of protection".

ARB.5.6 Means of implementation

ARB.5.6.1 *Australia – Salmon*, paras. 31, 33
(WT/DS18/9)

A certain difficulty arises in this case because of the divergent views of the parties as to what constitutes implementation. ...

...

Clearly, what constitutes a "reasonable period of time" depends upon the action which Australia takes under its legal system to implement the recommendations and rulings of the DSB. If implementation is effected by means of an administrative decision to repeal or modify the measure at issue or by means of a permit granted by the Director of Quarantine, the length of time needed to carry out such a process would be different from what it would be if Australia were to conduct a series of risk assessments.

ARB.5.6.2 *Australia – Salmon*, para. 38
(WT/DS18/9)

... Both parties also agree that the process involved in bringing the measure in dispute into conformity with Australia's obligations under the *SPS Agreement* is an administrative, not a legislative, process. As pointed out by the arbitrator in *European Communities – Hormones*, when implementation can be effected by administrative means, the reasonable period of time should be "considerably shorter than 15 months."

ARB.5.6.3 *Canada – Pharmaceutical Patents*, para. 49
(WT/DS114/13)

For example, if implementation is by *administrative* means, such as through a regulation, then the "reasonable period of time" will normally be shorter than for implementation through *legislative* means. It seems reasonable to assume, unless proven otherwise due to unusual circumstances in a given case, that regulations can be changed more quickly than statutes. To be sure, the administrative process can sometimes be long; but the legislative process can oftentimes be longer.

ARB.5.6.4 *Canada – Pharmaceutical Patents*, para. 51
(WT/DS114/13)

In addition, the *legally binding*, as opposed to the discretionary, nature of the component steps leading to implementation should be taken into account. If the law of a Member dictates a mandatory period of time for a mandatory part of the process needed to make a regulatory change, then that portion of a proposed period will, unless proven otherwise due to unusual circumstances in a given case, be reasonable. On the other hand, if there is no such mandate, then a Member asserting the need for a certain period of time must bear a much more imposing burden of proof....

ARB.5.6.5 *US – Hot-Rolled Steel*, para. 32
(WT/DS184/13)

The temporal relationship between the legislative and the administrative implementing actions is an important consideration in the present arbitration. The United States and Japan agree that the relationship is not necessarily a linear, sequential one and that some administrative actions may well be taken, or at least commenced, concurrently with the initiation of the legislative implementing effort.

ARB.5.6.6 *Chile – Price Band System*, footnote 86 to para. 33
(WT/DS207/13)

. . . I note that both parties in this arbitration argue that new legislation is necessary for implementation of the recommendations and rulings of the DSB, and therefore, appear to agree that "immediate" compliance by Chile is impracticable. The impracticability of Chile's immediate compliance has not been raised as an issue for decision in this arbitration.

ARB.5.6.7 *Chile – Price Band System*, paras. 36–37
(WT/DS207/13)

. . . Whether elimination of the PBS, in so far as it impacts upon the relevant products, is the "only appropriate" means of implementation (as opposed to a modification of the PBS) is not an issue for decision in this arbitration. As discussed above, the focus of my inquiry and determination relates to the period of *time* needed to implement the recommendations and rulings of the DSB, not to the *manner* in which Chile intends to implement them. . . .

The fact that an Article 21.3(c) arbitration focuses on the period of time for implementation, however, does not render the substance of the implementation, that is, the precise means or manner of implementation, immaterial from the perspective of the arbitrator. In fact, the more information that is known about the details of the implementing measure, the greater the guidance to an arbitrator in selecting a reasonable period of time, and the more likely that such period of time will fairly balance the legitimate needs of the implementing Member against those of the complaining Member. Nevertheless, the arbitrator should still avoid deciding what a Member must do for proper implementation. . . .

ARB.5.6.8 *Chile – Price Band System*, para. 38
(WT/DS207/13)

. . . I find the intricacy of the lawmaking process relevant to my determination, and I agree with the observation of previous arbitrators that implementation through legislation is likely to require a longer time for implementation than administrative rulemaking or other exclusively Executive action.

ARB.5.6.9 *US – Offset Act (Byrd Amendment)*, para. 57
(WT/DS217/14, WT/DS234/22)

. . . As a general rule, absent evidence to the contrary, implementation by legislative measures will, more often than not, require a longer period of time than implementation by means of administrative measures. . . .

ARB.5.6.10 *US – Offset Act (Byrd Amendment)*, para. 59
(WT/DS217/14, WT/DS234/22)

I do not consider the existence of numerous options to implement the recommendations and rulings of the DSB, as invoked by the United States, to be relevant to my determination of the "reasonable period of time" for implementation of the recommendations and rulings of the DSB. The weighing and balancing of the respective merits of various legislative alternatives is one of the key functions and aspects of any legislative process. The mere fact that implementation of the recommendations and rulings of the DSB necessitates the choice between several, or even a large number of, alternative options is generally not, in my view, in and of itself, a particular circumstance that would inform my determination of the shortest period possible to implement the recommendations and rulings of the DSB in this case.

ARB.5.6.11 *EC – Tariff Preferences*, para. 42
(WT/DS246/14)

It is not unusual for domestic or other legal systems to follow procedural conventions that are not explicitly mandated by legal instruments. Moreover, I find relevant that the Council has sought an opinion from the European Parliament and the ECOSOC before adopting the great majority of regulations related to the European Communities' GSP scheme over the years. The European Communities has also suggested that the consequences of failing to seek such opinions in the present implementation process would be a matter to be determined by the Court of Justice of the European Communities. It appears, therefore, that adoption of the regulation in question without seeking opinions from the European Parliament and the ECOSOC would be an "extraordinary" procedure. I agree with previous arbitrators that implementing Members are not required to adopt "extraordinary legislative procedures" in every case. In my view, seeking the opinions of the European Parliament and the ECOSOC should be included in determining the reasonable period of time for implementation.

ARB.5.6.12 *EC – Tariff Preferences*, para. 51
(WT/DS246/14)

I note that the Arbitrator in *Korea – Alcoholic Beverages* determined that it was reasonable to include in the reasonable period of time the "thirty-day grace period for enforcement of certain . . . instruments" provided in a Korean statute. The Arbitrator in *EC – Bananas III* also appears to have taken into account the European Communities' statement that "any change in legislation which directly affects the customs treatment of products in connection with importation or exportation, enters into force either on 1 January or 1 July of the relevant year" in determining the reasonable period of time in that dispute. In the present case, I regard the administrative practice of the European Communities, as it pertains to advance publication of tariff changes and the date on which such changes take effect, as a relevant factor in determining the reasonable period of time for implementation.

ARB.5.6.13 *US – Oil Country Tubular Goods Sunset Reviews*, para. 26
(WT/DS268/12)

. . . the nature of the steps to be taken for implementation has a bearing on the "reasonable period of time" required to fully implement the recommendations and rulings of the DSB. The implementation may require amendments to laws or regulations that may involve legislative action, or it may require amendments to administrative guidelines or procedures that may not involve such action. Implementation may also involve only the remedying of the deficiencies in a particular determination. Previous arbitration awards under Article 21.3(c) have recognized that when implementation requires legislative action, the "reasonable period of time" required may be longer than in cases where only administrative action is required to amend guidelines or procedures or to remedy the deficiencies in particular determinations....

ARB.5.6.14 *US – Oil Country Tubular Goods Sunset Reviews*, para. 50
(WT/DS268/12)

The United States considers that the waiver provisions of the USDOC Regulations must first be amended to bring them into conformity with the DSB's recommendations and rulings, and that only after the amended regulations are issued could they be applied to a new determination to remedy the "as applied" violation in this dispute. In this regard, I note two aspects of this dispute: first, one of the reasons for the Panel finding the "as applied" violation was that WTO-inconsistent waiver provisions were applied to Argentine exporters other than Siderca; and, second, an amendment of the waiver provisions of the USDOC Regulations is in any event required to remedy the "as such" violations in this dispute. The United States has explained why it considers an *in seriatim* approach to be necessary in this case to ensure that the redetermination is in conformity with its own legal system....

ARB.5.7 Structural adjustment

ARB.5.7.1 *Indonesia – Autos*, para. 23
(WT/DS54/15, WT/DS55/14, WT/DS59/13, WT/DS64/12)

Indonesia also requests an additional period of nine months following the issuance of its implementing measure (i.e., to 23 October 1999) as a "transition" period to allow the affected companies/industries to make structural adjustments. I do not view structural adjustments of Indonesia's affected industries as a "particular circumstance" which may be taken into account under Article 21.3(c) of the DSU. In virtually every case in which a measure has been found to be inconsistent with a Member's obligations under the GATT 1994 or any other covered agreement, and therefore, must be brought into conformity with that agreement, some degree of adjustment by the domestic industry of the Member concerned will be necessary. This will be the case regardless of whether the Member concerned is a developed or a developing country. Structural adjustment to the withdrawal or the modification of an inconsistent measure, therefore, is not a "particular circumstance" that can be taken into account in determining the reasonable period of time under Article 21.3(c).

ARB.5.7.2 *Canada – Pharmaceutical Patents*, para. 52
(WT/DS114/13)

. . . in my view, the "particular circumstances" mentioned in Article 21.3 do *not* include factors unrelated to an assessment of the shortest period possible for implementation within the legal system of a Member. Any such unrelated factors are irrelevant to determining the "reasonable period of time" for implementation. For example, as others have ruled in previous Article 21.3 arbitrations, any proposed period intended to allow for the "structural adjustment" of an affected domestic industry will not be relevant to an assessment of the legal process. The determination of a "reasonable period of time" must be a legal judgement based on an examination of relevant legal requirements.

ARB.5.7.3 *Argentina – Hides and Leather*, para. 41
(WT/DS155/10)

It thus appears that the concept of compliance or implementation prescribed in the DSU is a technical concept with a specific content: the withdrawal or modification of a measure, or part of a measure, the establishment or application of which by a Member of the WTO constituted the violation of a provision of a covered agreement. Compliance within the meaning of the DSU is distinguishable from the removal or modification of the underlying economic or social or other conditions the existence of which might well have caused or contributed to the enactment or application of the WTO-inconsistent governmental measure in the first place. Those economic or other conditions might, in certain situations, survive the removal or modification of the non-conforming measure; nevertheless, the WTO Member concerned will have complied with the DSB recommendations and rulings and with its obligations under the relevant covered agreement. To my mind, it is *inter alia* for the above reason that the need for structural adjustment of the industry or industries in respect of which the WTO-inconsistent measure was promulgated and applied, has generally been regarded, in prior arbitrations under Article 21.3(c) of the DSU, as *not* bearing upon the determination of a "reasonable period of time" for implementation of DSB recommendations and rulings.

ARB.5.8 Economic and financial collapse

ARB.5.8.1 *Indonesia – Autos*, para. 24
(WT/DS54/15, WT/DS55/14, WT/DS59/13, WT/DS64/12)

. . . Indonesia has indicated that in a "normal situation", a measure such as the one required to implement the recommendations and rulings of the DSB in this case would become effective on the date of issuance. However, this is not a "normal situation". Indonesia is not only a developing country; it is a developing country that is currently in a dire economic and financial situation. Indonesia itself states that its economy is "near collapse". In these very particular circumstances, I consider it appropriate to give full weight to matters affecting the interests of Indonesia as a developing country pursuant to the provisions of Article 21.2 of the DSU. I, therefore, conclude that an additional period of six months over and above the six-month period required for the completion of Indonesia's domestic rule-making process constitutes a reasonable period of time for implementation of the recommendations and rulings of the DSB in this case.

ARB.5.8.2 *Argentina – Hides and Leather*, para. 49
(WT/DS155/10)

A final point that should be made is that to build into the concept of a "reasonable period of time" to comply with DSB recommendations and rulings, time or opportunity to control and manage economic or social conditions which antedate or are contemporaneous with the adoption of the WTO-inconsistent governmental measure, may, in the generality of instances, be to defer to an indefinitely receding future the duty of compliance. The implications for the multilateral trading system as we know it today, of such an interpretation of "reasonable period of time" for compliance are clear and far-reaching and ominous. Such an interpretation would tend to reduce the fundamental duty of "immediate" or "prompt" compliance to a figure of speech.

ARB.5.8.3 *Argentina – Hides and Leather*, para. 51
(WT/DS155/10)

. . . I agree that under Article 21.2 of the DSU in conjunction with Article 21.3(c), account may appropriately be taken of the circumstance that the WTO Member which must comply with the DSB recommendations and rulings is a developing country confronted by severe economic and financial problems. That those problems in the case of Argentina are real is not disputed, although there may be debate as to whether Argentina's economy is "near collapse".

ARB.5.9 Economic impact of existing measure. *See also* Relevance of contentiousness (ARB.5.5)

ARB.5.9.1 *Canada – Patent Term*, paras. 46–48
(WT/DS170/10)

A second point of convergence between the parties concerns the significance, under Article 21.3(c) of the DSU, of the economic consequences of the expiry of certain patents during the "reasonable period of time" for the implementation of the recommendations and rulings of the DSB. I recall the United States' assertion that, if Canada is permitted to delay its implementation of the recommendations and rulings of the DSB, thousands of patents will continue to expire "prematurely", causing irreparable harm to patent owners; on average, 1,149 patents will fall into the public domain each month during 2001.

At the oral hearing, Canada accepted the statistics presented by the United States, but submitted that they are misleading as they fail to indicate whether or not the "prematurely" expiring patents have any commercial significance. . . .

Canada advanced the argument about the small number of patents with commercial value for the first time at the oral hearing. It is obvious that this argument would raise a major procedural problem if the commercial value of the patents expiring during the "reasonable period of time" had any relevance as a "particular circumstance" for the determination of the length of the "reasonable period of time" in this case. However, in my view, this is not so. Measures taken by Members, which are inconsistent with one of the covered agreements will, naturally, or at least very often, cause irreparable harm to economic operators who are nationals of other Members. In this respect, violations of the *TRIPS Agreement* will generally not differ from violations of one of the other covered agreements. The precise assessment of damage caused to a group of economic operators or to single individuals, or companies, may well be more difficult to evaluate than in the present case. However, this does not distinguish the present case from other cases involving violations of covered agreements for the purposes of determining the "reasonable period of time", under Article 21.3(c). I note that this view corresponds to the position taken by the United States at the oral hearing according to which the argument of urgency was raised to provide context. The United States acknowledged that the commercial value of the expiring patents is not relevant to the determination of the shortest period possible, within the Canadian legal system.

ARB.5.9.2 *US – Offset Act (Byrd Amendment)*, paras. 79–80 (WT/DS217/14, WT/DS234/22)

. . . economic harm suffered by foreign exporters does not, and cannot, by definition, impact on what is the "shortest period possible within the legal system of the Member to implement the recommendations and rulings of the DSB". The particular circumstances, within the meaning of Article 21.3(c), can only be of such nature as will influence the evolution and unfolding of the implementation process itself. Factors external to the legislative process itself are of no relevance for the determination of the reasonable period of time for implementation.

I do not wish to imply that economic harm, caused by the WTO-inconsistent measure, to economic agents of the Complaining Parties, or any other WTO Members, is irrelevant in the context of the implementation of the recommendations and rulings of the DSB. Many WTO-inconsistent measures will cause some form of economic harm to exporters of WTO Members. However, the need, and urgency, to remove WTO-inconsistent measures, and to remove the harm to economic agents caused by such measures, is, in my view, already reflected in the principle of "prompt compliance" under Article 21.1. The same concern, in my view, underlies the well established principle, under Article 21.3(c), that the reasonable period of time for implementation be the shortest time possible within the legal system of the Member. Thus, it would be supererogatory, and incongruous, to accord renewed consideration to the issue of economic harm when determining the shortest period possible for implementation within the legal system of the implementing Member.

ARB.5.10 Developing countries

ARB.5.10.1 *Indonesia – Autos*, para. 24
(WT/DS54/15, WT/DS55/14, WT/DS59/13, WT/DS64/12)

. . . Indonesia is a developing country. In that context, I note that Article 21.2 of the DSU requires that:

> Particular attention should be paid to matters affecting the interests of developing country Members with respect to measures which have been subject to dispute settlement.

Although the language of this provision is rather general and does not provide a great deal of guidance, it is a provision that forms part of the context for Article 21.3(c) of the DSU and which I believe is important to take into account here. . . . Indonesia is not only a developing country; it is a developing country that is currently in a dire economic and financial situation. Indonesia itself states that its economy is "near collapse". In these very particular circumstances, I consider it appropriate to give full weight to matters affecting the interests of Indonesia as a developing country pursuant to the provisions of Article 21.2 of the DSU. I, therefore, conclude that an additional period of six months over and above the six-month period required for the completion of Indonesia's domestic rule-making process constitutes a reasonable period of time for implementation of the recommendations and rulings of the DSB in this case.

ARB.5.10.2 *Chile – Alcoholic Beverages*, para. 44
(WT/DS87/15, WT/DS110/14)

Chile has also referred to Article 21.2, where the DSU, immediately after stressing that "prompt compliance" with the recommendations and rulings of the DSB is essential for the WTO dispute settlement system, provides:

> Particular attention should be paid to matters affecting the interests of developing country Members with respect to measures which have been subject to dispute settlement.

Chile has submitted that account must be taken of the specific interests of Chile as the developing country Member whose measure has been the subject of dispute settlement. However, Chile has not been very specific or concrete about its particular interests as a developing country Member nor about how those interests would actually bear upon the length of "the reasonable period of time" to enact necessary amendatory legislation.

ARB.5.10.3 *Chile – Alcoholic Beverages*, para. 45
(WT/DS87/15, WT/DS110/14)

It is not necessary to assume that the operation of Article 21.2 will essentially result in the application of "criteria" for the determination of "the reasonable period of time" – understood as the *kinds* of considerations that may be taken into account – that would be "qualitatively" different for developed and for developing country Members. I do not believe Chile is making such an assumption. Nevertheless, although cast in quite general terms, because Article 21.2 is in the DSU, it is not simply to be disregarded. As I read it, Article 21.2, whatever else it may signify, usefully enjoins, *inter alia*, an arbitrator functioning under Article 21.3(c) to be generally mindful of the great difficulties that a developing country Member may, in a particular case, face as it proceeds to implement the recommendations and rulings of the DSB.

ARB.5.10.4 *Chile – Price Band System*, paras. 55–56
(WT/DS207/13)

. . . I agree with the following statement by the arbitrator in *Chile – Alcoholic Beverages* that "an arbitrator functioning under Article 21.3(c) [must] be *generally mindful* of the great difficulties that a developing country Member may, in a particular case, face as it proceeds to implement the recommendations and rulings of the DSB." This arbitration is, however, the first arbitration under Article 21.3(c) to include developing countries as both complainant *and* respondent. The period of time for implementation of the recommendations and rulings of the DSB in this case is thus a "matter[] affecting the interests" of both Members: the general difficulties facing Chile as a developing country in revising its longstanding PBS, and the burden imposed on Argentina as a developing country whose access to the Chilean agricultural market is impeded by the PBS, contrary to WTO rules.

Furthermore, Chile has not pointed to additional *specific* obstacles that it faces *as a developing country* under present circumstances. This is a matter which I should take into account in evaluating whether a longer period of time may be needed for implementation. The absence of presently-existing, concrete difficulties in Chile's position as a developing country stands in contrast to previous arbitrations, wherein Members have identified, not simply their positions as developing countries, but also "severe" or "dire" economic and financial situations existing at the time of the proposed period of implementation. In contrast, the acuteness of Argentina's burden as a developing country complainant that has been successful in establishing the WTO-inconsistency of a challenged measure, is amplified by Argentina's daunting financial woes at present. Accordingly, I recognize that Chile may indeed face obstacles as a developing country in its implementation of the recommendations and rulings of the DSB, and that Argentina, likewise, faces continuing hardship as a developing country so long as the WTO-inconsistent PBS is maintained. In the unusual circumstances of this case, therefore, I am not swayed towards either a longer or shorter period of time by the "[p]articular attention" I pay to the interests of developing countries.

ARB.5.10.5 *US – Offset Act (Byrd Amendment)*, para. 81
(WT/DS217/14, WT/DS234/22)

. . . I note that, by its wording, Article 21.2 does not distinguish between situations where the developing country Member concerned is an implementing or a complaining party. However, I also note that the Complaining Parties have not explained *specifically* how developing country Members' interests should affect my determination of the reasonable period of time for implementation. It is useful to recall, once again, that the term "reasonable period of time" has been consistently interpreted to signify the "shortest period possible within the legal system of the Member". Therefore, I have some difficulty in seeing how the fact that several Complaining Parties are developing country Members should have an effect on the determination of the shortest period possible within the legal system of the United States to implement the recommendations and rulings of the DSB in this case.

ARB.5.10.6 *US – Oil Country Tubular Goods Sunset Reviews*, para. 52 (WT/DS268/12)

...for my determination of the reasonable period of time, Argentina requests me to use as "context" the fact that Argentina is a developing country Member. Having regard to the implementation process involved in this dispute, I consider that, beyond the fundamental requirement that the implementation process should be completed in the shortest period possible within the legal and administrative system of the United States, the "reasonable period of time" for implementation is not affected by the fact that Argentina, as the complaining Member, is a developing country.

ARB.5.11 Calendar of Legislative Body

ARB.5.11.1 *US – Offset Act (Byrd Amendment)*, paras. 69–70 (WT/DS217/14, WT/DS234/22)

...The fact that at any given point in the Congressional schedule there would be a "greater opportunity" to pass legislation than at another point in time, is not a particular circumstance relevant for my determination of the reasonable period of time for implementation in this case. The obligation to implement promptly and, if impracticable to do so immediately, then within a reasonable period of time, the recommendations and rulings of the DSB is an international treaty obligation of the United States; the specific content and meaning of this international legal obligation cannot be affected by non-legal considerations related to the United States Congressional schedule.

This is not to say that the schedule of the United States Congress (or any other legislative body of any implementing Member) can never be a relevant particular circumstance; for instance, previous arbitrators have given consideration, in their determination of the reasonable period of time for implementation, to circumstances where a draft bill could not be introduced into Congress for a number of months because a new Congress had not yet convened at the time when the arbitration was initiated. However, these circumstances do not arise in the present proceedings. The United States has *not* argued that it would not be possible to pass the implementing legislation at another point in time, for instance at the end of the Congressional session when the majority of bills are enacted, or at any other time during the Congressional session.

ARB.5.12 Flexibility of Implementation Process

ARB.5.12.1 *US – 1916 Act*, para. 39
(WT/DS136/11, WT/DS162/14)

Turning to the complexity of the United States' legislative process, I note that the United States has explained, in sufficient detail, the multiple and time-consuming steps involved in the enactment of legislation within the specific context of the legislative system of the United States. It is generally accepted that certain of these steps are not required by law, and that the majority of these steps are not subject to compulsory minimum time limits. In other words, the United States' legislative process, while complex, is characterized by a considerable degree of flexibility. That this flexibility is exercised to achieve the prompt passage of legislation when this is considered necessary and appropriate is revealed by the fact that bills have been passed by the United States Congress within short periods of time, using its "normal" legislative process. The United States has stated that it "will make every effort to promptly implement the DSB's recommendations and rulings" in this case. Since this is a case where the United States has to enact a piece of legislation to bring it into compliance with its international treaty obligations under the covered agreements, the United States Congress may reasonably be expected to use all the flexibility available within its normal legislative procedures to enact the required legislation as speedily as possible.

ARB.5.12.2 *Canada – Patent Term*, paras. 63–64
(WT/DS170/10)

Canada has described, in detail, in its written submission the different steps of the legislative phase of its law making process. The passage of legislation requires, in essence, three readings in both Houses of the Canadian Parliament, that is, the House of Commons and the Senate. The process includes an examination of the proposed legislation by committees, which normally takes place between the second and the third reading. Once the House of Commons has considered the bill, it is sent to the Senate for its consideration. After approval by the Senate, the bill is given Royal Assent by the Governor-General. The different steps in this process and their sequence are clearly structured and defined. With respect to timing and scheduling, however, the process is flexible, as Canada acknowledged at the oral hearing. Use of this flexibility does not require recourse to extraordinary procedures. Following earlier arbitration awards, I consider this flexibility to be an important element in establishing the "reasonable period of time".

Ultimately, the "reasonable period of time" appears to be a function of the priority which Canada attributes to the amendment of its *Patent Act* in order to bring it into conformity with its obligations under Article 33 of the *TRIPS Agreement*. I recognize that in all democratic societies, legislative initiatives designed to satisfy different needs and wishes compete with each other. I share, however, the view expressed in a recent arbitration award concerning another Member, which I adopt only to the extent that it fits the present case concerning Canada; it seems to me that this is the type of matter for which the Canadian Parliament should try to comply with the international obligations of Canada as soon as possible, taking advantage of the flexibility that it has in its normal legislative procedures.

ARB.5.12.3 *EC – Tariff Preferences*, para. 36
(WT/DS246/14)

As several previous arbitrators have noted, flexibility in a Member's legislative system may enable the Member to effect a legislative amendment in a shorter period of time than might otherwise be possible. In the present case, India submits that the European Communities' legislative system "is characterised by considerable flexibility". I agree, in the sense that no mandatory minimum time periods are imposed for any particular step in the implementation process as outlined by the European Communities. The European Communities has used this flexibility to modify Regulation 2501 (modifying or extending the GSP scheme) promptly in the past. I take into account, as a relevant matter, the flexibility in the European Communities' legislative system; but it does not, of itself, determine the question of the reasonable period of time for implementation.

ARB.6 Burden of Proof

ARB.6.1 *EC – Hormones*, para. 27
(WTDS26/15, WT/DS48/13)

In my view, the party seeking to prove that there are "particular circumstances" justifying a shorter or a longer time has the burden of proof under Article 21.3(c). In this arbitration, therefore, the onus is on the European Communities to demonstrate that there are particular circumstances which call for a reasonable period of time of 39 months, and it is likewise up to the United States and Canada to demonstrate that there are particular circumstances which lead to the conclusion that 10 months is reasonable.

ARB.6.2 *Canada – Pharmaceutical Patents*, para. 47
(WT/DS114/13)

. . . as immediate compliance is clearly the preferred option under Article 21.3, it is, in my view, for the implementing Member to bear the burden of proof in showing – "[i]f it is impracticable to comply immediately" – that the duration of any proposed period of implementation, including its supposed component steps, constitutes a "reasonable period of time". And the longer the proposed period of implementation, the greater this burden will be.

ARB.6.3 *Canada – Pharmaceutical Patents*, para. 55
(WT/DS114/13)

However, certain of the time periods specified by Canada for certain steps toward implementation are not fixed by either law or regulation. Rather, they have been estimated by Canada for purposes of this proceeding. As these estimates are not fixed by either law or regulation, but are only estimates, Canada bears a greater burden of proof in demonstrating their accuracy and legitimacy. And here Canada, in my view, has fallen short.

ARB.6.4 *US – 1916 Act*, para. 33
(WT/DS136/11, WT/DS162/14)

The parties do not dispute that "immediate" implementation is "impracticable" in this case. I, therefore, consider that the United States bears the burden of proof in showing that the period of 15 months proposed by it is the "shortest period possible" within its legislative system to implement the recommendations and rulings of the DSB in this particular case. I wish to emphasize that my task as an Arbitrator is to determine the "reasonable period of time" in light of the facts and circumstances of *this particular case*.

ARB.6.5 *US – Offset Act (Byrd Amendment)*, para. 44
(WT/DS217/14, WT/DS234/22)

. . . I also agree with statements by previous arbitrators that it is for the implementing Member to establish that the duration of the implementation period it proposes constitutes the "shortest period possible" within its legal system to implement the recommendations and rulings of the DSB. Where the implementing Member fails to establish that the period of time requested by it is indeed the shortest period possible within its legal system, the arbitrator must determine the "shortest period possible" for implementation, which will be shorter than proposed by the implementing Member, on the basis of the evidence presented by all parties in their submissions, and taking into account the 15-month guideline provided by Article 21.3(c).

ARB.6.6 *US – Offset Act (Byrd Amendment)*, para. 66
(WT/DS217/14, WT/DS234/22)

I recognize that estimating the duration of the various steps involved in a domestic legislative process is not an exact science. It would be unrealistic to expect an implementing Member to provide, as the basis for its request for a reasonable period of time, a definitive day-by-day schedule of the prospective implementing legislative process. Some of the steps in a legislative process, such as pre-legislative consultations, by their very nature, may prove particularly difficult to estimate. At the same time, however, I fail to see how it would be possible to arrive at a reasoned, and non-speculative, estimate of the total duration of a process without referring, at a minimum, to rough estimates of the time periods required for at least the key component steps of this process. Logically, the total time required for any process must be the sum of the time periods required for each of the component steps of this process. If the request for a total time period of 15 months, as argued by the United States, is based on "logical" and "rigorous" factors, such as the complexity of implementing legislation, or the general experience under the United States' legislative system, then I believe that such factors would necessarily provide the same relevant, and non-speculative, guidance with respect to at least some of the component steps of the legislative process. Put differently, I do not agree that an estimate of the total duration of the legislative process can be qualified as "logical" and "rigorous" if such an estimate is not based, at least to some extent, on an accumulation of the timeframes for the component steps. Moreover, if any possible estimates of the time periods required under the various component steps of the legislative process would be, as the United States stated at the oral hearing, mere "speculation", then it appears difficult to see how the total time period of 15 months, requested by the United States, would equally constitute anything other than "speculation".

ARB.6.7 *EC – Tariff Preferences*, para. 27
(WT/DS246/14)

India has argued that the implementing Member – in this case, the European Communities – bears the burden of demonstrating that the period it proposes is reasonable and that "the already great burden becomes even greater" if this period is more than 15 months. In my view, the European Communities must demonstrate that the period it proposes is reasonable; but I do not find it necessary in this arbitration to determine whether the burden of proof becomes greater if the period proposed is more than 15 months. I have found the evidence and arguments presented by both the European Communities and India very helpful in determining whether, in the particular circumstances of this case, the period of time for implementation should be 15 months or a shorter or longer period.

Annex A

Terms of Office of Current and Former Appellate Body Members

Terms of Office of Current Appellate Body Members

Name	Nationality	Term of Office
Georges Michel Abi-Saab	Egypt	1 June 2004 to 31 May 2008 1 June 2000 to 31 May 2004
Luiz Olavo Baptista	Brazil	12 December 2005 to 11 December 2009 11 December 2001 to 11 December 2005
Arumugamangalam Venkatachalam Ganesan	India	1 June 2004 to 31 May 2008 1 June 2000 to 31 May 2004
Merit E. Janow	United States	11 December 2003 to 10 December 2007
John S. Lockhart	Australia	12 December 2005 to 11 December 2009 11 December 2001 to 11 December 2005
Giorgio Sacerdoti	Italy	12 December 2005 to 11 December 2009 11 December 2001 to 11 December 2005
Yasuhei Taniguchi – Chairman (17 December 2004–16 December 2005)	Japan	11 December 2003 to 10 December 2007 1 June 2000 to 10 December 2003

Terms of Office of Former Appellate Body Members

Name	Nationality	Term of Office
James Bacchus	United States	1999–2003
		1995–1999
Christopher Beeby*	New Zealand	1999–2000
		1995–1999
Claus-Dieter Ehlermann	Germany	1997–2001
		1995–1997
Said El-Naggar	Egypt	1999–2000
		1995–1999
Florentino P. Feliciano	Philippines	1997–2001
		1995–1997
Julio Lacarte-Muró	Uruguay	1997–2001
		1995–1997
Mitsuo Matsushita	Japan	1999–2000
		1995–1999

* Mr. Beeby passed away in Geneva on 19 March 2000, before completing his term, and was replaced by Mr. Yasuhei Taniguchi.

Annex B
Biographies of Current Appellate Body Members

Georges Michel Abi-Saab (Egypt) (2000–2008)

Born in Egypt on 9 June 1933, Georges Michel Abi-Saab is Honorary Professor of International Law at the Graduate Institute of International Studies in Geneva (having taught there from 1963 to 2000), Honorary Professor at Cairo University's Faculty of Law, and a Member of the Institute of International Law.

Professor Abi-Saab served as consultant to the Secretary-General of the United Nations for the preparation of two reports on "Respect of Human Rights in Armed Conflicts" (1969 and 1970), and for the report on "Progressive Development of Principles and Norms of International Law Relating to the New International Economic Order" (1984). He represented Egypt in the Diplomatic Conference on the Reaffirmation and Development of International Humanitarian Law (1974 to 1977), and acted as advocate and Counsel for several governments in cases before the International Court of Justice (ICJ) as well as in international arbitrations. He has also served twice as judge *ad hoc* on the ICJ and as Judge on the Appeals Chamber of the International Criminal Tribunals for the Former Yugoslavia and for Rwanda. He is a Commissioner of the United Nations Compensation Commission and a Member of the Administrative Tribunal of the International Monetary Fund and of various international arbitral tribunals.

Professor Abi-Saab is the author of numerous books and articles, including: "Les exceptions préliminaires dans la procédure de la Cour internationale: Etude des notions fondamentales de procédure et des moyens de leur mise en oeuvre" (Paris, Pedone, 1967), "International Crises and the Role of Law: The United Nations Operation in Congo 1960–1964" (Oxford University Press, 1978); "The Concept of International Organization" (as editor) (Paris, UNESCO, 1981; French edition, 1980); and of two courses at the Hague Academy of International Law: "Wars of National Liberation in the Geneva Conventions and Protocols" (Recueil des cours, vol. 165 (1979–IV)) and the "General Course of Public International Law" (in French) (Recueil des cours, vol. 207 (1987–VII)).

Luiz Olavo Baptista (Brazil) (2001–2009)

Born in Brazil in 1938, Luiz Olavo Baptista is currently Professor of International Trade Law at the University of São Paulo Law School. He has been a Member of the Permanent Court of Arbitration at The Hague since 1996, and of the

International Chamber of Commerce (ICC) Institute for International Trade Practices and of its Commission on Trade and Investment Policy, since 1999. In addition, he has been one of the arbitrators designated under Mercosur's Protocol of Brasilia since 1993. Professor Baptista is also senior partner at the L.O. Baptista Law Firm, in São Paulo, Brazil, where he concentrates his practice on corporate law, arbitration and international litigation. He has been practicing law for almost 40 years advising governments, international organizations and large corporations in Brazil and in other jurisdictions. Professor Baptista has been an arbitrator at the United Nations Compensation Commission (E4A Panel), in several private commercial disputes and State–investor proceedings, as well as in disputes under Mercosur's Protocol of Brasilia. In addition, he has participated as a legal advisor in diverse projects sponsored by the World Bank, the United Nations Conference on Trade and Development (UNCTAD), the United Nations Centre on Transnational Corporations (UNCTC), and the United Nations Development Programme (UNDP). He obtained his law degree from the Catholic University of São Paulo, pursued postgraduate studies at Columbia University Law School and The Hague Academy of International Law, and received a Ph.D in International Law from the University of Paris II. He was Visiting Professor at the University of Michigan (Ann Arbor) from 1978 to 1979, and at the University of Paris I and the University of Paris II between 1996 and 2000. Professor Baptista has published extensively on various issues in Brazil and abroad.

Arumugamangalam Venkatachalam Ganesan (India) (2000–2008)

Born in Tirunelveli, Tamil Nadu, India on 7 June 1935, Arumugamangalam Venkatachalam Ganesan was a distinguished civil servant of India. He was appointed to the Indian Administrative Service, a premier civil service of India, in May 1959, and served in that service until June 1993. In a career spanning over 34 years, he has held a number of high level assignments, including Joint Secretary (Investment), Department of Economic Affairs, Government of India (1977–1980); Inter-Regional Adviser, United Nations Centre on Transnational Corporations (UNCTC), United Nations Headquarters, New York (1980–1985); Additional Secretary, Department of Industrial Development, Government of India (1986–1989); Chief Negotiator of India for the Uruguay Round of Multilateral Trade Negotiations and Special Secretary, Ministry of Commerce, Government of India (1989–1990); Civil Aviation Secretary of the Government of India (1990–1991); and Commerce Secretary of the Government of India (1991–1993). He represented India on numerous occasions in bilateral, regional, and multilateral negotiations in the areas of international trade, investment, and intellectual property rights. Between 1989 and 1993, he represented India at the various stages of the Uruguay Round of Multilateral Trade Negotiations.

After his retirement from civil service, Mr. Ganesan served as an expert and consultant to various agencies of the United Nations system, including the United Nations Conference on Trade and Development (UNCTAD), the United Nations Industrial Development Organization (UNIDO) and the United Nations Development Programme (UNDP), in the field of international trade, investment and intellectual property rights. He has also spoken extensively to the business, managerial, scientific and academic communities in India on the scope and substance of the Uruguay Round negotiations and Agreements and their implications. Until his appointment to the Appellate Body of the WTO in 2000, he was a Member of the Government of India's High Level Trade Advisory Committee on Multilateral Trade Negotiations. He was also a Member of the Permanent Group of Experts under the *Agreement on Subsidies and Countervailing Measures*, and a Member of a dispute settlement panel of the WTO in 1999–2000 in the *United States – Section 110(5) of the* US *Copyright Act* case.

Mr. Ganesan has written numerous newspaper articles and monographs dealing with various aspects of the Uruguay Round Agreements and their implications. He is also the author of many papers on trade, investment and intellectual property issues for UNCTAD and UNIDO, and has contributed to books published in India on matters concerning the Uruguay Round, including intellectual property rights issues.

Mr. Ganesan holds M.A. and M.Sc. degrees from the University of Madras, India.

Merit E. Janow (United States) (2003–2007)

Born in the United States on 13 May 1958, Ms. Merit E. Janow has been Professor in the Practice of International Economic Law and International Affairs at the School of International and Public Affairs of Columbia University since 1994. She teaches advanced law courses in international trade and comparative antitrust law along with courses on international trade policy. From 1997 to 2000, while at Columbia University, Ms. Janow served as Executive Director of the first international competition policy advisory committee to the Attorney General and the Assistant Attorney General for Antitrust of the United States Department of Justice. Before joining Columbia's faculty in 1994, Ms. Janow was Deputy Assistant United States Trade Representative for Japan and China (1990–93), and worked as a corporate lawyer specializing in mergers and acquisitions with the law firm Skadden, Arps, Slate, Meagher & Flom in New York (1988–90). Ms. Janow is the author of several books and has contributed chapters to more than a dozen books. She grew up in Tokyo, Japan, and speaks Japanese. Ms. Janow served as a WTO panelist from September 2001 to May 2002 in the dispute *European Communities – Trade Description of Sardines* (WT DS231).

John S. Lockhart (Australia) (2001–2009)

Born in Australia on 2 October 1935, John S. Lockhart was Executive Director at the Asian Development Bank (ADB) in the Philippines from July 1999 to 2002, working closely with developing member countries on the development of programmes directed to poverty alleviation through the promotion of economic growth. His other duties for the ADB included the development of law reform programmes and assisting in the provision of advice on legal questions, notably the interpretation of the ADB's Charter, international treaties, and United Nations instruments.

Prior to joining the ADB, Mr. Lockhart served as Judicial Reform Specialist at the World Bank focusing on strengthening legal and judicial institutions and working closely with developing countries and economies in transition in their projects of judicial and legal reform.

Since graduating in arts and law from the University of Sydney in 1958, Mr. Lockhart's professional experience has included Judge, Federal Court of Australia (1978–1999); President of the Australian Competition Tribunal (1982–1999); Deputy President of the Australian Copyright Tribunal (1981–1997); and Queen's Counsel, Australia and the United Kingdom Privy Council (1973–1978). He was appointed an Officer of the Order of Australia in 1994 for services to the law, education and the arts.

Giorgio Sacerdoti (European Communities – Italy) (2001–2009)

Born on 2 March 1943, Giorgio Sacerdoti has been Professor of International Law and European Law at Bocconi University, Milan, Italy, since 1986.

Professor Sacerdoti has held various posts in the public sector, including Vice-Chairman of the Organisation for Economic Co-operation and Development (OECD) Working Group on Bribery in International Business Transactions until 2001, where he was one of the drafters of the "Anticorruption Convention of 1997". He has acted as consultant to the Council of Europe, the United Nations Conference on Trade and Development (UNCTAD), and the World Bank in matters related to foreign investments, trade, bribery, development, and good governance. In the private sector, he has often served as arbitrator in international commercial disputes and at the International Centre for Settlement of Investment Disputes (ICSID).

Professor Sacerdoti has published extensively on international trade law, investments, international contracts and arbitration.

After graduating from the University of Milan with a law degree *summa cum laude* in 1965, Professor Sacerdoti gained a Master in Comparative Law from Columbia University Law School as a Fulbright Fellow in 1967. He was admitted to the Milan bar in 1969 and to the Supreme Court of Italy in 1979. He is a Member of the Committee on International Trade Law of the International Law Association.

Yasuhei Taniguchi (Japan) (2000–2007)

Born in Japan on 26 December 1934, Yasuhei Taniguchi is currently Professor of Law at Tokyo Keizai University, and Attorney at Law in Tokyo. He obtained a law degree from Kyoto University in 1957 and was fully qualified as a jurist in 1959. His graduate degrees include LL.M., University of California at Berkeley (1963) and J.S.D., Cornell University (1964). He taught at Kyoto University for 39 years and has been Professor Emeritus since 1998. He also has taught as Visiting Professor of Law in the United States (University of Michigan, University of California at Berkeley, Duke University, Stanford University, Georgetown University, Harvard University, New York University, and University of Richmond), in Australia (Murdoch University and University of Melbourne), at the University of Hong Kong, and at the University of Paris XII.

Professor Taniguchi is former president of the Japanese Association of Civil Procedure and currently vice-president of the International Association of Procedural Law. He is affiliated with various academic societies and arbitral organizations as arbitrator, including the International Council for Commercial Arbitration; the International Law Association; the American Law Institute; the Japan Commercial Arbitration Association; the Chartered Institute of Arbitrators; the American Arbitration Association; the Hong Kong International Arbitration Center; the Chinese International Economic and Trade Arbitration Commission; the Korean Commercial Arbitration Board; and the Cairo Regional Centre of Commercial Arbitration. He has also been an active arbitrator in the International Chamber of Commerce (ICC) Court of International Arbitration.

Professor Taniguchi has written numerous books and articles in the fields of civil procedure, arbitration, insolvency, the judicial system and legal profession, as well as comparative and international law related to these fields. His publications have been published in Japanese, Chinese, English, French, Italian, German, and Portuguese.

Annex C Information on Appellate Body Reports

1996

Report	Short Title	Document Symbol	Adoption Date	Minutes of DSB[1] Meeting where adopted	DSR[2] Reference
United States – Standards for Reformulated and Conventional Gasoline, AB-1996-1	*US – Gasoline*	WT/DS2/AB/R	20 May 1996	WT/DSB/M/17	1996:I, 3
Japan – Taxes on Alcoholic Beverages, AB-1996-2	*Japan – Alcoholic Beverages II*	WT/DS8/AB/R WT/DS10/AB/R WT/DS11/AB/R	1 November 1996	WT/DSB/M/25	1996:I, 97
United States – Restrictions on Imports of Cotton and Man-made Fibre Underwear, AB-1996-3	*US – Underwear*	WT/DS24/AB/R	25 February 1997	WT/DSB/M/29	1997:I, 11
Brazil – Measures Affecting Desiccated Coconut, AB-1996-4	*Brazil – Desiccated Coconut*	WT/DS22/AB/R	20 March 1997	WT/DSB/M/30	1997:I, 167

[1] Dispute Settlement Body.

[2] World Trade Organization, *Dispute Settlement Reports* (Cambridge University Press, 2000–2004) Vols. DSR 1996:1 to DSR 2000:XIII. The *Dispute Settlement Reports* of the World Trade Organization (the "WTO") include panel and Appellate Body reports, as well as arbitration awards, in disputes concerning the rights and obligations of WTO Members under the provisions of the *Marrakesh Agreement Establishing the World Trade Organization*. The *Dispute Settlement Reports* are available in English only. Starting with 2002, each volume contains a cumulative index of published disputes.

1997

Report	Short Title	Document Symbol	Adoption Date	Minutes of DSB Meeting where adopted	DSR Reference
United States – Measure Affecting Imports of Woven Wool Shirts and Blouses from India, AB-1997-1	*US – Wool Shirts and Blouses*	WT/DS33/AB/R and Corr.1	23 May 1997	WT/DSB/M/33	1997:I, 323
Canada – Certain Measures Concerning Periodicals, AB-1997-2	*Canada – Periodicals*	WT/DS31/AB/R	30 July 1997	WT/DSB/M/36	1997:I, 449
European Communities – Regime for the Importation, Sale and Distribution of Bananas, AB-1997-3	EC – Bananas III	WT/DS27/AB/R	25 September 1997	WT/DSB/M/37	1997:II, 591
EC Measures Concerning Meat and Meat Products (Hormones), AB-1997-4	*EC– Hormones*	WT/DS26/AB/R WT/DS48/AB/R	13 February 1998	WT/DSB/M/42	1998:I, 135
India – Patent Protection for Pharmaceutical and Agricultural Chemical Products, AB-1997-5	*India – Patents (US)*	WT/DS50/AB/R	16 January 1998	WT/DSB/M/40	1998:I, 9

1998

Report	Short Title	Document Symbol	Adoption Date	Minutes of DSB Meeting where adopted	DSR Reference
Argentina – Measures Affecting Imports of Footwear, Textiles, Apparel and Other Items, AB-1998-1	*Argentina – Textiles and Apparel*	WT/DS56/AB/R and Corr.1	22 April 1998	WT/DSB/M/45	1998:III, 1003
European Communities – Customs Classification of Certain Computer Equipment, AB-1998-2	*EC – Computer Equipment*	WT/DS62/AB/R WT/DS67/AB/R WT/DS68/AB/R	22 June 1998	WT/DSB/M/46	1998:III, 1003
European Communities – Measures Affecting the Importation of Certain Poultry Products, AB-1998-3	*EC – Poultry*	WT/DS69/AB/R	23 July 1998	WT/DSB/M/47	1998:V, 2031
United States – Import Prohibition of Certain Shrimp and Shrimp Products, AB-1998-4	*US – Shrimp*	WT/DS58/AB/R	6 November 1998	WT/DSB/M/50	1998:VII, 2755
Australia – Measures Affecting Importation of Salmon, AB-1998-5	*Australia – Salmon*	WT/DS18/AB/R	6 November 1998	WT/DSB/M/50	1998:VIII, 3327
Guatemala – Anti-Dumping Investigation Regarding Portland Cement from Mexico, AB-1998-6	*Guatemala – Cement I*	WT/DS60/AB/R	25 November 1998	WT/DSB/M/51	1998:IX, 3767
Korea – Taxes on Alcoholic Beverages, AB-1998-7	*Korea – Alcoholic Beverages*	WT/DS75/AB/R WT/DS84/AB/R	17 February 1999	WT/DSB/M/55	1999:I, 3
Japan – Measures Affecting Agricultural Products, AB-1998-8	*Japan – Agricultural Products II*	WT/DS76/AB/R	19 March 1999	WT/DSB/M/57	1999:I, 277

1999

Report	Short Title	Document Symbol	Adoption Date	Minutes of DSB Meeting where adopted	DSR Reference
Brazil – Export Financing Programme for Aircraft, AB-1999-1	*Brazil – Aircraft*	WT/DS46/AB/R	20 August 1999	WT/DSB/M/67	1999:III, 1161
Canada – Measures Affecting the Export of Civilian Aircraft, AB-1999-2	*Canada – Aircraft*	WT/DS70/AB/R	20 August 1999	WT/DSB/M/67	1999:III, 1377
India – Quantitative Restrictions on Imports of Agricultural, Textile and Industrial Products, AB-1999-3	*India – Quantitative Restrictions*	WT/DS90/AB/R	22 September 1999	WT/DSB/M/68	1999:IV, 1763
Canada – Measures Affecting the Importation of Milk and the Exportation of Dairy Products, AB-1999-4	*Canada – Dairy*	WT/DS103/AB/R WT/DS113/AB/R and Corr.1	27 October 1999	WT/DSB/M/70	1999:V, 2057
Turkey – Restrictions on Imports of Textile and Clothing Products, AB-1999-5	*Turkey – Textiles*	WT/DS34/AB/R	19 November 1999	WT/DSB/M/71	1999:VI, 2345
Chile – Taxes on Alcoholic Beverages, AB-1999-6	*Chile – Alcoholic Beverages*	WT/DS87/AB/R WT/DS110/AB/R	12 January 2000	WT/DSB/M/73	2000:I, 281
Argentina – Safeguard Measures on Imports of Footwear, AB-1999-7	*Argentina – Footwear (EC)*	WT/DS121/AB/R	12 January 2000	WT/DSB/M/73	2000:I, 515
Korea – Definitive Safeguard Measure on Imports of Certain Dairy Products, AB-1999-8	*Korea – Dairy*	WT/DS98/AB/R	12 January 2000	WT/DSB/M/73	2000:I, 3
United States – Tax Treatment for "Foreign Sales Corporations", AB-1999-9	*US – FSC*	WT/DS108/AB/R	20 March 2000	WT/DSB/M/77	2000:III, 1619

2000

Report	Short Title	Document Symbol	Adoption Date	Minutes of DSB Meeting where adopted	DSR Reference
United States – Imposition of Countervailing Duties on Certain Hot-Rolled Lead and Bismuth Carbon Steel Products Originating in the United Kingdom, AB-2000-1	*US – Lead and Bismuth II*	WT/DS138/AB/R	7 June 2000	WT/DSB/M/83	2000:V, 2595
Canada – Certain Measures Affecting the Automotive Industry, AB-2000-2	*Canada – Autos*	WT/DS139/AB/R WT/DS142/AB/R	19 June 2000	WT/DSB/M/84	2000:VI, 2985
Brazil – Export Financing Programme for Aircraft, Recourse by Canada to Article 21.5 of the DSU, AB-2000-3	*Brazil – Aircraft (Article 21.5 – Canada)*	WT/DS46/AB/RW	4 August 2000	WT/DSB/M/87	2000:VIII, 4067
Canada – Measures Affecting the Export of Civilian Aircraft, Recourse by Brazil to Article 21.5 of the DSU, AB-2000-4	*Canada – Aircraft (Article 21.5 – Brazil)*	WT/DS70/AB/RW	4 August 2000	WT/DSB/M/87	2000:IX, 4299
United States – Anti-Dumping Act of 1916, complaint by the European Communities, complaint by Japan, AB-2000-5, AB-2000-6	*US – 1916 Act*	WT/DS136/AB/R WT/DS162/AB/R	26 September 2000	WT/DSB/M/89	2000:X, 4793
Canada – Term of Patent Protection, AB-2000-7	*Canada – Patent Term*	WT/DS170/AB/R	12 October 2000	WT/DSB/M/90	2000:X, 5093

Korea – Measures Affecting Imports of Fresh, Chilled and Frozen Beef, AB-2000-8	*Korea – Various Measures on Beef*	WT/DS161/AB/R WT/DS169/AB/R	10 January 2001	WT/DSB/M/96	2001:I, 5
United States – Import Measures on Certain Products from the European Communities, AB-2000-9	*US – Certain EC Products*	WT/DS165/AB/R	10 January 2001	WT/DSB/M/96	2001:I, 373
United States – Definitive Safeguard Measures on Imports of Wheat Gluten from the European Communities, AB-2000-10	*US – Wheat Gluten*	WT/DS166/AB/R	19 January 2001	WT/DSB/M/97	2001:II, 717
European Communities – Measures Affecting Asbestos and Asbestos-Containing Products, AB-2000-11	*EC – Asbestos*	WT/DS135/AB/R	5 April 2001	WT/DSB/M/103	2001:VII, 3243
Thailand – Anti-Dumping Duties on Angles, Shapes and Sections of Iron or Non-Alloy Steel and H-Beams from Poland, AB-2000-12	*Thailand – H-Beams*	WT/DS122/AB/R	5 April 2001	WT/DSB/M/103	2001:VII, 2701
European Communities – Anti-Dumping Duties on Imports of Cotton-Type Bed Linen from India, AB-2000-13	*EC – Bed Linen*	WT/DS141/AB/R	12 March 2001	WT/DSB/M/101	2001:V, 2049

2001

Report	Short Title	Document Symbol	Adoption Date	Minutes of DSB Meeting where adopted	DSR Reference
United States – Safeguard Measures on Imports of Fresh, Chilled or Frozen Lamb Meat from New Zealand and Australia, AB-2001-1	*US – Lamb*	WT/DS177/AB/R WT/DS178/AB/R	16 May 2001	WT/DSB/M/105	2001:IX, 4051
United States – Anti-Dumping Measures on Certain Hot-Rolled Steel Products from Japan, AB-2001-2	*US – Hot-Rolled Steel*	WT/DS184/AB/R	23 August 2001	WT/DSB/M/108	2001:X, 4697
United States – Transitional Safeguard Measure on Combed Cotton Yarn from Pakistan, AB-2001-3	*US – Cotton Yarn*	WT/DS192/AB/R	5 November 2001	WT/DSB/M/112	2001:XII, 6027
United States – Import Prohibition of Certain Shrimp and Shrimp Products, Recourse to Article 21.5 of the DSU by Malaysia, AB-2001-4	*US – Shrimp (Article 21.5 – Malaysia)*	WT/DS58/AB/RW	21 November 2001	WT/DSB/M/113	2001:XIII, 6481
Mexico – Anti-Dumping Investigation of High Fructose Corn Syrup (HFCS) from the United States, Recourse to Article 21.5 of the DSU by the United States, AB-2001-5	*Mexico – Corn Syrup (Article 21.5 – US)*	WT/DS132/AB/RW	21 November 2001	WT/DSB/M/113	2001:XIII, 6675

Canada – Measures Affecting the Importation of Milk and the Exportation of Dairy Products, Recourse to Article 21.5 of the DSU by New Zealand and the United States, AB-2001-6	*Canada – Dairy (Article 21.5 – New Zealand and US)*	WT/DS103/AB/RW WT/DS113/AB/RW	18 December 2001	WT/DSB/M/116	2001:XIII, 6829
United States – Section 211 Omnibus Appropriations Act of 1998, AB-2001-7	*US – Section 211 Appropriations Act*	WT/DS176/AB/R	1 February 2002	WT/DSB/M/119	2002:II, 589
United States – Tax Treatment for "Foreign Sales Corporations", Recourse to Article 21.5 of the DSU by the European Communities, AB-2001-8	*US – FSC (Article 21.5 – EC)*	WT/DS108/AB/RW	29 January 2002	WT/DSB/M/118	2002:I, 55
United States – Definitive Safeguard Measures on Imports of Circular Welded Carbon Quality Line Pipe from Korea, AB-2001-9	*US – Line Pipe*	WT/DS202/AB/R	8 March 2002	WT/DSB/M/121	2002:IV, 1403

2002

Report	Short Title	Document Symbol	Adoption Date	Minutes of DSB Meeting where adopted	DSR Reference
India – Measures Affecting the Automotive Sector, AB-2002-1	*India – Autos*	WT/DS146/AB/R WT/DS175/AB/R	5 April 2002	WT/DSB/M/122	2002:V, 1821
Chile – Price Band System and Safeguard Measures Relating to Certain Agricultural Products, AB-2002-2	*Chile – Price Band System*	WT/DS207/AB/R	23 October 2002	WT/DSB/M/134	2002:VIII, 3045
European Communities – Trade Description of Sardines, AB-2002-3	*EC – Sardines*	WT/DS231/AB/R	23 October 2002	WT/DSB/M/134	2002:VIII, 3359
United States – Countervailing Duties on Certain Corrosion-Resistant Carbon Steel Flat Products from Germany, AB-2002-4	*US – Carbon Steel*	WT/DS213/AB/R and Corr.1	19 December 2002	WT/DSB/M/139	2002:IX, 3779
United States – Countervailing Measures Concerning Certain Products from the European Communities, AB-2002-5	*US – Countervailing Measures on Certain EC Products*	WT/DS212/AB/R	8 January 2003	WT/DSB/M/140	2003:I, 5
Canada – Measures Affecting the Importation of Milk and the Exportation of Dairy Products, Second Recourse to Article 21.5 of the DSU by New Zealand and the United States, AB-2002-6	*Canada – Dairy (Article 21.5 – New Zealand and US II)*	WT/DS103/AB/RW2 WT/DS113/AB/RW2	17 January 2003	WT/DSB/M/141	2003:I, 213
United States – Continued Dumping and Subsidy Offset Act of 2000, AB-2002-7	*US – Offset Act (Byrd Amendment)*	WT/DS217/AB/R WT/DS234/AB/R	27 January 2003	WT/DSB/M/142	2002:I, 375

2003

Report	Short Title	Document Symbol	Adoption Date	Minutes of DSB Meeting where adopted	DSR Reference
European Communities – Anti-Dumping Duties on Imports of Cotton-Type Bed Linen from India, Recourse to Article 21.5 of the DSU by India, AB-2003-1	*EC – Bed Linen (Article 21.5 – India)*	WT/DS141/AB/RW	24 April 2003	WT/DSB/M/148	2003:III, 965
European Communities – Anti-Dumping Duties on Malleable Cast Iron Tube or Pipe Fittings from Brazil, AB-2003-2	*EC – Tube or Pipe Fittings*	WT/DS219/AB/R	18 August 2003	WT/DSB/M/154	2003:VI, 2613
United States – Definitive Safeguard Measures on Imports of Certain Steel Products, AB-2003-3	*US – Steel Safeguards*	WT/DS248/AB/R WT/DS249/AB/R WT/DS251/AB/R WT/DS252/AB/R WT/DS253/AB/R WT/DS254/AB/R WT/DS258/AB/R WT/DS259/AB/R	10 December 2003	WT/DSB/M/160	2003:VII, 3117
Japan – Measures Affecting the Importation of Apples, AB-2003-4	*Japan – Apples*	WT/DS245/AB/R	10 December 2003	WT/DSB/M/160	2003:IX, 4391
United States – Sunset Review of Anti-Dumping Duties on Corrosion-Resistant Carbon Steel Flat Products from Japan, AB-2003-5	*US – Corrosion-Resistant Steel Sunset Review*	WT/DS244/AB/R	9 January 2004	WT/DSB/M/162	
United States – Final Countervailing Duty Determination with Respect to Certain Softwood Lumber from Canada, AB-2003-6	*US – Softwood Lumber IV*	WT/DS257/AB/R and Corr.1	17 February 2004	WT/DSB/M/165	

2004

Report	Short Title	Document Symbol	Adoption Date	Minutes of DSB Meeting where adopted	DSR Reference
European Communities – Conditions for the Granting of Tariff Preferences to Developing Countries, AB-2004-1	*EC – Tariff Preferences*	WT/DS246/AB/R	20 April 2004	WT/DSB/M/167	
United States – Final Dumping Determination on Softwood Lumber from Canada, AB-2004-2	*US – Softwood Lumber V*	WT/DS264/AB/R	31 August 2004	WT/DSB/M/175	
Canada – Measures Relating to Exports of Wheat and Treatment of Imported Grain, AB-2004-3	*Canada – Wheat Exports and Grain Imports*	WT/DS276/AB/R	27 September 2004	WT/DSB/M/176	
United States – Sunset Reviews of Anti-Dumping Measures on Oil Country Tubular Goods from Argentina, AB-2004-4	*US – Oil Country Tubular Goods Sunset Reviews*	WT/DS268/AB/R	17 December 2004	WT/DSB/M/180	
United States – Subsidies on Upland Cotton, AB-2004-5	*US – Upland Cotton*	WT/DS267/AB/R	21 March 2005	WT/DSB/M186	

2005

United States – Measures Affecting the Cross-Border Supply of Gambling and Betting Services, AB-2005-1	*US – Gambling*	WT/DS285/AB/R	20 April 2005	WT/DSB/M/188	
European Communities – Export Subsidies on Sugar (complaints by Australia, Brazil, and Thailand), AB-2005-2	*EC – Export Subsidies on Sugar*	WT/DS265/AB/R WT/DS266/AB/R WT/DS283/AB/R	19 May 2005	WT/DSB/M/189	
Dominican Republic – Measures Affecting the Importation and Internal Sale of Cigarettes, AB-2005-3	*Dominican Republic – Import and Sale of Cigarettes*	WT/DS302/AB/R	19 May 2005	WT/DSB/M/189	

Annex D

Arbitration Awards under Article 21.3(c) of the DSU:[1] 1997–2005[2]

Reasonable Period of Time Awarded by the Arbitrator

Article 21.3(c) of the DSU provides:

Article 21

Surveillance of Implementation of Recommendations and Rulings

(c) a period of time determined through binding arbitration within 90 days after the date of adoption of the recommendations and rulings. In such arbitration, a guideline for the arbitrator should be that the reasonable period of time to implement panel or Appellate Body recommendations should not exceed 15 months from the date of adoption of a panel or Appellate Body report. However, that time may be shorter or longer, depending upon the particular circumstances. (footnotes omitted)

Short Title Document Symbol DSR Reference	Arbitrator	Agreed by Parties or Appointed by DG	Date of Adoption of Report	Date of Circulation of Award	Nature of Change Envisaged	Reasonable Period of Time
Japan – Alcoholic Beverages II WT/DS8/15, WT/DS10/15, WT/DS11/13 (DSR 1997:I, 3)	Julio Lacarte-Muró	DG	01/11/1996	14/02/1997	Legislative	15 months
EC – Bananas III WT/DS27/15 (DSR 1998:I, 3)	Said El-Naggar	DG	25/09/1997	07/01/1998	Legislative	15 months and 1 week
EC – Hormones WT/DS26/15, WT/DS48/13 (DSR 1998:V, 1833)	Julio Lacarte-Muró	DG	13/02/1998	29/05/1998	Legislative	15 months
Indonesia – Automobiles WT/DS54/15, WT/DS55/14 WT/DS59/13, WT/DS64/12 (DSR 1998:IX, 4029)	Christopher Beeby	Parties	23/07/1998	07/12/1998	Legislative	12 months

[1] *Understanding on Rules and Procedures Governing the Settlement of Disputes.*

[2] There were no Arbitration Awards circulated under Article 21.3(c) of the DSU in 1995 or 1996.

Short Title Document Symbol DSR Reference	Arbitrator	Agreed by Parties or Appointed by DG	Date of Adoption of Report	Date of Circulation of Award	Nature of Change Envisaged	Reasonable Period of Time
Australia – Salmon WT/DS18/9 (DSR 1999:I, 267)	Said El-Naggar	Parties	06/11/1998	23/02/1999	Regulatory	8 months
Korea – Alcoholic Beverages WT/DS75/16, WT/DS84/14 (DSR 1999:II, 937)	Claus-Dieter Ehlermann	Parties	17/02/1999	04/06/1999	Legislative	11 months and 2 weeks
Chile – Alcoholic Beverages WT/DS87/15, WT/DS110/14 (DSR 2000:V, 2583)	Florentino P. Feliciano	Parties	12/01/2000	23/05/2000	Legislative	14 months and 9 days
Canada – Pharmaceutical Patents WT/DS114/13 (DSR 2002:I, 3)	James Bacchus	Parties	07/04/2000	18/08/2000	Regulatory	6 months
Canada – Autos WT/DS139/12, WT/DS142/12 (DSR 2000:X, 5079)	Julio Lacarte-Muró	Parties	19/06/2000	04/10/2000	Regulatory	8 months
US – Section 110(5) Copyright Act WT/DS160/12 (DSR 2001:II, 657)	Julio Lacarte-Muró	Parties	27/07/2000	15/01/2001	Legislative	12 months
US – 1916 Act WT/DS136/11, WT/DS162/14 (DSR 2001:V, 2017)	A.V. Ganesan	Parties	26/09/2000	28/02/2001	Legislative	10 months
Canada – Patent Term WT/DS170/10 (DSR 2001:V, 2031)	Claus-Dieter Ehlermann	Parties	12/10/2000	28/02/2001	Legislative	10 months
Argentina – Hides and the Leather WT/DS155/10 (DSR 2001:XII, 6013)	Florentino P. Feliciano	Parties	16/02/2001	31/08/2001	Regulatory	12 months and 12 days
US – Hot-Rolled Steel WT/DS184/13 (DSR 2002:IV, 1389)	Florentino P. Feliciano	Parties	23/08/2001	19/02/2002	Regulatory / Legislative	15 months
US – Line Pipe WT/DS202/17 (DSR 2002:V, 2061)	Yasuhei Taniguchi	DG	8/03/2002	26/07/2002[3]	N/A	N/A
Chile – Price Band System WT/DS207/13 (DSR 2003:III, 1237)	John Lockhart	Parties	23/10/2002	17/03/2003	Legislative	14 months
US – Offset Act (Byrd Amendment) WT/DS217/14, WT/DS234/22 (DSR 2003:III, 1163)	Yasuhei Taniguchi	DG	27/01/2003	13/06/2003	Legislative	11 months
EC – Tariff Preferences WT/DS246/14	John Lockhart	DG	20/04/2004	20/09/2004	Legislative	14 months and 11 days
US – Softwood Lumber V WT/DS264/13	John Lockhart	Parties	31/08/2004	13/12/2004[4]	N/A	N/A
US – Oil Country Tubular Goods Sunset Reviews WT/DS268/12	A.V. Ganesan	Parties	17/12/2004	7/06/2005	Regulatory	12 months

[3] Parties reached an agreement on the reasonable period of time for compliance during the proceedings. Therefore, the Arbitrator issued a brief report noting that it was not necessary to issue an award.

[4] Parties reached an agreement on the reasonable period of time for compliance during the proceedings. Therefore, the Arbitrator issued a brief report noting that it was not necessary to issue an award.

Annex E Articles of Covered Agreements Addressed in Appellate Body Reports

Appellate Body Report	WTO	GATT 1994	Agriculture	SPS	ATC	TBT	TRIMS	Anti-Dumping	Preship. Insp.	ROO	Import Licensing	SCM	Safeguards	GATS	TRIPS	DSU
US – Gasoline WT/DS2/AB/R		XX (chapeau) XX(g)														
Japan – Alcoholic Beverages II WT/DS8/AB/R WT/DS10/AB/R WT/DS11/AB/R		III:1 III:2 Ad III:2 GATT 1994 (par. 1(b)(iv))														
US – Underwear WT/DS24/AB/R		X:2 XIII:3(b)			6.10											
Brazil – Desiccated Coconut WT/DS22/AB/R		I II VI										10 32.1 32.3				7.3
US – Wool Shirts and Blouses WT/DS33/AB/R and Corr.1	IX	XXIII			6 6.10											3.2 3.8 3.9 11 19.2
Canada – Periodicals WT/DS31/AB/R		III:2 III:8(b)														
EC– Bananas III WT/DS27/AB/R		I:1 III:2 III:4 X:3(a) XIII XXIII	4.1 21.1								1.3 3.2 3.3			I I:2 (c) II XVII XXVIII (c)		3.7 6.2 7

(*cont.*)

(*cont.*)

Appellate Body Report	WTO	GATT 1994	Agriculture	SPS	ATC	TBT	TRIMS	Anti-Dumping	Preship. Insp.	ROO	Import Licensing	SCM	Safeguards	GATS	TRIPS	DSU
India – Patents (US) WT/DS50/AB/R															64.2 70.8 70.9	3.2 6.2 7 19.2
EC – Hormones WT/DS26/AB/R WT/DS48/AB/R				2.2 2.3 3.1 3.2 3.3 5.1 5.2 5.5 5.6 5.7 5.8 11.2												9.3 11 12.1 13.2 Appendix 3
Argentina – Textiles and Apparel WT/DS56/AB/R and Corr.1		II:1 VIII														11 13
EC – Computer Equipment WT/DS62/AB/R WT/DS67/AB/R WT/DS68/AB/R		II:1 II:5														6.2
EC – Poultry WT/DS69/AB/R		X XIII XIII (chapeau) XIII:2 XIII:2(d) XXVIII	5.1(b) 5.5								1.2 3.2					11

Australia – Salmon WT/DS18/AB/R				2.2 2.3 5.1 5.5 5.6 Annex A (par. 4)												11 12.1 12.2
US – Shrimp WT/DS58/AB/R	Preamble	XX XX (chapeau) XX(g)														12 13
Guatemala – Cement I WT/DS60/AB/R								17 17.3 17.4 17.5								1.1 1.2 6.2 7
Korea – Alcoholic Beverages WT/DS75/AB/R WT/DS84/AB/R		III:1 III:2 Ad III:2														11 12.7
Japan – Agricultural Products II WT/DS76/AB/R				2.2 5.1 5.6 5.7 7 Annex B (par 1)												13

(cont.)

(*cont.*)

Appellate Body Report	WTO	GATT 1994	Agriculture	SPS	ATC	TBT	TRIMS	Anti-Dumping	Preship. Insp.	ROO	Import Licensing	SCM	Safeguards	GATS	TRIPS	DSU
Brazil – Aircraft WT/DS46/AB/R												3.1(a) 4 4.7 27 27.2(b) 27.4 Annex I (item (k))				4 6 6.2 11.2 17.10 18.2
Canada – Aircraft WT/DS70/AB/R												1.1(b) 3.1(a) 14 Annex V				13 13.1
India – Quantitative Restrictions WT/DS90/AB/R		XV:2 XXIII XVIII:11 XVIII B XXIII:12 Ad XVIII:11 *BOP Und.* (fn. 1)														1.1 11 13
Canada – Dairy WT/DS103/AB/R WT/DS113/AB/R and Corr.1		II:1(b)	1(c) 3 8 9.1(a) 9.1(c) 9.1(e) Annex 2 (par. 5)													

Turkey – Textiles WT/DS34/AB/R		XXIV XXIV:4 XXIV:5 (chapeau) XXIV:8(a)														
Chile – Alcoholic Beverages WT/DS87/AB/R WT/DS110/AB/R		III:2 Ad III:2														3.2 12.7 19.2
Korea – Dairy WT/DS98/AB/R	II:2	XIX											2.1 4 4.2 5.1 11.1(a) 12.2			6.2
Argentina – Footwear (EC) WT/DS121/AB/R		XIX XXIV GATT 1994 (par. 1)											2.1 4 4.1(c) 4.2			11
US – FSC WT/DS108/AB/R		GATT 1994 (par. 1(b)(iv))	1(e) 3.3 8 9.1(d) 10.1									1.1 3.1(a) 4.2 (fn. 59) Annex I, (item (e))				4.4 17.6
US – Lead and Bismuth II WT/DS138/AB/R		VI:3						17.6				1.1(b) 14 19 21 21.2				3 11

(*cont.*)

(*cont.*)

Appellate Body Report	WTO	GATT 1994	Agriculture	SPS	ATC	TBT	TRIMS	Anti-Dumping	Preship. Insp.	ROO	Import Licensing	SCM	Safeguards	GATS	TRIPS	DSU
Canada – Autos WT/DS139/AB/R WT/DS142/AB/R		I:1										1.1 1.1(a)(1) (ii) (fn. 1) 3.1(a) 3.1(b)	I:1 II:1			7.1 11
Brazil – Aircraft (Article 21.5 – Canada) WT/DS46/AB/RW												3.1(a) 4.7 Annex I (item (k))				
Canada – Aircraft (Article 21.5 – Brazil) WT/DS70/AB/RW												3.1 (a)				21.5
US – 1916 Act WT/DS136/AB/R WT/DS162/AB/R	XVI:4	VI VI:1 VI:2 XXIII:1(a)						17.1 17.2 17.3 17.4 18.1 18.4	2							1.1 10 12.1
Canada – Patent Term WT/DS170/AB/R															33 62.2 70 70.1 70.2	
Korea – Various Measures on Beef WT/DS161/AB/R WT/DS169/AB/R		III:4 XX(d)	1(a)(ii) 3.2 6 7.2(a) Annex 3 (par. 8)													

US – Certain EC Products WT/DS165/AB/R		II:1(a) II:1(b)														3.2 3.7 21.5 22.6 23.1 23.2(a)
US – Wheat Gluten WT/DS166/AB/R													2.1 2.2 3.1 4.2(a) 4.2(b) 8.1 12.1 12.1(c) 12.2 12.3			11
EC – Bed Linen WT/DS141/AB/R								2.1 2.2.2 (cha- peau) 2.2.2(ii) 2.4 2.4.2 17.6(ii)								
Thailand – H-Beams WT/DS122/AB/R								3.1 3.4 3.7 5.2 5.3 12 17.5 17.6(i) 17.6(ii)								6.2 17.6 17.10 18.2

(*cont.*)

(*cont.*)

Appellate Body Report	WTO	GATT 1994	Agriculture	SPS	ATC	TBT	TRIMS	Anti-Dumping	Preship. Insp.	ROO	Import Licensing	SCM	Safeguards	GATS	TRIPS	DSU
EC – Asbestos WT/DS135/AB/R		III:1 III:2 III:4 XX(b) XXIII:1(b)				Annex 1.1										11
US – Lamb WT/DS177/AB/R WT/DS178/AB/R		XIX:1(a)											1 2.1 3.1 4.1(a) 4.1(b) 4.1(c) 4.2(a) 4.2(b) 11.1(a)			11
US – Hot-Rolled Steel WT/DS184/AB/R	XVI:4							2.1 2.2.1 2.4 2.4.2 3 3.1 3.4 3.5 5.10 6.1.1 6.8 6.13 6.14 9.4 17.6(i) 17.6(ii) Annex II					4.2(b)			11

US – Cotton Yarn WT/DS192/AB/R					6.2 6.4											11 22.4
US – Shrimp (Article 21.5 – Malaysia) WT/DS58/AB/RW		XX (chapeau)														11 21.5
Mexico – Corn Syrup (Article 21.5 – US) WT/DS132/AB/RW								3.1 3.4 3.7 17.5 17.6(i) 17.6(ii)								3.7 4.3 4.7 6.2 12.7 21.5
Canada – Dairy (Article 21.5 – New Zealand and US) WT/DS103/AB/RW WT/DS113/AB/RW			9.1(c) 10.1 13(c)(ii)									3.1 Annex I (items (j) & (k))				
US – FSC (Article 21.5 – EC) WT/DS108/AB/RW		III:4	1(e) 8 10.[illegible]									1.1(a)(1)(ii) 3.1 3.1(a) 4.7(fn. 59 (fifth sentence))		I:1		10.3 12.1 21.5 Appendix 3

(*cont.*)

(*cont.*)

Appellate Body Report	WTO	GATT 1994	Agriculture	SPS	ATC	TBT	TRIMS	Anti-Dumping	Preship. Insp.	ROO	Import Licensing	SCM	Safeguards	GATS	TRIPS	DSU
US – Section 211 Appropriations Act WT/DS176/AB/R															1.2 2.1 3.1 4 15.1 15.2 15.3 15.4 16 16.1 19.1 41.1 42 64.1 *Paris Conv.* (2(1), 6, 6*quin-quies* A(1), 8)	6 17.6 11
US – Line Pipe WT/DS202/AB/R		XIX XXIV						3.5					2 2.1 2.2 3.1 4.1(a) 4.1(b) 4.2(b) 4.2(c) 5.1 5.2(b) 8.1 9.1 12.3			22.4

India – Autos WT/DS/146/AB/R WT/DS/175/AB/R																Appeal With-drawn
Chile – Price Band System WT/DS207/AB/R		II:1(b)	4 4.2 (fn. 1)													3.4 6.2 11
EC – Sardines WT/DS231/AB/R						2 2.4 2.5 2.6 Annex 1.1 (par. 1, par. 2)										11 10.2 17.4 17.9
US – Carbon Steel WT/DS213/AB/R and Corr.1	XVI:4											1 10 11 11.6 11.9 15 15.3 (fn. 45) 21 21.1 21.2 21.3 22.1 22.7 27.10 27.11 32.5				6.2 7 11

(*cont.*)

(*cont.*)

Appellate Body Report	WTO	GATT 1994	Agriculture	SPS	ATC	TBT	TRIMS	Anti-Dumping	Preship. Insp.	ROO	Import Licensing	SCM	Safeguards	GATS	TRIPS	DSU
US – Countervailing Measures on Certain EC Products WT/DS212/AB/R	XVI:4	VI										1.1 10 14 19.1 21.1 21.2 21.3 32.5				3.2 11
Canada – Dairy (Article 21.5 – New Zealand and US II) WT/DS103/AB/RW2 WT/DS113/AB/RW2			3.3 8 9.1(c) 10.3													
US – Offset Act (Byrd Amendment) WT/DS217/AB/R WT/DS234/AB/R	XVI:4	VI:3						5.4 18.1 (fn. 24) 18.4				1 5.4 10 (fn. 35) 11.4 32.1 (fn. 56) 32.5				3.8 9.2 17.6

EC – Bed Linen (Article 21.5 – India) WT/DS141/AB/R								2.1 3.1 3.2 3.3 3.5 6.10 9 9.4 17.6 (i) 17.6(ii)								11 21.5
EC – Tube or Pipe Fittings WT/DS219/AB/R		VI:2						1 2.1 2.2 2.2.2 2.4.2 3.1 3.2 3.3 3.4 3.5 6.2 6.4 17.6(i)								
US – Steel Safeguards WT/DS248/AB/R WT/DS249/AB/R WT/DS251/AB/R WT/DS252/AB/R WT/DS253/AB/R WT/DS254/AB/R WT/DS258/AB/R WT/DS259/AB/R		XIX:1(a)											2.1 3.1 4.2 9.1			11 12.7

(*cont.*)

(*cont.*)

Appellate Body Report	WTO	GATT 1994	Agriculture	SPS	ATC	TBT	TRIMS	Anti-Dumping	Preship. Insp.	ROO	Import Licensing	SCM	Safeguards	GATS	TRIPS	DSU
Japan – Apples WT/DS245/AB/R				2.2 5.1 5.7 Annex A (par. 4)												11
US – Corrosion-Resistant Steel Sunset Review WT/DS244/AB/R	XVI:4							2.1 2.4 6.10 11.3 17.3 18.4								
US – Softwood Lumber IV WT/DS257/AB/R		VI:3										1.1(a)(1)(iii) 10 (fn. 36) 14 14 (d) 19.3 19.4 32.1				
EC – Tariffs Preferences WT/DS246/AB/R		I:1 Enabling Clause (par. 1, par. 2(a) (fn. 3), par. 2(d), par. 3(a), par. 3(c))														

US – Softwood Lumber V WT/DS264/AB/R		VI:2						2.2 2.2.1 2.2.1.1 2.4 2.4.2 9.2 9.4 17.6(ii)								3.2
Canada – Wheat Exports and Grain Imports WT/DS276/AB/R		I II:4 III VI Ad Note to XI, XII, XIII, XIV XVII XVII:1 Ad Note to: XVII:1 XVII:1(a) XVII:1(b) XVII:1(c) XVII:3. Ad Note to: XVIII														3.2 6.2 7 11 12 17.9 19.1

(*cont.*)

(*cont.*)

Appellate Body Report	WTO	GATT 1994	Agriculture	SPS	ATC	TBT	TRIMS	Anti-Dumping	Preship. Insp.	ROO	Import Licensing	SCM	Safeguards	GATS	TRIPS	DSU
US – Oil Country Tubular Goods Sunset Reviews WT/DS268/AB/R		X:3(a)						3 3 (fn. 9) 3.1 3.3 3.7 11.3								6.2 11
US –Upland Cotton WT/DS267/AB/R		XVI:3	1(e) 6 6.3 9.1 9.1(a) 10 10.1 10.2 10.3 10.4 13(a)(ii) 13(b)(ii) 21.1 Annex 2 (par. 1, par. 6, par. 11) Annex 3 (par. 10) Annex 3 (para.7)									3.1 3.1(a) 3.1(b) 3.2 4.2 5(c) 6.3(c) 6.3(d) 6.8 7.8				3.2 3.3 3.4 3.7 4.2 4.4 4.6 6 6.2 7 11 12.7 17.5 17.6 19.1

US –Gambling WT/DS285/AB/R		XX												I:1 XIV Chapeau XIV(a) XIV(c) XVI:1 XVI:2(a) XVI:2(c) XX:3		3.3 3.10 4.2 6.2 11 22.3(f)
EC – Export Subsidies on Sugar WT/DS265/AB/R WT/DS266/AB/R WT/DS283/AB/R		II:1(b) General Interpreta-tive Note to Annex 1A	3.1 3.3 8 9.1 9.1(a) 9.1(b) 9.1(c) 9.2 9.2(a) 9.2(b)(iii) 9.2(b)(iv) 10.1 10.3 21									3 3.1 3.2(a) 4.7				3.3 3.7 3.8 3.10 6.2 7.2 11 17.6 19.1
Dominican Republic – Import and Sale of Cigarettes WT/DS302/AB/R		III:4 XX(d)												XIV		6.2 11

Annex F

Working Procedures for Appellate Review[1]

Definitions

1. In these *Working Procedures for Appellate Review,*

"appellant"
means any party to the dispute that has filed a Notice of Appeal pursuant to Rule 20;

"appellate report"
means an Appellate Body report as described in Article 17 of the DSU;

"appellee"
means any party to the dispute that has filed a submission pursuant to Rule 22 or paragraph 4 of Rule 23;

"consensus"
a decision is deemed to be made by consensus if no Member formally objects to it;

"covered agreements"
has the same meaning as "covered agreements" in paragraph 1 of Article 1 of the DSU;

"division"
means the three Members who are selected to serve on any one appeal in accordance with paragraph 1 of Article 17 of the DSU and paragraph 2 of Rule 6;

"documents"
means the Notice of Appeal, any Notice of Other Appeal and the submissions and other written statements presented by the participants or third participants;

"DSB"
means the Dispute Settlement Body established under Article 2 of the DSU;

[1] WT/AB/WP/5, 4 January 2005. This document replaces the *Working Procedures for Appellate Review* circulated 1 May 2003. It is a consolidated, revised version, and reflects amendments to Rules 1, 18(5), 20, 21, 23, 27 and to Annex I, as well as the addition of a new Rule 23*bis* and a new Annex III, as discussed in WT/AB/WP/W/8 and WT/AB/WP/W/9. The *Working Procedures for Appellate Review* consolidated in this document will be applied to appeals initiated after 1 January 2005.

"DSU"
means the *Understanding on Rules and Procedures Governing the Settlement of Disputes* which is Annex 2 to the WTO *Agreement*;

"Member"
means a Member of the Appellate Body who has been appointed by the DSB in accordance with Article 17 of the DSU;

"other appellant"
means any party to the dispute that has filed a Notice of Other Appeal pursuant to paragraph 1 of Rule 23;

"participant"
means any party to the dispute that has filed a Notice of Appeal pursuant to Rule 20, a Notice of Other Appeal pursuant to Rule 23 or a submission pursuant to Rule 22 or paragraph 4 of Rule 23;

"party to the dispute"
means any WTO Member who was a complaining or defending party in the panel dispute, but does not include a third party;

"proof of service"
means a letter or other written acknowledgement that a document has been delivered, as required, to the parties to the dispute, participants, third parties or third participants, as the case may be;

"Rules"
means these *Working Procedures for Appellate Review*,

"*Rules of Conduct*"
means the *Rules of Conduct for the Understanding on Rules and Procedures Governing the Settlement of Disputes* as attached in Annex II to these Rules;

"SCM Agreement"
means the *Agreement on Subsidies and Countervailing Measures* which is in Annex 1A to the *WTO Agreement;*

"Secretariat"
means the Appellate Body Secretariat;

"service address"
means the address of the party to the dispute, participant, third party or third participant as generally used in WTO dispute settlement proceedings, unless the party to the dispute, participant, third party or third participant has clearly indicated another address;

"third participant"
means any third party that has filed a written submission pursuant to Rule 24(1); or any third party that appears at the oral hearing, whether or not it makes an oral statement at that hearing;

"third party"
means any WTO Member who has notified the DSB of its substantial interest in the matter before the panel pursuant to paragraph 2 of Article 10 of the DSU;

"WTO"
means the World Trade Organization;

"WTO Agreement"
means the *Marrakesh Agreement Establishing the World Trade Organization,* done at Marrakesh, Morocco on 15 April 1994;

"WTO Member"
means any State or separate customs territory possessing full autonomy in the conduct of its external commercial relations that has accepted or acceded to the WTO in accordance with Articles XI, XII or XIV of the *WTO Agreement;* and

"WTO Secretariat"
means the Secretariat of the World Trade Organization.

PART I

MEMBERS

Duties and Responsibilities

2. (1) A Member shall abide by the terms and conditions of the DSU, these Rules and any decisions of the DSB affecting the Appellate Body.
   (2) During his/her term, a Member shall not accept any employment nor pursue any professional activity that is inconsistent with his/her duties and responsibilities.
   (3) A Member shall exercise his/her office without accepting or seeking instructions from any international, governmental, or non-governmental organization or any private source.
   (4) A Member shall be available at all times and on short notice and, to this end, shall keep the Secretariat informed of his/her whereabouts at all times.

Decision-Making

3. (1) In accordance with paragraph 1 of Article 17 of the DSU, decisions relating to an appeal shall be taken solely by the division assigned to that appeal. Other decisions shall be taken by the Appellate Body as a whole.
   (2) The Appellate Body and its divisions shall make every effort to take their decisions by consensus. Where, nevertheless, a decision cannot be arrived at by consensus, the matter at issue shall be decided by a majority vote.

Collegiality

4. (1) To ensure consistency and coherence in decision-making, and to draw on the individual and collective expertise of the Members, the Members shall convene on a regular basis to discuss matters of policy, practice and procedure.

(2) The Members shall stay abreast of dispute settlement activities and other relevant activities of the WTO and, in particular, each Member shall receive all documents filed in an appeal.
(3) In accordance with the objectives set out in paragraph 1, the division responsible for deciding each appeal shall exchange views with the other Members before the division finalizes the appellate report for circulation to the WTO Members. This paragraph is subject to paragraphs 2 and 3 of Rule 11.
(4) Nothing in these Rules shall be interpreted as interfering with a division's full authority and freedom to hear and decide an appeal assigned to it in accordance with paragraph 1 of Article 17 of the DSU.

Chairman

5. (1) There shall be a Chairman of the Appellate Body who shall be elected by the Members.
(2) The term of office of the Chairman of the Appellate Body shall be one year. The Appellate Body Members may decide to extend the term of office for an additional period of up to one year. However, in order to ensure rotation of the Chairmanship, no Member shall serve as Chairman for more than two consecutive terms.
(3) The Chairman shall be responsible for the overall direction of the Appellate Body business, and in particular, his/her responsibilities shall include:
(a) the supervision of the internal functioning of the Appellate Body; and
(b) any such other duties as the Members may agree to entrust to him/her.
(4) Where the office of the Chairman becomes vacant due to permanent incapacity as a result of illness or death or by resignation or expiration of his/her term, the Members shall elect a new Chairman who shall serve a full term in accordance with paragraph 2.
(5) In the event of a temporary absence or incapacity of the Chairman, the Appellate Body shall authorize another Member to act as Chairman *ad interim*, and the Member so authorized shall temporarily exercise all the powers, duties and functions of the Chairman until the Chairman is capable of resuming his/her functions.

Divisions

6. (1) In accordance with paragraph 1 of Article 17 of the DSU, a division consisting of three Members shall be established to hear and decide an appeal.
(2) The Members constituting a division shall be selected on the basis of rotation, while taking into account the principles of random selection, unpredictability and opportunity for all Members to serve regardless of their national origin.
(3) A Member selected pursuant to paragraph 2 to serve on a division shall serve on that division, unless:
(i) he/she is excused from that division pursuant to Rules 9 or 10;
(ii) he/she has notified the Chairman and the Presiding Member that he/she is prevented from serving on the division because of illness or other serious reasons pursuant to Rule 12; or
(iii) he/she has notified his/her intentions to resign pursuant to Rule 14.

Presiding Member of the Division

7. (1) Each division shall have a Presiding Member, who shall be elected by the Members of that division.
   (2) The responsibilities of the Presiding Member shall include:
      (a) coordinating the overall conduct of the appeal proceeding;
      (b) chairing all oral hearings and meetings related to that appeal; and
      (c) coordinating the drafting of the appellate report.
   (3) In the event that a Presiding Member becomes incapable of performing his/her duties, the other Members serving on that division and the Member selected as a replacement pursuant to Rule 13 shall elect one of their number to act as the Presiding Member.

Rules of Conduct

8. (1) On a provisional basis, the Appellate Body adopts those provisions of the *Rules of Conduct for the Understanding on Rules and Procedures Governing the Settlement of Disputes*, attached in Annex II to these Rules, which are applicable to it, until *Rules of Conduct* are approved by the DSB.
   (2) Upon approval of *Rules of Conduct* by the DSB, such *Rules of Conduct* shall be directly incorporated and become part of these Rules and shall supersede Annex II.
9. (1) Upon the filing of a Notice of Appeal, each Member shall take the steps set out in Article VI:4(b)(i) of Annex II, and a Member may consult with the other Members prior to completing the disclosure form.
   (2) Upon the filing of a Notice of Appeal, the professional staff of the Secretariat assigned to that appeal shall take the steps set out in Article VI:4(b)(ii) of Annex II.
   (3) Where information has been submitted pursuant to Article VI:4(b)(i) or (ii) of Annex II, the Appellate Body shall consider whether further action is necessary.
   (4) As a result of the Appellate Body's consideration of the matter pursuant to paragraph 3, the Member or the professional staff member concerned may continue to be assigned to the division or may be excused from the division.
10. (1) Where evidence of a material violation is filed by a participant pursuant to Article VIII of Annex II, such evidence shall be confidential and shall be supported by affidavits made by persons having actual knowledge or a reasonable belief as to the truth of the facts stated.
   (2) Any evidence filed pursuant to Article VIII:1 of Annex II shall be filed at the earliest practicable time: that is, forthwith after the participant submitting it knew or reasonably could have known of the facts supporting it. In no case shall such evidence be filed after the appellate report is circulated to the WTO Members.
   (3) Where a participant fails to submit such evidence at the earliest practicable time, it shall file an explanation in writing of the reasons why it did not do so earlier, and the Appellate Body may decide to consider or not to consider such evidence, as appropriate.

(4) While taking fully into account paragraph 5 of Article 17 of the DSU, where evidence has been filed pursuant to Article VIII of Annex II, an appeal shall be suspended for fifteen days or until the procedure referred to in Article VIII:14–16 of Annex II is completed, whichever is earlier.

(5) As a result of the procedure referred to in Article VIII:14–16 of Annex II, the Appellate Body may decide to dismiss the allegation, to excuse the Member or professional staff member concerned from being assigned to the division or make such other order as it deems necessary in accordance with Article VIII of Annex II.

11. (1) A Member who has submitted a disclosure form with information attached pursuant to Article VI:4(b)(i) or is the subject of evidence of a material violation pursuant to Article VIII:1 of Annex II, shall not participate in any decision taken pursuant to paragraph 4 of Rule 9 or paragraph 5 of Rule 10.

(2) A Member who is excused from a division pursuant to paragraph 4 of Rule 9 or paragraph 5 of Rule 10 shall not take part in the exchange of views conducted in that appeal pursuant to paragraph 3 of Rule 4.

(3) A Member who, had he/she been a Member of a division, would have been excused from that division pursuant to paragraph 4 of Rule 9, shall not take part in the exchange of views conducted in that appeal pursuant to paragraph 3 of Rule 4.

Incapacity

12. (1) A Member who is prevented from serving on a division by illness or for other serious reasons shall give notice and duly explain such reasons to the Chairman and to the Presiding Member.

(2) Upon receiving such notice, the Chairman and the Presiding Member shall forthwith inform the Appellate Body.

Replacement

13. Where a Member is unable to serve on a division for a reason set out in paragraph 3 of Rule 6, another Member shall be selected forthwith pursuant to paragraph 2 of Rule 6 to replace the Member originally selected for that division.

Resignation

14. (1) A Member who intends to resign from his/her office shall notify his/her intentions in writing to the Chairman of the Appellate Body who shall immediately inform the Chairman of the DSB, the Director-General and the other Members of the Appellate Body.

(2) The resignation shall take effect 90 days after the notification has been made pursuant to paragraph 1, unless the DSB, in consultation with the Appellate Body, decides otherwise.

Transition

15. A person who ceases to be a Member of the Appellate Body may, with the authorization of the Appellate Body and upon notification to the DSB, complete the disposition of any appeal to which that person was assigned while a Member, and that person shall, for that purpose only, be deemed to continue to be a Member of the Appellate Body.

PART II

PROCESS

General Provisions

16. (1) In the interests of fairness and orderly procedure in the conduct of an appeal, where a procedural question arises that is not covered by these Rules, a division may adopt an appropriate procedure for the purposes of that appeal only, provided that it is not inconsistent with the DSU, the other covered agreements and these Rules. Where such a procedure is adopted, the division shall immediately notify the parties to the dispute, participants, third parties and third participants as well as the other Members of the Appellate Body.

(2) In exceptional circumstances, where strict adherence to a time-period set out in these Rules would result in a manifest unfairness, a party to the dispute, a participant, a third party or a third participant may request that a division modify a time-period set out in these Rules for the filing of documents or the date set out in the working schedule for the oral hearing. Where such a request is granted by a division, any modification of time shall be notified to the parties to the dispute, participants, third parties and third participants in a revised working schedule.

17. (1) Unless the DSB decides otherwise, in computing any time-period stipulated in the DSU or in the special or additional provisions of the covered agreements, or in these Rules, within which a communication must be made or an action taken by a WTO Member to exercise or preserve its rights, the day from which the time-period begins to run shall be excluded and, subject to paragraph 2, the last day of the time-period shall be included.

(2) The DSB Decision on "Expiration of Time-Periods in the "DSU", WT/DSB/M/7, shall apply to appeals heard by divisions of the Appellate Body.

Documents

18. (1) No document is considered filed with the Appellate Body unless the document is received by the Secretariat within the time-period set out for filing in accordance with these Rules.

(2) Except as otherwise provided in these Rules, every document filed by a party to the dispute, a participant, a third party or a third participant shall be

served on each of the other parties to the dispute, participants, third parties and third participants in the appeal.

(3) A proof of service on the other parties to the dispute, participants, third parties and third participants shall appear on, or be affixed to, each document filed with the Secretariat under paragraph 1 above.

(4) A document shall be served by the most expeditious means of delivery or communication available, including by:

(a) delivering a copy of the document to the service address of the party to the dispute, participant, third party or third participant; or

(b) sending a copy of the document to the service address of the party to the dispute, participant, third party or third participant by facsimile transmission, expedited delivery courier or expedited mail service.

(5) Upon authorization by the division, a participant or a third participant may correct clerical errors in any of its documents (including typographical mistakes, errors of grammar, or words or numbers placed in the wrong order). The request to correct clerical errors shall identify the specific errors to be corrected and shall be filed with the Secretariat no later than 30 days after the date of the filing of the Notice of Appeal. A copy of the request shall be served upon the other parties to the dispute, participants, third parties and third participants, each of whom shall be given an opportunity to comment in writing on the request. The division shall notify the parties to the dispute, participants, third parties and third participants of its decision.

Ex Parte Communications

19. (1) Neither a division nor any of its Members shall meet with or contact one party to the dispute, participant, third party or third participant in the absence of the other parties to the dispute, participants, third parties and third participants.

(2) No Member of the division may discuss any aspect of the subject matter of an appeal with any party to the dispute, participant, third party or third participant in the absence of the other Members of the division.

(3) A Member who is not assigned to the division hearing the appeal shall not discuss any aspect of the subject matter of the appeal with any party to the dispute, participant, third party or third participant.

Commencement of Appeal

20. (1) An appeal shall be commenced by notification in writing to the DSB in accordance with paragraph 4 of Article 16 of the DSU and simultaneous filing of a Notice of Appeal with the Secretariat.

(2) A Notice of Appeal shall include the following information:

(a) the title of the panel report under appeal;

(b) the name of the party to the dispute filing the Notice of Appeal;

(c) the service address, telephone and facsimile numbers of the party to the dispute; and

(d) a brief statement of the nature of the appeal, including:
   (i) identification of the alleged errors in the issues of law covered in the panel report and legal interpretations developed by the panel;
   (ii) a list of the legal provision(s) of the covered agreements that the panel is alleged to have erred in interpreting or applying; and
   (iii) without prejudice to the ability of the appellant to refer to other paragraphs of the panel report in the context of its appeal, an indicative list of the paragraphs of the panel report containing the alleged errors.

Appellant's Submission

21. (1) The appellant shall, within 7 days after the date of the filing of the Notice of Appeal, file with the Secretariat a written submission prepared in accordance with paragraph 2 and serve a copy of the submission on the other parties to the dispute and third parties.
(2) A written submission referred to in paragraph 1 shall
(a) be dated and signed by the appellant; and
(b) set out
   (i) a precise statement of the grounds for the appeal, including the specific allegations of errors in the issues of law covered in the panel report and legal interpretations developed by the panel, and the legal arguments in support thereof;
   (ii) a precise statement of the provisions of the covered agreements and other legal sources relied on; and
   (iii) the nature of the decision or ruling sought.

Appellee's Submission

22. (1) Any party to the dispute that wishes to respond to allegations raised in an appellant's submission filed pursuant to Rule 21 may, within 25 days after the date of the filing of the Notice of Appeal, file with the Secretariat a written submission prepared in accordance with paragraph 2 and serve a copy of the submission on the appellant, other parties to the dispute and third parties.
(2) A written submission referred to in paragraph 1 shall
(a) be dated and signed by the appellee; and
(b) set out
   (i) a precise statement of the grounds for opposing the specific allegations of errors in the issues of law covered in the panel report and legal interpretations developed by the panel raised in the appellant's submission, and the legal arguments in support thereof;
   (ii) an acceptance of, or opposition to, each ground set out in the appellant's submission;

(iii) a precise statement of the provisions of the covered agreements and other legal sources relied on; and
(iv) the nature of the decision or ruling sought.

Multiple Appeals

23. (1) Within 12 days after the date of the filing of the Notice of Appeal, a party to the dispute other than the original appellant may join in that appeal or appeal on the basis of other alleged errors in the issues of law covered in the panel report and legal interpretations developed by the panel. That party shall notify the DSB in writing of its appeal and shall simultaneously file a Notice of Other Appeal with the Secretariat.
(2) A Notice of Other Appeal shall include the following information:
(a) the title of the panel report under appeal;
(b) the name of the party to the dispute filing the Notice of Other Appeal;
(c) the service address, telephone and facsimile numbers of the party to the dispute; and either
(i) a statement of the issues raised on appeal by another participant with which the party joins; or
(ii) a brief statement of the nature of the other appeal, including:
(A) identification of the alleged errors in the issues of law covered in the panel report and legal interpretations developed by the panel;
(B) a list of the legal provision(s) of the covered agreements that the panel is alleged to have erred in interpreting or applying; and
(C) without prejudice to the ability of the other appellant to refer to other paragraphs of the panel report in the context of its appeal, an indicative list of the paragraphs of the panel report containing the alleged errors.
(3) The other appellant shall, within 15 days after the date of the filing of the Notice of Appeal, file with the Secretariat a written submission prepared in accordance with paragraph 2 of Rule 21 and serve a copy of the submission on the other parties to the dispute and third parties.
(4) The appellant, any appellee and any other party to the dispute that wishes to respond to a submission filed pursuant to paragraph 3 may file a written submission within 25 days after the date of the filing of the Notice of Appeal, and any such submission shall be in the format required by paragraph 2 of Rule 22.
(5) This Rule does not preclude a party to the dispute which has not filed a submission under Rule 21 or a Notice of Other Appeal under paragraph 1 of this Rule from exercising its right of appeal pursuant to paragraph 4 of Article 16 of the DSU.
(6) Where a party to the dispute which has not filed a submission under Rule 21 or a Notice of Other Appeal under paragraph 1 of this Rule exercises its right to appeal as set out in paragraph 5, a single division shall examine the appeals.

Amending Notices of Appeal

23*bis*. (1) The division may authorize an original appellant to amend a Notice of Appeal or an other appellant to amend a Notice of Other Appeal.

(2) A request to amend a Notice of Appeal or a Notice of Other Appeal shall be made as soon as possible in writing and shall state the reason(s) for the request and identify precisely the specific amendments that the appellant or other appellant wishes to make to the Notice. A copy of the request shall be served on the other parties to the dispute, participants, third participants and third parties, each of whom shall be given an opportunity to comment in writing on the request.

(3) In deciding whether to authorize, in full or in part, a request to amend a Notice of Appeal or Notice of Other Appeal, the division shall take into account:

(a) the requirement to circulate the appellate report within the time-period set out in Article 17.5 of the DSU or, as appropriate, Article 4.9 of the *SCM Agreement*; and,

(b) the interests of fairness and orderly procedure, including the nature and extent of the proposed amendment, the timing of the request to amend a Notice of Appeal or Notice of Other Appeal, any reasons why the proposed amended Notice of Appeal or Notice of Other Appeal was not or could not have been filed on its original date, and any other considerations that may be appropriate.

(4) The division shall notify the parties to the dispute, participants, third participants, and third parties of its decision. In the event that the division authorizes an amendment to a Notice of Appeal or a Notice of Other Appeal, it shall provide an amended copy of the Notice to the DSB.

Third Participants

24. (1) Any third party may file a written submission containing the grounds and legal arguments in support of its position. Such submission shall be filed within 25 days after the date of the filing of the Notice of Appeal.

(2) A third party not filing a written submission shall, within the same period of 25 days, notify the Secretariat in writing if it intends to appear at the oral hearing, and, if so, whether it intends to make an oral statement.

(3) Third participants are encouraged to file written submissions to facilitate their positions being taken fully into account by the division hearing the appeal and in order that participants and other third participants will have notice of positions to be taken at the oral hearing.

(4) Any third party that has neither filed a written submission pursuant to paragraph (1), nor notified the Secretariat pursuant to paragraph (2), may notify the Secretariat that it intends to appear at the oral hearing, and may request to make an oral statement at the hearing. Such notifications and requests should be notified to the Secretariat in writing at the earliest opportunity.

Transmittal of Record

25. (1) Upon the filing of a Notice of Appeal, the Director-General of the WTO shall transmit forthwith to the Appellate Body the complete record of the panel proceeding.
(2) The complete record of the panel proceeding includes, but is not limited to:
(a) written submissions, rebuttal submissions, and supporting evidence attached thereto by the parties to the dispute and the third parties;
(b) written arguments submitted at the panel meetings with the parties to the dispute and the third parties, the recordings of such panel meetings, and any written answers to questions posed at such panel meetings;
(c) the correspondence relating to the panel dispute between the panel or the WTO Secretariat and the parties to the dispute or the third parties; and
(d) any other documentation submitted to the panel.

Working Schedule

26. (1) Forthwith after the commencement of an appeal, the division shall draw up an appropriate working schedule for that appeal in accordance with the time-periods stipulated in these Rules.
(2) The working schedule shall set forth precise dates for the filing of documents and a timetable for the division's work, including where possible, the date for the oral hearing.
(3) In accordance with paragraph 9 of Article 4 of the DSU, in appeals of urgency, including those which concern perishable goods, the Appellate Body shall make every effort to accelerate the appellate proceedings to the greatest extent possible. A division shall take this into account in drawing up its working schedule for that appeal.
(4) The Secretariat shall serve forthwith a copy of the working schedule on the appellant, the parties to the dispute and any third parties.

Oral Hearing

27. (1) A division shall hold an oral hearing, which shall be held, as a general rule, between 35 and 45 days after the date of the filing of a Notice of Appeal.
(2) Where possible in the working schedule or otherwise at the earliest possible date, the Secretariat shall notify all parties to the dispute, participants, third parties and third participants of the date for the oral hearing.
(3) (a) Any third party that has filed a submission pursuant to Rule 24(1), or has notified the Secretariat pursuant to Rule 24(2) that it intends to appear at the oral hearing, may appear at the oral hearing, make an oral statement at the hearing, and respond to questions posed by the division.
(b) Any third party that has notified the Secretariat pursuant to Rule 24(4) that it intends to appear at the oral hearing may appear at the oral hearing.
(c) Any third party that has made a request pursuant to Rule 24(4) may, at the discretion of the division hearing the appeal, taking into account

the requirements of due process, make an oral statement at the hearing, and respond to questions posed by the division.

(4) The Presiding Member may set time-limits for oral arguments.

Written Responses

28. (1) At any time during the appellate proceeding, including, in particular, during the oral hearing, the division may address questions orally or in writing to, or request additional memoranda from, any participant or third participant, and specify the time-periods by which written responses or memoranda shall be received.

(2) Any such questions, responses or memoranda shall be made available to the other participants and third participants in the appeal, who shall be given an opportunity to respond.

(3) When the questions or requests for memoranda are made prior to the oral hearing, then the questions or requests, as well as the responses or memoranda, shall also be made available to the third parties, who shall also be given an opportunity to respond.

Failure to Appear

29. Where a participant fails to file a submission within the required time-periods or fails to appear at the oral hearing, the division shall, after hearing the views of the participants, issue such order, including dismissal of the appeal, as it deems appropriate.

Withdrawal of Appeal

30. (1) At any time during an appeal, the appellant may withdraw its appeal by notifying the Appellate Body, which shall forthwith notify the DSB.

(2) Where a mutually agreed solution to a dispute which is the subject of an appeal has been notified to the DSB pursuant to paragraph 6 of Article 3 of the DSU, it shall be notified to the Appellate Body.

Prohibited Subsidies

31. (1) Subject to Article 4 of the *SCM Agreement*, the general provisions of these Rules shall apply to appeals relating to panel reports concerning prohibited subsidies under Part II of that *Agreement*.

(2) The working schedule for an appeal involving prohibited subsidies under Part II of the *SCM Agreement* shall be as set out in Annex I to these Rules.

Entry into Force and Amendment

32. (1) These Rules shall enter into force on 15 February 1996.

(2) The Appellate Body may amend these Rules in compliance with the procedures set forth in paragraph 9 of Article 17 of the DSU.

(3) Whenever there is an amendment to the DSU or to the special or additional rules and procedures of the covered agreements, the Appellate Body shall examine whether amendments to these Rules are necessary.

Annex I

Timetable for Appeals[1]

	General Appeals	Prohibited Subsidies Appeals
	Day	Day
Notice of Appeal[2]	0	0
Appellant's Submission[3]	7	4
Notice of Other Appeal[4]	12	6
Other Appellant(s) Submission(s)[5]	15	7
Appellee(s) Submission(s)[6]	25	12
Third Participant(s) Submission(s)[7]	25	12
Third Participant(s) Notification(s)[8]	25	12
Oral Hearing[9]	35–45	17–23
Circulation of Appellate Report	60–90[10]	30–60[11]
DSB Meeting for Adoption	90–120[12]	50–80[13]

[1]Rule 17 applies to the computation of the time-periods below. [2]Rule 20.
[3]Rule 21(1). [4]Rule 23(1). [5]Rule 23(3). [6]Rules 22 and 23(4). [7]Rule 24(1).
[8]Rule 24(2). [9]Rule 27. [10]Article 17:5, DSU.
[11] Article 4:9, *SCM Agreement*. [12]Article 17:14, DSU.
[13] Article 4:9, *SCM Agreement*.

Annex II

Rules of Conduct for the Understanding on Rules and Procedures Governing the Settlement of Disputes

I. Preamble

Members,

Recalling that on 15 April 1994 in Marrakesh, Ministers welcomed the stronger and clearer legal framework they had adopted for the conduct of international trade, including a more effective and reliable dispute settlement mechanism;

Recognizing the importance of full adherence to the Understanding on Rules and Procedures Governing the Settlement of Disputes ("DSU") and the principles for the management of disputes applied under Articles XXII and XXIII of GATT 1947, as further elaborated and modified by the DSU;

Affirming that the operation of the DSU would be strengthened by rules of conduct designed to maintain the integrity, impartiality and confidentiality of proceedings conducted under the DSU thereby enhancing confidence in the new dispute settlement mechanism;

Hereby establish the following Rules of Conduct.

II. Governing Principle

1. Each person covered by these Rules (as defined in paragraph 1 of Section IV below and hereinafter called "covered person") shall be independent and impartial, shall avoid direct or indirect conflicts of interest and shall respect the confidentiality of proceedings of bodies pursuant to the dispute settlement mechanism, so that through the observance of such standards of conduct the integrity and impartiality of that mechanism are preserved. These Rules shall in no way modify the rights and obligations of Members under the DSU nor the rules and procedures therein.

III. Observance of the Governing Principle

1. To ensure the observance of the Governing Principle of these Rules, each covered person is expected (1) to adhere strictly to the provisions of the DSU; (2) to disclose the existence or development of any interest, relationship or matter that that person could reasonably be expected to know and that is likely to affect, or give rise to justifiable doubts as to, that person's independence or impartiality; and (3) to take due care in the performance of their duties to fulfil these expectations, including through avoidance of any direct or indirect conflicts of interest in respect of the subject matter of the proceedings.

2. Pursuant to the Governing Principle, each covered person, shall be independent and impartial, and shall maintain confidentiality. Moreover, such persons shall consider only issues raised in, and necessary to fulfil their responsibilities within, the dispute settlement proceeding and shall not delegate this responsibility to any other person. Such person shall not incur any obligation or accept any benefit that would in anyway interfere with, or which could give rise to, justifiable doubts as to the proper performance of that person's dispute settlement duties.

IV. Scope

1. These Rules shall apply, as specified in the text, to each person serving: (a) on a panel; (b) on the Standing Appellate Body; (c) as an arbitrator pursuant to the provisions mentioned in Annex "1a"; or (d) as an expert participating in the dispute settlement mechanism pursuant to the provisions mentioned in Annex "1b". These Rules shall also apply, as specified in this text and the relevant provisions of the Staff Regulations, to those members of the Secretariat called upon to assist the

panel in accordance with Article 27.1 of the DSU or to assist in formal arbitration proceedings pursuant to Annex "1a"; to the Chairman of the Textiles Monitoring Body (hereinafter called "TMB") and other members of the TMB Secretariat called upon to assist the TMB in formulating recommendations, findings or observations pursuant to the WTO Agreement on Textiles and Clothing; and to Standing Appellate Body support staff called upon to provide the Standing Appellate Body with administrative or legal support in accordance with Article 17.7 of the DSU (hereinafter "Member of the Secretariat or Standing Appellate Body support staff"), reflecting their acceptance of established norms regulating the conduct of such persons as international civil servants and the Governing Principle of these Rules.

2. The application of these Rules shall not in any way impede the Secretariat's discharge of its responsibility to continue to respond to Members' requests for assistance and information.

3. These Rules shall apply to the members of the TMB to the extent prescribed in Section V.

V. Textiles Monitoring Body

1. Members of the TMB shall discharge their functions on an *ad personam* basis, in accordance with the requirement of Article 8.1 of the Agreement on Textiles and Clothing, as further elaborated in the working procedures of the TMB, so as to preserve the integrity and impartiality of its proceedings.[1]

VI. Self-Disclosure Requirements by Covered Persons

1. (a) Each person requested to serve on a panel, on the Standing Appellate Body, as an arbitrator, or as an expert shall, at the time of the request, receive from the Secretariat these Rules, which include an Illustrative List (Annex 2) of examples of the matters subject to disclosure.

(b) Any member of the Secretariat described in paragraph IV:1, who may expect to be called upon to assist in a dispute, and Standing Appellate Body support staff, shall be familiar with these Rules.

2. As set out in paragraph VI:4 below, all covered persons described in paragraph VI.1(a) and VI.1(b) shall disclose any information that could reasonably be expected to be known to them at the time which, coming within the scope of the Governing Principle of these Rules, is likely to affect or give rise to justifiable doubts as to

[1] These working procedures, as adopted by the TMB on 26 July 1995 (G/TMB/R/1), currently include, *inter alia*, the following language in paragraph 1.4: "In discharging their functions in accordance with paragraph 1.1 above, the TMB members and alternates shall undertake not to solicit, accept or act upon instructions from governments, nor to be influenced by any other organizations or undue extraneous factors. They shall disclose to the Chairman any information that they may consider likely to impede their capacity to discharge their functions on an *ad personam* basis. Should serious doubts arise during the deliberations of the TMB regarding the ability of a TMB member to act on an *ad personam* basis, they shall be communicated to the Chairman. The Chairman shall deal with the particular matter as necessary".

their independence or impartiality. These disclosures include the type of information described in the Illustrative List, if relevant.

3. These disclosure requirements shall not extend to the identification of matters whose relevance to the issues to be considered in the proceedings would be insignificant. They shall take into account the need to respect the personal privacy of those to whom these Rules apply and shall not be so administratively burdensome as to make it impracticable for otherwise qualified persons to serve on panels, the Standing Appellate Body, or in other dispute settlement roles.

4. a. All panelists, arbitrators and experts, prior to confirmation of their appointment, shall complete the form at Annex 3 of these Rules. Such information would be disclosed to the Chair of the Dispute Settlement Body ("DSB") for consideration by the parties to the dispute.

b. (i) Persons serving on the Standing Appellate Body who, through rotation, are selected to hear the appeal of a particular panel case, shall review the factual portion of the Panel report and complete the form at Annex 3. Such information would be disclosed to the Standing Appellate Body for its consideration whether the member concerned should hear a particular appeal.

(ii) Standing Appellate Body support staff shall disclose any relevant matter to the Standing Appellate Body, for its consideration in deciding on the assignment of staff to assist in a particular appeal.

(c) When considered to assist in a dispute, members of the Secretariat shall disclose to the Director-General of the WTO the information required under paragraph VI:2 of these Rules and any other relevant information required under the Staff Regulations, including the information described in the footnote.[**]

5. During a dispute, each covered person shall also disclose any new information relevant to paragraph VI:2 above at the earliest time they become aware of it.

6. The Chair of the DSB, the Secretariat, parties to the dispute, and other individuals involved in the dispute settlement mechanism shall maintain the confidentiality

[**] Pending adoption of the Staff Regulations, members of the Secretariat shall make disclosures to the Director-General in accordance with the following draft provision to be included in the Staff Regulations:

"When paragraph VI:4(c) of the Rules of Conduct for the DSU is applicable, members of the Secretariat would disclose to the Director-General of the WTO the information required in paragraph VI:2 of those Rules, as well as any information regarding their participation in earlier formal consideration of the specific measure at issue in a dispute under any provisions of the WTO Agreement, including through formal legal advice under Article 27.2 of the DSU, as well as any involvement with the dispute as an official of a WTO Member government or otherwise professionally, before having joined the Secretariat.

The Director-General shall consider any such disclosures in deciding on the assignment of members of the Secretariat to assist in a dispute.

When the Director-General, in the light of his consideration, including of available Secretariat resources, decides that a potential conflict of interest is not sufficiently material to warrant non-assignment of a particular member of the Secretariat to assist in a dispute, the Director-General shall inform the panel of his decision and of the relevant supporting information."

of any information revealed through this disclosure process, even after the panel process and its enforcement procedures, if any, are completed.

VII. Confidentiality

1. Each covered person shall at all times maintain the confidentiality of dispute settlement deliberations and proceedings together with any information identified by a party as confidential. No covered person shall at any time use such information acquired during such deliberations and proceedings to gain personal advantage or advantage for others.

2. During the proceedings, no covered person shall engage in *ex parte* contacts concerning matters under consideration. Subject to paragraph VII:1, no covered person shall make any statements on such proceedings or the issues in dispute in which that person is participating, until the report of the panel or the Standing Appellate Body has been derestricted.

VIII. Procedures Concerning Subsequent Disclosure and Possible Material Violations

1. Any party to a dispute, conducted pursuant to the WTO Agreement, who possesses or comes into possession of evidence of a material violation of the obligations of independence, impartiality or confidentiality or the avoidance of direct or indirect conflicts of interest by covered persons which may impair the integrity, impartiality or confidentiality of the dispute settlement mechanism, shall at the earliest possible time and on a confidential basis, submit such evidence to the Chair of the DSB, the Director-General or the Standing Appellate Body, as appropriate according to the respective procedures detailed in paragraphs VIII:5 to VIII:17 below, in a written statement specifying the relevant facts and circumstances. Other Members who possess or come into possession of such evidence, may provide such evidence to the parties to the dispute in the interest of maintaining the integrity and impartiality of the dispute settlement mechanism.

2. When evidence as described in paragraph VIII:1 is based on an alleged failure of a covered person to disclose a relevant interest, relationship or matter, that failure to disclose, as such, shall not be a sufficient ground for disqualification unless there is also evidence of a material violation of the obligations of independence, impartiality, confidentiality or the avoidance of direct or indirect conflicts of interests and that the integrity, impartiality or confidentiality of the dispute settlement mechanism would be impaired thereby.

3. When such evidence is not provided at the earliest practicable time, the party submitting the evidence shall explain why it did not do so earlier and this explanation shall be taken into account in the procedures initiated in paragraph VIII:1.

4. Following the submission of such evidence to the Chair of the DSB, the Director-General of the WTO or the Standing Appellate Body, as specified below, the procedures outlined in paragraphs VIII:5 to VIII:17 below shall be completed within fifteen working days.

Panelists, Arbitrators, Experts

5. If the covered person who is the subject of the evidence is a panelist, an arbitrator or an expert, the party shall provide such evidence to the Chair of the DSB.

6. Upon receipt of the evidence referred to in paragraphs VIII:1 and VIII:2, the Chair of the DSB shall forthwith provide the evidence to the person who is the subject of such evidence, for consideration by the latter.

7. If, after having consulted with the person concerned, the matter is not resolved, the Chair of the DSB shall forthwith provide all the evidence, and any additional information from the person concerned, to the parties to the dispute. If the person concerned resigns, the Chair of the DSB shall inform the parties to the dispute and, as the case may be, the panelists, the arbitrator(s) or experts.

8. In all cases, the Chair of the DSB, in consultation with the Director-General and a sufficient number of Chairs of the relevant Council or Councils to provide an odd number, and after having provided a reasonable opportunity for the views of the person concerned and the parties to the dispute to be heard, would decide whether a material violation of these Rules as referred to in paragraphs VIII:1 and VIII:2 above has occurred. Where the parties agree that a material violation of these Rules has occurred, it would be expected that, consistent with maintaining the integrity of the dispute settlement mechanism, the disqualification of the person concerned would be confirmed.

9. The person who is the subject of the evidence shall continue to participate in the consideration of the dispute unless it is decided that a material violation of these Rules has occurred.

10. The Chair of the DSB shall thereafter take the necessary steps for the appointment of the person who is the subject of the evidence to be formally revoked, or excused from the dispute as the case may be, as of that time.

Secretariat

11. If the covered person who is the subject of the evidence is a member of the Secretariat, the party shall only provide the evidence to the Director-General of the WTO, who shall forthwith provide the evidence to the person who is the subject of such evidence and shall further inform the other party or parties to the dispute and the panel.

12. It shall be for the Director-General to take any appropriate action in accordance with the Staff Regulations.[***]

[***] Pending adoption of the Staff Regulations, the Director-General would act in accordance with the following draft provision for the Staff Regulations: "If paragraph VIII:11 of the Rules of Conduct for the DSU governing the settlement of disputes is invoked, the Director-General shall consult with the person who is the subject of the evidence and the panel and shall, if necessary, take appropriate disciplinary action".

13. The Director-General shall inform the parties to the dispute, the panel and the Chair of the DSB of his decision, together with relevant supporting information.

Standing Appellate Body

14. If the covered person who is the subject of the evidence is a member of the Standing Appellate Body or of the Standing Appellate Body support staff, the party shall provide the evidence to the other party to the dispute and the evidence shall thereafter be provided to the Standing Appellate Body.

15. Upon receipt of the evidence referred to in paragraphs VIII:1 and VIII:2 above, the Standing Appellate Body shall forthwith provide it to the person who is the subject of such evidence, for consideration by the latter.

16. It shall be for the Standing Appellate Body to take any appropriate action after having provided a reasonable opportunity for the views of the person concerned and the parties to the dispute to be heard.

17. The Standing Appellate Body shall inform the parties to the dispute and the Chair of the DSB of its decision, together with relevant supporting information.

...

18. Following completion of the procedures in paragraphs VIII:5 to VIII:17, if the appointment of a covered person, other than a member of the Standing Appellate Body, is revoked or that person is excused or resigns, the procedures specified in the DSU for initial appointment shall be followed for appointment of a replacement, but the time-periods shall be half those specified in the DSU.[****] The member of the Standing Appellate Body who, under that Body's rules, would next be selected through rotation to consider the dispute, would automatically be assigned to the appeal. The panel, members of the Standing Appellate Body hearing the appeal, or the arbitrator, as the case may be, may then decide after consulting with the parties to the dispute, on any necessary modifications to their working procedures or proposed timetable.

19. All covered persons and Members concerned shall resolve matters involving possible material violations of these Rules as expeditiously as possible so as not to delay the completion of proceedings, as provided in the DSU.

20. Except to the extent strictly necessary to carry out this decision, all information concerning possible or actual material violations of these Rules shall be kept confidential.

IX. Review

1. These Rules of Conduct shall be reviewed within two years of their adoption and a decision shall be taken by the DSB as to whether to continue, modify or terminate these Rules.

[****] Appropriate adjustments would be made in the case of appointments pursuant to the Agreement on Subsidies and Countervailing Measures.

Annex 1a

Arbitrators acting pursuant to the following provisions:

Articles 21.3(c); 22.6 and 22.7; 26.1(c) and 25 of the DSU;

Article 8.5 of the Agreement on Subsidies and Countervailing Measures;

Articles XXI.3 and XXII.3 of the General Agreement on Trade in Services.

Annex 1b

Experts advising or providing information pursuant to the following provisions:

Article 13.1; 13.2 of the DSU;

Article 4.5 of the Agreement on Subsidies and Countervailing Measures;

Article 11.2 of the Agreement on the Application of Sanitary and Phytosanitary Measures;

Article 14.2; 14.3 of the Agreement on Technical Barriers to Trade.

Annex 2

Illustrative List of Information to be Disclosed

This list contains examples of information of the type that a person called upon to serve in a dispute should disclose pursuant to the Rules of Conduct for the Understanding on Rules and Procedures Governing the Settlement of Disputes.

Each covered person, as defined in Section IV:1 of these Rules of Conduct has a continuing duty to disclose the information described in Section VI:2 of these Rules which may include the following:

(a) financial interests (e.g. investments, loans, shares, interests, other debts); business interests (e.g. directorship or other contractual interests); and property interests relevant to the dispute in question;
(b) professional interests (e.g. a past or present relationship with private clients, or any interests the person may have in domestic or international proceedings, and their implications, where these involve issues similar to those addressed in the dispute in question);
(c) other active interests (e.g. active participation in public interest groups or other organizations which may have a declared agenda relevant to the dispute in question);
(d) considered statements of personal opinion on issues relevant to the dispute in question (e.g. publications, public statements);
(e) employment or family interests (e.g. the possibility of any indirect advantage or any likelihood of pressure which could arise from their employer, business associates or immediate family members).

Annex 3

Dispute Number:________

World Trade Organization Disclosure Form

I have read the Understanding on Rules and Procedures Governing the Settlement of Disputes (DSU) and the Rules of Conduct for the DSU. I understand my continuing duty, while participating in the dispute settlement mechanism, and until such time as the Dispute Settlement Body (DSB) makes a decision on adoption of a report relating to the proceeding or notes its settlement, to disclose herewith and in future any information likely to affect my independence or impartiality, or which could give rise to justifiable doubts as to the integrity and impartiality of the dispute settlement mechanism; and to respect my obligations regarding the confidentiality of dispute settlement proceedings.

Signed: Dated:________

Annex III

Table of Consolidated and Revised Versions of the Working Procedures for Appellate Review

Document Number	Effective Date	Rules Amended	Working Documents/ Explanatory Texts	Principal DSB Meeting(s) at which Amendments Discussed, Minutes
WT/AB/WP/1	15 February 1996	N/A	WT/AB/WP/W/1	31 January 1996, WT/DSB/M/10 and 21 February 1996, WT/DSB/M/11
WT/AB/WP/2	28 February 1997	Rule 5(2) and Annex II	WT/AB/WP/W/2, WT/AB/WP/W/3	25 February 1997, WT/DSB/M/29
WT/AB/WP/3	24 January 2002	Rule 5(2)	WT/AB/WP/W/4, WT/AB/WP/W/5	24 July 2001, WT/DSB/M/107
WT/AB/WP/4	1 May 2003	Rules 24 and 27(3), with consequential amendments to Rules 1, 16, 18, 19, and 28, and Annex I	WT/AB/WP/W/6, WT/AB/WP/W/7	23 October 2002, WT/DSB/M/134
WT/AB/WP/5	1 January 2005	Rules 1, 18, 20, 21, 23, 23 *bis*, and 27, and Annexes I and III	WT/AB/WP/W/8, WT/AB/WP/W/9	19 May 2004, WT/DSB/M/169

Abbreviations used in the Table of References to the Covered Agreements and other Instruments and in the Indexes

AB	Appellate Body
AD	Anti-Dumping Agreement (Agreement on Implementation of Article VI of GATT 1994)
AG	Agreement on Agriculture
ARB	Arbitration Award under Article 21.3(c) of the DSU
ATC	Agreement on Textiles and Clothing
DSU	Understanding on Rules and Procedures Governing the Settlement of Disputes
GATS	General Agreement on Trade in Services
GATT 1947	General Agreement on Tariffs and Trade 1947
GATT 1994	General Agreement on Tariffs and Trade 1994
LA	Agreement on Import Licensing Procedures
SCM	Agreement on Subsidies and Countervailing Measures
SG	Agreement on Safeguards
SPS	Agreement on the Application of Sanitary and Phytosanitary Measures
TBT	Agreement on Technical Barriers to Trade
TRIPS	Agreement on Trade-Related Aspects of Intellectual Property Rights
VC	Vienna Convention on the Law of Treaties (1969)
WP	Working Procedures for Appellate Review
WTO	Marrakesh Agreement Establishing the World Trade Organization

Table of References to the Covered Agreements and other Instruments by Article

Subject Index

[1] Specific terms and phrases relating only to a specific Agreement or particular topic are listed under those headings.

Subject Index by Case (Appellate Body Reports)

Canada – Patent Term (WT/DS170/AB/R)

EC – Asbestos (WT/DS135/AB/R)

EC – Bananas III (WT/DS27/AB/R)

US – 1916 Act (WT/DS136/AB/R; WT/DS162/AB/R)

US – FSC (WT/DS108/AB/R)

US – FSC (Article 21.5 – EC) (WT/DS108/AB/RW)

US – Lead and Bismuth II (WT/DS138/AB/R)

US – Line Pipe (WT/DS202/AB/R)

Subject Index by Case (Arbitration Awards under Article 21.3(c) of the DSU)